D0107853

New Zealand

Peter Turner
Jeff Williams
Nancy Keller
Tony Wheeler

New Zealand

9th edition

Published by
Lonely Planet Publications
Head Office: PO Box 617, Hawthorn, Vic 3122, Australia
Branches: 150 Linden St, Oakland, CA 94607, USA
                10a Spring Place, London NW5 3BH, UK
                1 rue du Dahomey, 75011 Paris, France

Printed by
The Bookmaker Pty Ltd
Printed in China

Photographs by

Vicki Beale	Dolphin Discoveries	NZ Tourism Board,	Trust Bank, Royal
Coastal Kayakers	Adam Fry	Dunedin	Albatross Centre, NZ
DOC (Department	Gabrielle Green	Doc Ross	Peter Turner
of Conservation,	Charlotte Hindle	Soren Larsen	David Wall
New Zealand)	Holger Leue	Ray Stamp	Tony Wheeler
	Richard Nebesky	Richard Timbury	Jeff Williams

Front cover: Detail from a carved house, Otago Museum, Dunedin (David Wall)

First Published
December 1977

This Edition
September 1998

Although the authors and publisher have tried to make the information as
accurate as possible, they accept no responsibility for any loss, injury or
inconvenience sustained by any person using this book.

National Library of Australia Cataloguing in Publication Data

Turner, Peter.
    New Zealand.

    9th ed.
    Includes index.
    ISBN 0 86442 565 1.

    1. New Zealand – Guidebooks. 2. New Zealand – Description and travel.
    I. Williams, Jeff, 1954 Dec 15-. II. Title.

919.30437

Peter Turner

Peter Turner was born in Melbourne and after various forays around the world and a variety of occupations joined Lonely Planet in 1986 as an editor. Now a full-time travel writer, he works mostly in South-East Asia. Peter has contributed to LP's *Malaysia, Singapore & Brunei, Indonesia, South-East Asia on a shoestring* and is the author of the *Jakarta city guide* and *Singapore city guide*.

Jeff Williams

Jeff is a Kiwi from Greymouth on NZ's wild west coast who now lives with his wife Alison and son Callum in a seaside suburb of Brisbane in Queensland, Australia. He predominantly works as a writer for Lonely Planet and has authored, co-authored or contributed to LP's *New Zealand, Australia, Tramping in New Zealand, Outback Australia, Western Australia, South Africa, Lesotho & Swaziland, USA, Washington DC & The Capital Region, West Africa* and *Africa on a shoestring*. He is now out there somewhere, probably beside you, searching for 42.

Nancy Keller

Nancy was born and raised in Northern California, and worked in the alternative press for several years, doing every aspect of newspaper work from editorial and reporting to delivering the papers. She returned to university to earn a master's degree in journalism, finally graduating in 1986 after many breaks for extended stays on the west coast of Mexico. Since then she's been travelling and writing in Mexico, Israel, Egypt, Europe, various South Pacific islands, New Zealand and Central America. She has worked on several LP books, including *Central America, Rarotonga & the Cook Islands, Tonga, Mexico* and *California & Nevada*.

Tony Wheeler

Tony was born in England but grew up in Pakistan, the Bahamas and the USA. He returned to England to do a degree in engineering at Warwick University, worked as an automotive design engineer, returned to university to complete an MBA in London, then dropped out on the Asian overland trail with his wife, Maureen. Eventually settling down in Australia, they've been travelling, writing and publishing guidebooks ever since, having set up Lonely Planet Publications in the mid-1970s.

From Peter

Thanks to the New Zealand Tourism Board in Sydney and New Zealand, and to the many helpful information centres and tourism operators throughout New Zealand who were generous with their time and knowledge.

Thanks also to the 'in-laws' and everyone else for their hospitality and help. Above all thanks to my wife, Lorraine, who first introduced me to New Zealand and the wonders of things Kiwi. And last but not least a dedication to my daughters, Ruby and Madeleine, who loved New Zealand, their second homeland.

From Jeff

There are many to thank for making my research trips to New Zealand so fruitful. Thanks to Whitebait's family (Myra, Linda & Winston, Rosemary & Bernard) in Greymouth; Malcolm, Lynne, Taane & Eric Guiden in Tauranga (and Taanc for company from Cape Reinga to Taupo); Alison Hunter and Callum Williams both at home and on the road; the extended family of Adrienne Costanzo and Rob van Driesum at Lonely Planet in Melbourne; and co-author Peter Turner for writing advice and computing support.

Thanks also to Gaynor Stanley of the New Zealand Tourism Board in Sydney; Peter and Kerry of Mainstreet Backpackers, Kaitaia; Sharmila Patel of Fullers, Auckland; the many staff of Tourism Auckland and the Auckland Visitor Information Centre; Geoff of Sunkist Lodge, Thames, and the Stray Possum on Great Barrier Island (I enjoy your family's company immensely); the one and only Trout of Taupo Central Backpackers; the Pol's at the sublime Arataki Country Villa; Mark Dumble of Rainbow Lodge (and the *Blue Book*) in Taupo; the on-to-it staff of the Taupo Visitor Centre; Gordon Lidgard, NZ Motorcycle Rentals; Cam and the staff at ACB, the Pipi Patch (especially Mary Jo) and Hot Rocks (yes, you Kim); Damian Schroeder of Adrenalin Adventures, Auckland; the well-organised staff at Tourism Rotorua; the guys at Hill Hoppers and Longridge Jet near Te Puke; the ab-zorbing Zorb brothers at Ngongotaha; Steve Brennan at Waikato River Lodge; Michelle Houlihan, Whangarei Visitors Bureau; Neil and Alison at A2B Rentals, Auckland; the Animal Party – the answer to 'NZ Thirst' (Donkey – Minister for Spiritous Liquors, Gaming & Womens' Affairs, Rabbit – Minister for Dodgy Transport, and Rat – Roving Ambassador without Portfolio & VIP) in Auckland; Rory & Barbara at Tamara Backpackers, Wanganui; Klaus & Lillian in Opotiki; Jim Ogden of the Palmerston North Visitor Centre; Jules at Georgia Parkside, Auckland; Mark Clayton & Rae Piva in Havelock North; the Drabbles in Havelock North; Mary Mackey at the Gisborne Visitor Centre; Lance at the Tauranga Visitor Centre; Lynne at the Mt Maunganui Visitor Centre; Beth Richards at the Taumarunui Visitor Centre; Richard McCabe at the Cal-Neva Bar, Auckland; the friendly people at the Maungarongo Marae, Ohakune (a special thanks for your hospitality and the explanation of the significant features of the marae – and great breakfasts); and to the hundreds of others who contributed to this book in a significant way.

This Book

Tony Wheeler did the 1st edition of this book back in 1977 and the next two were updated by Simon Hayman. The 4th edition was updated by Mary Covernton, and Tony updated the 5th edition with Robin Tinker. The 6th edition was updated by Nancy Keller, who updated the 7th edition with Jeff Williams. Peter Turner and Jeff updated the 8th edition (and produced the Fauna & Flora guide) and this, the 9th, edition. Peter updated the Wellington and South Island chapters, while Jeff revised the North Island chapters.

Thanks to the many travellers who took the time to write, giving us their opinions and comments. We've taken all suggestions on board and tried to accommodate as many as possible. A list of your names is included on pages 687-8.

From the Publisher

The production of this edition was coordinated by Rachel Black (mapping and design) and Rebecca Turner (editorial).

Rachel, Jacqui Saunders and Ann Jeffree drew the maps and Ann also created some new illustrations. Rachel steered the book through layout.

This edition was edited by Rebecca, Paul Harding, Liz Filleul and Craig MacKenzie. Rebecca, Paul, Liz, Miriam Cannell, Wendy

Owen and Katie Cody proofread the chapters.

Thanks to Margie Jung for the cover, and to Katie and Jane Hart for their support.

Warning & Request

Things change – prices go up, schedules change, good places go bad and bad places go bankrupt – nothing stays the same. So, if you find things better or worse, recently opened or long since closed, please tell us and help make the next edition even more accurate and useful.

We value all of the feedback we receive from travellers. Julie Young coordinates a small team who read and acknowledge every letter, postcard and email, and ensure that every morsel of information finds its way to the appropriate authors, editors and publishers.

Everyone who writes to us will find their name in the next edition of the appropriate guide and will also receive a free subscription to our quarterly newsletter, *Planet Talk*. The very best contributions will be rewarded with a free Lonely Planet guide.

Excerpts from your correspondence may appear in new editions of this guide; in our newsletter, *Planet Talk*; or in updates on our Web site – so please let us know if you don't want your letter published or your name acknowledged.

Contents

Boxed Asides

Map Legend

BOUNDARIES

.... International Boundary
.... Provincial Boundary
.... Disputed Boundary

ROUTES

..... Freeway, with Route Number [A25]
.... Major Road
.... Minor Road
.... Minor Road - Unsealed
.... City Road
.... City Street
.... City Lane
.... Train Route, with Station
.... Cable Car or Chairlift
.... Ferry Route
.... Walking Track

AREA FEATURES

.... Building
.... Cemetery
.... Desert
.... Market
.... Park, Gardens
.... Pedestrian Mall
.... Reef
.... Urban Area

HYDROGRAPHIC FEATURES

.... Canal
.... Coastline
.... Creek, River
.... Lake, Intermittent Lake
.... Rapids, Waterfalls
.... Salt Lake

SYMBOLS

✪ CAPITAL	.... National Capital	✈	.... Airport	⚓	.... National Park
◉ CAPITAL	.... Provincial Capital	⁘	.... Archaeological Site	←	.... One Way Street
● CITY	.... City	⚲	.... Beach	P	.... Parking
● Town	.... Town	⛫	.... Castle or Fort	)(	.... Pass
● Village	.... Village	◠	.... Cave	⛽	.... Petrol Station
		⛪ 🏛	.... Church	★	.... Police Station
■	.... Place to Stay	⁓	.... Cliff or Escarpment	✉	.... Post Office
⚑	.... Camping Ground	◪	.... Dive Site	❖	...... Shopping Centre
⛺	.... Caravan Park	◔	.... Embassy	⚞	.... Skiing
⌂	.... Hut or Chalet	🦤	.... Fauna Park	🏊	.... Swimming Pool
		⊕	.... Hospital	☎	.... Telephone
▼	.... Place to Eat	☀	.... Lookout	☉	.... Toilet
⚐	.... Pub or Bar	⛩	.... Marae	❶	..... Tourist Information
		▲	.... Mountain or Hill	☕	.... Transport

Note: not all symbols displayed above appear in this book

Map Index

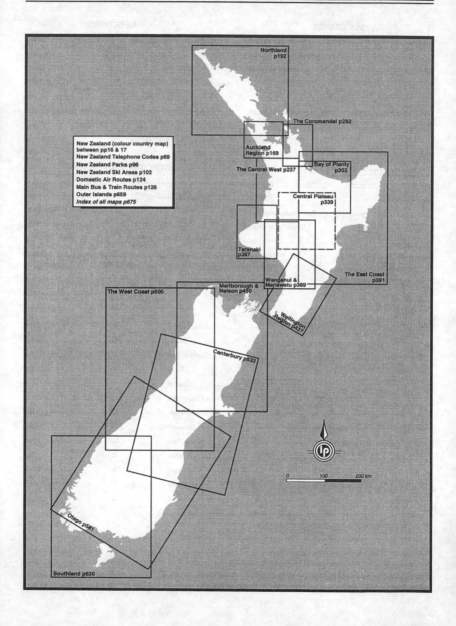

New Zealand (colour country map) between pp16 & 17
New Zealand Telephone Codes p69
New Zealand Parks p96
New Zealand Ski Areas p102
Domestic Air Routes p124
Main Bus & Train Routes p126
Outer Islands p659
Index of all maps p675

Northland p192
The Coromandel p282
Auckland Region p169
Bay of Plenty p302
The Central West p237
Central Plateau p339
Taranaki p267
The East Coast p391
Wanganui & Manawatu p369
Marlborough & Nelson p450
The West Coast p500
Wellington Region p437
Canterbury p533
Otago p581
Southland p630

0   100   200 km

Introduction

Fresh air, magnificent scenery and outdoor activities are the feature attractions of New Zealand. It's not a big country but for sheer variety it's hard to beat. Visitors who come expecting a pristine, green, well-organised little country are not disappointed and the county's reputation for being 'clean and green' is well deserved.

New Zealand is like a microcosm of all the world's attractions. You can tramp on the sides of active volcanoes, or in remote, rugged patches of virgin rainforest, through thermal areas of geysers and boiling mud, or kauri forests with some of the largest and oldest trees on earth. You can swim with dolphins, watch whales, see glaciers descending into rainforests, fish for trout in cold, pristine streams and see fur seals and penguins swimming around your boat as you cruise on remote fiords. The adventurous can go white-water rafting, cave rafting, rock and mountain climbing, tandem skydiving, bungy jumping, skiing down long glaciers, and much more. Plus there are many chances to experience the fascinating Maori culture and the warmth of New Zealand's friendly people.

The major cities each have their own unique character, a growing cultural life with some great nightlife, live theatre, dancing and arty cafes. Arts and crafts are popular and these cities have fine galleries.

Getting around is easy and cycling through the country is a popular way to travel. Finding affordable accommodation is also easy, although it's a good idea to book ahead in the

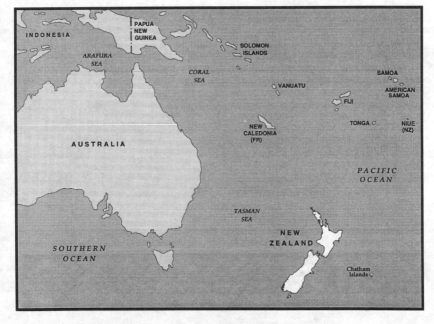

high season. The food is fresh and there's plenty of it, and even the wine is excellent.

Travellers do have one consistent complaint about New Zealand, though: that they haven't allowed themselves enough time in the country. Look at the map of the world and it doesn't appear to be a big country. However, once you arrive in New Zealand, it soon becomes apparent how much there is to see and do.

If time is no object, we'd recommend allowing at least six weeks for a visit. Of course you can still enjoy New Zealand in less time and some travellers make a mad dash through the country, rushing from activity to activity, and have a great time.

This book will help to show you all there is to see and do in New Zealand, and to plan your travels. Have a great time. It's a beautiful country.

Facts about the Country

HISTORY

New Zealand's history has two distinct phases – a pre-European era and the recent history since the arrival of Europeans.

Pre-European History

The original inhabitants of NZ were known until fairly recently as Moriori, or moa hunters. Recent evidence indicates that Polynesians arrived in NZ in a series of migrations and that the Moriori were an early wave of these Polynesians, not a separate race from the Maori, who came later. It's estimated that these first Polynesians arrived over 1000 years ago, possibly around 800 AD or earlier.

The reason for the great voyage across the ocean in canoes remains unknown but, whether by accident or design, the first settlers found temperate islands far larger than any islands of the Pacific. They named it Aotearoa, or the land of the long white cloud. Apart from bats, the land was devoid of mammals for hunting but the sea provided abundant food resources. Of the birdlife, the most spectacular was the huge flightless moa, up to 3.7m tall.

This initially plentiful food supply became the staple of early Polynesians, especially in the South Island, where the moa was hunted for its food and feathers until it became extinct. Agriculture was not well developed in this early 'Archaic' period of settlement, perhaps because of the colder climate. The agricultural societies based on imported Polynesian crops of kumara (sweet

---

Maori Legend – Creation of the Earth & Sky

In the beginning there was nothingness. Before the light, there was only darkness.

Rangi nui, the Sky, dwelt with Papa tu a nuku, the Earth. The two were united and bore many children. Papa's nakedness was covered with many things begotten from her union with Rangi — land, trees, animals of the sea and many other created things — so that she would not be naked. But all lived in utter darkness.

Rangi (Sky-Father) and Papa (Earth-Mother) had six important children. They were Tawhiri matea, god of winds and storms; Tangaroa, god of the sea and of all things living in it; Tane mahuta, god of the forest and of all things that live in the forest; Haumia tiketike, god of wild plants that give food for humankind, including the fern root, berries and many others; Rongo ma Tane, god of cultivated food, including the kumara and all other plants cultivated for food by humankind; and Tu matauenga, the god of war.

After aeons and aeons of living in darkness, because their parents were joined together and no light had ever yet come between them, the children of Rangi and Papa could take it no longer; they wanted light. They debated what they should do. Eventually they decided that they should separate their parents, so that light could enter the world.

They each tried, and failed, to separate Rangi and Papa. Finally it was Tane mahuta's turn to try, and he pushed and strained, his shoulders to the ground and his feet to the sky, and finally succeeded in forcing his parents apart. Light flooded into the world. Thus Tane mahuta became father of the day.

The two parents were grief-stricken at having been separated. They have been separated ever since, but their love for one another has never faded. In the beginning, Rangi shed so many tears that much of the land that had been revealed to light became covered by sea. Finally some of their children turned Papa over onto her stomach, so that Rangi and Papa would not always be looking at one another and grieving. Rangi still cries for his wife, but not as much as before when there was a danger that all the land would be drowned because of his tears; his tears now are the drops of dew that form every night on Papa's back. The mists that form in the mornings in the valleys, and rise towards the heavens, are Papa's sighs of longing for her husband. ■

Maori Legend – Creation of New Zealand

A long time after the creation of the world – after Tane mahuta had created a woman out of red earth, breathed life into her nostrils, mated with her and had a daughter, who also became his wife and bore him other daughters, and after many other things had happened – the demigod Maui, who lived in Hawaiki, went out fishing with his brothers.

They went further and further out to sea. When they were a long way out, Maui took out his magic fish-hook (the jaw of his sorcerer grandmother), tied it to a strong rope, then dropped it over the side of the canoe. Soon he caught an immense fish and, struggling mightily, pulled it up.

This fish became the North Island of NZ, called by the ancient Maori Te ika a Maui (the fish of Maui) or sometimes Te ikaroa a Maui (the big fish of Maui). The Mahia Peninsula, at the north end of Hawke Bay on the east coast of the North Island, was known as Te matau a Maui (the fish-hook of Maui), since it was the hook with which he caught the giant fish.

The South Island was known as Te waka a Maui, or the canoe of Maui, in which he was sitting when he caught the fish. Kaikoura Peninsula, on the north-east coast of the South Island, was the seat of the canoe. Another name for the South Island was Te wai Pounamu (the water greenstone), since much greenstone (jade, or *pounamu*) was found in the rivers there.

Stewart Island, south of the South Island, was known as Te punga a Maui (the anchor of Maui). It was the anchor that held the canoe as Maui hauled in the giant fish. ■

potato), taro and yams came later; this second era of settlement is known as the 'Classic Maori' period.

Maori oral histories tell of the discovery of NZ by the navigator Kupe, ascribed to the year 950 AD, but tribes have differing legends of the settlement of NZ. The widely believed story is that Kupe sailed to Aotearoa from Hawaiki, the 'ancestral homeland' for many Polynesian peoples. Despite the similar names, Hawaiki is not Hawaii. The location of Hawaiki is unknown, though some experts believe it may have been an island in the Marquesas in what is now French Polynesia.

The same legends tell of the Great Migration of around 1350, when a fleet of canoes left catastrophe-stricken Hawaiki for Aotearoa. The new immigrants from the great fleet soon established themselves in their adopted home, displacing or assimilating with the previous residents. This 'history' is now believed to be a dubious adaptation of Maori legends by early western historians, but it does point to a long period of migration from Polynesia.

Maori societies revolved around the *iwi* (tribe) or *hapu* (sub-tribe). Ancestor worship was important and long genealogies (*whakapapa*), often stretching back to one of the canoe groups of the Great Migration, were committed to memory. The societies were hierarchical, with positions of leadership largely hereditary.

The hapu were further divided into *whanau*, extended family groups that combined to form communal villages centred around the *marae* (sacred ground in front of the meeting house where the tribe's ancestral spirits live). There ceremonies were held and elders and others of authority addressed the community. Various local chiefs were under the authority of the *ariki*, or supreme chief of the entire tribe. At the bottom of the pecking order were the slaves taken from opposing tribes in battle.

Maori religion was complex, with a variety of gods representing the sea, sky, mountains, war, agriculture etc. The priests, or *tohunga*, could communicate with the gods and knew the rituals associated with offerings, but were also responsible for maintaining the history, genealogy, stories and songs of the tribe.

Essential to Maori religion and society were the notions of *mauri* (life force) and *wairua* (spirit) that reside in all things, and *mana* (spiritual power or prestige). *Tapu* (taboo) applied to forbidden objects, such as sacred ground or a chief's possessions, and

ADAM FRY

HOLGER LEUE

HOLGER LEUE

HOLGER LEUE

JEFF WILLIAMS

HOLGER LEUE

Maori culture is an integral part of New Zealand life

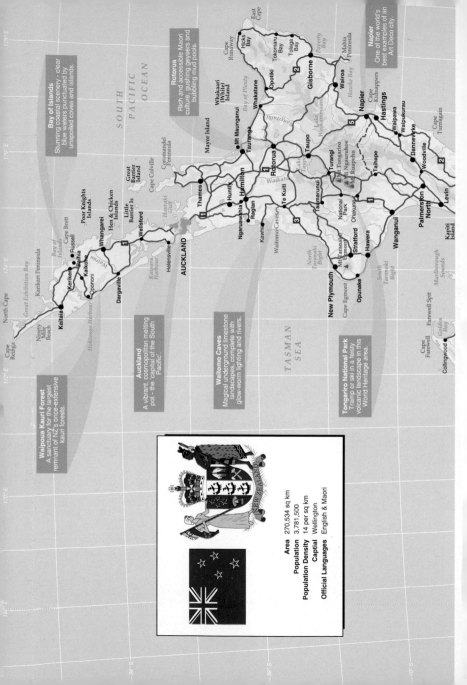

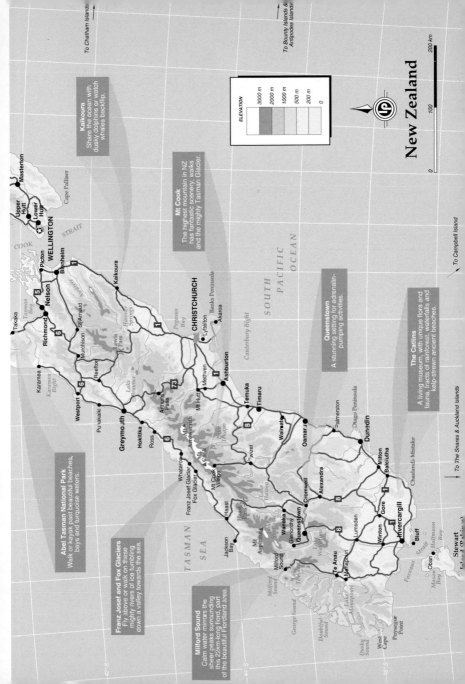

New Zealand

ELEVATION
- 3000 m
- 2000 m
- 1000 m
- 500 m
- 200 m
- 0

0   100   200 km

Abel Tasman National Park
Walk or kayak past beautiful beaches, bays and turquoise waters.

Kaikoura
Share the ocean with dusky dolphins or watch whales backflip.

Mt Cook
The highest mountain in NZ has fantastic scenery walks and the mighty Tasman Glacier.

Franz Josef and Fox Glaciers
Fly above or walk on these mighty rivers of ice tumbling down a valley towards the sea.

Milford Sound
Calm water mirrors the sheer peaks surrounding this 22km-long fiord, part of the beautiful Fiordland area.

Queenstown
A stunning setting for adrenalin-pumping activities.

The Catlins
A living museum, with unique flora and fauna, tracts of rainforest, waterfalls and kelp-strewn ancient beaches.

To Chatham Islands

To Bounty Islands & Antipodes Islands

To Campbell Island

To The Snares & Auckland Islands

COOK STRAIT

TASMAN SEA

SOUTH PACIFIC OCEAN

Masterton
Upper Hutt
Lower Hutt
WELLINGTON
Cape Palliser
Picton
Blenheim
Nelson
Richmond
Takaka
Tasman Bay
St Arnaud
Murchison
Kaikoura
Hanmer Springs
Pegasus Bay
Karamea
Reefton
Lewis Pass
Karamea Bight
Westport
Punakaiki
Hokitika
Ross
Greymouth
Arthur's Pass
Lake Brunner
CHRISTCHURCH
Lyttelton
Banks Peninsula
Akaroa
Methven
Mt Hutt
Ashburton
Temuka
Timaru
Waimate
Oamaru
Palmerston
Otago Peninsula
Dunedin
Milton
Balclutha
Chaslands Mistake
Franz Josef Glacier
Fox Glacier
Mt Cook Village
Mt Cook
Twizel
Lake Tekapo
Lake Pukaki
Haast
Haast Pass
Jackson Bay
Mt Aspiring
Wanaka
Lake Hawea
Lake Wanaka
Cromwell
Alexandra
Glenorchy
Queenstown
Te Anau
Manapouri
Lake Te Anau
Lake Manapouri
Milford Sound
George Sound
Doubtful Sound
Dusky Sound
West Cape
Puysegur Point
Lumsden
Winton
Gore
Invercargill
Bluff
Foveaux Strait
Mason Bay
Oban
Halfmoon Bay
Stewart Island
West Point
Canterbury Bight
42°S
46°S

DAVID WALL

DAVID WALL

COASTAL KAYAKERS

DAVID WALL

A	B
C	D

Activities

A: Jet-boating on the Shotover
   River near Queenstown
B: Climbing in Mt Cook National Park

C: Sea kayaking
D: Bungy jumping on the Kawarau River

In traditional Maori society, tattoos adorned members of the upper class

also to actions or even people proscribed by the tribe.

One of the best ways to promote the mana of a tribe was through battle, so the Maori had a highly developed warrior society. War had its own worship, sacrifices, rituals, dances and art forms. Tribes engaged in numerous battles over territory, for *utu* (revenge) or for other reasons, with the losers often becoming slaves or food. Eating an enemy not only delivered the ultimate insult but also passed on the enemy's life force or power. The Maori built defensive villages, or *pa*, to which they retreated when attacked. These fortresses were built on terraced hill tops with concentric defensive walls. If the outer wall was breached the defenders could retreat to the next fortified inner terrace.

Despite remaining a Neolithic culture (it would have been difficult to get beyond that stage in NZ, since there are few metals apart from gold) the Maori evolved elaborate artistic traditions. Facing the marae, ornate meeting houses were built featuring power-ful wooden carvings depicting ancestors, as well as woven flax wall panels and symbolic paintings.

The higher classes were decorated with intricate tattoos – women only had *moko* (facial tattoos) on their chins, while high-ranking men not only had tattoos over their entire face but also over other parts of their body (especially their buttocks).

The Maori made clothing from dog fur, flax, feathers and other materials; warm fur cloaks decorated with feathers are in some NZ museums. Woodcarving became increasingly refined, culminating in the period immediately before European intervention. They also made greenstone (jade) ornaments and *mere* (war clubs), and beautifully carved war canoes, as well as a variety of household items. Expeditions were mounted to the South Island to find jade, but otherwise most tribes stayed on the much warmer North Island.

European Exploration

In 1642 Dutch explorer Abel Tasman, who had just sailed around Australia from Batavia (modern-day Jakarta, Indonesia), sailed up the west coast of NZ but didn't stay long after his only landing attempt resulted in several of his crew being killed and eaten. He christened the land Niuew Zeeland, after the Netherlands province of Zeeland.

The Dutch, after this first uncomfortable look, were none too keen to return and NZ was left alone until British navigator and explorer Captain James Cook sailed around it in the *Endeavour* in 1769.

Because Tasman had only sailed up the west coast, there had been speculation that this could be the west coast of the fabled great southern continent. In the logical European cosmology, it was thought that a large southern land must exist to balance the large landmasses in the northern hemisphere.

Cook sailed right around the coast of NZ on three voyages altogether, mapping as he went, and many places still bear the names he gave them. He made friendly contact with the Maori many times after he discovered his Tahitian interpreter could communicate with

Captain James Cook

them. He was impressed with their bravery and spirit, and with the potential of this lightly populated land. After finishing his sail around the coasts of both the North and South islands and determining that it was not the large southern continent, Cook claimed the entire land for the British Crown and continued on to Australia.

Another European, the French explorer Jean-François Marie de Surville, was sailing around NZ at the same time as Cook but the two never did bump into one another. They came close, off the coast of the North Island, but each was unaware of the other's presence.

When the British started their antipodean colonising they opted for the larger and even more lightly populated Australia. New Zealand's first European settlers were temporary – sealers (who soon reduced the seal population to next to nothing) and then whalers (who did the same with the whales). They introduced diseases and prostitution,

created such a demand for preserved heads that Maori chiefs began chopping off their slaves' heads to order (before they'd only preserved the heads of warriors who had died in battle) and, worst of all, brought in European firearms. When they exchanged green-stone meres for muskets, the Maori soon embarked on wholesale slaughter of one another. The Ngapuhi tribe from Northland, led by Hongi Hika, embraced the new technology and sent raiding parties throughout the central North Island as far south as Hawkes Bay on the East Coast and Taranaki in the west.

By 1830 the Maori population was falling dramatically.

European Settlement

The first missionary, Samuel Marsden, brought Christianity to NZ in 1814, and other missionaries soon followed. The Bible was translated into Maori – the first time the Maori language had been written. By the middle of the 19th century tribal warfare had abated, cannibalism was fairly well stamped out and the raging impact of European diseases also curbed. But the Maori people now found themselves spiritually assaulted and much of their tradition and culture was irrevocably altered. Their numbers continued to decline.

During the early 19th century European settlers, or Pakeha, arrived in increasing numbers, some on settlement campaigns organised from Britain; in the 1830s entrepreneurs from Australia raced to carve out holdings in the new land. Growing lawlessness from less savoury settlers and a deterioration in Maori-Pakeha relations resulted in petitions for British intervention.

The British were not keen on further colonising – what with burning their fingers in America, fighting in Canada and stretching their involvement in other places, not to mention having Australia to worry about. The need to establish law finally prompted them to dispatch James Busby as the British Resident in 1833. It was a low-key effort, illustrated by poor Busby having to pay his own fare from Australia. Once he'd set up shop in Kororareka (now called Russell) in Northland, his efforts to protect the settlers and keep law and order were made somewhat difficult without the support of forces, arms and authority. He was soon dubbed 'the man of war without guns'.

Treaty of Waitangi

In 1838 the lawlessness problem, unscrupulous 'purchases' of Maori land and the threat of a French colonising effort at Akaroa in the South Island all stirred the British to seek annexation of NZ. Captain William Hobson was sent to replace Busby and persuade the Maori chiefs to relinquish their sovereignty to the British Crown.

A treaty was drawn up in 1840 within a few days of Hobson's arrival in NZ and on 5 February over 400 Maori gathered in front of Busby's residence at Waitangi in the Bay of Islands to hear the treaty read. The Maori chiefs had some objections, so the treaty was amended and they withdrew across the river to debate the issue throughout the night. The following day, with a truly British display of pomp and circumstance, the treaty was signed by Hobson and 45 Maori chiefs, mostly from the Bay of Islands region.

Over the next seven months the treaty was carried throughout NZ by missionaries and officials, eventually being signed by over 500 chiefs. Hobson proclaimed British sovereignty and established his capital at Kororareka but moved it to Auckland a year later.

Though the treaty was short and seemed to be simple, it was a controversial document that is still hotly debated in modern-day NZ. Under the terms of the treaty, the chiefs ceded their sovereignty to the Queen of England in exchange for the Queen's protection and the granting to Maori people of all citizenship rights, privileges and duties enjoyed by citizens of England. The treaty guaranteed the Maori possession of their land and stipulated that they could only sell their land to the Crown. The Queen's agent would then sell the land to settlers in an orderly and fair fashion.

The treaty seemed to promise benefits for both sides, but when settlers arrived and needed land and the Maori didn't want to sell, conflict inevitably resulted. The admirable idea that the government should be a go-between in all Maori-Pakeha deals to ensure fairness fell apart when the government was too tightfisted to pay the price.

Maori Wars

The first visible revolt came when Hone Heke, the first chief to sign the Treaty of Waitangi, chopped down the flagpole at Kororareka which flew the British flag. Despite new poles and more guards, Hone Heke or his followers managed to chop the pole down four times; on the last occasion it was covered with iron to foil further attempts. In 1845, Hone Heke burnt down the town of Kororareka. In the skirmishes that followed, the British governor posted a £100 reward for his head, to which the chief responded by offering a matching £100 for the governor's head.

This was only one in a long series of conflicts between the Maori and Europeans. The original benign intent of the Treaty of Waitangi began to ebb under the pressure of ever-increasing numbers of European settlers. Many land sales were disputed, as local chiefs sold land which belonged to the whole tribe or sold land of other tribes, resulting in a new development of tribal conflict.

The government pressed on with developing the colony. The Constitution Act of 1852 divided the country into six provinces that administered local government and took over the responsibility for land purchases and sales. Alarmed Maori became increasingly reluctant to sell land. In the Waikato region, a number of tribal chiefs united to elect a Maori 'King' in 1859 and resisted land sales and European settlement in the Waikato and King Country region until the 20th century.

Pressures between Maori and European finally escalated into fully fledged wars. Known collectively as the Maori Wars, fighting took place in many parts of the country between 1860 and 1865. The most bitterly fought conflicts were in Taranaki. The force of arms enabled imperial troops to vanquish

The Maori war canoe was once a fearsome sight to enemies

government abolished the provincial governments and centralised power in Wellington, which had become the capital in 1865.

European settlement and influence grew and NZ became a productive agricultural country. Sheep farming, the backbone of modern NZ, flourished as refrigerated ships made it possible to sell NZ meat in Europe. New Zealand became what has been called 'an efficient offshore farm' for England, exporting agricultural products, especially mutton, wool, sheepskin and dairy products, and importing manufactured goods.

Towards the end of the 19th century NZ went through a phase of sweeping and unprecedented social change. Women were given the vote in 1893, 25 years before Britain or the USA and 75 years before Switzerland. An eminent leader at the time, Richard John 'King Dick' Seddon, and the Liberal Party were responsible for many of the reforms. Their far-sighted social reforms and pioneering legislation included old-age pensions, minimum wage structures and the introduction of arbitration courts and child health services.

Meanwhile the Maori people suffered. New Zealand grew through immigration (a selective policy), but by 1900 the Maori population had dropped to an estimated 42,000. The Maori were given the vote in 1867, but continued to lose the struggle to hold on to their culture and ancestral lands.

the Taranaki tribes, but later skirmishes erupted in the East Coast region with the rise of Hauhauism, a Maori religious movement which aimed to oust the Europeans. Also around the region, Te Kooti led raiding parties against European settlements until he finally retreated to the King Country in 1872.

After the Maori Wars the government confiscated huge parcels of Maori land, which, with new legislation allowing private land sales, resulted in the loss of the prime Maori land over the rest of the 19th century.

Late 19th Century

While development in the North Island languished because of the conflicts, the South Island prospered. First farming and then the discovery of gold helped the South Island become the main area of settlement. After 1870, the North Island economy began to recover but it remained the poorer cousin until the 20th century. In 1876 the colonial

Early 20th Century

New Zealand had became a self-governing British colony in 1856 and a dominion in 1907. By the 1920s it controlled most of its affairs, but it was not a fully independent country until 1947.

Meanwhile NZ fought for the British in the Boer War of 1899-1902 and in WWI. The Kiwi soldiers earned a reputation for skill and bravery, but also suffered heavy losses, with one in every three men aged between 20 and 40 killed or wounded fighting for Britain in WWI. NZ troops also helped the British in WWII, fighting in the European and Middle East arenas. But after 1941, when war was declared in the Pacific and NZ was directly threatened, a division was also established in the south-west Pacific.

The postwar years were good to NZ, as the world rebuilt and prices for agricultural products were high. New Zealand had one of the highest per-capita incomes in the world and a social welfare system envied by many countries.

During the Korean War (1950-53), NZ again sent troops as part of a Commonwealth brigade. Australia, NZ and the USA signed the ANZUS defence pact, pledging mutual aid in the event of any attack. In response to the perceived threat of communism, NZ also joined the anti-communist SEATO (South-East Asia Treaty Organisation).

During the 1960s and 70s an increased amount of NZ aid was directed to Pacific countries and in 1971 NZ joined the South Pacific Forum, designed for Pacific governments to discuss common problems.

Recent History

New Zealand's economy, along with much of the rest of the world, took a nose dive in the 1970s and 80s. The closure of much of its traditional European market for agricultural products, combined with the oil-crisis price hikes of many of its mineral and manufactured imports, caused a dramatic deterioration in the country's economy. Robert Muldoon's National Party government of the day tried to buy NZ's way out of trouble by running up large foreign debts and investing in wayward industrial development programs.

In 1984 a Labour government was elected and, in a reversal of political roles, set about a radical restructuring of the economy; the finance minister, Roger Douglas, instituted his 'Rogernomics'. While the reforms produced some economic gains, they also resulted in rising unemployment, which increasingly threatened Labour's chances of re-election. As the finance minister pressed on with the privatisation of state industries and proposals of a flat income tax rate and deregulation of the labour market, Prime Minister David Lange decided enough was enough and sacked him. After the party rein-

stated Douglas, Lange shocked the nation by resigning in 1989. Labour was in disarray, and the National Party led by Jim Bolger swept to power in 1990.

The 1970s and 80s also saw a resurgence of Maori culture, as Maori leaders and activists pushed for social justice and highlighted Maori grievances. In 1975 the Treaty of Waitangi, which in 1877 was ruled 'a simple nullity', was reconsidered. The parliament passed the Treaty of Waitangi Act, establishing a Waitangi Tribunal to investigate Maori claims against the British Crown dating from 1975. In 1985 the act was amended to include claims dating back to the original signing of the treaty in 1840. Financial reparations were made to many Maori tribes whose lands were found to have been unjustly confiscated. See Maori Culture & Race Relations in the Society & Conduct section for more details on race relations.

In 1983 Australia and NZ signed the Closer Economic Relations Trade Agreement, permitting free and unrestricted trade between the two countries. As NZ increasingly saw itself as a Pacific nation, rather than an 'efficient offshore farm' for the UK, its UK trade declined in proportion to its increased trade with Australia, the USA, Japan and the rest of Asia.

In 1984 New Zealand took a strong stand on nuclear energy issues by refusing entry to nuclear-equipped US warships. In response, the USA suspended its obligations to NZ within the ANZUS defence pact. Although this brave policy has caused many problems for the Kiwis they have continued to stick by it.

New Zealand also became a leader in the Pacific in its opposition to nuclear testing by the French at Mururoa atoll in French Polynesia. In 1985 French secret service agents sank the Greenpeace ship *Rainbow Warrior* in Auckland Harbour (see the boxed text entitled The *Rainbow Warrior* Trail in the Northland chapter). In 1995 the French restarted testing in French Polynesia despite worldwide condemnation. NZ was again at the forefront of international protests and dispatched the frigate HMNZS *Tui* with a protest flotilla to Mururoa; the NZ Ambassador to France was recalled as a mark of NZ's outrage. After a number of pointless and controversial detonations the French finally stopped testing.

In the 1990s the National Party government pressed on with Labour's free-market economics, with greater privatisation, there were substantial cuts in welfare and a deregulation of the labour market that emasculated unions. Its majority was slashed in the 1993 elections and it held government by just one seat. Through a referendum in 1993 the population elected to adopt a Mixed Member Proportional (MMP) system based on the German model (see the Government & Politics section later in the chapter for an explanation of this system).

In the 1996 election the National Party formed a government in coalition with the minority NZ First Party, giving that party's leader, Winston Peters, the dual positions of deputy prime minister and treasurer. Public expectations were that NZ First would side with Labour. In late 1997 National PM Jim Bolger was ousted in a bloodless coup and replaced by Jenny Shipley, NZ's first woman PM.

Perhaps the most significant event of the 1990s – at least the greatest cause for national celebration – was NZ boat *Black Magic*'s historic win in the America's Cup yachting race in 1995 (see the boxed text entitled America's Cup 2000 in the Auckland chapter).

GEOGRAPHY

New Zealand stretches 1600km from north to south. It consists of two large islands around which are scattered some smaller islands, plus a few far-flung islands hundreds of kilometres away. NZ's territorial jurisdiction extends to the mostly uninhabited islands of Chatham, Kermadec, Tokelau, Auckland, Antipodes, Snares, Solander and Bounty, and to the Ross Dependency in Antarctica.

The North Island (115,000 sq km) and the South Island (151,000 sq km) are the two major landmasses. Stewart Island, with an area of 1700 sq km, lies directly south of the South Island. The country is 10,400km south-west of the USA, 1700km south of Fiji and 2250km east of Australia, its nearest large neighbour. Its western coastline faces the Tasman Sea, the part of the Pacific Ocean which separates NZ and Australia.

NZ's land area (268,000 sq km) is greater than that of the UK (244,800 sq km), but smaller than that of Japan (377,800 sq km). With only 3,540,000 people, almost 70% of whom live in the five major cities, NZ has a lot of wide open spaces. Its coastline, with many bays, harbours and fiords, is long compared with its landmass.

A notable feature of NZ's geography is the great number of rivers. There's a lot of rainfall in NZ and all that rain has to go somewhere. The Waikato River in the North Island is NZ's longest river (425km).

Also in the North Island, the Whanganui River is the country's longest navigable river, which has always made it an important waterway. New Zealand also has many beautiful lakes; Lake Taupo is the largest and lakes Waikaremoana and Wanaka are two of the most beautiful.

GEOLOGY

Both the North Island and South Island have some high mountains, formed by two distinct geological processes associated with the westward movement of the Pacific tectonic plate.

When one tectonic plate slides underneath another one, it forms a subduction zone. The North Island is on the southern reaches of the subduction zone where the oceanic Pacific plate is sliding underneath the continental plate. The resulting volcanic activity has created a number of large volcanoes and thermal areas, and some equally impressive volcanic depressions.

A rough 'line' of volcanoes, some of which are still active, extends south from the steaming Whakaari (White) Island in the Bay of Plenty past Mt Putauaki (Edgecumbe) and the highly active thermal areas in and around Rotorua and Lake Taupo. The latter, New Zealand's largest lake, was formed by a gigantic volcanic explosion in 186 AD and still has thermal areas bubbling away nearby. South of Lake Taupo are the North Island's spectacularly large volcanoes Tongariro, Ruapehu, Ngauruhoe and the smaller Pihanga. Further south-west is the lone volcanic cone of Mt Taranaki/Egmont. Port Nicholson, Wellington's harbour, was formed by a giant crater, now filled by the sea. Other parts of the North Island also have evidence of volcanic activity; in Auckland, for example, there are over 50 volcanic cones, including most of its famous 'hills' (One Tree Hill, Mt Eden etc) that rise up from the plains.

The North Island has some ranges of hills and mountains produced by folding and uplift, notably the Tararua and Ruahine ranges in the southern part of the North Island. In general, though, most of the high places of the North Island were formed by volcanic activity. In the centre there's a high plateau.

In the South Island the geological process is different. Here the two tectonic plates are smashing into each other, resulting in a process called 'crustal shortening'. This has caused the Southern Alps to rise as a spine, virtually extending along the entire length of the South Island. Thrust faulting, folding and vertical slips all combine to create a rapid uplift of the Southern Alps. Though the Southern Alps receive a lot of rainfall, and hence a lot of erosion, their rate of uplift is enough to keep pace and they are continuing to rise, as much as 10mm a year. Most of the east side of the South Island is a large plain known as the Canterbury Plains. Banks Peninsula, on the east coast, was formed by volcanic activity and joined to the mainland by alluvial deposits washed down from the Southern Alps.

CLIMATE

Lying between 34°S and 47°S, NZ is in Roaring Forties latitude, meaning it has a prevailing wind blowing over it from west to east year-round, ranging from gentle, freshening breezes to occasional raging gales in winter. Coming across the Tasman Sea, this breeze is relatively warm and moisture-laden. When the wind comes up from the south, it's coming from Antarctica and is icy; a southerly wind always means cold weather.

Because of their different geological features, the North and South islands have two distinct rainfall patterns. In the South Island, the Southern Alps act as a barrier for the moisture-laden winds coming across the Tasman Sea, creating a wet climate on the west side of the mountains and a dry climate on the east side: the annual rainfall on the west side is over 7500mm but is only about 330mm on the east.

The South Island's geography also creates a wind pattern in which the prevailing wind, after losing its moisture, blows eastwards as a dry wind, gathering heat and speed as it blows downhill and across the Canterbury Plains towards the Pacific coast. In summer this katabatic or föhn wind can be hot, dry and fierce. In the Grey River valley on the South Island's west coast there's another kind of downhill wind, locally called 'the Barber'.

In the North Island, the western sides of the high volcanoes get a lot more rain than the eastern sides but the rain shadow is not as pronounced, as there is not such a complete barrier as the Alps. Rainfall is more evenly distributed over the North Island, which averages around 1300mm per year.

It is a few degrees cooler in the South Island than the North Island. Winter is from June to August and summer from December to February. But there are regional variations: it's quite warm and pleasant up in the Northland region at any time of year. Higher altitudes are always considerably cooler, and it's usually windy in Wellington, which catches the winds whistling through the Cook Strait.

Snow is mostly seen in the mountains, though there can be snowfalls, even at sea level, in the South Island, particularly in the extreme south. Some of the plains and higher plateaus also receive snow in winter, notably the Canterbury Plains in the South Island and the high plateau around the Tongariro National Park in the North Island, especially

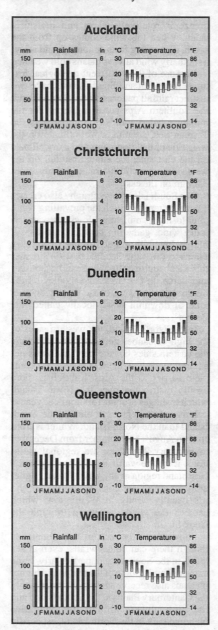

on the 'desert' (east) side. Snow is seldom seen near sea level on the west coasts and not at all in the far north.

One of the most important things travellers need to know about the NZ climate is that it's a maritime climate, as opposed to the continental climate typical of larger landmasses. This means the weather can change with amazing rapidity. If you're tramping at high altitudes, for example, the extreme changeability of the weather can be a life-or-death matter (see the Tramping section in the Outdoor Activities chapter for more details).

ECOLOGY & ENVIRONMENT
The colour Fauna & Flora section following this chapter outlines the sad story of the decimation of many bird species. It also focuses on the brave attempts to bring some species back from the brink of extinction. The Department of Conservation (DOC) administers national parks and reserves.

GOVERNMENT & POLITICS
The governmental structure of NZ is modelled on the British parliamentary system, with elections based on universal adult suffrage. The minimum voting age is 18 and candidates are elected by secret ballot. The maximum period between elections is three years and the government day can call an early election. Voting is not compulsory, but more than 80% of eligible voters usually do.

Also like the UK, NZ is a constitutional monarchy. The traditional head of state, the reigning British monarch, is represented by a resident governor-general, who is appointed for a five-year term. An independent judiciary makes up another tier of government.

The difference between the British Westminster system and the NZ model is that NZ has abolished the upper house and governs solely through the lower house. Known as the House of Representatives, it has 120 member's seats. The government runs on a party system. The party that wins a majority of seats in an election automatically becomes the government and its leader the prime minister (PM). The main parties are the National (conservative) and Labour parties.

The two-party system has traditionally made it difficult for other parties to gain much power. But in the 1993 election the Alliance party, including the Greens, Labour groups and former National Party MPs, gained 18% of the vote. Election results in 1993 were so close that the National Party was only voted in by a one-seat majority, ahead of the Labour Party and the smaller Alliance and NZ First parties, both with two seats.

After a 1993 referendum on electoral reforms, New Zealanders voted overwhelmingly for proportional representation. The government introduced the MMP (Mixed Member Proportional) electoral system, a limited form of proportional voting based on the German electoral system.

Under MMP, electors have two votes: one vote for a candidate in their electorate and the second for a political power. NZ has 60 general electorates and five Maori electorates, in which Maori voters can use their electorate vote. The remaining 55 seats are allocated to the parties according to the percentage of party votes received.

After the country's first MMP elections, in 1996, the minority NZ First Party and the National Party formed the country's first coalition government, even though the Labour Party achieved the highest number of votes. The Labour Party had denied the mercurial Tauranga MP Winston Peters the treasurer's position, so he and his party did a back-flip after the elections (and after holding the country's breath for an inordinate amount of time). During the election he had led voters to believe that his party was pro-Labour. Labour's Helen Clark was denied the opportunity to become the country's first woman PM, National leader Jim Bolger was returned as PM and Winston Peters became the coalition treasurer and deputy PM.

The Nationals plotted Bolger's demise while he was overseas in November 1997. He returned to find that he no longer had a majority of support within the party and that Jenny Shipley, the transport minister, was to take his place by the end of the year. Bolger went quietly but Peters was certainly not happy about it – and who knows which way he will turn in the future. Shipley became the country's first woman PM and quickly began to fill the front bench with her supporters. The government stumbles on in the uncertainties created by MMP.

ECONOMY

New Zealand is a modern country which enjoys a standard of living equivalent to that of other 'developed' countries.

The NZ economy has undergone a radical restructuring from 1984, first under Labour and then the current National government, moving from a welfare-state, government-involved economy towards a private open-market economy.

By the 1980s NZ had lost its traditional UK market for agricultural produce, had incurred huge foreign debts and the economy was stagnant and restricted by government controls.

First the financial market was deregulated by floating the NZ dollar and abolishing exchange controls. Restrictions on overseas borrowing and foreign investment were also reduced. Tariffs were lowered, agricultural subsidies abolished and the taxation system was reformed by introducing a goods and services tax (GST), while lowering company and personal income taxes.

The initial changes resulted in a drop in the NZ dollar, an influx of foreign capital, even larger capital speculation, and an increase in private foreign debt. Inefficient, government-protected industries faced with foreign competition went to the wall.

The bubble burst in 1987 with the worldwide stock market collapse, which hit NZ's speculation boom the hardest. Inflation and unemployment topped 10%, growth was nonexistent and the country questioned the restructuring. The main engineer of the economic reforms, Labour finance minister Roger Douglas, pressed on with a program of privatisation.

With the economy in the doldrums and the country enduring all the pain but no gain from the reforms, Labour was booted out of office in 1990. The incoming National government continued with the free-market reforms, tackling areas a Labour government never could. Welfare programs were cut (the state-funded health insurance system was abolished), privatisation was increased and, most significantly, the labour market was deregulated.

The economy continued to languish in the early 1990s but recently has shown dramatic improvement. The government is running a budget surplus, and public debt, though still high at around 45% of GDP, or $40 billion, has dropped from 50% of GDP in 1992. The economy is enjoying unprecedented growth of around 4%, inflation is under 2% and unemployment is around 6%. New Zealand is receiving plaudits from around the world for its market reforms, and business confidence is bursting.

The reforms have had a major effect on the NZ economy and society. Though still overwhelmingly reliant on agriculture for export income, NZ has made progress in its efforts to diversify its economy. Business efficiency and profit has increased in the manufacturing, finance and service industries. New Zealand also has a broader world outlook, both in its trade and in general. Since 1960, when Britain bought over half of NZ's exports, NZ has shifted its focus elsewhere, especially to Asia. Australia is now NZ's single-largest trading partner, accounting for 20.3% of all trade, but Asia takes 30% of exports, the USA 9.9% and the UK only 6.4%. New Zealand is also attracting greater investment from Asia, especially Japan and Singapore, and the Auckland property boom is spurred by Asian money.

The reforms have also had their pitfalls. As the corporate philosophy engulfs NZ, the once-sacrosanct ideals of equality in society have taken a back seat. Income disparity has grown substantially. In the new user-pays NZ, social services have been cut back, or rather sold off to private enterprise, resulting in higher charges and the axing of some nonprofitable services.

Tourism, service industries, manufacturing, small-scale industry and agriculture are important in the NZ economy. In a recent count the sector of trade, restaurants and hotels accounted for the largest proportion of GDP, followed by the sector of financing, insurance, real estate and business services, then by manufacturing and then agriculture.

With all the sheep, cattle and farms you see around NZ (the country is reckoned to have around 48 million sheep and 8.8 million cattle, including 3.8 million dairy and 5 million beef) it's not surprising that agriculture is an important part of the economy. In strictly dollar amounts it accounts for only about 10% of the entire GDP and employs about the same percentage of the country's workforce, but over 50% of all land in the country is devoted to pasture. Agricultural products from sheep, cattle, fish and forestry are NZ's chief exports. Farming is a scientific proposition in NZ, with constant research carried out and the most modern scientific farming methods used.

Principal exports, in order of importance, are: meat (beef and veal bring in slightly more revenue than lamb and mutton), dairy products, fish, forest products (primarily pine logs and timber products from nonnative trees), fruits and vegetables (especially kiwi fruit, apples and pears) and wool. Main imports are machinery and mechanical appliances, electrical machinery and equipment, textiles, motor cars and other goods.

Tourism is also a major source of foreign revenue. Tourist arrivals numbered 1.45 million in 1996. The tourism industry aimed to increase this number to three million by 2000, but current arrivals, and the downturn in the Asian economies, indicate that this will not be achieved.

POPULATION & PEOPLE

Of New Zealand's population of around 3.8 million, 72% are NZ European, 15.1% are NZ Maori, 5.8% are Pacific Island Polynesian and about 5% are Asian.

Many Pacific islands are experiencing a rapid population shift from remote and undeveloped islands to the 'big city'. Auckland is very much the big city of the South Pacific, with the greatest concentration of Polynesians on earth. It sometimes causes a great deal of argument, discussion and tension, and much of it is not between the recent Pacific immigrants and the Pakeha population, but between the islanders and the Maori, or among the various islander groups themselves.

Asian migration is also increasing. NZ has a sizable Indian community, mostly from Fiji, and has attracted East Asian migrants, many of them through NZ's recent immigration incentives.

With only about 13.7 people per sq km, NZ is lightly populated by many countries' standards but is more densely populated than Australia with its stretches of empty country and 2.3 people per sq km. Over the last 20 years or so the economic situation has led to a mass exodus of New Zealanders to Australia and further afield, though improving economic conditions have helped slowed emigration.

The South Island once had a greater population than the North Island but is now the place to go for elbow room – its population is barely more than that of Auckland. The nation's capital is Wellington but Auckland is the largest city. The six biggest urban regions – the only ones in the country with populations over 100,000 – are:

City	Population
Greater Auckland	992,000
Greater Wellington	334,100
Christchurch	325,300
Hamilton	131,300
Napier-Hastings	112,800
Dunedin	111,000

Despite its rural base, NZ is very much an urban country. Altogether, the population of the 15 largest 'urban areas' is nearly 70% of NZ's population – Auckland alone has 27% of the entire population.

EDUCATION
New Zealanders place a high value on education and virtually all of them are literate. Education is mandatory and free for all children between the ages of six and 15; in fact most children start school by the age of five and many have also attended preschools before then, all subsidised by the state. Correspondence education is available for children who live in remote places.

New Zealand has seven universities (including Lincoln which concentrates on agriculture) and a number of teachers colleges and polytechnics.

New Zealand is gaining a reputation, especially in Asian countries, as a good place to learn English. But this trend may be affected by the recent downturn in the Asian economies. There are numerous language schools throughout NZ (but most are in Auckland) and some student visas permit foreign students to study for up to four years.

ARTS
New Zealand has a multifaceted arts scene, with both Maori and Pakeha engaged in all kinds of traditional and modern arts. Although there are distinct 'Maori arts' and 'European arts', there is rarely a ruling over who can practise particular arts. For example, there are Pakeha who enjoy carving

Ceremonial adzes (*toki*) with greenstone blades were carried by Maori chiefs as symbols of authority

in bone and painting in traditionally Maori styles; Maori songs, *poi* dances and a little bit of Maori language are taught in all schools. Likewise, there are many Maori who excel in the traditionally European arts such as theatre and music. Dame Kiri Te Kanawa, a Maori, is one of the world's best-known operatic divas (see the boxed text entitled Dame Kiri Te Kanawa in The East Coast chapter).

Though the written word was not traditionally a part of Maori culture, NZ is experiencing a movement of dynamic Maori writing in fiction, nonfiction and poetry.

Maori Arts

Maori arts are dramatic in many ways and include various arts that people of European backgrounds might not be familiar with.

Traditionally the Maori did not keep a written history; their history was kept in long, specific and stylised songs and chants. As in many parts of the world where oral history has been practised, oratory, song and chant developed to become a magnificent art in Maori culture. The many rituals associated with Maori protocol are also quite stylised – if you visit a marae and are greeted with the traditional *haka* (war chant) and *wero* (challenge), you will appreciate how artistic they are. The Maori arts of song and dance include some special features, such as the poi dance and action songs. Martial arts, using a variety of traditional weapons and movements, are highly developed.

Other Maori arts include crafts such as wood, bone and jade carving, basketry and weaving, including a distinctive form of wall panelling, known as *tukutuku*, seen on marae and in Maori churches. You'll see woodcarvings, tukutuku and distinctive styles of painting (especially on the rafters and ceilings) in most Maori meeting houses.

Theatre & Dance

New Zealanders take part in all the traditional European-based art forms. There's a lively literary scene (see under the Literature heading later in this section), poetry readings, many dance styles and live theatre.

Poupou, carved wooden figures, decorate many meetings houses throughout New Zealand

Wellington is particularly known for its theatre scene, with traditional as well as improvisational and avant-garde live theatre companies. Other major centres – Auckland, Palmerston North, Christchurch and Dunedin – also have active theatre and dance scenes. Smaller towns often actively support a community theatre group.

Music

As with theatre, so with music – the major centres have the liveliest music scenes but even smaller towns can have some interesting music. There's plenty of opportunity for going out in the evening and hearing live music in the larger centres, with a choice of everything from a symphony concert and the ballet to a rock, jazz or blues band. Irish music – both the acoustic ballad minstrel variety and the rousing Irish dance-band style – is very popular in NZ.

Rock New Zealand rock music doesn't begin and end in Dunedin, though over the last 10 years you could be forgiven for thinking so. In terms of innovative and alternative music, Dunedin is NZ's music capital. (See the boxed text entitled The Dunedin Sound in the Otago chapter.)

In the 1970s and 80s, Split Enz was NZ's best-known and most successful band. Originally an unusual and eccentric group, their style became more mainstream in the 80s. Ridiculously enough, their completely apolitical song *Six Months in a Leaky Boat* was banned in England during the Falklands war of 1982.

Like many other NZ bands who achieved success, Split Enz based themselves in Australia and found themselves referred to as 'a great Australian band'. After its break-up in the mid-1980s, band member Neil Finn formed another successful 'Australian' band, Crowded House (at least Crowded House had some Australian members). For more details on the origins of Split Enz, see the boxed text entitled 'A Blind Date with Destiny' in the Central West chapter.

NZ bands have long been renowned not only for their 'alternative' feel but also for their imaginative names. Examples (all of which are or were quite good bands) include Sneaky Feelings, Straitjacket Fits, Look Blue Go Purple and the Jean-Paul Sartre Experience. Possibly the prize example, however, is an outfit called the Great Unwashed, who later renamed themselves The Clean – signifying a major change in musical direction, perhaps?

Visual Arts
The larger centres have a variety of museums and art galleries with contemporary and tra-

ditional art, and smaller towns often have a gallery, which may combine arts and crafts. All the visual arts are represented in NZ, including painting, sculpture, ceramics, pottery and a wide variety of handicrafts.

Literature
New Zealand has an active literary scene. Probably the most internationally known NZ writer is Katherine Mansfield (1888-1923), who was born and raised in NZ and later moved to England, where she spent most of her short adult life and did most of her writing (see the boxed text entitled Katherine Mansfield in the Wellington chapter). Her short stories are in many volumes, including *The Stories of Katherine Mansfield: Definitive Edition* edited by Antony Alpers.

Frank Sargeson (1903-82) is another classic NZ author. Within the country he is probably as well known as Mansfield, especially for his three-volume autobiography, novels and many short stories. But, since he lived all his life in NZ, his work did not become as widely known overseas.

For short stories see the *Oxford Book of New Zealand Short Stories* edited by Vincent O'Sullivan, and *Some Other Country: New Zealand's Best Short Stories* chosen by Marion McLeod & Bill Manhire. For a wide-ranging collection of fiction by NZ women, try *In Deadly Earnest* compiled by Trudie McNaughton.

For students of NZ literature there's the *Oxford History of New Zealand Literature in English* edited by Terry Sturm, or the *Penguin History of New Zealand Literature* by Patrick Evans.

Maurice Shadbolt is the author of several fine historical novels about NZ – so far he's published nine novels, four collections of short stories and several nonfiction books. His best-known novel is probably *The Season of the Jew*, which won the NZ Wattie Book of the Year Award in 1987 and was chosen by the *New York Times* as one of the best books of that year. This book follows a dispossessed band of Maori who identify with the Jews of ancient Israel.

Janet Frame is another popular novelist, poet and short-story writer. Her three-volume autobiography (*To the Island*, *An Angel at my Table* and *Envoy from Mirror City*) became famous after the film *An Angel at my Table* by acclaimed local director Jane Campion. *Janet Frame: An Autobiography* is a fascinating insight into her life. Frame's many works are widely available.

Shonagh Koea is another popular author; her better-known works include *The Woman Who Never Went Home*, *The Grandiflora Tree*, *Staying Home and Being Rotten* and *Fifteen Rubies by Candlelight*.

Other favourite authors include Maurice Gee, whose novel *Going West* won the NZ Wattie Book of the Year Award in 1993; Fiona Kidman *(The Book of Secrets)*; Owen Marshall *(Tomorrow We Save the Orphans)*; Philip Temple *(Beak of the Moon)*; and Dame Ngaio Marsh, who writes murder mysteries.

Maori & Pacific Literature Two books of the series *Te Ao Marama – Contemporary Maori Writing*, edited by Witi Ihimaera, have been published. *Volume One: Te Whakahuatanga o te Ao – Reflections of Reality* is an anthology of written and oral Maori literature; *Volume Two: He Whakaatanga o te Ao – The Reality* (1993) has prominent Maori authors examining the crucial issues affecting Maori people. Witi Ihimaera is a prolific Maori author of novels and short stories. Some of his better-known novels include *The Matriarch*, *Tangi* and *Pounamu, Pounamu*. His *Bulibasha* is a zany look at the life of Maori sheep-shearing gangs in the East Coast region of the North Island.

Keri Hulme received international acclaim when *The Bone People* won the British Booker McConnell Prize for fiction in 1985. She has published several other novels and books of poetry.

Alan Duff is a controversial author who writes about Maori people in modern NZ society. His two novels and one nonfiction book have all generated heated debate. His first novel, *Once Were Warriors*, was made into the eponymous film which received international acclaim; his second novel was *One Night Out Stealing*. In 1993 his non fiction *Maori: The Crisis and the Challenge* sparked a rage of controversy.

Other significant Maori authors include novelists Apirana Taylor and Patricia Grace *(Potiki)*, and poet Hone Tuwhare.

NZ also has some important Pacific islander authors. Albert Wendt, a Samoan author who is a professor of English at the University of Auckland, is one of the finest. His novels include *Leaves of the Banyan Tree*, *Pouliuli*, *Sons for the Return Home*, *Ola* and *Black Rainbow*; he has also published two poetry books and two collections of short stories.

The excellent *The Shark that Ate the Sun: Ko e Ma go ne Kai e La* by Niuean John Puhiatau Pule is about the Pacific islanders' experience in NZ.

Children's Literature This is a particularly fertile area of writing, with many NZ writers achieving international success.

David Hill deals with the sensitive subject of children with disabilities in *See Ya, Simon*. Rural life is the setting for Jack Lasenby's *Uncle Trev* and *Harry Wakatipu*. Sports, especially sailing and swimming, are the impetus for some of Tessa Duder's novels (the *Alex* series, *Jellybean* and *Night Race to Kawau*), while William Taylor's novels, aimed at 11 and 12-year-olds, focus on the plight of the underdog.

One of NZ's most successful writers is Margaret Mahy, author of over 100 titles and winner of the international Carnegie Medal for *The Changeover* and *The Haunting*. A favourite children's book is *The Terrible Taniwha of Timberditch* by Joy Cowley (illustrated by Rodney McRae).

Poetry James K Baxter, who died in 1972, is possibly the best-known NZ poet. Others include RAK Mason, Allen Curnow, Denis Glover, Hone Tuwhare and the animated Sam Hunt. *Contemporary New Zealand Poetry Nga Kupu Titohu o Aotearoa* edited by Miriama Evans, Harvey McQueen & Ian Wedde is an excellent collection of NZ poetry written both in English and Maori.

Wedde and McQueen also edited the comprehensive *Penguin Book of New Zealand Verse*.

Cinema

The history of NZ film doesn't really begin until the late 1970s. From some early stumbling attempts, notable feature films have survived the test of time and launched the careers of NZ directors and actors.

Sleeping Dogs (1977) is an accomplished psychological drama that was at the forefront of the new film industry; it also launched the careers of actor Sam Neill and director Roger Donaldson.

Bad Blood (1981) is a British-NZ production about the gun-toting psychosis of macho NZ, based on the true story of Stan Graham, a nutter oddly afforded hero status in NZ, who went berserk in a rural town during WWII. *Smash Palace* (1981), about a marriage break-up and custody chase, was a local success. *Came a Hot Friday* (1984), directed by Ian Mune, is one of NZ's better comedies.

Other films of note are *Utu* (Revenge; 1983), an amateurish but breakthrough Maori film; *Meet the Feebles* (1989), a sick piece of splatter puppetry but not without innovation; and *The Quiet Earth* (1985), an end-of-the-world sci-fi movie with wit and imagination. *Goodbye Pork Pie* (1980), an exuberant NZ road movie directed by Geoff Murphy, was a box office hit in NZ, as was the later *Footrot Flats* (1986), starring NZ's favourite cartoon character, The Dog.

New Zealand films moved into art-house cinemas with Vincent Ward's *Vigil* (1984), a brooding film about a girl's coming of age in the rain-drenched backblocks of NZ. It proved too ponderously artistic for many Kiwi film-goers but wowed them at Cannes. Ward's follow-up *The Navigator* (1988) is a strange modern/medieval hunt for the Holy Grail.

New Zealand's best-known director is Jane Campion. Her greatest films explore NZ themes. *An Angel at My Table* (1990), based on Janet Frame's autobiography, shows the fine character development typical of her films. Campion's masterpiece, *The Piano* (1993), about the trials of a mute woman in NZ's pioneer days, received Cannes and Academy Award success.

Suddenly the world noticed NZ's already accomplished movie industry. *Once Were Warriors* (1994), a brutal tale of modern urban Maori life, stunned movie-goers around the world. Peter Jackson's *Heavenly Creatures* (1994) also achieved critical acclaim. It's based on a famous 1950s case of matricide by two schoolgirls.

SOCIETY & CONDUCT

Maori culture has always been an integral part of NZ and is a strong and growing influence, although New Zealand culture is essentially European, transplanted by the British to these far-off islands.

European New Zealanders used to hold so strongly to their British traditions that they earned the tag of 'South Seas Poms'. While British culture is still a strong focus for many, a growing diversity of migrants and a wider global outlook has seen a distinct change in NZ society in recent years. Resurgent Maori culture and the new corporate philosophy have also helped to shape a new world view. New Zealand has always been proud of its traditions, but more than ever the country is exploring its identity.

Though the majority of NZ's population comes from English stock, other notable early influences were the Dalmatians, who came from Croatia to dig kauri gum in Northland. Scottish immigrants came in large numbers and their influence is most evident in the far south, where Scottish games are held, the bagpipes still blow and a distinct Scottish brogue can be heard.

More recently, Polynesians have brought their cultures with them. In Auckland you can go to a Samoan rugby match on Saturday afternoon, dance the *tamure* at a Cook Islands nightclub that night and go to a Tongan-language church service on Sunday. The Indians and Chinese are NZ's other two major immigrant groups.

Through a common history and culture based on British traditions and a strong geographical link, NZ shares many cultural attributes with, and has long been influenced by, neighbouring Australia. Many New Zealanders have migrated to Australia, or at least travelled to and worked there, but Kiwis are keen to distance themselves from their brasher and patronising cousins across the Tasman.

New Zealanders are intensely proud of their country. Aware of their country's small size and relative insignificance on the world stage, national achievements, particularly world-beating sporting achievements, are greeted with great fanfare. New Zealand also values its independence and is not afraid to take on the world, as it has done in its anti-nuclear stance, a policy so widely supported that not even conservative governments have been game to reverse it despite intense international pressure.

New Zealand's European population values hard work, resourcefulness, honesty, fairness, independence and ruggedness – legacies of their pioneering history. For the visitor, perhaps the most immediately obvious trait of all New Zealanders is their friendliness.

Maori Culture & Race Relations

The Maori are the original Polynesian settlers of NZ, migrating from the islands of the South Pacific around 800 AD. As such, Maori language and culture is closely related to that of other Polynesian peoples.

The ancestors of the Polynesians came from South-East Asia to the Pacific some 2500 years ago. The Austronesians, the common ancestors of South-East Asians and Polynesians, brought with them their animals and plants, though the existence of the kumara shows that contact was made between Polynesia and South America. Polynesian languages show linguistic similarities to those of the Malay peoples; other similarities exist in their arts and traditional religion.

The term Maori has only applied to NZ Polynesians since the arrival of the Europeans. Maori society was tribal and the Maori referred to themselves in terms of their iwi, such as Ngati Kahu, or 'descendent of Kahu'. The tribes were headed by a supreme chief, but often of more relevance was the hapu, and the village structure based around family groups. (Incidentally the largest iwi in 1996 was the Ngapuhi with 96,000 members, the Ngati Porou with 55,000, the Ngati Kahungunu with 45,000 and Ngai Tahu, the South Island iwi, with 29,000.)

Whakapapa determines everyone's place in the tribe, so ancestral and family ties are critical. The marae is the focus of Maori culture because it is where the tribe gathers. It is here that ancestors are as present as the current generations.

The history of the Maori parallels the history, or decline, of other indigenous peoples in colonised countries. The introduction of diseases and guns, which escalated tribal warfare, saw the decimation of their population. Missionary activity, increasing foreign settlement and the appropriation of land helped destruct traditional society.

The most important event in the history of New Zealand race relations was the signing of the Treaty of Waitangi in 1840. Though it signalled the annexation of the country by Britain, its motives – to stop lawlessness and the rampant grab for Maori land – were at least partly humanitarian. In exchange for granting sovereignty over NZ to Britain, the Maori chiefs were promised full exclusive and undisturbed possession of their lands, forests, fisheries and other properties, and the same rights and privileges as British subjects.

As settlement progressed, the terms of the treaty were increasingly ignored. Disputes over land resulted in the wars of the 1860s, which eventually broke the back of Maori resistance. Maori land was appropriated and the treaty, which was never ratified by a NZ parliament, was all but dead.

Despite romantic notions of the Maori people, partly inspired by the 'noble savage' sentiments fashionable in the 19th century, Europeans remained largely separate from

Maori society. Though intermarriage was common, for the most part the Maori retreated to the more isolated rural areas.

At the turn of the century, when race relations looked their bleakest, the Maori began to organise and develop leaders skilled in Pakeha and Maori affairs. The setting aside of Maori seats in parliament gave the Maori a political voice. In the South Island the Ngai Tahu people petitioned parliament over land

grievances. They also elected members of parliament specifically to lobby on these issues. The Young Maori Party, composed of Pakeha-educated Maori, pressed for greater education and health services for Maori communities.

Apirana Ngata was an inspiring Maori leader who became Minister of Native Affairs in 1928, establishing Maori land development schemes and stressing the

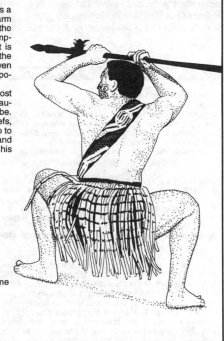

The Haka

The haka is the Maori war chant that precedes a battle. Delivered with fierce shouting, flexing arm movements that resemble fists pummelling the side of someone's head, and thunderous stamping to grind whatever is left into the dust, it is indeed a frightening sight. Made famous by the All Blacks national rugby team, it can scare even the spectators in the stands, let alone the opponents on the field.

Each tribe had its own haka, but the most famous and widely used comes from Te Rauparaha (1768-1849), chief of the Ngati Toa tribe. He was one of the last great warrior chiefs, carving a course of mayhem from the Waikato to the South Island, where European settlers and many southern Maori were slaughtered by his advance. Te Rauparaha's haka is:

Ka mate, ka mate
    It is death, it is death
Ka ora, ka ora
    It is life, it is life
Ka mate, ka mate
    It is death, it is death
Ka ora, ka ora
    It is life, it is life
Tenei te tangata puhuruhuru
    This is the hairy man
Nana i tiki mai whakawhiti te ra
    Who caused the sun to shine again for me
Upane, upane
    Up the ladder, up the ladder
Upane kaupane
    Up to the top
Whiti te ra
    The sun shines

It is said to have originated when Te Rauparaha was fleeing from his enemies. A local chief hid him in an underground kumara store, where Te Rauparaha waited in the dark, expecting to be found. When the store was opened and the sun shone in, it was not his enemies but the hairy local chief telling him they had gone. Te Rauparaha climbed the ladder to perform this victorious haka. ■

importance of Maori culture. Other Maori politicians lobbied the Labour Party and when Labour achieved power in 1935, the government introduced legislation guaranteeing equality in employment, and increased spending on health, housing and education. Though the Maori were conspicuous on the rugby field and keen to sign up to defend the realm in times of war, up until WWII interaction between Pakeha and Maori communities remained minimal.

Despite disparities in education, wealth and power-sharing between Maori and Pakeha, Maori people did enjoy greater acceptance and equality under the law than the indigenous peoples of other European colonised countries. New Zealanders are proud of their record of racial harmony. *Return to*

Paradise by James Michener tells of the outraged local reaction when WWII GIs stationed in NZ tried to treat the Maori like American blacks.

The postwar economic boom saw the greatest change in Maori society, as Maori migrated to the cities with the promise of jobs. Urban Maori mixed with Europeans as never before, as the government pursued the policies of assimilation fashionable at the time. But assimilation meant the dominance of European culture and though Maori culture survived, particularly in rural areas, Maori lost contact more than ever with their language and traditions.

In the late 1960s a new Maori voice arose and called for a revival in Maoritanga (Maori culture). Young activists combined with tra-

---

Marae Etiquette

Visitors to New Zealand will have several opportunities to experience interesting aspects of Maori culture. Perhaps the best place to gain some understanding of Maoritanga is by visiting a marae. The marae is the open area in front of the *whare hui* (meeting house), but the term is often loosely used to describe the buildings as well. Either way, it is a place which is sacred to the Maori and should be treated with great respect.

Some of the many customs and conventions of the marae include:

- that it is a place to stand (*Turangawaewae*)
- that it is a place of kinship (*Whanau-ngatanga*), friendship (*Manaakitanga*), love (*Aroha*), spirituality (*Wairua*) and the life force (*Mauri*)
- respect for elders (*Whakarongo kii nga kaumatua*)
- that it is a place where life and death merge, where the living (*te hunga ora*) give great honour to the dead (*te hunga mate*)
- the preservation and use of the Maori language (*Maori reo*)

A welcoming ritual (*Te Powhiri Ki Te Manuhiri*) is followed every time visitors (*manuhiri*) come onto the marae. They bring with them the memories of their dead. The hosts (*tangata whenua*) pay their respects to the deceased of the manuhiri, likewise the manuhiri to the tangata whenua. The ceremony removes the *tapu* (taboo) and permits the manuhiri and tangata whenua to interact. The practice varies from marae to marae. Note that shoes must be removed before entering a whare hui.

Te Powhiri Ki Te Manuhiri may proceed as follows: a welcoming call (*karanga*) by women of the tangata whenua to the manuhiri. It could also include a ceremonial challenge (*taki* or *wero*).The manuhiri reply to the karanga and proceed on to the marae. They pay their respects and sit where indicated, generally to the left (if facing outwards) of the whare hui.

Welcoming speeches (*mihi*) are given by the tangata whenua from the threshold (*Taumata Tapu*) in front of the meeting house. Each speech is generally supported by a song (*waiata*), generally led by the women. When the mihi is finished the manuhiri reply. The tapu is deemed to have been lifted from the manuhiri when the replies are finished. The manuhiri then greet the tangata whenua with handshakes and the pressing of noses (*hongi*). In some places the hongi is a single press, in others it is press, release, press.

ditional leaders to provide a new direction, calling for the government to address Maori grievances. The contentious Treaty of Waitangi, always on the Maori agenda, came to the fore as never before. Increasing radicalism saw the Maori take to the streets and engage in land occupations. In the 1970s, historic land disputes involved Raglan golf course, and Bastion Point in Auckland. The rise of black power groups and gangs such as the Mongrel Mob, a prominent Maori biker group, unsettled many in the European community.

The focus on Maori issues spurred the government to give the Maori language greater prominence in schools and the media, to institute the Race Relations Act banning discrimination and to introduce the Waitangi Tribunal in 1975 to investigate Maori land claims. Though some claims have resulted in the return of Maori land, the implications for private land ownership has seen claims delayed for many years.

In an attempt to extricate itself from the terms of the tribunal, the government in 1994 proposed a massive once and for all 'fiscal envelope' of $1 billion to pay out all Maori land claims over the following 10 years. Settlements have already been made, including the notable $170 million reparation to the Tainui in 1995 for lands confiscated in 1884 and agreement between the Crown and Ngai Tahu in 1997.

Perhaps the greatest effect of the Maori revival has been the growing interest in Maoritanga. Maori language, literature, arts

Before the manuhiri leave the marae they make farewell speeches (*poroporoaki*) which take the form of thanks and prayer.

The important thing to remember, as a visitor, is that once invited you are extremely welcome on the marae, as a cornerstone of Maori culture is hospitality. Once protocol has been satisfied you have become part of an extended family and the concern of the tangata whenua is you – the manuhiri. They want to see you fed and looked after, almost spoiled, because you are a guest. Such hospitality is fantastic and lucky visitors to New Zealand are increasingly being given the opportunity to enjoy it, either as a guest or on one of the marae tours that are becoming popular. If you do receive hospitality such as food and lodging, it is customary to offer a *koha*, or donation, to help towards the upkeep of the marae. When the roles are reversed and you are the tangata whenua, remember that the care of *your* guests becomes your first concern. ∎

and culture are experiencing a renaissance. The establishment of *Te Kohanga Reo* (language nests) in schools, with sessional or all-day immersion in Maori language and culture, is a strong step towards the preservation of Maori identity. The Maori population is now overwhelmingly urban and largely integrated into European society, but the loss of traditional culture is being redressed as more and more Maori learn the language and return to the marae. The 1996 census figures show that a quarter of all Maori (26%) cannot name their iwi (but that the number has risen since the previous census). Many, however, are now attempting to trace their whakapapa.

The marae is the main focus for Maoritanga and many Maori are re-establishing contact with the marae of their tribe. But even the marae are subject to the winds of change. Traditional tribal leadership has evolved into today's trust boards, whose power base is the maraes in rural areas. The trust boards are under increasing attack from young, urban Maori who see the old leaders as too conservative and exclusive. With their adherence to traditional etiquette and Maori language, many urban Maori not brought up on the marae feel excluded and want a greater say in tribal affairs and negotiations with the government.

Many Pakeha also have a growing awareness of Maori culture. Certainly government and intellectuals have embraced the new Maori revival and see an understudying of Maori culture and at least a basic knowledge of Maori as an advantage. However, there is an undercurrent of unease in the wider community, especially with radical Maori aspirations that call for Maori sovereignty – the establishment of a separate Maori government and judicial system.

The Maori occupation of the Moutoa Gardens in Wanganui in 1995, which created great acrimony in the town and other parts of NZ, points to the difficulties of adjustment for the dominant European culture. Though NZ is not the utopia of racial harmony it is sometimes portrayed to be, there is no denying the genuine attempts by the European community to accommodate Maori aspirations. The overall good relations between both communities continues, and NZ's record on race relations remains strong.

RELIGION

The most common religion in NZ is Christianity. Twenty-four per cent of the population is Anglican (Church of England), 18% is Presbyterian and 15% is Roman Catholic. Other denominations include the Methodist and Baptist churches, the Church of Latter-Day Saints, Jehovah's Witnesses, the Pentecostal church, Assemblies of God and the Seventh-Day Adventist church. Other faiths, including Hinduism, Judaism, Islam and the Baha'i faith, are also represented. The Ratana and Ringatu faiths, with significant followings, are Maori forms of Christianity. About 20% of Kiwis have no religion.

LANGUAGE

New Zealand has two official languages: English and Maori. English is the language you will usually hear spoken, but Maori, long on the decline, is making a comeback. You can use English to speak to anyone in NZ, as Maori people speak English. There are some occasions, though, when knowing a little Maori would be useful, such as visiting a marae, where often only Maori is spoken. Maori is also useful to know since many places in NZ have Maori names.

Kiwi English

Like the people of other countries in the world who speak English, New Zealanders have a unique way of speaking the language. The elision of vowels is the most distinctive feature of Kiwi pronunciation. The NZ treatment of 'fish and chips' – 'fush and chups' – is an endless source of delight for Australians. In the North Island sentences often have 'eh!' attached to the end. In the far south a rolled 'r' is practised widely, a holdover from that region's Scottish heritage – it is especially noticeable in Southland. See the glossary at the back of this book for an explanation of Kiwi English words and phrases.

A *Personal Kiwi-Yankee Dictionary* by Louis S Leland Jr is a fine and often hilarious book of translations and explanations of quirks between the Kiwi and Yankee ways of speaking English. Yanks will love it.

Maori

The Maori have a vividly chronicled history, recorded in songs and chants which dramatically recall the Great Migration and other important events. Early missionaries first recorded the language in a written form by using only 15 letters of the English alphabet, with all syllables ending in a vowel.

This language is related to other Poly-nesian languages (including Hawaiian, Tahitian and Cook Islands Maori) and has some similarity to dialects found in Indonesia. It's a fluid, poetic language, and surprisingly easy to pronounce if you just remember to split each word (and some can be amazingly long) into separate syllables.

Although the Maori language was never dead – it was always used in Maori ceremonial events – in recent years there has been a revival of interest in the language, an important part of the renaissance of Maoritanga. Many Maori people who had heard the language on the marae all their lives but had not spoken it in day-to-day living are studying

---

Place Names

Many place names have a clear Maori influence. These include:

anatoki – axe or adze in a cave; cave or valley in the shape of an axe
awa – river or valley
ika – fish
iti – small
kahurangi – treasured possession; special greenstone
kai – food
kainga – village
kare – rippling
kotinga – boundary line
koura – crayfish
manga – branch, stream or tributary
mangarakau – plenty of sticks; a great many trees
manu – bird
maunga – mountain
moana – sea or lake
moko – tattoo
motu – island
nui – big
o – of
one – beach, sand or mud
onekaka – red-hot or burning sand
pa – fortified village
papa – flat, broad slab
parapara – the soft mud used for dyeing flax
patarua – killed by the thousands; site of early tribal massacres

pohatu – stone
puke – hill
rangi – sky, heavens
rangiheata – absence of clouds; a range seen in the early morning
repo – swamp
roa – long
roto – lake
rua – hole, two
takaka – killing stick for parrot, or bracken
tane – man
tata – close to; dash against; twin islands
te – the
totaranui – place of big totara trees
uruwhenua – enchanted objects
wahine – woman
wai – water
waikaremumu – bubbling waters
waingaro – lost; waters that disappear in certain seasons
wainui – big bay or many rivers, the ocean
waka – canoe
wero – challenge
whanau – extended family
whanga – bay or inlet
whare – house
whenua – land or country

Try a few – Whanga-roa is 'long bay', Roto-rua is 'two lakes', Roto-roa is 'long lake' and Wai-kare-iti is 'little rippling water'. All these names with 'wai' in them – Waitomo, Waitara, Waioru, Wairoa, Waitoa and so on – are associated with water.

However, words don't always mean the sum of their components. If you're interested, *A Dictionary of Maori Place Names* by AW Reed is an excellent reference. ∎

Maori and speaking it fluently. Maori is now taught in schools throughout NZ, some TV programs and news reports are broadcast in Maori and many of the English place names are being renamed in Maori. Even government departments have been rechristened with Maori names: the Inland Revenue Department is also known as Te Tari Taake (the last word is actually *take*, meaning levy, but the department has chosen to stress the long *a* by spelling it '*aa*').

In many places, Maori people have got together to provide instruction in Maori language and culture for young children, so they will grow up speaking Maori and English, and be familiar with Maori tradition. It is a matter of some pride to have fluency in the language. On some marae only Maori can be spoken, to encourage everyone to speak it and to emphasise the distinct Maori character of the marae.

Pronunciation Most consonants in Maori – h, k, m, n, p, t and w – are pronounced much the same as in English. The Maori *r* is a flapped sound with the tongue near the front of the mouth, but not rolled. It is closer to the English *l* in pronunciation.

Two combinations of consonants require special attention. *Ng*, pronounced as in the English suffix '-ing' (singing, running etc), can be used at the beginning of words as well as at the end. It's easy to practise this sound – just say the '-ing' over and over, isolate the *ng* part of it and then practise using it to begin a word rather than end one.

The *wh* also has a unique pronunciation in Maori – generally like a soft English *f*. This pronunciation is used in many place names in NZ, especially in the North Island, where there are place names such as Whangarei, Whangaroa and Whakapapa (all pronounced as if they begin with a soft *f*). There is some regional variation, however: in the region around the Whanganui River, for example, the *wh* is pronounced the same as in English (as in when, why etc).

When learning to speak Maori the correct pronunciation of the vowels is all-important. To really get it right, you will have to hear someone pronounce it correctly. What is written here is only a rough guideline. Each vowel has both a long and a short sound. The approximate sounds are:

a	as in 'large' (long *a*)
a	as in 'but' (short *a*)
e	a sort of combination sound, between 'get' and 'bait' (long *e*)
e	as in 'get' (short *e*)
i	as in 'weed' (long *i*)
i	as in 'it' (short *i*)
o	as in 'pork' (long *o*)
o	a shorter sound than *o*
u	as in 'moon' (long *u*)
u	as in 'foot' (short *u*)

The approximate pronunciation of the diphthongs is:

ae & ai	as in 'sky'
ao & au	as in 'how'
ea	as in 'lair'
ei	as in 'bay'
eo	eh-oh
eu	eh-oo
ia	as in 'beer'
ie	as the 'ye' in 'yet'
io	as the 'ye o' in 'ye old'
iu	as in 'cue'
oa	as in 'roar'
oe	as in 'towing'
oi	as in 'toy'
ou	as in 'sow'
ua	as in 'fewer'

Each syllable ends in a vowel and there is never more than one vowel in a syllable. There are no silent letters.

There are many Maori phrasebooks, grammar books and Maori-English dictionaries if you want to study the language. Learning a few basic greetings is an excellent thing to do, especially if you plan to go onto a marae, where you will be greeted in Maori.

The *Collins Maori Phrase Book* by Patricia Tauroa is an excellent book for starting to speak the language, with sections on every-day conversation and also on how the language is used in a cultural context, such as on a marae. *Say it in Maori* compiled by Alan Armstrong is a pocket-sized book. *He Whakamarama: A New Course in Maori* by John Foster is an introductory language course and has an accompanying cassette.

Other English-Maori dictionaries include the *English-Maori Maori-English Dictionary* by Bruce Biggs, and the authoritative *Reed Dictionary of Modern Maori* by PM Ryan, one of the most authoritative.

Greetings & Small Talk Maori greetings are finding increased popularity; don't be surprised if you're greeted on the phone or on the street with 'Kia ora'. Try these ones:

Haere mai!
     Welcome!
Haere ra.
     Goodbye, farewell. (from the person staying to the one going)

E noho ra.
     Goodbye, farewell. (from the person going to the person staying)
Kia ora.
     Hello, good luck, good health.
Tena koe.
     Hello. (to one person)
Tena korua.
     Hello. (to two people)
Tena koutou.
     Hello. (to three or more people)
Kei te pehea koe?
     How are you? (to one person)
Kei te pehea korua?
     How are you? (to two people)
Kei te pehea koutou?
     How are you? (to three or more people)
Kei te pai.
     Very well, thank you; that is OK.
Ka pai.
     Thank you.

F una & Flor

R COLBORNE, DOC

Kea on southern rata

A s is the case for most Pacific islands, New Zealand's native flora and fauna are, for the most part, not found anywhere else in the world. And, like other Pacific islands, NZ's native ecosystem has been dramatically affected and changed by plants and animals brought by settlers, mostly in the last 200 years. Wild pigs, goats, possums, wallabies, rabbits, dogs, cats and deer have all made their mark on the native wildlife, and blackberries, gorse, broom and agricultural weeds have infested huge areas of land.

New Zealand is believed to be a fragment of the ancient southern continent of Gondwanaland which became detached over 100 million years ago allowing many ancient plants and animals to survive and evolve in isolation. As a result, most of the NZ flora and fauna is indigenous/endemic. It has the world's largest flightless parrot (kakapo), the only truly alpine parrot (kea), the oldest reptile (tuatara), some of the biggest earthworms, the smallest bats, some of the oldest trees, and many of the rarest birds, insects, and plants in the world. The first Maoris brought some rats and the now extinct Maori dog (*kuri*) with them but the only indigenous mammals at that time were bats.

Much of New Zealand's unique flora and fauna has survived, but today over 150 native plants – 10% of the total number of native species – and many native birds are threatened with extinction.

41

FAUNA

Birds

The endemic avifauna of New Zealand is not immense but it evolved in relative peace with very little threat, and no large competitors. So ground-dwelling parrots, kiwis and moas not only survived but thrived.

The balance was altered by the arrival of humans – first the Maori, then the Pakeha, as well as the predatory species which both groups introduced. Many species vanished in a 'blink of the eye' relative to NZ's evolutionary history.

So the NZ bird you *won't* see is the famous moa, a sort of oversized ostrich. Originally there were numerous types and sizes, the largest of them – the giant moas – as tall as 4m. They had been extinct for a few centuries by the time Europeans arrived, but you can see moa skeletons and reconstructions in many NZ museums. Similarly, the huia, with its remarkable differentiation and function in male and female bills, is extinct.

Kiwi

There are three species of kiwi: the brown kiwi (*Apteryx australis*), of which there are several subspecies; the little spotted kiwi (*A. owenii*); and the great spotted kiwi (*A. haastii*). The best known of NZ's birds, the kiwi has become the country's symbol.

R MORRIS, DOC   Great spotted kiwi

It's a small, tubby, flightless bird and, because it's nocturnal, is not easy to observe. Kiwis have defunct vestigial wings, feathers that are more like hair than real feathers, short sight and a sleepy nature, but strong legs. Most active at night, they are fairly lazy, sleeping for up to 20 hours a day. They spend the rest of the time poking around for worms, which they sniff out with the nostrils on the end of their bill.

The female kiwi is larger than the male and much fiercer. She lays an egg weighing up to half a kilogram, huge in relation to her size and about 20% of her body weight. After performing that mighty feat, she leaves the male to hatch it while she guards the burrow. When the kiwi hatches, it associates with its father, completely ignoring its mother.

R MORRIS, DOC   North Island brown kiwi

The kiwi is a threatened species but is not endangered. Brown kiwis can be seen on Stewart Island, at Waitangi State Forest, Little Barrier Island, Fiordland, Paparoa National Park and Mt Otanewainuku near Tauranga. Little spotteds are seen on Kapiti Island and the great spotted kiwi in the Paparoa National Park.

Royal Albatross

These large birds (*Diomedea epomorphora*; Maori: *toroa*) range throughout the world and breed on a number of the island groups to the south and east of NZ. There is one mainland breeding colony, at Taiaroa Head on the Otago Peninsula. They breed from October to September.

GR CHANCE, TRUST BANK, ROYAL ALBATROSS CENTRE
Royal albatross

There is nothing quite like seeing these enormous birds swoop past at eye level. On land, however, they are lumbering creatures. In winter you may see a wandering albatross (*Diomedea exulans*) over NZ waters.

Westland Black Petrel

Near Punakaiki, Westland, are the world's only breeding grounds of the largest burrowing petrel (*Procellaria westlandica*). Westland black petrels come to land only during the breeding season from March to December. Eggs are laid in May and chicks hatch in July/August. From August to November chicks are fed by one of the parents every three days. In December the fledglings leave the colony, not to return for seven years to breed.

Their daily flights to and from feeding grounds are best observed near Punakaiki in the South Island. They fly out individually each morning but congregate offshore for the flight in at dusk. During the breeding season thousands can be seen at the colony en masse. (See the Paparoa National Park section in the West Coast chapter.)

R MORRIS, DOC
Westland black petrel

Fiordland Crested Penguin

This penguin (*Eudyptes pachyrhynchus*; Maori: *pokotiwha*) lives around the south-west coast of the South Island and around Stewart Island. Believed to be the rarest species of penguin in the world, it is timid and identifiable by its yellow crest, which distinguishes it from the yellow-eyed penguin. You are most likely to see these birds when you're travelling down the West Coast in the World Heritage region, especially near the beach by Lake Moeraki, and in Milford Sound.

A MUNN, DOC
Fiordland crested penguins

Little Blue Penguin

The little blue penguin (*Eudyptula minor*; Maori: *korora*) is common in coastal waters from the top of the North Island to Stewart Island. The smallest species of penguin, it can often be seen coming ashore at night, most notably at Oamaru in Otago. Its upper parts are blue, underparts white and bill black. In Australia it is known as the little penguin.

Yellow-Eyed Penguin

The yellow-eyed penguin (*Megadyptes antipodes*; Maori: *hoiho*) is the world's second-rarest species of penguin, its numbers having diminished because of the loss of its coastal habitat. It can still be seen along the south-eastern coast of the South Island (see Oamaru, Otago Peninsula and the Catlins in the Otago chapter). A streaked yellow head and eye are its most conspicuous characteristics.

R MORRIS, DOC
Little blue penguin

Australasian Gannet

This gannet (*Morus serrator*; Maori: *takapu*) is becoming increasingly common around NZ waters and there are three mainland breeding colonies (Farewell Spit in the South Island, and Muriwai and Cape Kidnappers in the North Island). The juveniles migrate to Australia and return in four years to breed. These birds dive from

NZ TOURISM BOARD, DUNEDIN
Yellow-eyed penguin

P BLOK, DOC

Australasian gannet

R MORRIS, DOC

Spotted shags

MF SOPER, DOC

White heron

M WILLIAMS, DOC

Male blue duck

great heights, with wings folded back, to catch fish. Their yellow head against a white body is their most obvious feature. On land they are ungainly but in the air – poetry in motion.

Cormorants or Shags

Cormorants or shags are generally referred to as 'shags' in NZ, and seldom is the distinction made between the seven species. The black shag (*Phalacrocorax carbo novahollandiae*; Maori: *kawau*), NZ's largest shag, is common on inland lakes and along sheltered parts of the coastline. It is seen in flocks near shellbanks and sandspits or perched on rocks.

Three other species of *Phalacrocorax* are found in NZ: the pied shag (*P. varius varius*; Maori: *karuhiruhi*), sometimes referred to as the pied cormorant; the little black shag (*P. sulcirostris*); and the little shag (*P. melanoleucos brevirostris*; Maori: *kawaupaka*). The little black is distinguished from the immature little shag by its long, narrow bill.

A separate genus of shags is *Leucocarbo*. The New Zealand king shag (*L. carunculatus*) is one of the rarest shags in the world and only found in coastal waters on the southern side of Cook Strait. Pink feet are its distinguishing feature. The Stewart Island shag (*L. chalconotus*) is found in coastal waters from the Otago Peninsula to Stewart Island. The spotted shag (*Stictcarbo punctatus punctatus*; Maori: *parekareka*) is recognised by the black spots on its back. It is found in coastal waters around Auckland, in the Marlborough Sounds and on the Otago and Banks peninsulas.

White Heron

This heron (*Egretta alba modesta*; Maori: *kotuku*) is to NZ what the flamingos are to the Galápagos – it is widely spread throughout the world but seen in relatively few numbers in NZ.

It is believed that there are only 200 of these birds in the country. The sole breeding colony is on the banks of the Waitangi-Taona River on the west coast of the South Island (near Okarito) and the best time to see them is from September to November. After that, they scatter to wetlands and tidal lagoons throughout NZ. Their scarcity led the Maori to believe that seeing them was a once-in-a-lifetime experience.

Blue Duck

This endemic and threatened species of duck (*Hymenolaimus malacorhynchos*; Maori: *whio*) is found in fast-flowing rivers of the high country of the North and South islands, but no farther north than East Cape.

You can almost be certain that it is a blue duck if it is seen surfing and feeding in fast-flowing, turbulent water.

Weka

The four subspecies of weka are found in a wide range of habitats, usually in scrub and on forest margins. The North Island weka (*Gallirallus australis greyi*) is found on Kapiti Island, in Northland and Poverty Bay. The western South Island weka (*G. australis australis*) is found in the north and western regions of the South Island, while the eastern South Island weka (*G. australis hectori*) is found in the drier east. The Stewart Island weka (*G. australis scotti*) has been introduced to Kapiti Island. The flightless weka is most active at dusk, but can be seen scrounging during the day in areas where humans leave rubbish.

New Zealand Falcon

The falcon (*Falco novaeseelandiae*; Maori: *kearea*) is distinguished from the larger Australasian harrier by its rapid flight and longer tail. It inhabits high country in the Southern Alps and Fiordland and the forests of Westland and the North Island; it is rarely seen north of the central North Island. It has a rapid 'kek-kek-kek' call and feeds on smaller passerine birds.

Pukeko

This bird (*Porphyrio porphyrio melanotus*) is common throughout the wetter areas of NZ, especially near swamps and lake edges where there are clumps of rushes; it is a good swimmer. Pukekos have very large feet and emit a high-pitched screech when disturbed.

Black Stilt

The Mackenzie country of south Canterbury is the home of the black stilt (*Himantopus novaezelandiae*; Maori: *kaki*), one of the world's rarest wading birds. It is found in swamps and beside braided riverbeds in South Island river systems. A single remnant population of 70 adults (11 breeding pairs) survives in the wild.

The Department of Conservation (DOC) has established a captive breeding and release program for this endangered species near Twizel. About 30 juvenile birds have also been hand-reared (isolated from predators) and will be released into the wild at nine months

RICHARD TIMBURY

Weka

R MORRIS, DOC

Immature New Zealand falcon

CR VEITCH, DOC

Black stilt

R MORRIS, DOC

Pukeko

R MORRISON, DOC
South Island takahe

M SOPER, DOC
New Zealand dotterel

CR VEITCH, DOC
Male wrybill on nest

CR VEITCH, DOC
Kakapo

of age. Public viewing of these captive birds is welcome and guided tours leave daily from the DOC information centre in Twizel. The centre has a specially designed hide, which allows visitors to view the breeding birds without disturbance. It also has displays on the program.

South Island Takahe

The takahe (*Porphyrio mantelli hochstetteri*) disappeared and was believed extinct at the time Europeans arrived in New Zealand. It was found again in the Murchison Mountains of Fiordland in 1948. Its numbers were estimated in 1991 to be about 160, including some in captivity, mostly at Te Anau Wildlife Centre, Mt Bruce National Wildlife Centre and Maud Island in the Marlborough Sounds. It is a flightless bird that feeds on tussock shoots, alpine grasses and fern roots, and whose habitat is tussock and small patches of beech forest.

New Zealand Dotterel

The dotterel (*Charadrius obscurus*; Maori: *tuturiwhatu*) is a threatened species found north of the Bay of Plenty and Raglan and occasionally on Stewart Island. There are accessible breeding colonies on the sandy beaches of the eastern side of the Coromandel. Its nest is a simple sand scrape, sometimes lined with dry grass; the birds nest from August to December. Listen for the 'pweep' when they are disturbed – then back off, as you are too close.

Wrybill

If you fail to recognise this bird with its unique bill with its tip bent to the right, put your binoculars away and take up stamp collecting. Wrybills (*Anarhynchus frontalis*; Maori: *ngutuparore*) migrate within NZ, first nesting in the shingly riverbeds of Canterbury and Otago and then moving north to spend autumn and winter in the warmer estuaries and mudflats of the North Island. The wrybill swings its bill sideways through mud to trap marine organisms from the sludge.

Kakapo

The kakapo *(Strigops habroptilus)* is severely endangered. The remaining populations are on the predator-free Little Barrier and Codfish islands. The largest parrot in the world (males sometimes weigh up to 3kg), it is nocturnal and flightless, although it uses its wings for balance. There are probably only 50 or so birds left. You will only observe this bird with the assistance of DOC.

Kaka

There are two distinct subspecies of kaka. The North Island kaka (*Nestor meridionalis septentrionalis*) inhabits lowland forest in the North Island and forested offshore islands. The South Island kaka (*N. meridionalis meridionalis*) inhabits forest in Nelson, the West Coast, Fiordland and Stewart Island. The South

Island kaka is slightly larger and has a whitish (sometimes grey) crown; both birds are generally bronze in colour with crimson tones on their underparts.

Kea

The kea (*Nestor notabilis*) is a large parrot decked out in unparrot-like drab green except for bright red underwings. They inhabit South Island high-country forests and mountains and are amusing, fearless, cheeky and inquisitive birds. There are plenty of opportunities to observe them at the Fox and Franz Josef glaciers. At the car park at the terminal of the glaciers they hang around waiting for tourist hand-outs. Signs warn you of their destructive tendencies.

Parakeets

There are two species of indigenous parakeet – the yellow-crowned (*Cyanoramphus auriceps auriceps*) and red-crowned (*C. novaezelandiae novaezelandiae*); both are known to the Maori as kakariki. The yellow-crowned is seen high in the canopy of forests in the North, South and Stewart islands, and on many outlying islands. The red-crowned is not likely to be seen on the mainland but rather in the lowland forests on many offshore islands. Both species lay their eggs from October to January and the males help feed the chicks.

Morepork

The endemic owl (*Ninox novaeseelandiae novaeseelandiae*; Maori: *ruru*) is found throughout NZ, with the exception of the east of the South Island. It is the only endemic owl and differs from the introduced little owl (*Athene noctua*) in that it has a rounded head and larger tail. It gets its name from its cry of 'quor-quo', which, with imagination, sounds like 'more pork'. It would probably eat this meat if offered, but favours insects such as moths and wetas, with the occasional side dish of small birds and mice.

CR VEITCH, DOC

Kaka

R MORRIS, DOC

Kea

JL KENDRICK, DOC

Red-crowned parakeet

CR VEITCH, DOC

Morepork

JL KENDRICK, DOC
New Zealand pigeon

MF SOPER, DOC
Rifleman

New Zealand Pigeon

When you first encounter the New Zealand pigeon (*Hemiphaga novaeseelandiae novaeseelandiae*; Maori: *kereru*) in the forest, it is likely that you will be startled by its thumping, whistling wingbeat as it flies from tree to tree.

The bird is widespread in NZ forests and is occasionally seen eating in open fields. A large bird, it is the only endemic species of pigeon. The West Coast, the Catlins, Fiordland and Stewart Island are good places to see them.

Rifleman

There are two subspecies of rifleman, NZ's smallest bird. The South Island rifleman (*Acanthisitta chloris chloris*; Maori: *titipounamu*) is found throughout the island, especially in mountainous beech forests. The North Island rifleman (*A. chloris granti*) is found on the Barrier Islands and in forests south of Te Aroha. The rifleman has a short tail and short, spiralling flight, flitting from tree to tree when feeding.

Rock Wren

This bird (*Xenicus gilviventris*) inhabits subalpine and alpine fields in the South Island. Not much larger than the rifleman, it is recognised by its long legs and curious habit of bobbing up and down. It literally jumps from rock to rock, looking for insects and spiders. During winter it lives in rock crevices under the snow.

Fantail

There are two subspecies of fantail, the North Island (*Rhipidura fuliginosa placabilis*; Maori: *piwakawaka*) and South Island (*R. fuliginosa fuliginosa*); both are common in forests, scrubland and suburban gardens. The South Island fantail has more white on its outer tail feathers. Why do they follow you through the bush? They are attracted to the insects you disturb as you brush past the undergrowth.

R MORRIS, DOC
Rock wren

D CROUCHLEY, DOC
Fantail

Whitehead & Mohua (Yellowhead)

The whitehead (*Mohoua albicilla*; Maori: *popokatea*) inhabits forest and scrubland in the North Island. Like the mohua, its most conspicuous feature is the single colour of the head. It doesn't occur north of Te Aroha, except on Tiritiri and Little Barrier islands.

The mohua (*M. achrocephala*), or yellowhead, is about the size of a house sparrow and fairly hard to find. It is unmistakable in a forest because of its bright yellow head; you'll find it in the ancient forests of Arthur's Pass National Park, Fiordland or the Catlins State Forest Park (all in the South Island). If you see a similar bird in open grassland, it is most likely that it is the introduced yellowhammer.

M F SOPER, DOC
Mohua (yellowhead)

Chatham Island Black Robin

In 1976 there were only seven black robins (*Petroica traversi*) left in the world, all on Little Mangere Island in the Chatham Islands. In the next few years attempts were made to transfer the birds to safer habitats on other islands. These relocations were largely unsuccessful and in 1980 there were only five black robins left. Such a small population would usually spell extinction of the species but, as a last resort, wildlife authorities began a cross-fostering program using endemic warblers and, later, tom tits.

The robins must have sensed that the time for their emergence was right. By the end of summer 1984 there were 19 robins, and at the end of the following summer 38. The tom tits were ideal foster parents. The future of the black robin is no longer bleak and one the most courageous attempts to save an endangered species has succeeded.

D MERTON, DOC
Chatham Island black robin

North Island Kokako

The depletion of its habitat and the introduction of predators have severely endangered populations of the North Island kokako (*Callaeas cinerea wilsoni*). It is a member of the wattle-bird family and distinguished by its blue wattle (the skin hanging from its throat).

It is a weak flier and would most likely be seen bounding and gliding through the unmodified lowland forest of the central North Island, Taranaki, Northland and Coromandel. The South Island kokako, orange-wattled, may well be extinct by now.

R LALBOURNE, DOC
North Island kokako

Tui

The tui (*Prosthemadera novaeseelandiae novaeseelandiae*) is found throughout NZ's forests. Conspicuous by its white throat feathers (hence its common name, 'parson bird'), it has an extremely large repertoire of sounds and can mimic many other birds.

You can see them around much of the country. Pelorus Sound, Ulva Island and Oban (Stewart Island) are particularly fertile spotting grounds.

CR VEITCH, DOC
Tui

Bellbird

Saddleback

Bellbird

The bellbird (*Anthornis melanura melanura*; Maori: *makomako*) is common in both native and exotic forests and is easily identified by its beautiful bell-like call. It is found all over NZ, except Northland. Both sexes have curved honeyeater bills and short tail feathers.

Saddleback

There are two subspecies of saddleback, (you've guessed it by now!) the North Island (*Philesturnus carunculatus rufusater*, Maori: *tieke*) and South Island (*P. carunculatus carunculatus*). The first is found on islands off the East Coast region and Kapiti Island, and the second on small islands off the coast of Stewart Island. They differ in that the North Island saddleback has a narrow, buff-coloured band in front of the saddle. Both are weak fliers and tend to flit through the forest in short rapid movements. You will often be greeted into their territory with their distinctive chattering call.

Marine Mammals

Perhaps one of the greatest delights of a trip to New Zealand, especially the South Island, is a chance to observe the wealth of marine mammals. There are 76 species of whales and dolphins on this globe and New Zealand, as small as it is, is blessed with 35 of these species. Kaikoura is particularly blessed, as nearly half of that number of whales and dolphins have been seen in waters off its shores.

Of the 66 species of toothed whales and dolphins, the largest and the smallest are seen in NZ waters – the sperm whale and the Hector's dolphin. There are also baleen whales, seals and sea lions.

No longer does the blood of these species stain NZ waters. The whales, dolphins, seals and sea lions attract not the bludgeon and harpoon but the entranced

Bottlenose dolphin

eyes of foreign and local observers. The tourist dollars pouring into Kaikoura and elsewhere are worth many times the money made by the previous slaughter for oil and skins.

Humpback Whale

Sadly, sightings of the humpback (*Megaptera nova-engliae)* are rare. There is a group which migrates from Tonga to Antarctic waters via the coast of NZ. Once there were an estimated 100,000 in the world's oceans, now the number is believed to be about 2000. These whales sieve their food through baleen (fine whale-bones), hence their classification as Mysticeti (baleen whales). The males are a little smaller than the females, who usually reach 16m in length and about 50 tonnes in weight. Humpbacks have unique tail fluke patterns, long flippers (up to one third of their length) and throat grooves.

Sperm Whale

This whale (*Physeter macrocephalus*) is the largest of the toothed whales – the male often reaches up to 20m in length, while the female is much smaller with a maximum length of 12m. This is the whale 'watchers' come to Kaikoura to see, or they at least see 10% of the whale – all that is seen from the boats until the whale dives and exposes its tail flukes. Males weigh from between 35 and 50 tonnes and females just over 20 tonnes; both live for up to 70 years. They dive for long periods (around 45 minutes).

They are hard to locate in the open ocean and the only real giveaway is a blow from their spout or their sonar clicks, detected with hydrophones. Because they each require a huge feeding area whales are normally seen singly. The sperm whales have a single blowhole, offset on the left side of their head.

JEFF WILLIAMS

A sperm whale diving

Orca (Killer Whale)

Orca (*Orcinus orca*) are the largest of the dolphins and among the largest predators on earth, feeding on other dolphins and whales, as well as seals, sea birds, penguins and sharks. They are classified as members of the Odontoceti (toothed whales and dolphins). They grow up to 9.5m in length (females 7m) and to 8000kg in weight (females 4000kg).

They are distinguished by their huge dorsal fins, often reaching nearly 2m high. The NZ pods (groups) have not been extensively studied. Both sexes have up to 12 pairs of teeth in each jaw. The orca vocalises both for socialising and to keep contact when foraging for food. There is no record of an unprovoked attack by an orca, as powerful as it is, on humans.

Long-Finned Pilot Whale

Of the two species of pilot whale, the long and short-finned, it is the long-finned (*Globicephala melas*) which is seen the most in NZ waters. This is the species which has become notorious for large-scale 'strandings'. Long-finned pilot whales grow to over 6m in length (females 5.5m) and to 3000kg in weight (females 2500kg).

Bottlenose Dolphin

This is the 'Flipper' dolphin. It is one of the larger species, often reaching 4m in length, although those seen in NZ waters are about 3.5m. The bottlenose (*Tursiops truncatus*) is gregarious but occasionally goes 'solo'.

The bottlenose is the most recorded dolphin in history, probably because of its commensal fishing activities with people. They are also known to feed cooperatively among themselves after encircling a shoal of fish.

Dusky Dolphin

Dusky dolphins (*Lagenorhynchus obscurus*) can reach lengths of over 2m, but usually average 1.6m to 1.8m. What they lack in size they make up for in spirit. These are the most playful dolphins and those which 'dolphin swimming' participants are most likely to encounter. While in the water, you will see them executing head-first re-entry leaps, noisy leaps and somersaults.

They feed on small schooling fish and often round up hundreds of fish in a tight ball, from which members of the pod take turns at feeding. They congregate near the shore from late October to May; after that the pods break up, as winter comes on, and the dolphins move offshore.

Hector's Dolphin

This dolphin (*Cephalorhynchus hectori*) is confined to NZ waters. They have a rather dumpy shape, a distinctive rounded fin and reach a length of only 1.4m. Like the dusky dolphin they feed on small schooling fish, but they stay relatively close to shore year-round. Even

I JISSER, DOC
Stranded long-finned pilot whales

DOLPHIN DISCOVERIES
Common dolphin

though they are the world's rarest dolphin there is a good chance you will see them when travelling in the South Island. Kaikoura, Banks Peninsula and Porpoise Bay (Southland) are all good locations.

Some years back Greenpeace reported that 230 Hector's, about 30% of the population of the area, had been killed in gill nets around Banks Peninsula over a four-year period. Fortunately, DOC has since declared Banks Peninsula a marine mammal sanctuary.

Common Dolphin

This dolphin (*Delphinus delphis*) is the most wide-spread of dolphins, found all around the world. They grow up to 2.5m long, although they are likely to average just over 2m. They dive to nearly 300m and can stay underwater for five or so minutes.

Near Kaikoura, they are often seen alongside pods of duskys, but are considered more an offshore (pelagic) species. Common dolphins are recognised by the golden coloration on their sides. Squid is their favoured food.

F BRUEMMER, DOC
Female Hooker's sea lion

Hooker's Sea Lion

These sea lions *(Neophoca hookeri)* are visitors to the South Island and you are most likely to see them on beaches in the Catlins and on the Otago Peninsula. They are much larger than the NZ fur seal. When a pup was born on the Otago Peninsula in 1995 it was an incredible event – it was believed this hadn't occurred on the mainland for about 700 years.

New Zealand Fur Seal

This seal (*Arctocephalus forsteri*) is most commonly seen in NZ waters. Mature male seals (bulls) are about 2m in length and females (cows) are about 1.6m; their average weight is about 140kg. Once slaughtered for their dense, luxuriant two-layered skins, fur seals are now thriving as a protected species. You can see them basking on rocks, but they will probably enter the safety of the water if you get too close. Fur seals differ from sea lions in that they have a broader bear-shaped head, prominent ears and larger front flippers.

You can swim with them in a number of locations, especially near Kaikoura. They are a popular distraction for sea kayakers in the Abel Tasman National Park region, and you will see them from boats in Milford and Doubtful sounds.

P MOORE, DOC
New Zealand fur seal

Elephant Seal

This seal (*Mirounga leonina*), with a distinctive trunk-like nose, is not commonly seen in NZ. There is a small breeding colony at the Nuggets in the fauna-rich Catlins. The seals are found in their thousands on NZ's subantarctic islands. The male grows to over 4m long and can weigh more than 4000kg, making it the largest seal species.

C ROBERTSON, DOC
Male southern elephant seal

Other Fauna

The **tuatara** (*Sphenodon punctatus*) is a lizard-like reptile dating back to the age of the dinosaurs and perhaps before (260 million years?). Active at night, it eats insects, small mammals and birds' eggs. It also has a rudimentary 'third eye', grows to up to 60cm in length and may live for well over 100 years. The tuatara is found on protected offshore islands (eg The Brothers and Stephens Island in the Marlborough Sounds) for which you need special permission to visit. Some specimens are kept in captivity in places such as the Wellington Zoo, Otorohanga Kiwi House, and Southland Museum in Invercargill (where they have been successfully bred).

New Zealand has no snakes and only one spider that is dangerous to humans, the rare **katipo**, a close relative of the North American black widow and the Australian redback.

If you hear something croaking during the night, you can be sure it's not one of the three species of NZ **frogs** – they lack a vocal sac, so can only produce a high-pitched squeak. They're also remarkable in not having a free-swimming tadpole stage, instead undergoing metamorphosis in a capsule. One species of frog is restricted to the high parts of the Coromandel Peninsula, another to the summit of Stephens Island, Marlborough Sounds, and the other is only found in remnant rainforest in the Marlborough Sounds.

The **sandfly** (*Austrosimulium spp;* Maori: *te namu*) is the most ubiquitous of nuisances and leaves its impression on every traveller to NZ, especially those who venture to South Westland and Fiordland. Only the females bite, needing the blood they take from you to reproduce. The bite is extremely itchy, so do all you can to avoid being bitten in the first place, or try not to scratch the bite.

There are a number of species of **wetas**, quite large invertebrates with a fearsome appearance. The cave weta has long legs and a small body, perfectly adapted for movement on cave walls. In contrast, the bush weta has a large body. But males of both species look fearsome with a large head and snapping mandibles. The wingless alpine weta, also known as the 'Mt Cook flea', lives in rock crevices above the snowline.

There are two species of native (indigenous) **bat**, NZ's only mammals before the arrival of humans – the long-tailed and the short-tailed bat. You may see both species flitting around forest margins at sunset seeking insects. Bats were the only mammals to reach NZ, which was isolated from other land masses prior to mammalian expansion.

All of the introduced species of mammals have done their fair share of damage. Probably the most infamous is the **brush-tailed possum** (*Trichosurus vulpecula*). Also prevalent are the rabbit, chamois, thar, Virginia (white-tailed) deer, red deer, wild pigs and goats.

And **fish**. New Zealand is renowned as an angler's paradise, largely due to the introduction of rainbow and brown trout, perch, carp, Atlantic salmon and quinnat

P MORRISON, DOC

Tuatara

M AUSS, DOC

Giant weta

JL KENDRICK, DOC

Long-tailed bat

salmon to its rivers and estuaries. The native NZ grayling is believed to be extinct.

Sitting at a major confluence of warm and cold ocean currents, NZ's offshore waters have a great variety of tropical and cold-water species of fish, and its thousands of kilometres of coastline are home to tasty crustaceans such as the crayfish (lobster; Maori: *koura*).

FLORA

When the first Europeans arrived in the 1800s, about 70% of NZ was covered in native forest. Much of it was soon cleared for timber (like the large kauri forests) or to make way for farming.

Despite that, NZ still has some magnificent areas of native forest and bush. About 10% to 15% of its total land area is native flora, much of it in protected parks and reserves.

The variety of vegetation in NZ is enormous. Heading south from the giant kauri forests of Northland, there are the luxuriant lowland kohekohe forests of the Bay of Plenty; the rainforests dominated by rimu, various beeches, tawa, matai and rata, and a great range of tree ferns; the podocarp and hardwood forests of the lower parts of the North Island, with its kahikatea, tawa, rimu, rata, and kohekohe; the summer-flowering alpine and subalpine herb fields; and the windswept scrub of the smaller islands.

In the South Island the vegetation changes dramatically as you climb into the mountains. The lowland supplejacks give way to rimu, miro, and then tree ferns at about 800m. Above 1000m the totara, wineberry, fuchsias, rata and kaikomako are gradually left behind, to be replaced by subalpine scrub. At about 1200m the scrub gives way to the tussock grasses and alpine herb fields, and at the extreme heights only some hardy lichens hang on to the exposed rock.

Like the Australian species, most of the 72 NZ orchids are not large or brilliantly coloured; one exception is the beautiful *Earina autumnalis*, which has perfumed cream flowers.

Various introduced species have been planted in large tracts for the timber industry. The most obvious imports are the massive plantations of radiata or Monterey pine and Douglas fir (Oregon).

The Maori language has bestowed marvellous names on some of the native plants of NZ, names that are almost unpronounceable to Pakeha – tawhairauriki, kowhai ngutukaka, whauwhaupaku, mingimingi, hangehange, kumarahou, and pua o te reinga, to name a handful. Some of the English names are nearly as colourful and it's interesting to speculate about their derivation – gum digger's soap, wild Irishman, seven-finger, bog pine, flower of Hades and Dieffenbach's Spaniard.

Dracophyllum species
L MOLLOY, DOC

Mt Cook lily
RICHARD TIMBURY

T LILLEBY, DOC

Mangrove tree

Trees

The progenitors of NZ's two major forest groups, the podocarps and the southern beeches, were found in the ancient supercontinent of Gondwanaland. When the continents drifted apart and the land bridges were eventually lost, over 60 million years ago, NZ's flora evolved in isolation. Of the country's 2000 or so flowering plants, about 75% are only found in New Zealand.

The podocarps are part of an ancient family, Podocarpaceae, which evolved before flowering plants. Fossil pollen indicates that trees very similar to kahikatea and rimu have been here for more than 60 million years. The *Nothofagus* (beech) species found in NZ are very similar to those found in the south of South America, adding weight to the Gondwanaland theory.

For more information, see these books: *Which Native Tree* and *Which Native Fern* by Andrew Crowe and *New Zealand Trees and Ferns* by Murdoch Riley.

Kahikatea

L MOLLOY, DOC

Kahikatea forest

The white pine (*Dacrycarpus dacrydioides*) is NZ's tallest tree, reaching 60m, and maturing to hundreds of years. An adult tree has green scaly leaves. The immature fruit is yellow, ripening into an orange-red berry that bears a seed at its tip – favoured by the native pigeon (kereru) and the Maori. It is not surprising that the Maori also snared many pigeons on this tree.

Kamahi

Pronounced 'car-my', the hardy black birch (*Weinmannia racemosa*) is found throughout NZ, from Auckland down to Stewart Island. It grows to a height of 25m and attains a diameter of over 1m. It has grey bark with white blotches, glossy, dark-green leaves, small lilac-coloured flowers and rusty red seeds.

Kauri

Kauris (*Agathis australis*) only grow in Northland and on the Coromandel Peninsula. These large native trees were once ruthlessly cut down for their excellent

P de JAGER, DOC

Kauri

D CROUCHLEY, DOC

Kamahi in flower

timber and Northland is covered with evidence of the kauri days (see the Northland chapter).

Kauri gum was found to be an important ingredient for making varnish and at one time there were many 'gum diggers' who roamed the forests, poking in the ground for hard lumps of kauri gum.

Kauris grow to 30m and are believed to attain an age of about 2000 years. They have distinctive blotchy mosaic on their bark which feels as good as it looks.

Kowhai

This tree (*Sophora microphylla*) grows to about 11m and has small green leaves and groups of bright yellow flowers. There are three species of this, NZ's national flower, and all are similar in appearance. The tree is found in open areas, near rivers and on the edge of forests. They're popular trees with birds, especially tuis, which seek honey from the flowers.

Matai

The black pine (*Prumnopitys taxifolia*) is one of the most majestic of NZ's trees and is found throughout the North and South islands. It grows to 30m and often with a very wide girth (one easily seen at Lake Ianthe in Westland). Its thick, grey bark falls off to reveal blotchy red patches underneath. It has small, flat leaves, male and female flowers on the same long yellow spikes and produces purple edible berries.

Miro

The miro (*Prumnopitys ferrugineus*), another member of the pine family, grows to 25m. It is found throughout lowland forests in NZ. Very slow-growing, it may take 500 years to reach maturity. It has pointed leaves which could be mistaken for matai.

Pohutukawa

This beautiful tree (*Metrosideros excelsa*) is predominantly found in the north of the North Island but has been successfully planted throughout the South Island. Its magnificent crimson flowers appear in December, making it popularly known as the 'Christmas tree'; thin brown seeds appear in May. It grows to up to 20m in height and 2m across at its base, and is found close to the sea; good places to see it are East Cape and the Coromandel Peninsula.

Rata

The rata is another tree with beautiful crimson flowers like the pohutukawa, except that its leaves are shiny and pointed at both ends. The northern rata (*Metrosideros robusta*), reaching a height of 25m, grows in the North Island and in Nelson in the South Island. Southern rata (*M. umbellata*) predominates in the South Island but is also found in Northland.

This tree starts as a climber (epiphyte) on a host tree which it eventually strangles. When this happens the aerial roots disappear and the tree takes on a gnarled appearance.

J GREENWOOD, DOC
Kowhai flowers

J GREENWOOD, DOC
Pohutukawa

J GREENWOOD, DOC
Pohutukawa flowers

CR VEITCH, DOC
Rata

Rimu

The red pine (*Dacrydium cupressinum*), the most easily recognised of the podocarps, is found throughout NZ in areas of mixed forest. It grows to a height of more than 50m with a girth of about 1.5m. The narrow, prickly leaves drape down and often have little red cones at the tips of the leafy clusters. The fruit appears as a black nut at the tip of the seed.

It was once the most common of the lowland podocarps but its popularity as a building timber has drastically led to its depletion.

Cabbage Tree

The beautiful broad-leafed mountain cabbage tree (*Cordyline indivisa*; Maori: *toii*) is found in moist mountain areas where there is plenty of light. It grows to 20m and, when mature, its stems hang downwards. Captain Cook and his crew gave the cabbage tree its name – the shoots they ate reminded them of cabbage.

Beeches

NZ has several species of beech (*Nothofagus spp*). The silver beech (*Nothofagus menziesii*; Maori: *tawhai*) is found in stands in mixed forest on both islands and occurs in subalpine regions. It grows to up to 30m and has a silver-grey trunk of up to 2m in diameter. The small rounded leaves have serrated edges, the flowers are small and green and brown, and the fruit is small and woody. It is closely related to the other beeches, including the red beech (*N. fusca*) and black beech (*N. solandri var. solandri*).

L MOLLOY, DOC
Rimu

M WILLIAMS, DOC
Cabbage tree

M WILLIAMS, DOC
Cabbage tree flowers

The beautiful mountain beech (*Nothofagus solandri var. cliffortioides*; Maori: *tawhairauriki*) occurs in mountain and subalpine areas from the central North Island plateau to the far south of the South Island. It grows to 22m high in favoured sites (but usually to about 15m) and its trunk is about 1m in diameter. Its leaves are dark and pointy, as opposed to the light leaves of the tawhai. It has small red flowers and woody fruit. It is seen in splendour in Arthur's Pass National Park and near the Lewis Pass.

Totara

This tree (*Podocarpus totara*) has special significance in NZ, as it was favoured for Maori war canoes because of its soft wood. It can grow to be extremely old, attaining an age of 1000 years or more. It has long, pointy leaves, and the male and female cones occur on separate trees. Its red-and-pink stalks attract birds.

Nikau

The nikau (*Rhapalostylis sapida*) is found throughout lowland areas of the North Island and the north of the South Island, as far south as Banks Peninsula. The best place to see nikau is on the north of the West Coast, from Punakaiki to Karamea; their appearance there could fool you into thinking you are in the tropics. They can grow to 10m in height and their fronds were interwoven and used for roofing material by the Maori.

L MOLLOY, DOC

Silver beech forest

L MOLLOY, DOC

Totara

CR VEITCH, DOC

Nikau grove

T LILLEBY, DOC

Ponga

Ferns

One of the prominent features of the NZ bush is the proliferation of tree ferns which are intertwined with the undergrowth. There are over 80 species of fern and five species of soft fern. Perhaps the most interesting are the mauku (hen and chickens fern; *Asplenium bulbiferum*) and the raurenga (Kidney fern; *Trichomanes reniforme*), and the rarest would be the para (horseshoe or king fern; *Marattia salicina*). A common sight on NZ hillsides is the bracken fern (*Pteridium aquilinum*), growing to 3m or more.

The mamaku (black tree fern; *Cyathea medullaris*) is the largest of the NZ ferns and grows to a height of 20m, with the fronds extending to 7m. It grows throughout the country, common in damp forest gullies.

The ponga (silver tree fern; *Cyathea dealbata*) is the national symbol which adorns the jumpers of many of NZ's sports representatives. It grows to up to 10m in height and the fronds, which extend up to 4m, are white on the underside and dull green on the upper side.

The piupiu (crown fern; *Blechnum discolor*) is found throughout the country and is noticeable because its bright green fronds, up to 1.5m in length, often form a significant part of the ground cover. When the frond is turned over it reveals a silvery-grey side. Interestingly, it is the colour of the two types of fronds of *Blechnum* species, one brown and one green, which denotes whether they are fertile or sterile. The brown fronds look as though they are dead or dying, but they produce the reproductive spores. Other ferns produce spores seen as brown spots on the underside of green fronds.

T LILLEBY, DOC

Piupiu

Facts for the Visitor

PLANNING

When to Go

New Zealand's busiest tourist season is during the warmer months from around November to April, with some exceptions – ski resort towns, obviously, will be packed out in winter.

The peak travel time in NZ is the summer school holidays from 20 December to late January. During these holidays, when both New Zealanders and international visitors are out on the road, transport and every type of accommodation is likely to fill up, especially the more economical places, so book as far ahead as possible. It may be more pleasant to visit NZ either before or after this hectic period, when the weather is still warm. To a lesser extent the Easter weekend, Labour Day weekend in late October and the mid-year school holidays are also busy.

The main tourist season for overseas visitors is December, February and March, when accommodation can still be hard to find in the tourist areas, transport services are in demand, tramping trails can be crowded etc. Accommodation should be booked at least a day or two in advance. January and February are the best beach-weather months, but December and March are usually warm and even hot at times in some areas.

November and April are slightly cooler and the beach weather has passed but these months are noticeably quieter and accommodation is easier to find; in many ways they are the best months to travel.

October and May are even quieter and cheaper months to travel. Though snow falls at higher altitudes, the weather is cool but mild in much of the country. The main tourist industry starts to wind down; while most services and activities still operate, a few close.

June to September is a paradise for winter sports enthusiasts but, away from the busy ski areas, some accommodation, transport services and activities close due to lack of patronage. Some of the tramping trails are closed because of snow and ice, as are some of the pass roads. However, NZ is not like some countries where the weather is so miserable that there's no point in going. Winter is cold – freezing in the far south and at higher altitudes – but parts of the North Island, particularly Northland, and the Nelson region of the South Island have mild winters where nights are cold but days can be sunny and pleasant. You'll need warm clothes but there are many things to see and do in NZ year-round.

Maps

Many excellent maps are widely available in New Zealand – everything from street maps and road atlases to detailed topographical maps.

Automobile Association members (or members of affiliate organisations) can present their cards at any AA office and get many free maps. The AA city, town, regional and highway maps are some of the best available. For car touring off the beaten track, pick up a set of its superb 1:350,000 district maps. You don't have to be a member to buy its road atlases and large maps of the North and South islands. The Shell road atlas, Wises maps and road atlases, and the Minimap series are also excellent and available at AA offices and bookshops.

Land Information NZ (formerly known as DOSLI) publishes several excellent map series – street, country and holiday maps, maps of national parks and forest parks, detailed topographical maps for trampers, and more. Its maps are available at Land Information NZ offices, some bookshops and Department of Conservation (DOC) offices.

What to Bring

New Zealand may be a small, compact country but it has widely varying and changeable weather. A T-shirt-and-shorts day at the Bay of Islands can also bring snow and sleet to a high pass in the Southern Alps. In fact, on any of New Zealand's mountains you can often meet T-shirt and snow-gear weather on the same day. So be prepared – if you're tramping, proper gear can save your life. Good camping and sports equipment is available in NZ but is expensive, although it can be hired quite cheaply.

Bring waterproof gear and a warm down sleeping bag even if you're not camping or tramping. A sleeping bag will save a lot of money in budget accommodation where linen costs extra.

Come prepared for New Zealand's 'dress standards' too. An amazing number of restaurants, bars, clubs and pubs have draconian dress rules, so bring a set of 'smart casual' clothes.

New Zealand is a modern, well-organised country and you should be able to find most requirements, from film to pharmaceuticals. Clothing and luxury items are expensive by world standards though, so it is usually cheaper to bring them with you.

SUGGESTED ITINERARIES

New Zealand's nine or 10 big attractions on everyone's itinerary can be seen in under three weeks. But if you have limited time it pays to drop a couple and spend more time discovering the 'real New Zealand' away from the tourist traps. NZ has so much to see and do that it is easy to spend months travelling from one end to the other.

NZ's main drawcard for visitors is its wonderful scenery and rugged outdoors. You can whiz by the scenery, but you need more time to explore the outdoors, either on a tramp or simply to get there if you don't have your own transport.

Most visitors with limited time concentrate on one island. The South Island, with its magnificent Alps and fiords, is the first choice for most visitors. The North Island, however, also has fine scenery, especially the coastal landscape of the north and the volcanoes. Maori culture is overwhelmingly concentrated in the North Island.

The following nine-day itineraries are general suggestions for those with limited time, in which case you should rent a car or take a few tours. Add more days if you're doing the following by public transport. Those with special interests, particularly tramping and other outdoor activities, should also see the Outdoor Activities chapter. Tramping is the highlight of a NZ trip for many visitors.

North Island

Day 1
  Auckland – wander around the central city and waterfront; have dinner in Ponsonby

Day 2
  Auckland – cruise Parnell and visit the Auckland Museum; visit one of the lookout hills or ride to the top of the Sky Tower; take a ferry to Devonport

Day 3
  Auckland to Rotorua via the Waitomo Caves

Day 4 & 5
  Rotorua – visit Whakarewarewa's mud pools, geysers and Maori Arts & Crafts Institute; attend a Maori *hangi* and concert one evening; take a lake cruise; bathe at the Polynesian Spa; or see the Buried Village, Agrodome, Rainbow Springs & Farm Show and take a gondola ride

Day 6
  Rotorua to the Bay of Islands via the east coast

Day 7
  Cruise around the Bay of Islands on the Cream Trip or travel to the Hole in the Rock; visit the Waitangi National Reserve

Day 8
  Swim with the dolphins, sail or fish in the Bay of Islands or visit Cape Reinga and Ninety Mile Beach (this can be done as a day tour by bus but if you're driving you should spend the night somewhere on the west coast)

Day 9
  Return to Auckland via the ancient Waipoua Kauri Forest

To this itinerary you can add the lakeside resort of Taupo and its many outdoor activities (one or two days), the volcanoes and tramps of Tongariro National Park (one to five days) and Mt Taranaki (two to five days), the superb coastal scenery and beaches of Coromandel (two days), the Art Deco city of Napier (one day) and Wellington (one or two days). It's easy to spend extra days in the main destinations.

Tramping highlights include the Lake

Waikaremoana walk (four days), Tongariro Crossing walk (one to two days), Tongariro Northern Circuit (four days). You can canoe on the Whanganui River (four or five days).

The main North Island outdoor activity centres are Taupo, for adrenalin-buzz activities, and the Bay of Islands, for water-based activities; Auckland and Rotorua also offer many activities.

South Island

Day 1
Christchurch – walk or punt along the River Avon; visit the Arts Centre, gardens and museum; see the Wizard in Cathedral Square

Day 2
Christchurch to Mt Cook via Lake Tekapo – take a scenic flight over the Southern Alps

Day 3
Mt Cook to Queenstown via Arrowtown (stop at the Kawarau Bridge for a bungy leap or just to watch)

Day 4 & 5
Queenstown – take a gondola ride; cruise on the lake on the TSS *Earnslaw*; take a Skippers Canyon tour, jet-boat ride or try any of the activities – white-water rafting, tandem skydiving, parapenting etc

Day 6
day trip to Milford Sound (best done by coach tour from Queenstown, but if you're travelling by car leave Queenstown on the afternoon of Day 5 and spend the night in Te Anau)

Day 7
Queenstown to Fox or Franz Josef glaciers, taking the scenic route via the Haast Pass

Day 8
in the morning visit the glaciers (a guided walk is recommended) and in the afternoon continue along the West Coast and spend the night in Hokitika or Greymouth.

Day 9
Greymouth to Christchurch via Arthur's Pass (another stunning route)

The add-ons to this itinerary are numerous. The 'French' village of Akaroa is a good day trip from Christchurch. Then there's Dunedin and the wildlife of the Otago Peninsula (two to three days), the Catlins coastal drive (two days), Doubtful Sound (one day), scenic Wanaka and its many activities (one to two days), whale-watching and dolphin swimming at Kaikoura (one to two days), the wineries and beautiful waterways of Marl-

borough (two days), sunny Nelson and the coastal Abel Tasman National Park (two or more days) and the hot springs at Hanmer Springs (one day).

The South Island is a paradise for trampers. Highlights include the Routeburn (three days), Milford Track (four days), the Abel Tasman Coastal Track (three days walk or kayak). There's the Kepler, Heaphy, Greenstone, Caples, Rakiura and Queen Charlotte walks, as well as a host of less crowded but fine walks.

Queenstown and Wanaka are the main activities centres, with Kaikoura a must if you want to interact with marine mammals, but the South Island has a huge array of options.

HIGHLIGHTS

New Zealand has so many superb physical features that you tend to take the country's beauty for granted after a while. With hundreds of kilometres of rugged coastline and sandy beaches, lush native forest, rugged mountains and volcanoes, abundant wildlife and many other beautiful natural features, NZ has highlights practically everywhere you turn. Here's our list of not-to-be-missed sights or things to do in NZ, from north to south:

- Northland. The best of this region includes the magnificent Waipoua Kauri Forest on the west side, home of some spectacular giant 1500-year-old kauri trees; isolated beaches; the Bay of Islands on the east side; and the trip to Cape Reinga at its tip.
- Visiting museums for an insight into NZ culture, both Maori and Pakeha. The museums at Auckland, Wellington, Christchurch, Hamilton and Wanganui are among the best, but there are also interesting museums in smaller, out-of-the-way places such as the Otamatea Kauri & Pioneer Museum at Matakohe and the Wagener Museum at Houhora, both in Northland. A visit to a marae may be what you'll consider your warmest memory.
- Waitomo Caves, south of Hamilton. The Waitomo area is riddled with limestone caves with stalactites and stalagmites; the Waitomo Cave has the added attraction of a magnificent glow-worm grotto. Waitomo also offers amazing and unusual activities including cave rafting, abseiling expeditions in the caves, horse trekking and more.

- Rotorua, Bay of Plenty. This is one of NZ's most interesting areas. Go there for the thermal activity (boiling mud pools, hissing geysers and eerie volcanic landscapes) and Maori culture (don't miss the night-time Maori concerts or a hangi).
- Tongariro National Park, Central Plateau. A World Heritage area with some of the best mountain/volcano scenery in the country, excellent tramping tracks and skiing in winter.
- Kaikoura, east coast of the South Island. Whale-watching trips and swimming with dolphins have made this place famous, and there are many other activities.
- Fox and Franz Josef glaciers, west coast of the South Island. Nowhere else do glaciers so close to the equator come so close to sea level. Steep mountains and heavy rainfall are the scientific answer but sitting in subtropical rainforest, looking at so much ice, drives the easy answers out of your head. To experience their full majesty, get above them in a plane or helicopter or walk on them.
- Mt Cook, west coast of the South Island. The highest mountain in NZ has fantastic scenery, good walks and skiing, and the mighty Tasman Glacier.
- Queenstown, South Island. This main resort town of the South Island offers a host of activities in a fantastic setting.
- Fiordland, south-west coast of the South Island. Milford Sound is one of the most spectacular NZ fiords (similar to the fiords of Norway), with towering Mitre Peak. You won't forget the dolphins frolicking in the boat's bow wave and the absolute silence of night in this unique wilderness.
- The Catlins, south coast of the South Island. This place is a living museum, with an amazing array of flora and fauna including species not found elsewhere, tracts of rainforest, waterfalls and magnificent kelp-strewn ancient beaches. A must!
- A farmstay. Farm life, especially sheep farming, is what rural NZ is all about.
- Outdoor activities. NZ has some of the finest tramping in the world and great skiing. Activities range from boat trips and sheep station visits to shooting rapids upstream in jet-boats or downstream in inflatables, or you can white-water sledge/raft/boogey board, tandem sky dive, rap jump, mountain bike and bungy jump.

TOURIST OFFICES
Local Tourist Offices
Almost every city or town has a tourist information centre – any town big enough to have a pub and a corner shop seems to have one. Many are united by VIN, the Visitor Information Network, affiliated with the New Zealand Tourism Board (NZTB). These bigger information centres have trained staff, abundant information on local activities and attractions, and free brochures and maps. Staff also act as travel agents, booking almost all activities, transport and accommodation. Use the centres: they are an excellent resource for travellers everywhere in New Zealand.

Their only problem is that they can be understaffed and some are too busy. They may devote most resources to their booking facilities because self-funding is the name of the game in NZ and these centres rely on the 10% they take from bookings. Most operators prefer you to book directly with them. Also, a few (very few) operators don't pay to be listed with the centres, so information on their services may not be available.

Smaller tourist offices funded by local councils or business communities don't have the resources of the VIN network and are usually staffed by volunteers. Though the staff may not take bookings, they can answer most queries and are helpful.

Tourist Offices Abroad
The NZTB, whose role is to promote tourism to NZ, has representatives in various countries around the world. Its head office is at PO Box 95, Wellington, New Zealand (☎ (04) 472 8860) and its overseas offices include:

Australia
(☎ (02) 9247 5222) Level 8, 35 Pitt St, Sydney NSW 2000
Germany
(☎ (69) 9 71 21 10) Friedrichstrasse 10-12, D-60323 Frankfurt am Main
Hong Kong
(☎ 2526 0141) Unit 1601 Vicwood Plaza, 199 Des Voeux Road C
Japan
(☎ (6) 268-8335) Meiji Seimei Sakaisuji Honmachi Building, 2nd Floor, 1-7-15 Minami Honmachi, Chuo-ku, Osaka-shi 541
(☎ (3) 5381-6331) Shinjuku Monolith 21st Floor, 2-3-1 Nishi Shinjuku, Shunjuku-ku, Tokyo 163-09
Singapore
(☎ 738 5844) 391 Orchard Rd, Ngee Ann City, 15th Floor, Tower A, Singapore

UK
    (☎ (0171) 930 1662) New Zealand House, The Haymarket, London SW1Y 4TQ
USA
    (☎ (310) 395-7480) 501 Santa Monica Blvd, No 300, Santa Monica, CA 90401
    (☎ (212) 832-8482) 780 Third Avenue, Suite 1904, New York, NY 10017-2024

VISAS & DOCUMENTS
Passport
Everyone needs a passport to enter New Zealand. If you enter on an Australian or New Zealand passport, or a passport containing an Australian or New Zealand residence visa, your passport must be valid on arrival. All other passports must be valid for at least three months beyond the time you intend to stay in NZ, or one month beyond the intended stay if the issuing government has an embassy or consulate in NZ able to issue and renew passports.

Visas
Australian citizens or holders of current Australian resident return visas do not need a visa or permit to enter New Zealand and can stay indefinitely if they do not have any criminal convictions. Australians do not require a work permit.

Citizens of the UK, and other British passport holders who can show they have permanent UK residency, do not need a visa; they are issued on arrival with a visitor permit to stay for up to six months.

Citizens of the following countries do not need a visa and are given a three-month, extendable visitor permit upon arrival:

Austria, Belgium, Brunei, Canada, Czech Republic, Denmark, Finland, France, Germany, Greece, Iceland, Indonesia, Ireland, Italy, Japan, Kiribati, South Korea, Liechtenstein, Luxembourg, Malaysia, Malta, Monaco, Nauru, the Netherlands, Norway, Portugal, Singapore, South Africa, Spain, Sweden, Switzerland, Thailand, Tuvalu, USA.

Citizens of all other countries require a visa to enter New Zealand, available from any NZ embassy or consular agency. Visas are normally valid for three months.

To qualify for a visitor permit on arrival or for a visa, you must be able to show:

- Your passport, valid for three months beyond the time of your intended stay in NZ.
- Evidence of sufficient funds to support yourself for the time of your intended stay, without working. This is calculated to be NZ$1000 per month (NZ$400 per month if your accommodation has been prepaid) and can be in the form of cash, travellers cheques, bank drafts or American Express, Bankcard, Diners Club, MasterCard or Visa credit cards.
- Onward tickets to a country where you have right of entry, with firm bookings if travelling on special rate air fares.

Evidence of sufficient funds can be waived if a friend or relative in NZ sponsors you (ie will guarantee your accommodation and maintenance). Requirements can change, so always check the situation before departure.

Work & Student Visas It is illegal to work on a visitor permit. If you have an offer of employment, you should apply for a work permit valid for up to three years before arriving in NZ. Permission to work is granted only if no NZ job seekers can do the job you have been offered. A work permit can be applied for in NZ after arrival but, if granted, it will only be valid for the remaining time you are entitled to stay as a visitor.

Citizens of Canada, Japan and the UK aged 18 to 30 years can apply for a Working Holiday Work Visa, which is valid for a 12-month stay. It allows you to work while travelling around the country, but must be applied for in your home country before you enter NZ; it is only issued to those seeking a genuine working holiday, not for permanent work.

You can study on a visitor permit if it is one single course not more than three months long. For longer study, you must obtain a student permit.

Visa Extensions Visitor permits can be extended for stays of up to nine months, if you apply for further permits and meet normal requirements. 'Genuine tourists' and a few other categories of people can be granted stays of up to 12 months.

Apply for extensions at any New Zealand Immigration Service office in Auckland, Manukau, Hamilton, Palmerston North, Wellington, Christchurch and Dunedin.

Be careful not to overstay which will result in you being subject to removal from the country. Extensions are easy to get provided you meet the requirements.

Documents

No special documents other than your passport are required in New Zealand. Since no vaccinations are required to enter New Zealand, an international health certificate is not necessary.

Bring your driver's licence. A full, valid driver's licence from your home country is all you need to rent and drive a car in NZ. Members of automobile associations should bring their membership cards – it can be useful if recognised by the AA.

An ISIC card (International Student Identity Card) entitles you to certain discounts, particularly on transport. Even better is an International Youth Hostel card (YHA card), which is well worth having even if you don't intend staying in hostels. This card provides a 50% discount on domestic air travel and a 30% discount on major buslines, plus dozens of discounts on activities. A VIP Backpackers Card offers the same benefits and can be bought in NZ or Australia from VIP hostels.

EMBASSIES & CONSULATES
NZ Embassies & Consulates

New Zealand embassies and consulates in other countries include:

Australia
    (☎ (02) 6270 4211; fax 6273 3194) High Commission, Commonwealth Ave, Canberra, ACT 2600
    (☎ (02) 9247 1999; fax 9247 1754) Consulate-General, 14th Floor, Gold Fields Building, 1 Alfred St, Circular Quay, Sydney, NSW 2000/GPO Box 365, Sydney, NSW 2000

Canada
    (☎ (613) 238-6097; fax 238-5707) High Commission, Suite 727, Metropolitan House, 99 Bank St, Ottawa Ont K1P 6G3
    (☎ (604) 684-7388; fax 684-7333) Consulate-General, Suite 1200-888 Dunsmuir St, Vancouver BC V6C 3K4

France
    (☎ 01 45 00 24 11; fax 01 45 01 26 39) Embassy, 7ter, rue Léonard de Vinci, 75116 Paris

Germany
    (☎ (228) 22 80 70; fax 22 16 87) Embassy, Bundeskanzlerplatz 2-10, 53113 Bonn
    (☎ (40) 4 42 55 50; fax 4 42 555 49) Consulate-General, Heimhuderstrasse 56, 20148 Hamburg

Ireland
    (☎ (1) 676 2464; fax 676 2489) Consulate-General, 46 Upper Mount St, Dublin 2

Netherlands
    (☎ (70) 346 9324; fax 363 2983) Embassy, Carnegielaan 10, 2517 KH The Hague

UK
    (☎ (171) 930 8422; fax 973 0370) High Commission, New Zealand House, The Haymarket, London SW1Y 4TQ

USA
    (☎ (202) 328-4848; fax 667-5227) Embassy, 37 Observatory Circle NW, Washington, DC 20008
    (☎ (310) 207-1605; fax 207-3605) Consulate-General, Suite 1150, 12400 Wilshire Blvd, Los Angeles, CA 90025
    (☎ (206) 525-9881; fax 525-0271) Consulate, 6810 51st Ave NE, Seattle, WA 98115

Embassies & Consulates in NZ

Foreign embassies in NZ are in Wellington (see the Wellington chapter for details). Many countries also have consulates in Auckland and Christchurch (see the Auckland chapter and the Christchurch section of the Canterbury chapter).

CUSTOMS

Customs allowances are 200 cigarettes (or 50 cigars or 250g of tobacco), 4.5L of wine or beer and one 1125ml bottle of spirits or liqueur.

Goods up to a total combined value of NZ$700 are free of duty and GST. Personal effects are not normally counted. If you do not exceed your $700 passenger concession, and do not have any alcohol or tobacco in your possession, you can import two extra bottles of duty-free liquor.

As in most places the customs people are fussy about drugs.

MONEY
Costs

While it is possible to travel quite economically in New Zealand, it's just as easy to spend up big. If you stay in hostels, it will cost around $14 to $20 per person, per night. In motor camps, costs are about $20 for singles or $30 for two in simple cabins, and about half that for camping. Basic DOC camp sites are even cheaper. Guesthouses, farmstays, homestays and B&Bs charge around $70 a night for two, but it *can* be that much per person. Cheaper hotels charge about $35/50 for singles/doubles, while motels start at $60 to $70 for two.

Hostels, motor camps and motels have kitchens for guests' use, allowing you to cook – a big money saver. Eating out can cost anywhere from around $5 for a simple takeaway meal to around $50 or $60 for two for dinner at most medium-priced restaurants.

The average long-distance (three to five-hour) bus ride might cost around $30, or 30% less with an approved Backpacker/YHA card. For a few people travelling together, hiring or buying a car may be just as economical. Hitchhiking and cycling are popular and free ways of getting around.

Some of the many outdoor activities which attract people to NZ cost nothing, such as tramping, swimming and birdwatching. But the activities industry is huge and activities can end up being a major part of the travel budget.

Carrying Money

Travellers cheques are always the safest way to carry money and their exchange rate is slightly better than that for cash in New Zealand. American Express, Visa, Master-Card and Thomas Cook travellers cheques are widely recognised.

Credit cards are also a convenient way to carry money, if you avoid interest charges by always keeping your account in the black

and your bank doesn't charge exorbitant fees. Get a card with a PIN number attached for ATM withdrawals.

For long stays, it may be worth opening a bank account. Westpac and the Bank of New Zealand (BNZ) have many branches around the country and you can request a card for 24-hour ATM access.

ATMs & Credit Cards

Some banks allow ATM access to overseas savings accounts, via networks such as Cirrus and Plus, but check with your bank before departure to see if this facility will be available to you in NZ. You can get cash advances over the counter at banks or through the many 24-hour ATMs that display Visa or MasterCard symbols.

Visa, MasterCard and Australian Bankcard credit cards are the most widely recognised and are honoured by thousands of retail outlets. American Express is less widely recognised – for cash you must go to one of their offices in the main cities. Money can be sent by telegraphic transfer, bank to bank, or is more easily done through a credit card.

Currency

New Zealand's currency is dollars and cents. There are $5, $10, $20, $50 and $100 notes and 5c, 10c, 20c and 50c, $1 and $2 coins. Unless otherwise noted, all prices quoted in this book are in NZ dollars.

There are no limitations on the import or export of foreign currency. Unused NZ currency can be changed to foreign currency before you leave the country.

Currency Exchange

The currencies of Australia, the UK, USA, Germany and Japan are all easily changed, and at consistently good rates, in New Zealand. Most banks, found throughout the country, will exchange these and up to 30 other currencies, but exchange rates may be slightly lower for less frequently changed currencies.

Australia	A$1	=	NZ$1.16
Canada	C$1	=	NZ$1.24
France	1FF	=	NZ$0.30
Germany	DM1	=	NZ$0.99
Ireland	IR£1	=	NZ$2.53
Japan	¥100	=	NZ$1.37
Singapore	S$1	=	NZ$1.22
United Kingdom	UK£1	=	NZ$2.97
United States	US$1	=	NZ$1.78

Changing Money

Banks are open from 9 am to 4.30 pm from Monday to Friday. Exchange rates may vary a few cents between banks. At most banks there's no service charge for changing travellers cheques.

Moneychangers work in the major tourist areas and at airports. They have slightly longer weekday hours and are usually open on Saturday and sometimes Sunday. Rates may be competitive but are usually less than the banks. Thomas Cook offices have competitive rates and change a wider variety of currencies than most banks.

Tipping

Tipping is becoming more widespread, although many Kiwis still regard it as a rather odd, foreign custom and something to be discouraged. Nevertheless, it is on the increase, principally in the major tourist centres. You should tip in a restaurant (not in a simple cafe) if you feel you have received exceptional service. The tip should be about 5% to 10% of the bill.

Taxes

GST (Goods and Services Tax) adds 12.5% to the price of just about everything in New Zealand. Prices quoted almost invariably include GST, but look out for any small print announcing that the price is GST exclusive, such as for hire cars and some top-end hotels.

POST & COMMUNICATIONS
Post

NZ post shops are open from 9 am to 5 pm on weekdays. You can have mail addressed to you care of 'Poste Restante, CPO' in whichever town you require (CPO stands for Chief Post Office). Mail is usually held for 30 days.

Within New Zealand, standard post costs 45c for medium letters and postcards, and 80c for letters larger than 120mm by 235mm; delivery time is two days between major centres, and a bit longer for rural areas. Or there's Fast Post, promising next-day delivery between Auckland, Wellington and Christchurch, and two-day delivery for rural areas. Fast Post costs 80c/$1.20 for medium/large letters. In both cases the maximum thickness is 20mm.

For international mail, use Fast Post; just affix a Fast Post sticker or use a Fast Post envelope. This way it costs $1 to send postcards anywhere in the world.

The cost and average delivery times for airmail international letters with a maximum weight/thickness of 200g/20mm (prices given are for medium/large/extra large letters) to various destinations are:

Australia and South Pacific islands
    $1/1.50/3, three to eight days delivery
North America and East Asia
    $1.50/2.50/5, four to 10 days delivery
Europe
    $1.80/3/6, six to 12 days delivery
Rest of the world
    $1/4/7, six to 12 days delivery

Telephone

The phone system has been deregulated and opened to competition. Telecom still operates the public phone and local call networks, and the benefits of competition only affect NZ subscribers. From private phones, local calls cost 20c for unlimited time or are free for those subscribers who pay higher rent, while rates for long- distance calls through the various suppliers are competitive but constantly changing.

The big losers are those forced to use pay phones. Local calls cost a minimum of 39c, then 20c per minute or part thereof, out-of-area calls start at around 50c per minute, international calls have a minimum charge of $3 and the cost builds up at an alarming rate.

Almost all pay phones in NZ are now card-operated. Card phones accept $5, $10,

New Zealand Telephone Codes

$20 or $50 cards, available from visitor information centres, newsagencies, hostels and larger hotels or shops displaying the lime-green 'phonecards available here' sign. The larger cities have some credit-card phones. Long-distance and international calls can be dialled directly from pay phones. For international calls dial ☎ 00, then the country code, area code and number.

To avoid the high charges of making long-distance calls from public phones, use the various callcards available. These prepaid phonecards (to values of $10 to $50) offer discounted rates. Usually, you dial an ☎ 0800 (freephone) number and then follow the instructions before making overseas calls. Companies offering the cards include Eziphone and Smartel. The cards are available from many hostels and some retail outlets.

Many places to stay also have card phones for guests which you can receive calls on. You can make a short call to someone long

distance or overseas and get them to ring you straight back. Alternatively, you could make a reverse-charge call (see under the Reverse-Charge & Country Direct heading in this section).

Another option for long-distance telephone calls is the call-back service. Dial ☎ 013 before dialling the number (within NZ) and an operator will ring back immediately after you hang up to tell you how much it cost. For international price-required calls, dial ☎ 0160 rather than ☎ 00 to begin the call. This service costs $2.80 on top of the price for the call, but is useful because hotels may allow you to place long-distance calls from their telephones if you pay on the spot.

Emergency calls are not charged. Toll-free numbers in NZ are preceded by the ☎ 0800 code, but card phones may require you to insert a card, even though the call is not charged. Mobile phone numbers are preceded by the ☎ 025 code and are charged at a higher rate.

Useful numbers include:

☎ 64 – New Zealand country code
☎ 00 – international direct dial access code
☎ 010 – local and national operator
☎ 018 – directory assistance in NZ
☎ 0172 – international directory service
☎ 0170 – reverse-charge international calls
☎ 111 – emergency (police, ambulance, fire brigade)

NZ Area Codes All cities and towns on the South Island and Stewart Island have the ☎ 03 area code. The North Island has various regional area codes: ☎ 09 in Auckland and Northland, ☎ 07 in the Coromandel Peninsula, Bay of Plenty, Waikato and Central Plateau, ☎ 06 in the East Coast, Wanganui, Manawatu and Taranaki regions, and ☎ 04 in and around Wellington. If dialling within a region you still have to use the area code between towns, often for a town just a few kilometres down the road.

Reverse-Charge & Country Direct Dial ☎ 0170 for an operator-connected, reverse-charge international call, which will cost you $4.84.

The toll-free Country Direct service enables you to phone directly to an operator in an overseas country for reverse-charge calls, bypassing the NZ operator. The connection fee and call is then charged to the number you dial. Details, including Country Direct numbers, are listed in the front of telephone directories or from the NZ international operator. The access number varies, depending on the number of phone companies in the country you call, but is usually ☎ 000 9 (followed by the country code).

Telecards and call-back services from your telephone company, allowing you to make calls to anywhere in the world and have them charged to your home account, usually work out cheaper than Country Direct dialling. Inquire before you leave.

Fax

Many hotels, motels and even hostels have fax machines. Most centres of any size have a business offering fax services, as do post shops. The charge to send a fax is about $5, plus the telephone toll charges. Receiving a fax costs around $1 per page.

Email & Internet Access

Many businesses are on the Internet and more are jumping on the bandwagon, which means that you can send and receive email at some hotels, hostels and even camping grounds. A small fee usually applies. Checking your own email box is trickier, unless you or the owner of the terminal knows how to reconfigure the software and can change the settings back when you have finished. Various computer stores and Internet providers in even the smaller cities offer email services, which are usually more expensive. Internet cafes are rare.

INTERNET RESOURCES

A Web search on New Zealand will turn up dozens of useful sites and hundreds of useless ones, most of them advertising for the tourist industry. Good starting points are:

- www.govt.nz/
  New Zealand Government Online, with general information on the country, government services and regulations (immigration and census figures)
- www.lincoln.ac.nz/libr/nz/
  AraNui, a great links site to just about everything
- url.co.nz/nzl.html
  Destination New Zealand, with extensive lists of NZ travel resources; it's the best place to start looking for info on accommodation, transport, activities etc
- www.nztb.govt.nz/
  the New Zealand Tourism Board's site with highlights, itineraries, events, links etc
- nz.com/NZ/
  Akiko has news, general information and lots of links
- www.whitepages.co.nz/
  telephone directories for the country
- soc.culture.new-zealand
  the usual newsgroup trivia, but the soc.culture.new-zealand FAQ has extensive and interesting general information and cultural insights

CD ROM

One of the more interesting CD ROMs on NZ is the *TVNZ New Zealand Encyclopedia*, covering history, culture and many other topics, with over 2300 illustrations, 54 maps and 20 minutes of videos. Of interest to birdwatchers, *Birds of New Zealand* covers all NZ birds. Other CD ROMs include *Coast to Coast*, an interactive tourist guide.

Order them from New Zealand Video Tours (☎ 09 415 9343; www.nzvt.co.nz), PO Box 34-422, Auckland 10.

BOOKS

For details of New Zealand literature, including poetry, children's books and contemporary Maori and Pacific islander literature, see the Arts section in the Facts about the Country chapter. Whitcoulls and London Bookshops are two large chains with a wide variety of books, including sections specialising in NZ books. The larger cities have a good selection of other general and specialist bookshops. Most books are published in different editions by different publishers in different countries, but most of the books listed in this section will be available in NZ bookshops.

Lonely Planet

In *Tramping in New Zealand* Jim DuFresne describes nearly 50 walks in all parts of New Zealand.

Guidebooks

Innumerable specialist travel guides have been written about tramping, skiing, cycling, scuba diving, surfing, fishing, birdwatching and many other activities. See the Outdoor Activities chapter for details.

The *Mobil New Zealand Travel Guides* by Diana & Jeremy Pope are excellent resources for history, background information and interesting stories about the places you visit. They come in two volumes – *North Island* and *South Island*.

The Reader's Digest *Guide to New Zealand* was written by Maurice Shadbolt, one of the country's pre-eminent authors, who provides wonderful insights into New Zealand's history, culture and attractions. The coffee-table format is packed with wonderful photographs by Brian Brake, as well as historical pics.

History

A History of New Zealand by Keith Sinclair is a readable and entertaining general history, from the Maori account of the creation to the present. *The People and the Land – Te Tangata me Te Whenua: An Illustrated History of New Zealand 1820-1920* by Judith Binney, Judith Bassett & Erik Olssen is also good.

The *New Zealand Historical Atlas: Visualising New Zealand* – Ko Papatuanuku e Takoto Nei – is the most exciting NZ publication (1997) for years. Numerous colour spreads cover the prehistory, history and demography of the islands in detail. The text is easy to read and the graphs, diagrams, maps and illustrations highlight interesting aspects of the country's development – Maori migration, the kauri harvest, the sheep-meat industry, sport and leisure, women in paid work, suburban streets etc. The atlas is well worth the $74.95 price tag.

Two Worlds: First Meetings between Maori and Europeans 1642-1772 by Anne Salmond is an account of the first points of contact between the Maori and the European explorers. It's a fascinating anthropological history telling the story as it was experienced by both sides.

The 19th century land wars between Europeans and Maori are looked at in a new and interesting way in *The New Zealand Wars* by James Belich. Christopher Pugsley's *Anzac* is a pictorial account of NZ troops' involvement in the ill-fated Gallipoli campaign in 1915 during WWI, an important part of the national psyche.

Maori: A Photographic and Social History by Michael King is an excellent illustrated history of the Maori people.

The Old-Time Maori by Makereti is an important historical document. First published in London in 1938, the book was the first ethnographic account of the Maori people written by a Maori scholar. It's fascinating reading.

One of the most controversial elements of NZ history is the Treaty of Waitangi. Many books have been written about the treaty and the debates surrounding it. One of the best is *The Treaty of Waitangi* by Claudia Orange. Other books about the treaty by the same author include *An Illustrated History of the Treaty of Waitangi*.

Several books have been written about the Greenpeace ship, *Rainbow Warrior*, sunk by the French government in Auckland Harbour in 1985. *Making Waves: The Greenpeace New Zealand Story* by Michael Szabo tells the story of this and other Greenpeace activities in NZ and the Pacific, with lots of colour illustrations.

Biography

Some of the most fascinating history has been told through biography. *The Dictionary of New Zealand Biography* is a multivolume collection of hundreds of short NZ biographies.

A People's History: Illustrated Biographies from The Dictionary of New Zealand Biography, Volume One, 1769-1869 edited by WH Oliver contains over 100 biographies of early New Zealanders, illustrated by historic photos.

Three biographies about Maori elders are particularly interesting. *Eruera: The Teachings of a Maori Elder* by Eruera Stirling, as told to Anne Salmond, won the NZ Wattie Book of the Year Award, one of NZ's highest literary awards. *Te Puea* by Michael King tells the story of Te Puea Herangi, one of the most influential women in modern Maori history. *Whina*, also by King, tells the story of Whina Cooper, another important Maori figure, who organised her first public protest at 18 and welcomed an international audience to the XIV Commonwealth Games in Auckland in 1990 at 95.

The Book of New Zealand Women – Ko Kui Ma Te Kaupapa edited by Charlotte Macdonald, Merimeri Penfold & Bridget Williams is a large anthology of over 300 biographical essays of NZ women – a great resource.

Contemporary Autobiography Check out *The Life and Times of a Good Keen Man* by Barry Crump. One of New Zealand's favourite characters, Barry Crump is an alcoholic, writer and rugged adventurer, more the Bukowski than the bastard of the bush. He is the author of many popular books including *A Good Keen Man* (1960), *Hang On a Minute Mate* (1961) and many others published after them, which still sell even after all these years.

Being Pakeha by Michael King is the autobiography of one of New Zealand's foremost Maori historians, who is a Pakeha. *An Autobiography* by the poet Lauris Edmonds is a frank account of an emergent writer's life.

Mihi Edwards is a contemporary Maori elder who writes readable books telling the story of her life growing up Maori in Pakeha culture and how they were punished if they spoke their language in school. Her books include *Mihipeka: Early Years* and *Mihipeka: Time of Turmoil*.

Maori Culture
In recent years New Zealand has experienced a renaissance of interest in Maori culture, a subject covered by many excellent books. Language books are mentioned in the Language section of the Facts about the Country chapter.

Te Marae: A Guide to Customs & Protocol by Hiwi & Pat Tauroa is a useful little 'how-to' book for non-Maori visiting a marae for the first time.

Hui: A Study of Maori Ceremonial Gatherings by Anne Salmond is an excellent, more scholarly book about Maori gatherings on the marae with insights into Maori culture.

Te Ao Hurihuri: Aspects of Maoritanga edited by Michael King is a collection of writings on many aspects of Maori culture, written by a number of respected Maori authors.

Tikanga Whakaaro: Key Concepts in Maori Culture by Cleve Barlow is a book in English and Maori in which the author explains 70 terms central to Maori culture.

Maori Customs and Crafts compiled by Alan Armstrong is only a small book in the Pocket Guide series but describes and illustrates many different Maori customs and crafts.

A number of good books have been written about the rich legends, myths and stories of the Maori people. An excellent one is the illustrated *Maori Myths and Tribal Legends* retold by Antony Alpers. Another smaller volume is the illustrated *Maori Myth and Legend* by AW Reed.

Traditional Maori Stories, introduced and translated by Margaret Orbell, is a fine book of Maori stories in English and Maori.

Chatham Islands
Moriori: A People Rediscovered by Michael King tells about the Moriori people of the Chatham Islands and debunks some of the common notions about them. King also wrote *A Land Apart: The Chatham Islands of New Zealand*, with photographs by Robin Morrison, which is a good book of photographs, history and stories of these remote islands.

Photography

There are innumerable coffee-table books of NZ photographs. You'll find at least a dozen in almost any large bookstore in NZ, with titles like *New Zealand – the Glorious Islands*, *New Zealand – A Special Place*, *Beautiful New Zealand* and so on. Two of New Zealand's best photographers, Craig Potton and Robin Morrison, have published a number of books.

Art & Architecture

There are plenty of high-quality art books on NZ's well-known artists and Maori arts and crafts. The magnificent *Taonga Maori: A Spiritual Journey Expressed through Maori Art* by the Australian Museum (Sydney) has colour photographs and insightful text on some of the best Maori art.

Architecture is not what people usually think of when contemplating New Zealand, but the book *The New Zealand House* by Michael Fowler (architect) & Robert van de Voort (photographer) is a fascinating presentation of an amazing variety of NZ home architecture, with colour photos of everything from grand Victorian palaces to homemade rolling caravan inventions.

Cartoons

No overview of NZ publishing could be complete without mention of New Zealand's favourite comic strip, *Footrot Flats* by Murray Ball. Many books have been published of the adventures of the focal character, The Dog, a mongrel black-and-white sheepdog, and his master Wal, the farmer. It's a delightful look into rural NZ farming life as told from the sheepdog's point of view.

FILMS

See the Arts section of the Facts about the Country chapter for details of NZ films.

NEWSPAPERS & MAGAZINES

There is no national paper although the *New Zealand Herald* (Auckland), the *Dominion* (Wellington) and the *Press* (Christchurch) have wide circulations. Backing up the city newspapers are numerous local dailies, some OK, some not. The closest to a national weekly newsmagazine is the *Listener*, an excellent publication which provides a weekly TV and radio guide, plus articles on the arts, social issues and politics. International publications such as *Time* and *Newsweek* are available almost anywhere.

RADIO & TV

There are four commercial TV stations (only a couple may be received in some areas) plus Sky, a subscriber television service with news, sports, movie and documentary channels.

Many regional or local commercial stations broadcast on the AM and FM bands.

PHOTOGRAPHY & VIDEO

Photographic and video supplies, equipment and maintenance are all readily available in New Zealand, but prices are generally higher than in other countries. Video recorders in NZ operate on the PAL system.

Fuji and Kodak are the most popular films, with Agfa also available. Film and processing prices can vary, so it pays to shop around. For prints, one-hour photo developing shops are all over NZ. Slide film is very expensive and processing usually takes about a week.

The native bush in New Zealand is dense and light levels can be very low – 400 ASA film will help.

TIME

Being close to the international date line, New Zealand is one of the first places in the world to start the new day. New Zealand is 12 hours ahead of GMT (Greenwich Mean Time) and UTC (Universal Time Coordinated) and two hours ahead of Australian Eastern Standard Time.

In summer NZ observes daylight-saving time, where clocks are put forward by one hour on the last Sunday in October; clocks are wound back on the first Sunday of the following March. Ignoring daylight-saving time, when it is noon in NZ it is: 10 am in Sydney, 9 am in Tokyo, 8 am in Singapore, midnight in London, 8 pm the previous day in New York and 5 pm the previous day in San Francisco.

ELECTRICITY

Electricity is 230V, 50Hz, as in Europe and Australia; Australian-type flat three-prong plugs are used. Appliances designed for DC supply or different voltages need a transformer.

WEIGHTS & MEASURES

New Zealand uses the metric system, but you will still encounter vestiges of the imperial system, in use until 1967. If you go sky diving they'll take you up to 9000ft rather than 2743m and if you ask someone how much they weigh, the answer may be in kilograms, pounds or stones (a stone is 14 pounds).

LAUNDRY

Laundrettes are rare in NZ, but virtually every accommodation place provides a coin-operated washing machine and dryer, with which you can wash a full load of clothes for about $2 and dry it for $2, using coins or tokens.

HEALTH

There are no vaccination requirements to enter New Zealand. New Zealand is largely a clean, healthy, disease-free country with few health concerns. Medical attention is of a high quality but the state-subsidised health system has long since disappeared. A visit to a general practitioner costs around $35 and hospital services are expensive – take out travel insurance with decent medical coverage.

The same health precautions apply as in other developed countries. Of extra note for trampers in NZ is the presence of giardia in some lakes, river and streams, but it is rare. There is also a risk of catching amoebic meningitis if you bathe in natural hot thermal pools.

New Zealand has no dangerous animals, no snakes and only one poisonous spider (the rarely encountered katipo).

Trampers face the usual health dangers,

especially hypothermia. Many of New Zealand's most popular tramps are in alpine conditions and walkers must be well-equipped against the rain and cold. Good equipment can save your life, as can good advice. Consult DOC before undertaking walks and heed its warnings.

Predeparture Preparations

Health Insurance A travel insurance policy to cover theft, loss and medical problems is a good idea. There is a wide variety of policies and your travel agent will have recommendations. The international student travel policies handled by STA or other student travel organisations are usually good value. Check the small print: some policies specifically exclude 'dangerous activities', which can include scuba diving, motorcycling, even tramping. If such activities are on your agenda you don't want that sort of policy.

You may prefer a policy which pays doctors or hospitals direct rather than you having to pay on the spot and claim later. If you have to claim later make sure you keep all documentation. Some policies ask you to call back (reverse-charge) to a centre in your home country where an immediate assessment of your problem is made.

Check if the policy covers ambulances or an emergency flight home. If you have to stretch out you will need two seats and somebody has to pay for them!

Medical Kit A small, straightforward medical kit is a wise thing to carry. A possible kit list includes:

- aspirin or paracetamol – for pain or fever
- antihistamine (such as Benadryl) – useful as a decongestant for colds and allergies, to ease the itch from insect bites or stings, or to help prevent motion sickness
- rehydration mixture – for treatment of severe diarrhoea; this is particularly important if you're travelling with children
- antiseptic such as povidone-iodine (eg Betadine), which comes as a solution, ointment, powder or impregnated swabs – for cuts and grazes
- calamine lotion, antihistamine or anti-itch cream – to ease irritation from bites or stings

- bandages and adhesive plasters – for minor injuries
- scissors, tweezers and a thermometer (mercury thermometers are prohibited by airlines)
- insect repellent (for those sandflies), sunscreen, chapstick
- water purification tablets or another water purification system if you'll be camping in the bush

Health Preparations Make sure you're healthy before you start travelling. If you are embarking on a long trip make sure your teeth are OK.

If you wear glasses take a spare pair and your prescription. Losing your glasses can be a real problem, although in NZ new spectacles can be made up quickly and competently (but not cheaply).

If you require a particular medication take an adequate supply, as it may not be available locally. Take the prescription, with the generic rather than the brand name (which may not be available), as it will make getting replacements easier. It's a wise idea to have the prescription with you to show you legally use the medication – it's surprising how often over-the-counter drugs from one country are illegal without a prescription or even banned in another.

Immunisations You don't need any vaccinations to visit New Zealand. It's always a good idea to keep your tetanus immunisation up to date no matter where you are – boosters are necessary every 10 years and protection is highly recommended.

Other Considerations

Water Tap water is clean, delicious and safe to drink in New Zealand. Water in lakes, rivers and streams is often OK, but the parasitic protozoan *Giardia lamblia* has been found in these sources. DOC can advise on the occurrence of giardia in national parks and forest areas it administers. Giardia is not common but, to be certain, water from these sources should be purified before drinking.

Water Purification The simplest way of purifying water is to boil it thoroughly. Vigorously boiling for five minutes should be satisfactory; however, at high altitude water boils at a lower temperature, so germs are less likely to be killed.

Simple filtering will not remove all dangerous organisms, so if you can't boil water treat it chemically. Chlorine tablets (Puritabs, Steritabs or other brand names) will kill many pathogens, but not those pathogens causing giardia. Iodine is very effective in purifying water and is available in tablet form (such as Potable Aqua), but follow the directions carefully and remember that too much iodine can be harmful.

If you can't find tablets, tincture of iodine (2%) or iodine crystals can be used. Four drops of tincture of iodine per litre or quart of clear water is the recommended dosage; the treated water should be left to stand for 20 to 30 minutes before drinking. Iodine crystals can also be used to purify water but this is a more complicated process, as you have to first prepare a saturated iodine solution. Iodine loses its effectiveness if exposed to air or damp, so keep it in a tightly sealed container. Flavoured powder will disguise the taste of treated water and is a good idea if you are travelling with children.

Sunburn You can get sunburnt surprisingly quickly on the beach, in the snow and at high altitudes, even through cloud. The sun is particularly dangerous in New Zealand, where the ozone layer is said to be considerably thinner than in other parts of the world. Use sunscreen and take extra care to cover areas which don't normally see sun eg feet. A hat provides added protection and you can also use zinc cream or some other barrier cream for your nose, lips and ears. Calamine lotion is good for mild sunburn.

Hypothermia Too much cold can be dangerous, particularly if it leads to hypothermia. Hypothermia is a real and present danger in New Zealand, due to the country's extremely changeable weather. Visitors die from hypothermia every year, mostly because they have gone out walking without adequate preparation, not realising that within the space of a few minutes a bright, warm day can change to freezing winds, rain and hail. Always be prepared for cold, wet or windy conditions even if you're just out walking or hitching; it's especially important if you're tramping out in the bush, away from civilisation.

Hypothermia occurs when the body loses heat faster than it can produce it and the core temperature of the body falls. It is surprisingly easy to progress from very cold to dangerously cold with a combination of wind, wet clothing, fatigue and hunger, even if the air temperature is above freezing. It is best to dress in layers; silk, wool and some of the new artificial fibres are good insulating materials. A hat is important, as a lot of heat is lost through the head. Take a strong, waterproof outer layer, as keeping dry is vital. Carry basic supplies, including food containing simple sugars to generate heat quickly, and lots of fluids. A space blanket is something all travellers in cold environments should carry.

Symptoms of hypothermia are exhaustion, numb skin (particularly toes and fingers), shivering, slurred speech, irrational or violent behaviour, lethargy, stumbling, dizzy spells, muscle cramps and violent bursts of energy. Irrationality may take the form of sufferers claiming they are warm and trying to take off their clothes.

To treat mild hypothermia, first get the person out of the wind and/or rain, remove their clothing if it's wet and replace it with dry, warm clothing. Give them hot liquids – not alcohol – and some high-kilojoule, easily digestible food. Do not rub victims, but instead allow them to slowly warm themselves. This should be enough to treat the early stages of hypothermia. The early recognition and treatment of mild hypothermia is the only way to prevent severe hypothermia, which is a critical condition.

Giardiasis The parasite causing this intestinal disorder is present in contaminated water. The symptoms are stomach cramps, nausea, a bloated stomach, watery and foul-smelling diarrhoea and frequent gas. Giardiasis can appear several weeks after you have been exposed to the parasite. The symptoms may

disappear for a few days and then return; this can go on for several weeks. Tinidazole, known as Fasigyn, or metronidazole (Flagyl) are the recommended drugs for treatment.

Amoebic Meningitis This very serious disease can be a danger if you bathe in natural hot thermal pools. Fortunately, it's no danger if you know how to protect yourself from it.

The amoeba that causes the disease can enter your body through the orifices of your head, usually the nose but occasionally the ears as well. Once it gets inside the nose it bores through the tissues and lodges in the brain. It's easy not to catch the disease – just keep your head out of water!

Symptoms of amoebic meningitis may have a slow onset – it could be several days or even several weeks before the first symptoms are noticed. Symptoms may be similar to the flu at first, later progressing to severe headaches, stiffness of the neck, hypersensitivity to light and then even coma. It can be treated with intravenous anti-amoebic drugs.

Bee & Wasp Stings Wasps are a problem in some places in New Zealand. They are attracted to food, especially at picnic sites; late summer is the worst time of year for them. There are many wasps in beech forests.

Bee and wasp stings are usually painful rather than dangerous. Calamine lotion will give relief; ammonia is also an effective remedy. Ice packs or antihistamine cream will reduce the pain and swelling. If you are allergic to bee or wasp stings, carry your medication with you.

Mosquitoes & Sandflies Mosquitoes appear after dusk. They are not a big problem in some parts of the country but in certain places – notably the west coast of the South Island and especially in summer – they can come in clouds. Avoid bites by covering bare skin and using an insect repellent. Insect screens on windows and mosquito nets on beds offer good protection, as does burning a mosquito coil or using a pyrethrum-based insect spray. Mosquitoes may be attracted by perfume, aftershave or certain colours. They can bite you through thin fabrics or on any small part of your skin not covered by repellent.

Another NZ insect that can drive you wild is the sandfly, a tiny black creature found in inland areas as well as around the coast, where it lives in bushes, trees or grasses. Sandfly bites can be even more irritating than mosquito bites; since the insects live on the ground, sandfly bites are mainly on the feet and ankles. Wearing shoes, thick socks and plenty of insect repellent is not only advisable but practically a necessity where sandflies are present.

The most effective insect repellent is called DEET (N,N-Diethylmetatoluamide), an ingredient in many commercially available repellents. Look for a repellent with at least a 28% concentration of DEET. Note that DEET breaks down plastic, rubber, contact lenses and synthetic fabrics, so be careful what you touch after using it. It poses no danger to natural fibres.

DOC gave us a few other recommendations for keeping away the sandflies and mosquitoes. It says that eating plenty of vitamin B1 is an effective deterrent to sand flies and we've heard it does the same thing to mosquitoes too. DOC also recommends making up a half-and-half mixture of Dettol (the antiseptic) and baby oil, and wiping it over parts of your skin where sandflies may bite.

Other good insect repellents include Off! and Repel, which comes in a stick or a spray and will not eat through plastic the way DEET-containing repellents do.

Spiders Of New Zealand's many spiders, by far the most famous is the only poisonous one, the retiring little katipo spider (*Latrodectus katipo*). Its poisonous bite can be fatal, but rarely is, even though mention of its name strikes fear into the hearts of brave souls. Only a few deaths have ever been recorded, most of them a long time ago. Antivenin is now available from most hospitals and it's effective even if administered as long as three days after being bitten.

The katipo is found in all NZ coastal areas except for the far south. It lives in areas just back from the high-tide zone, weaving a small, dense web in driftwood, grasses or any other suitable place close to the ground. The katipo is not aggressive and only bites if disturbed.

Only the mature female spider is venomous; she has a shiny black body, about 6mm long, with a bright red patch on the rear of the abdomen. The non-venomous mature male is identified by the presence of white markings on both sides, in addition to the red patch; the white markings are also present on the immature spiders of both sexes.

WOMEN TRAVELLERS
New Zealand is quite an easy country for women travellers, with very few hassles. Women should, however, exercise the same degree of caution as they would in most other countries. We recommend that you observe all the commonsense habits of safety, such as not walking through isolated urban areas alone when it's dark, not hitchhiking alone etc.

GAY & LESBIAN TRAVELLERS
Legislation decriminalising sex between consenting male adults aged 16 and older was finally passed in 1985. The Human Rights Act 1993 makes it unlawful to discriminate against a person on the grounds of their sexual orientation, in regards to employment, access to public places, provision of goods and services, accommodation and education facilities.

Numerous gay and lesbian organisations are found throughout the country, with the biggest concentration in Auckland. Auckland is also home to the HERO festival held annually in February. Various cultural events are held and up to 200,000 people line the streets to witness the parade. The Devotion Festival in November is Wellington's biggest gay and lesbian pride celebration.

NZ has a Gay & Lesbian Tourism Association (☎ (04) 384 1877; fax 384 5187; Box 11-582, Wellington 6001) to promote gay and lesbian tourism to NZ. Travel Gay New

Zealand (fax (04) 382 8246; webnz.com/tpac/gaynz/) is an information and reservation service covering gay destinations and accommodation.

For further contacts and gay and lesbian venues, see the Auckland and Wellington chapters.

DISABLED TRAVELLERS

NZ generally caters well for disabled travellers. Most hostels, hotels, B&Bs etc have wheelchair access and disabled bathrooms, as required by law for new establishments. Many government facilities and tourist attractions are similarly equipped. Disabled travellers usually receive discounts on transport.

A good contact point is the Disability Information Service (☎ (03) 366 6189; fax: 379 5939; 314 Worcester St, Christchurch/PO Box 32-074, Christchurch).

SENIOR TRAVELLERS

Senior travellers over 60 receive a discount on most transport; proof of age may be required. Discounts on attractions, activities and other services may also be available but sometimes only for NZ citizens.

Life for many NZ seniors revolves around the bowling club and the garden (NZ has many wonderful private gardens open to the public, if you're interested), but many seniors are also active. It is not uncommon to meet septuagenarians on the tramping tracks, and many clubs and activities cater for seniors. NZ retirees are out in force touring their country, often pulling a caravan or driving a motor home, and many B&Bs are run by older couples delighted to meet like-minded travellers from overseas.

TRAVEL WITH CHILDREN

New Zealand is an ideal country to travel with children. Health problems are not a major issue, getting around is easy and many attractions and activities cater for children. However, all those theme attractions with hands-on activities and rides for the kids can be very expensive for families.

Family passes are usually available at attractions, though. Childrens prices are quoted in this book, but usually apply to children from four to 14 years of age. For children younger than four, admission is often free or only a token amount applies.

Hostels don't really cater for children, but also don't discourage them. YHA hostels are better set up for families and often have specific family rooms set aside, but families can also get a four-bed share room to themselves in most backpackers. At isolated hostels, you might get the whole place to yourself. B&Bs are mostly for couples and some even ban children. Motels, and particularly camping grounds, are well set up for children and often have playgrounds and games rooms. Children cost extra on top of double rates, but the charge is usually half the per extra adult rate at motels and camping grounds, and the real 'littlies' may be free. Holiday homes and self-contained cottages are ideal for families. They are more spacious and often better value than tourist flats or motel units. The best way to find them is to head straight to the information centre when you hit town.

Major car hire companies, at least, have car seats for children but they are not always high quality. Good cradle restraints for babies are hard to get – you're better off bringing your own. If you can get a good deal on a motor home, it can be an economical and enjoyable way of seeing the country.

DANGERS & ANNOYANCES

Violent crime occurs but is not common in New Zealand. The newspapers report on murders and bashings in great detail, but this is more a reflection of the lack of crime (or perhaps lack of news). Auckland is the 'crime capital' of the country, but very safe by most standards. Of course, normal precautions should be taken in rough areas and around drunken yahoos on Saturday nights.

Theft, primarily from cars, can be a problem and is on the rise. Don't leave any valuables in a car, either outside accommodation or, particularly, at tourist parking areas, such as car parks at the start of walks.

If you must leave your belongings in the car, make sure they are hidden from view.

The biggest dangers in NZ, though, may come not from your fellow humans but from nature. Remember to take all the recommended precautions when tramping, especially in the mountains; see the Tramping section in the Outdoor Activities chapter for advice on tramping safety and follow the advice!

Sharks exist in NZ waters but are well fed by the abundant marine life and rarely pose a threat to humans. However attacks do occasionally occur. Take notice of any local warnings when swimming, surfing or diving.

LEGAL MATTERS
'New Zealand Green', the local sobriquet for marijuana, is widely indulged in but illegal. Don't get caught with it – fines can be stiff. Penalties for importing illegal drugs are severe. Despite widespread campaigns, drink-driving still seems to be a national sport, but penalties are tough and you'll find yourself in the lockup if you are caught over the limit.

The legal dictum is pretty much 'buyer beware'. There's been so much deregulation that consumer rights are minimal and regulatory authorities, where they exist, often have little power. Fortunately most Kiwi businesses are honest, but you should always read the fine print carefully.

The Commerce Commission, with offices in Auckland, Wellington and Christchurch, oversees the Fair Trading Act and can offer advice. The Citizens Advice Bureau, with offices in Wellington, Auckland, Rotorua and Christchurch, is a referral service for legal, consumer and other advice. Like most British-based legal systems, lawsuits in NZ are prohibitively expensive and weighted against small complainants – this isn't the USA.

BUSINESS HOURS
Office hours are generally Monday to Friday from 9 am to 5 pm. Most government offices are open from Monday to Friday from around 8.30 am to 4.30 pm. Shops are usually open from Monday to Friday from 9 am to 5 pm plus Saturday morning (9 am to 12.30 pm), with late-night shopping to 9 pm one night of the week, usually Thursday or Friday. Many small convenience stores (or dairies) stay open for much longer hours and many of the larger supermarkets are open seven days a week until 8 pm or later.

PUBLIC HOLIDAYS & SPECIAL EVENTS
People from the northern hemisphere never seem to become completely familiar with upside-down seasons. To them Christmas simply doesn't fall in the middle of summer and how is it possible to have mid-winter cold in August? But it's worth remembering, since Christmas is in the middle of the summer school holidays, which means lots of crowds and higher prices. Shorter school breaks during the year are less hectic but also busy.

Public holidays include:

January
    New Year's Day and the next day (1st and 2nd)
February
    Waitangi Day or New Zealand Day (6th)
March/April
    Good Friday and Easter Monday (variable dates)
April
    Anzac Day (25th)
June
    Queen's Birthday (1st Monday)
October
    Labour Day (4th Monday)
December
    Christmas Day and Boxing Day (25th and 26th)

Each province has its own anniversary-day holiday. Province holidays (dates can vary) include: Wellington, 22 January; Auckland, 29 January; Northland, 29 January; Nelson, 1 February; Otago, 23 March; Southland, 23 March; Taranaki, 31 March; Hawkes Bay, 1 November; Marlborough, 1 November; Westland, 1 December; and Canterbury, 16 December.

When these holidays fall between Friday and Sunday, they are usually observed the following Monday; if they fall between Tuesday and Thursday, they are held on the preceding Monday.

Some of the more noteworthy cultural events and festivals include:

January
>   *Auckland Anniversary Day Regatta*, Auckland
>   *Summer City Program*, Wellington (beginning of January to end of February) – two months of festivals and entertainment around the city

February
>   *Marlborough Food & Wine Festival*, Blenheim (2nd weekend)
>   *Art Deco Festival*, Napier (3rd weekend) – balls, dinners, fancy dress and Art Deco tours
>   *International Festival of the Arts*, Wellington (even-numbered years) – a month of national and international culture
>   *Aotearoa Traditional Maori Performing Arts Festival*, Wellington (odd-numbered years)

March
>   *Golden Shears Sheep Shearing Competition*, Masterton – a major event in this rather sheepish country!
>   *Ngaruawahia Regatta for Maori Canoes*, Hamilton
>   *Wildfoods Festival*, Hokitika – tasty and healthy wild food from the land and sea
>   *Pasifika Polynesian Festival*, Auckland – traditional arts, entertainment, sports and food celebrating Auckland's Pacific communities

April
>   *Highland Games*, Hastings

June
>   *NZ Agricultural Field Days*, Hamilton – a major agricultural show at Mystery Creek

September
>   *NZ Trout Festival*, Rotorua – fishing contest

November
>   *Canterbury Show Week*, Christchurch

December
>   *Festival of Lights*, New Plymouth – annual light-up of the town and lighting display at Pukekura Park over Christmas

There are many smaller annual events held all over NZ; each little town seems to have its annual fair (or show), often involving simple sports like racing horses on the beach, wheelbarrow and sugar bag races, woodchopping and sheep-shearing contests.

ACTIVITIES

For details on New Zealand's wide range of adventure activities, see the Outdoor Activities chapter.

LANGUAGE COURSES

People from around the world, especially Asia and the Pacific countries, come to New Zealand to study English. Typically each language school arranges for its students to live with New Zealand families, so that English is used outside as well as inside the classroom. Schools also arrange a variety of extracurricular evening and weekend activities for students.

Auckland has the highest concentration of language schools, but there are a few in other parts of the country as well. The Auckland Visitor Information Centre keeps a complete, up-to-date list.

WORK

New Zealand has a moderately high unemployment rate, so it's fussy about foreigners taking jobs from its citizens. An ordinary visitor permit or visa does not give you the right to work in NZ – so if you work you are breaking the law. Apply for a work permit before arriving in NZ or within the country at any New Zealand Immigration Service office. Generally you need to be sponsored by an employer with an offer of definite employment in an occupation that is in demand. Special working holiday visas are available to citizens of Canada, Japan and the UK aged 18 to 30, and Australians can work; see the earlier Visas section.

Fruit picking is readily available and popular work for visitors. Apples, kiwi fruit and other types of fruit and vegetables are picked in summer and early autumn; pay rates are so low that many New Zealanders won't touch this work. The main picking season is from around January to April, though there may be some agricultural work year-round. Picking is hard work and you are paid according to the amount you pick.

ACCOMMODATION

New Zealand has a wide range of accommodation but there is one catch: the Kiwis are great travellers. A greater proportion of New Zealanders have passports than the residents of any other country and when they are not jaunting around overseas they'll be jaunting around at home. So book ahead during the holiday season, particularly in the main tourist areas at peak times: the summer holidays from Christmas to the end of January, and Easter. At these times prices rise in the beach resorts and other popular destinations, and finding a room can be difficult. International tourism also puts a strain on accommodation and is at its busiest from October to April, particularly during February and March.

Accommodation Guides

It's worthwhile picking up some of the accommodation guides, especially if they're free.

The *AA Accommodation Guide*, also available as separate guides to the North and South islands, is revised yearly. Mostly motels are listed, but you might find some hotels, motor camps, and a few guesthouses and B&Bs. Once *the* accommodation guide to NZ, it is still useful but is less comprehensive and full of advertising. The guide costs $9.95 in bookshops but is free at AA offices for members or members of an affiliated automobile association overseas.

Jason's accommodation directories are similar commercially produced guides, available for free from motels and motor camps, but you'll have to pay for them at bookshops. They have the most complete listings in two guides, *Jason's Motels & Motor Lodges* and *Jason's Budget Accommodation*, which lists motor camps and camping grounds.

Other publications useful for the latest listings of hostels, DOC camping grounds, and B&Bs are listed in this section.

One of the best resources for accommodation information is the local information centre, found in almost every town of any size. Most also act as booking agents for accommodation; you can fax them from overseas for information and accommodation bookings.

Camping & Cabins

New Zealand is a great place for camping. For the tent camper, Kiwi camping grounds are some of the best in the world, and motor camps have excellent facilities for tent campers, caravans and campervans, plus on-site vans and cabins of different degrees of luxury.

, Camping grounds and motor camps are found all over the country and often in prime locations – right on the beach or next to a babbling brook in mountain areas. They are well equipped: most have kitchens and dining areas where the cooker, hotplates, kettles and toasters are provided, though occasionally you may have to supply your own pots and pans, utensils, plates etc. They're great places to meet people – you talk with other people while you fix your food and carry on when you share a table to eat – and also have laundry facilities and, often, TV rooms. Though it's best to bring your own sleeping bag, most places also hire linen if you're staying in cabins.

Camp or caravan sites are usually charged at a per-person rate, typically around $7 to $9 per adult, half-price for children. But rates may be for a minimum of two people and then an additional charge for each extra person, or are sometimes just a straight site charge. A powered site for a caravan or campervan is usually a dollar or two more per person.

At most sites the kitchen and showers are free but a few have coin-operated hotplates and hot showers. At most sites laundry facilities are coin-operated.

Camping becomes less practical in NZ in winter, especially in the south.

A good guide is the *New Zealand Camping Guide* by Noni Hansen, covering almost every motor camp, and DOC and regional camping ground throughout the country, with maps showing their location.

DOC Camping Grounds DOC operates over 120 camping grounds around NZ, often in beautiful locations. Its camping grounds are in reserves and national parks, maritime parks, forest parks and farm parks – DOC offices have lists.

Standard DOC camping grounds are h~ , with minimal facilities including cold running water, toilets, fireplaces and not much else, but they also have minimal charges (around $2 to $6 per adult). Informal camping grounds are free, but have almost no facilities, apart from a cold-water tap and places to pitch tents. Some DOC camping grounds are fully serviced like motor camps and have on-site managers.

Local DOC offices have details on facilities, what you need to take and whether you should book in advance. Standard and informal camping grounds operate on a first come, first served basis, and fees are paid by a self-registration system. Since the low fees are used for the maintenance of the camping grounds, it's important to pay them (usually into an honesty box) even when there's no warden.

Back Country Huts DOC also operates numerous back country huts, most of which can only be reached on foot. See the Tramping section in the Outdoor Activities chapter for more information.

Cabins & Tourist Flats Many camping grounds and motor camps have cabins. Standard cabins are simply freestanding rooms with bare mattresses. You provide your own sleeping gear (a sleeping bag is fine) and towels, or linen can usually be hired. Rooms cost around $25 to $30 for two, making them better value than backpacker hostels. The minimum rate is generally per double, plus so much for each additional person, but some charge per cabin and some per person, making them cheap for singles.

Many motor camps now offer hostel-style bunkrooms, often a cabin filled with dorm beds, but they are cheap at around $12 per person and often empty. Alternatively, backpacker beds are offered in two, three or four-bed cabins.

Better equipped cabins are called 'tourist flats'. Closer to motel standard, they have kitchens and/or bathrooms and may be serviced, with linen provided. On-site caravans (trailer homes in US parlance) are another camping-ground possibility. Many camping

grounds also have regular motel rooms or an associated motel complex.

Hostels
Hundreds of hostels offer cheap accommodation all over NZ. At a hostel you rent a bed, usually for around $14 to $16 a night. Bunkrooms may be for 10 or more people, sometimes segregated, sometimes not. Other hostels have smaller bunkrooms or 'share rooms' with three or four beds, and almost all have at least a few twin or double rooms. Sometimes single rooms are offered, though they are rare and, unless the hostel is empty, you'll have to pay for a double. All hostels have a communal kitchen, laundry, dining area and lounge area.

Hostels are divided into two camps – YHA hostels and private hostels or backpackers. Due to intense competition, the YHA in New Zealand has gone to great lengths to change its image. Gone are the chores and curfews, as well as many of the fuddy-duddy managers traditionally associated with YHAs. YHA hostel offices are typically closed during the day, but the hostels are open all day for guests' use; if you arrive outside office hours, you can leave your baggage there and use the communal facilities until the office opens for you to check in.

Hostels vary enormously. Purpose-built YHA hostels tend to be more consistent in standards, with adequate facilities for the numbers of people they handle. Private hostels range from new, purpose-built facilities that offer excellent standards of accommodation to converted family homes designed for six people but housing 20 or more. Some lack sufficient bathroom facilities, good communal areas and adequate kitchens, which are essential to a good hostel.

On the other hand, some YHA hostels may have an institutional feel, making the home atmosphere of private hostels more attractive. Ultimately it boils down to the managers – some are just not in tune with backpackers, but many are right on the ball, promote a congenial atmosphere and offer travel information, tours, activities etc.

Many of the hostels, YHA and private, are just brilliant.

In the peak season, it is essential to book at least a day in advance, especially for double or twin rooms, which are limited compared with the more financially lucrative dormitories. Even dormitories fill up, despite the tendency of some hostels to cash in and pack the dorms to overflowing with beds.

Many hotels, motor camps and even some motels are cashing in on the backpacker boom and also offer backpacker accommodation, often at cheaper rates than the hostels. They can be good value but are often anonymous and lack the atmosphere of a hostel. Many motor camps though, especially in the main tourist areas, have good communal areas where travellers meet and you might also meet a few congenial Kiwis.

Take a sleeping bag. At independent backpackers bedding usually costs extra. YHA hostels provide bedding for free; you just have to ask for it.

YHA Hostels The YHA in New Zealand produces the free annual *YHA Accommodation Guide* with details on all its NZ hostels; it is available at all NZ YHA hostels and travel centres. Otherwise try your national YHA or the NZ YHA national office (☎ (03) 379 9970; fax 365 4476; PO Box 436, Christchurch). The YHA also goes under the banner of Hostelling International (HI), but the term YHA is still more common in NZ.

YHA hostels are only open to members. Join the YHA in your home country or in NZ at any YHA hostel for $24. Nonmembers can also stay at hostels by paying an extra instalment of $4 per night on a membership card. After six nights stay you become a full member. If you have a YHA card make sure you bring it, even if you don't want to stay in hostels. Flashing your YHA card will bring discounts on buses (usually a 30% discount), airlines and for many activities.

New Zealand also has a number of Associate YHA Hostels – privately owned premises affiliated to the YHA – which are also open to nonmembers at the same rates.

Hostels can be booked ahead directly by phone, through the New Zealand YHA offices, or through another hostel (for a $1 fee). But reservations must be paid in full in advance at a hostel or by credit card over the phone. If you cancel your reservation, rules state that full refunds are only given for a 'valid reason'.

Backpackers The many backpackers (private or independent hostels) have about the same facilities and prices as YHA hostels – fully equipped communal kitchens, common areas, laundry facilities and so on.

A couple of handy brochures are useful for the latest listings of the many backpackers springing up around the country. Hostels pay to be listed in these brochures, so they are not independent assessments or regulated organisations, but the brochures are up-to-date and well prepared.

Budget Backpackers Hostels New Zealand is an excellent publication, commonly known as the BBH guide, put out by Budget Backpackers Hostels. Available through member hostels and some information centres, it has details, prices and the biggest selection of backpackers throughout NZ. Backpackers' BPP rating, based on guest assessments, is an interesting and usually accurate grade for hostels. You can also get a copy through the Rainbow Lodge (☎ /fax (07) 377 1568; 99 Titiraupenga St, Taupo) or Foley Towers (☎ /fax (03) 379 3014; 208 Kilmore St, Christchurch).

The *VIP Backpackers Accommodation Guide* also lists a wide range of hostels including most of the large, city hostels. All the backpackers listed are members of the VIP network; a VIP Card ($25) gives you $1 off at VIP hostels, plus discounts similar to those offered on a YHA card. The VIP accommodation guide is available at VIP hostels and information centres, or you can request one from VIP Backpackers Resorts at Auckland Central Backpackers (☎ (09) 358 4852; fax (09) 358 4872; 9 Fort St, Auckland).

YMCA & YWCA Hostels YMCA and YWCA hostels in larger cities offer rooms, from the no-frills to quite luxurious, and are generally reasonably priced. A few are single-sex only but most take both men and women. Although the emphasis is on long-term accommodation for young people coming to study or work in the 'big city', they do provide accommodation in the crowded summer season when their long-term residents go home or on holiday. Accommodation is often in single or twin rooms.

B&Bs & Guesthouses

B&B accommodation in private homes is by far the biggest category of accommodation and B&Bs are sprouting everywhere. Everyone with a spare room in their house seems to be getting in on the act.

The best publication for B&B listings is the *New Zealand Bed & Breakfast Book* by J & J Thomas, available in NZ bookstores and updated annually. Though the blurbs are the overstated rantings of the owners, it has by far the biggest listing of B&Bs, with prices and details on facilities. Local visitor information centres also have lists of B&Bs.

Although breakfast is definitely on the agenda at the real B&B places, it may or may not feature at guesthouses. Breakfast may be 'continental' (ie not much) or a substantial meal of fruit, eggs, bacon, toast, tea and coffee. Many guesthouses pride themselves on the size, quality and 'traditional value' of their breakfasts. If you like to start the day heartily it's worth considering this when comparing prices. A big breakfast is worth at least $10 per person.

Guesthouses may be spartan, cheap, ultra-basic 'private' (unlicensed) hotels. Most are comfortable, relaxed but low-key places, patronised by people who don't enjoy the impersonal atmosphere of many motels. Others are very fancy indeed.

Guesthouses are often slightly cheaper than B&Bs. B&Bs usually start at around $40 a single, if available, or $60 a double – that will get you a standard room with share bathroom. Doubles with attached bathroom start at around $80. B&Bs can be very luxurious and cost well over $100.

Many B&Bs also offer an evening meal for an extra charge. A few B&Bs have a kitchen where guests can do their own cooking.

Farmstays (Farm Holidays)

New Zealand has been called the world's most efficient farm, so a visit to a farm is an interesting way of getting to grips with the real New Zealand. Farmstays are popular and many offer guests the chance to 'have a go' at all the typical farm activities and be treated as one of the household. Choose from dairy, sheep, high country, cattle or mixed farming farms.

Costs vary widely. Some have rooms in the homestead for $100 or more a double including meals, but most offer B&B for more like $80 per day, with an extra $20 or so for dinner. Some farms have separate cottages where you fix your own food and others are more like backpackers in basic shearers cottages. Information centres have listings of farmstays, which can often be cheaper than the advertised farmstays.

Other places offer accommodation and meals for nothing or at cheap rates in exchange for work on the farm. Though some travellers have reported the occasional labour camp, many farms offering accommodation on this basis provide an excellent chance to work on a farm, learn about farm life and save money.

Farm Hosting in NZ (FHINZ; ☎ (06) 376 4582; fax 358 1092; Kumeroa Lodge Stud, RD1 Woodville) produces a booklet ($15) that lists farms throughout NZ providing lodging in exchange for four hours work per day.

WWOOF An economical way of staying on a farm and doing some work is joining Willing Workers on Organic Farms (WWOOF). Membership provides you with a list of over 300 organic farms throughout the country where, in exchange for your 'conscientious work', the farm owner will provide food, accommodation and some hands-on experience in organic farming. You must contact the farm owner or manager by telephone or letter; you cannot simply turn up at a farm without warning.

To join WWOOF and receive the booklet, contact Janet and Andrew Strange (☎ (03) 544 8695; PO Box 1172, Nelson).

Homestays

Increasing numbers of households offer rooms. Most are B&B arrangements (see under the B&Bs & Guesthouses heading in this section), but several of the agencies which handle farmstays are combination farm-homestay services. Visitor information centres throughout NZ, especially in the smaller towns, keep lists of homestays in their areas.

Motels

NZ motels have all the facilities of motels everywhere, and more. Many motel units have fully equipped kitchens, though some studio units only have a fridge, and tea and coffee-making equipment. Most motels provide you with a small carton of fresh milk and often have a laundry for guests.

Many visitors find NZ motels a definite notch below international standards. Many motels date from the 1960s and look like it. Though comfortable enough, they are drab, prefabricated affairs. Newer motels are often cheap constructions but usually brighter with better decor, and some are definitely luxurious.

Motel rooms typically cost around $60 to $70 a double, and then $10 to $15 for every extra person. The more luxurious new motels charge around $80 and up. The difference in price between a single or double room, if there is one, is usually minimal. In tourist towns, motels can really hike prices in the main tourist season. On the other hand, when it is quiet they may give discounts, especially if it looks like you will walk out the door.

A motor inn is part motel, part hotel, offering motel-style accommodation and usually a bar and restaurant.

Hotels

Many traditional, older-style pubs have rooms, but they are often just a sideline enterprise and the main emphasis is on the bar. At the other end of the scale are the five-star hotels in the big cities. At the cheapest pubs, singles/doubles might cost as low as $20/30, though $30/50 is more common, while at the most luxurious new establishments a room could cost $200 or more.

The pubs can be good value and often have plenty of character. Some now also have 'backpackers rooms' that usually cost about half the normal hotel rate. These are regular hotel rooms without the frills – no TV, radio etc – and towel and bedding are not provided or cost extra. They may also be the rooms that are awaiting renovation ie very shabby indeed.

Many economical older hotels are listed in the free *Pub Beds* brochure, which brings a good discount when presented at participating hotels. It's published by Pub Beds (PO Box 101 291, North Shore Mail Centre) and is available at many NZ hotels and information centres.

Holiday Homes & Cottages

Holiday homes (baches) or self-contained cottages can be rented in many country areas. They can be good for longer stays in one area, although many can be rented for only one or two nights. Prices are usually reasonable – typically $60 to $120, which, for a whole house or self-contained bungalow, is good value.

Information centres keep listings and will arrange bookings. *Baches & Holiday Homes to Rent* is an annual guide, with a wide selection of listings, sold in NZ bookshops.

FOOD

Though the typical Kiwi diet is still based on meat and boiled vegetables, the country's culinary horizons have broadened immeasurably in recent years. The major cities and tourist towns have restaurants serving Italian, Middle Eastern, Indian, Thai and Mexican food, as well as other cuisines, and plenty of fashionable cafes.

In the hinterlands, Chinese restaurants still predominate over any other sort of international cuisine but, while hearty meals are

Kiwi Fruit

New Zealand's most famous fruit, the kiwi fruit, is a marvel of NZ agricultural know-how. NZ took this obscure fruit, once known as the Chinese gooseberry, developed new strains suitable for local conditions and then marketed it internationally under the name kiwi fruit. In the 1980s, when no self-respecting nouvelle cuisine chef was without this colourful fruit on hand, the country was overtaken in the kiwi fruit rush that saw vines planted everywhere. The rich volcanic soils and temperate climate of the Bay of Plenty region were particularly suited to kiwi fruit, and millionaires were made overnight.

HOLGER LEUE

This is kiwi fruit country – Te Puke, Bay of Islands

Since those heady days, other countries have started to grow the kiwi fruit and the price has dropped. However, NZ produces the largest and juiciest variety, which still accounts for two-thirds of the kiwi fruit grown in the world. NZ kiwi fruit exports are worth more than $400 million a year.

Imported from the Yangtze Valley in China, the first kiwi fruit climbers were grown as ornamental garden vines. It was only around 50 years ago that the first attempts were made to grow them commercially. The industry grew slowly at first; only in the last couple of decades has it assumed the economic importance it enjoys today.

The NZ agricultural industry is always on the lookout to develop other exotic fruit, such as nashi pears and persimmons, which are also widely exported. Perhaps one of the most delightful fruits you'll find in NZ, grown in backyards all over the country for decades but never really developed commercially, is the sweet, highly perfumed feijoa, a South American import. ■

---

offered, many Chinese in NZ have lost contact with their rich culinary roots and the Kiwi version can be a bland travesty of the real thing.

There's not much of a national cuisine – no moa and chips or Auckland fried kiwi. They're big meat eaters though and a NZ steak is every bit as good as an Aussie or American one. Lamb, of course, is top quality and available everywhere, with venison found in the better restaurants. New Zealand is also renowned for its dairy products – its milk, cheese and ice cream are excellent.

With all that coastline it's not surprising that NZ's seafood is excellent. Green-lipped mussels, available all over NZ, are easily the best in the world and cheap. Oyster fans shouldn't leave NZ without tasting the superb oysters (the best come from Bluff on the South Island). Scallops are also good eating. Crayfish (lobster) is a speciality in some areas, though most of it is exported and hard to find. Other exotics include the now-rare

and expensive shellfish toheroa or slightly less pricey tuatua. In some places, such as Ninety Mile Beach in the North Island, and in the right season, a few minutes of digging in the sand at the beach can yield bucketfuls of shellfish, including tuatuas, pipis and periwinkles.

Saltwater fish favourites include hoki, hapuka, groper, snapper, and kingfish. New Zealand also has good freshwater fish, with incredibly large rainbow and brown trout, in rivers and lakes all over the country. You can't buy trout in the shops but there are many opportunities to catch one yourself.

Eels, plentiful in NZ's rivers and creeks, are another local delicacy, especially smoked eels. Smoked fish is also quite popular.

Perhaps the only things that visitors find lacking, particularly away from the cities, is good bread (Europeans will kill for a slice of solid rye or sourdough after a few weeks) and decent coffee (more fashionable cafes have espresso machines and they sometimes know how to use them, but Americans may

Fast Food

New Zealand has plenty of fast-food joints, including those symbols of US culinary imperialism: McDonald's, Pizza Hut and KFC. Or try traditional Kiwi favourites: fish and chips, and hot meat pies.

Fish and chips is an English institution that New Zealand excels at. Not only can you get some superb fresh fish, deep fried in batter, but fish and chip shops also offer mussels, scallops, oysters, paua fritters and other seafood delights, served with hot, crisp chips. (For Americans, 'chips' in NZ are thickly cut french fries.) Try kumara chips for a variation. Unlike in Australia, where frying up fish and chips seems to be an Italian or Greek occupation, in NZ it's very often a Chinese one.

New Zealanders are just about as tied to the meat pie as Australians but they probably do a better job of them. The meat pie has as great a cultural significance to New Zealanders as the hot dog has to a Noo Yorker – and is as frequently reviled for not being what it once was. Georgie Pie, a chain of pie shops, has now fallen into this culinary void.

Other snacks popular in NZ include nachos, potato skins and hamburgers like the great 'Kiwi burger' with a fried egg, beetroot and salad.

Cafes & Tearooms

New Zealand's traditional cafes or coffee shops, called tearooms, are nothing to get excited about. They're usually open on weekdays from around 9 am to 5 pm and perhaps on Saturday morning, serving fare such as tea, scones and white bread sandwiches. Devonshire teas, which include a pot of tea, one or two scones, jam and whipped cream, are served at morning and afternoon tea time (around 10 am and 3 pm).

In the larger cities, more fashionable cafes have espresso (or cappuccino, cafe latte etc), croissants, sinfully rich desserts and baked focaccia with a variety of ingredients. These cafes are also often popular late-night hangouts for espresso or wine, light meals and music.

Pub Food

Pubs offer some of the best value for money. Counter meals (pie and chips, stews etc) have more or less died out, though some bars still sell pies from a pie warmer. A lot of pubs now have bistro meals – simple but good food like schnitzel, steak, roasts or fish with chips and salad or coleslaw. Average main courses range from $8 to $12 and they are usually excellent value. The Cobb & Co chain offers pub-style food in locations all over NZ.

Restaurants

Stodgy, English-inspired roasts or plates of 'meat and three veg' used to be the order of the day in NZ restaurants, but the restaurant scene is now much more innovative. The main cities have a variety of international cuisines and top quality restaurants, but even the small towns often have fashionable bar-restaurants with varied menus.

A lot of restaurants now offer main meals that are marinated, smoked, sautéed or provençal, doused in booze and accompanied by a variety of colourful things you're not really meant to eat. Menus in better NZ restaurants almost invariably feature venison, lamb, beef and fish dishes. With such excellent fresh produce, it is hard to go wrong, but the chefs are not always as innovative as their menus, especially in the smaller towns. The new international influence on menus may be limited to pasta, 'gourmet' pizzas, a bland Thai dish or two, or the ever-present nachos. That said, even in the countryside, you will find some real gems, but expect to pay $20 or more for a main course in better restaurants. With an entrée (appetiser) dessert and drinks, a meal in a good restaurant will cost around $50 per person.

Fully licensed restaurants are now more common, but many restaurants are still BYO, where you 'bring your own' wine, beer etc. Food prices are generally lower than in licensed restaurants.

Vegetarian New Zealand has a number of great vegetarian restaurants, mainly in the big cities. Auckland has several cheap and excellent vegetarian restaurants, including Gopals run by the Hare Krishnas. In Christchurch the Mainstreet Cafe is more expensive but the food, especially dessert, is superb.

Self-Catering

As many places to stay provide cooking facilities for guests, buying and cooking your own food will save you a lot of money travelling around NZ.

New Zealand has several large supermarket chains – Pack 'N Save, New World and Woolworths for example – and they're usually open seven days a week until around 8 pm. Large supermarkets are found in the cities and towns that serve a large rural community.

When the supermarkets are shut, the good old corner dairy is the place to go. A dairy is a small shop found on many street corners throughout New Zealand, selling milk, food, newspapers, chocolate, sweets – a bit of everything, but mostly food. They're open longer hours than other shops and are more widespread, but their selection is usually not as good as a larger shop and their prices are higher.

DRINKS
Beer

New Zealanders are great drinkers, and both the beer and the pubs are pretty good. Almost all the beer is now brewed by only two companies, NZ Breweries and DB Breweries. Steinlager, the various types of DB (Bitter, Export etc) and Lion Red are probably the most popular beers. Down in the deep south you'll come across some different labels such as Speights. Monteith's, from the South Island's wild west coast, is as dark as the bituminous coal dug by the miners who drink it.

Small boutique breweries are popular and found in the main cities and towns. Probably the best of the boutique beers are from Marlborough and Nelson – Pink Elephant and Mac's. 'Dark' drinkers will appreciate the Black Mac. If your constitution is up to it seek out Hooker's Ale, a beer with a kick like an enraged moa.

Cans aren't popular and most beer is sold in bottles anyway, which is cheaper. In a pub the cheapest beer is on tap. You can ask for a 'seven', originally seven fluid ounces but now a 200ml glass, the closest metric equivalent; a 'handle', a half-litre or litre mug with a handle and often called a pint or half-pint (old ways die hard); or a jug, which is just that.

Drinks at public bars are the cheapest, while lounge or fancier bars tend to mark their drinks up more, but prices vary widely.

In public bars you can pretty much wear anything, but lounge bars have a lot of 'neat dress required' signs. The bars with entertainment are normally lounge bars, which can sometimes make things awkward for the traveller with jeans, sandals and T-shirt.

Wine

New Zealand has a thriving wine-producing industry and many wineries have established international reputations, particularly for their whites.

A few notable wine-producing areas are Henderson near Auckland, Martinborough in the Wairarapa, Hawkes Bay, Blenheim in the Marlborough region of the South Island, and Central Otago. Winery visits and tours are popular in these places and, of course, there's free wine tasting. New wineries are constantly opening, as NZ wine continues to achieve a better reputation. The best-known regions are Marlborough, noted for its sauvignon blanc, and Hawkes Bay, noted for its chardonnay.

An unusual NZ speciality is kiwi fruit wine. There are lots of different varieties – still and bubbly, sweet and dry – and even a liqueur. You may not like it, but New Zealand's the best place to try it.

ENTERTAINMENT

As in many countries, there's plenty of nightlife in the major cities but not much in the small towns, where everything seems to shut with a bang after dark, except the pub and the Chinese takeaway, and even they might be closed by around 9 or 10 pm. In the cities there's plenty of entertainment, with cinemas, theatre, discos, live-music venues, late-night cafes and plenty more.

SPECTATOR SPORTS

Rugby union is practically a national mania, with cricket taking a distant second place. New Zealand also excels at hockey and netball, which attract few spectators.

It seems little boys in NZ learn to play rugby about as soon as they can walk and continue to play it as late in life as they can manage. As you travel you'll see matches played everywhere by teams of all ages. In rugby season, when they're not playing, they're inside watching it on television. The All Blacks, New Zealand's national rugby team, are national heroes. A variant of the game, rugby league, is also very popular.

All cities have major stadiums, where you can see top national, and sometimes international, rugby teams. Just front up to a game (usually held on a Saturday or Sunday in winter) and buy your ticket at the gate.

New Zealanders are also big punters and breed fine racehorses. Almost every town worth its salt has a racetrack with weekend meets at various times of year.

SHOPPING

You don't go to New Zealand intending to come back with a backpack full of souvenirs – a photograph of some flawless moment may be your best reminder – but there are some things worth checking out.

Woollen Goods

New Zealand produces beautiful woollen gear, particularly jumpers (sweaters) made from hand-spun, hand-dyed wool. Hand-knitted jumpers are something of an art form in NZ and although not cheap – they sell in tourist shops for around $150 to $300 – they are of the highest quality. Other knitted goods include hats, gloves, scarves and mufflers.

Woollen Swann-Dri jackets, shirts and pullovers are so practical and warm that they're just about the NZ national garment in the countryside, especially for farmers. Most common are the red-and-black or blue-and-black plaid ones, though they do also come in a few solid colours. You can buy Swann-Dris (affectionately called 'Swannies') in better outdoor-gear shops and again, though not cheap – a good pullover could cost you around $200 – but they're top quality and should keep you warm for at least the next decade.

Sheepskins are also popular buys – the ones sold in the top tourist shops are beautiful and pure white, with long, thick, straight combed wool. Numerous other sheepskin goods include toasty warm slippers.

Greenstone (Pounamu)

Jade, called greenstone or pounamu in New Zealand, is made into ornaments, brooches, earrings, cuff links and *tiki*. The latter are tiny, stylised Maori figures, usually depicted with their tongue stuck out in a warlike challenge, worn on a thong or chain around the neck. They've got great *mana*, or power, but they also serve as fertility symbols, so beware!

Bone Carvings

Maori bone carvings are another fine Maori art form undergoing something of a renaissance. Maori artisans have always made bone carvings, but nowadays they feed the tourist industry. Tiki, very interesting human and animal figures, such as dolphins and sea birds, are carved from bone. Bone fish-hook pendants, carved in traditional Maori and modernised styles, are most common and worn on a thong or a chain around the neck.

Paua (Abalone)

Abalone shell, called paua in NZ, is carved into some beautiful (and some tacky) ornaments and jewellery. Shells are used as ashtrays in places where paua is plentiful, but it's illegal to take natural paua shells out of NZ. Only processed ornaments can be taken with you.

A National Obsession

No book about NZ would be complete without mention of the national obsession – Rugby Union football. Try to escape the euphoria when the All Blacks, the national team, steamroll their international opponents into the mud of Eden Park in Auckland. Look at the fear on the faces of the opposition as the All Blacks perform the fearsome haka at the start of a match for which they have become famous.

According to tradition, rugby had its beginnings in 1823, when William Webb Ellis picked up the ball during a game of soccer at Rugby School in England. The illegality of this move led to the popularity of such handling of the ball and the game was born. The Rugby Union was formed in 1871 and rugby was carried to the far outposts of the British Empire by British citizens travelling and living abroad.

The NZ Football Union was founded in 1892 and the country became a stronghold of the game. Interprovincial championships began in 1902 with play for the Ranfurly Shield, which was donated by the governor-general of the time, the Earl of Ranfurly. New Zealand first played in Great Britain in 1888-89.

The highest level of competition for rugby is now the World Cup, first held in 1987 and hosted jointly by Australia and NZ. New Zealand won the inaugural World Cup, went out in the semi-final stages of the 1991 tournament and lost 15-12 to South Africa in the 1995 final.

The Bledisloe Cup competition (instigated by Lord Bledisloe, the former NZ governor-general) has been contested by NZ and Australia since 1931. By 1997 NZ had nearly three times as many wins (and four draws).

The game is played on a quadrangular field. The maximum distance between the goal lines is 100m, the field is 69m wide and goalposts are 5.6m apart, with the crossbar 3m above the ground. The object is to get the ball across the opponents' goal line and ground it (called a try and worth four points), or kick it over the goal posts (called a conversion and worth two points, a penalty worth three or a drop goal from the field worth three).

There are 15 players in each side – eight forwards and seven backs. The backs include a fullback, left wing, right wing, outside centre, inside centre, fly half and scrum half. They usually have slender builds and can move quickly with the ball. Looking at a number of forward packs, you could be forgiven for thinking that brawn is a prerequisite. There are two burly props, a hooker to rake the ball in the scrum, two second rowers or locks, two flankers (or breakaways) and the last man down (No 8). The last three are referred to as loose forwards.

The oval ball is leather and weighs 440g. It is kicked off from the centre and then, by a combination of maul, ruck and scrum, is taken by one team. Without getting offside and without passing forward, they attempt to get the ball to the opponents' line. Play stops only for: a lineout, when the ball has gone out and is thrown back in to a line of players; a scrum, when opposing players pack down against each other; a penalty or conversion; or a respite to remove an injured player. Get the full bottle from someone in the pub.

There are about 11,000 clubs in NZ. The All Blacks have had many great players over the years, such as the famous lock forward Colin 'Pine Tree' Meads – 55 caps (representing NZ) and 133 appearances between 1957 and 1971; the great winger Brian Williams; fullback extraordinaire Don Clarke; fly half Grant Fox; scintillating loose forward Ian Kirkpatrick; the great Waka Nathan; and the sensation of the 1995 World Cup, winger Jonah Lomu, nicknamed the 'human bulldozer'.

Seven-a-side competition is now popular with the advent of the Hong Kong sevens tournament, which the All Blacks won in 1995.

If you're interested and are there at the right time, make sure you see a game at Eden Park. Tickets are available at the park and it's best to buy them well in advance.

Rugby league, with 13 instead of 15 players and slightly different rules, is also popular, especially in Auckland (the Warriors play in the Australian Super League competition), but not as revered as rugby union. NZ reached the semi-final of the 1995 Rugby League World Cup. ∎

Woodcarvings

Another distinctive Maori art form, wood-carvings are worth checking out, particularly in Rotorua. Carvers produce tremendous forms such as leaping dolphins, as well as the sometimes highly intricate traditional Maori carvings. Expect to pay a small fortune for high-quality work. Of course, many poor examples are turned out for the tourist trade and they tend to dominate the market.

Other Arts & Crafts

New Zealanders have a reputation as great do-it-yourselfers and there are a lot of excellent shops selling art and craft, with everything from hand-painted scarves and ceramics to homemade jams and preserves. The quality of the pottery and weaving is particularly fine; they make good presents to take back home and don't take up much room in your luggage. Nelson, in particular, is noted for its excellent pottery and the quality of its local clay.

Fashion

City Kiwis have an independent flair when it comes to fashion and consequently there are some great little clothes shops around. In Auckland, check out Ponsonby Rd, the markets and in the centre around High and O'Connell Sts. The more mainstream designers congregate around the central city

and Parnell districts in Auckland. Thornton Hall is a successful women's label you'll find in all the major cities.

The outdoor clothing market has also become very competitive and the durable yet stylish Canterbury sports clothing label is known internationally. New Zealand is making quite a name for itself with high-quality outdoor fashion.

Camping Equipment & Souvenirs

New Zealand manufactures some excellent camping gear – packs, tents, sleeping bags, boots, fleece and rain jackets – but their prices are very high. You will get some of the world's best quality gear, but generally it will be cheaper overseas. Count on paying up to double what you would in the USA, for example. The large cities have second-hand sports shops where you can sometimes pick up reasonably priced gear.

Books of NZ photography are sold in bookshops; the Whitcoulls chain has a large selection. Or how about a book of *Footrot Flats* cartoons?

Of course there are also plenty of silly souvenirs, with Kiwi or sheep dominating. How about a little tin can that goes 'baaaa' like a sheep when you turn it over? Or a miniature sheep? Then there are the snow-domes with a flock of sheep trapped in a perpetual snow shower.

Outdoor Activities

New Zealand is a haven for visitors who seek to combine adventure with the wide open spaces. The land, air and water are not sacrosanct, and the Kiwis and their visitors move over or through these media in just about every way imaginable. They jet-boat, white-water sledge, raft, boogey board, canoe, kayak, surf, surf raft, scuba dive and ski through the water; bungy jump, parapente, skydive, abseil, fly, helicopter and barrel roll through the air; and tramp, mountain bike, ski, horse ride, rock climb, 'zorb' and ice climb across and up terra firma. And beneath the surface caving, cave rafting, *tomo* (hole or entrance to a cave) exploring and hydro-sliding are all pursued.

For an indication of the lengths to which Kiwis will go to experience something different, read *Classic New Zealand Adventures* by Jonathan Kennett et al. It has every adventure from a sedate paddle down a river to wharf jumping on a bicycle, pillocking (or 'surfing') across mud flats on a rubbish-bin lid, and bridge swinging.

The various adrenalin-pumping activities do have an element of risk. Perceived danger is part of the thrill but real danger has crept into an industry reeling from a number of recent deaths and serious accidents in activities such as white-water rafting, tandem skydiving, ballooning, cave rafting, jet-boating and even bungy jumping, which had an unblemished record until a couple of recent (non-fatal) accidents. Travellers should be aware that adventure sports, particularly those on fast-flowing rivers such as rafting and kayaking, do entail risk. Chances of a mishap are perhaps minuscule, but make sure that the company you choose takes adequate safety precautions.

But one sport with a high accident rate is tramping. Almost every year tourists die because of inexperience or inadequate equipment. Some trails are only for the experienced, and weather conditions are changeable, making high-altitude walks subject to snow and ice even in summer. Always check weather conditions. Consult and register your intentions with a Department of Conservation (DOC) office before heading off on the longer walks. Above all, heed their advice.

TRAMPING

Tramping (that's Kiwi for hiking or trekking) is the best way to experience NZ's natural beauty and is very well organised. The country has thousands of kilometres of tracks – many well marked, some only a line on the map. Tramping is made easy by NZ's excellent network of huts, enabling trampers to avoid lugging tents and cooking gear. Many tracks are graded, though others are only for experienced, fit walkers.

This section should open your eyes to the possibilities of tramping, but before attempting any track you should consult the appropriate authority for the latest information. There are literally hundreds of tracks to be enjoyed all over NZ. The famous ones – Milford, Routeburn, Abel Tasman – attract many visitors (and crowds) while equally fine but unknown tracks are all but deserted.

The so-called Great Walks are the most popular tracks. Their beauty does indeed make them worth experiencing, but please don't go and then be upset that they are crowded. Of *course* these tracks are sometimes crowded, especially in summer, when people from all over the world come to tramp.

The most walked tracks in NZ are the Abel Tasman Coastal Track, the Routeburn, the Milford, the Tongariro Northern Circuit, the Kepler, and Lake Waikaremoana.

If you want to avoid the crowds, DOC offices and park headquarters can advise and help you plan some enjoyable walks on lesser known tracks. DOC offices are in every city and in dozens of towns, and give free information about tramping in their areas. Every national park, forest park and maritime park has its own DOC headquarters.

There are also council parks, farm parks, regional parks and more, all of which have walks (in NZ a walk is defined as a fairly easy day walk or less, often suitable for families, while a tramp is a longer trek that requires you to be suitably equipped and where some experience may be necessary).

When to Go

The most crowded season is during the school summer holidays, two weeks before Christmas to the end of January – a good period to avoid. The best weather is from January to March, though most tracks can be walked enjoyably any time from about November to April. June and July in the middle of winter are not the time to be out on the tracks. Some are closed in winter because of avalanche danger. It's best to time your walks so that the most southerly are done in midsummer.

Surprisingly, most people on the tracks are from outside NZ. It's common to have a ratio of only one Kiwi out of 10 people in a hut, although on the Milford Track it can reach 50/50. Kiwis do tramp, but they tend to avoid the popular tracks, seeking the really wild and untouched regions.

What to Bring

For an enjoyable tramp the primary consideration is your feet and shoulders. Make sure your footwear is adequate and that your pack is not too heavy. Having adequate, waterproof rain gear is also important, especially on the South Island's West Coast where you can get drenched to the skin in minutes if your rain gear is not up to the challenge.

Equipment This list is for someone who will be sticking to the main tracks, staying in huts and tramping during the summer months. It is inadequate for snow country or winter.

Boots – light to medium with good ankle support are recommended. The boots should be broken in to avoid painful blisters. Cover your heels with

moleskin before you start if you think there is any chance of blisters.

Alternative footwear – thongs (jandals/flipflops) or running/tennis shoes for strolling around the huts or if the boots become just too painful to wear.

Socks – three heavy polypropylene or woollen pairs; two to be worn at once to reduce the chance of blisters. Frequent changes of socks during the day also reduces the chance of blisters but isn't too practical.

Shorts, light shirt – for everyday wear; swimsuits for the immodest.

Woollen sweater/jersey, woollen trousers – essential in case of cold weather. Some of the modern synthetics, such as polypropylene and polar fleece, are just as good as wool.

Waterproof raincoat and overtrousers – a combination of wet and cold can be fatal.

Dishes & cutlery – knife, fork, spoon, cup, plate, soup bowl. (You can cut this back to knife, spoon and bowl – a bowl is multipurpose: you can eat or drink out of it, and mix things in it.)

Pot/billy (one) – 1.5 to 2l capacity is sufficient.

Pans (two) – 15cm across and 5cm deep is plenty. The pot and pans are adequate for two to three-course meals for two people. Preferably the pots should fit into each other and be made of aluminium for lightness.

Pot scrubber and tea towel – washing up is usually done in cold water, making pot cleaning pretty difficult.

Camping stove – take one along, even if you'll be staying in huts. Many huts don't have cookers.

Matches/lighter – for cooking and lighting candles. Matches are difficult to keep dry.

Candle – half to one candle per day. Some huts have lanterns supplied.

Torch (flashlight) – for nocturnal toilet visits and late arrival at the hut.

Small first-aid kit, toilet paper and insect repellent – see the Health section in the Facts for the Visitor chapter for information on first-aid kits and insect repellents.

Small towel (or plas chamois cloth) – should dry quickly.

Sleeping bag – warm down or Hollofill, light to medium weight, including a light stuff bag for rapid and easy packing.

Pen/pencil and paper.

Map and compass.

Water purifier (see the Health section in the Facts for the Visitor chapter).

Sun protectors – hat, cream, glasses.

Camera, binoculars, reference books.

Food Take food which is nourishing, tasty and lightweight:

Breakfast – the most important meal of the day:
  tea/coffee, sugar, instant milk
  muesli/porridge (quick cooking) – good with sultanas (raisins)
  bacon and eggs – bacon in vacuum pack will last for days
  bread, butter/margarine, Vegemite/Marmite or honey
Lunch – normally eaten between huts and therefore should not require too much preparation:
  bread/crackers, butter or margarine (nice wholemeal crackers are available, but 'Cabin Bread' is larger and stronger and so will stand up to being crammed into a pack)
  cheese – tasty, not bland
Dinner – must be hot and substantial:
  instant soups – help to whet the biggest appetites
  fresh meat – good for the first two days
  dehydrated meals – Alliance is excellent, Vesta is OK
  dehydrated vegetables, instant mashed potatoes (check preparation time: 20 minutes is the limit)
  rice – goes with everything (couscous as a substitute)
  dessert – easy to cook dishes such as tapioca, custard or instant puddings
Snacks – important source of energy while tramping:
  chocolate – 100g per person per day
  raisins, sultanas, dried fruit
  scroggin – combination of all the above (make it yourself)
  glucose – in the form of barley sugar, glucose tablets or powder from chemists; it gives almost instant energy
  biscuits – great before bed with tea or coffee; get a recipe for 'Tararuas', an indestructible, calorie-packed life saver
  cordial concentrate – powder; a great thirst quencher, adds flavour to purified water
  instant noodles

This list of food is by no means complete for a long trek, but it should get you through the first tramp without suffering from withdrawal symptoms. For a three-day tramp, one loaf of bread, 200 to 300g of butter/margarine and 200g of instant dried milk (required for many dishes) are sufficient for one person.

As all rubbish should be carried out, ensure that everything is in suitable containers. Don't take glass bottles – transfer the ingredients into light containers. Extra lightweight metal and plastic containers are available from supermarkets and some chemists.

All your gear should be kept in plastic bags, preferably two, for protection from the elements. Clothes must be kept dry under all circumstances. Plastic pack liners, 'survival bags', made by the NZ Mountain Safety Council, are sold in outdoors shops for about $5 and are an excellent investment. Made of thick plastic that will not tear, a survival bag is large enough to climb into for survival if need be, or you could split it and make a shelter. If you can't find one, you could use large green plastic rubbish bags. Put the lot into a lightweight, waterproof backpack.

The total weight of your backpack should not exceed 14kg for a three-day tramp.

Department of Conservation (Te Papa Atawhai)

DOC looks after parks, tracks, walkways, huts and general tramping facilities. It also administers hundreds of scenic, historic, scientific and nature reserves, and wildlife refuges and sanctuaries. It also has responsibility for the Subantarctic Islands and the two World Heritage areas – Tongariro National Park and Te Wahipounamu (southwest NZ, which incorporates Fiordland, Mt Aspiring, Mt Cook and Westland national parks).

The local DOC office is usually the best place for information on nature and outdoor attractions in any area. DOC produces excellent pamphlets on almost any natural attraction. In some towns the visitor centres have the same information and a collection of DOC pamphlets. Also check out www.doc.govt.nz on the Web.

Conservation Volunteer Program DOC has a volunteer program for conservation projects. Work might include counting certain species of birds, guarding and protecting nesting areas, track and/or hut maintenance or any number of other activities. You don't get paid but you do get a chance to go to some wild out-of-the-way places and get hands-on experience in conservation. You can volunteer for any length of time; check with DOC regional offices or on the Web.

National Parks

New Zealand has many parks: 13 national, 19 forest, three maritime and two marine, plus a few other types of parks and reserves.

DOC information centres for national and maritime parks are found at:

Abel Tasman National Park – Totaranui, Nelson, Motueka, Takaka

Arthur's Pass National Park – Arthur's Pass township

Bay of Islands Maritime & Historic Park – Russell

Egmont National Park – Dawson Falls and North Egmont on Mt Taranaki/Egmont

Fiordland National Park – Te Anau

Hauraki Gulf Maritime Park – Auckland

Kahurangi National Park – Karamea, Motueka, Takaka, Nelson

Marlborough Sounds Maritime Park – Picton, Blenheim, Havelock

Mt Aspiring National Park – Wanaka, Makarora

Mt Cook National Park – Mt Cook Village

Nelson Lakes National Park – St Arnaud, Lake Rotoroa

Otago Goldfields Park – Dunedin, Alexandra

Paparoa National Park – Punakaiki

Stewart Island Stewardship Area – Oban (Halfmoon Bay)

Te Urewera National Park – Aniwaniwa, Lake Waikaremoana

Te Wahipounamu World Heritage Area – Haast township

Tongariro National Park – Whakapapa on Mt Ruapehu, Ohakune Mountain Road

Westland National Park – Franz Josef and Fox glaciers

Whanganui National Park – Pipiriki, Taumarunui, Wanganui

In addition to the national parks there are numerous forest areas. The excellent pamphlet *Exploring New Zealand's Parks* outlines the national, maritime and forest parks.

Books

DOC produces very good books with detailed information on the flora and fauna, geology and history of NZ's national parks. DOC leaflets outline thousands of walking tracks throughout the country.

Jim DuFresne's *Tramping in New Zealand* is another Lonely Planet guide, with descriptions of nearly 50 walks, of various lengths and degrees of difficulty, in all parts of the country. *New Zealand's Top Ten Tracks* by

Mark Pickering contains many of the obvious ones (Milford, Routeburn etc). *101 Great Tramps* by Mark Pickering & Rodney Smith has 101 suggestions for two-day to six-day tramps around the country. Also worth a scan is *Walking Tracks of NZ's National Parks*.

Tramping in North Island Forest Parks by Euan & Jennie Nicol and *Tramping in South Island Forest Parks* by Joanna Wright are good for shorter walking and tramping possibilities, from half-hour walks to tramps taking several days. The descriptions of flora, fauna and history in these books are outstanding.

The Forest and Bird Book of Nature Walks by David Collingwood & EV Sale, revised by Joanna Wright, has good suggestions for short walks.

BP (Penguin) publishes a series of pocket-sized paperback guides to several of NZ's most popular walking tracks. There's also a series of Shell guides to the more popular tracks.

Moir's Trampers' Guide to the Southern Lakes & Fiordland by the New Zealand Alpine Club is the definitive work on tracks in the south of the South Island. It comes in two volumes – *Northern Section: Lake Wakatipu to the Ohau Watershed* and *Southern Section: Hollyford Valley South*.

Maps

Land Information NZ's topographical maps are the best, but bookshops don't usually have a good selection. It has map sales offices in the main cities and major towns. The local DOC often sells Land Information NZ's maps of the tracks in its immediate area.

Land Information NZ (formerly known as DOSLI) has various series of maps. Park maps cover national, state and forest parks, and Trackmaps cover some of the more popular walking tracks. There are also Holiday-maker maps, Touringmaps, Terrainmaps and Streetfinder maps and larger Aotearoa and Pacific maps covering all of NZ and many Pacific islands. The most

New Zealand Parks

0   100   200 km

Bay of Islands Maritime & Historic Park

Kaitaia

Russell

Poor Knights Islands Marine Reserve

Northland Forest Park

Whangarei

Hauraki Gulf Maritime Park

Commandel Forest Park

Auckland

Thames

Raukumara State Forest

Kaimai-Mamaku Forest Park

Hamilton

Tauranga

Whakarewarewa Forest Park

Pirongia Forest Park

Rotorua

WHANGANUI NATIONAL PARK

Pureora Forest Park

Whirinaki Forest Park

TE UREWERA NATIONAL PARK

Gisborne

Sugar Loaf Islands Marine Park

Taupo

New Plymouth

Turangi

Kaimanawa Forest Park

Kaweka Forest Park

TONGARIRO NATIONAL PARK

Napier

Hastings

EGMONT NATIONAL PARK

Wanganui

Ruahine Forest Park

ABEL TASMAN NATIONAL PARK

Marlborough Sounds Maritime Park

Rimutaka Forest Park

Palmerston North

Tararua Forest Park

TASMAN SEA

Takaka

KAHURANGI NATIONAL PARK

Nelson

Picton

WELLINGTON

Haurangi Forest Park

Westport

Victoria Forest Park

Mt Richmond Forest Park

St Arnaud

NELSON LAKES NATIONAL PARK

PAPAROA NATIONAL PARK

LEWIS PASS NATIONAL PARK

Greymouth

Lake Sumner Forest Park

Hanmer Springs National Park

Hokitika

ARTHUR'S PASS NATIONAL PARK

SOUTH PACIFIC OCEAN

WESTLAND NATIONAL PARK

Craigeburn Forest Park

Christchurch

TE WAHIPOUNAMU WORLD HERITAGE AREA

MT COOK NATIONAL PARK

Banks Peninsula

MT ASPIRING NATIONAL PARK

Timaru

Milford Sound

Milford

Wanaka

Otago Goldfields Park

Queenstown

Te Anau

Dunedin

FIORDLAND NATIONAL PARK

Catlins State Forest Park

Invercargill

Oban

Stewart Island (Rakiura)

National & Forest Parks

World Heritage Areas

detailed are the Topomaps series of topographical maps, but you may need two or three maps to cover one track. The maps cost about $12.50 each.

Track Classification

Tracks are classified according to their difficulty and many other features – how they are marked, degree of steepness etc. In this chapter we loosely refer to the level of difficulty (easy, medium, hard and difficult). The widely used track classification system is:

Path – easy and well formed; allows for wheelchair access or constructed to 'shoe' standard. Suitable for people of all ages and fitness levels.

Walking Track – easy and well formed; constructed to 'shoe' standard. Suitable for people of most ages and fitness levels.

Tramping Track – requires skill and experience; constructed to 'boot' standard. Suitable for people of average physical fitness.

Route – requires a high degree of skill, experience and route-finding ability. Suitable for well-equipped trampers.

Track Safety

It's very important that you learn and follow some basic rules of safety when tramping in NZ. Thousands of Kiwis and overseas visitors tramp in NZ every year without incident, but every year a few die in the mountains. Most fatalities could have been avoided if simple safety rules had been observed.

The main thing to be aware of is the extremely changeable weather. New Zealand has a maritime climate, which means that the degree and frequency of climate changes is much more severe than large land masses with a continental climate (eg Australia, North America, Europe).

Always be mentally and physically prepared for all kinds of weather and the possibility of sudden changes. Heavy rain, snow and high winds can hit mountain areas *even in summer*, and it can happen in a matter of minutes even on a warm, sunny day. Take along warm clothes, waterproof rain gear (raincoat and overtrousers) and a waterproof pack liner. If you should find your clothing

and footwear are not adequate for the conditions, it's best to turn back.

Weather forecasts should be watched but taken with a grain of salt. New Zealand's prevailing weather comes from the southwest, an area which has no inhabited land and very little sea or air traffic, making accurate reporting difficult. In Fiordland it is considered that the forecast weather hits the area a day before it is forecast.

Hypothermia is the main health hazard when tramping. Be aware of what causes it so you can avoid it, and know what to do about it if it does occur. (Hypothermia is covered under Health in the Facts for the Visitor chapter.)

Drowning was once called the 'New Zealand disease'. Never attempt to cross a river when it is in flood. Many tracks have an emergency wire crossing upstream. If there is no emergency crossing, backtrack to shelter or wait until the creek or river subsides. You would be well advised to learn and practise river crossing techniques.

Getting lost is another very real danger, so stick to the tracks. The native bush is very dense. People have become hopelessly lost even when having set off to do something as simple as a 15-minute walk, and have only been found many days later or not at all. People frequently go missing in the bush and it's not always overseas visitors – it's often experienced trampers who know the area they're tramping in.

Always make sure someone responsible knows where you're going, what route you intend to take, when you expect to come out, and that they must notify the police if you don't come out. Don't forget to let them know when you've come out safely!

Fill out an intentions and/or help form at the DOC office, national park headquarters or visitors centre at the start of the trip, and write in the logbooks of huts along the way, giving the names of the members of your party and details of arrival and intended departure. Do this even if you don't stay in the huts – it will make it far easier to find you if you should go missing.

For safe tramping make sure you:

- Choose a track that suits your level of fitness and experience.
- Find out what to expect on the track. Always seek local advice about current track and weather conditions from the proper authority – the local DOC office, national park headquarters etc – before you set out.
- Go with at least one other person, and stay on the track.
- Be sure to purify river or lake water before drinking it.
- Take along a first-aid kit and everything else you're supposed to – water purifier, warm clothes etc.
- If you meet heavy rain, and rivers in your path have risen, stay where you are until the rivers go down, retrace your tracks, or take another route. Don't ever cross a flooding river unless you are absolutely certain you can get across safely.

The NZ Mountain Safety Council has published a number of pamphlets with good information on tramping including *Bushcraft, Mountaincraft, Outdoor First Aid, Hypothermia, Survival* etc. They are widely available at information centres and hostels. DOC can also give you excellent safety advice. It's worth talking to them about it.

Going with tramping clubs can be a great way to tramp in NZ, as you'll be with like-minded people who know about the bush. Federated Mountain Clubs (PO Box 1604, Wellington) has information on local clubs all around NZ.

Accommodation & Wardens
The following notes on huts and wardens apply only to the popular 'tourist' tracks. Keep these factors in mind:

- When walking allow about 4km per hour on easy ground.
- Huts are usually placed three to four hours apart.
- Huts usually cater for 24 or more, and beds are thick foam mattresses on bunks.
- Huts on the more popular tracks usually have wood stoves for heating and gas burners for cooking.
- There is a two-night limit on huts if they are full.

If you venture off the popular tracks onto any other tracks, things will be quite different. For example, it may take you an hour to cover 1km, huts may be eight hours or so apart, there won't be any wardens and you will have to be much better prepared.

Camping on tracks is allowed on all except the Milford Track. On Great Walks tracks, where the huts can fill up, camping areas are provided beside all the huts for overflow. On the Milford and Routeburn tracks numbers are regulated so huts don't get overloaded.

The NZ Environmental Care Code has guidelines for camping (it is reproduced in this chapter). Always leave firewood in huts for the next group, in case they arrive in heavy rain or after dark.

In the last decade or so, the conditions of tracks and huts have improved dramatically. Tracks are administered by DOC officers and wardens; the former are permanent staff, well trained and very knowledgeable. The wardens are temporary, usually employed for the summer season to keep an eye on and maintain the huts, to provide track information and first aid, to collect hut fees and to help trampers.

Wardens in the national parks collect hut fees when they're on duty, from November to April. Whether a warden is present or not, it's important that you always pay your hut fees, which are used to maintain the huts. Most DOC offices in the regional centres near the start of tracks sell back country hut tickets (see later in this section). Check with wardens or DOC staff in the regional offices for weather forecasts and track information.

Hut & Camping Fees DOC has a network of back country huts (over 950 at last count) in the national, maritime and forest parks. Hut fees range from $4 to a maximum of $30 per night for adults, paid with tickets purchased in advance at any DOC office or park visitors centre. The tickets cost $4 each (you can buy them in booklets) and are valid for 15 months. Children under 11 years of age can use all huts free of charge. Children 11 years and older are charged half-price and use a special 'youth ticket'. If you plan to do a lot of tramping, DOC also sells an Annual Hut Pass, available at all huts except the Great Walks huts.

New Zealand's Environmental Care Code
Toitu te whenua – Leave the land undisturbed.

- **Protect plants and animals.** Treat New Zealand's forests and birds with care and respect. They are often unique and rare.
- **Remove rubbish.** Litter is unattractive, harmful to wildlife and can increase vermin and disease. Plan your visits so as to reduce rubbish, and carry out what you carry in.
- **Bury toilet waste.** In areas without toilet facilities, bury your toilet waste in a shallow hole well away from waterways, tracks, camp sites and huts.
- **Keep streams and lakes clean.** When cleaning and washing, wash well away from the water source. Because soaps and detergents are harmful to water life, drain used water into the soil to allow it to be filtered. If you suspect the water may be contaminated, either boil it for at least three minutes, filter it, or chemically treat it.
- **Take care with fires.** Portable fuel stoves are less harmful to the environment and are more efficient than fires. If you do use a fire, keep it small, use only dead wood and make sure it is out by dousing it with water and checking the ashes before leaving.
- **Camp carefully.** When camping, *leave no trace of your visit.*
- **Keep to the track.** By keeping to the track, you lessen the chance of damaging fragile plants.
- **Consider others.** People visit the back country and rural areas for many reasons. Be considerate of other visitors who also have a right to enjoy the natural environment.
- **Respect cultural heritage.** Many places in New Zealand have a spiritual and historical significance. Treat these places with consideration and respect.
- **Enjoy your visit.** Enjoy your outdoor experience. Take a last look before leaving an area: will the next visitor know that you have been there?

Protect the environment for your own sake, for the sake of those who come after you, and for the environment itself. ■

Huts are classed into four categories and, depending on the category, a night's stay may use one or two tickets, except on Great Walks where special passes are needed. When you arrive at a hut, date the tickets and put them in the box provided. Accommodation is on a first come, first served basis.

The best (category one) huts have cookers and fuel, bunks or sleeping platforms with mattresses, toilet and washing facilities, and a water supply. They may also have lighting, heating, radio communications, drying facilities, and a duty hut warden. The huts, found on Great Walks, are from $6 to $30 a night (youths half-price; off-season $4 to $8).

Category two (intermediate) huts have bunks or sleeping platforms with mattresses, toilet and washing facilities, and a water supply. They may also include cooking and heating facilities, but you may have to provide your own cooker and fuel. The cost is $8 (two tickets) per night. Category three huts are basic, with bunks or sleeping platforms (but no mattresses), toilet and water supply only. You provide your own cooker and fuel. These huts are $4 (one ticket) per night. There is no fee for category four huts, which are usually just simple shelters.

Camping is permitted outside the huts (but not on the Milford); the cost is $6 ($9 on the Routeburn), $4 to $8 in the off-season.

A list of all huts and their categories is available at any DOC office. The Milford and Routeburn tracks operate on a system of their own and are best booked in Te Anau.

The Great Walks
All of the Great Walks are described in this book. The descriptions are designed to whet your appetite rather than deluge you with information. The walks are covered in detail in the pamphlets provided by DOC offices (and information centres) and in Lonely Planet's *Tramping in New Zealand* by Jim DuFresne. For information on a particular walk, see the relevant section of this book –

eg the Lake Waikaremoana Circuit is covered under Te Urewera National Park in The East Coast chapter. The Great Walks are:

Abel Tasman Coastal Track, Abel Tasman National Park (South Island) – an easy, two to three-day walk along the coast and close to beaches and bays. NZ's most popular walk is inundated with people, but to control numbers DOC plans to introduce a booking system in 1998.

Heaphy Track, Kahurangi National Park (South Island) – a four to five-day, medium to hard tramp of 77km through forest and limestone (karst) landscape. The last day provides one of the great beach walks.

Kepler Track, Fiordland National Park (South Island) – this 67km, four to five-day walk is a medium to hard tramp. It climbs to the top of a mountain and includes alpine, lake and river valley scenery.

Lake Waikaremoana Track, Te Urewera National Park (North Island) – a three to four-day, easy to medium tramp with great views of the lake and surrounding bush-clad slopes. Plans have been mooted to introduce a booking system.

Milford Track, Fiordland National Park (South Island) – this 54km, four-day walk is one of the best known in the world. It includes views of river valleys, glaciers, waterfalls and an alpine pass crossing. Bookings are essential.

Rakiura Track (Stewart Island) – a three-day tramp, mostly on duckboards, for which medium fitness is required. The track goes along the coast and through forest.

Routeburn Track, Mt Aspiring and Fiordland national parks (South Island) – a medium, 40km, three-day walk through stunning alpine scenery. It must be booked.

Tongariro Northern Circuit, Tongariro National Park (North Island) – a four-day, medium to hard tramp through an active volcanic landscape. Part of this tramp can be done as the one-day Tongariro Crossing.

The canoe trip down the Whanganui River in Whanganui National Park in the North Island is obviously not a walk – they call it the Whanganui Journey – but it, too, is one of the Great Walks (the Matemateonga Walkway is nearby).

Accommodation All Great Walks require a special Great Walks Pass, sold at DOC offices, national park offices and other places in the vicinity of each walk. Lake Waikaremoana, the Heaphy and Rakiura

tracks do not require a Great Walks Pass in the off season.

Prices differ between the walks, but are generally not expensive. They allow you either to use the huts or to camp in the designated camping grounds, whichever you prefer. Bring camping gear, since at peak times (summer, Easter weekend etc) the huts can fill up.

Other Tracks

In addition to the Great Walks there are numerous other tramping possibilities in all forest and national parks. These are merely some of the possibilities:

North Island

Coromandel Track (Coromandel Peninsula) – an easy to medium, three-day walk near the Pinnacles at the top of Kauaeranga Valley in the Coromandel Forest Park.

Great Barrier Forest Track (Great Barrier Island) – a four-day, easy to medium loop walk. There is the opportunity to see historic kauri dams, regenerating forest and hot springs.

Mt Holdsworth Circuit & Totara Flats Track (Holdsworth, Tararua Forest Park) – two three-day tramps. The first tramp is a medium to hard walk through forest and over the top of alpine Mt

Holdsworth. The second is a medium tramp mostly along the Totara River Valley, with three low saddles to cross.

Ninety Mile Beach-Cape Reinga Walkway (Northland) – a 50km, three day, easy tramp. There are no huts but there are plenty of places to camp on this beach walk.

Round the Mountain, Mt Taranaki/Egmont (Egmont National Park) – a 55km walk of four days or more (depending on which of the many side trips you do). It is medium to hard tramping through forest and mountainous country.

Tongariro Crossing (Tongariro National Park) – a long one-day, medium tramp designed to introduce the fit tramper to this active volcanic landscape.

South Island

Arthur's Pass tramps (Arthur's Pass National Park) – there are many walks to choose from in this park including Goat Pass, Three Passes, Harper Pass and Cass-Lagoon Saddle. Most tramps in this great park are difficult.

Banks Peninsula Walk (private/public land near Akaroa) – a two-day (medium) or four-day (easy) walk over the hills and along the coast of Banks Peninsula. You have to book accommodation in advance.

Dusky & George Sound tracks (Fiordland National Park) – just a couple more examples of the great wealth of tramping in this World Heritage region. The Dusky is a very challenging tramp, as is the George Sound route – you need lots of time if you plan to tramp in this region.

Greenstone/Caples tracks (Stewardship land just outside Fiordland National Park) – these two tracks are close to the Routeburn and a good way to finish this popular track.

Hollyford Track (Fiordland National Park) – there are several variants on this track but it will take eight days if you walk in and walk out, four days if you fly one way. It traverses through low level forest, often on muddy tracks, and includes lake, alpine, rainforest and coastal scenery.

Inland Pack & Croesus tracks (Paparoa National Park) – the first of these walks, a medium tramp, follows river valleys through the karst landscape near Punakaiki on the West Coast. The second walk is a medium two-day crossing of the Paparoa Range from Blackball to Barrytown.

Kaikoura Coast Track (private/public land near Amuri, 50km south of Kaikoura) – three-day walk along spectacular coast; nights are spent in farm cottages.

Matukituki Valley walks (Mt Aspiring National Park) – there are a number of good walks in the Matukituki Valley near Wanaka. The difficult Cascade Saddle Route joins this region with the Rees-Dart valleys.

Mt Somers Subalpine Walkway (Canterbury Foothills) – a medium, three-day walk through river valleys, subalpine forest and pastures. There are harder variations for the fitter tramper.

North-West Circuit (Stewart Island) – this eight to 10-day route is just one of the many possibilities on Rakiura. The whole island offers the chance for wilderness walks.

Queen Charlotte Track (Marlborough Sounds) – a three to four-day, medium walk from which you get great views of the Sounds and pass many historic places.

Rees-Dart Track (Mt Aspiring National Park) – a 70km, four to five-day, hard walk through river valleys and over an alpine pass.

St James Walkway (Lake Sumner Forest Park/Lewis Pass Reserve) – this 66km, five-day, medium walk passes through subalpine scenery.

Travers-Sabine Circuit & D'Urville Valley Track (Nelson Lakes National Park) – these are five to six-day circular tracks for experienced trampers only. The first is 80km long and includes alpine passes and river valleys. The second is about 65km and also includes a high-altitude pass.

Wangapeka & Leslie-Karamea tracks (Kahurangi National Park) – the first is a four to five-day, medium tramp through river valleys and over passes (a good return walk after the Heaphy). The second is a 90-100km, five to seven-day tramp for the experienced only. It includes river valleys, gorges and passes.

Getting There & Away

Getting to and from tracks can be a real problem, except for the most popular, which are serviced by trampers' transport. Having a vehicle only simplifies the problem of getting to one end of the track. Otherwise you have to take public transport or hitch in, and if the track starts or ends at the end of a dead-end road, hitching will be difficult.

Leave excess luggage behind or send it on to a point near the end of the track. Camping grounds and other accommodation places will often hold luggage for free. Bus companies will carry excess luggage at a very reasonable price and will hold it in their offices until it is picked up.

SKIING & SNOWBOARDING

New Zealand is one of the most popular places for skiing and snowboarding in the southern hemisphere. In addition to downhill (alpine) skiing, there are ample opportunities

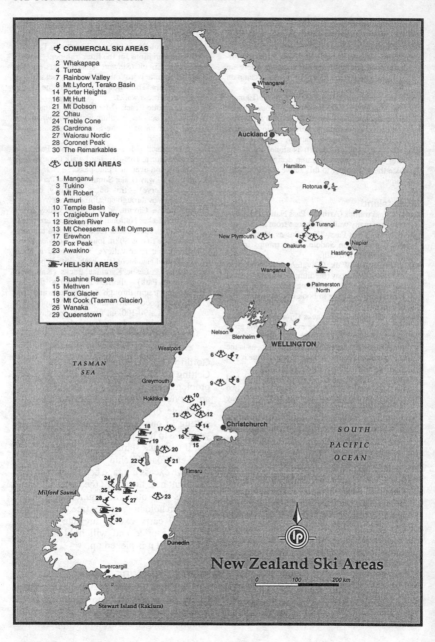

COMMERCIAL SKI AREAS

2 Whakapapa
4 Turoa
7 Rainbow Valley
8 Mt Lyford, Terako Basin
14 Porter Heights
16 Mt Hutt
21 Mt Dobson
22 Ohau
24 Treble Cone
25 Cardrona
27 Waiorau Nordic
28 Coronet Peak
30 The Remarkables

CLUB SKI AREAS

1 Manganui
3 Tukino
6 Mt Robert
9 Amuri
10 Temple Basin
11 Craigieburn Valley
12 Broken River
13 Mt Cheeseman & Mt Olympus
17 Erewhon
20 Fox Peak
23 Awakino

HELI-SKI AREAS

5 Ruahine Ranges
15 Methven
18 Fox Glacier
19 Mt Cook (Tasman Glacier)
26 Wanaka
29 Queenstown

New Zealand Ski Areas

0   100   200 km

for cross-country, ski touring and ski mountaineering. One ski area, the Waiorau Nordic Ski Area in the Pisa Range near Wanaka, specialises in Nordic skiing, but many of the downhill ski areas offer cross-country possibilities.

Heli-skiing is another attraction. In winter helicopters are used to lift skiers up to the top of long, isolated stretches of virgin snow, or even onto glaciers.

New Zealand's commercial ski areas are generally not very well endowed with chalets, lodges or hotels. Accommodation is usually in surrounding towns, sometimes quite a long distance from the slopes, but daily transport shuttles to and from the main ski areas. A good variety of accommodation is usually on offer, from cheap hostels to high-class hotels and ski lodges.

Club ski areas are open to the public and much less crowded than the commercial ski fields. Although nonmembers pay a slightly higher rate, they are still usually a cheaper alternative. Many have lodges you can stay at, subject to availability. Winter holidays and weekends will be fully booked, but midweek you'll have no trouble.

At the major ski areas, lifts cost from $30 to $60 a day and two-hour group lessons are around $35/20 an hour for adults/children. These costs are much lower at the smaller resorts. All the usual equipment can be bought or hired in NZ; for between $25 and $30/15 an adult/child can be fitted out. Snowboard hire is from $30 to $40.

The ski season is generally from June to October, although it varies considerably from one ski area to another. Snow-making machines assist nature at some areas.

There are plenty of ski-package tours both from Australia and within NZ. Information centres in NZ, and the NZTB internationally, have brochures on the various ski areas and packages available, and can make bookings.

The *NZ Ski & Snowboard Guide* by Brown Bear is an excellent (free) annual reference filled with information on all the commercial and club ski areas in NZ. It has colour illustrations of the ski areas and ski runs, and information on heli-skiing and glacier skiing. On the Web, try www.snow.co.nz for information on the ski fields, and www.borderzone.co.nz for snowboarding.

North Island

Whakapapa Whakapapa ski area, the largest in NZ with over 30 groomed runs and 23 lifts, is 6km above Whakapapa Village on Mt Ruapehu in Tongariro National Park. It's the end of the road – known as the Top of the Bruce – and has the most popular ski slopes in NZ, including a downhill course dropping nearly 675m over 4km. There are chairlifts, T-bars, platters and rope tows, and plenty of possibilities for snowboarding including excellent pipes off the far western T-bar, cross-country, downhill, ski touring, and paragliding. The normal season is from the end June to mid-November.

Accommodation can be found at Whakapapa Village within the national park (see Tongariro National Park in the Central Plateau chapter), or in nearby towns including National Park (12km away), Turangi (50km) and Ohakune (74km). Accommodation bookings are very heavy during the ski season, especially on weekends.

You can drive yourself up to the slopes or you can take a shuttle minibus from Whakapapa Village, National Park or Turangi; a taxi service is available from Ohakune.

Contact: Ruapehu Alpine Lifts Ltd, Private Bag, Mt Ruapehu (☎ (07) 892 3738, snowphone (07) 892 3833).

Turoa Around the other side of Mt Ruapehu from the Whakapapa ski area, the Turoa ski area on the south-western side of Ruapehu is the country's second largest ski area. Quad and triple chairlifts, T-bars and platters take you up to the beginning of a 4km run. There's also a beginners lift, snowboarding and cross-country skiing. There is no road toll or parking fee and daily ski area transport is available from Ohakune, 17km away, where there's plenty of accommodation – once again, accommodation bookings can be heavy during the ski season, especially for the more economical places, so make sure you plan ahead.

Ohakune has the liveliest après-ski scene in the North Island. There are three cafeterias, plus a snack shack and bar on the ski area. Skis can be hired on the slopes or at many places around Ohakune. The season lasts from June to November.

Contact: Turoa Ski Resort Ltd, PO Box 46, Ohakune (☎ (06) 385 8456, snowphone 0900 99 444).

Tukino This club-operated ski area is on the eastern side of Mt Ruapehu, 50km from Turangi. It's quite remote – 14km of gravel road from the sealed Desert Rd (SH1), and you need a 4WD vehicle to get in (or make a prior arrangement to use the club transport). Because access is so limited, the area is uncrowded, but most runs are beginner or intermediate with only a couple of advanced runs. It has a short season (July to October) because it is on the opposite side of the mountain from prevailing winds.

Accommodation at the lodges must be arranged in advance: *Desert Alpine Club* (☎ (09) 420 5339); *Christiana Club* (☎ (07) 855 4749); and *Aorangi Club* (☎ (04) 478 7055). For information call the mountain manager (☎ (06) 387 6294).

Manganui Ski Area, Mt Taranaki There's more volcano-side skiing on the eastern slopes of Mt Taranaki in the Egmont National Park at the Manganui club ski area, 22km from Stratford. The ski area is a 20-minute walk along the scenic Manganui Gorge from the car park. It has a T-bar and three rope tows, and there is a day-visitor canteen. The season here is from mid-June to October. There is limited accommodation on the ski area and at the Stratford Mountain House, with more accommodation available in Stratford and New Plymouth.

Early summer skiing is possible off the summit of Mt Taranaki; when conditions permit, it is an invigorating two-hour climb to the crater but an exhilarating 1300m descent.

Contact: Stratford Mountain Club, care of 32 Mountain Rd, RD2 Stratford (snowphone (06) 765 7669).

South Island
Coronet Peak New Zealand's southernmost slopes, near Queenstown, are rated the best in New Zealand and are comparable to any in the world. The season, mid-June to October, is reliable because of a multimillion dollar snow-making system. Access to the ski area is from Queenstown, 18km away, and there's a shuttle bus service in the ski season. The rich often catch a helicopter.

Chairlifts, T-bars and beginners lifts take you up the slopes. The treeless slopes and good snow provide excellent skiing – the chairlifts run to altitudes of 1585 and 1620m. Consistent gradient and the many undulations make this a snowboarder's paradise.

The ski area is operated by the Mt Cook Group and it has a licensed restaurant, overnight ski storage, a ski repair shop and ski lessons. For accommodation see the Queenstown section in the Otago chapter; there's a multiplicity of après-ski possibilities.

Contact: Mt Cook Group, PO Box 359, Queenstown (☎ (03) 442 4640, snowphone (0900) 99766).

The Remarkables Like Coronet Peak, The Remarkables ski area is near Queenstown (23km away), with shuttle buses running from Queenstown during the season (late June to late October). It, too, has beginner, intermediate and advanced runs, with chairlifts and beginners tows.

Both Coronet Peak and The Remarkables have designated ski school areas, with group, private, and children's lessons. The Remarkables also offers a Nordic ski school with cross-country lessons. Snowboarding instruction is also available.

Contact: as for Coronet Peak.

Treble Cone The season at Treble Cone, 29km from Wanaka in the southern lake district, is from mid-June to early October. Reliability has been improved with the extension of snow-making to the top of the Deliverance chair. The highest of the areas in the southern lake area, Treble Cone is spectacularly situated overlooking Lake Wanaka. Slopes are steep and best for intermediate to advanced skiers. It has a chairlift, two T-bars and one learner tow, as well as a lift-serviced, natural half-pipe for snowboarding. Accommodation is available in Wanaka and shuttle buses run from there or from Queenstown, 1½ hours away.

Contact: Treble Cone Ski Area, PO Box 206, Wanaka (☎ (03) 443 7443, snowphone 0900 34 444).

Cardrona Cardrona, 25km from Wanaka, is open from mid-June to mid-October. It has three chairlifts, beginners tows and a radical half-pipe for snowboarders. Numerous gentle runs over variable terrain are suitable for beginners and intermediate skiers. Buses run from Wanaka during the ski season, or from Queenstown, about 1½ hours away. There is a licensed bistro, two cafes and four luxury apartments on the slopes.

Cardrona has acquired a reputation for its services offered to disabled skiers and it is the first resort in the South Island to have an on-field crèche.

Contact: Cardrona Ski Resort, PO Box 117, Wanaka (☎ (03) 443 7411, snowphone 0900 34 444).

Waiorau Nordic Area New Zealand's only commercial Nordic ski area is 26km from Wanaka, on the Pisa Range high above Lake Wanaka. There are 25km of groomed trails and thousands of hectares of open rolling country for the ski tourer. Huts with facilities are dotted along the top of the Pisa Range. So whatever Nordic discipline you are into is catered for here. The season is from late June to late September.

Contact: Waiorau Nordic Ski Area, Cardrona Rd, Wanaka (☎ (03) 443 7542).

Awakino This club ski area is on Mt St Mary in the Waitaki Valley, 11km from Kurow and 45km from Oamaru. Awakino is known to get the odd powder blast during southerly storms but essentially it is for intermediate skiers. The season is from July to October. Although it has just three rope lifts and one access tow, most runs are for intermediate and advanced skiers. Good cross-country

touring is available nearby. There's accommodation 500m below the main rope lift or at Kurow, Oamaru or Omarama. Access to the area is by 4WD.

Contact: Waitaki Ski Club, PO Box 191, Oamaru (☎ (03) 434 5110).

South Canterbury Region There are three ski areas in South Canterbury – Ohau, Mt Dobson and Fox Peak. The Mt Dobson and Fox Peak ski areas are between Fairlie and Tekapo, on the main Christchurch to Mt Cook road. Both towns are good bases for skiing in this region.

The most distant from Christchurch, the **Ohau** commercial ski area is on Mt Sutton, 52km from Twizel, and has the longest T-bar lift in NZ. It has a large percentage of intermediate and advanced runs, plus excellent terrain for snowboarding, cross-country and ski touring to Lake Dumb Bell. Accommodation is available at the Lake Ohau Lodge, 15 minutes from the slopes, or in Twizel and Omarama, 52km away. The ski season is from July to October.

Contact: Ohau Ski Area, PO Box 51, Twizel (☎ & snowphone (03) 438 9885).

With a 3km-wide basin, **Mt Dobson**, a commercial ski area 26km from Fairlie, caters for learners and has NZ's largest intermediate area and advanced runs. From the summit of Mt Dobson, on a clear day, you can see Mt Cook and the Pacific Ocean. Accommodation is in Fairlie and Lake Tekapo. The season is from late June to October.

Contact: Mt Dobson Ski Area, 30 Alloway St, Fairlie (☎ (03) 685 8039, snowphone 0900 39 888).

The **Fox Peak** club ski area, 29km from Fairlie in the Two Thumb Range, has four rope tows and the learners tow is free. There is good ski touring from the summit of Fox Peak and parapenting is also popular here. There's accommodation at the ski area at Fox Lodge, 3km below the ski area, or in Fairlie. The season is from early July to late September.

Contact: Fox Peak Ski Club, PO Box 368,

Timaru (☎ (03) 688 1870, snowphone (03) 688 0044).

Mt Hutt Mt Hutt is one of the highest ski areas in the southern hemisphere and is rated as one of the best in NZ. It's 118km west of Christchurch, close to the local accommodation centre of Methven or reached by bus from Christchurch.

Mt Hutt has beginner, intermediate and advanced-level slopes, with a quad and a triple chairlift, three T-bars, various other lifts, and heli-skiing from the car park to slopes further afield. Instruction is offered at all levels, and there's also racing and racing instruction. The wide open faces are good for those learning to snowboard.

The ski season is very long, usually from early May to mid-October, and is made reliable by extensive snow-making facilities. There's a variety of accommodation in Methven, 26km away, or you can stay at Ashburton, 61km away, or Christchurch.

Contact: Mt Cook Group, PO Box 14, Methven (☎ (03) 302 8811, snowphone 0900 99 766).

Erewhon The Erewhon club ski area must be one of the best gems in NZ. It is based on Mt Potts, above the headwaters of the Rangitata River, and is about 75km from Methven. It has four rope lifts and one learners lift. Accommodation and meals are available from a lodge at Mt Potts, 8km from the ski area. It has a good mix of beginner, intermediate and advanced slopes, with snowboarding and cross-country also popular. Transport by 4WD is essential, and can be arranged through the club. The season is from June to September.

Contact: Erewhon Ski Club, care of Mt Somers Station, Mt Somers (snowphone (03) 308 7091).

Porter Heights The closest commercial ski area to Christchurch, Porter Heights is 96km away on the Arthur's Pass road. The 720m-long 'Big Mama' is the steepest run in NZ. There are three T-bars, one platter lift and a learners tow. There's a half-pipe for snow-

boarders, plus good cross-country areas, and ski touring out along the ridge. The season runs from mid-June to mid-October. Accommodation is available at the area or in neighbouring Springfield. There is a $6 toll on the access road.

Contact: Porter Heights Skifield, PO Box 536, Christchurch (☎ (03) 379 7087, snowphone 0900 34 444).

Arthur's Pass & Craigieburn Regions
There are five ski areas in the Arthur's Pass and Craigieburn regions.

The most distant from Christchurch, **Temple Basin** is a club area just 4km from the Arthur's Pass township. It is a 45-minute walk uphill from the car park to the lift area with four rope tows. From the summit of Mt Temple, on a clear day, spectacular views extend all the way from the Tasman Sea to the Pacific Ocean. At night there's floodlit skiing. Accommodation is at two on-field lodges, or in Arthur's Pass. The season is from June to October. There are good back-country runs for snowboarders.

Contact: Temple Basin Ski Club, PO Box 1228, Christchurch (☎ (03) 377 7788, snowphone (03) 366 6644 ext 1104).

The **Craigieburn Valley** ski area, centred on Hamilton Peak, is 40km from Arthur's Pass, 48km from Springfield and 110km from Christchurch. It is one of NZ's most challenging club areas, with intermediate and advanced runs and a shredder's 'soggy dream'. It is a pleasant 10-minute walk through beech forest from the car park to the ski area. The season is from early July to October.

Contact: Craigieburn Valley Ski Club, PO Box 2152, Christchurch (☎ (03) 365 2514, snowphone (03) 366 6644).

It is possible to ski from Craigieburn to the **Broken River** club ski area, 50 minutes away; it will take twice that time to ski back, so plan accordingly. Otherwise access to Broken River is unsealed for the last 6km, after which it's a 15-minute walk to the lodges and a further 10-minute walk to the ski area. Accommodation is available in three lodges, or you can stay in Springfield,

40 minutes away; it's 1½ hours to Christchurch. The season is from late June to October.

Contact: Broken River Ski Club, PO Box 2718, Christchurch (☎ (03) 318 7270, snowphone (03) 366 6644).

Another good club area in the Craigieburn Range is **Mt Cheeseman**, 112km from Christchurch. The ski area, based on Mt Cockayne, is in a wide, sheltered basin with mostly intermediate and advanced runs. Accommodation is at two lodges in the area, or in Springfield. The season is from early July to late September. Southern Excursions (☎ (03) 358 9249) has transport to Cheeseman and Porter Heights.

Contact: Mt Cheeseman Ski Club, PO Box 22178, Christchurch (☎ (03) 379 5315, snowphone (03) 366 6644).

The fifth ski area is **Mt Olympus**. Hard to find, but worth the search, Mt Olympus, is 66km from Methven and 12km from Lake Ida. This club area has four tows which lead to a number of intermediate and advanced runs. The southerly aspect on the south side of the Craigieburn Range makes for good powder. Snowboarding is accepted, there are good cross-country areas and ski-touring trails to other areas. Accommodation is on the field and in a lower lodge, or in Methven; 4WD is advisable from the bottom hut. The season is from early July to October.

Contact: PO Box 25055, Christchurch (☎ (03) 366 6644, ext 1108).

Hanmer Springs Region There are three ski areas near Hanmer Springs. **Amuri**, a club area based on Mt St Patrick, is 17km from Hanmer Springs and has a poma and two rope tows leading to mostly intermediate and advanced runs. Accommodation is on-field, or you can stay in Hanmer Springs, 45 minutes away. The season is from early July to September.

Contact: Amuri Ski Area, PO Box 129, Hanmer Springs (☎ (03) 315 7201, snowphone (03) 366 6644).

Mt Lyford is 60km from Hanmer Springs or Kaikoura, and 4km from Mt Lyford Village where accommodation is available.

The Lake Stella field has skiing at all levels, basin and off-piste cross-country skiing, 15km of groomed trails for ski touring, and a natural pipe for snowboarding. It is open from May to October; a $5 toll applies on the access road.

The nearby **Terako Basin** ski field has advanced skiing and is linked by rope tow to Mt Lyford.

Contact: Mt Lyford Ski Area, Private Bag, Waiau, North Canterbury (☎ (03) 315 6178, snowphone (03) 366 6644).

Nelson Region In the north, near St Arnaud in Nelson Lakes National Park, there are two ski areas. The **Rainbow Valley** commercial ski area is just outside the park. There is a double chair and a T-bar which lift skiers to the top of a spacious bowl, two learners tows, and there's good cross-country ski touring. Accommodation is available in St Arnaud or in Nelson or Blenheim, each 1½ hours away. The season is from mid-June to October.

Contact: Rainbow Valley Ski Area, Private Bag, St Arnaud (☎ (03) 521 1861, snowphone 0900 34 444).

Inside the park, 15km from St Arnaud, **Mt Robert** is a club area with two lodges right at the ski area, but it's a two-hour walk from the car park, 7km from St Arnaud, to reach it. On weekends a helicopter lift runs from the car park (about $35 per person). This area is known for its powder and many cross-country opportunities for those suitably equipped. The season is from mid-June to October.

Contact: Nelson Ski Club, PO Box 344, Nelson (snowphone (03) 548 8336).

Heli-Skiing & Glacier Skiing

New Zealand is a great place to try heli-skiing. Harris Mountains Heli-Skiing, based in Wanaka and Queenstown, has been suggested by many as the pick of the bunch. It operates from July to October over a wide area with over 100 peaks and 200 runs to choose from in The Remarkables, the Harris Mountains, the Buchanans Range, and the Branches, plus the Tyndall Glacier. They can be contacted at 99 Ardmore St, Wanaka

(☎ (03) 443 7930). Four runs in a day will cost $655, seven runs $830.

Other heli-skiing companies in the South Island include:

Alpine Guides Mt Cook (☎ (03) 435 1834), based in Mt Cook Village
Methven Heli-ski (☎ (03) 302 8108)
Mt Hutt Heli-Ski, based in Rakaia (☎ (03) 302 8401)
Southern Lakes Heliski (☎ (03) 442 6222), based in Queenstown

In the North Island, Snowrange Heli-skiing does guided heli-ski trips to the Ruahine Ranges, south-east of Mt Ruapehu. It is based in Taihape (☎ (06) 388 1696).

The **Tasman Glacier** is a ski resort for the jetsetter – to ski 10 to 12km down from the upper reaches of the Tasman Glacier first requires a flight up from Mt Cook airfield in a ski-plane. You need to be a competent skier as well as a rich one to savour this unique skiing experience. The lower reaches of the glacier are almost dead flat and are usually covered in surface moraine so you must either walk out – or fly once again. Count on around $600 for a flight up, the guide fee, two runs down the glacier and the flight back. The season is from mid-July to late October.

MOUNTAINEERING

New Zealand has a rich history of mountaineering, providing an ideal training ground for greater adventures overseas. The Southern Alps offer a great number of challenging climbs, and are studded with a number of impressive peaks. This very physical and highly challenging pursuit is not for the uninitiated, and contains a number of dangers – fickle weather, storms, winds, extreme cold, loose rock, rockfalls and equipment failure.

But if you have to climb 'because it's there', proper instruction and training will enable you to make commonsense decisions that enhance your safety and get you up among those beautiful mountain peaks.

The Mt Cook region has always been the focus of climbing in NZ. On 2 March 1882, William Spotswood Green and two Swiss alpinists, after a 62-hour epic, failed to reach the summit of Cook (Aoraki). Two years later three local climbers, Tom Fyfe, George Graham and Jack Clarke, spurred into action by the news that two well-known European alpinists, Edward Fitzgerald and Matthias Zurbriggen, were coming to attempt Cook, set off to climb it before the visitors. On Christmas Day 1884 they ascended the Hooker Glacier and north ridge, a brilliant climb in those days, and stood on the summit.

In 1913 Freda du Faur, an Australian, was the first woman to reach the summit. In 1948 Edmund Hillary's party climbed the south ridge. (Hillary went on to become, with Tenzing Norgay, the first to reach the summit of Mt Everest in the Himalaya.) Since then most of the daunting face routes have been

Following in Sir Edmund Hillary's footsteps...

climbed. The Mt Cook region has many great peaks – Sefton, the beguiling Tasman, Silberhorn, Elie de Beaumont, Malte Brun, Aiguilles Rouges, Nazomi, La Perouse, Hicks, De la Beche, Douglas and the Minarets. Many of the peaks can be ascended from Westland National Park, and there is a system of climbers' huts on both sides of the divide.

Mt Cook is only one of a number of outstanding climbing areas. The others extend along the spine of the South Island from Tapuaenuku (in the Kaikouras) and the Nelson Lakes peaks, in the north, to the rugged mountains of Fiordland.

Arthur's Pass has a number of challenging routes on Mt Rolleston and 'away from it all' climbs on Mts Carrington and Murchison. To the south lie the remote Arrowsmiths, with true wilderness climbing possibilities.

Beyond the Cook region is Mt Aspiring National Park, centred on 'the Matterhorn of the South', Mt Aspiring, and the Volta, Thermae and Bonar ice fields which cling to its sides. This is the second centre of mountaineering in NZ, with possibilities for all levels of climbs on Aspiring, Rob Roy, Avalanche, Liverpool, Barff, and peaks around the Olivine Ice Plateau. To the south, in the Forbes Mountains, is Mt Earnslaw, flanked by the Rees and Dart rivers.

Fiordland is not without its impressive peaks. The mightiest of these is Tutoko, the centrepiece of the Darrans Range, just to the north of Milford Sound. There are some walks in this area but, generally, if you wish to explore the Darrans you are forced to climb up sheer granite walls. This is the remotest and most daunting region of NZ, and the domain of the skilled, confident mountaineer.

The NZ Alpine Club (☎ (03) 377 7595; Level 6, Manchester Courts, on the corner of Manchester and Hereford Sts, Christchurch) provides information and produces the annuals *NZ Alpine Journal* and *NZ Climber*. For those seeking to learn the necessary skills, the following companies provide expert instruction, mountaineering courses and private guiding:

Mt Cook & Westland National Parks
  Alpine Guides Mt Cook (☎ (03) 435 1834)
  PO Box 20, Mt Cook Village
  Alpine Guides (Westland) (☎ (03) 751 0825)
  PO Box 38, Main Rd, Fox Glacier
  Alpine Recreation (☎ (03) 680 6736)
  PO Box 75, Lake Tekapo

Mt Aspiring National Park
  Mt Aspiring Guides (☎ (03) 443 9422)
  PO Box 345, Wanaka
  Mountain Recreation (☎ (03) 443 7330)
  PO Box 204, Wanaka

ROCK CLIMBING

This sport has increased in popularity in New Zealand. No longer just considered practice for mountaineering, it is now an activity in its own right. A number of companies take beginners out for their first climbs, with all attention paid to safety.

In the North Island, popular climbing areas include the Mt Eden Quarry in Auckland, Whanganui Bay and Motuoapa in the vicinity of Lake Taupo, Piarere near Cambridge and, about 20km south-east of Te Awamutu, the Wharepapa Rock Climbing Field.

The South Island has a great number of rock-climbing areas. The Port Hills above Christchurch has a number of climbs, and 100km away on the road to Arthur's Pass is Castle Hill and a number of great friction climbs. North of Dunedin is Long Beach. For the adventurous there are the long, extreme routes of the Darrans in Fiordland.

RAP JUMPING

Rap jumping is a variation on abseiling or rappelling – instead of the traditional face to the wall, feet first approach of descent, you go almost head first, face out. Auckland offers urban rap jumping above the shoppers.

CAVING

Caving opportunities abound as this is another activity popular among local outdoor enthusiasts. Auckland, Westport and Waitomo are all areas where you'll find both active local clubs and organised tours. One of the most spectacular caving experiences is the 100m abseil into the 'Lost World' tomo near Waitomo. For more information contact the NZ Speleological Society (NZSS; ☎ (07) 878 7640; PO Box 18, Waitomo Caves).

MOUNTAIN BIKING & CYCLE TOURING

New Zealand, with its great scenery and off-road possibilities, is great biking country. Most towns have mountain bikes for hire, and excellent cycling books are available (see the Bicycle section in the Getting Around chapter).

For downhill fans, various companies will take you up to the tops of mountains, hills and volcanoes (Mt Ruapehu, Christchurch's Port Hills, The Remarkables) so that you can hurtle down without the usual grunt of getting uphill beforehand.

Many routes which were traditionally walked are now being cycled. One thing to remember, though, is *never* to bicycle on walking tracks in national parks unless it has been permitted. DOC will fine you if you're caught. Contact the NZ Mountain Bike Association (NZMBA; ☎ (07) 378 9552; PO Box 371, Taupo).

WATER ACTIVITIES
Jet-Boating

New Zealand is the home of the amazing jet-boats, invented by CWF Hamilton in 1957. An inboard engine sucks water into a tube in the bottom of the boat, and an impeller driven by the engine blows it out a nozzle at the stern in a high-speed stream. The boat is steered simply by directing the jet stream.

The boats are ideal for use in shallow water and white water because there are no propellers to damage, there is better clearance under the boat, and the jet can be reversed instantly for quick braking. The instant response of the jet enables the boats to execute 360° spins almost within the length of the boat. All that adds up to some hair-raising rides on NZ rivers.

The Shotover and Kawarau rivers near Queenstown and the Buller near Westport are renowned jet-boating rivers in the South Island; the Dart River is less travelled but also good. In the North Island, the Whanga-

JEFF WILLIAMS

New Zealand's rivers and jet-boats can be a hair-raising combination

nui, Manganui-a-te-Ao, Motu, Rangitaiki, Kaituna and Waikato rivers are excellent for jet-boating. At Waitomo you can drive your own mini jet-boat and at Broadlands, Waikato, you can ride as a passenger in an exhilarating sprint jet.

Just about every riverside and lakeside town throughout NZ has a jet-boat company that runs trips, sometimes in combination with other adventure activities such as bungy jumping, aerial sightseeing, rafting and tramping.

Rafting

There are almost as many white-water rafting possibilities as there are rivers in NZ. And there is no shortage of companies to take you on a heart-pounding, drenching, exhilarating and spine-tingling ride down some wild, magnificent rivers. The Shotover and Kawarau rivers in the South Island, popular for jet-boating, are also popular for white-water rafting. Canterbury has the Rangitata River, considered one of NZ's best.

The north of the South Island has great rafting possibilities, such as the Buller, Karamea, Mokihinui and Gowan rivers. Details about all the companies offering trips can be found in the respective sections. The West Coast has the Hokitika and Waiho rivers, plus many other rafting possibilities.

In the North Island there are plenty of rivers, like the Rangitaiki, Wairoa, Motu, Tongariro, Rangitikei and Ngaruroro, that are just as good. There is also the Kaituna

Cascades near Rotorua, with the 7m Okere Falls as its highlight. This is perhaps NZ's bumpiest raft ride, with 15 drops in 40 minutes. The drop over the 6m Tawhai Falls in Tongariro National Park is another dramatic plunge

Rivers are graded from I to VI, with VI meaning 'unraftable'. The grading of the Shotover canyon varies from III to V+ depending on the time of year, the Kawarau River is rated IV, and the Wairoa River is graded III to V. On the rougher stretches there's usually a minimum age limit of 12 or 13 years. The rafting companies supply wet suits and life jackets.

Rafting trips take anything from one hour to three days and cost between about $75 and $130 per person per day, depending on whether or not helicopter access is involved. Spring and summer are the most popular rafting times.

Be aware that people have been killed in rafting accidents – check at local tourist offices for the best and safest times for rafting. There are risks in all such adventure activities, but safe rafting will always to some extent depend on your fellow crew, ie the other amateurs in the boat with you.

Cave Rafting

Yet another variation on the rafting theme is not true rafting at all, but it is very unusual and exciting. It's known as 'tumu tumu toobing' and 'black-water rafting' at Waitomo in the North Island, as 'underworld rafting' at Westport and 'adventure caving' at Greymouth in the South Island.

It involves donning a wet suit, a lighted hard hat and a black inner tube and floating on underground rivers through some spectacular caves. An added attraction is seeing glow-worms, twinkling like a Milky Way of stars in the bowels of the earth.

Canoeing & Kayaking

An open two-person canoe is called a 'Canadian canoe' in NZ. A kayak, a smaller, narrower one-person craft which is covered except for a hole for the paddler to sit in, is often called a 'kayak' in NZ but it can also

be called a 'canoe'. Specify whether you mean a 'Canadian canoe' or a 'kayak' when talking about river trips in NZ.

Many companies offer canoeing and kayaking trips on the same rivers where rafting is popular. You can go for a few hours of quiet paddling or white-water excitement in hired canoes or kayaks without a guide, or take longer solo or guided camping trips with fishing and other activities thrown in.

Canoeing is especially popular on the Whanganui River in the North Island, where you can hire a canoe for days at a time. It's also popular on lakes, notably Lake Taupo, and on lakes near Christchurch.

Kayaking is a very popular sport. Commercial trips (for those without their own equipment) are offered on a number of rivers and lakes in the North and South islands. One of the best is with Alpine River Guides on the Matukituki and Makarora rivers near Wanaka. Contact the NZ Canoeing Association (NZCA), PO Box 3768, Wellington.

Sea Kayaking Sea kayaking is very popular. Renowned sea kayaking areas are the Hauraki Gulf, Bay of Islands and Coromandel in the North Island and, in the South Island, the Marlborough Sounds and along the coast of the Abel Tasman National Park, where sea kayaking has become a viable alternative to walking the Abel Tasman Coastal Track (see those sections for further details).

Fiordland has become a popular destination for those wishing to hone their sea kayaking skills. Tour operators in Te Anau, Milford and Manapouri arrange spectacular trips in the lakes and on the fiords.

River Sledging

Discard the raft, kayak, canoe, Lilo or inflated inner tube if you think they lack manoeuvrability. Instead, grasp a responsive polystyrene sled or a modified boogey board, flippers, wet suit and helmet, a positive attitude, and go for it.

In the South Island, rivers around Queenstown and Wanaka offer this thrill (see those sections in the Otago chapter).

Sailing

Auckland is appropriately named the City of Sails – the insular nature of NZ throws up the world's best mariners and the Kiwis have swept the world before them in international yachting races. Most recently Kiwi sailors have dominated the Whitbread around the world race and, in May 1995, Russell Coutts' *Black Magic* captured the America's Cup from Dennis Conner's *Young America* team in a 5-0 finals 'sail'-over. See the boxed text entitled America's Cup 2000 in the Auckland chapter for details of NZ's defence of the cup.

There are plenty of opportunities for travellers to experience sailing in NZ. The Bay of Islands (and Whangaroa to the north), the southern lakes (Te Anau and Wakatipu) and the cities of Auckland and Dunedin are good venues to experience the thrill of the wind in the sails.

Scuba Diving

The Bay of Islands Maritime and Historic Park and the Hauraki Gulf Maritime Park in the North Island, and the Marlborough Sounds Maritime Park in the South Island, are obvious attractions but both islands have many more diving possibilities. Even Invercargill, with its notoriously cold water, has a club!

New Zealand has two marine parks for interesting diving. The Poor Knights Islands, off the coast near Whangarei, is reputed to have the best diving in NZ and the late Jacques Cousteau rated it one of the 'top 10' diving spots in the world. The Sugar Loaf Islands, another interesting reserve, is off Back Beach in New Plymouth, not far from the city centre.

Fiordland in the South Island is most unusual because the extremely heavy rainfall leaves a layer of freshwater, often peaty brown, over the saltwater. You descend through this murky and cold freshwater into amazingly clear and warmer saltwater. The freshwater cuts out light which discourages the growth of seaweed and this provides ideal conditions for the growth of black coral (*Antipathes fiordensis*). Fiordland also has snake stars which symbiotically live on the black coral, and brachiopods, true living fossils.

Coastal Fishes of New Zealand: A Diver's Identification Guide by Malcolm Francis is a field guide to all the fish a diver in NZ is likely to encounter. For more information contact the NZ Underwater Association (NZUA; ☎ (09) 849 5896); PO Box 875, Auckland).

Surfing

With its thousands of kilometres of coastline, NZ has excellent surfing possibilities. Swells come in from every angle and, while any specific beach will have better surfing at some times of the year than at others, there's good surfing to be found *somewhere* in NZ at any time of the year.

Raglan's 2km long left-hander is NZ's most famous wave, but areas closer to Auckland also have great surfing. Dunedin is one of the best spots in the South Island, especially in summer and autumn, but there are hundreds of possibilities. Among the guidebooks on surfing in NZ, look out for *The New Zealand Surfing Guide* by Mike Bhana and *A Guide to Surf Riding in New Zealand* by Wayne Warwick.

A few spots recommended by surfers are:

North Island
Auckland area
    West coast: Muriwai, Piha
    East coast: Matakana Island, Whangamata
Gisborne
    city beaches, Mahia Peninsula
Hamilton area
    Raglan
Taranaki
    Greenmeadows Point, Puniho Rd, Stent Rd
Wellington
    Castlepoint, Palliser Bay, Titahi Bay

South Island
Dunedin
    Lobsters near Akatore River, Long Point, Sandfly Bay
Greymouth
    Blaketown, Cobden breakwater
Kaikoura
    Mangamanu Reef, Mangawhau Point, Meatworks
Westport
    Westport beaches, Tauranga Bay

Windsurfing

As soon as windsurfing took off it had thousands of Kiwi adherents and plenty of popular spots to catch the wind. The lakes of both main islands are popular. Auckland harbour and the Hauraki Gulf, the Bay of Islands, Oakura near New Plymouth and 'windy' Wellington Harbour are just some of the outstanding coastal locations. There are many places from where you can hire boards and receive NZ Windsurfing Association-approved instruction.

Fishing

New Zealand is renowned as one of the great sportfishing countries of the world, thanks largely to the introduction of exotic rainbow trout, brown trout, quinnat salmon, Atlantic salmon, perch, char and a few other fish. The lakes and rivers of central North Island are famous for trout fishing, especially Lake Taupo and the rivers that feed it. The rivers and lakes of the South Island are also good for trout, notably the Mataura River, Southland. The rivers of Otago and Southland also have some of the best salmon fishing in the world.

Saltwater fishing is also a big attraction for Kiwi anglers, especially in the warmer waters around the North Island where surfcasting or fishing from boats can produce big catches of grey mullet, trevally, mao mao, porae, John Dory, gurnard, flounder, mackerel, hapuku, tarakihi, moki and kahawai. The Ninety Mile Beach and the beaches of the Hauraki Gulf are good for surfcasting. The Bay of Islands and Whangaroa in Northland, Tutukaka, near Whangarei, Whitianga on the Coromandel and Mayor Island in the Bay of Plenty are noted big game fishing areas.

The colder waters of the South Island, especially around Marlborough Sounds, are good for snapper, hake, trumpeter, butterfish, ling, barracouta and blue cod. The Kaikoura Peninsula is great for surfcasting.

Fishing gear can be hired in areas like Taupo and Rotorua, and a few sports outlets in other towns rent it out, but serious enthusiasts may wish to bring their own. Rods and tackle may have to be treated by NZ quarantine officials, especially if they are made with natural materials such as cane or feathers.

A fishing permit is required to fish on inland waters. They cover particular regions and are available for a day, a month or a season; these are sold at sport shops. Local visitor information centres and DOC offices have more information about fishing licences and regulations.

Many books have been written about fishing in NZ. John Kent has written the *North Island Trout Fishing Guide* and the *South Island Trout Fishing Guide*. Tony Orman, a renowned NZ fisherman and author, has written *21 Great New Zealand Trout Waters* as well as *Fishing the Wild Places of New Zealand*, telling not only how to catch fish but also relating some of the author's adventures fishing in many of NZ's wilderness areas. For surfcasting, check out *Surfcasting: A New Zealand Guide* by Gil Henderson.

Marine-Mammal Watching

Kaikoura, on the north-eastern coast of the South Island, is the country's centre for marine-mammal watching. The main attraction is whale-watching tours, and there is swimming with dolphins and seals.

The sperm whale, the largest toothed whale, is seen but other wildlife to be sighted on the tours include: Hector's dolphin (the smallest and rarest of all dolphins), the dusky dolphin (found only in the southern hemisphere, often in huge groups), the NZ fur seal, the orca or killer whale (the largest of all dolphins), common dolphin and pilot whale.

Nature being what it is, there's no guarantee of seeing any specific animal on any one tour. In general, the sperm whales are most likely to be seen from October to August, and orcas from December to March. Most of the other animals are seen year-round.

Dolphin swimming is common across NZ, with dolphins in the North Island at Whakatane, Paihia and Whitianga, and in the Marlborough Sounds and Fiordland in the South Island.

AERIAL ACTIVITIES
Bungy Jumping

Bungy jumping was made famous by Kiwi AJ Hackett's bungy dive from the Eiffel Tower in 1986. He teamed up with NZ's champion speed skier, Henry van Asch, and looked for a way to make commercial jumping safe. This company alone has sent many thousands of people hurtling earthward from bridges over the Shotover and Kawarau rivers near Queenstown, in Normandy, France, and even from a tower in Cairns, Australia, with nothing between them and

kingdom come but a gigantic rubber bungy cord tied to their ankles.

The jump begins when you crawl into the preparation area, get your ankles strapped up with a towel for padding, and have adjustments made to the cord depending on your weight. You then hobble out to the edge of the jumping platform, stand looking out over thin air, and get ready to jump. The crew shout out 'five, four, three, two, ONE!' and you dive off and are flying, before soaring upwards again on the bungy.

After bobbing up and down like a human yo-yo, the crew down below pull you into a rubber raft. No doubt about it, it's a daredevil sport, and the adrenalin rush can last for days. But it's all very well organised, with every possible precaution and attention to safety.

The historic Kawarau Suspension Bridge near Queenstown, attracts the most jumpers; it's 43m above the Kawarau River. A more spectacular dive spot is Skippers Canyon Bridge, 71m above a narrow gorge on the Shotover River, also near Queenstown. Highest of the lot near Queenstown is the 102m Pipeline where the first bounce brings you up to the height of the Skipper's Bridge! You can also bungy off the Waiau River Bridge near Hanmer Springs, close to Christchurch and the cheapest at $89.

Jumping is also done in the North Island at Taupo, 45m above the scenic Waikato River, and from an 80m bridge over the Rangitikei River near Mangaweka.

A new variation is the bungy rocket, for a bounce in a tandem capsule, at Tauranga and Christchurch.

Parapenting & Paragliding

This is perhaps the easiest way for humans to fly, without the problems faced by Icarus. After half a day of instruction you should be able to do limited solo flights. Before you know it you could be doing flights from 300m.

The best place to learn the skills necessary to operate your parapente/paraglider is Wanaka with the Freeflight Parapenting School (see Wanaka and Queenstown in the Otago chapter). Initial instruction is conducted at Mt Iron, just outside the town, and the long jumps are from the road up to the Treble Cone ski field (often up to six minutes air time).

Tandem flights, where you are strapped to an experienced paraglider, are offered all over the country. Perhaps the most popular is from the top of the gondola hill in Queenstown.

Aerial Sightseeing

All over NZ, planes and helicopters offer sightseeing trips (called 'flightseeing' by the locals), a great way to see the incredible contrast in scenery and the spectacular mountain ranges.

Some of the best trips are around the Bay of Islands, the Bay of Plenty, Tongariro National Park and Mt Taranaki in the North Island, and Mt Cook and the West Coast glaciers and fiords in the South Island.

Aerial sightseeing companies operate from the local aerodrome, and a flight can often be arranged on the spot. Ask at the local tourist office for information.

A far more sedate way to see the countryside is from a hot-air balloon. A company operating from near Methven takes you up to an altitude where you get spectacular views of the Southern Alps.

Skydiving

A lot of the aerial sightseeing companies also operate skydiving courses and trips. Many visitors take the 'ultimate' jump in tandem with a fully qualified instructor. It is not cheap, usually around $175, but the thrill is worth every dollar.

Tandem skydiving can be tried in the North Island at Taupo, Rotorua, at Parakai near Auckland, Paraparaumu near Wellington and Hastings near Napier. In the South Island there's tandem skydiving at Nelson, Christchurch, Wanaka and Queenstown.

A bonus is that you also get in some great aerial sightseeing, so pick the views you really want to see.

PETER TURNER

Tandem skydive into a scenic place like Wanaka, Otago.

OTHER ACTIVITIES

New Zealand is the home of invention when it comes to activities, like Zorbing (rolling downhill in a transparent plastic ball – see Rotorua) and Fly By Wire (a self-drive flying machine dangling from a wire – see Paekakariki). A variation on a traditional theme, quad bikes (4-wheel farm bikes) are a fun way to traverse the countryside and are popping up everywhere (see Rotorua, Taupo, Nelson and Hanmer Springs). Mazes are another thing that Kiwis do with a different slant. The original three-dimensional maze at Wanaka in the South Island can take hours to work through (see also Rotorua), and the idea has been exported to Japan.

Horse Riding

Horse riding is offered almost everywhere, and unlike some other parts of the world where beginners only get led around a paddock, in NZ you can get out into the countryside. Horse rides range from half-hour rides to 12-day treks. In the South Island, all-day adventure rides on horseback are a great way to see the surrounding country in Kaikoura, around Mt Cook, Queenstown and Dunedin. There are many treks offered in Westland, from all-day rides at Punakaiki, and excursions up to 12 days long at the Waitaha Valley, Ross.

In the North Island, Taupo has options for wilderness horse trekking and for rides in the hills overlooking the thermal regions. The Coromandel Peninsula, Waitomo, South Kaipara and Pakiri are also good places for horse trekking.

The informative *Where to Ride In New Zealand* pamphlet produced by the ILPH (☎ (07) 849 0678) PO Box 10-368, Pukete Rd, Te Rapa, is available from information centres.

Birdwatching

New Zealand is a birdwatcher's paradise in a relatively small area, with many unique endemic species, interesting residents and wave upon wave of visitors. It is as famous for extinct and point-of-extinction species as it is for common species.

The extinct species can't be 'watched' but a tour through museums, into caves where their bones are found and into former habitats is fascinating. These were the islands of the giant 4m-tall moa and the Haast's eagle which was large enough to have preyed upon it; and the remarkable huia with its vastly different male and female beaks. The number of species on the point of extinction

and the frenzied efforts to rebuild their populations is also a captivating story.

Any visiting birdwatcher will not be disappointed by the more accessible species. The kiwi is probably the species most sought after by birdwatchers and you are guaranteed to see the Stewart Island subspecies at all times of the year. Other sought-after birds are the royal albatross, the white heron (kotuku), the cheeky kea which ranges throughout the Southern Alps, the yellowhead (mohua), Fiordland crested penguin, yellow-eyed penguin, Australasian gannet, wrybill and, in the forests, the kereru (NZ pigeon), rifleman, tui, kaka and saddleback. See the colour Fauna & Flora section for more details on New Zealand's birds.

Some of the best places for birdwatching are Ulva Island (Stewart Island), the Catlins Forest Park and south-east coast, Fiordland and the forests of Westland, Otago Peninsula, Cape Farewell, Marlborough Sounds, Te Urewera National Park, the Firth of Thames and the Coromandel, Tiritiri Matangi and Little Barrier islands, and the forests and coasts of Northland. A number of islands are wildlife refuges where threatened birds are protected; special permission is needed to visit.

Two good guides are *A Field Guide to New Zealand Birds* by Geoff Moon and *Birds of New Zealand: Locality Guide* by Stuart Chambers. Both have excellent colour photos of the birds in their natural environments and lots of good information; the *Locality Guide* also gives practical information on how and where to find each species.

Getting There & Away

The overwhelming majority of visitors to New Zealand arrive by air. Apart from cruise ships, no regular sea services to NZ are available. However you travel, it's worth taking out travel insurance.

AIR
Airports & Airlines

New Zealand has six airports that handle international flights – Auckland, Wellington, Palmerston North and Hamilton in the North Island, and Christchurch and Dunedin in the South Island. Most international flights go through Auckland. Wellington airport has limited runway capacity and international flights to Australia. Flights from Christchurch are also mainly to Australia, although there are some connections to other countries. Freedom Air is a budget service that flies from Dunedin, Palmerston North and Hamilton.

Buying Tickets

As in Australia, STA and Flight Centre are popular travel agents specialising in discount fares. Flight Centre has some of the cheapest fares and there are branches throughout NZ. STA has offices in Auckland, Hamilton (Waikato University), Palmerston North, Wellington, Christchurch and Dunedin.

Here are some sample discount fares offered from Auckland, quoted in NZ dollars:

Auckland to:	one way	return
Bangkok/Hong Kong	1120	1550
Buenos Aires	3000	2200
Cairns	810	960
Fiji	750	820
Frankfurt	1570	2870
Honolulu	1080	1400
London	1570	2870
Los Angeles/San Francisco/Vancouver	1400	2000
New York	1900	2600
Singapore	1020	1380
Sydney/Melbourne/Brisbane	560	560
Tokyo	2580	1780

Round-the-World & Circle Pacific Tickets

Round-the-World (RTW) tickets have become popular in recent years; basically there are two types – airline tickets and agent tickets.

The airline RTW tickets are often real bargains and can work out to be no more expensive or even cheaper than an ordinary return ticket. This ticket is issued by two or more airlines that have joined together to market a ticket which takes you around the world on their combined routes. It lets you fly pretty well anywhere you choose using their combined routes as long as you don't backtrack, ie keep moving in approximately the same direction east or west.

Other restrictions are that you (usually) must book the first sector in advance and cancellation penalties then apply. There may be restrictions on how many stops you are permitted and usually the tickets are valid for 90 days up to a year.

The other type of RTW ticket, the agent ticket, is a combination of cheap fares strung together by an enterprising travel agent. These may be cheaper than airline RTW tickets, but the choice of routes will be limited.

Circle Pacific tickets use a combination of airlines to circle the Pacific – combining Australia, NZ, North America and Asia. As with RTW tickets, there are advance purchase restrictions and limits to your number of stopovers. Air New Zealand sometimes offers good deals on tickets involving departure from Los Angeles that don't include Asia but do include NZ, Australia and many small Pacific islands.

The USA & Canada

Most flights between the USA and NZ are

Air Travel Glossary

Apex Tickets Apex stands for Advance Purchase Excursion fare. These tickets are usually between 30% and 40% cheaper than the full economy fare, but have restrictions. You must purchase the ticket at least 21 days in advance (sometimes more) and must be away for a minimum period and return within a maximum period. Stopovers are not allowed and, if you have to change your dates of travel or destination, there will be extra charges to pay. These tickets are not fully refundable – if you cancel your trip, the refund is often considerably less than what you paid for the ticket. Take out travel insurance to cover yourself in case you have to cancel your trip unexpectedly – for example, due to illness.

Baggage Allowance This will be written on your ticket; you are usually allowed one 20kg item to go in the hold, plus one item of hand luggage. Some airlines which fly transpacific and transatlantic routes allow for two pieces of luggage (there are limits on their dimensions and weight).

Bucket Shops At certain times of the year and/or on certain routes, many airlines fly with empty seats. This isn't profitable and it's more cost-effective for them to fly full, even if that means having to sell a certain number of drastically discounted tickets. They do this by off-loading the tickets onto bucket shops (UK) or consolidators (USA), travel agents who specialise in discounted fares. The agents, in turn, sell them to the public at reduced prices. These tickets are often the cheapest you'll find, but you can't purchase them directly from the airlines. Availability varies widely, so you'll not only have to be flexible in your travel plans, but you'll also have to be quick off the mark as soon as an advertisement appears in the press. Bucket-shop agents advertise in newspapers and magazines and there's a lot of competition, so it's a good idea to telephone first.

Bumped Just because you have a confirmed seat doesn't mean you're going to get on the plane – see Overbooking.

Cancellation Penalties If you have to cancel or change an Apex or other discount ticket, there may be heavy penalties involved; insurance can sometimes be taken out against these penalties. Some airlines impose penalties on regular tickets as well, particularly against 'no show' passengers.

Check In Airlines ask you to check in a certain time ahead of the flight departure (usually two hours on international flights). If you fail to check in on time and the flight is overbooked, the airline can cancel your booking and give your seat to somebody else.

Confirmation Having a ticket written out with the flight and date on it doesn't mean you have a seat until the agent has confirmed with the airline that your status is 'OK'. Prior to this confirmation, your status is 'on request'.

Courier Fares Businesses often need to send their urgent documents or freight securely and quickly, so they use courier companies. These companies hire people to accompany the package through customs and, in return, offer a discount ticket which is sometimes a phenomenal bargain. In effect, what the courier companies do is ship their freight as your luggage on the regular commercial flights. This is a legitimate operation – all freight is completely legal. There are two shortcomings, however: the short turnaround time of the ticket, usually not longer than a month, and the limitation on your luggage allowance.

Discounted Tickets There are two types of discounted fares – officially discounted (see Promotional Fares, and Apex Tickets) and unofficially discounted (see Bucket Shops). The latter can save you more than money – you may be able to pay Apex prices without the associated Apex advance booking and other requirements. The lowest prices often impose drawbacks, such as flying with unpopular airlines, inconvenient schedules, and unpleasant routes and connections.

Economy Class Tickets Economy-class tickets are usually not the cheapest way to go, though they do give you maximum flexibility and are valid for 12 months. If you don't use them, most are fully refundable, as are unused sectors of a multiple ticket.

Full Fares Airlines traditionally offer first class (coded F), business class (coded J) and economy class (coded Y) tickets. These days there are so many promotional and discounted fares available that few passengers pay full fare.

Lost Tickets If you lose your airline ticket, an airline will usually treat it like a travellers cheque and, after inquiries, issue you with a replacement. Legally, however, an airline is entitled to treat it like cash, so if you lose a ticket, it could be forever. Take good care of your tickets.

MCO An MCO (Miscellaneous Charges Order) is a voucher for a value of a given amount, which resembles an airline ticket and can be used to pay for a specific flight with any IATA (International Air Transport Association) airline. MCOs, which are more flexible than a regular ticket, may satisfy the irritating onward ticket requirement, but some countries are now reluctant to accept them. MCOs are fully refundable if unused.

No Shows No shows are passengers who fail to show up for their flight for whatever reason. Full-fare no shows are sometimes entitled to travel on a later flight.

Open Jaw Tickets These are return tickets which allow you to fly to one place but return from another, and travel between the two 'jaws' by any means of transport at your expense. If available, this can save you backtracking to your arrival point.

Overbooking Airlines hate to fly with empty seats and, since every flight has some passengers who fail to show up (see No Shows), they often book more passengers than they have seats available. Usually the excess passengers balance those who fail to show up, but occasionally somebody gets bumped. If this happens, guess who it is most likely to be? The passengers who check in late.

Promotional Fares These are officially discounted fares, such as Apex fares, which are available from travel agents or direct from the airline.

Reconfirmation You must contact the airline at least 72 hours prior to departure to 'reconfirm' that you intend to be on the flight. If you don't do this, the airline can delete your name from the passenger list and you could lose your seat.

Restrictions Discounted tickets often have various restrictions on them, such as necessity of advance purchase, limitations on the minimum and maximum period you must be away, restrictions on breaking the journey or changing the booking or route etc.

Stand-by This is a discounted ticket where you only fly if there is a seat free at the last moment. Stand-by fares are usually only available directly at the airport, but sometimes may also be handled by an airline's city office. To give yourself the best possible chance of getting on the flight you want, get there early and have your name placed on the waiting list. It's first come, first served.

Student Discounts Some airlines offer student-card holders 15% to 25% discounts on their tickets. The same often applies to anyone under the age of 26. These discounts are generally only available on ordinary economy-class fares.

Tickets Out An entry requirement for many countries is that you have an onward or return ticket, in other words, a ticket out of the country. If you're not sure what you intend to do next, the easiest solution is to buy the cheapest onward ticket to a neighbouring country or a ticket from a reliable airline which can later be refunded if you do not use it.

Transferred Tickets Airline tickets cannot be transferred from one person to another. Travellers sometimes try to sell the return half of their ticket, but officials can ask you to prove that you are the person named on the ticket. This may not be checked on domestic flights, but on international flights tickets are usually compared with passports.

Travel Periods Some officially discounted fares, Apex fares in particular, vary with the time of year. There is often a low (off-peak) season and a high (peak) season. Sometimes there's an intermediate or shoulder season as well. At peak times, when everyone wants to fly, both officially and unofficially discounted fares will be higher, or there may simply be no discounted tickets available. Usually the fare depends on your outward flight – if you depart in the high season and return in the low season, you pay the high-season fare. ■

---

to/from the USA's west coast. Most travel through Los Angeles but some are through San Francisco. If you're coming from some other part of the USA, your travel agent can arrange a discounted 'add-on' fare to get you to the city of departure.

Excursion (round-trip) fares are available from various airlines but are more expensive than those from travel agents. Cheaper 'short life' fares are frequently offered for limited periods. The easiest way to get a cheap air fare from the USA is through a travel agency selling discounted fares; these fares can be about US$650 return from Los Angeles or about US$1050 return from New York. For as little as $100 extra you can fly from Los Angeles to Australia with a stopover in New Zealand.

The Sunday travel sections of papers like the *New York Times*, the *Chicago Tribune*, the *Los Angeles Times* or the *San Francisco Chronicle/Examiner* always have plenty of ads for cheap airline tickets; there are often good deals on flights across the Pacific, especially in the west-coast papers. If you don't live in these areas, you can have the tickets posted to you.

Two of the most reputable discount travel agencies in the USA are STA and CIEE. Both are international travel agencies with many offices throughout the USA and in other countries. The magazine *Travel Unlimited*

(PO Box 1058, Allston, MA 02134) publishes details of the cheapest air fares and courier possibilities departing from the USA for destinations all over the world.

If you want to visit other Pacific destinations on your way to or from NZ, compare carefully the stopover possibilities offered by each airline. Air New Zealand flights offer an excellent variety of stopover options on its route between Los Angeles and Auckland. You can tack on stopovers in Honolulu, Tahiti, Rarotonga, Western Samoa, Tonga and Fiji quite cheaply. Other airlines fly to NZ for the same price, or sometimes cheaper, but with more limited stopover options.

In Canada, the *Vancouver Sun* and the Toronto *Globe & Mail* carry travel agents' ads. The magazine *Great Expeditions* (PO Box 8000-411, Abbotsford BC V2S 6H1) is also useful. Much of the same advice about travel between the USA applies to Canada, especially stopover options.

Australia

The NZ cities with flights to Australia are Auckland, Christchurch, Wellington, Dunedin, Palmerston North and Hamilton (the last three have Freedom Air flights only). Australian cities with flights to NZ are Brisbane, Cairns, Melbourne, Perth and Sydney. Air New Zealand, Qantas Airways and United Airlines (Sydney and Melbourne only) are the main carriers. Smaller carriers include Garuda Indonesia and EVA Airways (Taiwan) from Brisbane and Aerolíneas Argentinas, Thai Airways International, Royal Tongan Airlines and Polynesian Airlines from Sydney.

The fare depends on the day you fly out as well as where you fly to and from. The year is divided into peak and off-peak (low) times, which can vary between airlines. The main peak season is over the summer school holidays (10 December to 15 January). Typical low-season, rock-bottom fares from a travel agent specialising in discount tickets from Sydney cost around A$515/550 one-way/return to Auckland, Christchurch or Wellington with the main carriers, or A$420/470 return from Sydney/Brisbane to Hamilton, Palmerston North and Dunedin in K Class (a no-frills version of economy class) with Freedom Air. From Melbourne the equivalent fare is around A$580/620 to Auckland, Christchurch or Wellington. Return fares in the high season cost around A$200 more, while tickets valid for two months or longer are also more expensive.

If you're travelling from Australia to the US west coast via New Zealand, the high season varies but is generally during the US summer (June, July and August). Low-season fares start at around A$1400/2000 one-way/return, high-season fares are more like A$2400 return.

RTW fares departing from Australia, which can include a stopover in New Zealand, vary with the season. The northern hemisphere summer (June, July and August) is usually the high season for RTW fares; tickets cost around A$2300 (with Philippine Airlines) to A$3000 (with Air New Zealand) in the high season, but can be around A$1800 in the low season.

In Australia, STA and Flight Centre are major dealers in cheap air fares and have branches in all major cities. Otherwise, check the travel agents' ads in the *Yellow Pages*.

The UK

London-Auckland return tickets can be found in London bucket shops for around £800. Some stopovers are permitted on this sort of ticket. Depending on which airline you travel with, you may fly across Asia or across the USA. If you come across Asia you can often make stopovers in places like India, Bangkok, Singapore and Australia; in the other direction, stopover possibilities include places like New York, Los Angeles, Honolulu or a variety of Pacific islands. Stopover options vary depending on the airline you use.

Since New Zealand is about as far from Europe as you can get, it's not much more to continue round the world rather than backtracking. Agents can organise you an RTW route through the South Pacific from around £750.

There has been cut-throat competition between London's many bucket shops; London is an important European centre for cheap fares. Although there are some untrustworthy operators most of them are fine.

Check the travel page ads in the *Times*, *Business Traveller*, the weekly 'what's on' magazine *Time Out* or give-away papers like *TNT*. Good, reliable low-fare specialists are Trailfinders at 194 Kensington High St, London W8 (☎ (0171) 938 3939) or 46 Earls Court Rd, London W8 (☎ (0171) 938 3366), and STA at 86 Old Brompton Rd, London SW7 (☎ (0171) 937 9962) or 117 Euston Rd, London NW1 (☎ (0171) 465 0484). Also worth trying are Quest Worldwide (☎ (0181) 547 3322) and Bridge the World (☎ (0171) 911 0900).

Most British travel agents are registered with ATOL (Air Travel Organiser's Licence), administered by the Civil Aviation Authority. If you pay an ATOL-registered agent who then goes out of business, the CAA will guarantee a refund or an alternative. Unregistered bucket shops are riskier but also sometimes cheaper.

Continental Europe

Frankfurt is the major arrival and departure point for NZ flights, with connections to other European centres.

There are many bucket shops on mainland Europe where you can buy discounted air tickets. The international student and discount travel agencies STA and Council Travel also have a number of offices in various European countries. Any of their offices can give you the details on which office might be nearest you. In Amsterdam, make sure your travel agent has an 'SGR' certificate or you may never see your money again.

Asia

There are far more flights to NZ from Asia than there were only a few years ago. There are direct flights to Auckland from Tokyo, Hong Kong, Singapore, Denpasar/Bali and Taipei, and connecting flights to most other places. Many of the connecting flights have stopovers in Australia. There are also a few direct flights to Christchurch including flights from Tokyo and Singapore.

Ticket discounting is widespread in Asia, particularly in Hong Kong, Singapore and Bangkok; Hong Kong is probably the discount air ticket capital of the region. There are a lot of fly-by-nights in the Asian ticketing scene so a little care is required. STA, which is reliable, has branches in Hong Kong, Tokyo, Singapore, Kuala Lumpur and Bangkok.

SEA

Cruise ships aside, there are no longer any regular passenger ship services to NZ. Even arranging to work your way across the Pacific as crew on a yacht is much more difficult than it used to be. There are many yachts sailing around the Pacific but nowadays they're usually only willing to take on experienced yachties as crew.

To try your luck finding a yacht, you have to go to the appropriate port at the appropriate time. There are lots of favourite islands, ports and harbours where you're likely to find yachts, such as Sydney and Cairns in Australia; Bali in Indonesia; various ports in Fiji or Tahiti; and Hawaii, San Diego or San Francisco in the USA. In NZ, popular yachting harbours include the Bay of Islands and Whangarei (both in Northland), Auckland and Wellington.

There are certain times when you're more likely to find yachts. From Fiji, October to November is a peak departure season as cyclones are on their way. March-April is the main departure season for yachts heading to Australia; be prepared for rough seas and storms crossing the Tasman Sea.

DEPARTURE TAXES

There's a $20 departure tax from Auckland, Wellington and Dunedin airports, and a $25 tax from Christchurch, Hamilton and Palmerston North, payable at the airport.

ORGANISED TOURS

As well as the host of tours you can arrange

in NZ, many can be arranged from outside the country. The New Zealand Tourism Board can provide details of tour companies; its offices around the world are listed in the Tourist Offices section in the Facts for the Visitor chapter. If you just want to add accommodation or car or campervan hire to your air ticket, travel agents can often get better deals than those available on arrival.

WARNING

The information in this chapter is particularly vulnerable to change: international travel prices are volatile, routes are introduced and cancelled, schedules change, special deals come and go, and rules and visa requirements are amended. Airlines and governments seem to take a perverse pleasure in making price structures and regulations as complicated as possible. You should check directly with the airline or a travel agent to make sure you understand how a fare (and ticket you may buy) works. The travel industry is highly competitive and there are many lurks and perks.

The upshot of this is that you should get opinions, quotes and advice from as many airlines and travel agents as possible before partings with your hard-earned cash. The details given in this chapter should be regarded as pointers and are not a substitute for your own careful, up-to-date research.

Getting Around

New Zealand has an extensive air service, reasonable bus networks and a limited, but useful, train service. The main cities and tourist areas are well covered and easy to reach. Smaller communities and many interesting out-of-the-way places are not so easy, often impossible, to reach by public transport.

Transport is privately run in New Zealand; when the government services were sold off, unprofitable runs were axed and prices rose. But private competition has thrown up some useful services, such as the many small shuttle buses which often pick up and drop off travellers at their accommodation.

Transport can be expensive, but discounts are almost always available. You need to be a travel agent to work out the complicated fare structures, which are often deliberately vague, but the rules for cheaper travel are: always assume a discount is available, book as far in advance as possible, and get yourself a discount card.

The most readily available discounts are for backpackers; cards issued by the hostel associations, such as a YHA card, International Student Identity Card (ISIC) card or VIP Backpackers Card, can bring reductions of around 30% to 50% on some services without pre-booking.

The discount system disadvantages independent travellers. If you are not on a fixed schedule and don't want to be tied down by bookings, you'll end up paying more for transport. But flexibility has its advantages and pre-booked discount fares often have nasty penalty or no-refund clauses if you change your mind.

Flexibility and the ability to reach so many delightful places away from the tourist hordes make car travel the best way to see New Zealand. Competition between the many small rental car operators makes for cheap car hire, but beware of insurance policies. For stays of a couple of months or more, it is worth considering buying a car and reselling it when you leave. Hiring or buying a car can actually be the cheapest transport in some instances. New Zealand is also very well set up for cyclists.

Pedestrians have to be careful in New Zealand. Unless crossing the street at a level crossing or traffic lights, pedestrians must give way to cars. New Zealand drivers not only won't slow down for you, some think it is their duty to gun down jaywalkers.

AIR

Although New Zealand is a compact country and ground transport is generally quite good, flying can sometimes make a lot of sense, particularly if you've already done the same journey by land. Great views can be enjoyed, particularly over the mountains or volcanoes. Discounted flights can make flying in New Zealand quite economical.

Domestic Air Services

New Zealand's major domestic airlines are Air New Zealand and Ansett New Zealand. With a host of connecting flights, the Air New Zealand network covers the country quite completely. Ansett's coverage is more limited but it, too, has many useful flights. Smaller airlines, such as Mt Cook Airline, Eagle Air and Air Nelson, are partly owned or booked by Air New Zealand and come under its 'Air New Zealand Link' umbrella.

Apart from the major operators, there are many local and feeder airlines. Services of interest include Southern Air's economic hop between Invercargill and Stewart Island, which is cheaper than the boat services and a favourite with trampers; flights to Great Barrier Island off Auckland; or flights to the Chatham Islands from Christchurch or Wellington with Air Chatham. Flights between the North and South islands are a popular alternative to the ferry services (see under the Getting There & Away heading in the Wellington section of the Wellington Region chapter).

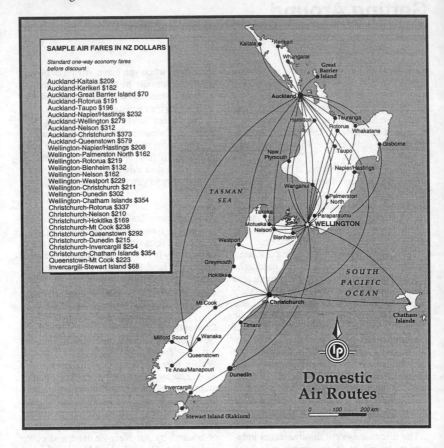

SAMPLE AIR FARES IN NZ DOLLARS

Standard one-way economy fares
before discount

Auckland-Kaitaia $209
Auckland-Kerikeri $182
Auckland-Great Barrier Island $70
Auckland-Rotorua $191
Auckland-Taupo $196
Auckland-Napier/Hastings $232
Auckland-Wellington $279
Auckland-Nelson $312
Auckland-Christchurch $373
Auckland-Queenstown $579
Wellington-Napier/Hastings $208
Wellington-Palmerston North $162
Wellington-Rotorua $219
Wellington-Blenheim $132
Wellington-Nelson $162
Wellington-Westport $229
Wellington-Christchurch $211
Wellington-Dunedin $302
Wellington-Chatham Islands $354
Christchurch-Rotorua $337
Christchurch-Nelson $210
Christchurch-Hokitika $169
Christchurch-Mt Cook $238
Christchurch-Queenstown $292
Christchurch-Dunedin $215
Christchurch-Invercargill $254
Christchurch-Chatham Islands $354
Queenstown-Mt Cook $223
Invercargill-Stewart Island $68

Domestic Air Routes

0   100   200 km

Discount Fares

Air New Zealand and Ansett New Zealand have regular listed economy fares, but also discounts which make it virtually unnecessary to ever pay the full fare.

Various discounts apply for domestic tickets bought before arrival in New Zealand. Air New Zealand's Visit New Zealand fares, which can only be bought outside the country, offer a 10% discount from 1 October to 30 April and 20% during the other months. However, better discounts often apply to tickets bought in conjunction with an international flight (on any airline),

depending on the country you are flying from; consult your travel agent. From Australia, 35% discounts are available on NZ domestic flights with no booking restrictions.

On the other hand, the various discount fares, which can only be booked and purchased in NZ, are up to 50% cheaper than the regular fare, but restrictions apply – no-refund rules may apply for cancellations and the fares may not be available on some peak services. Ansett's discount rules are: book two days in advance and save 10%, a week in advance and save 30%, 10 days and save

40%, and 14 days and save 50%. Air New Zealand follows a similar formula but its discount rules are more vague.

Air New Zealand and Ansett offer 50% discounts on stand-by flights for ISIC holders, YHA and VIP card holders. There's usually no problem getting a seat, except at the busiest times, such as school holidays and Monday morning commuter flights.

Other discounts and one-off specials may be available. Always ask about discounts when booking domestic tickets at airline offices, or go through a travel agent.

Air Passes

Air New Zealand offers an Explore New Zealand Pass for residents of other countries. Valid for all Air New Zealand and Link flights, it can be bought overseas or in New Zealand on presentation of an international ticket, but in New Zealand a 12.5% GST (Goods and Services Tax) is added.

The tickets are in the form of coupons and represent one sector (ie a single flight with just one flight number). Flights use between one and three coupons, depending on how many transfers are involved. The pass can be excellent value for long-distance, direct or through flights eg Auckland-Dunedin, but shorter hops involving transfers make it less attractive. The passes are issued in conjunction with an international ticket (with any airline) and valid for the life of that ticket. Your itinerary must be decided when you buy the pass and cannot be changed, but the dates for each flight can be changed at no extra charge.

The cost of passes varies according to the number of coupons involved:

Pass	Price (NZ$)
three coupons	$495
four coupons	$660
five coupons	$775
six coupons	$990
seven coupons	$1155
eight coupons	$1320

BUS

Bus travel in NZ is relatively easy and well organised, but can be expensive and time-consuming. The main bus company in both the North and South islands is InterCity. With a few exceptions, InterCity buses go to almost all bigger towns and the main tourist areas.

Newmans is the other main bus company, with a good North Island network and a more limited South Island service that runs along the east coast from Nelson to Invercargill.

Smaller bus companies include Mt Cook Landline, running between Christchurch, Queenstown and Milford in the South Island. White Star, on both islands, runs Wellington-Palmerston North-Wanganui-New Plymouth services with other connections, as well as a link between Nelson and Christchurch via the Lewis Pass, with connections to Picton and Westport.

Local operators offer more limited services. Both the North and South islands have small shuttle services and there's also a network of backpackers buses (see under the Backpackers Buses section later in this chapter).

Buses on main routes usually run at least daily, although on weekends on some routes the buses may run less frequently or not at all. InterCity buses will usually operate more often if there is competition on the route. The Getting There & Away sections for each town have more bus information.

Discount Fares

Although fares vary between companies, they are generally similar. Knowing the discounts available from various companies can cut travel costs by as much as 50% – you'll never have to pay full fare. All bus companies have free timetable booklets detailing discounts and schedules. Most of the following discounts apply only to trips that would otherwise cost $20 or more.

InterCity and Newmans offer a 30% discount to seniors (over 60) and anyone with recognised backpackers cards. These discounts are easy to get and have no special restrictions.

Fares booked in advance (five days before with InterCity and the day before with Newmans) have a 30% discount, but limited

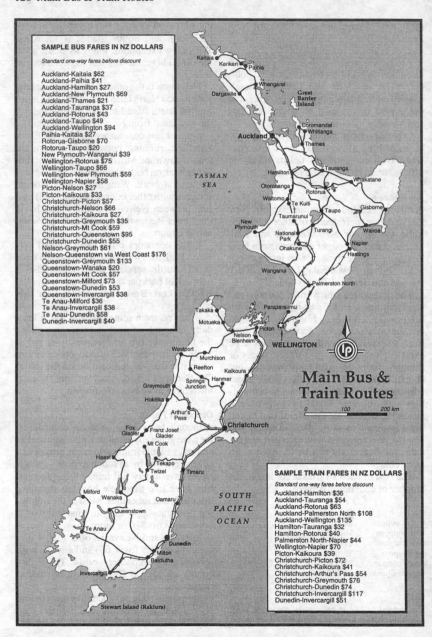

SAMPLE BUS FARES IN NZ DOLLARS

Standard one-way fares before discount

Auckland-Kaitaia $62
Auckland-Paihia $41
Auckland-Hamilton $27
Auckland-New Plymouth $69
Auckland-Thames $21
Auckland-Tauranga $37
Auckland-Rotorua $43
Auckland-Taupo $49
Auckland-Wellington $94
Paihia-Kaitaia $27
Rotorua-Gisborne $70
Rotorua-Taupo $20
New Plymouth-Wanganui $39
Wellington-Rotorua $75
Wellington-Taupo $66
Wellington-New Plymouth $59
Wellington-Napier $58
Picton-Nelson $27
Picton-Kaikoura $33
Christchurch-Picton $57
Christchurch-Nelson $66
Christchurch-Kaikoura $27
Christchurch-Greymouth $35
Christchurch-Mt Cook $59
Christchurch-Queenstown $95
Christchurch-Dunedin $55
Nelson-Greymouth $61
Nelson-Queenstown via West Coast $176
Queenstown-Greymouth $133
Queenstown-Wanaka $20
Queenstown-Mt Cook $57
Queenstown-Milford $73
Queenstown-Dunedin $53
Queenstown-Invercargill $38
Te Anau-Milford $36
Te Anau-Invercargill $38
Te Anau-Dunedin $58
Dunedin-Invercargill $40

Main Bus & Train Routes

0   100   200 km

SAMPLE TRAIN FARES IN NZ DOLLARS

Standard one-way fares before discount

Auckland-Hamilton $36
Auckland-Tauranga $54
Auckland-Rotorua $63
Auckland-Palmerston North $108
Auckland-Wellington $135
Hamilton-Tauranga $32
Hamilton-Rotorua $40
Palmerston North-Napier $44
Wellington-Napier $70
Picton-Kaikoura $39
Christchurch-Picton $72
Christchurch-Kaikoura $41
Christchurch-Arthur's Pass $54
Christchurch-Greymouth $76
Christchurch-Dunedin $74
Christchurch-Invercargill $117
Dunedin-Invercargill $51

seats are available at this rate. InterCity also has Super Saver fares offering a 50% discount. Discounts for return fares are from 10% to 20%.

Cancellation penalties on any sort of fares are high – 10% if you cancel 12 or more hours before departure and 50% within 12 hours, while no refunds are given after departure.

Travel Passes

The major bus lines offer discount travel passes valid from around 14 days to three months. InterCity, with the biggest network, has the most options. As with any unlimited travel passes, you have to do lots of travelling to make them pay – they're best for people who want to see a lot within a short time. Book ahead on the buses to be sure of a seat.

InterCity, in conjunction with the Tranz Scenic rail network and the *Interislander* ferry, also offers a 3-in-1 Travelpass covering nationwide bus/train/ferry travel. Five days travel taken over 10 days costs $360 (children $240), eight days travel over three weeks $485 ($323), 15 days travel over five weeks $610 ($406) and 22 days travel over eight weeks $710 ($473).

The main travel passes (available at visitor information centres and bus depots) include:

InterCity Passes
InterCity has numerous North Island passes including: Auckland-Wellington and points between ($99, children $66); Auckland-Napier via Rotorua and the east coast ($149, $99). Its South Island passes include: Picton-Invercargill, including Queenstown and Te Anau ($132, $88); and Queenstown-Nelson via the West Coast ($125, $84). Combo passes combine the various options for either island. Passes covering both islands cost from $370 (children $248) to $585 ($392). Passes are usually valid for three months and reservations cost $3 per sector (or you can see if stand-by seats are available).

Newmans Stopover Pass
This pass ($95) covers 14 days travel in all parts of the North Island except Northland; you can travel only in one direction (ie no backtracking).

Northliner Express
This company offers several discount backpackers passes for the Northland which are valid for

14 days from date of purchase and provide unlimited travel on various routes. The Bay of Islands pass costs $49, the Northland Freedom pass $109 and the Top Half Pass $79.

Shuttle Buses

Small shuttle bus companies offer useful services throughout the country. Typically these buses are smaller, cheaper and have a friendlier atmosphere than the regular large buses. Some of them are designed with foreign travellers and/or backpackers in mind and have lots of little extras that make them attractive: some will pick up and drop off at accommodation or leave from central destinations (often a town's visitor information centre).

Everyone who has a minibus seems to offer a shuttle service. As such, small operators tend to come and go. Most offer an excellent service, but a few seem to go only when they feel like it ('Sorry, not running today. It's my wife's birthday.').

The South Island has a plethora of shuttles, particularly on the Picton-Christchurch and Queenstown-Christchurch routes. Following are a few examples of the more useful or extensive services on both islands:

North Island

Alpine Scenic Tours (☎ (07) 378 6305) – services between Turangi and National Park, with useful stops for trampers in the Tongariro National Park, and extension services up to Taupo and Rotorua

Bellbird Connection (☎ (07) 386 8281) – services the ends of the Tongariro Crossing from Turangi

Coachrite Connections (☎ (06) 868 9969) – Gisborne-Wairoa and Napier-Hastings

Geyserland Express (☎ (09) 357 6616) – Auckland-Rotorua

Hot Water Beach Conxtions – Ferry Landing-Hahei and Hot Water Beach on the Coromandel Peninsula

Little Kiwi Bus Co (☎ 0800 759 999) – Auckland-Hamilton

Northliner Express (☎ (09) 307 5873) – Auckland-Paihia and a loop around Northland

On Ground Airlines (☎ (0800) 755 575) – Palmerston North-Napier (a good option for someone on a bus pass that doesn't include Napier)

Thermal Connection (aka Pink Bus; ☎ (07) 377 6067) Taupo-Rotorua via Waimangu and Waiotapu thermal areas

Waitomo Wanderer (☎ (07) 873 7559) – Waitomo-Rotorua-Taupo loop

West Coaster/Pioneer (☎ (09) 438 3206; Whangarei) – passes through Dargaville completing the Northland loop (in conjunction with InterCity and Northliner)

White House Backpackers Shuttle (☎ (07) 866 8468) – Coromandel-Fletchers Bay

South Island

Atomic Shuttles (☎ (03) 322 8883) – three services between Christchurch, Dunedin, Picton and Queenstown

Bottom Bus (☎ (03) 366 9830) – Dunedin to Invercargill via the scenic Catlins route, then on to Manapouri and Te Anau and back to Dunedin via Gore

Catch-a-Bus (☎ (03) 453 1480) – between Dunedin, Queenstown, Wanaka, Te Anau and Invercargill, and Blenheim-Picton-Nelson

Coast to Coast (☎ 0800 800 847) – Christchurch-Hokitika/Greymouth via Arthur's Pass

Cunningham's (☎ (03) 789 6617) – Karamea-Westport for the southern end of the Heaphy Track

East West (☎ 0800 500 251) – Christchurch-Westport via Reefton daily

Golden Bay Book-a-Bus (☎ 0800 259 864) – Takaka-Collingwood/Christchurch/Nelson with connections to Totaranui and Heaphy by arrangement

Kiwi Discovery (☎ 0800 505 504) – Queenstown-Milford

Ko-op Shuttles (☎ (03) 366 6633) – Christchurch to Picton, Dunedin and Greymouth (daily)

Nelson Lakes Transport (☎ (03) 521 1887) – Nelson-St Arnaud (for the Nelson Lakes National Park)

Sounds to Coast (Blenheim Taxis; ☎ 0800 802 225) – Picton-Greymouth via St Arnaud (Monday, Wednesday and Friday)

Southern Link Shuttles (☎ (03) 358 8355) – Christchurch to Queenstown, Picton and Dunedin

Backpackers Buses

Bus companies which cater for backpackers sell passes lasting from several days to weeks for various parts of the country. In some places, notably the west coast of the South Island, these passes can be the best way of seeing the area, as hitchhiking is difficult and the more conventional bus services simply whiz past many of the most attractive spots. They offer a degree of flexibility, some more than others, allowing you to get off the bus for independent travel and then catch the next bus. In summer it can be difficult to get a seat on a crowded bus, so advance bookings are necessary.

The buses are comfortably fitted out, their atmosphere is casual and there are plenty of sightseeing stops along the way, plus stops for walks, picnics, shopping and activities such as sky diving, bungy jumping and white-water rafting. The bus companies often get good discounts on activities for their passengers.

If you have limited time, can't be bothered arranging transport connections, want to see a number of spots en route and sample a wide variety of activities, these buses may be ideal. They are also a great way to meet like-minded people, but are very much like tours. Some travellers come away disappointed because they mistakenly thought the backpackers buses were normal buses with just a few stops at scenic spots on the way. The buses have set itineraries and you go along with the group – if some passengers want to go bungy jumping en route, everyone tags along. The only real independent travel is when you get off the bus.

Accommodation costs are extra; low-cost overnight accommodation is pre-booked, usually at hostels, with an option to camp if you have your own tent. The exception is Flying Kiwi, where accommodation, on the bus or in tents, is included.

The main companies, with extensive networks throughout New Zealand, are Kiwi Experience and Magic Bus. Kiwi Experience has a reputation for a party atmosphere with socialising based around the pub. It tends to favour large hostels to keep groups together, though you can book other hostel accommodation. The Magic Bus, affiliated with InterCity, is similar but slightly more flexible. Passengers are encouraged to pre-book their accommodation in the hostel of their choice.

A few others run specialised routes with varying degrees of flexibility. Except for the Southern Explorer, which operates only from November to May, all the buses operate year-round, with more frequent departures in summer.

All companies have pamphlets detailing

itineraries, departure times and costs; they require advance booking and usually a deposit. Be sure you understand the refund policy in case you decide to cancel. The main companies (and their routes, prices and details) include:

Flying Kiwi – Specialising in outdoor tours, Flying Kiwi's 'rolling travellers home' includes bunks, tents, hot shower and kitchen; it carries mountain bikes, a Canadian canoe, a windsurfer, fishing gear and more. South Island trips include 10-day ($575) and 17-day ($890) trips. In the North Island options include a seven-day trip ($390) and a two-day Northern Express trip ($89). A 24-day, all-NZ tour is $1190. Contact the business at Koromiko in Blenheim (☎ (03) 573 8126; 0800 692 396).

Kiwi Experience – This service operates on the North and South islands, offering 17 routes, with from one to 23 days allowed to complete one route; most passes are valid for six months. Trips include: limited North Island or South Island loops (minimum seven days each; around $240); all-NZ tours (minimum 14 days; around $400); and the Whole Kit & Caboodle trip (minimum 23 days; $879). Useful small loops where other services are limited include Awesome Adventures and Top Bit around Northland and to Cape Reinga, and the link with Bottom Bus along the Catlins and Southern Scenic Route. These are more like shuttles than backpackers buses. For reservations contact its offices in Auckland (☎ (09) 366 9830), Wellington (☎ (04) 385 2153), Christchurch (☎ (03) 377 0550), Queenstown (☎ (03) 442 9708), and Sydney, Australia (☎ (02) 9368 1766).

Magic Bus – Affiliated with InterCity buses, Magic Bus operates on the North and South islands. Its network is extensive but does not include Northland. It has shorter North or South island loops (around $250) and all-NZ tours for 12/14/16-day minimums ($388/399/499). Book at any hostel or by phoning its offices in Auckland (☎ (09) 358 5600), Wellington (☎ (04) 387 2018), Nelson (☎ (03) 548 3290), Queenstown (☎ (03) 442 8178) and Christchurch (☎ (03) 377 0951).

Southern Explorer – This company services the South Island. Its tours include a four-day trip from Queenstown to Dunedin via Te Anau, Milford Sound, the 'southern scenic route' to Invercargill, through the Catlins and on to Dunedin ($140); for $170 you can continue on from Dunedin to Queenstown or Te Anau. One-day sections are available for individual day prices ($25 to $45). Book in Queenstown at the Backpacking Specialists (☎ (03) 442 8178) or in Te Anau (☎ (03) 249 7820).

West Coast Express – This service also covers the South Island. It has a six-day Nelson to Queenstown via the West Coast route ($99); you can depart from either end of the line. For bookings in Nelson contact Paradiso Backpackers (☎ (03) 546 6703); in Queenstown call the Backpacking Specialists (☎ (03) 442 8178).

TRAIN

New Zealand's privately owned rail network covers just a few main routes: Auckland-Rotorua/Tauranga/Wellington, Wellington-Napier, Picton-Christchurch and Christchurch-Greymouth/Invercargill. There are more details on these routes in the relevant regional chapters. The Tranz Scenic fares and timetables booklet is available at railway stations and visitor centres throughout the country.

NZ trains are modern and comfortable, and the elimination of many smaller halts has made train travel reasonably speedy, usually a little quicker than the buses. Some routes are scenic and trains are certainly more comfortable than buses, but train travel is expensive unless you can get a big discount.

Tranz Scenic has a nationwide central reservations centre (☎ 0800 802 802; free fax 0800 101 525) which is open every day from 7 am to 9 pm (call ☎ 64 4 498 3303 from overseas). Reservations can also be made at most railway stations, travel agents and information centres.

Like the buses, discounts are available for trains. YHA and VIP card holders get a 30% discount, students 20%, seniors 30% and disabled travellers 50%. A limited number of other discounted seats are set aside on each train – advance booking is required. Discount fares are: Super Saver (50% discount), Saver (30%) and Economy Fare (20%).

The 3-in-1 Travelpass is a rail pass that also includes InterCity bus travel and the *Interislander* ferry (see under the earlier Bus heading for details).

CAR & MOTORCYCLE

Driving around New Zealand is quite easy – distances between towns are short, traffic is light and the roads are usually in good condition. Petrol (gasoline) is expensive at about $1 a litre (US$3 a gallon). Petrol prices vary slightly from station to station and from city to countryside, but only by a few cents; the average costs per litre in large cities is 93c for unleaded and 56c for diesel.

Driver courtesy is reasonably good in the towns, except for perhaps Auckland, but the highways are full of cowboys. Driving 20km/h over the speed limit and aggressive tailgating are common, despite the forever twisting and narrow roads. Autobahns don't exist – apart from the occasional overtaking lane, highways are single lane in either direction and pass through the towns. Traffic is generally light, but it is easy to get stuck behind a truck or campervan. Count on covering about 80km for every hour of driving on the highways.

Unsealed, back-country roads are another hazard for the uninitiated. Many visitors lose control by moving onto the loose gravel verges and skidding into ditches.

Kiwis drive on the left, as in the UK, Australia, Japan and much of Asia. For those used to driving on the right – take care. Every year almost 100 serious or fatal accidents involve foreign drivers, many of them driving on the wrong side of the road.

A 'give way to the right' rule applies. This is interpreted in a rather strange fashion when you're turning left and an oncoming vehicle is turning right into the same street. Since the oncoming vehicle is then on your right you have to give way to them.

Speed limits on the open road are generally 100km/h; in built-up areas the limit is usually 50km/h. An LSZ sign stands for Limited Speed Zone, which means that the speed limit is 50km/h (although the speed limit in that zone is normally 100km/h) when conditions are unsafe due to bad weather; limited visibility; pedestrians, cyclists or animals on the road; excessive traffic; or poor road conditions.

Pick up a copy of *The Road Code*, a wise investment that will tell you all you need to know. It's available at NZ Automobile Association (AA) offices and bookshops. There is a similar book for motorcyclists.

A valid, unrestricted drivers' licence from your home country is required to rent and drive a car in New Zealand. The AA staff can advise if you wish to obtain a New Zealand driver's licence. To drive a motorcycle you must have a motorcycle licence or special endorsement on your home-country driver's licence.

Excellent road maps are readily available in New Zealand, and good maps are essential for exploring off the highways where signposting is not always good. The best of the lot are AA's 1:350,000 district maps ($3.50; free to members).

Members of an equivalent automobile association overseas may qualify for reciprocal benefits from the AA in New Zealand; remember to bring your card. Otherwise AA membership (☎ 0800 500 222) is good insurance if you buy a car. Apart from free maps and publications, membership entitles you to free emergency breakdown service, free advice on traffic tickets and accidents, and various discounts on services and accommodation.

Theft from cars is a problem in New Zealand, particularly at isolated parking areas at scenic spots and walks. The North Island tends to be worse than the South Island, but wherever you park, don't leave valuables in the car and hide your gear if you can't take it with you.

Rental

Car Usually you must be at least 21 years old to rent a car in New Zealand (sometimes 25) and under 25s often incur a larger insurance excess.

The major car-hire companies offer new cars, country-wide networks, more reliability, better insurance and high prices. The many smaller companies are much cheaper, have mostly older cars, and contracts and insurance policies have to be looked at closely.

Because rental car accidents (usually minor) are so common in New Zealand, insurance premiums are very high. Bigger companies will remove the excess for around $10 a day extra, but smaller operators offering cheap rates often have a compulsory insurance excess of around $700. Insurance coverage for all hire cars is invalid on certain roads, typically beaches and unsealed roads in major tourist areas.

The big operators – Avis, Budget, Hertz – have extensive fleets of cars with offices in most towns. Unlimited kilometre rental of a small car (a late-model Japanese car of 1600cc or less) starts at around $70 per day, more for rental of only a few days. For driving around town without an unlimited kilometre option, expect to pay about 30c a kilometre. Medium-sized cars are typically around $100 per day with unlimited kilometres. A drop-off fee applies if you're not returning the car to the city of hire. Overseas travel agents can often get better deals in hiring new cars through major operators than you can hunt out yourself in New Zealand.

A huge number of smaller companies undercut the big operators, but there may be more restrictions on use and one-way rentals may not always be possible. Some budget operators, such as Pegasus and Shoestring, have national networks.

Car rental is competitive in the major cities, but Auckland is the cheapest place to rent a car. The surplus of operators means that you can often get special deals for longer rentals, especially outside the peak summer months. Shop around by phone – quoting a competitor's rates may bring a reduction, even from the major companies. In peak season you may get a good, reasonably current model for $55 a day (all inclusive) for rentals of more than four days, while in off-peak periods the cost may drop to $45.

Many smaller operators have older, second-hand cars, advertised for as little as $20 per day, but you get what you pay for. Advertised rates (and even quotes over the phone) are often misleading, and business practices can leave a lot to be desired. Always check kilometre rates, if the price includes GST, minimum hire periods, the age of the car, bonds and insurance coverage. Always read the rental agreement before you sign.

Rock-bottom rates usually apply to minimum one-month hire in the off season for a beat-up car over 10 years old with limited or even no insurance. Full payment in advance and a credit-card bond is usually required. Insurance from the cheaper rental agencies is usually subject to a $700 excess for any accident or damage to the car (some even include tyre replacement and puncture repairs), even if it is not your fault. Most, however, will cash your bond but refund it later if the other driver's blame can be proved and they have insurance (don't count on it).

If you are prepared to risk the insurance excess, second-hand car hire can be good value. By shopping around, you can hire a 1990 model Japanese import for a month in the off season for as little as $30 a day or a more recent model for $40 a day (sometimes less). Prices are up to 50% higher in the peak season and also higher outside Auckland.

Campervan Campervans (also known as mobile homes, motor homes or, in US parlance, Winnebago's or RVs) are an enormously popular way of getting around New Zealand. In tourist areas of the South Island almost every other vehicle seems to be a campervan. Campervans combine transport and accommodation in one neat package and you've also got your own kitchen on wheels.

Many companies rent out campervans and their costs vary with the type of vehicle and the time of year. A small van, suitable for two people, typically has a sink, hot and cold water, gas cooker, 12V fridge and 240V heater. The dining table and seats fold down to form a double bed. Usually they are of minivan size with a 2L unleaded petrol engine, easy to drive, manoeuvrable around town and with enough pep for the hills. Slightly larger varieties may have their own toilets and showers. Others may be kitted-out kombi vans or 4WDs, or even station wagons with pop-up tents fitted on top.

Four to six-berth campervans are of light-truck size and usually contain the works. They are very comfortable with an extra double sleeping cabin at the front, microwave, toilet, shower etc. Fuel consumption is about the same as for the smaller vans but they may run on much cheaper diesel fuel.

The only drawback is their size – it makes them not much fun to drive in the cities and sluggish on the hills. They are high (around 3.3m), so the top is easily scraped by the inexperienced, especially on signs or verandahs when parking on the camber of a road.

Campervans usually have 240V power systems (just plug them in at a motor camp) with backup 12V systems, so you can still camp in luxury out in the wild or at basic campsites. Dispose of waste water properly; toilets must be emptied at designated dumping stations, found at motor camps or provided by some councils.

Usual rates through the main companies for two/four/six-berth vans are around $150/ 220/250 a day, dropping to $90/130/ 150 in winter (May to September) and slightly less again for more than three weeks hire. But price wars have seen rates drop to as low as $65 a day for a four- berth van. Overseas travel agents can also get good discounts.

Maui and Brits New Zealand are two of the biggest operators and the main car hire companies also rent campervans. For details on companies renting campervans see the Auckland chapter and the Christchurch section in the Canterbury chapter. Smaller operators rates start at around $40 per day for kitted out minivans.

Motorcycle It's also possible to hire a motorcycle for touring in New Zealand. Most of the motorcycle-hire shops are in Auckland, but Christchurch has a few too; see the Auckland chapter and Christchurch section in the Canterbury chapter for details. You can hire anything from a little 50cc moped (niftyfifty) for zipping around town to a big 750cc touring motorcycle.

Remember you will need a motorcycle licence; a car licence will get you by if you want to tootle around on a moped, but to hire a regular motorcycle (rental bikes are usually from 250cc to 750cc in size) requires a motorcycle licence.

NZ Motorcycle Tours (☎ 0800 245 386 877; 360 Flume Rd, Cambridge) has two, three and five-day tours around New Zealand.

House Trucks

When you're travelling around New Zealand, watch out for colourful and exotic house trucks. These individually built constructions look like a collision between an elderly truck and a timber cottage, sometimes complete with shingle roof and bay windows. Many of these uniquely Kiwi contraptions look far too fragile for road use but seem to travel all over the country and are often parked for days or even months in the most idyllic settings. ■

Purchase

Car For a longer stay and/or for groups, buying a car and then selling it again at the end of your travels can be one of the cheapest and best ways of seeing New Zealand. You're not tied to the bus schedules, nor do you find yourself waiting by the roadside with your thumb out looking for a ride.

Auckland, as the largest city and main gateway to New Zealand, is the easiest place to buy a car. Christchurch is the next-best for overseas visitors, but a distant second. One of the easiest ways to buy a cheap car is to scour the notice boards of hostels, where other travellers sell their cars before moving on. You can pick up an old car for only a few hundred dollars. The really cheap backpackers specials, beat-up 15 to 20-year-old cars that somehow are still running after many circuits of New Zealand, are so cheap that it may be worth taking the risk that they will finally die on you.

Otherwise, cars are advertised in the newspapers just like anywhere else in the world. Auckland also has a number of popular auctions and car fairs, where people bring their cars to sell (see the Auckland chapter). These events have lots of cars from around $1000 to $4500. The cars sold at these are older, cheap cars; a good, later model used car from a dealer may start at around $8000. Cheap, Japanese secondhand imports, shipped to NZ, are numerous and getting spares is no longer a problem. The cheapest prices are generally at the auctions and the next-cheapest prices are at the car fairs, where you have more time to browse.

Another option is the 'buy-back system', where the dealer guarantees to buy the car back from you at the end of your travels. The buy-back amount varies, but may be 50% less than the purchase price. Hiring or buying and selling it yourself is usually much better value.

Make sure any car you buy has a WOF (Warrant of Fitness) and that the registration lasts for a reasonable period. A WOF certificate, proving that the car is roadworthy, is valid for six months but must be less than 28 days old when you buy a car. To transfer registration, both you and the seller fill out a form which can be filed at any post office. Papers are sent by mail within 10 days. It is the seller's responsibility to transfer ownership and pay the costs involved. If needed, registration can be purchased for either six months or a year (around $200 per year). Third-party insurance, covering the cost of repairs to another vehicle in an accident that is your fault, is also a wise investment.

Car inspections are highly recommended and the cost may well save you in repair bills later. Various car inspection services will check any car you intend to buy for around $80. They stand by at car fairs and auctions for on-the-spot inspections, or will come to you. The AA also offers a mobile inspection service – it is slightly cheaper if you bring the car to an AA-approved mechanic. AA checks are thorough, but most garages will look over the car for less.

Another wise precaution before you buy a car is to ring for a credit check (☎ 0800 658 934). With the licence plate and chassis numbers, the ownership of the car can be confirmed and you can find out if any outstanding debts are owed on it.

BICYCLE

Touring cyclists are almost everywhere in New Zealand, especially in summer. The many hills make for hard going at times, but it's a compact country with plenty of variety. Many cyclists call New Zealand a cyclists' paradise – it's clean, green, uncrowded,

friendly, there are numerous camping options and cheap hostels, plenty of fresh water, the climate is not too hot or too cold, the roads are good, and bikes and cycling gear (to rent or buy) are readily available, as are bicycle repair services.

Cycle Touring in New Zealand by Bruce Ringer is full of useful information for cyclists, like where the steep hills are! The excellent *Pedallers' Paradise* booklets by Nigel Rushton cover the North and South islands, and include city maps and elevation profiles of the routes. *Classic New Zealand Mountain Bike Rides* by Paul, Simon & Jonathan Kennett is another good cycling book, suggesting a wide variety of short and long rides all over New Zealand.

Occasionally a cyclist may resort to public transport. The major bus lines and trains only take bicycles on a 'space available' basis (meaning they may not get on) and charge up to $10. Some of the shuttle or backpackers buses, on the other hand, make sure they always have storage space for bikes and often carry them for free.

Many international airlines will carry your bicycle at no additional cost as 'sporting equipment'. Except on the smallest planes, domestic airlines take bicycles for $20. Remember to bring your helmet, as NZ regulations require that you wear one.

The Kiwi Experience bus people offer a bus-bike combination called Wild Cycles; for more details ring ☎ (09) 366 1445. Adventure South (☎ (03) 332 1222; PO Box 33-153, Christchurch) has back-road cycle tours in the South Island. Pedaltours NZ (☎ (09) 302 0968; 4/156 Parnell Rd, Auckland) has a variety of guided bicycle tours throughout New Zealand.

Rental

Many bicycle rental operators in New Zealand offer daily and weekly bicycle hire, with negotiable monthly rates. Bicycle rental is listed in the Getting Around sections of cities and towns in this book. Costs vary widely – rates can be anywhere from around $10 to $25 a day, from $50 to $125 a week and from around $120 to $360 a month; they depend on what kind of bike you get and where you get it from. Time spent comparing prices is time well spent. Most rental companies also offer bicycle touring gear and repair kits.

Purchase

Bicycles can be readily bought in New Zealand, but prices are high for new bikes. You're better off bringing one with you or buying a used one. Hostel notice boards frequently have signs offering mountain bikes for sale, or check the newspaper ads.

HITCHING

Hitching is never entirely safe in any country in the world and we don't recommend it. The well-publicised murder of two Swedish hitchhikers a few years ago highlights the fact that even in relatively safe New Zealand hitchhiking can be a risky undertaking. But many people do choose to hitch, and the advice that follows should help to make their journeys as fast and safe as possible.

New Zealand is a great place for hitching and, although almost anybody who does a fair amount of hitching will get stuck somewhere uncomfortable for an uncomfortably long time, most travellers rate it highly. It's pretty safe and the roads are not crowded, but there are just enough cars to make things fairly easy and the locals are well disposed towards hitchhikers.

The usual hitching rules apply. Pick your hitching spot so drivers can see you easily and stop safely. A 50km/h rather than a 100km/h speed zone is easier for cars to stop. Some hitchhikers claim it is better to walk along the road than stand in one spot, but drivers like to see your face. Chances are usually better earlier in the day.

In larger towns it pays to take a bus or walk out of town before starting to hitch. You may pick up a lift on the way out, but don't count on it. It's much harder to get a ride in town with a pack than on the open road, where it's a lot easier if you have a pack. Learn which rides not to take – not just rides from crazy drivers but also those that leave you at inconvenient locations; wait for the right one.

Dress for the occasion – not in your fancy

clothes ('they can afford to take the bus') or too shabbily ('don't want them in my car'). If someone else is already hitching on the same stretch of road, remember to walk ahead of them so they get the first ride, or leave the road until they get a ride. Most importantly, be careful – there are some unpleasant people on the road in New Zealand just as anywhere else in the world.

Hitching on the main North Island routes is generally good. In the South Island hitching down the east coast from Picton through Christchurch to Invercargill is mostly good. Elsewhere in the South Island, hundreds of kilometres of main roads have very little traffic. Expect long waits – even days – in some places. If it gets too much (eg you find yourself hurling abuse at drivers that don't stop), catch a bus, but you may have to get into the next town first.

It's easier hitching alone if you are male. Unfortunately, even though New Zealand is basically a safe country for women, a woman on her own may experience some tricky – if not dangerous – situations. It is better to hitch with someone else if possible. Many hostels have local hints for hitching (such as what bus to get out of town and where to hitch from) on their notice boards.

BOAT

Inter-Island Ferries

The *Interislander* ferry and the *Lynx* services, operating between Wellington in the North Island and Picton in the South Island, are covered in detail in the Wellington Region chapter.

Other regularly scheduled inter-island ferry services in New Zealand include those to the various islands off Auckland (see the Auckland chapter). A ferry also connects Stewart Island with the South Island at Bluff, near Invercargill.

Other Water Transport

Transport can be more convenient by water than by land, especially in the Marlborough Sounds where many places to stay can only be reached by water. Regular launch and water-taxi services also operate along the coast of the Abel Tasman National Park.

Other convenient ferry services include the ferries in the Bay of Islands, such as the Russell-Paihia passenger ferry and the car ferry crossing over from Opua. On the west side of the Northland is the convenient car ferry from Rawene to Kohukohu.

In other places, transport over lakes is a significant way to get around and see things, such as at Wakatipu, Taupo and Waikaremoana. Sometimes the most interesting things to see are reached by water rather than by land; cruises on Milford and Doubtful sounds in Fiordland in the South Island and on the Bay of Islands in the Northland are especially popular.

LOCAL TRANSPORT
Bus & Train
Most of the urban buses have been privatised and only operate on profitable runs ie hardly at all. Larger cities have bus services but, with a few honourable exceptions, they are mainly daytime, weekday operations and departures are infrequent. On weekends, particularly on Sunday, bus services can be hard to find or stop altogether. Some small cities that once had government-funded buses now have nothing.

The only city with a good suburban train service is Wellington.

Taxi
The main cities have plenty of taxis and even small towns may have a local service. Taxis cruise the busy areas in Auckland, Wellington and Christchurch, but otherwise you usually either have to phone for one or go to a taxi rank.

ORGANISED TOURS
Tours can sometimes be a useful way of getting around New Zealand, especially in otherwise hard-to-reach areas, when your time is limited or when you want the benefit of commentary.

Backpackers often use the 'alternative' buses as a sort of informal tour (see under the Backpackers Buses heading in the Bus section earlier in this chapter). New Zealand Nature Safaris (☎ 09 358 4874) is similar, with an emphasis on wildlife, wilderness areas and walks. Nine-day North Island tours cost $585 and 10-day South Island tours are $650. Food and accommodation (camping, cabins etc) cost extra.

Otherwise there is a variety of more conventional tours. Thrifty Tours, operated by InterCity, is indeed thrifty, using a combination of tour buses and public transport to create a variety of short and long tours all over New Zealand. Gray Line (☎ 0800 800 904) is another major tour operator, offering different one-day tours in various cities and towns, plus inter-city tours. All of these are major companies which can be contacted through virtually any travel agent or visitor information centre in New Zealand, or through travel agents or the New Zealand Tourism Board (NZTB) before you arrive in the country.

Specific, worthy and interesting tours (some several days long) have been listed in the regional chapters under the towns from where they depart.

Bushwise Women (☎ (03) 332 4952; PO Box 28 010, Christchurch) specialises in trips for women only. The trips range from working on conservation projects to tramping but all provide a good opportunity to meet other women travellers.

North Island

Auckland

The name Auckland (Maori: Tamaki-makau-rau) refers both to a region, stretching roughly from the Bombay Hills in the south to the towns of Wellsford and Warkworth in the north, and a city, nestled between Waitemata and Manukau harbours.

Administratively, Auckland city consists of a number of cities, which form one vast urban sprawl. Auckland City proper lies between Waitemata and Manukau harbours. North Shore City, centred around Takapuna, is just over the harbour bridge. Manukau City is to the south of Auckland, around the airport, and Waitakere City is to the west.

Auckland city, with a population approaching one million (992,000), is one of the world's most exciting waterside cities. A mere stroll down its main artery Queen St is not enough. You have to explore its heart – the magnificent harbour – reminiscent of Sydney, San Francisco, Hong Kong and Cape Town. Auckland has lots of enthusiastic yachties; it's very much the 'the City of Sails' and the site of the America's Cup defence in 2000 (see the boxed text entitled America's Cup 2000).

Auckland is surrounded by water and covered in volcanic hills, replete with pa indicating a 1000-year occupation. So many islanders from NZ's Pacific neighbours have moved to Auckland that it now has the largest concentration of Polynesians in the world. More recently it has attracted immigrants from Asia. These foreign influences help give Auckland a much more cosmopolitan feel than other NZ cities.

The main entry point for international visitors, Auckland also has a wide range of accommodation and entertainment.

HIGHLIGHTS

- Cruising on the harbour
- Enjoying the view from the Skytower
- Exploring Auckland Museum and its Maori collection
- Strolling and eating in one of Auckland's genteel inner suburbs like Parnell and Ponsonby
- Visiting historic Devonport by ferry
- Discovering the islands of the Hauraki Gulf, including the volcanic Rangitoto, Waiheke (a village extension of Auckland) and the wild and remote Great Barrier Island
- Walking through the rugged forest of the Waitakeres
- Touring the wineries in West Auckland

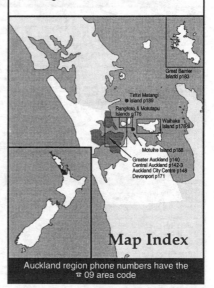

Great Barrier Island p183
Tiritiri Matangi Island p189
Rangitoto & Motutapu Islands p176
Waiheke Island p178-9
Motuihe Island p188
Greater Auckland p140
Central Auckland p142-3
Auckland City Centre p148
Devonport p171

Map Index

Auckland region phone numbers have the ☎ 09 area code

History

Maori settlement in the Auckland area dates from as early as 1350 AD. Other Maori peoples wanted the fertile land in succeeding years and eventually the volcanic cones were topped by *pa* (fortified Maori villages).

Tribal warfare and epidemics ravaged the settlements and by 1840, when Europeans came, the area was almost deserted.

From early colonial times the administrative centre of the country had been at Russell

AUCKLAND

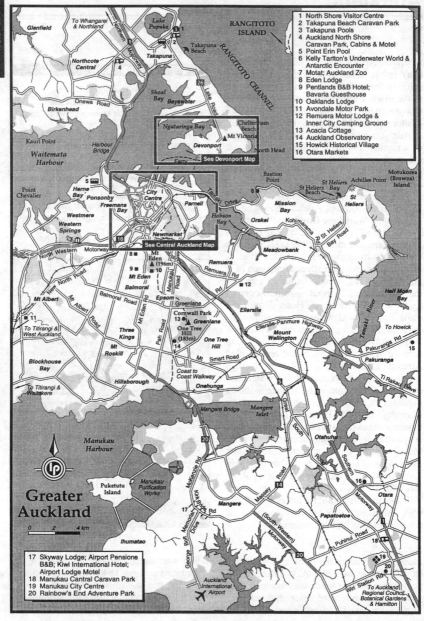

1 North Shore Visitor Centre
2 Takapuna Beach Caravan Park
3 Takapuna Pools
4 Auckland North Shore
   Caravan Park, Cabins & Motel
5 Point Erin Pool
6 Kelly Tarlton's Underwater World &
   Antarctic Encounter
7 Motat; Auckland Zoo
8 Eden Lodge
9 Pentlands B&B Hotel;
   Bavaria Guesthouse
10 Oaklands Lodge
11 Avondale Motor Park
12 Remuera Motor Lodge &
   Inner City Camping Ground
13 Acacia Cottage
14 Auckland Observatory
15 Howick Historical Village
16 Otara Markets

Greater
Auckland

0   2   4 km

17 Skyway Lodge; Airport Pensione
   B&B; Kiwi International Hotel;
   Airport Lodge Motel
18 Manukau Cantral Caravan Park
19 Manukau City Centre
20 Rainbow's End Adventure Park

in the Northland but, after the signing of the Treaty of Waitangi in 1840, Captain William Hobson, New Zealand's first governor, moved the capital south to a more central position. The site of Auckland was chosen principally for its fine harbour and good soil. In September 1840 officials came down from Russell to formally proclaim Auckland the NZ capital. Hobson named the settlement after Lord Auckland, then viceroy of India.

The new settlement did not get off to a good start and 25 years later the capital was moved again, this time south to Wellington.

Since the turn of the century Auckland has been NZ's fastest-growing city and its main industrial centre. While political deals may be done in Wellington, Auckland remains the dominant commercial centre.

Orientation

The commercial heart of the city is Queen St, which runs from Queen Elizabeth II Square (usually called QE II Square) near the waterfront and uphill to Karangahape Rd (K Rd), passing Aotea Square with the visitor centre nearby.

While the commercial district has much of the accommodation, many restaurants and most of Auckland's nightlife, it suffers from the 'dead heart' syndrome of many cities. Parnell, just east of the city centre, is a fashionable area of renovated wooden villas. Parnell Rd is lined with restaurants and boutiques, and continues to fashionable Broadway. Just west of the city centre is Ponsonby Rd, packed with cafes and bars.

Maps The Minimap series is handy. You can get good maps from the visitor centre, the Automobile Association (AA), Land Information NZ and bookshops. Jason's has a free series of *Official Auckland Region* guides. Land Information NZ at 99 Albert St sells a full selection of AA maps; it's open on weekdays from 8 am to 4.30 pm. Wises map shop is at 58 Albert St.

Information

Tourist Offices The Auckland Visitor Information Centre (☎ (09) 366 6888; fax 366 6893), 24 Wellesley St West just off Queen St, can answer most queries and make bookings for transport, tours, activities and accommodation in Auckland and farther afield. The office is open on weekdays from 8.30 am to 5.30 pm (until 6 pm in summer) and from 9 am to 5 pm on weekends and holidays. It also has an information kiosk, open from 9 am to 5 pm daily, on QE II Square.

The Airport Visitor Centre (☎ (09) 275 6467) in the International Terminal answers queries and make bookings. There is also a small information booth in the Domestic Terminal.

Other information centres include the North Shore Visitor Centre (☎ (09) 486 8670) on Hurstmere Rd in Takapuna, on the North Shore, and the Devonport Information Centre (see the Devonport section).

DOC and Auckland Regional Parks have a combined information centre (☎ (09) 366 2166) at the Ferry Building, open daily from 8.30 am to 6 pm in summer, and from 8.30 am to 5 pm weekdays at other times. They have brochures on NZ parks and natural attractions. The main DOC office (☎ (09) 307 1465) is in the Sheraton complex on K Rd.

The free tourist information booklets *Auckland A-Z Visitors Guide*, Jason's *Auckland: What's On* and *Auckland Great Time Guide* contain maps of the city. Another good free map is Budget's *Auckland City Visitor Map*.

The Hero Project (☎ (09) 307 1057) at 12 Kent St and the *Out! Bookshop* (☎ (09) 377 7770) at 45 Anzac Ave are good contact points for the gay and lesbian community. *Out!* is NZ's leading gay newspaper, with a complete guide to gay Auckland.

The *Auckland Tourist Times: What's Happening* is a useful free weekly for visitors. The *New Zealand Herald* is the Auckland morning daily.

The AA (☎ (09) 377 4660) is at 99 Albert St. Members of an overseas auto club have reciprocal rights; it has accommodation directories and excellent maps. It's open on weekdays from 8.30 am to 5 pm.

AUCKLAND

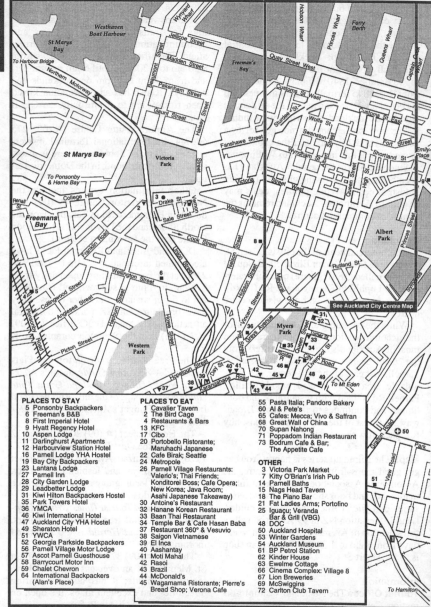

PLACES TO STAY
5 Ponsonby Backpackers
6 Freeman's B&B
8 First Imperial Hotel
9 Hyatt Regency Hotel
10 Aspen Lodge
11 Darlinghurst Apartments
12 Harbourview Station Hotel
16 Parnell Lodge YHA Hostel
19 Bay City Backpackers
23 Lantana Lodge
27 Parnell Inn
28 City Garden Lodge
29 Leadbetter Lodge
31 Kiwi Hilton Backpackers Hostel
35 Park Towers Hotel
36 YMCA
46 Kiwi International Hotel
47 Auckland City YHA Hostel
49 Sheraton Hotel
51 YWCA
52 Georgia Parkside Backpackers
56 Parnell Village Motor Lodge
57 Ascot Parnell Guesthouse
58 Barrycourt Motor Inn
59 Chalet Chevron
64 International Backpackers
   (Alan's Place)

PLACES TO EAT
1 Cavalier Tavern
2 The Bird Cage
4 Restaurants & Bars
13 KFC
17 Cibo
20 Portobello Ristorante;
   Maruhachi Japanese
22 Cafe Birak; Seattle
24 Metropole
26 Parnell Village Restaurants:
   Valerio's; Thai Friends;
   Konditorei Boss; Cafe Opera;
   New Korea; Java Room;
   Asahi Japanese Takeaway)
30 Antoine's Restaurant
32 Hanane Korean Restaurant
33 Baan Thai Restaurant
34 Temple Bar & Cafe Hasan Baba
37 Restaurant 360° & Vesuvio
38 Saigon Vietnamese
39 El Inca
40 Aashantay
41 Moti Mahal
42 Rasoi
43 Brazil
44 McDonald's
45 Wagamama Ristorante; Pierre's
   Bread Shop; Verona Cafe

55 Pasta Italia; Pandoro Bakery
60 Al & Pete's
65 Cafes: Mecca; Vivo & Saffran
68 Great Wall of China
70 Supan Nahong
71 Poppadom Indian Restaurant
73 Bodrum Cafe & Bar;
   The Appetite Cafe

OTHER
3 Victoria Park Market
7 Kitty O'Brian's Irish Pub
14 Parnell Baths
15 Nags Head Tavern
18 The Piano Bar
21 Fat Ladies Arms; Portofino
25 Iguacu; Veranda
   Bar & Grill (VBG)
48 DOC
50 Auckland Hospital
53 Winter Gardens
54 Auckland Museum
61 BP Petrol Station
62 Kinder House
63 Ewelme Cottage
66 Cinema Complex: Village 8
67 Lion Breweries
69 McSwiggins
72 Carlton Club Tavern

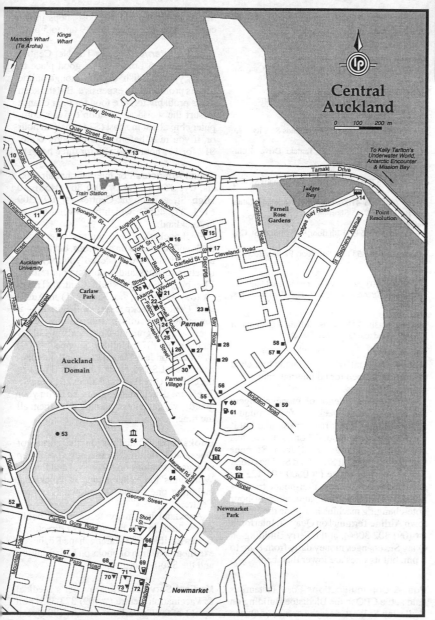

Central Auckland

Marsden Wharf (Te Aroha)

Kings Wharf

0   100   200 m

Tooley Street

Quay Street East

To Kelly Tarlton's
Underwater World,
Antarctic Encounter
& Mission Bay

Tamaki Drive

Judges Bay

Parnell Rose Gardens

Point Resolution

Train Station

The Strand

Ronayne St.

Augustus Tce

York St.

Earle

Charlton

Garfield St.

Cleveland Road

Gladstone Road

Judges Bay Road

St Stephens Avenue

Parnell Rise

Heather Street

Bath

St Georges

Auckland University

Grafton Road

Stanley Street

Carlaw Park

Windsor St.

Akaroa

Falcon St.

Cheshire Street

Parnell

Bay Road

Parnell Road

Auckland Domain

Parnell Village

Mausell Rd.

Parnell Road

Short St.

George Street

Carlton Gore Road

Newmarket Park

Ayr Street

Brighton Road

Mountain Road

Khyber Pass Road

Broadway

Newmarket

Foreign Consulates Consulates in Auckland include:

Australia
(☎ (09) 303 2429) Union House, 32-38 Quay St, City
Canada
(☎ (09) 309 3690) 9th floor, Jetset Centre, 48 Emily Place, City
Cook Islands
(☎ (09) 366 1100) 1/127 Symonds St, City
France
(☎ (09) 528 6122) 229 Tamaki Drive, Kohimarama
Germany
(☎ (09) 377 3460) 5th floor, 52 Symonds St, City
Japan
(☎ (09) 303 4106) 6th floor, National Mutual Building, 37-45 Shortland St, City
Netherlands
(☎ (09) 379 5399) 7th floor, 90 Symonds St, City
Sweden
(☎ (09) 373 5332) 18th floor, 92-96 Albert St, City
UK
(☎ (09) 303 2973) Fay Richwhite Building, 151 Queen St/corner of Queen and Wyndham Sts, City
USA
(☎ (09) 303 2724) General Building, corner of Shortland and O'Connell Sts, City

Money The Bank of New Zealand branch at the airport is open for all international arrivals and departures.

Queen St has plenty of moneychangers and banks open on weekdays from around 9 am to 4.30 pm. Their rates are similar but it pays to shop around. Thomas Cook has bureaux de change on Queen St near Customs St and near Shortland St. The Amex Travel Services office (☎ 0800 801 122) is at 101 Queen St. For after-hours transactions, a Thomas Cook automatic 24-hour note-changing machine is outside the Downtown Airline Terminal on Quay St. Interforex (☎ (09) 302 3066), at the Ferry Building on Quay St, changes money daily from 8 am to 8 pm, but its rates are lower than banks.

Post & Communications Poste restante is held at the CPO in the Bledisloe Building on Wellesley St West, near the corner of Queen St. There are several NZ post shops in the city open on weekdays from 9 am to 5 pm.

Email & Internet Access The Net Central Cybercafe at 5 Lorne St is a good place to satisfy your 'nerdish' urges, although online time is prohibitively expensive. But the keen nerds probably forsake food for their chance to surf the world and couldn't give a computer chip about the cost ($7 for half an hour or, if you're in before 11 am or after 6 pm, $12 for 1½ hours and $20 for three hours).

Travel Agencies For international air tickets, try: STA Travel (☎ (09) 309 0458), 10 High St, and Flight Centres (☎ (09) 309 6171, 377 4655), which has several offices in Auckland.

Backpackers travel centres offer good deals and discounts on activities, but remember if activities are cancelled you may have to return to Auckland to collect your refund. The biggest is Auckland Central Travel (☎ (09) 358 4874; fax 358 4971) in Auckland Central Backpackers at 9 Fort St – it seems to have information on just about every activity going in New Zealand. Others include the YHA Holiday Shoppe (☎ (09) 379 4224) on Jean Batten Place and Independent Travel Services (☎ (09) 303 3442) in the Central City Backpackers at 26 Lorne St. There are disreputable agents, so be on your guard – we get letters warning us of them all the time.

Bookshops Whitcoulls on the corner of Queen and Victoria Sts is a huge bookshop with good sections on NZ, travel and fiction. Whitcoulls has other shops in Auckland, including one in the Downtown Shopping Centre.

Auckland has many second-hand bookshops (look in the *Yellow Pages* directory). Books Pasifika, 283 Karangahape Rd, has an excellent selection of books on Maori culture and the South Pacific islands.

Medical Services The Traveller's Medical & Vaccination Centre (☎ (09) 373 3531) on level 1 of the Canterbury Arcade, 170 Queen

St, is open from 9 am to 6 pm on weekdays and from 9 am to 2 pm on Saturday. Travelcare (☎ (09) 373 4621) is on the 5th Floor of the Dingwall Building at 87 Queen St.

Auckland Museum

In the Domain, the museum has a great display of Maori artefacts and culture: pride of place goes to a magnificent 25m-long war canoe (the *waka Te Toki a Tapiri*). The museum also houses a fine collection of South Pacific items and NZ wildlife, including a 3m-tall giant moa model and exhibits from around the world.

Pounamu Ventures runs an excellent 1½-hour program which includes a guided tour of the Maori exhibits, followed by a half-hour performance of **Maori music and dance**. This excellent introduction to Maori culture begins at 11 am and 1.30 pm daily ($7, children $2).

The museum is open daily from 10 am to 5 pm; entry is free but entry to special exhibits is from $5 to $7 (children $3 to $5). It's about a 25-minute walk from Queen St through the Domain or you can catch the Link or Explorer buses to Parnell Rd.

The Skytower

The imposing Skytower on the corner of Federal and Victoria Sts is part of the Harrah's Sky City complex (a 24-hour casino, revolving restaurant, cafes and bars). It is NZ's tallest structure at 328m (and bigger than the Eiffel Tower). A lift takes you from the ground up to the observation decks in 40 seconds and in a 200km/h wind the top of the building sways up to 1m.

From the preliminary observation levels you can see ant-like humans scurrying along Auckland's CBD. For techno-junkies, there are all sorts of interactive displays, audio guides, powerful binoculars and weather monitors. Catching the skyway lifts costs $15 ($3 extra to go to the ultimate viewing level); the spectacular views are well worth the extra cost.

New Zealand National Maritime Museum

This museum (☎ (09) 358 3010) on the downtown waterfront is dedicated to one of NZ's national obsessions – sailing. This extensive museum explores 1000 years of NZ's seafaring history. Dozens of sailing craft and displays are exhibited, including the huge 25m (76ft) outrigger canoe *Taratai* that modern navigator Jim Siers constructed using 1000-year-old methods and sailed across the Pacific. Outside is **KZ1**, the America's Cup challenger.

Other exhibits illuminate the Maori and European discovery of and migration to NZ; there's even a recreation of an old immigrant ship, complete with swaying movement and creaking floorboards. There are exhibits on navigation, fishing, oral history and even a NZ seaside dairy, not to mention the Hall of NZ Yachting, the world's first jet-boat (the *Hamilton Jet*) invented in New Zealand in 1957, sailing school, boat-builders and sailmakers.

It is open daily from 9 am to 5 pm (to 6 pm in summer); entry is $10 (children $5, family $25). Guided tours are conducted – usually at 11 am or 2 pm – as are sailing trips at 1 pm. A one-hour 'Salty Sam' lunch-time cruise on Waitemata Harbour on the *Ted Ashby* is $15/10.

Kelly Tarlton's Underwater World & Antarctic Encounter

On Tamaki Drive, 6km east of downtown Auckland, this unique aquarium is housed in old stormwater holding tanks. An acrylic tunnel runs through the aquarium and you travel through on a moving footpath, with the fish swimming all around. Step off at any time to take a better look – it is designed to recreate the experience of scuba diving around the NZ coast. The aquarium was the inspiration of diver Kelly Tarlton.

The big attraction now is the Antarctic Encounter. It includes a walk through a replica of Scott's 1911 Antarctic hut, a ride aboard a heated Snow Cat through an environment where a penguin colony lives at -7°C, a simulated attack by an orca and a very cold below-the-ice aquarium. Finally, there's

America's Cup 2000

On 14 May 1995 a crew of NZ yachties on *Black Magic*, skippered by Russell Coutts, won the fifth straight race against *Young America*, skippered by US defence stalwart Dennis Conner. The 5-0 victory in this final challenge series off San Diego entitled the Kiwis to take the America's Cup (affectionately known as the 'Auld Mug') out of the USA for only the second time in 144 years. And it was only NZ's third cup challenge.

The cup has a long and illustrious history. In 1851 the *America* sailed to England, participated in and won the Round the Isle of Wight Race. A silver pitcher was presented to the skipper of *America*, taken back to the USA and, in 1857, entrusted to the New York Yacht Club (NYYC). It was first challenged for (unsuccessfully) in 1870-71 by the British.

Challenge after challenge was mounted but the cup seemed to be cemented safely in its case at the NYYC. The Australians had been peppering away with challenges and in 1983 *Australia II*, with its now legendary winged keel, beat the NYYC's *Liberty* 4-3, taking the cup out of the USA for the first time. Conner, skipper of the unsuccessful defender, was flabbergasted and vowed to get it back. He was true to his word and in 1987 wrested the cup from the Aussies off Fremantle, Western Australia.

New Zealand's first real challenge was mounted in 1988 in San Diego. Amid legal wrangling, the defender's *Stars and Stripes* beat challenger *KZ1*. In 1992 the cup was again successfully defended by the San Diego Yacht Club.

After *Black Magic's* 1995 win, the defence of the cup fell to Team New Zealand/Royal NZ Yacht Squadron. After some indecision, Auckland and the Hauraki Gulf were chosen as the defence site. Auckland has all the facilities of Westhaven and the Viaduct Basin and the gulf has a time-honoured course for match racing.

The magnetism of the Auld Mug is immense. Syndicates from such places as Hong Kong, Spain, Japan, Italy, Britain, the Virgin Islands, Switzerland, France, Australia and Russia will challenge. Obviously the Americans want it back – the St Francis, Waikiki and San Francisco yacht clubs are mounting challenges. And Dennis Conner – the nemesis of modern challenges and defences – will represent the Cortez Racing Association.

Auckland city and harbour will be buzzing from the moment challenger eliminations start in 1999 until the match races end in 2000 (these start on 26 February) and probably long before as well. Find out more at www.americascup2000.org.nz.

(Perhaps the cup needs defence of a different sort – in 1997 a protester walked into the room where the cup was on display and smashed it with a sledgehammer. It has since been repaired.) ∎

---

a visit to an Antarctic scientific base of the future and exhibits on the history of Antarctica.

One ticket gives you entry to all parts of Underwater World ($20, children $10). It's open daily in summer from 9 am to 9 pm (to 6 pm in winter). On Tuesday, Thursday and Sunday, you can see the shark-feeding frenzy at 2 pm. Get there on bus Nos 72 to 76 from the downtown terminal, or on the Explorer bus. The *Harbour Explorer* ferry also stops here.

Auckland City Art Gallery

The Auckland City Art Gallery is in two parts. The old building is two blocks east of Queen St, on the corner of Wellesley St East and Kitchener St, beside Albert Park. This heritage gallery has an extensive collection of NZ art, including many works by Colin McCahon and Frances Hodgkins (entry is free). The new gallery across the road is for changing special exhibits ($3, children $1). Both galleries are open daily from 10 am to 5 pm.

Museum of Transport & Technology

This museum (known as Motat) is out at Western Springs near the zoo, just off the Great North Rd. Motat is in two sections. Motat I has exhibits on transport, communications and energy, including one about pioneer aviator Richard Pearse. This eccentric South Island farmer may have flown before the Wright brothers. During his life he produced a steady stream of inventions and devices, but he was a lousy farmer! Also at Motat I is the infotainment Science Centre, with hands-on exhibits.

Motat II at Sir Keith Park Memorial Airfield features displays of rare and historic aircraft. Exhibits include a V1 flying bomb and Lancaster bomber from WWII, but pride of place goes to the huge Solent flying boat that ran a Pacific islands loop in the luxury days of flying.

Motat is open from 10 am to 5 pm. Entry to Motat I and II is $8 (children $4) or $4 ($2) for Motat II only. Electric trams run regularly from Motat I around to the zoo and Motat II.

Motat is signposted just off the North Western Motorway and can be reached by a Pt Chevalier bus No 045 departing from Customs St East in the city, or the Explorer bus.

Auckland Zoo

The Auckland Zoo is on Motions Rd off Great North Rd in the same area as Motat. Though not a large zoo, it is beautifully landscaped and a continuing renovation program has replaced many of the old animal houses with more spacious, naturalistic compounds. The **primate exhibit** is particularly well done.

In the nocturnal house you can see kiwis foraging for worms. There's also a large walk-through aviary of native birds, and the rare tuataras, prehistoric NZ reptiles. The usual lions, hippos, rhinos etc can also be seen. Tui Farm is a favourite with children.

The zoo is open daily from 9.30 am to 5.30 pm (last admission 4.15 pm); entry is $11 (children $6). The Pt Chevalier bus No 045 from Customs St East will get you to both Motat and the zoo, as will the Explorer bus.

Historic Buildings

There are numerous restored and preserved colonial-era historic buildings in the city. The oldest of these is **Acacia Cottage** in Cornwall Park at the foot of One Tree Hill. Built in 1841, the cottage was originally where Shortland St is today.

Highwic at 40 Gillies Ave, Epsom, and **Alberton** at 1 Kerr-Taylor Ave, Mt Albert, were both large houses of wealthy mid-Victorian New Zealanders. They were built in the 1860s and extended over time. In Parnell, **Ewelme Cottage** at 14 Ayr St was built from fine native kauri by a clergyman in the 1860s. All are open daily from 10.30 am to noon and from 1 to 4.30 pm. A visit to Ewelme Cottage is $3 (children $1).

Just five doors from Ewelme, **Kinder House** (1857) at 2 Ayr St is a fine example of early architecture and contains two galleries of the artwork and memorabilia of the Rev Dr John Kinder. The restored home is open from 11 am to 3 pm ($1, children 50c).

Renall St, off Ponsonby Rd, has been declared a conservation area and is a registered place of historic interest for its 19th century atmosphere. The houses along this block are not open to the public, but you can stroll along and admire the 20 or so early artisans' houses.

In south-east Auckland, **Howick Historical Village** (☎ (09) 576 9506) in Lloyd Elsmore Park on Bells Rd, Pakuranga, is a restored village of the 1840 to 1880 period on the old military settlement of Howick. The restored buildings include a thatched sod cottage, forge, village store and settlers' houses. It's open daily from 10 am to 4 pm (until 5 pm in summer); entry is $9 (children $3.50, family $20). Take the Howick bus from the Downtown Bus Terminal.

Parnell

Parnell is an old inner suburb, only 2km from the centre, where there was a concerted effort to stave off the office developers and restore the old houses and shops, many of them with a decidedly eccentric touch.

Parnell Rd is one of the most appealing streets in NZ with lots of art and craft shops, good (and expensive) restaurants, galleries and trendy Kiwis.

Parnell Village is an interesting area – a unified cluster of restored shops and houses, linked by paved alleyways, courtyards and boardwalks. Browse in the exclusive shops even if you can't afford to buy. The Elephant House at 237 Parnell Rd has one of the largest and most innovative arrays of crafts, while the Cupboard boutique at No 333 wins the Most Pretentious Award for its sign: 'Clothes for those that understand the difference.'

Farther east on Gladstone Rd, the Parnell Rose Gardens have harbour views and are in bloom from November to March.

The handy Link bus stops in Parnell.

Mt Eden & One Tree Hill

Auckland is built across more than 50 extinct volcanoes, and many of the volcanic cones that dot the city provide parkland retreats and fine views.

The view from Mt Eden, the highest volcanic cone in the area at 196m, is superb. You can see the entire Auckland area – all the bays and both sides of the isthmus – or look 50m down into the volcano's crater. The summit crater is sacred to the Maori and known as *Te Ipu a Mataaho* (bowl of Mataaho) after the god of volcanoes. You can drive to the top or take bus No 274 or 275 from Customs St East and then walk.

One Tree Hill (183m) is a distinctive bald hill, topped only by a lone pine tree and a huge obelisk dedicated to the Maori. It was the largest and most populous of the Maori pa, and the terracing and dugout storage pits are visible. It was named after a sacred totara tree which stood here until 1876 and has since been replaced by a (now huge) pine tree, which is looking decidedly sick after a chainsaw attack by a Maori protester. Get there on a bus beginning with No 30 or 31 from the corner of Queen and Victoria Sts.

Auckland Observatory

The Auckland Observatory (☎ (09) 624 1246) in the One Tree Hill Domain, off Manukau Rd, is open to the public every

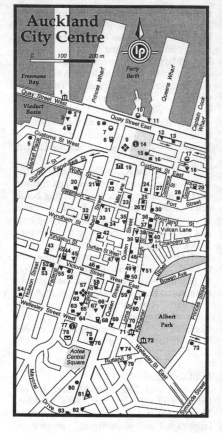

Tuesday, Thursday and Saturday from 7.30 pm on clear nights for telescope viewing and help in finding southern hemisphere constellations ($3, children $1).

The **Stardome Show** is held from Tuesday to Sunday at 3 and 4 pm and, except on Wednesday, also at 6.30, 7.30 and 8.30 pm ($9, children $4.50).

Markets

On Victoria St West, opposite Victoria Park, is the large **Victoria Park Market**, open from 9 am to 6 pm (till 7 pm on weekends). It's an alternative, renovated market concentrating

PLACES TO STAY

6	Copthorne Harbour City
13	Quay Royale Apartments
16	Novotel Hotel
20	Federal Place Apartments
22	Stamford Plaza Hotel; Ariake
24	Downtown Queen St Backpackers & Park in the Bar
25	Auckland Central Backpackers (ACB), Auckland Central Travel, Cafe at the World's End, Rat's Bar & CBD Cafe
28	City Backpackers Hotel
36	De Brett's International Backpackers
46	The President's Appartments; A Little Italy
53	Sky City Hotel
54	Albion Hotel
61	Albert Park Backpackers & Sub Station
62	Centra Hotel
63	City Central (formerly Abby's) Hotel
70	Central City Backpackers (CCB), Independent Travel Services & Embargo
75	Aotea Central Square Backpackers Hostel
83	Parkview Apartments

PLACES TO EAT

3	Gault's on Quay; Kermadec & Viaduct Quay
11	Cin Cin on Quay
12	Daikoku
18	McMahons Restaurant
26	White Lady
27	The 24-Hour Casino
31	Toki Japanese Food & Bar
35	BNZ Tower & Food Hall
38	Vulcan Cafe; Sushi Factory; Papa Jack's Voodoo Lounge; Occidental Hotel; Rupin's; Apicius & Melba Café
41	Baritone Bar & Brasserie
45	Mai Thai; Mexican Cafe; Cafe Midnight Express
47	Finance Plaza Food Hall
49	Hard to Find Mexican Restaurant
51	Simple Cottage Restaurant; Paneton; Lemon Moose Cafe; Wofem Bros Bagelry
55	Sultan's Table
60	Tony's Restaurant
64	Okonomo-yaki Japanese; Middle East Restaurant & Tony's Steak & Seafood
65	Daikoku
66	Strand Arcade: New Orient Chinese Restaurant
67	Mid City Food Hall
69	Countrywide Bank Centre Food Hall
74	Green Elephant Cafe & Bar; Public Library
76	Gopals Vegetarian Restaurant
79	Green Elephant Café & Bar
82	Merchant Mezze Bar; Caravanserai Tea House

OTHER

1	New Zealand National Maritime Museum
2	Cruising Auckland
4	The Loaded Hog
5	Turners & Growers Building; Watershed Theatre
7	Downtown Airline Terminal; Waterfront Bar & Restaurant
8	Cal-Neva Bar
9	Downtown Shopping Centre & Downtown Food Court
10	Ferry Building (Ferries to Devonport & Gulf Islands) & DOC
14	Queen Elizabeth II (QE II) Square & Information Kiosk
15	Urban Rap Jumping
17	Downtown Bus Terminal
19	Old Customs House
21	Club U4ria
23	Travelcare
29	Rose & Crown
30	YHA Travel (Holiday Shoppe)
32	Shakespeare Tavern & Brewery
33	Wises Mapshop
34	Pride Centre
37	STA Travel
39	Deschlers
40	Squid Bar
42	The Crow Bar
43	The Dispensary
44	The Palace
48	Travellers' Medical & Vaccination Centre
50	Whitcoulls
52	Sky City Casino & Restaurants (Cafe Fortuna, Tamarind, The Deli, Compass Brasserie, Orbit), Skytower & Bus Terminal
56	Automobile Association (AA) & Land Information NZ
57	The Atrium
58	Chili Lounge; Margarita's
59	Net Central Cybercafe
68	Civic Tavern: London Bar, Murphy's Irish Bar & Younger's Tartan Bar
71	New Art Gallery
72	Auckland City Art Gallery
73	Maidment Theatre
77	Auckland Visitor Information Centre & Town Hall
78	Central Post Office
80	Town Hall
81	Queen's Head Tavern

mostly on crafts, souvenirs and clothes. It also has outdoor cafes, entertainers and a concentration of New Age eclectics. It's a 20-minute walk west from the city centre, or you can take Bus No 005 from Customs St West (weekdays only), the Link or Explorer buses.

Auckland also has traditional markets selling fruit, vegetables and everyday goods. The biggest and most interesting is the **Otara Markets**, held every Saturday from around 6 am to noon in the car park between the Manukau Polytech and the Otara town centre on Newbury St. Otara Markets in one of the main Polynesian residential areas has a great atmosphere.

There are other markets selling food, art and craft, antiques and clothing in the city and surrounding suburbs; the visitor centre keeps a current list.

Auckland Suburbs

The suburban sprawl stretches almost 60km north to south and 30km east to west. Like many cities, much of it is suburban conformity, but parts are interesting for their history, vistas or character.

Auckland's most prestigious and historic real estate is found around the city's delightful bays and beaches. For architecture buffs, the older suburbs have fine, 19th-century wooden villas, built mostly of durable kauri.

Just south of the central city area, straight up the hill from Queen St, is **K Rd**. After WWII, the area around K Rd was a popular inner suburb for Maori and then Polynesian residents. With its South Pacific clubs, it maintains its Polynesian feel but now also has a strong Indian presence. It was once a disreputable area, but the strip clubs and sex shops are giving way to restaurants and renovation.

K Rd runs south-west to Ponsonby Rd in fashionable **Ponsonby**. Behind historic shopfronts, Ponsonby Rd's many restaurants are abuzz with the chatter of diners, the hiss of cappuccino machines and the bleep of mobile phones. Ponsonby has many fine old houses, though the adjoining **Herne Bay**,

right on the harbour, has some of Auckland's best Victorian houses.

Just south of Parnell is **Newmarket**, a lively and increasingly trendy shopping area along Broadway. Newmarket is well known for its furniture and clothes shops, particularly those selling designer outdoor fashion.

Tamaki Drive, which starts at the train station, runs east past sheltered bays to the wealthy suburbs facing Rangitoto Island. From the city centre, Tamaki Drive crosses Hobson Bay and first reaches **Orakei**, which contains Auckland's most expensive real estate. Parakai Drive in Orakei is millionaires' row, with great views across the city. Tamaki Drive continues on to **Bastion Point**. A 19th-century fort was built here to protect the entrance to the harbour, but Bastion Point is best-known for the Maori land occupation of 1977-78. The squatters were eventually evicted in a huge police operation, but the protest halted further subdivision of the point.

Tamaki Drive leads farther around to chic **Mission Bay**, Auckland's smaller answer to California's Santa Monica. Mission Bay is most popular in summer, with a park area, sidewalk cafes and a pleasant, calm beach. Farther on, **St Heliers Bay** is similar but smaller. Farther east along Cliff Rd, the **Achilles Point Lookout** has dramatic views of the city, harbour and Hauraki Gulf. Bus Nos 715 and 765 run along Tamaki Drive from the Downtown Bus Terminal.

Rainbow's End Adventure Park

This large amusement park on the Great South Rd (corner of Wiri Station Rd) at Manukau is open daily from 10 am to 5 pm (until 8 pm in January). Super passes for $30 (children $20) are good for unlimited rides all day; otherwise, a $15 entry buys three rides.

Take bus No 327, 347, 447, 457, 467, 487 or 497 from the Downtown Bus Terminal or take the Manukau exit off the Southern Motorway and drive 400m to the park.

Lion Breweries

Lion Breweries (☎ (09) 377 8840) is NZ's

largest multinational brewery and gives free tours of the plant at 368 Khyber Pass Rd in Newmarket. See the process, guzzle a Steinie and try other popular commercial beers. Free tours are held on request at 10.30 am and 2 pm; bookings are essential.

Parks & Gardens

Covering about 80 hectares, the **Auckland Domain**, right near the centre of the city, is a lovely public park that contains the museum and the Winter Gardens with its hot-house fernery.

Popular for jogging, picnics and walks, **Cornwall Park**, adjoining One Tree Hill on Greenlane Rd, is an extensive pastoral retreat only 6km south of the city centre. It has sportsgrounds, fields of grazing sheep, a visitor centre, Acacia Cottage and a restaurant.

Eden Garden, on the slopes of Mt Eden, is noted for its camellias, rhododendrons and azaleas. Entry is via Omana Ave and costs $3.

The extensive and relatively new **Auckland Regional Council Botanical Gardens** are 27km south of the city. Take the Southern Motorway to the Manurewa turnoff (the one past Rainbow's End).

Get the Auckland Regional Parks guide from the Auckland Visitor Information Centre or the DOC-Auckland Regional Parks information centre.

Walking

The Auckland Visitor Information Centre and the DOC-Auckland Regional Parks office have pamphlets on walks in and around Auckland. *Inner City Strolling* outlines self-guided walks along the waterfront, Tamaki Drive and Parnell. DOC's *Auckland Walkways* pamphlet has a good selection of forest and coastal day walks outside the metropolitan area.

The *Coast to Coast Walkway* covers the walk marked out between the Waitemata Harbour and the Manukau Harbour. The four-hour walk encompasses Albert Park, the university, the Domain, Mt Eden, One Tree Hill and other points of interest, keeping as much as possible to reserves rather than city streets.

Swimming & Surfing

Auckland is known for its fine and varied beaches dotted around the harbours and the coast.

The east coast beaches along Tamaki Drive, including Mission Bay and St Heliers Bay, are very popular. At most east coast and harbour beaches, swimming is better at high tide. Popular North Shore beaches include Takapuna and Milford. To get to them, take Bus No 83 or 85 from Victoria St West.

For good surf less than 50km from the city, try Te Henga (Bethells) on the west coast where the water is often very rough. You should also check out Karekare, Muriwai and Whatipu. Most of the surfing beaches have surf clubs and lifeguards. Farther afield, but possible as day trips, Piha and Raglan on the west coast and Tawharanui, near Warkworth, have some of NZ's best waves.

City swimming pools include the Olympic Pool in Newmarket; the Parnell Baths on Judges Bay Rd, with a saltwater pool on the waterfront (closed in winter); the heated Point Erin pool on Shelly Beach Rd, Herne Bay; and Takapuna Pools on Killarney St, Takapuna.

Outside the city, hot pool and swimming complexes include the **Aquatic Park** at Parakai near Helensville, and Waiwera Thermal Pools, 48km to the north; for details see the Around Auckland section.

Urban Rap Jumping

For the most exhilarating view of Auckland's skyline, rap jump (face-down abseil) from the top of the Novotel Hotel on QE II Square. The crowd gathered below samples some of your fear, especially when you are dropped six storeys in a spread-eagled free fall – you can actually hear their gasps. You can even see your folly reflected in nearby skyscrapers.

The cost is $50 for a single jump; it's best to do three for $75 – this gets an initial heart starter, a second spinning jump, and a third where you free fall, spin and go 'hog wild'. Phone Adrenalin Adventures (☎ (09) 373 3559) to book.

Sea Kayaking

Auckland has a host of sea kayaking operators with trips on the harbour and out to the islands. They include Auckland Wilderness Kayaking (☎ (09) 630 7782), with half-day trips to Motukorea ($50), a full-day harbour tour ($95), night kayaking ($55) and an overnight trip to Mahurangi ($175); Ferg's Kayaks (☎ (09) 529 2230), with evening trips to Rangitoto and day rentals; and Ross Adventures (☎ (09) 357 0550) with moonlight trips from Waiheke Island. Mainly Kayaking (☎ (09) 817 4560) has week-long kayaking trips with a German-speaking guide.

Other Activities

The *Auckland Adventure* booklet from the Auckland visitor centre lists activities and operators.

The Parakai Parachute Centre (☎ 0800 753 000) at Parakai, near Helensville, does **tandem skydiving** daily, weather permitting. It charges $195 for a jump from 12,000ft with about a minute's free fall; for an extra $10 they'll provide transport to and from Auckland. The centre has a good reputation for accelerated free-fall courses.

Scuba diving trips are organised by the Dive Centre (☎ (09) 444 7698) in Takapuna, Orakei Scuba Centre (☎ (09) 524 2117) and other operators.

Sailboards, mountain bikes and camping equipment can be hired from Windsurf Kiwi (☎ (09) 629 0952). Windscene Windsurf (☎ (09) 528 5277) has **windsurfing** courses and rentals.

Horse riding is available at South Kaipara Head with South Kaipara Horsetreks (☎ (09) 420 2835) which caters for experienced riders (a full-day ride with a sumptuous picnic lunch is $80 and a two-day 'overnighter' $200), or at Pakiri (☎ (09) 420 7269) near Wellsford.

Mountain bike rentals and tours abound. Trails range from the very easy at Cornwall

Park in the city to the very strenuous at Dome Valley, near Warkworth. Auckland Adventures (☎ (09) 379 4545) has a full-day mountain-biking experience near Muriwai Beach ($75, less $20 if you bring your own bike).

Cliffhanger Adventures (☎ (021) 661 851) has an **abseiling** trip to the Waitakere Ranges; ring for costs. Balloon Safaris (☎ (09) 415 8289) does **hot-air balloon** flights for $195. There are also many possibilities for fishing, tennis, golf and other sports in and near Auckland; ask at the visitor centre.

Language Courses

People from around the world, especially Asia and the Pacific, come to NZ to study English. Auckland has the highest concentration of language schools, and the visitor centre keeps a complete, up-to-date list (check in *Auckland A-Z*).

Organised Tours

You can tour the major Auckland attractions in a United Airlines Explorer Bus (☎ 0800 727 892) for $15 (children $7, adult two-day pass $25). It departs daily from the Ferry Building on the hour and goes to Mission Bay, Kelly Tarlton's, Parnell Rose Gardens, Auckland Museum, Parnell Village, Victoria Park Market and back to the Ferry Building. At the museum you can pick up its Satellite Link (from October to April) to Mt Eden, St Lukes shopping mall, Auckland Zoo, Motat and the visitors centre.

Auckland has many tour operators. Three-hour tours will typically drive around the city centre, over the harbour bridge and out along Tamaki Drive, including stops at Mt Eden, the Auckland Museum and Parnell, for about $38/19. Other tours do the above and include a harbour cruise for $80. ABC Tours (☎ 0800 222 868) and Scenic Tours (☎ (09) 303 3123) are both reputable. Hotel pick-up and drop-off is usually included in the price.

Trips to West Auckland take in the gannet colony at Muriwai and/or the Waitakere Ranges for around $50 (half day) to $80 (full day). Bush & Beach Nature Tours (☎ 0800 423 224) offers small-group nature tours to

West Auckland. You see the magnificent kauri, an ethereal bush cascade and Muriwai Beach; half/full-day trips cost $55/99 (including a hearty picnic lunch on the day trip). (They will show you where the movie *The Piano* and episodes of the cult TV classics *Xena: Warrior Princess* and *Hercules* were filmed.)

Less sedate but undeniably exhilarating are 4-Track Adventures' (☎ 0800 487 225) four-wheel 300cc bike safaris to the tracks of the Muriwai Forest and the untracked sands of Muriwai Beach; a one/two/three-hour blast is $85/145/185 (snacks included).

Other specialised tours around Auckland include golf, fishing and garden tours – try Golf Plus Tours (☎ 0800 788 848).

Tours depart from Auckland for Waitomo, Rotorua and the Bay of Islands and, in winter to the North Island ski areas; the visitor centre has details.

Scenic Flights There are scenic flights over Auckland, the Gulf Islands and the Coromandel; try Great Barrier Airlines (☎ 0800 900 600). The Helicopter Line (☎ (09) 377 4406) and Downtown Helicopters (☎ (09) 309 0234) do heli-flights over the city; the visitor centre has details.

Harbour Cruises The best ways to appreciate the City of Sails is to take to the water. Fullers Cruises (☎ (09) 367 9111) has the largest selection of cruises and operates almost all the ferries.

The cheapest option is to take the short ferry ride to picturesque Devonport. Ferries also go to many of the nearby islands in the Gulf. Rangitoto and Waiheke are easy to reach and make good day or half-day trips from Auckland. See the Devonport and Hauraki Gulf Islands sections for details.

Cruising Auckland (☎ (09) 366 7000; 0800 227 847) has a coffee/luncheon cruise from 12.30 to 2 pm daily ($25/45), a sunset/dinner cruise from 6.30 to 8.30 pm ($30/65). The 25m cruiser *Tiger IV* is based opposite the Maritime Museum, Viaduct Harbour.

Fullers also has popular tours around the inner harbour, including a 1½ hour coffee cruise $20 (children $10), and a 1½ hour luncheon cruise ($38). The *Harbour Explorer* loops from Devonport to Kelly Tarlton's, Rangitoto Island and back to

---

The *Soren Larsen*

Nothing epitomises Auckland Harbour more than the tall ship *Soren Larsen*, a square-rigged, 19th-century brigantine beauty with 12 sails.

The *Soren Larsen* was built out of oak in Nykøbing Mors in Denmark and achieved fame as the star of the TV series *The Onedin Line*. It returned to NZ and the Pacific in October 1994 after a circumnavigation of the globe.

You can sail on it for a day, or half a day, and realise the exhilaration it must have been to be part of the crew when it sailed into the world's most exotic ports. Haul on the lines and peer out to the modern harbour, dominated by the Skytower.

Speak to the people at Contact Squaresail Pacific (☎ (09) 411 8755; tallship@voyager.co.nz) for more information on day sailing, and extended NZ and Pacific voyages. ∎

After an exotic life, the *Soren Larsen* has retired to Auckland Harbour.

SOREN LARSEN

Devonport, with connecting ferries to the Ferry Building. An all-day Harbour Explorer pass, allowing you to get on and off at will, is $20 (children $10) or for $69 ($49) you can buy the Harbour Explore Super Ticket, a two-day pass that includes entry to Hobson Wharf, Tarlton's and the Rangitoto shuttle.

Plenty of other companies offer cruises and sailing trips – the visitor centre has details. The Pride of Auckland (☎ (09) 373 4557) has three daily trips, the best of which is their Sailing the NZ Way from 12.30 to 2.30 pm ($49). Westhaven Sailing School (☎ (09) 575 5051) have morning, afternoon and moonlight cruises. For the best trip on the harbour see the boxed text entitled The Soren Larsen.

Among the most interesting cruises are those offered by the 1909 wooden auxiliary schooner Te Aroha, sailing from the Marsden Wharf in central Auckland every few days from October to April. Their nature-oriented tours go around the islands of the Hauraki Gulf and farther afield to the Coromandel, Bay of Islands and Bay of Plenty. Popular day trips to Tiritiri Matangi run at least once a week in January and February ($30).

Special Events

The visitor centre keeps a list of the many annual and current events held in Auckland and supplies exact dates. Some of the more important ones follow:

January
    Open Tennis Championships; Opera in the Park; Auckland Anniversary Day Regatta
February
    Symphony under the Stars; Devonport Food & Wine Festival; HERO Festival, Parade & Party
March/April
    Dragonboat Races; Around the Bays Fun Run; Ironman Competition; Pasifika Polynesian Festival; Royal NZ Easter Show; Sky Show, Waitemata Harbour
May
    Auckland to Suva Yacht Race
June
    NZ Boat Show
July
    Rally of New Zealand
December
    Great NZ Crafts Show; NZ Golf Open

Places to Stay

Camping & Cabins North of the city, the four-star *Auckland North Shore Caravan Park, Cabins & Motel* (☎ (09) 418 2578) is at 52 Northcote Rd in Takapuna, 4km north of the Harbour Bridge; take the Northcote Rd exit and it's 700m west of the motorway, beside Pizza Hut. Tent and powered sites are $18/25 for one/two, cabins are from $45 to $55, tourist flats are $73, leisure lodges are $95 for four and motel units are $80 a double.

The *Takapuna Beach Caravan Park* (☎ (09) 489 7909), 22 the Promenade, Takapuna, is 8km north of the city centre and right on the beach, with a view of Rangitoto Island. It's an easy walk to the shops and central Takapuna, and a 10-minute ride into downtown Auckland. Tent sites are $18, powered sites are from $23 to $27, cabins $32 and on-site vans $40 (prices are for two).

Farther north of Auckland, the *Tui Glen Motor Camp* (☎ (09) 838 8978) is beside the swimming pool complex at Henderson, 13km north-west of Auckland. Tent/powered sites are $8/10 per person, cabins are $38 for two and tourist flats are $48.

The closest camping ground to the city is the quiet and secure *Remuera Motor Lodge & Inner City Camping Ground* (☎ (09) 524 5126) at 16 Minto Rd, off Remuera Rd. It's 8km south of downtown Auckland; take bus No 64 or 65 from the Downtown Bus Terminal. It has plenty of trees, a large pool and is just 100m from the shops and bus stop. Tent/powered sites are $24/27 for two, a self-contained bunkroom with beds costs $20 per person and tourist flats are $69 for two.

The *Avondale Motor Park* (☎ (09) 828 7228) at 46 Bollard Ave, off New North Rd, is 9km south-west of central Auckland and close to Motat and the zoo. Tent/powered sites are $18/20, on-site vans are $35, cabins are $45 and tourist flats are $55 (prices are for two).

South Auckland has many caravan parks, such as the *Manukau Central Caravan Park* (☎ (09) 266 8016) at 902 Great South Rd, Manukau, a quiet place away from the motorway. *Meadowcourt Motor Camp*

(☎ (09) 278 5612) at 630 Great South Rd is close to Manukau city and the airport. Tent/powered sites are $12/14 for two.

The Auckland Regional Council has camping grounds in the regional parks around Auckland, many in coastal areas. Some are accessible by vehicle, others are reached by tramping. Contact the DOC-Auckland Regional Parks information centre (☎ (09) 303 1530) for information and bookings.

Hostels Auckland has plenty of hostels in the city centre and inner suburbs. Prices given here are for summer. Despite the large number, they may still fill up in summer and it pays to book, especially if you want a single or double. In winter it's not so hectic and most hostels give discounts. All hostels have kitchens; some have cafes and even bars. Beware: there are some atrocious, filthy hostels.

City Centre At 9 Fort St, near the corner of Queen St, the *Auckland Central Backpackers* (ACB) (☎ (09) 358 4877) is Auckland (and NZ's) largest hostel, with room for 300 people. Amenities include made-up beds, two cafes, a lively rooftop bar (*Rat's*), a dairy downstairs, a video theatre and an excellent backpackers' travel agency. A bed in a three or four-bed dorm costs $16; singles/doubles are $25/40, with linen and duvet. Its location and facilities compensate for its impersonal 'big hostel' feel.

Right opposite at 4 Fort St is *Downtown Queen St Backpackers* (☎ (09) 373 3471). Uncertainty about the noisy Park in the Bar disco downstairs may herald its demise. Dorms cost from $17 and singles/doubles are $26/40.

At 38 Fort St is the new 200-bed *City Backpackers Hotel* (☎ 0800 220 198), which provides apartment-style accommodation in the heart of the red-light district. The dorm rooms are from $17 to $20 per person, deluxe rooms are $55 and a two-bedroom serviced apartment is from $120 to $150. Not far away, on the corner of High and Shortland Sts, is *De Brett's International Backpackers*

(☎ (09) 377 2389); dorms are $17, singles $30 and twins and doubles $40.

Just off Queen St and behind the Sheraton Hotel, the *Auckland City YHA Hostel* (☎ (09) 309 2802) on the corner of City Rd and Liverpool St is one of Auckland's biggest hostels. Comfortable, multi-share rooms cost $19 per person and double and twin rooms are $44. It is open 24 hours and has a shop and luggage safes.

The basic *Kiwi Hilton Backpackers Hostel* (☎ (09) 358 3999), nearby at 430 Queen St, charges from $13.50 for dorms and $36 for doubles. Its cousin in 'cheap', the *Aotea Central Square Backpackers Hostel* (☎ (09) 303 3350) at 295 Queen St, is also basic. It charges $14 in the dorms or $36 for a double. Both these doss houses (temporary accommodation) are the haunts of 'permanents'.

Far better is the new *Albert Park Backpackers* (☎ (09) 309 0336) at 27-31 Victoria St East and only 50m from Queen St and the eateries of High St. It has all the necessary facilities and a rooftop BBQ area was in preparation when we visited. It can store luggage and make bookings for activities. Dorms are $17, singles are $30 and twins and doubles $40.

Another good, large hostel is the *Central City Backpackers* (CCB; ☎ (09) 358 5685) at 26 Lorne St. Though large, it manages to maintain a homey feel, and the rooms are spotless, if a little dark. It sleeps 160 and has all the usual amenities, including a travel agency. The cost is $16 in 10-bed dorms, $18 in four-bed dorms and $40 in twins and doubles. Downstairs is the *Embargo* bar, which has a backpackers' night on Tuesdays.

The smaller but conveniently located *Bay City Backpackers* (☎ (09) 303 4768), formerly *Downtown*, is at 6 Constitution Hill, near Auckland University. It needs some work, but has a good atmosphere; parking is available and the houses have a small garden. It is $13 in a dorm and $30 in a double.

The *Georgia Parkside Backpackers* (☎ (09) 309 8999) is at 189 Park Rd on the corner of Carlton Gore Rd, Grafton, overlooking the Domain. This rambling old place has been upgraded and boasts a variety of comfortable rooms. Dorms cost from $13 to $16 and doubles from $34 to $38 for more private rooms.

Though the hostels are a better option, the YWCA and YMCA also have beds and often have rooms in summer when everything else is full. The *YWCA* (☎ (09) 379 4912), 10 Carlton Gore Rd, Grafton, charges $20 per person (women only) in singles or twins, linen included. The *YMCA* (☎ (09) 303 2068) is on the corner of Pitt St and Greys Ave. It takes both sexes in singles/twins for $27/49, linen included.

Parnell From the city, stylish Parnell is a 20-minute walk or you can take the Link bus.

International Backpackers (Alan's Place) (☎ (09) 358 4584), 8 Maunsell Rd, is in a quiet residential location near the museum. The large brick building has plenty of individual rooms, a commercial-style kitchen, lounge, TV room, dining area and reading room, plus off-street parking. Dorms cost $16, though most beds are in doubles and twins ($38, singles $25).

The friendly *Parnell Lodge YHA Hostel* (☎ (09) 379 3731), 2 Churton St on the corner of Earle St, sleeps 70; the cost is $17 in dorms ($15 in winter) and $40 for doubles and twins. It has a nice outdoor area and a huge, fully equipped kitchen.

There are a few backpackers on St Georges Bay Rd. The *City Garden Lodge* (☎ (09) 302 0880) at No 25 is a fine hostel in a large, elegant old home originally built for the queen of Tonga. It has undergone a facelift and is one of the best in Parnell; costs are $17 in dorms, $27 for singles and $38 for doubles or twins. Farther down the hill at No 60, *Lantana Lodge* (☎ (09) 373 4546) is a friendly, neat and well-run place; the cost is $17 in dorms, $40 for doubles and twins (duvets are provided). There are good views of the city from the rear of the lodge. A dorm at the basic *Leadbetter Lodge* (☎ (09) 358 0665) at No 17 costs $17.50.

Other Suburbs Mt Eden, a pleasant residential area 4km south of the city centre, has

hostels which tend to be the last to fill up in summer. Bus Nos 274 and 275 run from the Downtown Bus Terminal to Mt Eden Rd.

The *Eden Lodge* (☎ (09) 630 0174), 22 View Rd, is upmarket, set in a huge colonial-era home and surrounded by gardens. The rooms are comfortable and the house has large, pleasant communal areas. Dorms cost $15 and twin or double rooms $36. Buses stop on the corner of Mt Eden and View Rds. Farther up the hill, *Oaklands Lodge* (☎ 0800 222 725) is at 5A Oaklands Rd in a quiet tree-lined street at the foot of Mt Eden; the bus stops at the Mt Eden shops, 100m away. It charges from $16 to $19 for dorms, $44 for twins and doubles and $30 for singles.

Ponsonby, like Parnell, is another happening area close to the city. *Ponsonby Backpackers* (☎ (09) 360 1311), 2 Franklin Rd, is in a historic house only a street from Ponsonby Rd. Dorms cost $13 or $14, singles are $20 and doubles or twins $34 or $36. The rooms vary in quality and the bathroom facilities are light on, but this is a good place.

The *Budget Tourist Lodge* (☎ (09) 278 8947) at 558 Great South Rd, Manukau, is a cheap option close the airport (and even provides a free shuttle). The accommodation includes bunk beds for $19, singles for $42 and doubles and twins for $52 (or $65 with en suite). Another motel near the airport offering cheap beds is the *Skyway Lodge* (☎ (09) 275 4443) at 30 KirkBride Rd, Mangere; it has limited backpacker facilities for $20 per person.

B&Bs & Guesthouses B&Bs and guesthouses are popular. Those mentioned here are reliable, with a 'home away from home' feeling and include breakfast in the rate.

In the city centre, *Aspen Lodge* (☎ (09) 379 6698) looks out on a delightful little park at 62 Emily Place, about a five-minute walk from Queen St. It has a convivial dining/common area; singes/doubles are $49/69.

About a 10-minute walk from Queen St, the *Freeman's B&B* (☎ (09) 376 5046) at 65 Wellington St, Freemans Bay, has a private garden area behind the house and 12 rooms at $45/75 and self-contained apartments at $95 a double.

The fashionable Parnell district has two good guesthouses, both with private bath in every guest room. The *Ascot Parnell Guesthouse* (☎ (09) 309 9012) at 36 St Stephens Ave, off Parnell Rd, is a long-running favourite, with 11 guest rooms in a restored historic home; it charges $79/117. Nearby, *Chalet Chevron* (☎ (09) 309 0291) at 14 Brighton Rd has beautiful harbour views; it charges $68 for singles and $98 for doubles or twins.

Mt Eden also has attractive guesthouses. The *Bavaria Guesthouse* (☎ (09) 638 9641) at 83 Valley Rd is a lovely place with a private sun deck and garden; both English and German are spoken. Rooms, all with private bath, are $69/99. Also in Mt Eden, the *Pentlands B&B Hotel* (☎ (09) 638 7031) at 22 Pentland Ave, off Valley Rd, has large grounds, a BBQ area and picnic tables, and a lounge with a pool table and open fire; it charges $49/79 (a triple family unit is from $89 to $119).

Really classy is the *Great Ponsonby B&B* (☎ (09) 376 5989), a tastefully decorated turn-of-the-century villa at 30 Ponsonby Terrace. But chic is not cheap; rooms start at $125 and studios from $150.

The *Airport Pensione B&B* (☎ (09) 275 0533) on the corner of KirkBride and Westney Rds, Mangere, is close to the airport; singles/doubles are $50/60. For B&Bs in Devonport see the Around Auckland section.

Motels Auckland has over 100 motels and costs start from around $65/75 for singles/doubles. Several areas reasonably close to the city have a good selection.

Parnell Village Motor Lodge (☎ (09) 377 1463) at 2 St Stephens Ave, on the corner of Parnell Rd, has studio units from $88, and a range of units for $130 for two with a kitchen. All are self-contained, and reasonably priced for the good location. The only down side was the unfriendly reception when we arrived. The *Parnell Inn* (☎ (09) 358 0642) at 320 Parnell Rd is another reasonably priced motel with studio units for

from $75/80 ($90 with kitchen for two). The *Barrycourt Motor Inn* (☎ (09) 303 3789) at 10-20 Gladstone Rd has plenty of single/double units in its south wing for $110/145 ($150/160 in the north wing).

Another alternative is Jervois Rd in Herne Bay, after its junction with Ponsonby Rd. A number of motels are on, or just off, Jervois and Shelly Beach Rds, close to the southern end of the Harbour Bridge. At 6 Tweed St, the *Harbour Bridge Motel* (☎ (09) 376 3489) has units for from $68, with larger family units for $75 a double. It's an 1886 building full of character, with a more recent extension. With an outdoor BBQ and an attractive garden, it is in a convenient location.

Also in Herne Bay, the *Sea Breeze Motel* (☎ (09) 376 2139) at 213 Jervois Rd is near beaches, fishing areas, restaurants and shops; it has studio units for $89 and one-bedroom units for $98. The *Abaco Spa Motel Apartments* (☎ (09) 376 0119) at 59 Jervois Rd has units from $99 to $109.

Remuera just past Newmarket, 5km from the city, has a motel row along Great South Rd. This includes the *Siesta* (☎ (09) 520 2107) at No 70, *Aaberdeen* (☎ (09) 524 5381) at No 76, *Double Tree* (☎ (09) 522 2011) at No 80 and the *Ascot Motor Lodge* (☎ (09) 523 3794) at No 92. *Hansen's* (☎ (09) 520 2804) at No 96 and the *Tudor Court* (☎ (09) 523 1069) at No 108 are two of the cheapest, with units for from $65.

Across the Harbour Bridge, Takapuna and Birkenhead have plenty of motels. Out near the airport, Mangere has dozens, particularly along KirkBride Rd and McKenzie Rd.

Near the airport, the *Kiwi International Hotel* (☎ (09) 256 0046) at 150 McKenzie Rd has standard units from $89. The *Airport Lodge Motel* (☎ (09) 275 4084) at 294 KirkBride Rd has single/double units with fully equipped kitchen for $85/95. Both places offer courtesy airport transport.

Hotels Several hotels are conveniently situated in the city heart. The *Albion Hotel* (☎ (09) 379 4900) on the corner of Hobson and Wellesley Sts has 20 rooms in an old restored building; singles/doubles with private bath are $70/75. On the corner of Albert and Wellesley Sts, *City Central Hotel* (☎ (09) 307 3388), formerly *Abby's*, is close to the information centre and Skytower. The clean rooms are a little cell-like, especially those beside the internal lightwell, and thus not good value from $89/130 for standard/ studio rooms. The *Kiwi International Hotel* (☎ (09) 379 6487) on Queen St is an old place tarted up slightly; economy rooms with shared bathroom are $39/49 and better rooms are $89.

More expensive, but an excellent place to stay, the *First Imperial Hotel* (☎ (09) 357 6770) at 131-139 Hobson St has 61 rooms, with private bath and other amenities, priced from $180.

The *Park Towers Hotel* (☎ (09) 309 2800) at 3 Scotia Place, just off Queen St, has rooms with simple, student-like decor and private bath for $146 for two.

Directly opposite the train station, the *Harbourview Station Hotel* (☎ (09) 303 2463) at 131 Beach Rd looks a bit decrepit on the outside but the interior has been renovated. Rooms with private bath and telephone cost $50/70.

Auckland's best business hotels charge from around $200 per room, but substantial discounts are usually available. The *Copthorne Harbour City* (☎ (09) 377 0349), 96-100 Quay St West, and the *Novotel Hotel* (☎ (09) 377 8920), 8 Customs St East, are older luxury hotels and, hence, cheaper. Next up the rung are the *Hyatt Regency Hotel* (☎ (09) 366 1234) on the corner of Princes St and Waterloo Quadrant and the *Centra Hotel* (☎ (09) 302 1111), 128 Albert St.

Auckland's best hotels are the *Sheraton* (☎ (09) 379 5132) at 83 Symonds St; the *Stamford Plaza Hotel* (☎ (09) 309 8888) on Albert St, where double rooms are around $360 a night; and the top-of-the-heap *Sky City Hotel* (☎ 0800 777 102) with 300 rooms, 50 or so suites and all the facilities expected for the exorbitant cost.

The Park Central group (☎ (09) 377 4848) has apartment-style hotels around the city centre. *The President's Apartments* is at 27-35 Victoria St ($150), *Federal Place Apartments* at 18 Federal St ($120), *Quay Royale Apartments* at 48 Quay St ($220), *Parkview* at 363 Queen St ($150) and the *Darlinghurst Apartments* in Parliament St ($100 to $120).

Places to Eat

Because of its size and greater ethnic diversity, Auckland has the best range of dining possibilities in the country. Japanese and Korean restaurants are everywhere, a reflection of current tourism trends.

In the city centre, High St/Lorne St and, perpendicular to it, Vulcan Lane are haunts for lunch-time cafe society, while those up on Queen St towards K Rd are full of character.

The highest concentrations of cafes and restaurants are in Ponsonby and Parnell. Other suburban areas, such as Newmarket, Mt Eden and Herne Bay, have smaller enclaves. Devonport (see the Around Auckland section), replete with cafes and bars, is only a short ferry ride away.

Restaurants The *Dining Guide*, sponsored by Diners Club, lists restaurants by category and the *Aucklander Dining Guide* contains over 120 restaurants (which pay to be listed).

City Centre Tony's Steak & Seafood at both 27 Wellesley St West and 32 Lorne St must be doing something right because it's been carrying on unchanged while other places have come and gone. It has a basic steakhouse menu which also features lamb dishes and pastas; steaks cost around $24 for dinner, but less for lunch.

For cheap Italian food, *A Little Italy* at 43 Victoria St West has good pizza and pasta.

For Mexican food, the *Mexican Cafe* upstairs at 67 Victoria St West has a fun, casual atmosphere. It has equally popular bar and restaurant sections, and offers vegetarian and meat dishes. Another fine Mexican restaurant, the tiny *Hard to Find Cafe* at 47 High St has a bright Mexican decor and healthy food. It is indeed hard to find, tucked away in an off-street arcade. Main courses are around $15 at either place.

Chinese restaurants range from cheap

takeaways to flash eateries that attract wads of HK$. For value, the *New Orient Chinese Restaurant* in the Strand Arcade on Queen St does a great yum cha daily and buffet dinners on Wednesday and Thursday ($18) and Sunday ($19).

Auckland has a significant Indian community – mostly from Fiji – and plenty of good, cheap Indian restaurants, a number of them along K Rd. The *Aashantay* at No 309 has excellent North Indian food and the *Moti Mahal* at No 271 has curries from $10 to $12. *McMahon's Restaurant* at 34 Customs St is an old-fashioned, dowdy Indian restaurant that scores low on ambience but high on value. Lunch buffets ($10) and weekend dinner buffets ($13) are good value.

Middle Eastern fare – usually Turkish – is also cheap and popular. The *Middle East Restaurant* at 23A Wellesley St West is tiny and often crowded – the food is excellent and reasonably priced. For authentic Turkish food, try the similarly priced *Cafe Midnight Express* at 59 Victoria St West, near the Mexican Cafe; it's open until 11 pm. Another good Turkish place is the *Sultan's Table* at 68 Victoria St West.

For vegetarian food, *Gopals Vegetarian Restaurant*, run by the Hare Krishnas, is on the 1st floor at 291 Queen St near Aotea Square. This relaxed, comfortable place has Indian vegetarian snacks and unbeatable value buffets. It's open for dinner from 5 to 8.30 pm nightly and for lunch from noon to 2.30 pm from Monday to Saturday. The *Simple Cottage Restaurant* at 50 High St is another popular vegetarian place with good, economical vegetarian food and some fine desserts; it's open until 9 pm.

Auckland has many Japanese restaurants, including two branches of *Daikoku* at 48 Quay St and 39 Elliott St, the *Ariake* on Swanson St alongside the Stamford Plaza and *Toki Japanese Food & Bar* at 12-26 Swanson St (with dinner mains from $10 to $16). At the *Okonomo-yaki Japanese* on Wellesley St West, you sit around a teppan (hot plate) with a spatula and chopsticks while the meal is cooked in front of you.

There are many Thai choices in the city

(and in the suburbs). The *Green Elephant Cafe & Bar* at 27 Rutland St is adjacent to the Auckland public library – soups are $7.50 and mains around $16. *Mai Thai* is on the corner of Albert St and Victoria St West near Sky City.

For great views of the city, try the revolving *Restaurant 360°* on the top floor of the Telecom Building in Hereford St, just behind the Karangahape Plaza on K Rd. Buffets cost $22 for lunch, while dinner is $30 to $35 (with entertainment). In the same building, the *Vesuvio* Italian restaurant doesn't revolve, but the views are great and you'll get some of the best Italian food in town for about $25.

For fine views of the ferries and harbour, *Cin Cin on Quay* in the Ferry Building at 99 Quay St is an innovative and stylish restaurant that attracts the glitterati and visiting VIPs. It's not cheap but isn't outrageously expensive for the quality. In a similar vein, *Kermadec* in the Viaduct Quay complex on Quay St and the nearby *Gaults on Quay* serve top-quality seafood; see the *Auckland Waterfront Dining Out Guide* for prices and menus.

Upstairs in the Downtown Airline Terminal on Quay St, the *Waterfront Bar & Restaurant* is more upmarket and serves lunch (a full buffet is $12) and dinner, both inside and out on the patio.

The most spectacular views in town are from the Skytower. Here you will find *Cafe Fortuna* for a 24-hour buffet, the *Tamarind* for Pacific Rim food, the *Deli* for snacks and the á la carte *Compass Brasserie*. The top place (in height and cost) is the exclusive *Orbit* with million dollar views.

Parnell The Parnell Village has some good medium-priced restaurants hidden away, several with tables in open courtyards. There's *Valerio's* for Italian food or *Thai Friends* for good Thai food at reasonable prices. The bright and pleasant *Konditorei Boss* German pastry shop/cafe is highly enjoyable for European pastries, espresso and light meals; it's also great for people-watching on a sunny day. Combine these with *Cafe Opera*, *New Korea*, *Java Room* and *Asahi Japanese Takeaway* and you have lots of choice.

Parnell is particularly good for Italian food. The *Portobello Ristorante* at 131 Parnell Rd is a small, quality restaurant with imaginative pasta dishes (entrées are $12.50, mains $17.50). Other Italian places along Parnell Rd include the popular *Portofino* at No 156, where pasta mains and gourmet pizzas average $19, *Pasta Italia* at No 397, and the *Pandoro Bakery* on the corner of Parnell Rd and St Stephens Ave.

Cafe Birak at 161 Parnell Rd is another trendy place with an eclectic menu, though moderately priced. The large *Maruhachi Japanese* on the corner of Parnell Rd and Akaroa St is a Japanese restaurant with a sushi bar, tempura, teppanyaki and big, reasonably priced salmon rolls.

Antoines Restaurant at 333 Parnell Rd is one of Auckland's finest restaurants. In a renovated house, it is one of those silver service, gold credit card emporiums where the best local produce is tantalisingly presented in the French way – mains are about $30.

Ponsonby This is Auckland's busiest restaurant district, strung out over many blocks along Ponsonby Rd. You can walk along here in the daytime or evening and see what captures your fancy. On Saturday nights, get there early or book.

Heading down Ponsonby Rd from the corner of Jervois Rd, a couple of fine eateries are one block down on the corner of Pompallier Terrace. *Freiya's* is a Parsee place, the Parsees (or Zoroastrians) being Persians who migrated to India. It has atmosphere, music and good food, but is really just an expensive Indian restaurant. Opposite Freiya's, *Java Jive* has a reasonably priced menu with a selection of meat and vegetarian dishes, plus strong coffees and good desserts (also see under the Entertainment heading); the cafe opens nightly at 6 pm.

Café Cézanne at 296 Ponsonby Rd is a small, casual place with a great atmosphere and good food at good prices. Breakfasts,

light meals, gourmet burgers and unusual pies are served all day, all for around $7.50, and there's a good dinner menu. Next door at No 294, the *Turkish Cafe* is one of the cheapest restaurants in Ponsonby, with main courses for around $16 or a mixed platter for two at $20. The food is good and the service excellent. Across the road are *Hasan Baba* at No 263, another cheap Turkish cafe with good lunch specials and, at No 268, *The Ain't No Cure Cafe* – '...for what?', we ask.

Two of the trendiest eating spots in Auckland are the *Tuatara* at 198 Ponsonby Rd and *SPQR* at No 150. The *Tuatara* has straightforward, well-prepared food and good coffee. The tables outside are popular during the day, but this place also packs them in until late at night. The smaller *SPQR* is similar, with stylish decor, hearty breakfasts ($12) and a good range of moderately priced snacks and light meals. The food is a prelude or complement to the wine quaffing, which goes on into the early hours. Opposite SPQR, the *Atomic Cafe* at No 121 is a breakfast and day-time hang-out, with arguably the best coffee in town (its roasters supply many other cafes).

The fully licensed *Ponsonby Fire Station* at 1 Williamson Ave features modern NZ and continental cuisine; it is open from Tuesday to Friday for lunch and for dinner nightly.

Ponsonby Rd also has several good Asian restaurants. For Thai, try the *Sawadee* at No 42A, the *Thai Palace* at No 244 and the *Thai Classic* at No 282. Indian food, such as $12.50 vegetarian thalis, can be found at the *Masala Cafe & Bar* at No 169, while Indian balti cooking (and a sense of wellbeing) is served at the *Karma* at No 107. You'll find Malaysian at the *Mutiara* at No 64 and Korean at *Koreana* at No 29.

Other Suburbs Just west of Ponsonby, along Jervois Rd, the Herne Bay shopping centre has a small selection of good cafes and restaurants. *Sierra Coffee* at 50 Jervois Rd is good for a coffee and a cheap light meal. *Andiamo* at No 194 is licensed, trendy and open until midnight. Of the other Herne Bay eateries, *Vinnie's* at No 166 has an innovative

Auckland Region
Top: Rangitoto Island, as seen from Cheltenham Beach
Middle: The view of the Auckland skyline from Mt Victoria
Bottom: City of Sails – the view from Westhaven Marina

GABRIELLE GREEN

ADAM FRY

HOLGER LEUE

HOLGER LEUE

A	B
	C
	D

Auckland Region
A: Pretty Piha Beach, near Auckland
B: Ferry Building, Auckland

C: Te Henga (Bethells) beach, near Auckland
D: Gannet colony at Muriwai Beach, near Auckland

menu – bottled figs with grilled goats cheese for $12.95, for example. A few doors up at No 170 is the lively *Copacabana*.

The busy Newmarket shopping district also has a small enclave of good, cheap restaurants on Khyber Pass Rd, near Broadway. *Poppadom Indian Restaurant* at No 471 is a long-running favourite, with curries for around $16, cheaper vegetarian dishes and banquets. For Chinese food, there's the licensed *Great Wall of China* at No 410 with banquets for from $20. At No 440, the *Supan Nahong* serves good Thai food. Around the corner at 4 Osborne St is the *Appetite Cafe* which uses organically produced ingredients in its dishes. Next door at No 2 is the Turkish *Bodrum Cafe & Bar* which has meals for around $15. There is a collection of nice cafes around Short St including *Mecca*, *Vivo* and *Saffran*.

Tamaki Drive in Mission Bay has a string of good places: the oh-so-sweet *Death by Chocolate* at No 91; the *Jewel of India* at No 3/33; the Italian places *Positano*, at No 97, and *Santa Lucia*, at No 51; the *Business* at No 95, for Mediterranean food; and the superb award-winning *Saints Waterfront Brasserie* at No 425 in St Heliers.

Cafes The ever reliable *Paneton* at 60 High St, near the corner of High St and Victoria St East, has focaccia breakfast platters for $6.50 and French toast for $7.50. Next door is the *Lemon Moose Cafe*, which has footpath tables and chairs and tasty food (with discounts for backpackers). Also close is the trendy *Wofem Bros Bagelry*.

Vulcan Lane is a paved alleyway between High and Queen Sts. The *Vulcan Cafe* is a fashionable lunch-time cafe. Close by is the excellent *Sushi Factory*, where you select inexpensive sushi dishes from a revolving conveyor belt – we get out of here replete for about $12 (and the healthy green tea is free). The *Rupin Cafe* just across High St has breads, pastries, pizza and pasta; it's open daily from 7 am until early evening (late on Friday). Other cafe choices here are *Apicius* and the *Melba Café*. Around the corner at 2 Freyberg Place is the swish *Baritone Bar &*

Brasserie with an impressive array of designer pizzas, fish dishes and coffees. The perfect setting to sip chardonnay and watch the lunch-time crowd.

Several other good places are up the hill on Queen St, between Aotea Square and K Rd. The *Caravanserai Tea House* at No 430 is a casual, relaxing Middle Eastern caravanserai (way-station) to revitalise weary travellers. You can get cheap lunches – like a chicken kebab for $10 – or just hang out over coffee. Next door is the more upmarket *Merchant Mezze Bar*, a haunt of young professionals at lunch time, and a little farther uphill is the reliable *Hanane Korean Restaurant*.

Keep going up Queen St for more good cafes and restaurants. The *Baan Thai Restaurant* at 456 Queen St on the corner of Turner St is open for dinner nightly. Farther up the block, the *Temple Bar* at 486 Queen St is a hip little cafe featuring 'cool coffee, kai and music' (also see the Entertainment section).

On K Rd, the *Verona Cafe* at No 169 is a popular cafe open long hours. Though not dirt cheap, you can get excellent, innovative NZ fare for around $16 a main course. At No 173, *Wagamama Ristorante* is the place for sit-down meals, and *Pierre's Bread Shop* has takeaway delicacies.

Rasoi at No 211 is a straightforward, vegetarian Indian place with laminex tables. Its thali, starting at $3.50 and going up to $13 (all you can eat), are tasty and great value for lunch or dinner. Farther down K Rd, on the corner of Mercury Lane, is the suitably cavernous *Brazil*, a long way from the beaches of Rio – but the pervading aroma of brewed coffee is the same.

Other K Rd choices are the Latin American *El Inca* above Camerons Tavern at No 373 and the *Saigon Vietnamese*, with good vegetarian choices, at No 450.

The *Cafe at the World's End* on the 7th floor of ACB at 9 Fort St is a good, cheap cafe next to the bar, catering primarily for backpackers with nightly specials such as Cajun fish for $6. On the ground floor of ACB is the *CBD Cafe*, an excellent lunch spot with a variety of hot meals.

Pub Food The various city pubs are another economical eating possibility, particularly for lunch. The *Shakespeare Tavern & Brewery* on the corner of Wyndham and Albert Sts boasts the title of 'NZ's first micro brewery' but also serves food (while you enjoy its Willpower Stout and Sir Toby Belch's ginger ale). The bistro of the *London Bar* on the 1st floor at Wellesley St West also serves large pub meals. Farther up Queen St is the *Queen's Head Tavern* with large meals for around $15.

In Ponsonby, try the *Bronze Goat* at 108 Ponsonby Rd which features NZ specialities including venison, whitebait, lamb and oysters; it is open for lunch on weekdays and dinner nightly. There is also the *Harp and Crown* at 106 Ponsonby Rd and the *Cavalier Kitchen* in the Cavalier Tavern at 68 College Hill Rd. The *Bird Cage* on the corner of Victoria St West and Franklin Rd, opposite the Victoria St Market, is a fancier pub that serves meals but it is mainly noted for its good value $5 breakfasts.

Fast Food Food halls in central Auckland are mostly open during shopping hours only. The Downtown Shopping Centre on QE II Square, on the corner of Queen St and Customs St West, has the *Downtown Food Court*. Other food halls are on the lower ground floor of the BNZ Tower on the corner of Queen and Swanson Sts, and on the 4th floor of the Finance Plaza on the corner of Queen and Durham Sts. On the 4th floor of Countrywide Bank Centre at 280 Queen St down from Wellesley St there's an international food hall with kebabs, fish and chips, Chinese, Japanese (the *Fujiyama* for sushi) and traditional cafes. The Atrium on Elliott St also has seven international outlets in a food hall.

For Asian fare, you can't beat *Mid City Food Hall* between Elliott and Queen Sts. Excellent, authentic Thai, Chinese, Malay, Korean and Japanese meals cost $5 to $7 (sushi is $6.90 and udon $6.50); it's open daily from 10 am to 10 pm.

The Victoria Park Market has several restaurants, cafes and a food hall.

If *McDonald's* – especially the tasty Kiwiburger – is a favourite; you'll find it in the Downtown Food Court, on Queen St and K Rd. There's a *Wendy's* upstairs on Queen St, just down from Wellesley St. In the same block but a bit farther down the hill, opposite McDonald's, there's a *Pizza Hut* downstairs in the Strand Arcade. Nearby on the westside is a *Burger King*. There's a *KFC* on Quay St East and a *Georgie Pie* on Finance Plaza.

The cheap eats and late nights quandry can be solved by the *White Lady* mobile hamburger stand, an Auckland institution. It's on Shortland St just off Queen St and is open in the evenings until around 3 am during the week, and 24 hours on weekends and holidays. It's a good place for burgers, toasted sandwiches or a steak. The *24-Hour Casino* on the corner of Fort and Commerce Sts has cheap breakfasts – the hearty special is $5.50.

Locals swear by the hamburgers from *Al & Pete's*, near the BP petrol station on the corner of Parnell and Gladstone Rds.

Entertainment

Auckland has a good variety of places to go to after the sun sets. The entertainment section in the Saturday *Herald* has a limited run-down on events, mostly movies. Gig guides tend to come and go – the *Lava* is a current example; the visitor centre will have copies. *What's Happening*, a free monthly magazine, lists major events. The weekly *Alive & Happening* and *Live and Loud* pamphlets from the Auckland Visitor Centre also list the latest events, music, concerts, theatre, opera, dance and sports.

The biggest entertainment venue is the new Sky City casino complex on the corner of Victoria and Hobson Sts. The main attraction here is, of course, the gambling, but it also has a 700-seat theatre, restaurants, bars, a hotel and observation decks.

Cinema & Performing Arts

Arthouse films can be seen at the University, or at the *Vogue, Academy, Capitol* or *Bridgeway* (in Northcote) theatres. Many good cinemas around the city show first-run films; check the newspapers.

Live theatre venues around the city centre include the *Maidment Theatre* (☎ (09) 308 2383) on the corner of Princes and Alfred Sts, the *SiLO Theatre* on Lower Greys Ave and the *Sky City Theatre* in the casino complex.

The *Stables* (☎ (09) 525 3336) on the corner of Main Highway and Arthur St, Ellerslie, features alternative theatre.

The Aotea Centre on Aotea Square on Queen St is a venue for all kinds of performances and concerts; stop by or phone for their current schedule (☎ (09) 309 2677). Also check out the Auckland Philharmonia Orchestra (☎ (09) 638 7073), the NZ Symphony Orchestra (☎ (09) 358 0952) and the NZ Ballet Company (☎ (09) 358 3580). The revamped *Town Hall* is becoming a focus for the arts and performances.

Auckland University has a restaurant, pub, live music, plays, film series, lectures and more.

Pubs, Music & Dancing Auckland has plenty of convivial pubs and bars, many with music, though live bands are disappearing in favour of cheaper DJs and taped music. Big-name rock concerts are held at the *Powerstation* at 33 Mt Eden Rd, Mt Eden.

Nightlife tends to be quiet during the week. On weekends the popular spots are full to overflowing and dress standards apply at many of the fancier bars, where a beer costs around $4.

The *Kiwi Tavern* at 3 Britomart Place, just off Customs St East, is popular with backpackers (and travel writers). It has the Moa Bar on the ground floor and the Loft Bar upstairs, where you can hang out, relax, play pool or darts, have a coffee or beer, read newspapers, check out the notice board and generally relax. It is open daily until late, with a great travellers' Tuesday with the 'Taste of NZ' (six beers for $6).

Rat's Bar in ACB on Fort St is a lively and popular backpacker hangout. It has low prices and is always active, even during the week. It has an outdoor 7th-floor rooftop deck, plus an indoor cafe and a bar with weekly pool competitions.

Across the road on Fort St, the noisy *Park in the Bar* in the Downtown Queen St Backpackers is a popular Friday pick-up spot with suburbanites.

Margarita's at 18 Elliott St is a popular bar with backpackers. Staff serve cheap $5 meal specials and have free entry on Monday when they have a beer special (eight beers for $5). Above is the classy *Chili Lounge*, an open arena encased in rimu with big windows, friendly staff and an eclectic menu.

The *Loaded Hog*, at Viaduct Quay down by the waterfront on Quay St, is currently one of the most popular pubs in town. This pub brewery is favoured by the cellular phone brigade and enforces dress codes, but has a good atmosphere and is always lively.

The *Civic Tavern* at 1 Wellesley St West near the corner of Queen St has three bars on three floors, each specialising in a different part of the British Isles. *Murphy's Irish Bar* is on the ground floor, *Younger's Tartan Bar* is downstairs, and upstairs is the *London Bar*, an English-style pub. On weekends, the London Bar features jazz combos while Murphy's has higher-energy bands.

Kitty O'Brian's Irish Pub at 2 Drake St, Freemans Bay, on the corner of Wellesley St, always packs them in and has the best reputation for pouring a good Guinness. Live music, including Irish, is featured nightly. Another great and lively Irish bar, with live music most nights, is the *Dog's Bollix* on the corner of K and Newton Rds.

The *Rose & Crown*, another renovated pub on Customs St East, has occasional bands, especially on Saturday night.

The *Squid Bar* at 17 O'Connell St has guest DJs every night – it specialises in rave, techno and house music. The *Sub Station*, underneath Albert Park Backpackers on Victoria St East, is a regular basement bar with live music on weekends. Farther along, *Embargo* at 26 Lorne St, another basement bar underneath a backpackers, gives travellers the chance to meet an interesting regular clientele.

Small Vulcan Lane, between Queen and

High Sts, is also lively on weekends. The upstairs bar *Papa Jack's Voodoo Lounge* at the Vulcan Cafe turns up the volume and attracts a mixed crowd with a bent for alternative music. Or you can head bang at the *Occidental Hotel* opposite. Just around the corner on High St is *Deschlers*, a trendy cafe and bar, popular for lunches and after dark.

Albert St is another area to cruise for music and bars. In the Downtown Airline Terminal, the *Waterfront Bar & Restaurant*, upstairs on the corner of Albert and Customs Sts, attracts a younger, moneyed crowd at weekends. The chic *Cal-Neva Bar* (formerly *Sam Bucca's*) near the corner of Wolfe and Albert Sts is an expansive bar with a good selection of the excellent Monteith's (a West Coast, South Island beer) on tap. It's a popular spot, featuring live music on weekends and serves great food, including ceviche for $7.50. At the hill end of Victoria St West, across from the Skytower, are two late-night bars, the *Palace* and the *Dispensary*.

The *Temple Bar* at 486 Queen St is a hip little cafe with live music, usually folk, several nights a week. The *Crow Bar* at 26 Wyndham St is another place which has cleverly woven 'bar' into its title – this place really hums on the weekend.

In Parnell, the *Nags Head Tavern* at the northern end of St George's Bay Rd near the Strand is a popular English-style pub, with meals served in a restaurant section off to one side. *Iguaçu* at 269 Parnell Rd is a very trendy bar/restaurant where it's a challenge to squeeze through the door on Friday nights. You will also find the popular *Fat Ladies Arms* at 144 Parnell Rd; *Seattle* on the corner of Tilden St and Parnell Rd, a shiny bar and upmarket cafe (about $15 for a main course); the height-enhanced *Veranda Bar & Grill (VBG)*, uphill from the village; the height-challenged *Metropole*, downhill from the village; and the architecturally challenged but fun *Piano Bar* at the top of Parnell Rise.

The *Carlton Club Tavern* on the corner of Broadway and Khyber Pass Rd in Newmarket is a renovated pub with a popular rugby/sports bar. It's a good place to watch an Auckland Warriors game on the weekend. *McSwiggins*, just across the road, is another popular Newmarket watering hole.

Java Jive at 12 Pompallier Terrace, just off Ponsonby Rd in Ponsonby, is one of those rarities that has live music every night, mostly jazz and blues. Other Ponsonby choices – and an eclectic mix they are – are the *Cavalier Tavern* at 68 College Hill Rd; the *Chill Bar & Cafe* at 116 Ponsonby Rd; *One Red Dog* at No 151; the *Tuatara* at No 198; and the *Alhambra*, a good jazz venue, at No 283.

Club U4ria in the large, glossy building on the corner of Albert and Wolfe Sts is happening on Saturday night (entry is free before 10 pm, $3 between 10 pm and midnight and $5 after then). The *@Luna* at 178 Symonds St features new Kiwi rock music most nights.

Gay & Lesbian Venues Auckland is undoubtedly NZ's gay capital, with dozens of gay organisations and venues, ranging from bowling to tramping groups.

Gay nightlife is concentrated around K Rd and Albert St. *Staircase* at 340 K Rd is a very popular gay nightclub, disco and bar. *Legend* on the other side of K Rd at No 335 opposite the Staircase is another gay bar. At No 373 you have the *K Bar* and, upstairs on the 1st floor, *Sinners* nightclub.

Ponsonby Rd is another 'gay way' with meeting places like the gay bar *Surrender Dorothy* at No 3/175 and the *Olé Restaurant & Bar* at No 161. In the suburbs is *Karacters* at 21 George St, Papatoetoe.

Spectator Sport

For a well-rounded look at NZ, Auckland is a good place to see a rugby match. Eden Park is the home of rugby union in Auckland. The Mt Smart Stadium is the home of the Auckland Warriors rugby league team, and their matches against visiting Australian teams are guaranteed to attract an enthusiastic crowd.

Getting There & Away

Air Auckland is the major arrival and departure point for international flights. See the

Getting There & Away chapter for more information.

International airlines represented in Auckland include (the phone number shown is for reservations and reconfirmations):

Aerolíneas Argentinas
(☎ (09) 379 3675) ASB Centre, 135 Albert St
Air France
(☎ (09) 379 4455) represented by World Aviation, 6th Floor, Trust Bank Building, 229 Queen St
Air New Zealand
(☎ (09) 357 3000) corner of Queen and Customs Sts; 139 Queen St
Air Pacific
(☎ (09) 379 2404) 404 Queen St
British Airways
(☎ (09) 356 8690) corner of Queen and Customs Sts
Cathay Pacific
(☎ (09) 379 0861) 191 Queen St
Freedom Air International
(☎ 0800 600 500) PO Box 109698, Newmarket
Japan Airlines
(☎ (09) 379 9906) 120 Albert St
Polynesian Airlines
(☎ (09) 309 5396) 283 Karangahape Rd
Qantas Airways
(☎ (09) 357 8900, 0800 808 767) 154 Queen St
Singapore Airlines
(☎ (09) 303 2129) West Plaza Building, corner of Albert and Fanshawe Sts
Thai Airways International
(☎ (09) 377 3886) 22 Fanshawe St
United Airlines
(☎ (09) 379 3800) 7 City Rd

Air New Zealand, Ansett New Zealand and Mt Cook Airline connect Auckland with the other major centres in NZ. See the Getting Around chapter for fare details. Local operators also have flights into and out of Auckland.

Domestic airlines operating from Auckland include:

Air New Zealand
(☎ (09) 357 3000) corner of Queen and Customs Sts; 139 Queen St
Ansett New Zealand
(☎ (09) 302 2146) 75 Queen St; 50 Grafton Rd
Great Barrier Airlines
(☎ (09) 275 9120) Auckland Domestic Terminal
Waiheke Air Services
(☎ (09) 372 5001) Ostend, Waiheke Island

Mt Cook Airline
(☎ (09) 309 5395) 34 Queen St; Downtown Airline Terminal

Bus InterCity buses have services from Auckland to just about everywhere in NZ; see individual destinations for details. InterCity buses operate from the Sky City Coach Terminal at 102 Hobson St. For inquiries and reservations, call ☎ (09) 357 8400. The ticket office is open on weekdays and Sunday from 7.30 am to 6.15 pm and on Saturday from 7.30 am to 2.30 pm.

Newmans (☎ (09) 309 9738) buses also operate from the Sky City Terminal and go just about everywhere in the North Island. Northliner Express (☎ (09) 307 5873) buses also operate from the Sky City Terminal, with services heading north from Auckland to Whangarei, the Bay of Islands and Kaitaia.

Smaller services are the Geyserland Express (☎ (09) 357 6616) to Rotorua, C Tours (☎ (06) 758 1777) to New Plymouth, and the Little Kiwi Bus Co (☎ 0800 759 999) to Hamilton.

Backpacker buses operate in and from Auckland; both Kiwi Experience (☎ (09) 336 9830; fax 366 1374) and Magic Bus (☎ (09) 358 5600) offer door-to-door service, picking up and dropping off at any Auckland hostel. For more details see the Getting Around chapter.

Train Trains arrive at and depart from the train station (☎ 0800 802 802) on Beach Rd, about 1km east of the city centre. A number of readers have written saying that they felt intimidated at the station at night. You can check reservations and information daily from 7 am to 9 pm.

Two trains operate between Auckland and Wellington. The *Overlander* train runs daily, departing from both cities in the morning and arriving around dinner time. The *Northerner* is an overnight train operating nightly, except Saturday, and departing from both cities in the evening and arriving early in the morning.

The *Geyserland* operates daily between Auckland and Rotorua and the *Kaimai*

Express operates daily between Auckland and Tauranga, both stopping in Hamilton on the way.

Hitching As usual, it's easier to get a lift from out of town, but if you want to hitch from central Auckland, use the Beaumont St motorway ramp near Victoria Park to go north and the Grafton Bridge ramp behind the hospital to go south.

Otherwise, to start hitching northwards, take a bus from the Downtown Bus Terminal to Waiwera (bus No 895), Hatfields Beach (bus No 894), Orewa (bus No 893) or Silverdale (bus No 899). Each has departures about six times a day and charges about $6.50. Alternatively, you can take one of the hourly buses to Albany and start hitching from there.

Going south, take any southbound long-distance bus and get off at the Bombay Hills crossroads. Buses leave many times daily; the cost is around $10.

Getting Around

To/From the Airport
The Auckland airport is 21km south-west of the centre. It has two terminals (international and domestic), each with a tourist information centre. A free shuttle service operates between the two and there's also a signposted footpath.

At the international terminal there's a free-phone for accommodation bookings, and many places to stay also provide a free shuttle to/from the airport. A bank is open to change money for all arriving and departing flights, but charges a $3 transaction fee. Both terminals have left-luggage facilities and car rental desks, though you get better rates from companies in town.

The AirBus shuttle runs every 20 minutes between the airport and the Downtown Airline Terminal (☎ (09) 275 9396), 86 Quay St, starting at 6.10 am and finishing at 8.50 pm, with scheduled stops along the way. The cost is $10 one way (children 5 to 15, $3) and the trip takes 40 minutes (allow an hour during rush hour).

Door-to-door shuttles also run to and from the airport, and competition is cut-throat.

The two main operators are Super Shuttle (☎ (09) 307 5210) and Johnston's Shuttle Link (☎ (09) 275 1234). The cost between the airport and the city centre is around $10/18 one way/return per person, but all sorts of deals are available. Super Shuttle's rates are as low as $9 for backpackers going to or from a hostel.

A taxi to the airport from the city will cost around $35.

Bus Local bus routes operate daily from around 6.30 am to 10.30 pm, finishing around 7 pm on Sunday.

The Downtown Bus Terminal is on Commerce St, between Quay St and Customs St East, but not all buses leave from here. Local bus route timetables are available from the bus terminal, newsagents, the visitor centre, or you can phone Buz a Bus (☎ (09) 366 6400) for information and schedules. Buses operate from 7 am to 7 pm on weekdays, until 9 pm on Friday, from 8 am to 7 pm on Saturday and from 8 am to 6 pm on Sunday. The bus information kiosk at the Downtown Bus Terminal is open from 7 am to 6.30 pm from Monday to Saturday and from 9 am to 5 pm on Sunday. The Bus Place at 67 Victoria St West is another source of information and is open from 8.15 am to 5 pm on weekdays. The *Auckland Busabout Guide*, available at information centres and the bus information kiosk, shows bus routes and departure points for the city's major attractions.

Inner-city fares cost 40c, while fares for farther distances cost from $1. Busabout passes are available for unlimited daily bus use from 9 am onwards (anytime on weekends) for $8 (children $4, families $12). The passes can be bought on the bus. Weekly passes are also available.

The Link is a great new bus service which travels clockwise and anti-clockwise around a loop which includes Queen St, the casino, Ponsonby Rd, K Rd, the university, Newmarket, Parnell, the train station and QE II Square. The service frequency is every 10 minutes from 6 am to 6 pm on weekdays (every 30 minutes after 6 pm until 10 pm or 11 pm on Friday) and every 30 minutes from

7 am to 11 pm on weekends. The all-white buses are easily spotted and the fare is only $1 (for the entire loop if you wish).

Train There's a limited Cityrail (☎ (09) 270 5143, 0800 103 080) train service, with just two main lines running west to Waitakere and south to Papakura. The first stop out from the main train station is at Newmarket. Trains run roughly every hour from 6 am to 7 pm.

Car, Motorcycle & Campervan Auckland is crawling with car and campervan hire operators and is the best city in which to hire a vehicle for touring NZ. Some good deals can be had for long-term hire, but be warned that cheapest is not necessarily the best.

The major companies – Avis, Budget, Hertz and Thrifty – are the most reliable, offer full insurance and have offices at the airport and all over the country. They are expensive, but rates are often negotiable for longer rentals.

If you are prepared to take limited insurance and risk losing an excess of around $700, then the cheaper operators offer some pretty good deals. Prices vary with the season, the age of the car and length of rental. In the off-season, for rental of a month or more, a good 1990 model car costs as little as $30 per day. For shorter rentals in the high season, expect to pay $50 or more a day. A campervan or kitted-out minibus starts at around $70 per day.

Ignore prices quoted on brochures and shop around by phone. Always read the rental agreement thoroughly before you sign. See the Getting Around chapter for a full discussion of car hire and its pitfalls.

Auckland had over 60 rental operators at last count. The following are either the larger operators or can offer drop-off in the South Island, usually Christchurch.

A2B	☎ (09) 377 0825, 0800 222 929
Ace*	☎ 0800 502 277
Adventure*	☎ 0800 866 500
Avis	☎ (09) 379 2651
Avon/Percy*	☎ (09) 303 1122
Brits NZ*	☎ 0800 839 100
Budget*	☎ (09) 375 2270
Hertz	☎ (09) 309 0989, 0800 654 321
Letz	☎ (09) 275 6890
Maui*	☎ (09) 275 3013, 0800 651 080
McDonalds	☎ (09) 276 8574
Nationwide	☎ 0800 803 003
Northpark Rentals	☎ (09) 537 0991
Pegasus*	☎ (09) 275 3222, 0800 803 580
Quality Rentals	☎ (09) 270 0155
Thrifty	☎ (09) 309 0111, 0800 737 070
Wagon Rentals	☎ (09) 412 9189
Camping Holidays**	

* Rents out campervans as well as cars.
** Specialises in station wagons with camping equipment.

You can rent a small scooter for $25 for 24 hours; only a car licence is needed. For larger motorcycles, some places will rent them out and others will sell it on a buy-back system. They usually hire anything from 250cc to 750cc.

New Zealand Motorcycle Rentals (☎ (09) 358 2252; 85 Customs St West, Auckland; nzmr@cybernet.co.nz) rents out 225cc to 1100cc motorcycles on both a short-term and long-term basis. Rates (which include bike insurance, unlimited kilometres and sales tax) range from $79/69/59 for three to six days/seven to 20 days/21 days-plus for a Yamaha SR250 to $130/120/110 for a Yamaha XJ600 to $265/245/195 for a BMW R1100RT.

Graeme Crosby (☎ (09) 376 3320) at 299 Great North Rd hires out motorcycles as well as arranging buy-backs.

Buying a Car For stays of two months or more, many people look at buying a car. You can buy through dealers on the buy-back scheme at car fairs or though ads in the newspapers. The hostels in Auckland also have notice boards where travellers leaving the country advertise their cars, and the visitor centre on Wellesley St West has a similar board.

For newspaper listings, cars are advertised in the *NZ Herald* on Wednesday, the *Trade & Exchange* on Monday and Thursday, and the *Auto Trader* magazine.

Buy-backs, where the dealer agrees to buy

back your car for an agreed price, are not usually a great deal but are an easier option. Dealers who work on this system include:

Budget Car Sales	☎ (09) 379 4120
Downtown Rentals	☎ (09) 303 1847
Geraghty McGregor Motors	☎ (09) 307 6700
Rex Swinburne Motors	☎ (09) 620 6587
Rock Bottom Rentals	☎ (09) 622 1592

The most popular way to buy a car is through the car fairs, where people bring their cars to sell. Manukau is the biggest and best, but the Ellerslie Racecourse car fair is also good. In the city centre, there is a car fair next to the old Oriental Markets, but it is relatively small. Arrive early, between 8.30 and 9.30 am, for the best choice of cars – the car fairs are over by about midday. For a credit check phone ☎ 0800 658 934; quote chassis and licence plate numbers. Mechanical inspection services, credit agencies and Auto Check details are all on hand at the car fairs, which are listed below:

Ellerslie Racecourse (☎ (09) 810 9212) near the Greenlane roundabout on Sunday from 9 am to noon

Manukau City, South Auckland (☎ (09) 358 5000) in the car park of the giant shopping mall near the Manukau motorway offramp on Sunday from 8.30 am to 1 pm

Old Oriental Markets (☎ (09) 524 9183) on Beach Rd in the city centre on Saturday from 9 am to noon

Alternatively, you could try the car auctions. Two of the best-known are:

Hanmer Auctions (☎ (09) 579 2344; 830 Great South Rd, Penrose) also holds auctions several times a week, with Monday, Wednesday and Friday at 6 pm set aside for budget vehicles

Turner's Car Auction (☎ (09) 525 1920; McNab St, Penrose) has auctions several times a week, with Wednesday at 11.30 am set aside for budget vehicles

Taxi Deregulation is the name of the game in NZ and, when the taxi industry was deregulated, small companies cropped up all over the place offering cut-price fares. Now the companies have gotten together to 'self-regulate' (set) prices, though driver training

still seems to be nonexistent. Flagfall is $2 and then around $1.50 per kilometre.

There are many taxis in Auckland which usually work from ranks but also cruise popular areas. You often have to phone for a taxi – Auckland Taxi Co-op (☎ (09) 300 3000) is one of the biggest companies.

Bicycle Several companies around Auckland hire out bicycles, usually mountain bikes, by the day, week, month or longer. They also hire gear you may need for longer journeys – helmets, panniers and tents.

A handy place in the city centre is *Adventure Cycles* (☎ (09) 309 5566) at 1 Fort Lane, just off Fort St. Mountain bike rentals with panniers and a bike kit start at $25/100/250 per day/week/month.

The Penny Farthing Cycle Shop (☎ (09) 379 2524, 379 2002) on the corner of Symonds St and Khyber Pass Rd hires out mountain and hybrid bikes. Pack 'n Pedal (☎ (09) 522 2161) at 436 Broadway in Newmarket hires out mountain bikes at $25 per day, sells bikes on the buy-back system (buy-backs at half-price) and sells cycling gear and camping equipment. Another buyer and seller of new and used bikes is the Outside Adventure Exchange (☎ (09) 366 1445) at 16 Shortland St. All of the above places will advise on cycling routes, and organised and supported cycling trips.

Boat Fullers (☎ (09) 367 9111 for schedules) is the main ferry operator to Devonport and the Hauraki Gulf islands. Ferries to Devonport ($7 return) leave roughly every 30 minutes and about a dozen ferries a day go to Waiheke ($23 return). See the Hauraki Gulf Islands section later in this chapter for transport to other islands. All Fullers ferries depart from the Ferry Building.

Around Auckland

REGIONAL PARKS
The Auckland Regional Council administers 21 regional parks around the Auckland

region, all within 15 to 90km of the city. There are several coastal and beach parks with swimming and surfing beaches, plus bush parks, a kauri park, the Waitakeres west of Auckland, the Hunua Catchment east of Auckland and a gannet colony at Muriwai. The parks have good walks and tramping tracks, ranging from 20 minutes to several hours in length; camping is allowed in several parks.

An Auckland Regional Parks pamphlet with a list of facilities in each park is available from the Auckland visitor centre, or the DOC-Auckland Regional Parks information

centre (☎ (09) 303 1530) at the Ferry Building in Auckland.

DEVONPORT

Devonport is an attractive suburb on the tip of Auckland's North Shore peninsula. One of the earliest areas of European settlement, it retains a 19th-century atmosphere with many well-preserved Victorian buildings. It's touristy, only 15 minutes away by ferry and has lots of small shops, art and craft galleries and cafes.

The helpful Devonport Information Centre (☎ (09) 446 0677) on Windsor

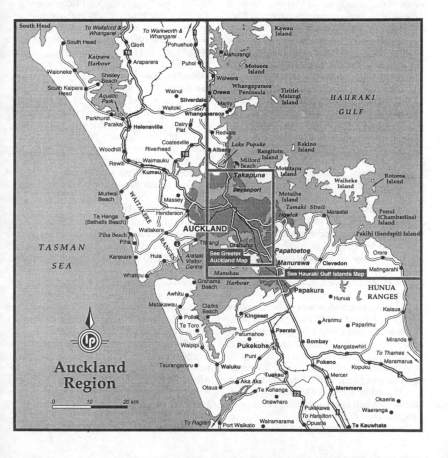

Auckland Region

Reserve is open from 10 am to 4 pm daily. Get a copy of *Old Devonport Walk* which outlines the many historic buildings in this antique port.

Things to See

Devonport also has several points of interest. Two volcanic cones, **Mt Victoria** and **North Head**, were once Maori pas – you can see the terracing on the sides of the cones. Mt Victoria is the higher of the two, with a great 360° view and a map at the top pointing out all the landmarks and giving the names of the many islands you can see. You can walk or drive to the summit of Mt Victoria; the road is open at all times except from 6 pm to 7 am on Thursday, Friday and Saturday.

North Head, on the other cone, is a historic reserve riddled with old tunnels built at the end of the last century in response to fears of a Russian invasion. The fortifications were extended and enlarged during WWI and WWII but dismantled after WWII. Some of the old guns are still here and a ranger is on hand with historical information. The reserve is open to vehicles daily from 6 am to 6 pm and to pedestrians until 10 pm.

The **waterfront promenade**, with a fine view of the city, makes a good stroll. Near the ferry wharf is a children's playground and a large lawn area where families picnic on sunny days.

Walk west from the wharf along the promenade (left as you come out of the wharf building) for about five blocks until you reach the navy base, then turn right into Spring St. At the end of the street is the small **Naval Museum**, open from 10 am to 4.30 pm daily (entry is free).

The **Devonport Museum** on Mt Cambria Reserve, just east of Mt Victoria, chronicles Devonport's history and is open on weekends from 2 to 4 pm. **Jackson's Muzeum** at 10 Victoria Rd (the main drag) is filled with automobiles and old bric-a-brac. It is open on Sunday; entry is a stiff $10 (children $6).

Just north of the foot of North Head, **Cheltenham Beach** is a lovely little beach with a superb view of Rangitoto.

Devonport Cinemas, in an Art Deco build-ing at 48-56 Victoria St, are a welcome escape (for some) from the scent of coffee.

Organised Tours

Devonport Tours (☎ (09) 357 6366) meets the ferry hourly from 10 am to 3 pm and an enjoyable minibus tour takes you around the sights, including the summits of North Head and Mt Victoria, which are quite a climb otherwise. The tour takes about an hour and costs $15 (or $22 including the ferry from the city).

The *Kestrel*, a historic ferry, cruises back and forth across the harbour from Auckland to Devonport, currently on Friday evening. There's a jazz band for dancing, a restaurant for dining, and all in all it's a very pleasant cruise. Reservations are recommended (☎ (09) 367 9111).

Places to Stay

Devonport is an enjoyable and convenient place to stay, and has several good, small B&B guesthouses to choose from. Pride of place goes to the *Peace & Plenty Inn* (☎ (09) 445 2925) at 6 Flagstaff Terrace, just a one-minute walk from the ferry wharf, facing the little triangular grassy park on Victoria Rd. In a restored, historic kauri house, it's one of the most artistically and unusually decorated places we've seen. It charges $180/210 for single/double B&B.

Also in Devonport are the *Aniwaniwa Cottage Homestay* (☎ (09) 445 4454) at 20 Hastings Parade ($70/100); *Baker's Place* (☎ (09) 445 4035) at 30 Hastings Parade (a cottage for $120); *Badger's of Devonport Quality Accommodation* (☎ (09) 445 2099) at 30 Summer St ($89/119); *Devonport Villa Inn Luxury B&B* (☎ (09) 445 8397) at 26 Tainui Rd (from $135 to $185 for two); the *Villa Cambria* (☎ (09) 445 7899) at 71 Vauxhall Rd (from $85 to $160 depending on room and facilities); and the *Devonport Village Inn B&B* (☎ (09) 445 8668) at 9 Albert Rd (from $60/100).

At Cheltenham Beach, *Cheltenham by the Sea B&B* (☎ (09) 445 9437) at 2 Grove Rd, just off Wairoa Rd, is a guesthouse in a family home; the cost is $55/80 for B&B in one of three rooms, each with private entrance but sharing bathroom facilities (an ensuite room is $100 for two).

The historic, beautifully renovated *Esplanade Hotel* (☎ (09) 455 1291) is directly opposite the ferry dock at 1 Victoria Rd. The rooms are simple but stylish with TV and phone, and the bathrooms range from big to huge. Singles cost $65 with shared facilities, doubles with private bathroom are from $85, and suites are from $220.

Places to Eat

Most of Devonport's restaurants and cafes

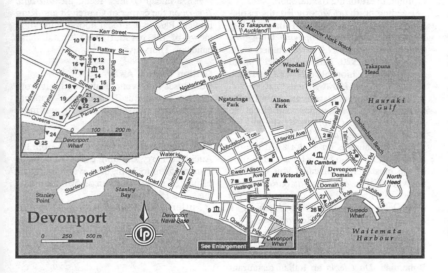

Devonport

PLACES TO STAY
1   Cheltenham by the Sea B&B
2   Villa Cambria
3   Devonport Villa Inn Luxury B&B
5   Devonport Village Inn B&B
6   Aniwaniwa Cottage Homestay
7   Baker's Place
8   Badger's of Devonport Quality Accommodation
15 Peace & Plenty Inn
20 Esplanade Hotel & Grapevine Wine Bar

PLACES TO EAT
10 Da Ciccio ; Bohemian Mediterranean
12 Portofino Bar & Restaurant; Devonport Delicatessan Espresso Bar; Skoozi of Devonport Café; Devonport Cafe; Star Fish;
14 Windsor Tea & Coffee Shop

16 Pizza Delissimo; New Delhi Indian; Monsoon; Koumi Japanese
17 Manuka Woodfired Pizza
18 Stone Oven Bakery & Cafe
19 Catch 22 Fish Shop; Abide in the Vine Cafe; Devonport Bar & Brasserie; Java House
24 Food Hall, Port-O-Call, Torpedo Bay & America's Cup Bar
27 The Watermark Restaurant & Bar

OTHER
4   Devonport Museum
9   Naval Museum
11 Devonport Cinemas
13 Jackson's Museum
21 Devonport Information Centre
22 Library & Public Toilets
23 Windsor Reserve
25 Devonport Wharf & Ferry Terminal
26 Masonic Tavern & Joe's

are strung out along Victoria Rd, the main street leading from the ferry wharf.

The ferry building itself has a small food hall with fast-food places and dining facilities (avoid the greasy pizza). Upstairs are two popular bar/restaurants, *Port-O-Call* – with the *America's Cup Bar* – and *Torpedo Bay*, where you can dine inside or out, day or night, overlooking the harbour.

Heading north up Victoria Rd, the Esplanade Hotel has a couple of flash dining rooms, including the *Grapevine Wine Bar*, which has varied NZ fare; dinner costs around $15 to $20. Farther up Victoria Rd are plenty of fashionable cafes and bars such as the *Devonport Bar & Brasserie* at No 5-7, the trendy *Skoozi of Devonport* at No 14, the *Devonport Delicatessen Espresso Bar* at No 16, the *Devonport Cafe* at No 18, and the *Abide in the Vine Cafe* at No 41.

Good restaurants on Victoria Rd are the BYO *Java House* in the WJ Scott Mall (one of the most delightful cafes you will find anywhere); the *Portofino Bar & Restaurant* at No 26 with good pasta dishes; the BYO *New Delhi Indian* and *Koumi Japanese*, a Japanese sushi bar and takeaway, at No 59; *Monsoon* at No 71 with reasonably priced Thai and Malaysian curries or the *Bohemian Mediterranean* at No 99. Next door to the Bohemian, *Da Ciccio* an Italian restaurant and pizzeria, is open for dinner daily (and for lunch on weekends).

For great views, *McHugh's of Cheltenham*, 46 Cheltenham Rd, is on the beach directly opposite Rangitoto. Buffet lunches cost $20 on weekdays and $25 on weekends; book ahead on ☎ (09) 445 0305. Also good for the city skyline and a harbour studded with yachts is the *Watermark Restaurant & Bar* at 33 King Edward Parade; the emphasis is on seafood and it is open for dinner nightly and from 9 am on weekends.

For takeaway fish and chips to eat down at the waterfront, the *Catch 22* fish shop at 19 Victoria Rd has a good selection, as does *Star Fish* – hopefully not on the menu – at 26 Victoria Rd. Pizza lovers will be well satisfied at *Pizza Delissimo*, next door to the New Delhi, and *Manuka Woodfired Pizza* at

No 49 (we didn't try the pizzas, but the idea of firing the oven with scented manuka, or NZ tea tree, leaves us wondering). The *Stone Oven Bakery & Cafe* at 5 Clarence St is a local institution – the perfect place for breakfast – and the *Windsor Tea & Coffee Shop* at 8 Victoria Rd is for those who can't choose between a flat white or a short black.

For a cheap counter meal, the *Masonic Tavern* on the corner of Church St and King Edward Parade is a local boozer with good views of the harbour; *Joe's* upstairs has bands on Thursdays.

Getting There & Away

Bus Buses to Devonport run regularly from the Downtown Bus Terminal in Auckland, but the ferry crossing is quicker and more enjoyable.

Boat The Devonport ferry departs from the Auckland Ferry Building every 30 minutes from 6.15 am to 7 pm, then every hour until 11 pm ($7 return, children $3.50); the crossing takes 15 minutes.

Fullers' *Harbour Explorer* stops at Devonport, Kelly Tarlton's and Rangitoto; an all-day pass entitles you to jump on and off the boat wherever you like. Ring Fullers (☎ (09) 367 9111) for information.

WEST AUCKLAND

No more than an hour's drive from the city, West Auckland has excellent surf beaches, nature reserves and the Waitakere Ranges, which offer good walking and temperate rainforest. West Auckland is also the place to go for vineyards and craft outlets.

Vineyards

New Zealand wine has a worldwide reputation and there are numerous vineyards in the West Auckland area. The *Winemakers of West Auckland* pamphlet – available from the visitor centre – details the vineyards, their addresses and opening hours. Some, such as Delegat's and Corbans, are within walking distance of Henderson, which can be reached by bus or Cityrail from Auckland. Other large and well-known vineyards, such as

Matua Valley, House of Nobilo and Coopers Creek, are farther out near Kumeu.

Some of the wineries have excellent restaurants. For fine dining in a beautiful setting, the *Hunting Lodge* (☎ (09) 411 8259) at Matua Valley is open from Friday to Sunday for lunch and dinner. Other restaurants are *de Vines* at Lincoln Vineyards, the *cafe* at Pleasant Valley Wines and *Allely House* at Selaks Vineyard.

Waitakere Ranges

These scenic ranges once supported important kauri forests, but these were logged almost to extinction in the 19th century, though a few stands of kauri and other mature trees such as rimu survive. The **Centennial Memorial Park** now protects many native plants in the regenerating forest. Bordered to the west by the beaches on the Tasman Sea, the park's sometimes rugged terrain with steep-sided valleys is the most significant forest area close to Auckland and is popular for picnics and walks.

The **Arataki Visitor Centre** (☎ (09) 817 7134) on SH24, 6km north-west of Titirangi on Scenic Drive, is a good starting point for exploring the ranges. As well as providing a host of information on the area, this impressive centre with its Maori carvings (which include more than a fair share of oversized phalluses) and spectacular views is an attraction in its own right. The nature trail at the centre indicates native species and contains mature kauris.

The visitor centre has pamphlets, including the excellent *Nga Tohu a Nga Tupuna* (indicating the carved ancestors of Te Kawerau a Maki) and maps for walking over 200km of trails in the ranges, or you can also get information from the DOC-Auckland Regional Parks Information Centre in Auckland. Noted walks are the **Karamatura Loop Walk** near Huia, leading to waterfalls and northern rata forest, and the **Cascade Falls Walk** at the north of the park, which passes mature kauri.

Piha & Whatipu

Piha, about 40km west of Auckland at the edge of Centennial Memorial Park, is a small seaside village inhabited by many artists, craftspeople and alternative types. It comes alive in summer with hundreds of beachgoers, holidaymakers and surfers. In summer, in addition to the beach life, there's tennis, lawn bowls, live bands at the surf club on weekends, and lots of partying. Surfing competitions are held in Piha and there are many good bushwalks through the surrounding Waitakere Ranges and along the rocky coastline. It's a very enjoyable, picturesque spot – a refreshing change from Auckland. Karekare, south of Piha, has a surf-pounded beach and, nearby, rain-drenched forest. It was the location for the award-winning film *The Piano*.

The *Piha Domain Motor Camp* (☎ (09) 812 8815) right on the beach is open year-round and has tent/powered sites for $14/15 for two and on-site vans at $25. Non-campers will find private homestays, baches and caravans in Piha.

Another attractive spot is Whatipu, on the northern side of Manukau Harbour at Manukau Heads, 40km from Auckland via Titirangi and Huia, and about a 50-minute drive from the city. The *Whatipu Lodge* (☎ (09) 811 8860), set in a quiet and isolated area good for tramping and fishing, has basic camp sites at $8 per vehicle (up to four people), plus hostel-style accommodation with single, twin and double rooms at $18 per person. Take the bus to Huia and they'll come to pick you up.

Muriwai Beach & Gannet Colony

The road to Muriwai Beach is well signposted at Waimauku on SH16. Apart from the renowned **surf beach**, the main attraction here is the colony of Australasian gannets. The colony was once confined to a nearby rock stack but has now overflowed to the shore cliffs, even past the barriers erected to keep observers out. If you haven't seen these beautiful birds at close range before, take the opportunity to see them here.

A good way to explore the beach and forest around Muriwai is on a horse trek through the Muriwai Beach Riding Centre (☎ (09) 411 8480).

Places to Stay At the small settlement of Muriwai, the *Muriwai Waterfront Camp* (☎ (09) 411 9262) is adjacent to the beach; tent and powered sites are $16 for two and on-site vans are $20. A small shop and cafe, the only one in Muriwai, is at the entrance to the camp. The *Muriwai Beach Motel* (☎ (09) 411 8780) on Motutara Rd has single/double one-bedroom units for $55/80.

Helensville

This town is less than an hour's drive from Auckland, 4km inland from the southern end of Kaipara, NZ's biggest harbour.

Helensville itself is no great attraction, but you can take interesting **harbour cruises** on the MV *Kewpie Too* (☎ (09) 420 8466) – advance bookings are essential. Tours range from a four-hour cruise ($12) to an all-day cruise ($35, children $15) that lands at Pouto Point on the northern head of the harbour and joins a 4WD sand dune tour from Dargaville.

Four kilometres north-west of Helensville, at Parakai, **Aquatic Park** is a huge hot pool/swimming complex with indoor and outdoor hot mineral pools and various waterslides. The centre is open from 10 am to 10 pm daily; entry is $9 (children $6) and waterslides cost extra. The Helensville bus from Auckland continues on to Parakai and stops at the front of Aquatic Park.

Tandem skydiving at Parakai Parachute Centre is also popular (see Other Adventure Activities in the Auckland section).

Places to Stay & Eat The turn-of-the-century kauri villa *Malolo House* (☎ (09) 420 7262) at 110 Commercial Rd has dorms for $14 and doubles and twins for $34. The friendly owners explain the regional attractions and book local trips and adventures. The *Point of View Backpackers* (☎ (09) 420 7331) is a small, no-frills place a long way from town; it charges $15 per person.

The *Grand Hotel* (☎ (09) 420 8427) on Railway St has singles/doubles for $25/50 and a restaurant. The best options are the various homestays and farmstays in the area. The small Helensville Information Centre (☎ (09) 420 7468) on the main street has listings.

Out at Parakai, the *Aquatic Park Holiday Camp* (☎ (09) 420 8884) is adjacent to the thermal complex. Here a tent site is $8.50 per person, with the added incentive of free admission to the hot pools. Parakai also has three motels, one with basic backpacker accommodation.

Hauraki Gulf Islands

The Hauraki Gulf off Auckland is dotted with islands (Maori: *motu*). Some are within minutes of the city and popular as day trips. Waiheke, a favourite weekend escape, has become almost a dormitory suburb. It also has some fine beaches and hostels, so it's a popular backpacker destination. Great Barrier, once a remote and little-visited island, is also becoming a popular destination and can be used as a stepping stone to the Coromandel. The islands are generally accessible by ferry or light aircraft. There are also some 'getting there is half the fun' possibilities, like the elderly wooden auxiliary schooner *Te Aroha* and light plane from Paihia.

There are 47 islands in the Hauraki Gulf Maritime Park, administered by DOC. Some are good-sized islands, others are simply rocks jutting out of the sea. The islands are loosely put into two categories: recreation and conservation. The recreation islands can be visited, transport to them is available, and their harbours are dotted with yachts in summer. The conservation islands, on the other hand, have severely restricted access. Special permits are required to visit some and others cannot be visited at all, since these islands are refuges for the preservation of plants and animals, especially birds, often extremely rare or even endangered species.

Information

The Hauraki Gulf Islands are administered

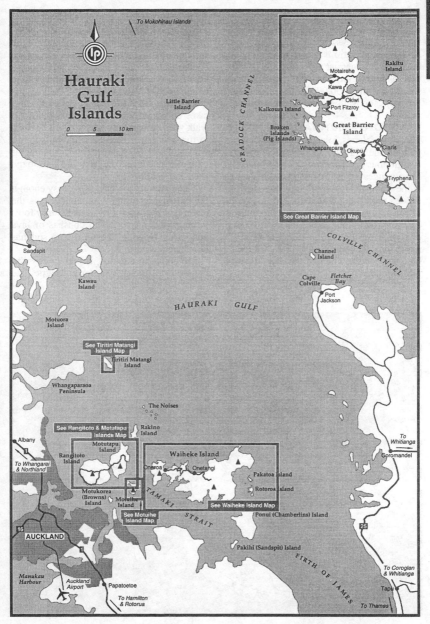

by DOC, whose information centre in Auckland has the best information about natural features, walkways and camping. The Auckland Visitor Centre is where to learn about the more commercial aspects of the islands, such as hotels, ferry services etc. Trampers should get the 1:50,000 Land Information NZ maps for Waiheke and Great Barrier.

RANGITOTO & MOTUTAPU ISLANDS

These two islands, joined by a causeway, are part of the Hauraki Gulf Maritime Park. Rangitoto is just 10km north-east of the city. The youngest of the 50 or so volcanic cones in the Auckland region, Rangitoto rose from the sea only about 600 years ago in a series of volcanic explosions. The last eruption was 250 years ago. Rangitoto is the short version of Nga Rangi-itotongia-a-Tama-te-kapua, a name meaning 'the days of Tamatekapua's bleeding', as the chief of the *Arawa* canoe was wounded here.

Rangitoto is a good place for a picnic. It has lots of pleasant walks, a saltwater swimming pool, BBQs and a great view from the summit of the 260m cone. Lava caves are another attraction. There's an information board with maps of the walks and a shop which opens for the ferries.

The hike from the wharf to the summit takes about an hour. Up at the top, a loop walk goes around the crater's rim. The walk to the lava caves branches off the summit walk and takes 30 minutes (return). A tractor train tour also meets the ferry and goes to the summit for $12.

There are other walks, some easy enough for kids. Bring water – on sunny days the black lava gets pretty hot – and sturdy footwear, as the whole island consists of lava with trees growing through it (no soil has developed as yet).

Motutapu, in contrast, is mainly covered in grassland, grazed by sheep and cattle. The

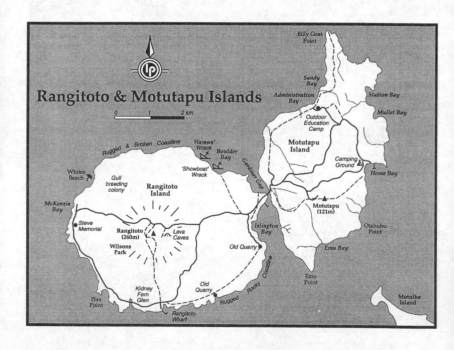

island was bought from the Maori in 1842 for 10 empty casks, four double-barrelled shotguns, 50 blankets, five hats, five pieces of gown material, five shawls and five pairs of black trousers. There's an interesting three-hour round-trip walk between the wharf at Islington Bay and the wharf at Home Bay. Islington, the inlet between the islands, was once known as 'Drunken Bay' because sailing ships would stop here to sober up crews who had overindulged in Auckland.

There's a DOC camping ground at Home Bay on Motutapu Island. Facilities are basic, with only a water tap and toilet provided at this rudimentary camping ground. Bring your own cooking equipment, as open fires are not permitted; camping fees are $3 per night. For more information, contact the island's senior ranger (☎ (09) 372 7348) or DOC in Auckland.

Getting There & Away
The ferry trip to Rangitoto Island from the Ferry Building in Auckland takes about an hour. Fullers (☎ (09) 367 9111) has ferries leaving daily at 9.30 and 11.30 am (and 2 pm in summer). They depart from Rangitoto for the return trip at 12.30 and 3 pm, with an extra boat leaving the island at 5 pm in summer. The return fare is $18 (children $9). Fullers' *Harbour Explorer* ferry stops at Rangitoto.

WAIHEKE ISLAND
Waiheke is the most visited of the gulf islands and at 93 sq km is one of the largest. It's reputed to be sunnier and warmer than Auckland and has plenty of picturesque bays and beaches.

The island attracts all kinds of artistic folk, who exhibit their work in galleries and craft shops on the island. There is also an increasing number of retirees and commuters. While it is slowly becoming an Auckland suburb, it is still a relaxed, rural retreat.

Waiheke was originally discovered and settled by the Maori. Legends relate that one of the pioneering canoes came to the island. Traces of an old fortified pa can still be seen

on the headland overlooking Putiki Bay. Europeans arrived with the missionary Samuel Marsden in the early 1800s and the island was soon stripped of its kauri forests.

Orientation & Information
The island's main settlement is Oneroa, at the western end of the island. From there the island is fairly built up through to Palm Beach and Onetangi in the middle. But beyond this the eastern end of the island is lightly inhabited. The coastline is a picturesque mixture of coves, inlets and private beaches.

The Waiheke Island Visitor Information Office (☎ (09) 372 9999; fax 372 9919) is at the Artworks complex, on the main road, Ocean View Rd, in Oneroa, 1km from the ferry dock. It has maps and information, and makes bookings for tours and accommodation. It is open from 9 am to 5 pm daily (until 4 pm in winter).

The *Gulf News* ($1) is a weekly newsmagazine of island events. *Waiheke Island – A Tour* ($1.50), an interesting little booklet produced by the Waiheke Historical Society, is available at the information office. The annual *Island Time – a visitor's guide to Waiheke* is another useful book, as is the monthly magazine the *Waihekean*.

Oneroa has a post office, banks and 24-hour ATMs. The annual Waiheke Jazz Festival is held at Easter, and the Waiheke Arts & Crafts Fair in October.

Things to See
The **Artworks** centre is home to a variety of art and craft galleries, other businesses and community groups. Artworks is on Ocean View Rd on the corner of Kororoa Rd, between Oneroa and Matiatia Wharf; it's open daily from 10 am to 4 pm. *Whitaker's Musical Experience* in the Artworks Centre is your chance to savour antique instruments; casual entry to the 1½-hour show is $7 (children $5).

On the road to Onetangi, between the airstrip and the golf club, is the small **Historic Village** and **Waiheke Island Museum**. The Historic Village is just an old cottage, an old woolshed and a couple of baches, but the little museum is interesting enough, with photos and relics of the old days on the island. It is open from 11 am to 2 pm on weekends most of the year and usually daily during school holidays.

Waiheke has nearly 30 **vineyards**, but you can only visit four of them on a tour or by arrangement. Some will charge you for tours and tastings. The information office has brochures.

Water Sports

Popular beaches with good sand and swimming include Oneroa Beach and the adjacent Little Oneroa Beach, Palm Beach in a lovely little cove, and the long stretch of sand at Onetangi Bay. A number of the beaches have shady pohutukawa trees. There are nudist beaches at Palm Beach and on the west end of Onetangi Bay. Surf skis and boogie boards can be hired on Onetangi; there's snorkelling at Hekerua Bay.

Sea Kayaking

Waiheke's many bays and central position in the Hauraki Gulf make it an ideal spot for sea kayaking. Half-day guided kayaking trips cost around $40, depending on numbers, and

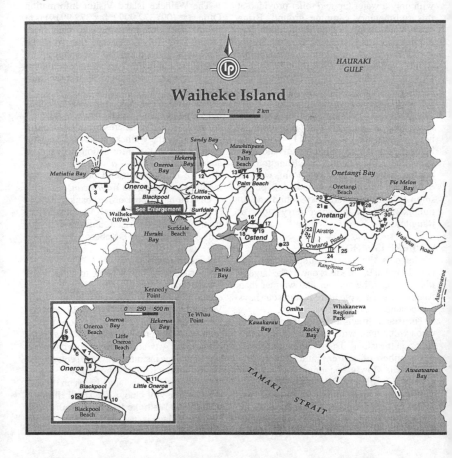

longer excursions are offered. Moonlight kayaking is becoming popular. Operators include Gulf Adventures (☎ (09) 372 7262) and Ross Adventures (☎ (09) 357 0550), based at Matiatia; a two to three hour trip is around $55.

Walking

Waiheke has a system of walkways, outlined in the *Waiheke Islands Walkways* pamphlet, which is available on the island or at the DOC-Auckland Regional Parks office in Auckland.

In Onetangi there's a forest and bird re-serve with several good walks, one of them going up to three large kauri trees. For coastal walks, a good, well-marked track leads right around the coast from Oneroa Bay to Palm Beach. It's about a two-hour walk; at the Palm Beach end you can jump on a bus back to town. Another good coastal walk begins at the Matiatia ferry wharf.

The best walks are in the less-developed eastern part of the island. The **Stony Batter Walk**, leading through private farmland, derives its name from the boulder-strewn fields. From Man o' War Bay Rd, the track leads to the old gun emplacements with their

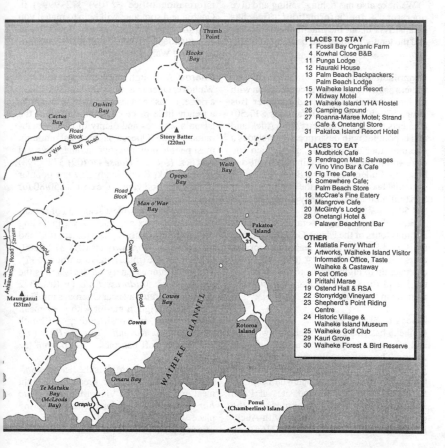

PLACES TO STAY
1 Fossil Bay Organic Farm
4 Kowhai Close B&B
11 Punga Lodge
12 Hauraki House
13 Palm Beach Backpackers;
   Palm Beach Lodge
15 Waiheke Island Resort
17 Midway Motel
21 Waiheke Island YHA Hostel
26 Camping Ground
27 Roanna-Maree Motel; Strand
   Cafe & Onetangi Store
31 Pakatoa Island Resort Hotel

PLACES TO EAT
3 Mudbrick Cafe
6 Pendragon Mall: Salvages
7 Vino Vino Bar & Cafe
10 Fig Tree Cafe
14 Somewhere Cafe;
   Palm Beach Store
16 McCrae's Fine Eatery
18 Mangrove Cafe
20 McGinty's Lodge
28 Onetangi Hotel &
   Palaver Beachfront Bar

OTHER
2 Matiatia Ferry Wharf
5 Artworks, Waiheke Island Visitor
   Information Office, Taste
   Waiheke & Castaway
8 Post Office
9 Piritahi Marae
19 Ostend Hall & RSA
22 Stonyridge Vineyard
23 Shepherd's Point Riding
   Centre
24 Historic Village &
   Waiheke Island Museum
25 Waiheke Golf Club
29 Kauri Grove
30 Waiheke Forest & Bird Reserve

connecting underground tunnels and sweeping views; from there you can continue north to Hooks Bay or south to Opopo Bay.

Other Activities

The Shepherd's Point Riding Centre (☎ (09) 372 8104) at 6 Ostend Rd, between Ostend and the airstrip, has guided **horse riding** for from $20 for one hour and $70 for a day ride; it also offers farmstays and residential riding holidays.

Scenic flights, starting at $30, are operated by Waiheke Airservices (☎ (09) 372 5000).

Waiheke also has fishing, sailing and dive operators – the information office has details. Ask about the nine-hole golf course and the tennis, croquet and badminton facilities.

Organised Tours

Fullers has a host of tours in conjunction with its ferry service. The Island Explorer Bus Tour ($7, children $3.50, families $17.50) connects with the 10 am ferry from Auckland and is popular with daytrippers. It includes a one-hour tour of the island, after which you can explore the island at will with an all-day bus pass. Fullers also has a Back & Beyond Tour that takes in more of the eastern half for $18 (children $9) and a vineyard tour for $33 ($8.50).

Several small local operators also offer minibus tours of the island. Gulf Adventures (☎ (09) 372 7262) has reasonably priced tours. The 'Postie Run' (☎ (09) 372 9166) can take up to eight people to the far end of the island for $15 per person; the trip runs from 8 am to 1 pm.

Places to Stay & Eat

Waiheke has two good hostels, a few hotels and motels, a lodge and a couple of posh resorts. The only camping on the island is at Rocky Bay, at the far end of the beach off Gordon's Rd in the Whakanewha Regional Park (and there are limited sites at Palm Beach Backpackers). Bookings for the camping ground must be made with Auckland Regional Parks (☎ (09) 366 2166) and at the information office (☎ (09) 372 9999) before arrival; Whakanewha is $5 (children $2).

To get away from it all, call in at the *Fossil Bay Organic Farm* (☎ (09) 372 7569) at 58 Korora Rd near Oneroa. Its staff can pick you up from the wharf and guarantee a peaceful stay on their farm; singles are $20, and twins and doubles are $38. You can also camp here for $10. Fully self-contained units sleeping four/six are $60/80.

Waiheke has nearly 100 homestays, farmstays, B&Bs, baches or flats for rent, costing anything from $15 to $200 a night. Phone the information office (☎ (09) 372 9999) in Oneroa and someone will help to match you with the type of place you are looking for. The Auckland Visitor Centre lists accommodation on Waiheke.

Oneroa Although the principal town of Waiheke, Oneroa is not very big. Straddling a ridge, it has sea views on both sides and is a trendy little place containing most of the island's services and plenty of good restaurants. While Oneroa is pleasant enough, most people prefer to stay on other bays and beaches. *Hauraki House* (☎ (09) 372 7598) at 50 Hauraki Rd in Sandy Bay is a popular B&B with good views; the cost is $50/80 for singles/doubles.

Oneroa has the widest selection of restaurants, snack bars and takeaways, including *Taste Waiheke*, a good place for a coffee, and the upmarket *Castaway* (☎ (09) 372 8209) in April Arcade (main meals are around $17). The most famous eatery on the island is the sophisticated *Mudbrick Cafe* (☎ (09) 372 9050) at Church Bay near Oneroa; sample its cabernet sauvignon merlot with your meal. Near the cafe, in a bush setting on Church Bay Estate, is *Kowhai Close B&B* (☎ (09) 372 6763); staff can pick you up from the ferry.

In the Pendragon Mall is the licensed *Salvages*, a good place for breakfast, a light meal or snack. In the View Mall, *Vino Vino Bar & Cafe* is a popular bar and gathering place with good food and an outdoor deck offering great views over Oneroa Bay.

The *Fig Tree Cafe* is near the waterfront on the corner of the Esplanade and Moa Ave in Blackpool, between Surfdale and Oneroa. This small, attractive and popular place has meat, seafood and vegetarian dishes for around $20; reservations are recommended (☎ (09) 372 6363).

Little Oneroa Just east of Oneroa, Little Oneroa has a reasonable beach and one of the island's few areas of native bush. The *Punga Lodge* (☎ (09) 372 6675) at 223 Ocean View Rd is in a tranquil bush setting. The summer rate is $55/85 for B&B singles/doubles.

Palm Beach Palm Beach is in a beautiful little cove with a pleasant beach. *Palm Beach Backpackers* (☎ (09) 372 8662) at 54 Palm Rd is a sprawling place with a school camp feel, but it's right on the beach and rents out windsurfers, kayaks, mountain bikes etc. The cost is $16 per person in dorms, $40 for double rooms and $10 per person for camping.

A few streets back, the *Palm Beach Lodge* (☎ (09) 372 7763) is much more upmarket with double rooms at $240, which includes an assortment of activities.

On the hill overlooking Palm Beach, the *Waiheke Island Resort* (☎ (09) 372 7897) at 4 Bay Rd is posh. Chalets with their own private decks and beautiful sea views cost from $159 per person. It has a restaurant and entertainment in summer.

Right by the beach, the *Somewhere Cafe* at 39 Palm Rd has a cheap cafe menu with a salad bar. Next door, the general store offers takeaways and groceries.

Ostend This village has shops and a couple of places to eat but it is a fair way from the beach. On the main road, the *Midway Motel* (☎ (09) 372 8023), 1 Whakarite Rd, has nice units for from $65 a double.

In the centre of Ostend village, the *RSA* serves good, cheap pub food and the cheapest beer on the island; opposite this is a Chinese takeaway. The *Mangrove Cafe* also comes recommended, as does *McCrae's*

Fine Eatery (formerly *Nutters*) at 40 Wharf Rd, the only BYO on the island.

Onetangi Onetangi's long, sandy beach is one of the best on the island – it's popular in summer for swimming, surfing, windsurfing and other activities. Surf skis, surfboards and boogie boards can be hired at the store or on the beach in summer.

The popular *Waiheke Island YHA Hostel* (☎ (09) 372 8971) is on Seaview Rd in Onetangi, on the hill overlooking the bay. The cost is $16 per person and most of the rooms are twins; doubles cost $32 and $35, and a self-contained flat is $65. Bicycles, kayaks and surfboards can be hired.

On the beach, the *Roanna-Maree Motel* (☎ (09) 372 7051) has a swimming pool, spa pool and well-equipped units for $85 to $110 (in high season).

The Onetangi Hotel (☎ (09) 372 8239) is opposite the beach; it has good value meals in its *Palaver Beachfront Bar* and is the place to see the many bands which visit in summer. At Onetangi Beach Store, the *Strand Cafe* does takeaways and sit-down meals, with seating inside or outside; it's open daily year-round. *McGinty's Lodge* is open for dinner on Friday and Saturday.

Getting There & Away

Air Waiheke Air Services (☎ (09) 372 5000) and Great Barrier Airlines (☎ (09) 275 9120) have flights to/from Waiheke.

Boat Fullers' (☎ (09) 367 9111) high-speed ferry service takes about half an hour from Auckland's Ferry Building to Matiatia Wharf ($23 return, children $10.50). Ferries depart from Auckland at 5.50, 6.30, 8.15 and 10 am, noon, 2, 4, 5, 5.30, 6.30, 7.30 and 9.30 pm daily, returning 45 minutes later; extra services are provided at some times of the year (on Friday there is a departure at 11.15 pm, returning at midnight). Fullers buses connect with the arriving and departing ferries.

Subritzsky Shipping Co (☎ (09) 534 5663) operates a vehicle ferry between Kennedy Point on Waiheke and Half Moon

Bay in Auckland. Ferries leave from two to four times daily, and the voyage takes 1½ hours. The cost is about $60 each way ($110 return) for a car and driver, $30 for motorcycles each way and $10 for passengers (children $5).

Getting Around

Bus Two bus routes operate on the island, both connecting with the arriving and departing ferries. The Onetangi bus goes from Matiatia Wharf, through Oneroa, Surfdale and Ostend, to Onetangi. The Palm Beach bus goes from Matiatia through Oneroa, Blackpool, Little Oneroa, Palm Beach and Ostend, to Rocky Bay. Return bus fares (children's are half-price) from Matiatia Wharf are: Oneroa $2, Palm Beach $6, Rocky Bay $6 and Onetangi $6. You can buy bus tickets from Fullers when you buy your ferry ticket. For $12, the Island Explorer bus tour includes a one-hour tour and an all-day bus pass.

Car, Scooter & Bicycle Cycling is a good way to explore the island, though the hills make it tough-going in places. Most fun are the little nifty-fifty scooters, favoured by Auckland daytrippers who buzz around and scare the island's residents witless.

Waiheke Rental Cars (☎ (09) 372 8635) has an office by the ferry wharf at Matiatia Bay. It hires out cars, Jeeps and utes (pick-up trucks) for $45 per day plus 40c per kilometre. Automatic nifty-fifty scooters are $30 for a full day and motor bikes are from $35. The scooters are easy to ride and only a car licence is required, but be careful when riding, especially on gravel. Drivers must be 21 and need a driver's licence (foreign licences accepted).

Bicycles can be rented at various places, including at the ferry wharf and the visitor centre. The going rate is $25 per day. Pick up a copy of the *Bike Waiheke* pamphlet, available from Fullers or the visitor centre.

Taxi Taxi services are provided by Waiheke Taxis (☎ (09) 372 8038) and Dial-a-Cab (☎ (09) 627 9666). If you have a group of four, a taxi may cost about the same as the bus. A taxi from the wharf to Onetangi is about $17.

PAKATOA ISLAND

Pakatoa is a small tourist resort 36km from Auckland and just off the east coast of Waiheke. The resort has a restaurant, one of the nation's 'choicest' bars, cafe, pool and other sporting facilities. There are views of the gulf and across to the Coromandel from the island's high point.

The *Pakatoa Island Resort Hotel* (☎ (09) 372 9002, 0800 666 200) is the island's only accommodation. The resort mainly offers packages, such as two nights for $230 per person twin share, including meals and ferry transport.

GREAT BARRIER ISLAND

Great Barrier, 88km from the mainland, is the largest island in the gulf. It is a rugged scenic island, resembling the Coromandel Peninsula to which it was once joined.

With a population of around 1200 living on the 110 sq km island, there's plenty of open space. Great Barrier has hot springs, historic kauri dams, a forest sanctuary and myriad tramping tracks. Because there are no possums on the island, the native bush is lush.

The island's main attractions are its beautiful beaches and its fine tramping. The west coast has safe sandy beaches; the east coast beaches are good for surfing. The best tramping trails are in the Great Barrier Forest between Whangaparapara and Port Fitzroy, where there has been much reafforestation. Cycling, swimming, fishing, scuba diving, boating, sea kayaking and just relaxing are other popular activities on the island.

Named by Cook, Great Barrier Island later became a whaling centre. The island implemented the world's first airmail postal service in 1897 (using pigeons) – the centenary was celebrated with the release of hundreds of birds. It has also been the site of some spectacular shipwrecks, including the SS *Waira-rapa* in 1894 and the *Wiltshire* in 1922. There's a cemetery at Katherine Bay,

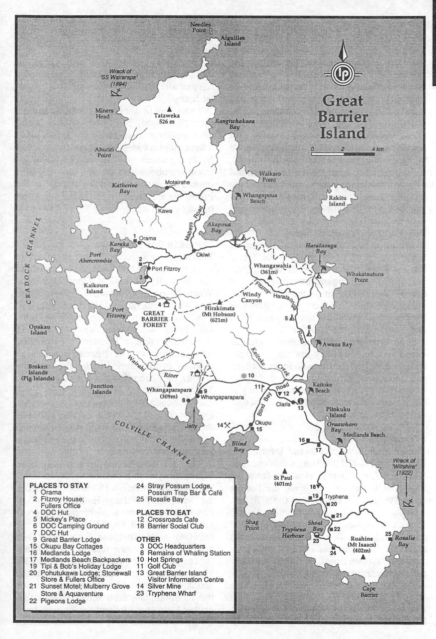

Great Barrier Island

0   2   4 km

PLACES TO STAY
1 Orama
2 Fitzroy House;
  Fullers Office
4 DOC Hut
6 Mickey's Place
7 DOC Hut
9 Great Barrier Lodge
15 Okupu Bay Cottages
16 Medlands Lodge
17 Medlands Beach Backpackers
19 Tipi & Bob's Holiday Lodge
20 Pohutukawa Lodge; Stonewall
   Store & Fullers Office
21 Sunset Motel; Mulberry Grove
   Store & Aquaventure
22 Pigeons Lodge

24 Stray Possum Lodge,
   Possum Trap Bar & Café
25 Rosalie Bay

PLACES TO EAT
12 Crossroads Cafe
18 Barrier Social Club

OTHER
3 DOC Headquarters
8 Remains of Whaling Station
10 Hot Springs
11 Golf Club
13 Great Barrier Island
   Visitor Information Centre
14 Silver Mine
23 Tryphena Wharf

where victims of the *Wairarapa* wreck were buried.

Great Barrier Island is decidedly isolated. Only two hours by ferry from Auckland, the Barrier (as it is called locally) is 20 years away. The island has no electricity supply, only private generators, most roads are unpaved and it has only a few shops.

Tryphena is the main settlement and arrival point for the ferries. It consists of a few dozen houses, shops, card phone (hidden away by the storage shed at the wharf), toilets, a school, a ferry wharf and a handful of accommodation places dotted around the harbour. From the wharf it is a couple of kilometres to the Mulberry Grove Store, and then another 1km over the headland to Pa Beach and the Stonewall Store.

The airport is at **Claris**, a small settlement with a shop (Kaitoke Store), the Great Barrier Island Information Centre, motels and petrol. **Whangaparapara** is an old timber town and the site of the island's 19th-century whaling activities. **Port Fitzroy** is the other main town; it is also very small, but is the home of the DOC office.

From around mid-November to Easter the island is a busy holiday destination, especially during the Christmas holidays until the end of January, Easter and the Labour Day long weekend. At these times make sure you book transport, accommodation and activities in advance.

Information

The new Great Barrier Island Information Centre (☎ (09) 429 0033), an offshoot of the Auckland City Council, is across from the airport in Claris. In Tryphena, the Fullers office (☎ (09) 429 0004), next to the Stonewall Store, is a mine of information. Talk to Tamara, who can provide information and make bookings. The office maintains an extensive list of homestays and lodges. In summer it is open from 8.30 am to 5 pm daily and in winter from 9 am to 3 pm.

On the island, the main DOC office (☎ (09) 429 0044; fax 429 0071) is in Port Fitzroy, a 15-minute walk from the ferry landing. It has information and maps on the

island, collects fees and sells hut tickets, and has a good camping ground. It's open on weekdays from 8 am to 4 pm – if there's enough tourist interest, it also opens on weekends in summer. Whangaparapara also has a small DOC post, which opens at irregular hours.

There's no power on the island, so bring a torch (flashlight). Most people on the island generate their own power by using solar, wind or diesel energy, but there are no street lights anywhere. The Barrier has an automatic telephone service and card-operated phones are dotted around the island. See the Places to Eat section for information on buying groceries.

Things to See & Do

Medlands, with its wide sweep of white sand, is one of the best **beaches** on the island and is easily accessible from Tryphena. Whangapoua is a fine surfing beach, while Kaitoke, Awana Bay and Harataonga are also good. Whangapoua has an excellent right-hand break, while Awana has both left and right-hand breaks. Tryphena's bay, lined with pohutukawa, has sheltered beaches.

Many people come just for the **walks** – beware they are often not well signposted. The Great Barrier Forest walks are most easily reached from Whangaparapara or Port Fitzroy. You can take the ferry to either of these destinations and walk 45 minutes to one of the two huts that can be used as bases for exploring the forest.

The most spectacular short walk is from Windy Canyon to Hirakimata (Mt Hobson). **Windy Canyon**, only a 15-minute walk from the main road (Fitzroy-Harataonga road), has spectacular rock outcrops and great views of the island. From Windy Canyon, an excellent trail continues for another 1½ hours through scrubby forest to **Hirakimata** (621m), the highest point on the island with views across to the Coromandel Peninsula and Auckland on a fine day. Near the top of the mountain are lush forests and a few mature kauri that survived the logging days. From Hirakimata it is two hours though forest to the hut closest to Port Fitzroy and then 45 minutes to Port Fitzroy itself.

Many other trails traverse the forest. From the road outside Whangaparapara you can also walk to the **hot springs**, though the trail is usually very muddy and not well maintained. There is also a good, four-hour walk west from Tryphena to Okupu Bay that eventually joins the Blind Bay Rd.

Mountain biking is popular on the island. There is diverse scenery, and biking is not too difficult here, even though the roads are unsealed. A popular ride is to cycle from Tryphena to Medlands Beach in about an hour, stop for a swim, then cycle another hour to the hot springs; from there it's another half-hour to accommodation in Whangaparapara. You could catch the ferry out from Whangaparapara, or spend another day cycling through the forest up to Port Fitzroy, stopping on the way for a hike up to the kauri dams on a good, well-marked 4WD track. It's about a three hour ride, not counting stops; allow all day for the dams. (The easiest way to organise it would be with a 'Possum Pursuits Pass' from the Stray Possum Lodge in Tryphena.)

Great Barrier provides some of the most varied **scuba diving** in NZ. There's pinnacle diving, shipwreck diving, lots of fish and over 33m (100ft) visibility at some times of year; February to April is probably the best time. Aquaventure (☎ (09) 429 0033) in Tryphena conducts diving trips and also offers diving instruction.

Aquaventure also rent kayaks for **sea kayaking**, as do many of the accommodation places. Fitzroy House (☎ (09) 429 0091) staff in Port Fitzroy will guide kayaking groups for $70 per day and rent out kayaks for $35 per day. Tryphena Kayaking (☎ (09) 429 0551) has a twilight mystery tour with a BBQ afterwards ($45). Aotea Sea Kayaking Adventures (☎ (09) 429 0664) hires out kayaks for $25/45 for a half/full day with guiding.

Horse treks can be arranged through Fitzroy House (☎ (09) 429 0091), Adventure Horse Treks (☎ (09) 429 0274) and Nagle Cove Horse Treks (☎ (09) 429 0212).

A number of operators offer boat and fishing trips. Safari Tours (☎ (09) 429 0448), and Tipi & Bob's (☎ (09) 429 0550) have informative tours around the island for $40 per person. Fishing charters work out about $60/110 for a half/full day, based on four people.

Places to Stay

Most accommodation is in Tryphena, but places are scattered all over the island. Prices are steep in summer, but rates drop dramatically outside the peak period. Summer prices are quoted here.

Camping & Huts There are DOC camping grounds at Harataonga Bay, Medlands Beach, Akapoua Bay and Awana Bay, all with basic facilities including water and pit toilets. Fires are only permitted in the designated fireplaces in the camping grounds, using only the firewood provided by DOC. It's a good idea to bring your own cooker. Camping is not allowed outside the camping grounds without a permit. Camping costs $5 per adult ($2.50 if you bring your own cooker).

As well as the camping grounds, DOC has two huts in the Great Barrier forest near Port Fitzroy and Whangaparapara, each a 45-minute walk from the nearest wharf. Each hut sleeps up to 24 in bunkrooms; facilities include cold water, pit toilets and a kitchen with a wood stove. Bring your own sleeping bag and cooking equipment. The cost is $8 (two tickets). From November to January the huts are very busy; accommodation is first come, first served, so be early! Readers recommend camping at *Mickey's Place* at Awana ($3 per person).

Hostels The *Stray Possum Lodge* (☎ (09) 429 0109, 0800 767 786) in Tryphena is the best backpackers on the island (and is YHA associate), providing quality accommodation in a lovely bush setting. Dorms cost $16 and $18 and twins and doubles are $50; there is also limited camping space for $12 per person.

Two great self-contained chalets are also

available for $85/100 for two/three people ($15 per extra person); each has a spiral staircase leading to a mezzanine sleeping space. The Stray Possum has a bus for transport around the island and snorkelling gear, boogie boards, mountain bikes etc for hire. A Possum Pursuits Pass ($45) will get you access to most of the island's delights during your stay.

Pohutukawa Lodge (☎ (09) 429 0211) in Tryphena has some incredibly tight-fitting little rooms. The oddly shaped bunks are $15 per night; linen is an extra $5 and evening meals are $15. A separate lodge has self-contained doubles costing $85 with breakfast.

Medlands Beach Backpackers (☎ (09) 429 0320) is on Mason Rd, just inland from the main road at Medlands Beach. The hostel is fairly basic and expensive at $20 per person ($14 in off season) in shared rooms, but it's close to the superb beach.

Guesthouses & Motels *Pigeons Lodge* (☎ (09) 429 0437) at Shoal Bay on the beachfront is in a bush setting. It charges $90 for two, but caters mostly for pre-sold packages.

The *Sunset Motel* (☎ (09) 429 0568) in Tryphena has motel units, which sleep up to six, for $95 a double. It also has a well-equipped hostel section with good lounge and kitchen facilities for $15 per person in two, four and six-bed rooms.

Tipi & Bob's Holiday Lodge (☎ (09) 429 0550) has motel-style accommodation 50m from the sea, with a garden bar and restaurant. Good self-contained units, most with great sea views, cost from $90 a double. An older cottage sleeping up to eight costs $85 a double ($15 per extra person).

The *Medlands Lodge* (☎ (09) 429 0352) on Mason Rd, Medlands Beach, is set on four hectares of park-like grounds at the foot of the hills inland from the beach. Excellent self-contained units sleeping four cost $90 for two and there's also a five-bed bunkroom. You can cook or order meals.

At Whangaparapara, the *Great Barrier Lodge* (☎ (09) 429 0488) at the water's edge

is a big place overlooking the inlet. It has a restaurant and bar; rooms cost from $45 to $90 for two in self-contained cabins.

Fitzroy House (☎ (09) 429 0091) is on the other side of the bay from the ferry wharf at Port Fitzroy. This old homestead offers fine views of the bay and two self-contained cottages starting at $100 a double. This is a particularly good place for organising activities such as horse riding, sea kayaking, sailing and tramping, as transport to the trails is arranged.

At Karaka Bay, the next bay north of Port Fitzroy, *Orama* (☎ (09) 429 0063) is a Christian fellowship hostel that has self-contained flats for $100 in summer. Staff will pick you up from the Port Fitzroy ferry wharf. It has good facilities, including a swimming pool, but no alcohol is permitted.

Remoter possibilities abound. The quaint *Okupu Bay Cottages* (☎ (09) 429 0025) at Allom Bay can be accessed by boat or walking track; they are good value at $100/120 for two/four people. The Aquarian generation will find solace at the *Flower House* (☎ (09) 429 0464), where the meals are organic and the fresh olives and cheese are mouthwatering.

Baches Great Barrier Island has a big array of holiday baches, all privately owned and maintained. The going rate is around $60 to $80 a double and many sleep four or more. Fullers (☎ (09) 429 0004) keeps a list (and will mark them on the map), so check with them. Baches include:

The Granny Flat	☎ (09) 429 0451
Hi Look Cottage	☎ (09) 429 0537
Lovell's Holiday Bach	☎ (09) 429 0468
Macadamia Heights	☎ (09) 429 0497
Mulberry Cottage	☎ (09) 429 0537
Nancy's Nest	☎ (09) 429 0433
Ollies Cottage	☎ (09) 429 0478
Sherwood Orchids	☎ (09) 429 0445
Tom & Rose Bone	☎ (09) 429 0292
Valley View Cottage	☎ (09) 429 0298
Whale Cottage	☎ (09) 429 0107

Places to Eat

Restaurants are few, so all the places to stay

provide meals or cooking facilities, or both. *Tipi & Bob's* and the *Possum Trap Bar & Café* in the Stray Possum, both in Tryphena, are the only fully fledged restaurants (each has a bar).

The *Barrier Social Club* in Tryphena has good value meals and cheaper bar prices; it is open on Wednesday, Friday and the weekend from 4 pm for good meals (fish, chips and salad is about $12). Claris also has a social club and you can get a meal at the golf club. For pies, coffee and groceries there is the *Crossroads Cafe*, 1km north-west of Claris.

Tryphena has two grocery stores, the Mulberry Grove Store and the Stonewall Store, but food is more expensive than on the mainland. Claris, Whangaparapara and Port Fitzroy have general stores. Wash down any meal with bush honey Island Mead, available from the local stores.

Getting There & Away

Air Great Barrier Airlines (GBA; ☎ (09) 275 9120), the main airline servicing the island, flies twice daily from the Air New Zealand domestic terminal at Auckland airport to Claris and Okiwi. The flight from Auckland takes half an hour and costs $75/150 one way/return. Special deals are often available in the off-season or there's a fly-boat combination, where you fly one way and go by boat the other way for $120. The airline operates a transfer bus ($10) from Claris to Tryphena and from Okiwi to Port Fitzroy. GBA also flies to Whitianga, Tauranga, Rotorua and Whangarei on Wednesday, Friday and Sunday.

Trans Island Air (☎ 0800 359 723) has daily flights to/from Auckland.

Boat Fullers has high-speed ferries departing from the Auckland Ferry Building to Tryphena on Friday at 6.30 pm; it departs from Tryphena at 8.45 pm, arriving in Auckland at 11 pm. On Sunday the ferry goes directly to Port Fitzroy at 11 am; it departs from Port Fitzroy for Whangaparapara at 2 pm and Whangaparapara for Tryphena at

2.45 pm. It finally departs from Tryphena at 4 pm, arriving in Auckland at 6.15 pm.

Travelling by ferry is good when used in com- bination with the fly-boat option ($110 return). The voyage takes two hours and costs $89 return (children $44.50). Fullers also has a day-trip package for $57 (children $28.50). Ferries sail subject to weather conditions; cancellations are rare but they do happen.

The cheapest way to get to Great Barrier is with Gulf Trans (☎ (09) 373 4036, 0800 GULF TRANS), which operates a car and passenger service from Auckland's Wynyard Wharf to Tryphena every Tuesday at 7 am, returning from Fitzroy every Wednesday at 8 am. The crossing by the *Tasman* takes six hours, costs $20 (children $10) and the ferry has a lounge bar. The faster *Sealink* is $40/65 one way/return (children $20/35). A weekender special, which includes a small vehicle and three passengers, is $299.

An Explorer Pass ($110) includes the Fullers or *Sealink* ferry from Auckland to Great Barrier return, transfers to and accommodation in the Stray Possum, and transport to the tramping trails (or to the hot pools). For another $20 you can get to or from the island by boat, then fly to Whitianga in the Coromandel (or vice versa). The Coromandel-Auckland leg is by InterCity bus. Certain conditions exist for these deals; contact ☎ 0800 767 786.

Another popular way to visit the island is to travel overland with InterCity from Auckland to Paihia in the Bay of Islands (via Waipoua Kauri Forest). You then fly from Paihia to Great Barrier Island (Claris). From the Barrier you fly the next leg to Whitianga on the Coromandel Peninsula. You then have the option of returning to Auckland via Waitomo Caves or travelling on to Wellington via Taupo. This superb trip is exceptional value at $250 and can also be done in the reverse order.

Getting Around

From Tryphena in the south to Port Fitzroy in the north is 47km by gravel road, or 40km via Whangaparapara using the walking tracks. The roads are graded but rough.

Great Barrier Travel (☎ (09) 429 0568) has a bus that meets the ferry and takes passengers into Tryphena for $5. In theory it continues through Medlands Beach and Claris to Port Fitzroy, but unless enough passengers want to go you will have to charter. Many of the places to stay will come to pick you up if notified in advance; the Stray Possum has a bus for its guests. In summer the best option for getting between Fitzroy and Tryphena is the daily Fullers boat ($10).

Bob's Rentals (☎ (09) 429 0050) has 4WD vehicles for $95 per day and Wheels Down Under (☎ (09) 429 0110) has small Suzuki Samurais for $85. Great Barrier Lodge (☎ (09) 429 0488) in Whangaparapara and Aotea Tours (☎ (09) 429 0055) in Fitzroy also have rental cars. All these rental car places act as taxi services.

Mountain bikes are readily available for hire for $20 to $25 per day. Most places to stay also rent out bikes and may give discounts.

MOTUIHE ISLAND

Halfway between Auckland and Waiheke, small Motuihe Island was once a quarantine station, and the cemetery at the north-western tip has the graves of victims of the 1918 influenza epidemic. In WWI it was used as a prisoner-of-war camp, from where that the German captain Count Felix von Luckner made a daring but ultimately unsuccessful escape.

The peninsula pointing out to the north-west has fine sandy beaches on both sides, so one side is always sheltered from the wind. The beaches make it popular with daytrippers. There are several walking tracks on the island – it takes about three hours to walk around it.

If you want to stay overnight, ask DOC about its basic camping ground and farmhouse. You can reach it at the kiosk on the island (☎ (09) 534 5419), or check with the Auckland DOC office.

Getting There & Away

Fullers stops at Motuihe on its Wednesday, Friday (leaving 6.30 pm) and Sunday mail run leaving Auckland at 9.30 am and also stopping at Rangitoto, Motutapu and Rakino. There are extra sailings in summer; the fare is $18 return (children $9).

RAKINO ISLAND

This small island, just to the north of Motutapu Island, was originally known as Hurakia and was purchased from its Maori owners in 1840. At one point the island was used for prisoners taken in the Maori Wars. The island has sandy beaches, rugged coastlines and deep-water coves. Beyond Rakino there is a cluster of tiny islands collectively known as The Noises.

Fullers stops at Rakino on its Wednesday, Friday and Sunday mail run ($20, children $5, including Motuihe).

TIRITIRI MATANGI ISLAND

Part of the Hauraki Gulf Maritime Park, this island – about 4km off the coast of the Whangaparaoa Peninsula – is about halfway between the islands close to Auckland and Kawau Island.

The island is an 'open sanctuary' where native wildlife is protected but visitors are permitted. It has some original coastal broadleaf forest with large pohutukawa and some re-vegetated forest. Native birds, including many rare species, thrive here and are practically tame, since there is nothing to threaten them. They include the rare takahe, black robins, bellbirds, parakeets, whiteheads, saddlebacks and little spotted kiwis. The island attracts ornithologists from all over the world.

There are a number of good **walks**. Starting from the wharf there are one to three-hour walks, and in a day you could explore most of the coast and ridges.

Camping is absolutely prohibited on the island to protect the wildlife, but it may be possible to stay overnight in the lighthouse keeper's house; contact DOC (☎ (09) 479 4490). A guided tour with DOC is $5 (children $2.50).

Getting There & Away
A ferry from Whangaparaoa Peninsula (☎ (09) 424 5561 for details) leaves at 9.45 am on Sunday and Thursday and 10.15 am on Saturday from the Gulf Harbour Marina, returning at 3.30 pm; the trip costs $25/15 for adults/children. These trips depart from Auckland on Thursday at 8.30 am and Saturday on 9.30 am ($30/18). The *Te Aroha* schooner also comes here (see Organised Tours in the Auckland section).

OTHER ISLANDS
Dotted around Rangitoto, Motutapu and Waiheke, and farther north, are many smaller islands.

South of Rangitoto, the small island of **Motukorea** (Island of the Oystercatcher), is also known as Browns Island. The island had three fortified Maori pa on the volcanic cones by 1820; it was purchased from the Maori by John Logan Campbell and William Brown in 1839, before the founding of Auckland, and used as a pig farm. It's now part of the Hauraki Gulf Maritime Park; access is unrestricted.

Rotoroa, a Salvation Army alcohol reha-

bilitation clinic, is just south of Pakatoa. **Ponui**, also known as Chamberlins Island, is a larger island just south of Rotorua. It has been farmed by the Chamberlin family ever since they purchased it from the Maori in 1854. South again is **Pakihi**, or Sandspit Island, and the tiny Karamuramu Island.

Little Barrier, 25km north-east of Kawau Island, is one of NZ's prime nature reserves and the only area of NZ rainforest unaffected by humans, deer or possums. Several rare species of birds, reptiles and plants live in the varied habitats on the volcanic island.

Access to the island is strictly restricted and a DOC permit, which is very difficult to obtain, is required before any landing is made on this closely guarded sanctuary. The easiest way to gain access is to come on a *Te Aroha* cruise (see Organised Tours in the Auckland section).

Motuora Island is halfway between Tiritiri Matangi and Kawau. There is a wharf

AUCKLAND

and camping ground on the west coast of the island but there is no regular ferry service. Get a camping permit from the ranger (☎ (09) 422 8882) on Kawau, or from the caretaker on Motuora.

The most remote islands of the Hauraki Gulf Maritime Park are the **Mokohinau Islands**, 23km north-west of Great Barrier. They are all protected nature reserves and visitors require landing permits.

See the Northland chapter for details on **Kawau Island**.

Northland

Geographically, this region is shaped like a finger pointing north from Auckland. Northland is the cradle of modern New Zealand: it was where Europeans first made permanent contact with the Maori; the first squalid sealers' and whalers' settlements were formed; and the Treaty of Waitangi between the settlers and the Maori was signed. To this day Northland has a greater proportion of Maori in its population than elsewhere in NZ.

The big attraction of Northland is the beautiful Bay of Islands, though scenic, sheltered bays and superb, but far less touristy, beaches are all along the east coast.

The west coast is a long stretch of sand pounded by the surf of the Tasman Sea. It also has scenic harbours, such as Hokianga, but the main attraction is the 'Kauri Coast', where the best remaining stands of NZ's once mighty kauri forests can be seen

Kaitaia and the Far North feature some great beaches and are home to Maori communities, offering travellers the chance to learn about Maori lifestyle and culture.

Getting Around

There are two main routes – east and west – through Northland to the top of New Zealand. To reach Northland, go through Helensville or Warkworth to Wellsford and then on to Brynderwyn, 112km north of Auckland. From here, the simplest and fastest route is to head straight up through Whangarei on the eastern side of the peninsula and through the Bay of Islands to Kaitaia.

The west coast route is longer and slower, though the road is now sealed virtually all the way. It goes along the Kauri Coast through Matakohe, Dargaville, the Waipoua Kauri Forest and the remote and scenic Hokianga Harbour.

The two main bus lines serving Northland are Northliner Express (☎ (09) 307 5873; Auckland), leaving from the Downtown Airline Terminal in Auckland, and InterCity

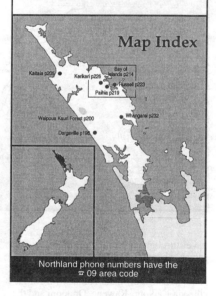

HIGHLIGHTS

- Exploring the Bay of Islands, with the most beautiful of Northland's wonderful coastal scenery
- Visiting the ancient kauri forests of the Kauri Coast
- Travelling through the desolate landscapes of Ninety Mile Beach and Cape Reinga
- Swimming at the beaches near Whangarei, Doubtless Bay and the Hokianga Harbour
- Deep-sea fishing anywhere on the coast, but especially Tutukaka, the Bay of Islands and Whangaroa

Map Index

Kaitaia p205
Kerikeri p226
Bay of Islands p214
Russell p223
Paihia p219
Waipoua Kauri Forest p200
Whangarei p232
Dargaville p196

Northland phone numbers have the ☎ 09 area code

(☎ (09) 357 8400), leaving from the Sky City Coach Terminal in Auckland. These services follow the east coast from Auckland to Whangarei, the Bay of Islands and Kaitaia, but connect with the West Coaster service for the west coast. Northliner has bus passes costing from $49, for travel between Auckland and the Bay of Islands, to $109, for

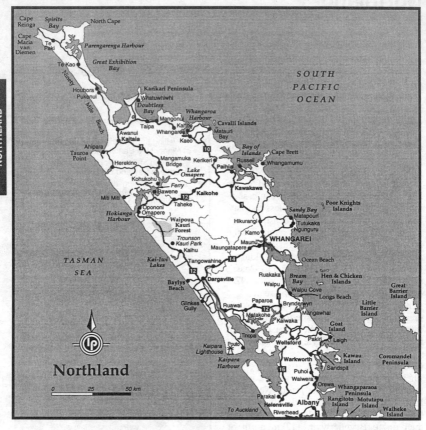

Northland

0   25   50 km

travel throughout Northland. InterCity bus passes can be used in Northland.

The West Coaster/Pioneer (☎ (09) 438 3206; Whangarei) links Paihia with Dargaville via Kaikohe, Rawene, Opononi and the Waipoua forests, allowing time for photo stops at the big trees. It leaves Paihia at 9 am for Auckland, Sunday to Friday, arriving in Auckland at 5.30 pm. On weekdays it also leaves from Dargaville at 9 am, arriving in Auckland at 12.45 pm.

The main backpacker connection running through Northland is Kiwi Experience's Awesome Adventures. See the Auckland and Getting Around chapters for more details on tour possibilities.

Auckland to Whangarei

While many visitors do this trip along SH1 in just a few hours in their haste to get to the Bay of Islands, the east coast between Auckland and Whangarei has many delightful bays and beaches.

Just north of Auckland, the Hibiscus Coast between Whangaparaoa and Warkworth is a

HOLGER LEUE

ADAM FRY

HOLGER LEUE

JEFF WILLIAMS

Northland
A: Coastside living in Russell, Bay of Islands
B: Kerikeri

C: Farmer Bill Kerr and his dog Tom, near Te Kaeo
D: Cape Reinga lighthouse

HOLGER LEUE

HOLGER LEUE

Taranaki
Top: No shortage of beer choices in New Plymouth
Bottom: View of Mt Taranaki from Lake Mangamahoe

favourite with Auckland holiday-makers in summer. It is also becoming an extension of Auckland as more people move out to enjoy the beaches and semi-rural lifestyle within commuting distance of Auckland. Heading further north, the coast is less developed and less accessible but no less beautiful.

WHANGAPARAOA PENINSULA

Now virtually a suburb of Auckland, the Whangaparaoa Peninsula – just north of Auckland off SH1 – is good for water-based activities: windsurfers flock to Manly Beach, boaties leave from the Weiti River and Gulf Harbour, and swimmers find great beaches around the tip of the peninsula at **Shakespeare Regional Park**. Many native bush birds and waders can be seen, and the native forests of the park contain karaka, kowhai and old puriri. A number of walking tracks traverse the park. The park is just beyond the huge Gulf Harbour Marina development, an upmarket real estate blot on the landscape.

Whangaparaoa has a small **narrow gauge railway** with steam trains offering rides ($3, children $1.50) on the weekends. Whangaparaoa is also the place for boats to Tiritiri Matangi Island (see the Hauraki Gulf Islands section in the Auckland chapter).

OREWA

Orewa (population 6000) is another Auckland satellite suburb with a large mall-style shopping centre. Its main attraction is the great beach that runs next to the highway. The town also has a statue of Sir Edmund Hillary, one of the first two people to stand on top of Mt Everest (the other was Tenzing Norgay). City buses from Auckland run to Orewa, so it is an easy first stop out of Auckland going north.

The Hibiscus Coast Information Centre (☎ (09) 426 0076; fax 426 0086) is on the highway south of town, next to KFC. Pick up a copy of *Walks of the Hibiscus Coast*, outlining many good walks in the area. Orewa Cycle Works at 278 Main Rd has proved indispensable for cyclists heading up around Northland; staff hire out bikes, do repairs and sell parts.

Places to Stay & Eat

A good reason to stop in Orewa is the *Marco Polo Backpackers Inn* (☎ (09) 426 8455) at 2a Hammond Ave, Hatfields Beach, just off the highway on the northern outskirts of Orewa; take Auckland city bus No 893, 894, 895, 897 or 899. At this purpose-built hostel, nestled into hillside greenery, tent sites are $9, dorm beds are $14 and singles/doubles are from $25/32. Staff can arrange a variety of trips, including snorkelling trips to Goat Island ($25), and can also organise bone-carving courses.

The *Pillows Travellers Lodge* (☎ (09) 426 6338), 412 Hibiscus Coast Highway, is a flash hostel providing excellent accommodation for $15 in a dorm, $28 for singles, $34 for twins and doubles and $49 with en suite. It is conveniently located near the centre of Orewa – opposite the beach and right on the highway – and boasts a spa.

Orewa has a dozen motels and three camping ground/motor camps. *Puriri Park* (☎ (09) 426 4648) on Puriri Ave is a well-equipped motor camp with a pool in a quiet setting. Camp sites are $9.50 per person, cabins are $35 for two, tourist flats are $56 for two and motels are $64.

Cafes abound. Try *Kotuku Cafe Life* in Hillary Square, the *Corner Cafe* in Westpac Plaza, *Cafe 328* on Hibiscus Highway or *Teacups* at 354 Main Rd. Nightlife is confined to the *Three Lamps Tavern* at 326 Hibiscus Coast Highway or the *Slipped Disc*, a few vertebrae down.

WAIWERA

The coastal village of Waiwera, 48km north of Auckland (bus No 895 from the Downtown Bus Terminal), is noted for its thermal pools. This huge complex of hot pools, spa pools, waterslides etc is open daily from 9 am to 10 pm (till 11 pm on Friday and Saturday); entry is $12 (children $7). A private spa costs $10. Horse riding is offered by Ti Tree Hills (☎ (09) 426 7003) for $20 an hour.

Just north of Waiwera is **Wenderholm Regional Park**, a coastal farmland park with a good beach, estuary and walks.

NORTHLAND

Places to Stay & Eat

Near the hot pools is a range of accommodation choices. The grand hotel that was a popular escape from Auckland earlier this century has gone, but the present *Waiwera Resort Hotel* (☎ (09) 426 4089) has motel-style units for $75 a double or large, self-contained family units for $120. The *Waiwera Motel* (☎ (09) 426 5153) at 25 Weranui Rd is nestled in a peaceful valley; doubles are from $68 to $85.

PUHOI

North of Waiwera, 1km off SH1, Puhoi is a picturesque historic village that claims to be NZ's first Bohemian settlement. The small **Puhoi Bohemian Museum** is open irregular hours, but the main point of interest is the historic pub, crammed with old artefacts. Sadly, the phlegmatic barman who hurled insults at some unsuspecting customers has gone.

At Puhoi you can hire canoes (☎ (09) 422 0891) for $12 per hour for a paddle down the river to Wenderholm Regional Park on the coast. The area is also great for mountain biking. *Puhoi Cottage*, 500m past the Puhoi Store, has delicious Devonshire teas and home-cooked goodies.

WARKWORTH

Just off the main highway, nestled by the Mahurangi River, this pretty town (population 1750) was once connected to Auckland by steamships that docked at the town's old wharf. Now Warkworth is mainly a lunch stop on the drive north, but the surrounding area is a popular summer holiday destination.

The Warkworth Visitor Information Centre (☎ (09) 425 9081, 425 9299), 1 Baxter Street, near the river and bus station, has a complete run-down on the area. It is open from 9 am to 5.15 pm on weekdays and 9 am to 3 pm on weekends.

On the outskirts of town, the **Parry Kauri Park** has short forest walks and a couple of monstrous mature kauri, including the 800-year-old McKinney kauri. Also at the park, the small **Warkworth Museum**, open from

9 am to 4 pm in summer (until 3.30 pm in winter), has well-presented pioneering exhibits ($4, children 50c).

Places to Stay & Eat

The *Boss Lodge* (☎ (09) 425 8185), 26 View Rd, is an excellent hostel about 1km west of the highway on a hill overlooking surrounding farmland. The two-storey hostel has good communal areas (TV room and pool tables), dorm beds for $16 and double rooms for $36.

Warkworth's historic pub, the *Warkworth Inn* (☎ (09) 425 8569) on Queen St, has typical old pub rooms with shared facilities for $35/64 a single/double including a continental breakfast. Next to the river on Elizabeth St, the *Bridge House Lodge* (☎ (09) 425 8351) is a part-old, part-new establishment with some style. Rooms with attached bathroom start at $65. Those with extra cash can treat themselves at *Saltings B&B* (☎ (09) 425 9670), 1210 Sandspit Rd; a beautiful room is from $85.

In Wellsford, 19km north of Warkworth, is *Sun Valley Motor Lodge* (☎ (09) 423 8829) at 22 Port Albert Rd. Singles/doubles are $65/75 and backpackers beds are $20.

The licensed *Riverbank Cafe* on Wharf St (with a fine selection of wines) and *Ducks Crossing* in Riverview Plaza both have fine outlooks over the river and the old wharf. *Gypsy Fare* on Neville St is a quaint cafe with a good selection of coffees.

Getting There & Away

Gubbs Motors (☎ (09) 425 8348) has three daily buses on weekdays to Silverdale (which connect with the Yellow Bus Company going to the Auckland Downtown Bus Terminal; $15). A connection from Warkworth to Sandspit, for Kawau Island, can be arranged for $12 per taxi load.

AROUND WARKWORTH

The biggest unabashedly touristy attraction is 4km north of Warkworth on SH1. **Sheepworld** demonstrates many aspects of NZ sheep farming, including sheepdog manoeuvres, shearing and things you can try for yourself, such as carding, spinning, weaving and feeding tame sheep and lambs. It's open daily from 9 am to 5 pm, with shows at 11 am and 1 pm, and an extra show in January at 3 pm ($9, children $4.50).

The **Dome State Forest**, 10km north of Warkworth on SH1, is a regenerating forest which was logged about 90 years ago. A walking track to the Dome summit (336m) and its great views leads from the car park and takes about an hour return. A three-hour walk leads beyond the summit to the **Waiwhiu Kauri Grove**, an unlogged stand of 20 mature kauri trees.

Six kilometres south of Warkworth, the **Earth Satellite Station** has an information centre with hands-on exhibits explaining satellite communications; it was a Kiwi astrophysicist from Warkworth who in 1970 pinpricked the location of the disabled Apollo 13 in outer space, enabling NASA ground crew to bring it home. The station is open to the public from 9 am to 4 pm.

To the east of Warkworth on the scenic Mahurangi Peninsula is **Sandspit**, from where the ferry departs for Kawau Island. To the south of Sandspit are the new beach suburbs of **Snells Beach**, with a trendy 'ye olde' English pub, shopping centre, motel and B&Bs, and **Algies Bay**. These shallow bays are pleasant enough but, 3km further, **Martins Bay** is the pick of the beaches and has a motor camp.

KAWAU ISLAND

Directly east of Warkworth, Kawau Island's main point of interest is **Mansion House**, an impressive historic house built in 1846 by Sir George Grey, an early NZ governor. It was a hotel for many years before being restored and turned into a museum.

Kawau has many beautiful walks, starting from Mansion House and leading to beaches, an old copper mine and a lookout. An unusual sight are the numerous wallabies, introduced from Australia.

Vivian Bay is the only sandy bay with accommodation on the island; attractions include a white, sandy beach, swimming, fishing, snorkelling and bush walks.

Places to Stay

There are several places to stay at Vivian Bay, on the north side of Kawau Island, and a couple of others on Bon Accord Harbour.

Kawau Island Cottages for Couples (☎ (09) 422 8835) has three chalets on the beach; the cost is $190 a double, with all meals included. Also right on the beach, *St Clair Lodge* (☎ (09) 422 8850) is another upmarket B&B, charging from $200 a double, including all meals. The St Clair beachfront units cost from $140.

Bon Accord Harbour's accommodation is mostly homestays such as *Katie Clark Units: Harris Bay* (☎ (09) 422 8835) and the *Cedar Lodge* (☎ (09) 422 8700) on the waterfront at Smelting Cove. *Pah Farm* (☎ (09) 422 8765) at Moores Bay has camping.

Getting There & Away

Two ferry companies operate trips to Kawau from Sandspit (one hour). The Kawau Kat (☎ (09) 425 8006) has trips to Mansion House at 2 pm daily for $18 return (children $9) – there are more sailings in summer. The mail-run cruise, departing from Sandspit at 10.30 am on the fast Kawau Kat, delivers the mail, stopping at Mansion House and many coves, bays and inlets ($25, children $10).

Matata Cruises (☎ (09) 425 6169) has a coffee cruise to Kawau for $20 (children $10) return at 10 am daily. It also offers a combined three-hour lunch-Mansion House cruise for $35.

Fullers (☎ (09) 367 9111) has cruises to Kawau from Auckland (from January to March) at 10 am, returning at 4.30 pm ($40, children $20).

WARKWORTH TO BREAM BAY

Less frequented than the main road north to Whangarei is the scenic route from Warkworth out to Leigh on the east coast, and then north via Mangawhai and Waipu to Bream Bay. This route has a number of places where you can relax off the not-so-beaten path.

The first good beach, **Omaha**, is a short detour from the Leigh road and has a sweeping stretch of white sand, good surf and a lifesaving club. For a pleasant, sheltered beach, try **Mathesons Bay** just before you enter the small town of Leigh. **Leigh** sits above a picturesque harbour dotted with fishing boats. It has a motel, a sometimes lively pub popular with fishers, and a great fish and chip shop that cooks up the fresh, local catch.

Further north, around the cape from Leigh, **Goat Island** is the site of the Cape Rodney-Okakari Point Marine Reserve, where Auckland University has a marine laboratory. The reserve is teeming with fish that can be hand fed in the water or viewed from a glass-bottomed boat (☎ (09) 422 6334) that operates in summer for $18 (children $9). Snorkelling and diving gear can be hired at Seafriends (☎ (09) 422 6212), 1km before the beach. Seafriends also has a good, inexpensive restaurant and a small aquarium. *Goat Island Camping* (☎ (09) 422 6185) has a few tent/powered sites for $16/20 for two.

Continuing along the coast, a gravel road leads to **Pakiri**, a tiny rural settlement with a white-sand surf beach. A good way of seeing the unspoilt beach and the forests behind is on horseback. Pakiri Beach Horse Rides (☎ (09) 422 6275) on Rahuikiri Rd has popular rides along the beach; these cost from $25 for a one-hour ride to $85 for all-day treks. Staff arrange farmstays for $70 per person including meals.

From Pakiri, the gravel road via Tomatara eventually meets the sealed road to Mangawhai. You rejoin the coast at **Mangawhai Heads**, a growing summer resort town with a great surf beach and a lifesaving club. The **Mangawhai Cliffs Walkway** (1½ to two hours one way) starts at the beach and affords extensive views inland and out to the Hauraki Gulf islands. Mangawhai has motels and caravan parks.

A particularly scenic part of the road goes over the headland to Langs Beach and then on to Waipu.

WAIPU & BREAM BAY

Near the mouth of the Waipu River is an estuary which provides a home for many species of wader birds, including the rare NZ dotterel, variable oyster-catchers and fairy terns. The *Ebb & Flow Backpackers* (☎ (09) 432 0217) is well situated overlooking the Waipu River estuary on Johnson Point Rd. A bunk bed costs $13 to $14, and twins and doubles are $34. The Ebb & Flow overlooks the estuary, and views from the verandah include the Hen & Chicken Islands and Sail Rock. At Waipu Cove there's a motel (☎ (09) 432 0348) and caravan park (☎ (09) 432 0410).

At Uretiti, DOC has a camping ground ($5); book on ☎ (09) 438 0299. You can buy supplies from the Waipu Four Square supermarket.

In Waipu there's an unusual, small museum, the **House of Memories** (☎ (09) 432 0745), which has displays relating to the early Nova Scotian settlers of Waipu and the surrounding district; it is open from 9.30 am to 4 pm daily. About 10 minutes drive west of Waipu is North River Treks (☎ (09) 432 0565), offering a variety of rides along rivers, through farmland and on beaches.

Kauri Coast

Heading towards Whangarei, you can turn off SH1 past Wellsford and travel along SH12 to the area known as the Kauri Coast. At the northern end of the Kaipara Harbour and extending along the west coast to Hokianga, the Kauri Coast is so-called because of the Kauri timber and gum industry that flourished here in the 19th century, generating much of NZ's wealth. The massive kauri forests are all but gone; however, the Waipoua Kauri Forest has untouched kauri forest and is the best place in NZ to see these magnificent trees. A prior visit to Matakohe is worthwhile for an understanding of kauri and the kauri industry.

MATAKOHE

Turning off at Brynderwyn for Dargaville, you pass through Matakohe, where the **Matakohe Kauri Museum** has a strange and wonderful collection of kauri gum. It also has lifelike displays of various aspects of the life of the kauri bushpeople and an extensive photographic collection. It's a superb museum, worth the short detour to see it.

The museum shop has some excellent bowls and other items crafted from kauri wood. They're expensive but very well made. Look for the items made of 'swamp kauri', ancient kauris which lay in swamps for thousands of years, their gum-saturated wood still in good condition. The museum is open daily from 9 am to 5.30 pm (until 5 pm in winter); entry is $6 (children $2).

Facing the museum is the **Matakohe Pioneer Church**, built in 1867 of local kauri. The tiny church served both Methodists and Anglicans, and also acted as the town hall and school for the pioneer community.

Places to Stay

Near Matakohe are two backpackers. The *Old Post Office Guesthouse* (☎ (09) 431 7453) is at Paparoa, 7km from Matakohe. It is a very pleasant hostel with all the facilities; a share room is $13.50 and singles/doubles are $18/33. The pleasant outdoor area overlooks a sylvan valley and its staff arrange transport to the museum. At Ruawai, west of Matakohe on the main road to Dargaville, is the small *Ruawai Travellers Lodge* (☎ (09) 439 2283). All beds cost $15 in this clean place; the only drawback is its position on the main road. Pluses are free linen and laundry facilities.

DARGAVILLE

Founded in 1872 by Joseph McMullen Dargaville, this once-important river port thrived on the export of kauri timber and gum. As the kauri forests were decimated, Dargaville declined, and today it is a quiet backwater servicing the agricultural Northern Wairoa area.

With a population of 7750, Dargaville is the main town on the Kauri Coast and the access point for the Waipoua kauri forests to the north. Dargaville's only other claim to fame is its title as the 'kumara capital of NZ'.

The helpful information centre (☎ /fax (09) 439 8360) on Normanby St is open in winter from 8.30 am to 5 pm on weekdays, and in summer from 8 am to 5.30 pm on weekdays and 9 am to 3 pm on weekends. It can help with tours, bus tickets and accommodation in Dargaville and has a list of homestays and farmstays in the area. It is also the AA office.

Harding Park & Maritime Museum

On a hill overlooking the town and the sweeping Wairoa River, Harding Park is the site of an old Maori *pa*, Po-tu-Oterangi. Tucked into the bottom of the hill is an early European cemetery.

On top of the hill, the small Maritime Museum has an eccentric collection of anything over 50 years old, including settlers' items, kauri gum samples and a huge slab of kauri. The maritime section has models of ships built or repaired in the Kaipara Harbour, notorious for its shipwrecks, and a massive Maori war canoe. Nearly 18m long, the 18th-century canoe is the only surviving example from pre-European times. In front of the museum are the masts from the *Rainbow Warrior*, the Greenpeace flagship bombed by the French in 1985. The museum is open from 9 am to 4 pm daily ($3, children 50c).

Organised Tours

The information centre has details on tours to the Waipoua Kauri Forest, the Trounson Kauri Park, Kai-Iwi Lakes, and 4WD tours along the beach to the Kaipara Lighthouse, returning to Dargaville or connecting with a boat ride south to Shelley Beach.

Places to Stay

Selwyn Park (☎ (09) 439 8296) on Onslow St has tent/powered sites for $14/18, simple cabins for $28 and fully equipped tourist cabins for $39 for two.

The YHA associate *Greenhouse Backpackers Hostel* (☎ (09) 439 6342), 13 Portland St, charges $15 for dorms and $25/34 for singles/doubles. It has a pool table, rents out bicycles and arranges Baylys Beach horse rides and walks in the Waipoua Kauri Forest.

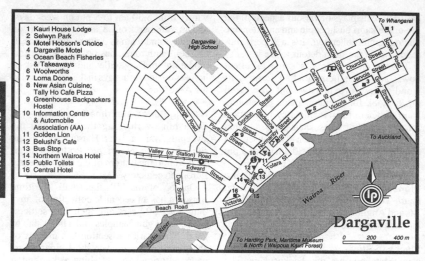

1 Kauri House Lodge
2 Selwyn Park
3 Motel Hobson's Choice
4 Dargaville Motel
5 Ocean Beach Fisheries & Takeaways
6 Woolworths
7 Lorna Doone
8 New Asian Cuisine; Tally Ho Cafe Pizza
9 Greenhouse Backpackers Hostel
10 Information Centre & Automobile Association (AA)
11 Golden Lion
12 Belushi's Cafe
13 Bus Stop
14 Northern Wairoa Hotel
15 Public Toilets
16 Central Hotel

Dargaville

The *Central Hotel* (☎ (09) 439 8034), an old kauri building at 18-22 Victoria St, has rooms for from \$30/55. Local motels range from the straightforward *Dargaville Motel* (☎ (09) 439 7734) at 217 Victoria St with doubles from \$65 to the well-appointed *Motel Hobson's Choice* (☎ (09) 439 8551), 212 Victoria St, with a pool and a variety of studio, one and two-bedroom units starting at \$85 a double.

The delightful *Kauri House Lodge* (☎ (09) 439 8082) on Bowen Rd is a rambling colonial homestead furnished with antiques. This fine B&B, set on 40 hectares, has only two double rooms (bookings essential) for from \$125 to \$140, and a pool.

Places to Eat

All these are on Victoria St. *Ocean Beach Fisheries & Takeaways* at No 164 is the place for fish and chips. For moderately priced Chinese food, try the *Golden Lion*, or the brighter *New Asian Cuisine* at No 114. At No 116 is the *Tally Ho Cafe Pizza*, open daily from 11 am for dining in or takeaway.

Belushi's Cafe at No 102 is Dargaville's answer to cafe society, with such bohemian offerings as cappuccino, bagels and crois-

sants. The *Northern Wairoa Hotel* has pub food, a Friday night smorgasbord and huge Sunday roasts. The *Lorna Doone* on the corner of Victoria and Gladstone Sts, opposite Woolworths, is a fancy restaurant, open daily for lunch and dinner.

Getting There & Away

The bus stop is on Kapia St. Main Coachlines has a bus to/from Auckland (\$20) via Matakohe every day except Saturday. Pioneer Coachlines, which comes under the InterCity umbrella, also does this run.

The West Coaster bus service runs from Paihia to Dargaville via Kaikohe, Rawene, Opononi and Waipoua daily except Saturday, and from Dargaville to Paihia on Tuesday, Thursday and Saturday. On Monday, Wednesday and Friday it goes from Dargaville to Whangarei and Paihia, looping back to Dargaville and then on to Matakohe, Brynderwyn and return.

AROUND DARGAVILLE
Kaipara Lighthouse

A worthwhile trip from Dargaville, if you can find a way to get there, is the 71km run south-east to Kaipara Lighthouse; the last

6.5km is on foot along the foreshore. If you don't have wheels check with the information centre about tours that go there. Built in 1884, the lighthouse has been restored.

Baylys Beach & Ripiro Ocean Beach

Only a 15-minute drive from Dargaville is Baylys Beach, lying on the 100km-long Ripiro Ocean Beach which is backed by high, yellow sand dunes. This stretch of surf-pounded coast is the site of many shipwrecks, including a French man o' war and an ancient Portuguese ship.

Ripiro Ocean Beach is a gazetted highway and you can drive along its hard sands at low tide, although it is primarily for 4WD vehicles. Ask locals about conditions before venturing out onto the sands. There is also access at Glinks Gully, Mahuta Gorge and Omamari.

Horse rides on Baylys Beach are popular. Baylys Beach Horse Treks (☎ (09) 439 6342) offers regular half-day beach rides for $30.

The *Baylys Beach Motor Camp* (☎ (09) 439 6349) at Baylys Beach, 14km from Dargaville, has sites for $17 and cabins from $28 for two. The *Ocean View Home Stay* (☎ (09) 439 6356) is a small, simple bach-turned-B&B for $60 a double.

DARGAVILLE TO HOKIANGA

En route to the big trees from Dargaville you can make a number of excursions. There are many walks you can undertake in Waipoua Kauri Forest and the smaller reserves. Any visit to this area should be preceded by a visit to the kauri museum in Matakohe. Get the DOC brochure *Waipoua Kauri Forests* from the Dargaville information centre.

Kai-Iwi Lakes

Only 34km north of Dargaville are three freshwater lakes called the Kai-Iwi Lakes (Taharoa Domain), which are popular for swimming, trout fishing and boating. The lakes are Kai-Iwi, Taharoa and Waikere. The largest of the lakes, Taharoa, has deep blue water fringed with gleaming white-sand beaches and pine groves. Activities are out-lined in the *Taharoa Domain: Kai-Iwi Lakes* pamphlet available from information centres throughout Northland. You can rent kayaks at Lake Taharoa.

A three-hour return **walk** from the lakes leads to the coast, then north along the beach to the base of Maunganui Bluff. You can also climb the summit (three hours return) or continue north for the three-day walk to Omapere (see under the Opononi heading).

Places to Stay There are two rustic camping grounds at the Kai-Iwi Lakes, one at Pine Beach right on the main lake and another at Promenade Point (book these at Kai-Iwi Lakes or at Dargaville's information centre). They have toilets, cold showers, fireplaces, and no power, and cost $7 (children $5).

Waterlea (☎ (09) 439 0727) is a farm with self-contained accommodation right at the entrance to the lakes. The owners organise trout fishing tours ($35 per hour for two) and other activities.

Trounson Kauri Park

Heading north from Dargaville you can take a route passing by the 573-hectare Trounson Kauri Park, 40km north of Dargaville. There's an easy half-hour walk leading from the parking and picnic area by the road, passing through beautiful forest with streams and some fine kauri stands, a couple of fallen kauri trees and the 'four sisters' – two trees each with two trunks. There's a ranger station and camp sites.

Guided night-time nature walks are organised through the Kauri Coast Holiday Park. These excellent, informative walks cost $9 and explain the flora and nightlife. Trounson has recently been set aside as a mainland refuge for threatened species; the first bird introduced was the kokako. You might see a kiwi if you're lucky; you will certainly see possums.

Places to Stay The turn-off for the Trounson Kauri Park is 32km north of Dargaville. Just after the turn-off, the *Kauri Coast Holiday Park* (☎ (09) 439 0621) is in a lovely riverside spot central to the lakes and the kauri forest. Bushwalks, pony rides, river, lake and sea fishing can be organised. Tent or powered sites cost $18, basic cabins are from $30 and a tourist flat is $55.

The DOC camping ground at the Trounson Kauri Park (☎ (09) 439 0605) is only open in summer. It's a beautiful place, ringed by superb kauris. Sites are $6 per person, with or without power. Cabins cost $8 per person or $60 a week.

On SH12, 2km north of the Trounson turn-off, the *Kaihu Farm Hostel* (☎ (09) 439 4004) has dorms for $15, and twins and doubles for $17 per person. The rooms out the back have the best views. Get breakfast/dinner for $6/10 and enjoy the view from the back patio while dining. Rent a mountain bike ($12 per day) or take a walk to its secret glow-worm grotto.

Waipoua Kauri Forest

The highlight of a west-coast visit, this superb forest sanctuary – proclaimed in 1952 after much public pressure and antagonism at continued milling – is the largest remnant of the once extensive kauri forests of northern NZ. There is no milling of mature kauri trees nowadays, except under extraordinary circumstances such as for the carving of a Maori canoe.

The road through the forest passes by some splendid huge kauris. Turn off to the forest lookout just after you enter the park – it was once a fire lookout and offers a spectacular view. A little further north, the park visitor centre (☎ (09) 439 0605) has plenty of information and excellent exhibits on kauri trees, native birds and wildlife. A fully grown kauri can reach 60m and have a trunk 5m or more in diameter. They are slow growing and some kauris are 2000 years old.

Several huge trees are easily reached from the road. **Te Matua Ngahere**, the 'father of the forest', has a trunk over 5m in diameter, believed to be the widest girth of any kauri tree in NZ. This massive tree is a short drive then a 20-minute walk from the car park. Close by are the **Four Sisters**, a graceful collection of four tall trees in close proximity. Also near Te Matua Ngahere is the

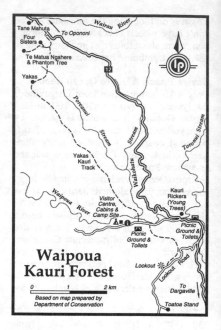

Waipoua Kauri Forest

Based on map prepared by Department of Conservation

Phantom Tree, believed to be the second largest in the forest. In the past, theft from cars has been a problem – the car park is guarded voluntarily (a $2 donation ensures that your car is not broken into).

From the same access path you can follow a half-hour walking track to the **Yakas Tree**, the eighth largest kauri in NZ, and continue on the whole two-hour trek to the park information centre.

Further up the road is **Tane Mahuta**, 'lord of the forest', the largest kauri tree in NZ, which stands close to the road and is estimated to be 1200 years old. At 52m, it's much higher than Te Matua Ngahere but doesn't have the same impressive bulk – although its cubic volume is said to be even greater.

On the south-eastern boundary of the Waipoua Kauri Forest is the 250-hectare **McGregor Memorial Reserve**. It contains regenerating kauri and podocarp forest and is the habitat of the kiwi and kauri snail. As manuka (tea tree) is an ideal cover under which native trees grow, it is being planted over former grassland in the reserve. To reach the reserve, turn off SH12 onto Marlborough Rd, about 1km south of Katui Homestead. The entrance to the reserve is 4km down Marlborough Rd.

Places to Stay Right in the heart of the forest, next to the Waipoua River and just past the information centre, camp sites (with shared showers and toilets) cost $6. Cabins with showers and kitchen facilities cost $10/5 for adults/children (four-bed cabins) and $14/7 (two-bed cabins). A furnished three-bedroom lodge is also available; bookings are made with DOC (☎ (09) 439 0605).

On SH12 at the southern edge of the forest, 48km north of Dargaville, *Waipoua Lodge* (☎ (09) 439 0422) is a fine old homestead with B&B for $85 a double. In Waimamaku, just north of the forest, the pleasant *Solitaire Guesthouse* (☎ (09) 405 4891) is a B&B in a well-restored old kauri house and charges $40/65 (dinner is $20).

Hokianga

Further north from the Kauri Coast, the road winds down to the Hokianga Harbour and the tiny twin townships of Omapere and Opononi. Hokianga is a depressed rural area with no industry and little development, but the harbour is beautiful, and the area is unspoilt – much less commercial than the Bay of Islands. It is a good place to take time-out and drift for a while, as plenty of alternative lifestylers have found out.

As you come up over the hill from the south, the rest stop on **Pakia Hill** has a great view of the harbour and is worth a stop.

Further down the hill, 2km west of Omapere, Signal Station Rd leads out to the **Arai-Te-Uru Recreation Reserve**, on the South Head of the Hokianga Harbour. It's about a 30-minute walk from Omapere or, if you're driving, a five-minute walk from the car park to Signal Station Point. This over-

looks the harbour entrance, the massive sand dunes of North Head and the turbulent confluence of the harbour and the open sea. There's a swimming beach, people fish off the rocks and it's also the northern end of the superb Hokianga-Waipoua Coastal Track.

OMAPERE

Omapere has a tiny museum, on the main road through town, which also houses the Hokianga Information Centre (☎ (09) 405 8869). It's open daily in summer from 9 am to 5 pm (10 am to 2 pm on Sunday).

Places to Stay & Eat

Globe Trekkers (☎ (09) 405 8183) is a good, well-run hostel on the main road in Omapere overlooking the harbour. Dorm beds cost $15, twins and doubles are $37 and there is ample space for tents. It offers a variety of activities and the Northland hostel special – bone-carving courses. The oft-vacant *Green Cafe Guest House* (☎ (09) 405 8193) is across from the beach and has great views; a dorm bed is $14.

The *Motel Hokianga* (☎ (09) 405 8847) has units for $75 a double and the *Omapere Tourist Hotel & Motel* (☎ (09) 405 8737) has a variety of accommodation, ranging from camp sites for $9 per person to motels units at $80 a double (in high season). *Whaley B&B* (☎ (09) 405 8641) is on the way to the heads on Signal Station Rd; it is reasonably priced at $30 per person.

For a splurge the fancy *Harbourmaster's Restaurant* is at the Omapere Tourist Hotel & Motel, where you can eat outside, watching the boats and all activity in the bay. The *Omapere Tearooms* is the fast-food choice. The *Ports Cafe & Tearooms* has a panoramic view of the harbour; it serves light meals and has a separate dinner menu.

OPONONI

Only 3.5km past Omapere the road passes through the tiny settlement of Opononi. The stone walls along Opononi's seafront were constructed from rock ballast used in timber ships which were sailed out from Sydney by convicts.

Back in 1955 a dolphin paid so many regular, friendly visits to the town that it became a national attraction. Opo, as the dolphin was named, played with children and learned to perform numerous tricks with beach balls. Unfortunately, Opo was killed, some say accidentally, by illegal dynamite fishers. A **sculpture of Opo** marks the dolphin's grave outside Opononi's pub. You can see a video of Opo at the Hokianga Information Centre in Omapere.

Walking

The **Hokianga-Waipoua Coastal Track** leads south from South Head at the entrance of Hokianga Harbour along the coast: it's four hours to the Waimamaku Beach exit; six hours to the Kawerua exit which also has a camping ground and hut; 12 hours to the Kerr Rd exit, where there's a camping ground at Waikara Beach; or you could continue the entire 16 hours (allow about three days) to the Kai-Iwi Lakes. Pick up a brochure from any local information centre or DOC office.

From Cemetery Rd on the eastern outskirts of Opononi, a half-hour climb leads up **Mt Whiria**, one of the oldest unexcavated pa sites, with a splendid view of the harbour.

Two kilometres east of Opononi the Waiotemarama Gorge road turns south for 6km to the **Waiotemarama bush track**, the best short walk from Opononi. This track climbs to Mt Hauturu (680m). It's a four-hour walk to the summit (six hours return), but there's a shorter loop walk starting from the same place which takes only about two hours and passes kauri trees and a picturesque waterfall. The highest point in Northland, Te Raupua (781m), is nearby but there is no regular track.

Between Waima and Taheke is the **old Waoku coach road**, once the sole route to Dargaville and, because of the rainfall, only open during summer. This is a more adventurous walk, muddy and not well marked, so proper gear and preparation are required. Get information from DOC.

The **Six Foot Track** at the end of Mountain Rd (near Okopako Lodge) gives access to many Waima Range walks.

Other Activities

The MV *Sierra* is a 12m (40ft) boat built of local Hokianga kauri in 1912, at the end of the logging boom. The boat recreates the historic 'mail run' around the harbour in summer ($20, children free). The *Alma* (☎ (09) 405 7704) also has cruises on the harbour at 10 am on Saturday ($20).

The fishing and shellfishing are excellent around the Hokianga Harbour. Fishing trips are easily arranged; even fishing off the wharf or the rocks near the harbour entrance is not bad. Okopako Pony Trekking (☎ (09) 405 8815) at Okopako Lodge has two-hour horse treks ($30) and longer rides through the bush of the Waima Hills.

Places to Stay

The *Opononi Holiday Park* (☎ 405 8791) has powered and non-powered sites at $10 per adult, tourist cabins from $45 for two, and standard cabins and on-site caravans from $30 to $45 for two.

The *Opononi YHA* at Pakanae was recently burnt out by a fire but may have reopened by now. The *House of Harmony* (*Te Rangimarie*) (☎ /fax (09) 405 8778) is conveniently located and charges $15 per person in dorms or double rooms. It's up the steep driveway beside the South Hokianga War Memorial Hall in the centre of Opononi.

Five kilometres east of Opononi, off the highway just before Whirinaki on Mountain Rd, *Okopako* (☎ (09) 405 8815) is a peaceful farm and backpackers lodge with good views. Dorm beds cost $15, doubles and twins are $38 and family rooms are available. Horse rides in the nearby hills (especially along the Six Foot Track) and harbour activities can be arranged.

More isolated, but well worth the effort to get to, is *Manaia Hostel & Treks* (☎ (09) 409 5347) at Mitimiti on the north-western side of the harbour. A bed is $20 and the horse treks, with Jack's Horse Trekking (☎ (09) 409 5003), are $30 for two hours. They pick up from Rangi Point which is reached by water taxi from Opononi.

In central Opononi, the *Opononi Resort Hotel* (☎ (09) 405 8858) has one-bedroom motel units for $80 and two-bedroom units for $90. Most of the hotel rooms have shared facilities and cost $25/35. The *Dunes Motel* (☎ (09) 405 8824) has one-bedroom units from $60 and two-bedroom units from $80 (prices are for two).

Places to Eat

Opononi has cafes and takeaways, and the restaurant at the *Opononi Resort Hotel* provides basic food at moderate prices. Seafood is the local speciality and it's excellent; try *Opononi Takeaways by the Sea*. The *South Hokianga RSA* (☎ (09) 405 8723) accepts nonmembers – attractions are the cheap beer and a kitbag of reminiscences.

Getting There & Away

West Coaster buses stop at Omapere and Opononi on their Sunday-to-Friday run from Paihia to Dargaville. From Dargaville to Paihia, InterCity (Pioneer) buses only go on Tuesday, Thursday and Saturday.

RAWENE

Rawene is a tiny settlement on a point on Hokianga Harbour, from where ferries cross to Kohukohu for the pleasant back route to Kaitaia. The shallow waters around Rawene become mud flats at low tide but, while it lacks beaches, Rawene is full of history.

While you wait for the ferry you can visit historic **Clendon House**, built in the late 1860s by James Clendon, the resident magistrate. It is open from 10 am to 4 pm daily in summer but only on weekends in winter ($2, children $1). In addition to Clendon House, the **Wharf House** (now a restaurant) is the oldest building in town and Rawene's hotel dates from the 1870s.

Further up Hokianga Harbour, 3km west of Horeke, **Mangungu Mission** is another historic building dating from 1839. The Hokianga chiefs signed the Treaty of Waitangi here in 1840.

Places to Stay

Rawene has a motor camp (☎ (09) 405 7720) on Marmon St just off Manning St with tent/powered sites at $8/9 per person and cabins at $15 per person. The *Masonic Hotel* (☎ (09) 405 7822), just a few steps up from the ferry landing, has rooms for from $25/35. B&Bs include *Hokingamai* (☎ (09) 405 7782) on Bundry St with singles/doubles for $40/60, and *Searell Homestay* (☎ (09) 405 7835) on Nimmo St ($40/60). The *Riverhead Guest House* (☎ (09) 401 9610) in Horeke is an 1871 kauri house furnished in period style ($60 for two).

Getting There & Away

The ferry departs from Rawene roughly every hour on the half-hour between 7.30 am and 5.45 pm, and from the Narrows on the Kohukohu side at 7.45 am until 8 pm in summer (until 6 pm in winter). The crossing takes 15 minutes, and fares are $8 for cars ($12 return) and $1 for passengers.

KOHUKOHU

This pleasant town is in a very quiet backwater on the north side of Hokianga Harbour. It is a good example of a completely preserved town with a number of historic kauri villas over 100 years old and other fine buildings including the Masonic Lodge, the Anglican Church and an old school.

Travellers are spoilt at the *Kohukohu Tree House* (☎ (09) 405 5855), one of the finest backpackers in the country. Constructed of wood and stained glass, it is nestled in the hills not far from the waters of Hokianga Harbour and 2km from the northern ferry terminus. Dorms cost $16 per person and doubles, including three private sleep-outs, are from $36 to $38 (the one with the highest elevation has superb views of Hokianga Harbour). This is a good place to relax, go mountain biking, kayaking, walking or try bone-carving.

B&Bs include *Yarborough House* (☎ (09) 405 5896), a wonderful old homestead on Yarborough St which charges $35/65 for singles/doubles, and *Kohukohu Farmstay*

(☎ (09) 405 5534) on Hawkins Rd, which charges $25/50.

KAIKOHE

Kaikohe (population 3700) is the main town of central Northland, with strong Maori traditions. A centre for the Ngapuhi tribe, it was the scene of bloody battles during the Maori land wars. Hone Heke eventually settled in Kaikohe and died here in 1850. His monument lies on the western outskirts of town on **Kaihoke Hill**, with fine views across Hokianga Harbour.

Kaikohe's only real tourist attraction is the **Pioneer Village** on the back road through town. The village houses a historic court house, cottage, school, jail, general store, fire station and saw mill, and features various memorabilia, farm machinery and steam engines. It is open from 10 am to 4 pm on weekdays in summer but only on weekends in winter. Admission of $5 (children $1) includes a guided tour.

The Kaikohe information centre (☎ (09) 401 1693) is on the main road. The *Mid North Motor Inn* (☎ (09) 401 0149) at 158 Broadway and the *New Haven Motel* (☎ (09) 401 1859) at 36 Raihara St both have singles/doubles for about $55/70. And for a meal, you can't pass up the eclectic fare at *ET's Maori Food and Chinese Restaurant* on Lower Broadway.

PUKETI & OMAHUTA FORESTS

North of Kaikohe, the Puketi and Omahuta forests consist of one large forest area with kauri sanctuaries and other native trees, camping and picnic areas, streams and pools, and viewpoints. Kauri milling in Puketi was stopped some years back to protect not only the kauri but also the rare kokako.

The two forests are reached by several entrances and contain a network of walking tracks varying in length from 15 minutes (the Manginangina Kauri Walk) to two days (the Waipapa River Track). A pamphlet detailing the tracks and features of the forests is available from any DOC office. Camping is permitted and there are basic trampers huts and a camping ground at the Puketi Recre-

ation Area on the Waiare Rd, 28km north of Kaikohe. Book at the DOC office in Kerikeri (☎ (09) 407 8474); a camp site is $5.

The Far North

KAITAIA

Kaitaia, a large northern commercial centre (population 4800), is the jumping-off point for trips up Ninety Mile Beach to Cape Reinga and offers a good chance to participate in aspects of Maori culture.

Entering Kaitaia you'll see a welcome sign in three languages – Welcome, Haere Mai (Maori) and Dobro Dosli (Dalmatian) – as many Maoris and Dalmatians live in the area. Both groups are culturally active, with a Maori marae and a Yugoslav Cultural Club the focus of activities.

Every year a special marathon is conducted along the length of Ninety Mile Beach, celebrating the legend of Te Houtaewa. This great runner ran the length of the beach from near Ahipara to steal kumara from the Te Rarawa people, returning with two full baskets after being angrily pursued. The marathon celebrates the return of the kumara – reconciliation for a past deed.

Information

The Northland Information Centre (☎ (09) 408 0879) in Jaycee Park on South Rd has information on Kaitaia and all the Far North, and books accommodation, tours and activities. It is open from 8.30 am to 5 pm daily (9.30 am to 1 pm on winter weekends).

Far North Regional Museum

The Far North Regional Museum, near the information centre, houses an interesting collection, including a giant moa skeleton, various bits and pieces from shipwrecks and the Northwood Collection – photographs taken around 1900 by a professional photographer. The giant 1769 de Surville anchor, one of three the explorer lost in Doubtless Bay, is one of the museum's prizes. It's open on weekdays from 10 am to 5 pm with

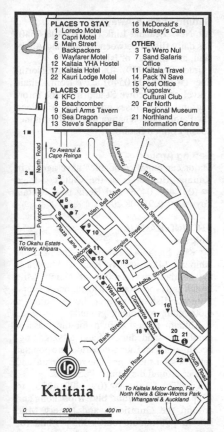

PLACES TO STAY
1 Loredo Motel
2 Capri Motel
5 Main Street
  Backpackers
6 Wayfarer Motel
12 Kaitaia YHA Hostel
17 Kaitaia Hotel
22 Kauri Lodge Motel

PLACES TO EAT
4 KFC
8 Beachcomber
9 Kauri Arms Tavern
10 Sea Dragon
13 Steve's Snapper Bar

16 McDonald's
18 Maisey's Cafe

OTHER
3 Te Wero Nui
7 Sand Safaris
  Office
11 Kaitaia Travel
14 Pack 'N Save
15 Post Office
19 Yugoslav
  Cultural Club
20 Far North
  Regional Museum
21 Northland
  Information Centre

Kaitaia

0   200   400 m

To Awanui &
Cape Reinga

North Road

Pukepoto Road

To Okahu Estate
Winery, Ahipara

Awanui River

Allen Bell Drive

Dunn Street

Empire Street

Plaza Lane

Balcove St

West Lane

Melba Street

Commerce Street

Bank Street

Redan Road

South Road

To Kaitaia Motor Camp, Far
North Kiwis & Glow-Worms Park,
Whangarei & Auckland

extended summer hours ($2.50, children 50c).

Te Wero Nui

The locals in Kaitaia have banded together to build an excellent cultural centre in the heart of this very Maori town. Entitled Te Wero Nui (the ultimate challenge), this is a tourist-focused learning centre. It offers an opportunity to participate in cultural activities and practical crafts such as herbal medicines, weaving, bone and woodcarving, and the spiritual side of life.

The centre (☎/fax (09) 408 4884) is

behind KFC on Commerce St. It is possible to stay on the marae and to participate in all activities. A week-long stay is $240 plus accommodation ($15 per night) and *hangis* are arranged for groups of 20 or more. There is an arts and craft shop which sells authentic items crafted on the premises.

Other Things to See & Do

The Aero Club (☎ (09) 406 7320) has scenic flights to Cape Reinga. Sailing and fishing trips can be arranged from Kaitaia.

Kaitaia is a centre for tours to surrounding areas, notably Cape Reinga and the gumfields of Ahipara (see under the Cape Reinga & Ninety Mile Beach and Around Kaitaia headings).

The **Ancient Kauri Kingdom** in Awanui is worth a visit. Here 30,000 to 50,000 year-old kauri stumps, which have been dragged from swamps, are fashioned into furniture and woodcraft products; the factory is open daily from 8.30 am to 5.30 pm (entry is free).

Okahu Estate (☎ (09) 408 0888), 3.5km south of Kaitaia, is NZ's most northerly winery. Enjoy its great selection from December to June from 10 am to 6 pm.

Places to Stay

Camping, Cabins & Hostels The *Kaitaia Motor Camp* (☎ (09) 408 1212) at 67 South Rd on the southern end of town, and the basic *Pine Tree Lodge Motor Camp* (☎ (09) 409 4864), 18km west at Ahipara, have tent or powered sites for $8.50 per person.

The *Park Ninety Mile Beach* (☎ (09) 406 7298) is 18km north on the Cape Reinga road at Waipapakauri Ramp and has tent and powered sites for $20, basic cabins for $35 and fully equipped tourist cabins for $50 (prices are for two). There's a licensed restaurant.

At 235 Commerce St, *Main Street Backpackers* (☎ (09) 408 1275) is a good hostel that organises many activities. The live-in owner, Peter, is active in the Maori community and takes visitors to see the local marae. It's a good place to stay and its rates are $12 or $13 for shared rooms, and singles/doubles are $25/32. You can do your own bone-carving for $10, equipment supplied.

It is rumoured that the *Kaitaia YHA Hostel* (☎ (09) 408 1840) at 160 Commerce St is closing. At present, the cost is $15 for a dorm bed and $18/30 for singles/doubles.

Motels & Hotels Motels (and their prices for doubles, which are less in winter) include the *Kauri Lodge* (☎ (09) 408 1190), 15 South Rd ($65); *Capri* (☎ (09) 408 0224), 3 North Rd ($75); *Loredo* (☎ (09) 408 3200), 25 North Rd ($80); and the *Wayfarer* (☎ 0800 118 100), 231 Commerce St ($78).

In Ahipara, there are the *Baylinks* (☎ (09) 409 4694) at 115 Takahe St and the *Adriaan Lodge* (☎ (09) 409 4888) on Reefview Rd (they have backpackers beds for $20 per person). Awanui, 6km north of Kaitaia, has the *Norfolk Motel & Campervan Park* (☎ (09) 406 7515) with units from $65.

The *Kaitaia Hotel* (☎ (09) 408 0360) on Commerce St is a venerable hotel with 30 rooms at $35/48, all with bathroom. Right in the centre of town, the hotel is a Kaitaia institution.

Places to Eat

The pickings are pretty slim. *Steve's Snapper Bar* at 123 Commerce St is a good and economical takeaway – it has fish and chips and pizzas. There is a *KFC* on Commerce St, next to Mainstreet Backpackers, and a *McDonald's* on Matthews Ave. The *Kauri Arms*, *Collard's Tavern* and the *Kaitaia Hotel* serve pub food and have live bands on weekends.

Maisey's is the closest you get to a 'chic' cafe – it sells Auckland favourites such as potato wedges ($4) and nachos ($6).

The *Sea Dragon* on Commerce St is a reasonable BYO Chinese restaurant; filling smorgasbords are $10 per diner. Kaitaia's top restaurant by far is the licensed *Beachcomber* on Commerce St, featuring good seafood.

The gigantic Pack 'N Save on the main drag is the cheapest place for self-caterers.

Getting There & Away

Air New Zealand Link (☎ (09) 408 0540) has daily flights between Kaitaia and Auckland, and the Bay of Islands.

InterCity (☎ (09) 408 0540) and Northliner (☎ (09) 408 0540) leave from Kaitaia Travel on Blencowe St and from the information centre. Buses go daily to Auckland via Paihia and Whangarei (but Northliner doesn't run on Saturday).

Getting Around

Major car rental companies have agents in Kaitaia: Budget is at the Caltex Garage (☎ (09) 408 0453) and Hertz is at Kaitaia Toyota (☎ (09) 408 2920).

AROUND KAITAIA
Ahipara

It's easy hitching a ride out to the beach at Ahipara, 14km west of Kaitaia. Ahipara is the southernmost section of Ninety Mile Beach and is popular with locals and visitors. It offers fishing, surfing, horse riding, a motor camp and picnic grounds.

Ahipara is best known for the massive gumfields sand dunes. Sand tobogganing, beach safaris and quad-bike rides are popular activities on the dunes above Ahipara and further around the Tauroa Peninsula.

Tua Tua Tours (☎ (09) 409 4875) in Ahipara operates **quad bike trips** along and around the Gumfields and Ninety Mile Beach; a 90-minute tour is $65 per bike (or $80 with a passenger), and three hours is $105 (or $150). You can go alone by hiring a quad bike from Adriaan Lodge (☎ (09) 409 4888); it's $40/70 for one/two hours.

A **walk** through the Ahipara gumfields gives you the chance to find ancient moa crop stones, to search for pieces of kauri gum in the sand and to gaze out to Ninety Mile Beach stretching far to the north. Get a good 'mud map' ($1) from Mainstreet Backpackers in Kaitaia.

Herekino

This remote spot, 29km south of Kaitaia, is a great getaway. Its salient pluses are its isolation and country pub (known for drinkin', and talkin' of shearin', crutchin' and dockin'). The *Tui Inn* (☎ (09) 409 3883) on Puhata Rd (just past the pub) is not flash (yeah, basic) but is a great place to stay and learn about the 'bush', real 'Kiwis', ridin', huntin', fishin' and shootin'. A bed is $12 per person and likely you will be cookin' and eatin' somethin' you have caught or shot (and gutted, filleted or skinned) yourself.

Kaitaia Region Walks

The **Kaitaia Walkway**, on the edge of the Herekino Forest, makes a good day trip and has excellent views. Originally planned as a road, the track has a gentle gradient along its 9km and you should allow four hours to walk it. To get there head south from Kaitaia on SH1 for 3km, then turn right into Larmer Rd and follow it to the end.

More challenging is the **Mangamuka Walkway** which connects the Takahue Valley south of Kaitaia with the Mangamuka Gorge. The 9km track through the Raetea and Maungataniwha forests requires good bush skills to negotiate and could take up to six hours. You can best reach the walk from SH1 at the top of the range picnic area.

There are many tough **mountain-biking** trips in the region. Get information on walks from the local DOC office (☎ (09) 408 2100), 127 North Rd, Kaitaia; also get a free copy of its *Kaitaia Area Walks* for more ideas.

Far North Kiwis & Glow-worms Park

In Fairburn, about a 30-minute drive from Kaitaia, this nocturnal park (☎ (09) 408 4100) is open from 9 am to 5 pm in June and July and from 9 am to 10 pm the rest of the year (hours may change). The main attraction is a glow-worm grotto beside a waterfall; at night there are trips to see the glow-worms in their natural habitat. There's also a nocturnal kiwi house and areas for daytime picnics. Entry is $8 (children $3).

To reach the park from Kaitaia, travel 8km south-east on SH1, turn left at the Fairburn signpost and continue for 9km along the gravel road.

CAPE REINGA & NINETY MILE BEACH

At the tip of the long Aupouri Peninsula, Cape Reinga is at the northern tip of NZ. As such it is a pilgrimage site for those who want to travel from one end of the country to the other. Contrary to popular belief, Cape Reinga is not the northernmost point of the country – that's Surville Cliffs on North Cape, 30km to the east. Nor is it the most western part of the North Island – Cape Maria van Diemen, just one bay around, claims that title. But standing at the windswept **Cape Reinga lighthouse** and looking out over the endless sea certainly has an end-of-the-world feel to it. Directly below the lighthouse is the Columbia Bank maelstrom, where the waters of the Tasman Sea and Pacific Ocean meet, generating waves up to 10m high in stormy weather.

The Aupouri Peninsula is known to the Maori as *Te Hika o te Ika* (tail of the fish) from the creation legend that tells of how Maui hauled a great fish from the sea, which

The Cape Reinga lighthouse overlooks the often stormy meeting of the Tasman Sea and Pacific Ocean

became the North Island. The peninsula is a rugged, desolate landscape dominated by high sand dunes and flanked by Ninety Mile Beach. If they metricate it to Ninety Kilometre Beach the name will be a lot more accurate.

The **Aupouri Forest**, about 75km long and 5km wide, covers two-thirds of the western side of the peninsula. It's an exotic forest, mostly pine, planted for timber. Kauri forest used to cover the area; in fact, traces have been found of three separate growths of kauri which were buried and then grew up again. This was a fruitful area for gumdiggers. On the northern edge of the Aupouri Forest, a volcanic rock formation called **The Bluff** is part of a private reserve used for fishing by the Maori tribe living in nearby Te Kao. A colony of white-fronted terns can be seen just past The Bluff on a prominent sandspit.

North of The Bluff, the Te Paki Reserves are public land with free access; just leave the gates as you found them and don't disturb the animals. There are about 7 sq km of giant sand dunes on either side of where the Te Paki Stream meets the sea; a stop to take flying leaps off the dunes is a highlight of the locally operated tours.

Bus tours travel along the hard sands of Ninety Mile Beach to Cape Reinga, or vice versa, depending on the tides. Private vehicles can also do the beach trip but all hire-car agreements prohibit use on the beach. The usual access point for vehicles is Waipapakauri, just north of Kaitaia. Tours go as far as Te Paki Stream, though most cars only go as far as The Bluff. The beach 'road' is only for the well-prepared with rugged vehicles. Cars have hit soft sand and been swallowed by the tides – you may see the roof of an unfortunate vehicle poking through the sands.

Motorcycling on the beach is OK but take it slow and be extra careful: a few bikers were killed when they suddenly rode into washouts or soft sand.

DOC has a shop at Cape Reinga serving snacks (seasonal) and this tiny outpost even has a post office.

Wagener Museum

This museum at Houhora houses an unrelated collection of oddities but the sheer number of items makes it astonishing. Exhibits include stuffed animals and birds, Maori artefacts, antique gramophones and washing machines, a huge commode collection, pianolas and other musical instruments that the guide will play for you.

The museum has a cafe and is open daily from 8 am to 5.30 pm ($6, children $2). All Cape Reinga tours stop here. For an extra $3 (children $1.50) you can also visit the **Subritzky Homestead** next door. Dating from 1862, the homestead is constructed of local kauri.

Walking

The coastline is scattered with beautiful beaches, connected by a network of tracks. You can walk the **Ninety Mile Beach** but you'll need to be prepared as there are no huts.

From Cape Reinga you can walk along Te Werahi Beach to **Cape Maria van Diemen** in about five hours return. Beautiful **Tapotupotu Bay** is a two-hour walk east of Cape Reinga, via Sandy Bay and the cliffs. From Tapotupotu Bay it is about an eight-hour walk to **Kapowairua** at the eastern end of Spirits Bay. Both Tapotupotu Bay and Kapowairua have camping grounds and road access. For details of walking tracks in the area, inquire at the information centre in Kaitaia.

Organised Tours

Bus tours go from Kaitaia, Doubtless Bay and the Bay of Islands. Tours from Kaitaia or Doubtless Bay are preferable since they're much closer to Cape Reinga. Tours from the Bay of Islands are larger, more commercial, and involve considerably more travel at each end of the day.

Competition has reduced prices significantly. From Kaitaia, Sand Safaris (☎ (09) 408 1778), 221 Commerce St, and Harrison's Cape Runner (☎ (09) 408 1033), 123 North Rd, have small buses for day trips taking in the main features of the cape and sand tobogganing. The cost is $30 (children $20), including a picnic lunch, but these prices may not last too long! Paradise Connexion (☎ (09) 406 0460) operates from Mangonui for $50 per person.

Fullers, King's, Dune-Rider and Northern Exposure tours emanate from the Bay of Islands (see that section for details).

The northern beaches are great for horse riding; contact Manuka Treks (☎ (09) 409 8848) or Puketutu Pony Rides & Bushwalks (☎ (09) 408 0979). Expect to pay about $25 per hour.

Places to Stay & Eat

DOC has several camping grounds in the Cape Reinga area. There's a site at Kapowairua on Spirits Bay ($4 per person), with cold water and limited toilet facilities, and another at Tapotupotu Bay ($5), with toilets and showers; neither has electricity. Bring a cooker as fires are not allowed. Both bays have mosquitoes and biting sandflies, so come prepared with repellent. The Rarawa Beach camping ground ($5), 3km north of Ngataki, has water and toilet facilities only (no prior bookings, no open fires).

At Waitiki Landing, the last settlement before the cape, *Waitiki Landing Cabins* (☎ (09) 409 7508) is the northernmost accommodation in NZ. A bunk bed is a reasonable $17 and twin or double cabins are $50. Waitiki Landing has a shop and a restaurant which makes great pizzas.

North Wind Lodge Backpackers (☎ (09) 409 8515) is 6km down an unsealed road at Henderson Bay on the peninsula's east side. It is small, quiet, friendly and near a great stretch of beach. A dorm bed costs $14 and twin rooms are $30.

The *Pukenui Lodge Motel & Hostel* (☎ (09) 409 8837) is in a lovely setting overlooking the harbour. The motel has units for from $69 to $89 and some backpackers beds for $14. Follow Lambs Rd west for about 500m to the *Pukenui Holiday Camp* (☎ (09) 409 8803) with camp sites at $8 per person, backpackers beds at $14 per person and on-site vans from $30 for two.

Further on, almost at the end of Lambs Rd

is the *Pukenui Farmstay* (☎ (09) 409 7863), a delightful cottage with all the amenities and a verandah from which you see memorable sunsets. It charges $13 per person or $30 for a twin room; camping is $8. Staff will pick up from the Pukenui shop and let visitors collect their own eggs and vegetables.

The *Houhora Heads Motor Camp* (☎ (09) 409 8564) is next to the Wagener Museum. It has limited facilities but tent/powered sites are $10.50/15 for two. At the turn-off to the museum, on the highway, the *Houhora Chalets Motel* (☎ (09) 409 8860) has A-frame units for from $50 to $70 a double, depending on the season.

KARIKARI PENINSULA

Remote Karikari Peninsula forms the western end of Doubtless Bay. Roads are mostly unsealed and facilities are limited, but the peninsula's beaches are among Northland's finest.

Rangiputa has lovely white-sand beaches that are easy to reach. A turn-off on the road to Rangiputa takes you to remote **Puheke Beach** with white sand dunes and long, lonely windswept beaches.

On the east coast of the peninsula, **Tokerau Beach** is a depressed place, while, further north, **Whatuwhiwhi** is more attractive. But loveliest of all is **Matai Bay** with its tiny 'twin coves'.

Places to Stay

Rangiputa is a small settlement. The *White Sands Motor Lodge* (☎ (09) 408 7080) has an attached shop; pleasant, modern units cost $125 for two in summer or only $50 in the off season. *Rangiputa Beach B&B* (☎ (09) 406 7667) is right on the beach and worth considering.

DOC has a camping ground at Matai Bay (☎ (09) 402 2100). During the Christmas holidays it is popular, but at other times is usually not full ($6, children $3). A good walking track goes from the end of the beach up onto the southern peninsula.

The *Whatuwhiwhi Holiday Park* (☎ (09) 408 7202) is at the end of Whatuwhiwhi Rd. A camp site is $20 for two and cabins are

NORTHLAND

from $35 to $45. The *Tokerau Beach Backpackers* (☎ (09) 406 7943), at the junction of the Inland and Tokerau Beach Rds, looked comfortable enough from the outside (it was closed when we visited). A dorm bed is $15. There is a shop/liquor store across the road.

DOUBTLESS BAY

The bay gets its unusual name from an entry in Captain Cook's logbook, where he wrote that the body of water was 'doubtless a bay'. Lying between the Bay of Islands and Kaitaia, Doubtless Bay has picturesque bays, coves and beaches. The whole area is great for fishing and shellfishing, boating, swimming and other water sports.

The principal town, Mangonui, is a charming historic village. Stretching west around the bay are the modern, popular beach resorts of Coopers Beach, Cable Bay and Taipa. With its glorious climate and beautiful beaches, Doubtless Bay is a go-ahead area, attracting moneyed retirees and other rat race escapees.

Doubtless Bay competes with Kaitaia as a good base for exploring the Far North. On the northern and western sides the bay is bounded by the Karikari Peninsula. Paradise Connexions (☎ (09) 406 0460) in Mangonui has tours to Cape Reinga; see that section.

Mangonui

Mangonui is a small, picturesque fishing village – the name means 'big shark' – with numerous old kauri buildings lining the shallow Mangonui harbour. It has all the basic services.

The **Mangonui Courthouse** is a historic reserve and the nearby Wharf Store has a variety of art and craft. The area attracts many craftspeople and Doubtless Bay has plenty of craft outlets.

Also at Mangonui is attractive **Mill Bay**, dotted with tiny boats; you can take Silver Egg Rd out to Mill Bay's Mangonui Cruising Club and an assortment of historical markers. This was the spot where Mangonui's first European settler made his base, and the whaling boats replenished their water from the stream.

Between Mangonui and Coopers Beach is the **Rangikapiti Pa Historic Reserve**, with ancient Maori terracing and a spectacular, sweeping view of Doubtless Bay. There's a walkway from Mill Bay, west of Mangonui, to the top of the pa.

Beaches

The first beach west of Mangonui is **Coopers Beach**, a fine sweep of sand lined with pohutukawa trees. Coopers Beach is quite developed and has a small shopping centre. The next bay along, less-developed **Cable Bay**, was once home to the longest cable in the world: a cable stretched 3500 nautical miles from here to Queensland, Australia, from 1902 to 1912. It closed in 1912 when another cable was laid between Sydney and Auckland.

Across the river from Cable Bay, **Taipa** is another popular summer destination. According to Maori legend, Taipa is the place where Kupe first set foot on the new land. Today it has a fine beach, a harbour where the Taipa River meets the sea, and several motels and motor camps.

Dolphin Swimming

Doubtless Bay Adventures (☎ (09) 406 0538) runs two trips daily out to the bottlenose dolphins (weather permitting) from Mangonui. The trips are four hours long and leave at 8 am and 1 pm; the cost is $70/50 for adults/children and all equipment is provided. Mac 'n' Mo, the operators, provide a commentary on the flora, fauna and history of the Karikari Peninsula and Doubtless Bay.

Places to Stay

Camping & Cabins The closest place to Mangonui is the *Hihi Beach Motor Camp* (☎ (09) 406 0307) with tent/powered sites for $10/12 for two and cabins from $55 (less in winter). Taipa is a more attractive destination than Hihi. The *Taipa Caravan Park* (☎ (09) 406 0995) on the river close to the beach has camp sites from $9 per person and cabins for $30.

Hostels & Guesthouses The *Old Oak Inn* (☎ (09) 406 0665), 19 Waterfront Drive, in Mangonui is a pleasant 1861 kauri house. A dorm bed in this hostel costs $15 and doubles are from $45.

Mac 'n' Mo's (☎ (09) 406 0538), on the highway in Coopers Beach, has singles/doubles for $35/55.

Just off the road to Hihi, 2km from the highway, *Abraham Lincoln's B&B* (☎ (09) 406 0090) is a pleasant farmstay high on a hill with expansive views across Mangonui Bay; doubles are $60.

Motels & Hotels There are many motels in the area costing around $60 to $80 a double, but most charge $100 or more from Christmas to the end of January. Motels include the *Mangonui Motel* (☎ (09) 406 0346) in Mangonui (German is spoken), the *Blue Pacific Motel* (☎ (09) 406 0010) and *Taipa Sands Motel* (☎ (09) 406 0446) in Taipa. The *Taipa Resort Hotel* (☎ (09) 406 0656) on Taipa Point Rd is superbly situated; it costs a lot more than the others ($195 for two) but you get what you pay for. The *Driftwood Lodge* (☎ (09) 406 0418) in Cable Bay is a standard motel but right on the beach.

In Mangonui the historic *Mangonui Hotel* (☎ (09) 406 0003) is comfortable and has been refurbished, with regular rooms at $45 for a single and doubles with bathroom for $90 (breakfast included).

Places to Eat
In Mangonui the licensed *Cafe Nina* is a cosy little cafe with good Mediterranean food (such as delicious lamb shanks for $18.50) – an ideal place to drink cappuccino and have a game of chess or backgammon.

Similar in style, but a touch classier, the *Slung Anchor* is opposite the local supermarket. Snacks during the day will set you back around $5 and the dinner menu features seafood. The award-winning *Mangonui Fish Shop*, near the wharf, is on stilts over the water. You can eat your fish and chips on tables overlooking the bay. Shellfish, seafood salads and smoked fish are also sold here.

The *Mangonui Hotel* has a restaurant with a pleasant outdoor garden area to one side; it has bands on the occasional weekend.

Getting There & Away
InterCity buses pass through Mangonui once a day on the Bay of Islands-Kaitaia route. Northliner buses do the same run, stopping at Mangonui, Coopers Beach and Taipa, daily except Saturday.

WHANGAROA

Whangaroa Harbour is a picturesque inlet of small bays and bright green water, surrounded by high, rugged cliffs and curious hills. The area was once well known for its kauri forests. The timber was milled at Whangaroa and across the harbour at Totara North, often ending up as sailing vessels.

The small town of Whangaroa, 6km off the main road (SH10), is now a popular gamefishing centre. This is a very quiet town but good tours and activities are available. Totara North, on the other side of the bay, is even sleepier and has an old timber mill.

The Boyd Gallery (☎ (09) 405 0230), the general store in Whangaroa, is also an informal tourist information office.

Walking
For walks, the domed, bald summit of St Paul's offers fine views. It is a half-hour walk above Whangaroa to the south. The Wairakau track north to Pekapeka Bay (90 minutes) begins near the church hall on Campbell Rd in Totara North and passes through farmland, hills, shoreline, Wairakau Stream and Bride's Veil Falls before arriving at DOC's Lane Cove Cottage.

Organised Tours
Many travellers rave about the yacht *Snow Cloud* (☎ (09) 405 0523), which operates out of Whangaroa Harbour (Te Ngaere) to the Cavalli Islands, where there are excellent beaches, diving spots (including the wreck of the *Rainbow Warrior*), snorkelling and walks. The cost is a mere $50 per person (minimum two) for this excellent day trip.

Sea Fever Cruises has harbour cruises, and

several other boats are available for deep-sea fishing, water-skiing and diving. Book boats through the Boyd Gallery or Marlin Hotel.

The area around Whangaroa Harbour is ideal for sea kayaking. Northland Sea Kayaking (☎ (09) 405 0381) is located east on the coast, past Tauranga Bay (pick-up from Kaeo can be arranged for $5 return). This coast is magical, with bays, beaches, sea caves, tunnels and islands to explore. The kayak tours 'comb' the coast for a very reasonable $60 per day, including accommodation.

Places to Stay
Camping & Cabins The *Whangaroa Harbour Motor Camp* (☎ (09) 405 0306) charges $8/10 per person for tent/powered sites and from $30 for cabins. The camp is about 2.5km before the wharf.

DOC's *Lane Cove Cottage*, reached by the Wairakau track or by boat, charges $8 per night. It has showers and flush toilets but you have to bring your own cooker. Book through DOC in Kerikeri (☎ (09) 407 8474).

Hostels The *Sunseeker Lodge* (☎ (09) 405 0496) is up on a hill about 500m beyond the wharf, with a great view of the harbour. It charges $14 for dorms, $20 for singles and $35 for doubles and twins. Motel units are $70 a double, although one is set aside for backpackers at $20 per person.

At Totara North, the *Historic Gumstore Hostel* (☎ (09) 405 1703) dates from 1890 and has dorms for $17 and doubles/twins for $50/60. The town is a backwater (literally, as the mangrove-fringed creek is right beside the old store) but you can rent dinghies and go fishing.

Just west of the Totara North turn-off, 12km north of Kaeo, the pleasant *Kahoe Farm Hostel* (☎ (09) 405 1804) has dorm beds for $16, and doubles or twins for $37. It is run by fifth-generation Kiwis – although the Italian chef doesn't qualify for this status (yet!). The enthusiastic owners organise activities like soccer competitions, walks, horse treks, kayaking and sailing. Meals of the day include genuine 'Italian' pizza ($12 to $15 for a large).

Motels & Hotels The *Whangaroa Motel* (☎ (09) 405 0022) and the *Truant Lodge Motel* (☎ (09) 405 0133) have motel rooms from about $70.

At the exclusive *Kingfish Lodge* (☎ (09) 405 0164), reached by boat, the cost is about $140 per person including transfers.

Right by the wharf the *Marlin Hotel* (☎ (09) 405 0347) has share-facility rooms at $30/40 for singles/doubles; the hotel is the social centre of the town.

Places to Eat
The *Marlin Hotel* does dinner, breakfast and lunch, or visitors can gain temporary membership at the *Big Gamefish Club*, opposite the pub, where fish, of course, features heavily on the menu. Come during the summer and see them weigh in the marlin.

AROUND WHANGAROA
For a scenic drive, you can visit the beautiful bays and fine beaches east of Whangaroa. From the SH10, just south-east of Kaeo, the road via Otoroa is sealed almost all the way to Matauri Bay, except for the final descent to the beach. From Matauri Bay through to Whangaroa the road is unsealed almost all the way, but the great scenery makes the strain on the nerves worthwhile!

The trip out to **Matauri Bay** is one of *the* surprises of Northland. Matauri Bay is Maori land, home to the Ngati Kura people, and this superb stretch of beach sees few tourists. The view from the ridge above the bay is spectacular with the beach, Cavalli Islands and headland way down below. At the top of the headland in Matauri Bay is a monument to the *Rainbow Warrior*. (The boat itself lies offshore in the waters of the Cavalli Islands.) *Rainbow Warrior* dives can be arranged at Matauri Bay Holiday Park or in Paihia.

Heading west from Matauri Bay, the road leads to **Te Ngaire**, a small settlement with a lovely quiet beach, then to nearby **Wainui Bay** for cast fishing. You can then detour to **Mahinepua Bay** or continue on to **Tauranga**

Bay, another fine sweeping beach with good surf and accommodation.

Places to Stay

The *Matauri Bay Holiday Park* (☎ (09) 405 0525) has sites for $18 and cabins from $30. The *Oceans Beachfront Holiday Village* (☎ (09) 405 0417) at the end of the road has comfortable units from $80 a double; it also has a licensed restaurant. DOC has a very basic hut at Papatara Bay on Motukawanui Island (sleeps eight), one of the Cavallis; book through DOC in Kerikeri.

The *Tauranga Bay Holiday Park* (☎ (09) 405 0436), on the beach at Tauranga Bay, has tent/powered sites for $8/9 per person and cabins for $30 for two; four-person minimum rates apply in summer. The *Tauranga Bay Motel* (☎ (09) 405 0222) is a plain but comfortable motel for $50 a double (from $100 in summer).

Bay of Islands

Long famed for its stunning coastal scenery, the Bay of Islands is one of the country's major attractions. The bay is punctuated by dozens of coves and its clear waters range in hue from turquoise to deep blue. Dotted with nearly 150 islands, the Bay of Islands is aptly named. The islands have escaped development as the townships are all on the mainland.

The Bay of Islands is also of enormous historical significance. As the site of NZ's first permanent English settlement, it is the cradle of European colonisation. It was here that the Treaty of Waitangi was drawn up and first signed by 46 Maori chiefs in 1840; the treaty remains the linchpin of race relations in modern-day NZ.

Paihia is the centre of the Bay of Islands. Though only a small town, its population swells dramatically in summer. Waitangi Reserve is within walking distance.

Only a short passenger ferry ride away, Russell has all the character that Paihia lacks. Though also a popular tourist destination,

historic Russell is a smaller, sleepier town with many fine old buildings and a delightful waterfront.

To the north is Kerikeri – 'so nice they named it twice', claim the tourist brochures. Kerikeri is more like a real town and much less touristy.

Organised Tours & Activities

As a major tourist centre, the Bay of Islands has a mind-boggling array of activities and tours. Many are water-based to make the most of the natural surroundings. Backpackers discounts are available for many activities and tours, and the hostels arrange cheap deals.

Cruises The best introduction to the area is a cruise. Fullers (☎ (09) 402 7421) and Kings Tours & Cruises (☎ (09) 402 8288) operate popular regular cruises. There are also smaller operators.

Best known is Fullers' 'Cream Trip', which started back in 1920 when one Captain Lane picked up dairy products from the many farms around the bay. As more roads were built and the small dairy farms closed, the service became more of a tourist trip. The trip takes about five hours and costs $65 (children $33). It leaves daily in the main season, and on Monday, Wednesday, Thursday and Saturday from June to September.

Other Fullers cruises include the Hole in the Rock (passing through it) off Cape Brett ($55, children $28) and the *R Tucker Thompson* tall sailing ship cruise ($79, children $40). Most tours stop at Otehei Bay on Urupukapuka Island, where westerns writer Zane Grey went big game fishing and a tourist submarine, the *Nautilus*, is submerged. To go underwater costs $10 (children $5).

Kings has a Day in the Bay cruise for $69/35 with a stopover on either Waewaetorea or Urupukapuka island. It also has a Hole in the Rock cruise for $50/25.

Also very popular are the high-speed Hole in the Rock trips, which are a neck-snapping jet-boat ride of the adrenalin-pumping, rather than the camera-priming, kind. Exitor

(☎ (09) 402 7020) runs trips at 10 am and 2 pm for $50 (children $25). Kings has a Mack Attack at 9.15 am and 1.35 pm ($50, children $25).

All cruises depart first from Paihia and then from Russell about 15 minutes later.

Sailing A very pleasant way to explore the Bay of Islands is on a sailing trip. Operators include:

A Place in the Sun (☎ (09) 403 7615), which organises cruises for $40 for a half-day or longer ($65).

Carino (☎ (09) 402 8040), a 42ft catamaran offering full-day sailings for $60 and the only licensed charter to offer swimming with dolphins.

Great Escape Charters (☎ (09) 407 8920) in Opua, with bareboat yacht charters (5m two-berth/6m three-berth/6.3m four-berth yachts cost $70/90/130 for 24 hours).

Gungha (☎ (09) 407 7930), a 14m ocean-going sloop departing from Kerikeri and picking up in Russell (full-day cruises are $65/40).

Straycat (☎ (09) 407 6130), with day trips in a catamaran departing from Russell, Kerikeri and Paihia for $65, including lunch.

Vigilant (☎ (09) 403 7596), with full-day cruises (you help to sail it) for $65 including lunch.

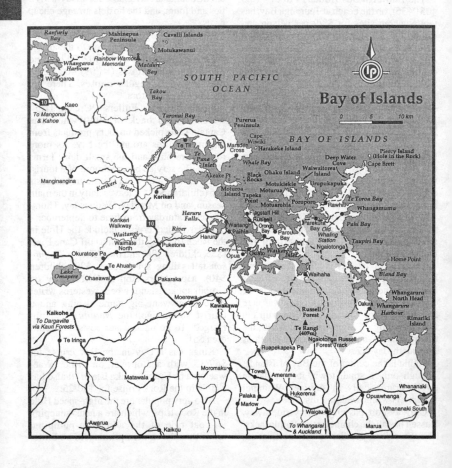

Dolphin Swimming Although Kaikoura in the South Island is still the premier destination for swimming with the dolphins, trips from the Bay of Islands are becoming increasingly popular. The big plus for Bay of Islands trips is that they also operate in winter.

The Bay of Islands trips have a high success rate, and operators have offered another, free trip if dolphins are not sighted. Dolphin swims are subject to weather and sea conditions.

Dolphin Discoveries (☎ (09) 402 8234) got this activity under way in this region in 1991. It operates with small groups and provides all necessary equipment ($85 for adults).

Heritage Trails (☎ (09) 402 6288) has daily trips in summer and trips on Tuesday, Thursday and Sunday in winter. The good thing about this trip is that Maori culture, myths and legends pertinent to the bay are explained. Fullers, the big tour conglomerate, is not to be outdone and also runs Dolphin Encounters for the same price.

Sea Kayaking Coastal Kayakers (☎ (09) 402 8105) does a trip from Waitangi around the mangrove forests up to Haruru Falls, passing right underneath the falls, and out to Motumaire Island all in one day. The full-day trip costs $60 or shorter four-hour trips cost $40. Kayaks and gear can be rented for $10/25/35 per hour/half-day/full day. Kayaks can also be hired at Bay Beach Hire (☎ (09) 402 7905) on the beach.

Over in Russell, Kaptain Kayak (☎ 025 766 896) on the corner of Matauwhi Rd and Florence Ave hires out kayaks and canoes in addition to mountain bikes and windsurfers.

Scuba Diving Paihia Dive Hire (☎ (09) 402 7551) on Williams Rd hires full sets of scuba gear to qualified divers. It also offers scuba and snorkelling courses, tank filling and scuba gear servicing, and diving trips, including expeditions to the sunken *Rainbow Warrior* ($145), and has a dive shop

Matauri Cat Charters (☎ (09) 405 0525), near the Oceans Motel at Matauri Bay, has a

two-dive package on the *Rainbow Warrior* for $135.

Other Activities The Bay of Islands is noted for its **fishing**, particularly snapper and kingfish. Fishing charter boats abound and can be booked at the Maritime Building in Paihia or at Russell wharf. One recommended operation is Serious Fun (☎ (09) 402 6015); a snapper fishing trip in the bay is about $65 per person (backpackers $60). A full-day kingfish trip will cost about $200 per person.

Surprisingly inexpensive are the **scenic flights**: you can take a short aerial tour (about 15 minutes) for around $45. Bay of Islands Aero Club (☎ (09) 407 8400) at Kerikeri has scenic flights or you can take seaplane flights ($95) from the Paihia wharf (☎ (09) 402 8338).

Sky-Hi Tandem Skydive (☎ 025 756 758) operates from the Watea (Haruru Falls) airport; the cost is $170 (30 seconds of free fall).

There is an excellent barbecue cruise (☎ (09) 402 7848) up the Waitangi River; fresh panfried fish and T-bone steak are served ($25).

There are a couple of **horse riding** operators – with Big Rock Horse Springs (☎ (09) 407 5999) you swim the horses; a full-day trip, including pick-up from Paihia, is $65. Horse Treks Bakewell (☎ (09) 407 5517) in Kerikeri has one-hour rides for $25.

Organised Tours It's easier to make trips to Cape Reinga and Ninety Mile Beach from Kaitaia or Doubtless Bay. However, a few trips leave from the Bay of Islands.

King's Tours & Cruises (☎ (09) 402 8288) has trips departing from Paihia with pick-ups in Kerikeri daily at 7.30 am, returning at 6.30 pm. The tour also stops at Puketi Kauri Forest and Wagener Museum. The cost is $75 (children $40). Fullers (☎ (09) 402 7421) charges $89/50 for a similar trip with lunch thrown in. Kings has an express trip which leaves at 8.15 am for Cape Reinga ($60/40).

A popular tour with the younger set is the 4WD Dune Rider (☎ (09) 402 8681), which

The *Rainbow Warrior* Trail

New Zealand is seldom mentioned on the world stage. With a population of three and half million and its relative isolation, NZ is in many eyes a small, almost inconsequential Pacific nation. In 1985 an explosion in Auckland Harbour made world headlines and put NZ on the map.

The Greenpeace flagship *Rainbow Warrior* lay anchored in Auckland Harbour, preparing to sail north of Tahiti to protest against French nuclear testing.

The *Rainbow Warrior* never left Auckland. French saboteurs, with the backing of the French government, attached explosives to the side of the ship and sank her. In the explosions one green campaigner, Fernando Pereira, was killed.

It took some time to find out exactly what had happened, but in inquisitive, rural NZ the comings and goings of foreigners are not easily forgotten. Two of the saboteurs were captured, tried and found guilty, while the others have never been brought to justice.

The incident caused an uproar in France – not because the French government had conducted a wilful and lethal act of terrorism on the soil of a friendly nation, but because the French secret service had bungled the operation and been caught. The French used all their political and economic might to force NZ to release the two saboteurs, and in a farcical turn of events the agents were imprisoned on a French Pacific island as if they had just won a trip to Club Med. Within two years, and well before the end of their sentence, they returned to France to receive a hero's welcome.

Northland was the stage for this deadly mission involving several secret service agents. Explosives for the sabotage were delivered by a yacht (which had picked them up from a submarine) from Parengarenga Harbour in the far north. They were driven to Auckland in a Kombi van, by French agents posing as tourists. Bang! An innocent man dead, and international outrage – Auckland Harbour was in the news.

The skeletal remains of the *Rainbow Warrior* were taken to the waters of the beautiful Cavalli Islands. The masts of this oceanic crusader were sent to the Maritime Museum in Dargaville. The memory of the Portuguese photographer and campaigner who died endures in a peaceful bird sanctuary in Thames. A haunting memorial to the once-proud boat sits in peace atop a Maori pa site at Matauri Bay.

The world again focused on the *Rainbow Warrior* in 1995. Ten years after the sinking the French announced that they were resuming nuclear testing in the Pacific, and Greenpeace's new flagship bearing the name of its ill-fated predecessor set sail for the Mururoa test site. It entered the exclusion zone and was stormed by French marines. ■

costs \$75. Kiwi Experience's (☎ (09) 366 9830) Awesome Adventures Pass (minimum four days; \$167) includes a trip to the cape – it is well recommended.

Getting There & Away

Air Air New Zealand Link (☎ (09) 407 8419) has daily flights to Kerikeri from Auckland. Great Barrier Airlines has daily flights in summer from Auckland to Watea (Haruru Falls) airstrip then on to Great Barrier Island and Whitianga in the Coromandel.

Bus All buses serving Paihia arrive at and depart from the Maritime Building by the wharf.

InterCity has buses daily from Auckland to the Bay of Islands, via Whangarei and Opua. The trip takes about four hours to Paihia and goes to Kerikeri before continuing north to Kaitaia.

Northliner has an Auckland-Whangarei-Bay of Islands-Kaitaia bus service. It departs from the Downtown Airline Terminal in Auckland and stops in Paihia, Haruru Falls and Kerikeri. There's a connecting service to Russell and also a direct Whangarei-Russell service.

Pioneer Coachlines has a four-hour trip from Paihia to Dargaville via the Waipoua Forest on weekdays (and a Sunday service in summer); see under the Getting Around heading at the beginning of this chapter.

Getting Around

Passenger ferries connect Paihia with Russell, running from around 7 am to 7 pm (to 10 pm from October to June). Three ferries, the large Fullers ferry and two local services, operate on average every 20 minutes from Russell to Paihia in summer. The fare is \$3 one way; return tickets offer no saving and are less flexible.

To get to Russell with your car, cross from Opua to Okiato Point using the car ferry (see under the Russell heading).

There's also a water taxi (☎ (09) 403 7123) for getting around the bay islands.

BAY OF ISLANDS MARITIME & HISTORIC PARK

The maritime and historic park consists of some 40 different sites extending all the way from Mimiwhangata Bay in the south to Whangaroa Harbour in the north. Marked walks of varying levels of difficulty (many very easy) take anywhere from 10 minutes to 10 hours and include tramps around islands, pas and other historical sites, scenic, historic and recreational reserves, and the Mimiwhangata Marine Park.

The Bay of Islands Maritime & Historic Park Visitor Centre is at Russell (☎ (09) 403 7685). DOC Kerikeri (☎ (09) 407 8474) can also help with information. DOC's *The Story of the Bay of Islands Maritime & Historic Park* is indispensable and has a haunting frontispiece: '*Whatungarongaro te tangata toitu te whenua* (People are perishable but the land endures).' You can also get the useful *Urupukapuka Island Archaeological Walk* and *Bay of Islands Walks* pamphlets from the DOC visitor centre.

Development of islands in the Bay of Islands is limited, though **Urupukapuka Island** has camping facilities.

Places to Stay

The DOC office in Russell (☎ (09) 403 7685) has details of accommodation in the park. The *Cape Brett Hut* is a very popular destination. You can arrange to walk there and stay in the hut by ringing ☎ (09) 403 7923. A *koha* (donation) should be made to the local Maori landowners.

Camping is permitted at most of the bays on Urupukapuka Island but you need food, stove, fuel, and a shovel for digging a toilet; the cost is \$4 per person. For Urupukapuka Island, take a Fullers tour, get off at Otehei Bay and arrange to catch the tour on another day.

Also popular is *Mimiwhangata Cottage & Lodge* in Mimiwhangata Coastal Park (see the Russell Road section).

PAIHIA & WAITANGI

The main town in the area, Paihia (population 2000) was settled by Europeans as a mission station in 1823 when the first raupo (bullrush) hut was built for the Reverend Henry Williams. Paihia still has a very pretty setting but the missionary zeal has been replaced with an equally fervent tourist industry. It's basically an accommodation, eating and tours centre.

Adjoining Paihia to the north is Waitangi, the site of the historic signing on 6 February 1840 of the treaty between the Maori people and the representatives of Queen Victoria's government.

The Treaty of Waitangi is a momentous document that on the one hand saw the Maori tribes accept British governorship, but on the other granted the Maori citizenship and land rights. The treaty lies at the heart of Maori grievances and land claims today.

Information

Most of the information places are conveniently grouped together in the Maritime Building right by the wharf in Paihia. Here you'll find the Bay of Islands Visitor Information Centre (☎ (09) 402 7345; fax 402 7314) on Marsden Rd, which can give information, advice and make bookings.

Also here are the Fullers, King's and other offices for cruises and tours, fishing boat bookings, the bus station, and terminal for the ferry to Russell. The offices are open from 8 am to 5 pm daily.

Close by is **Aquatic World** (☎ (09) 402 6220), which struggles to make an ordinary aquarium interesting. It is open from 9 am to 5.30 pm daily ($6.50, children $3.50).

Waitangi National Reserve

The Treaty House in Waitangi has special significance as the start of the European history of NZ. Built in 1832 as the home of British Resident James Busby, it was eight years later the setting for the signing of the historic treaty. The house, with its beautiful sweep of lawn running down to the bay, is preserved as a memorial and museum.

Just across the lawn, the magnificently detailed Maori **Whare Runanga** (meeting house) was completed in 1940 to mark the centenary of the treaty. The carvings represent the major Maori tribes.

Down by the cove is the largest war canoe in the world – the Maori canoe *Ngatokimatawhaorua*, named after the canoe in which the Maori ancestor Kupe discovered NZ. It too was built for the centenary, and a photographic exhibit details how the canoe was made from two gigantic kauri logs. Traditionally the canoe was launched every year on 6 February (New Zealand Day) for the annual treaty-signing commemoration ceremonies, when dignitaries gathered and Maori activists protested. For the Maori, the treaty remains a symbol of the expropriation of their land and highlights the failure of the government to honour its responsibilities under the treaty. After a 1995 protest, when the governor-general was spat at by protesters, the prime minister announced that a lower key ceremony would be held in Parliament Gardens in Wellington.

Beyond the Treaty House a road climbs Mt Bledisloe, from where there are commanding views. Beginning from the visitor centre, a **walking track** takes off through the reserve, passing through the mangrove forest around Huia Creek and on to Haruru Falls. The walkway has a boardwalk among the mangroves so you can explore them without getting wet feet. The walk to the falls takes about 1½ hours each way.

Entry to Waitangi Reserve is $8 (children under 12 free); it's open from 9 am to 5 pm daily. At the visitor centre an audiovisual presentation relating the story of the developments surrounding the signing of the treaty begins every half-hour.

Kelly Tarlton's Shipwreck Museum

Beached beside the bridge over the Waitangi River is the barque *Tui*, an old sailing ship imaginatively fitted out as a museum of shipwrecks. It's open from 9 am to 5.30 pm daily, longer during holidays ($6, children under 16 $2.50). Recorded sea chants, creaking timbers and swaying lights accompany the collection of over 1000 bits and pieces the late Kelly Tarlton dragged up from wrecks.

NORTHLAND

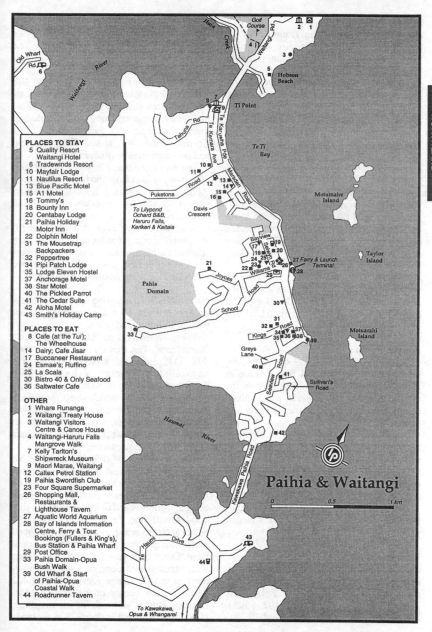

PLACES TO STAY
5 Quality Resort
  Waitangi Hotel
6 Tradewinds Resort
10 Mayfair Lodge
11 Nautilus Resort
13 Blue Pacific Motel
15 A1 Motel
16 Tommy's
18 Bounty Inn
20 Centabay Lodge
21 Paihia Holiday
  Motor Inn
22 Dolphin Motel
31 The Mousetrap
  Backpackers
32 Peppertree
34 Pipi Patch Lodge
35 Lodge Eleven Hostel
37 Anchorage Motel
38 Star Motel
40 The Pickled Parrot
41 The Cedar Suite
42 Aloha Motel
43 Smith's Holiday Camp

PLACES TO EAT
8 Cafe (at the *Tui*);
  The Wheelhouse
14 Dairy; Cafe Jisar
17 Buccaneer Restaurant
24 Esmae's; Ruffino
25 La Scala
30 Bistro 40 & Only Seafood
36 Saltwater Cafe

OTHER
1 Whare Runanga
2 Waitangi Treaty House
3 Waitangi Visitors
  Centre & Canoe House
4 Waitangi-Haruru Falls
  Mangrove Walk
7 Kelly Tarlton's
  Shipwreck Museum
9 Maori Marae, Waitangi
12 Caltex Petrol Station
19 Paihia Swordfish Club
23 Four Square Supermarket
26 Shopping Mall,
  Restaurants &
  Lighthouse Tavern
27 Aquatic World Aquarium
28 Bay of Islands Information
  Centre, Ferry & Tour
  Bookings (Fullers & King's),
  Bus Station & Paihia Wharf
29 Post Office
33 Paihia Domain-Opua
  Bush Walk
39 Old Wharf & Start
  of Paihia-Opua
  Coastal Walk
44 Roadrunner Tavern

Paihia & Waitangi

0   0.5   1 km

Haruru Falls

A few kilometres upstream from the *Tui* are the attractive Haruru Falls, also accessible via the walkway through Waitangi National Reserve. At the foot of the falls there's good swimming, several motor camps, a licensed restaurant and a tavern. If you wish to kayak to the base of the falls, see under the Sea Kayaking heading earlier in this section.

Walking

Just behind Paihia is the **Opua Forest**, a regenerating forest with a small stand of kauris and a number of walking tracks ranging from 10 minutes to three hours. If you walk up from School Rd for about 20 minutes, you'll find a couple of good lookouts. DOC publishes pamphlets with details on all the Opua Forest walks. You can also drive into the forest by taking the Oromahoe Rd west from Opua.

There is a variety of good short and long walks around the Bay of Islands and on the islands themselves. The park information centre in Russell and DOC Kerikeri have lots of information on walks.

Special Events

This region celebrates many special events. In January there is a **Tall Ships Race** at Russell. February has Waitangi Day on the 6th and a 10-day **arts festival**, with exhibits of touchable art, plays, music, comedy and dance.

There is a **Country Music Festival** in early May and a **Jazz & Blues Festival** in mid-August. September is 'foodies' month, with Russell's **Oyster Festival** and the very popular **Wine & Food Festival** in Paihia, on the Waitangi foreshore.

In October, the Auckland to Bay of Islands **Weekend Coastal Classic** – NZ's largest yacht race – is held.

Places to Stay

Camping & Cabins There are many camping grounds around Paihia and Waitangi, most of them near Haruru Falls. The *Tradewinds Resort* (☎ (09) 402 7525), beside the river and facing the falls, has

powered sites at $9 per person in peak season, and motel units at $89 to $97 in peak season but $59 to $63 at other times. The camp is well equipped with a large swimming pool, bar and restaurant.

The *Twin Pines Tourist Park* (☎ (09) 402 7322) on Puketona Rd at the falls has tent/powered sites at $7.50/8 per person, cabins and on-site caravans from $40 a double and tourist flats from $50. Next door, the *Falls Caravan Park* (☎ (09) 402 7816) has tent and powered sites at similar rates.

The *Bay of Islands Holiday Park* (☎ (09) 402 7646) is 3km from the falls, 6.5km from Paihia on Puketona Rd. It has tent/powered sites at $8.50/9.50 per person and cabins at $35 for two.

Smith's Holiday Camp (☎ (09) 402 7678) is a lovely spot right at the waterside, 2.5km south of Paihia towards Opua. Powered sites are $10 per person, cabins are $45 for two and motel units are from $85 a double.

Hostels Paihia has a good selection of backpackers hostels; all make bookings for activities at discounted prices.

There are several on Kings Rd, Paihia's 'hostel row'. The *Pipi Patch Lodge* (☎ (09) 402 7111; pipipatch@acb.co.nz) at No 18 is an excellent backpackers; it charges $16 for dorm beds, $40 for twins/doubles and $25 per person in units which sleep four. Each room has kitchen and bathroom facilities. There is also a pool, spa and bar with an outdoor patio, a great place for backpackers in the 'strip' to congregate.

The *Mousetrap* (☎ (09) 402 8182) at No 11 is comfortable and laid-back with spacious meeting areas and a verandah shaped like a ship's bridge. It costs $15 for dorm beds, and doubles and twins are $32. Another good hostel, the *Peppertree* (☎ (09) 402 6122) at No 15 is a sparkling, well-equipped place with good communal areas and a pool table. Dorm beds cost $16 or $18 in rooms with attached bathroom; doubles with bathroom cost $42. *Lodge Eleven* (☎ (09) 402 7487) on the corner of Kings and MacMurray Rds is a modern, clean place, charging $16 a night in dorms, $36 for twins and $38 for doubles. Each room has its own toilet and shower.

Just around the corner from Kings Rd, the *Pickled Parrot* (☎ (09) 402 6222) on Greys Lane is a good place in a nice setting with a pleasant outdoor area (and a 'pickled parrot'); dorms are $16 and doubles $38.

The *Centabay Lodge* (☎ (09) 402 7466) at 27 Selwyn Rd, in a good position just behind the shops, is part-hostel, part-tourist lodge. The standards of accommodation remain high and reasonably priced. Bunkrooms cost from $16 per person, doubles are $39, twin units with en suite are $49 and self-contained studios are from $50 to $75 (prices are seasonal).

The newcomer in town is *Tommy's* (☎ (09) 402 8668) on Davis Crescent. This is another purpose-built place with tidy dorm rooms for $16 per person ($20 in peak season), and twins and doubles for $34.

Down at the Waitangi end of Paihia the *Mayfair Lodge* (☎ (09) 402 7471) at 7 Puketona Rd has bunk beds from $15, and doubles for $36 in winter (extra in summer). It's well equipped with kitchen and lounge facilities, billiards, a barbecue and spa pool.

B&Bs & Guesthouses Several B&Bs are found around Paihia and the Bay of Islands; the information centre makes referrals and bookings. *Lilypond Orchard B&B* (☎ (09) 402 7041) on Puketona Rd is reasonable at $35/70 for singles/doubles. The *Cedar Suite* (☎ (09) 402 8516), 5 Sullivans Rd, is a slice of luxury at $88 for two for a self-contained studio apartment.

Motels In Paihia motels stand shoulder to shoulder along the waterfront; doubles are around $120 during the peak summer season, dropping to $80 or so during low season. Places to try (high-season rates are listed, winter rates will be considerably lower) are:

Al Motel (☎ (09) 402 7684) 46 Davis Crescent ($120 for doubles)
Aloha Motel (☎ (09) 402 7540) 36-38 Seaview Rd (doubles from $135)

Anchorage Motel (☎ (09) 402 7447) 2 Marsden Rd ($195 for doubles)
Ash Grove Motel (☎ (09) 402 7934) Blackbridge Rd, Haruru Falls ($101 for doubles)
Blue Pacific Motel (☎ (09) 402 7394) 166 Marsden Rd ($120 for doubles)
Bounty Inn (☎ (09) 402 7088) corner of Selwyn and Bayview Rds ($135 for doubles)
Dolphin Motel (☎ (09) 402 8170) 69 Williams Rd (singles/twins for $80/110)
Nautilus Resort (☎ 402 8604) Puketona Rd (price on application)
Star Motel (☎ (09) 402 7064) 78 Seaview Rd ($120 for doubles)

Hotels Paihia also has quite luxurious tourist hotels. The *Quality Resort Waitangi* (☎ (09) 402 7411) is in a nice setting, north across the bridge, with an excellent restaurant, bar and heated pool; standard rooms start from $160.

The *Paihia Holiday Motor Inn* (☎ (09) 402 7911) on Joyces Rd has a pool and well-equipped rooms from $102 a double.

Places to Eat
The *Blue Marlin Diner*, in the shopping mall overlooking the bay, is a no-frills greasy spoon but has cheap, filling breakfasts and other snacks and grills. The *Cafe Over the Bay*, upstairs in the shopping mall, has a good view of the bay and good, reasonably priced food too, with lots of European snacks and dishes (mostly French and Italian).

In the lane that runs though the shopping mall, *King Wah* is a licensed Chinese restaurant with dark décor and reasonably priced banquets and buffets ($15). Also here is the *Sidewalk*, a good place for a drink or meal at the tables out on the pavement.

The licensed *La Scala* restaurant on Selwyn Rd is a pricey place with a mixed seafood platter, including lobster, for two at about $75. The *Buccaneer*, to the north on Selwyn Rd, has good home-cooked meals at a reasonable price. The *Saltwater Cafe* at 14 Kings Rd is licensed and BYO, and open daily. It has an innovative blackboard menu; expect to pay about $25 each for a main meal, corkage and coffee.

At 41 Williams Rd, *Esmae's* is a fancy, licensed restaurant with interesting nouvelle

Kiwi cuisine at around $22 a main dish. Upstairs at 39 Williams Rd, *Ruffino* is a little pizza cafe with cheap meals; pastas and small pizzas are around $9.

Bistro 40 and *Only Seafood* are in a converted old home at 40 Marsden Rd with attractive décor and areas indoors and out overlooking the sea. Both have good food, with Only Seafood getting the best marks for moderately priced, excellent seafood.

The best value place in town is *Cafe Jisar* on the corner of Marsden Rd and Davis Crescent. Seafood chowder is $7.50, fish of the day is $17.50 and meat dishes are from $19 to $24. There is a courtesy vehicle from the hostel strip (☎ (09) 402 7779).

There are two places to eat at Kelly Tarlton's *Tui* – a simple cafe and the more stylish *Wheelhouse*.

Entertainment

The *Lighthouse Tavern* upstairs in the shopping mall on Marsden Rd has a restaurant and a pub, and features live bands ($3 cover charge). At Haruru Falls the *Twin Pines* has a tavern with house brews on tap and entertainment on weekends. The *Roadrunner* pub is a five-minute drive south of Paihia.

The barn-like *Paihia Swordfish Club* on Marsden Rd allows nonmembers when it suits them; it is a far cry from the intimate little clubhouse that once stood on this spot.

RUSSELL

Russell (population 1100) is a short ferry ride across the bay. It was originally a fortified Maori settlement which spread over the entire valley, then known as Kororareka.

Russell's early European history was turbulent. In 1830 it was the scene of the 'war of the girls', when two Maori girls from different tribes each thought they were the favourite of a whaling captain. This resulted in conflict between the tribes, which the Maori leader, Titore, who was recognised as the chief of chiefs in the area, attempted to resolve by separating the two tribes and making the border at the base of the Tapeka Peninsula. A European settlement quickly sprang up in place of the abandoned Maori village.

In 1845 the government sent in soldiers and marines to garrison the town when the Maori leader Hone Heke threatened to chop down the flagstaff – symbol of Pakeha authority – for the fourth time. On 11 March 1845 the Maoris staged a diversionary siege of Russell. It was a great tactical success, with Chief Kawiti attacking from the south and another Maori war party attacking from Long Beach. While the troops rushed off to protect the township, Hone Heke felled the hated symbol of European authority on Maiki Hill for the final time. The Pakeha were forced to evacuate to ships lying at anchor off the settlement. The captain of HMS *Hazard* was wounded severely in the battle and his replacement ordered the ships' cannons to be fired on the town – most of the buildings were razed.

Russell today is a peaceful and pretty little place which justifiably features 'romantic' in its self-promotion. It's a marked contrast to the hustle of Paihia across the bay.

Information

There is no information office. Fullers (☎ (09) 403 7866) at the land end of the pier may reluctantly proffer information. Get a copy of *Russell: Kororareka* from the Bay of Islands Visitor Information Centre in Paihia.

The excellent Bay of Islands Maritime & Historic Park Visitor Centre (☎ (09) 403 7685) is in Russell – see under the Bay of Islands Maritime & Historic Park heading earlier in this section. The free *Russell Heritage Trails* pamphlet includes walking and driving tours.

Russell Museum

The Russell Museum was built for the bicentenary of Cook's Bay of Islands visit in 1769. It's small but it houses maritime exhibits, displays relating to Cook and his voyages, and a fine 1:5 scale model of his barque *Endeavour* – a real working model – in addition to a collection of early settlers' relics. The museum is open from 10 am to 4 pm daily ($2.50, children 50c).

Pompallier House

Close by, and on a lovely waterfront site, is Pompallier House, built to house the printing works for the Roman Catholic mission founded by the French missionary Bishop Pompallier in 1841. It also served as a tannery and in the 1870s was converted to a private home. One of the oldest houses in NZ, it has a small museum. It is open from 10 am to 5 pm daily, but is closed on weekends from June to October ($5).

Maiki (Flagstaff Hill)

Overlooking Russell is Maiki (Flagstaff Hill), where Hone Heke made his attacks – this, the fifth flagpole, has stood for a lot longer than the first four. The view is well worth the trouble to get up there, and there are several routes to the top. By car take Tapeka Rd, or on foot take the track west from the boat ramp along the beach at low tide, or up Wellington St at high tide. Alternatively, simply walk to the end of Wellington St and take the short track up the hill, about a 30-minute climb.

Long Beach

About 1km behind Russell to the east is

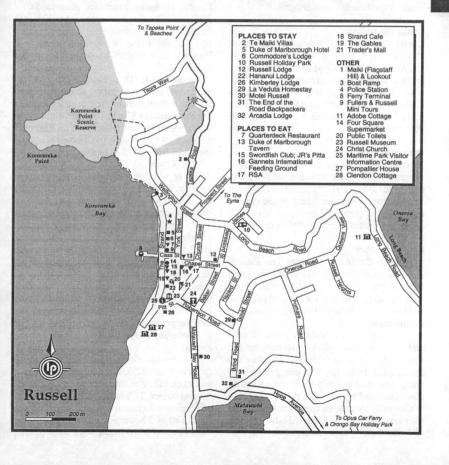

PLACES TO STAY
2   Te Maiki Villas
5   Duke of Marlborough Hotel
6   Commodore's Lodge
10 Russell Holiday Park
12 Russell Lodge
22 Hananui Lodge
26 Kimberley Lodge
29 La Veduta Homestay
30 Motel Russell
31 The End of the Road Backpackers
32 Arcadia Lodge

PLACES TO EAT
7   Quarterdeck Restaurant
13 Duke of Marlborough Tavern
15 Swordfish Club; JR's Pitta
16 Gannets International Feeding Ground
17 RSA
18 Strand Cafe
19 The Gables
21 Trader's Mall

OTHER
1   Maiki (Flagstaff Hill) & Lookout
3   Boat Ramp
4   Police Station
8   Ferry Terminal
9   Fullers & Russell Mini Tours
11 Adobe Cottage
14 Four Square Supermarket
20 Public Toilets
23 Russell Museum
24 Christ Church
25 Maritime Park Visitor Information Centre
27 Pompallier House
28 Clendon Cottage

Russell

0   100   200 m

Oneroa Bay, with a beautiful beach known variously as Oneroa Bay Beach, Donkey Bay Beach or Long Beach. There is an interesting adobe house here. It's about a 15-minute walk from the Russell wharf, heading over the hill on Long Beach Rd. When you reach the hill's summit, at the intersection with Queen's View Rd, there's a tiny graveyard with benches and a good view of Oneroa Bay. Take a turn here and go about one block up Queen's View Rd to where it meets Oneroa Rd and the view is even better – a sweeping vista of the peninsula. There's an unofficial nudist beach past the rocky outcrops at the beach's northern end.

Other Attractions
Christ Church on Robertson Rd is the oldest church in NZ. Built in 1835, it is suitably scarred with musket and cannon ball holes, and has an interesting graveyard.

Clendon Cottage was built by James Clendon, US Consul in 1839, who later moved to Rawene (see that section) as resident magistrate.

Organised Tours
Russell Mini Tours (☎ (09) 403 7866) departs from Fullers, fronting the pier, several times daily and charges $12 (children $6) for a one-hour tour. Many of the cruises out of Paihia pick up passengers at Russell about 15 minutes after their Paihia departure.

Places to Stay
Camping, Cabins & Hostels The *Russell Holiday Park* (☎ (09) 403 7826) on Long Beach Rd has tent/powered sites at $8/10 per person, cabins with kitchen from $56 for two and tourist flats from $89 a double; prices are for the high season.

The *Orongo Bay Holiday Park* (☎ (09) 403 7704) is 3km south of Russell on the road to the Opua car ferry. Orongo Bay has backpacker beds for $15 per person and camp sites at $8 per person. There's a swimming pool and a TV/games room.

Centrally located on the corner of Beresford and Chapel Sts, *Russell Lodge* (☎ (09) 403 7640) has budget units, each with four bunks and private toilet, at $16 per person most of the year, or you can get the whole unit for $48 for two. There is a large, fully equipped kitchen, a pool table and a separate TV lounge. The motel units, sleeping four to six people, range from $75 to $105.

The *End of the Road* (☎ (09) 403 7632) is a small but comfortable backpackers at the end of Brind St; a bed in a share room is $16 and the one double room is $36.

B&Bs, Motels & Hotels Good B&Bs include: the very swish *Villa Helios* (☎ (09) 403 7229) at 44 du Fresne Place, Tapeka Point, with double/executive villas for $160/225; *La Veduta Homestay* (☎ (09) 403 8299), on the corner of Gould and Hazard Sts; and the *Eyrie* (☎ (09) 403 7306) at 7 Prospect St, a modern home with rooms for $65/85.

Arcadia Lodge (☎ (09) 403 7756) on Florance Ave has great views over Matauwhi Bay; in summer, B&B is from $85 for two (larger suites are $140). The free-standing *Te Maiki Villas* (☎ (09) 403 7046) on Flagstaff Rd have awesome views of Russell Harbour; they cost from $145 a double.

The *Commodore's Lodge* (☎ (09) 403 7899) is a stylish old building right on the waterfront. Well-equipped units with kitchens sleeping up to six people cost $190 in summer. There is a pool in the central courtyard; rates are halved in the off season. Similar, though more modern, is the *Hananui Lodge* (☎ (09) 403 7875), which backs on to the waterfront. Self-contained motel units cost from $75 up to $180 in the peak season. Russell also has a range of other motels. The *Motel Russell* (☎ (09) 403 7854) has doubles for $125 ($65 in the off season). The top place in town (with a price to match) is *Kimberley Lodge* (☎ (09) 403 70900) on Pitt St.

The fine old *Duke of Marlborough Hotel* (☎ (09) 403 7829), right on the waterfront, would certainly be the place to stay if money was no object. This is a place with some real old-fashioned charm. It has 'budget' rooms from $80 and better rooms with waterfront views (up to $210 in the high season). All rooms have private facilities, including tea and coffee-making equipment and a colour TV.

Places to Eat

Russell has several cafes and takeaways, including the waterfront *Strand* with sandwiches, snacks, a courtyard at the back and a verandah in front. Close by is the small *JR's*, where you get excellent lamb pitta bread rolls for $6.50 (and an impressive collection of sauces). In the Traders Mall, *Penny's Place* is a licensed cafe and takeaway with Chinese food and pizzas.

The *Duke of Marlborough Tavern* has typical pub food in its family section, with main dishes costing around $15. More refined dining can be had in the restaurant at the *Duke of Marlborough Hotel* on the waterfront, or the lounge bar and tables out front are a great place for a drink on a sunny day.

Also on the waterfront are the more upmarket *Quarterdeck* and licensed *Gables*, with main courses for around $20. *Gannets International Feeding Ground* on the corner of York and Chapel Sts is a quality brasserie with a blackboard menu and good seafood choices.

Entertainment

The *Duke of Marlborough Tavern* was the first pub in NZ to get a licence, back on 14 July 1840. Its three predecessors all burnt down. The tavern, in the block behind the hotel, has both a family room and a more serious, perhaps 'rougher', bar. If you want cheaper beer then go to the friendly *RSA*; a member will sign you in. The *Swordfish Club* is also worth a visit; again you need to be signed in by a member.

Getting There & Away

Your choices are to come on the passenger ferry from Paihia ($3 each way), to drive or hitch in via the Opua car ferry, or take the Northliner bus.

Fullers runs a continuous shuttle service during the day from Opua to Okiato Point, still some distance from Russell. This ferry operates from 6.50 am to 9 pm (10 pm on Friday). The one-way fare is $7 for a car and driver, $12 for a campervan and driver, $3.50 for a motorcycle and rider, plus $1 for each additional adult passenger. There's a much longer dirt road which avoids the Opua ferry, but it's a long haul.

OPUA

As well as being the car ferry terminus, Opua is a deep-sea port from which primary produce (meat, wool and butter) is exported. The town was established as a coaling port in the 1870s, when the railway line was constructed. Before the wharf was built, after WWI, the coal was transported out to ships on lighters (flat-bottomed barges). Today, the occasional cruise ship may be seen alongside the wharf, as well as many local and foreign yachts during summer.

The **Opua Forest**, for the most part a regenerating forest, is open to the public. There are lookouts up graded tracks from the access roads and a few large trees have escaped axe and fire, including some fairly big kauris. You can enter the forest by walking in from Paihia on School Rd (see under the Paihia & Waitangi heading), driving in from Opua on the Oromahoe Rd, or a couple of other access roads. The Bay of Islands Visitor Information Centre in Paihia has leaflets.

The *Ferrymans Restaurant & Bistro* by the car ferry is a great place to sit out by the waterside and enjoy a light meal. *Opua General Stores* has filling rolls for $3.50 and huge ice-cream cones for 90c.

Vintage Railway

There's a historic steam train service that operates from Opua to Kawakawa, running from Saturday to Tuesday in winter and daily except Friday in summer. The trip takes 45 minutes each way and a one-way/return ticket costs $10/16 (children $6/10).

KERIKERI

At the northern end of the bay, Kerikeri (population 1700) is a laid-back provincial town. It has plenty of accommodation and can be used as a base for exploring the Bay

NORTHLAND

of Islands, but is primarily a service town for the surrounding agricultural district.

The word *kerikeri* means 'to dig' and it was right here, in 1820, that the first agricultural plough was introduced to NZ, and also that the Maori grew large crops of kumara (sweet potato) before the Pakeha arrived. Today it is still primarily an agricultural region, with kiwi fruit, citrus and other

orchards. Large numbers of itinerant farm-workers congregate in Kerikeri for the six-week kiwi fruit harvest beginning in early May, but orchard work of one kind or another is usually available year-round.

Kerikeri is significant in NZ history. It became the site of the country's second mission station when the Reverend Samuel Marsden chose the site at the head of the

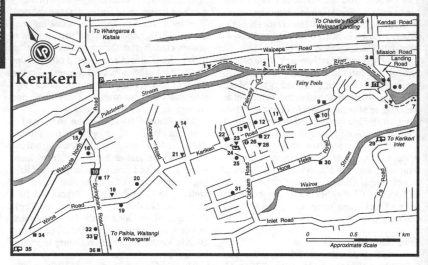

PLACES TO STAY

3	Glenfalloch Homestay B&B
9	Kerikeri YHA Hostel
11	Abiline Motel
14	Aranga Holiday Park
17	Kerikeri Farm Hostel
22	Central Motel
27	Cottle Court Motel
29	Pagoda Lodge Caravan Park
30	Hone Heke Lodge
34	The Trekker's Rest
35	Hideaway Lodge & Adventure Park
36	Puriri Park

PLACES TO EAT

1	Friends Restaurant
8	Stone Store Tearooms & Restaurant
18	Rocket Cafe; Robb's Winery
21	Gourmandise Restaurant
23	Black Olive
28	Raptures Organic Cafe; Blue Indonesian

OTHER

2	Rainbow Falls
4	Scenic Reserve & Car Park
5	Kemp House; Stone Store
6	Rewa's Maori Village & Visitors Centre
7	Kororipo Pa
10	Red Barn Pottery
12	Price Choppers
13	New World Supermarket
15	Origin Art & Craft Cooperative
16	Blue Gum Pottery
19	Spectrum Glass
20	The Kauri Workshop
24	Post Office; Bus Station
25	Cathay Cinema & Restaurant
26	Public Toilets
31	Keriblue Ceramics
32	The Orange Centre
33	Annie's Bar & McCrae's Hotel

Kerikeri inlet under the protection of the Maori chief, Hongi Hika. In November 1819 the Reverend John Butler arrived at the site and set up the mission headquarters. New Zealand's oldest wooden building, Kemp House, and its oldest stone building, the Stone Store, were established as part of this mission.

The visitor centre at Rewa's Maori Village has pamphlets. Get information on walks in the area from DOC (☎ (09) 407 8474) on Landing Rd.

Stone Store & Kemp House
The Stone Store is the oldest stone building in NZ; construction began in 1833 and was completed in 1836. The river in front of the Stone Store is subject to flooding, and floods and time have taken their toll on the building. Long-standing renovations are still in progress and the building is closed.

Kemp House is NZ's oldest surviving building, a remarkable fact given that it is made of wood. It was erected in 1821 by the Reverend John Butler, who was the first head of the Church Missionary Society's new station. Still complete with original fittings and chattels, it's open daily from 10 am to 6 pm in summer (less frequently in winter); entry is $5 (students $2).

Rewa's Maori Village
Just across the river from the Stone Store, Rewa's Maori Village is built on a site thought to have been occupied at one time by Chief Rewa. The various buildings are part of an authentic reproduction of a *kainga*, a pre-European unfortified Maori village, with various dwellings, kitchen buildings, storerooms and so on, and exhibits of the many plants the Maori used. It's open daily ($2, children 50c).

Waimate North Mission House
This is NZ's second oldest surviving house. Built of kauri between 1831 and 1832, it was the Anglican Waimate Mission from 1832 to 1841 and the home of NZ's first Anglican bishop, Bishop Selwyn, from 1842 to 1844. It can be reached from SH1 between Ohaea-

wai and Okaihau by turning off at Te Ahuahu, or from SH10 by turning off at Puketona. It is open daily, except Thursday and Friday, from 10 am to 4.30 pm. Adjacent to the building is the Church of St John the Baptist (1871). An entry fee is charged.

Art & Craft Shops
The Kerikeri area is home to many artists and artisans. Several shops display their work, and in most you can see work in progress, especially pottery. On Kerikeri Rd at the northern end of town is Red Barn Pottery; at the south side, also on Kerikeri Rd, is Spectrum Glass (stained/leaded glass) and the Kauri Workshop. On SH10 there are several good shops, including the Origin Art & Craft Cooperative with many kinds of craft, and Blue Gum Pottery. At 13 Mill Lane, in town, is Keriblue Ceramics.

Walking
Just up the hill behind the Stone Store is a marked Historical Walk which takes about 10 minutes and leads to **Kororipo Pa**, the fortress of Maori chief Hongi Hika. Huge warfaring parties of Maori once departed from here on raids, terrorising most of the North Island. The walk emerges near the St James Anglican church, built in 1878.

Across the bridge from the Stone Store is a scenic reserve with several marked tracks. There's a 4km Kerikeri River track leading to Rainbow Falls, passing by the Wharepoke Falls (Fairy Pools) along the way. Alternatively, you can reach the Rainbow Falls from Waipapa Rd, in which case it's only a 10-minute walk to the falls. The Fairy Pools are great for swimming and picnics and can be reached from the dirt road beside the YHA hostel if you aren't up to the hike along the river. Get the free *Kerikeri Basin Walks* from the Bay of Islands Visitor Information Centre in Paihia.

Places to Stay
Camping & Cabins The *Pagoda Lodge Caravan Park* (☎ (07) 407 8617) is on Pa Rd at the inlet near the Stone Store. Powered

sites are $10 per person and tourist flats are $60 for two.

The *Aranga Holiday Park* (☎ (09) 407 9326) is on Kerikeri Rd in a lovely setting beside the Puketotara River, only five minutes walk from town. Tent/powered sites are $8/9 per person, cabins are $30 for two and a tourist flat with private facilities is $56 for two. The *Hideaway Lodge* (☎ (09) 407 9773) on Wiroa Rd has tent sites for $7.50 per person (see also Hostels).

Hostels Kerikeri's hostels attract both tourists and itinerant workers, catered for in large dorms; some will help to find orchard work.

The *Kerikeri Farm Hostel* (☎ (09) 407 6989) on SH10, 1.5km north of the Kerikeri turn-off, holds the record for readers letters this edition. It is a pleasant farm and the friendly owners encourage you to participate in farm activities – squeeze your own organic orange juice or crack a bowl of macadamia nuts. Dorms are $15, twins and doubles are $34 and a self-contained unit is $60.

Along Wiroa Rd, 3km from Kerikeri, the *Trekkers Rest* (☎ (09) 407 7270) is a small, friendly place in nice surroundings; a dorm bed is $14 and twins or doubles are $36. They will pick you up from Kerikeri.

The *Kerikeri YHA Hostel* (☎ (09) 407 9391) on Kerikeri Rd charges $14 for a dorm or $34 for doubles. The *Hone Heke Lodge* (☎ (09) 407 8170), an itinerant picker's haven, is on Hone Heke Rd in a quiet residential area; the cost is $12 to $14 in bunkrooms and $34 to $40 for twin or double rooms. It has a new games room but the rest of the place looks tired.

The *Hideaway Lodge* (☎ (09) 407 9773) is on Wiroa Rd, west of the SH10 junction. It's 4km out but offers free rides to town. Dorms are $12, twin or double rooms are from $30, and there's a field where tent sites are $7.50 per person. It has a pool, barbecue and games room.

B&Bs & Guesthouses The Paihia visitor centre has details on B&Bs in the area. *Stoneybroke* (☎ (09) 407 7371) on Edmonds Rd, 12km east of Kerikeri near Kerikeri inlet,

has singles/doubles for $35/60. *Puriri Park* (☎ (09) 407 9818) on SH10 is a comfortable cottage offering double B&B for $75. It also has two-bedroom self-contained units from $55. A place recommended by readers is *Glenfalloch Homestay B&B* (☎ (09) 407 5471) on Landing Rd, which charges from $95 to $125 for a double.

Motels The *Abilene Motel* (☎ (09) 407 9203) at 136 Kerikeri Rd has a swimming pool and 10 units, two with private spa pools, from $78 for two.

The *Central Motel* (☎ (09) 407 8921) on Main Rd has units with features like a waterbed suite, swimming and spa pools, colour TVs and so on. Summer rates start at $75 for two, dropping to $65 in winter. The *Cottle Court Motel* (☎ (09) 407 8867) on Kerikeri Rd is reasonably priced, charging from $68/70 a single/double.

Places to Eat

Cafes and restaurants in town include *Raptures Organic Cafe*, with a wholefood menu including pastas for $15; the *Black Olive*, which has medium/large gourmet pizzas for $15/20; and the *Blue Indonesian*, with succulent dishes for $13.50 (such as pak prik Thai chilli and King Po chicken).

Across from the Stone Store the *Stone Store Restaurant* is open daily from 9 am to 9 pm. It's a lovely spot to eat indoors or out on the verandah overlooking the inlet.

More expensive places include the licensed *Friends Restaurant*, five minutes out of town on Waipapa Rd, which features music on some nights; the *Rocket Cafe* in Robb's Fruit Winery, which is one of the best cafes in Northland; and the upmarket *Gourmandise*, opposite the BP service station on Kerikeri Rd.

If you are after a drink, *Annie's Bar* in McCrae's Hotel on SH10 is a good choice; relax next to the big open fire. Dine in at the restaurant at the atmospheric Cathay Cinema before taking in a current movie.

Getting There & Away

InterCity and Northliner Express buses come

and go from Kerikeri Holiday Shoppe (☎ (09) 407 8013) on Cobham Rd, just off Kerikeri Rd in the town centre; see the Getting Around section at the start of the chapter. Both companies have buses departing from Kerikeri in the morning for the half-hour trip to Paihia, returning in the evening.

Paihia to Whangarei

There are two very scenic drives out on the east coast: the back road from Russell to SH1, and the drive out to Tutukaka from Hikurangi on SH1, which loops around to Whangarei. Out to sea are the Poor Knights Islands.

RUSSELL ROAD

The back road from Russell skirts around the coast before joining SH1 at Whakapara. The road is long, unsealed and rough for the most of the way but scenic. It is for those with their own transport, plenty of time and a desire to get off the beaten track.

From Russell, the road starts near Orongo Bay and skirts along the Waikare Inlet before reaching the Waikare Rd to Waihaha. This turn-off eventually leads back to the highway and Paihia, about a 90-minute drive all up from Russell.

Continuing along the Russell Road past the Waihaha turn-off, there's access to the **Ngaiotonga Scenic Reserve**, which preserves the mixed forest that was once predominant throughout Northland. There are two short walks, suitable for families. The 20-minute **Kauri Grove Nature Walk** and the 10-minute **Twin Bole Kauri Walk** both provide opportunities to see these majestic trees.

Another side trip from the Russell Road is to take the northern Manawaora Rd, which passes many small bays, including **Parekura Bay**, where there is accommodation and boat rental. Further on is the turn-off to isolated **Rawhiti**, a small Maori settlement where life still revolves around the marae. Past the

marae on the headland is the *Rawhiti Motor Camp*, which has a small shop, camp sites, some on-site vans and stunning views of the Bay of Islands. Boat hire and dive refills are available.

Rawhiti is also the starting point for the trek to **Cape Brett**, a hard 7½-hour walk to the top of the peninsula, where overnight stays are possible in the Cape Brett Hut. Book the hut and get information on the walk at the Bay of Islands Maritime & Historic Park Visitor Centre (☎ (09) 403 7685) in Russell.

Closer to the Rawhiti turn-off, a shorter one-hour walk leads through Maori land and over the headland to Whangamumu Harbour. At the main beach on the harbour, the **Whangamumu Scenic Reserve** has a 'back to nature' camping ground. There are over 40 prehistoric sites on the peninsula and the remains of an unusual whaling station. A net, fastened between the mainland and Net Rock, was used to ensnare or slow down whales so the harpooners could get an easy shot in. The whales taken were mainly humpbacks; in 1927 over 70 whales were trapped in this fashion.

Further south, another side road leads to the **Whangaruru North Head Scenic Reserve**, which has beaches, camping grounds, walks and fine coastal scenery in a farmland park setting; camping is $5 per person. Pohutukawa, puriri and kowhai abound and many bird species can be seen in the area. The small settlement of Whangaruru North, just before the reserve, also has a motor camp, as does Oakura on the other side of the harbour.

The *Whangaruru Harbour Backpackers Beach House* (☎ (09) 433 6806) gives the budget-conscious the option to stop in this magnificent isolated region; the cost is $15 per person.

At Helena Bay, Russell Road returns to tarseal and leads back to SH1. About 8km from Helena Bay along a rough, winding side road is the **Mimiwhangata Coastal Park**. This is a truly scenic part of the coastline, with coastal dunes, pohutukawa, jutting headlands and picturesque beaches. DOC has a luxurious lodge sleeping 10 that costs $550 per week ($450 in winter) and a simpler but comfortable cottage for eight at $350 per week ($250 in winter); camping is also possible ($4). Book with DOC in Whangarei or Russell.

TUTUKAKA COAST

At Hikurangi on SH1 you can turn off and take a very scenic route to Whangarei. From Hikurangi, the first place on the coast is Sandy Bay surf beach, where you can horse trek on a little-frequented piece of the east coast. There is a succession of idyllic bays from here on – Woolley's, Whale (with some excellent walks), Matapouri, Church, Kowharewa, Pacific, Dolphin and Whangaumu (Wellingtons). All have scope for walking, boating, swimming and, most popularly, fishing.

Small, exclusive **Tutukaka** is the home of the Whangarei Deep Sea Anglers Club and the beautiful harbour is cluttered with yachts and fishing boats. The tiny yacht club here launched a multi-million dollar challenge for the 1995 America's Cup, eventually won by Auckland-based *Black Magic*.

Tutukaka is best known as a premier gamefishing destination, and late in the day marlin and other catch are weighed in. The well-organised Tutukaka Charter Boat Association (☎ (09) 434 3818) at the marina handles fishing, diving and cruise charters.

Ngunguru, a few kilometres south of Tutukaka, has food outlets, accommodation, petrol, a laundrette and a sports complex. You can get from Whangarei to Ngunguru ($6, children $3) and Tutukaka ($7, children $3.50) on weekdays with Tuatara Transit (☎ 025 529 722).

Places to Stay & Eat

At Sandy Bay, *Whananaki Trail Rides* (☎ (09) 433 8299) has backpackers farmhouse beds for $15, a three-berth caravan for $25 and camping for free. Horse trekking is $30 for two hours, or a two-day trek is $150.

The *Tutukaka Hotel* (☎ (09) 434 3854) charges $60 a double. *Pacific Rendezvous* (☎ (09) 434 3847) is an exclusive resort on its own headland just south of Tutukaka; one to three-bedroom, self-contained chalets are from $110 in summer ($85 in winter).

If you love seafood, Tutukaka is paradise. The places to go for a meal are the *Tutukaka Hotel*, *Scnappa Rock* and the *Blue Marlin* (☎ (09) 434 3909) in the Whangarei Deep Sea Anglers Club.

At Ngunguru, the motor camp (☎ (09) 434 3851) on Papaka Rd has camp sites at $20 for two and on-site vans from $35. The *Chalet Court Motel* (☎ (09) 434 3786) charges from $60 a double, while the well-situated *Brimar Lodge* (☎ (09) 434 3844) on Ngunguru Rd charges from $75 with breakfast.

POOR KNIGHTS ISLANDS MARINE RESERVE

This marine reserve, 24km off Northland's east coast near Tutukaka, was established in 1981. It is reputed to have the best scuba diving in NZ and has been rated as one of the top diving spots in the world.

The two large islands, Tawhiti Rangi and Aorangi, were once home to members of the Ngati-wai tribe but, since a massacre in the early 1800s by a raiding party, the islands have been *tapu* (sacred). You're *not* allowed to land on the islands but you can swim near them.

Since the northern islands are bathed in a subtropical current, varieties of tropical and subtropical fish not seen in other coastal waters are observed. The waters are clear and there are no problems with sediment. The underwater cliffs drop steeply (about 70m) to a sandy bottom, where there is a labyrinth of archways, caves and tunnels, packed with a bewildering variety of fish.

As the islands are relatively isolated from the mainland they have acted as a sanctuary for flora and fauna – the most famous example is the prehistoric tuatara.

Diving trips depart from Whangarei, Tutukaka and elsewhere. A sightseeing day trip on the boats costs around $75 (children $55). Divers should count on $125 for full diving equipment and two dives.

Operators in Tutukaka are Knight Line

(☎ (09) 434 3733), the Tutukaka Charter Boat Association (☎ (09) 434 3818), Pacific Hideaway (☎ (09) 434 3675) and Aqua Action Adventures (☎ (09) 434 3867). In Whangarei, contact the Dive Shop (☎ (09) 438 3521) on Water St, the Dive Connection (☎ (09) 430 0818) at 140 Lower Cameron St and Sub Aqua Dive (☎ (09) 438 1075) at 41 Clyde St. The MV *Wairangi* (☎ (09) 434 3350) has interesting ecotourism trips along the coast and to the islands; ring for costs and itineraries.

Whangarei

Whangarei (population 45,000) is the major city of Northland and a haven for yachts. It is a pleasant, thriving city with an equable climate, though its main attractions are in the surrounding area. The beaches at Whangarei Heads, about 35km east of town, are incredibly scenic and have many tiny bays and inlets.

The climate and soil combine to make Whangarei a gardener's paradise – many parks and gardens thrive in this city.

Information
The helpful and friendly Whangarei Visitors Bureau (☎ (09) 438 1079; fax 438 2943) is at Tarewa Park on Otaika Rd, on SH1 at the southern entrance to town. It's open daily in summer from 8.30 am to 6.30 pm; in winter, it's open on weekdays from 8.30 am to 5 pm and weekends from 10 am to 3 pm. There is a cafe which overlooks a 'kid-friendly' park, with weekend toy train rides.

The AA office (☎ (09) 438 4848) is on the corner of Robert and John Sts. DOC (☎ (09) 438 0299), next door to the visitors bureau, has information on camping, recreational activities, maps and hut tickets, as well as an environmental shop with souvenirs.

Things to See & Do
Boats from around the world are moored in **Town Basin**, an attractive area right on the edge of the town centre along Quay St. The waterfront along the river has been renovated and includes the **Clapham Clock Museum** (☎ (09) 438 3993), which has an awesome 1300 timepieces, all ticking away furiously. Don't worry, clepsydra, skeleton, speaker's, 'nark', chess, gravity, tower, coconut, balloon, grandfather, 400 day and hickory dickory dock are all clocks. It is open from 10 am to 5 pm daily ($5, children $3, including a guided tour).

Also at the Town Basin is the **Museum of Fishes**, open from 10 am to 4 pm daily ($3.50, children $1.50). Fishing enthusiasts will appreciate the stuffed game fish – otherwise forget it.

Spanning a stream in the centre of town, **Cafler Park** has well-tended flowerbeds, and the Margie Maddren Fernery & Snow Conservatory, NZ's only all-native fernery with over 80 varieties on display. Both are open daily from 10 am to 4 pm (entry is free).

The Northland Craft Trust, known simply as **The Quarry**, is about 500m west of town in an old quarry. This artists cooperative has studios where you can observe work in progress or buy craft at the showroom. It is open daily from 10 am to 4 pm.

West of Whangarei, 5km out on the Dargaville road at Maunu, is the **Whangarei Museum**, open from 10 am to 4 pm daily. The museum includes a kiwi house, the 1885 Clarke Homestead and the Exhibition Centre museum, which houses European relics and an impressive collection of Maori artefacts (including superb feather cloaks).

The museum park also has an old locomotive, which runs in summer, and an abandoned mercury mine. Entry is $7 (children $3.50), or $3 for any one of the venues.

Scenic Reserves & Walks
The 26m-high **Whangarei Falls** are very photogenic, with water cascading over the edge of an old basalt lava flow. Next to the Ngunguru Rd, in the suburb of Tikipunga, 5km north of the town centre, the falls can be reached by Tikipunga bus (weekdays only). The surrounding domain has three natural pools in the river and numerous picnic spots.

The **AH Reed Memorial Kauri Park**

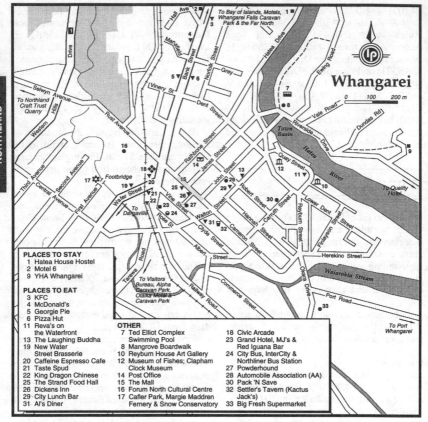

Whangarei

0   100   200 m

PLACES TO STAY
1 Hatea House Hostel
2 Motel 6
9 YHA Whangarei

PLACES TO EAT
3 KFC
4 McDonald's
5 Georgie Pie
6 Pizza Hut
11 Reva's on
   the Waterfront
13 The Laughing Buddha
19 New Water
   Street Brasserie
20 Caffeine Espresso Cafe
21 Taste Spud
22 King Dragon Chinese
25 The Strand Food Hall
26 Dickens Inn
29 City Lunch Bar
31 Al's Diner

OTHER
7 Ted Elliot Complex
   Swimming Pool
8 Mangrove Boardwalk
10 Reyburn House Art Gallery
12 Museum of Fishes; Clapham
   Clock Museum
14 Post Office
15 The Mall
16 Forum North Cultural Centre
17 Cafler Park, Margie Maddren
   Fernery & Snow Conservatory

18 Civic Arcade
23 Grand Hotel, MJ's &
   Red Iguana Bar
24 City Bus, InterCity &
   Northliner Bus Station
27 Powderhound
28 Automobile Association (AA)
30 Pack 'N Save
32 Settler's Tavern (Kactus
   Jack's)
33 Big Fresh Supermarket

spans a pretty stream and has a waterfall, several easy walkways and over 50 kinds of native trees including punga, totara and large kauris (some up to 3m in diameter). It's 5km north-east of town, out on Whareora Rd.

The **Waimahanga Walkway** in Onerahi is an easy walk along an old railway embankment. It takes two hours and passes through mangrove swamps and over a 300m timber truss harbour bridge. The free *Whangarei Walks* describes more walks.

Activities

The Whangarei Visitors Bureau provides a leaflet on activities and attractions. Whangarei is a popular centre for diving and fishing, mostly organised out of Tutukaka. The Whangarei Tramping Club (☎ (09) 436 1441) welcomes visitors. Northland Districts Aero Club (☎ (09) 436 0890) has scenic flights; Whangarei City Riding Centre (☎ (09) 437 5710) runs horse treks; Northland Coastal Adventures (☎ (09) 436 0139) has a variety of trips – beach and bush walks, kayaking, fishing and snorkelling included (ring for details); and Farm Safaris (☎ (09) 432 3794) has quad bike trips through a working farm at Maungakaramea

($40 per person; one hour; minimum of four people).

The Ted Elliot complex on Ewing Rd has indoor and outdoor pools, saunas and spas. Entry is $2.50 (children $1).

Places to Stay

Camping & Cabins The *Alpha Caravan Park* (☎ (09) 438 9867) at 34 Tarewa Rd is centrally located, less than 1km from town. Tent and powered sites are $14 for two and self-contained motel units are $60 for two. The *Whangarei Holiday Park & Cabins* (☎ (09) 437 6856) on Mair St, 2.5km from the town centre by Mair Park, has tent or powered sites at $8 per person and cabins at $28 for two.

The *Otaika Motel & Caravan Park* (☎ (09) 438 1459), 136 Otaika Rd, is at the southern entrance to Whangarei, with tent and powered sites at $8 per person and well-equipped tourist flats at $38/45 for singles/doubles.

The *Whangarei Falls Caravan Park* (☎ (09) 437 0609, 0800 227 222), 5km from town, is a good place with swimming and spa pools and cheap backpacker accommodation. There are tent and caravan sites at $9 per person, bunk beds at $13 and cabins at $32/42 for two/three.

Other camping and caravan sites include *Kamo Springs Caravan Park* (☎ (09) 435 1208) at 55 Great North Rd, Kamo, and the *Blue Heron Holiday Park* (☎ (09) 436 2293) on Tamaterau Beach.

Hostels The *YHA Whangarei* (☎ (09) 438 8954), 52 Punga Grove Ave, is a small, easygoing hostel with fine views. A bed costs $14 in a dorm or $16 in a twin or double room. It's a short walk from town, but the final climb is up a steep hill – take the signposted short cut from Dundas Rd if walking.

Hatea House Hostel (☎ (09) 437 6174), 67 Hatea Drive, has bunk beds for $14 and twins/doubles for $34/38.

Motels & Hotels Whangarei's budget motels generally charge from around $60 to $80 a double. The following are good: *Motel 6*

(☎ (09) 438 9219), 153 Bank St; *Burgundy Rose* (☎ (09) 437 3500), 100 Kamo Rd; *Redwood Lodge* (☎ (09) 437 6843) on the corner of Hatea Drive and Drummond St; *San Jose* (☎ (09) 438 7459), 10 Cross St (with budget units for $50); *Cypress Court* (☎ (09) 437 6193), 29 Kamo Rd; and the *Continental Motel* (☎ (09) 437 6359), 67 Kamo Rd.

The *Quality Hotel* (☎ (09) 438 0284) is 500m from the city on Riverside Drive; a standard double is $115 and a suite is $155.

Places to Eat

Restaurants The *Eating Out* guide, available from the visitor centre, has a comprehensive rundown on Whangarei's many restaurants. *Reva's on the Waterfront* in the Town Basin has a Tex-Mex and seafood menu; a dinner main is from $8.50 to $23. It often has live music.

The *King Dragon Chinese*, 11-13 Lower Bank St, is good for Cantonese banquets and does lunch buffets on weekdays. The *Laughing Buddha*, 79 Walton St, is a gourmet vegetarian cafe, open daily for lunch and from Thursday to Saturday for dinner.

The *New Water Street Brasserie*, 24 Water St, has a typical lamb/fish/venison/steak menu and a reputation as one of Whangarei's best restaurants. Try the Vietnamese fried fish with tamarind and coriander for $20. *MJ's* in the Grand Hotel at 2 Bank St is also pretty reliable.

The *Topsail Cafe* (☎ (09) 436 0529) on the 1st floor of the Onerahi Yacht Club is a must for crayfish.

Pub Food The Settler's Tavern in the town centre has a number of bars, of which *Kactus Jack's* is the best. Steak and fish dishes cost around $10 to $12. The restaurant in the *Stage Coach Hotel*, 567 Kamo Rd, about 2km north of the town centre, has a family menu. The *Dickens Inn* on Cameron St is open seven days for all meals; a lunch costs about $7.

Cafes & Fast Food During the day the Strand Food Hall has *Long John Silver* for fish and chips, the *Strand Cafe* for coffee and lunches and, upstairs, the classy *Robert Harris Cafe Shop* has balcony tables. Other choices are *Espresso Cafe* on Water St and the *City Lunch Bar* on Walton St.

Taste Spud on Water St has about 20 different kinds of baked potatoes and a few Mexican and Indian snacks.

Just north of the centre, Bank St is fast food alley with *McDonald's*, *KFC*, *Pizza Hut* and *Georgie Pie*. *Al's Diner* on Walton St is modelled on an American diner and serves fish and chips and hamburgers.

For self-catering, the huge Pack 'N Save supermarket is central, or Big Fresh at the Okara shopping centre on Port Rd is even bigger with a large fresh food section.

Entertainment
Kactus Jack's, behind the Settler's, is always popular with the locals and features local bands. The *Red Iguana Bar* in the Grand Hotel has live music on weekends. *Reva's on the Waterfront* is another restaurant with live music on most weekdays. The *Powderhound* on Vine St is a popular local nightclub. Out of town, the *Tutukaka Hotel* on the north-east coast and the *Parua Bay Hotel*, south-east of town at Whangarei Heads, are popular on weekends.

Getting There & Away
Air Air New Zealand Link and Ansett have flights between Auckland and Whangarei daily, with onward connections. Great Barrier Airlines flies twice a week to/from the island.

Bus The InterCity bus depot (☎ (09) 438 2653) is on Rose St. InterCity has frequent buses between Auckland and Whangarei, continuing north to Paihia, Hokianga Harbour and Kaitaia, with another route to Dargaville.

Northliner has a Auckland-Whangarei-Bay of Islands service daily, with a route to Kerikeri via Paihia or directly to Russell on the Opua ferry. It operates from the Northliner Terminal (☎ (09) 438 3206), 11 Rose St.

Hitching Whangarei is a very busy spot for hitchhikers going north and south. Heading north, the best hitching spot is on SH1 just after the Three Mile Bush Rd intersection, in Kamo, 5km north of town; any Kamo bus will drop you there. Heading south, the best spot is on SH1 opposite Tarewa Park or about 500m further south, by the supermarket.

Getting Around
The Whangarei Airport Shuttle (☎ (09) 437 0666) has a door-to-door service for $7.

Whangarei Bus Services (☎ (09) 438 3104) operates a limited local bus service. On Saturday the problem is particularly acute; there are no buses on Sunday. The Onerahi bus route serves the airport on the same schedule.

Avis (☎ (09) 438 2929), Budget (☎ (09) 438 7292) and Rent-a-Cheepy (☎ (09) 438 7373) are represented. There are plenty of taxis. Pro Drive (☎ (09) 438 7977) returns you and your car home safe after a night out drinking.

AROUND WHANGAREI
Whangarei Heads
From Whangarei, Heads Rd winds its way around the northern shore of Whangarei Harbour, passing picturesque coves and bays on its way to the heads at the harbour entrance. This drive (there is no bus) has magnificent scenery and passes small settlements such as Parua Bay, McLeod Bay and McKenzie Bay. There are great views from the top of 419m **Mt Manaia**, a sheer rock outcrop above McLeod Bay, but it is a hard, steep climb.

Urquarts Bay near the heads has good views (blighted by the oil refinery on the other side) and from adjoining Woolshed Bay it is a 30-minute walk over the headland to the delightful beach at Smugglers Cove.

You can also make a detour from Parua Bay to beautiful **Pataua**, a sleepy fishing settlement that lies on a shallow inlet. A footbridge leads to the small offshore island, which has a surf beach.

Marsden Point Refinery Model

New Zealand's oil refinery is at Marsden Point, across the harbour from Whangarei Heads.

At the information centre (☎ (09) 432 8194) there is a 130 sq m scale model of the refinery, accurate down to the last valve and pump. The centre, on Marsden Point Rd, Ruakaka, is open daily from 10 am to 5 pm (entry is free).

The Central West

The Central West, predominantly the Waikato and King Country regions, lie to the
south and west of Auckland.

The Waikato, one of the world's richest
dairy, thoroughbred and agricultural areas, is
about one hour's drive from central Auckland. It includes four fertile plains and
Hamilton, New Zealand's fifth-largest city,
as its major centre. The region also encompasses the central and lower reaches of New
Zealand's longest river, the Waikato, which
starts in the central North Island, flows out
from Lake Taupo and meets the sea on the
west coast.

Further south is a historic region known
as the King Country, extending roughly from
the towns of Otorohanga in the north to
Taumarunui in the south, and from western
Lake Taupo to the coast.

Waikato

The Waikato region was cultivated by the
Maori in pre-European times, with archaeological evidence showing that thousands of
hectares were under cultivation with kumara
(sweet potatoes) and other crops.

When the Europeans settled in Auckland
in 1840, relations with the local Maori were
peaceful at first; missionaries in the 1830s
introduced European crops and farming
methods to the Waikato region, and by the
1840s the Maori were trading their agricultural produce with the European settlers in
Auckland.

Relations between the two cultures soured
during the 1850s, largely due to the Europeans' eyeing of Maori land for settlement.
By the early 1860s the Waikato Maori had
formed a 'King Movement' and united to
elect a king. The movement probably
stemmed both from a need for greater organisation of Maori tribes against the Pakeha
and from a desire to have a Maori leader

HIGHLIGHTS

- Experiencing adventure activities at Wai-
  tomo Caves
- Surfing at Raglan beaches
- Exploring the coastal backwaters of Kawhia
  and Mokau
- Enjoying the rich agricultural lands of the
  Waikato, the English-style settlements of
  Cambridge and Te Aroha and the secluded
  reaches of the Waikato River

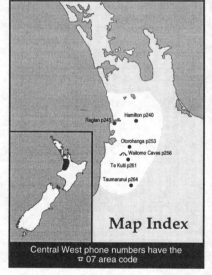

Raglan p245   Hamilton p240

Otorohanga p253

Waitomo Caves p256

Te Kuiti p261

Taumarunui p264

Map Index

Central West phone numbers have the
☎ 07 area code

equivalent to the British queen when dealing
with the Pakeha.

Potatau Te Wherowhero, was a paramount
high chief of the Waikato tribes when he was
made the first Maori king in 1859. He died
one year later aged about 85 and was succeeded by his son, the second and most
widely known Maori king, Matutaera Te
Wherowhero – commonly known as King
Tawhiao – who ruled for the next 34 years
until his death.

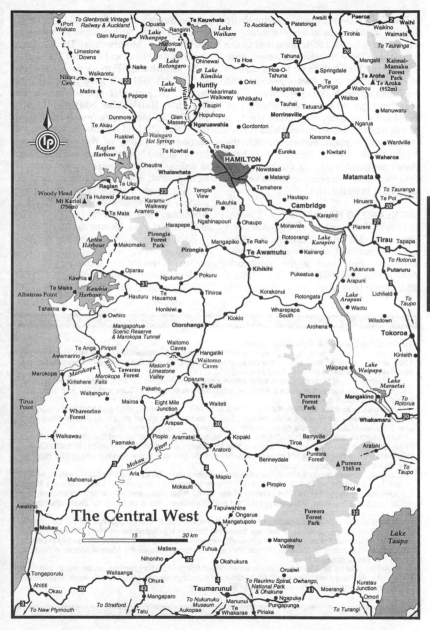

THE CENTRAL WEST

The King Movement was a nationalistic step for the Maori, who were unwilling to sell or otherwise lose their homeland to the Europeans. The Europeans, however, were equally unwilling to take no for an answer. In July 1863 they sent a fleet of gunboats and small craft up the Waikato River to put down what they regarded as the 'open rebellion' of the Maori King Movement. After almost a year of warfare, known as the Waikato Wars and involving many historic battles, the Pakeha finally won in April 1864 and the Maori retreated south to the now King Country, where Europeans dared not venture for several more decades.

AUCKLAND TO HAMILTON

The trip to Hamilton by road from Auckland takes about 1½ hours and there are a few points of interest along the way. Steam train enthusiasts can pause at the **Glenbrook Vintage Railway** (☎ (09) 236 3546), where 12km steam train rides for $8 (children $3)

run on Sunday and public holidays. To get there follow the yellow signs after leaving the Southern Motorway at Drury, 31km south of Auckland, and head for Waiuku.

Te Kauwhata, 67km south of Auckland and just off SH1, is a good place for wine tasting. Of particular interest here is the **Rangiriri Battle Site Heritage Centre** (☎ (07) 826 3663), open from 9 am to 5 pm daily. New Zealand is a little bereft in representing the history of the wars between European and Maori – this is a small attempt to redress the imbalance. Wander over the battleground, including cemetery and redoubts, where a small group of warriors made a stand against the British forces in November 1863. Nearby sites of interest are at Whangamarino, Mercer and Meremere.

From Rangiriri the road follows the Waikato River all the way to Hamilton. Along the way is **Huntly**, a coal-mining town with the large Huntly Power Station (☎ (07) 828 9590) which can be visited by appointment;

Te Arikinui Dame Te Atairangikaahu

The Maori King Movement, in which local chief Te Wherowhero was elected as the first Maori king in 1859, is still very much alive among the Waikato Maori tribes. Te Arikinui Dame Te Atairangikaahu, the Maori queen, is sixth in the line of succession.

Her father, Koroki Mahuta, was the fifth Maori king. When he died in 1966, there was widespread concern over his successor, since he had no sons but two daughters, Tura and Piki, and there had never been a Maori queen.

According to ancient tradition, if an *ariki* (first-born of a noble family) died and had no sons, office would be passed on to a close male relation. This posed a major question: should it be passed on to one of Koroki Mahuta's female descendants or bestowed upon someone else?

After much discussion and debate, the Maori chiefs and elders decided that the office should pass to his daughter Piki. Princess Piki became the first Maori queen on 23 May 1966. In 1970 Queen Elizabeth II gave her the title of Dame Commander of the British Empire, and her official title became Te Arikinui Dame Te Atairangikaahu.

Many westerners misunderstand her position, believing her to be queen of the New Zealand Maori; in fact Te Arikinui Dame Te Atairangikaahu is queen only of the tribes who united to form the Maori King Movement in the 1850s. She is head of the Tainui tribal confederation, which consists of four major tribes: the Waikato, Maniapoto, Hauraki and Raukawa. This is one of New Zealand's largest Maori confederations.

Te Arikinui Dame Te Atairangikaahu's marae is the magnificent Turangawaewae Marae, beside the Waikato River in Ngaruawahia. If you are travelling through Ngaruawahia on SH1, you can see the marae as you cross the bridge over the river. The queen has houses in various places significant to her people – for example, there is a house for the Maori queen beside the Maketu Marae in Kawhia, where the *Tainui* canoe is buried.

Te Arikinui Dame Te Atairangikaahu is an eloquent speaker and a gracious leader much loved by her people. She uses her influence to try to promote equality between Maori and Pakeha, and mutual understanding and respect for each culture. ■

free two-hour guided tours are offered to groups.

The lookout on SH1, 2km north of the town, has a restaurant, craft shop and the **Pukeroa Native Timber Museum**, open from 9.30 am to 5 pm daily, with samples of woodturning and all kinds of NZ and exotic timbers. Also at Huntly is the **Huntly Mining & Cultural Museum** at 26 Harlock Place, open from 10 am to 3 pm daily (except Monday).

South of Huntly the road enters Taupiri Gorge, a gap through the ranges. On the left, as you emerge from the gorge, is a Maori cemetery on the hillside.

Ngaruawahia, 19km north of Hamilton on SH1, is an important centre for the Waikato Maori people and the home of the Maori queen, Te Arikinui Dame Te Atairangikaahu. About 300m off SH1, beside the river on River Rd, is the impressive **Turangawaewae Marae**.

If you're fit, the top of Taupiri Mountain has excellent views, and the **Hakarimata Walkway** on the opposite side of the river also has good views. The northern end leads off Parker Rd, which can be reached by crossing the river at Huntly and following the Ngaruawahia-Huntly West Road. The southern end meets the Ngaruawahia-Waingaro Road just out of Ngaruawahia. To walk the length of the track takes seven hours.

A shorter walk, and easier to get to if you have no transport, is the three-hour return trek from Brownlee Ave, Ngaruawahia, to Hakarimata Trig (371m). The top part of this is fairly steep but the view is rewarding. Tracks from each access point meet at the trig.

HAMILTON

New Zealand's largest inland city, Hamilton (population 112,800) is 129km south of Auckland. Built on the banks of the Waikato River, it is the Waikato region's major centre and in the past few decades has undergone spectacular growth.

Archaeological evidence shows that the Maori had long been settled around the Hamilton area but, when the Europeans arrived, the site was deserted. European settlement was initiated by the 4th Regiment of the Waikato Militia, who were persuaded to enlist with promises of an acre (less than half a hectare) in town and another 50 in the country. The advance party, led by Captain William Steele, travelled up the Waikato River on a barge drawn by a gunboat and on 24 August 1864 went ashore at the deserted Maori village of Kirikirioa. The township built on that site was named after John Fane Charles Hamilton, the popular commander of HMS *Esk* who had been killed in Tauranga at the battle of Gate Pa four months earlier.

The Waikato River was once Hamilton's only transport and communication link with other towns including Auckland, but it was superseded by the railway in 1878 and later by roads.

Orientation & Information

Running north to south a block from the Waikato River, Victoria St is the main commercial thoroughfare with most essential services.

The Hamilton Visitor Centre (☎ (07) 839 3580; fax 839 3127) is in the municipal building in Garden Place, between Victoria and Anglesea Sts. It's open from 9 am to 4.45 pm on weekdays and 10 am to 2 pm on weekends and public holidays. It has information on the Hamilton, Waitomo and Waikato regions and also sells bus and train tickets.

DOC (☎ (07) 838 3363) is in BDO House at 18 London St near the river. The Map Shop (☎ (07) 834 6725), 820 Victoria St, operated by Land Information NZ, has maps of every description on NZ and most parts of the world. The Automobile Association (AA; ☎ (07) 839 1397) is at 14 Barton St and the post shop is on Victoria St (opposite Garden Place).

Waikato Museum of Art & History

This museum is in a modernistic building on the corner of Victoria and Grantham Sts near the river. It has a good Maori collection, with carvings and the impressively large and intricately carved *Te Winika* war canoe, dating

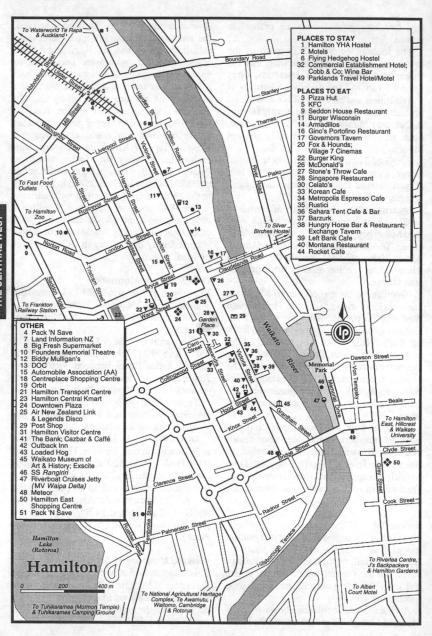

PLACES TO STAY
1 Hamilton YHA Hostel
2 Motels
6 Flying Hedgehog Hostel
32 Commercial Establishment Hotel;
Cobb & Co; Wine Bar
49 Parklands Travel Hotel/Motel

PLACES TO EAT
3 Pizza Hut
5 KFC
9 Seddon House Restaurant
11 Burger Wisconsin
14 Armadillos
16 Gino's Portofino Restaurant
17 Governors Tavern
20 Fox & Hounds;
Village 7 Cinemas
22 Burger King
26 McDonald's
27 Stone's Throw Cafe
28 Singapore Restaurant
30 Celato's
33 Korean Cafe
34 Metropolis Espresso Cafe
35 Rustici
36 Sahara Tent Cafe & Bar
37 Barzurk
38 Hungry Horse Bar & Restaurant;
Exchange Tavern
39 Left Bank Cafe
40 Montana Restaurant
44 Rocket Cafe

OTHER
4 Pack 'N Save
7 Land Information NZ
8 Big Fresh Supermarket
10 Founders Memorial Theatre
12 Biddy Mulligan's
13 DOC
15 Automobile Association (AA)
18 Centreplace Shopping Centre
19 Orbit
21 Hamilton Transport Centre
23 Hamilton Central Kmart
24 Downtown Plaza
25 Air New Zealand Link
& Legends Disco
29 Post Shop
31 Hamilton Visitor Centre
41 The Bank; Cazbar & Caffé
42 Outback Inn
43 Loaded Hog
45 Waikato Museum of
Art & History; Exscite
46 SS Rangiriri
47 Riverboat Cruises Jetty
(MV Waipa Delta)
48 Meteor
50 Hamilton East
Shopping Centre
51 Pack 'N Save

Hamilton

from 1836. The canoe has been beautifully restored, a project displayed in photos along the wall. It's open from 10 am to 4.30 pm daily ($2, children 50c, families $4.50) and has free entry on Monday. The attractive *Museum Cafe* is good for a snack.

Also at the museum is **Exscite**, the Science and Technology Exhibition Centre with science exhibits and hand-on activities ($5, children $3).

Mormon Temple

This temple at Tuhikaramea, 12km from the Hamilton city centre, is worth visiting, if just for pondering how and why it became the first to be established by the Church of Latter-Day Saints in the South Pacific. Salt Lake City, USA, is far removed in tenor and texture from the contemporary Waikato landscape. The best time to visit the temple is at night over Christmas; its visitor centre is open from 9 am to 9 pm daily.

Parks & Gardens

The huge **Hamilton Gardens** complex contains about 100 different theme gardens – rose gardens, a riverside magnolia garden, a scented garden, cacti and succulents, vegetable and glasshouse gardens, carnivorous plants, and many more, with new ones still under construction. The complex is on Cobham Drive on the east side of Cobham Bridge, and can be reached by walking south from the city along the river walkway. The gardens are always open (admission is free).

Other relaxing spots are **Hamilton Lake (Rotoroa)** and the green domains along the **Waikato River**. Walkways pass through verdant parks and bushy areas on both sides of the river through the city centre all the way south to Cobham Bridge. The area below the traffic bridge (Bridge St) is particularly attractive. Embedded in the riverbank walkway are the remains of the gunboat SS *Rangiriri*, which played a part in the Maori Wars.

Hamilton Zoo

New, more natural pens, walkways and a program to house endangered species from around the world has made this zoo one of NZ's best. Though still relatively small, it is well laid out with spacious grounds. It is 8km from the city – take SH23 west towards Raglan, turn right at Newcastle Rd and then right again onto Brymer Rd. It is open from 9 am to 5 pm daily ($7, children $3.50).

Activities

The historic paddleboat MV *Waipa Delta*, which made its first voyage on the Waikato River in 1877, runs popular river cruises from Memorial Park, on the riverbank opposite the town centre. Cruises range from afternoon tea ($20) to dinner cruises ($40, on Saturday $50). Reservations are recommended (☎ 0800 472 335).

The visitor centre supplies details on many things to do around Hamilton, including river and lake amusements, horse riding, ice skating, a Grand Prix raceway, tenpin bowling and more. It also has a free map of the walkways around the lake, along the river and down to Hamilton Gardens. DOC has information on other walks in and around Hamilton.

Waterworld Te Rapa (☎ (07) 849 4389) on Garnett Ave in Te Rapa, 4km north of the centre, is a large place with several indoor and outdoor pools and waterslides.

Skivys Tours (☎ (07) 856 2005) has good half-day tours of Hamilton ($30) and day tours to Waitomo ($85).

Places to Stay

Camping & Cabins Hamilton has a couple of camping grounds on the eastern side of the river, 2 or 3km from the city centre. The *Municipal Motor Camp* (☎ (07) 855 8255) on Ruakura Rd in Claudelands, 2km east, has tent/powered sites for $14/17 for two, standard cabins at $24 and family/tourist cabins at $34/42. The *Hamilton East Tourist Court* (☎ (07) 856 6220) on Cameron Rd, 3km east, has tent/powered sites at $13/16 for two and cabins from $16/30 up to $35/45 for singles/doubles.

Hostels The *Flying Hedgehog* (☎ (07) 839 3906), 8 Liverpool St, is a large two-storey house with bright rooms for $16 in the dorms and $35 for doubles and twins. It has been extensively renovated and even boasts a petanque court in the landscaped garden. It provides a good, simple free city map.

The plain *Hamilton YHA Hostel* (☎ (07) 838 0009) at 1190 Victoria St is beside the river a few blocks north of the centre, a pleasant 15-minute walk along the river. It charges $15/17 in dorms/doubles.

About 2km south of the museum, *J's Backpackers* (☎ (07) 856 8394) is at 8 Grey St. This cosy hostel in a suburban house has dorm beds for $15 or twins for $35. Just over 2km out of town is the *Silver Birches* (☎ (07) 855 6260) at 182 Tramway Rd; it charges $15 for a passable dorm and $55 to $70 for self-contained units. The *Parklands Travel Hotel/Motel* (see Hotels) has budget backpackers rooms at $20 per person, including linen.

Farmstays, Homestays & B&Bs The visitor centre lists farmstays, homestays and B&Bs in the Waikato region.

Motels There are many motels, particularly along Ulster St, the main road from the north. They include:

Albert Court Motel (☎ (07) 856 3090), 15 Albert St; swimming pool ($60/70 for singles/doubles)
Aquarius Motor Inn (☎ (07) 839 2447), 230 Ulster St; indoor heated swimming pool ($95/130)
Bavaria Motel (☎ (07) 839 2520), 203-207 Ulster St; spa pool ($63/75)
Classic Motel (☎ (07) 849 6588), 451 Ulster St; swimming and spa pools (from $70/75)
Gardena Court Motel (☎ (07) 838 1769), 257 Ulster St; swimming and spa pools (from $75)
Glenview Motor Hotel (☎ (07) 843 6049), 16005 Ohaupo Rd; swimming pool (from $86.50/110)

Hotels The *Parklands Travel Hotel/Motel* (☎ (07) 838 2461), just across the river at 24 Bridge St, has hotel rooms at $25 a single or $55 a double with bathroom. The motel has studio units from $67 a double with kitchen.

Right in the city centre on Victoria St near the corner of Collingwood St, the *Commercial Establishment* (☎ (07) 839 1226) has

private-facility rooms at $45/55 for singles/doubles and shared-facility rooms at $25/40. Also here are a *Cobb & Co* restaurant and a wine bar.

Places to Eat
Restaurants Hamilton has plenty of good restaurants. The *Stone's Throw Cafe* at 10 Alma St has a great atmosphere and serves large portions of international food. *Gino's Portofino* at 8 Bryce St is a bit more expensive but it's popular with the yuppie crowd for its Continental cuisine.

Pizza lovers will enjoy the choice of gourmet pizzas at *Barzurk*, 250 Victoria St – the New Orleans (with Cajun chicken, red onions, banana, cashew, yoghurt and mango chutney) for $15.90 is divine. At 592 Victoria St, trendy *Armadillos* specialises in Mexican food and American ribs.

The *Singapore Restaurant* on Garden Place is a good, licensed Chinese restaurant, but has little in the way of Singaporean cuisine. For some Middle Eastern flavour, the *Sahara Tent Cafe & Bar* at 254 Victoria St is a real surprise – it is not really 'Saharan' but you could be forgiven for thinking that you had just drifted in to a backstreet place in Istanbul.

More upmarket restaurants include the *Montana Restaurant* at 131 Victoria St with an excellent steak and seafood menu (mains are around $23); the old-fashioned *Seddon House* at 67 Seddon Rd; and the classy *Rustici* on the river at 312 Victoria St. At the latter try the mussel chowder ($7.50) and fish of the day in beer batter ($19.50).

Pub Food There's a popular *Cobb & Co* in the Commercial Establishment on the corner of Victoria and Collingwood Sts and, a block away, the similar *Hungry Horse Bar & Restaurant*.

The friendly, English-style *Fox & Hounds* on Ward St does pub lunches and ploughmans platters (items on the brasserie menu range from $6.50 to $8.50). Nearby, the *Governor's Tavern* on Bryce St by the river has indoor areas plus a riverside garden bar, which is pleasant in summer.

Fast Food The modern Centreplace shopping centre is good for a quick and cheap meal. On the ground floor is an international food hall with a variety of cuisines, including Italian, Chinese and Singaporean.

The Downtown Plaza across Ward St has a food hall with McDonald's, Asian food and pizza.

The *Korean Cafe* in the Farmers Building on Collingwood St on the corner of Alexandra St serves an unusual mix of Mexican snacks at cheap prices and Korean food. Nearby, the *Metropolis Espresso Cafe* at 241 Victoria St is a hip cafe with lunches, dinners and tempting desserts. A fair proportion of the clientele at the retro *Rocket Cafe* on the corner of Hood and Victoria Sts are students (who appreciate value).

In Garden Place on Victoria St, *Celato's* has pizza, coffee and gelati, while *Burger Wisconsin* at 789 Victoria St boasts gourmet chargrilled burgers.

KFC and *Pizza Hut* are on Ulster St. *McDonald's* is on the corner of Victoria St and Claudelands Rd, and on Greenwood St, while Burger King is on Ward St. Also on Greenwood St is another *KFC*, *Burger King* and NZ's own *Georgie Pie*.

Entertainment

Cinema & Theatre The *Village 7 Showcase*, upstairs on Ward St, has ten movie theatres showing latest releases. Live theatre venues in the city include the *Founders Memorial Theatre* (☎ (07) 838 6600) on Tristram St; the *Riverlea Centre* (☎ (07) 856 5450) on Riverlea Rd off Cambridge Rd; and the *Meteor* on Victoria St.

Music, Dancing & Pubs Hamilton has plenty of lively nightspots on weekends. Most have DJs and a few have bands.

Down on Hood St, the *Bank* is a trendy bar in a renovated historic building and is always a popular place for a drink. The dance floor gets active. Next door, the *Outback Inn* is popular with students and also has a lounge dance floor.

Biddy Mulligan's at 742 Victoria St is an Irish pub and one of the town's most popular

places. Live bands play regularly. The wine bar in the Commercial Establishment (see Places to Stay earlier) has live bands to dance to on weekend nights. The *Exchange Tavern* at 188 Victoria St has head-banging bands on the weekend. The *Cazbar & Caffé* in the Market Place on Hood St is another pleasant spot to enjoy a meal with a drink (before its metamorphosis into a late-night venue).

The *Fox & Hounds* on Ward St is a popular English-style pub with 27 varieties of imported beer, as well as Newcastle Brown, Guinness and cider on tap. It serves pub lunches and has live entertainment on Thursday and Saturday nights. The ubiquitous and popular drinking venue *Loaded Hog* can be found at 27 Hood St.

Legends, upstairs over the Air New Zealand Link office on Ward St, is a good, lively disco, as is *Orbit* on Bryce St.

Getting There & Away

Air Air New Zealand (☎ (07) 839 9835), 33-35 Ward St near Victoria St, has direct flights to Auckland, Christchurch, Dunedin, Gisborne, Napier, Palmerston North and Wellington, with onward connections.

Freedom Air (☎ (07) 834 3621) at Hamilton Airport has daily international flights to and from Australia (see the Getting There & Away chapter).

Bus All local and long-distance buses arrive at and depart from the Transport Centre on the corner of Anglesea and Ward Sts. Inter-City (☎ (07) 834 3457) and Newmans (☎ (07) 838 3114) are both represented.

Frequent buses make the connection between Hamilton and Auckland. Buses also leave for Thames, Tauranga, Whakatane, Opotiki, Rotorua, Taupo, New Plymouth and Wellington. InterCity has a daily Auckland-Hamilton-Waitomo-Rotorua tour bus. The Little Kiwi Bus Co (☎ 0800 759 999) runs between Hamilton and Auckland daily ($19 one way, children $11).

A number of local bus operators run regular services to nearby towns including Raglan, Huntly, Te Awamutu, Morrinsville,

Te Aroha and Thames. Kiwi Experience and Magic Bus stop at Hamilton.

Train Hamilton is on the main rail line and all trains between Auckland and Wellington, Rotorua and Tauranga stop at Hamilton's Frankton train station on Queens Ave, west of the city centre. Tickets can be bought at the Frankton train station, or conveniently at the Hamilton Transport Centre or the visitor centre.

Hitching Hamilton is spread out and it's a long walk to good hitching spots on the outskirts.

Heading south to Waitomo or New Plymouth, catch a Glenview bus to the outskirts. For hitching to Rotorua, Taupo, Tauranga or Wellington, catch a Hillcrest bus and get off by the Hillcrest School. Hitching north to Auckland is easiest if you take a Huntly bus to the outskirts.

Getting Around
To/From the Airport Hamilton Airport is 12km south of the city. The Airport Shuttle (☎ (07) 847 5618) offers a door-to-door service to/from the airport for $7 per person. Roadcat Transport (☎ (07) 856 7192) has a shuttle to Auckland airport for $40 ($75 for two).

Bus Hamilton's city bus system operates on weekdays only, with services from around 7 am to 5.45 pm (until 8.45 pm on Friday). All local buses arrive at and depart from the Hamilton Transport Centre.

For information and timetables of local city bus routes and local buses travelling further afield (to Huntly, Te Aroha, Thames, Raglan – see Getting There & Away in the Raglan section) consult the Hamilton Transport Centre or the visitor centre. For bus information, ring the visitor centre (☎ (07) 839 3360) or Busline (☎ (07) 856 4579).

Car The many car rental agencies include Waikato Car Rentals (☎ (07) 856 9908), Rent-a-Dent (☎ (07) 839 1049) and Cambridge Car Rentals (☎ 0800 278 333).

WAINGARO HOT SPRINGS
A popular day trip from Hamilton, Waingaro Hot Springs has three thermal mineral pools, private spa pools, giant waterslides, children's play areas and barbecues. The complex is open from 9 am to 10 pm daily ($5, children $2.50).

You can stay nearby in the *Waingaro Hot Springs Motel & Caravan Park* (☎ (07) 825 4761). Camp sites with power cost from $24 for two, on-site vans are $24 for two and motel units are $70. To get there, turn west at Ngaruawahia, 19km north of Hamilton, and travel for 23km; it is clearly signposted.

RAGLAN
On the coast 48km west of Hamilton, Raglan (population 1550) is Hamilton's closest and most popular beach. Raglan is world famous for its surfing, attracting top surfers from around the world to Manu Bay and Whale Bay, especially in summer when surfing competitions are held. It is named after Lord Raglan, a British officer who 'wiped out' seriously at the Charge of the Light Brigade.

Relaxed little Raglan lies on a beautiful sheltered harbour, good for windsurfing, boating and swimming. The famous black-sand surfing beaches are west of town.

Information
The Raglan Information Centre (☎ (07) 825 0556) on Bow St has heaps of information on the region. It is open daily from 10 am to 5 pm (until 4 pm on Sunday), closing for an hour at lunch time. There is a small, interesting museum on Wainui Rd; inquire at the information centre for opening times.

Beaches
The beach at the **Kopua Recreational Reserve** near the camping ground, a five-minute walk over the footbridge from town, is a safe, calm estuary beach popular with families. On the other side of the tiny peninsula is a popular windsurfing beach, reached via the camping ground (a day-use fee is charged). Other sheltered inner-harbour beaches close to town include **Cox's Bay**, reached by a walkway from Government Rd

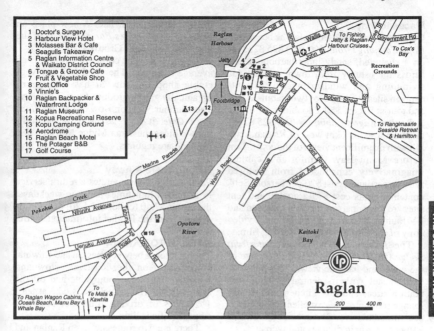

1 Doctor's Surgery
2 Harbour View Hotel
3 Molasses Bar & Cafe
4 Seagulls Takeaway
5 Raglan Information Centre
  & Waikato District Council
6 Tongue & Groove Cafe
7 Fruit & Vegetable Shop
8 Post Office
9 Vinnie's
10 Raglan Backpacker &
   Waterfront Lodge
11 Raglan Museum
12 Kopua Recreational Reserve
13 Kopu Camping Ground
14 Aerodrome
15 Raglan Beach Motel
16 The Potager B&B
17 Golf Course

Raglan

THE CENTRAL WEST

or from Bayview Rd, and **Puriri Park**, towards the end of Wallis St, a safe swimming spot at high tide.

Ngarunui Beach (Ocean Beach), about 5km west of town, is a popular surf swimming beach. Swim on the left side, away from the riptides, where lifeguards are posted in summer.

Manu Bay, 8km west of Raglan, is a world-famous surfing beach, said to have the longest left-hand break in the world. Featured in the 1966 cult surfing film *Endless Summer*, this beach was where a surfer rode a wave for 10 minutes. The very long, uniform waves at Manu Bay are created by the angle at which the ocean swell from the Tasman Sea meets the coastline. **Whale Bay**, a couple of kilometres further west, is another excellent surfing spot.There are some **tattooed rock faces** nearby; they are difficult to find so ask for directions.

Ruapuke Beach, a rugged stretch of coastline still further past Whale Bay, is good for surfcasting but not so good for swimming, due to treacherous cross-currents; it can be reached from Ruapuke Rd.

Activities

It is always pleasant and relaxing to walk down to the fishing jetty around sunset and meet the trawlers returning from the day's fishing. A few locals are often hanging around to inspect the day's catch. The jetty is four blocks west of the town centre along Wallis St.

Midway between Hamilton and Raglan, the Karamu Walkway goes through the Four Brothers Scenic Reserve. Other walking possibilities are in Pirongia Forest Park, south of Raglan.

Raglan Harbour Cruises (☎ (07) 825 0300) has 1½-hour cruises in summer for $15 (children $7.50). It also arranges fishing charters. The information centre can give information on canoeing and mountainbiking possibilities.

Places to Stay

Camping, Cabins & Hostels The beachside *Kopu Camping Ground* (☎ (07) 825 8283) is on a sheltered, sandy inner-harbour beach across the estuary from town, popular for swimming and windsurfing. It has tent/caravan sites at $14/16 for two, cabins at $40 and tourist flats at $50 a double.

Raglan Wagon Cabins (☎ (07) 825 8268) on Wainui Rd is 6km west of Raglan, on a hill with magnificent views of the coast, 2km before Manu Bay. Comfortable cabins, imaginatively constructed from restored railway carriages, cost $20 per person. Self-contained units cost $75 a double and tent sites are $8 per person. There's a kitchen and TV lounge. The friendly owner has a video copy of the *Endless Summer* surfing film.

The *Raglan Backpacker & Waterfront Lodge* (☎ (07) 825 0515) is on the edge of the water and has fine views. This purpose-built hostel with its central outdoor recreation area, spotless kitchen and comfy lounge room provides excellent standards of accommodation for $12 in shared rooms or $16 per person in doubles and twins.

B&Bs, Motels & Hotels The *Potager B&B* (☎ (07) 825 8722), 78 Wainui Rd, has comfortable singles/doubles for $30/55; and the *Rangimaarie Seaside Retreat* (☎ (07) 825 7567) on Greenslade Rd charges $40/60.

The *Harbour View Hotel* (☎ (07) 825 8010) on Bow St has single/double rooms at $35/50. Across the bridge on the west side of town, the peaceful *Raglan Beach Motel* (☎ (07) 825 8153) at 14 Wainui Rd is right on the shore of the estuary, with rooms at $65/70.

Places to Eat

Vinnie's on Wainui Rd serves great pizzas (regular/large/king size are $10.50/20/27) – they even taste good when they are overdone! The menu is innovative but the locals seem to go there for the fish and chips special ($7.50). Also on Wainui Rd, on the corner of Bow St, is the excellent *Tongue & Groove Cafe*, which serves hearty helpings of ethnic dishes; it is open from Thursday to Monday

from 10.30 am until late. A new place on Bow St, the *Molasses Bar & Cafe*, is of the ilk of the Tongue & Groove Cafe.

Seagulls, near the corner of Cliff St, is an average takeaway. The good fruit and vegetable shop on Bow St has a range of organically grown produce for self-caterers. The Harbour View on Bow St has the *Black Rock Cafe*. It also has bands – the well-known blues musician Midge Marsden and his band are regulars.

Getting There & Away

Pavlovich & Sons operates a return service to Hamilton four times daily on weekdays; the cost is $7.40 (children $4.20) one way. It departs from the Raglan information centre.

RAGLAN TO KAWHIA

The back roads between Raglan and Kawhia, 55km south on the coast, are slow and winding, but scenic, enjoyable and off the beaten track. The gravel roads take at least 1½ hours of driving time, not counting stops. Traffic is light.

There are two routes between Raglan and Kawhia. From Raglan you can head west along the coast, out past Ocean Beach, Manu Bay and Whale Bay, and keep following the coast road until it turns inland and meets the interior road at Te Mata, 20km south of Raglan. Along the way is the *Ruapuke Motor Camp* near the beach at Ruapuke. Alternatively, from Raglan head towards Hamilton and take the signposted Te Mata-Kawhia turn-off.

About 12km south-west of Raglan is **Mt Karioi**. You can take a good round-the-mountain drive, over mostly gravel roads, in a couple of hours from Raglan. Along this route the **Te Toto Track**, starting from the Te Toto car park on Whaanga Rd (the coast road) on the western side of Mt Karioi, is strenuous but scenic, ascending steeply to a lookout point (two hours) followed by an easier stretch up to Karioi summit (one hour). From the east side of the mountain, the **Wairake Track** is a steeper two-hour climb to the summit and meets the Te Toto Track.

Mt Karioi is in one part of the Pirongia Forest Park; a larger part lies within the triangle formed by the towns of Raglan, Kawhia and Te Awamutu, with the 959m summit of **Mt Pirongia** clearly visible throughout the district. Tracks going through the forest park lead to the summit of Mt Pirongia – the mountain is usually climbed from Corcoran Rd on the Hamilton side. There's a hut near the summit if you want to spend the night. Maps and information about Pirongia Forest Park are available from DOC in Hamilton. The township of **Pirongia** is 32km south-west of Hamilton. You can go horse riding on the slopes of the mountain with Mt Pirongia Horse Treks (☎ (07) 871 9960) – a one-hour ride is $20.

Near Te Mata, 20km south of Raglan, are the **Bridal Veil Falls**. From the car park it's an easy 10-minute walk through native bush to the top of the falls, with a further 10-minute walk leading down to the pool at the bottom, where it's possible to swim.

Marcus Vernon's Farmstays (☎ (07) 825 6892) is a friendly, easy-going place to learn about life on a sheep and cattle farm, high on a hill with stunning views. For $20 a day, and four hours help on the farm, you get a bed in the farmhouse with all meals. B & B with no work costs $35, or rooms with private facilities in a separate house can be rented (the whole house is $95). The farm is at the end of Houchen Rd, 4km off the main road just north of Te Mata.

KAWHIA

Kawhia is a sleepy, crumbling little port on the Kawhia Harbour. The harbour is large, with many extensions, but its entrance is narrow – the occupants of the *Tainui* canoe missed it on their first trip down the coast around 1350 AD and Captain Cook also missed it when he sailed past in 1770, naming Albatross Point on the southern side of the harbour but failing to note the harbour itself.

Today Kawhia is still easy to miss, though it gets a few fishing enthusiasts and bathers during summer.

Things to See & Do

The **Kawhia Museum** is in the historic former Kawhia County Building right near the wharf. It has interesting exhibits as well as pamphlets and information on the town. The museum is open irregular hours but if you ask around someone might open it for you. Marae visits can also be arranged through the museum.

From the museum and the wharf, a pleasant walk extends along the coast to the **Maketu Marae** with its impressively carved meeting house, Auaukiterangi. Through the marae grounds and behind the wooden fence, two stones, Hani and Puna, mark the burial place of the *Tainui* canoe. You need permission from a Maori elder to visit this marae.

Three kilometres behind the town and through the Tainui Kawhia Pine Forest is windswept **Ocean Beach** and its black dunes; swimming can be dangerous. Two hours either side of low tide you can find the **Puia Hot Springs** in the sands – just dig a hole for your own little natural spa. It is a lot less crowded than Hot Water Beach near Hahei on the Coromandel. There's a driveable track over the dunes.

Places to Stay & Eat

Kawhia's camping grounds fill up at busy periods in summer, so plan ahead. The *Forest View Motor Camp* (☎ (07) 871 0858) on Waiwera St has tent sites, van sites and cabins, as does the *Beachside Motor Camp* (☎ (07) 871 0727) on the beachfront. The *Kawhia Motor Camp* (☎ 871 0863) on Karewa St is smaller and simpler, with just tent and van sites.

The *Kawhia Motel* (☎ (07) 871 0865) is a friendly place on the corner of Jervois and Tainui Sts; units cost $57/67 for singles/doubles. Historic *Rosamond House* (☎ (07) 871 0681) on Rosamond Terrace has B&B for $40/60.

Kawhia has a general store, a pub, a fish and chip shop and a cafe. The latter is a couple of doors down from the serious drinker's retreat, *Lena's Bar*.

THE CENTRAL WEST

The *Tainui* Canoe

Though it's only a small town, Kawhia has an illustrious history. It was here that the *Tainui* canoe, one of the canoes of the Great Migration of around 1350 AD, made its final landing.

Before the *Tainui* canoe departed from the Maori homeland island of Hawaiki, the priests there prophesied that the departing canoe would eventually come to a favourable place where its people would make a new home, have a good life and prosper. Their prophecy went something like this:

Te Tauranga mou e Tainui	Your resting place Tainui
Ko te Taihauauru	Is the west coast
Ka whia te mataitai	(There is) an abundance of shellfish
Ka whia te ika	An abundance of fish
Ka whia te kai.	An abundance of food.

The priests told the leaders of the *Tainui* canoe which landmarks to look for so they would know they had arrived at the new home they were destined to find.

The *Tainui* canoe left Hawaiki, stopping at Easter Island, Raiatea (an island in French Polynesia) and Rarotonga (the principal island of the Cook Islands) as it crossed the Pacific. It landed in New Zealand at Maketu on the Bay of Plenty, accompanied by the *Arawa* canoe. The *Arawa* canoe stopped there, its people becoming the Arawa people, a large Maori tribe that still lives in the Bay of Plenty and Rotorua areas today.

The leaders of the *Tainui* canoe – Hoturoa, the captain, and Rakataura, the expert *tohunga* or high priest – knew that the *Tainui's* home was destined to be on the west coast. So the *Tainui* canoe continued on. The story of how it found its final resting place is a long and heroic one. Seeking, first one way and then another, to get to the west coast, the Tainui people finally dragged their canoe overland at Manukau Harbour, near Auckland. Setting off southwards in search of the prophesied landmarks, they journeyed all the way to the South Island, still without finding their place. They turned around and came north again, still searching, and finally recognised their prophesied new home at Kawhia Harbour.

When they landed the canoe, they tied it to a pohutukawa tree on the shore, naming the tree Tangi te Korowhiti. Though the tree is not marked, it still grows with a few other pohutukawa trees on the shoreline between Kawhia town and the Maketu Marae; you can easily see it. At the end of its long voyage, the *Tainui* canoe was dragged up onto a hill and buried. After burying the canoe, Hoturoa and Rakataura placed sacred stones at either end to mark its resting place. Hani, on higher ground, is the stone marking the bow of the canoe, and Puna, the lower stone, marks the stern. These sacred stones are still there, a powerful remembrance to the Tainui people. You can walk up behind the marae and see the stones behind a wooden fence.

The prophecy that this place would be a good home for the long-journeying Tainui people did come true. Kawhia Harbour was abundant with shellfish, fish and food. Today the Tainui tribe extends over the entire Waikato region, over the Coromandel Peninsula, north to Auckland and south to Lake Taupo and south past Mokau on the coast. Kawhia, the Maketu Marae and the burial place of the *Tainui* canoe are supremely sacred to all the Tainui people.

Another point of historical significance for Kawhia is that it was once the home of Te Rauparaha, the great Maori warrior. When pushed out of Kawhia by warring Waikato tribes in 1821, Te Rauparaha moved southwards, making his base on Kapiti Island off the west coast of the southern end of North Island, from there making raids all the way down to the South Island. See the Kapiti Coast section in the Wellington chapter for more on Te Rauparaha. ■

Getting There & Away

Kawhia Bus & Freight (☎ (07) 871 0701) takes passengers on the freight run to Te Awamutu daily except Sunday.

The 50-minute drive to Kawhia from Te Awamutu or Otorohanga is a scenic route offering fine views of the harbour. Along the way is the Te Kauri Park Nature Reserve, with a one-hour walk from the road to a kauri grove – the harbour probably marks the southernmost 'boundary' of where kauri grow naturally.

You can drive or cycle down the mostly unsealed coastal back roads all the way from Raglan in the north to Awakino and Mokau in the south, finally coming to New Plymouth (or vice versa). It's slow going but scenic.

TE AWAMUTU

Te Awamutu (population 8150) is a service town for the local dairy-farming community. It is noted for its rose gardens, hence its title 'the Rose Town of New Zealand'. Brothers Tim and Neil Finn of the popular band Split Enz (and later of Crowded House) came from here (see the boxed text on this page).

Te Awamutu was an important site in the Waikato wars – you can still see the flat-topped hill where there was a fort. After the wars, it became a frontier town. The name Te Awamutu means 'river cut short', since the river above this point was unsuitable for canoes.

The Te Awamutu Information Centre (☎ (07) 871 3259) on the corner of Gorst Ave and SH3, opposite the Rose Garden, is open from 9 am to 4.30 pm on weekdays and from 10 am to 3 pm on weekends.

Things to See

The **Te Awamutu Rose Garden** has over 2000 rosebushes. The garden is on the main road, opposite the information centre. The roses are at their best from November to April; a rose show is held every November.

Beginning behind the Rose Garden, the Pioneer Walk goes beside the river for about 1.5km to Memorial Park and the **Aotearoa Centre**, where there's a Maori carving and weaving institute.

The **Te Awamutu Museum** in the Civic Centre on Roche St houses a fine collection of Maori *taonga* (treasures), the centrepiece of which is the Uenuku, a totara carving, said to have been brought to NZ on the *Tainui* canoe. It is open from Tuesday to Friday from 10 am to 4 pm and on weekends from 2 to 4 pm (entry is free). There is now a small exhibit of Finn brothers memorabilia.

Every Thursday from around 10 am to 3 pm, farm animals are auctioned off at the **Te Awamutu Sale**, held at the saleyard on Gorst Ave, near the information centre. It's a rural event which urban visitors find fascinating.

The **Wharepapa Rock Climbing Field**, with over 50 rock climbs ranging from beginner to advanced, is 22km south-east of Te Awamutu.

'A Blind Date with Destiny'

Fans of Split Enz, NZ's most famous pop music export, can trace the early lives of its two most well-known members – the Finn brothers, Neil and Tim. They allude to their beginnings in this humble NZ town in their songs (such as the Crowded House song *Mean to Me*) and keen fans of the band (and also Crowded House) can analyse the brothers' roots by taking a walk through Te Awamutu (the information centre provides a keyed map).

Included on the walk is 588 Teasdale St where the brothers lived when they were young; St Patricks School, which both attended; Te Awamutu College, which Neil attended from Form 4; Martins Electrical Store, where Neil worked (and played piano outside on Friday nights); Craft Shop Pot Pourri (now Trade Aid Shop), where Neil often played guitar; Hammond, Finn & Chaplin, the firm in which their father Dick was a partner (he and his wife now live in Cambridge); and Albert Park, where the brothers performed for the Te Awamutu Centennial in 1984. ■

Places to Stay & Eat

The *Road Runner Motel & Holiday Park* (☎ (07) 871 7420) at 141 Bond Rd has tent and powered sites for $8.50 per person and on-site vans/cabins for $27/35 for two. The *Old Mangapiko School* (☎ (07) 871 6599) at 21 Bruce Rd has been converted to comfortable self-contained accommodation; it charges $85 a double. The *Farmstay Foxhill* (☎ (07) 870 2266) at 106 Herbert St, Kihikihi, has singles/doubles for $30/50 – the owners speak German, English and French.

Motels in Te Awamutu include the *Rosetown Motel* (☎ (07) 871 5779) at 844 Kihikihi Rd with singles/doubles for $62/72, the *Road Runner* (☎ (07) 871 7420; see earlier in this section) and the *Park Lodge Motel* (☎ (07) 871 5179) at 387 Ohaupo Rd with rooms for $55/65.

Te Awamutu has a selection of eateries on Alexandra St, the town's main commercial street, including a *KFC* and the *Gold Star* for Chinese food. A popular place for good, cheap grills is the *Rose & Thorn*, 32 Arawata St. Nearby, at No 39, is the *Robert Harris Coffee Shop*, open daily.

Getting There & Away

Buses and trains between Auckland and Wellington stop at Te Awamutu. There's local buses between Te Awamutu and Hamilton.

MORRINSVILLE

About 33km north-east of Hamilton, Morrinsville (population 5300) is a centre for the Waikato dairy industry. Its tourist literature boasts that 'there are more cows within a 25km radius of Morrinsville than in any other part of the world'!

Information Morrinsville (☎ (07) 889 5575) on Thames St, the main thoroughfare, is open from 9.30 am to 5 pm on weekdays and 10 am to 4 pm on weekends. It can arrange accommodation in farmstays and homestays; alternatively, Morrinsville has a camping ground, hotel and motel. For a meal visit the trendy *Council Bar & Cafe* on Canada St.

CAMBRIDGE

On the Waikato River 20km south-east of Hamilton, Cambridge (population 8520) is a small, peaceful town with a charming rural English atmosphere. Cricket is played on the village green in the centre of town and the avenues are lined with broad, shady European trees, at their best in autumn. The Cambridge region is famous for the breeding and training of thoroughbred horses. One well-known Cambridge-bred horse is Charisma, winner of the Olympic three-day event in both 1984 and 1988, ridden by New Zealander Mark Todd.

Information

The Cambridge Information Centre (☎ (07) 827 6033) on the corner of Victoria and Queen Sts is open from 8 am to 4.30 pm on weekdays. Get a copy of its free *Cambridge Welcomes You* and *Cambridge and Heritage Tree Trails* pamphlets.

Things to See & Do

Cambridge has a number of arts and crafts and antiques shops, adding to the town's twee atmosphere. Best-known is the award-winning **Cambridge Country Store**, in an old church on SH1. Another old church worth seeing, also on SH1, is the 100-year-old **St Andrew's Anglican Church**, a white church with a beautiful wooden interior, fine stained-glass windows and a high steeple sheathed in copper. The outside is beautiful but it's still a surprise to see the beauty of the interior.

The **Cambridge Museum**, occupying the former Cambridge Courthouse building (1909) on Victoria St, is open from Tuesday to Saturday from 10 am to 4 pm and on Sunday from 2 to 4 pm (summer only). **Te Koutu Lake** at the Te Koutu Park in the centre of town is a peaceful bird sanctuary.

The **Cambridge Thoroughbred Lodge**, ideal for horse lovers, is 3km south of town on SH1. It's a magnificent horse stud that has tours at 3.30 pm daily for $10 (children $5). The thoroughbreds are brought out on show with commentaries and there are show jumping and dressage exhibitions.

Activities

Other attractions in Cambridge include jetboat rides and canoeing on the Waikato River and walking on tracks along both sides of the river and around Te Koutu Lake. The information centre has free pamphlets showing the town's walking tracks. Camjet Riverboat Tours (☎ 025 711 878) has 45-minute rides along a scenic section of the Waikato ($40 per person).

There are also walks further afield. From SH1 take the turn-off at Cambridge and in about a five-minute drive you'll reach the Maungakawa Scenic Reserve, a regenerating forest with some exotic timber species and a fairly easy short bush walk. From the eastern side of Mt Maungakawa, a track suitable for experienced trampers ascends from Tapui Rd; it takes half a day to walk there and back. Also about a five-minute drive from town, Mt Mungatautri is another good walking spot; it takes about 1½ hours to climb to the summit.

Places to Stay

The *Cambridge Motor Camp* (☎ (07) 827 5649) at 32 Scott St, Leamington, about

1.5km from town, has tent and powered sites at $8.50 per person and cabins at $26 for two.

The *Cambridge Country Lodge Backpackers* (☎ (07) 827 8373) is a pleasant hostel in a rural setting on a small farm 100m down Peake Rd, a turn-off from the SH1 1km north of Cambridge. It provides courtesy transport and bicycles. You can do your own cooking, or home-prepared meals are available. The cost is $14 in dorms, $30 in twins and doubles.

Motels in Cambridge include the *Cambrian Lodge Motel* (☎ (07) 827 7766) at 63 Hamilton Rd and the *Captains Quarters Motor Inn* (☎ (07) 827 8989) at 57A Hamilton Rd, both charging $70/80 for singles/doubles. The *Colonial Court Motel* (☎ (07) 827 5244), 37 Vogel St, has units from $65/70 and the *Leamington Motel* (☎ (07) 827 4057), 90 Shakespeare St, charges $58/70. The classy *Mews Motor Inn* (☎ (07) 827 7166), 20 Hamilton Rd, has rooms for $100.

Cambridge also has good B&Bs. *Birches* (☎ (07) 827 6556) on Maungatautari Rd charges $40/60 and *Park House* (☎ (07) 827 6368), overlooking the town square at 70 Queen St, charges $80/100. The information centre has a full list of other B&Bs and farmstays.

Places to Eat

Cambridge is a popular lunch spot. Trendy places are the *Alphaz Restaurant & Wine Bar* at 72 Alpha St and *Sazarac Caffé* at 35 Duke St. For an elegant dinner there is *Souter House* at 19 Victoria St – salmon fillets and the snapper Provençale for $12.50 are excellent entrée choices.

The *Prince Albert Tavern* in the Victoria Plaza off Halley's Lane, an old English-style pub with open fires and an outdoor garden area, serves pub meals.

Getting There & Away

Lying on SH1, Cambridge is well connected by bus. Most long-distance buses from Hamilton to Rotorua or the Bay of Plenty stop in Cambridge. Cambridge Travel Lines (☎ (07) 827 7363) and Cresswell Motors (☎ (07) 827 7789) both have weekday services between Cambridge and the Hamilton Transport Centre.

MATAMATA

This town (population 5,500), 23km northeast of Cambridge and nestled beneath the Kaimai-Mamaku Ranges, is the apotheosis of NZ rural living. It is one of the premier thoroughbred training and breeding centres in the world, producing many great champions. Of particular interest in town is the **Firth Tower** built in 1882 by Yorkshireman Josiah Clifton Firth. Firth spoke Maori fluently and was respected by the regional Maori leaders with whom he negotiated with during the Maori Land Wars. He must have had some doubts about his standing, however, as the tower, with its 24-rifle loopholes and 45cm thick walls, was built long after the wars had ended.

The information centre (☎ (07) 888 7260) at 45 Broadway, open on weekdays from 8.30 am to 5 pm and weekends from 10 am to 3 pm, provides a list of places to stay (especially homestays and farmstays). Staff also give details of how to reach attractions such as **Wairere Falls** and **Opal Hot Springs**, and on parachuting, gliding, jetboating and the many **walking tracks** through the ranges.

KARAPIRO

Karapiro, the furthest downstream of a chain of hydroelectric power stations and dams on the Waikato River, is 28km south-east of Hamilton, 8km past Cambridge, just off SH1. The road passes over the dam and the lake is popular for aquatic sports. For camping at the lake, the Karapiro Lake Domain (☎ (07) 827 4178) beside the lake has tent sites, powered sites and bunkrooms.

The King Country

The King Country is named after the Maori King Movement, which developed in the Waikato in the late 1850s and early 1860s.

When King Tawhiao and his people were forced to move from their Waikato land after the Waikato Wars of 1863 to 1864 against British troops, they came south to this region, which was as yet unaffected by European encroachment. Legend has it that King Tawhiao placed his white top hat, symbol of the kingship, on a large map of NZ and declared that all the land it covered would be under his *mana*, or authority. The area coincided roughly with the present-day districts of Otorohanga, Waitomo and Taumarunui, extending westwards to the coast and eastwards as far as Lake Taupo.

For several decades the King Country remained the stronghold of King Tawhiao and other Maori chiefs, who held out against the Europeans longer than other Maori elsewhere in NZ. This area was forbidden to the Europeans by Maori law until the 1880s, and was even then not much penetrated by Europeans until, with the consent of the Maori chiefs, the Auckland-Wellington Main Trunk Railway line entered the region in 1891. The earliest Europeans to settle in Otorohanga were timber millers, the first of them arriving in 1890. The laying of the railway to form a continuous line from Auckland to Wellington in 1908 marked the end of the region's isolation, though even today a powerful Maori influence pervades.

From 1884, when Pakeha were allowed into the district, until 1955, the King Country was 'dry' (alcohol was prohibited). This condition was apparently imposed by Maori chiefs when they agreed to the Europeans building the railway through their country, opening it up even more to the outside world. Needless to say there are now hotels everywhere, so you won't go thirsty.

OTOROHANGA

Otorohanga (population 2770), in the upper Waipa basin, is on SH3, 59km south of Hamilton and 16km from Waitomo. A dairy and sheep-farming community, it is the northernmost township of the King Country. Otorohanga's only real tourist attraction is its impressive kiwi house.

The name Otorohanga means 'food for a long journey'. Legend says that a Maori chief who was on his way to Taupo passed through Otorohanga carrying little food, but through magic incantations was able to make the food last for the journey.

For rural atmosphere, the local stock and farm auction, the Otorohanga Sale – the biggest in the King Country, is held every Wednesday at the saleyards from around 10 am to 2 pm. The Otorohanga County Fair is held on the second Saturday in February.

The Visitor Information Centre (☎ (07) 873 8951) on the corner of Maniapoto and Tuhoro Sts is open on weekdays from 9 am to 5.30 pm and on weekends from 10 am to 5 pm. It is also the AA agent, is home to the post shop and sells bus, ferry and train tickets. There is a small museum on Kakamutu Rd.

Otorohanga Kiwi House

'Not another kiwi house,' you may groan – but this one is worth a visit. In a kiwi house night and day are reversed, so you can watch the kiwis in daytime under artificial moonlight. There are also various other native birds, including some keas, which more than live up to their reputation for being inquisitive. The walk-in aviary is the largest in NZ. Other birds include morepork owls, hawks and wekas. Tuataras are also on display.

It is open from 10 am to 5 pm daily (from 10 am to 4 pm from June to August). The last entry is half an hour before closing time ($7.50, children $2.50).

Places to Stay

The *Otorohanga Kiwitown Caravan Park* (☎ (07) 873 8214) is on Domain Rd, adjacent to the Kiwi House – you can hear the kiwis calling at night. There's a barbecue area, with free wood; tent/powered sites are $13/15 for two and on-site vans are $27.

Also near the kiwi house, *Oto-Kiwi Lodge* (☎ (07) 873 6022), 1 Sangro Crescent, is a well-equipped backpackers. It's has four-bed dorms at $15 per person, and twins and doubles for $37. It operates day bushwalking trips near Waitomo and fishing trips near Kawhia – these are both $40.

The *Royal Hotel* (☎ (07) 873 8129) on Te

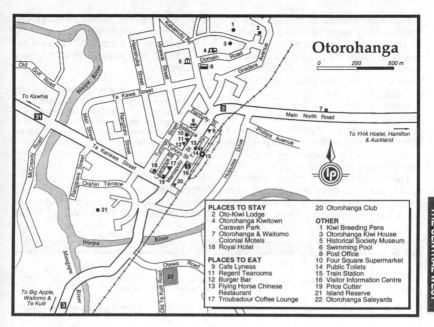

Otorohanga

0   250   500 m

PLACES TO STAY
2 Oto-Kiwi Lodge
4 Otorohanga Kiwitown
   Caravan Park
7 Otorohanga & Waitomo
   Colonial Motels
18 Royal Hotel

PLACES TO EAT
9 Cafe Lyness
11 Regent Tearooms
12 Burger Bar
13 Flying Horse Chinese
   Restaurant
17 Troubadour Coffee Lounge

20 Otorohanga Club

OTHER
1 Kiwi Breeding Pens
3 Otorohanga Kiwi House
5 Historical Society Museum
6 Swimming Pool
8 Post Office
10 Four Square Supermarket
14 Public Toilets
15 Train Station
16 Visitor Information Centre
19 Price Cutter
21 Island Reserve
22 Otorohanga Saleyards

THE CENTRAL WEST

Kanawa St has singles/doubles at $35/50 ($65 with en suite). The *Otorohanga & Waitomo Colonial Motels* (☎ (07) 873 8289) on Main North Rd about 1km from town has rooms from $60/69.50.

The visitor information centre keeps a list of B&Bs and farmstays in the area.

Places to Eat

Maniapoto St has many takeaways and coffee shops. The *Regent Tearooms* is a pleasant place open during the day and the *Troubador Coffee Lounge* serves typical country fare. Also along here is the *Flying Horse Chinese Restaurant*; *Cafe Lyness*, Oto's trendiest spot, with designer sandwiches from $3.50; and the *Burger Bar*, a hole-in-the-wall fast-food takeaway which is open until late.

The *Otorohanga Club* has a restaurant and the *Royal Hotel* on Te Kanawa St has bistro meals, a licensed restaurant, a pub and a lounge bar with entertainment on weekends.

The *Big Apple*, a barn-like complex with a large restaurant, is on the highway south of town just before the Waitomo turn-off.

Getting There & Away

InterCity buses arrive at and depart from the visitor information centre, which sells tickets. There are several buses a day in each direction (via Hamilton there are connecting services to Rotorua and Tauranga). C Tours also has an on-demand Auckland-New Plymouth bus that stops at Otorohanga.

To get to Waitomo, change buses in Otorohanga. The Waitomo Shuttle (☎ 0800 808 279) runs to and from Waitomo for $7; book through the information centre.

The train station is in the centre of town. The day and evening Auckland-Wellington trains stop at Otorohanga.

WAITOMO

Waitomo is famous for its limestone caves, and the whole region is riddled with caves and limestone formations. Tours through the Waitomo Cave (more commonly known as the Glow-worm Cave) and the Aranui Cave have been feature attractions for decades and are still one of the North Island's main tourist attractions. Eight kilometres west of SH3, it is a great place to chill out.

Visitors used to stop for an hour or a day, just to see the caves; now there's plenty to do during a longer stay. Waitomo has a host of activities – organised caving expeditions, rafting through caves, abseiling, horse trekking, canoeing and more.

The name Waitomo comes from *wai* (water) and *tomo* (hole or shaft). It's aptly named: dotted throughout the countryside are a number of tomos, shafts dropping abruptly through the surface of the ground into underground cave systems.

JN Jennings, in *Karst* (ANU Press, Canberra, 1971), is a good reference for these phenomena:

Rivers going underground, great springs emerging from the ground, independent hollows and basins instead of connecting valleys, deep potholes and vast caves, isolated tower-like hills ... these are some of the distinctive features of karst, the name given to the kinds of country that owe their special characteristics to the unusual degree of solubility of their component rocks in natural waters.

Information

The information centre is at the Museum of Caves (☎ (07) 878 7640; fax 878 6184),

---

Enter the Lost World

If it's adventure you're after, then Waitomo is the place to be. The caves offer many challenging activities, from abseiling and rock climbing to black-water rafting and canoeing.

Lost World And now ... to try to describe the indescribable. This is what the first explorers had to say:

'We had fallen upon a 'wonderland'. The sight that met our view was enchanting. Fairyland was before us. Away down, near what appeared to be its very depths was a large plateau of moss and ferns, but so far down that they appeared only small topped matter showing all the tints of green. As we looked we more than half expected to see the pixies come dancing out. This is no imagination. It was fairyland without fairies.'

King Country Chronicle, 16 December 1906.

We LP researchers found it the same when we went through. With 100m (300ft) of free-hanging abseiling to get into the Lost World cave, it's right up there as one of the most amazing things you can do in this country. And you don't even need prior abseiling or caving experience.

The principal trip to Lost World is a 1½-day affair, including a half-day abseiling instruction on the first day and then a full day at Lost World. This is when you abseil down into the cave, then, by a combination of walking, rock climbing, spider-walking, inching along narrow rock ledges, wading and swimming through a subterranean river, you take a three-hour journey through a 30m-high cave to get back out, passing glow-worms, amazing rock and cave formations, waterfalls and more. The cost is $395.

The other option is a tandem abseil into the cave, with a guide right beside you on another rope, so you don't need the first day's detailed instruction. At the bottom, you walk for half an hour into the cave, and exit via another vertical cavern back to the surface, without doing the underground river trip. The tandem trip is the brainchild of Waitomo Adventures (☎ 0800 924 866) based in the Cavelands Cafe. It takes four hours and costs $195.

Haggas Honking Holes Yet another amazing trip presented by the Lost World people, this four-hour caving trip includes professional abseiling instruction followed by a caving trip with four abseils, rock climbing, and going along a subterranean river with waterfalls. Along the way you see glow-worms and a variety of cave formations – including stalactites, stalagmites, columns, flowstone and cave coral. It's a good experience for seeing real caving in action, using caving equipment and going through caverns of various sizes, squeezing through some tight spots and narrow passageways as well as traversing huge caverns.

which is also the post office and a booking agent for most activities. It's open daily from 8.30 am to 5.30 pm (until 5 pm in winter from Easter to the end of October, and until around 8 pm, in January).

Serious cavers can get more information from the Tomo Group Hut (see Places to Stay).

Groceries are available at the store next to Cavelands Cafe, but the choice is wider at nearby Otorohanga or Te Kuiti.

Waitomo Caves

Glow-worm Cave had been known to the local Maori for a long time, but the first European to explore it was English surveyor Fred Mace, who was shown the cave in December 1887 by Maori chief Tane Tinorau. Mace prepared an account of the expedition, a map was made and photographs given to the government, and before long Tane Tinorau was operating tours of the cave.

The Glow-worm Cave is just a big cave with the usual assortment of stalactites and stalagmites – until you board a boat and swing off onto the river. As your eyes grow accustomed to the dark you'll see a Milky Way of little lights surrounding you – these are the glow-worms. You can see them in other caves and in other places around Waitomo, and in other parts of NZ, but the ones in this cave are still something special to see; conditions for their growth here are

The name of the adventure derives from a local farmer, 'Haggas', and characters in a Dr Seuss story, 'honking holers'. The cost is \$125; or the 'Gruesome Twosome' combines this with the Lost World tandem abseil for \$295.

Tumu Tumu Toobing Waitomo Adventures also operates a physical four-hour tubing trip for the adventurous traveller through the Tumu Tumu Cave (for the type of trip see Black Water Rafting I & II). If you combine this with either the Lost World or Haggas Honking Holes adventures you get \$20 off the tubing trip.

Black Water Rafting I & II Black Water Rafting introduced the sport of cave tubing to the unsuspecting traveller in 1987 – it soon became one of NZ's most popular adventures.

Black Water Rafting I is a three-hour trip down a subterranean river through the Ruakuri Cave. First you put on a wetsuit and caver's helmet with a light on the front, grab a black inner tube, and you're off on a trek through the cave which involves leaping over a small waterfall, floating through a long, glow-worm-covered passageway, and plenty of joking and laughs. At the end of the journey there's a hot shower and soup to warm up your innards, but in the wetsuit you probably won't get too cold. The cost is \$65.

Black Water Rafting II is even more adventurous. This all-day caving expedition goes through a different part of the Ruakuri Cave and includes all the features of BWR I but also involves a 30m abseil. The trip takes five hours and costs \$125.

Trips leave from the Black Water Cafe (☎ 0800 228 464) several times daily. Both trips include entry to the Museum of Caves.

Waitomo Down Under Waitomo Down Under (☎ (07) 878 6577), next door to the Museum of Caves, operates 'float through' caving adventures, similar to Black Water Rafting. In its main adventure, you go through the Te Ana Roa cave (long cave) in inner tubes, going over *two* waterfalls (one on a slide) and getting a good close-up view of some glow-worms along the way. It includes a visit to the local marae; the cost is \$65. Its Adventure II is a 50m abseil down into the 'Baby Grand' tomo (it is also \$65).

Canoeing Yes, you can even canoe the caves. The fully qualified guides of Waitomo Wilderness Tours (☎ (07) 878 7640, after hours ☎ (07) 873 8012) combine a good mix of activities in their underground trips. You first abseil 27m into a cave stream from where you canoe with the glow-worms. After exploring the cave on foot you exit via a belayed rock climb. These adventurous trips cost \$95, including soup and toast afterwards. ■

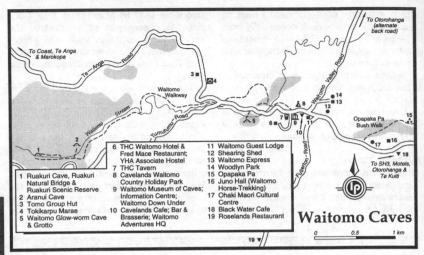

Waitomo Caves

1 Ruakuri Cave, Ruakuri
   Natural Bridge &
   Ruakuri Scenic Reserve
2 Aranui Cave
3 Tomo Group Hut
4 Tokikarpu Marae
5 Waitomo Glow-worm Cave
   & Grotto

6 THC Waitomo Hotel &
   Fred Mace Restaurant;
   YHA Associate Hostel
7 THC Tavern
8 Cavelands Waitomo
   Country Holiday Park
9 Waitomo Museum of Caves;
   Information Centre;
   Waitomo Down Under
10 Cavelands Cafe; Bar &
   Brasserie; Waitomo
   Adventures HQ

11 Waitomo Guest Lodge
12 Shearing Shed
13 Waitomo Express
14 Woodlyn Park
15 Opapaka Pa
16 Juno Hall (Waitomo
   Horse-Trekking)
17 Ohaki Maori Cultural
   Centre
18 Black Water Cafe
19 Roselands Restaurant

0   0.5   1 km

THE CENTRAL WEST

just about perfect, so there is a remarkable number of them. The tour takes 45 minutes.

The Glow-worm Cave is the most popular cave, crammed with tourists being shuttled through, one tour after the other. The big tour buses peak around lunchtime; try to go on the first tour of the day.

Aranui Cave is 3km further up the road from the Glow-worm Cave. The cave has no river running through it and hence no glow-worms. It is a large cave with thousands of tiny, hollow 'straw' stalactites hanging from the ceiling. It takes about 45 minutes to tour this cave. Various scenes in the formations are pointed out and photography is permitted. Transport to the cave is not included with the tour ticket.

Nearby Ruakuri Cave is open only for black-water rafting (see the boxed text entitled Enter the Lost World).

Tours & Tickets The Waitomo and Aranui caves can be visited individually or with a combined ticket. Tickets are sold at the entrance to the Glow-worm Cave. Entry to the Glow-worm Cave is $17.50 (children under 13 $10), the Aranui Cave costs $17.50 ($10) or a combined two-cave ticket is $27

($14). The 'museum-cave special' includes the Glow-worm Cave tour and the Museum of Caves for $19.

The 45-minute tours of the Glow-worm Cave leave daily on the half-hour from 9 am to 5 pm. From late October to Easter there's also a 5.30 pm tour, with more at the height of the summer season. Aranui Cave tours go at 10 and 11 am, 1, 2 and 3 pm, and also take about 45 minutes.

Museum of Caves

This museum has excellent exhibits about how caves are formed, the flora and fauna that live in caves, the history of caves and cave exploration.

Displays include a cave model, fossils of extinct birds and animals that have been discovered in caves, and a cave crawl for the adventurous. There are also audiovisual presentations about caving, glow-worms and the many other natural attractions in the Waitomo area.

It is open from 8.30 am to 5.30 pm daily (until 5 pm in winter from Easter to the end of October, and until around 8 pm in January). Entry is $3.50 (children free); free entry is often included with various activities or

Glow-worms

Glow-worms are the larvae of a type of gnat called a fungus gnat, which looks much like a large mosquito without mouth parts. The larvae glow-worms have luminescent organs which produce a soft, greenish light. Living in a sort of 'hammock' suspending from an overhang, they weave sticky threads which trail down and catch unwary insects attracted by their lights. When an insect flies towards the light, it gets stuck in the threads and becomes paralysed, after which the glow-worm reels in the thread and eats the insect.

The larval stage lasts for six to nine months, depending on how much food the glow-worm gets – the more food, the quicker it can mature. When the glow-worm has grown to about the size of a matchstick it goes into a pupa stage, much like a cocoon. The adult fungus gnat emerges about two weeks later.

The adult of the species may be caught and eaten by the larval glow-worm. Even if it avoids that fate, the adult insect does not live very long because it does not have a mouth; it emerges, mates, lays eggs and dies, all within about two or three days. The sticky eggs, laid in groups of 40 or 50, hatch in about three weeks to become larval glow-worms.

Glow-worms thrive in moist, dark caves, but they can survive anywhere if they have the requisites of moisture, an overhang to suspend from, and insects to eat. Waitomo is famous for its glow-worms but you can see them in many other places around New Zealand, both in caves and outdoors. Similar glow-worms exist in south-eastern Australia but the New Zealand variety is a distinct species, *Arachnocampa luminosa*.

When you come upon glow-worms, don't touch their hammocks or hanging threads, try not to make loud noises and don't shine a light right on them. In daylight their lights fade out, and if you shine a torch right on them they will dim their lights. It takes the lights a few hours to become bright again, during which time the glow-worm will catch no food. The glow-worms that shine most brightly are the hungriest. ■

you can get a 'museum-cave special' (see Waitomo Caves earlier).

Other Attractions

Waitomo's newest attraction is one of its best. **Woodlyn Park** (☎ /fax (07) 878 6666) is the realisation of a dinkum Kiwi's dream. Barry Woods, ex-shearer, puts on a helluva show, in which he cleverly integrates a history lesson into his inimitable humorous piece of theatre.

It is a New Zealand farm show with a difference, with many introduced, trained animals. Sheepdog Jed (a lady), cows, bulls, sheep, pigs (including the Josie the Captain Cooker and Sam the kunekune) and a Kiwi bear (possum) work in cohorts with Barry and his simple, manual 'virus-free' computer to explain the country's early European heritage. The shows are riotous fun and the audience are deliberately involved. It is well worth the entry of $9.50 (children $4.50). Woodlyn Park is 600m up the Waitomo Valley Road.

The **Ohaki Maori Cultural Centre** is a replica of a pre-European Maori pa, with traditional Maori arts and crafts on sale. Demonstrations and displays of Maori weavngs are put on for groups. The centre is open daily from 10 am to 4.30 pm. Entry to the village is $3 (children $2), while entry to the weaving demonstration costs $6 (children $2).

The **Shearing Shed** exhibits products made with the fur of Angora rabbits. It's open daily from 9 am to 5 pm (entry is free).

Mason's Limestone Valley is a private farm with limestone caves that can be visited on a three-hour tour for $60 (a family $120); a shorter trip is $30 (school groups are $20 per person). The cave tour includes a boat trip along the underground river where you will see glow-worms, and a tour of the farm on a tractor trolley. Bookings are by appointment (☎ (07) 878 7622) and tours go at 9.30 am and 1.30 pm.

To get there, take SH3 north of Te Kuiti for 3km, then take the turn-off to Oparure, 4km away. The farm is on the Boddie Rd, 3km past Oparure.

Activities

For details on cave activities see the boxed text entitled Enter the Lost World.

The Museum of Caves has free pamphlets on various walks in the area. The walk from the Aranui Cave to the Ruakuri Cave is an excellent short walk. From the Glow-worm Cave ticket office, it's a 15-minute forest walk to a grove of California redwood trees. Also from here, the 5km, three-hour Waitomo Walkway takes off through farmland and follows Waitomo Stream to the Ruakuri Scenic Reserve, where a half-hour return walk passes by the river, caves and a natural limestone bridge.

A one-hour return walk, the **Opapaka Pa Bush Walk** takes off from the car park of the Otaki Maori Cultural Centre, leading up to a pre-European pa site on a hill. Plaques along the way describe traditional Maori medicines found in the forest, traditional forest lore and the pa site itself.

Many other good walks are west of Waitomo on the Marokopa Road; see the Marokopa Road section.

Waitomo Horse-Trekking (☎ (07) 878 7649) operates from the Juno Hall hostel (see Places to Stay), with a variety of rides through Waitomo wilderness areas. The cost is $25 for a one-hour ride, $35 for two hours, $60 for a half-day, $100 for a full-day ride and $200 for overnight treks.

At Woodlyn Park (see Other Attractions) you can drive a powerful jet-boat, capable of 100hp, around a specially designed course – this is the only operation of its type in NZ and a thrilling experience. Seven laps cost $27 (a parent could take a child in a family boat – five laps cost $30). The course is open from November to April from 9.30 am to 6.30 pm (until 5 pm from May to October).

Places to Stay

Camping, Cabins & Hostels The *Cavelands Waitomo Country Holiday Park* (☎ (07) 878 7639) is opposite the museum. Tent/powered sites cost $15/18 for two, while cabins which sleep four are $35. The new chalets are also good value.

The *Waitomo Caves Associate YHA Hostel* (☎ (07) 878 8227) is at the THC Waitomo Hotel in the centre of Waitomo, in a separate building that was the staff quarters. It charges $16 per night or $17 for non-YHA members.

Juno Hall (☎ (07) 878 7649) is on the main road in from the highway to the caves, about 1km before the Museum of Caves. Its communal area has the feel of a ski lodge and it offers good standards of accommodation. The cost is $16 in dorms, $39 in twins with private facilities and $49 in doubles. You can camp for $7.50 per person. Activities include horse trekking, hunting and fishing trips.

Two kilometres further on past the Glow-worm Cave, the *Tomo Group Hut* (☎ (07) 878 7442) is the clubroom of the Hamilton Tomo Group, the largest caving club in NZ. They welcome visitors, and the cost of $10 for the first night and $8 for each successive night helps to support the club. The hut is quite 'rustic' but has good lounge and kitchen areas, even if the beds in the shared rooms are hard. Bring your own sleeping bag. The helpful caretaker can tell you about walks and free activities in the area, or if you're lucky you may be invited on a caving trip, particularly on weekends when cavers come to the hostel.

Guesthouses & Farmstays *Waitomo Guest Lodge* (☎ (07) 878 7641) is conveniently situated just 100m from the Museum of Caves. It's a pleasant, friendly B&B. Rooms, each with private bath, cost $40/70 for singles/doubles, including breakfast.

At Woodlyn Park (see Other Attractions) you can stay in the *Waitomo Express* (☎ (07) 873 8657), a converted railcar which has all mod-cons – kitchen, shower, toilet, three bedrooms and comfortable lounge. It is an absolute bargain at $70/80 ($10 for each extra person).

Several homes and farms in the area offer lodging and B&B for around $40/65. Check with the Museum of Caves, where many are listed.

Motels & Hotels There are a couple of motels on SH3 at Hangatiki at the junction of the Waitomo turn-off, 8km from Waitomo.

The *Glow Worm Motel* (☎ (07) 873 8882) has doubles for $69 and $73 and one-bedroom units for $97/109 for three/four people. About 100m south on SH3, the *Caves Motor Inn* (☎ (07) 873 8109) has a variety of accommodation including a lodge at $20 per person on a shared basis and standard units at $65/75. There is also a bar and restaurant.

The *THC Waitomo Hotel* (☎ (07) 878 8227), high on the hill in the centre of the village, was built in 1908 and was *the* place to stay. This grand old hotel is not quite as sophisticated or as expensive as it looks. Though one wing has refurbished rooms for $140, many of the rooms are economy with one set of bunks. The budget twin rooms, $40 with en suite, are popular, so book ahead.

Places to Eat

The store beside the Museum of Caves is open daily, with the *Cavelands Cafe, Bar & Brasserie* off to one side, where you can get inexpensive meals to take away or eat in. The *Black Water Cafe*, 2km from the caves out towards SH3, has both indoor and patio seating and is open daily from 9 am to 5 pm for breakfast, lunch and Devonshire teas.

The *THC Tavern* near the Museum of Caves is excellent value for light meals and snacks (around $6). Drinks are reasonably priced and bands also play sometimes on weekends.

For more elegant and expensive dining the *THC Waitomo Hotel* has the *Fred Mace Restaurant*, which in addition to its regular menu also does lunch and Sunday night buffets for around $25.

The upmarket *Roselands Restaurant* is open for lunch, with an ample barbecue of steak or fish, a salad buffet, dessert and coffee. It is in an attractive setting with garden, verandah or indoor seating. From Waitomo village, go 400m east towards SH3, then follow the signs for 3km.

Getting There & Away

The Waitomo Shuttle (☎ 0800 808 279) operates between Waitomo and Otorohanga ($7 one way).

InterCity has round-trip bus services to the Glow-worm Cave from Auckland and Rotorua. You only get to spend an hour at the caves so it's a very rushed trip. If you are already in Otorohanga you can catch the InterCity bus to the caves as it passes through at about noon. Magic Bus and Kiwi Experience also come to Waitomo.

The Waitomo Wanderer (☎ (07) 873 7559 Waitomo, (07) 348 5179 Rotorua, (07) 378 9000 Taupo) operates a useful daily loop around the Central North Island. It departs from Waitomo at 4 pm, Rotorua at 6.15 pm, Taupo at 7.30 pm and returns to Waitomo at 9.15 pm ($25, children $15).

Hitching to Waitomo from the turn-off on SH3 is usually pretty easy, as is hitching around Waitomo once you're there. Hitching out towards Te Anga and Marokopa can be more difficult because there's so little traffic.

MAROKOPA ROAD

Heading west from Waitomo, the Marokopa Road follows a rewarding and scenic route with a couple of natural beauties worth visiting. DOC produces a useful *West to Marokopa* pamphlet, or *A Trip Through Time* by Peter Chandler, available from the Waitomo Museum of Caves, outlines a geological driving tour of the 53km road from Waitomo to Kiritehere on the coast, with suggestions for walks.

On weekdays Perry's Bus runs from Taharoa on the coast along the Marokopa Road to Te Kuiti via Te Anga and Waitomo. It departs from the Te Kuiti train station at 1 pm for the return trip.

The **Tawarau Forest**, about 20km west of Waitomo village, has various walks outlined in a DOC pamphlet, including a one-hour walk to the Tawarau Falls from the end of Appletree Rd. The Alpiger Hut shown in the DOC pamphlet is now closed.

The **Mangapohue Natural Bridge Scenic Reserve**, 26km west of Waitomo, is a 5½-hectare reserve with a giant natural limestone bridge formation; this is a 20-minute walk from the road on a wheelchair-accessible pathway. You can easily walk to the summit. On the far side, big rocks full of oyster fossils jut up from the grass. At night you'll see glow-worms.

Not far from Natural Bridge, the **Marokopa Tunnel** is another massive limestone formation – a natural tunnel 270m long and 50m high at its highest point, going through a limestone hill. Limestone formations, fossils and glow-worms can be seen.

The tunnel is on private land, owned by a friendly farming couple who run Marokopa Tunnel Treks (☎ (07) 876 7865). They conduct guided walks through the tunnel, departing from their farmhouse near the Natural Bridge car park and leading on a bush walk beside the Marokopa River, then up a small tributary to the tunnel ($18, students $10). A picnic lunch and afternoon tea are provided; plan to spend about 3½ to four hours. Torches are provided.

About 4km further west is **Piripiri Caves Scenic Reserve**, where a 30-minute track leads to a large cave containing fossils of giant oysters. Bring a torch.

The impressive 36m **Marokopa Falls** are 32km west of Waitomo. You can view them from the road above, or walk to the bottom on a track starting just downhill from the roadside vantage point.

The falls are near **Te Anga**, where you can stop for a drink at the pleasant Te Anga Tavern. From Te Anga you can turn north to Taharoa or Kawhia, 53km away, or southwest to **Marokopa**, a small village on the coast, 48km from Waitomo. The whole Te Anga-Marokopa area is riddled with caves. The bitumen road ends just out of Marokopa at Kiritehere, but it is possible to continue, on a difficult but scenic road, 60km further south until you meet SH3 at Awakino (see the Te Kuiti to Mokau section). About 20km south of Marokopa is the **Whareorino Forest**, which has forest walks and overnight accommodation at Leitch's Hut (inquire at DOC in Te Kuiti).

Places to Stay In Te Anga, the *Bike 'n' Hike* (☎ (07) 876 7362) is a small backpackers operated by an outdoorsy fellow knowledgeable about caving, geology and fossils; he

organises activities and rents out mountain bikes.

About 10km south of Te Anga on the road to Marokopa, *Hepipi Farm* (☎ (07) 876 7861) offers B&B and also has three self-contained units at the beach in Marokopa for $45 per unit, each sleeping four or five people. Also at the beach in Marokopa is the basic *Marokopa Motor Camp* (☎ (07) 876 7546).

TE KUITI

This small, provincial town (population 5070), south of Otorohanga, is another base for visiting Waitomo, 19km away. Te Kuiti probably comes from Te Kuititanga, meaning 'the narrowing in', referring not only to the narrowing of the Mangaokewa Valley here but also to the confiscation of Maori property after the Waikato wars. Locals will proudly tell you, however, that the town is named for Te Kooti, a prominent Maori rebellion leader who settled here in 1872, seeking refuge from the Pakeha, and stayed for a number of years. The magnificently carved Te Tokanganui-o-noho Marae, overlooking the south end of Rora St, was Te Kooti's gift to his hosts, the Ngati Maniapoto people.

Te Kuiti, home to many champion sheep shearers, is known as 'the Shearing Capital of the World'. A 'big shearer' statue is the most prominent feature of the town.

Information

The Te Kuiti Visitor Information Centre (☎ (07) 878 8077; fax 878 5280) on the main drag, Rora St, is open from 9 am to 5 pm daily (from 10 am to 4 pm on weekends in winter). It has information on Waitomo and the surrounding area as well as Te Kuiti, homestays and farmstays; it's also the AA agent.

The DOC office (☎ (07) 878 7297) is at 78 Taupiri St.

Things to See & Do

Apart from the big shearer, Te Kuiti's main attraction is the **Te Kuiti Muster**, held on the first weekend in April (or the following

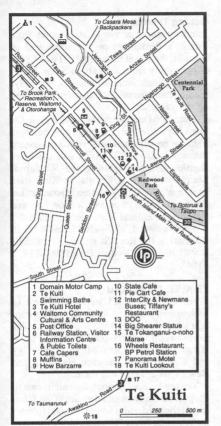

1 Domain Motor Camp
2 Te Kuiti
  Swimming Baths
3 Te Kuiti Hotel
4 Waitomo Community
  Cultural & Arts Centre
5 Post Office
6 Railway Station, Visitor
  Information Centre
  & Public Toilets
7 Cafe Capers
8 Muffins
9 How Barzarre
10 State Cafe
11 Pie Cart Cafe
12 InterCity & Newmans
   Buses; Tiffany's
   Restaurant
13 DOC
14 Big Shearer Statue
15 Te Tokanganui-o-noho
   Marae
16 Wheels Restaurant;
   BP Petrol Station
17 Panorama Motel
18 Te Kuiti Lookout

Te Kuiti

THE CENTRAL WEST

If you're a garden fan, ask the information centre for its King Country Gardens brochure, which gives details on 20 private gardens you can visit in the region.

The **Mangaokewa River** winds through the town, with a pleasant riverside walkway. Beside the river, the **Mangaokewa Scenic Reserve**, 3km south of town on SH30, has picnic and barbecue areas, a waterhole for safe swimming and overnight camping.

On the north-western boundary of Te Kuiti, the attractive **Brook Park Recreation Reserve** has walking tracks leading to the summit of the Ben Lomond Hill. Besides affording a fine view, the hill is the site of the historic Matakiora Pa, constructed in the 17th century by Rora, son of Maniapoto. Camping is permitted.

The **Te Kuiti Lookout** on Awakino Rd (SH3) as it climbs out of town heading south, provides a great view over the town, especially at night with the sparkling lights stretching out below.

Places to Stay & Eat

The *Domain Motor Camp* (☎ (07) 878 8966) on Hinerangi St on the north side of town beside the Mangaokewa River, about 800m north of the information centre, is a peaceful camping ground with tent/powered sites at $11/13 for two, on-site vans at $20 and cabins at $25 for two.

Camping is also permitted at the *Brook Park Recreation Reserve* on the north-western boundary of Te Kuiti, and at the *Mangaokewa Scenic Reserve* beside the river (see Things to See & Do); both have barbecues, picnic areas and toilets, but no other facilities. Payment is by donation.

On Mangarino Rd, just north of town, is the *Casara Mesa Backpackers* (☎ (07) 878 6697). This farmstay has great views over the town from its verandah and is well worth the $15 per person for a bed with linen (a continental/cooked breakfast is $5/8 extra). The owner picks up and drops off in Te Kuiti and arranges tours further afield to Waitomo.

On Rora St in the town centre, the *Te Kuiti Hotel* (☎ (07) 878 8172) has singles/doubles with private facilities costing $45/55. The

weekend, if Easter falls then). This popular event has all kinds of entertainment including sheep and goat-shearing championships, a country parade, arts and crafts, live music, sheep races, Maori culture groups, barbecues and hangis, a duathlon and a town-wide bargain day.

Tours can be arranged to **Te Tokanganui-o-noho Marae**. The marae protocol and Maori teachings are explained at the meeting house, along with the importance of the carvings. Entry is by *koha* (donation); contact the information centre.

Te Kuiti has some fine gardens and parks.

Panorama Motel (☎ (07) 878 8051) at 59 Awakino Rd (SH3), about 1.5km south of town, has a pool and units from $60/70. For a list of the many B&Bs and farmstays contact the information centre.

Te Kuiti has daytime cafes on Rora St, or the *State Cafe* is open until 8 pm for standard takeaways and the *Pie Cart Cafe* is open until very late (and serves delectable ham off the bone). Also on Rora St, *Tiffany's Restaurant* is open late or *Wheels Restaurant*, beside the BP Petrol Station, is a friendly, casual restaurant. It has both Continental and Chinese food, with a restaurant and a takeaway section.

Cafe Capers, across from the information centre, is also a good choice with a selection of 'real' coffees and a varied lunch menu, as is *Muffins* on King St. Te Kuiti's one nightspot, *How Barzarre* on the corner of King and Taupiri Sts, serves snacks such as nachos ($7) before it transforms into a late-night venue.

Many NZ sheep stations welcome visitors and put on sheep-shearing and sheepdog displays

Getting There & Away

InterCity buses arrive at and depart from Tiffany's Restaurant on the south end of Rora St; the ticket office (☎ (07) 878 8872) is open daily from 8.30 am to 5 pm. Long-distance buses include those to New Plymouth, Taumarunui or north to Hamilton and on to Auckland.

Buses also operate in the local region. On weekdays the Perry's bus runs between Taharoa on the coast and Te Kuiti, passing through Waitomo, Te Anga and the other scenic attractions along the Waitomo-Marokopa Road. It departs Te Kuiti train station at 1 pm. The Waitomo Wanderer (see Waitomo earlier) operates a loop between Rotorua, Taupo and Waitomo via Te Kuiti.

The Auckland-Wellington trains stops in Te Kuiti at the Rora St station. Get tickets from Tiffany's or Budget Travel (☎ (07) 878 8184).

TE KUITI TO MOKAU

From Te Kuiti, SH3 runs south-west to Mokau on the rugged west coast before continuing on to New Plymouth in Taranaki. The road runs through a lightly populated farming area and is very scenic in parts. InterCity and C Tour buses between Hamilton and New Plymouth take this route.

The road passes through the small town of **Piopio**, which has a small museum, and then tiny **Mahoenui**, from where the road follows the Awakino River. The road along the river is the most spectacular part of the route. Through a short road tunnel you enter the steep **Awakino Gorge**, lined with dense bush and giant pongas.

The road follows the river all the way to **Awakino**, a small settlement on the coast where boats shelter on the river estuary away from the windswept coast. Awakino can also reached via the Marokopa Road from Waitomo. Just south of Awakino is the **Manioroa Marae**, which contains the anchor stone of the *Tainui* canoe, whose descendants populated the King Country. Ask at the organic farm opposite the marae on SH3 for permission to enter. Marae protocol should be observed.

Five kilometres further south, the little town of **Mokau** is at the edge of the King Country before you enter Taranaki. The town's Tainui Museum, open from 10 am to 4 pm, has a fascinating collection of old photographs from the time when this once-isolated outpost was a coal and lumber shipping port for pioneer settlements along the Mokau River. Mokau River Cruises (☎ (06) 752 9775) has good three-hour trips up the river in the historic *Cygnet* for $30 in summer. Mokau is otherwise just a speck on the map, but it does have a fine stretch of wild beach and good fishing. The river mouth hides some of the best whitebait in the North Island.

Places to Stay

The *Awakino Hotel* (☎ (06) 752 9815) has singles/doubles for $40/70 and offers backpackers accommodation for $13 per person. The *Palm House* (☎ (06) 752 9081) in Mokau is a good little hostel on SH3 and close to the beach. Dorms are $15, twins or triples $34 or a double is $40. Inquire next door if no one is around (but beware of the unfriendly canine). Mokau also has two motor camps and the *Mokau Inn Motel* (☎ (06) 759 9725), which charges $50/60.

TAUMARUNUI

Taumarunui is a quiet little town (population 6630) on SH4, 82km south of Te Kuiti and 43km north of National Park. Its name, meaning 'big screen', comes from an episode in the town's history when a Maori chief, Pehi Taroa, was dying and asked for a screen to shade him from the sun. They say that he died before the screen was in place, still asking for it with his final words – '*taumaru nui*'.

In winter Taumarunui operates as a ski town, but is really too far from the snow to be convenient. In summer it is one of the main access points for canoeing on the Whanganui River (see the Whanganui National Park section in the Wanganui & Manawatu chapter for details).

History

At the confluence of the Whanganui and Ongarue Rivers, both major transport waterways, Taumarunui was already an important settlement in pre-European days. It was also significant as the historical meeting place of three important Maori tribes: the Whanganui, the Tuwharetoa and the Maniapoto.

Pakeha did not settle in the area until the 1880s, but even then their influence was minimal until the Main Trunk Railway Line came south from Te Kuiti in 1903. In the same year, the riverboat service coming from the coast at Wanganui was extended up the Whanganui River to Taumarunui. Taumarunui flourished as the rail link, running all the way to Auckland, became a much-travelled route and timber from the area's sawmills was freighted out.

Information

The Taumarunui Information Centre (☎ (07) 895 7494; fax 895 6117) is at the train station on Hakiaha St in the town centre. It's open from 9 am to 4.30 pm on weekdays and on weekends from 10 am to 4 pm. It's also the agent for AA and for InterCity bus and train tickets. It is worth a stop just for a look at the operating model of the Raurimu Spiral ($2).

The DOC office (☎ (07) 895 8201) at Cherry Grove, beside the river, is the place to go for information on the Whanganui National Park and canoeing the river.

Raurimu Spiral

The Raurimu Spiral is a feat of rail engineering that was declared a 'wonder of the world' when it was completed in 1908. The spiral's three horseshoe curves, one complete circle and two short tunnels, allowed the Main Trunk Railway coming south from Auckland and north from Wellington to finally be joined at Horopito. The information centre has an excellent working model of the spiral and pamphlets explaining its construction. At Raurimu, 37km south of Taumarunui, you can see the real thing from a lookout just off the highway.

Rail buffs can experience the spiral on any train between Wellington and Auckland. For

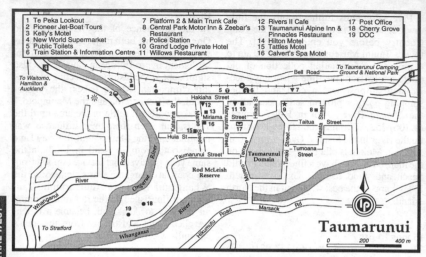

1 Te Peka Lookout	7 Platform 2 & Main Trunk Cafe	12 Rivers II Cafe	17 Post Office
2 Pioneer Jet-Boat Tours	8 Central Park Motor Inn & Zeebar's	13 Taumarunui Alpine Inn &	18 Cherry Grove
3 Kelly's Motel	Restaurant	Pinnacles Restaurant	19 DOC
4 New World Supermarket	9 Police Station	14 Hilton Motel	
5 Public Toilets	10 Grand Lodge Private Hotel	15 Tattles Motel	
6 Train Station & Information Centre	11 Willows Restaurant	16 Calvert's Spa Motel	

Taumarunui

THE CENTRAL WEST

a day trip, you can take the train from Taumarunui to National Park and return to Taumarunui the same day – the information office has all the relevant schedules.

Nukunuku Museum

This private museum (☎ (07) 896 6365) is devoted to the Whanganui River and the area around it, with Maori and pioneer artefacts, and pioneer buildings. The museum is at Nukunuku, 17km down the Whanganui River from Taumarunui. It can visited by river or via Saddlers Rd, off the Whanganui River Road. It is open by appointment only (entry by donation).

Stratford-Taumarunui Heritage Trail

See the Taranaki chapter for details on this route between Taumarunui and Stratford (note that 25km of this is unsealed).

Walking

The information centre has suggestions for several enjoyable walks around Taumarunui. A pleasant walkway extends east along the Whanganui River from Cherry Grove to the Taumarunui Camping Ground, about 3km away. Another track leads to the Rangaroa

Domain with a good view over the town, its rivers and mountains; go over the train line, up The Incline and through the native bush behind the scout den to reach it. The Te Peka Lookout across the Ongarue River on the western side of town is another good vantage point.

For even better views extending to Tongariro National Park in the south, climb flat-topped Mt Hikurangi (770m), north-east of the town. The curious hill can be seen from far and wide. Before climbing, you must ask permission from the owner (☎ (07) 895 3031).

The Ohinetonga Scenic Reserve on the banks of the Whakapapa River, 26km south of town at Owhango, has bush walks lasting from one to three hours.

Places to Stay

The *Taumarunui Camping Ground* (☎ (07) 895 9345) is on the banks of the Whanganui River near SH4, 3km east of town. Tent/powered sites are $14/16 for two, cabins are $25 a double and a family unit is $45. Features of the camp include kayaks and bicycles for hire, bush walks, overnight tramping and guided tours. For those who have just finished a river journey, there is a laundry.

Taumarunui has no hostels, but the *Grand Lodge Private Hotel* (☎ (07) 895 7876) on the main drag, Hakiaha St, is a private hotel with basic singles/doubles for $25/37; it has kitchen facilities.

A better bet is the *Taumarunui Alpine Inn* (☎ (07) 895 7033) on the corner of Marae and Miriama Sts. This is basically a large pub with a name change to attract ski groups, but the rooms are clean, comfortable and good value. It has backpackers rates of $20/32 for singles/doubles (linen extra) or regular rooms with attached bathroom for $35/45. It has a restaurant and lounge bar with entertainment, and small kitchens for guests to cook in. The motel across the road, *Calvert's Spa* (☎ (07) 895 8500), has good units for $50/75; there are some private spas and a light breakfast is included.

On SH4 at the west end of town, *Kelly's Motel* (☎ (07) 895 8175) has studio singles/doubles at $48/70, plus two-bedroom family units. The more luxurious *Central Park Motor Inn* (☎ (07) 895 7132) on Maata St has a pool and *Zeeber's Restaurant*. Other motels include the *Hilton Motel* (☎ (07) 895 7181/2) on Hakiaha St ($52/75) and *Tattles Motel* (☎ (07) 895 8063) on the corner of Marae and Huia Sts ($50/66). Contact the information centre for a list of B&Bs (charging around $60 per adult).

Places to Eat

The *Main Trunk Cafe* on Hakiaha St on the east end of town is in a brightly painted, red, 1913 railway passenger car, now restored and converted to a cheerful cafe. It's open 24 hours, with a menu of fish and chips, burgers, sandwiches and the like. Adjacent is *Platform 2*, a pleasant coffee bar with a varied lunch menu.

There are other tearooms, takeaways and cafes along Hakiaha St and down the side streets, including two Chinese restaurants and the *Rivers II Cafe* on the corner of Marae St – the latter is an upmarket coffee bar with an excellent selection of vegetarian dishes.

The licensed *Pinnacles Restaurant* at the Taumarunui Alpine Inn has reasonably priced meals. The *Willows Restaurant* upstairs on Hakiaha St opposite the train station is also licensed. The lounge bar at the Alpine Inn has live music (or the dreaded karaoke) occasionally.

Getting There & Away

Buses and trains travelling between Auckland and Wellington all stop at the train station at Taumarunui. The station also houses the information centre, where you can buy tickets.

Hitching is easy heading north or south on SH4. It is a lot more difficult to hitch on the lightly trafficked Stratford-Taumarunui Road.

Taranaki

The Taranaki region juts out into the Tasman Sea on the west coast of the North Island, about halfway between Auckland and Wellington. The region is named after the large Mt Taranaki volcano, also called Mt Egmont, whose massive cone dominates the landscape. Conditions are excellent for agriculture, with rich volcanic soil and abundant rainfall.

The names Taranaki and Egmont are both widely used in the region. Taranaki is the traditional Maori name for the volcano and Egmont is the name James Cook gave it in 1770, after the Earl of Egmont, who had encouraged his expedition. Today the region is called Taranaki, the cape is called Cape Egmont, and the waters on either side of the cape are called the North and South Taranaki bights. Egmont National Park remains the name of the national park, but in 1986 the NZ government ruled that Mt Taranaki and Egmont are *both* official names for the volcano.

In addition to the obvious attraction of Taranaki – the 'most climbed' mountain in NZ – the region is popular for its world-class surfing and windsurfing beaches.

NEW PLYMOUTH

Principal centre of the Taranaki region, New Plymouth (population 66,500) is about equidistant from Auckland (373km) and Wellington (357km). A coastal city, with Mt Taranaki towering behind it and surrounded by rich agricultural and dairy lands, New Plymouth is a good base for visiting Egmont National Park. In parts it is attractive, featuring fine parks and the spectacular backdrop of Mt Taranaki, but near the sea the city's industrial installations blight the landscape.

History

Archaeological evidence shows that the region was settled by the Maori from early times. In the 1820s the Taranaki Maori took off to the Cook Strait region in droves to

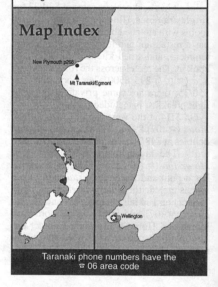

HIGHLIGHTS

- Walking, mountain climbing or skiing on the awe-inspiring Mt Taranaki volcano
- Visiting Maori and European historical sites
- Windsurfing or surfing the beaches of Oakura, Opunake and New Plymouth
- Driving along the Stratford-Taumarunui Heritage Trail

Map Index

New Plymouth p268

Mt Taranaki/Egmont

Wellington

Taranaki phone numbers have the ☎ 06 area code

avoid a threatened attack by the Waikato tribes, but it was not until 1832 that the Waikato tribes attacked and subdued the remaining Te Ati-awa tribe, except at Okoki Pa (New Plymouth) where whalers had joined in the battle. So when the first European settlers arrived in the district in 1841, the coast of Taranaki was almost deserted. Initially it seemed there would be no opposition to land claims, so the New Zealand Company was able to buy extensive tracts from the Te Ati-awa who had stayed.

When other members of the Te Ati-awa

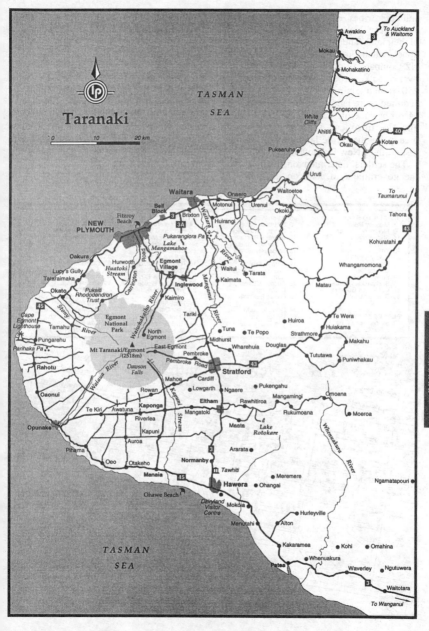

and other tribes returned after years of exile and slavery they objected strongly to the sale of their land. Their claims were substantially upheld when Governor Fitzroy ruled that the NZ Company was only allowed to retain just over 10 sq km around New Plymouth of the 250 it had claimed. The Crown slowly acquired more land from the Maori, but the Maori became increasingly reluctant to sell and the European settlers increasingly greedy for the fertile land around Waitara, just north of New Plymouth.

The settlers' determination finally forced the government to abandon its policy of negotiation, and in 1860 war broke out. For 10 years the Maori kept the military engaged in guerrilla warfare. During this time, settlers moved in on Waitara and took control there, but the Maori came and went as they pleased throughout the rest of the province. The Taranaki chiefs had not signed the Treaty of Waitangi and did not recognise the sovereignty of the British queen, so they were treated as rebels. By 1870 over 500 hectares of their land had been confiscated and much of the rest acquired through extremely dubious transactions.

The Taranaki province experienced an

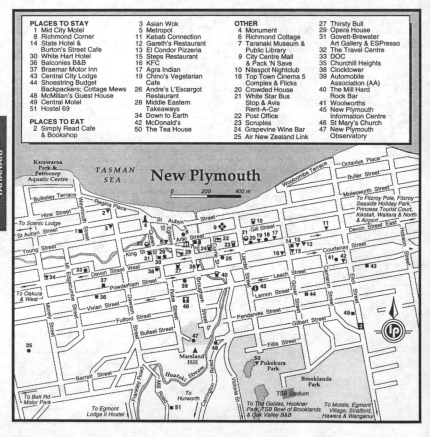

PLACES TO STAY
1 Mid City Motel
8 Richmond Corner
14 State Hotel & Burton's Street Cafe
30 White Hart Hotel
36 Balconies B&B
37 Braemar Motor Inn
43 Central City Lodge
44 Shoestring Budget Backpackers; Cottage Mews
48 McMillan's Guest House
49 Central Motel
51 Hostel 69

PLACES TO EAT
2 Simply Read Cafe & Bookshop
3 Asian Wok
5 Metropol
11 Kebab Connection
12 Gareth's Restaurant
13 El Condor Pizzeria
15 Steps Restaurant
16 KFC
17 Agra Indian
19 Chino's Vegetarian Cafe
26 Andre's L'Escargot Restaurant
28 Middle Eastern Takeaways
34 Down to Earth
42 McDonald's
50 The Tea House

OTHER
4 Monument
6 Richmond Cottage
7 Taranaki Museum & Public Library
9 City Centre Mall & Pack 'N Save
10 Nitespot Nightclub
18 Top Town Cinema 5 Complex & Flicks
20 Crowded House
21 White Star Bus Stop & Avis Rent-A-Car
22 Post Office
23 Scruples
24 Grapevine Wine Bar
25 Air New Zealand Link
27 Thirsty Bull
29 Opera House
31 Govett-Brewster Art Gallery & ESPresso
32 The Travel Centre
33 DOC
35 Churchill Heights
38 Clocktower
39 Automobile Association (AA)
40 The Mill Hard Rock Bar
41 Woolworths
45 New Plymouth Information Centre
46 St Mary's Church
47 New Plymouth Observatory

TARANAKI

economic boom with the discovery of natural gas and oil at Kapuni in 1959 and more recently at the Maui natural gas field off the coast of South Taranaki.

Information

Devon St (East and West) is the main street; its central section is a mall. The New Plymouth Information Centre (☎ (06) 759 6080; fax 759 6073) on the corner of Liardet and Leach Sts is open from 8.30 am to 5 pm on weekdays and 10 am to 3 pm on weekends, with a computerised information line operating 24 hours a day. The staff are helpful and the informative brochures – *Options* and *Taranaki for Free* – are good.

The DOC office (☎ (06) 758 0433; fax 758 0430) at 220 Devon St West is open from 8 am to 4.30 pm on weekdays. The Automobile Association (AA) office (☎ (06) 757 5646) is at 49-55 Powderham St and the main post office is on Currie St.

Museums & Galleries

The **Taranaki Museum** on Ariki St, between Brougham and Egmont Sts, has a collection of Maori artefacts, wildlife exhibits including moa and whale skeletons, and an early colonists' exhibition. It is open from 10.30 am to 4.30 pm on weekdays and 1 to 5 pm on weekends (entry is free, but donations are welcome).

The **Govett-Brewster Art Gallery**, on the corner of Queen and King Sts, is a renowned contemporary art gallery with a good reputation for its adventurous shows. Fans of abstract animation on film should seek out the films of Len Lye, pioneer animator of the 1930s, whose works are held here and shown from time to time. It's open from 10.30 am to 5 pm daily (entry is free, except during special exhibitions).

Historic Places

If you like historic sites, pick up a free *Heritage Walkway* leaflet from the information centre, which outlines a self-guided tour of 30 historic sites around the city.

Richmond Cottage on Ariki St on the corner of Brougham St was built in 1853.

Unlike most early cottages, which were made of timber, Richmond Cottage was sturdily built of stone. From June to October it's open from 2 to 4 pm on Friday and 1 to 4 pm on weekends. Otherwise it's also open on Monday, Wednesday and Friday from 2 to 4 pm ($1, children 20c).

St Mary's Church on Vivian St between Brougham and Robe Sts, built in 1846, is the oldest stone church in NZ. Its graveyard has headstones of early settlers and of soldiers who died during the Taranaki wars. Impressed by their bravery, the British also buried several Maori chiefs here.

On Devon St at the eastern end of the city is the **Fitzroy Pole**, erected by the Maori in 1844 to mark the point beyond which Governor Fitzroy had forbidden settlers to acquire land. The carving on the bottom of the pole depicts a sorrowful Pakeha topped by a cheerfully triumphant Maori.

Marsland Hill & Observatory

The New Plymouth Observatory is on Marsland Hill off Robe St. Public nights are held every Tuesday and include a planetarium program and viewing through a 6 inch refractor telescope if the weather is clear; opening times are 7.30 to 9.30 pm from March to October and 8 to 10 pm from November to March ($2, children $1).

Paritutu & Other Viewpoints

Above the power station is Paritutu, a steep hill with a magnificent view from the top. The name means 'rising precipice' and it's worth the tiring but quick scramble to the summit. Not only do you look down on the station but also out over the city and the rocky Sugar Loaf Islands rising just offshore.

Another good viewpoint is Churchill Heights, with a trig marker on top showing directions and distances to places near and far. You can walk up from Morley St or drive up from the entrance on Cutfield St.

Parks

New Plymouth is renowned for its superb parks. **Pukekura Park**, a 10-minute walk from the city centre, is worth a visit, with 49 hectares of gardens, bush walks, streams, waterfalls, ponds and a kiosk cafe. Display houses with orchids and other exotic plants are open daily from 10 am to noon and 1 to 4 pm. Rowing boats on the lake can be hired on weekends, holidays and summer evenings. The lights and decorations in Pukekura Park from mid-December to early February are worth making a special trip to see. The park also has a delightful cricket oval in the English tradition.

Adjoining Pukekura is the lovely **Brooklands Park** and, between the two, the Bowl of Brooklands, an outdoor sound-shell in a bush and lake setting. Brooklands Park was once the land around an important early settler's home; the fireplace and chimney are all that remain of the house after the Maori burnt it down. Highlights include a 2000-year-old puriri tree, a rhododendron dell with over 300 varieties, and a children's zoo open daily from 9 am to 6 pm.

On the waterfront is **Kawaroa Park**, with green areas, squash courts and the Petrocorp Aquatic Centre, which has a waterslide, an outdoor pool and an indoor pool (open all year). Also on the waterfront in the central city area is Pukeariki Landing, an historic area with sculptures.

Sugar Loaf Islands Marine Park

This marine park, established in 1986, includes the rocky islets offshore from the power station, Back Beach on the west side of Paritutu, and the waters up to about 1km offshore. The islands, eroded volcanic remnants, are a refuge for seabirds, NZ fur seals and marine life; the greatest number of seals present is from June to October but some are there year-round.

Activities in the park include boating and sailing, diving, birdwatching, pole fishing, surfing and beach walks. Boat trips to the islands are popular in summer. Happy Chaddy's Charters (☎ (06) 758 0228) depart from Lee Breakwater hourly from 8.30 am to 5.30 pm ($20, children $10).

Walking

The information centre has leaflets on good walks around New Plymouth, including coastal walks and others through local reserves and parks, in addition to the Heritage Walkway already mentioned. The Te Henui Walkway, extending from the coast at East End Reserve to the city's southern boundary, is one of the most interesting and varied. The Huatoki Valley walkway, following the Huatoki Stream, makes an attractive walk to the city centre. There are many walks on Mt Taranaki; the New Plymouth Tramping Club (☎ (06) 757 9622, 756 7497) may help visiting walkers.

Surfing & Windsurfing

Besides being beautiful to look at, the Taranaki coastline is a world-class surfing and windsurfing area. In the New Plymouth area, Fitzroy and East End beaches are at the eastern end of the city. Fitzroy is a surfing beach and can be reached by bus from New Plymouth. There's also good surf at Back Beach, by Paritutu at the western end of the city, and at Oakura, 15km west of New Plymouth. There are no buses to Oakura but hitchhiking is easy.

The Sirocco Windsurfing Shop & School, also called the Coastal Surf Shop (☎ (06) 752 7562), on SH45 just before Oakura, hires out surfboards and sailboards and offers instruction. Vertigo Total Surf (☎ (06) 752 7363) is also on the Main Rd in Oakura. Both are good sources of up-to-the-minute information on wind and surf conditions.

Aerial Sightseeing

Several operators offer scenic flights around the area including flights over the snow-capped summit of Mt Taranaki – superb if the weather's clear. They include Air Taranaki (☎ (06) 745 4375), the New Plymouth Aero Club (☎ (06) 755 0500) and the Stratford Aero Club (☎ (06) 756 6628/7771).

Organised Tours

Neuman's Sightseeing Tours (☎ (06) 758 4622) at 78-80 Gill St has a variety of tours, ranging from a $30 half-day scenic city tour to a full-day tour around Mt Taranaki ($40) or down the Stratford-Taumarunui Heritage

Trail ($60). Tubby's Tours (☎ (06) 753 6306), operating a daily shuttle service to Mt Taranaki, offers city tours for from $30 for three hours. Cruise NZ Tours (☎ (06) 758 3222) comes highly recommended; its city tour is $35.

Places to Stay

Camping & Cabins The *Belt Rd Motor Camp* (☎ (06) 758 0228) at 2 Belt Rd is on a bluff overlooking the port, 1.5km west of the centre. Tent and powered sites are $17 for two, backpackers cabins are $22 per person and other cabins range from $30 to $40 for two, depending on facilities.

In Fitzroy, 3.5km east of the centre, the *Fitzroy Seaside Holiday Park* (☎ (06) 758 2870) is at the end of Beach St beside a good surfing beach. It has tent and powered sites at $16 for two and cabins/on-site caravans at $33/38. Also in Fitzroy, *Princess Tourist Court* (☎ (06) 758 2566) at 29 Princes St has tent/powered sites at $16/18 for two, cabins ranging from $25 to $30 for singles or $30 to $35 for doubles, tourist flats at $40/49 and motel units at $50/59.

Heading around the coast in the other direction, the *Oakura Beach Motor Camp* (☎ (06) 752 7861) is an attractive camping ground right on Oakura, a beautiful beach for surfing and windsurfing. The turn-off to the beach is 1km west of Oakura, which is 15km west of New Plymouth. The cost for two is $14/16 for tent/powered sites.

Hookner Park (☎ (06) 753 9506/9168) at 551 Carrington Rd is a quiet, peaceful camp on a commercial dairy farm 10km south of the centre. Campers are welcome to join in the farm life. The cost for two is $17 in tent and powered sites, $28 in cabins or $30 in on-site vans.

Hostels The YHA-associate *Egmont Lodge* (☎ (06) 753 5720) at 12 Clawton St is a tranquil hostel in large, park-like grounds with a stream running through. It's a fair way (1.5km) from town – a 15-minute walk on a pleasant streamside walkway or phone for free pick-up from the bus station. The hostel is well set up for information on walks and

other activities. The cost is $15 in dorms, $25 in singles, twins and doubles are $36, or you can pitch a tent.

About the same distance from the centre, *Hostel 69* (☎ (06) 758 7153) at 69 Mill Rd is a small, pleasant hostel with services including free mountain bikes, free pick-up when you arrive and rides to good hitching spots when you leave. It's a friendly place with a large, well-kept garden and, when it's clear, stunning views of Mt Taranaki. It charges $13 in dorms, $13/28 for singles/doubles, and $7 per person to camp in the beautiful, secluded garden.

More central, the *Shoestring Budget Backpackers* (☎ (06) 758 0404) at 48 Lemon St is in a large, stately old home; it charges $13 in dorms, $25 in singles and $32 in doubles or twins (with TV it's $40). It's a well-equipped, friendly place with an outside patio, and the rooms are excellent. The *Central City Lodge* (☎ (06) 758 0473) at 104 Leach St is on a busy road but has off-street parking. Singles/twins are $25/40, backpackers beds are $15 (linen hire is $5 extra) and B&B is $40/60. The *Richmond Corner* (☎ (06) 759 0050), 25 Ariki St, is an old converted hotel with a great barbecue area, central location and sea views. Backpackers beds are $15 (in an eight-bed dorm) and singles/doubles are $26/48.

The *Scenic Lodge* (☎ (06) 751 3310) at 199 Centennial Drive is the former quarters for the power station; singles/doubles are $20/40 (there are weekly rates) and backpackers beds are $10.

B&Bs *Balconies B&B* (☎ (06) 757 8866) at 161 Powderham St is a fine place with singles/doubles at $50/70. *McMillan's B&B* (☎ (06) 758 2375), 32 Carrington St, near Pukekura Park, is also quite central. It's a good guesthouse with rooms at $40/60.

Other recommended B&Bs include: *Kirkstall* (☎ (06) 758 3222) at 8 Baring Terrace ($45/65); the stunning *Treehouse* (☎ (06) 757 4288) at 75 Morley St ($45/70); and the farmlet *Oak Valley* (☎ (06) 758 1501) at 248 Junction Rd ($65/95, dinner is $25). The information centre lists homestays and farmstays in the area.

Motels & Hotels New Plymouth has plenty of motels, charging from around $55/60 and up. The *Mid City Motel* (☎ (06) 758 6109) on the corner of St Aubyn and Weymouth Sts is reasonably central, with singles/doubles for $60/70. The *Central Motel* (☎ (06) 758 6444) at 86 Eliot St, a few blocks east of the centre, is small but convenient, with units at $65/75. The *Timandra Lodge Motels* (☎ (06) 758 6006) at 31B Timandra St off Coronation Ave, the extension of Eliot St, charges $60/70. The *Cottage Mews* (☎ (06) 758 0404), next door to the Shoestring Budget Lodge at 50 Lemon St, is good value, with tidy rooms from $55/60 (an extra adult is $10).

Other motel choices are *Coronation Court* (☎ (06) 757 9125), 226 Coronation Ave, with rooms at $65/75 (two-bedroom units are $105, an extra adult is $10) and the clean, friendly *Saddle & Sulky* (☎ (06) 757 5763), 188 Coronation Ave, with rooms at $68/78 (an extra adult is $15 and family units are from $88).

There are several old-style hotels around central New Plymouth. The *White Hart Hotel* (☎ (06) 757 5442) on the corner of Devon St West and Queen St has singles/doubles for $25/40. Or there's the *State Hotel* (☎ (06) 758 5373) on the corner of Devon St East and Gover St, with rooms for $42/55 and a family restaurant. More modern, the *Braemar Motor Inn* (☎ (06) 758 0859) at 157 Powderham St has singles/ doubles for $30/40 or doubles with private facilities for $50.

Places to Eat

Restaurants The BYO *Steps Restaurant* at 37 Gover St is a popular Mediterranean place offering good lunches and dinners and a pleasant atmosphere (the succulent sesame fish is $17.50).

The *Asian Wok* on the corner of St Aubyn and Dawson Sts has great value smorgasbords of Chinese, Thai and Indonesian food for $10 (a Thai green curry is $16.50). It's a

pleasant little cafe, open evenings only. For authentic, good Indian food try the *Agra Indian* at 151 Devon St East; it is open daily from 5.30 pm until late (for lunch on Thursday and Friday).

Chino's Vegetarian Cafe at 117 Devon St is a trendy BYO with blackboard menu (also featuring meat and fish dishes) which is open daily from 7 am to midnight. The *Metropol* on the corner of King and Egmont Sts is the place to taste NZ and Pacific Rim dishes.

Quality licensed restaurants include *Gareth's* at 182 Devon St East (with whitebait entrees for $13.50), or the 'genuinely French' *Andre's L'Escargot* in a historic building at 37-39 Brougham St. At the latter beef mains are from $25.

Pub Food The *Mill Hard Rock Bar* on Courtenay/Powderham St on the corner of Currie St, popular for its evening entertainment, has a dining area with bar meals always available; it's open from 11 am until late daily, except Sunday.

The licensed *Burton's Street Cafe* in the State Hotel (see Places to Stay) is open daily for all meals.

Fast Food New Plymouth is a small city but the *McDonald's* on the corner of Leach and Eliot Sts is absolutely huge. There's an equally large *KFC* on the corner of Courtenay and Gover Sts. There are plenty of Chinese takeaways around the centre, especially on Devon St, and a *Burger Wisconsin*, also on Devon St.

El Condor Pizzeria on Devon St East near the corner of Gover St is a trendy little pizza and pasta place with a difference. It's Argentinian and open from Tuesday to Sunday for dinner – mini/medium/large pizzas are $7/14/20. In the same block, the *Kebab Connection* at No 211A features doner kebab and other Middle Eastern fare. On Devon St West, between Egmont and Brougham Sts, is the ever reliable *Middle Eastern Takeaways*.

In the City Centre shopping mall on Gill St there's a food hall with Chinese and Italian food, seafood, wholefood, sandwich and dessert counters, and a *Robert Harris Coffee Shop* upstairs (with superb sea views). Also in the City Centre shopping mall is the large *Pack 'N Save* supermarket for groceries. *Woolworths* is on Leach St between Eliot and Cameron Sts, beside McDonald's. *Down to Earth* is a bulk wholefood grocery on the corner of Devon St West and Morley St with 'healthy takeaways'.

Simply Read Cafe & Bookshop on the corner of Dawson and Hine Sts is a bookstore cafe and an ideal place for a coffee (a bottomless cup is $1.50) and snack during the day with views across the sea. Vegetarian lunches are around $5. Other good cafes are *ESPresso* in the Govett-Brewster Art Gallery, *Flicks* in the Top Town Cinema 5 complex on Devon St East, and the *Kiosk* (aka the *Tea House*) in Pukekura Park.

Entertainment

The *TSB Bowl of Brooklands* at the entrance to Brooklands Park is a large, fine outdoor theatre where concerts are held; the information centre will have current schedules and prices. The *Opera House* on Devon St West stages a variety of performances.

The *Mill Hard Rock Bar* (see Places to Eat) is a popular place for a night out, with a section for bands from Wednesday to Saturday night and a separate disco. Bar meals are available and it's known for having something enjoyable for all ages. The *White Hart Hotel* on the corner of Devon St West and Queen St has live bands in the bar on Friday night.

Other popular night spots include *Crowded House* and *Scruples*, both on Devon St; the *Thirsty Bull* on Devon St West; and the *Grapevine Wine Bar* on the corner of Currie and Devon Sts. The latter is open from 5 pm from Monday to Saturday and also serves meals (entrées $10, mains $20).

Getting There & Away

Air Air New Zealand Link (☎ (06) 757 9057), 12-14 Devon St East, has direct flights to Auckland, Hamilton, Nelson, Wanganui and Wellington, with onward connections.

Bus InterCity (☎ (06) 759 9039) stops at the Travel Centre on the corner of Queen and King Sts. It has several buses daily heading north to Hamilton and Auckland, and southeast to Wanganui and Palmerston North, from where buses proceed south to Wellington or east to Napier and Gisborne.

White Star (☎ (06) 758 3338) buses depart from the Avis Rent-A-Car office at 25 Liardet St. They operate daily except Saturday, with two buses a day heading to Wellington ($65) via Wanganui and Palmerston North.

C Tours (☎ (06) 758 1777) has buses, on demand, to Auckland ($69) via Otorohanga and Hamilton.

Hitching For hitching north, a good spot is on Courtenay St about 1.5km east of the centre; anywhere from about Hobson St eastwards is good, the further out the better.

South towards Wanganui, a good hitching spot is on the corner of Coronation Ave and Cumberland St, about 1.5km south of the centre.

To hitch west around the Taranaki coast towards Oakura, head west out of town on Devon St West, which becomes South Rd.

Getting Around

The New Plymouth airport is 11km east of the centre. Withers (☎ (06) 751 1777) operates a door-to-door shuttle to and from the airport ($10).

City buses operate daily except Sunday. The information centre has local timetables.

Tubby's Tours (☎ (06) 753 6306) operates an on-demand shuttle service from New Plymouth to Mt Taranaki; for details see the Mt Taranaki/Egmont section.

AROUND NEW PLYMOUTH

Egmont National Park, of course, is the primary attraction of the New Plymouth area, but there are several other places of interest, all within about 20km of New Plymouth. Hurworth, the Pouakai Zoo Park and the Pukeiti Rhododendron Trust can all be reached by heading south from the centre on Carrington Rd.

Tupare

Tupare, 7km south of New Plymouth, is a fine three-storey Tudor-style house surrounded by 3.6 hectares of lush English garden. It's part of the National Trust; look for it at 487 Mangorei Rd on the Waiwhakaiho River. The garden is open from 9 am to 4 pm daily on 1 September to 31 March ($5, children free).

Hurworth

This early homestead at 552 Carrington Rd, about 8km south of New Plymouth, dates from 1856. Its pioneer builder and first occupant, Harry Atkinson, was later to become New Zealand premier four times. The house was the only one at this site to survive the Taranaki wars and is today owned by the Historic Places Trust. It's open from 10 am to 4 pm from Wednesday to Sunday ($3.50, children $1).

Pukeiti Rhododendron Trust

This trust is a 4 sq km garden surrounded by native bush and internationally renowned for its large collection of rhododendrons and azaleas. Peak flowering of rhododendrons generally takes place from September to November, though the garden is worth seeing at any time of year.

Pukeiti is 20km south of New Plymouth; to get there, just keep following Carrington Rd all the way from town. The road passes between the Pouakai and Kaitake ranges, both part of Egmont National Park, but separated by the trust. Pukeiti is open daily from 9 am to 5 pm ($6, children free).

Lake Mangamahoe & TATATM

If you're heading out towards Stratford or North Egmont on SH3, stop at Lake Mangamahoe, 9.5km south of New Plymouth. It is a great setting for photographs of Mt Taranaki, reflected in its waters.

Opposite the lake, on the corner of SH3 and Kent Rd, is the Taranaki Aviation, Transport & Technology Museum (TATATM), with vehicles, railway and aviation exhibits, farm equipment and household items. It's open from 10.30 am to 4.30 pm on Sunday and public holidays ($4, children 50c).

Inglewood

This small village (population 2850), 13km south of New Plymouth, is worth a stop to visit *MacFarlane's Caffé*. This fine restaurant on Matai St is a real surprise with heaps of dining treats. Kids love the Moo's Fluffy ($1), all coffees are $2.50, teas are $2 and the fine house wines are $3. Particularly tasty are its South of the Border ribs ($15) and oven-baked lamb shanks ($15.50).

The *Forrestal Lodge* (☎ (06) 756 7242) at 23 Rimu St has backpackers beds for $15, and single/twin B&B for $25/45.

Waitara

Waitara is 13km east of New Plymouth on SH3. If you turn off SH3 at Brixton, just before Waitara, and head 7km south, you'll reach the site of the Pukerangiora Pa. It's beautifully situated on a high cliff by the Waitara River, but historically it was a particularly bloody battle site.

Rafting and canoeing on the Waitara and Mokau rivers are popular local activities. For details of times and costs, phone Camp 'n' Canoe (☎ (06) 764 6738).

Just beyond Waitara on SH3 heading east from New Plymouth is the Methanex NZ's Motunui Plant (☎ (06) 754 8009). Opened in 1986, it was the world's first plant to convert natural gas to petrol (gasoline) and remains the world's largest methanol production facility. Natural gas is piped here from the Maui natural gas field, 34km offshore from Cape Egmont; the synthetic fuel produced here meets a third of NZ's petrol needs. You can stop by the visitor centre near the plant's main entrance to see exhibits; it's open from 8 am to 5 pm daily (entry is free).

North via SH3

Heading north towards Waikato from New Plymouth, SH3 is a scenic route. This is the route to take for Waitomo, and buses heading north go this way to Hamilton. Get the free *Scenic 3 Highway* pamphlet from the

Otorohanga and New Plymouth visitor centres.

Heading past Waitara the highway follows the west coast with its high sand dunes and surf beaches. **Urenui**, 16km past Waitara, is a popular beach destination in summer. *Urenui Beach Motor Camp* (☎ (06) 752 3838) has a variety of accommodation right next to the beach and sand dunes. About 5km past Urenui, you can sample natural beers at the **White Cliffs Brewing Company**, a boutique brewery open during the week and from 10 am to 5 pm on Saturday (except Wednesday, 3 to 5 pm).

The brewery is near the turn-off to Pukearuhe and the **White Cliffs**, huge cliffs resembling their namesake in Dover. The cliffs dominate the coastal landscape and contain two-million-year-old marine sediments. A walkway along the cliffs leads from Pukearuhe to Tongaporutu via a tunnel from the beach, accessible only at low tide. On a fine day the full-day walk has superb views of the coastline and of Mts Taranaki and Ruapehu.

SH3 continues further north from Tongaporutu to Mokau, on the border of Taranaki and the Waikato. Mokau has a backpackers and other accommodation (see The Central West chapter).

MT TARANAKI/EGMONT

The Taranaki region is dominated by the massive cone of 2518m Taranaki – a dormant volcano that looks remarkably like Japan's Mt Fuji or the Philippines' Mayon.

Geologically, Mt Taranaki is the youngest of a series of three large volcanoes on one fault line, the others being Kaitake and Pouakai. Mt Taranaki last erupted 350 years ago, but is regarded as being dormant rather than extinct. The top 1400m is covered in lava flows and a few descend to 800m above sea level. An interesting feature is the small subsidiary cone on the flank of the main cone and 2km south of the main crater, called Fantham's Peak (1962m).

There's a saying in Taranaki that if you can see the mountain it's going to rain and if you can't see the mountain it's already raining!

The mountain is one of the wettest spots in NZ, with about 7000mm of rain recorded annually at North Egmont (compared with 1584mm in New Plymouth), as it catches the moisture-laden winds coming in from the Tasman Sea and sweeps them up to freezing heights. Still, it doesn't *always* rain there and the volcano is a spectacular sight on a clear day.

History

Mt Taranaki was supremely sacred to the Maori, both as a burial site for chiefs and as a hideout in times of danger.

According to legend, Taranaki was once a part of the group of volcanoes at Tongariro. He was forced to leave rather hurriedly when Tongariro caught him with the beautiful Pihanga, the volcano near Lake Taupo who was Tongariro's lover.

So angry was Tongariro at this betrayal that he blew his top (as only volcanoes can when upset) and Taranaki took off for the coast. Fleeing south in anger, pain and shame, the defeated Taranaki gouged a wide scar in the earth as he fled, meeting the sea at Wanganui and then moving still further west to his current position, where he's remained in majestic isolation ever since.

The Maori did not settle the area between Taranaki and Pihanga very heavily, perhaps because they feared the lovers might be reunited, with dire consequences. Most of the Maori settlements in this district were clustered along the coast between Mokau and Patea, concentrated particularly around Urenui and Waitara.

The Egmont National Park was created in 1900 and is the second-oldest national park in the country.

Information

If you plan to tramp in Egmont National Park, get hold of local information about current track and weather conditions before you set off. DOC operates two visitor information centres on the mountain, offering maps and advice on weather and track conditions. The North Egmont Visitor Centre (☎ /fax (06) 756 0990) is the closest to New

TARANAKI

Plymouth and therefore the most visited. It is open from 9 am to 5 pm daily from 1 December to 30 April. Otherwise it's open from 9 am to 4 pm on weekdays (except Tuesday, when it is closed) and 9 am to 5 pm on weekends. On the other side of the mountain, the Dawson Falls Visitor Centre (☎ 025 430 248) is open from 9 am to 5.30 pm from Thursday to Monday.

Other places for maps and information on the mountain include DOC's Stratford Field Centre (☎ (06) 765 5144) on Pembroke Rd, coming up the mountain from Stratford, and the DOC office in New Plymouth (☎ (06) 759 6080). There are also information centres around the mountain in New Plymouth (☎ (06) 758 6086), Stratford (☎ (06) 765 6708) and Hawera (☎ (06) 278 8599).

Tramping & Skiing

In winter, the mountain is popular with skiers, while in summer it can be climbed in one day. There are a number of excellent tramping possibilities, including hikes to the summit or right round the mountain. Shorter tracks ranging from easy to difficult and in length from 30 minutes to several hours start off from the three roads heading up the mountain.

Due to its easy accessibility, Mt Taranaki ranks as the 'most climbed' mountain in NZ. Nevertheless, tramping on this mountain holds definite dangers and should not be undertaken lightly.

The principal hazard is the erratic weather, which can change from warm and sunny to raging gales and white-out conditions amazingly quickly and unexpectedly; snow can come at any time of year on the mountain, even in summer. There are also precipitous bluffs and steep icy slopes. In good conditions tramping around the mountain, or even to the summit, can be reasonably easy, but the mountain has claimed over 50 lives. Don't be put off, but don't be deceived.

If you intend to go tramping, get a map and consult a conservation officer for current weather and track conditions before you set off. Some tracks marked on maps have been closed and other planned ones may have

opened. Be sure to register your tramping intentions and some emergency contact numbers with a DOC office. Read and heed its pamphlet *Taranaki: The Mountain*.

Make sure you get *Walks in Egmont National Park* ($1.50); if you intend to walk or climb for any distance or height then get the Infomap No 273-09.

A trip to the North Egmont Visitor Centre is worthwhile for the view, and there are numerous long and short tracks and bush walks as well. The centre has interesting displays on the park and the mountain, and screens an audiovisual.

The roads to the Stratford Mountain House Motor Lodge, East Egmont and Dawson Falls also have many worthwhile tracks and bush walks. From the Mountain House Motor Lodge, Pembroke Rd continues 3km to the Stratford Plateau and from there a 1.5km walk takes you to the Manganui ski area. Skiing equipment can be hired at the Mountain Lodge in Stratford (see Places to Stay).

There are two main routes to the summit. The safest and most direct route takes off from the North Egmont Visitor Centre; allow about six to eight hours for the return trip. This route on the north side of the mountain loses its snow and ice earliest in the year. Another route to the summit, taking off from the Dawson Falls Visitor Centre, requires more technical skill and keeps its ice longer; if you go up this way, allow seven to 10 hours for the return trip.

The round-the-mountain track, accessible from all three mountain roads, goes 55km around the mountain and takes from three to five days to complete. You can start or finish this track at any park entrance. There are a number of huts on the mountain.

If you are an inexperienced climber or want other people to climb or tramp with, DOC can put you in contact with tramping clubs and guides in the area. MacAlpine Guides (☎ (06) 751 3542) provides guided trips to the summit year-round; it also has abseiling trips to Dawson Falls. Another reliable operator is Chris Prudden (☎ (06) 758 8261).

Places to Stay
Camping, Cabins & Hostels There are many tramping huts scattered about the mountain, administered by DOC and reached only by trails. Most cost $8 a night (for two tickets, purchased from DOC offices), but some cost $4 (one ticket). You provide your own cooking, eating and sleeping gear, they provide bunks and mattresses, and no bookings are necessary – it's all on a first-come, first-served basis.

By the Dawson Falls Visitor Centre (☎ 025 430 248), *Konini Lodge* has bunkhouse accommodation at $18/12 for adults/children. Bring your own sleeping bag, food and kitchen utensils.

There are motor camps at New Plymouth, Stratford, Eltham, Hawera, Opunake, Waitara and Oakura, but camping is not encouraged within the park itself – you're supposed to use the tramping huts.

You will come to no 'arm at the *Missing Leg* (☎ (06) 752 2570), a small backpackers at 1082 Junction Rd in Egmont Village. It has dorm beds for $13 and doubles for $30. You can hire bikes for $10 per day and there are comprehensive horse-riding lessons for $15 per half-hour.

Guesthouses The *Dawson Falls Tourist Lodge* (☎ (06) 765 5457) beside the visitor centre is an attractive alpine-style lodge with lots of carved wood and painted decorations, good views, comfortable rooms and sitting rooms and a spacious dining room. It has singles/doubles for $80/110 (extra adults are $40); a four-course dinner is $35. A courtesy car will meet public transport in Stratford.

On the east side of the mountain, *Mountain Lodge* (☎ (06) 765 6100) on Pembroke Rd about 15km from Stratford, has rooms from $95 and chalet cabins with kitchens at $85 (breakfast is $9). You can hire skis in winter for use at the Manganui ski area.

Getting There & Away
There are several points of access to the park, but three roads lead almost right up to where the heavy bush ends. Closest to New Plymouth is Egmont Rd, turning off SH3 at Egmont Village, 12km south of New Plymouth, and heading another 16km up the mountain to the North Egmont Visitor Centre. Pembroke Rd enters the park from the east at Stratford and ascends 18km to East Egmont, Stratford Mountain House, the Plateau car park and Manganui ski area. From the south-east, Manaia Rd leads up to Dawson Falls, 23km from Stratford.

Public buses don't go to Egmont National Park but Tubby's Tours in New Plymouth (☎ (06) 753 6306) operates an on-demand door-to-door shuttle bus from New Plymouth to the mountain. The cost is $10 one way or $10/15 one way/return ($20 for less than three people), whether you return on the same or a different day.

AROUND MT TARANAKI/EGMONT
Mt Taranaki is the principal attraction but there are also other places of interest around the Taranaki region.

There are two principal highways around the mountain. SH3, on the inland side of the mountain, is the most travelled route, heading south from New Plymouth for 70km until it meets the coast again at Hawera. The coast road, SH45, heads 105km around the coast from New Plymouth to Hawera, where it meets up again with SH3. A round-the-mountain trip on both highways is 175km, although short cuts can be taken. Get a Taranaki Heritage Trails booklet, available free from information centres and DOC offices.

Stratford
Stratford, 40km south of New Plymouth on SH3, is named after Stratford-upon-Avon in England, Shakespeare's birthplace, and almost all of its streets are named after a Shakespearian character. The town (population 10,100) has a good visitor information centre (☎ (06) 765 6708) on Broadway, the main street; a DOC field centre (☎ (06) 765 5144) on Pembroke Rd, heading up to Mt Taranaki; and an AA office (☎ (06) 765 7331) at 298 Broadway North.

On SH3, 1km south of the centre, the **Taranaki Pioneer Village** is a four-hectare outdoor museum with 50 historic buildings.

It's open daily from 10 am to 4 pm ($5, children $2).

At Stratford is the turn-off for Pembroke Rd, heading up the mountain for 18km to East Egmont, the Stratford Mountain House and the Manganui ski area. It is also the southern end of the Stratford-Taumarunui Heritage Trail.

Places to Stay & Eat The *Stratford Holiday Park* (☎ (06) 765 6440) on Page St beside the King Edward Park has tent sites, powered sites, cabins, tourist flats and a backpackers bunkhouse with dorms for $16 per person, a kitchen/lounge area and an indoor heated pool.

The *Country Class Crafts & Green Cheese Cafe* in nearby Tariki has been recommended for its fine country fare.

Stratford-Taumarunui Heritage Trail

From Stratford, the Whangamomona-Tangarakau Gorge route (SH43) heads off towards Taumarunui in the central North Island. The route has been designated a Heritage Trail, passing by many historic sites, including historic **Whangamomona** village, Maori pa sites, small villages, waterfalls, abandoned coal mines and small museums. You can pick up a free Heritage Trails booklet from information centres or DOC offices in Stratford, Taumarunui or New Plymouth giving details of places of interest along the route; keep an eye out for the blue-and-yellow Heritage Trail signs along the way, with explanatory plaques.

It takes a minimum of 2½ to three hours to drive the 150km from Stratford to Taumarunui (or vice versa), as the road winds through hilly bush country and 30km of it is unsealed. Nevertheless it's a good trip if you can put up with the road. It's best to start early in the day; allow at least five hours for the trip if you plan to make stops to see the historic sites. Fill up with petrol from the Stratford or Taumarunui ends, as petrol stations are limited once you're on the road. This road is definitely off the beaten track.

Eltham & the Lakes

About 10km south of Stratford is Eltham, well known for its cheeses. You can get information from the Eltham Public Library (☎ (06) 764 8838) on High St; it is open from 9.30 am to 5.30 pm on weekdays.

Eleven kilometres south-east down the Rawhitiroa Rd is Lake Rotokare' (rippling lake), the largest stretch of inland water in Taranaki, where there's a 1½ to two-hour walk around the lake through native bush. The nearby artificial Lake Rotorangi, 46km long, is popular for boating and fishing.

On Manaia Rd 3km north of Kaponga, which is about 13km west of Eltham on the road to Opunake, is the large **Hollard Gardens**, administered by the National Trust. It's most colourful from September to November when the rhododendrons bloom but many other plants provide colour year-round. The vast array of rare plants makes it a horticulturist's delight, with posted half and one-hour walks through various gardens. It's open from 9 am until dusk daily from 1 September to 31 March ($5, children free).

Hawera

Hawera is on the coast 70km south of New Plymouth and 90km from Wanganui. The town (population 8400) has the Information South Taranaki office (☎ (06) 278 8599) at 55 High St, beside the dominating water tower. The AA office (☎ (06) 278 5095) is at 121 Princes St.

Elvis fans might be interested in visiting the **Kevin Wasley Elvis Presley Memorial Room** (☎ (06) 278 7624) at 51 Argyle St, which has a collection of Elvis records (over 2000) and souvenirs. Please ring (☎ (06) 278 7624) before you arrive (entry by donation).

The excellent **Tawhiti Museum** houses a private collection of remarkable exhibits, models and dioramas covering many aspects of Taranaki heritage. The lifelike human figures were cast from real people around the region; it's quite an unusual museum. A bush railway operates on the first Sunday of each month and every Sunday during school holidays. It is on Ohangai Rd near the corner of

Tawhiti Rd, 4km from town. It's open from 10 am to 4 pm from Monday to Friday, but on Sunday only from June to August ($5, children $1).

Two kilometres north of Hawera on Turuturu Rd are the remains of the pre-European **Turuturumokai Pa**. The reserve is open to the public daily. The Tawhiti Museum has a model of the pa.

Taranaki's newest attraction is **Dairyland** (☎ (06) 278 4537), an 'udder' delight on the corner of SH3 and Whareroa Rd, 2km south of Hawera. It has interactive and audiovisual displays (including a dairy tanker on its collection route) covering all aspects of the dairy industry. The licensed *cafe* revolves, simulating a rotary cowshed floor.

Places to Stay The *King Edward Park Motor Camp* (☎ (06) 278 8544) on Waihi Rd, adjacent to the park, gardens and municipal pool, has tent and powered sites, cabins and on-site vans.

Hawera has two farm backpackers beyond the Tawhiti Museum. *Ohangai Backpacker Farm* (☎ (06) 272 2878) on the Urupa Rd in Ohangai is a 300 milking cow dairy farm with a well-equipped backpackers in the paddocks. The cost is $14 in good four-bed rooms or $32 for twin rooms. German and French are spoken. Free pick-up from Hawera is offered, or take the Tawhiti Rd from Hawera, turn right in front of the museum and follow the signs for 5km.

Wheatly Downs (☎ (06) 278 6523) is another good farmstay backpackers also past the Tawhiti Museum – don't turn right but keep going straight on the Ararata Rd (the extension of Tawhiti Rd) for 4km beyond the museum. Dorm beds are $15 and twins/doubles are $36/40.

Oakura

If you're starting round the mountain from New Plymouth on the coast road, SH45, the first settlement you'll come to is tiny Oakura, 15km west of New Plymouth, known for its beautiful beach, which is great for swimming, surfing and windsurfing. Oakura has a craft shop called the Crafty Fox that is open daily, and a surfing and windsurfing shop.

The *Oakura Beach Motel* (☎ (06) 752 7680) on Wairau Rd charges $52/67. The *Wave Haven* (☎ (06) 752 7800) on the corner of Ahuahu and Main South Rds isn't far from the beach and is extremely popular with wave riders; dorms are $10/15 without/with linen and singles/doubles in shared rooms are $15/30.

The local pub has an attractive beer garden and there's the popular *Burnt Toast* diner and pizzeria for snacks.

Lucy's Gully

Lucy's Gully, 23km from New Plymouth on SH45, is one of the few places where exotic trees are being maintained in a national park. A pleasant picnic area, it is also the start of a couple of tracks into the Kaitake Ranges. Further along SH45, turn west at Pungarehu onto Cape Rd to reach **Cape Egmont Lighthouse** – it's closed to visitors.

Parihaka

Inland 2km from Pungarehu is the Maori village of Parihaka, formerly the stronghold of the Maori prophet and chief Te Whiti and once one of the largest Maori villages in NZ. Te Whiti led a passive resistance campaign against the ruthless land confiscation that was taking place with the expansion of European settlement. In the last military campaign in Taranaki, Te Whiti was defeated and jailed, and in 1881 Parihaka was razed. The heavily armed troops were opposed only by dancing children.

The spirit of Te Whiti lives on and his descendants and followers meet at Parihaka annually; it is not open to the public.

Opunake

Opunake (population 2100) is the largest town on the west side of the mountain. There's a fine beach in the small Opunake Bay, a peaceful place good for swimming and surfing. The information office (☎ (06) 761 8663) is in the Egmont Public Library & Cultural Centre on Tasman St.

Right on the beach, the *Opunake Beach*

Camp Resort (☎ (06) 761 8235) has tent/powered sites for \$7.50/8.50 per person, on-site caravans, and backpackers beds for \$13. In town, the *Opunake Motel & Backpackers*

(☎ (06) 761 8330), 36 Heaphy Rd, has motel units for \$55/70, a cottage and a large house for backpackers out the back where dorm beds cost \$18.

The Coromandel

The Coromandel is a rugged, densely forested peninsula where rivers force their way through gorges and pour down steep cliffs to the sea. The peninsula, with its beautiful coastal scenery and fine beaches, gets very busy in summer. Small towns and holiday resorts are scattered up and down the coast on both sides of the peninsula. The Coromandel Forest Park stretches almost the entire length of the peninsula and the landscape gets more rugged and more isolated further north. The peninsula is one of the best parts of the scenic Pacific Coast Highway which links Auckland with Napier.

South of the Coromandel Peninsula are the pancake-flat Hauraki Plains and, to the west, the birdwatchers' heaven, the Firth of Thames.

Getting There & Away

Air Great Barrier Airlines (☎ 0800 900 600) services the Coromandel Peninsula with its scheduled Auckland-Paihia-Great Barrier Island-Coromandel route. Its excellent Barrier Island and Coromandel Pass ($130) includes a flight from Whitianga to Great Barrier, or vice versa, on Wednesday, Friday and Sunday. Also included are a boat trip across to the Barrier and a bus trip to or from Auckland to Whitianga.

Air Coromandel (☎ 0800 275 912) has two flights daily between Whitianga and Auckland.

Bus Thames is the transport hub of the Coromandel. InterCity (☎ 0800 731 711) has daily buses from Auckland to Thames ($21), continuing on to Paeroa, Waihi, Tauranga and Rotorua. The InterCity bus travels daily in a loop from Thames to Coromandel, Whitianga, Tairua and back to Thames; it is $45 (inclusive with a Busplan). A $79 Coromandel Busplan, however, allows you to travel from Auckland to Thames and then do a loop of the peninsula. Once back in Thames, you have the choice of returning to

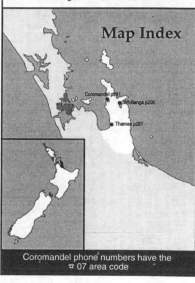

Map Index

Coromandel p291
Whitianga p295
Thames p287

Coromandel phone numbers have the ☎ 07 area code

Auckland or heading south to Rotorua or Tauranga. From Thames, this bus (Murphy-Turley) leaves for Coromandel at 10.15 am from the old train station and picks up at Sunkist Lodge; it costs $14.

Coromandel Bus Service/Carter Tours (☎ (07) 866 8598) runs daily (except Wednesday) from Coromandel to Thames return; it's $14/25 one way/return. A daily shuttle operates between Whangamata,

THE COROMANDEL

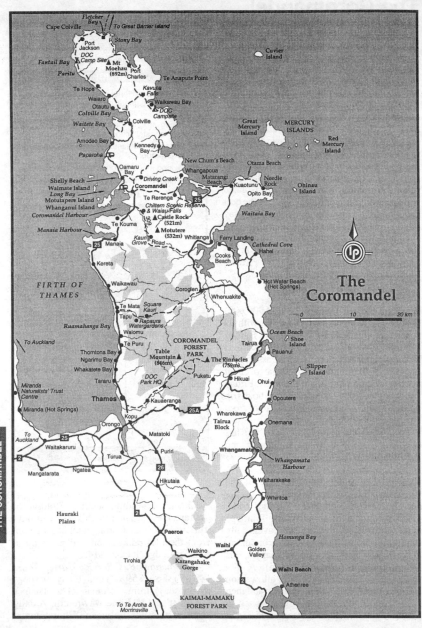

The Coromandel

Opoutere and Hikua, south of Tairua. There is also a connection from Whangamata (☎ (07) 865 8613) to Waihi and Tauranga. Three days a week, there is a service from Opoutere to Whitianga; bookings are essential and schedules vary for all these services.

Hitching Hitching is good on most of the peninsula but be prepared for long waits from Coromandel to Colville or across to Whitianga. Traffic on the east coast is busy during holiday periods, but otherwise light.

Boat The ferry from Princes Wharf, Auckland to Coromandel town is an on-again, off-again sort of thing; for a crystal ball appreciation of it all ring ☎ (09) 379 9072 or (07) 866 7084. If it happens, it's $29/55 one way/return.

Hauraki Plains

The pancake-flat Hauraki Plains are drained by the Piako and Waihou rivers, which flow into the Firth of Thames.

Birdwatching on the Firth at Miranda, and hot springs at Miranda and Te Aroha help slow the traveller down. To the east of the rural centre of Paeroa is the historic Karangahake Gorge and the mining town of Waihi.

MIRANDA

Avid birdwatchers will love this area, one of the most accessible for studying birds. It's off the Thames/Pokeno Rd, only an hour's drive from Auckland. The vast mudflat on the western side of the Firth of Thames is teeming with aquatic worms and crustacea which attract thousands of Arctic-nesting shore birds over the Arctic winter.

The two main species are the bar-tailed godwit and the lesser knot, but it isn't unusual to see turnstones, curlew sandpipers, sharp-tailed sandpipers and the odd vagrant red-necked stint and terek sandpiper.

Miranda also attracts internal migrants after the godwits and knots have departed,

including the pied oystercatcher and the wrybill from the South Island, and banded dotterels and pied stilts from both main islands. For more information, visit the Miranda Naturalists' Trust Centre; pick up a copy of *Shore Bird Migration to and from Miranda*.

The **Miranda Hot Springs** complex (☎ (07) 867 3955) has open and covered hot pools, private spas, play areas, and powered camp sites. It's open from 9 am to 9 pm daily ($5, children $2.50).

Places to Stay

The *Miranda Naturalists' Trust Centre* (☎ (09) 232 2781) has clean and modern rooms at its education centre. A bed here is a reasonable $15 for nonmembers ($10 for members), and an apartment costs $45/35. Membership of the trust is $20 per year.

Not far south of the centre, next to the hot springs, is the tidy *Miranda Holiday Park* (☎ (07) 867 3205), where tent and caravan sites are $12 per person, on-site vans $40 and the leisure lodge $70 for two.

PAEROA

The Maori name for the Coromandel range was Te Paeroa-o-Toi (the long range of Toi) and local Maori are believed to be descendants of the *Arawa* and *Tainui* canoes of the Great Migration fleet. In the days before the plains were drained, Paeroa (population 3670) was a thriving port and evidence of this can be seen in the Paeroa Historical Maritime Park. The double paddle steamer, *Kopu*, once operated between Paeroa and Auckland.

Lemon & Paeroa, New Zealand's own 'internationally famous in NZ' soft drink had its beginnings in this town but all that remains is one discarded giant empty bottle (left here after Gulliver's travels?).

The Paeroa Information Centre (☎ (07) 862 8636) is on Belmont Rd (SH2) and is open daily. The town has a small museum, open from 10.30 am to 3 pm on weekdays.

Karangahake Gorge

The Karangahake Gorge Historic Walkway,

along the Ohinemuri River, commenced when the Paeroa to Waihi railway line was closed in 1979. Waikino is at the eastern end of the gorge and, after floods in 1981, the only building left standing was the Waikino Hotel.

The visitor centre in Waikino, now the terminus of the 6km Waihi-to-Waikino vintage railway, has information on the history and walks of the area. The booklet *Karangahake Gorge Historic Walkway* by Derek Beisly and the DOC pamphlet of the same name outline several easy walks and suggest harder ones.

Three highlights of the walkway are the **Owharoa Falls** and the Talisman and Victoria **gold battery sites**. There's a small museum and a craft shop in Waikino ($5, children $1).

Places to Stay & Eat

The *Paeroa Hotel* (☎ (07) 862 7099), *Casa Mexicana Motel* (☎ (07) 862 8216), *Paeroa Motel* (☎ (07) 862 8475) and *Racecourse Motel* (☎ (07) 862 7145) are accommodation choices.

On Belmont Rd, you'll find the *Belmont Bakery* at No 15, the *Tui Coffee Lounge* at No 18 and the *Four Seasons Chinese* at No 70. On Normanby Rd (SH2) is the *Cosy Kitchen Tearooms*. The *Talisman Tearooms & Crafts* at Waikino serves light lunches.

TE AROHA

Te Aroha, 55km north-east of Hamilton on SH26, is at the foot of the mountain of the same name. Te Aroha means 'love', and Kahu-mata-momoe, sitting on the mountain summit, was filled with love for the land and people of Te Paeroa-o-Toi. It's well worth the climb.

In European times, Te Aroha became a favourite spa resort and the hot mineral and soda pools in the Domain are still a favourite place to relax after a walk in the area.

Orientation & Information

The Domain, a large park on Whitaker St a block or two south of the clocktower, has most of the town's attractions, including the Te Aroha Museum, the hot spa baths, a geyser, walking tracks to Mt Te Aroha, a restaurant and the information centre and DOC offices.

The Te Aroha Information Centre (☎ (07) 884 8052) in the Domain is open on weekdays from 9 am to 5 pm and on weekends from 10 am to 3 pm. It also serves as the town's Automobile Association (AA) agent and sells maps and provides information on Mt Te Aroha and the Kaimai-Mamaku Forest Park (on behalf of DOC).

Things to See

The **Te Aroha Museum** in the Cadman Building in the Domain, occupying the town's original bathhouse building, has exhibits on the mining and agricultural development of the town. It's open from 1 to 3 pm on weekends, daily during the school summer holidays (entry is by donation).

History buffs might also like to see NZ's oldest **organ**, the 1712 Renatus Harris pipe organ, in St Mark's church.

The **Hot Soda Water Baths** in the Domain have two types of thermal water: hot soda water and hot mineral water. All the baths are in private hot-tub pools; the cost is $6 (children $3) for half an hour. The baths are open daily from 11 am to 9 pm from Monday to Wednesday (until 10 pm from Thursday to Sunday); they're popular so book in advance on the weekend (☎ (07) 884 8717).

Behind the pools is the 3.5m **Mokena Geyser**, said to be the only hot soda-water geyser in the world. It's quite active, going off about every half-hour or so.

Walking

The walking tracks up Mt Te Aroha start at the rear of the Domain from behind the hot pools. It takes about an hour on a relatively easy track to ascend to the Bald Spur Lookout, also called the Whakapipi Lookout (350m); after that it's another two hours steep climbing to reach Te Aroha's summit (950m). The view is magnificent. The Wairere Falls, two waterfalls 73m and 80m high, are 26km south of Te Aroha.

Places to Stay & Eat

The *Te Aroha Holiday Park* (☎ (07) 884 9567), about 2km west of Te Aroha on Stanley Rd, has a swimming pool and tennis courts. Tent/powered sites are $17/18 for two, cabins start at $30 and tourist flats cost $52 a double.

The *Te Aroha YHA* (☎ (07) 884 8739) on Miro St is a pleasant small hostel (cottage) and charges $13 a night. Double rooms and free bicycles are available. Another budget option is *4 Seasons Lodge* (☎ (07) 884 9306) at 21 Waihou Rd; it has tent sites and single and double rooms.

The *Te Aroha Motel* (☎ (07) 884 9417) at 108 Whitaker St has units at $57/68. The information centre can provide referrals for farmstays and B&Bs in the area.

At the surprisingly trendy and licensed *Caffé Banco* at 174 Whitaker St, shop for collectables while lunching. The *Domain House Restaurant*, in a heritage building at 1 Wilson St, is more formal but a perfect spot for lunch.

Getting There & Away

Turley-Murphy Connections (InterCity ☎ 0800 468 372) has buses between Hamilton and Thames, stopping in Te Aroha daily except Saturday. These connect with InterCity services in Hamilton.

WAIHI

Waihi, once a booming gold-mining town, has a number of architectural reminders of its heyday. Gold was first discovered in 1878 and the Martha mine became the richest gold mine in the country and was worked until 1952. It has since been reopened (but not to the public).

The Waihi Information Centre (☎ (07) 863 6715) is on Seddon St next to the towering old Martha Hill Cornish pumphouse.

Things to See & Do

The interesting **Waihi Arts Centre & Museum** on Kenny St has superb models and displays about the local Martha Hill mine and is open from 10 am to 4 pm on weekdays and from 1.30 to 4 pm on weekends ($2, children $1).

Railway buffs from the **Goldfields Steam Train Society** (☎ (07) 863 8251) have repaired 8km of track between Waihi and Waikino and run trains between the two. To get to the train station turn off SH2 at Wrigley St and proceed to the end. The train runs daily at 11 am, 12.30 and 2 pm from Waihi and 11.45 am, 1.15 and 2.45 pm from Waikino ($8, children $4).

Waihi Beach, 11km east, is a small, expanding town with a fine surf beach which is popular in summer.

Places to Stay & Eat

The *Waihi Motor Camp* (☎ (07) 863 7654) is at 6 Waitete Rd in Waihi. At Waihi Beach is the *Athenree Motor Camp* (☎ (07) 863 5600) on Waihone Ave; the *Beachhaven Camp & Caravan Park* (☎ (07) 863 5505) on Leo St; and the *Bowentown Motor Camp* (☎ (07) 863 5381) at Waihi Beach South.

The *Golden Cross* (☎ (07) 863 6306) on the corner of Rosemount and Kenny Sts is an old pub offering backpackers beds for $15 in shared rooms, doubles and twins. The *Palm Motel* (☎ (07) 863 8461) on Parry Palm Ave and *Waihi Motel* (☎ (07) 863 8094) on SH2 have singles/doubles from $60/70.

At Waihi Beach, the *Waihi Beach Motel Hotel* (☎ (07) 863 5402) is a modern, beer barn-style pub with rooms from $60 with private facilities. The *Shalmar Motel* (☎ (07) 863 5439), 40 Seaforth Rd, has units for $85 a double.

The information centre has an up-to-date list of B&Bs and homestays in the area, such as *Pohutukawa Sands* (☎ (07) 863 4566) at 9 Glen Isla Place and the *Waihi Beach B&B* (☎ (07) 863 5250) at 16 Mayorview Terrace, both in Waihi Beach.

The country-style and licensed *Grandpa Thorn's* is at 4 Waitete Rd, Waihi; *Wings Cafe*, in an old cargo plane at the airport, and *Cactus Jacks* are at Waihi Beach; and the *Waitete Orchard*, which is home to all sorts of organic delights and fruit wines, is out on Waitete Rd.

THE COROMANDEL

Coromandel Peninsula

The Coromandel Peninsula has some of the North Island's finest coastal scenery and beaches. It is very much a bastion for those seeking an alternative lifestyle away from the bustle of Auckland, a serenity only briefly punctuated by the hordes of Christmas holiday-makers.

The west coast of the peninsula, bounded by the shallow Firth of Thames, is scenic and contains the picturesque historic towns of Thames and Coromandel, though the most spectacular coastal scenery is on the east coast. The east coast is the main resort area.

As a backdrop to this beautiful coastline, a rugged, forest-clad mountain range runs along the peninsula's spine, with many good opportunities for tramping.

History

Maori have lived on the peninsula since the first settlers arrived and the sheltered areas of the east coast supported a large population. This was one of the major moa-hunting areas of the North Island although other food sources included fishing, sealing, bird-hunting and horticulture.

The history of European colonisation on the peninsula and the plains to the south is steeped in gold-mining, logging and gum-digging. Gold was first discovered in NZ at Coromandel in 1852 by Charles Ring, but the rush was short-lived once the miners found it was not alluvial gold but gold to be wrested from the ground by pick and shovel. More gold was discovered around Thames in 1867 and over the next few years other fields were proclaimed at Coromandel, Kuaotunu and Karangahake. In 1892 the Martha mine at Waihi began production and by the time it closed in 1952 around $60 million of gold had been extracted. The area is rich in semi-precious gemstones like quartz, agate, amethyst, jasper, chalcedony and carnelian.

Kauri logging was big business on the peninsula for around 100 years. Allied to the timber trade was ship-building, which took off after 1832 when a mill was established at Mercury Bay. By the 1880s Kauaeranga, Coroglen (Gumtown) and Tairua were the main suppliers of kauri to Auckland mills. Things got tougher once the kauri around the coast became scarce due to indiscriminate felling, and the loggers had to penetrate deeper into the bush for the timber. Getting the logs out became more and more difficult. Some logs were pulled out by bullock teams, others had to be hauled to rivers and floated out after dams had been built, and tramways were built on the west coast. But by the 1930s the logging of kauri on the peninsula had all but finished.

A useful brochure entitled *Coromandel Peninsula: Heritage Trails* outlines urban heritage trails in Thames, Coromandel and Whitianga.

THAMES

Thames (population 6500) is the gateway to and main town of the Coromandel, lying on the shallow Firth of Thames. Its streets are lined with old wooden houses and pubs dating from the 19th century, when the gold rush and kauri trade made it one of the biggest towns in NZ.

Most visitors merely pass through Thames on their way to the scenic bays and beaches to the north and east.

Information

The Thames Information Centre (☎ (07) 868 7584) basks in its impractical isolation in the old train station on Queen St. It is open from 8.30 am to 5 pm daily in summer, with shorter weekend hours (9 am to 4 pm) in winter. Pick up a copy of the useful *Coromandel Directory*. Another excellent publication is *The Coromandel Travellers Guide*, available from the information centre or Sunkist Lodge.

The DOC office (☎ (07) 868 6381) in the Kauaeranga Valley is open from 8 am to 4 pm during the week. There's an AA office at 424 Pollen St, and the post office is also on Pollen St.

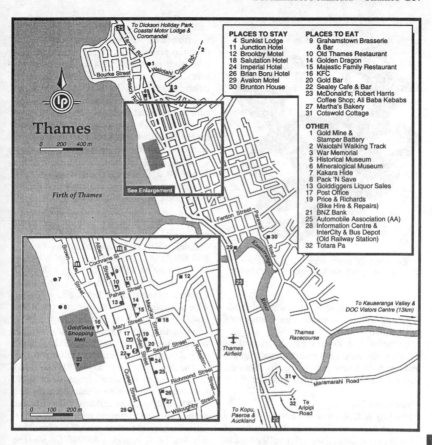

PLACES TO STAY
4 Sunkist Lodge
11 Junction Hotel
12 Brookby Motel
18 Salutation Hotel
24 Imperial Hotel
26 Brian Boru Hotel
29 Avalon Motel
30 Brunton House

PLACES TO EAT
9 Grahamstown Brasserie & Bar
10 Old Thames Restaurant
14 Golden Dragon
15 Majestic Family Restaurant
16 KFC
20 Gold Bar
22 Sealey Cafe & Bar
23 McDonald's; Robert Harris Coffee Shop; Ali Baba Kebabs
27 Martha's Bakery
31 Cotswold Cottage

OTHER
1 Gold Mine & Stamper Battery
2 Waiotahi Walking Track
3 War Memorial
5 Historical Museum
6 Mineralogical Museum
7 Kakara Hide
8 Pack 'N Save
13 Golddiggers Liquor Sales
17 Post Office
19 Price & Richards (Bike Hire & Repairs)
21 BNZ Bank
25 Automobile Association (AA)
28 Information Centre & InterCity & Bus Depot (Old Railway Station)
32 Totara Pa

Things to See & Do

At the northern end of town, visit the **gold mine and stamper battery** for a look at the town's gold-mining history. The Hauraki Prospectors' Association has set up a working stamper battery, as well as displays and photographs, and tours of the mine are conducted twice daily. It is open from 9 am to 4 pm, but usually closed in winter ($5, children $2, families $13).

The **Mineralogical Museum** on the corner of Brown and Cochrane Sts has a full collection of NZ rocks, minerals and fossils. It's open from 11 am to 4 pm daily. The local

historical museum, on the corner of Cochrane and Pollen Sts, has pioneer relics, rocks and old photographs of the town. It is open from 1 to 4 pm in summer ($2, children 50c).

The large concrete phallus overlooking the town on Monument Hill is in fact the **WWI Peace Memorial**, with good views of Thames and the surrounding countryside. Another good vantage point is the **Totara Pa**, once occupied by the Ngati Maru tribe until its defeat by Hongi Hika in 1821. It is now a cemetery, but careful observation will reveal the remains of fortifications and deep trenches.

THE COROMANDEL

Entwined tiki are a symbol of good luck –
these are an example from the Ngati Maru tribe

The **Kakara Hide** is an excellent bird-watching hide at the edge of the mangroves just off Brown St.

Bicycles and kayaks can be rented in Thames, the aero club offers scenic flights, and jet-boat tours run along the Waihou River – the information centre has details.

Places to Stay

Camping & Cabins The *Dickson Holiday Park* (☎ (07) 868 7308) is 3km north of Thames in an attractive, quiet valley beside a stream. Tent/powered sites cost $8/9 per person. The backpackers bunkroom (a YHA associate) costs from $12 to $15 per person, cabins start from $39 a double, a tourist flat with bathroom and colour TV costs $56 for two and motel units are $70.

See the North of Thames section for camp sites on the coast north of Thames.

Hostels *Sunkist Lodge* (☎ (07) 868 8808), 506 Brown St, is a relaxed hostel in a historic building that was the Lady Bowen Hotel from 1868 to 1952; it's said to have a resident ghost (we haven't been lucky enough to see it). Dorm beds cost $14 and $16 and twins

and doubles are $35. The upstairs verandah is a fine place to laze and watch the sunset over the placid Firth of Thames; there is a definitive pool table in the lounge downstairs. The manager, Geoff, is a mine of information on the Coromandel and you can arrange all your transport around the peninsula and to Great Barrier Island from here.

B&Bs & Guesthouses The information centre keeps a list of B&Bs and homestays. Of note for its historic charm is *Brunton House* (☎ (07) 868 5160), 210 Parawai Rd, a large house with verandahs and a swimming pool; singles/doubles are $40/75.

Motels & Hotels Motels abound in Thames and north along the coast towards Coromandel. The plain *Brookby Motel* (☎ (07) 868 6663) at 102 Redwood Lane is one of the cheapest at $52/58 for singles/doubles. The *Avalon* (☎ (07) 868 7755) on Jellicoe Crescent is more upmarket at $82 a double. The *Coastal Motor Lodge* (☎ (07) 868 6843), 3km north of Thames on SH25, is considerably more expensive with cottages from $95 for two or chalets for $115, but it's very attractive and pleasantly situated.

The *Brian Boru Hotel* (☎ (07) 868 6523), 200 Richmond St, on the corner of Pollen St, has double rooms with a bathroom for $66 to $88, with some imaginatively decked out as theme rooms complete with indoor waterfalls. The motel section next to the hotel has the best beds, charging $65/96 for singles/doubles.

The town's other hotels also have standard pub rooms. The *Imperial Hotel* (☎ (07) 868 6200) on the corner of Sealey and Pollen Sts has singles/doubles at $28/55 without bath. Desperados can try the *Junction Hotel* (☎ (07) 868 6008) on the corner of Pollen and Pahau Sts and the *Salutation* (☎ (07) 868 6488), 400 Mary St.

Places to Eat

Pollen St, reputed to be one of the longest straight shopping streets in NZ, has plenty of takeaways and coffee lounges, such as *Martha's Bakery*, for baked goodies. *KFC* is

The Coromandel
Top: Pauanui as seen from Paku Hill in its twin town, Tairua
Middle: Estuary sunrise, Opoutere
Bottom: West coast beach

HOLGER LEUE

HOLGER LEUE

HOLGER LEUE

HOLGER LEUE

The Coromandel
A: Cathedral Cove, near Hahei
B: Seaweed, Fletcher Bay

C: Opportunity shop staff, Coromandel
D: Lambs, Coromandel Peninsula

close to the Goldfields Mall, and in the mall itself is a *Robert Harris Coffee Shop* and the excellent *Ali Baba Kebabs*; at the latter, dwarfed by the nearby *McDonald's*, you get a great kebab for $6.

For value, the licensed *Old Thames Restaurant* on Pollen St is popular for moderately priced steaks, seafood and pizzas ($12 for a small, from $16 for a large); it's open daily from 5 pm. The *Majestic Family Restaurant*, 640 Pollen St, has a fish and chip takeaway at the front and good seafood meals in the restaurant around the back from $12, with slightly cheaper steaks. The *Golden Dragon* is the place for a cheap Chinese meal or takeaways.

The fancy restaurant at the *Brian Boru Hotel* serves three-course dinners, or you can dine à la carte. The restaurant features flounder, a Thames speciality, and the bar serves this with chips for $14.

Bars and cafes are proliferating. Most fashionable is the *Grahamstown Brasserie & Bar* at 719 Pollen St in a beautifully restored building. The food is expensive but good. The *Gold Bar*, on the corner of Sealey and Pollen Sts, is *the* place at the moment – apart from its grip on the nightlife you can get good Tex-Mex meals here. The entrée scallops are superb at $10.50. The *Sealey Cafe & Bar*, 109 Sealey St, is another fine establishment for a meal or just a drink. It has a pleasant courtyard out the front.

Just out of town on Maramarahi Rd, *Cotswold Cottage* is fully licensed and the menu combines seafood and game caught locally; a three-course meal is $35.

Getting There & Around

Thames is the main transport hub for the Coromandel; see Getting There & Away at the beginning of this chapter. Buses depart from the old train station (☎ (07) 868 7251), which sells tickets. Sunkist Lodge (☎ (07) 868 8808) also sells tickets and the Coromandel Busplan.

For local exploration, hire mountain bikes from Price & Richards on Pollen St for $15 per day.

COROMANDEL FOREST PARK

There are over 30 walks and tramps through Coromandel Forest Park, covering the area from the Maratoto Forest, near Paeroa, to Cape Colville. The most popular region is the Kauaeranga Valley which cuts into the Colville Range behind Thames. There are old kauri dams in the valley, including the Tarawaere, Waterfalls, Dancing Camp, Kauaeranga Main, Moss Creek and Waterfalls Creek dams; do not climb on them.

Walks in the Kauaeranga Valley, especially on weekends, have become so popular that DOC has built an 80-bed hut at the Pinnacles to accommodate trampers. One of the best, most accessible walks is through the valley to the Pinnacles. The three to four-hour hike through regenerating forest to the jagged limestone outcrop is rewarded with great views. Other walks can be done in the area, though some trails are hazardous and have been closed – check with DOC.

Information

The DOC Visitor Centre (☎ (07) 868 6381) is in the Kauaeranga Valley about 15km from Thames. It is open from 8 am to 4 pm on weekdays, and on weekends in summer. DOC has a pamphlet outlining mountain-biking tracks on the peninsula. Sunkist Lodge in Thames also has information about walks.

Places to Stay

DOC camping grounds are scattered throughout the Coromandel Forest Park. You'll find them on the west coast and northern tip of the peninsula at Fantail Bay, Port Jackson and Fletcher Bay, and at Stony Bay and Waikawau Bay on the east coast. All charge only a nominal fee; it isn't necessary to book.

Camping grounds ($5, children $2.50) are all along the Kauaeranga Valley Rd past the visitors centre. From the end of the road it is a two-hour walk to the Moss Creek camp site (camping fees are $6, children $3) or the Pinnacles Hut; the latter has bunks, toilets, cooking and washing facilities. Bring your own cooking gear. The cost for the hut is

$12/6; buy tickets from DOC or the Thames Information Centre.

Getting There & Away

The headquarters and main entrance to the park are reached from the southern edge of Thames along Kauaeranga Valley Rd. Sunkist Lodge in Thames has a bus going on demand to the end of the Kauaeranga Valley Rd for $17/34 one way/return. Hitching in and out is reputed to be easy.

NORTH OF THAMES

As you travel north from Thames, SH25 snakes along the coast for 32km past lots of pretty little bays and calm beaches. Fishing and shellfishing are excellent all the way up the coast and the landscape turns crimson when the pohutukawa blooms in summer.

Along the way you pass through Whakatete, Ngarimu Bay, Te Puru, Tapu and other small settlements. The **Rapaura Watergardens**, 6km inland from Tapu on the Tapu-Coroglen road, are open from 10 am to 5 pm daily in summer ($5, children $1) and there are tearooms. Also on the Tapu-Coroglen Rd is the huge 'square' kauri, estimated to be 1200 years old.

Places to Stay

The *Boomerang Motor Camp* (☎ (07) 867 8879) in Te Puru, 11km north of Thames, has camping, cabins and on-site vans. Nearby is the *Puru Park Motel* (☎ (07) 868 2686) and the luxurious *Te Puru Coast View Lodge* (☎ (07) 868 2326), a Mediterranean-style villa with singles/doubles for $90/140.

A few kilometres north is the *Waiomu Bay Holiday Park* (☎ (07) 868 2777) which has camping, on-site vans, cabins, tourist flats and motel units. The *Seaspray Motel* (☎ (07) 868 2863) is also in Waiomu; it charges $60/78.

At Tapu, 22km north of Thames, the *Tapu Motor Camp* (☎ (07) 868 4837) has camp sites, on-site vans and cabins. The backpackers rate is $12 per person in bunkrooms and cabins and caravans are $29 for two. Also in Tapu, the improved *Te Mata Lodge* (☎ (07) 868 4834) has rustic, hostel-style accommodation set in the bush at $12/24 for singles/doubles. There are plenty of bush walks, including one to the beach, and the rivers are good for swimming. To reach Te Mata Lodge, go 1.5km north past Tapu on the coast road, turn inland past the concrete bridge down Te Mata Creek Rd, and follow the road to the end.

COROMANDEL

At Wilsons Bay the road leaves the coast and cuts through hills and valleys until it reaches the next major town, Coromandel, 55km north of Thames. It was named after HMS *Coromandel*, which visited in 1820 to pick up a load of kauri spars for the navy. It was here, on Driving Creek, 3km north of the township, that Charles Ring discovered gold in 1852. At the height of the gold rush the town's population rose to over 10,000, but today it's a soporific little township of fewer than 1000 souls and is noted for its crafts and alternative lifestylers.

Information

The Coromandel Information Centre (☎ (07) 866 8598) is in the District Council building on Kapanga Rd. It's open from 9 am to 5 pm daily (in winter, weekend hours are 10 am to 2 pm). The centre has many useful leaflets on the surrounding area and takes bookings for accommodation. The DOC field centre in the building has information on parks and walks.

Things to See

The small **Coromandel Mining & Historic Museum** on Rings Rd has gold mining and colonial era exhibits. It's open daily from 10 am to 4 pm in summer ($2, children 50c). In winter, it is usually open on weekends.

The **Coromandel Stamper Battery** (☎ (07) 866 8765), also on Rings Rd, demonstrates the process of crushing ore, the first step in extracting gold, and shows various amalgamation processes. It is open daily in summer and on Friday and weekends in winter; there's a nominal entry fee.

Driving Creek (☎ (07) 866 8703), 3km north of Coromandel, is the site of various

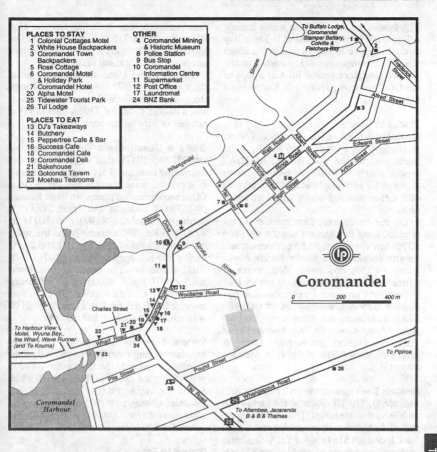

PLACES TO STAY
1. Colonial Cottages Motel
2. White House Backpackers
3. Coromandel Town Backpackers
5. Rose Cottage
6. Coromandel Motel & Holiday Park
7. Coromandel Hotel
20. Alpha Motel
25. Tidewater Tourist Park
26. Tui Lodge

PLACES TO EAT
13. DJ's Takeaways
14. Butchery
15. Peppertree Cafe & Bar
16. Success Cafe
18. Coromandel Cafe
19. Coromandel Deli
21. Bakehouse
22. Golconda Tavern
23. Moehau Tearooms

OTHER
4. Coromandel Mining & Historic Museum
8. Police Station
9. Bus Stop
10. Coromandel Information Centre
11. Supermarket
12. Post Office
17. Laundromat
24. BNZ Bank

Coromandel

fascinating enterprises masterminded by one of Coromandel's leading artists, Barry Brickell. A potter who discovered excellent clay on his land, Brickell had to work out a way of moving it down the hill to his kiln. So he built his own railway to do it! The **Driving Creek Railway** travels up steep grades, across four high trestle bridges, along two spirals and a double switchback, and through two tunnels. It's an hour-long round trip and Brickell takes visitors up to the top at 10 am and 2 pm daily, with extra runs at noon and 4 pm in summer ($10, children $5).

For crafts, Coromandel has interesting **craft shops** along Kapanga Rd, or, if you want to explore farther afield, pick up a copy of the *Coromandel Craft Trail* pamphlet from the information centre.

Walking

Coromandel is in the middle of a region abounding in natural beauty, scenic reserves, and attractive bush walks. The information centre has a big map on the wall showing all the scenic reserves and the two farm park recreation reserves with camping (at Cape Colville and Waikawau Bay).

A few of the more notable walks include a 3km walk from Coromandel to Long Bay through a grove of large kauris and a climb through Whangapoua State Forest to the 521m Castle Rock on 309 Rd. Get a copy of the DOC pamphlet *Walking in Coromandel* ($1).

Places to Stay

Camping & Cabins The *Coromandel Motel & Holiday Park* (☎ (07) 866 8830), 400m north-east of the post office, has tent/ powered sites at $9/10 per person. Cabins cost $36 for two people and motel units cost $85. Off-season and family tariffs are available.

On the beachfront, 3km west of Coromandel, *Long Bay Motor Camp* (☎ (07) 866 8720) has sites from $8.50 per person and on-site caravans. At *Shelly Beach Motor Camp* (☎ (07) 866 8988), 5km north of Coromandel, tent/powered sites are $8/11.

North of Coromandel are the *Oamaru Bay Tourist Flats & Caravan Park* (☎ (07) 866 8735) on Oamaru Bay (7km north); *Papaaroha Motor Camp* (☎ (07) 866 8818) at Papaaroha (12km); and *Angler's Lodge & Motor Park* (☎ (07) 866 8584) at Amodeo Bay (18km).

Hostels The *Tidewater Tourist Park* (☎ (07) 866 8888), 270 Tiki Rd near the harbour, is an YHA associate hostel. This friendly, spotless place has new hostel cabins and tourist flats. It charges $15 ($14 for YHA members) in dorms, and twins or doubles are $17 per person. Self-contained two-person tourist flats cost $70 and studio units $80. Cycles are rented out for $10 per day.

Tui Lodge (☎ (07) 866 8237), 600 Whangapoua Rd, is a quiet hostel 10 minutes walk from town. The Whitianga bus will stop at the gate or there's free pick-up on request. The backpackers house has a variety of accommodation; it charges $14 in the dorms or $30 for twins and doubles.

The *White House Backpackers* (☎ (07) 866 8468) on the corner of Frederick St and Rings Rd is based on three houses. Dorm rooms are $14 and twins and doubles $34. It

runs peninsula trips including tours to Hot Water Beach for $35 (two people $50). On Monday and Thursday it operates a free bus one way from Auckland ($20 return).

The tidy and clean *Coromandel Town Backpackers* (☎ (07) 866 8327), 327 Rings Rd, is a small hostel with dorm beds for $14 and a double room for $30. It also offers a number of trips on the peninsula.

B&Bs & Guesthouses The *Rose Cottage* (☎ (07) 866 7047) is on Pagitt St opposite the mining museum. This simple guesthouse in a private home charges $55 per person. Other recommended places are *Wave Runner* (☎ (07) 866 8956) at 240 Pagitt St ($75 a double); *Allambee* (☎ (07) 866 8011) at 1720 Tiki Rd ($70 a double); and the well-appointed *Buffalo Lodge* (☎ (07) 866 2933) on Buffalo Rd, open in summer only (from $180 a double). The peaceful *Jacaranda B&B* (☎ (07) 866 8002) is an imposing house set back off the highway 3km south of town; it has B&B for $75 a double or $110 with a queen-sized bed. Dinner is $25.

Motels & Hotels Coromandel has many motels charging from $65 to $85 a double. Possibilities include the *Wyuna Bay* (☎ (07) 866 8507), the *Harbour View* (☎ (07) 866 8690), the *Alpha* (☎ (07) 866 8709) and *Colonial Cottages* (☎ (07) 866 8856). The *Coromandel Hotel* (☎ (07) 866 8760) has rooms for $50 for two.

Places to Eat

For cheap meals, try the *Bakehouse* on Wharf Rd and its lasagne with smoked snapper and oysters for $9; the bistro bar at the *Coromandel Hotel*; the *Golconda Tavern*; the *Moehau Tearooms*; *DJ's Take-aways*; and the *Coromandel Cafe* for sandwiches and hot meals. The latter is open for breakfast, lunch and, during summer, great dinners.

On Kapanga Rd, the *Success Cafe* serves light lunches and has a full menu at night; the *Coromandel Deli* has inexpensive snacks (nachos from $5), sandwiches, coffees and a garden area out the back (Monday is pizza

THE COROMANDEL

night with large serves for $12); and the *Peppertree Cafe & Bar* has excellent seafood meals in the dining room or the more casual bar. The latter has fat and juicy Coromandel scallops for $24, snapper is about the same, and homemade feijoa ice cream for $7.50.

You can't buy provisions beyond Colville so stock up before you go. Or buy fish from the butchery and cook it yourself.

Getting There & Around

The shuttle to Fletcher Bay, operated by White House Backpackers (☎ (07) 866 8468), runs daily on demand at 11.30 am in summer; it is $16/30 one way/return. Also see the Getting There & Away section at the beginning of the chapter.

AROUND COROMANDEL
North of Coromandel

The road heading north is sealed up to the town of **Colville**, 85km north of Thames. Tiny Colville was formerly known as Cabbage Bay, named by Captain Cook who insisted that his crew eat the leaves of native cabbage trees, to guard against scurvy. Now it is home to alternative lifestylers; there is a small wholefood cafe and a quaint cooperative store which sells just about everything.

North of Colville the roads are rough and hitching may not be so easy. From Colville you can head north along the west coast to Fletchers Bay or head over the ranges to Port Charles.

Port Charles is just a small collection of holiday baches on a scenic bay with a pleasant beach. The road leads to another small bay with more holiday houses and then over a headland with fine views to **Stony Bay** with its pebble beach and DOC camping ground. From Stony Bay, tracks lead to Fletcher Bay and Mt Moehau.

Following the west coast road, 12km north of Colville, you will find Te Hope and the start of the walk to **Mt Moehau** (892m), the peninsula's highest peak. This is a demanding three to four-hour walk but is rewarded with fine views of Coromandel and the Hauraki Gulf. The trail continues on to Stony Bay – it's a full day's walk to cross the peninsula.

The west coast road leads eventually to **Fletcher Bay** – a real land's end. This is a magical place with deserted beaches, forest and coastal walks, sea kayaking, fishing trips, mountain biking and splendid views across to Great Barrier, Little Barrier and Cuvier islands.

From Fletcher Bay, it's about a three-hour walk to Stony Bay on the east coast. Sometimes groups who have access to transport drive as far as possible and walk the rest of the way, with a driver meeting them on the other side. A lot of people elect to walk both ways. It is an easy, pleasant walk with great coastal views and then an ambling section across open farmland. Mountain bikers must use the longer and tougher marked stock route that runs along the flank of Mt Moehau.

Places to Stay DOC has camping grounds at Fletcher Bay, Waikawau Bay and Stony Bay on the eastern side of the peninsula, and at Port Jackson and Fantail Bay on the western side.

Colville Backpackers & Farmstay (☎ (07) 866 6820) is on a farm where you can join in with the activities. A bed in the backpackers cottage is $14 to $16 per person, doubles are $32, the bush lodge is $12 per person or it's $55 for the whole place. Camping costs from $5 to $9.

The *Fletcher Bay Backpackers* (☎ (07) 866 8989) is a small, comfortable 16-bed place perched up on a hill overlooking a farm and beach; it has all facilities but you must bring food. It charges $16 per person and is closed from 1 June to 1 September.

SH25 to Whitianga

There are two possible routes from Coromandel south-east to Whitianga. SH25 is longer (46km, 1¼ hours) and much of it is still gravel but it's the more scenic route, following the coast and offering exquisite beach views. The other road is the unsealed 309 Rd.

If you continue on the much improved SH25 east of Coromandel you come to Te

Rerenga, almost on the shore of Whanga-poua Harbour. The road has some sections of dirt and tight corners on which you have to take care. It forks here; if you head north you come to the end of the road at Whangapoua. From Whangapoua you can walk along the rocky foreshore to the isolated and pristine **New Chum's Beach**. The walk takes about 30 minutes and starts by the picnic area at the end of the road.

Continuing east you can visit the beach-side towns of Matarangi, Kuaotunu, Otama and Opito before heading south to Whitianga. This whole stretch has beautiful beaches. **Matarangi** has a good beach but it is a dull real estate development, which seems to be the fate of parts of the Coromandel. **Kuaotunu** is a small settlement with a delightful beach and a camping ground. Off Opito Bay is the spectacular **Needle Rock**, so named because the hole through the rock is tapered like the eye of a needle.

Highway 309

Highway 309 (known locally as 309 Road) is the shorter way to Whitianga (32km, 45 minutes) but it's rather rough going as the road is unsealed. It's a bush road and is generally not as scenic as SH25, unless you want to get out and do some walking. It does have some excellent spots including the **Chiltern Scenic Reserve**, **Waiau Falls**, a grove of large kauri trees and a two-hour return walking track to the summit of **Castle Rock**. The **kauri grove** is particularly interesting as there is a Siamese kauri which forks just above the ground. The roots of the kauri are protected by a system of boardwalks.

The *309 Honey Cottage* (☎ (07) 866 5151) is about 12km from Whitianga on 309 Rd. It's a lovely place, relaxing and scenic, with farm and bush. The cost is $15 a night in an old kauri cottage beside a river, or you can camp for $5 ($10 if you use cottage facilities).

WHITIANGA

The pleasant Whitianga area of Mercury Bay has a long history by NZ standards. The Polynesian explorer Kupe landed near here around 950 AD and the area was called Te Whitianga-a-Kupe (the crossing place of Kupe). Prior to that, the land was abundant with moas and there is evidence that there were moa hunters here 2000 years ago.

Mercury Bay was given its modern name by Captain Cook when he observed the transit of Mercury while anchored in the bay in November 1769.

Whitianga is the main town on Mercury Bay. Buffalo Beach, the principal frontage onto the attractive bay, takes its name from HMS *Buffalo*, wrecked there in 1840. The beach itself is reasonable and there are seven good beaches all within easy reach of town.

The town is a big game-fishing base for tuna, marlin, mako (blue pointer shark), thresher shark and kingfish. It is very much a tourist town and its small population (2200) swells to mammoth proportions during the January holidays.

The Whitianga Information Centre (☎ (07) 866 5555), 66 Albert St, is open from 9 am to 5 pm on weekdays and 10 am to 3 pm on weekends.

Museum

The little museum opposite the ferry wharf has many historic photos of Mercury Bay and the kauri logging era, and exhibits on mining, blacksmithing, the colonial era, Maori carvings, the HMS *Buffalo* and other shipwrecks. The jaws of a 1350kg white pointer shark caught in the Hauraki Gulf in 1959 hang on the wall, overlooking all.

The museum is open daily in summer from 10 am to 3 pm (in winter 11 am to 2 pm four days a week); entry is $2 (children 50c).

Ferry Landing

From the Narrows, on the southern side of town, a passenger ferry crosses over to Ferry Landing, site of the original township on the southern side of Mercury Bay. The wharf at Ferry Landing was built in 1837 and the stone for it came from Whitianga Rock, a *pa* (fortified Maori village) site of which Captain Cook said 'the best engineers in Europe could not have chosen a better site for a small band of men to defend against a greater

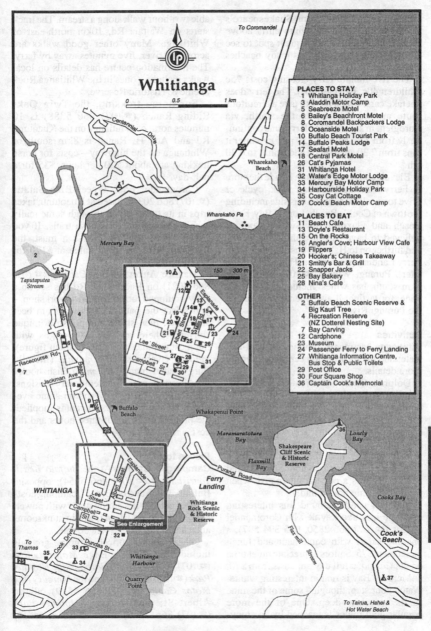

Whitianga

0   0.5   1 km

PLACES TO STAY
1   Whitianga Holiday Park
3   Aladdin Motor Camp
5   Seabreeze Motel
6   Bailey's Beachfront Motel
9   Coromandel Backpackers Lodge
9   Oceanside Motel
10 Buffalo Beach Tourist Park
14 Buffalo Peaks Lodge
17 Seafari Motel
18 Central Park Motel
26 Cat's Pyjamas
31 Whitianga Hotel
32 Water's Edge Motor Lodge
33 Mercury Bay Motor Camp
34 Harbourside Holiday Park
35 Cosy Cat Cottage
37 Cook's Beach Motor Camp

PLACES TO EAT
11 Beach Cafe
13 Doyle's Restaurant
15 On the Rocks
16 Angler's Cove; Harbour View Cafe
20 Flippers
20 Hooker's; Chinese Takeaway
21 Smitty's Bar & Grill
22 Snapper Jacks
25 Bay Bakery
28 Nina's Cafe

OTHER
2   Buffalo Beach Scenic Reserve &
    Big Kauri Tree
4   Recreation Reserve
    (NZ Dotterel Nesting Site)
7   Bay Carving
12 Cardphone
23 Museum
24 Passenger Ferry to Ferry Landing
27 Whitianga Information Centre,
    Bus Stop & Public Toilets
29 Post Office
30 Four Square Shop
36 Captain Cook's Memorial

0   150   300 m

THE COROMANDEL

number'. The view from Shakespeare's Lookout, on top of the white cliffs above Ferry Landing, is lovely, a great spot to see all of Mercury Bay with its many beaches and coves.

The five-minute ferry crossing costs 75c (children 40c, bicycles 40c). The ferry does not take cars, which have to take a circuitous route around the bay to the south, via Coroglen. In summer, the ferry runs continuously from 7.30 am to 10.30 pm; in winter it runs from 7.30 am to noon and from 1 to 6.30 pm.

Bicycles can be hired from beside the store in Ferry Landing. You can walk, cycle or drive to excellent spots on this side including the town of Cook's Beach, Lonely Bay, Front Beach and Flaxmill Bay (where Cook is believed to have careened the *Endeavour*), and further on to Hahei. A bus also runs from Ferry Landing (see Getting There & Around later). Purangi Winery (☎ (07) 866 3724), 6km south, has wines, including kiwi fruit wine, for tasting; it also operates cruises on the Purangi River.

Activities

Whitianga has many activities on land and water and the information centre can supply more details.

Dolphin Quest (☎ (07) 866 5555) organises **swimming with dolphins**. The bottlenose dolphins were once regular visitors close inshore but now are not so common and the tours are dependent on definite sightings. Wet suits, snorkels and flippers are supplied; the cost is $75 for a three-hour trip. The three-hour Seven Island Seafari ($70) is a popular alternative when the dolphins are not around.

You can paddle around this interesting coastline in a **sea kayak** with Coromandel Safaris (☎ (07) 866 2850, 025 394 597); a one-day safari with equipment and lunch included is $75. Sailors appreciate quiet time on the *Carino*; a full day out costs from $70.

Mercury Bay is rich in interesting **walks**. Watch your step, though – some of the mine shafts are quite deep. One of the more popular gold mines is reached by an enjoy-

able two-hour walk along a stream. The track starts on Waitaia Rd, 10km north-east of Whitianga. Many other good walks are across the river, five minutes away by ferry. The information centre has details on local walks including ones in the Whitianga Rock Scenic & Historic Reserve.

For **horse trekking**, the Twin Oaks Riding Ranch (☎ (07) 866 5388) is 10 minutes north of Whitianga on the Kuaotunu Rd and Ace Hi Ranch is 8km south of Whitianga on the highway – costs for horse trekking are about $20 per hour, $35 for a half-day.

Coromandel Four Wheel Bike Safaris (☎ (07) 866 2034), based at Kuaotunu, takes trips in its **quad bikes** through some really scenic and adventurous bush trails. If you haven't done this before it's a must; the four-hour trips are good value at $120 for two people.

Maurice Aukett of Bay Carving (☎ (07) 866 4021) on Racecourse Rd has set up a fully equipped **bone carving** workshop – you select the pattern to carve (from beef shinbone), then shape and polish a unique souvenir. There are over 100 designs, with the most popular being *tiki* (human figure), *taniwha* (water spirit), *manaia* (literally 'bird-headed man'), *hei matu* (fish hook), wildlife and more contemporary designs. The studio is open daily and on some evenings. Tuition and all equipment is supplied, the process takes about three hours and the cost is from $25 to $45.

Places to Stay

Camping & Cabins At the *Buffalo Beach Tourist Park* (☎ (07) 866 5854), opposite Buffalo Beach and on Eyre St, camping costs $10 per person; it's a little more with power. Shared accommodation is $14 in bunkrooms and chalets are from $40 a double.

Other similarly priced camping grounds include the *Water's Edge Motor Lodge* (☎ (07) 866 5760), the *Harbourside Holiday Park* (☎ (07) 866 5746) and the *Mercury Bay Motor Camp* (☎ (07) 866 5579), all on Albert St; the *Whitianga Holiday Park* (☎ (07) 866 5896) at the northern end of

Buffalo Beach; the *Aladdin Motor Camp* (☎ (07) 866 5834) on Bongard Rd; and the Cooks Beach Motor Camp (☎ (07) 866 5469).

Hostels The new *Buffalo Peaks Lodge* (☎ (07) 866 2933) at 12 Albert St interweaves portraits of Kiwi legends into its decor (*sans* Te Rauparaha). The lodge is being expanded but already includes a spa, barbecue and patios. It is a fine backpackers and charges $5 for camping, $15.50 in dorms, $16.50 for single, and $35 for twins and doubles. The *Cat's Pyjamas* (☎ (07) 866 4663) at 4 Monk St is a friendly place with all the facilities. It is run by an aeroplane building enthusiast (ask to see the unfinished product) and his wife; dorms are $15, camping is $10, and twins and doubles with en suite are $20 per person. They arrange trips to Hot Water Beach for $15 return (you can spend all day in your self-made pool).

Coromandel Backpackers Lodge (☎ (07) 866 5380), 46 Buffalo Beach Rd, is a converted seaside motel. This is a good hostel with a wonderful, sunny aspect. There are free kayaks, surfboards and fishing gear, plus bicycles for hire. It is $15 in a dorm and doubles and twins are $35 (with made-up beds and towels).

B&Bs The small and pleasant *Cosy Cat Cottage* (☎ (07) 866 4488), 41 South Highway, is unusual – it's absolutely loaded with cat art. Cats are portrayed on everything from the sheets to the place mats at the dinner table and there are literally hundreds of cat statues. Singles/doubles cost from $50/80. The information centre has several other B&Bs on its books.

Motels & Hotels Whitianga has about 20 motels. Most charge $70 a double and more in summer, although there's substantial reductions in winter. Cheaper motels include the *Seafari Motel* (☎ (07) 866 5263) and the *Central Park Motel* (☎ (07) 866 5471) opposite each other on Mill Rd, and *Bailey's Beachfront Motel* (☎ (07) 866 5500) at 66

Buffalo Beach. Many others are along Buffalo Beach Rd including the *Seabreeze* (☎ (07) 866 5570) at Nos 71-72 and the ritzier *Oceanside* (☎ (07) 866 5766) at No 32.

The *Whitianga Hotel* (☎ (07) 866 5818) on Blacksmith Lane has doubles and twins for $45 to $75 in low season and from $85 to $95 in high season.

Places to Eat
There's a range of budget places – pizzas at the *Bay Bakery*; good pub food at the *Whitianga Hotel*; a Chinese takeaway on Albert St; fresh seafood meals and the most popular takeaway fish and chips in town from *Snapper Jacks* on Albert St. There's also the hard-to-find (but worth it) *Nina's Cafe*, with a Thai night on Thursday, near the intersection of Victoria and Coghill Sts.

On the Esplanade with sea views is *Angler's Cove*, with main meals from $15 and an adjoining ice-cream parlour, and the *Harbour View Cafe*, which is good value. *Doyle's* at No 21 has fancier dining in a restored, two-storey house; try a Thames flounder for $16 or a salmon steak for $18. At the beach end of Albert St is the BYO *Beach Cafe*, recommended for its pasta.

The 'in' places at the moment are *On the Rocks* on the Esplanade, with succulent scallops for $23 and mussels for $19 a dozen; and *Smitty's* on Albert St with wedges for $5 and gut-busting burgers for $12-plus. Both places continue to party long after your meal is finished. *Hookers* on Albert St is both a restaurant and nightclub, the place to be after the others close.

Getting There & Around
Hot Water Beach Conxtions runs a bus from Ferry Landing at 7.30 and 10 am, 12.30, 3 and 4.30 pm to Cook's Beach, Hahei and Hot Water Beach, with some services continuing to Dalmeny Corner on the highway for connection with buses to Auckland and Whitianga. It has a $15 explorer pass which allows you to get on and off along the way.

HAHEI & HOT WATER BEACH

This popular section of coast is accessible from the Stone Steps Wharf at Ferry Landing and from the highway. The offshore islands provide protection for the beaches around Hahei, which are arguably the best of the Coromandel's many fine beaches. The waters offshore and the islands have been incorporated as a **marine park** and are excellent for diving.

At the eastern end of Hahei beach is a former Maori pa, Te Pare Point, which still has much evidence of the elaborate terracing used as fortifications. The tiny town of Hahei revolves around the general store where you can get information. Just north of Hahei is **Cathedral Cove** (Te Whanganui a Hei), accessible only at low tide through a gigantic arched cavern which separates it from Mares Leg Cove. This headland was also the site of a Maori pa.

To the south of Hahei is the Hot Water Beach where thermal waters are brewing just below the sand. Two hours before and after low tide, you can dig a hole in the sand (with a shovel, as the water is hot) and sit in your own little natural spa pool; allow about 15 minutes to prepare your pool. If you want to take a cooling dip in the ocean afterwards, be very careful – several people have drowned here due to the strong rips and big surf.

The *Hahei Explorer* (☎ (07) 866 3910), a rigid inflatable boat, operates scenic trips to Cathedral Cove and Hot Water Beach daily from Hahei – landings are made whenever the sea allows. It leaves at 10 am, noon, 2 pm and 4 pm in summer.

Places to Stay

Sites at the *Hot Water Beach Motor Camp* (☎ (07) 866 3735) cost $10 per person, more if you want power. The *Hahei Holiday Resort/Cathedral Cove Lodge Backpackers* (☎ (07) 866 3889) is right on the beach and has camp sites from $9 per person, cabins from $33 and tourist flats from $62. The backpackers has beds from $15 and twins only for $36.

The *Tatahi Lodge* (☎ (07) 866 3992) on Grange Rd behind the Hahei Store is a motel

with a sparkling, purpose-built backpackers building. The excellent facilities are $15 in the bunkrooms, or $36 for twin rooms. Classy, self-contained, two-bedroom motel units cost $92 a double (less in winter). The lodge lends shovels for Hot Water Beach and arranges transport.

At the luxury end of the market is *Hay-Lyn Park Lodge* (☎ (07) 866 3888) at Hahei Beach. It charges $100 a double in winter, considerably more in summer; it also has a coffee shop.

The excellent *Breakers Restaurant* close to Tatahi Lodge fills the culinary void; succulent Cajun chicken is $20.

TAIRUA & PAUANUI

This schizophrenic twin-town is separated by Tairua Harbour. A passenger ferry links the two, otherwise it is a long drive. Tairua is small, older and lies on the highway; its tourist highlight is the climb to the top of Paku (an old pa site whose name, in Maori , is 'women's breasts'), which provides great views. If you climb Paku, legend has it that you will return in seven years. Most of the attractions on this side of the harbour are natural and thus free.

Conversely, Pauanui is a sprawling, real estate agent's dream with canal-side homes for the rich. Pauanui has the pretty harbour on one side, a great surf beach on the other and pine-clad mountains behind. The only problem is that it's a boring, suburban development.

The area has a number of **walks,** including the Broken Hills, and activities include game fishing, canoeing and horse trekking.

The Tairua Information Centre (☎ (07) 864 7575) on SH25 is open from 9 am to 5 pm on weekdays and from 10 am to 1 pm on weekends. Pauanui Information Centre (☎ (07) 864 8138) on Pauanui Boulevard is open from Monday to Saturday from 10 am to 4 pm, and on Sunday from 10 am to 2 pm.

The ferry service (☎ (07) 864 8133 before 6 pm, 025 970 316 after hours) makes regular crossings between the two towns; it is $3/5 one-way/return (children $1/2 regardless of age, bikes $1).

Places to Stay & Eat

You have the choice of five motor camps in this area; a camp site is about $9 to $10 per person and each camping ground usually has on-site vans and cabins available. On SH25 in Tairua you'll find *The Flying Dutchman* (☎ (07) 864 8448), 305 Main Rd, a good hostel with a balcony area leading off the recreation room. The cost is $14 or $15 in shared rooms and $32 for twins and doubles. Closer to town, at 200 Main Rd in a Spanish-style villa, is the new *Tairua Backpackers Lodge* (☎ (07) 864 8345). This friendly place has people returning for the fresh fruit, vegetables and free-range eggs the owners provide for free. Dorms are $15, and twins and doubles $34; sightseeing tours on the owners' dive boat to the Alderman Islands are good value at $20 per person.

The *Sir George Grey Hotel* (☎ (07) 864 8451) on Main Rd in Tairua has singles for $25. There are at least ten motels or lodges in Tairua and Pauanui. A good choice is the classy *Pacific Harbour Motor Lodge* (☎ (07) 864 8581) on the main road; singles/doubles in this island-style resort are from $75/100. For five-star luxury, *Puka Park Lodge* (☎ (07) 864 8088) in snooty Pauanui is favoured by visiting dignitaries and hotel-trashing rock stars; it charges from $295 up to an astronomical $1500.

In Tairua, the *Out of the Blue Cafe* is open daily for innovative food (not your usual pies and sausage rolls) and a good selection of coffee. *Shells*, attached to the Pacific Harbour and specialising in Pacific Rim fare, is also open daily. If you are extremely wealthy, then the *Puka Park Restaurant* and *Hunting Room Cafe* in upmarket Pauanui are probably troughs of choice.

OPOUTERE

Opoutere has a fine beach and, about a 15-minute walk from the road, the Wharekawa Wildlife Refuge – breeding ground of the endangered NZ dotterel and the variable oystercatcher. (Keep dogs out of here and don't cross into the roped-off area during the breeding season.) There is a weekday Waihi to Opoutere shuttle – it leaves at noon.

The *Opoutere YHA Hostel* (☎ (07) 865 9072) is a fine place to get right away from it all. It's in a country setting, almost encircled by native bush and overlooking Wharekawa Harbour. You can take one of the hostel's kayaks and paddle around, and there are plenty of bushwalks. The cost is $15 in dorms, $17 per person in doubles, or you can camp on the extensive lawn. The management is friendly and informative. Just down the road from the Opoutere Hostel is *Opoutere Park* (☎ (07) 865 9152) with camp sites from $8 per person.

WHANGAMATA

Whangamata is a sprawling hotch-potch of single-storey buildings but its saving grace is the great 4km surf beach with an excellent break by the bar. This well equipped resort town has a population of 4000 but gets 10 times that number of visitors in summer.

The Whangamata Information Centre (☎ (07) 865 8340) on Port Rd, the main street, is open from 9 am to 5 pm daily in summer, with shorter weekend hours in winter.

Things to See & Do

Whangamata has a number of **craft** outlets outlined in a pamphlet available from the information centre.

The area has some excellent **walks**. The most popular is the Wentworth Falls walk, which takes one hour (one way) through beautiful bush. To get to the track, take the highway south for 3km to the turn-off and then 4km to the camping ground. From the falls, a harder trail (get advice at the camping ground) leads to the top of the ranges and on to Marakopa Rd. There are plans for a three-day walk, the **Whangamata Track**, similar to the walk in the Kauaeranga Valley – it will be guided, but freedom walkers will also be permitted.

Horse riding, game fishing, kayaking, windsurfing and mountain biking can be arranged. The information centre has details.

Places to Stay

The *Pinefield Holiday Park* (☎ (07) 865 8791) on Port Rd has powered and tent sites for $20 for two, and cabins and tourist flats from $40 a double. Similarly, the *Whangamata Motor Camp* (☎ (07) 865 9128) on Barbara Ave has sites for $8 per person and cabins for $33 for two. The DOC-owned *Wentworth Valley Campground* (☎ (07) 865 7032) is in a beautiful valley setting at the start of the trek to Wentworth Falls, 7km from Whangamata. It has gas barbecues and cold showers; camping is $8 (children $4) in summer.

The *Bedshed Motor Lodge* (☎ (07) 865 9580) on the corner of Port Rd and Mayfair Ave is a combined backpackers and motel about 1km from the shopping centre, as you head south. It has excellent accommodation for $16 in shared rooms and $40 for doubles and twins. Motel units cost from $65, or $105 with kitchen, in summer. This new, pristine hostel has everything, including a small video theatre.

Tukere House (☎ (07) 865 8009) on Tukere Drive is an attractive B&B in an A-frame lodge charging $40/85, or families can rent the whole unit. It's 2km north of town, over the bridge. Right near the start of the Wentworth Valley walk, *Wentworth Valley Retreat* (☎ (07) 8657210) has excellent homestay accommodation in a beautiful setting for $85/110.

Places to Eat

Whangamata has plenty of takeaways and coffee lounges but is not overly endowed with restaurants. *Gingers Health Food & Cafe*, 601 Port Rd, is the best option for vegetarians and they bake great breads here. On Port Rd, *Cedarwood* at No 413 is an ideal family place and *Pinky's* at No 703, open daily, is an unpretentious place with moderately priced meals.

Bay of Plenty

The sweeping Bay of Plenty is blessed with a good climate, fine beaches and is a thriving agricultural district most noted for kiwi fruit. The bay stretches from the main city of Tauranga on the west to Whakatane and Opotiki, the main focal points of the east.

Just inland in this region is one of New Zealand's premier tourist attractions, Rotorua. The Rotorua region is famous around the world for its geysers, hot springs, mud pools, shimmering lakes, trout fishing, tramping and a host of other activities.

The region is also of great significance to the Maori, whose presence dates back to the area's discovery and exploration in the 14th century.

Rotorua

Rotorua (regional population 68,000) is the most popular tourist area of the North Island. Nicknamed 'Sulphur City', it has the most energetic thermal activity in the country with bubbling mud pools, gurgling hot springs, gushing geysers and evil smells. Rotorua also has a large Maori population whose cultural activities are among the most interesting and accessible in NZ.

The city itself is thriving, buoyed by the huge influx of tourism (earning another local nickname: 'Roto-Vegas'); it's also scenically located 280m above sea level on the shores of Lake Rotorua, which teems with trout. The area has some interesting trout springs and wildlife parks.

History
The district of Rotorua was probably first settled during the middle of the 14th century by descendants of the navigators from Hawaiki who arrived at Maketu in the central Bay of Plenty in the *Arawa* canoe. Originally, they were of the Ohomairangi tribe but soon after they reached Maketu they

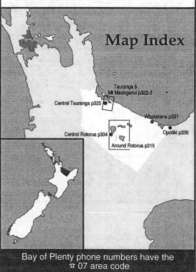

Map Index

Bay of Plenty phone numbers have the ☎ 07 area code

changed their tribal name to Te Arawa to commemorate the vessel that had brought them safely so far.

Much of the inland forest was explored in the late 14th century by Ihenga, who discovered and named the lakes of Rotorua and many other geographical features of the area. The name Rotorua means 'the second lake'

Bay of Plenty

(*roto* means lake; *rua* means two) as it was the second lake that Ihenga discovered.

In the next few hundred years, various sub-tribes spread into the area and, as they grew in numbers, they split into more sub-tribes and began to fight over territory. In 1823 the Arawa lands were invaded by the Ngapuhi chief, Hongi Hika, of Northland. The Arawa managed to rout the Northlanders and forced them to withdraw.

During the 1850s, wars erupted between the Arawa and the Waikato tribes. In 1867 the Waikato tribes attacked, in retaliation for the part the Arawa played in preventing the

east coast reinforcements getting through for the Maori King Movement. During these wars the Arawa threw in their lot with the government, gaining the backing of their troops.

With the wars virtually over in the early 1870s, European settlement around Rotorua took off with a rush, particularly as the army and government personnel involved in the struggle had broadcast the scenic wonders of the place. People came to take the waters in the hope of cures for all sorts of diseases, and Rotorua's tourist industry was thus founded. The town's main attraction was the fabulous

Pink and White Terraces, formed by the sinter deposits of silica from volcanic activity. Considered at the time among the seven natural wonders of the world, they were destroyed in the 1886 Tarawera eruption.

Orientation & Information

The main shopping area is down Tutanekai St, the central part of which is a parking area and pedestrian mall. Fenton St starts by the Government Gardens near the lake and runs all the way to Whakarewarewa (just say 'Whaka') thermal area 2km away. It's lined with motels for much of its length.

Tourism Rotorua (☎ (07) 348 5179; fax 348 6044) is at 67 Fenton St on the corner of Haupapa St. It has information, makes bookings for everything around Rotorua and has a travel agency. The Map and Track shop is also here, as well as a cafe and other services for travellers, including showers, luggage storage, fishing licences, phonecards and stamps. It's open from 8 am to 5.30 pm daily. There is also a currency exchange, open from 8 am to 5.30 pm daily.

The Automobile Association (AA; ☎ (07) 348 3069) is on Amohau St. American Express is at Blackmore's Galaxy Travel (☎ (07) 347 9444) at 411 Tutanekai St. Thomas Cook has a forex desk in the Air New Zealand office and there are plenty of banks that will change foreign currencies. The post office is on Hinemoa St between Tutanekai and Amohia Sts and a laundrette is at 89 Fenton St, opposite the police station.

A transport service for the disabled (wheelchairs) is available on the hour from Allison's Unichem Pharmacy in the City Plaza, opposite DEKA supermarket.

Thermal Air is a useful free weekly tourist publication and the annual free *Rotorua Visitors Guide* is indispensable. The excellent

---

Pokarekare ana

Pokarekare ana is New Zealand's most cherished traditional song. Though most people probably think its origin is more ancient, the song was actually adapted from a poem by Paraire Henare Tomoana (1868-1946) of the Ngati Kahungunu tribe. His original lyrics were not about Rotorua, but rather Waiapu. Nevertheless, the words seemed to fit the story of Hinemoa and Tutanekai so perfectly that in popular song the lake's name was changed to Rotorua, and the song is thought to be about the two lovers.

Almost anyone from NZ can sing this song for you. Often you will hear only the first verse and the chorus sung, but there are several verses. If you want to sing along, it goes like this:

Pokarekare ana nga wai o Rotorua.	Troubled are the waters of Rotorua.
Whiti atu koe, e hine, marino ana e.	If you cross them, oh maiden, they will be calm.
CHORUS:	
E hine e, hoki mai ra,	Come back to me, maiden,
Ka mate ahau i te aroha e.	I love you so much.
E kore te aroha e maroke i te ra.	My love will never dry in the sun.
Makuku tonu i aku roimata e.	It will always be wet with my tears.
Tuhi atu taku reta, tuku atu taku ringi.	I have written my letter, I have sent my ring.
Kei kite to iwi, raruraru ana e.	If your people see them, there will be trouble.
CHORUS	
Kua whati taku pene, kua pau aku pepa,	My pen is broken, my paper is all used up.
Engari te aroha, mau tonu ana e.	But my love for you will always remain. ■

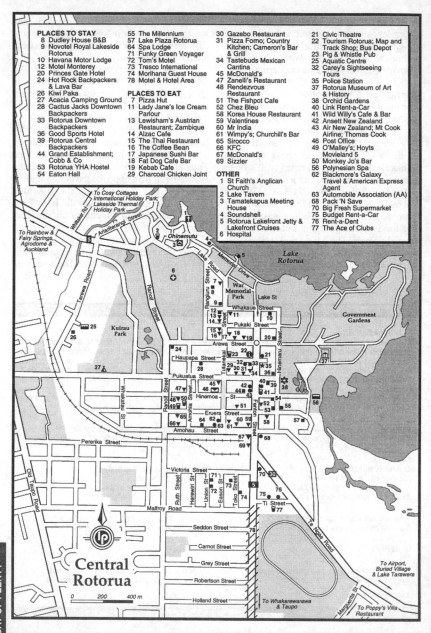

PLACES TO STAY
8 Dudley House B&B
9 Novotel Royal Lakeside Rotorua
10 Havana Motor Lodge
12 Motel Monterey
20 Princes Gate Hotel
24 Hot Rock Backpackers & Lava Bar
26 Kiwi Paka
27 Acacia Camping Ground
28 Cactus Jacks Downtown Backpackers
33 Rotorua Downtown Backpackers
36 Good Sports Hotel
39 Rotorua Central Backpackers
44 Grand Establishment; Cobb & Co
53 Rotorua YHA Hostel
54 Eaton Hall
55 The Millennium
57 Lake Plaza Rotorua
64 Spa Lodge
71 Funky Green Voyager
72 Tom's Motel
73 Tresco International
74 Morihana Guest House
78 Motel & Hotel Area

PLACES TO EAT
7 Pizza Hut
11 Lady Jane's Ice Cream Parlour
13 Lewisham's Austrian Restaurant; Zambique
14 Alzac Cafe
15 The Thai Restaurant
16 The Coffee Bean
17 Japanese Sushi Bar
18 Fat Dog Cafe Bar
19 Kebab Cafe
29 Charcoal Chicken Joint
30 Gazebo Restaurant
31 Pizza Forno; Country Kitchen; Cameron's Bar & Grill
34 Tastebuds Mexican Cantina
45 McDonald's
47 Zanelli's Restaurant
48 Rendezvous Restaurant
51 The Fishpot Cafe
52 Chez Bleu
58 Korea House Restaurant
59 Valentines
60 Mr India
61 Wimpy's; Churchill's Bar
65 Sirocco
66 KFC
67 McDonald's
68 Sizzler

OTHER
1 St Faith's Anglican Church
2 Lake Tavern
3 Tamatekapua Meeting House
4 Soundshell
5 Rotorua Lakefront Jetty & Lakefront Cruises
6 Hospital
21 Civic Theatre
22 Tourism Rotorua; Map and Track Shop; Bus Depot
23 Pig & Whistle Pub
25 Aquatic Centre
32 Carey's Sightseeing Tours
35 Police Station
37 Rotorua Museum of Art & History
38 Orchid Gardens
40 Link Rent-a-Car
41 Wild Willy's Cafe & Bar
42 Ansett New Zealand
43 Air New Zealand; Mt Cook Airline; Thomas Cook
46 Post Office
49 O'Malley's; Hoyts Movieland 5
50 Monkey Jo's Bar
56 Polynesian Spa
62 Blackmore's Galaxy Travel & American Express Agent
63 Automobile Association (AA)
68 Pack 'N Save
70 Big Fresh Supermarket
75 Budget Rent-a-Car
76 Rent-a-Dent
77 The Ace of Clubs

Gateway to Geyserland map, available for $1 at Tourism Rotorua, includes a good map of the city and surrounding area.

Lake Rotorua

Lake Rotorua is the largest of 12 lakes in the Rotorua district. It was formed by an eruption and subsequent subsidence of the area. Various cruises on the lake depart from the Rotorua lakefront jetty at the end of Tutanekai St daily in summer (and most days in winter).

The *Lakeland Queen* paddle steamer (☎ (07) 348 6634) does one-hour breakfast ($24), luncheon ($26) and dinner cruises ($42.50) on the lake daily, or morning ($16) and afternoon tea ($18) cruises; children pay half-price. The *Scatcat* motorised catamaran does cruises to Mokoia Island ($25) and two-lake cruises over Lake Rotorua and through the Ohau Channel to Lake Rotoiti ($49).

The *Hovershuttle* hovercraft cruises cost $30 (children $15) and the *Supa Jet* (☎ 025 813 209) supervised guided trips around Lake Rotorua are $25 per person.

A number of fishing boats also operate from the jetty. Self-drive speed boats from Lake Front Boat Hire (☎ 025 813 209) are $45 for 15 minutes, $70 for 25 minutes.

Ohinemutu

Ohinemutu is a lakeside Maori village. Its name means 'the place of the young woman who was killed' – and was given by Ihenga in memory of his daughter.

The historic Maori **St Faith's Anglican Church** by the lakefront has a beautiful interior decorated with Maori carvings, woven tukutuku panels, painted scrollwork and stained-glass windows. An image of Christ wearing a Maori cloak is etched on a window so that he appears to be walking on the waters of Lake Rotorua. Seen from this window, it's surprising how much Lake Rotorua does resemble the Sea of Galilee. The church is open daily from 8 am to 5 pm.

Opposite the church is the impressive **Tamatekapua Meeting House**, built in 1887. Named for the captain of the *Arawa* canoe, this is an important meeting house for all Arawa people. The Magic of the Maori Concert (see Maori Concerts & Hangis) is held here.

Rotorua Museum of Art & History

This impressive museum (☎ (07) 349 8334), better known as the Bath House, is in a Tudor-style building in the Government Gardens. The building was an elegant spa retreat, built in 1908. The museum has small but fascinating exhibits on the local Te Arawa Maori people; the 1886 Mt Tarawera eruption, with videos about how it happened; the Pink and White Terraces; the history of this building; and changing displays. It's open from 9.30 am to 5 pm daily ($5, children $2).

In the gardens around the Bath House are typical English touches like croquet lawns, and rose gardens – not to mention steaming pools and a petanque ring.

A good **craft market** is held every second weekend at the Soundshell.

Orchid Gardens

The Orchid Gardens in Hinemaru St contain an extensive hothouse of orchids which bloom year-round as well as a Micro-world display where you can get a microscopic view of living reptiles and insects. There is also a big water organ, really a huge fountain, with over 800 jets. It's a magnificent 15-minute show of water which swirls, leaps and generally makes graceful, ballet-like movements up to 4m high. It plays every hour on the hour from 9 am to 5 pm. The complex is open from 8.30 am to 5.30 pm daily ($9, children $3).

Te Whakarewarewa

This is Rotorua's largest and best known thermal reserve and a major Maori cultural area. It's pronounced Faka-raywa-raywa – most call it simply 'Whaka'. On the other hand, even the name Whakarewarewa is short for Te Whakarewarewatangaoteopetauaawahiao, which means 'the gathering together of the war forces of Wahiao'.

Hinemoa & Tutanekai

The story of Hinemoa and Tutanekai is one of the most well known lovers' tales in New Zealand. It is not a legend but a true story, though you may hear one or two variations. The descendants of Hinemoa and Tutanekai still live in the Rotorua area today.

Hinemoa was a young woman of a sub-tribe that lived on the western shore of Lake Rotorua. Tutanekai was a young man of the sub-tribe that lived on Mokoia Island, on the lake.

The two sub-tribes sometimes visited one another, and that was how Hinemoa and Tutanekai met. But though both were of high birth in their respective tribes, Tutanekai was illegitimate and so, while the family of Hinemoa thought he was a fine young man and could see that the two young people loved one another, they were not in favour of them marrying.

At night, Tutanekai would play his flute on the island, and sometimes the wind would carry his melody across the water to Hinemoa. In his music she could hear his declaration of love for her. Her people, meanwhile, took to tying up the canoes at night to make sure she could not take off and go to him.

Finally, one night, as she heard Tutanekai's music wafting over the waters, Hinemoa was so overcome with longing that she could stand it no longer. She peeled off her clothes to get rid of the weight and set off to swim the long distance from the shore to the island. In some versions of the story she also buoyed herself up with calabash gourds.

When she arrived on Mokoia, Hinemoa was in a quandary. She had had to shed her clothing in order to swim to the island, but now there, she could scarcely walk into the settlement naked! She sought refuge in a hot pool and tried to figure out what to do next.

Time passed and eventually a man came to fetch water from a cold spring beside the hot pool. In a deep man's voice, Hinemoa called out, 'Who is it?' The man replied that he was the slave of Tutanekai, come to fetch water. Hinemoa reached out of the darkness, seized the calabash and broke it. This

The gateway of the model village of Te Whakarewarewa depicts the two lovers entwined

happened a few more times, until finally Tutanekai himself came to the pool and demanded that the interloper identify himself. He was amazed when it turned out to be Hinemoa.

Tutanekai stole Hinemoa into his hut. In the morning, when Tutanekai was sleeping very late, a slave was sent to wake him and came back reporting that someone else was also sleeping in Tutanekai's bed! The two lovers emerged, and when Hinemoa's efforts to reach Tutanekai had been revealed, their union was celebrated. ∎

Whakarewarewa's most spectacular geyser is **Pohutu** (Maori for 'big splash' or 'explosion'), an active geyser which usually erupts at least once an hour. Pohutu spurts hot water about 20m into the air but sometimes shoots up over 30m in brief 'shots'. The average eruption lasts about five to 10 minutes, though the longest is reputed to have lasted for 15 hours! You get an advance warning because the Prince of Wales' Feathers geyser always starts off shortly before Pohutu.

Other Whaka attractions include the **Maori Arts & Crafts Institute** (☎ (07) 348 9047) with working craftspeople, an art gallery, a replica Maori village, kiwi house and a Maori concert ($11) held daily at 12.15 pm.

Whaka is 2km south of the city centre, straight down Fenton St. City buses drop you near a rear entrance, or the Sightseeing Shuttle bus will drop you at the main gate. Whaka is open daily from 8 am to 5 pm (last entry 4.30 pm); entry for the day is $11 (children $4).

Close to town is **Kuirau Park**, an area of volcanic activity which you can wander around for free. It has a crater lake and pools of boiling mud. Those wishing to swim in hot water can visit **Kerosene Creek**, out on SH5. Turn left on the old Waiotapu Rd and follow it for 3km; this is one of the few places where the public can bathe in natural thermal pools for free.

Thermal Pools

The popular **Polynesian Spa**, off Hinemoa St in the Government Gardens, is open daily from 6.30 am to 11 pm. The first building in Rotorua, a bath house, was opened at these springs in 1886 and people have been swearing by the health-giving properties of the waters ever since. The modern complex has several pools at the lake's edge. Entry to the main pools is $8.50 (children $3), private pools are $9 (children $3) per half-hour. Towels and swimsuits can be hired, as can the sauna, or an Aix massage (under jets of hot water) is available by appointment.

The **Waikite Valley Thermal Pool** (☎ (07) 333 1861) is an open-air natural mineral pool (39°C) with medicinal mineral waters. To get there, go 30km south on SH5 (the highway to Taupo) to a signposted turn-off which is opposite the turn-off to Waiotapu. The pool is another 6km down this road. It is open from 10 am to 9.30 pm daily ($4, children $2).

Maori Concerts & Hangis

Maori culture is a major attraction in Rotorua and, although it has been commercialised, it's worth investing in the experience. The two big activities are concerts and *hangi* (meals cooked in an earth oven). Often the two are combined.

The concerts are put on by locals. Chances are, by the time the evening is over you'll have been dragged up on stage, experienced a Maori *hongi* (nose-to-nose contact), have joined hands for a group sing-in, and thought about freaking out your next-door neighbour with a *haka* (war dance) when you get home. Other features of a Maori concert are *poi* dances, action songs and hand games.

Poi dances are performed by women only and consist of whirling round the flax poi balls on lengths of string. Action songs are a recent addition to the Maori activities – story-songs illustrated by fluid hand and arm movements. There are also hand games – a reaction-sharpening pastime.

For a concert only, one of the best performances is presented daily (8 pm) at **Tamatekapua Meeting House** in Ohinemutu, opposite St Faith's Church down by the lake ($15). You can show up at the door for the Magic of the Maori Concert; book directly (☎ (07) 349 3949) or with Tourism Rotorua.

Another option is the daily concert starting at 12.15 pm at Whakarewarewa – (see that section).

For a combined concert and hangi, Tamaki Tours (☎ (07) 346 2823) does an excellent Twilight Cultural Tour to a marae and Maori village complex. They pick you up at your accommodation and along the way explain the traditional protocol involved in visiting a marae and a 'chief' is chosen among the group to represent the visitors. The concert is followed by a hangi. It costs $52.

Big hotels which also offer Maori concerts and hangis include:

	Concert only	Concert & Hangi
International Plaza Hotel, Froude St (☎ (07) 348 1189)	$18	$47
Lake Plaza, Eruera St (☎ (07) 348 1174)	$17.50	$40
Millennium, Eruera St (☎ (07) 348 1234)	$16	$43
Quality Hotel, Fenton St (☎ (07) 348 0199)	$17	$43 $29*
Sheraton Rotorua, Fenton St (☎ (07) 348 7139)	$25	$49

* Hangi only

Zorbing

Like the bungy, zorbing is another of those unusual Kiwi innovations. Rotorua is the only place where you can do it. The rules are simple – climb into an inflated double plastic sphere (the two spheres are held together with shock cords), strap in and then roll downhill for about 150m, rotating within the sphere, and eventually come to a stop. To cure a hangover, skip the tying in and ask for a couple of buckets of cold water to be tossed inside the sphere – you literally slip downhill. The guys who invented it were looking for a way to walk on water. They found it. Zorb dry for $30 (or for $45 if you have two rides, the second one wet); book through Mountain Adventures (☎ (07) 348 6423) or Zorb HQ (☎ 025 850 628). The zorb orbit is at the base of Mt Ngongotaha, 6km north of Rotorua, near Rainbow Springs.

White-Water Rafting

Several rafting companies make white-water rafting trips on the Rangitaiki River (Grade III to Grade IV). Day trips, with a barbecue lunch, cost around $85. The trips depart from the Rangitaiki River Bridge in Murupara; they'll provide transport from Rotorua for an extra $5. Contact River Rats (☎ (07) 347 6049), the Rafting Company (☎ (07) 348 0233) or the White-Water Excitement Co (☎ (07) 345 7182).

Most popular are the shorter and more dramatic rafting trips on the Kaituna River over the 7m Okere Falls, off SH33 about 16km north-east of Rotorua. Kaituna Cascades (☎ (07) 357 5032) was the first company to make this trip and it's still going strong. Time on the river is about 40 minutes. You go over the 7m falls, then over another 3m drop, as well as over various rapids ($58). All Rotorua's rafting companies do a Kaituna trip, including Great Kiwi White Water (☎ (07) 348 2144) and Raftabout (☎ (07) 345 4652). There is a heli-raft option with KiwiKopters and Raftabout for $85 per person.

Kaituna Cascades also conducts an extreme **tandem kayak** trip in which a passenger who weighs less than 85kg, with no prior experience, can negotiate a series of Grade V drops on the Kaituna. Many of the paddlers are world champions. Trips leave Rotorua at 9am, 11.45 am and 2.30 pm daily ($95).

Fishing

You can hire guides to trout fish or go it alone but a licence is essential and there's various regulations. Guided fishing trips cost about $70 per hour per boat but you are almost guaranteed to catch a fish. Plan to spend about two to three hours on the trip. Ask at Tourism Rotorua or at the Rotorua lakefront for fishing operators.

You can wander down to the lakefront and fish if you have a fishing licence and it's the fishing season (October to June). Get your fishing licence directly from a fishing guide or the Map and Track shop. Licences cost $12 per day, $25 per week or $62 for the season.

Other Activities

You can go **tandem skydiving** from the Rotorua airport (☎ (07) 345 7520) for $195. The initial flight includes some amazing views over the lakes and volcanoes of the region.

Waka Hikoi (☎ (07) 362 7878) operates half-day guided **kayaking** trips on Lake Rotoiti and other lakes for $49 per person. Adventure Kayaking (☎ (07) 348 9451) has a half-day trip on Lake Rotorua (which includes the Ohau Channel) for $35, full-day trips on Lake Tawawera for $50 and rents out tandem kayaks for $80 per day.

Operators doing **horse treks**, for $25 per hour, are Paradise Treks (☎ (07) 348 8195), the Farmhouse (☎ (07) 332 3771) and Foxwood Park (☎ (07) 345 7003).

Mountain Adventures (☎ (07) 348 6423), 6km north of town near Rainbow Springs, takes trips over Mt Ngongotaha in **quad bikes**. The 90-minute trip includes 15 minutes of instruction and some great bush tracks ($70). They can also arrange for you to **rap jump** with Extreme Limits (☎ (07) 362 7603) from a rocky outcrop on the side of Mt Ngongotaha; three jumps from the 30m cliff cost $50.

Off Road NZ: You Drive (☎ (07) 332 5748) on Amoore Rd (20-minute drive west of Rotorua) is a buzz place. Here you can 4WD to your heart's delight for $60 for an hour, or slide and spin on an off-roader for

12 laps for $20 (passengers free). It is open daily from 9 am to 5 pm (rain or shine).

About 45km south of Rotorua, on the Waikato River, you can go **jet-boating** and sprint jet-boating with River Glen Tours (☎ (07) 333 8165) – see Around Taupo in the Central Plateau chapter. At Longridge Park, Paengaroa, near Te Puke (40km north of Rotorua), you can jet-boat up the Kaituna River with Longridge Jetboat (☎ (07) 533 1515) and 4WD over a great course with Hill Hoppers (☎ (07) 533 1818) – see Around Tauranga.

Organised Tours

Rotorua offers a mind-boggling array of tours – Tourism Rotorua can book any tours, as can hostels and hotels.

Carey's Sightseeing Tours (☎ (07) 347 1197), 18 Haupapa St, has a large range. Carey's Capers visits most of Rotorua's favourite volcanic and thermal attractions, with a dip in an isolated hot-water stream along the way (from $55/95 for a half-day/full-day tour). Other Carey's tours take in the main attractions in a variety of combinations, including the thermal reserves, trout springs, lake cruises, Kaituna River rafting (4WD 'Mud and Mayhem' trips, $115) and 4WD tours to Mt Tarawera ($65, children $40, for a half-day).

Its 'World Famous' Waimangu Round Trip, well-known in these parts since 1902, is one of the best. Focusing on the 1886 Mt Tarawera eruption, it includes the Waimangu Volcanic Valley, a cruise on Lake Rotomahana past the site of the Pink and White Terraces, another cruise on Lake Tarawera, a visit to the Buried Village, and a dip in the Polynesian Spa ($140, children $80, for the full day).

4WD tours are popular. Three-hour tours cost around $65 and full-day tours are $140 (children 40% of adult price). Mt Tarawera 4WD Tours (☎ (07) 348 2814), Tarawera Mountain Sightseeing Tours (☎ (07) 348 9333) and Mountain Magic (☎ (07) 348 6399) go to Mt Tarawera. 4WD Bush Safaris (☎ (07) 332 5748) has wheel-spinning, mud-throwing and rut-gouging tours over some

very rugged tracks through native bush. You can drive yourself or they can drive.

Other tours go to the Agrodome, thermal areas etc; InterCity, Gray Line and Taylor's are three established companies (Tourism Rotorua provides details of them and others). We have had good reports about Shamrock Magic Tours (☎ (07) 332 3075); its full-day spectacular is $97 (with lunch at Freo's Cafe) and its 'Rotorua at its Best' is $55.

Scenic Flights Flights over the city and lake start at around $50. Tarawera flights start at $100. Otherwise head further afield to White Island and even down to Mt Ruapehu and Mt Ngauruhoe in the Tongariro National Park.

Volcanic Wunderflites (☎ (07) 345 6079) are particularly popular for flights over the awesome chasm of Mt Tarawera. A Rotorua flightseeing favourite is White Island Airways (☎ (07) 345 9832), which does Tiger Moth flights. Both companies operate from the airport, as does Lakeside Aviation (☎ (07) 345 4242), Scenic Air Tours (☎ (07) 345 4004) and Scenic Flight Wharehouse (☎ (07) 345 6749).

Volcanic Air Safaris (☎ (07) 348 9984/4069) does helicopter and floatplane flights departing from the Rotorua lakefront. Other helicopter operators include Marine Helicopters (☎ (07) 357 2512), based at the Agrodome, Tarawera Helicopters (☎ (07) 348 1223) at Whaka, and KiwiKopters (☎ (07) 345 5460) at the airport.

Places to Stay

Camping & Cabins The *Acacia Camping Ground* (☎ (07) 348 1886) at 129-137 Pukuatua St is beside Kuirau Park. Tent/powered sites cost $8/9 per person and tourist flats cost from $45 for two (higher rates in the summer peak). The *Cosy Cottage International Holiday Park* (☎ (07) 348 3793) at 67 Whittaker Rd may be the only place in the world with heated tent sites – the ground warmth gradually warms your tent at night. They also have a mineral pool, a heated swimming pool, canoes, bicycles and fishing tackle for hire. Tent/powered sites are

$18/20 for two, tourist cabins cost $36 a double and tourist flats are from $46 to $55.

The *Lakeside Thermal Holiday Park* (☎ (07) 348 1693) at 54 Whittaker Rd has hot mineral pools and spas. Tent/powered sites are $16/18, tourist cabins $35, tourist flats $50 and chalets $55 (all prices for two).

The *Rotorua Thermal Holiday Park* (☎ (07) 346 3140), on the southern end of the Old Taupo Rd, is a large camping ground with hot mineral pools and a heated swimming pool. Tent and caravan sites are $8.50 per person, cabins cost from $35 and tourist flats $60 a double. There is also a lodge with B&B at $26 per person, linen included.

A little further out, the *Holdens Bay Holiday Park* (☎ (07) 345 9925) at 21 Robinson Ave is about 500m from Lake Rotorua, 6.5km from central Rotorua on SH30. The *Blue Lake Holiday Park* (☎ 362 8120) is on Tarawera Rd, 10km from town. Kayaks, canoes, fishing boats and bicycles are available for hire.

Other possibilities are:

All Seasons Holiday Park (☎ (07) 345 6240), 7.5km from the city centre on Lee Rd, Hannahs Bay, off SH30

Fisherman's Lodge Family Holiday Park (☎ (07) 362 8754), a two-minute drive from Lake Tarawera and surrounded by native bush

Greengrove Holiday Park (☎ (07) 357 4429), corner of Hall and School Rds, Ngongotaha

Lake Rotoiti Lakeside Holiday Park (☎ (07) 362 4860), 21km from Rotorua on Okere Rd, Okere Falls, on the shore of Lake Rotoiti

Ohau Channel Lodge (☎ (07) 362 4761), 17.5km from Rotorua on Hamurana Rd, at the northern end of Lake Rotorua

Rainbow Resort (☎ (07) 357 4289), 8km from the city centre at 22 Beaumonts Rd, Ngongotaha

Redwood Holiday Park (☎ (07) 345 9380), 3km from the city centre at 5 Tarawera Rd, Ngapuna, at the intersection of Te Ngae Rd

Waiteti Trout Stream Holiday Park (☎ (07) 357 5255), beside Waiteti Stream at 14 Okona Crescent, Ngongotaha

Hostels The pick of the backpackers is the *Hot Rock* (☎ (07) 347 9469) at 118 Arawa St. It is a former motel and a number of the thermally heated, spacious rooms have en suites and kitchen facilities. The friendly, efficient staff arrange sightseeing tours and trips to Maori cultural performances. There are three hot pools (indoor and outdoor) on the premises. Shared dorms start at $15, made-up rooms sleeping four are $17 per person, and twins and doubles are around $40 per room (or $20 per person); all rooms have a bathroom. The popular Lava Bar is adjacent.

The smallest and one of the nicest of Rotorua's hostels is the funky little *Funky Green Voyager* (☎ (07) 346 1754) at 4 Union St. In a tranquil residential neighbourhood close to the centre, the hostel is comfortable and casual with a spacious backyard and a pleasant sunny conservatory. The cost is $15 in dorms or $36 for double and twin rooms.

The new *Rotorua Downtown Backpackers* (☎ (07) 346 2831), on the corner of Haupapa and Fenton Sts, is near the tourism centre and bus station. It has dorms from $15 to $16, twins for $34 and doubles for $36. There is a large kitchen area, guest bar and barbecue facilities.

Rotorua Central Backpackers (☎ (07) 349 3285) at 10 Pukuatua St has spacious rooms and a spa pool in a classic older building. The cost is $15 per person in dorms, $32 in twins and $36 in doubles. It's centrally located and quiet.

Rotorua YHA Hostel (☎ (07) 347 6810) on the corner of Eruera and Hinemaru Sts has plenty of twin and family rooms and a thermal spa pool. It charges $17 in dorm rooms and $38 for a double room.

The *Spa Lodge* (☎ (07) 348 3486) at 69 Amohau St is old and cramped but the rooms are thermally heated; it charges $15 in dorms, $25/36 for singles/doubles.

Cactus Jacks Downtown Backpackers (☎ (07) 348 3121) is central at 54 Haupapa St (but should, by rights and design, be somewhere like Taos, New Mexico). It has rooms or cabins and there are spas for guests; it charges $14.50 in dorms, and $27/33/37 in singles/twins/doubles.

The *Kiwi Paka* (☎ (07) 347 0931) at 60 Tarewa Rd, a fair walk from the city centre, caters for the local bus crowd. It charges $14 in four-bed shared rooms; twins and doubles are $36. You can camp on the lawn for $7.

Its thermal pool is jam-packed when buses are in but it has a nice cafe and the Under Canvas bar.

B&Bs & Guesthouses Toko St is quiet and well away from the tourist hustle of central Rotorua. At No 3 there's the *Tresco International* (☎ (07) 348 9611), where B&B costs $48/75 for singles/doubles. There are sinks in the rooms and it's a neat, tidy and comfortable place. The same can be said for the *Morihana Guest House* (☎ (07) 348 8511) a bit further down at No 20; singles/doubles are $48/85 with breakfast. Both places have hot mineral pools.

Central *Eaton Hall* (☎ (07) 347 0366) at 39 Hinemaru St, opposite the Quality Resort, is a comfortable, homey guesthouse with B&B at $48/80 (less in the off season). Book ahead in summer as this is a popular place.

The Tudor-style *Dudley House B&B* (☎ (07) 347 9894) at 6 Rangiuru St is recommended by our readers as being extra good value at $40/60 (at quiet times $30/50).

Tourism Rotorua has listings for nearly 50 homestays and farmstays and can make bookings.

Motels Rotorua has over 80 motels and Fenton St, as it heads south from town past the Big Fresh supermarket, has wall-to-wall motels as far as the eye can see. In the off season they compete, with discounts displayed. Good motels include:

Aywon Motel (☎ (07) 347 7659), 18 Trigg Ave; studio and one-bedroom units from $79, spa units from $115.
Bel Aire Motel (☎ (07) 348 6076), 257 Fenton St; $60 a double.
Forest Court Motel (☎ (07) 346 3543), 275 Fenton St; from $56 a double.
Havana Motor Lodge (☎ (07) 348 8134), 12 Whakaue St; $65/75 for singles/doubles.
Heywoods Motor Lodge (☎ (07) 349 5586), 249 Fenton St; $65 to $130 a double.
Kiwi International Villas (☎ (07) 347 3333), 11 Tryon St; Half-price specials (on presentation of discount card) for $40 include an excellent suite and access to spas and pools.
Kiwi Lodge Motel (☎ (07) 349 1991), 279 Fenton St; $50/65.

Kiwi Paka (☎ (07) 347 0931), 60 Tarewa Rd; from $44 to $48 for two.
Motel Monterey (☎ (07) 348 1044), 50 Whakaue St; $60 to $75 a double.
Tom's Motel (☎ (07) 347 8062), 6 Union St; $66/78.
Travellers Motor Lodge (☎ (07) 348 5998), 15 Fenton St; $70 a double.
Wylie Court Motor Lodge (☎ (07) 347 7879), 345 Fenton St; from $112 a single.

Hotels Right in the centre, on the corner of Hinemoa and Fenton Sts, the *Grand Establishment* (☎ (07) 348 2089) has singles/doubles with private facilities for $50/65. Rooms have tea and coffee-making facilities and there's a sauna, restaurant, bar and nightclub. Conveniently situated on the corner of Hinemaru and Pukuatua Sts, the *Good Sports Hotel* (☎ (07) 348 1550) has typical pub rooms for $45/55. It has a large thermal pool and Dobbo's Sports Bar.

The *Princes Gate Hotel* (☎ (07) 348 1179) at 1 Arawa St on the corner of Hinemaru St is a luxurious hotel with crystal chandeliers, canopies over the beds, an elegant restaurant and bar, a health facility and much more. It charges $105/140.

Rotorua has some big hotels. In a rough progression of price and quality are the *Regal Geyserland* (☎ (07) 348 2039), *Rotorua International Plaza* (☎ (07) 348 1189), *Lake Plaza Rotorua* (☎ (07) 348 1174) and then a definite jump to *Rydges* (☎ 0800 654 994), the *Sheraton* (☎ (07) 349 5200) and the *Millennium* (☎ (07) 348 0199). Prices start at $120 a double and go up to around $250 a double at the Sheraton.

The new *Novotel Royal Lakeside Rotorua* (☎ (07) 346 3888) at 9-11 Tutanekai St is the pinnacle of luxury, if you can afford it. And if expense is no obstacle, Rotorua has a few exclusive and secluded lodges such as the *Solitaire Lodge* (☎ (07) 362 8208) at Lake Tarawera and the *Woodlands Country Lodge* (☎ (07) 332 2242) on Hamurana Rd, Ngongotaha, where doubles cost $550, including meals.

Places to Eat
Restaurants The *Alzac Cafe* on Tutunekai St is a European-style cafe where you can

come for a meal or just to hang out over coffee. The menu is 'California-style', emphasising fresh ingredients and eclectic international dishes. *Valentines*, on the corner of Amohau and Fenton Sts, and *Sizzler* at 209 Fenton St have a range of hearty family meals from $16.

Lewisham's Austrian Restaurant at 115 Tutanekai St specialises in traditional Austrian and Hungarian food. *Zanelli's*, at 23 Amohia St, is a popular Italian dinner house, with good gelati. The popular *Gazebo Restaurant* at 45 Pukuatua St features European and Asian food. There are good lunch specials or more expensive evening meals. *Sirocco* at 86 Eruera St is a Mediterranean cafe/bar which is open daily for lunch and dinner; a meal costs about $15.

For genuine Pacific Rim cuisine featuring innovative use of local ingredients try the *Rendezvous Restaurant* at 116 Hinemoa St; it is open from Tuesday to Saturday for dinner. Also highly recommended for its Kiwi fare is *Poppy's Villa* at 4 Marguerita St; main courses are about $25. Both of these restaurants are in atmospheric old villas.

Rotorua also has the *Thai Restaurant* at 187 Tutanekai St, with good Thai meals from $15 to $23; it is open Monday to Saturday for lunch and daily for dinner. *Mr India* at 45 Amohau St is moderately priced and has all the authentic subcontinental favourites such as vindaloo, korma, naan and vegetarian dishes.

The *Korea House Restaurant* at 16 Eruera St is a pleasant, large and fancy place serving Korean food. Japanese tastes are satisfied at the *Japanese Sushi Bar* at 184 Tutanekai St; a sushi main is $13, tempura is also $13 and a small sashimi plate is $8.

Pub Food *Cobb & Co*, in the Grand Establishment on Hinemoa St between Tutanekai and Fenton Sts, has its usual dinner menu.

Churchill's Bar at 426 Tutanekai St is another good place for a meal. A comfortable English-style bar, it serves up a lot of lunches and finger food in big, satisfying portions; food is always available. *Cameron's Bar & Grill*, upstairs on the corner of Fenton and

Pukuatua Sts, serves snacks and light meals for lunch and dinner for under $10.

Fast Food *Tastebuds Mexican Cantina* at 93 Fenton St, near the corner of Pukuatua St, serves up the usual cheap and tasty Tex-Mex fare to take away or eat there. The *Charcoal Chicken Joint* at 286 Tutanekai St has chargrilled chicken and hot carvery sandwiches. The *Robert Harris Coffee House* opposite at No 227 has good coffee, pastries and cakes.

Pizza Forno at 31 Pukuatua St makes pretty good pizzas, to eat there or take away; phone for free delivery (☎ (07) 347 9854). Two doors away, *Country Kitchen* does good sandwiches. The *Coffee Bean* at 189 Tutanekai St also makes good sandwiches and 'hangover-cure' breakfasts – bacon, eggs, toast, coffee (about $7); it's open during the day, daily except Sunday.

The *Kebab Cafe* at 67 Arawa St has a good selection of Middle Eastern and Indian dishes including vegetarian selections; lunch will cost about $6 and dinner about $15 and there are also takeaways. For fish and chips try the *Fishpot Cafe* on Eruera St – a fishermans basket is $20, while oysters and scallops are $20.

Most of the tourist attractions have cafes but the one at the *Orchid Gardens* on Hinemaru St is especially enjoyable and not expensive.

Chez Bleu on Fenton St near the corner of Hinemoa St is said to make the best burgers in town. It's open until the wee hours on weekends. *Wimpy's* on Tutanekai St near Amohau St serves not so much hamburgers as good, old-fashioned filling lunches and dinners at cheap prices. The roasts are good value.

McDonald's is on the corner of Fenton and Amohau Sts, on Tutanekai St and out on Fairy Springs Rd. The latter has a shop called the *Happy Homestead*, which specialises in merchandise and collectables – the kids will go wild. *KFC* is on Amohau St and Fairy Springs Rd and *Pizza Hut* is on Tutanekai St, up near the lake. *Lady Jane's Ice Cream*

Parlour near the lake end of Tutanekai St is also popular with children.

Entertainment

The happening place at the moment is the *Lava Bar* in the Hot Rock Backpackers at 118 Arawa St. Here you can mix with an international and local crowd, play pool and listen to good sounds.

The popular *Pig & Whistle* on the corner of Haupapa and Tutanekai Sts is a renovated police station with a number of brews on tap including its own Swine Lager. Guzzle a Swiney and listen to bands on weekend nights.

Monkey Jo's on Amohia St is a trendy bar and popular pick-up spot that packs them in most nights of the week. *Churchill's Bar* at 426 Tutanekai St is a safe, relaxed, English-style bar with plenty of different beers on tap, NZ wines and meals. *Cameron's Bar & Grill*, upstairs on the corner of Fenton and Pukuatua Sts, sometimes has live music. It, too, serves food and has Guinness on tap and a huge range of whiskies. The *Fat Dog*, a cafe and bar at 69 Arawa St, is a good place to while the evening away with an espresso (the aroma may cancel out Rotorua's unique smell).

Other good bars are *Wild Willy's*, a 'Wild West' bar at 134 Fenton St, and *O'Malley's*, an Irish pub at 85 Eruera St. Both have live music on Friday and Saturday nights and O'Malley's menu includes Irish stew and cottage pie for $8.50. *Zambique* on Tutanekai St has also been recommended as a 'palace of good times'.

The Grand Establishment has *Wheeler's Nightclub*, a disco popular with the young crowd. *Bar Zazu* in the Millennium, *Clarke's Bar* in the Novotel and *Cards Bar* in the Sheraton are open daily from 4 pm until late. *Dobbo's Bar* at the Good Sports Hotel on the corner of Hinemaru and Pukuatua Sts is a sports bar with live bands on weekends. The *Ace of Clubs* on Ti St attracts the nocturnals wanting to party on; it's open until 4.30 am. The rougher set will like the *Lake Tavern* on Lake Rd.

Getting There & Away

Air The Air New Zealand and Mt Cook Airline office (☎ (07) 347 9564) on the corner of Fenton and Hinemoa Sts is open on weekdays from 8.30 am to 5 pm; it also has a counter at the airport (☎ (07) 345 6175) open daily. It offers daily direct flights to Auckland, Christchurch, Mt Cook, Queenstown, Taupo and Wellington, with onward connections.

Ansett New Zealand (☎ (07) 347 0596) has a city office at 113 Fenton St and an airport ticket counter (☎ (07) 345 5348). Ansett offers daily direct flights to Christchurch, Queenstown, Invercargill and Wellington, with connections to other centres.

Bus All major bus companies stop at the Tourism Rotorua centre (☎ (07) 348 5179) on Fenton St, which handles bookings.

InterCity has daily buses to and from Auckland, Wellington, Taupo, Tauranga, Whakatane and Hamilton, and Opotiki. On the east coast routes, InterCity goes daily to Gisborne via Opotiki, to Napier via Taupo.

Newmans buses go from Rotorua to Hamilton, Auckland, Taupo, Wellington, Palmerston North, Tauranga and Napier. Magic Bus and Kiwi Experience backpackers buses also stop in Rotorua.

The Thermal Connection (aka the Pink Bus; ☎ (07) 377 6067, 0800 222 231) has a daily service to Taupo ($14/28 one way/return). See Taupo in the Central Plateau chapter.

Geyserland Express (☎ (07) 357 6616), not to be confused with the train of the same name, has an Auckland return service ($28).

Train The train station is on the corner of Railway Rd and Lake Rd, about 1km northwest of the centre. The station opens only when trains are leaving or arriving. Buy train tickets at Tourism Rotorua, not the station.

The *Geyserland Express* train operates daily between Auckland and Rotorua, stopping at Hamilton. It departs from Rotorua at 1.05 pm and arrives at Auckland at 5.15 pm. In the other direction, it leaves Auckland at 8.20 am and arrives at Rotorua at 12.25 pm.

Hitching Hitching to Rotorua is generally not bad, except on SH38 from Waikare-moana – past Murupara the road is unsealed and traffic is very light. The problem hitching out of Rotorua is often the sheer number of backpackers leaving town. You may have to join the queue and wait.

Getting Around
To/From the Airport The airport is about 10km out of town, on the eastern side of the lake. Airport Shuttle (☎ (07) 346 2386) and Super Shuttle (☎ (07) 349 3444) offer a door-to-door service to/from the airport for $8 for the first person and $2 for each additional passenger. A taxi from the city centre is about $15.

Bus Rotorua Sightseeing Shuttle (☎ 025 957399) makes a constant loop daily from 8.15 am to 5.10 pm. The route begins at Tourism Rotorua and goes to Whakare-warewa, back to Tourism Rotorua, then on to the Orchid Gardens, Polynesian Spa, museum, lakefront, Skyline Skyrides, Rainbow Springs, Agrodome and back to Tourism Rotorua. Half-day passes for up to five hours cost $15, full-day passes are $22 (children half-price), and you can jump on and off wherever you like. Ring for hotel pick-up.

The Pink Bus (also The Thermal Connection; ☎ (07) 348 2302, 0800 222 231) has a service to Waiotapu and Waimangu thermal areas about 9 am, picking up at Tourism Rotorua and some accommodation places; buses return at 12.30 pm. The buses to Waiotapu are $30 (including admission) and to Waimangu are $25 (bus only).

Reesby Coachlines (☎ (07) 347 0098) operates several suburban bus routes week-days, with a limited Saturday service. Route 3 runs to Whakarewarewa, Route 2 to Rainbow Springs.

Car Rotorua has a host of car rental companies. The competition is fierce and they all seem to offer 'specials' to try to undercut the others. Rent-a-Dent (☎ (07) 349 1919) on Ti St and Link Rent-a-Car (☎ (07) 347 8063) at 108 Fenton St are two economical companies. Ask about relocating cars to Auckland; you drive to Auckland for them and pay only for insurance and fuel.

Bicycle Rotorua is fairly spread out and public transport is not very good, so a bicycle is worthwhile. Lady Jane's (☎ (07) 347 9340), on the corner of Tutanekai and Whakaue Sts, hires out bikes from $15 per day; a deposit is required. Another good place is the Rotorua Cycle Centre (☎ (07) 348 6588), which is also good for repairs and cycle parts.

AROUND ROTORUA
Hell's Gate
Hell's Gate (Tikitere), another highly active thermal area, is 16km east of Rotorua on the road to Whakatane (SH30). The reserve covers 10 hectares, with a 2.5km walking track to the various attractions including the largest hot thermal waterfall in the southern hemisphere. It's open daily from 8.30 am to 5 pm ($10, children $5).

George Bernard Shaw visited Hell's Gate in 1934. 'I wish I had never seen the place,' he said. 'It reminds me too vividly of the fate theologians have promised me.'

Waimangu Volcanic Valley
The Waimangu Volcanic Valley is another interesting thermal area, created during the eruption of Mt Tarawera in 1886. A walk through the valley (an easy downhill stroll) first passes the Waimangu Cauldron (a pale blue lake steaming quietly at 53°C) then many other interesting thermal and volcanic features. Waimangu means 'black water', as much of the water here was a dark, muddy colour. In this valley the Waimangu Geyser used to perform actively enough to be rated the 'largest geyser in the world'. Between 1900 and its extinction in 1904 it would occasionally spout jets nearly 500m high!

The walk continues down to Lake Roto-mahana (warm lake), from where you can either get a lift back up to where you started or take a half-hour boat trip on Lake

To Tauranga
• The Farmhouse
To Tauranga
Kaituna River
33
To Tauranga
Okere Falls
Lake Rotoiti Lakeside Holiday Park
Hamurana Springs ◉
Ohau Channel Lodge
Hongi's Track
Lake Rotoehu
Ohau Channel
Lake Rotoiti
Merge Lodge
Tikitere (Hell's Gate)
Ruato
To Whakatane & Gisborne
30
Lake Rotokawau
To Agrodome, Hamilton & Auckland
5
Lake Rotorua
Greengrove Holiday Park
Rainbow Resort
Mountain Adventures, Zorbing, Rap Jumping
Rainbow Springs & Skyline Skyrides
The Happy Homestead
Mokoia Island
Te Ngae Maze
Lake Rotokawau
Airport
Fairbank Maze
Western Okataina Walkway
Eastern Okataina Walkway
Lake Okataina
Tarawera River
Mt Ngongotaha
See Central Rotorua Map
30
All Seasons Holiday Park; Holdens Bay Holiday Park
To Paradise Valley Springs
5
Rotorua
Tarawera Road
Lake Okareka
Lake Tarawera
Redwood Holiday Park
Whakarewarewa
Whakarewarewa Forest Park
Blue Lake Holiday Park
Blue Lake
Fisherman's Lodge Family Holiday Park
Tarawera Landing
30
5
Green Lake
Te Wairoa (Buried Village)
Mt Tarawera (erupted 1886)
Crater Chasm
Whakarewarewa State Park
Waimangu Round Trip
Site of White Terraces (destroyed 1886)
Site of Pink Terraces (destroyed 1886)
Patiti Island
Lake Rotomahana
Waimangu Volcanic Valley
Waimangu Rd
Lake Okaro
Lake Rerewhakaaitu
Lake Opouri
Waikite Thermal Mineral Baths
5
Rerewhakaaitu Road
Ash Pit Road
Old Waiotapu Rd
38
Mud Pools
Kerosene Creek Thermal Area
Lady Knox Geyser
Waiotapu Thermal Area
KAINGAROA STATE FOREST
Around Rotorua
To Taupo
To Lake Waikaremoana
0   5   10 km

The Eruption of Mt Tarawera

In the 19th century, Lake Tarawera near Rotorua was a major tourist attraction. It brought visitors from around the world to see the Pink and White Terraces: large and beautiful terraces of multi-levelled pools, formed by silica deposits from thermal waters which had trickled over them for centuries. The Maori village of Te Wairoa, on the shores of the lake, was NZ's principal tourist resort. From here Sophia, a Maori guide, took visitors on boat trips over the lake to view the terraces, which were regarded as one of the seven wonders of the world. Mt Tarawera towered silently over the lake, although the Maori believed that a powerful fire spirit lived inside it.

One day in June 1886, Sophia took a party out on the lake as usual, to go to see the terraces. As they were on the lake, they suddenly saw a phantom Maori war canoe gliding across the water, the Maori boatmen inside it paddling rapidly. It was an ancient war canoe of a kind which had never existed on this lake. It was seen by all the people in the tourist boat, both Maori and Pakeha.

To Maori people, the appearance of a phantom Maori war canoe is an omen of impending disaster. Back at Te Wairoa, an old tohunga, Tuhoto Ariki, said the sighting of the canoe foretold disaster. He predicted that the village would be 'overwhelmed'.

Four days later, on 10 June 1886, in the middle of the night, there were earthquakes and loud sounds and the eruption of Mt Tarawera suddenly lit up the sky, with fire exploding from many places along the top of the mountain. By the time it was finished, six hours later, over 8000 sq km had been buried in ash, lava and mud, the Maori village of Te Wairoa was obliterated, the Pink and White Terraces were destroyed, 153 people were killed, Mt Tarawera was sliced and opened along its length as if hit with a huge cleaver, and Lake Rotomahana was formed.

Excavations were carried out at Te Wairoa to rescue the survivors. The guide Sophia became a heroine because she saved many people's lives, giving them shelter in her house.

The old tohunga, however, was not so fortunate. His house was buried in volcanic ash, and he was trapped inside. The Maori people working to rescue the survivors refused to dig him out. They feared he had used his magic powers to cause the eruption – he had been saying for some time that the new orientation of the villagers towards tourists and a money economy were not traditional, and that neglect of the old traditions would anger the fire spirit inside the mountain. Finally, after four days had passed, he was dug out alive by Europeans, who took him to be cared for in Rotorua. He died a week later, aged around 104. ■

Rotomahana, past steaming cliffs and the former site of the Pink and White Terraces.

The Waimangu Volcanic Valley is open daily from 8.30 am to 5 pm. The cost is $11 (children $5) for the valley walk only; it's $29 (children $7) for both the valley walk and boat trip. It's a 20-minute drive from Rotorua, going 19km south on SH5 (the road towards Taupo) and then 5 to 6km from the marked turn-off.

Waiotapu

Also south of Rotorua, Waiotapu (sacred waters) is perhaps the best of the thermal areas to visit. It has many interesting features including the large, boiling Champagne Pool, craters and blowholes, colourful mineral terraces and other rock formations, and the Lady Knox Geyser which spouts off (with a little prompting) punctually at 10.15 am and gushes for about an hour.

It opens daily at 8.30 am, closing at 5 pm (last entry 4 pm), but is usually open later in summer ($10, children $4). To get there, go 30km south on SH5 (the road towards Taupo), turn at the marked turn-off and go 2km. (The turn-off for the Waikite Thermal Mineral Baths is also there; see Thermal Pools in the Rotorua section.)

Trout Springs

Several trout springs run down to Lake Rotorua and the trout, lured perhaps by the free feeds waiting for them from the tourists, swim up the streams to the springs. They are not trapped there; if you watch you may see a trout leaping the little falls to return to the lake or come up to the springs.

The **Rainbow Springs Trout & Wildlife Sanctuary** is the best known of the trout springs. There are a number of springs (one with an underwater viewer), an aviary and a nocturnal kiwi house. It's a pleasant walk through the pongas and native bush to see the trout in the streams. Pick up your bag of trout feed at the entrance and watch the trout feeding frenzy – unless a tour bus has gone through and the trout have already pigged out. The springs also have a wildlife area with eels, wallabies, deer, birds, sheep, wild pigs and other native and introduced animals, now all found in the wild in NZ.

Across the road, the Rainbow Farm Show is part of Rainbow Springs and has shows at 10.30 and 11.45 am, 1 and 2.30 pm (extra shows in summer at 9 am and 4 pm) with sheep shearing and sheep dogs.

Rainbow Springs is 4km north of central Rotorua, on the west side of Lake Rotorua – take SH5 towards Auckland or Hamilton, or catch the Sightseeing Shuttle Bus. It is open 8 am to 5 pm daily ($10, children $5); the farm shows cost $7.80 ($3.50) or a combined ticket is $13.50 ($6).

Paradise Valley Springs are similar, set in an attractive 6-hectare park with various animals. The springs, 13km from Rotorua on Paradise Valley Rd, at the foot of Mt Ngongotaha, are open daily from 9 am to 5 pm ($10, children $5).

Skyline Skyrides

Skyline Skyrides is on the west side of Lake Rotorua, near the Rainbow and Fairy Springs. Here you can take a gondola ride up Mt Ngongotaha for a panoramic view of the lake area and, once there, fly 900m back down the mountain on a luge (a sort of toboggan) or a flying fox, coming back up again on a chairlift. There is a cafe and restaurant for twilight dining on top of the mountain. The gondola costs $12 (children $5) for the return trip and the luge is $4.50 for one ride, less for multiple trips (eg five rides cost $16). The gondola operates from 10 am daily. At night you can get a combination gondola and one-ride luge package for $9 ($6).

There is also a flight simulator, shooting range, mini-golf course and other attractions to spend your money on at the top. There are walking tracks around the mountain.

Agrodome

If seeing the millions of sheep in the NZ countryside has stimulated your interest in these animals, visit Agrodome. Going to see a bunch of sheep seems a rather strange thing to do in NZ, but for $10.50 (children $5) you get an interesting, educational and entertaining one-hour show at 9.30 am, 11 am and 2.30 pm daily. There are sheep-shearing and sheepdog displays; by the time you're

Performing to Schedule

How does the Lady Knox Geyser manage to perform so neatly to schedule? Simple – it's blocked up with some rags so the pressure builds up, then a couple of kilos of soap powder is shoved in in to decrease the surface viscosity. And off it goes.

This scientific principle of the relation of soap powder to surface viscosity of geysers was discovered by some early Europeans who thought it would be a great idea to use the hot water in the ground to wash their clothes. ■

through you may even be able to tell the difference between some of the 19 breeds of sheep on show. A dairy display, farmyard nursery and cow milking are also included.

You can hire horses for a guided tour or take a farm buggy tour of the 120-hectare farm ($10, children $5). Agrodome is 7km north of Rotorua on SH1.

Mazes

Near the airport are a couple of large mazes. The **Fairbank Maze**, opposite the airport, is the largest hedge maze in NZ, with a 1.6km pathway. There are also gardens, ponds, an orchard, picnic areas, birds and animals. The maze is open from 9 am to 5 pm daily ($4, children $2).

Te Ngae Park, 3km beyond the airport, is a 3-D, 1.7km wooden maze similar to the original Wanaka maze on the South Island. It's open daily from 9 am to 5 pm ($4, children $2).

Buried Village

The Buried Village is reached by a 15km scenic drive along Tarawera Rd, which passes the Blue and Green Lakes. On display are many artefacts and excavated buildings from the village which was buried in ash by the Mt Tarawera eruption. Of particular interest is the story of Tuhoto Ariki who foretold the destruction; his house has been excavated and is on display. There's a good bush walk through the valley to Te Wairoa Falls which drops about 80m over a series of falls.

The village is open from 8.30 am to 5 pm daily, until 6 pm in summer ($9, children $2).

Lake Tarawera

About 2km past the Buried Village is Tarawera Landing on the shore of Lake Tarawera. Tarawera means 'burnt spear', named by a visiting hunter who left his birdspears in a hut and, on returning the following season, found both the spears and hut had been burnt.

Tarawera Launch Cruises (☎ (07) 362 8595) has a cruise at 11 am crossing over Lake Tarawera towards Lake Rotomahana. It stays on the other side for about 45

minutes, long enough for people to walk across to Lake Rotomahana, then returns to Tarawera Landing. The trip takes two hours and costs $20. A shorter 45-minute, $15 cruise on Lake Tarawera leaves at 1.30, 2.30 and 3.30 pm. Boats from Tarawera Landing can also provide transport to Mt Tarawera and to Hot Water Beach on Te Rata Bay. The beach has hot thermal waters and a basic DOC camping ground.

Whirinaki Forest Park

About 50km east of Rotorua, signposted off the main road, is the 609 sq km Whirinaki Forest Park. Access is off SH38 on the way to Te Urewera National Park; take the turn-off at Te Whaiti to Minginui. The park is noted for the sheer majesty and density of its native podocarp forests; it has walking tracks, scenic drives, camping and huts, lookouts, waterfalls, the Whirinaki River, and some special areas, including the Oriuwaka Ecological Reserve and the Arahaki Lagoon. For more information about this excellent forest park get a copy of the booklet *Tramping & Walking in Whirinaki Forest Park*.

The DOC has a field centre in the sawmill village of Minginui, but the park headquarters' office is the Ikawhenua Visitor Centre (☎ (07) 366 5641) in Murupara.

Ask for details on the fine Whirinaki Track walk, an easy two-day walk that can be combined with Te Hoe Loop Walk for a four-day walk with seven huts that starts in some of NZ's finest podocarp forest and proceeds along a series of river valleys.

Places to Stay Just before Minginui is the *Whirinaki Recreation Camp* (☎ (07) 366 3601) and in Minginui is the *Ohu Forest Users' Camp*; both charge $5 (children $2). Down by the Whirinaki River, at the Mangamate Waterfall, there is an informal camping area; a camp site is $5. The forest has nine back country huts costing $4 per person. Murupara has all types of accommodation as well as food outlets.

Walking

Check in at the Map and Track shop for pamphlets and excellent maps outlining the many fine walks in the area.

On the south-east edge of town, **Whakarewarewa State Forest Park** was planted earlier this century as an experiment to find the most suitable species to replace NZ's rapidly dwindling and slow-growing native trees. The Forestry Corporation Visitor Information Centre (☎ (07) 346 2082) in the park is open daily and has a woodcraft shop, displays and an audiovisual on the history and development of the forest. Check in here if you want to go walking. Walks range from half an hour to four hours, including some great routes to the Blue and Green Lakes. Several walks start at the Visitor Centre, including a half-hour walk through the **Redwood Grove**, a grove of large Californian redwood trees.

Other walks in the Rotorua area include the 22.5km **Western Okataina Walkway** through native bush from Lake Okareka to Ruato, on the shores of Lake Rotoiti. There's public transport past the Ruato end only; the whole walk takes about six hours and you need good boots or stout shoes.

The **Eastern Okataina Walkway** goes along the eastern shoreline of Lake Okataina to Lake Tarawera – about a 2½-hour, 8km walk. A connecting track makes it possible to do a two-day walk from either Lake Okataina or Ruato to Lake Tarawera and camp overnight at a DOC camping ground ($5 per site), from where you can walk another hour to the Tarawera Falls.

To go tramping on **Mt Tarawera**, the easiest access is from Ash Pit Rd at the northern end of Lake Rerewhakaaitu, but there is no public transport. Mt Tarawera is Maori Reserve land and permission should be obtained. DOC can tell you how to arrange it in Rotorua, but in summer there is usually someone on the track to collect the $2 fee. From the parking area it is a two-hour walk along a 4WD track to the crater chasm and Ruawhaia Dome. From here, most walkers return along the same route but it is possible to follow another track leading to Lake Rotomahana and Lake Tarawera. You can complete a loop if you can arrange to be dropped off on the Ash Pit Rd and time your return to meet the Tarawera Launch at the Tarawera outlet for transport back to the Tarawera Landing.

It is essential to take water and wear good tramping shoes – it's easy to slip on the volcanic scoria. The weather on Mt Tarawera can be very changeable, so bring warm and waterproof clothing to protect against wind and rain.

The **Okere Falls** are about 16km north-east of Rotorua on SH33 – the turn-off is well signposted. It's about a 30-minute walk through native podocarp forest to the falls. These are the 7m falls that the rafting companies take people over. There are several other walks, including walks up the Kaituna River to Hinemoa's Steps and to some caves.

Just north of Waiotapu on SH5, a good trail leads to **Rainbow Mountain** with its small crater lakes and fine views. It is a good, short, but fairly strenuous 1½-hour walk to the Maungakakatamea Lookout.

Other short walks can be made around Lake Okataina, Mt Ngongotaha (just north of Rotorua) and Lake Rotorua.

Western Bay of Plenty

The western Bay of Plenty extends from Katikati and Waihi Beach to Te Puke on the coast and south to the Kaimai Ranges.

Captain Cook sailed into the Bay of Plenty on the *Endeavour* in October 1769, naming it for the number of thriving settlements of friendly Maori he encountered (and the amount of supplies they gave him). It was a sharp contrast to the 'welcome' he received from the Maori of Poverty Bay several weeks earlier, when lives were lost and no food was available.

The area is not as popular with tourists as the far more commercial Bay of Islands but in summer it hums along nicely. It enjoys one of the highest proportions of sunny days in New Zealand, the climate is consistently mild year-round and in summer the coastal beaches are popular with Kiwis.

The region is rapidly becoming the horticultural centre of NZ and its main exports are kiwi fruit and timber products, including logs and woodchips. There is a growing mineral water industry, with springs being 'tapped' all over the place. Naturally there are several hot mineral spas around.

TAURANGA

Tauranga (population 87,000) is the principal city of the Bay of Plenty and its port – one of the largest export ports in NZ – ships out the produce from the rich surrounding region. The days of the overnight kiwi fruit millionaires have gone but the area is still thriving economically and draws increasing numbers of retirees attracted by the temperate climate and a city well supplied with facilities. Tauranga is indeed a pleasant place to live but its tourist attractions are limited mostly to the beaches and headland scenery of Mt Maunganui across Tauranga Harbour.

Tauranga is Maori for 'resting place for canoes', for this was where some of the first Maori to arrived.

As the centre of NZ's principal kiwi fruit region, work is available when kiwi fruit is being picked (May and June) but you may be able to find some orchard work at almost any time. Check with the hostels for orchard work contacts.

Information

The Tauranga Information & Visitors Centre (☎ (07) 578 8103; fax 577 6235) has moved from the waterfront to 80 Dive Crescent next to the Mt Maunganui harbour bridge roundabout. It's open in summer on weekdays from 7 am to 5.30 pm and on weekends from 8 am to 4 pm. Get the free *What's to See and Do?* publication.

The DOC office (☎ (07) 578 7677) on the corner of McLean and Anson Sts is open from 8 am to 4.30 pm on weekdays. The AA office (☎ (07) 578 2222) is on the corner of Devonport Rd and First Ave.

Things to See

The **Historic Village** (☎ (07) 578 1302) on Seventeenth Ave features restored period buildings, vintage vehicles, farming equipment, an 1877 steam locomotive, an old tugboat, a Maori culture section and relics from the gold-mining era. It's open from 9 am to 5 pm daily ($6, children $2.50).

Te Awanui, a fine replica Maori canoe, is on display in an open-sided building at the top end of the Strand, close to the centre of town. Continue uphill beyond the canoe to **Monmouth Redoubt**, a fortified site during the Maori Wars. A little further along is **Robbins Park**, with a rose garden and hothouse.

The **Elms Mission Station House** on Mission St was founded in 1835 and the present house was completed in 1847 by a pioneer missionary. It is furnished in period style. The grounds contain gardens and several historic buildings. It is open from 11 am to 2 pm on Sunday.

Walking

There are many walking possibilities in the region. A good number of these are outlined in the free pamphlet *Walkways of Tauranga*, available from visitor centres. Ten walks in Tauranga and Mt Maunganui (including the fascinating **Waikareao estuary**) and further afield are described. Each is accompanied by a handy map.

The backdrop to the western Bay of Plenty is the rugged 70km-long **Kaimai-Mamaku Forest Park**, with tramps for the more adventurous; DOC can provide more detailed information on walks in this area. **McLaren Falls**, in the Wairoa River valley, 11km from Tauranga just off SH29, is worth a visit. There's good bushwalking, rock pools and the falls.

Sea Activities

Charter and fishing trips operate from Tauranga year-round. During the summer the place comes alive with sea activities of all kinds including jet-skiing, swimming with the dolphins, water-skiing, windsurfing, parasailing, sea kayaking, diving,

TONY WHEELER

TONY WHEELER

CHARLOTTE HINDLE

Bay of Plenty
Top: The Bath House (Rotorua Museum of Art and History), Rotorua
Bottom Left: Mt Tarawera, near Rotorua
Bottom Right: Hell's Gate (Tikitere), near Rotorua

ADAM FRY

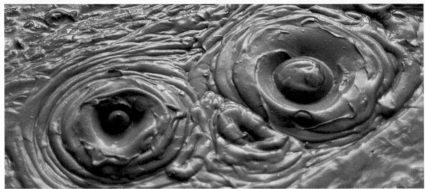
HOLGER LEUE

ADAM FRY

HOLGER LEUE

ADAM FRY

A	B
C	
D	E

Bay of Plenty
A: Historic Village, Tauranga
B: Pohutu Geyser erupts at least once an hour

C: Mud Pools, Te Whakarewarewa
D: Champagne Pool, Waiotapu Thermal Reserve
E: Surf beach, Mt Maunganui

surfing, swimming, line fishing, deep-sea fishing and sailing. Ask at the visitor centre for details and see the Around Tauranga section for details of trips to Mayor Island.

Recommended activities include sailing on Tauranga Harbour on the *Slipstream* yacht (☎ (07) 576 1841), from $30 for 1½ hours to $80 for a full day. Gemini Galaxsea (☎ (07) 578 3197) has dolphin-swimming experiences from a motorised yacht for $75 per day. Even if you don't meet the dolphins (they claim a high success rate) it is good value for a day cruise and you get to snorkel on the reefs. Fishing charters are available – get a copy of the *Gateway to the Magic Triangle* from the visitor centre.

White-Water Rafting

White-water rafting is popular around Tauranga, particularly on the Wairoa River, which has some of the best falls and rafting in NZ. It's definitely a rafting trip for thrill-seekers – one highlight of the trip is a plunge over a 4m waterfall! The water level is controlled from a dam, so the Wairoa can only be rafted on a few days of the year. Contact Wet 'N' Wild Rafting (☎ (07) 578 4093) for more information; it has trips on other rivers.

Flying & Skydiving

The Tauranga airport in Mt Maunganui is the base for a number of air clubs. Scenic flights can be arranged at the airport. The Tauranga Glider Club (☎ (07) 575 6768) flies every weekend, weather permitting, and an instructor will take you gliding and give you a flying lesson as you go. You can also do a flight in a microlight (a sort of powered hang-glider) with Microlight Training Flights (☎ (07) 575 8944). Tandem skydiving is extremely popular and costs $190 with Tandem Skydiving (☎ (07) 576 7990); there is a $10 discount for backpackers and a free photo. A different way to fly is on the **Bungy Rocket** – shoot above the Strand Reclamation car park for $25 per person (two at a time); it fires from 10 am until late.

Places to Stay

Camping & Cabins The *Mayfair Caravan Park* (☎ (07) 578 3323) is on Mayfair St, off Fifteenth Ave, beside the harbour. Powered sites cost $9 per person and cabins cost $30 a double. Tent facilities are limited.

The *Silver Birch Motor Park & Thermal Pools* (☎ (07) 578 4603) is at 101 Turret Rd (the extension of Fifteenth Ave) by the Hairini Bridge. Powered sites cost $9, cabins cost from $40 for two and there are also tourist/motel flats from $50/60 for two. It has thermal pools, boat ramp, dinghies and other recreational facilities.

At the *Palms Caravan Park* (☎ (07) 578 9337), 162 Waihi Rd, about 4km south of the city centre, sites cost from $9 per person and on-site vans cost $30 for two. The *Bayshore Leisure Park* (☎ (07) 544 0700) on SH29 (6km from the city centre) has tent and powered sites from $9 per person and cabins for $30 for two. This place has its own hot mineral pools.

Hostels Tauranga has a good selection of hostels, which fill up in the kiwi fruit picking season. The *Waireinga YHA Hostel* (☎ (07) 578 5064), 171 Elizabeth St, is conveniently close to the city centre, next to the motorway and the Waikareao Estuary. It's a cosy hostel charging $15 per person in dorms or twin rooms and $34 for a double; tent sites are $8. If you're coming into town by bus, ask to get off at First Ave.

The *Bell Lodge* (☎ (07) 578 6344) at 39 Bell St, 4km from town, is a newer, purpose-built hostel, pleasantly situated on three hectares of land. This friendly hostel is well equipped with heating in all the rooms, a big kitchen and lounge with fireplace. Bunk beds cost $15, singles/doubles with en suite cost from $28/36, or you can pitch a tent for $8 per person. It is very popular and crowded in the picking season when weekly rates are offered. Phone for free pick-up.

The *Apple Tree Cottage* (☎ (07) 576 7404), 47 Maxwell St, Pillans Point at Otumoetai, is a small, friendly hostel in a private house with a basic bunkroom bungalow at the back (and a hot spa), costing $13.50 per person; singles/doubles are

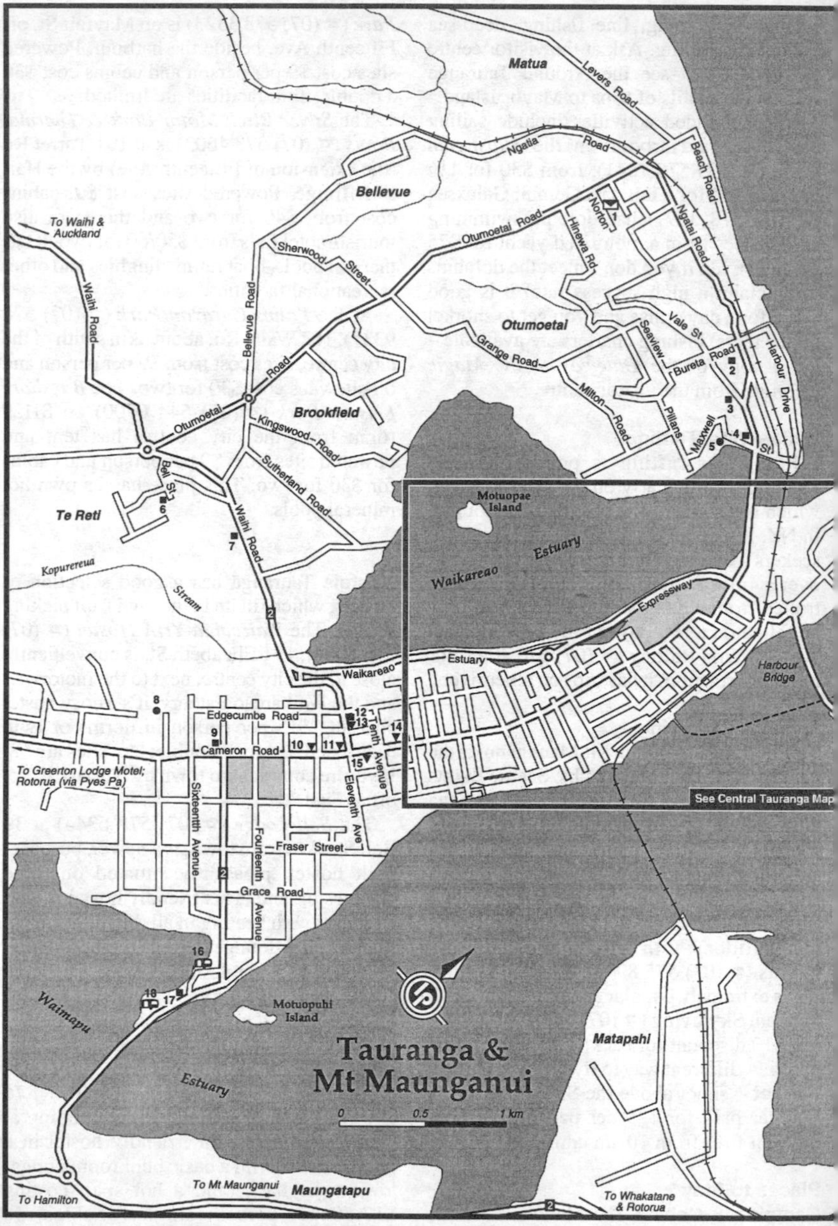

Matua
Levers Road
Ngatai Road
Beach Road
Bellevue
Norton
Hinewa Rd
Ngatai Road
To Waihi & Auckland
Otumoetai Road
Sherwood Street
Bellevue Road
Waihi Road
Otumoetai
Grange Road
Vale St
Seaview
Bureta Road
Harbour Drive
Milton Road
Pillans
Maxwell
St
Road
Otumoetai
Brookfield
Kingswood Road
Sutherland Road
Bell St
Te Reti
Waihi Road
Motuopae Island
Estuary
Waikareao
Kopurereua
Stream
Expressway
Estuary
Waikareao
Harbour Bridge
Edgecumbe Road
Cameron Road
Tenth Avenue
Eleventh Ave
To Greerton Lodge Motel; Rotorua (via Pyes Pa)
Sixteenth Avenue
Fourteenth Avenue
Fraser Street
Grace Road
See Central Tauranga Map
Waimapu
Motuopuhi Island
Estuary
Matapahi
Tauranga & Mt Maunganui
0
0.5
1 km
To Mt Maunganui
Maungatapu
To Hamilton
To Whakatane & Rotorua
1
2
3
4
5
6
7
8
9
10
11
12
13
14
15
16
17
18

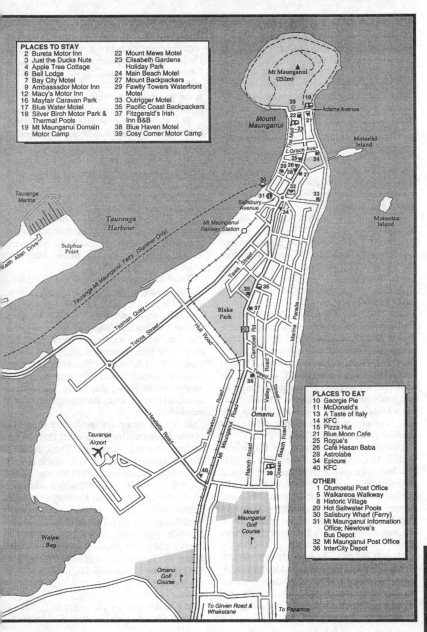

PLACES TO STAY
2 Bureta Motor Inn
3 Just the Ducks Nuts
4 Apple Tree Cottage
6 Bell Lodge
7 Bay City Motel
9 Ambassador Motor Inn
12 Macy's Motor Inn
16 Mayfair Caravan Park
17 Blue Water Motel
18 Silver Birch Motor Park & Thermal Pools
19 Mt Maunganui Domain Motor Camp
22 Mount Mews Motel
23 Elisabeth Gardens Holiday Park
24 Main Beach Motel
27 Mount Backpackers
29 Fawlty Towers Waterfront Motel
33 Outrigger Motel
35 Pacific Coast Backpackers
37 Fitzgerald's Irish Inn B&B
38 Blue Haven Motel
39 Cosy Corner Motor Camp

PLACES TO EAT
10 Georgie Pie
11 McDonald's
13 A Taste of Italy
14 KFC
15 Pizza Hut
21 Blue Moon Cafe
25 Rogue's
26 Café Hasan Baba
28 Astrolabe
34 Epicure
40 KFC

OTHER
1 Otumoetai Post Office
5 Waikareoa Walkway
8 Historic Village
20 Hot Saltwater Pools
30 Salisbury Wharf (Ferry)
31 Mt Maunganui Information Office; Newlove's Bus Depot
32 Mt Maunganui Post Office
36 InterCity Depot

Mt Maunganui (232m)

Mount Maunganui

Adams Avenue

Moturiki Island

The Mall

Grace Ave

Motuotau Island

Tauranga Marina

Tauranga Harbour

Sulphur Point

Keith Allan Drive

Tauranga-Mt Maunganui Ferry (Summer Only)

Salisbury Avenue

Mt Maunganui Railway Station

Tasman Quay

Totara Street

Hull Road

Blake Park

Tawa Street

Marine Parade

Campbell Rd

Tweed Street

Valley Road

Omanu

Hewletts Road

Newton Road

Tauranga Airport

Mt Maunganui Road

Ranch Road

Ocean Beach Road

Mount Maunganui Golf Course

Waipu Bay

Omanu Golf Course

To Given Road & Whakatane

To Papamoa

$32/36. Ask about its Coast with the Most trips ($25).

Nearby, *Just the Ducks Nuts* (☎ (07) 576 1366), 6 Vale St, is another small hostel (20 beds) but with plenty of space, a laid-back atmosphere and good communal areas. It provides good accommodation for $15 in the dorms, or twins/doubles cost $32/36 (weekly dorm rate $84); they drop off and pick up.

Motels & Hotels There are over 30 motels around Tauranga. The biggest concentrations are on Waihi Rd to the north, and Fifteenth Ave on the Rotorua Road, where you'll find many older motels.

Cheap, central motels include the old *Strand Motel* (☎ (07) 578 5807), 27 the Strand. It's plain and straightforward but conveniently located with singles/doubles for $60/68 ($75 with sea views). The *Roselands Motel* (☎ (07) 578 2294) at 21 Brown St is central in a quiet location and charges from $75 for two.

The *Blue Water Motel* (☎ (07) 578 5420), 59 Turret Rd, has doubles with a sitting room from $79. There's also a tepid thermal swimming pool, private spa pool and children's play area. The *Greerton Lodge Motel* (☎ (07) 578 7040), 1222 Cameron Rd, 4km from the centre, is a good place with swimming and spa pools and charges $60/70. The *Harbour View Motel* (☎ (07) 578 8621) at 7 Fifth Ave East is in a quiet waterside spot and singles/doubles cost from $65/75.

Upmarket places (around the $90 mark) include the *Ambassador Motor Inn* (☎ (07) 578 5665), on the corner of Cameron Rd and Fifteenth Ave; *Macy's Motor Inn* (☎ (07) 577 9764), on the corner of Eleventh Ave and Edgecumbe Rd; *Bay City* (☎ (07) 578 0588), 166 Waihi Rd; and the *Tauranga Motel on Second Avenue* (☎ (07) 578 7079), 1 Second Ave.

The *Hotel St Amand* (☎ (07) 578 8127), 105 the Strand, has singles/doubles with shared facilities for $35/50 or singles with a bath for $20. The St Amand has live bands on weekends, which is great for entertainment but not for sleep.

Places to Eat

Restaurants One of the most popular 'ethnic' restaurants is the reasonably priced *Collar & Thai* upstairs in the Goddards Centre, 21 Devonport Rd. The food is Thai and the dress is casual. At 62 Devonport Rd is the gourmet *Mediterraneao*, a European-style restaurant with great cakes and coffee.

The *Baywatch Brasserie & Bar*, on the corner of the Strand and Wharf St, is one of Tauranga's most popular restaurants. The menu is innovative, with interesting treatments of local produce, and the desserts are great. Nearby is the *Shiraz* for Middle Eastern fare such as babaganoush ($5.50) and generous shawarma platters ($14.50).

For Italian food, *A Taste of Italy* is a very popular licensed and BYO restaurant on the corner of Eleventh Ave and St John St, with entrée pastas for $9 and mains like veal marsala for around $20.

You can dine inside or outside, overlooking the water, at the *Harbourside Brasserie & Bar* at the Strand Extension, from 11.30 am until late. A three-course meal costs from $35 to $40 but the choice of dishes is good and combines a variety of local produce; there's a supper menu as well. Not far away, sandwiched between the Strand and Devonport Rd is *Beach Street*, a top restaurant with an innovative menu; don't miss the roasted kumara, orange brie, bacon and avocado salad ($12.50).

In a tight group on the Strand (roughly across from the Bungy Rocket) there is an enclave of good restaurants. These include the *Mongolian Feast* at No 63, which has an all-you-can-eat option for $18.50; the *Globe Cafe & Wine Bar* at No 59, with a selection of 30 wines by the glass; *Forrest*, a 'natural cuisine' restaurant at No 51 (its only drawback being that awful practice of charging for side vegetables, rice and salad separately); and the *Amphora Cafe Bar* at No 43, which serves beautiful shak-shuka (eggplant and capsicum fritters) for $7 and pizzas from a wood-fired oven.

Fast Food Tauranga has plenty of fast-food options including *Pizza Hut*, *McDonald's*,

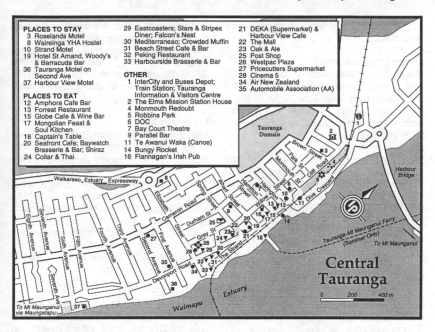

PLACES TO STAY
3 Roselands Motel
8 Waireinga YHA Hostel
10 Strand Motel
19 Hotel St Amand, Woody's & Barracuda Bar
36 Tauranga Motel on Second Ave
37 Harbour View Motel

PLACES TO EAT
12 Amphora Cafe Bar
13 Forrest Restaurant
15 Globe Cafe & Wine Bar
17 Mongolian Feast & Soul Kitchen
18 Captain's Table
20 Seafront Cafe; Baywatch Brasserie & Bar; Shiraz
24 Collar & Thai

29 Eastcoasters; Stars & Stripes Diner; Falcon's Nest
30 Mediterraneao; Crowded Muffin
31 Beach Street Cafe & Bar
32 Peking Restaurant
33 Harbourside Brasserie & Bar

OTHER
1 InterCity and Buses Depot; Train Station; Tauranga Information & Visitors Centre
2 The Elms Mission Station House
4 Monmouth Redoubt
5 Robbins Park
6 DOC
7 Bay Court Theatre
9 Parallel Bar
11 Te Awanui Waka (Canoe)
14 Bungy Rocket
16 Flannagan's Irish Pub

21 DEKA (Supermarket) & Harbour View Cafe
22 The Mall
23 Oak & Ale
26 Post Shop
27 Westpac Plaza
27 Pricecutters Supermarket
28 Cinema 5
34 Air New Zealand
35 Automobile Association (AA)

Central Tauranga

0   200   400 m

KFC and *Georgie Pie*, all on Cameron Rd. The *Crowded Muffin* in Devonport Rd gets rave reviews for its inexpensive lunches.

Down by the wharf, the *Captain's Table* has fish and chips as well as other standard cafe-bar fare. Nearby on the Strand, the *Seafront Cafe* never fails to deliver a hearty breakfast, good coffee and a smile.

Upstairs in the DEKA department store is the *Harbour View Cafe*, an enjoyable and inexpensive cafeteria with a sweeping harbour view. They serve tasty food at great prices; lunch costs about $5.

Devonport St has a concentration of dining opportunities. The West Plaza at 75 Devonport St has the *Stars & Stripes Diner* for burgers, tortillas and other Kiwi Americana. *Falcon's Nest* is a good little cafe-bar with meals in the $12 range. Above Falcon's Nest, *Eastcoasters* is a spacious place serving Mexican and Tex-Mex food, light meals, burgers and huge sandwiches. There is also a *Kebab House* here. Across the street, the

Peking is a better-than-usual Chinese place with a takeaway section, à la carte meals or a set menu costing $22.

Entertainment

The Bay Court Theatre hosts an eclectic mix of highbrow entertainment. Several hotel bars have live entertainment nightly from Thursday to Saturday, such as the *Barracuda Bar* in the Hotel St Amand. The *Oak & Ale* is a pleasant English-style pub in the Mall with a wide range of beers and occasional bands. *Flannagan's Irish Pub* at 14 Hamilton St is similar and you can also get a meal.

Other late night choices are *Harington's Nightclub* at 10 Harington St, *Abbey Road* at 22a Devonport Rd, which has live music on Friday and Saturday, and the *Parallel Bar* on Wharf St, which features alternative dance music. The *Soul Kitchen* on the Strand above the Mongolian Feast, has an eclectic mix of music; it is open on weekends until late.

Tauranga's bar-restaurants (see Places to

BAY OF PLENTY

Eat) are also lively and stay open late on weekends.

Getting There & Away
Air Air New Zealand Link (☎ (07) 578 0083) has an office on the corner of Devonport Rd and Elizabeth St. It has direct flights to Auckland, Rotorua and Wellington, with connections to other centres. Tauranga's airport is in Mt Maunganui.

Bus InterCity (☎ (07) 578 2825), in the information centre on Dive Crescent, and Newmans are the main buslines serving Tauranga. InterCity connects Tauranga with Auckland, Hamilton, Thames and Rotorua, and with Gisborne via Whakatane and Opotiki. Newmans runs to Hamilton (Friday and Sunday), Auckland, New Plymouth, Rotorua, Taupo and Napier. Supa Travel (☎ (07) 571 0583) is a local company with buses to Auckland ($31) daily except Saturday. Newmans and Supa Travel stop at the visitor centre, which also handles bookings for these buses. Most buslines continue to Mt Maunganui after stopping in Tauranga.

Call-a-Bus (☎ 0800 100 550) has a door-to-door service to Auckland for $45.

Train The *Kaimai Express* to Auckland departs from Tauranga at 8.05 am; transfers and other connections can be made in Hamilton before it goes on to Auckland. It departs from Auckland for Tauranga at 5.40 pm, arriving in Tauranga at 9.05 pm; there is a bar on board and snacks are served. The visitor information centre handles bookings.

Getting Around
The Tauranga Airport Shuttle (☎ (07) 578 6086) charges $7 for a door-to-door airport service.

Tauranga has a local bus service which provides transport to most locations around the area, including Mt Maunganui ($3 one way) and Papamoa ($4).

Several car rental agencies have offices in Tauranga, including Budget and Avis. An economical choice is Rent-a-Dent; the visitor centre has more details. The harbour

bridge has a $1 toll in each direction for cars, but it's free for bicycles and pedestrians.

The local taxi companies are: Citicabs (☎ (07) 577 0999), Tauranga Taxis (☎ (07) 578 6086) and Coastline (☎ (07) 578 8095).

The ferry service to Mt Maunganui operates in summer ($5).

MT MAUNGANUI
The town of Mt Maunganui (Maunganui means 'large mountain') stands at the foot of the 232m hill of the same name (also called 'the Mount' – 'Mauao'). It's just across the inlet from Tauranga and its fine beaches make it a popular holiday resort for Kiwis. Like Tauranga, the town of Mt Maunganui is built on a narrow peninsula.

The downside of the drive to the mount is the industrial area that the road goes through, reminiscent of the factory-pocked towns of the eastern US seaboard.

Information
The Mt Maunganui Information Office (☎ (07) 575 5099) on Salisbury Ave is open on weekdays from 9 am to 5 pm (until 4 pm on weekends); it is closed on Sunday in winter.

Things to See & Do
Walking trails go around and up Mt Maunganui for magnificent views. You can climb around on the rocks on Moturiki Island, which is actually joined to the peninsula; see *Walkways of Tauranga*. The beach between Moturiki and Maunganui is good for surfing and swimming.

There are excellent **hot saltwater pools** at the foot of the Mount on Adams Ave – the hot pools are open daily from 6 am to 10 pm, but from 8 am to 10 pm on Sunday ($2.50, children $1.50). Entry to the private pools is $3.50 (children $2.50).

Places to Stay
Camping & Cabins Mt Maunganui is a popular summer resort, so there are plenty of camping grounds. At the foot of the Mount, the *Mt Maunganui Domain Motor Camp* (☎ (07) 575 4471) has waterfront sites for

$16 for two, and cabins and on-site vans from $40.

At the *Cosy Corner Motor Camp* (☎ (07) 575 5899), 40 Ocean Beach Rd, camp sites cost $10 per person, on-site caravans are $36 for two and tourist flats are $50. At 75 Girven Rd, the *Golden Grove Motor Park* (☎ (07) 575 5821) has sites for $10 per person, and tourist cabins from $35 for two.

On the Mall, overlooking Pilot Bay on the Tauranga side of the peninsula, the *Elisabeth Gardens Holiday Park* (☎ (07) 575 5787) has tent and powered sites for $10 per person. Cabins cost $45 for two, while motel rooms are from $85 for two.

Hostels Both backpackers are on Maunganui Rd.

The *Mount Backpackers* (☎ (07) 575 0860) at No 87 has dorms for $15, and two doubles for $35.

The new *Pacific Coast Backpackers* (☎ (07) 574 9601) at No 432 is much larger with dorms from $15 to $16, twins and doubles for $38 and two singles for $29. They run Action Stations (☎ 0800 666 622), an adventure travel operation which organises activities such as dolphin swimming ($95 with two nights accommodation), sailing on the *Slipstream* ($25), rafting on the Wairoa ($75) and diving (day trip $85 with two dives, Divemaster courses with accommodation and transfers $595).

Motels & Hotels Mt Maunganui has fewer motels than Tauranga and prices spiral outrageously in summer to over $100. At other times of the year prices are around the usual $85/95 a single/double. Motels include *Fawlty Towers Waterfront Motel* (☎ (07) 575 5883) at 28 the Mall, *Blue Haven Motel* (☎ (07) 575 6508) at 10 Tweed St, *Main Beach Motel* (☎ (07) 574 4050) on Marine Parade and the overpriced *Outrigger Motel* (☎ (07) 575 4445), 48 Marine Parade.

The *Mount Mews Motel* (☎ (07) 575 7006), 8 Maunganui Rd, is an excellent motel and a definite cut above the rest. Well-appointed units cost $95 a double or units

with spa bath are $115; these rates apply year-round.

The only hotel is the rather expensive *Bayfair Motor Inn* (☎ (07) 575 5089), Girven Rd, where the weekday tariff for a double is from $105. There are a few B&Bs: *Fitzgerald's Irish Inn B&B* (☎ (07) 575 4013), 463 Maunganui Rd, is a place saturated with character; a double is $70.

Places to Eat
In the oceanside twin towers, the BYO *Blue Moon Cafe* is a handy little eatery; it has an innovative lunch menu with most dishes costing less than $10. At 16 Pacific Ave is *Café Hasan Baba* for Turkish food.

For fancier dining, the *Epicure* and *Rogue's*, both on Maunganui Rd, are bistro-style, licensed restaurants with Pacific Rim menus. *Astrolabe* at 82 Maunganui Rd is a bar and cafe open until late; it occasionally has live music in the summer. You can get sushi and sashimi for $12.50 and an Astrolabe seafood stack for $20.

The shopping centre along Maunganui Rd has plenty of takeaways and restaurants. Fast-food addicts can go to *KFC* on the corner of Newton St and Hewletts Rd or *McDonald's* in the Bayfair Centre and in the downtown (Phoenix) shopping centre.

Getting There & Away
Tauranga airport is at Mt Maunganui; see the Tauranga section.

Newmans and Supa Travel buses serving Tauranga also stop at Mt Maunganui, in front of the visitor centre. InterCity stops outside its agent, Davies Drycleaners (☎ (07) 575 4669), 409 Maunganui Rd. Newlove's buses run from Wharf St in Tauranga to the Mount, stopping outside the information centre and the hot pools; the fare is $3.

You can reach Mt Maunganui across the harbour bridge from Tauranga ($1 toll in each direction), or from the south via Te Maunga on SH2.

There's a boat in summer from Salisbury Wharf in Mt Maunganui to Tauranga ($5).

AROUND TAURANGA
Matakana Island
Sheltering Tauranga Harbour, this elongated island is a quiet rural retreat just across the harbour from Tauranga. Two-thirds of the island is pine forest, providing the main industry, and the rest is farmland on the western side. Matakana has 24km of pristine white-sand surf beach on its east shore and is also good for windsurfing, kayaking and fishing. An ideal way to explore the island is by bicycle, which you can take across on the ferry. The island has a general store and social club but not much else – bring your own supplies.

Matakana Island Backpackers Retreat (☎ (07) 578 0375) at the southern end of the island on the harbour side is a large house with backpackers beds for $18 and single or double rooms for $25 per person. They have bicycles, surfboards and windsurfers and will pick up from the ferry landing. There is a kitchen, or meals are provided by arrangement.

It is possible to stay in one of the island's three maraes – Rangiwaea, Te Rangihouhiri and Opureora – by prior arrangement; check at the Tauranga visitor centre.

Getting There & Away The main ferry (☎ 025 927251) departs from Omokoroa at 7.45 am and 4 pm for the western side of the island. It costs $2 for the 15-minute crossing. You can also take the *Forest Lady* (☎ 025 937426), a barge for the logging trucks that runs from the docks at Sulphur Point in central Tauranga to the south end of the island. It shuttles across every weekday, but there is no fixed schedule. The island has no public transport. There is a tour to Matakana on the first Sunday of the month, departing from Coronation Pier at 10 am and returning at 3.30 pm ($65, children $25).

Omokoroa
This town is 22km west of Tauranga and is on a promontory which protrudes well into the sheltered harbour with fine views of the harbour and Matakana. It is a popular summer destination and has two caravan parks.

From Omokoroa you can visit Matakana on the regular ferry service.

Katikati
In the past few years Katikati (to locals, Catty-Cat) on the Uretara River has become an open-air art gallery and many of its buildings are adorned with **murals**. Get the *Mural Town: Katikati* brochure from the Mural Town Information Centre (☎ (07) 549 1658) on Cherry Court.

Morton Estate is one of NZ's bigger wineries on SH2, 8km south of Katikati. Tastings and tours are popular and the vineyard also has a good restaurant.

Places to Stay & Eat The *Sapphire Springs Holiday Park* (☎ (07) 549 0768) backs on to the Kaimai Ranges. Tent/powered sites are $12/14, cabins $30, tourist flats $50 and a motel room $65; all prices are for two. A bunk bed in the lodge is $12.50; the springs are free to visitors but private spas are available. The *Katikati Naturist Park* (☎ (07) 549 2158) at 149 Wharawhara Rd is well set up for those who prefer to remove their clothes; a day visit is $6 and an overnight stay is $10 per person for a tent or powered site, or on-site vans are $35/40 for singles/doubles. The *Katikati Motel* (☎ (07) 549 0385) in town has singles/doubles for $60/74.

The information centre has a list of homestays and farmstays in the area, many providing budget accommodation from $14. Good choices include *Jacaranda Cottage* (☎ (07) 549 0616) with B&B singles/doubles for $30/50 and budget beds for $12; at the other end of the scale, *Fantail Lodge* (☎ (09) 376 0700) on Rea Rd does B&B for $269 per person.

Good lunches are served at the *Balcony Cafe* on the main street. For elegant afternoon teas and fine dining, try the *Twickenham Homestead* on the corner of SH2 and Mulgan St.

Tuhua Island
Tuhua (Mayor) Island is a dormant volcano about 40km north of Tauranga in the Bay of Plenty. There are walking tracks through the

now overgrown crater valley and an interesting walk around the island. The north-west corner is a marine reserve, but specialist groups can ask for permission to land. (Get permission from the Maori Trust Board – inquire at the Tauranga visitor centre.) Day/overnight visitors pay a $10/6 landing fee (children $3).

The only place you can camp is at Opo Bay (☎ (07) 577 0531); per person, a site is $6, bunk units are $12, a unit with toilet and wash basin $14 and a unit with toilet and shower $20.

Getting There & Away Ferries to the island operate three or four days a week from Christmas Day until the end of January. They depart from Coronation Pier in Tauranga, going out via Mt Maunganui at 7 am and returning at 4 pm. The trip takes about three hours in each direction. The cost is $40 (children $25) for a day trip, or $60 ($40) if you go out for more than the day.

Minden Lookout
From Minden Lookout, about 10km from Tauranga, there's a superb view back over the Bay of Plenty. To get there, take SH2 to Te Puna and turn off south on Minden Rd; the lookout is about 4km up the road.

Papamoa
Papamoa, 13km south of Mt Maunganui, is blessed with miles of beaches; digging for tuatua is popular when the tide is right. There are a couple of motor camps at Papamoa, all of them along Papamoa Beach Rd. The *Papamoa Beach Holiday Park* (☎ (07) 542 0816) and *Beach Grove Holiday Park* (☎ (07) 542 1337) have tent/powered sites for about $10/12 and basic cabins for $40. You can get takeaway food from places on Beach Rd, and the *Blue Biyou on the Beach* at 559 Beach Rd is known for fine meals and enormous Sunday brunches.

Te Puke
Hailed as the 'Kiwi Fruit Capital of the World', Te Puke is not as bad as its civic plaudits have made it sound. There is much native bush nearby and the town is not far from several good beaches and exciting rivers. Te Puke gets busy in the kiwi fruit-picking season when there's plenty of work. The information office (☎ (07) 573 9172) is at 72 Jellicoe St.

Things to See & Do The Bay of Plenty is kiwi fruit country and here you can learn a little more about this fruit that is so important to NZ's economy. Gardening enthusiasts can visit many private gardens in the area.

Kiwi Fruit Country (you won't miss the garish 'big kiwi fruit' sign, which looks like a green-dyed, sectioned human kidney) is on SH33, 6km east of Te Puke and 36km from Tauranga. You can visit the orchards and the shop, watch a video about kiwi fruit and sample some kiwi fruit or kiwi fruit wine. The complex is also a theme park – it's all quite tacky but the kids might enjoy it. Including a 'kiwi-kart' ride through the orchards and an exhibition on how the fruit is grown and packed, entry costs $8.50 (children $4). Kiwi Fruit Country is open daily from 9 am to 5 pm.

Next to Kiwi Fruit Country is the **Vintage Auto Barn** (☎ (07) 573 6547), with over 50 vintage cars on display. It is open from 8.30 am to 5 pm daily ($5, children $2).

At Longridge Park, Paengaroa, near Te Puke, you can take a thrilling half-hour jet-boat ride up the winding and bush-clad Kaituna River with Longridge Jetboat (☎ (07) 533 1515) for $55 ($35).

Afterwards, 4WD over a challenging series of tracks with Hill Hoppers (☎ (07) 533 1818). You get to drive, even blind-folded at one stage, for $45 (younger unlicensed passengers are $15). You can combine both jet-boating and four-wheel driving for $89 ($45). More sedate are the Longridge kiwi fruit and farm park tours for $10 ($5). There is an excellent cafe on the premises.

Places to Stay The *Te Puke Holiday Park* (☎ (07) 573 9866) has sites from $9 per person, hostel-style accommodation for $12, and on-site caravans and cabins for $32 for two. The *Beacon Motel* (☎ (07) 573 7825) at 173 Jellicoe St has singles/doubles from $58/75.

De Haven (☎ (07) 533 1025) at Paengoroa, about 8km east of Te Puke, is a small hostel with beds for $16 per person. Another option is *Lodore Lodge* (☎ (07) 573 8258) at 51 Atahua Way, 4.5km from Te Puke; B&B is $18 per person.

Maketu

There's a Maori *pa* site at Town Point, near the township of Maketu, north-east of Te Puke. Maketu was the landing site of the *Arawa* canoe, more than 600 years ago, and there is a stone monument on the foreshore which commemorates this. The name Maketu comes from a place in Hawaiki. The information centre (☎ (07) 533 2343) shouldn't be missed – a beautiful mural decorates its front.

To get to Maketu from Tauranga, take SH2 through Te Puke and turn left into Maketu Rd just past Rangiuru.

Eastern Bay of Plenty

The eastern Bay of Plenty extends from Maketu and Pukehina to Opotiki in the far east of the bay and takes in Whakatane, Opotoki and Ohope.

WHAKATANE

Whakatane (population 18,000) lies on a natural harbour at the mouth of the Whakatane River. The *Mataatua* canoe landed at the mouth of the river in about 1350, during the Great Migration, and Whakatane became an important Maori centre. Only around the beginning of the 20th century did Europeans discover the richness of the land and settle in any numbers. Whakatane today is the principal town for the eastern Bay of Plenty and a service centre for the Rangitaiki agricultural and milling district.

Whakatane is a pleasant town in one of the sunniest parts of the North Island. Many visitors are attracted to the nearby beaches, especially in summer, and two major attractions are offshore – Whakaari (White Island), NZ's most active volcano, and dolphin swimming tours.

Information

The organised information centre (☎ /fax (07) 308 6058) is on Boon St, half a block off the Strand, and is open from 9 am to 5 pm on weekdays and 9 am to 1 pm on Saturday. The staff can provide brochures on just about everything and make tour bookings. The AA office is opposite the information centre on Boon St. The DOC office (☎ (07) 308 7213) is being relocated to the new Regional Council Building.

Things to See

The **Whakatane Museum** on Boon St is one of the more interesting regional museums, with photographic and artefact exhibits on early Maori and European settlers and the natural environment, including the smoking Whakaari (White Island) volcano just offshore. It's also a centre of historical research, with an archive of historical publications. It's open from 10 am to 4.30 pm on weekdays, 11 am to 1.30 pm on Saturday, 2 to 4.30 pm on Sunday ($1.50, children 75c).

Just to one side of the traffic circle on the corner of the Strand and Commerce St is **Pohaturoa**, a large rock outcrop and important Maori sacred site. The coastline used to come right up to here and there's a tunnel in the rock where baptisms and other rites were performed. Today the rock is set apart in a little park, with a plaque explaining its historical and religious significance. Also in the park are a Maori canoe, carved benches and a monument to a Mataatua chief.

The **Whakatane Astronomical Observatory** (☎ (07) 304 9193; chris@BOPRC. govt.nz, beetee@wave.co.nz) on Hurunui Ave, Hillcrest, opens to the public every Tuesday evening, weather permitting. The small **botanical gardens** are at the river end of McGarvey Rd, beside a children's playground.

PLACES TO STAY
8 Commercial Hotel
10 Whakatane Hotel & Why Not Cafe
25 Whakatane Backpackers Lodge
28 Camelia Court Motel
29 Bay Hotel
31 Whakatane Motor Camp & Caravan Park
32 Alton Lodge
34 Barringtons Motor Lodge
35 Livingston Inn
36 Tourist Court Motel
38 Cortez Motor Inn
39 NauMai Motel

PLACES TO EAT
1 The Reef Licensed Cafe
5 Wharf Shed Bar & Brasserie
9 Harbourside Restaurant; Dago's Famous Pizzeria
14 Wedgewood Food Court; Barnacles Seafood Restaurant
16 Go Global
18 New Hong Kong Chinese Restaurant
20 Neptune's Takeaway
23 Deja Vu Italian Restaurant
26 KFC
27 McDonald's

OTHER
2 Public Toilets
4 Muriwai Cave
4 Mataatua Park
6 Regional Council Buildings (DOC); Public Toilets
7 Dolphins Down Under
11 Puketapu Lookout
12 Wairere Falls
13 Papaka Redoubt
15 Pohaturoa Rock
17 Visitor Information Centre; Public Toilets
19 Automobile Association (AA)
21 Museum & Gallery
22 InterCity Bus Depot (Bay Coachlines)
24 Whakatane Astronomical Observatory
30 Botanical Gardens
33 Pack 'N Save
37 Motu River Rafting

Dolphin Swimming

Dolphins Down Under (☎ (07) 308 4636), 92 the Strand, run popular trips year-round (subject to weather) to swim with the dolphins. They have a high success rate for dolphin spotting in summer, when there are up to three trips a day for $85 (children $50). All necessary equipment, including a wet suit, is supplied. In winter the dolphins move further offshore and trips are subject to demand.

Walking

The information centre and DOC have lots of details on walks. An interesting 2½-hour town centre walk encompasses a number of scenic and historic spots including Muriwai Cave, Wairere Falls, Puketapu Lookout, Hapaka Redoubt, Pohaturoa and a big game fishing facility.

Other notable walks include the 3½-hour **Kohi Point Walkway**, Nga Tapuwae-o-Toi (Sacred Footsteps of Toi), which extends through the Kohi Point Scenic Reserve, passing many attractive sites including lookouts and the Pa of Toi, reputedly the oldest pa site in NZ. Other walkways are the Ohope Bush Walk, the Mokorua Scenic Reserve,

Latham's Track and the Matata Walking Track. The 300m White Pine Bush Walk, starting about 10km from Whakatane, is suitable even for people in wheelchairs and the elderly.

Other Activities

Check with the visitor information centre about the wide variety of activities in and around Whakatane. Possibilities include hunting trips, horse treks, bushwalking, trout or sea fishing, diving and kayak trips, windsurfing and jet-boating.

Motu River Rafting (☎ (07) 308 5449) does white-water **rafting** trips on the Motu and other rivers, and parasailing in summer; a three-day 4WD/raft/jet-boat combination is $350. Another rafter on the Motu is Wet 'n' Wild (☎ (07) 578 4093), which is based in Opotiki.

Pohutukawa Tours (☎ (07) 308 6495) operates a variety of flexible half-day, full-day and overnight tours. Full-day **fishing** charters on the *Charmaine* are $30 (with a $15 tackle hire fee).

Kiwi Jet Boat Tours (☎ (07) 307 0663) has a 1¼-hour **jet-boat** trip along the Rangitaiki River from Matahina Dam to Aniwhenua Falls at $55 (children $45).

Places to Stay

The information centre has a list of homestays and farmstays in the area. Nearby Ohope Beach also has accommodation.

Camping & Hostels The *Whakatane Motor Camp & Caravan Park* (☎ (07) 308 8694) on McGarvey Rd beside the Whakatane River has recreational facilities, including a swimming pool and a spa pool. Tent or powered sites are $8 per person, a bed in the backpackers is $12.50 or cabins are $30.

Whakatane Backpackers Lodge (☎ (07) 308 0406), 11 Merritt St, is a friendly backpackers in a large old house. A dorm bed is $15 and twins and doubles are $34. The Whakatane and Commercial hotels (see under Hotels) have backpackers rooms.

Motels Most motels are on or just off Landing/Domain Rd. In the $65/75 a single/double range is the fading *Tourist Court Motel* (☎ (07) 308 7099) and, opposite, the better *NauMai Motel* (☎ (07) 308 6422) or the slightly more expensive *Cortez Motor Inn* (☎ (07) 308 4047). The *Camelia Court Motel* (☎ (07) 308 6213), 11 Domain Rd, has more style and charges $75/83, while the newer and well-appointed *Alton Lodge* (☎ (07) 308 5438) has a heated swimming pool and charges from $70/80.

Newer places on Landing Rd include the *Livingston Inn* (☎ (07) 308 6400) at No 42, with rooms from $90 to $130; and *Barringtons Motor Lodge* (☎ (07) 308 4273) at No 34, with studio/one-bedroom units from $90/100.

Hotels The old Art Deco *Whakatane Hotel* (☎ (07) 308 8199) on the Strand has dreary singles/doubles with shared facilities for $25/35 and a couple of basic rooms are set aside for backpackers at $14 per person. The rooms with private facilities for $35/45 are much better. The *Commercial* (☎ (07) 308 7399) on the Strand East is a better class of pub but bands on the weekend can be very noisy. Singles/doubles cost $25/32 or $35/45 with attached bathroom. The *Bay Hotel* (☎ (07) 308 6788) at 90 McAllister St is a better private hotel/guesthouse with rooms from $40/50 (more with private bathroom).

Places to Eat

Most of Whakatane's eating places are in the shopping area along the Strand. You can get an adequate meal at the *Wedgewood Food Court*, or *McDonald's* and *KFC* are both near the intersection of Commerce St and Domain Rd. Try *Neptune's Takeaway* in Boon St for fish and chips or burgers with the lot, or the unfortunately named *Dago's Famous Pizzeria* for crusty pizza base adorned with Super Special mix.

The *New Hong Kong Restaurant* on Richardson St has Chinese food, with a separate counter for takeaways which is a block behind in Boon St; chow mein is $7.50 and barbecued pork is from $8.50.

You can get a hearty steak meal at the *Harbourside*, between the Quay and the Strand, Italian dishes from *Deja Vu* at 64 Commerce St, and continental food at *Go Global* on the corner of Commerce St and Shapley Place. At the latter, Kashmiri lamb is $20 and delectable devilled prawns $22.

The popular *Why Not Cafe*, in the Whakatane Hotel, has a better class of pub fare, while the licensed *Barnacles Seafood Restaurant* has upmarket fish and chips.

The hippest place in town at the moment is the *Wharf Shed Bar & Brasserie* on Muriwai Drive; a main course here costs around $20. At The Heads is the popular *Reef Licensed Cafe*, known for its seafood (a reef and beef combination is $23.50); it's open daily for lunch and dinner.

Getting There & Around

Air New Zealand Link (☎ 0800 737 000) has daily flights linking Whakatane to Auckland and Wellington, with connections to other centres.

A taxi (☎ 0800 807 038) to or from the airport costs $10; there is no bus service.

The InterCity bus depot (☎ (07) 308 6169) is on Pyne St (Bay Coachlines). InterCity has buses connecting Whakatane with Rotorua and Gisborne, with connections to other places; all buses to Gisborne go via Opotiki. Courier services around East Cape originate from Opotiki and Gisborne (see East Cape in the East Coast chapter).

OHOPE BEACH

The town of Ohope and its fine beach is 7km 'over the hill' from Whakatane. It is a pleasant area in which to spend a few days, with all types of accommodation available, and there are a number of walks in the area.

The *Ohope Backpackers* (☎ (07) 312 5173), 1A West End, has bunks for $15 or double rooms for $32. This place is a grand three-storey building near the beach and has fine sea views from the verandah.

The *Ohope Beach Holiday Park* (☎ (07) 312 4460) on Harbour Rd has sites for $12, cabins for $30 and $35, tourist flats for $50 and motels from $60 (all prices are for two).

There are about eight motels, most of them along West End, charging about $65 for doubles, and a number of homestays.

If you are after takeaways, try the *Pink Caddyshack*. The restaurant at *Ohope Beach Resort* has superb ocean views.

WHAKAARI

Whakaari, or White Island, is NZ's most active volcano, smoking and steaming away just 50km off the coast from Whakatane. It's a small island of 324 hectares formed by three separate volcanic cones, all of different ages. Erosion has worn away most of the surface of the two older cones and the youngest cone, which rose up between the two older ones, now occupies most of the centre of the island. Hot water and steam continually escape from vents over most of the crater floor and temperatures of 600°C to 800°C have been recorded. The highest point on the island is Mt Gisborne at 321m. Geologically, Whakaari is related to Whale Island and Mt Putauaki (Edgecumbe), as they all lie along the same volcanic trench.

The island is privately owned and the only way you can land on it is with a helicopter or boat tour which has arranged permission. The island has no jetty so boats have to land on the beach, which means that boat landings are not possible in rough seas. A visit to Whakaari is an unforgettable, if disconcerting, experience, but the constant rumblings and plumes of steam do not necessarily mean that it is about to blow up.

History

Before the arrival of Europeans the Maori caught sea birds on the island for food. In 1769 Captain Cook named it White Island because of the dense clouds of white steam hanging above.

The first European to land on the island was a missionary, the Reverend Henry Williams, in 1826. The island was acquired by Europeans in the late 1830s and changed ownership a number of times after that. Sulphur production began but was interrupted in 1885 by a minor eruption and the following year the island was hurriedly abandoned in the wake of the Tarawera eruption. The island's sulphur industry was resumed in 1898 but only continued until 1901, when production ceased altogether.

In the 1910s, further mining operations were attempted and abandoned due to mud flows and other volcanic activity, and ownership of the island continued to change. In 1953 White Island was declared a Private Scenic Reserve.

The island was at its most active between 1976 and 1981 when two new craters were formed and 100,000 cubic metres of rock was ejected.

Getting There & Away

Trips to Whakaari include a one or two-hour tour on foot around the island. A landing by boat is definitely weather dependent. Operators include the following:

East Bay Flight Centre (☎ (07) 308 8446) operates flightseeing tours over the island ($95, minimum of two people).
Kahurangi (☎ (07) 323 7829) offers a good five-hour trip in a 20ft (6m) foil cat ($95 per person, minimum of four people).
Pee Jay (☎ 0800 733 529) has good tours on a 40ft (12m) sportscruiser ($95 per person, including lunch). It operates daily, year-round, weather permitting.
White Island Volcano Adventure (☎ 0800 804 354) offers 2½-hour helicopter flights ($275 per person, minimum of four people, and $575 ex-Rotorua). This is the only sure way to be able to land on the island.

All trips (except for fixed-wing flightseeing) incur a $10 landing fee; it may be included in the quoted price.

MOUTOHORA

Moutohora, or Whale Island, so-called because of its shape, is 9km north of Whakatane and has an area of 414 hectares. It's another volcanic island, on the same volcanic trench as White Island, but much less active, and along its shore are hot springs which can reach 93°C. The summit is 350m high and the island has several historic sites including an ancient pa site, an old quarry and a camp.

Whale Island was settled by Maori before the 1769 landing by Captain Cook. In 1829 there was a Maori massacre of sailors from the trading vessel *Haweis* while it was anchored at Sulphur Bay, followed by an unsuccessful whaling venture in the 1830s. In the 1840s the island passed into European ownership and is still privately owned, although since 1965 it has been an officially protected wildlife refuge administered by DOC.

Whale Island is principally a haven for sea and shore birds, some of which are quite rare. Some of the birds use the island only for nesting at certain times of the year, while others are present year-round. The island has a large colony of grey-faced petrels, estimated to number 10,000.

The island's protected status means landing is restricted. Contact the Whakatane DOC office and inquire about tours to the island operated at Christmas time.

WHAKATANE TO ROTORUA

Travelling along SH30 from Whakatane to Rotorua you'll come to the **Awakeri Hot Springs**, 16km from Whakatane, with hot springs, spa pools, picnic areas and a holiday park (☎ (07) 304 9117). At the latter, powered sites are $18, tourist flats $50 and motels $70 (prices are for two).

Lying just off SH30, **Kawerau** is a timber town surrounded by pine forest and dependent on the huge Tasman Pulp & Paper Mill. Kawerau has an information centre (☎ (07) 323 7550) on Plunket Street in the centre of town, and a selection of accommodation, but the only real reason to come here is to visit the waterfalls outside town. You can visit the **mill** for a 1½-hour tour; bookings are essential (☎ (07) 308 6058).

Tawerau Falls are a half-hour drive from Kawerau along a well-graded road through the pine forests (watch out for the logging trucks). From the end of the road it is a 15-minute walk through native forest to the falls, which emerge from a hole in the canyon wall. The track continues another two hours up to the top of the falls and on to

Lake Tarawera – a good walk with views of the lake and Mt Tarawera.

Also near Kawerau, **Mt Putauaki (Edgecumbe)** is a commanding volcanic cone with panoramic views of the entire Bay of Plenty from the top. You'll need a permit; contact Tasman Forestry (☎ (07) 323 4599).

OPOTIKI

Opotiki, the easternmost town of the Bay of Plenty, is the gateway to the East Cape and the rugged forests and river valleys of the Raukumara and nearby ranges. The town itself is nothing special, but many visitors stop over on the way to the East Coast and there are some reasonable surf beaches, such as Ohiwa and Waiotahi, nearby. Opotiki is very much a model of Maori tradition – the main street is lined with the works of mastercarvers.

The Opotiki area was settled from at least 1150, which was 200 years before the Great Migration. In the mid-1800s Opotiki was the centre of Hauhauism, a Maori doctrine which advocated, among other things, the extermination of Europeans. In 1865, the Rev Karl Volkner was murdered in his church, St Stephen the Martyr, which led to the church being used as a fort by government troops.

Information

The Opotiki Information Centre (☎ (07) 315 8484; fax 315 6102), on the corner of St John and Elliott Sts, is open on weekdays from 8.30 am to 4.30 pm. DOC (☎ 315 8484) has an office in the same building. The centre does bookings for a range of activities and can organise visits to a local marae.

Hukutaia Domain

Just over 7km from the town centre is the fascinating Hukutaia Domain, which has one of the finest collections of native plants in NZ, many of the species rare and endangered. One example, a puriri tree – named Taketakerau – is estimated to be over 2000 years old. The remains of the distinguished dead of the Upokorere sub-tribe of the Whakatohea were ritually buried beneath it.

The tree is no longer *tapu* (sacred) as the remains have been re-interred elsewhere.

Other Things to See & Do

The old-fashioned **cinema** on Church St is fun to visit; a movie is $7.50 (children $4).

The **Historical & Agricultural Society Museum** on Church St contains historic local items; hours are extremely variable.

Readers recommend beach horse trekking with Tirohanga Beach Treks (☎ (07) 315 7490); a two-hour ride is $35 per person.

Places to Stay

Camping & Cabins The *Opotiki Holiday Park* (☎ (07) 315 6050) on Potts Ave has tent and powered sites for $8 per person, cabins at $28 for two and tourist flats at $40.

There are several beachfront camping grounds near Opotiki. The *Island View Family Holiday Park* (☎ (07) 315 7519) on Appleton Rd 4km from town has camp sites and cabins. The *Tirohanga Beach Motor Camp* (☎ (07) 315 7942) on the East Coast Rd 6km from town has camp sites, cabins and tourist flats. Also on the East Coast Rd, 12km from Opotiki, the *Opape Motor Camp* (☎ (07) 315 8175) has camp sites and an on-site caravan.

Hostels *Central Oasis Backpackers* (☎ (07) 315 5165), 30 King St, is in the centre of town in an old cottage. It's a delightful, friendly and small hostel with dorm beds for $14 and $15, twins and doubles for $32. On Waiotahi Beach, about five minutes west of Opotiki, is the *Opotiki Backpackers Beach House* (☎ (07) 315 5117). It is a nice, small place with adjoining kitchen and recreation room; the $12 beds are in the loft and there are doubles for $28. The adjoining *Beachhouse Cafe* is open from November to April; quiches, nachos, cakes and salads are all about $6 each and good coffee is $2.

Motels & Hotels The *Ranui Motel* (☎ (07) 315 6669) at 36 Bridge St has singles/doubles for $58/70, and the *Magnolia Court Motel* (☎ (07) 315 8490), on the corner of

PLACES TO STAY
2 Opotiki Holiday Park
5 Masonic Hotel
6 Opotiki Hotel
12 Central Oasis Backpackers
18 Magnolia Court Motel
19 Ranui Motel

PLACES TO EAT
8 Elliot Street Bar & Brasserie
13 The Fish & Chip Shop
14 Aggie's
15 Flying Pig
16 Dannie's
17 Shooter's Diner
22 Peddler's Crafts & Cafe

OTHER
1 Wharf and Boat Ramp
3 Cinema
4 Opotiki Historical & Agricultural Society Museum
7 Hickey's Sport (Bike Repairs)
9 InterCity Bus Depot
10 Visitor Information Centre & DOC
11 Post Office; Public Toilets
20 New World Supermarket
21 Waioweka Rest Area

Bridge and Nelson Sts, charges from $73 for a double.

Opotiki has a couple of nondescript hotels with budget accommodation: the *Opotiki Hotel* (☎ (07) 315 6078) and the *Masonic Hotel* (☎ (07) 315 6115), both on Church St.

Places to Eat

Although not exactly the gourmet capital of the Bay, Opotiki does have a small range of places to eat.

Dannie's, near the corner of St John and Bridge Sts, is a fast-food place. The *Fish & Chip Shop* on Church St does battered mussels and chips. For a hearty breakfast go to *Shooter's Diner* on Bridge St – they also serve full meals at other times.

On Church St are two good cafes: *Aggie's* is good for vegetarian quiches and lasagne and the BYO *Flying Pig* serves kebabs and other delights in pitta bread for about $6 to $10. The *Elliot Street Bar & Brasserie* on Elliot St was described to us as 'upmarket in Opotiki terms'; mains are around $20. The quaint *Peddlers Crafts & Cafe* at 92 Hikutaia Rd is open from Thursday to Sunday from 10.30 am to 4 pm for lunches and afternoon teas.

Getting There & Away

Travelling east from Opotiki there are two routes to choose from. SH2 crosses the spectacular Waioeka Gorge. There are some fine walks of one day and longer in the **Waioeka Gorge Scenic Reserve**. The gorge gets progressively steeper and narrower as you travel inland, before the route crosses typically green, rolling hills, dotted with sheep, on the descent to Gisborne.

The other route east from Opotiki is SH35 around the East Cape, described fully in the East Coast chapter.

The InterCity bus depot (☎ (07) 315 6450) is on Elliot St. InterCity has daily buses connecting Opotiki with Whakatane, Rotorua and Auckland. Heading south, the buses connect Opotiki with Gisborne, Wairoa and Napier on Wednesday, Friday and Sunday.

Central Plateau

The Central Plateau is at the heart of the North Island and is the centre of New Zealand's volcanic activity. The country's main volcanic area, the Taupo Volcanic Zone, stretches in a line from White Island, north of the Bay of Plenty, through Rotorua and down to the Tongariro National Park.

The Central Plateau was at its most active some 2000 years ago. The remaining volcanoes do not match the destructive fury of some of the world's other hot spots, but still put on spectacular shows from time to time. Since 1995 Mt Ruapehu has exploded in a series of eruptions, spewing forth rock and clouds of ash and steam.

Taupo is the main resort town of this volcanic plateau and lies on large Lake Taupo, itself a remnant of a massive volcanic explosion. Taupo caters for a range of tastes, from trout fishing to bungy jumping. The plateau extends southwards to the majestic, snow-capped volcanoes in the Tongariro National Park, one of NZ's premier parks with many fine walks.

Lake Taupo

New Zealand's largest lake, Lake Taupo, is in the very heart of the North Island. Some 606 sq km in area and 357m above sea level, the lake was formed by one of the greatest volcanic explosions the world has experienced. Accounts of darkened skies in the daytime and blood-red sunsets were recorded around 186 AD in places as distant as China and Rome, and are believed to refer to the effects of the Taupo explosion in the atmosphere. Pumice from this explosion is found as far away as Napier and Gisborne and forms a layer (just 1cm thick in some places and metres thick in others) over a vast area of the central North Island. The area is still volcanically active and, like Rotorua, has thermal areas to visit.

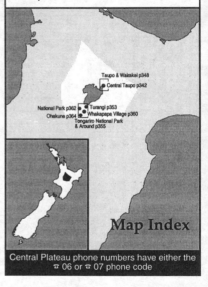

HIGHLIGHTS

- Visiting Tongariro National Park, dominated by smoking Mt Ruapehu
- Walking the famous Tongariro Crossing and the Northern Circuit
- Trout fishing or boating at Lake Taupo
- Exploring Wairekei Park and its thermal regions, and the Huka Falls
- Skiing at Whakapapa and Turoa
- Tandem skydiving or bungy jumping at Taupo

Central Plateau phone numbers have either the ☎ 06 or ☎ 07 phone code

Today serene Lake Taupo is claimed to be the world's trout-fishing capital. If you thought those trout in the Rotorua springs looked large and tasty, they're nothing compared to the monsters found in Lake Taupo. All New Zealand's rainbow trout descend from a single batch of eggs brought from California's Russian River nearly a century ago. International trout-fishing tournaments are held on Lake Taupo each year on the

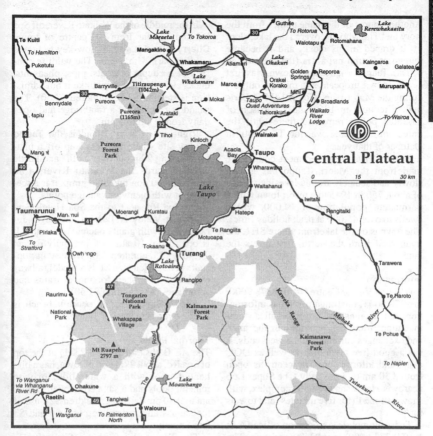

Central Plateau

0   15   30 km

Anzac Day long weekend (on or around 25 April).

TAUPO

Taupo lies on the north-east corner of Lake Taupo and has scenic views stretching across the lake to the volcanic peaks of Tongariro National Park. This relaxed resort is the main town of the area and makes a good base to explore the local attractions. Activities in Taupo range from fishing and boating on the lake to adrenalin-pumping bungy jumping and skydiving to even 'swimming with the trout'.

Lake Taupo is also the source of NZ's longest river, the Waikato, which leaves the lake at the township, flows through the Huka Falls and the Aratiatia Rapids, and then through the heart of the northern part of the North Island to the west coast just south of Auckland.

History

Back in the mists of time, a Maori chief named Tamatea-arikinui visited the area and, noticing that the ground felt hollow and his footsteps seemed to reverberate, called the place Tapuaeharuru (resounding footsteps).

Another source of the name comes from the story that Tia, who discovered the lake, slept by it draped in his cloak, and it became known as Taupo-nui-a-Tia (the great cloak of Tia). Taupo, as it became known, was first occupied by Europeans as a military outpost during the Maori Wars. Colonel JM Roberts built a redoubt in 1869 and a garrison of mounted police remained there until the defeat of the rebel warrior Te Kooti in October of that year.

In the 1870s the government bought the land from the Maori. Taupo has grown slowly and sedately from a lakeside village of about 750 in 1945 to a resort town with a permanent population of 19,000, which swells to over 45,000 at peak holiday times. The town is on the lakefront where SH1, the main road from the north, first meets the lake.

Information

The Taupo Visitor Centre (☎ (07) 378 9000; fax 378 9003) on Tongariro St has information and handles bookings for all accommodation, transport, activities in the area, and exchanges currency on the weekends. It has a good free town map as well as DOC maps and information. The centre is open from 8.30 am to 5 pm daily. The Super Loo nearby is a large shower-toilet complex, with showers for $1 (for five minutes) and towels for $1.

The Automobile Association office (AA; ☎ (07) 378 6000) is at 93 Tongariro St. The post office is on the corner of Horomatangi and Ruapehu Sts.

Things to See

Taupo's main attractions, such as the Wairakei Park and thermal regions, are north of town. But in town, on Story Place, near the visitor centre on Tongariro St, the **Taupo Regional Museum & Art Gallery** has many historical photos and mementoes of the 'old days' around Lake Taupo. Exhibits also include Maori carvings, a moa skeleton and a rundown on the trout industry. It is open daily from 10.30 am to 4.30 pm (entry is free).

In the middle of the Waikato River, off Spa Rd and not far from the centre of town, **Cherry Island** is a small, low-key trout and wildlife park with a cafe. The wildlife consists of a couple of goats, pigs, pheasants, ducks etc – the kids might like it but admission is steep at $7.50 (children $3.50). The island is reached by a footbridge and open daily from 9 am to 5 pm.

Right near Cherry Island is the **Taupo Bungy** site where jumpers leap off a platform jutting 20m out over a cliff and hurtle down towards the Waikato River, 45m below. If you don't want to jump, it is a scenic spot with plenty of vantage points.

On Spa Rd, next to the Spa Hotel, **Spa Dinosaur Valley** is Taupo's answer to Jurassic Park with giant concrete dinosaurs. It is open from 10 am to 4 pm daily except Tuesday ($5, children $3). **Trainsville**, upstairs at 35A Heu Heu St, is a model railway exhibition in a shop for model trains and aeroplanes ($3, children $1.50).

Acacia Bay, a pleasant, peaceful beach, is a little over 5km west of Taupo.

Thermal Pools

The AC Baths (☎ (07) 378 7321) at the top of Spa Rd, about 2km east of town, has a big, heated pool with a waterslide, private mineral pools and a sauna. It's open from 8 am to 9.30 pm daily ($4, children $2); use of the saunas and waterslide costs $4 and $3 respectively.

The Taupo Hot Springs (formerly De Bretts; ☎ (07) 378 0541) are on the Taupo-Napier Highway (SH5), 1km from the lake. There are also large outdoor pools, a big hot waterslide and private pools. The pools are open from 8 am to 9.30 pm daily and entry is $6 (children $2.50). Private pools are $8 per person.

Fishing

A number of fishing guides and charter boats operate in Taupo; check with the visitor centre. A trip costs about $60 per person on a share basis. Boats can also be hired from the launch office (☎ (07) 378 3444), starting at $65 per hour for a boat taking up to six people and going up to around $120 per hour for the larger boats. The hostels also book fishing boat trips. Count on a fishing trip lasting around two or three hours. If you go on a boat trip they'll supply all the gear and organise a fishing licence.

Taupo is world-famous for its trout fly fishing. Fly fishing is the only fishing you can do on all rivers flowing into the lake, and within a 300m radius of the river mouths. Spin fishing is allowed on the Waikato River (flowing *out* of the lake) and on the Tokaanu tail race, flowing into the lake from the Tokaanu Power Station. Both spin fishing and fly fishing are allowed on the lake. Several fly-fishing guides operate around Taupo, some of whom are very good. The price is reasonable when you consider you are paying for years of local knowledge – around $250 a day, everything included.

If you're going to do it on your own, Bob Sullivan's Taupo Sports Depot (☎ (07) 378 5337) on Tongariro St by the waterfront and the Fly & Gun Shop (☎ (07) 378 4449) on Heu Heu St have fishing tackle for hire, which costs $8 (you buy your own lures).

Fishing licences are available from the visitor centre or the launch office. Licences for fishing on Lake Taupo and the nearby rivers cost $12 per day, $25 per week, $35 per month or $52 for the year.

Make sure you always have your fishing licence and obey the rules listed on it when fishing – there are huge fines for violations.

Water Sports

The Acacia Bay Lodge (☎ (07) 378 6830) at 868 Acacia Bay Rd in Acacia Bay hires out motorboats at $24 per hour, rowing boats and Canadian canoes at $12 per hour, and kayaks at $10 per hour. It takes an hour from there in a motorboat to reach the Maori rock carvings.

The Sail Centre (☎ (07) 378 3299) at Two Mile Bay, south of Taupo, hires out Canadian canoes, windsurfers, catamarans and sailboats in summer. Bruce Webber Adventures (☎ (07) 378 4715) has a good name for his kayak school and kayaking trips. A guided two-hour trip on the Waikato is $25.

During summer there are lots of activities on Lake Taupo including swimming, water skiing, windsurfing, paragliding and sailing. The visitor centre has details. Gear can be hired at the lakefront.

Several white-water rafting companies operate from Taupo and offer one-day trips on the Tongariro and Rangitaiki rivers, and longer trips on other rivers (from grades II to IV). Book these trips through the hostels or the visitor centre. The float trips on local rivers such as the Waikato are ideal for children ($45, children $20).

A little different and popular is drift diving, which provides the chance to let the current of the Waikato River do the work, and swim with the trout. Contact the Dive Inn (☎ (07) 378 1926), 26 Spa Rd, for more details; it charges $65, including hire of gear.

Bungy Jumping

The bungy jump in Taupo is the most popular on the North Island, largely because of its scenic setting on the Waikato River. It costs $90 for a jump but there is a bewildering array of discounts. The Taupo Bungy office (☎ (07) 377 1135) is open daily from 9 am to 5 pm.

Tandem Skydiving

This is one of the popular Taupo adrenalin-rushes. In addition to the skydiving itself, at the cheapest rate in NZ, you get a brilliant view over Lake Taupo and the entire region. Both Great Lake Skydive Centre (☎ 0800 373 335) and Taupo Tandems (☎ 025 428 688) do tandem skydives for $165.

Flightseeing & Gliding

You can go for a scenic flight on the float-plane (☎ (07) 378 7500) next to Taupo Boat Harbour; a number of operators also go from the airport. All offer similar flights for similar prices, ranging from about $30 for a short flight over town to about $120 for flights across the lake and Tongariro National Park.

Helistar Helicopters (☎ (07) 374 8405) on Huka Falls Rd offers a variety of scenic

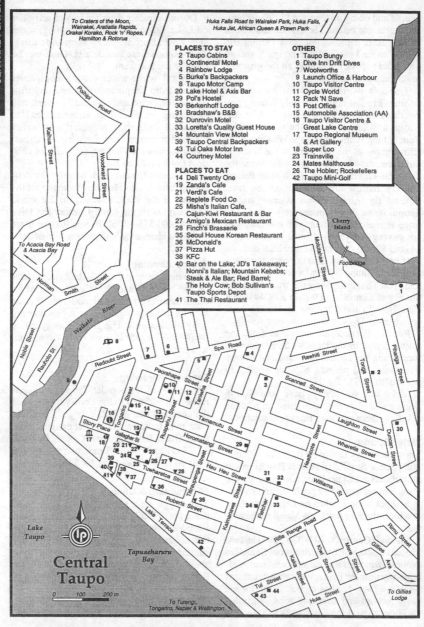

PLACES TO STAY
2 Taupo Cabins
3 Continental Motel
4 Rainbow Lodge
5 Burke's Backpackers
8 Taupo Motor Camp
20 Lake Hotel & Axis Bar
29 Pol's Hostel
30 Berkenhoff Lodge
31 Bradshaw's B&B
32 Dunrovin Motel
33 Loretta's Quality Guest House
34 Mountain View Motel
39 Taupo Central Backpackers
43 Tui Oaks Motor Inn
44 Courtney Motel

PLACES TO EAT
14 Deli Twenty One
19 Zanda's Cafe
21 Verdi's Cafe
22 Replete Food Co
25 Misha's Italian Cafe,
    Cajun-Kiwi Restaurant & Bar
27 Amigo's Mexican Restaurant
28 Finch's Brasserie
35 Seoul House Korean Restaurant
36 McDonald's
37 Pizza Hut
38 KFC
40 Bar on the Lake; JD's Takeaways;
    Nonni's Italian; Mountain Kebabs;
    Steak & Ale Bar; Red Barrel;
    The Holy Cow; Bob Sullivan's
    Taupo Sports Depot
41 The Thai Restaurant

OTHER
1 Taupo Bungy
6 Dive Inn Drift Dives
7 Woolworths
9 Launch Office & Harbour
10 Taupo Visitor Centre
11 Cycle World
12 Pack 'N Save
13 Post Office
15 Automobile Association (AA)
16 Taupo Visitor Centre &
    Great Lake Centre
17 Taupo Regional Museum
    & Art Gallery
18 Super Loo
23 Trainsville
24 Mates Malthouse
26 The Hobler; Rockefellers
42 Taupo Mini-Golf

Central
Taupo

0   100   200 m

helicopter flights, including a 10-minute flight over Taupo ($75).

The Taupo Gliding Club (☎ (07) 378 5627) goes gliding on Sunday and Wednesday afternoons (when the weather is suitable) at Centennial Park on Centennial Drive, about 5km up Spa Rd from the town centre. A flight costs from $40.

De Bretts Aviation (☎ 0800 800 207) has a variety of flights in the area, including scenic biplane rides from $125. There are three fixed-wing flightseeing companies; ask at the visitor centre.

Horse Trekking

Taupo Horse Treks (☎ (07) 378 0356) on Karapiti Rd (the road leading to Craters of the Moon) has a good reputation for treks, which are off-road and go through some fine forest with good views over the Craters of the Moon. An hour's ride is $20, while two hours is $35.

Off-Road Riding

If you don't make it to Arataki (see Places to Stay) then Taupo Quad Adventures (☎ (07) 377 6404) has fully guided off-road trips. It's at the turn-off to Orakei Korako on SH1. A bike is $60/80 for 1½/2½ hours and seats two (twilight or night rides are available).

'Rock 'n' Roping'

The masochist from R 'n' R (☎ (07) 374 8111) who dreamt up this diabolical confidence course must lurk furtively in bush near Taupo – obviously he/she led a Tarzan/Jane-like existence as a kid. Enough said – leap to your death (only to be saved by a rope), swing into oblivion, be a 'flying fox' and generally have a good time. The cost depends on how daring you are. What did these guys do before kernmantel ropes? A swing is $15, a combo (swing, flying fox and trapeze) is $30 and a half-day blast is $50. It is near Deerworld on SH5, 30km north of Taupo.

Walking

You can walk from Taupo to Aratiatia. From the centre of town head up Spa Rd, passing the Taupo Bungy site. Turn left at County

Ave and continue through Spa Thermal Park at the end of the street, past the skateboard bowl and over the hill, following the rough roadway to the left until you hit the track.

The track follows the river to Huka Falls, crossing a hot stream and riverside marshes en route. It's about a one to 1½-hour walk from the centre of Taupo to Huka Falls. From the falls you continue straight ahead along the 7km Taupo Walkway to Aratiatia (another two-plus hours). There are good views of the river, Huka Falls, and the power station across the river. It's easy walking. Alternatively, you can drive out to the falls and park, cross the bridge and walk out to Aratiatia.

Another walk worth mentioning is Mt Tauhara, with magnificent views from the top. Take the Taupo-Napier Highway (SH5) turn-off, 2km south of the Taupo town centre. About 6km along SH5, turn left into Mountain Rd. The start of the track is signposted on the right-hand side. It will take about two hours to the top, walking slowly.

A pleasant walkway goes from the Taupo lakefront to Four Mile Bay. It's a flat, easy walk along public-access beaches. Heading south from Taupo, there's a hot water beach on the way to Two Mile Bay. At Two Mile Bay the walkway connects with the Lions Walk, going from Two Mile Bay (3.2km south of Taupo) to Four Mile Bay (6.4km). Anywhere along here you can easily get back to SH1, the lakeside road.

There are plenty of other good walks and tramps in the area; the visitor centre has the relevant DOC pamphlets ($1).

Organised Tours

Walter's Backpackers Tours, run by a delightful, spry old fellow, include three-hour tours of the local sights ($20) and full-day trips further afield to Tongariro ($40) and Waitomo ($50). Book with Walter (☎ (07) 378 5924) at hostels or the visitor centre.

Paradise Tours (☎ (07) 378 9955) does 2½-hour tours to the Aratiatia Rapids, Geothermal Centre, Craters of the Moon and Huka Falls for $25 (children $12). Rapid Sensations (☎ (07) 378 7902) does guided three-hour mountain-bike tours through the geothermal areas ($45).

Wilderness Escapes (☎ (07) 378 3413) has a number of trips; guided walks are from $30 and full-day kayak trips from $90.

Lake Cruises Four boats specialise in cruises on the lake: the *Barbary*, the *Spirit of Musick*, the *Ernest Kemp* and the faster *Cruise Cat*. The *Barbary*, built in 1926, is a 15m ocean-going racing yacht once owned by actor Errol Flynn. 'Barbary Bill', the skipper, is much loved by tourists and locals and his trip is probably the most popular. The *Spirit of Musick* is an elegant 44ft (13m) ketch. The *Ernest Kemp* is a replica 1920s steam ferry.

All four boats offer similar cruises, visiting a modern Maori rock carving beside the lake. The carving is on private land so it cannot be reached by foot; the only way to see it is by boat. All four also offer morning, afternoon and evening cruises in summer; these last about 2½ to three hours (the *Cruise Cat* is out for about 1½ hours). The cost is $20 (children $10) on all boats, except the *Cruise Cat* ($24, children $12).

All the boats leave from the wharves at the Taupo Boat Harbour, off Redoubt St. Bookings can be made at the visitor centre or at the launch office by the wharves (☎ (07) 378 3444).

Places to Stay
Camping & Cabins Camping is free beside the river at *Reid's Farm* about 1.5km south of the Huka Falls towards Taupo; it is popular, and colourful house trucks are often parked there.

The *Taupo Motor Camp* (☎ (07) 377 3080) on Redoubt St by the river has tent/powered sites at $9/9.50 per person, cabins at $35 for two, and on-site caravans at $45 for two. Rates are lower outside the holidays. *Taupo Cabins* (☎ (07) 378 4346) at 50 Tonga St has a variety of cabins. The most basic are $30 a double, tourist cabins with cooking facilities are $40 and self-contained tourist flats are $50.

The *All Seasons Holiday Park* (☎ (07) 378

4272) is at 16 Rangatira St. It, too, is about 1.5km from the town centre. It has a hot thermal pool and a variety of accommodation including tent sites at $10 per person, standard cabins and rooms in a 40-bed lodge at $15 per person, tourist cabins at $40 for two, and tourist flats at $55 for two.

The *De Bretts Leisure Park* (☎ (07) 378 8559) is beside the De Bretts Pools, 1km from the lake on SH5. Camp sites are $12 per person, leisure lodges are $75 for two and motel-style units are $70 for two.

The *Hilltop Holiday Park* (☎ (07) 378 5247) at 39 Puriri St, off Taharepa Rd, has hot mineral spas and a cold pool. Tent/powered sites are $18/20, cabins are from $26, on-site vans are $33 and tourist flats are $49; all prices are for two.

The *Lake Taupo Holiday Park* (☎ (07) 378 6860) is on Centennial Drive, opposite the AC Baths. It's a 7-hectare park with tent and powered sites for $8 per person, cabins at $45 for two and tourist flats at $55.

Great Lake Holiday Park (☎ (07) 378 5159) on Acacia Bay Rd, 3km west of town, has tent and powered sites at $9 per person, cabins at $26 for two, on-site vans at $33 and tourist flats at $49.

The *Windsor Motel* (☎ (07) 378 6271) a. Waitahanui, 12km south on SH1, has tent sites at $12, caravans at $30 and cabins at $25 (prices for two).

Hostels *Taupo Central Backpackers* (☎ (07) 378 3206) at 7 Tuwharetoa St is the geographical pick of the town's hostels. As a former hotel it has an attached bathroom in every room (a big plus). It has a great rooftop bar, *Trout's* (named after its ebullient owner), and a barbecue/meeting area with superb views of the lake and the Central Plateau. Dorms cost $15, and doubles and twins are $40, including breakfast.

Rainbow Lodge (☎ (07) 378 5754) at 99 Titiraupenga St is a popular hostel with an excellent reputation among travellers (its owners Mark and Sue are veteran travellers). It has a large communal area, a sauna and a games area, and is on the ball with activities, tours and travel information. Mountain bikes, fishing tackle and camping gear are available for hire, and there's free luggage storage. It charges $14 to $16 in dorms, $26 in singles and $34 in doubles and twins.

The YHA associate hostel is *Pol's Hostel* (☎ (07) 378 3311) at 56 Kaimanawa St. This hostel has bright rooms, good views of the lake and roomy outside deck areas. The cost is $16 per bed in three and five-bed dorms, or $36 in double and twin rooms. Excellent tours, run by Kiwi Value Tours (☎ (07) 378 9662), start from here.

Sunset Lodge (☎ (07) 378 5962) at 5 Tremaine Ave, about 2km south of town, is a small, friendly hostel. It has a comfortable atmosphere and free services including pick-up, shuttles to attractions and an inflatable boat. It charges $13 or $14 in dorms; double or twin rooms are $32. To get there turn off from Lake Terrace into Hawai St, then into Pipi St – it is on the corner.

Burke's Backpackers (☎ (07) 378 9292), 69 Spa Rd, is a converted motel and each of the former units has a dorm with a double room off it and a shared bathroom. It charges $15 for a dorm or from $36 for twin and double rooms, including breakfast. It has a nice landscaped garden in its centre.

Berkenhoff Lodge (☎ (07) 378 4909), 75 Scannell St, is a rambling old place. It has a bar/games room (named after a resident canine), dining room (with $6 steak meals) and a spa. It charges $14 in dorms and $34 for twins or doubles (including a light breakfast). At the time of writing, the *Lake Hotel* (☎ (07) 378 6165) on Tongariro St was metamorphosing into a backpackers.

B&Bs & Guesthouses *Bradshaw's B&B* (☎ (07) 378 8288) at 130 Heu Heu St has a tearoom where meals are available; it charges $40/60 a single/double or $45/65 with private facilities. The pleasant *Gillies Lodge* (☎ (07) 377 2377), 77 Gillies Ave, is a well-appointed place with B&B for $65/85. *Loretta's Quality Guest House* at 135 Heu Heu St is good value for $67/77, including a continental breakfast. Absolute luxury is available at the three-bedroom *Greenwood Lodge* (☎ (07) 377 2421) at 183 Lake Terrace; the whole lodge, sleeping six, is yours for $395 for two nights. The visitor centre has a list of over 40 other homestay and farmstay places.

Motels & Hotels Taupo is packed with motels and the competition tends to keep prices down, though many of them have minimum rates during holiday periods. Economical, good-value motels include the *Dunrovin* (☎ (07) 378 7384) at 140 Heu Heu St, a 1950s-style motel with a classic '50s name. It's basic but smart and doubles cost from $65. The *Continental Motel* (☎ (07) 378 5836) at 9 Scannell St on the corner of Motutaiko St and the *Golf Course Motel* (☎ (07) 378 9415) at 123 Tauhara Rd are similarly priced.

The *Courtney Motel* (☎ (07) 378 8398) at 15 Tui St has a variety of units, including studios from $60 and one, two and three-bedroom units at $80 for two ($12 for each extra person). The *Mountain View Motel* (☎ (07) 378 9366), 12-14 Fletcher St, has doubles from $65 to $85.

The better motels line the lakefront along Lake Terrace. Typical of these is the *Tui Oaks Motor Inn* (☎ (07) 378 8305) on the corner of Tui St. It is a modern, well-appointed motel with doubles from $85 to $120. The *Oasis Beach Resort* (once *Manuel's*; ☎ (07) 378 9339), 241 Lake Terrace, has existed there in one form or another for as long as we can remember; the big plus is access to private grotto spa pools. Double rooms are from $85 to $135.

The *De Bretts Thermal Hotel* (☎ (07) 378 7080) is 3km from the town centre on SH5, right near the Taupo Hot Springs. It's a grand hotel (1889) with a variety of accommodation including budget rooms at $20/30 with shared bath and regular rooms with private bath, TV etc at $72/85.

If money is no object and you're looking for the height of understated luxury, one of NZ's most expensive hotels is just outside Taupo. The *Huka Lodge* (☎ (07) 378 5791) near Huka Falls costs a mint but we believe it is worth it.

Places to Eat

Restaurants *Amigo's* at 63 Heu Heu St is a popular restaurant/bar with good Mexican food and décor. There are a few not-so-Mexican selections on the menu too. It's open daily from 4 pm to 2 am, and can be a lively drinking hole. The *Seoul House* at 100 Roberts St is the sole Korean place in Taupo and worth a visit for the authentic barbecue-style food.

Tuwharetoa St is the main dining strip. *Misha's Italian Cafe* at No 28 has a good selection of pizza and pasta for around $16. The blackboard specials offer excellent, authentic Italian dishes such as scaloppine. *Finch's Brasserie* at No 64 is a great choice for meat dishes (from $16 to $28); the *Hobler* at No 42 is a casual place with an open fire and a good selection of NZ dishes; the *Cajun-Kiwi Restaurant & Bar* at No 38, open daily, serves those Louisiana favourites jambalaya, crawfish pie and filé gumbo (mains are around $20); and *Mates Malthouse* at No 22 has inexpensive meals and a casual atmosphere.

The Tongariro St-Lake Terrace corner has a collection of restaurants. On the Tongariro St side, upstairs at No 5, the *Bar on the Lake* has superb lake views and good food. *Nonni's* at No 3 is another good Italian place with pasta and speciality breads. The excellent *Steak & Ale Bar*, with its intimate booths and popular bar, has an eclectic menu featuring succulent steaks. Around the corner at 2 Roberts St, the *Thai Restaurant* cooks all the authentic Thai favourites; three courses will set you back about $30.

If you're going upmarket, the *Edgewater* at 243 Lake Terrace is an elegant and expensive but top-notch restaurant. Adjacent is *Pepper's Brasserie*, a more reasonably priced family place. Both restaurants have stunning views of the lake. *Reflections of the Lake* (☎ (07) 378 8305) in the Tui Oaks Motor Inn is for romantic candlelit dinners – specialties include seafood chowder, hapuka steaks and venison.

Fast Food The city centre has plenty of daytime cafes for a coffee and snack or a light meal. *Zanda's Cafe* has inexpensive food with both vegetarian and meat selections. It's in the Marama Arcade between Heu Heu and Horomatangi Sts. On Horomatangi St, the *Deli Twenty One* has a wide selection of sandwiches and snacks to eat there or take away. On Heu Heu St, *Verdi's Cafe* is slightly expensive but has excellent coffee.

Down by the lakefront is a *Pizza Hut*, *McDonald's* complete with DC3 aircraft, *KFC* and *Georgie Pie*; the fate of the latter is uncertain. On Tongariro St near the lakefront, *JD's Takeaways* does good fish and chips. *Mountain Kebabs* at the lake end of Tongariro St has a selection of inexpensive Middle Eastern food, with vegetarian and meat selections (medium/large kebabs are $6.50/8.50). *Replete Food Co*, a cafe near the corner of Heu Heu and Ruapehu Sts, is the place to chill out. People watch as you enjoy a hearty $6 lunch and great coffee.

For self-caterers, *Pack 'N Save* and *Woolworths* are open daily.

Entertainment

The focus of entertainment is the *Holy Cow*, upstairs at 11 Tongariro St, mainly because of the personalities of the owners and their selection of music. You can get good counter meals at reasonable prices. It hums until late even on the odd winter night and table dancing is permitted. Upstairs in the Taupo Central Backpackers is *Trout's Bar* – a dinky little bar with good selections of videos and music, Monteith's on tap, a covered barbecue area and, undeniably, the best views of the lake and mountains.

The *Red Barrel* on the lakefront near Tongariro St is a lively pub and good for socialising and dancing. It has live bands for dancing on Wednesday, Friday and Saturday nights. *Rockefellers* on Tuwharetoa St, a popular bar with friendly staff, stays open until late. *Mates Malthouse*, the *Hobler*, *Cajun-Kiwi Restaurant* and *Steak & Ale Bar* (see Places to Eat) all have lively moments.

On Tongariro St on the corner of Tuwharetoa St, the *Axis Bar* has live bands on Thursday, Friday and Saturday nights. *De Bretts Thermal Hotel* (see Places to Stay) and the *Spa Hotel*, 2km east of the town centre along Spa Rd, both have live bands on weekends. The Spa is the place to go if you've been kicked out of every other hotel in town.

The *Great Lake Centre* (☎ (07) 377 1200) on Tongariro St has a theatre and hall for performances, exhibitions and conventions. The visitor centre has the current schedule. The *Starlight Cinema Centre* is on Horomatangi St.

Getting There & Away

Air Air New Zealand Link and Mt Cook Airline (☎ 0800 800 737) have direct flights to Auckland, Christchurch, Rotorua and Wellington, with onward connections.

In Taupo, ticketing for both is handled through travel agencies: AA Travel Centre (see Information), Budget Travel (☎ (07) 378 9799) at 37 Horomatangi St and the James Holiday Shoppe (☎ (07) 378 7065) on the same block of Horomatangi St.

Bus Taupo is about halfway between Auckland and Wellington. InterCity, Newmans and Alpine Scenic Tours arrive at and depart from the Taupo Travel Centre (☎ (07) 378 9032) at 16 Gascoigne St. The travel centre also sells tickets for trains and the *Interislander* ferry.

InterCity and Newmans have several daily buses to Turangi, Auckland, Hamilton, Rotorua, Tauranga, Napier, Wanganui, Palmerston North and Wellington. Mount Cook Landline also stops at the visitor centre on its daily Auckland-Wellington run.

Shuttle services operate year-round between Taupo, Tongariro National Park and the Whakapapa Ski Area, a 1¼-hour trip. They travel daily and may include package deals for lift tickets and ski hire. Bookings can be made at the visitor centre or at the hostels. Kiwi Shuttle (☎ 025 503 654) leaves at 6.45 am for Turangi (and the start of the walking tracks) and returns from Turangi at 5 pm ($30 return from Taupo).

The Thermal Connection, a backpacker shuttle, passes two geothermal areas (Waiotapu and Waimangu) on the way to Rotorua ($14/28 one way/return – entry fees are extra). It departs from Taupo (door to door) at 8 am and returns from Rotorua at 3 pm. This service coincides with the Lady Knox Geyser's performances.

Getting Around

Taupo Taxis (☎ (07) 378 5100) and Stop Taxis (☎ (07) 378 9250) have door-to-door airport shuttle services for $8.

Taupo finally has a scheduled bus service. Adventure Link (☎ (07) 378 0227) departs from accommodation places in Taupo five times daily. It drops off at places to the north (including Aratiatia and Craters of the Moon), in Wairakei Park and as far south as the airport. A day pass is $10 or you pay $2.50/5 for one way/return, regardless of distance.

Hire mountain bikes from Cycle World (☎ (07) 378 6117) at 126 Ruapehu St, opposite the Pack 'N Save supermarket, and Ski Yer Heart Out (☎ (07) 378 7400) on Roberts St near Lake Terrace. Most hostels have bikes and the Rainbow Lodge will also rent them to non-guests for $15 per day or $3 per hour. Bikes are forbidden on the track from Spa Park to the Huka Falls due to track damage.

AROUND TAUPO
Wairakei Park

Crossing the river at Tongariro St and heading north from town on SH1, you'll arrive at the Wairakei Park area, also known as the Huka Falls Tourist Loop. Take the first right turn after you cross the river and you'll be on Huka Falls Rd, which passes along the river. At the end, turn left, back onto the highway, and you'll pass other interesting spots on your way back to town.

There's no public transport but tours go to a few places along here, otherwise walk or hire a mountain bike for the day.

En route look out for **Honey Hive New Zealand**, for all you ever wanted to know about bees, and **New Zealand Woodcraft**, where you can buy woodturned items made from native timbers. Both are open daily; entry to the Honey Hive is free and to the woodcraft centre is $2.

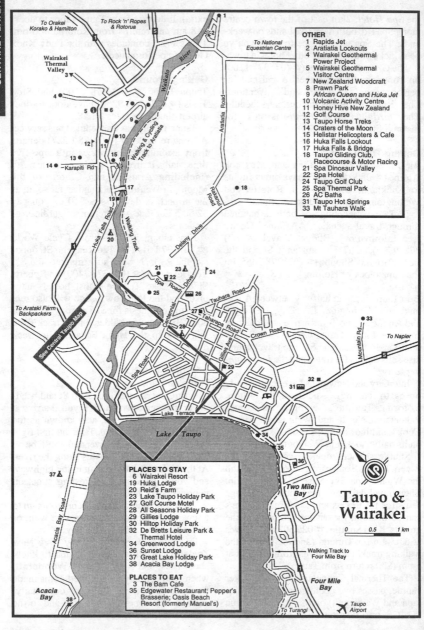

OTHER
1 Rapids Jet
2 Aratiatia Lookouts
4 Wairakei Geothermal Power Project
5 Wairakei Geothermal Visitor Centre
7 New Zealand Woodcraft
8 Prawn Park
9 *African Queen* and *Huka Jet*
10 Volcanic Activity Centre
11 Honey Hive New Zealand
12 Golf Course
13 Taupo Horse Treks
14 Craters of the Moon
15 Helistar Helicopters & Cafe
16 Huka Falls Lookout
17 Huka Falls & Bridge
18 Taupo Gliding Club, Racecourse & Motor Racing
21 Spa Dinosaur Valley
22 Spa Hotel
24 Taupo Golf Club
25 Spa Thermal Park
26 AC Baths
31 Taupo Hot Springs
33 Mt Tauhara Walk

PLACES TO STAY
6 Wairakei Resort
19 Huka Lodge
20 Reid's Farm
23 Lake Taupo Holiday Park
27 Golf Course Motel
28 All Seasons Holiday Park
29 Gillies Lodge
30 Hilltop Holiday Park
32 De Bretts Leisure Park & Thermal Hotel
34 Greenwood Lodge
36 Sunset Lodge
37 Great Lake Holiday Park
38 Acacia Bay Lodge

PLACES TO EAT
3 The Barn Cafe
35 Edgewater Restaurant; Pepper's Brasserie; Oasis Beach Resort (formerly Manuel's)

Taupo & Wairakei

0   0.5   1 km

Huka Falls Along Huka Falls Rd are the spectacular Huka Falls, known as *hukanui* in Maori, meaning 'great body of spray'. A footbridge crosses the Waikato River above the falls – a great torrent of water, more like a giant rapid – that plunges through a narrow cleft in the rock. The water here is clear and turquoise, particularly on a sunny day.

Volcanic Activity Centre This is the place for budding vulcanologists. The observatory monitors volcanic activity in the volatile Taupo Volcanic Zone, and the visitor centre has excellent displays on NZ's geothermal and volcanic activity.

Exhibits include a large relief map with push-button highlighters to show you the volcanic regions, and old documentaries about the eruptions of Ngauruhoe and Ruapehu in 1945, the largest in NZ this century. Pick up a monitoring report to tell you about recent earthquakes or to see if Ruapehu is about to erupt. The centre and bookshop are open daily from 10 am to 4 pm ($2).

If you wish to learn more about the region's volcanic activity, there are guided vulcanology tours (☎ (07) 378 5901) on the lake and to surrounding areas ($90). If you wish to see it all from the air with the same knowledgeable guide it will cost $170.

African Queen **& *Huka Jet*** Next along, 9km north of Taupo, Huka Jet and the African Queen share a dock on the river. Together they make strange bedfellows, exemplifying 'the old and the new' of NZ river boating.

The *African Queen* (☎ 0800 727 437) is actually the historic *Waireka*, a riverboat which once operated on the Whanganui River. It makes cruises daily at 11 am and 3 pm, and the Moonlight Glowworm Cruise goes at 9 pm in summer and 6 pm in winter. The cruises cost $18 (children $8).

Partly inspired by the engineering of river boats like the *Waireka*, which has a draught of only 30.5cm laden, Kiwi CWF Hamilton was inspired to invent the jet-boat. The *Huka Jet* (☎ (07) 374 8572) departs from the same dock for a 30-minute ride down to the

Aratiatia Dam and up to the Huka Falls. Half-hourly trips run all day long ($45, children $20, including transport from Taupo).

Prawn Park (☎ (07) 374 8474), near Huka Jet, is the world's only geothermally heated freshwater **prawn farm**. There are tours on the hour from 11 am to 4 pm in summer, less frequently in winter; it costs a massive $11.50 (which includes three prawns – 'raw' ones perhaps).

Aratiatia Rapids Two kilometres off SH5 is the Aratiatia Rapids, a spectacular part of the Waikato River until the government, in its wisdom, plonked a power house and dam down, shutting off the water. To keep the tourists happy they open the control gates at 10 am, noon and 2 pm daily, and also at 4 pm in summer. You can see the water flow through from three good vantage points (entry is free).

Rapids Jet (☎ (07) 374 8338) shoots up and down the lower part of the Aratiatia Rapids ($45). It's a sensational ride, rivalling the trip to Huka Falls. The jet-boats depart from the end of the access road to the Aratiatia lookouts.

Wairakei Thermal Valley This thermal valley, like Orakei Korako, gets its name from being the place where the waters were used as mirrors. This is the remains of what was once known as Geyser Valley. Before the geothermal power project started in 1959 this was one of the most active thermal areas in the world, with 22 geysers and 240 mud pools and springs. The neighbouring geothermal project has sucked off the steam, and only eight or so mud pools remain active. There's a bush walk to the Huiata pools but they're only active after a heavy rain. It's open daily from 8.30 am ($5, children $1). The quaint *Barn Cafe* is here.

Wairakei Geothermal Power Project New Zealand was the second country in the world to produce power from natural steam. If you dive into all that steam you will find yourself at the Wairakei Geothermal Power Project, which generates about 150,000kW, providing about 5% of NZ's electricity.

The visitor centre is close to the road, where you can make an educational stop between 9 am and 4 pm from Monday to Saturday. Information on the bore field and power house is available and an audiovisual ($2) is shown. You can drive up the road through the project and from a lookout see the long stretches of pipe, wreathed in steam.

Just south of here is the big Wairakei Resort and its international golf course.

Craters of the Moon Craters of the Moon is an interesting and unexploited thermal area. It's run by DOC, so it is less touristy than other commercially exploited thermal areas. Don't miss the lookout just before the car park – it's the best place for photos.

This thermal area sprang up in the 1950s. The power station lowered underground water levels, reducing the pressure of the heated water, and causing more vigorous boiling and steam. New mud pools and steam vents appeared, and you can wander through them on a plank-walk.

It is open from dawn to dusk. There is a small kiosk staffed by volunteers at the car park (they will keep an eye on your car). Entry is free but donations are appreciated.

Craters of the Moon is signposted on SH1 about 5km north of Taupo.

Broadlands

This beautiful and often unseen stretch of the mighty Waikato River, equidistant (40km) between Rotorua and Taupo, is worth visiting. To get there turn off SH5 onto Homestead Rd, just south of Reporoa. The stunning scenery is best seen by River Glen Tours jet-boat (☎ (07) 333 8165). You can travel downstream to the Orakei Korako thermal region ($65) through some magnificent steamy gorges or head upstream through the exciting Full James rapids to Aratiatia ($50).

The brave can take a spin with one of NZ's best drivers in a V8 Group A **sprint boat** on the specially designed slalom course on the Waikato; this two-minute, G-force pulling

adrenalin buzz is not easily forgotten and well worth the $30 per person cost.

Waikato River Lodge (☎ (07) 333 8165) is mainly for conference groups but has a popular self-contained Lockwood chalet which sleeps six ($20 per person).

Arataki & Pureora Forest Park

The dominating western ramparts of Lake Taupo largely comprise the huge Pureora Forest. Logging was eventually stopped in the park in the 1980s after long campaigns by conservationists.

There are long and short forest treks, including tracks to the summits of Mt Pureora (1165m) and the rock pinnacle of Mt Titiraupenga (1042m). DOC offices in Taupo and Te Kuiti have pamphlets, maps and information on the park. The north section of the park is designated for recreational hunting, but you must obtain a permit from park headquarters.

Arataki Country Villa (☎ (07) 882 8857, 025 819 145), nestled beside the picturesque Mangakino Stream, is one of those rare gems. There are activities galore here, including horse trekking, quad bikes, tramping and trout fishing on a secluded section of the stream. The house, surrounded by a working farm (where you can participate in daily activities), is fully equipped with comfortable beds. On the balcony is a barbecue and heated spa pool – enjoying the sunsets from here is a pure delight. The cost is a mere $17 per person, with a minimal fee charged for the many activities. To get there take SH30 from Te Kuiti, turn south on SH32 and follow the signs. From Taupo, take the Kinloch Rd to SH30, then turn north.

Orakei Korako

Between Taupo and Rotorua, Orakei Korako is one of the finest thermal areas of NZ but receives fewer visitors than the others because of its remote location.

After the destruction of the Pink and White Terraces by the Tarawera eruption, Orakei Korako was possibly the best thermal area left in NZ and one of the finest in the world. Although three-quarters of it now lies beneath the dam waters of Lake Ohakuri, the quarter that remains is the best part and still very much worth seeing.

A walking track takes you around the large, colourful silica terraces for which the park is famous, as well as geysers and Ruatapu Cave – a magnificent natural cave with a pool of jade-green water. The pool may have been used by Maori as a mirror during hairdressing ceremonies; Orakei Korako means 'the place of adorning'.

Entry is $12.50 (children $5), including a boat ride across Lake Ohakuri. It's open daily from 8.30 am to 4.30 pm. Canoes and dinghies are available for hire and there are two hot tubs.

Accommodation (☎ (07) 378 3131) is available in the *Geyserland Resort Lodge* which has a fully equipped kitchen. The cost is $18 per person in rooms with two to six beds. Tourist flats sleeping six cost $18 (children $12) and there is a minimum of $48 per night. Tent and caravan sites are free.

To get to Orakei Korako from Taupo, take SH1 to Hamilton for 23km, and then travel for 14km from the turn-off. From Rotorua the turn-off is on SH5, via Mihi.

TURANGI

Developed for the construction of the nearby hydroelectric power station in 1973, Turangi (population 4300) is Taupo's smaller cousin at the southern end of Lake Taupo. The town itself is 4km inland from the lake and access to the lake is from nearby Tokaanu.

Turangi's main attractions are its excellent trout fishing (on the Tongariro River) and access to the northern trails of nearby Tongariro National Park.

Information

The Turangi Information Centre (☎ (07) 386 8999), just off SH1, has a detailed relief model of the Tongariro National Park and is the place to stop for information on the park, Kaimanawa Forest Park, trout fishing, walks, and snow and road conditions during the ski season. The office also issues hut tickets, ski passes and hunting and fishing

licences, and acts as the AA agent. It is open from 8.30 am to 6 pm daily in summer (to 5 pm in winter).

DOC (☎ (07) 386 8607) is at the junction of SH1 and Ohuanga Rd. The post office and banks are in the Turangi shopping mall, opposite the information centre.

Tongariro National Trout Centre

Five kilometres south of Turangi on SH1 is the DOC-managed trout centre, an important hatchery. It's open from 9 am to 4 pm daily (entry is free). This landscaped centre has a self-guided walk to an underwater viewing area, keeping ponds and a picnic area. You can fish for trout in the Tongariro River, which runs close by.

Tokaanu

About 5km west of Turangi on the lake, this settlement has a collection of motels and fishing lodges.

The **Tokaanu Thermal Park** is an interesting thermal area with hot baths. A 15-minute boardwalk leads around the mud pools and thermal springs. In the park, the Thermal Pools has hot pools, a sauna and exhibits. The walk is free, while entry to the public pool costs $3 (children $1); entry to the private pools and sauna is $4. All are open daily from 10 am to 9 pm.

Walking

The DOC *Turangi Walks* leaflet outlines notable walks such as the Tongariro River Walkway (three hours return), Tongariro River Loop Track (one hour), Hinemihi's Track near the top of Te Ponanga Saddle (15 minutes return), a walk on Mt Maunganamu (40 minutes return) and a walk around Lake Rotopounamu, which abounds in birdlife (20 minutes to the lake, then 1½ hours around the lake).

Trout Fishing

February and March are the best months for brown trout and June to September are the best for rainbow trout, but the fishing is good most of the year. Don't forget a fishing licence.

Turangi has a variety of fishing guides who charge from around $45 to $50 per hour, including all gear. Or you can hire your own gear from Greig Sports (☎ (07) 386 7713) in the shopping mall.

Boats can be hired for lake fishing – aluminium dinghies cost $15 per hour from Braxmere Lodge just before Waihi, which rents out fishing gear.

Other Activities
River rafting is popular, and the Tongariro River has Grade III rapids or, for families, Grade I on the lower reaches in summer. The Rafting Centre (☎ 0800 101 024, (07) 386 6409) on Atirau Rd is the home of Tongariro River Rafting; its five-hour trip (half the time on the river) costs $75 per person. The family floats are $25 per person (minimum of four).

It's a Trout's Life

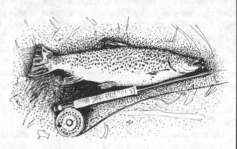

DOC operates three trout hatcheries in New Zealand – one in Wanaka in the South Island, one near Rotorua and one in Turangi. The Wanaka hatchery is more for salmon than trout, while the two North Island hatcheries are almost exclusively for rainbow trout. There are other private hatcheries, some of which obtain their eggs from DOC operations.

The first brown trout eggs arrived in NZ from Tasmania in 1867. They had originally come to Australia from England. Rainbow trout eggs first arrived from California in 1883. Hatcheries were established at that time to rear the first young fish and, while many fish are hatched naturally nowadays, there is still a need for artificial hatcheries. This is because some of NZ's lakes and rivers have insufficient good spawning grounds though they may be ideal for trout. Plus there's a lot of fishing going on (although there are tight limitations on the number of fish that can be caught).

In the wild, fully grown trout migrate each winter to suitable spawning beds. This usually means gravel beds in the upper reaches of rivers and streams. Here a female fish makes a shallow depression and deposits eggs which are quickly fertilised by an attendant male fish. The female fish then sweeps gravel over the eggs. Over two or three days this process is repeated to create a redd with several pockets of eggs. During this process the fish do not feed and a female fish may lose one-third of her body weight by the time she returns to the lake. Male fish are in even worse shape because they arrive at the spawning grounds before the females and leave afterwards.

Less than 1% of the eggs survive to become mature fish. The eggs may be damaged or destroyed by gravel movement and even when hatched they may be eaten by other fish, birds or rats. Even other trout will happily make a meal of them.

Because there were only a few shipments of eggs, from which all of today's trout are descended, NZ's rainbow trout are considered to be a very pure strain. The hatchery eggs are collected by capturing fish during their spawning run. Eggs are gently squeezed from a female fish and milt from males added and stirred together in a container. Incubator trays containing about 10,000 eggs are placed in racks and washed over by a continuous flow of water.

After 15 days the embryos' eyes start to appear and by the 18th day the embryos, previously very sensitive and frail, have become quite hardy. They need to be because on that day the eggs are poured from a metre height into a wire basket. Any weak eggs are killed off by this rough treatment, ensuring that only healthy fish are hatched out. The survivors are now placed 5000 to a basket and about 10 days later the fish hatch out, wriggle through the mesh and drop to the bottom of the trough. They stay there for about 20 days, living off the yolk sac.

When they have totally absorbed their yolk sac they are known as fry and although they can be released at this stage they are normally kept until they are 10 to 15cm long. At this time they are nine to 12 months old and are known as fingerlings. They are moved outside when they are about 4cm long and reared in ponds. Fingerlings are transported to the place where they will be released in what looks rather like a small petrol tanker, and simply pumped out the back down a large diameter pipe! ∎

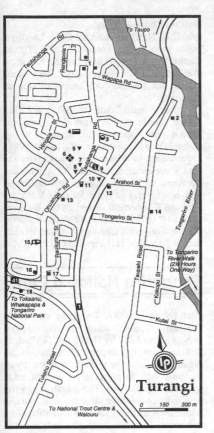

PLACES TO STAY
1   Bellbird Lodge
2   Sportsman's Lodge
12 Parklands Motor Lodge
13 Club Habitat
14 Creel Lodge
15 Turangi Cabins & Holiday Park
17 Anglers Paradise Resort Motel

PLACES TO EAT
5   Magee's Restaurant & Bar
7   Hong Kong Chinese Restaurant &
    Country Fried Chicken
8   Valentino's
10 Burger King (Shell Petrol Station)

OTHER
3   Turangi Bus & Travel Centre
4   Swimming Pool
6   Turangi Shopping Mall & CPO
9   Turangi Information Centre &
    Automobile Association (AA)
11 Huckleberry's Pub
16 DOC
18 The Rafting Centre

A highly recommended trip is the **wetlands ecotour** with Tongariro Eco Tours (☎ (07) 386 6409), based at the Rafting Centre. You will have the chance to see some 40 species of birdlife in the wetlands environment as you cruise around the lake edge on the *Delta Queen* ($40 per person, binoculars supplied).

The information centre also arranges horse treks, hunting and fishing trips, cruises and charter boats, mountain biking, kayaking, scenic flights and many other outdoor activities.

Places to Stay

Camping & Cabins *Turangi Cabins & Holiday Park* (☎ (07) 386 8754) is on Ohuanga Rd, off SH41. Tent/powered sites are $8/9 per person, pokey cabins are $15 per person and on-site vans are $35 for two. At one time this was the power station construction workers' quarters, which explains all the cabins. At Tokaanu the *Oasis Motel & Caravan Park* (☎ (07) 386 8569) on SH41 has tent/powered sites at $6.50/8 per person, cabins at $15 per person and motel units from $50 to $63 for two. It also has hot pools and spa pools.

Other motor camps north of Turangi on the lakeside road to Taupo are the *Tauranga-Taupo Fishing Lodge* (☎ (07) 386 8385), 11km north, and the *Motutere Bay Caravan Park* (☎ (07) 386 8963), 17km north.

Hostels *Bellbird Lodge* (☎ (07) 386 8281) at 3 Rangipoia Place is a small, friendly hostel with a spacious lounge area and kitchen. The cost is $8 to camp, $14 to $15 in dorms, or $32 in twins and doubles. This popular, well-run hostel is about the best

CENTRAL PLATEAU

reason to stay in Turangi. Ask Clint where the big fish can be found.

Club Habitat (☎ (07) 386 7492) on Ohuanga Rd is a huge complex (220 beds) with rooms scattered around the grounds. Camping is $7 per person, and backpackers beds are $15 in dorms or $38 in twins. The better-furnished cabins with kitchens and shared bath are adequate for $60, better en-suite motel units are $70 for two, and family units are $95. There is a big restaurant-bar-entertainment complex, and a sauna and spa.

Motels The *Sportsman's Lodge* (☎ (07) 386 8150) at 15 Taupehi Rd has rooms with shared kitchen and TV lounge at $50 a double. The *Creel Lodge* (☎ (07) 386 8081), 165 Taupehi Rd, has units from $75. The *Tokaanu Lodge* (☎ (07) 386 8572) has three private mineral pools, a covered outdoor pool, a fish cleaning area and a fish freezer/smoker. The cost is $72 for one-bedroom units and $105 for four-person units.

The *Anglers Paradise Resort Motel* (☎ (07) 386 8980), on the corner of SH41 and Ohuanga Rd, has studio/one-bedroom units from $89/135 for two; it also has a restaurant. *Parklands Motor Lodge* (☎ (07) 386 7515) on the corner of SH1 and Arahori St has tent/powered sites for $15/18 for two and studio/family units for $80/90 for two.

Places to Eat

The Turangi shopping mall has a large supermarket open daily. The *Hong Kong Chinese Restaurant*, *Country Fried Chicken* and *Magee's Restaurant & Bar* are all near the shopping mall. *Burger King* is at the Shell petrol station.

Also near the shopping mall is *Valentino's*, a good Italian restaurant and a solid reminder of the many Italian construction workers here when the power station was built. *Club Habitat* has a cafeteria-style restaurant with good, cheap meals. The restaurant in the Angler's Paradise specialises in seafood; entrée/main serves of prawn cutlet rolls are $9/22 and huge seafood baskets are $23.

Getting There & Away

InterCity, Newmans and Mt Cook Landline buses stop at the Turangi Bus & Travel Centre. Auckland-Wellington and Rotorua-Wellington buses running along the eastern side of the lake to/from Taupo all stop at Turangi.

Alpine Scenic Tours (☎ (07) 386 8918) runs a shuttle several times daily between Turangi and National Park, stopping at the Ketetahi and Mangatepopo trail heads, Whakapapa and, in winter, the Whakapapa ski area – an excellent service for skiers and trampers. It also has services to/from Taupo and a weekday service to/from Rotorua. Bellbird Connection, based at the Bellbird Lodge (☎ (07) 386 8281), provides a shuttle for the Tongariro Crossing/Whakapapa ski area ($20 return, children $25).

Tongariro National Park

Established in 1887, Tongariro was NZ's first national park. It was given to the country in September 1887 by Horonuku Te Heuheu Tukino, a far-sighted paramount chief of the Ngati Tuwharetoa people who realised it was the only way to preserve an area of such spiritual significance. The name Tongariro originally covered the three mountains of the park (Tongariro, Ngauruhoe and Ruapehu) and comes from *tonga* (south wind) and *riro* (carried away). The story goes that Ngatoro-i-rangi was stuck on the summit and had almost perished from the cold. He called to his sisters in Hawaiki for fire and his words were carried to them on the south wind.

With its collection of mighty (and still active) volcanoes, Tongariro is one of the country's most spectacular parks. In summer it has excellent walks and tramps, most notably the Tongariro Northern Circuit and the Tongariro Crossing. In the winter it's an important ski area.

Information

The Whakapapa Visitor Centre in Whakapapa Village, on the northern side of the park,

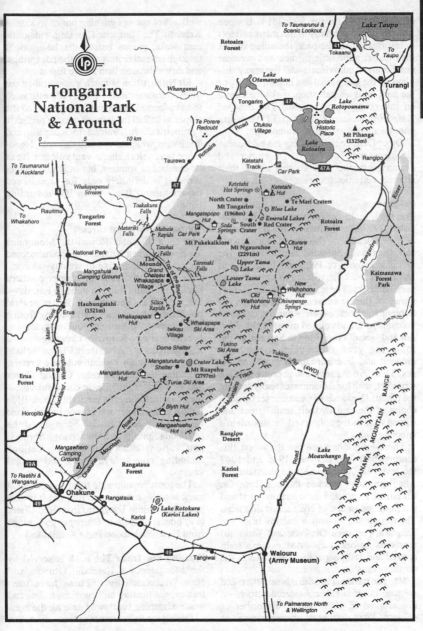

Tongariro National Park & Around

(☎ (07) 892 3729; fax 892 3814) is open from 8 am to 5 pm daily. It has maps and lots of information on the park, including walks, huts and current skiing, track and weather conditions. Audiovisuals and the many displays on the geological and human history of the park, plus a small shop, make the centre an interesting place to visit. The detailed *Tongariro National Park* map ($11) is worth purchasing before you go tramping.

Other DOC centres serving the park are in Ohakune and Turangi. In December and January, ask the park centres about their summer activities program.

Volcanoes

The long, multi-peaked summit of **Mt Ruapehu** (2797m) is the highest and most active of the volcanoes. The upper slopes were showered with hot mud and water in the volcanic activity of 1969 and 1975, and in December 1988 the volcano threw out some very hot rocks. These were just tame precursors to the spectacular eruptions of September 1995, when Ruapehu sprayed volcanic rock and emitted massive clouds of ash and steam. From June to September the following year, the mountain rumbled, groaned and sent ash clouds high into the sky. The 1996 ski season was pretty much a write-off, with local businesses really feeling the pinch. The locals in Ohakune set up deck chairs at the end of their main street and sipped wine as they observed the mountain's antics.

These eruptions were not the worst this century, however. Between 1945 and 1947 the level of Crater Lake rose dramatically when eruptions blocked the overflow. On Christmas Eve, 1953 the overflow burst and the flood led to one of NZ's worst disasters. The torrent swept away a railway bridge at Tangiwai (between Ohakune and Waiouru) moments before a crowded express train arrived and 153 people lost their lives in the resulting crash.

Mt Tongariro (1968m) is another old volcano but it is still considered active – it last erupted in 1926. It has a number of coloured lakes dotting its uneven summit as well as hot springs gushing out of its side at Ketetahi. The Tongariro Crossing, a magnificent walk, passes beside the lakes, right through several craters, on to the hot springs, and down through lush native forest.

Mt Ngauruhoe is much younger than the other volcanoes in the park – it's estimated to have formed in the last 2500 years and the slopes to its 2291m summit are still perfectly symmetrical. In contrast to Ruapehu and Tongariro, which have multiple vents, Ngauruhoe is a conical, single-vent volcano. It can be climbed in summer, but in winter (under snow) it is definitely only for experienced mountaineers. It's a steep but rewarding climb.

Tongariro Northern Circuit

The long, circular Round-the-Mountains Track embracing Ruapehu, Ngauruhoe and Tongariro requires five to six days to complete. More popular is the shorter northern circuit, normally done in three to four days. One of NZ's Great Walks, it has several possibilities for shorter walks taking from a few hours to overnight, and includes the famous one-day Tongariro Crossing.

Highlights of the Northern Circuit include tramping through several volcanic craters, including the South Crater, Central Crater and Red Crater; brilliantly colourful volcanic lakes including the Emerald Lakes, Blue Lake and the Upper and Lower Tama Lakes; the steaming Ketetahi Hot Springs and the cold Soda Springs and Ohinepango Springs; and various other volcanic formations including cones, lava flows and glacial valleys.

The most popular side trip from the main track is to Ngauruhoe summit, but it is also possible to climb Tongariro from Red Crater (1½ hours) or walk to Ohinepango Springs from New Waihohonu Hut (30 minutes).

Walking the Track The track is served by the Mangatepopo, Ketetahi, Oturere and New Waihohonu huts. These have mattresses, gas heating and cookers, toilets and water. Camping is allowed near all the huts.

During the full summer season – from late

October to 31 May – a Great Walks pass is required and must be bought in advance, whether you stay in the huts or camp beside them; the cost is $14 per night in huts or $6 for camping (children half-price). Ordinary back country hut tickets and annual passes cannot be used during these months. All park visitor centres sell passes.

At other times, ordinary back country hut passes or annual passes may be used; the cost is $8 per night (two tickets) for huts or $4 (one ticket) for camping. However, this track is quite different in winter, when it is covered in snow and is a tough alpine trek.

Estimated walking times are:

Mangatepopo car park to Mangatepopo Hut	15 minutes
Mangatepopo Hut to Emerald Lakes	three to four hours
Emerald Lakes to Ketetahi and Springs	two to three hours
Emerald Lakes to Oturere Hut	one to two hours
Oturere Hut to New Waihohonu Hut	two to three hours
New Waihohonu Hut to Whakapapa Village	five to six hours

Track Safety Check with one of the DOC offices for current track and weather conditions before you set out. The weather on the mountains is extremely changeable – it can change from warm brilliant sunshine to snow, hail or wind within a few minutes. Bring a rain coat and warm, woollen clothing.

Accidents occur on this track when people misjudge loose rocks or go sliding down the volcanic slopes – watch your step!

On Ngauruhoe, watch out for loose scoria, and be careful not to dislodge rocks onto people coming up behind. Around the Ketetahi Hot Springs, be careful of unstable ground caused by thermal activity.

In winter alpine or mountaineering experience is essential, especially to climb the peaks. If you don't know how to use ice axes, crampons and avalanche gear, come with an experienced guide.

Tongariro Crossing Often called 'the finest one-day walk in NZ', the Tongariro Crossing covers many of the most spectacular features of the Tongariro Northern Circuit between the Mangatepopo and the Ketetahi huts. On a clear day the views are magnificent. This is what many trampers do as day two of the Northern Circuit, with the extra walk along the Ketetahi track. Because of its popularity, shuttles are available to both ends of the track.

There are a couple of steep spots, but most of the track is not terribly difficult. However, it is a long, exhausting day's walk. It's billed as a seven to eight-hour walk, but expect it to take longer if you're not in top condition. Some prefer to do it as a two-day walk, especially if side trips are included.

The track passes through vegetation zones ranging from alpine scrub and tussock to places where there is no vegetation at all on the higher altitudes and to the lush podocarp forest as you descend from Ketetahi Springs to the end of the track.

Worthwhile side trips from the main track include ascents to the summits of Mt Ngauruhoe and Mt Tongariro. Mt Ngauruhoe can be ascended most easily from the Mangatepopo Saddle, reached near the beginning of the track after the first steep climb. The summit of Tongariro is reached by a poled route from Red Crater.

Walking the Track Near the start of the track is the Mangatepopo Hut, accessed by Mangatepopo Rd, or there's the Ketetahi Hut near the Ketetahi Hot Springs, a couple of hours before the end of the track. To stay at or camp beside either hut, you must have a Great Walks pass, purchased in advance and valid from the end of October until 31 May.

The Ketetahi Hut, beside the Ketetahi Hot Springs, is the most popular in the park. It has bunks to sleep 24 people, but regularly has 50 to 60 people trying to stay there on Saturday nights and at the busiest times of year (summer and school holidays). As bunks are claimed on a first come, first served basis, it's not a bad idea to bring camping gear, just in case. Campers can use all the hut facilities – except for bunks – which can make the kitchen crowded, especially at peak times.

Estimated walking times are:

Mangatepopo Rd end to Mangatepopo Hut	15 minutes
Mangatepopo Hut to Mangatepopo Saddle	1½ hours
(Side trip) Mangatepopo Saddle to summit of Mt Ngauruhoe	three hours return
(Side trip) Red Crater to Tongariro Summit	1½ hours return
Mangatepopo Saddle to Emerald Lakes	1½ to two hours
Emerald Lakes to Ketetahi Hut	two hours
Ketetahi Hut to Ketetahi Hot Springs	10 minutes
Ketetahi Hut to road end	two hours

Crater Lake

When Ruapehu is volcanically active, the area within 1.5 to 2km around Crater Lake is off-limits; check with DOC park offices for the latest information.

The walk to Crater Lake in the crater of Ruapehu begins at Iwikau Village, at the end of the Top of the Bruce Rd above Whakapapa Village, and takes about seven hours return (four hours up, three hours down). It's definitely not an easy stroll and the track isn't marked. Even in summer, there may be ice and snow to get through; in winter, forget it unless you are an experienced mountaineer. Check with the Whakapapa Visitor Centre for current weather conditions before you set off. Boots, sunglasses and windproofs are always essential, while ice axes and crampons may be needed.

From December to April you can use the chairlift at the Whakapapa Ski Area to get you up the mountain, cutting about three hours off the walk. Guided walks to Crater Lake go from the chairlift (☎ (07) 892 3738 for reservations) for $35 (children $25).

You can reach Crater Lake from the Ohakune side, but the track is steeper and ice axes and crampons are always necessary (to ascend a steep glacier). From this side, allow five hours to go up and three to come down.

Other Walks

The visitor centres at Whakapapa, Ohakune and Turangi have maps and information on interesting short and long walks in the park as well as track and weather conditions.

Keen trampers can do the entire **Round-the-Mountains Track** (five to six days). Definitely get a good map before walking this track (such as Parkmaps No 273-04).

A number of fine walks begin at or near the Whakapapa Visitor Centre and from the road leading up to it. Several other good walks take off from the road leading from Ohakune to the Turoa Ski Area (see Ohakune). DOC's *Whakapapa Walks* has walks from the visitor centre, including:

Ridge Track
  A 30-minute return walk, which climbs through beech forest to alpine shrublands for views of Ruapehu and Ngauruhoe.
Silica Rapids
  A 2½-hour, 8km loop track to the Silica Rapids, named for the silica mineral deposits formed here by the rapids on Waikare Stream, which passes interesting alpine features and, in the final 2km, back down the Top of the Bruce Rd above Whakapapa Village.
Tama Lakes
  A 16km track to the Tama Lakes (five to six hours return). On the Tama Saddle between Ruapehu and Ngauruhoe, the Tama Lakes are great for a refreshing swim. The upper lake affords fine views of Ngauruhoe and Tongariro. (Beware of winds on the saddle.)
Taranaki Falls
  A two-hour, 6km loop track to the 20m Taranaki Falls on Wairere Stream.
Whakapapa Nature Walk
  A 15-minute loop track suitable for wheelchairs, beginning about 200m above the visitor centre and passing through beech forest and gardens indicating the park's vegetation zones.

Both the Tongariro Northern Circuit and Crossing can be reached from Mangatepopo Road off SH47. Still more tracks take off from SH47, on the park's north side, and include:

Lake Rotoaira
  On the shores of Lake Rotoaira, on the north side of the park, are excavations of a pre-European Maori village site.

Lake Rotopounamu
> A beautiful, secluded lake set in podocarp forest on the saddle between lakes Rotoaira and Taupo, Rotopounamu can be reached by a 20-minute walk from SH47. The lake is on the west side of Mt Pihanga. To walk around the lake takes 1½ hours.

Mahuia Rapids
> About 2km north of the SH48 turn-off leading to Whakapapa, SH47 crosses the Whakapapanui Stream just below the rapids.

Matariki Falls
> A 20-minute return track to the falls takes off from SH47 about 200m from the Mahuia Rapids car park.

Skiing

The two main ski areas are the Whakapapa Ski Area, above Whakapapa Village, and the Turoa Ski Area, to the south near Ohakune. The Tukino Ski Area is on the eastern side of Ruapehu. The only accommodation at the ski fields is in private lodges, so most skiers stay at Whakapapa Village, National Park and Ohakune. (See Skiing in the Outdoor Activities chapter.)

Other Activities

The most popular activities in the park are tramping in summer and skiing in winter, but there are several other interesting activities.

The Grand Chateau in Whakapapa has a public nine-hole golf course and tennis courts and hires out golf clubs, tennis racquets etc. Even if you can't afford to stay at the hotel, stop in for a drink in the lobby just to savour the atmosphere.

The ski lifts at Whakapapa Ski Area (☎ (07) 892 3738) also operate for sightseeing and for trampers transport up the mountain from December to April (subject to weather). A return ride is $15 (children $7.50).

Mountain Air (☎ (07) 892 2812), with an office on SH47 near the SH48 turn-off to Whakapapa, has flights over the volcanoes (from $45).

Plateau Outdoor Adventure Guides (☎ (07) 892 2740), based at Raurimu 6km north of National Park township, offers a wide variety of activities around Tongariro and the Whanganui River. These include canoeing, white-water rafting, mountaineering, tramping and ski touring.

Places to Stay

Within the park itself, Whakapapa Village has an expensive hotel, a motel and a motor camp. Also in the park are two DOC camping grounds (near National Park and Ohakune) and the huts, accessible only by walking tracks. Towns near the park include National Park, Ohakune and Turangi (see these sections).

Camping & Cabins There are two basic DOC camping grounds in the park with cold water and pit toilets; the cost is low ($2) and you place your money in an honesty box. The *Mangahuia Camping Ground* is on SH47, between National Park and the SH48 turn-off heading to Whakapapa. The *Mangawhero Camping Ground* is near Ohakune, on Ohakune Mountain Rd.

The popular *Whakapapa Holiday Park* (☎ (07) 892 3897) is up the road from the Grand Chateau, opposite the visitor centre. It's in a pretty spot and couldn't be more conveniently located. Tent/powered sites cost $8/9 per person, cabins are $35 for two and tourist flats are $55 for two, with prices the same all year. From December to June there's also a special backpackers share rate of $14 in cabins.

Scattered around the park's tramping tracks are nine huts, with foot access only. The cost is $8 in huts, $4 for camping beside the huts, with back country hut tickets and annual hut passes both acceptable. However, in the summer season from the end of October to the end of May a Great Walks hut or camp-site pass is required for the four Tongariro Northern Circuit huts: Ketetahi, Mangatepopo, New Waihohonu and Oturere. The cost is $14 in huts and $6 for camping.

All park visitor centres have information on huts and can sell hut tickets or Great Walks passes.

Motels & Hotels At Whakapapa Village, the *Grand Chateau Hotel* (☎ (07) 892 3809) is

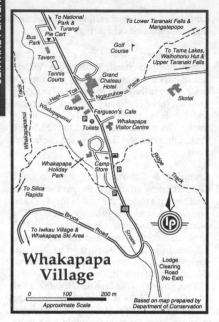

Whakapapa
Village

0   100   200 m
Approximate Scale

Based on map prepared by
Department of Conservation

cutlery), as well as a sauna, spa pool, gym, games room and restaurant.

Places to Eat

The *Whakapapa Camp Store* sells takeaway snacks and food for self-catering – as usual it's more expensive than elsewhere. During ski season, there's a takeaway food van (pie cart) at Whakapapa Village (burgers are about $5). The restaurant at the Top of the Bruce, where the lifts start, is for hungry skiers and sightseers over summer.

Ferguson's Cafe is reasonably priced for snacks, light meals and coffee, and its cakes are superb. The *Skotel* has a licensed restaurant and bar. The restaurant at the *Whakapapa Tavern* may be open only in winter.

Of course the fancy place to eat is at the *Grand Chateau Hotel*. Its Ruapehu Room is an elegant restaurant serving expensive à la carte meals, or the $35 Saturday night buffet or the $25 Sunday lunch buffet are both good value. Otherwise a food and drink bill for two will cost over $130. The downstairs family *Carvery* is less expensive.

Getting There & Away

Bus & Train Trains and InterCity buses stop at National Park village, the main gateway to Tongariro.

Alpine Scenic Tours (☎ (07) 386 8918) has an inexpensive shuttle departing from Turangi at 7.30 am and 3.30 pm – with an extra service at 11 am in summer – to Whakapapa Village, Mangatepopo car park (for the Tongariro Crossing), National Park and Ketetahi car park (end of the Tongariro Crossing) along the way. It goes up to the ski area at the Top of the Bruce by request; its services also continue north from Turangi to Taupo and Rotorua. Since seats are limited, book in advance to guarantee a spot.

From National Park village other shuttles run to Whakapapa, Mangatepopo and Ketetahi for the Tongariro Crossing (see the National Park section). Transport is also available from Ohakune (see that section).

Car & Motorcycle The park is encircled by roads. SH1 (at this point it's called the Desert

indeed a grand hotel. Apart from the Hermitage at Mt Cook, it is the best-known hotel in NZ. Built in 1929 in an opulent style, it has been well preserved and is priced accordingly. For most of the year, economy rooms are $118, standard rooms are $141 and premium rooms are $175. There are also more expensive suites and villas. In the ski season, standard rooms cost $262 on Friday and Saturday, $192 during the week, and various packages are offered. Discount packages are sometimes available.

Behind the Chateau is the *Skotel* (☎ (07) 892 3719) with both deluxe and budget accommodation. From the end of October to early July, hostel-style twin rooms are $40, standard rooms are $82 and deluxe rooms are $110. In the ski season, hostel rooms are $82 and other rooms are around 50% more. There are also self-contained chalets sleeping six people for $110 a double in summer ($230 in winter). There's a communal kitchen for the regular rooms (you provide crockery and

Road) passes down the eastern side of the park; SH4 passes down the western side; SH47 crosses the northern side; and SH49 crosses the southern side. The main road up into the park is SH48, which leads to Whakapapa Village, continuing further up the mountain to the Top of the Bruce and the Whakapapa Ski Area. Ohakune Mountain Rd leads up to the Turoa Ski Area from Ohakune in the south-west.

For the Tongariro Crossing, access is from the end of Mangatepopo Rd off SH47, and SH47A from the end of Ketetahi Rd off National Park Rd, which runs between SH1 and SH47. Theft from parked vehicles is a problem at both ends: don't leave valuables in your car.

NATIONAL PARK

At the gateway to Tongariro, this small settlement is at the junction of SH4 and SH47, 15km from Whakapapa Village. It caters to the ski season crowds, with plenty of accommodation but little else apart from great views of Ruapehu. In the quiet summer season it's a convenient base for the walks and attractions of the park. Several daily shuttles leave from here for both ends of the Tongariro Crossing and Whakapapa Village in summer, and the ski area in winter. It is also a base for other ventures, such as canoe trips on the Whanganui River.

A few kilometres south on SH4 at Horopito (pepper tree) is a monument to the Last Spike – the spike that marked the completion of the Main Trunk Railway Line between Auckland and Wellington in 1908.

Activities

Howard's Lodge, Pukenui Lodge and the Ski Haus hire out tramping boots and other gear for the Tongariro Crossing and other treks. The spa pools at Ski Haus and Pukenui Lodge can be hired by guests and non-guests.

Go For It Tours (☎ (07) 892 2705) at the Petticoat Junction building, which is also the train station, does guided off-road motor cycle tours and rents out mountain bikes for $12 per hour.

See Whanganui National Park in the

Wanganui & Manawatu chapter for details on canoe hire and operators on the Whanganui River.

Places to Stay

Prices increase dramatically in the ski season, when accommodation is tight and bookings are essential, especially on weekends.

Hostels The modern *Pukenui Lodge* (☎ 0800 785 368, (07) 892 2882) on Millar St specialises in DB&B (dinner, bed and breakfast) in winter; it charges $55 (children $45) in quad shared rooms or $60 (children $55) in twins and doubles. In summer a dorm bed is $17. The spacious lodge has an open fire, disabled facilities and a restaurant. It sells lift passes, organises transport and gives out free information.

The *Ski Haus* (☎ (07) 892 2854) on Carroll St has good amenities such as a spa pool, billiards table and a sunken fireplace in the large lounge. It has a house bar, a restaurant and a kitchen. Rooms are simple but comfortable. In summer a dorm bed costs $15, doubles and twins are $40 and you can camp for $8 per person. From June to the end of October, doubles start at $66/88 during the week/on weekends. It costs $7/12 for a continental/full breakfast.

Also on Carroll St, *Howard's Lodge* (☎ (07) 892 2827) is a good hostel with a spa pool, barbecue, ski hire and comfortable lounge and kitchen areas. You can do your own cooking year-round, and breakfasts ($10) are also available. In summer, a bed in the simple bunkhouse out the back costs $15 or a bed in the inside four-bed rooms costs from $17.50 (no bedding) to $22.50, while singles and doubles cost from $40 to $60. Winter rates are 50% higher.

Further down Carroll St, the *National Park Lodge* (☎ (07) 892 2993), an older-style ski lodge, has a large lounge area and comfortable rooms from $15 in shared rooms or from $60 for twins and doubles in the motel units. In winter, shared rooms are $25 per person and other rooms are 50% higher. The new *National Park Backpackers*

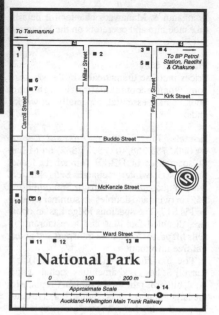

1	Eivin's Cafe
2	Pukenui Lodge
3	Schnapps Hotel & Restaurant
4	The Lodge Resort
5	National Park Backpackers
6	National Park Lodge
7	Fletcher's Ski Lodge & Motel
8	Howard's Lodge
9	National Park Store, Tearooms & Post Office
10	Ski Haus
11	National Park Hotel
12	Chalet on the Rocks
13	Chalet on the Rocks
14	Railway Station, Petticoat Junction & Go For It Tours

(☎ (07) 892 2870) on Findlay St has dorm beds for $12 and twins and doubles for $15. It has access to a full-sized climbing wall.

Escape the ski set at *Te Ruke Lodge* (☎ (07) 896 6231) at Owhango, 26km north of National Park. It's a cattle and sheep farm with a spa, horse riding and a chance to go mustering. A transfer from National Park is only $10 and the dorms from $12 to $15; the doubles for $36 are good value.

Chalets, Motels & Hotels The *National Park Hotel* (☎ (07) 892 2805) on Carroll St has bunk beds at $15 per person with linen included. Hotel rooms cost $20/45 for singles/doubles. Prices remain the same all year. There's a kitchen where guests can cook. Near the hotel and on Ward St, *Chalet on the Rocks* (☎ (07) 892 2938) has two self-contained three-bedroom houses with single and double rooms for $20 per person.

Fletcher's Ski Lodge & Motel (☎ (07) 892 2846) on Carroll St offers accommodation,

plus spa pools, billiards, volleyball, barbecue, fireplace, lounge etc. In summer, motel units are $50 or $60. In winter prices rise to $80 for studio units and $100 for motel units (more on weekends). In summer, guests can cook in the kitchen; in winter, you have to eat in the restaurant.

The *Mountain Heights Lodge* (☎ (07) 892 2833) on SH4, 2km south of National Park, has motel units for $50 in summer and $110 in winter. It also has a lodge which is only open during the ski season, with twin rooms and bunk rooms ($45 per person for dinner and B&B).

The *Discovery Motel & Caravan Park* (☎ (07) 892 2744) on SH47, between National Park and Whakapapa, has camp sites for $10. In summer, motel units and chalets are $76 and cabins sleeping two are $25. In winter, cabins are $40, and motel units and chalets range from $82 a double to $180 for six people. It has a spa pool, a restaurant and bar.

Places to Eat
All the places to stay in National Park provide either meals or kitchens for their guests, or both.

The bar and restaurant at the *Ski Haus* are open to guests and non-guests. Its restaurant is open year-round; several other places to stay have restaurants, such as *Schnapps* on the highway, but these are usually open only in winter. *Eivin's Cafe* on SH4, on the Carroll St corner, is good value with main meals from $14 to $20.

Getting There & Away

Bus Daily InterCity buses arrive at and depart from the National Park Store on Carroll St. Tickets are sold at the Ski Haus, Pukenui Lodge and Howard's Lodge. Journeys north to Auckland via Hamilton or south to Wellington via Palmerston North both take about five hours.

Alpine Scenic Tours (☎ (07) 386 8918) operates several daily shuttles making a round trip between Turangi and National Park, with stops at Whakapapa Village, Whakapapa Ski Area by request, the Mangatepopo and Ketetahi car parks (Tongariro Crossing), and on from Turangi to Taupo and Rotorua. For the track ends, make sure you arrange transport beforehand, as there are no phones at the trail heads.

Tongariro Track Transport (☎ (07) 892 3716), which trades as Whakapapa Shuttle in winter, operates a daily shuttle from behind the National Park BP petrol station to either end of Tongariro Crossing, stopping at Whakapapa Village on the way ($15 return). The Ski Haus, Pukenui Lodge and Howard's Lodge provide similar services for about $16.

Train Some trains running between Auckland and Wellington stop at National Park. *Interislander* ferry tickets and train tickets are sold not from the train station, but from the Ski Haus or Howard's Lodge, both on Carroll St.

OHAKUNE

Pretty Ohakune (population 1560) is the closest town to the Turoa Ski Area on the southern side of Ruapehu. It's very much a skiing town with lots of motels and even more restaurants. A lot of effort goes into catering for those snow-season big-spenders from mid-June to late October, and many places don't even bother opening up outside this season. Nevertheless, Ohakune tries to attract tourists year-round and many outdoor

activities can be organised in summer, including trips on the Whanganui River.

Ohakune's main commercial district is to the south of the town on the highway. The northern end of town by the train station (the 'junction') comes alive during the ski season but is quiet otherwise.

Check out the Big Carrot on SH49, paying homage to the town's primary product. Kids like the tank in the Clyde St park.

Information

The Ruapehu Visitor Centre (☎ (06) 385 8427), 54 Clyde St, has an excellent 3-D model of Tongariro National Park – great for tracing where you're going to walk. The staff make bookings for activities and accommodation, for InterCity buses and for the train. From June to October it's open from 8 am to 5 pm daily, but at other times on weekdays from 9 am to 4.30 pm and weekends from 10 am to 3.30 pm.

The Ohakune Ranger Station (☎ (06) 385 8578) is on Ohakune Mountain Rd, which leads to Turoa. It's open from 8 am to 4.30 pm on weekdays and daily in the ski season from 8 am to 2.30 pm. It offers maps, weather reports and advice about this side of the Tongariro National Park.

The Turoa Ski Area operates a phone line (☎ (07) 385 8456) with information on ski and road conditions.

Walking

Ohakune Mountain Rd travels 17km from the northern end of Ohakune to the Turoa Ski Area on Ruapehu. Several walking tracks lead off from this road into the Tongariro National Park. Stop by the ranger for maps and information about the tracks. Weather on the mountains is highly changeable, so come prepared and let someone know your intentions.

Two of the most delightful walks are the short 15-minute **Rimu Track** and the longer 1½-hour **Mangawhero Forest Walk**, both departing from opposite the Ohakune Ranger Station. They both pass through a lovely section of native forest; the Rimu

CENTRAL PLATEAU

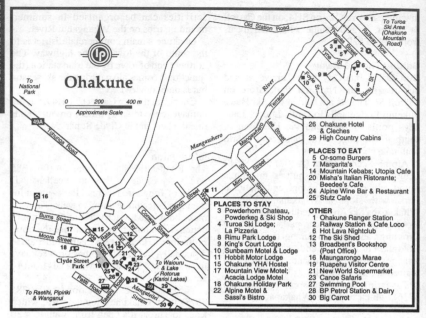

Ohakune

0   200   400 m
Approximate Scale

26 Ohakune Hotel
   & Cleches
29 High Country Cabins

PLACES TO EAT
5 Or-some Burgers
7 Margarita's
14 Mountain Kebabs; Utopia Cafe
20 Misha's Italian Ristorante;
   Beedee's Cafe
24 Alpine Wine Bar & Restaurant
25 Stutz Cafe

PLACES TO STAY
3 Powderhorn Chateau,
   Powderkeg & Ski Shop
4 Turoa Ski Lodge;
   La Pizzeria
8 Rimu Park Lodge
9 King's Court Lodge
10 Sunbeam Motel & Lodge
11 Hobbit Motor Lodge
15 Ohakune YHA Hostel
17 Mountain View Motel;
   Acacia Lodge Motel
18 Ohakune Holiday Park
22 Alpine Motel &
   Sassi's Bistro

OTHER
1 Ohakune Ranger Station
2 Railway Station & Cafe Loco
6 Hot Lava Nightclub
12 The Ski Shed
13 Broadbent's Bookshop
   (Post Office)
16 Maungarongo Marae
19 Ruapehu Visitor Centre
21 New World Supermarket
23 Canoe Safaris
27 Swimming Pool
28 BP Petrol Station & Dairy
30 Big Carrot

Track is marked with plaques pointing out various features of the forest.

Other popular tracks leading from Ohakune Mountain Rd include a 1¼-hour return walk to the **Waitonga Falls**, beginning 11km past the ranger station, and the five-hour return walk to **Lake Surprise**, beginning 15km past the ranger station. If you continue past the falls on Waitonga Falls track, you join the Round-the-Mountains Track (see the Tongariro National Park section). Other tracks taking off from Ohakune Mountain Rd include a 10-minute return walk to the **Mangawhero Falls** and a four to five-hour walk on the **Old Blyth Track**. You can get maps of these walks at the Ruapehu Visitor Centre.

There's no regularly scheduled transport up the mountain and traffic is light for hitching. Snowliner Shuttle (☎ (06) 385 8573) can be chartered to the tracks, but tends to be expensive. Mountain Transport (☎ (06) 385 9045) runs to the mountain for $5/10 one

way/return (at least six times each morning in winter). Or you could go to the top with a bicycle (see Cycling) and do some tramping on your way down.

Cycling

The Powderhorn Ski Shop (☎ (06) 385 8888) hires out mountain bikes at $10 per hour, $25 for half a day or $35 per day. A cheaper and highly enjoyable way to do some cycling in Ohakune is to go with Ride the Mountain (☎ (06) 385 8257). In summer it will take you in a van to the ski area at the top of Ohakune Mountain Rd and set you loose with a bicycle, helmet and all the other gear you need ($30).

Bicycles are not allowed on any trails in the national park.

Other Activities

Ask at the visitor centre about activities around Ohakune – horse trekking, whitewater rafting, fishing, canoeing, kayaking and jet-boat trips on the nearby Whanganui River, golf and more. You can swim in the Powderkeg restaurant-bar's hot pool.

Ohakune is a base to organise canoeing trips on the Whanganui River. Two local operators are Canoe Safaris (☎ (06) 385 9237), with an office on Miro St, and Yeti Tours (☎ (06) 385 8197). Raetihi Motor Camp (☎ (06) 385 4176) in Raetihi, 11km west of Ohakune, also has canoeing equipment and can arrange transport. See the Whanganui National Park section in the Wanganui & Manawatu chapter for more details.

Places to Stay

Finding a place to stay is no problem in summer, but during the ski season you should definitely book ahead. More places can be found in Raetihi, 11km west.

Camping & Cabins The *Ohakune Holiday Park* (☎ (06) 385 8561) at 5 Moore St is a pleasant camp beside a gurgling stream, with plenty of trees and green areas and a comfortable TV lounge-dining room. Tent/powered sites are $14/16 for two, while backpackers cabins or on-site vans are $16 per person ($32 each in the ski season).

The *Raetihi Motor Camp* (☎ (06) 385 4176) in Raetihi, 11km west of Ohakune, is a friendly place with tent and powered sites, on-site vans and cabins. It offers free glow-worm tours, and is also a popular and inexpensive place to hire canoes or kayaks for the Whanganui River.

The *Mangawhero Camp Site* is a simple DOC camp site ($4, children $2) on Ohakune Mountain Rd. Facilities include cold water and pit toilets.

Hostels The *Ohakune YHA Hostel* (☎ /fax (06) 385 8724) is on Clyde St, near the post office and visitor centre. It's a good hostel with twin, triple and bunk rooms; you have your own room key. During the ski season it is heavily booked. It charges $16 in dorms or $36 in twin rooms (a dorm bed in summer is $13).

Nearby, the *Alpine Motel* (see Lodges, Motels & Hotels) has a separate backpackers in the rear. It provides excellent accommodation in new, spotless rooms for $15 per person. In the ski season, rates are $19 during the week or $23 on weekends.

At the north end of town, the *Rimu Park Lodge* (☎ (06) 385 9023), 27 Rimu St, is a comfortable, restored 1914 villa in a secluded spot just a two-minute walk from the railway station, restaurants and nightlife. It's quiet and restful in summer and very popular with skiers in winter. The cost is $15 in dorm rooms, $34 in double rooms or $40 in cabins during summer. In the ski season it's a B&B, charging $30 per person in shared rooms or cabins. Chalets and units next to the house cost from $85 to $220 (sleeps 10) in winter. The quaint restored railway carriage is $95 in winter (less in summer).

At the old, Tudor-style *King's Court Lodge* (☎ (06) 385 8648) on Rimu St rooms with shared facilities are $30 per person ($40 with breakfast).

Lodges, Motels & Hotels At the southern end of town, the *Ohakune Hotel* (☎ (06) 385 8268) at 72 Clyde St has singles/doubles for $25/40; doubles with private facilities are from $60. Close by, the *Alpine Motel* (☎ (06) 385 8758) at 7 Miro St is a popular place, with studio units, family units, chalets (and a backpackers in the rear), plus a spa pool and a popular restaurant-bar. Double units are $70, or $110 in winter. Chalets sleeping up to four people are $75 a double and $10 for each extra person in summer, or $165 for four in winter.

Also at the southern end of town, the *Mountain View Motel* (☎ (06) 385 8675) at 2 Moore St has units from $50 in summer and $115 in the ski season. There is also a 14-bed bunkhouse for $12 per person ($16 in winter); bring your own sleeping bag and kitchen utensils. Next door, at 4 Moore St, the *Acacia Lodge Motel* (☎ (06) 385 8729) has kitchen units from $65 (add $20 midweek in winter and $40 on weekends).

Between the southern and northern ends of town, the *Hobbit Motor Lodge* (☎ (06) 385 8248) on the corner of Goldfinch and

CENTRAL PLATEAU

Wye Sts has single/double motel units for $75/85 in summer and $105/165 during the ski season. In summer, bunk beds are $17 (with own sleeping bag) or $20 (linen provided); in the ski season they're from $30 with linen provided.

The *Sunbeam Motel & Lodge* (☎ (06) 385 8470) at 178 Mangawhero Terrace has backpackers beds at $12 per person, lodge rooms at $40 a double or $60 with private facilities, studio units at $60 and motel units at $65. In winter, rooms and units range from $75 to $165.

The *Turoa Ski Lodge* (☎ (06) 385 8274) at 10 Thames St is at the 'junction', in the thick of the winter nightlife. It's open only during the ski season, with doubles for $90 and bunks for $25 per person.

Ohakune has a number of other lodges that come to life in the ski season. Top of the heap is the *Powderhorn Chateau* (☎ (06) 385 8888), the place to be for après ski, with new chalet rooms for $170 a double.

Four kilometres east of town on SH49 at Rangataua, the *Ruapehu Homestead* (☎ (06) 385 8799) has a variety of fancy rooms and a licensed restaurant; it also organises activities through Ruapehu Outback Adventures. It has lodge rooms at $35/50 per person in summer/winter, motel units at $85/135 a double and the bunk room is $20 per person year-round.

Places to Eat

The 'junction' is active during the winter with the après ski crowd, but little is open in summer. Places on the south side of town are open year-round.

On the south side, the pleasant *Stutz Cafe* on Clyde St is open daily from breakfast until dinner, with European and Chinese food, pizza and takeaways. Nearby, *Cleches* at the Ohakune Hotel on the Raetihi Rd corner is also open for long hours and has a better class of pub food. On the opposite corner, the *Alpine Wine Bar & Restaurant* is open for wining and dining every evening. A little further along is *Beedee's Cafe* for pre-ski breakfasts and, next door, *Misha's Italian Ristorante*, has small/large pizzas for $11/19

and vegetarian spaghetti for $11. Even further west on Clyde St is *Mountain Kebabs* with the chicken variety for $6.50, and the slightly hippie *Utopia Cafe*, which serves focaccia, vegetarian dishes (such as tofu Reubens for $12) and other innovative delights.

On Miro St, *Sassi's Bistro* at the Alpine Motel is also open for dinner daily; it's a pleasant place with a varied, changing menu with something to suit all budgets.

There are many popular restaurants along Thames St, including *La Pizzeria*, which cooks fairly reasonable pizzas. Next door is the appropriately named *Or-Some Burgers* for a late-night hunger buster (about $6). In winter there's a licensed restaurant at the *Turoa Ski Lodge* and, just around the corner, *Margarita's* has its usual brand of Tex-Mex food and lots of carousing patrons.

The most popular place on Thames St is the *Powderkeg* on the corner of Thames St and Mangawhero Terrace. Especially famed for its bar, a favourite après-ski hang-out, it's also known for its restaurant with good food and its indoor heated pool. It's hard to get in the door at times.

Entertainment

Ohakune is known as the good-fun nightlife place during the ski season; the rest of the year it's quiet. The *Hot Lava* nightclub on Thames St is a popular spot, open every night during the ski season, with live music on weekends and disco music on other nights (in winter it attracts some big-name bands).

Other places with live music in the ski season include the always popular *Powderkeg*, *Margarita's* and the *Turoa Ski Lodge* at the 'junction', and the *Ohakune Hotel* on Clyde St in the southern part of town.

Getting There & Away

InterCity buses serve Ohakune daily except Saturday, arriving at and departing from the Ruapehu Visitor Centre, which sells the tickets.

The Auckland-Wellington trains stop at Ohakune. Buy tickets at the Ruapehu Visitor Centre, not at the station.

Getting Around

In winter several companies have transport between Ohakune and the Turoa Ski Area, charging from $15 to $18 for round-trip door-to-door transport from wherever you're staying. The Ruapehu Mountain Tours bus also operates from the corner of Clyde and Goldfinch Sts for $10 return.

Snowliner Shuttle (☎ (06) 385 8573) offers a variety of transport around the area. In winter, the cost is $15 return to Turoa, $65 to the Chateau for three people and $85 (also for three) to Top of the Bruce.

LAKE ROTOKURA

Lake Rotokura is about 11km south of Ohakune on SH49, at Karioi in the Karioi Forest, about 1km from the Karioi turn-off. It's called Lake Rotokura on the map and the sign but it's actually two lakes not one – the locals call them the Karioi Lakes. Karioi means 'places to linger' and they couldn't be more aptly named. They are two little jewels,

one above the other, great for picnicking, fishing and relaxing.

WAIOURU

At the junction of SH1 and SH49, 27km east of Ohakune, Waiouru is primarily an army base. In a large grey concrete building with tanks out front, the **QEII Army Memorial Museum** tells the history of the NZ Army in times of war and peace, with an extensive collection of artefacts from early colonial times to the present and a 23-minute audio-visual. It's open from 9 am to 4.30 pm daily ($7, children $4).

SH1 from Waiouru to Turangi is known as the **Desert Road** and is often closed in winter because of snow, but can also close at other times of the year. It runs through the Rangipo Desert east of Ruapehu. It's not a true desert, but was named because of its desert-like appearance, caused by a cold, exposed and windswept location.

Wanganui & Manawatu

The Wanganui region is dominated by the Whanganui River, historically one of the most important rivers in New Zealand. Once the sole means of access to the region, it is the only way to reach the isolated interior of the Whanganui National Park. Apart from the national park, the main places of interest are Wanganui city and Palmerston North in the neighbouring Manawatu district.

The spelling difference between Whanganui and Wanganui is mostly a political issue. It was originally spelt Wanganui, because the Maori tribes of the river region do not pronounce 'wh' as an 'f', contrary to most Maori dialects. However, the sound is aspirated and strictly speaking should be 'Wh'. The 'h' has been officially restored to the name of the river and national park, but not to the city or the region as a whole. The difference in spellings is in many ways a reflection of the split in attitudes over Maori issues, which came to a head at Moutoa Gardens in Wanganui (see that section). Interestingly, the Pakeha-dominated town and region retain the old spelling, while the river area, very much Maori territory, takes the new spelling.

Wanganui

The main artery of the Wanganui district is the Whanganui River and the main highlight of the district is the Whanganui National Park, based around the river and the parallel River Road. The estuary, over 30km long, is the area known to the early Maori as Whanganui, meaning 'great estuary' or 'great wait'.

WHANGANUI NATIONAL PARK

Whanganui National Park's main attraction is the Whanganui River, which winds its way 329km from its source on the flanks of Mt Tongariro in the central North Island to the Tasman Sea at the city of Wanganui. The

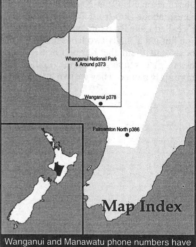

Whanganui National Park & Around p373

Wanganui p378

Palmerston North p386

Map Index

Wanganui and Manawatu phone numbers have either the ☎ 06 or ☎ 07 area code

river is not the longest in the country – that honour goes to the Waikato River – but the fact that it is the longest *navigable* river in the country has been shaping its destiny for centuries. Historically a major route for travel between the sea and the interior of the North Island, first by the Maori and then by the Pakeha, the route was eventually superseded by rail and road. But recently recreational canoe, kayak and jet-boat enthusiasts

368

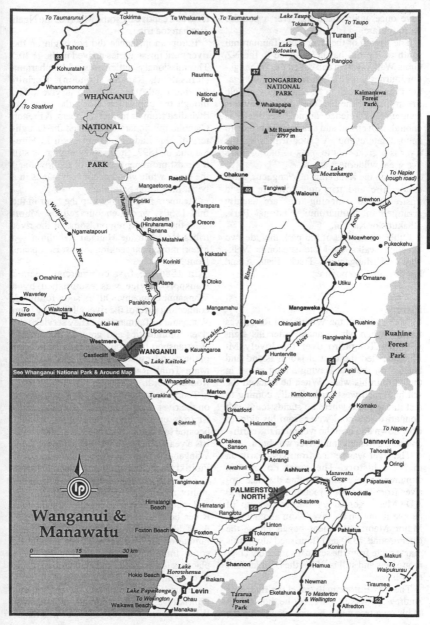

See Whanganui National Park & Around Map

Wanganui &
Manawatu

0   15   30 km

have once again made the river a popular thoroughfare.

The stretch of the river from Taumarunui south to Pipiriki has been added to the NZ Great Walks system and called the 'Whanganui Journey'. A Grade II river, the Whanganui is easy enough to be enjoyed by people of any age, whether they have previous canoeing experience or not, yet there is enough movement and small-sized rapids to keep it interesting. A canoe trip down the river is a great way to relax in one of NZ's last great wilderness areas.

Though the river ends at Wanganui, most canoe hire and trip operators are based upstream and canoeing trips are usually arranged in Taumarunui, National Park, Ohakune or Raetihi.

Other attractions of the park include two excellent walks, the Matemateaonga Walkway and Mangapurua Track. Fishing and hunting are also popular.

History

In Maori legend, the Whanganui River was formed when Mt Taranaki, after his fight with Mt Tongariro over the lovely Mt Pihanga, fled the central North Island and headed for the sea, leaving a long gouge in the earth in his wake. When he reached the sea he turned westwards, finally coming to rest in the place where he stands today. Mt Tongariro sent cool water from his side, to flow down and heal the wound in the earth – and so the Whanganui River was born.

The river was settled from very early on in NZ's history. The great Polynesian explorer Kupe explored some distance upriver from the river's mouth in around 900 AD. Maori genealogy traces a group of people living on the river from about 1100. Major Maori settlement began along the river around 1350 and flourished along this major route from the sea to the interior. Their motto was and still is: 'I am the river and the river is me.'

The first European to travel the river was Andrew Powers in 1831, but he didn't do it of his own free will – he was brought up the

river as a captive by some Maori of the Ngati Tuwharetoa tribe.

European influence did not begin on the river until missionaries arrived in the 1840s. The missionary settlements of Hiruharama (Jerusalem), Ranana (London), Koriniti (Corinth) and Atene (Athens) survive today, though the population along the river has dwindled from its former numbers. A French Catholic missionary established the Daughters of Our Lady of Compassion in Hiruharama in 1892. St Joseph's church is still the most prominent feature of the town and the large, white wooden convent stands in a beautiful garden beside it.

Steamers first voyaged up the river in the mid-1860s, when, encouraged by Maori from the Taranaki region, some of the river tribes joined in the Hauhau Rebellion – a Maori movement seeking to oust Europeans from NZ.

In 1886 the first commercial steamer transport service was established by a Wanganui company. Others soon followed, connecting parts of the river all the way from Wanganui to Taumarunui. They serviced the river communities and grew in importance as a transport link from the sea to the interior of the island, especially after 1903, when the Main Trunk Railway reached Taumarunui from the north.

Tourism was another major development on the river. Internationally advertised tourist trips on the 'the Rhine of Maoriland' became so popular that by 1905 12,000 tourists a year were making the trip upriver from Wanganui or downriver from Taumarunui to Pipiriki House (which burnt down in 1959).

The engineering feats and skippering ability required to operate the steamboats and paddle steamers on the Whanganui River became legendary, spawning something like the lore that Mark Twain made famous on the Mississippi River. It required some imaginative engineering in some places, such as cables and channelling of the river's currents.

Around 1918, land along the river above Pipiriki was given as grants to returning WWI soldiers. This rugged area was a major challenge to clear – some families struggled for years to make a go of their farms, but by the early 1940s only a few remained.

One of the most famous features of the river, the Bridge to Nowhere, was built in 1936 as part of a road from Raetihi to the river. It stands as mute testimony to the failed efforts to settle the region. The track from the Mangapurua Landing to the bridge, though now only a walking track, used to be a 4.5m-wide roadway leading down to the riverboat landing.

The Auckland-Wellington Main Trunk Railway line and improved roads gradually superseded the riverboats, the last of which made its final commercial voyage in 1959. Today only one vessel of the old fleet still operates on the river: the *Otunui* makes river cruises on the lower reaches of the river from Wanganui. Another of the old fleet, the MV *Ongarue*, is on display at Pipiriki, and the *Waimarie* has been raised and is undergoing restoration in Wanganui. The MV *Waireka* now operates tourist cruises at Huka Falls near Taupo.

Information

Maps, brochures and information about the park are available at the DOC offices in Wanganui (☎ (06) 345 2402), Taumarunui (☎ (07) 895 8201) and Pipiriki (☎ (06) 385 4631). Information centres in the area – at Taumarunui, Ohakune and Wanganui – also have information on the park.

Good books about the river include the *Guide to the Whanganui River* by the NZ Canoeing Association (good for canoe trips), and *The Wanganui River – a scenic, historic and wilderness experience* published by Land Information NZ. *In and Around Whanganui National Park*, a DOC booklet, is good if you want to do some walking or tramping.

Whanganui River

The native bush is thick podocarp-broadleaf forest, with many types of trees and ferns. Occasionally you will see poplar and other introduced trees along the river, evidence of

You may be startled by the screeching alarm call of the pukeko, a bird commonly found in the rushes of Whanganui River

where people planted them in settlements that have long since vanished.

There are also traces of former Maori settlement along the river in various places, with *pa* (fortified village) sites, old *kainga* (village) sites, and the unusual Hauhau *niu* poles of war and peace at Maraekowhai, at the confluence of the Whanganui and Ohura rivers. The Ratakura, Reinga Kokiri and Te Rerehapa falls, all near Maraekowhai on the Ohura River, were popular places for Maori to come to catch small 'tuna riki' eels (river, or freshwater, eel found in the Whanganui). Several of the landings marked along the Whanganui River's banks were once riverboat landings.

Canoeing & Kayaking The most popular section of the river for canoeing and kayaking is between Taumarunui and Pipiriki. Entry to the river is at Taumarunui (Cherry Grove), Ohinepane and Whakahoro (Wades Landing).

Taumarunui to Pipiriki is a five-day/four-night trip. Ohinepane to Pipiriki is a four-day/three-night trip and Whakahoro to Pipiriki is a three-day/two-night trip. Taumarunui to Whakahoro is a popular overnight

River Safety & Etiquette

At the height of summer, numerous canoes, kayaks and jet-boats ply the Whanganui River. There are a few simple 'rules of the road'. When an oncoming craft is approaching, keep to the right, unless you are already so far to the left that you'd have to cross in the path of the oncoming craft. The craft heading downriver has the right-of-way.

If you're in a canoe or kayak and a jet-boat is approaching from either direction, you should move to the true right of the river if possible.

When beaching a canoe or kayak, pull it well clear of the water and secure it tightly. Water levels can rise quickly.

Don't drink the river water unless it's boiled. Clean drinking (rain) water is available at huts and camping grounds. ■

trip, especially for weekenders, or you can do a one-day trip from Taumarunui to Ohinepane or Ohinepane to Whakahoro. From Whakahoro to Pipiriki, 88km downstream, there's no road access so you're committed to the river for a few days. Most canoeists stop in Pipiriki.

The season for canoe trips is usually from around September to Easter. Up to 5000 people make this trip each year, the majority of them doing it over the summer holidays from Christmas to the end of January. During winter the river is almost deserted, with good reason. The cold weather and shorter days deter most people, and the winter currents are swifter.

Canoe and kayak operators will provide you with everything you need for the journey, including life jackets and waterproof drums – essential if you capsize in the rapids. Prices range from about $20 per day for single-person kayaks to $35 per day for two-person Canadian canoes (transport not included). Transport in and out can be just as costly as the canoes themselves; the cost may be around $45 per person, depending where you're starting out from, sometimes much higher. Some operators include the transport cost when they hire out the canoes – ask

about transport in and out and figure this amount into the overall cost.

Another option is a fully guided canoe or kayak trip – typical prices are around $250 per person for a two-day guided trip and $550-plus per person for a five-day trip.

Operators that offer independent hiring and/or guided trips include:

Backcountry Lifestyle, Wanganui (☎ (06) 342 8116).
Transfers to the Flying Fox ($5) and upriver jet-boat trips from $25. Also three-day package with overnight at Koriniti Marae, canoe downriver, Ahu Ahu Valley walk and farmstay, Bushy Park and return to Wanganui ($295).
Canoe Safaris, 5 Miro St, Ohakune
(☎ (06) 385 9237). Guided trips only.
Hikoi-Wairua Tours, Pipiriki (☎ (06) 342 8084).
One-day tours around Pipiriki and Hiruharama. Also offers a $69 package which includes mail bus transport to Flying Fox in Koriniti, canoe trip and return by mail bus to Wanganui.
Kellys Motel, Taumarunui (☎ (07) 895 8175).
Hire only.
Pioneer Jet-Boat Tours, Taumarunui
(☎ (07) 895 8074). Hire only.
Plateau Outdoor Adventure Guides, Raurimu
(☎ (07) 892 2740). Guided trips and hire.
Raetihi Motor Camp, Raetihi (☎ (06) 385 4176).
Hire only.
Rivercity Tours, Wanganui (☎ (06) 344 2554).
Guided trips and hire.
Wades Landing Outdoors, Owhango
(☎ (07) 895 5995, mobile 025 797 238).
Guided trips, hire and jet-boat trips.
Whanganui River Experiences, Wanganui
(☎ (06) 345 7933). Guided trips and hire.
Yeti Tours, Ohakune (☎ (06) 385 8197).
Guided trips and hire.

Jet-Boat Trips Jet-boat trips give you a chance to see parts of the river in just a few hours that would take you days to cover in a canoe or kayak. These depart from Pipiriki, Taumarunui and Whakahoro. All operators provide transport to the river ends of the Matemateaonga Walkway and the Mangapurua Track.

Departing from Pipiriki, you can take a number of trips including a four-hour return trip to the Bridge to Nowhere for $60 (children half-price) with Bridge to Nowhere Jet Boat Tours (☎ (06) 385 4128).

From Taumarunui you can do anything

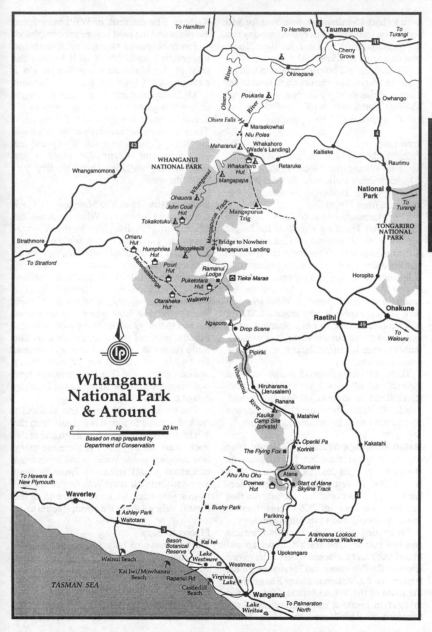

Whanganui
National Park
& Around

0   10   20 km

Based on map prepared by
Department of Conservation

from a short 15-minute jet-boat tour for $15 per person (minimum three) to a two-day run to Wanganui with Pioneer Jet-Boat Tours (see Canoeing & Kayaking).

Whakahoro is a bit off the beaten track – it's a long drive down an unsealed road to get there, whichever way you come – but Wades Landing Outdoors (☎ (07) 894 5995 has one-hour trips for $30 per person.

Tramping

Probably the most famous and best travelled track in Whanganui National Park is the 40-minute bush walk from the Mangapurua Landing to the Bridge to Nowhere, 30km upstream from Pipiriki.

The Matemateaonga Walkway and the Mangapurua Track are excellent for longer tramps. Both are one-way tracks beginning (or ending) at remote spots on the river, so you must arrange for jet-boat transport to or from these ends. Any jet-boat operator on the river will do this, but if they have to make a special trip from Pipiriki or Whakahoro to pick you up expect to pay around $200 for four people. If you arrive at Ramanui Lodge, and jet-boats are already there, it is substantially cheaper for the transfer to the Mangapurua trail head.

There are several good walks between Pipiriki and Wanganui; see the Whanganui River Road & Pipiriki section for details. The DOC offices in Wanganui, Pipiriki and Taumarunui have information and maps.

Matemateaonga Walkway Taking four days to complete, the 42km Matemateaonga Walkway has been described as one of NZ's best walks. Nevertheless it is not widely known and does not attract the crowds that can form on some of NZ's more famous tracks, probably due to its remoteness.

Penetrating deep into bush, wilderness and hill country, the track follows an old Maori track and a disused settlers' dray road between the Wanganui and Taranaki regions. It traverses the Matemateaonga Range along the route of the Whakaihuwaka Rd, started in 1911 to create a more direct link from Stratford to Raetihi and the Main Trunk

Railway. The outbreak of WWI interrupted the plans and the road was never completed.

The track passes through thick bush and regenerating bush. Much of it follows the crest of the Matemateaonga Range. On a clear day, a 1½ hour side trip to the summit of Mt Humphries affords a panoramic view of the Wanganui region all the way to Mt Taranaki and the volcanoes of Tongariro. There's a steep section between the Whanganui River (75m above sea level) and the Puketotara Hut (427m), but much of the track is easy walking. There are five huts along the way.

Mangapurua Track The Mangapurua Track is a 40km track between Whakahoro and the Mangapurua Landing, both on the Whanganui River. The track runs along the Mangapurua and Kaiwhakauka streams, both tributaries of the Whanganui River, passing through the valleys of the same names. Between these valleys a side track leads to the Mangapurua Trig, at 663m the highest point in the area, from where you can see all the way to the volcanoes of the Tongariro and Egmont national parks on a clear day. The route passes through land that was cleared for farming by settlers earlier this century and later abandoned. The Bridge to Nowhere is 40 minutes from the Mangapurua Landing end of the track.

The track takes 20 hours and is usually walked in three to four days. Apart from the Whakahoro Hut at the Whakahoro end of the track, there are no huts, but there are many fine camping spots. Water is available from numerous small streams. There is road access to the track at the Whakahoro end and from a side track leading to the end of the Ruatiti Valley-Ohura Rd (from Raetihi).

Places to Stay

The park has nine huts, a lodge and numerous camping grounds. Along the upper section of the river between Whakahoro and Pipiriki are three Category Two huts classified as Great Walk Huts: the Whakahoro Hut at Whakahoro, the John Coull Hut and the Tieke Hut. Tieke has been revived as a marae; you can stay here, but full marae protocol must be observed (see the boxed text entitled Marae Etiquette in the Facts about the Country chapter).

Alternatively, on the other side of the river near the Tieke Hut, the *Ramanui Lodge* (☎ (06) 385 4128) has accommodation for $57 per person, meals included; camping costs $4 per person. It's quite remote, 21km upriver from Pipiriki, near the Matemateaonga Walkway; the only way to get there is by river or by tramping. The lodge is run by Bridge to Nowhere Jet Boat Tours in Pipiriki, so it can arrange jet-boat transfers to/from Pipiriki and to the Mangapurua Track.

Along the Matemateaonga Walkway are five huts, but only two of them – the Puketotara and Pouri huts – are good Category Two huts. The others are simpler, with only two bunks. On the lower part of the river, Downes Hut is on the west bank, opposite Atene.

During the summer season from 1 October to 30 April, a Great Walks hut and camping pass is required for boat trips on the river involving overnight stays in the park between Taumarunui and Pipiriki; the rule applies only to this stretch of the river. The pass is valid for six nights and seven days and allows you to stay overnight in the huts, in camp sites beside the huts or in other designated camp sites along the river.

The Great Walks pass costs $25 if purchased in advance (otherwise $35). Children aged 11 and older are half-price (under 11 free). Jet-boaters who only spend one night in the park pay $8 (children $4). Passes are available at all DOC offices and information centres in the region, and some canoe operators also sell them. During this time, hut wardens are on duty and the river is patrolled by conservation officers, so bring your pass.

Great Walks passes are not required in the off-season from 1 May to 30 September. During this time, the cost is $8 in huts, $4 for camping beside the huts, and free for camping at designated river camp sites. Annual hut passes are acceptable during this time.

Getting There & Away

If you're going on a canoe or kayak trip, the canoe company will make some arrangement for transport to get you and the canoe to and from the river.

Camp 'n Canoe (☎ (06) 764 6737) in Kaponga, Taranaki, has guided trips and transport in and out to both ends of the Matemateaonga Walkway. You can check with the DOC and information centres at Stratford in Taranaki, and in the park, to see if anyone else is also offering this service.

There's road access to the river at Taumarunui, Ohinepane and Whakahoro. Whakahoro is a long drive in through a remote area, along a road that is unsealed for much of its distance; roads leading to Whakahoro take off from Owhango or Raurimu, both on SH4. There isn't any further road access to the river until you reach Pipiriki. From Pipiriki, the Whanganui River Road heads south for 79km to Wanganui and east for 28km to Raetihi.

The only public transport to any part of the river is at Taumarunui, served by buses and trains, and at Pipiriki, where the mail bus makes a round trip from Wanganui on weekdays. See the Wanganui section in this chapter and the Taumarunui section in the Central West chapter for details.

WHANGANUI RIVER ROAD & PIPIRIKI

The Whanganui River Road, running along the Whanganui River most of the way from Wanganui to Pipiriki, is a scenic and historic area worth making the detour to see. The Road meets SH4, the highway from Wanganui to the centre of the North Island, 14km north of Wanganui and again at Raetihi, 91km north of Wanganui.

It takes about 1½ to two hours to drive the 79km between Wanganui and Pipiriki – that's not counting stops. If you come on the mail-run bus from Wanganui to Pipiriki the trip will take most of the day, but you'll have the benefit of lots of social and historical commentary. The full circle from Wanganui to Pipiriki to Raetihi and back down SH4 through the scenic Paraparas and the Mangawhero River Gorge to Wanganui takes about four hours. The Whanganui River Road is also becoming increasingly popular with cyclists as an alternative route to SH4.

Information

Pick up a copy of the *River Road Scenic and Historic Drive* pamphlet, available at the DOC offices and information centres in Wanganui and Pipiriki. It gives a map and commentary about various interesting spots along the road. The Pipiriki DOC office (☎ (06) 385 4631) is open on weekdays from 8 am to 5 pm, but is not always staffed.

A *Motorist's Guide to the Wanganui River Road* by Judith Crawley is a 40-page booklet for $4.95 with much more detail.

Things to See

The main attraction of the drive is the scenery and lovely views of the Whanganui River. A few notable sights include the Maori villages of **Atene**, **Koriniti**, **Ranana** and **Hiruharama** (you can visit Hiruharama's historic Catholic church and the historic flour mill at Ranana); the Operiki Pa and other pa sites; the Aramoana hill from where there's a panoramic view; and Pipiriki.

Pipiriki is beside the river at the north end of the Whanganui River Road, 79km from Wanganui and 28km from Raetihi. This is the ending point for canoe trips coming down the Whanganui River, and for jet-boat rides (see the earlier Whanganui National Park section).

The **Colonial House** in Pipiriki is a historic house now converted to a museum with many interesting exhibits on the history of Pipiriki and the river. If it's locked, ask at the DOC office about entry.

Beside the Colonial House, some old steps and foundations are all that remain to mark the site of the old **Pipiriki House** hotel, a glamorous hotel once popular with tourists.

Pipiriki was once a bustling place served by river steamers and paddleboats. An interesting historic relic at Pipiriki is the **MV Ongarue**, a 20m, 65-passenger riverboat that was once one of the A Hatrick & Co riverboat fleet. Built by Yarrow & Co in

London in 1903 and shipped in sections to Wanganui where it was assembled, the riverboat plied the river from 1903 to 1959, when the Pipiriki House burned down and the riverboat fleet ceased operating. The vessel was restored in 1983 and is now on display on land, about 50m from the turn-off to the DOC office.

Walking

The Wanganui Information Centre and DOC office have brochures on a couple of good walks starting from the Whanganui River Road. Or ask for the DOC booklet *Walks In and Around Whanganui National Park*, with details on these and other walks along the river.

The **Aramoana Walkway** begins across the road a few metres south of the Aramoana Lookout, near the southern end of the Whanganui River Road, 3km north of its junction with SH4. A 7km, 2½-hour loop track, the walkway passes through farmland and forest to higher ground from where there's a panoramic view of the river area and all the way to Mt Ruapehu to the north, Mt Taranaki to the west and Kapiti Island to the south. Other features include fossilised cockle shell beds, evidence that this land – now 160m high – was once at the bottom of the sea. Take drinking water, warm clothing and be prepared for mud after wet weather. (It's closed during the lambing season in spring.)

The **Atene Skyline Track** begins at Atene, on the Whanganui River Road about 22km north of where it meets with the SH4. The 18km track takes six to eight hours and features native forest, sandstone bluffs and the 523m Taumata Trig, commanding broad views. The track ends back on river road, 2km downstream from where it began.

Places to Stay

At Pipiriki there's a DOC camping ground with toilets and cold water. Another basic DOC camping ground is the *Otumaire Camp Site* between Atene and Koriniti. Beside the river at Ranana, the *Kauika Camp Site* (☎ (06) 342 8133) has hot showers, a kitchen and a laundry. Tent sites are $6 for two and powered sites are $10.

There are various other places to stay along the Whanganui River Road. The *Flying Fox* (☎ (06) 342 8160) is a superb little getaway on the right bank of the river across from Koriniti; access is by flying fox, hence the name (a cableway crossing is $2.50). You can sleep in a loft above the Brewhouse ($20 per person; dinner and B&B is $50 per person) or camp ($8). The *Koriniti Marae*, on the left bank, also takes visitors for $13 per person, plus *koha* (a donation) – see the boxed text entitled Marae Etiquette in the Facts about the Country chapter. A few kilometres north is friendly *Operiki Farmstay* (☎ (06) 342 8159); dinner and B&B is $55 (children $25) – campervans are $15 and dinner is $20.

The *Ahu Ahu Ohu* (☎ (06) 345 5711) is a remote farming community about 4km up the Ahu Ahu Stream from where it meets the Whanganui River at the Te Tuhi Landing, between Atene and Koriniti on the other side of the river. This alternative community welcomes campers, WWOOFers and back-packers. Contact them before you arrive to be picked up at the Te Tuhi Landing.

The nuns at the Catholic church in Hiruharama take in travellers. A large room has been divided by curtains into cubicles; the cost is around $10.

Getting There & Away

One of the most convenient and congenial ways of travelling the Whanganui River Road is with the mail-run bus, which goes from Wanganui to Pipiriki on weekdays and takes passengers along with the mail for an interesting tour. See the Wanganui section.

If travelling the road by car, petrol is available at Raetihi (north) and at Upokongaro and Wanganui (south), but not in-between. This route is also becoming a favourite with cyclists, despite the steep hills.

WANGANUI

Midway between Wellington and New Plymouth, Wanganui is an attractive city on the banks of the Whanganui River. The town has many fine old buildings and the centre has been rejuvenated by the restoration of historic buildings on the main street, Victoria Ave, down by the river. The block from Taupo Quay and Ridgway St has many restored reminders of Wanganui's days as a prominent port.

History

Kupe, the great Polynesian explorer, is believed to have travelled up the Whanganui River for about 20km around 900 AD. There were Maori living in the area around 1100, and they fully established themselves soon after the great Polynesian migration from Hawaiki around 1350. By the time the first European settlers came to the coast around the late 1830s there were numerous Maori settlements scattered up and down the river.

European settlement at Wanganui was hastened along when the New Zealand Company was unable to keep up with the supply and demand for land around Welling-ton. In 1840 many Wellington settlers moved to Wanganui and founded a permanent set-tlement there; the deed was signed on the site now known as Moutoa Gardens. Initially called Petre after one of the directors of the New Zealand Company, the town's name was changed to Wanganui in 1844 (the name Kupe had given the river).

When the Maori understood that the gifts the Pakeha had given them were in exchange for the permanent acquisition of their land, seven years of bitter opposition followed. The Pakeha brought in thousands of troops to occupy Queen's Park, and the Rutland Stockade dominated the hill. Ultimately, the struggle was settled by arbitration and, when the Maori Wars were waged with the Tara-naki tribes, the Wanganui Maori assisted the Pakeha. The town today is still very much a centre for re-emergent Maori consciousness.

Information

The Wanganui Information Centre (☎ /fax (06) 345 3286) is on Guyton St between St Hill and Wilson Sts. It's open from 8.30 am to 5 pm on weekdays and from 10 am to 2 pm on weekends (extended hours during

WANGANUI & MANAWATU

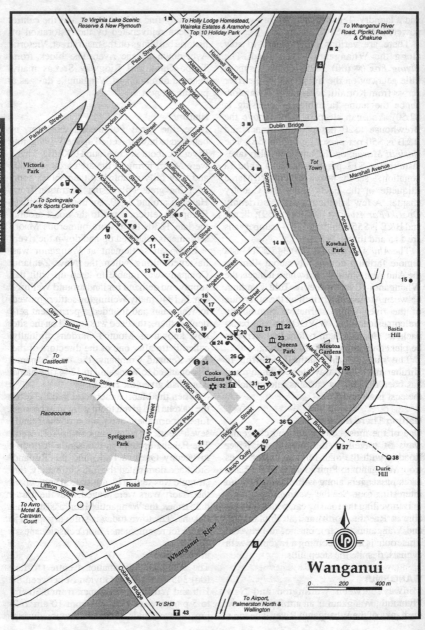

Wanganui

0   200   400 m

To Virginia Lake Scenic Reserve & New Plymouth

To Holly Lodge Homestead, Waireka Estates & Aramoho Top 10 Holiday Park

To Whanganui River Road, Pipriki, Raetihi & Ohakune

Peet Street

Halswell Street

Alexander Street

Pitt Street

Niblett Street

London Street

Glasgow Street

Liverpool Street

Keith Street

Dublin Bridge

Parsons Street

Campbell Street

Wolstead Street

Mulligan Street

Harrison Street

Dublin Street

Bell Street

Plymouth Street

Victoria Avenue

Grey Street

St Hill Street

Guyton Street

Ingestre Street

Somme Parade

Anzac Parade

Marshall Avenue

Kowhai Park

Victoria Park

To Springvale Park Sports Centre

Tot Town

Bastia Hill

To Castlecliff

Purnell Street

Wilson Street

Maria Place

Guyton Street

Ridgway Street

Taupo Quay

Queens Park

Moutoa Gardens

Market Place

Rutland St

Drews Ave

Cooks Gardens

City Bridge

Racecourse

Spriggens Park

Liffiton Street

Heads Road

To Avro Motel & Caravan Court

Durie Hill

Whanganui River

Cobham Bridge

To SH3

To Airport, Palmerston North & Wellington

	PLACES TO STAY				
1	River City Motel	19	Redeye Cafe	29	Whanganui Riverboat Centre
2	Acacia Park Motel	28	Rutland Arms Inn	31	Post Office
3	Astral Motel	30	Chamomile; Cables Restaurant & Bar	32	Opera House
4	Riverside Inn			33	Public Toilets
5	Manor Inn Wanganui		OTHER	34	Information Centre
14	Tamara Backpackers	6	Celtic Arms Pub	35	White Star Bus Stop
24	Grand Hotel & Cobb & Co Restaurant	7	Woolworths	36	Otunui Dock
42	Coachman's Lodge	10	Courtney's Bar & Cafe	37	Red Lion Inn
		15	Water Tower	38	Durie Hill Elevator
	PLACES TO EAT	18	DOC	39	Trafalgar Square Shopping Mall & Foodtown Supermarket
8	Wing-Wah Chinese Restaurant	20	One Jolly Bar Fat Kool Cafe		
9	McDonald's	21	Wanganui Regional Museum	40	Amadeus Riverbank Cafe
11	Michaels Restaurant	22	Sarjeant Art Gallery	41	Wanganui Travel Centre
12	Pizza Hut	23	War Memorial Hall	43	Putiki Church (St Paul's Memorial)
13	KFC	25	Air New Zealand		
16	Mid Avenue Fish & Chips	26	Wanganui-Taxi Bus		
17	Jabee's Kebabs	27	Automobile Association (AA)		

WANGANUI & MANAWATU

summer). The staff are helpful and there's a great model of the area from Wanganui right up to the Tongariro National Park.

The DOC office (☎ (06) 345 2402) on the corner of Ingestre and St Hill Sts is a good resource for maps, pamphlets and information on the Whanganui National Park and the river road.

The AA office (☎ (06) 345 4578) is at 78 Victoria Ave.

Wanganui Regional Museum & Serjeant Art Gallery

Opposite the War Memorial Hall on Wicksteed St, near Maria Place, is one of the largest and best regional museums in NZ, containing excellent Maori exhibits. The collection includes the magnificently carved Te Mata-o-Houroa *waka* (war canoe), other fine carvings and some nasty-looking *mere*, (elegant but lethal greenstone clubs). The museum also has good colonial and wildlife collections – the display of moa skeletons is particularly worth seeing. It is open from Monday to Saturday from 10 am to 4.30 pm and on Sunday from 1 to 4.30 pm ($2, children 60c).

On the hill beside the museum is the Serjeant Art Gallery, which has an extensive permanent exhibition, as well as frequent special exhibits. It's open on weekdays from 10.30 am to 4.30 pm and weekends from 1 to 4.30 pm (entry is free).

Parks & Gardens

Wanganui has several parks right in the city centre including the pleasant **Queens Park** in which the museum and gallery are situated.

Wanganui's most famous park is **Moutoa Gardens**, claimed as Maori land and subject to a four-month Maori occupation in 1995. The occupation signalled a new chapter in Maori-Pakeha relations and caused great acrimony in the town. The city council, abandoned by Wellington, fought the claim in the High Court, while angry Pakeha counter-demonstrated under the banner of 'One New Zealand' and police raids flamed Maori anger. When the claim was eventually rejected by the High Court, the country looked on, expecting violence, but the occupation was peacefully abandoned after a moving night-long meeting addressed by Maori leaders. The gardens have acquired a sacred status in the eyes of many Maori.

The **Virginia Lake Scenic Reserve (Rotokawau)**, about 1km north from the top end of Victoria Ave, is a beautiful reserve with a lake, theme gardens, a walk-in aviary, statues and the Higginbottom Fountain. The winter gardens and aviary are open from 9 am to 5 pm daily, and the rest of the reserve is always open.

Whanganui Riverboat Centre
On the riverbank beside Taupo Quay, the Whanganui Riverboat Centre (entry is free) houses the *Waimarie* side-paddle steamer, currently being restored. This vessel was launched on the Whanganui River in 1900 and plied the river for over 50 years until 1952, when it sank at its original berth. It remained submerged for another 40 years until raised for restoration; the goal is to get it on the river again.

Durie Hill
Across the river from the town centre is the carved gateway to the Durie Hill elevator. You can follow a tunnel into the hillside and then, for $1 (children 60c), ride up through the hill to the summit 65m above.

There are two viewpoints at the top: a lower one on the top of the lift machinery room and the higher War Memorial Tower, from where there's a fine view over the town all the way to Mt Taranaki, Mt Ruapehu or the South Island, if the weather is clear.

In summer the elevator operates from 7.30 am to 6 pm on weekdays, 10 am to 6 pm on Saturday and 11 am to 5 pm on Sunday.

Putiki Church
If you turn right after the Victoria Ave bridge and continue for 1km you come to Putiki Church, also called St Paul's Memorial Church. It's a plain little place from the outside but the interior is magnificent, completely covered in Maori carvings and *tuku-tuku* (wall panels). The church is usually open during the day but if it's locked you can ask for the key at the caretaker's house on the corner of Anaua St and SH3.

Holly Lodge & Waireka Estates
Six kilometres upstream from the Dublin St Bridge, the Holly Lodge Homestead is a historic homestead by the river. The homestead is open from 8 am to 8 pm daily (entry is free); you can reach it by road, or come by water on the *Otunui*.

Two kilometres further upstream, the Waireka Estate (☎ (06) 342 5729) is a 19th century homestead with a fascinating private museum. Interesting tours of the homestead are given to groups; phone for bookings. The *Otunui* may also continue on to Waireka.

Activities
The best way to get a feel for the Whanganui and its history is to take a **river cruise** on the 16m *Otunui* paddle steamer (☎ (06) 345 3513). Its long history began in 1907, when it was shipped in pieces from England and reassembled at Hatrick's Foundry in Wanganui. After plying the Whanganui River for 40 years, the vessel had a varied history, which included being sunken for 20 years, relocated to other parts of the North Island and finally returned to Wanganui in 1984, where it was restored. Cruises depart from the City Marina beneath the City Bridge. The paddle steamer usually leaves at 11 am daily. To go up the river as far as Holly Lodge is $20 (children $10).

A variety of other river trips are possible by canoe, kayak, jet-boat or motorised vessel, starting further up the river in the Whanganui National Park. Rivercity Tours (☎ (06) 344 2554) offers additional tours up the Whanganui River Road and on to the Drop Scene or the Bridge to Nowhere by jet-boat, returning to Wanganui via SH4. See the Whanganui National Park section for more details on river activities.

If you prefer sightseeing from the air, the Wanganui Aero Club (☎ (06) 345 0914) has a variety of **scenic flights** ($80 for 15 minutes) and Wanganui Aero Work (☎ (06) 345 3994) has Tiger Moth flights.

Organised Tours
A very interesting trip up the Whanganui River Road can be made with the weekday mail run, going up the river from Wanganui to Pipiriki on weekdays. You get picked up around 7.30 am for an all-day trip up the

river, stopping at many interesting and historic sites including the Kawana Flour Mill, Hiruharama church and Koriniti Marae; the river's past and present is related along the way. Coffee and tea is provided, but bring lunch (you return to town around 3 or 4 pm). The cost is $25 per person, with an optional half-hour jet-boat trip from Pipiriki to Drop Scene for another $40 or to the Bridge to Nowhere ($60, minimum of three people). Contact the mailman (☎ (06) 344 2554) for bookings.

Places to Stay

Camping & Cabins Closest in is the *Avro Motel & Caravan Court* (☎ (06) 345 5279) at 36 Alma Rd, 1.5km west of the city centre. It has powered sites at $18 for two, motel units at $65/72 and double family units from $80; there's an indoor spa pool and swimming pool but no kitchen facilities.

The *Aramoho Top 10 Holiday Park* (☎ (06) 343 8402) at 460 Somme Parade, 6km north of the Dublin St Bridge, is a peaceful, parklike camp on the town-side bank of the Whanganui River. It has tent and caravan sites at $16 for two, cabins from $23 to $32, tourist flats at $50 and motels at $60. Local Aramoho buses run there weekdays.

Other camps and cabins are at Castlecliff, a seaside suburb 8km north-west of Wanganui. The local Castlecliff bus runs there every day except Sunday. The *Castlecliff Motor Camp* (☎ (06) 344 2227) by the beach on the corner of Karaka and Rangiora Sts has tent/powered sites at $15/16 for two, backpackers cabins at $15/26 for one/two and larger cabins at $32 for two.

Also in Castlecliff, the *Alwyn Motel & Cabins* (☎ (06) 344 4500) opposite the beach at 65 Karaka St doesn't have camping but it does have cabins at $35, tourist flats at $48 and motels at $60.

Hostels The friendly *Riverside Inn* (☎ /fax (06) 347 2529) at 2 Plymouth St opposite the river is part-guesthouse and part-YHA hostel. The cost is $16 in dorms or $34 for double and twin rooms. The guesthouse half of the Riverside Inn is $45/60 for singles/

doubles, including a continental breakfast. Don't confuse it with the nearby Riverside Motel.

Also overlooking the river is *Tamara Backpackers* (☎ (06) 347 6300), 24 Somme Parade, a rambling old guesthouse-turned-hostel. It's a well run, friendly place with large recreational areas. Dorm beds cost $14 and $15, singles are $22, and doubles and twins are from $30 to $32. They organise three-day canoe trips on the Whanganui (DOC fees included) for $120.

Motels & Hotels The *River City Motel* (☎ (06) 343 9107) at 57 Halswell St is attractively situated on a quiet, tree-lined street at the foot of St John's Hill; it charges $65 a double. The *Coachman's Lodge* (☎ (06) 345 2227) at 30 Liffiton St beside the racecourse has singles/doubles from $55/65.

The *Astral Motel* (☎ (06) 347 9063) at 45 Somme Parade on the corner of Dublin St has units from $60. Across the river, the *Acacia Park Motel* (☎ (06) 343 9093) at 140 Anzac Parade has studio units at $60/70, or from $75 to $80 with kitchen. The *Manor Inn Wanganui* (☎ (06) 345 2180) at 63-65 Dublin St has studio units for $80 and luxury spa units for $99.

The *Grand Hotel* (☎ (06) 345 0955) at 99 Guyton St is about the only hotel of the old school still surviving in Wanganui; singles/doubles are $55/65 and all rooms have private facilities.

Places to Eat

Wanganui has several good restaurants. *Cables* on the corner of Victoria Ave and Ridgway St has plenty of atmosphere (mains are from $23); it is open from Tuesday to Saturday from 6 pm. If you want to pull out all the stops and splurge, head for *Michael's* (☎ (06) 345 2690) at 281 Wicksteed St on the corner of Dublin St. It's an award-winning and elegant restaurant in a classic converted home.

Chamomile on the corner of Victoria Ave and Ridgway St and the *Redeye Cafe* at 96 Guyton St are pleasant cafes with good light meals and snacks. For Mediterranean-style food, there's *Jabee's Kebabs* at the top end of Victoria Ave. The *Mid Avenue* on the corner of Victoria Ave and Ingestre St is a good place for fish and chips.

For pub food, *Cobb & Co* tucked away in the recesses of the Grand Hotel on the corner of Guyton and St Hill Sts, a block from Victoria Ave, has the usual Cobb & Co menu and hours. The *Rutland Arms Inn*, 48 Ridgway St, is one of Wanganui's most pleasant pubs for a meal or drink in a magnificently restored historic building.

The fast-food chains have outlets in Wanganui, within a couple of blocks on Victoria Ave. *Pizza Hut* is on the corner of Victoria Ave and Plymouth St, *KFC* is almost opposite, *McDonald's* is on the next block, between Dublin and Liverpool Sts, and *Eagle Boys Pizza* is not far away. For Chinese food, the *Wing-Wah* on Victoria Ave is popular and cheap.

Entertainment

The *Red Lion Inn* on Anzac Parade is a consistently good place, has a variety of entertainment and travellers are always made to feel welcome. Its *Top of the Red* bar and cafe is open from Wednesday to Sunday from 11.30 am to late (Saturday from 4 pm).

Other cafes or bars which are popular gathering places at night are the *Celtic Arms* at 432 Victoria Ave, open daily from 11 am; the *One Jolly Bar Fat Cool Cafe* on the corner of Guyton St and Victoria Ave, where there is a blackboard menu (open to 3.30 am on weekends); *Courtney's Bar & Cafe* in the Mid Town Motor Inn; and *Amadeus Riverbank Cafe* at 69 Taupo Quay, also with an innovative blackboard menu.

Getting There & Away

Air Air New Zealand Link (☎ (06) 345 4089) at 133 Victoria Ave has daily direct flights to Auckland and Wellington, with onward connections.

Bus InterCity and Newmans buses operate from the top end of Ridgway St. Both operate buses to Auckland via Hamilton, and to New Plymouth. Heading south, buses go to Palm-

erston North and on to Wellington or Napier. For services north to Tongariro, Taupo and Rotorua, you have to transfer at Bulls, on the way to Palmerston North.

White Star buses (☎ (06) 345 7612) operate from in front of Avis Rent-A-Car, 161 Ingestre St, with buses to New Plymouth, Palmerston North and Wellington.

The mail-run bus (☎ (06) 344 2554) heads up the Whanganui River Road to Pipiriki and back on weekdays (they pick up from hostels); see under Organised Tours in this section.

Car & Motorcycle Between Wanganui and the centre of the North Island the highway (SH4) passes through the Paraparas, an area of interesting *papa* (large blue-grey mudstone) hills with some beautiful views, and also passes close by the impressive Raukawa Falls and along Mangawhero River Gorge.

Alternatively you can take the Whanganui River Road – see the Whanganui River Road & Pipiriki section.

Getting Around

To/From the Airport The airport is about 4km from town, across the river towards the sea. Ash's Transport Services (☎ (06) 343 8319, 025 958 693) operates a shuttle to the airport, bus station and other points in town. It also operates a shuttle to Palmerston North airport.

Bus Wanganui Taxi-Bus (☎ (06) 343 5555) operates a limited local bus service on weekdays, including routes to Castlecliff and to Aramoho, all departing from the taxi-bus stop on Maria Place near Victoria Ave.

WESTMERE TO LAKE WIRITOA

Heading north-west from Wanganui on SH3 as if you were going to New Plymouth, after about 5.5km you reach Rapanui Rd. Turn towards the sea on this road and you come to some pleasant spots.

First is the **Westmere Reserve & Wildlife Refuge**, where there's lots of birdlife and a 40-minute walk around Lake Westmere. Next along, **Bason Botanical Reserve** is a

25-hectare reserve with a lake, conservatory, gardens of many kinds, lookout tower and an old homestead. The reserve is open every day from 9.30 am until dusk; the conservatory is open from 10 am to 4 pm on weekdays and 2 to 4 pm on weekends.

At the end of Rapanui Rd, 9km from the SH3 turn-off, the black-sand **Mowhanau Beach**, also called Kai Iwi Beach, is a beautiful beach. The Mowhanau Creek meets the sea here and provides a safe place for children to swim, and there's also a motor camp and scenic papa cliffs. You can walk back to Castlecliff along the coast (two to three hours).

Bushy Park

Bushy Park is 24km north-west of Wanganui. Following the signs as if you were going to New Plymouth, take SH3 to Kai Iwi, turn off where you see the signs and go 8km further on a sealed side road. Owned by the Royal Forest & Bird Protection Society, the park is a 96-hectare scenic reserve with spacious grounds, picnic and BBQ areas, bush walks and a historic 1906 homestead. It's open daily from 10 am to 5 pm ($3, children $1).

Accommodation is available (☎ (06) 342 9879) in the homestead; it's like staying in a well preserved museum. Singles/doubles are $75/90 for B&B. It also has a bunkroom at $15 per person, and caravan and tent sites at $15 for two.

Ashley Park

Ashley Park (☎ (06) 346 5917) at Waitotara, 34km north-west of Wanganui on SH3, is another attractive park, with gardens and trees surrounding a picturesque lake. Activities include fishing, eeling, birdwatching and kayaking. The park is open daily from 9 am to 5 pm (entry is free).

Accommodation is available and you can join in the farm activities, or go boating on the lake or hunting. B&B in the house is $35 per person (extra person $11), with dinner by arrangement. It also has basic cabins at $11 per person (children under 12 $6), powered sites for $10/14.50 for one/two people and tent sites for $3 per person. Remote Adventures (☎ (06) 346 5747) is a wilderness farmstay which organises bushwalks, jet-boating and scenic flights near Waitotara.

Lake Wiritoa

About 12.5km south-east of Wanganui, off SH3, Lake Wiritoa is popular for swimming and water-skiing. To get there, turn left at Lake Kaitoke and keep going past it to Lake Wiritoa.

Manawatu

The rich sheep and dairy farming district of Manawatu is centred around the provincial city of Palmerston North, dominated by Massey University, and includes the surrounding districts of Rangitikei to the north and Horowhenua to the south.

PALMERSTON NORTH

On the banks of the Manawatu River, Palmerston North (population 72,500) is the principal centre of the Manawatu region and a major crossroads. With Massey University, the second-largest university in NZ, and several other colleges, Palmerston North has the relaxed feel of a rural university town. Though not really a tourist destination, it is well ordered and pleasant.

Orientation & Information

The wide open expanse of the Square with its gardens and fountains is very much the centre of town. You can get your bearings from a lookout on top of the Civic Centre building on the Square, open on weekdays.

The Palmerston North Information Centre (☎ (06) 358 5003; fax 356 9841) in the Civic Centre on the Square has plenty of information on the area. It's open from 8.30 am to 5 pm on weekdays and 9 am to 5 pm on weekends.

The DOC office (☎ (06) 358 9004) is at 717 Tremaine Ave, on the north side of town. The AA office (☎ (06) 357 7039) is at 185 Broadway Ave, near Amesbury St.

Manawatu Gorge

About 15km north of Palmerston North, the SH2 to Napier runs through the spectacular Manawatu Gorge. Manawatu Jet Tours (☎ (06) 326 8190) operates jet-boat trips on the river and will arrange transport for small groups from Palmerston North for no extra cost ($25 for the shortest trip). The information centre and High Life at 475 Main St also have information on horse trekking, bridge swinging, abseiling, and drift rafting in the area.

Other Things to See & Do

The **Science Centre & Manawatu Museum** on the corner of Church and Pitt Sts has a museum specialising in the history of the Manawatu region, including its Maori history, culture and art. The Science Centre has rotating science exhibits and the hands-on displays are fun for kids and adults alike. It's open from 10 am to 5 pm daily. Entry to the museum is free, while the Science Centre costs $6 (children $4, family $15).

Around the corner is the modern, spacious **Manawatu Art Gallery** at 398 Main St West. It's open from 10 am to 4.30 pm on weekdays and 11.30 am to 4.30 pm on weekends (entry is free, but donations are welcome).

Rugby fans shouldn't miss the **New Zealand Rugby Museum** at 87 Cuba St, a few blocks from the Square. This interesting museum contains exhibits and memorabilia relating to the history of rugby in NZ from the first game played in the country, in Nelson in 1870, up to the present. It also has mementos from every country where rugby is played and videos of the most famous international games. The museum is open from Monday to Saturday from 10 am to noon and 1.30 to 4 pm, and on Sunday from 1.30 to 4 pm ($3, children $1).

The **Esplanade** is a beautiful park stretching along the shores of the Manawatu River, a few blocks south of the Square. The Manawatu Riverside Walkway & Bridle Track, extending 10km along the river, passes through the park.

Palmerston North is well supplied with sporting venues. The **Showgrounds** include the Manawatu Sports Stadium, other stadiums, rugby pitches, a stockcar track, concert halls and more. Other sports venues include the Awapuni Racecourse for thoroughbred horse racing, and the Manawatu Raceway on Pioneer Highway for trotting and greyhound racing. There is an indoor rock-climbing wall, **City Rock**, at 38a Grey St ($8).

Places to Stay

Camping, Cabins & Hostels The *Palmerston North Holiday Park* (☎ (06) 358 0349) at 133 Dittmer Drive, off Ruha Place, is pleasantly situated beside the Esplanade, about 2km from the Square. It has tent/powered sites at $17/20, cabins at $35 to $39 and tourist flats at $55; all prices are for two.

The *Peppertree Hostel* (☎ (06) 355 4054), a YHA associate at 121 Grey St, has a well appointed kitchen, off-street parking, open fireplace and a homey atmosphere. It charges $15 for a dorm, or $25 for singles and $35 for twins and doubles; it offers free pick-up from the bus/train station.

King St Backpackers (☎ (06) 358 9595), 95 King St, is a large, lifeless, run-down 70-bed hostel and very much a last resort. The cost is $14 per person in dorm and shared rooms, with reduced weekly rates.

About 25km north-west of the city, at the junction of SH3 and SH1, is Sanson. Here you will find a small backpackers (☎ (06) 329 3456) which has dorm beds for $12.

B&Bs & Guesthouses *Grey's Inn* (☎ (06) 358 6928) at 123 Grey St at the junction with Princess St is an attractive, homey guesthouse with B&B at $55/80; *Emma's Place* (☎ (06) 357 5143) at 250 Fitzherbert Ave charges $38.50/50; *Glenfyne* (☎ (06) 358 1626) at 413 Albert St charges $40/65; and *Iti Mara Homestay* (☎ (06) 354 2666), 3 Peters Ave, has self-contained units for $45/60 (with free pick-up).

Motels The *Consolidated Mid City Motel* (☎ (06) 357 2184) at 129 Broadway Ave is a fancy, central motel with singles/doubles from $61/68. Further along at 258 Broadway

Central Plateau
Top: Mt Ruapehu, Tongariro National Park
Bottom: Emerald Lakes, Tongariro Crossing, Tongariro National Park

The East Coast
Art Deco architecture, Napier

Ave, the *Broadway Motel* (☎ (06) 358 5051) is much the same, but charging $55/60.

There's a 'motel row' on Fitzherbert Ave, south of the Square; motels along here are a bit more expensive. They include the *Hibiscus* (☎ (06) 356 1411) at No 114 ($75/80), the *Avenue* (☎ (06) 356 3330) at No 116 ($75/85), the *Rose City* (☎ (06) 356 5388) at No 120 ($97 to $105), the *Coachman* (☎ (06) 357 3059) at No 134 ($99) and the *Tokyo* (☎ (06) 356 7074) at No 167 ($85/ 100). The best along the strip at the price is *Harrington's* (☎ (06) 354 7259) at No 301 ($85 for single, double or twin).

Hotels The *Empire Establishment* (☎ (06) 357 8002) on the corner of Princess and Main Sts has 9 rooms with private bath, off-street parking; singles/doubles are $60/ 65. The *Masonic Hotel* (☎ (06) 358 3480) at 249 Main St West is $39/44 with private facilities (twins are $6 extra).

The *Shamrock Inn B&B Hotel* (☎ (06) 355 2130) at 267 Main St West is a refurbished hotel with good budget rooms for $30/40 and double rooms with en suite for $55. The bar downstairs often has bands at weekends. Top of the range by far is the *Quality Hotel* (☎ (06) 356 8059), 110 Fitzherbert Ave, with doubles for $140. The entrance is on Ferguson St.

Places to Eat

Palmerston North has its fair share of cafes and bar/restaurants serving inexpensive fare to cater for the town's student population.

On Broadway Ave, the *Downtown Arcade* has a good food hall with counters serving Italian, Chinese, fish and chips, coffee, ice cream etc. It is open late to cater for moviegoers. Popular student bar/restaurants with reasonably priced meals and snacks are *Dr Jekyll's* at 113 Broadway Ave and the slightly fancier *Orleans Cafe & Bar* on Main St. At 49 the Square, the tiny *Truelife Bakery* specialises in wholefoods.

Also along the south-west side of the Square, *Puddleducks* at 42 the Square is a popular cafe for lunches and teas. Beside it, the *Cafe Ojakbashe* serves moderately

priced Turkish dishes, or for pizza there's *Pizza Piazza* at 16-17 the Square. *Oscar's Wine Bar* on the corner of Coleman Place and the Square is a fancy bar but the blackboard menu features inexpensive light meals. Next to it, *Bella's Cafe* is a popular lunch spot. *Deano's Bar & Grill* on Coleman Place is a popular older style bar and grill with good steaks from $14.

The chains are well represented, including *McDonald's*, *KFC*, *Pizza Hut*, and *Cobb & Co* in the Empire Establishment. For self-caterers, the *Foodtown* supermarket is on Ferguson St at the rear of the Plaza shopping centre. *Pack 'N Save* is a little further along. *Spostato Cafe*, upstairs at 213 Cuba St, the best Italian place in town, is open daily from 6 pm until late.

There's a new wave of fine cafes along Broadway Ave. *Aqaba* at No 186 is a great little bar with good bar snacks (from $5 to $12); *Cafe Vavasseur* at No 201 is a great atmospheric BYO but the meals are quite pricey; and the *Bathhouse* at No 161 has periodic jazz, a couple of big open fires for winter, or al fresco dining in summer.

Another trendy enclave is George St, behind the library. Here you'll find *Barista's Expresso Bar* with an international menu and range of coffees; the *George St Deli*; a Kurdish place, *Sinbad's*, with tasty kebabs and naan breads; and *Omni* with vegetarian meals (around $6.50) and folk music on Friday, the only night you can BYO.

Entertainment

Theatre and music performances are staged at the *Centrepoint Theatre*, *Globe Theatre* and the *Abbey Theatre*. The revamped *Regent Theatre* is due to open soon and will host big events. The city's people are avid movie-goers – the large *Downtown Cinema 7* complex, upstairs in the Downtown Arcade, shows the latest films and art house selections.

Nightlife fluctuates according to the student year and is quiet during the holidays.

The *Celtic Inn* in the Regent Arcade between Broadway Ave and King St is a small, pleasant, low-key Irish pub with live

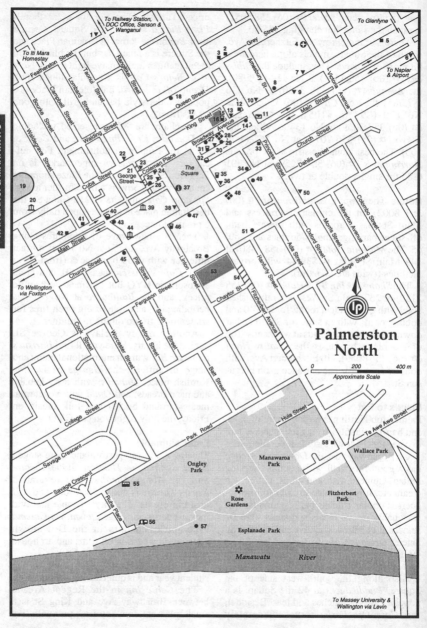

Palmerston North

WANGANUI & MANAWATU

PLACES TO STAY
2 Grey's Inn
3 Peppertree Hostel
5 Broadway Motel
12 Consolidated Mid City Hotel
17 King St Backpackers
33 Empire Establishment & Cobb & Co Restaurant
41 Shamrock Inn B&B Hotel
42 Masonic Hotel
53 Quality Hotel
54 Motel Strip
56 Palmerston North Holiday Park
58 Emma's Place

PLACES TO EAT
1 McDonald's
6 Pizza Hut
7 Cafe Vavasseur
9 Aqaba
10 Bathhouse
13 Dr Jekyll's Cafe Bar
21 George St Cafe Precinct: Barista's Espresso Bar; George St Deli; Sinbad's; Omni
22 Spostato Cafe

23 Deano's Bar & Grill
24 Bella's Cafe; Oscar's Wine Bar
26 Pizza Piazza
30 Orleans Cafe & Bar
36 McDonald's
38 Puddleducks; Cafe Ojakbashe; Truelife Bakery
50 KFC

OTHER
4 After-Hours Emergency Medical Centre
8 Automobile Association (AA)
11 Post Office
14 Ansett New Zealand
15 Celtic Inn
16 Regent Theatre
18 City Rock Rock Climbing Wall
19 Palmerston North Showgrounds
20 New Zealand Rugby Museum
25 Public Library
27 Air New Zealand
28 Downtown Arcade, Food Hall & Downtown Cinema 7

29 High Life
31 High Flyers Cafe
32 White Star & Local Bus Stop
34 Abbey Theatre
35 Bassline Nightclub
37 Information Centre & Civic Centre
39 Manawatu Art Gallery
40 Travel Centre (InterCity, Newmans)
43 Globe Theatre
44 Science Centre & Manawatu Museum
45 Centrepoint Theatre
46 Fat Ladies Arms
47 Square Edge Community Arts Centre
48 Plaza Shopping Centre
49 Municipal Opera House
51 Foodtown Supermarket
52 Pack 'N Save
55 Lido Swimming & Recreation Centre
57 Miniature Railway

music on weekend nights. The *Fat Ladies Arms* on the corner of Church and Linton Sts is a popular student watering hole. The cafes and bars along Broadway Ave and George St are all popular on weekends (see Places to Eat).

The *High Flyers Cafe*, on the corner of the Square and Main St, is for a more mature crowd, and the *Bassline Nightclub*, upstairs on the Square, has a big dance floor.

Getting There & Away

Air Milson Airport on the northern outskirts of town is a modern international airport; planes often get diverted here when the weather at Wellington is bad.

Air New Zealand (☎ (06) 351 8800) on Broadway Ave has daily direct flights to Auckland, Christchurch, Hamilton and Wellington, with onward connections. Ansett New Zealand (☎ (06) 355 2146) is at 50-52

Princess St. It has daily direct flights to Auckland, Christchurch, Invercargill, Nelson, Queenstown and Wellington, with connections to other centres. Freedom Air (☎ 0800 600 500) flies to Hamilton, as well as Brisbane and Sydney in Australia (see the Getting There & Away chapter).

Bus InterCity, Newmans and Tranzit Coachlines buses operate from the Palmerston North Travel Centre (☎ (06) 351 5633) on the corner of Main and Pitt Sts. InterCity and Newmans buses go from Palmerston North to most places in the North Island; Tranzit Coachlines operates one route, Palmerston North via Masterton to Wellington.

White Star buses (☎ (06) 358 8777) operate from a bus stop at the Courthouse, on Main St near the Square, with buses to Wellington, Wanganui and New Plymouth.

Many direct services between Auckland

and Wellington bypass Palmerston North, stopping instead at nearby Bulls. Wellington-Napier buses do stop at Palmerston North.

On Ground Airlines (☎ 0800 755 575) have a twice-daily service to Napier and return ($35; discounts are available).

Train The train station is off Tremaine Ave, about 12 blocks north of the Square. Trains between Auckland and Wellington stop here, as do trains between Wellington and Napier. The Auckland-Wellington trains run twice daily in each direction (morning and night). The Wellington-Napier train runs once daily in each direction.

Getting Around

Local minibuses operate from the bus stop in the middle of Main St, on the east side of the Square. They operate on weekdays from 7 am to 6 pm, Saturday until 1 pm and not at all on Sunday; all rides cost $1.50. The No 12 bus goes to Massey University but none go to the airport. One of the minibuses stops near the airport at the Milson shopping centre; from the terminal to the shopping centre is a 10 to 15-minute walk. A taxi costs $9 to the centre, or $11 to Massey.

RANGITIKEI

The Rangitikei region stretches from Taihape (the self-styled 'gumboot' capital) in the north to Bulls in the south (to the west of Palmerston North) and also includes the towns of Hunterville and Marton. In NZ terms it is very much an unsung region but there is great potential for tourism, only now being realised along the banks of the untamed Rangitikei River. Visit the Rangitikei Information Centre (☎ (06) 388 0350) on Hautapu St, Taihape, for more information and a free copy of the pamphlet *Rangitikei: The Undiscovered Secret.*

Just south of Taihape ('a gumboots throw from civilisation') is *River Valley Lodge* (☎ (06) 388 1444), on the banks of the Rangitikei. It is quite remote, in a pristine valley, and there are many activities to engage in – white-water rafting ($79), abseil-

ing ($20), kayaking ($40), horse trekking ($35 for two hours) and walking (free). A dorm bed in the lodge is $15, twins and doubles are $40. The lodge has a huge communal area with an open fire – grab a beer, relax and tell the person next to you about your NZ experiences.

Mangaweka

Located north on SH1, 52km south of Waiouru, Mangaweka's most noticeable attraction is the **Aeroplane Cafe**, a cafe in an old DC-3 plane right beside the highway, open daily. Beside the plane, Rangitikei River Adventures (☎ (06) 382 5747) offers various activities including a 80m bungy jump ('High Time') over the Rangitikei; it's $120 for a jump and photos.

It also does a number of Rangitikei River trips, including jet-boating and rafting ($99), and can arrange accommodation. Bookings are essential for all activities.

Gardens

The **Cross Hills Gardens**, with one of NZ's largest and most varied collections of rhododendrons and azaleas, is 5km north of Kimbolton, on SH54 about a 45-minute drive north of Palmerston North. It's open from 10.30 am to 5 pm daily during the bloom from September to April; there is a small entry fee.

Ohakea

Ohakea is a whistle-stop town, west of Palmerston North on SH1 near Bulls. It is dominated by a large air force base, where you'll find the **Ohakea Museum** dedicated to the exploits of the tiny Royal New Zealand Air Force. This small museum of air force memorabilia is open from Monday to Saturday from 7.30 am to 4.30 pm and on Sunday from 10 am to 4.30 pm ($5, children $2). The plus is the *Kites Kafé*, from where the kids can watch the ageing jets come and go.

HOROWHENUA

The Horowhenua region extends from Foxton in the north to Waikawa Beach in the south and it is bordered by the Tasman Sea to the west and the rugged Tararuas to the east. Included in the region is the provincial centre Levin, the beautiful lakes Papaitonga and Horowhenua, and Himatangi, Foxton, Waitarere and Hokio beaches.

Levin

Levin, 50km south of Palmerston North, is a sizeable town (pop 15,000) in the centre of the fertile Horowhenua agricultural region. The Horowhenua Visitor Information Centre (☎ (06) 368 7148) in Regent Court on Oxford St is open daily. The AA (☎ (06) 368 2988) is at 212 Oxford St. **Lake Papaitonga**, a few kilometres south of Levin and reached by Buller Rd, is a serenely beautiful place. Follow the boardwalk to the sacred lake which features heavily in the Maori chief Te Rauparaha's story.

There are plenty of motels, including the *Travelodge Motel* (☎ (06) 368 7173) at 98 Main Rd, with studio units from $66; *Totara Lodge* (☎ (06) 368 4114) at 15 Devon St, with singles/doubles for $45/78; and the *Ploughman Motel* (☎ (06) 368 7199) at 364 Oxford St, which charges from $55/65.

There are the usual fast-food outlets along the main road. For a change, *Cafe Extreme*, 7 Bath St, has a good salad selection, muffins, steaks and gourmet burgers.

Tokomaru Steam Engine Museum

The Tokomaru Steam Engine Museum, in Tokomaru on SH57 about 30km north of Levin, exhibits a large collection of working steam engines and locomotives. It's open daily from 9 am to noon and from 1 to 3.30 pm ($5, children $2).

WANGANUI & MANAWATU

The East Coast

The East Coast is an area full of interest, with the sea on one side and towering forested hills in the hinterland. It is also a place of contrasts, from the Art Deco and Spanish Mission-style architecture of bustling Hastings and Napier to the serene, primeval forests that girt Lake Waikaremoana in Te Urewera National Park.

The area includes three of the North Island's larger cities and their adjoining bays: Gisborne on Poverty Bay and Napier and Hastings on Hawkes Bay.

From Opotiki on the eastern Bay of Plenty, circling around to Gisborne, the East Cape is a rugged landscape with stunning coastal scenery and dense inland forest inland. This long-isolated region has retained its strong Maori influence, and remains largely undeveloped and well off the main tourist routes.

East Cape

The East Cape is a scenic, isolated and little-known region of the North Island. The small communities scattered along the coast are predominantly Maori and the pace of life is peaceful and slow. Geographically, the area has few natural harbours and, until the road network was completed, goods had to be loaded off the beaches onto waiting barges. The interior is still wild bush, with the Raukumara Range extending down the centre of the cape. The western side of the range is divided into several state forest parks: Ruatoria, Raukumara, Urutawa and Waioeka.

The coast is now circled by 330km of highway (SH35), which took decades to build. It is an excellent road (open year-round) which has made the coast more accessible than ever. The drive is worthwhile, if only for the magnificent views of this wild coast dotted with picturesque little bays, inlets and coves that change aspect

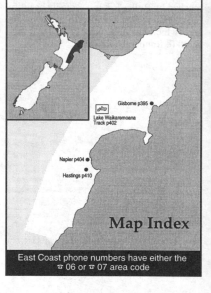

HIGHLIGHTS

- Exploring Napier, with its Art Deco architecture and seaside ambience
- Discovering Te Urewera National Park and its Lake Waikaremoana Great Walk
- Visiting the rugged East Cape and Raukumara Ranges
- Roaming over wild, windswept Mahia Peninsula
- Surfing at one of the East Coast's many remote beaches

Gisborne p395

Lake Waikaremoana Track p402

Napier p404

Hastings p410

Map Index

East Coast phone numbers have either the ☎ 06 or ☎ 07 area code

with the weather. On a sunny day the water is an inviting turquoise, at other times a layer of clouds hangs on the craggy mountains rising straight up from the beaches and everything turns a misty green. Dozens of fresh, clear streams flow through wild gorges to meet the sea. During the summer the coastline turns crimson with the blooming of the pohutukawa trees which line the seashore.

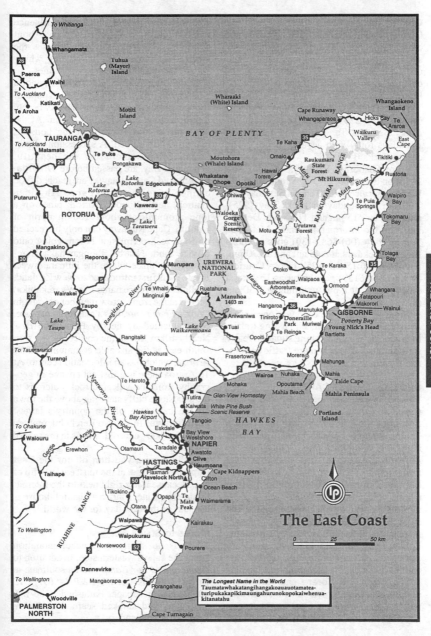

THE EAST COAST

The East Coast

0   25   50 km

The Longest Name in the World
Taumatawhakatangihangakoauauotamatea-
turipukakapikimaungahurunokopokaiwhenua-
kitanatahu

Getting There & Around

Getting around the East Cape by bus is not easy. The only options are the various courier services, which travel sections of the cape and take passengers. This situation might change, so contact the Opotiki or Gisborne information centres.

From Opotiki, Apanui Pony Express (☎ (07) 325 2700) leaves at 6.30 am for Hicks Bay and Te Araroa and returns on weekdays (only with advance notice). The cost to Hicks Bay is $35.

From Gisborne, Fastways (☎ (07) 868 9080) on the corner of Grey St and Awapuni Rd has a service at 9.30 am on Saturday and 7.30 am on Sunday to Hicks Bay ($25), returning at 1.15 pm and 11.15 pm. Departing from the information centre, Matakaoa Transport (☎ (06) 868 6139) goes to Hicks Bay on weekdays at 8.45 am and 12.30 pm, returning at 6.15 am ($25). Cooks Couriers (☎ (06) 868 6139) goes as far as Te Araroa on weekdays at 2 pm, returning at 7.30 am ($25).

Hitching around the cape was once notoriously slow, with not much passing traffic. Many locals say the hitching situation really isn't that bad. There is more traffic in summer than in winter.

OPOTIKI TO EAST CAPE

This trip is well described in *Opotiki & East Cape*, a comprehensive booklet available free from the Opotiki Visitor Information Centre. A number of activities are described in *Gisborne & East Cape: Guidebook to Adventure*. Along the first stretch of road from Opotiki there are fine views across to the steaming Whakaari (White Island) marine volcano. At the Waiaua River is the turn-off for the road to Gisborne via Toa Toa and the **Old Motu Coach Road**, probably more suited to mountain bikes. At Ruatama Enterprise (☎ (07) 315 4630) you can learn aspects of Maori culture on a marae stay; contact Mohi and Sonia for more details.

The beaches at **Torere** and **Hawai** are steeply shelved and covered with driftwood; they're good spots for seascape photography. Hawai is the boundary of the Whanau-a-Apanui tribe, whose sphere of influence extends north to Cape Runaway. About 45km from Opotiki the road crosses the **Motu River**, famed for its jet-boating, whitewater rafting and kayaking possibilities.

Some 25km further on is **Te Kaha**, once a whaling centre but now a small town popular for boating and fishing. It has a rocky beach, a pub, a store and accommodation. At the large marae, the Tukaki meeting house is magnificently carved. A succession of picturesque bays, including the beautiful Whanarua Bay, are passed before **Whangaparaoa** and Cape Runaway are reached. You cannot miss the Raukokore Anglican Church, nestled under Norfolk pines on a lone promontory, about 100km north of Opotiki. Cape Runaway can only be reached on foot; seek permission before going onto private land. Nearby Taungawhaka is reputedly the place where the kumara (sweet potato) was first introduced to New Zealand.

Hicks Bay (once named Te Wharekahika) gets its name from a crew member of Captain Cook's *Endeavour*. It is a magnificent place, complemented by nearby Horseshoe Bay. Nearly 10km 'round the corner' as you turn south-east is the sizeable community of **Te Araroa**, which has an information centre. At Te Araroa there is a distinct change in geography from the volcanic rock outcrops to the sandstone cliffs standing above the town on the bay. One of the country's largest **pohutukawa**, Te Waha o Rerekohu, reputed to be over 600 years old, stands in the school grounds.

At Te Araroa you turn off for the **East Cape lighthouse**, at the most easterly tip of NZ. Because it lies right next to the International Date Line, sunrise at the lighthouse is the start of the new day for the world.

Places to Stay & Eat

There is no shortage of accommodation along the cape's western side. In addition to *Tirohanga Motor Camp* and its soulmate at Opape, there is *Coral's B&B* (☎ (07) 315 8052), also in Opape. Famished? The fish and chips and smoked seafood at *Torere Seafoods* are legendary!

Te Kaha is the central point on the western side of East Cape. The *Te Kaha Holiday Park & Motels* (☎ (07) 325 2894) has camp sites, cabins and tourist flats, and 'luxury' backpackers accommodation from $12 per person. The revamped *Te Kaha Hotel* (☎ /fax (07) 325 2830) has double rooms (from $65 for two) and luxury beachside units. At pretty Whanarua Bay, *Rendezvous on the Coast* (☎ (07) 325 2899) has camp sites from $14 for two, and cabins from $30. Readers recommend *Robyn's Place* (☎ (07) 325 2904), a small backpackers ($14 per person) which has beach access and walks.

At Waihau Bay, the *Waihau Bay Holiday Park* (☎ (07) 325 3844) at Oruati Beach has camp sites, cabins and on-site caravans. *Waihau Bay B&B* (☎ (07) 325 3674) is opposite the beach and has doubles for $70. Equidistant between Whangaparaoa and Hicks Bay is the new *Lottin Point Motel* (☎ (06) 864 4455) with superb units from $80 for two.

Hicks Bay has a takeaway and a general store. If you take the dirt road around the peninsula from the Hicks Bay township, you'll come to the spic-and-span *Hicks Bay Backpackers Lodge* (☎ (06) 864 4731) on Onepoto Beach Rd. It's a small, friendly place with a backpackers bunkroom off to one side of the home, and fronts a beautiful beach, only 50m away. The nightly cost is $14 or $15 in dorms or $35 for a double room. It organises trips to the East Cape lighthouse. Also at Hicks Bay, on the hill overlooking the bay, is the *Hicks Bay Motel Lodge* (☎ (06) 864 4880) with doubles starting at $70.

Te Araroa Holiday Park (☎ (06) 864 4873), midway between Te Araroa and Hicks Bay, is another lovely spot. In a sheltered 15-hectare parklike setting near the beach, the park has lots of amenities, including a cinema. Tent/powered sites cost $8.50/9 per person, bunkroom accommodation is $10, cabins are $30 for two and tourist flats are $45.

EAST CAPE TO GISBORNE

Heading south from Te Araroa the first place

of interest you come to is **Tikitiki**. The Anglican Church is well worth visiting for its Maori architectural design.

A few kilometres off the road is **Ruatoria**, which has powerful Mt Hikurangi as a backdrop. Ruatoria is a very important Maori town – the centre of the Ngati Porou tribe and the home of many eminent Maori. Sir Apirana Ngata, a politician from the early 1900s to 1930, lived here, and the Maori war hero Lieutenant Ngarimu VC was born here.

About 25km south is **Te Puia Springs**, a pretty little town with hot springs nearby, and the pleasant **Waipiro Bay**. Another 10km further is **Tokomaru Bay**, a crumbling but picturesque town with a good beach and sweeping cliffs at the southern end of the bay.

Tolaga Bay is next and, although popular with surfers, is not particularly exciting when contrasted with Tokomaru or bays to the north. South of Tolaga Bay is a small settlement called **Whangara**, the setting for Witi Ihimaera's wonderful fictional work *The Whale Rider*. It is a great little book to read for a feel of the Maori culture and mythology of the area. After passing Tatapouri and Wainui beaches you reach Gisborne.

Places to Stay

Heading south along the east coast from Te Araroa you come to the Waiapu River and the town of Tikitiki, which has a hotel and caravan park. Ruatoria has the old *Manutahi Hotel* (☎ (06) 864 8437) with standard pub rooms. At Te Puia is the *Hot Springs Hotel* (☎ (06) 864 6861), a Historic Trust building, with singles/doubles for $35/55. Te Puia also has a motel and the information centre can tell you about homestays in the area.

At Waipiro Bay on the coast, *Waikawa Lodge* (☎ (06) 864 6719) on Waikawa Rd is a small, romantic backpackers cottage for getting away from it all (it receives heaps of fan mail at Lonely Planet). It has just four twins/doubles at $20 per person. The big plus here is the two-hour horse treks ($30) guided by Anne and Jimmy, two quintessential Kiwis. They will pick you up from Te Puia Springs.

On Potae St in Tokomaru Bay, the *House of the Rising Sun* (☎ 864 5858) is a small, comfortable and homey hostel about a block from the beach. Hiking, swimming, surfing, tennis, fishing, cycling, horse riding on the beach and visits to the new beachside pub are all popular activities. It charges $14 for a dorm and $30/32 for twins/doubles. Further south, the well-equipped *Tolaga Bay Motor Camp* (☎ (06) 862 6716) on Wharf Rd is on the beach, with sites from $17 for two and a variety of cabins from $34 for two. The historic *Tolaga Bay Inn* (☎ (06) 862 6550) on Cook St has singles/doubles for $35/55 and the *Tolaga Bay Motel* (☎ (06) 862 6888) on the corner of Cook and Monkhouse Sts has units from $55/65.

RAUKUMARA & WAIOEKA

Inland, the Raukumara Range offers tramping (the highest mountain in the range is Hikurangi at 1752m) and white-water rafting on the Waioeka and Motu rivers – contact Wet 'n' Wild Rafting (☎ (07) 578 4093) for more information on rafting. The most popular way of accessing this rugged, untamed region is via SH2 (the Waioeka Gorge Road), the 144km road which connects Opotiki to Gisborne at the base of the East Cape triangle.

There are many great walks in this region and DOC has plenty of information on possibilities. See its *Raukumara Forest Park* and *Waioeka Gorge Scenic Reserve* pamphlets. The rare blue duck may be seen in the Raukumara, and Hochstetter's frog (*Leiopelma hochstetteri*) is quite common in the park. Some parts of the region are penetrable by mountain bike, while others are certainly not. This region is one of New Zealand's last frontiers, as wild as sections of south Westland.

The *Riverview Cottage Farmstay* on SH2 (☎ (07) 315 5553) and the *Matawai Hotel* (☎ (06) 862 4874), also on SH2, are 16km and 76km from Opotiki respectively; the latter has backpackers beds for $15 and doubles for $55. The *Matawai Village Cafe* is the place to get a bite to eat.

Poverty Bay

GISBORNE

Gisborne (population 45,800) is NZ's most easterly city and one of the closest to the International Date Line. It was here that Captain Cook made his first landfall in NZ on 9 October 1769. He named it 'Poverty Bay', after deciding it had nothing to offer. It was an inauspicious first meeting – Cook's landing party was attacked and several Maori were killed in the altercation.

The fertile alluvial plains around Gisborne support intensive farming of subtropical fruits, market-garden produce and vineyards. Recently, kiwi fruit and avocados have been important crops. The city itself is right on the coast at the confluence of three rivers: the Turanganui, Waimata and Taruheru. Often described as 'the city of bridges', it is also noted for its fine parks.

Gisborne features strongly in Maori history. This part of the East Coast retains a definite Maori character with great emphasis placed on the retention of culture and traditions. It is here you will here Te Reo Maori (the Maori language) being spoken.

History

The Gisborne region has been settled for over 1000 years. Two skippers of sacred canoes of the Great Migration fleet – Paoa of the *Horo-uta* and Kiwa of the *Takitimu* – made an intermarriage pact which led to the founding of Turanganui a Kiwa (now Gisborne). The newly introduced kumara soon flourished in the fertile soil and Maori settlement spread to the hinterland.

European settlement of the region did not occur until the late 19th century. A man of considerable drive, John Williams Harris, was first to purchase a small area on the west bank of the Turanganui River. He set up the region's first whaling venture, and in 1839 began farming up the Waipaoa River near Matunuke.

As whaling became increasingly popular, missionaries also began to move into the

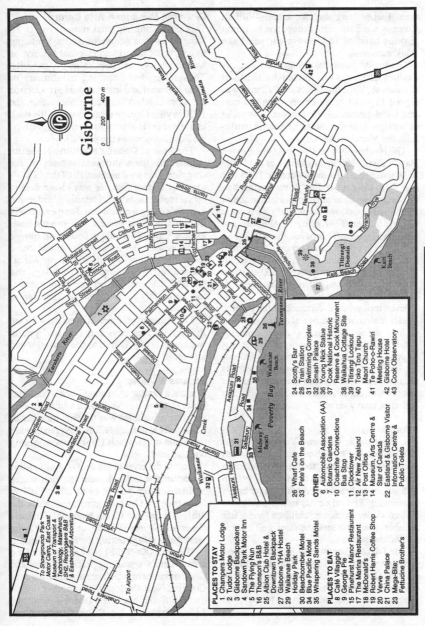

Gisborne

0   200   400 m

THE EAST COAST

PLACES TO STAY
1   Champers Motor Lodge
2   Tudor Lodge
3   Gisborne Backpackers
4   Sandown Park Motor Inn
5   The Flying Nun
16 Thomson's B&B
25 Albion Club Hotel &
    Downtown Backpacker
27 Gisborne YHA Hostel
29 Waikanae Beach
    Holiday Park
30 Beachcomber Motel
34 Blue Pacific Motel
35 Whispering Sands Motel

PLACES TO EAT
8   Café Villaggio
9   Georgie Pie
15 Pinehurst Manor Restaurant
17 The Marina Restaurant
18 McDonald's
19 Robert Harris Coffee Shop
20 Verve
21 China Palace
23 Mega-Bite;
    Fettucine Brother's

24 Scotty's Bar
28 Train Station
31 Swimming Complex
32 Smash Palace
36 Young Nick Statue
37 Cook National Historic
    Reserve & Cook Monument
38 Waikahua Cottage Site
39 Titirangi Lookout
40 Toko Toru Tapu
    Maori Church
41 Te Poho-o-Rawiri
    Meeting House
42 Gisborne Hotel
43 Cook Observatory

OTHER
6   Automobile Association (AA)
7   Botanic Gardens
10 Coachite Connections
    Bus Stop
12 Air New Zealand
13 Clocktower
14 Museum, Arts Centre &
    Star of Canada
22 Eastland & Gisborne Visitor
    Information Centre &
    Public Toilets
26 Wharf Cafe
33 Pete's on the Beach

area. Father Baty and Reverend William Colenso were the first Europeans to tramp into the heart of Te Urewera and see Lake Waikaremoana.

Gradually more Pakeha arrived but organised settlement was limited due to Maori resistance. When the Treaty of Waitangi was signed in 1840 many chiefs from the east coast did not acknowledge the treaty, let alone sign it. In the 1860s, numerous battles with the Maori broke out.

The Hauhau insurrection that began in the Bay of Plenty reached its height at the battle of Waerenga-a-hika in November 1865. By the following year the government had crushed opposition and transported a number of the survivors, including the charismatic Maori leader Te Kooti, to the remote Chatham Islands. This paved the way for an influx of Europeans, who brought with them their flocks of sheep. But in 1868 Te Kooti escaped and with an army of 200 exacted revenge on the settlement at Matawhero, killing 33 Europeans and 37 Maori.

Even today, however, much of the pasture land is leased from the Maori and a large part of it is under their direct control. Unfortunately, the pioneer farmers were so anxious to profit from the land that they ripped out far too much forest cover, with disastrous results. Massive erosion occurred as the steeply sloping land was unable to hold the soil after heavy rains.

Information

The Eastland & Gisborne Visitor Information Centre (☎ (06) 868 6139; fax 868 6138) is at 209 Grey St. Look for the fine Canadian totem pole beside it. It's open from 7.30 am to 5.30 pm daily in winter, with longer hours in summer. The office has useful brochures and good city maps, and children (and a fair number of adults) love the mini-golf course behind the centre.

The DOC office (☎ (06) 867 8531) at 63 Carnarvon St is open from 8 am to 4.30 pm on weekdays; you're requested to first seek information from the visitor centre. The Automobile Association (AA; ☎ (06) 868 1424) is at 363 Gladstone Rd.

Gisborne Museum & Arts Centre

This interesting regional museum is at 18 Stout St and has numerous displays relating to east coast Maori and colonial history, as well as geology and natural history exhibits. The gallery has changing exhibitions of local, national and international art. Outside are more exhibits – a sled house, stable, the 1870 Wyllie Cottage (first house on the site), and Lysnar House with working artists' studios (not open to the public).

The **Star of Canada Maritime Museum** behind the main museum is part of the complex. One wild night in 1912 the 12,000-ton ship *Star of Canada* was blown ashore on the reef at Gisborne. The ship's bridge and captain's cabin were salvaged and eventually installed in what became the town's best-known home. This unique house was moved to its present site, restored and made into a museum. There are displays on Maori canoes, early whaling and shipping, and Cook's Gisborne visit but the most interesting items relate, of course, to the *Star of Canada*.

The museum complex is open from 10 am to 4 pm on weekdays and 1.30 to 4 pm on weekends (entry is free to the museum and arts centre).

Statues & Views

There's a **statue** of 'Young Nick' (Nicholas Young), Cook's cabin boy, in a little park on the river mouth. He was the first member of Cook's crew to sight NZ. Across the bay are the white cliffs which Cook named 'Young Nick's Head'.

Across the river at the foot of Kaiti Hill is a **monument** to Cook, near the spot where he first set foot on NZ (9 October 1769 in 'ship time' in Cook's journal, but really the 8th). It's in the Cook National Historic Reserve. Nearby Waikahua Cottage once served as a refuge during the Hauhau unrest.

Titirangi (Kaiti Hill) has fine views of the area. There's a walking track up from the Cook monument which starts near Waikahua Cottage. Near the top is yet another monument to Cook, but it is a fine statue. At the 135m summit is the **Cook Observatory**, with a sign proclaiming it the 'World's Easternmost Observatory'. The Gisborne Astronomical Society (☎ (06) 868 8653) meets here at 7.30 pm on Tuesday; all are welcome.

Down on **Kaiti Beach**, low tide attracts a wealth of birdlife, including stilts, oyster-catchers and other pelagic visitors.

Te Poho-o-Rawiri

Also at the foot of Titirangi is Te Poho-o-Rawiri Maori meeting house, one of the largest in NZ. It has a richly decorated interior and its stage is framed by carved *maihi* (ornamental carved gable boards). The human figure kneeling on the right knee with right hand held upwards is the *tekoteko* (carved figure) representing the ancestor who challenges those who enter the marae. It is open all the time except when a function is in progress; seek permission before entering. A little Maori church, **Toko Toru Tapu**, stands on the side of Titirangi, not far from the meeting house.

The leaflet called *Tairawhiti – Heritage Trails: Gisborne District* is good for information on historic sites in this Maori ancestral land.

Other Attractions

The Gisborne area has a few attractive gardens to visit, including the huge **Eastwoodhill Arboretum** (☎ (06) 863 9800), 35km from town, which is open daily from 10 am to 4 pm ($5, children free). It contains the largest collection of northern hemisphere temperate trees, shrubs and climbers in NZ. To get there follow the Ngatapa-Rere Road; there is a 45-minute marked track through the trees. The visitor information centre has details on many other private gardens. The **Botanic Gardens** are in town beside the river off Aberdeen Rd.

Gisborne is a major wine-producing area, noted for its chardonnay. **Wineries** to visit: Parker Methode Champenoise, 24 Bank St; Matawhero Wines on Riverpoint Rd; Millton Wines in Manutuke; and Harvest Wines on Customhouse St in Gisborne. There are tours to the larger wineries such as Montana and Corbans. There is also a natural beer brewery, the Sunshine Brewing Company, at 109 Disraeli St.

Near the A&P Showgrounds in Makaraka is the **East Coast Museum of Transport & Technology (ECMOT)**. It is open daily from 9.30 am to 4.30 pm ($2, children 50c).

At Matawhero, a few kilometres south along SH2, the historic Presbyterian Church is the only building in the vicinity to have survived the conflicts of 1868.

Activities

You can swim at Waikanae Beach in the city. In fact there's good swimming, fishing and surfing all along the coast. Midway Beach has a swimming complex with a big waterslide and children's playground. Enterprise Pools on Nelson Rd is an indoor complex open to the public.

The Motu and Waioeka rivers are in the Gisborne district; ask at the visitor information centre about white-water rafting. The centre also has details on walks, horse trekking, fishing, hunting and tours.

A new walk of interest is the Te Kuri Walkway, a three-hour walk through farmland and some forest to a commanding viewpoint. The walk traverses the farm of Murray Ball, the cartoonist and creator of *Footrot Flats*, whose beloved hero is 'The Dog'. The walk starts 4km north of town at the end of Shelley Rd.

You can horse trek with Waimoana Horse Trekking (☎ (06) 868 8218) at Wainui; a trek is $25 for two hours.

Places to Stay

Camping & Cabins The *Waikanae Beach Holiday Park* (☎ (06) 867 5634) is on Grey St at Waikanae Beach. Camp sites cost $14 for two, cabins range from $22 for two, and tourist flats are $48.

The *Showgrounds Park Motor Camp* (☎ (06) 867 4101) at Makaraka is cheaper ($10.50 for two, $12.50 with power) but it's not so conveniently central. The cabins are also cheap at $15 to $20 for two ($9 an extra adult) but they're pretty spartan.

Hostels At 147 Roebuck Rd, the *Flying Nun Backpackers* (☎ (06) 868 0461) still awaits the right winds for Sister Bertrille. Backpackers with the right equipment (the hat and healthy habits, perhaps) can alight here in this good backpackers with all the facilities. It charges $13 in dorms, $30/35 in twins/doubles, and $17.50 in singles. Dame Kiri Te Kanawa (see the boxed text below) stretched her vocal chords and had her early singing lessons here.

The *Gisborne YHA Hostel* (☎ (06) 867 3269) is at 32 Harris St, 1.5km from the town centre across the river, in a big rambling old home with spacious grounds. The nightly cost is $14 in dorms and $32 for doubles or twins.

Gisborne Backpackers (☎ (06) 868 1000) is at 690 Gladstone Rd, about 2km from the town centre. This large, former orphanage has dorm rooms for $13 and $15, or singles/doubles for $20/35.

The *Downtown Backpack* (☎ (06) 867 9997), part of the Albion Club Hotel at 13 Gladstone Rd, is an absolute last resort; it charges $12 (earplugs not included) for basic rooms perched above a noisy bar.

B&Bs & Guesthouses The visitor information centre has full details. *Thomson's B&B* (☎ (06) 868 9675), 159 the Esplanade, is pleasantly situated in the historic riverfront district and charges $55 for two; *Tudor Lodge* (☎ (06) 867 7577), 573 Aberdeen Rd, charges $40/55 for singles/doubles; and *Repongaere* (☎ (06) 862 7717), near Patutahi, is an upmarket B&B in an historic homestead. This fine retreat charges from $120 to $150 a double (dinner can be arranged).

Motels & Hotels Most Gisborne motels start from around $70/80 for singles/doubles. Salisbury Rd, close to the city centre and right near the beach, is a good motel hunting ground. Motels here include the *Blue Pacific* (☎ (06) 868 6099) and *Whispering Sands* (☎ (06) 867 1319), on the beach, or the *Beachcomber* (☎ (06) 868 9349) across the street.

Other good choices include the *Coastland Motel* (☎ (06) 868 6464) at 114 Main Rd (from $66 a double), and the *Champers Motor Lodge* (☎ (06) 863 1515) at 811 Gladstone Rd (doubles and twins from $80 to

---

Dame Kiri Te Kanawa

One of the most famous Kiwis of all time (in international terms) is Dame Kiri Te Kanawa, the serenely beautiful opera diva. (The other well-known Kiwi is perhaps mountaineer Sir Edmund Hillary.)

It's hard to imagine that this lyrical soprano who graces La Scala and Covent Garden with aplomb had her beginnings in this motley neighbourhood; she was born in Gisborne in 1944. Her first major leading role was as the Countess in *Le Nozze di Figaro* at Covent Garden (1971), and she has since embraced the roles of Donna Elvira (*Don Giovanni*), Marguerite (*Faust*), Mimi (*La Bohéme*), Amelia (*Simon Boccanegra*) and Desdemona (*Otello*). There have been many famous commercial recordings – *West Side Story* with José Carreras, and the haunting calls across the valley of Canteloube's *Songs of the Auvergne*. She also sang at Charles and Diana's wedding in 1981.

The pressure is on Kiri to be in Auckland for the America's Cup in 2000. Gisborne's humble hope is that Kiri, supreme mistress of the *waiata* (song), will come for the dawn of the new millennium. Imagine the welcome her voice would give. ∎

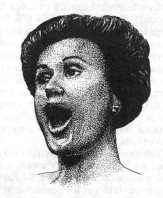

$120). The *Gisborne Hotel* (☎ (06) 868 4109) on the corner of Tyndall and Huxley Rd, Kaiti, is a tidy enough place if a little isolated (prices on application).

Places to Eat

Gisborne has the usual selection of sandwich places, particularly along Gladstone Rd – or you could try Peel St, where there is *Mega-Bite* with good hot lunches (quiche, samosas and the like), sandwiches, rolls, and drinks. Next door are the *Fettucine Brothers* – you guessed it, it's an Italian pasta place. Opposite and in the pedestrian mall leading to McDonald's, is the *Robert Harris Coffee Shop* with a good selection of sandwiches. *Georgie Pie* is on Gladstone Rd.

For Chinese food, the most popular place is *China Palace* on Peel St, which has a takeaway counter at front and a no-frills dining section. The BYO *Verve* at 121 Gladstone Rd has continental meals, an Internet connection and a nice ambience – it is open daily.

Down at Gisborne wharf, the *Wharf Cafe* serves meals, decadent desserts and wine by the glass. *Pete's on the Beach* is a seafood and steak place, open for lunch and dinner.

The top of the town's dining pile is the *Pinehurst Manor* at 4 Clifford St, a winner of several awards and justifiably so. Out of town, in Ballance St village, is the popular *Café Villaggio*, recognisable by its Art Deco look and with a good blackboard menu.

Entertainment

For a *Once Were Warriors* experience, the *Albion Club* on Gladstone Rd and the *Gisborne Hotel* on Huxley Rd, Kaiti, are rough pubs with live music most weekends.

The most interesting place in town is *Smash Palace*, set appropriately in the junkyard area of town at Bank St. A couple of beaten up old Morris Minor cars and the hulk of a long-grounded aircraft greet you outside, while inside is a veritable Aladdin's cave of junk from all parts of the globe and Kiwi memorabilia. But the place has atmosphere, a good selection of beers and wines, and light bar meals.

You'll find the young trendy set at *Scotty's Bar* on Gladstone Rd and a slightly older group of ragers at the *Irish Rover* on Peel St. During summer, bands, musicians and poets perform in the parks.

Getting There & Away

Air The Air New Zealand office (☎ (06) 867 9768) is at 37 Bright St. It has daily direct flights to Wellington, Napier, Hamilton and Auckland, with onward connections.

Bus The InterCity depot (☎ (06) 868 6196) is at the information centre. InterCity has at least one bus daily to Napier via Wairoa. From Napier there are connections to Palmerston North and Wellington. InterCity also runs buses between Gisborne and Auckland via Opotiki, Whakatane and Rotorua.

Coachrite Connections (☎ (06) 868 9969) has a 7.45 am bus daily, except Saturday, to Wairoa ($20), Napier ($35) and Hastings ($35), with student/backpacker discounts of around 20%. It departs from opposite Georgie Pie on Gladstone Rd.

Newmans buses depart from the information centre on Friday and Saturday at 7.15 am for Wellington via Napier ($79).

The much longer, but very scenic, East Cape route to Opotiki can be done by a combination of courier services (ask at the Opotiki or Gisborne information centre). Another route from Rotorua to Gisborne runs through the Te Urewera National Park, passing Lake Waikaremoana and joining the Napier route at Wairoa, 97km south of Gisborne; there is currently no bus on this service.

Hitching Hitching is OK from the south of the city, and not too bad through Waioeka Gorge to Opotiki – it's still best to leave early. To hitch a ride out, head along Gladstone Rd to Makaraka, 6km west, for Wairoa and Napier, or the turn-off to Opotiki and Rotorua. Hitching from Wairoa to Waikaremoana is hard going.

Getting Around

Gisborne City Buses (☎ (06) 868 6761) run

only on weekdays and until about 5.30 pm. Taxis include Gisborne Taxis (☎ (06) 867 2222) and Eastland Taxis (☎ (06) 868 1133). Link Shuttles (☎ (06) 868 8385) run to Gisborne airport ($10 from town). For cheap rentals, check out Scotties (☎ (06) 867 7947).

GISBORNE TO WAIROA

Heading south towards Napier you have two choices. The bus follows the SH2 coastal route before meeting SH36 in Wairoa. Inland SH36 is equally scenic.

The **coastal route** runs just inland most of the way south from Gisborne, before entering the Wharerata State Forest. At the southern edge of the state forest, 56km from Gisborne, Morere is a pretty little town noted for its hot springs. The **hot springs** are complemented by short walks of up to two hours through the beautiful native forest of the surrounding reserve. The hot springs are open from 10 am to 8 pm daily ($3, children $1.50, in the public pool; $4, children $2, in private pools).

You can stay in Morere at the delightful *Peacock Lodge* (☎ (06) 837 8824), about two minutes walk from SH2. Follow the road next to the tearooms across the stream. This colonial farmhouse has a spacious lounge, fully equipped kitchen and a large, wide verandah – it charges $15 in shared rooms, or $30 in doubles and twins. The *Morere Springs Tavern* has a small restaurant.

SH2 continues south to Nuhaka on the northern end of the sweep of Hawkes Bay, where you can head west to Wairoa or east to the superb, windswept and wild **Mahia Peninsula** (mahia translates as 'indistinct sounds', although the peninsula is said to be named after a place in Tahiti). There are long, curving beaches popular with surfers, clear water for diving and fishing, birdwatching at Mangawhio Lagoon and walks to a number of reserves. The isthmus was once an island, but sand accumulation has formed NZ's largest tombolo landform (where a sand or shingle bar ties an island to another island or the mainland). The Mahia is a magical, atmospheric place, majestic in either sun or storm.

Facilities are limited and you'll need your own transport to get around. The *Mahia Beach Motel & Holiday Park* (☎ (06) 837 5830) at Nuhaka has sites from $16 for two, cabins for $36 for two and motel-style units for $70. Some 6km from Opoutama is the *Tunanui Station Cottages* (☎ (06) 837 5790), which has a fully self-contained cottage sleeping six ($100) – the views over the peninsula from here are stupendous.

Along SH36, the **inland route** to Wairoa and Napier, there are also several things to see and do. You can climb up **Gentle Annie Hill** for a good view over the Poverty Bay area. **Doneraille Park** (53km from Gisborne), a native bush reserve, is a popular picnic spot with good swimming when the water is clear. There's fine trout fishing at **Tiniroto Lakes**, 61km from Gisborne, and, about 10km further, the **Te Reinga Falls** are worth a detour off the main road.

Hawkes Bay

Hawkes Bay (on some maps Hawke Bay) is, sadly, missed by many visitors to NZ. Napier (like Hastings) is one of the best holiday destinations in the country, with fine Art Deco architecture. The region also offers the 'perfect' village of Havelock North, wineries near Te Mata Peak and natural attractions such as the Cape Kidnappers gannet colony.

WAIROA

The two highways, SH2 and SH36, merge in Wairoa (population 10,680), 98km south of Gisborne. Wairoa has a reasonable beach and the town is the gateway to Te Urewera National Park. The reconstructed **lighthouse** by the river, built in 1877 of solid kauri, used to shine from Portland Island at the tip of the Mahia Peninsula. Not far east of Wairoa is the Whakaki Lagoon, an important wetlands area renowned for its bird populations.

The Wairoa Information Centre (☎ (06) 838 7440) is on the corner of SH2 and Queen

St. The DOC field centre (☎ (06) 838 8252) is at 272 Marine Parade.

Places to Stay & Eat
The *Riverside Motor Camp* (☎ (06) 838 6301) is a pleasant place on the banks of the Wairoa River with powered sites from $8 per person and cabins for $31 a double. Wairoa also has pub rooms at the *Clyde Hotel* (☎ (06) 838 7139) on Marine Parade, and the *Three Oaks Motel* (☎ (06) 838 8204), on the corner of Campbell St and Clyde Rd, has doubles for $75.

At Frasertown, 8km north of Wairoa, *Tipi Backpacker* (☎ (06) 838 7960) makes an excellent base for visiting Te Urewera National Park. This quiet, rural retreat is on SH38 – look for the big *tipi* (teepee) in the garden. A dorm bed in the well-equipped farmhouse costs $14, twins and doubles are $34 or in summer you can stay in the tipi for $12. The staff organise trips to Te Reinga Falls and local glow-worm caves, and arrange transport to the national park. They can pick up from Napier or Gisborne for $15 – ring for details. The hostel is closed in winter.

For food, try *Johanna's* in Clyde Court, or *Katz* and *Oslers Bakery*, both on Marine Parade.

Getting There & Away
All InterCity (☎ (06) 838 6049) and Coachrite Connections buses between Gisborne and Napier pass through Wairoa. Unfortunately the service to Rotorua via Te Urewera has ceased.

WAIROA TO NAPIER
There are some good reserves along this stretch of road, all accessible from SH2, to break the twisting drive.

Lake Tutira has a farmland setting; there are walkways around the lake and a bird sanctuary. The **Hawkes Bay Coastal Walkway** is 12km from SH2, down Waikari Rd. The walkway is 16km long, goes from the Waikari River to the Aropaoanui River, and involves equal portions of boulder hopping, track walking and beach walking.

Off Waipati Rd and 34km from Napier is

the **Waipatiki Scenic Reserve**. The **White Pine Bush Scenic Reserve**, 29km from Napier, is notable for the dominant kahikatea (white pine). The **Tangoio Falls Scenic Reserve**, 2km south of White Pine, has the Te Ana Falls, stands of ponga and whekiponga and podocarps. The White Pine and Tangoio Falls reserves are linked by the **Tangoio Walkway**, which follows Kareaara Stream.

TE UREWERA NATIONAL PARK
Te Urewera National Park is one of the country's most attractive parks. It is a marvellous area of lush forests, lakes and rivers, with lots of tramps ranging from half an hour to several days, and plenty of birds, trout, deer and other wildlife. The main focus of the park is the superbly scenic Lake Waikaremoana (sea of rippling waters). Most visitors to the park come to go boating on the lake or walk the Waikaremoana Track, one of New Zealand's Great Walks, but other walks are possible.

The park protects part of the largest untouched native forest area in the North Island. The rivers and lakes of the park offer good fishing for trout.

Information
The Aniwaniwa Visitor Centre (☎ (06) 837 3803) is within the park on the shores of the lake. It has interesting displays on the park's natural history and supplies information on the walking tracks and accommodation around the park. The Ikawhenua Visitor Centre (☎ (07) 366 5641) is the park's other main information centre and near Murupara on the park's western edge. Hut and camping ground passes for the Lake Waikaremoana Track can also be bought at DOC offices and visitor centres in Gisborne, Whakatane and Napier.

Lake Waikaremoana Track
This three to four-day tramp is one of the most popular walks in the North Island. The 46km track has spectacular views from the Panekiri Bluff, but all along the walk through fern groves, beech and podocarp forest there

are vast panoramas and beautiful views of the lake. The walk is rated as easy and the only difficult section is the climb to Panekiri Bluff. Because of its popularity it is very busy from mid-December to the end of January and at Easter.

The walk can be done year-round, but the cold and rain in winter deter most people and make conditions much more challenging. Because of the altitude, temperatures can drop quickly even in summer. Walkers should take portable stoves and fuel as there are no cooking facilities in the huts. It's not recommended that you park your car at either end of the track – there's been break-ins.

Five huts are spaced along the track, but at peak times it is wise to take a tent. Huts and camp sites are $6 (children $3).

Walking the Track The track can be done from either Onepoto in the south or Hopuruahine Landing in the north. Starting from Onepoto, all the climbing is done in the first few hours. Water on this section of the track is limited so make sure you fill your water bottles before heading off. For those with a car, it is safest to leave it at Waikaremoana and then take a boat to the trail heads.

Estimated walking times are:

Onepoto to Panekiri Hut	five hours
Panekiri Hut to Waiopaoa Hut	three to four hours
Waiopaoa Hut to Marauiti Hut	4½ hours
Marauiti Hut to Te Puna Hut	2¾ hours
Te Puna Hut to Whanganui Hut	two hours
Whanganui Hut to Hopuruahine	three hours

Other Walks
The other major walk in the park is the Whakatane River Round Trip. The three to five-day walk starts at Ruatahuna on SH38, 45km from the Aniwaniwa Visitor Centre towards Rotorua. The track follows the Whakatane River then loops back via the Waikare River, Motumuka Stream and the Whakatane Valley. The track has six huts.

DOC at Aniwaniwa has track notes for this walk and sells topographical maps.

Another good walk is the Lake Waikareiti Track, which begins near Aniwaniwa and leads to the Sandy Bay Hut. There are at least 20 other walks along the park's 600km of tracks.

Kayaking

Bay Kayaks (☎ (06) 837 3737) have guided kayaking trips on the lake starting at $90. There is a tramp-paddle option allowing you to, say, walk three sections of the track and kayak one for variety. Kayaks can also be rented for $35 a half-day, $45 per day or $175 for five days (sixth day free).

Places to Stay

There are various camps and cabins along SH38, including a camp, cabins and motel 67km inland from the Wairoa turn-off.

DOC has over 50 huts along the walkways throughout the national park. The five Lake Waikaremoana Track huts are rated as Great Walks huts and cost $6 per night, but other huts are $4 or free. DOC also has some minimal facility camping grounds, where it costs only $2 to camp. All the ranger stations have information on camping.

On the shore of Lake Waikaremoana is the *Waikaremoana Motor Camp* (☎ (06) 837 3826), the most popular place to stay. Camp sites cost $7.50 per person, $9 with power, while cabins are $30 for two, chalets are $55, motel units are $55 and a family unit costs $77 for four. The camp has a shop.

At Tuai, just outside the southern entrance to the park, there is a motor camp and the *Tuai Lodge*. The nearest hostel is the *Tipi Backpacker* at Frasertown, 42km south of Tuai (see Wairoa).

On the northern edge of the park there is a range of accommodation. There are motels at Ruatahuna, Taneatua and Murupara, which also has a hotel. At Galatea, on the Whakatane-Murupara Road, the *Galatea Estate Guest Cottage* (☎ (07) 366 4703) has doubles or twins for $65.

Getting There & Around

Most of the 120km road through the park between Frasertown and the town of Murupara is unsealed, winding and time-consuming. Traffic is light, making it slow for hitching. There is no longer an InterCity service between Wairoa and Rotorua.

The Waikaremoana Shuttle service (☎ (06) 837 3836) operates on demand from Tuai to Onepoto, the motor camp, visitor information centre, Mokau landing, and Hopuruahine. Depending on the number of people, the cost from Tuai is around $10 to Onepoto and $20 to Hopuruahine.

From Home Bay, Waikaremoana, a water taxi (☎ (06) 837 3737) will drop off at all parts of the lake. It charges $10 to Onepoto and $15 to Hopuruahine – you can get off at many secluded camping spots.

NAPIER

Lying on sweeping Hawkes Bay, Napier (population 54,000) is a fascinating, architecturally rich city, blessed with a Mediterranean climate, fine coastal position, attractive Marine Parade, good restaurants and a friendly population. It is a great city to visit but avoid domestic holidays, when it is crowded and accommodation is expensive.

History

Long before Captain Cook sighted the area in October 1769, the Maori found a plentiful source of food in the bay and the hinterland. The Otatara Pa, with its barricades now rebuilt, is one of the pre-European sites of habitation. The French explorer Jules Dumont d'Urville, using Cook's charts, sailed the *Astrolabe* into the bay in 1827. After whalers started using the safe Ahuriri anchorage in the 1830s, a trading base was established in 1839. The town was planned in 1854, named after the British general and colonial administrator, Charles Napier, and soon flourished as a commercial regional centre.

In 1931 Napier was dramatically changed when a disastrous earthquake, measuring 7.9 on the Richter scale, virtually destroyed it. In Napier and nearby Hastings over 250 people

THE EAST COAST

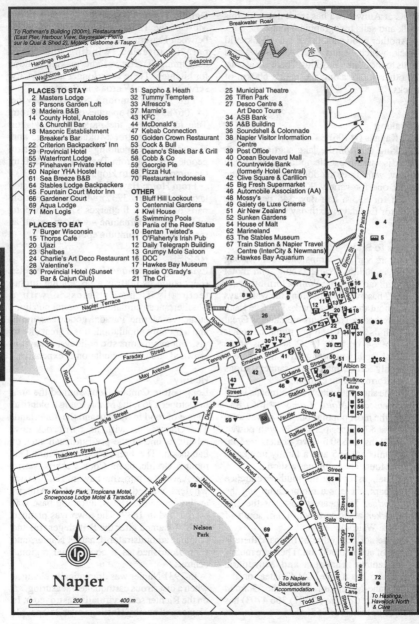

To Rothman's Building (300m), Restaurants
(East Pier, Harbour View, Bayswater, Pierre
sur le Quai & Shed 2), Motels, Gisborne & Taupo

PLACES TO STAY
2 Masters Lodge
8 Parsons Garden Loft
9 Madeira B&B
14 County Hotel, Anatoles
   & Churchill Bar
18 Masonic Establishment
   Breaker's Bar
22 Criterion Backpackers' Inn
29 Provincial Hotel
55 Waterfront Lodge
57 Pinehaven Private Hotel
60 Napier YHA Hostel
61 Sea Breeze B&B
64 Stables Lodge Backpackers
65 Fountain Court Motor Inn
66 Gardener Court
69 Aqua Lodge
71 Mon Logis

PLACES TO EAT
7 Burger Wisconsin
15 Thorps Cafe
20 Ujazi
23 Shelbes
24 Charlie's Art Deco Restaurant
28 Valentine's
30 Provincial Hotel (Sunset
   Bar & Cajun Club)

31 Sappho & Heath
32 Tummy Tempters
33 Alfresco's
37 Mamie's
43 KFC
44 McDonald's
47 Kebab Connection
50 Golden Crown Restaurant
53 Cock & Bull
56 Deano's Steak Bar & Grill
59 Georgie Pie
68 Pizza Hut
70 Restaurant Indonesia

OTHER
1 Bluff Hill Lookout
3 Centennial Gardens
4 Kiwi House
5 Swimming Pools
6 Pania of the Reef Statue
10 Bertan Twisted's
11 O'Flaherty's Irish Pub
12 Daily Telegraph Building
13 Grumpy Mole Saloon
16 DOC
17 Hawkes Bay Museum
19 Rosie O'Grady's
21 The Cri

25 Municipal Theatre
26 Tiffen Park
27 Desco Centre &
   Art Deco Tours
34 ASB Bank
35 A&B Building
36 Soundshell & Colonnade
38 Napier Visitor Information
   Centre
39 Post Office
40 Ocean Boulevard Mall
41 Countrywide Bank
   (formerly Hotel Central)
42 Clive Square & Carillion
45 Big Fresh Supermarket
46 Automobile Association (AA)
48 Mossy's
49 Gaiety de Luxe Cinema
51 Air New Zealand
52 Sunken Gardens
54 House of Malt
58 Marineland
63 The Stables Museum
67 Train Station & Napier Travel
   Centre (InterCity & Newmans)
72 Hawkes Bay Aquarium

THE EAST COAST

Napier

0   200   400 m

To Kennedy Park, Tropicana Motel,
Snowgoose Lodge Motel & Taradale

Nelson
Park

To Napier
Backpackers
Accommodation

To Hastings,
Havelock North
& Clive

died, and waterlocked Napier suddenly found itself 40 sq km larger. The quake heaved that amount of water-covered land above sea level, and in places the land level rose by over 2m. The Napier airport is built on that previously submerged area. The rebuilding program that followed has left one of the world's best examples of an Art Deco city.

Orientation

At the northern end of town Bluff Hill looms, acting as a natural boundary between the centre and the Ahuriri and port areas. The fine wooden villas on the hill that survived the quake give this district a genteel air. Marine Parade with its many attractions marks the eastern boundary and the main part of town is in this north-eastern corner.

The prime commercial streets are Hastings and Emerson Sts. Emerson St has been developed into a pedestrian thoroughfare with clever paving and street furniture to complement its many Art Deco features.

Information

Napier's helpful and well-informed visitor information centre (☎ (06) 834 1911; fax 835 7129) is at 100 Marine Parade. It's open from 8.30 am to 5 pm on weekdays and 9 am to 5 pm on weekends (extended over summer). The AA office is on Dickens St (but it is closed on weekends).

The DOC office (☎ (06) 835 0415) is also on Marine Parade, in the Old Courthouse. It has information on walkways around Napier, the Cape Kidnappers gannet colony, Te Urewera National Park, and the Kaweka and Ruahine forest parks, both about 50km west of Napier.

Art Deco Architecture

The earthquake and fire of 1931 resulted in the collapse of most of Napier's older brick buildings. Two frantic years of reconstruction from 1931 to 1933 meant that much of the city architecture dates from the peak years for Art Deco. Dr Neil Cossons, past president of the British Museums Association, said:

Napier represents the most complete and significant group of Art Deco buildings in the world, and is comparable with Bath as an example of a planned townscape in a cohesive style. Napier is without doubt unique.

The Napier Art Deco Trust promotes and protects the city's architectural heritage. Its excellent guided Art Deco walks cost $10 for adults and leave from the Desco Centre (☎ (06) 835 0022), 163 Tennyson St, at 2 pm on Wednesday, Saturday and Sunday (almost daily in the summer months). The walk takes 1½ hours, and is preceded by a half-hour introductory talk (and illustrative videos). The shop in the Desco Centre sells books, postcards and souvenirs.

Walk leaflets ($1.50; in German also) are available from the visitor centre, Desco Centre or the museum. There's also an Art Deco Scenic Drive map to the Art Deco and Spanish Mission-style architecture around Napier and Hastings ($2.50). The *Marewa Meander* ($1.50) leads you through a suburb transformed after the quake.

As you walk around town, look for Art Deco motifs on the buildings, such as zig-zags, lightning flashes, geometric shapes and rising suns. The soft pastel colours are another Art Deco giveaway, employed by restorers, though many of Napier's buildings were originally monochrome plaster.

Emerson St has some excellent examples of Art Deco, though many of the shopfronts have been modernised and you'll have to look up to the second storeys to see the fine Art Deco detail. Good examples on Emerson St are the **Provincial Hotel**, **Charlie's Art Deco Restaurant**, the **Esprit buildings**, the **Criterion Hotel** and the **ASB Bank**. On Dalton St the **Hotel Central** (which is now the Countrywide Bank) is a superb example of the style, both externally and internally (don't miss the foyer and stairs). Round the corner on Dickens St, look for the extravagant Moorish and Spanish Mission-style building which used to be the **Gaiety de Luxe Cinema**. On the corner of Dickens and Dalton Sts is the State Cinema (now a shopping complex).

Tennyson St has fine, preserved buildings. The recently restored **Municipal Theatre** is a must with its neon light fittings and wall decorations. The **Daily Telegraph Building** is one of the finest examples of Art Deco in Napier and the **Desco Centre** facing Clive Square is also impressive, despite some modifications. At the intersection of Tennyson and Hastings Sts are more fine buildings, particularly the block of **Hastings St** from Tennyson St to Browning St. On Marine Parade the **Soundshell** is Art Deco, as is the paving of the plaza. From here you can admire the Art Deco **clocktower** (neon lit at night) of the A&B building and also the **Masonic Hotel**, now the Masonic Establishment.

In the third week of February, Napier holds an Art Deco weekend, when there are dinners, balls and much fancy dress. The fifth Art Deco World Congress will be held here in 1999.

Marine Parade

Lined with Norfolk pines and some fine old wooden buildings that survived the quake, Marine Parade is one of NZ's premier seaside boulevards. It has retained its air of an old-fashioned English seaside resort complete with pebble beach, but the strong riptide makes for hazardous swimming.

Marine Parade has parks, sunken and scented gardens, and amusements including mini golf, swimming pools and a rollerblading rink. The statue of **Pania of the Reef**, a sort of Maori equivalent of Copenhagen's Little Mermaid, is at the parade's northern end.

Marineland has a collection of performing seals and dolphins; displays take place at 10.30 am and 2 pm, with an extra 4 pm show in summer ($8, children $4).

Not far away on the parade, the **Hawkes Bay Aquarium** has sharks, crocodiles, piranha, turtles and other animals including NZ's unique tuataras. It's open daily from 9 am to 5 pm and feeding time is 3.15 pm ($7, children $3.50).

Marine Parade also has a **Kiwi House**, open daily from 11 am to 3 pm ($3, children

$1.50). The **Stables Museum** at 321 Marine Parade covers the effects of the 1931 quake and is open 8 am to 6 pm daily ($6, children $2.50).

Hawkes Bay Museum & Cultural Trust

Also on Marine Parade is a well-run art gallery and museum. Quality Maori artefacts of the east coast's Ngati Kahungunu tribe are displayed, as well as European antiques and Art Deco items; there's also a dry but informative audiovisual of the 1931 earthquake.

The museum has regular exhibitions. The best at the moment is that of the dinosaurs found in Hawkes Bay. It records the struggle of an amateur palaeontologist, Jan Wiffen, who proved university-trained sceptics wrong and found several prehistoric species when they said there were none to be found.

The museum is open from 10 am to 4.30 pm daily ($4, children free). Its shop has good-quality souvenirs.

Bluff Hill Lookout

There's an excellent view over all of Hawkes Bay from Bluff Hill, 102m above the Port of Napier. It's a sheer cliff-face down to the port, however, and rather a circuitous route to the top. It's open daily from 7 am until one hour after sunset.

Activities

There are many water activities, including fishing, windsurfing, kayaking, canoeing, parasailing, jet-boating, water-skiing and tandem skydiving – ask at the information centre.

Although the beach along Marine Parade is not good for swimming, there's great swimming and surfing on the beach up past the port. The pool on Marine Parade ($1) is closed in winter. The Onekawa Complex is larger and fancier, with waterslides and other attractions.

More activities can be found at Riverland Outback Adventures (☎ (06) 834 9756), 50km north of Napier on SH5, where there's horse trekking, white-water rafting and backpacker accommodation. Hawkes Bay Jet Tours (☎ (06) 874 9703) organises trips on the scenic Ngaruroro River, which range from 30 minutes to one day.

Hawkes Bay Adventure Kayaking (☎ (06) 875 0341) does trips in the inner harbour and out to Cape Kidnappers.

Places to Stay

Camping & Cabins Napier has a number of camping grounds, but none are conveniently central. Closest to the centre is *Kennedy Park* (☎ (06) 843 9126) off Kennedy Rd at Marewa, 2.5km from the post office. Powered sites cost $18 for two. There are also some basic huts at $25 for two, cabins at $38, tourist flats at $56 and motel units for $60.

The *Westshore Holiday Camp* (☎ (06) 835 9456) is on Main Rd near Westshore Beach, 6km north of town. Camp sites here are $7 per person, cabins are $25 to $30 for two and there are tourist flats from $40.

At Taradale, 9.5km out, *Taradale Holiday Park* (☎ (06) 844 2732) at 470 Gloucester St has tent/powered sites from $7/7.50 per person, and on-site caravans and cabins from $40.

Hostels The *Napier YHA Hostel* (☎ (06) 835 7039), 277 Marine Parade, is a former guesthouse in an excellent location opposite the beach. It charges $15 a night in a dorm or twin room. The kitchen, dining room and recreation area are all separate, making it more spacious.

Right in the centre the *Criterion Backpackers' Inn* (☎ (06) 835 2059) at 48 Emerson St is upstairs in what was formerly the Criterion Hotel, a classy Art Deco building. It has the usual kitchen and dining facilities plus a large recreation area; downstairs are a bistro and bar. It charges $12 and $14 in the dorms, $30 for twin or double rooms.

The *Stables Lodge Backpackers* (☎ (06) 835 6242), 321 Marine Parade, is behind The Stables museum complex – you enter from Hastings St after hours. It's a modern hostel with spotless rooms and a good kitchen-dining area. A dorm is $15, and doubles and twins are $36 (cheaper in winter).

The *Aqua Lodge* (☎ (06) 835 4523) in a

converted house at 53 Nelson Crescent has a poolside barbecue, just the ticket on a balmy evening; dorms are $15, singles are $23, and doubles and twins are $36. They provide a free pasta meal on Thursday night in winter. The tiny *Napier Backpackers Accommodation* (☎ (06) 835 8901) at 19 McGrath St donates its profits to charity.

The *Glen-View Farm Hostel* (☎ (06) 836 6232) is a hill-country sheep and cattle station ($12 a night), where horse riding and walking are popular. You can join in with the farm activities. The hostel is 31km north of Napier off SH2, 2km along the Arapaoanui Rd towards the sea.

B&Bs & Guesthouses Since it is a summer resort of the old-fashioned variety, Napier has some good guesthouses along Marine Parade. However, as a major thoroughfare, it can be quite noisy. The *Pinehaven Private Hotel* (☎ (06) 835 5575) at No 259 has singles/doubles for $45/65; it's a strictly nonsmoking place. The front rooms have fine views of the seafront. The *Waterfront Lodge* (☎ (06) 835 3429) at No 217 is another old, wooden guesthouse offering B&B for $30/50, but it also has backpacker rooms for $15/32. At No 415 is the charming French-style *Mon Logis* (☎ (06) 835 2125), built in 1915 as a private hotel, but expensive at $150 a double. Opposite Marineland on the parade, the *Sea Breeze B&B* (☎ (06) 835 8067) has a lounge room with a great view and charges $40/70.

Another good hunting ground for B&Bs is on Bluff Hill, just a short walk down to the city (but a hard walk back); see the *Napier Hill Homestays* pamphlet. A number of fine wooden villas offer accommodation – the visitor information centre has listings. They include *Madeira B&B* (☎ (06) 835 5185), 6 Madeira Rd, at the end of a very steep street. It charges $75 a double and the upstairs balcony is *the* spot to take breakfast. Nearby, the *Parsons Garden Loft* (☎ (06) 835 1527), 29 Cameron Rd, is a fine old villa, with a new, self-contained flat at the back of the house costing $45/65. The *Masters Lodge* (☎ (06) 834 1946) at 10 Elizabeth Rd is the most upmarket place in Napier; it is the former home of the founder of the National Tobacco Co (now Rothmans), Gerhard Husheer. Swiss-style meals are served.

Motels Napier has plenty of motels, particularly around Westshore, on the Taupo Road. *Fairley Court* (☎ (06) 835 9633) at 1 Tareha St has singles/doubles from $70/90. The *Marineland Motel* (☎ (06) 835 2147), 20 Meeanee Quay, charges the same; it has an indoor pool.

The *Fountain Court Motor Inn* (☎ (06) 835 7387) at 209 Hastings St is conveniently located and charges $70/85. The *Snowgoose Lodge Motel* (☎ (06) 843 6083) at 376 Kennedy Rd charges $60/85, and at 335 Kennedy Rd, the *Tropicana Motel* (☎ (06) 843 9153) has units for $56/68. The *Gardener Court* (☎ (06) 835 5913), 16 Nelson Crescent, charges $60/75, and the *Harbour View* (☎ (06) 835 8077) on Hardinge Rd charges $70/90.

Hotels The fine old *Masonic Establishment* (☎ (06) 835 8689) on the corner of Marine Parade and Tennyson St is very central. The rooms with bathroom are $60/85 or singles without bath cost $40. Breaker's Bar is underneath so the rooms can be noisy.

For something special, the *County Hotel* (☎ (06) 835 7800), 12 Browning St, is a boutique hotel in a newly refurbished and converted building. Rooms offering real luxury start at $150.

Places to Eat
Restaurants & Cafes Napier has an excellent selection of restaurants, cafes and bars, and many places act as all three.

Alfresco's, upstairs at 65 Emerson St, has a good range of food and great liqueur coffees. On lower Emerson St *Sappho & Heath* is the place for good coffee and panini. *Anatoles* at the County Hotel on Browning St is a cafe-bar open for breakfast, lunch and dinner. This is the place to be seen and is upmarket but not outrageously expensive for good and varied food.

Ujazi on Tennyson St has great coffee and

a vegetarian selection; it is open in the evening on weekends. Coffee and a bagel is about $7. *Thorps Cafe* on Hastings St serves humungous sandwiches to order.

If you are hankering for satay or rendang head to *Restaurant Indonesia* at 409 Marine Parade. This is a licensed and BYO restaurant with attractive decor and interesting food. Its rijsttafels, that Dutch-Indonesian-smorgasbord blend, range from $24 to $30 per person.

The Ahuriri wharf precinct has a number of trendy new eateries-cum-bars. *Bayswater* and *East Pier* on Hardinge Rd, *Shed 2* on West Quay and *Pierre sur le Quai* at 63 West Quay are fine dining establishments. At Onekawa, in the complex at 120 Taradale Rd, is *Cafe Absolute*, a relaxing place to enjoy a coffee. The adjoining restaurant has an excellent à la carte menu.

Pub Food *Deano's Steak Bar & Grill* on Marine Parade serves good, old-fashioned pub food. Its excellent, large steaks and grills are very good value. On Marine Parade is the *Cock & Bull*, a pastiche English-style pub, complete with British soccer memorabilia and Guinness on tap.

Fast Food Emerson St has some good sandwich bars, including *Tummy Tempters* at 204 Emerson St for healthy sandwiches and snacks. *Kebab Connection* on Dickens St has huge kebabs for $7. There are plenty of Chinese places in Napier. Try the *Golden Crown* on Dickens St; the Wednesday to Friday lunch-time smorgasbord is unbeatable value at $8. On the small, pedestrianised Market St, *Shelbes* specialises in pizzas and is reasonably priced. At 10 Shakespeare Rd is *Burgers Wisconsin*, which makes gourmet burgers (eg chicken, camembert, cranberry for $8.90).

McDonald's, *KFC*, *Pizza Hut*, *Valentine's* (a family buffet chain in the style of Denny's in the USA) and *Georgie Pie* are all represented in Napier.

Entertainment
The *Cri* on Emerson St is always a good bar

for a drink and often has bands on Friday and Saturday. *Rosie O'Grady's* on the Hastings St side of the Masonic has Guinness on tap and occasional live music. *Mossy's* on Dickens St is a local venue for musicians who gather for impromptu jam sessions; it has a good range of food, coffees and beers. *Breaker's Bar* in the Masonic Establishment has a DJ from Wednesday to Saturday and *O'Flaherty's Irish Pub* on Hastings St is yet another Irish pub that packs them in with bands on weekends. In the County Hotel there is a smoking bar, *Churchill's*, where you can imitate the great man by sticking a big fat cigar in your mouth.

Serious drinking bars are the *House of Malt* and *Bentan Twisted's* on Hastings St, the *Provincial Hotel* on Emerson St and the *Grumpy Mole Saloon* (with its often grumpy and fisty clientele) on the corner of Hastings and Tennyson Sts.

Getting There & Away

Air Air New Zealand (☎ (06) 835 3288) is on the corner of Hastings and Station Sts. It has direct flights to Auckland and Wellington several times daily, and to Christchurch daily with connections to other centres.

Bus InterCity and Newmans both operate from the Napier Travel Centre (☎ (06) 834 2720) at the train station in Munro St. Inter-City has services to Auckland, Hamilton, Rotorua, Taupo, Tauranga, Gisborne, Palmerston North and Wellington. The Travel Centre is closed on the weekend and the information centre handles ticketing.

Newmans routes head north to Taupo, Rotorua and Tauranga, through Palmerston North and Wanganui to New Plymouth, and to Wellington via Palmerston North.

As well as InterCity, Coachrite Connections travels daily, except Saturday, between Gisborne, Wairoa and Napier.

Train The train station (☎ (06) 834 2720) is on Munro St. The Bay Express train operates daily between Napier and Wellington, with several stops including Hastings and Palmerston North.

Hitching If you're heading north catch a bus and get off at Westshore, or try thumbing closer in. If you're heading south stick to SH2. The alternative inland route (SH50) is much harder going, with less traffic.

Getting Around

The airport shuttle bus (☎ (06) 879 9766) charges $7, and Napier Taxi Service (☎ (06) 835 7777) charges about $12.

Nimbus (☎ (06) 877 8133) operates the suburban bus services on weekdays, with regular buses between Napier and Hastings via Taradale, plus other local services. There's no service on weekends. All the local buses depart from the corner of Dickens and Dalton Sts.

Napier Cycle & Kart Centre (☎ (06) 835 9528) at 104 Carlyle St hires out 10-speeds and tandems at $12 for a half-day and $17 per day.

HASTINGS

Hastings (population 64,370), only 20km south of Napier, shared the same fate as Napier in the 1931 earthquake and is also noted for its Art Deco and Spanish Mission-style architecture. The paved Civic Square is particularly attractive, with the Art Deco clocktower as its centrepiece (but watch out for those trains that hurtle through the square!).

Hastings is an agricultural centre. During the apple harvest season from February to April, it is popular with those seeking work (accommodation is tight at this time). There are many nearby wineries.

The Blossom Festival, a celebration of spring, is held in September/October, with parades, arts and crafts and visiting artists.

Information

The Hastings Visitor Information Centre (☎ (06) 878 0510) on Russell St is open from 8.30 am to 5 pm on weekdays and 10 am until 3 pm on weekends. The AA office is on Heretaunga St West.

Things to See & Do

The legacy of the 1931 earthquake is an

THE EAST COAST

impressive collection of **Art Deco and Spanish Mission buildings**. The *Self Drive: Art Deco Tour* pamphlet ($1.50) is available from the information centre to explore Hastings' architecture in depth. The highlights are undoubtedly the **Westerman's Building**, with its impressive bronze and leadlight shopfronts that have largely survived modernisation, and the magnificent **Municipal Theatre** on Hastings St, the most imposing example of Spanish Mission style in the region.

Travelling with children? In Windsor Park, 2km east of the town centre on Grove Rd, is **Fantasyland** leisure park. It has a miniature of the Disneyland castle, a Mother Hubbard's shoe, merry-go-round, pirate ship, Noddy Town, go-karts, bumper boats, other boats you can take out on the lake fronting the castle, a flying fox, narrow gauge train rides and much more. It's open from 9 am to 4.30 pm daily ($3, children free, but rides are extra).

The **Hawkes Bay Exhibition Centre** in the Civic Square on Eastbourne St hosts a wide variety of changing exhibitions. It's open from 10 am to 4.30 pm on weekdays, from noon to 4.30 pm on weekends.

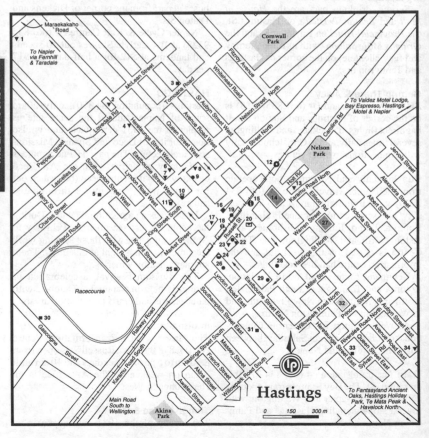

Hastings

THE EAST COAST

※▨※▨※▨※▨※▨※▨

There's Work if you Want it
Many overseas travellers come to this region to work so they can extend their trip to other parts of the country. The realities: if you are a competent picker you will make about $350 to $400 a week either apple picking or thinning (both back-breaking work). Top flight pickers can earn up to $700 but you have to be bloody good. Night packing can earn up to $8.50 an hour. There is usually work from November (in the summer apple season), followed by peach picking. The hostels usually find orchard contracting work if you are staying with them. Avoid short-term grape picking, as it doesn't pay that well. ■

※▨※▨※▨※▨※▨※▨

You can **tandem skydive** (☎ (06) 877 4558) at Bridge Pa Airport for $140.

Places to Stay
In Windsor Park, adjacent to Fantasyland, *Hastings Holiday Park* (☎ (06) 878 6692) has camp sites at $9 per person. Cabins start at $25 for two and tourist flats are $50 to $65. The camp is on Windsor Ave, 2.5km from the post office. The *Raceview Motel & Holiday Park* (☎ (06) 878 8837) at 307 Gas-

coigne St, adjacent to the racecourse, has camping at $14 for two.

Backpackers are busy in the harvest season. The *Hastings Backpackers Hostel* (☎ (06) 876 5888), 505 Lyndon Rd East, has dorm beds for $14, and doubles and twins for $26. It is in a suburban area, not far from the city centre. The staff organise cheap trips to the region's attractions, including rubber tubing on the Tuki Tuki River ($5). *AJ's Backpackers Lodge* (☎ (06) 878 2302), a spacious Edwardian house at 405 Southland Rd, is a tidy, well-run place charging $14 for a dorm and $36 a twin. It is staffed by travellers.

Travellers BakPak Hostel (☎ (06) 878 7108), 606 St Aubyn St West, is yet another hostel in a suburban house; it's crammed with fruit pickers during the season but is quiet otherwise. Camp sites are $8, dorm beds $14, twins and doubles are $36, and singles are $24. It is being extended with larger family-style units ($14 per person per bed).

The many motels include the *Hastings Motel* (☎ (06) 878 6243), 1108 Karamu Rd, charging from $65/72 a single/double, and *Mecca Motel* (☎ (06) 878 3192), 806 Heretaunga St East, which charges $75 a double.

THE EAST COAST

PLACES TO STAY		
3	Travellers BakPak Hostel	
5	AJ's Backpackers Lodge	
25	Portmans Motor Lodge	
30	Raceview Motel & Holiday Park	
31	Hastings Backpackers Hostel	
33	Mecca Motel	

PLACES TO EAT		
1	The Corn Exchange	
2	Rush Munro's Ice Cream Garden	
4	McDonald's	
6	La Pizza Forno	
7	Piccolo's	
8	Baksters	
13	Cat & Fiddle Alehouse	
14	Kmart Plaza, Muffs & Public Toilets	
17	St Vineés Wine Bar & Cafe	
22	Cobb & Co	
23	Robert Harris Coffee Shop	
34	Vidal Winery & Brasserie	

OTHER		
9	Automobile Association (AA)	
10	Shooter's	
11	Bentan Twisted's	
12	Train Station & Hastings Travel Centre	
15	Hastings Visitor Information Centre	
16	Air New Zealand	
18	Hastings Clocktower	
19	Public Toilets	
20	Post Office	
21	Westerman's Building	
24	Nimbus & Coachrite Connections Buses	
26	Hawkes Bay Exhibition Centre	
27	Hawkes Bay Brewery	
28	New World Supermarket	
29	Municipal Theatre	
32	Queen's Square	

New places include *Portmans Motor Lodge* (☎ (06) 878 8332), 401 Railway Rd ($90 to $130 for doubles), and the Spanish-style *Valdez Motor Lodge* (☎ (06) 876 5453) on Karamu Rd North (studios for $110 and two-bed units $150).

The information centre lists over 40 B&Bs, homestays and farmstays.

Places to Eat

The ice cream at *Rush Munro's Ice Cream Garden* on Heretaunga St West is a real treat; it's homemade, loaded with fresh fruit, and very rich. The ubiquitous family favourite *Cobb & Co* is on Heretaunga St.

The *Robert Harris Coffee Shop* on Russell St has the usual cafeteria-style pastries and cakes and *Muffs* in the Kmart Plaza is good for a muffin or quick takeaway. *St Vineés Wine Bar & Cafe*, 108 Market St South, provides both burger-type snacks and more substantial meals. The popular *Cat & Fiddle Ale House*, 502 Karamu Rd, has good pub food but be careful that the dish doesn't run away with the spoon. *Baksters* on Nelson St North has economical bar meals such as hearty serves of nachos ($8). Out of town, on Karamu Rd, is *Bay Espresso*, good for breakfasts and lunches. *Ancient Oaks*, on the way to Havelock North, makes good salads (Thai lamb salad is $12 and crabmeat and melon salad is $10.50).

The pleasant *Vidal Winery Brasserie*, open daily for lunch and dinner, is attached to the Vidal Winery at 913 Aubyn St. The best place in town if you can afford it is *Piccolo's*, a brasserie on the corner of Lyndon Rd and Nelson St; it is open Tuesday to Friday for lunch and Tuesday to Saturday for dinner. For a quiet drink and good food, try *La Pizza Forno* on Heretaunga St West.

Bentan Twisted's on Eastbourne St and *Shooter's* (with regular happy hours) on the corner of Eastbourne and King Sts are popular bars. The *Corn Exchange* at 118 Maraekakaho Rd is open daily for all meals, and has a sunny deck and intimate bar.

Getting There & Away

Nimbus (☎ (06) 877 8133) operates a frequent local bus service from Napier ($4) on weekdays. Coachrite Connections buses to Gisborne stop at the Nimbus bus stop on Eastbourne St. All InterCity and Newmans buses going to Napier continue to Hastings, stopping at the Hastings Travel Centre (☎ (06) 878 0213) at the train station on Caroline Rd. Nimbus provides a service to Havelock North ($2).

HAVELOCK NORTH

Havelock North, 5km east of Hastings, is a great holiday destination well worth a visit for its gardens, wineries, village atmosphere and the towering backdrop of Te Mata peak. If you have kids in tow, there's the miniature railway in beautiful Keirunga Gardens; it operates on the first and third Sunday of the month ($1 per ride).

Te Mata Peak

Te Mata Peak is about 11km from Hastings. It rises up in some dramatically sheer cliffs to the Te Mata trig, 399m above sea level, commanding a spectacular view over the Heretaunga Plains to Hawkes Bay. On a clear day you can see all of Hawkes Bay up to the Mahia Peninsula, and to Mt Ruapehu in the Tongariro National Park. You can also see oyster shells in the rocks at your feet!

Te Mata Peak is part of the 98-hectare Te Mata Park, with several walkways. You can drive right up to the trig at the summit.

The peak is a favourite spot for hanggliding. Gliders get remarkable possibilities from the updraughts breezing in from the Pacific Ocean, just a few hundred metres away. Peak Paragliding (☎ 025 441 572) offers tandem paragliding. You can 'Summit Plummet' for $45 ($60 with transport) down to the plains below, or climb to the clouds and return to the summit for $90 (conditions permitting).

Places to Stay & Eat

There are some superb places to stay, all reasonable considering the high standards and backdrop of vineyards. The *Havelock Motor Lodge* (☎ (06) 877 8627) at 7 Havelock Rd is within walking distance of the

THE EAST COAST

village cafes; doubles are from $95. But it is the quaint cottages and B&B that people come here for. These include: *Telegraph Hill Villa* (☎ (06) 877 5140) at 334 Te Mata Rd ($140 for two); *Providencia* (☎ (06) 877 2300), a gracious old building in a picturesque rural setting on Middle Rd; *Endsleigh Cottages* (☎ (06) 877 7588) on Endsleigh Rd ($90 to $140); the *Greenhouse* (☎ (06) 877 4904) on Te Mata Rd ($135); and the unbeatable historic *Rush Cottage* (☎ (06) 877 7985), adjacent to Lombardi Estate vineyard and with magnificent views over the vineyards, Napier Hill and the bay ($140).

The *Rose & Shamrock* is a great Irish pub in the centre of the village; meals, such as wedges and salad, are from $7 to $10. *Cafe Diva*, across the road, is good for relaxing over a light lunch and the nearby *Turk's Bar* and *Happy Tav* are popular for a drink. *Peak House* on Te Mata Rd is popular for both the spectacular view and the Sunday roast brunch ($20, children $10).

AROUND HAWKES BAY
Wineries & Arts and Crafts
The Hawkes Bay area is one of NZ's premier wine-producing regions, with many vineyards to visit. Hawkes Bay is very much the chardonnay capital of NZ, but cabernet sauvignon grapes from the area are highly regarded and many other varieties are produced.

Vineyards to visit include Brookfields at Meeanee, Mission at Taradale (the oldest in the country), Esk Valley Estate Winery, Vidal of Hawkes Bay, Ngatarawa Wines in Hastings and Church Road Winery in Taradale. Havelock North has a concentration of wineries, especially out on Te Mata Rd. Included are Te Mata Estate Winery, Bradshaw Estate, Akarangi Wines, Waimarama Estate and Lombardi Wines. A number of the wineries are open for lunch and offer excellent dining.

The Hawkes Bay Vintners produce a handy *Guide to the Hawkes Bay Wineries*. Every year around February, the Harvest Hawkes Bay weekend has activities focusing on food and wine. Around the same time an international

concert is held at the Mission and a special label is produced for each entertainer.

A fine way of visiting the wineries is by bicycle (hire one in Napier), since most of them are within easy cycling distance and it's all flat land. From Napier, Bay Tours (☎ (06) 843 6953) does four-hour winery tours for $30, Eastland Tours (☎ (06) 836 6705) has a similar tour, and Wine Tour Trails (☎ (06) 877 5707) also charges $30.

Some local craftspeople open their studios to the public. Get the informative *Hawkes Bay Arts & Crafts Guide* from the visitor information centres.

Cape Kidnappers Gannet Colony
From late October until late April the Cape Kidnappers gannet colony comes to life. These large birds usually make their nests on remote and inaccessible islands but here they nest on the mainland and are curiously unworried by human spectators.

The gannets usually turn up in late July after the last heavy storm of the month. Supposedly, the storm casts driftwood and other handy nest-building material high up the beach so very little effort has to be expended collecting it. In October and November eggs are laid and take about six weeks to hatch. By March the gannets start to migrate and by April only the odd straggler will be left.

You don't need a permit to visit the gannet sanctuary and the best time to see the birds is between early November and late February (the sanctuary is closed from June to October).

Three tour operators run to Cape Kidnappers (so named because Maori tried to kidnap a Tahitian servant boy from Cook's expedition here). Gannet Beach Adventures (☎ (06) 875 0898) at Te Awanga, 21km from Napier, has rides on a tractor-pulled trailer along the beach for $18 (children $12). From where they drop you, it's a 20-minute walk to the main saddle colony. The guided return trip takes about four hours. Unimog (☎ (06) 835 4446) departs from Napier and goes along the beach in a Mercedes Benz for $30 (children $20). The most exciting way of getting to the cape is with Quad Ventures

(☎ (06) 836 6652) which leaves from Sullivan's motor camp at Te Awanga; it is $90/140 for one/two people on a bike and the trip takes from three to four hours.

Alternatively, the 8km walk along the beach from Clifton, just along from Te Awanga, takes about two hours. You must leave no earlier than three hours after high tide and start back no later than 1½ hours after low tide. It's another 8km back and there are no refreshment stops so go prepared! All trips are dependent on the tides. The tide schedule is available from the Napier information centre. No regular buses go to Te Awanga or Clifton from Napier, but Kiwi Shuttle (☎ 025 475578) goes on demand for $15 per person. There is a rest hut, with refreshments, at the colony.

DOC, which administers the reserve, has a handy leaflet and booklets on the colony. Accommodation is available in Te Awanga at *Sullivan's Motor Camp* (☎ (06) 875 0334), which is also good for information. At Clifton, the *Clifton No 2 Reserve* has camp sites and cabins.

Inland Ranges

The main populated area of Hawkes Bay is concentrated around the Napier-Hastings. Regional Hawkes Bay does extend much further, however, both to the south and inland.

The inland region provides some of the best tramping on the North Island – in the remote, untamed Kaweka and Ruahine ranges. DOC has produced an excellent series of pamphlets on the ranges. See *North-east Kaweka*, *Makahu Saddle*, *Southern Kaweka*, *South-east Ruahine*, *Mid-east Ruahine* and *Western Ruahine*.

An old Maori track, now a road, runs from the bay into Inland Patea, a vast region which stretches from Ruapehu to Taihape and across to the gorges of the Wanganui River. The route heads from Fernhill near Hastings via Omahu, Okawa, Otamauri, Blowhard Bush and the Gentle Annie towards Taihape.

The Longest Place Name in the World
Hold your breath and then spit this out as fast as you can (it helps to split it into its component parts): Taumatawhakatangihangakoauauo tamateaturipukakapikimaungahoronukupokai whenuakitanatahu. According to the *Guinness Book of Records* it means: 'The place where Tamatea, the man with the big knees, who slid, climbed, and swallowed mountains, known as land eater, played his flute to his loved one.' ■

It is a three-hour return car journey from Fernhill to the top of the Kawekas.

Central Hawkes Bay

The main towns of central Hawkes Bay are Waipukurau (almost always 'Waipuk') and Waipawa. The Waipukurau information office is in Railway Esplanade.

Many visit this region to see the **longest place name in the world** (yes, longer than Llanfairpwllgwyngllgogerychwyrndrobwll llantysiliogogogoch in Wales) – see the boxed text above. From Waipukurau on SH2 you head towards Porangahau on the coast. Follow this road for 40km to the Mangaorapa junction and then follow the 'Historic Sign' indicators. The AA roadsign is a few kilometres up the hill from Mangaorapa station; the actual *maunga* (mountain) is on private property.

After contemplating its astronomic length you can stop off at the idyllic *Lochlea Farmstay* (☎ (06) 855 4816, 0800 186 506; lochlea.farm@xtra.co.nz) at 344 Lake Rd, Wanstead; twins and doubles on this laid back and friendly farm are from $15 per person. The *Porangahau Lodge* (☎ (06) 855 5386) is good value at $60 per person with all meals provided; they do 4WD trips to the longest place name ($35, children $20). In Waipawa stop for tea at the *Abbotslee Tearooms* and in Waipuk try the *Stray Cat Cafe* and *Dak's Bar & Grill*.

Wellington Region

Wellington, the capital of New Zealand, is on a beautiful harbour at the southern tip of the North Island. Approaching it from the north, you will pass through one of two regions – either the Kapiti Coast on the west side (SH1) or the Wairarapa on the east side of the North Island (SH2) – before entering the heavily populated Hutt Valley or the city itself. Both these areas have interesting activities and places to visit.

Wellington

Wellington takes part in friendly rivalry with larger Auckland. The city, with a regional population of 334,000, including 158,000 in the city itself, is hemmed in by its magnificent harbour, with wooden Victorian buildings on the steep hills. It prides itself as a centre for culture and the arts, has a plethora of restaurants, cafes, nightlife and activities, and is home to the country's government and national treasures. Apart from its importance as the capital, it's a major travel crossroads between the North and South islands.

The city's fine harbour was formed by the flooding of a huge crater. The city runs up the hills on one side of the harbour, and so cramped is it for space that many of its workers live in two narrow valleys leading north between the steep, rugged hills – one is the Hutt Valley and the other follows SH1 through Tawa and Porirua. The city's nickname is 'Windy Wellington'. You'll discover why!

History
Maori legend has it that the explorer Kupe was the first person to discover Wellington Harbour. The original Maori name was Te Whanga-Nui-a-Tara, Tara being the son of a Maori chief named Whatonga who had settled on the Hawkes Bay coast. Whatonga sent Tara and his half-brother to explore the

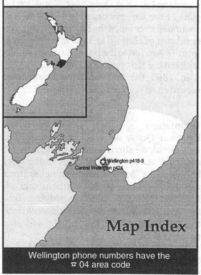

HIGHLIGHTS

- Enjoying Wellington Harbour, whether you are taking in the view from Mt Victoria, cruising across to Eastbourne or walking along the city foreshore
- Taking the exhilarating cable-car ride to the Botanic Gardens and then walking on trails through stands of native trees
- Seeing the Maori collection in Te Papa
- Discovering mystical Kapiti Island and the scenic Kapiti Coast
- Visiting the vineyards of the Wairarapa and the region's rugged coastline
- Exploring the Tararua Ranges

Wellington p418-9
Central Wellington p424

Map Index

Wellington phone numbers have the
☎ 04 area code

WELLINGTON REGION

southern part of the North Island. When they returned over a year later, their reports were so favourable that Whatonga's followers moved to the harbour, founding the Ngati Tara tribe.

The first European settlers arrived in the New Zealand Company's ship *Aurora* on 22 January 1840, not long after Colonel

William Wakefield arrived to buy land from the Maori. The idea was to build two cities: one would be a commercial centre by the harbour (Port Nicholson) and the other, further north, would be the agricultural hub. The settlers were to be allotted two blocks: a town section of an acre (less than half a hectare) and a back-country block worth £1 an acre. However, the Maori denied they had sold the land at Port Nicholson, or Poneke, as they called it. Founded on hasty and illegal buying by the New Zealand Company, land rights struggles followed and were to plague the country for the next 30 years and still affect it today.

Wellington began as a settlement with very little flat land. Originally the waterfront was along Lambton Quay, but reclamation of parts of the harbour began in 1852 and has continued ever since. In 1855 an earthquake razed part of Hutt Rd and the area extending from Te Aro flat to the Basin Reserve, which initiated the first major reclamation.

In 1865 the seat of government was moved from Auckland to Wellington.

Orientation

Lambton Quay, the main business street, wriggles along almost parallel to the seafront (which it once was). The heart of the city, known as the 'Miracle Mile', stretches from the train station, at the northern end of Lambton Quay, to Cambridge and Kent Terraces. Thorndon is the historic area immediately north of the centre and the embassy district.

The waterfront along Jervois Quay, Cable St and Oriental Parade is an increasingly revitalised area and now houses the huge, futuristic Te Papa (Museum of New Zealand). Renovated Queen's Wharf has ferries, restaurants and a few diversions, while Oriental Parade, past the Freyberg swimming pool, is Wellington's premier seafront boulevard and a pleasant place for a stroll.

Mt Victoria at the eastern edge of the city has hostels and cheap places to stay. Willis St, Cuba Mall, Manners Mall, Courtenay Place and Queens Wharf, as well as Lambton Quay, are important streets for shopping and restaurants.

Maps The Map Shop, on the corner of Vivian and Victoria Sts, carries Land Information NZ's complete line of maps, plus aerial photographs. It's open from 8.30 am to 5 pm on weekdays.

Information

Tourist Offices The Central Wellington Visitor Information Centre (☎ (04) 801 4000; fax 801 3030) is on Civic Square at 101 Wakefield St. It's open from 8.30 am to 5.30 pm on weekdays and from 9.30 am to 5.30 pm on weekends. Its staff book almost everything. The information centre at the airport (☎ (04) 388 5123) is open until around 6 or 7 pm daily and until 11.30 pm on Saturday.

The DOC Visitor Centre (☎ (04) 472 7356; fax 471 2075; PO Box 5086) in the government buildings facing Lambton Quay has information on walks, parks, outdoor activities and camping in the region. The office is open on weekdays from 9 am to 4.30 pm and from 10 am to 3 pm on weekends.

The Automobile Association (AA; ☎ (04) 473 8738) on the 1st floor at 342 Lambton Quay has the usual AA maps and services, and NZ travel books and maps. AA members receive a 10% discount.

Free tourist publications with events listings include *Wellington What's On* and the weekly *Capital Times* and *City Voice*. The *Dominion* and the *Evening Post* are the two local daily newspapers.

Embassies & Consulates As the capital city of NZ, Wellington houses consulates and embassies of many countries, including:

Australian High Commission
   (☎ (04) 473 6411) 72-78 Hobson St
Canadian High Commission
   (☎ (04) 473 9577) 61 Molesworth St
French Embassy
   (☎ (04) 384 2555) 34-42 Manners St
German Embassy
   (☎ (04) 473 6063) 90-92 Hobson St

WELLINGTON REGION

JEFF WILLIAMS

HOLGER LEUE

Reputedly known as the longest
place name in the world

**TAUMATAWHAKATANGI
HANGAKOAUAUOTAMATEA
TURIPUKAKAPIKIMAUNGA
HORONUKUPOKAIWHEN
UAKITANATAHU**

THE PLACE WHERE TAMATEA, THE MAN WITH
THE BIG KNEES, WHO SLID, CLIMBED, AND
SWALLOWED MOUNTAINS, KNOWN AS LANDEATER,
PLAYED HIS FLUTE TO HIS LOVED ONE
Guinness Book of Records

JEFF WILLIAMS

The East Coast
Top: The quirky interior of Smash Palace, Gisborne
Left: Fountain, Napier
Right: The longest place name in the world

Wellington Region
Top: The view from Castlepoint, the Wairarapa
Middle: Oriental Bay, Wellington
Bottom: A Wairarapa vineyard

Netherlands Embassy
(☎ (04) 473 8652) 10th Floor, Investment Centre, on the corner of Featherston and Ballance Sts
UK High Commission
(☎ (04) 472 6049) 44 Hill St, Thorndon
US Embassy
(☎ (04) 472 2068) 29 Fitzherbert Terrace, Thorndon

Money Banks around town exchange foreign currency and are open from 9 am to 4.30 pm on weekdays. Thomas Cook has a foreign exchange office at 358 Lambton Quay which is open from 9 am to 5.30 pm on weekdays and from 10.30 am to 2 pm on Saturday. The American Express office (☎ (04) 473 7766) in the Sun Alliance Centre on Lambton Quay at Grey St, near the lower cable-car terminal, is open from 9 am to 5 pm on weekdays.

Post & Communications The chief post office, or CPO, is in the train station lobby. Poste restante mail can be collected between 8.30 am and 5 pm on weekdays. Other post offices, including a post shop, are spread around the centre.

Travel Agencies Of the many travel agencies, The Hub (☎ (04) 385 3580) in the Trekkers Hotel at 213 Cuba St caters for backpackers and can book travel, activities and accommodation on both islands.

The YHA Travel Centre (☎ (04) 801 7238) is on the corner of Courtenay Place and Taranaki St. STA, specialising in air fares, has offices at 130 Cuba St (☎ (04) 385 0561), 37 Willis St (☎ (04) 472 8510) and in the Student Union building at Victoria University (☎ (04) 499 1017).

Bookshops Dymocks at 366 Lambton Quay opposite the BNZ Centre is one of Wellington's largest bookshops, with armchairs for browsers. Others with a good range of titles include Whitcoulls at 312 Lambton Quay and 91 Cuba St; London Bookshops at 310 Lambton Quay and 89 Cuba Mall; and Ahradsen's in the BNZ Centre. Unity Books, 119-125 Willis St, on the corner of Manners Mall, is something of a Wellington institution with an excellent fiction selection as well as a good general range.

Megazines on the ground floor of the Market at James Smith Corner, on the corner of Cuba and Manners Sts, has the most extensive range of magazines. Bellamy's at 106 Cuba St is a good second-hand bookshop, and there's more bookshops further south on Cuba St.

Cultural Centres The German cultural centre, the Goethe Institut (☎ (04) 499 2469), is at 150 Cuba St on the corner of Garrett St. It's open from 9 am to 5 pm from Monday to Thursday and from 9 am to 3 pm on Friday. The Alliance Française (☎ (04) 472 1272), 24 Johnson St, is open from 9 am to 5 pm on weekdays.

The Japan Information & Cultural Centre (☎ (04) 387 9386) at 113 Customhouse Quay, near the corner of Lambton Quay, is open from 9 am to 5 pm on weekdays.

The Beehive & Parliament
Three buildings on Bowen St form New Zealand's parliamentary complex. By far the most distinctive and well known is the modernist executive office building known as the Beehive – because that is just what it looks like. Designed by British architect Sir Basil Spence, its construction began in 1969 and was completed in 1980. Controversy surrounded its construction and, while it's not great architecture, it is the architectural symbol of the country.

Next door is the Old Parliamentary Building, completed in 1922. Expensive plans to extend the Old Parliamentary Building and move the Beehive were recently quashed after a public outcry in a country that doesn't like spending money on its politicians. Beside the Old Parliamentary Building, the neogothic Parliamentary Library building is the oldest in the complex.

Free public tours (☎ (04) 471 9503) of the Beehive and the House of Representatives are offered most days between 10 am to 4 pm. The public can also attend sessions of

WELLINGTON REGION

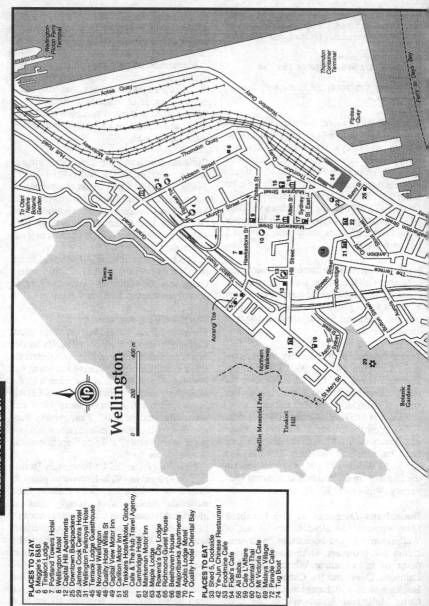

WELLINGTON REGION

Wellington

0   200   400 m

PLACES TO STAY
5 Maggie's B&B
6 Tinakori Lodge
7 Portland Towers Hotel
8 Wellington Motel
12 Capital Hill Apartments
25 James Cook Centra Hotel
29 Downtown Backpackers
31 Wellington Parkroyal Hotel
45 Terrace Lodge Guesthouse
46 Novotel West Plaza
48 Quality Hotel Willis St
49 Capital View Motor Inn
51 Carlton Motor Inn
55 Trekkers Hotel/Motel, Globe
   Cafe & The Hub Travel Agency
61 Cambridge Hotel
62 Marksman Motor Inn
63 Maple Lodge
64 Rowena's City Lodge
65 Richmond Guest House
66 Beethoven House
68 Majoribanks Apartments
70 Apollo Lodge Motel
71 Quality Hotel Oriental Bay

PLACES TO EAT
33 Shed 5, Dockside
42 Fe-Jun Chinese Restaurant
53 Yasmine Cafe
54 Fidel's Cafe
56 Ali Baba
59 Cafe L'Affare
60 Oriental Thai
67 Mt Victoria Cafe
69 Malaya Village
72 Parade Cafe
74 Tug Boat

To Otari Native Botanic Garden

Town Belt

Tinakori Hill

Stellin Memorial Park

Botanic Gardens

Northern Walkway

Aotea Quay

Thorndon Quay

Hobson Street

Murphy Street

Hawkestone St

Tinakori Road

Grant Road

Hutt Motorway

Hutt Road

Waterloo Quay

Thorndon Container Terminal

Wellington-Picton Ferry Terminal

Pipitea Quay

Ferry to Days Bay

Pipitea St

Mulgrave Street

Aitken St

Sydney St East

Molesworth Street

Bowen Street

Hill Street

The Terrace

Lambton Quay

Bunny St

Featherston Street

Stout Street

Aurora

Bolton Street

Aorangi Tce

St Mary St

Acorn St

Sydney St West

Footbridge

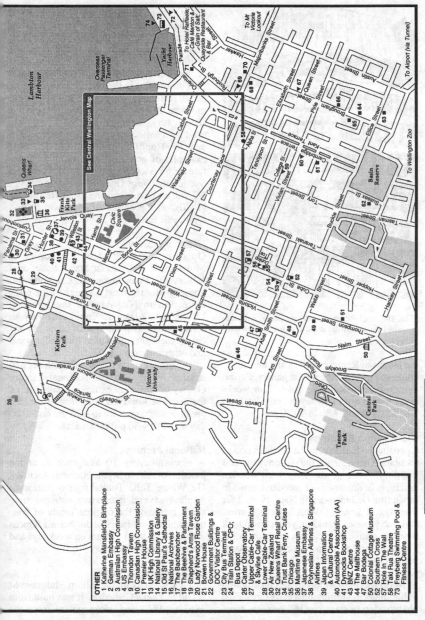

Lambton Harbour

Queens Wharf

Frank Kitts Park

Overseas Passenger Terminal

Yacht Harbour

To Hotel Raffaele;
Café Menton &
Grain of Salt;
Quayside Restaurant
& Bar

To Mt Victoria Lookout

To Airport (via Tunnel)

See Central Wellington Map

Civic Square

Kelburn Park

Victoria University

Central Park

Tanera Park

Basin Reserve

To Wellington Zoo

OTHER
1 Katherine Mansfield's Birthplace
2 German Embassy
3 Australian High Commission
4 US Embassy
9 Thorndon Tavern
10 Canadian High Commission
11 Premier House
13 UK High Commission
14 National Library & Gallery
15 Old St Paul's Cathedral
16 National Archives
17 The Backbencher
18 The Beehive & Parliament
19 Shepherd's Arms Tavern
20 Lady Norwood Rose Garden
21 Bowen House
22 Government Buildings &
   DOC Visitor Centre
23 City Bus Terminal
24 Train Station & CPO;
   Bus Depot
26 Carter Observatory
27 Upper Cable-Car Terminal
   & Skyline Cafe
28 Lower Cable-Car Terminal
30 Air New Zealand
32 Queens Wharf Retail Centre
34 Trust Bank Ferry, Cruises
35 Chicago
36 Maritime Museum
37 Japanese Embassy
38 Polynesian Airlines & Singapore
   Airlines
39 Japan Information
   & Cultural Centre
40 Automobile Association (AA)
41 Dymocks Bookshop
43 BNZ Centre
44 The Malthouse
47 The Opera
50 Colonial Cottage Museum
52 Southern Cross
57 Hole In The Wall
58 Taki Rua Theatre
73 Freyberg Swimming Pool &
   Fitness Centre

The statue of Richard Seddon, also known as 'King Dick', stands in front of the Beehive

the House of Representatives and are free to come and go from the public gallery. Parliament usually meets three out of four weeks every month from Tuesday to Thursday from 2 to 5.30 pm and 7.30 to 10.30 pm.

Old Wooden Buildings

Opposite the Beehive, at the northern end of Lambton Quay, stands the old **government buildings**, one of the largest all-wooden buildings in the world – a wooden temple in Japan (the Daibutsu-den in Nara) beats it for 'the biggest' honours. With its block corners and slab wooden planking, you have to look twice to realise that it is not made of stone. The building has been restored and houses various offices, including the DOC Visitor Centre.

Wood was used widely in the construction of buildings in Wellington's early days. Fine old **wooden houses** can still be seen, espe-cially along Tinakori Rd in the historic Thorndon area, Wellington's first suburb, just uphill from the parliament buildings. Pick up a copy of the *Thorndon Heritage Trail* brochure from the visitor information centre. Dating from 1843, **Premier House** on Tinakori Rd is the official prime ministerial residence. An early Labour prime minister, Michael Joseph Savage, spurned such luxury, however, and the house was used for a variety of purposes between 1935 and 1990 until it was restored. The best examples of genuine 19th-century architecture are on Ascot St, just off Tinakori Rd and Sydney Rd West. One of the oldest pubs in NZ still on its original site is the **Thistle Inn** (1840), on the corner of Mulgrave St and Sydney St East.

National Library

Opposite the Beehive on the corner of Molesworth and Aitken Sts, the National Library (Te Puna Matauranga o Aotearoa) houses by far the most comprehensive book collection in NZ. Also at the National Library is the Alexander Turnbull Library, an early colonial collection with many historical photographs, often used for genealogical and other research on NZ.

The library hosts free public lectures and cultural events and the National Library Gallery has different exhibits usually on NZ themes. The library is open from 9 am to 5 pm on weekdays, 9 am to 4.30 pm on Saturday and 1 to 4.30 pm on Sunday.

National Archives

A block away, at 10 Mulgrave St at the junction of Aitken St, the National Archives (Te Whare Tohu Tuhituhinga o Aotearoa) displays several interesting national treasures, including the original Treaty of Waitangi and other historical documents. Opening hours are 9 am to 5 pm on weekdays and 9 am to 1 pm on Saturday.

Old St Paul's Cathedral

Just a few doors up the hill on Mulgrave St is Old St Paul's Cathedral. It was built from 1863 to 1864 and looks quaint from the outside, but the interior is a good example of early English Gothic design in timber. Old St Paul's is open from 10 am to 5 pm from Monday to Saturday (admission by donation).

Museums

Te Papa (Museum of New Zealand) The country's national museum on Cable St, opened in 1998, is in a striking building that dominates the waterfront. Wellington's new pride and joy has an extensive Maori collection and its own marae. Natural history, the environment, European settlement, among other things New Zealand, are presented in impressive gallery spaces with a touch of interactive high-tech. It has excellent Maori and Pacific Islands collections, although the rest of the world gets a look-in with changing exhibits of international art. Shops, restaurants and an auditorium round off this impressive complex. It's open from 10 am to 6 pm daily and until 9 pm on Thursday (admission is free, except for special shows).

Maritime Museum On the corner of Jervois Quay and the renovated Queens Wharf, this museum has many maritime relics associated with the city, a fine three-dimensional model of the harbour and a collection of ship models. A corner is devoted to the interisland ferry *Wahine*, which sank in Wellington Harbour in 1968; this disaster has had a strong impression on the national psyche. Photo and video exhibits document the tragedy. The museum is open from 9.30 am to 4 pm on weekdays and from 1 to 4.30 pm on weekends ($2, children $1).

Katherine Mansfield's Birthplace This house at 25 Tinakori Rd is where the famous writer was born in 1888. The excellent video *A Portrait of Katherine Mansfield* screens there and the 'Sense of Living' exhibition displays photographs of the period alongside excerpts from her writing. A doll's house has been constructed from details in the short story of the same name. The house is open from 10 am to 4 pm daily, except Monday when its hours are 10 am to 2.30 pm ($4, children $1).

Other Museums The **Colonial Cottage Museum** at 68 Nairn St is one of the oldest

---

Katherine Mansfield

Katherine Mansfield is New Zealand's most distinguished author, known throughout the world for her short stories and often compared to Chekhov and Maupassant.

Born Katherine Mansfield Beauchamp in 1888, she left Wellington when she was 19 for Europe, where she spent the rest of her short adult life. She mixed with Europe's most famous writers, such as DH Lawrence, TS Eliot and Virginia Woolf, and married the literary critic and author John Middleton Murry in 1918. In 1923, aged 34, she died of tuberculosis at Fontainebleau in France. It was not until 1945 that her five books of short stories (*In a German Pension*, *Bliss*, *The Garden-Party*, *The Dove's Nest* and *Something Childish*) were combined into a single volume, *Collected Stories of Katherine Mansfield*.

She spent five years of her childhood at 25 Tinakori Rd in Wellington; it is mentioned in her stories *The Aloe* (which in its final form became *Prelude*) and *A Birthday* (a fictionalised account of her own birth). ∎

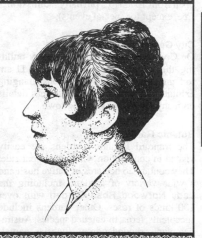

colonial cottages in Wellington. It was built in 1858 by carpenter William Wallis and lived in by his family until 1977. It's open from 10 am to 4.30 pm on weekdays and from 1 to 4.30 pm on weekends ($3, children $1).

Those familiar with the expressions 'silly mid on', 'leg spin' and 'maiden over' will gravitate to the **National Cricket Museum** at the Basin Reserve. Aficionados will be bowled over by the 1743 Addington bat (one of the oldest) and Australian cricketer Dennis Lillee's controversial aluminium bat banned in 1979. It's open from 10.30 am to 3.30 pm daily from October to April, but only on weekends the rest of the year ($3, children $1 or free if accompanied by an adult).

The **Alexander McKay Geological Museum** is in the Cotton Building at Victoria University. It's open from 9 am to 5 pm on weekdays (admission is free, but donations are appreciated).

Capital E This children's educational and entertainment centre on Civic Square has rotating exhibits, usually hands-on, a children's theatre company and a television studio. It's great for kids and the huge Hocus Pocus Toys shop alone is worth a visit; it's open from 10 am to 5 pm daily (admission is free, except for special events).

City Gallery Wellington

On Civic Square, in the Old Library building, the city art gallery is open from 11 am to 5 pm daily and features various changing exhibits. The information centre has details on many art galleries around town.

Botanic Gardens

The tranquil Botanic Gardens are easily visited in conjunction with a cable-car ride. They contain 26 hectares of native bush and a wide variety of gardens, including the **Lady Norwood Rose Garden** with over 100 kinds of roses. Other gardens include succulents, ferns, threatened species, Australian plants, rhododendrons, fuchsias, camellias, begonias and herbs. The large gardens

have an information centre with a World Wide Fund for Nature shop and a cafe.

The main entrance to the **Otari Native Botanic Garden** is at the junction of Wilton Rd and Gloucester St; get there with the No 14 bus (Wilton). Devoted to the cultivation and preservation of indigenous New Zealand plants, it has a number of walks through densely forested areas and flax clearings. There is also a fernery and an information centre.

Wellington Zoo

This zoo has a wide variety of native and non-native wildlife and has outdoor lion and chimpanzee parks, plus a nocturnal kiwi house also housing tuataras and giant wetas. The kiwis are on view from 10 am to 4 pm daily but the best time to see them is from 10 am to noon. The zoo is 4km from the city centre, at the end of the Newtown Park bus route No 10. It is open from 9.30 am to 5 pm daily ($8, children $4).

Cable Car

A Wellington icon and 'must-do' attraction is the cable car that runs from an arcade off Lambton Quay up to Kelburn, overlooking the city. The cable-car service began in 1902, carried nearly half a million passengers in its first year and by 1912 was transporting a million passengers a year. In the late 1970s the track was reconstructed and the two old wooden cable cars were replaced with shiny red Swiss-made ones.

A ride to the top costs $1.50 (children 70c) or $2.50 return (children $1.40). It operates at 10-minute intervals from 7 am to 10 pm on weekdays and from 9 am to 10 pm weekends and public holidays. The Skyline Cafe (open daily from 10 am to 4 pm) at the top offers great views over the city and harbour. From the top you can stroll back down through the Botanic Gardens or return to town by a series of steps which interconnect with roads.

The **Carter Observatory** is in the Botanic Gardens near the top cable-car terminal. It has displays and videos about astronomy and is open from 10 am to 5 pm on weekdays ($3, children $1.50). The best time to go is between noon and 5 pm on weekends ($5, children $3), when planetarium shows are held, or from 6.30 to 10 pm on Tuesday and Saturday night, when you can also view the night sky through the telescope (weather permitting).

Views

The best view of the city, harbour and surrounding region is from the lookout at the top of **Mt Victoria** (196m), east of the city centre. It's a taxing walk but well worth the effort; otherwise take bus No 20 on weekdays from the train station or Courtenay Place and walk or ride back down. To drive, take Oriental Parade along the waterfront and then Carlton Gore St. Alternatively, head up the hill on Majoribanks St and follow the 'Lookout' signs, turning left onto Hawker St.

Other good views are from the top cable-car terminal and from the Northern, Southern and Eastern walkways.

The **ECNZ wind turbine** on Brooklyn Hill also has good views. Take Victoria St to Brooklyn Rd, turn left into Ohiro Rd, then right into Todman St and follow the signposts. Bus No 7 is the closest public transport, but still leaves you with a stiff 2km walk.

Walking

Wellington has many enjoyable walks in the city and surrounds. The visitor information centre has brochures on the Eastern, Northern and Southern walkways, Red Rocks Coastal Walk and others.

The easy **Red Rocks Coastal Walk** follows the volcanic coast from Owhiro Bay to Red Rocks and Sinclair Head, where there is a seal colony. Take bus No 1 or 4 to Island Bay, then No 29 to Owhiro Bay Parade (or walk 2.5km along the Esplanade). From the start of Owhiro Bay Parade it is 1km to the quarry gate where the coastal walk starts.

The DOC Visitor Centre is another good source of information on walks. Its free brochure *Walking Around Wellington*, also available at the visitor centre, gives details of over 50 walks in the Wellington area including the city itself, the Kapiti Coast, Hutt Valley and Wainuiomata on the eastern side of the harbour.

Mountain Biking

City biking destinations include Mt Victoria, most of the Southern Walkway, along the ridgetop at Tinakori Hill, in firebreaks around Karori Reservoir and a track to Mt Kau Kau. Longer rides can be enjoyed (or endured) in Belmont, East Harbour and Kaitoke regional parks; up the Rimutaka

Windy Wellington

Wellington really can get windy. When the sun's shining it can be a very attractive city, but it's not called the windy city for nothing – one of the local rock stations even calls itself Radio Windy.

At the start of winter you've got a fair chance of experiencing some gale-force days – the sort of days when strong men get pinned up against walls and little old ladies, desperately clutching their umbrellas, can be seen floating by at skyscraper height. Seriously, the flying grit and dust can be uncomfortable to the eyes and the flying rubbish can be a real mess. I was walking back from a restaurant late one windy night when a sudden gust blew several bags of garbage out of a doorway, a passing car hit one and a veritable snowstorm of soft-drink cans, pizza boxes and assorted debris rushed down the street eventually overtaking the offending car!

One blustery day back in 1968 the wind blew so hard it pushed the almost-new Wellington-Christchurch car ferry *Wahine* on to Barrett's Reef just outside the harbour entrance. The disabled ship later broke loose from the reef, drifted into the harbour and then sank, causing the loss of 51 lives. The Wellington Maritime Museum has a dramatic model and photographic display of the disaster.

Nancy Keller

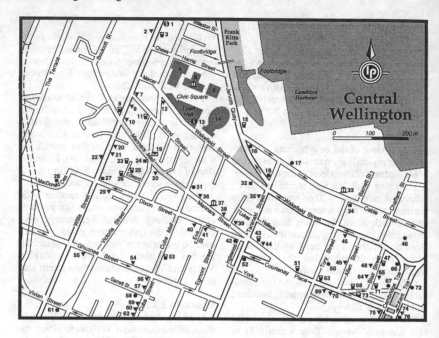

Incline to the Wairarapa and along Tunnel Gully; in Queen Elizabeth II Park on the Kapiti Coast; and in Battle Hill Forest Park. The visitor centre has free maps.

Water Sports

With all the wind and water, Wellington is a great place for **windsurfing** – choose from sheltered inlets, rough harbours and wave-beaten coastal areas, all within half an hour's drive of the city. Wild Winds Sail & Surf (☎ (04) 384 1010), Chaffers Marina, Oriental Bay, has windsurfing courses for beginners. Windsurfers and boats can be hired at the Days Bay Boatshed (☎ (04) 562 8150), opposite the pier in Eastbourne, over the harbour from Wellington.

For **kayaking** on the bay, Fergs Rock 'n' Kayak (☎ (04) 499 8898) at Shed 6, Queens Wharf, rents out kayaks, from $7 per hour up to $25 per day. Guided trips are offered, including night trips, usually via Somes

Island, for around $40. The 'rock' part of the name refers to the 14m indoor rock wall for rock climbing.

Good surfing breaks include one near the airport and the fine breaks on Palliser Bay, south-east of Wellington.

The Freyberg Swimming Pool at 139 Oriental Parade is the best pool close to the city centre. It's open from 6.30 am to 9 pm daily, except Friday when it closes at 5.30 pm.

In-Line Skating

You can't beat rollerblading along the waterfront on a sunny day. Cheapskates (☎ (04) 499 0455), 60 Cuba St, hires out rollerblades from its shop and from its roving van at the foot of Taranaki St by the waterfront on weekends. Fergs Rock 'n' Kayak (☎ (04) 499 8898) at Queens Wharf also rents out rollerblades for $10/15 for an hour/night.

Organised Tours

Bus Wally Hammond (☎ (04) 472 0869)

PLACES TO STAY		48	Exchange	14	Michael Fowler
24	Central City	49	Cafe India		Centre
	Apartments	54	Satay Village	15	St John's Bar
27	Abel Tasman	55	Flip Brasserie	16	The Film Centre
28	Rosemere	56	Krazy Lounge	17	Circa Theatre
	Backpackers	57	Zest	18	Wellington Market
32	Plaza International	59	Khmer Satay	19	Post Shop
34	Museum Hotel		Noodle House	23	Ruby Ruby
66	Wellington City YHA	60	Cafe Istanbul	25	La Strada
	Hostel	62	Midnight Espresso	26	ESCape
76	Halswell Lodge	64	Beacon	31	Market at James
		65	Mondo Cucina		Smith Corner
PLACES TO EAT		69	Cinta	33	Te Papa (Museum
2	Ye-Jun Chinese	70	Sahara Cafe		of New Zealand)
	Restaurant	74	Deluxe Cafe	37	State Opera House
7	South of the Border	75	Calzone	42	Phoenix Theatre
9	A Taste of France		Restaurant	43	Molly Malone's &
10	Kopi				The Dubliner
12	Lido Cafe	**OTHER**		46	New World
20	Armadillo	1	BNZ Centre		Supermarket
21	Satay Time	3	The Malthouse	47	One Red Dog
22	Turner's Steakhouse	4	Central Library &	50	Out! Bookshop
29	Chevy's		Continuum	51	The Big Easy
30	McDonald's; KFC		Theatre	52	YHA Travel Centre
35	Fujiyama Teppanyaki	5	City Gallery	53	Hotel Bristol
36	A Taste of France		Wellington	58	Goethe Institut
38	Java Indonesian	6	Capital Eè	61	The Map Shop
	Restaurant	8	Bouquet Garni Wine	63	The Planet Bar
39	Great India		Bar	67	Downstage Theatre
40	Angkor	11	The Loaded Hog	68	Kitty O'Shea's
41	La Casa Pasta	13	Central Wellington	71	Opera
44	Espressoholic		Visitor	72	Bats Theatre
45	Satay Kampong		Information Centre	73	Bus Stop

takes a 2½ hour city highlight tour at 10 am and 2 pm for $20 (children $10), including hotel pick-up and drop-off. The three-hour Kapiti Coast Tour ($55, children $26) runs daily at 9 am and 1.30 pm. Full-day Wairarapa and Palliser Bay tours ($110, children $48) leave at 9 am.

Newlands (☎ 0800 287 287) operates a city Wellington Explorer Tour at 10 am and 2 pm for $20 (children $10), with 10% discounts for YHA members.

Maori Tours (☎ (04) 560 4630) has tours to a marae in the Hutt area, explaining Maori culture and customs, and demonstrating Maori arts and crafts. Costs range from $49 to $85, plus transport, which can be arranged from Wellington for $15.

Tours further afield include 4WD safaris with ATA-All Terrain Adventures (☎ (04) 478 5099) and John Watson (☎ (04) 528 7033). A good, personalised historical tour of the Wellington hinterland is conducted by Attic Window Tours (☎ (04) 563 7596) and includes museums, the Takapuwahia Marae, homesteads, churches and wildlife reserves.

Harbour & Fishing Cruises Trips across the harbour to Days Bay are made on the *Trust Bank Ferry* (☎ (04) 499 1273). The ferry catamaran goes to and from Queens Wharf on a regular daily schedule. The one-way fare is $7 (children $3.50). It's a 30-minute trip to Days Bay, where there are beaches, a fine park and a couple of houses that Katherine Mansfield's family kept for summer homes; her story *At the Bay* recalls summer holidays at Days Bay. At least three ferries per day also call in at Somes Island ($14 return). Somes Island was a quarantine station until 1995 and has only just been opened to the public. Now a reserve managed by DOC, the island has walking trails and beach areas.

Other cruises and yacht charters go from Queens Wharf but they cater primarily to group charters.

Special Events

Wellington is always celebrating one event or another; various tourist publications and the information centre have current listings. Notable regular events include:

February
> *Dragon Boat Festival* – a festival with an international flavour held between Queens and Taranaki St wharves (towards the end of February)

February/March
> *International Festival of the Arts* – a biennial event involving a month of culture, including theatre, music, opera and a writers festival, with many top international artists performing (even-numbered years)

March
> *Wellington Fringe Festival* – innovative festival of the arts
>
> *Wellington Wind Festival* – kite flying, windsurfing, birdman contests and cultural events (just about anything related to Wellington's windy claim to fame)

April-May
> *ASB Bank Laugh Festival* – national and international comedians perform in venues around town
>
> *Wellington International Jazz Festival* – jazz concerts, workshops and street performances (odd-numbered years)

July
> *International Film Festival* – a two-week gala event

Places to Stay

Camping & Cabins Areas of green grass (or even no grass) for pitching a tent in the city are rarities. Closest is the *Hutt Park Holiday Village* (☎ (04) 568 5913) at 95 Hutt Park Rd in Lower Hutt, 13km north-east of the centre of Wellington. It has tent/powered sites for $17/20, standard/tourist cabins for $30/40, tourist flats for $58 and motel units for $78 (all prices are for two people). It is a 15-minute drive from the ferry terminal, a five-minute walk from the bus stop (take the Eastbourne bus) or a 20-minute walk from Woburn train station.

The *Harcourt Holiday Park* (☎ (04) 526 7400) at 45 Akatarawa Rd in Upper Hutt, 35km north-east of Wellington, is in a lovely native-bush setting. Sites are $18 for two, cabins $30 and tourist flats from $53 to $65.

Around 20km north of Wellington and 1km from SH1 in central Porirua, *Camp Elsdon* (☎ (04) 237 8987) at 18 Raiha St is a holiday camp catering mostly for youth groups, but has cabins, and plenty of tent and power sites for $16 for two.

Around 30km east of Wellington and south of Wainuiomata, the lovely *Rimutaka Forest Park* (☎ (04) 564 8551) off Coast Rd has camping ($4, children $2) at Catchpool Valley near DOC's Catchpool Visitor Centre. A shower block and coin-operated gas BBQs make this better than the usual basic DOC camp.

Hostels The *Wellington City YHA Hostel* (☎ (04) 801 7280), on the corner of Cambridge Terrace and Wakefield St, is conveniently situated, queer-friendly (in that it was the first in Wellington to 'come out') and quite a luxurious hostel. Most rooms have private bath and views right over the harbour. The cost is $17 and $19 in different-sized dorms, or $46 for twins and doubles.

Also convenient but further from the action is *Downtown Backpackers* (☎ (04) 473 8482) on the corner of Waterloo Quay and Bunny St, opposite the train station. It's a large hostel with a big-city feel, but amenities include a restaurant, bar with billiard table, huge kitchen, lounge facilities and a pub next door. All rooms have private bathroom; the cost is $18 for a dorm bed or $32/40 for singles/doubles.

Trekkers Hotel (☎ (04) 385 2153), 213 Cuba St, is in a lively area among the delights of Cuba St. It stretches through from Cuba St to Dunlop Terrace. It's a large hotel but also popular with backpackers. Good rooms with basins cost $30/38 for backpackers; hotel rooms are $45/59 for essentially the same rooms with linen provided. Hotel rooms with attached bathrooms, TV, phone etc are $59/79. Facilities include spa, sauna, laundry, kitchen, cafe (Globe Cafe), bar and The Hub travel agency.

The dilapidated *Rosemere Backpackers* (☎ (04) 384 3041) at 6 MacDonald Crescent is a short walk uphill from the centre. It's a fine old house with good city views but badly in need of an overhaul. The cost is $15 for dorms and $36 for doubles.

Several hostels are found on and near Brougham St in the pleasant Mt Victoria area, a quiet residential suburb close to the city. From the train station catch bus No 2 or 5 to Brougham St, or No 1 or 3 to the Basin Reserve stadium. The area is only a five-minute walk from Courtenay Place.

Beethoven House (☎ (04) 384 2226) at 89 Brougham St, Mt Victoria, is one of New Zealand's original backpackers and many people stay just for the company of the eccentric owner, Alan. All birthdays, including Ludwig's, the house's and yours, as well as Christmas are celebrated. Alan is helpful but straight-talking, which some find hard to take. The $15 or $16 for a dorm bed and $36 double-room rate includes the now-famous breakfast heralded by a wake-up call of classical music. There's no prominent sign outside.

Nearby, *Rowena's City Lodge* (☎ (04) 385 7872) at 115 Brougham St is a larger hostel, up a driveway above the street. It's friendly, well equipped and one of the better choices. Rates are $15 in dorms and $20/38 for singles/doubles.

Around the corner at 52 Ellice St is *Maple Lodge* (☎ (04) 385 3771), a smaller hostel with rates of $16 in dorms and $18/36 for singles/doubles. It has safe off-street parking, a confined kitchen, dining room, TV lounge and laundry facilities.

Wide World Backpackers (☎ (04) 383 9600) at 137 Happy Valley Rd (opposite a school) is 5km south of the city centre but a good choice if you have transport. This house has just three share rooms at $10 per person for the first night, dropping to $8 for subsequent nights.

Guesthouses Wellington has a wide selection of guesthouses. At 116 Brougham St in the Mt Victoria area, *Richmond Guest House* (☎ (04) 385 8529) is simple but clean and comfortable with a guests' kitchen. B&B is

$35/50 for share singles/doubles or $45/60 with private bath.

Also on the south side of town, the *Carillon Motor Inn* (☎ (04) 385 8795) at 33 Thompson St is a B&B in a classic house with motel-style units for $56/69 (twins $78). Continental breakfast is an extra $4 and there's a guests' kitchen.

The simple *Terrace Lodge Guesthouse* (☎ (04) 382 9506), 291 the Terrace, is a comfortable home-style guesthouse with singles/doubles for $45/65 ($55/75 with private bath). Breakfast is $6.50 ($12.50 for a cooked breakfast) and there's also a guests' kitchen.

A bit more luxurious, the *Tinakori Lodge* (☎ (04) 473 3478) at 182 Tinakori Rd in the historic Thorndon district offers attractive B&B rooms, each with TV, at $66/80 ($80/110 with en suite). Nearby, *Maggie's B&B*, 17 Aorangi Terrace, is a popular, reasonably priced B&B with rooms with TV and share bathroom for $50/70.

Motels *Halswell Lodge* (☎ (04) 385 0196), 21 Kent Terrace, has the best position. Hotel-style rooms with en suite cost $69/79 for singles/doubles or new units behind the main building cost $110 and some have spas. The *Wellington Motel* (☎ (04) 472 0334) at 14 Hobson St is clean and comfortable with studios for $95 or two-bedroom family units for $105.

Other recommended motels close to the centre include: *Marksman Motor Inn* (☎ (04) 385 2499) at 44 Sussex St, *Wallace Court Motels* (☎ (04) 385 3935) at 88 Wallace St, *Apollo Lodge Motel* (☎ (04) 385 1849) at 49 Majoribanks St, the *Capital View Motor Inn* (☎ (04) 385 0515) at 12 Thompson St, and *Adelaide Motel* (☎ (04) 389 8138) at 209 Adelaide Rd. All have units for around $95.

Hotels The popular, central *Trekkers Hotel* is a good cheaper option (see under Hostels earlier). *Cambridge Hotel* (☎ 385 8829), 28 Cambridge Terrace, has typical old pub rooms at $30 a single with shared bathroom or $55 a double with en suite.

Otherwise, Wellington is awash with

mostly mid-range hotels. Wellington is a business, rather than tourist, destination and weekend discounts from Friday to Sunday deliver good deals on quality hotels.

Portland Towers Hotel (☎ (04) 473 2208), 24 Hawkestone St, is one of the cheaper highrises with rooms for $135 during the week ($90 on weekends). The *Bay Plaza* (☎ (04) 385 7799) at 40-44 Oriental Parade charges $140/85 during the week/weekend. The *Museum Hotel* (☎ (04) 385 2809) at 80 Cable St, a five-storey motel above a car park, charges $164 to $186, dropping to a more reasonable $85 to $124 on weekends. The central *Abel Tasman* (☎ (04) 385 1304) on the corner of Willis and Dixon Sts has rooms from $93 on weekends, rising to $120 on weekdays.

The central *Quality Hotel Willis St* (☎ (04) 385 9819) at 355 Willis St has rooms for from $125 ($95 on weekends), but the *Quality Hotel Oriental Bay* (☎ (04) 385 0279) at 73 Roxburgh St is a standout for its harbour-view rooms from $139 ($95 on weekends).

The *Novotel Wellington* (☎ (04) 385 9829), 345 the Terrace, is one of the city's best hotels and has a swimming pool. Weekends rates are a particularly good deal, with rooms from $88, rising to $135 on weekdays. The *Hotel Raffaele* (☎ (04) 384 3450) at 360 Oriental Parade is also recommended; its doubles are $224 during the week (weekend specials are $95).

At the top end, with rooms in the $300 range, are the *James Cook Centra Hotel* (☎ (04) 499 9500) at 147 the Terrace, the *Wellington Parkroyal* (☎ (04) 472 2722) on the corner of Grey and Featherston Sts, and the *Plaza International* (☎ (04) 473 3900) at 148-176 Wakefield St; prices are around half on weekends.

Apartment Hotels Wellington also has some apartment hotels, a cross between an apartment and a hotel. You can rent them nightly and there's often discounts for long-term stays. *Majoribanks Apartments* (☎ (04) 385 7305) at 38 Majoribanks St has double apartments for $94 to $140 nightly; extra

adults are charged $15 each. The *Central City Apartments* (☎ (04) 385 4166) on the corner of Victoria and Edward Sts has studio units for $120 ($99 from Friday to Sunday). One and two bedroom units are also available.

Places to Eat

Wellington has numerous cafes and restaurants serving a wide selection of international cuisines. Courtenay Place and Cuba St in particular are packed with restaurants.

Restaurants Restaurants are found all around the city, but Courtenay Place is the entertainment centre of Wellington and has a large selection of fashionable restaurants. The Manners Mall-Willis St area also has a good range, as does Cuba St, while Oriental Parade is noted for a few seafood restaurants.

Asian Asian is the dominant international cuisine and Asian restaurants serve some of the cheapest food.

If you like spicy Malaysian food you're in luck because the city has nearly 30 Malaysian restaurants and the competition keeps prices down. At the bottom end of the scale, *Satay Time*, 143 Willis St, is a no-frills takeaway with a few tables, but the food is excellent and the prices (around $5 to $7 for a meal) are hard to beat.

Satay Kampong, 262 Wakefield St, is another basic and functional place with nothing over $8 on the menu; this tiny restaurant is enormously popular. It is open for lunch from 11 am to 2.30 pm daily and also from 6 to 9.30 pm from Monday to Saturday. *Satay Village*, 58 Ghuznee St, near Cuba St, is a brighter little place with good, cheap meals.

Malaya Village, 17-19 Majoribanks St, is more a real restaurant, with pleasant decor and authentic Malaysian hawker fare for around $10 a main. *Cinta* at 41 Courtenay Place is more stylish again, and more expensive.

Khmer Satay Noodle House, 148 Cuba St, is low on decor but great value. Noodle dishes for $5 to $7 are very tasty and a steaming dish of noodle soup with added chilli is guaranteed to clear the sinuses. It is open from 11 am to 9 or 10 pm daily. *Angkor* at 43 Dixon Street is more a real Cambodian restaurant, a rarity in New Zealand. You can sample such delights as mahope kari (a curry selection of chicken, lamb or prawn), amok trei (spicy steamed fish) and yao horn (a charcoal broiler steam boat). It is open for dinner daily.

Java Indonesian Restaurant, upstairs at 119 Manners St, is Wellington's only Indonesian restaurant and has reasonably priced mains from $9.50 to $12.50, and a bar.

The *Oriental Thai* at 58 Cambridge Terrace may well be the city's best Thai restaurant but is expensive.

Courtenay Place is Wellington's traditional Chinatown and, though it has now been taken over by fashionable restaurants and bars, many Chinese restaurants remain. One place stands out as particularly good value, but it's not on Courtenay Place. The *Ye-Jun* Cantonese restaurant upstairs at 40 Willis St has an all-you-can-eat 10-course dinner buffet for $12 and weekday lunches for $10. It's not gourmet food but the price and quantity make it especially popular with travellers.

The Indian subcontinent is also well represented. The *Great India* at 141 Manners St gets rave reviews from Wellingtonians and serves delicious tandoori specialities. *Cafe India*, 22 Allen St, is also popular and has mains for around $15.

For Japanese food, the more expensive *Sakura* restaurant is on the 3rd floor of the Japan Seamans' Insurance Hall at 181-195 Wakefield St and is open for lunch and dinner from Tuesday to Saturday. For teppanyaki, try the pricey *Fujiyama Teppanyaki* on lower Taranaki St.

Middle Eastern *Ali Baba* at 203 Cuba St is a very pleasant place to dine, with seating on Turkish pillows or chairs if you prefer. It's casual and great for an inexpensive meal, snack, or just a baklava and coffee, and is open from 10.30 am to 9 pm daily and until 10 pm on Friday. Also on Cuba St at No 156

is *Cafe Istanbul*, another Turkish restaurant-cafe, with pleasant Turkish decor and mains for around $15. The *Sahara Cafe* at 39 Courtenay Place has Turkish, Lebanese and Syrian food.

Tex-Mex *Armadillo* at 129 Willis St is a Wellington institution – a loud, Texas cowboy-style restaurant-bar specialising in American food like steaks, ribs, southern chicken and burgers in Texas-size portions. It's not cheap at $18-plus for mains, but the portions are big and the place, complete with John Wayne decor, is lots of fun.

Around the corner at 97 Dixon St, *Chevy's* is a colourful pseudo-US restaurant with fancy burgers and Tex-Mex food. *South of the Border* on the corner of Willis and Bond Sts had good-value $16 buffets from Monday to Wednesday.

Seafood The *Tug Boat*, as its name suggests, is in a boat moored on the water behind the Freyberg Swimming Pool on Oriental Parade. It has a mixed menu but is noted mainly for its seafood. Mains are around $20 to $28, while the seafood platter ($65 for two) includes lobster.

About 500m further east on Oriental Parade, the *Quayside Restaurant & Bar* has great harbour views, as it is built over the water in the old Oriental Bay Sea Baths. This is a more formal restaurant but the mains ($22 to $24) are reasonably priced for seafood.

The attractive, upmarket *Shed 5* and *Dockside* restaurants-bars on Queens Wharf are both fine places for seafood. They were opened as part of the city's waterfront revamp. *Shed 5* also has a cafe section, outdoor dining and dance music on weekends.

European & Other Italian food is served at several restaurants, including *La Casa Pasta* upstairs at 37 Dixon St, with home-style food. *Calzone* on the corner of Courtenay Place and Cambridge Terrace is a yuppie sort of place serving gourmet pizzas, pastas, salads and desserts; it's open from 10 am to 1 am daily.

Overlooking the harbour, *Café Menton*, 232 Oriental Parade, about 500m east of the Parade Cafe, is a rarity – a reasonably priced French restaurant with mains for around $20. Upstairs, *Grain of Salt* is a more formal and expensive nouvelle Kiwi restaurant with a lamb/salmon/venison menu.

If your wallet allows, head to *Mondo Cucina*, 15 Blair St, just north of Courtenay Place. It is open from 6 pm for dinner daily, and for brunch from Wednesday to Sunday. Blair St is at the centre of the Courtenay Place restaurant scene; other fashionable restaurants here include the *Exchange* at No 20 for steaks and innovative mains for around $25, and the slightly cheaper *Beacon* at No 8. On the corner of Blair St, at 14-16 Courtenay Place, is the very swish *Opera*, where 'overtures' are about $11, various 'acts' (pastas and mains) are around $22, and 'finales' (desserts) are $9.50.

For steaks, the licensed *Turner's Steakhouse* in the Willis St Village has an open BBQ. Their motto is 'If you leave us hungry, you've only got yourself to blame'. A huge steak, bottomless salad bowl and fries/baked potato is $20.50. It is open from 5.30 pm daily.

Cafes Wellington prides itself as a cultural centre and no literati could flourish without a decent cafe scene for a relaxed meal, snack, dessert or coffee. Good cafes are all around the city centre. Cuba St is one of the best cafe strips, favoured by alternative society, and Courtenay Place has more than its fair share of cafe-bars.

In the centre is the licensed and trendy *Lido Cafe* on the corner of Victoria and Wakefield Sts. The excellent *Clark's Cafe*, on the mezzanine floor of the Central Library on Victoria St, is open daily and worth a visit even if you weren't planning to go to the library. The small and pleasant *Kopi*, 103 Willis St, near Manners St, serves good coffee and light Malaysian meals.

There are a number of hip cafes where the decor is graffiti, the music is underground,

and the customers may include hipsters with spiky purple hair or dreadlocks down to their waists, international hitchhikers or librarians from Taupo. *Espressoholic* at 128 Courtenay Place near the corner of Taranaki St is trendy indeed and open long hours (from 8 am daily until well past 1 am most nights).

Cuba St has a string of good cafes. Check out the *Midnight Espresso* at 178 Cuba St near the corner of Vivian St or the *Globe Cafe* in Trekkers Hotel, 213 Cuba St. The *Krazy Lounge* on the corner of Cuba and Ghuznee Sts is one of the most popular cafes because of its good food and has is open until late. *Zesta*, a few doors along on Cuba St, is another good cafe-bar and a popular spot for a light meal ($12 to $15) for lunch or dinner.

Judging by the number of cabbies, the most popular cheap eatery in town (especially for cooked breakfasts) is the *Foodmine Cafe* on Cuba St near the corner of Abel Smith St. For something completely different, small *Fidel's Cafe* next door at No 234 is a cool hangout for coffee-craving, left-wing subversives.

The *Deluxe Cafe* at 10 Kent Terrace, beside the Embassy Theatre and facing Courtenay Place, is a smaller, quieter but very hip little cafe open from 7.30 am to midnight most days.

The *Mt Victoria Cafe* on the corner of Brougham and Queen Sts, in the Mt Victoria area at the southern end of town, is a pleasant vegetarian wholefood cafe, with delicious food and live jazz and board games on Sunday evening.

Down by the water, *Parade Cafe* on Oriental Parade is opposite the Freyberg Swimming Pool. This popular cafe has a mixed menu, reasonable prices and a few outside tables and chairs.

Cafe L'Affare on College St is out of the action but has a reputation for serving the best coffee in town. The stylish cafe is attached to a coffee warehouse, one of the main distributors of coffee in Wellington, and is open during the day.

Pub Food The *Hotel Bristol*, 131 Cuba St, has good old-fashioned pub fare at cheap prices. The *Backbencher*, *Loaded Hog*, *Shepherds Arms*, *Malthouse* and *Molly Malone's* are all a better class of pub serving bistro meals. *One Red Dog* on Blair St is a popular and stylish brewery restaurant with a varied menu. For addresses and details of these pubs, see the Entertainment section.

Fast Food The fast-food giants are well represented in Wellington. *McDonald's*, *KFC* and *Pizza Hut* are all in Manners Mall in the city centre. There's also a *KFC* on Kent Terrace on the corner of Pirie St, another *McDonald's* on Courtenay Place near the Cambridge Terrace junction and yet another on Lambton Quay near the lower cable-car terminal.

Wellington has a reasonable selection of food courts for cheap, varied dining but most are only open during shopping hours. The food court on the ground floor of the Market at James Smith Corner has Chinese, Mexican, Pizza and other fare and is open the longest – from 9 am to 8 pm on weekdays and until late on Friday and Saturday. The Gourmet Lane food centre in the basement level under the BNZ Centre at Willis St/ Lambton Quay is open until 5 pm from Monday to Saturday.

For sea views, the food court in the Queens Wharf Retail Centre is open from 10 am to 6 pm daily. It has Thai, Chinese and Turkish food, as well as a McDonald's. The food court in the Wellington Market on Wakefield has excellent Asian, including Indian food, but is only open from 10 am to 6 pm from Friday to Sunday.

There's some reasonably priced cafes and delis along Courtenay Place, Manners Mall, along Lambton Quay right in the centre, and along Cuba St and Cuba Mall.

At 101 Manners St, close to the Cuba St junction, *A Taste of France* French bakery has a variety of interesting sandwiches and baked goods. Another branch is on Willis St.

Ali Baba, 203 Cuba St, sells doner kebabs with salad and bread for around $8. *Sahara Cafe* at 39 Courtenay Place is another cheap Turkish place.

An important port like Wellington natu-rally has plenty of fish and chip specialists. The *Wellington Fish Supply* at 40 Moles-worth St, opposite the Beehive, has good fish and chips. *Shed 5* on the waterfront also has a fresh fish market next to the restaurant.

Entertainment
Cinemas There are plenty of cinemas: *Midcity* on Manners St, the *Hoyts 5* on Manners Mall and the *Embassy* on Kent St, which screens commercial films; the *Paramount* at 25 Courtenay Place, which has 'hard-edged' art-house movies; the *Penthouse* at 205 Ohiro Rd in Brooklyn, which screens 'middle of the road' art-house films; the *Film Centre* on Cable St, which boasts 'quality independent productions'; and the *Continuum* on Civic Square, which has 'alternative' movies.

The Wellington Film Society (☎ (04) 384 6817) presents interesting international and art films; phone for a schedule.

Performing Arts Wellington is the most active place in New Zealand for live theatre, supporting a number of professional theatre companies and quality amateur companies.

Downstage Theatre (☎ (04) 801 6946) presents plays in the Hannah Playhouse on the corner of Cambridge Terrace and Courtenay Place; the pleasant Encore cafe is here. *Circa Theatre* (☎ (04) 801 7992), near the corner of Cable and Taranaki Sts on the Lambton Harbour waterfront, presents a variety of drama. The *Bats Theatre* (☎ (04) 802 4175), 1 Kent Terrace, is a more avant-garde, alternative theatre.

The *Taki Rua Theatre* (☎ (04) 384 4531) at 12 Alpha St specialises in New Zealand drama, with new and Maori plays and local themes. The *Phoenix Theatre* (☎ (04) 385 4939) at 13 Dixon St is a community theatre company.

Reduced-price theatre tickets for the Bats, Circa and Downstage theatres are available at the information centre, subject to availability.

The Wellington City Opera (☎ (04) 384 4434) and the Royal New Zealand Ballet (☎ (04) 238 5383) both perform in town,

WELLINGTON REGION

usually at the State Opera House; ring for schedules.

The *State Opera House* (☎ (04) 385 0832) on Manners St, the *Michael Fowler Centre* (☎ (04) 801 4263) on Wakefield St, the *Wellington Town Hall* (☎ (04) 471 1573) on Wakefield St and the *Victoria University Theatre* (☎ (04) 473 3120) are all popular performance venues. The ritzy Michael Fowler Centre, part of the Civic Square complex, has its main entrance on Wakefield St. It hosts all sorts of performances, from bands to the New Zealand Symphony Orchestra. Check the newspapers or the information centre for current shows. The amphitheatre at Frank Kitts Park on the waterfront and the *Dell* in the Botanic Garden are popular venues for outdoor concerts and shows.

Music & Dancing For gig guides pick up a copy of *City Voice* or *Lava*, which are free papers available around town.

Courtenay Place is the undisputed nightlife centre of Wellington with numerous bars, and crowds on weekends. Along it you'll find the *Big Easy* (often referred to locally as the 'big sleazy'), a 'singles' venue with oversized bouncers on the door. *Kitty O'Shea's* is a more convivial pub-bar with rock bands. The *Planet Bar* on the corner of Courtenay Place and Tory St is large and pleasant with interesting decor, a long twisted bar and DJs from Thursday to Saturday. It's open from 11 am to 3 am, Sunday to Tuesday, and until 5 am on other days. The *Opera* on the corner of Blair St is similar, if slightly yuppier, and another popular late-night venue with DJ music.

Blair and Allen Sts, running off Courtenay Place, are also fertile hunting grounds for booze and music. On Blair St, the *Blue Room* has DJ dance music from Thursday to Saturday and occasional bands. The *Judder Bar* on Allen St also has DJs.

Queens Wharf is away from the main nightlife areas and less frenetic. *Chicago* has bands downstairs on weekends, doing mostly 1980s covers. The dance floor is lively or there is a quieter bar upstairs. *Shed 5* at Queens Wharf is popular with the yuppie set for more upmarket dancing (and dining) on weekends. The *St Johns Bar* at 5-9 Cable St, in the old St John's Ambulance building, not far from the wharf, is a good after-dark venue popular with locals.

Tiny Edward St, off Victoria St, has a few interesting bars, the pick of which is *ESCape* at No 9. DJs pump out the music from Thursday to Sunday, with African rhythms on Friday.

For original bands, the pick of the venues is *Bar Bodega*, 286 Willis St on the corner of Abel Smith St, and the *Hole in the Wall*, 154 Vivian St near Cuba St. Bar Bodega is a cool hangout popular with alternative types and is open from morning until late. Good local bands play every night of the week and on Tuesday and Sunday it is usually the last bar in town to shut. Tucked away among the seedy sex venues on Vivian St, Hole in the Wall is a good venue for alternative bands every night (except Sunday) from around 10 pm. For a change of pace, Monday is jazz night and there are drinks specials on Monday and Tuesday.

Pubs Brewery pubs are very popular. The *Loaded Hog* at 12-14 Bond St, just off Willis St, has a lively atmosphere, live music Wednesday to Sunday nights (no cover charge) and a good menu. It's open from 11 am till late daily and until 10 pm on Sunday. Not far from the corner of Lambton Quay and Willis St (No 47), the *Malthouse* is a good place for a meal but an absolute shrine for the lover of naturally brewed NZ beer. *One Red Dog* on Blair St is a chic variety of the brewery pub, very popular for a meal and late night drinking on the weekend.

Molly Malone's, an Irish pub at the Glass House on the corner of Courtenay Place and Taranaki St, is another rousing, popular pub. Live music is mostly Irish, playing Tuesday to Saturday nights with no cover charge; on Monday nights there's an Irish jam session. It's open from 11 am till late from Monday to Saturday and until 9 pm on Sunday. Traditional Irish fare is served upstairs in the *Dubliner*.

The *Backbencher* is on the corner of Molesworth St and Sydney St East, opposite the Beehive, so you might bump into a polly or two or overhear a coup. It does a thriving business at lunch time, serving large portions of food, and dinners are popular too. The atmosphere is casual, friendly and fun. It's open from 11 am until late daily.

Also on Molesworth St, a couple of blocks up the hill at No 110, the *Thorndon Tavern* is a sports bar with a big-screen sports TV, billiards, darts and TAB racing downstairs. It also has pub food and laid-back bands playing on weekends. A slightly suburban but stylish pub is the renovated *Shepherd's Arms Tavern* on Tinakori Rd, not far from the main entrance to the Botanic Gardens.

Wine buffs should check out the *Bouquet Garni Wine Bar*, on the corner of Willis and Boulcott Sts, in a historic building with a huge wine list and expensive bistro meals.

Gay & Lesbian Venues An always popular gay venue is *Caspers Bar* at 120 Victoria St on the ground floor of MRL House (opposite McDonald's). Nearby *ESCape*, upstairs at 9 Edward St, has gay, lesbian (last Saturday night of every month) and friends' nights, and special evenings on long weekends. Downstairs at 9 Edward St is *ESC*, a cool cafe and bar. Its motto is: 'It doesn't matter if you are black or white, straight or gay, leave your attitude on the outside and come on in and meet some really warm people.' Tiny Edward St is something of a gay way, and a few doors from Escape is the popular *Ruby Ruby*, open from 11 am to 3 am from Monday to Saturday. *La Strada* in the same street is a gay-friendly tapas bar.

Evergreen Coffee House, 144 Vivian St, is a popular gay and lesbian cafe open late, and *Flip Brasserie* in the RSA Building at 103 Ghuznee St (a great, but not cheap, place for good Mediterranean food and company) is a gay-friendly restaurant.

Out! Bookshop and men's cruise bar is at 15 Tory St, between Wakefield St and Courtenay Place, and *Unity Bookshop* on the corner of Willis and Manners Sts has a good gay and lesbian book section. If you are hoping to meet a friendly bunch of people when you arrive in Wellington try the Gay Switchboard (☎ (04) 385 0674) from 7.30 to 10 pm or the Lesbian Line (☎ (04) 389 8082) on Tuesday and Thursday from 7.30 to 10 pm. AIDS services include the NZ Aids Foundation Awhina Centre (☎ 801 6640) at Level 2, 45 Tory St.

Things to Buy

The Market at St James is in the Old St James building on the corner of the Cuba Mall and Manners St. Dozens of tiny shops upstairs sell African beads, Balinese jewellery, bongs, candles and other New Age stuff, but the food court on the ground floor is good. Wellington Market on Wakefield St is similar but mostly specialises in second-hand goods and furniture and is open Friday to Sunday from 10 am to 5 pm.

New Zealand's answer to Bloomingdale's or Harrods is Kirkcaldie & Stains on Lambton Quay.

The well-stocked New World supermarket, on the corner of Cambridge Terrace and Wakefield St, is open from 8 am to 10 pm daily.

Camping & Sports Gear The Kathmandu store, on the ground floor of the Rural Bank Building at 34 Manners St, has good-quality tramping clothing. Mainly Tramping at 39 Mercer St has high-quality camping gear, or Doyles next door is cheaper and has a large army surplus-style range. Second Wind Sports at 45 Cuba St sells both new and used sports and outdoor equipment of all kinds.

Getting There & Away

Air Wellington airport has a domestic and international terminal, each with restaurants, gift shops and its own information centres (☎ (04) 388 5123) open until around 6 or 7 pm daily and until 11.30 pm on Saturday. Left-luggage lockers are in the domestic terminal.

Air New Zealand and Ansett offer direct domestic flights to many places in NZ, with connections to other centres. Air New Zealand has direct flights to Auckland,

Blenheim, Chatham Islands, Christchurch, Dunedin, Gisborne, Hamilton, Napier, Nelson, New Plymouth, Palmerston North, Rotorua, Taupo, Tauranga, Timaru, Wanganui and Westport. Ansett has direct flights to Auckland, Blenheim, Christchurch, Dunedin, Hamilton, Invercargill, Nelson, Palmerston North and Rotorua.

The flight between Wellington and Picton in the South Island takes 25 minutes in a small plane. Some travellers take the ferry in one direction and fly in the other to experience both. The strait can be just as bumpy up above as it often is at sea level. Soundsair (☎ (04) 388 2594) has Wellington-Picton flights for $59 one way and also flies to nearby Blenheim for $65.

International flights serving Wellington are mostly Air New Zealand and Qantas flights to/from Sydney, Brisbane and Melbourne. Polynesian Airlines has limited direct flights to Melbourne and Sydney and is usually the cheapest. Travel agents are the best place to buy international tickets (see the earlier Information section).

International and domestic airlines with offices in Wellington include:

Air New Zealand
  (☎ (04) 474 8950) on the corner of Panama St and Lambton Quay
  (☎ (04) 495 2910) 79 Willis St
Ansett New Zealand
  (☎ (04) 471 1146) Shop 10, Harbour City Centre, Panama St
British Airways
  (☎ (04) 472 7327) Royal Insurance Building on the corner of Featherston and Panama Sts
Malaysia Airlines
  (☎ 0800 657 472) 10th Floor, 111 the Terrace
Polynesian Airlines
  (☎ 0800 800 993) 3-11 Hunter St
Qantas Airways
  (☎ (04) 472 1100; 0800 808 767) ASB Bank Tower, 2 Hunter St
Singapore Airlines
  (☎ (04) 473 9749) 3-11 Hunter St
United Airlines
  (☎ (04) 472 0470) 26 Brandon St

Bus Wellington is an important junction for bus travel, with buses to Auckland and all major towns in-between.

Buses from the two main companies, InterCity (☎ (04) 472 5111) and Newmans (☎ (04) 499 3261), depart from Platform 9 at the train station, as well as from the *Interislander* ferry terminal. Tickets for these buses are sold at the travel reservations and tickets centre in the train station. City to City: White Star (☎ (04) 478 4734) buses depart from Bunny St, near Downtown Backpackers opposite the train station, and run along the west coast of the North Island to Palmerston North, Wanganui and New Plymouth.

Train Wellington train station (☎ (04) 498 3413; 0800 802 802) is a large station with a travel centre offering reservations and tickets for trains, buses, the *Interislander* ferry, airlines, tours and more. Luggage lockers are open daily from 6 am to 10 pm.

A free shuttle bus runs between the train station and the ferry terminal, departing from the station 35 minutes before each ferry leaves and meeting each arriving ferry.

Trains operate between Wellington and Auckland, running through the central North Island. The daily, daytime *Overlander* departs from each end in the morning. The overnight *Northerner* runs daily except Saturday, departing from each city in the evening and arriving early the next morning. The *Bay Express*, between Wellington and Napier, departs from Wellington in the morning, arriving in Napier in the early afternoon; it leaves from Napier an hour later to arrive back in Wellington in the evening.

Hitching It's not easy to hitch out of Wellington because the highways heading out of the city, SH1 up the Kapiti Coast and SH2 up the Hutt Valley, are motorways for a long distance and hitching is illegal on motorways. Catch a bus or train out to the Kapiti Coast or to Masterton and hitch from there.

Boat The *Interislander* (☎ 0800 802 802) ferries shuttle back and forth between Wellington and Picton. The trip takes around three hours and sailing times (subject to change) are:

Leaves Wellington	Leaves Picton
1.30 am*	5.30 am*
9.30 am	10.30 am
2.30 pm	1.30 pm
5.30 pm	6.30 pm
10.30 pm	9.30 pm

* Tuesday to Sunday only

It's best to do the trip in daylight, if the weather's good, to see Wellington Harbour and the Marlborough Sounds. Sailing can be rough in adverse weather but ferries are large and well equipped, with various lounges, cafes, bars, a movie theatre and an information centre for bookings. Fares are:

	Standard	Economy	Sailaway Saver	Super Saver
Adult	$46	$39	$32	$23
Child	$28	$23	$19	$14
(4 to 14)				
Motorbikes	$46	$39	$32	$23
Cars	$165	$140	$116	$83
Campervans	$190	$162	$133	$95

Children under four years travel for free and bicycles cost $10. All discount fares *must* be booked in advance. Only standard fares are available on the day of departure. Discounts are subject to availability and may not be available during peak travel times, such as day sailings in January and other domestic holiday periods. The cheapest fares are available only when no one else wants to travel, like at night and in the middle of winter, and refund restrictions apply. Economy fares are more readily available and more flexible. Various day-excursion, family and group fares are also offered.

At peak periods you should book well ahead – the ferries can be booked solid at certain popular holiday times, especially for the limited vehicle space. At other times passengers can usually get on the same day and those transporting cars can give limited notice but it's wise to book.

You can book up to six months in advance, either directly (☎ 0800 802 802) or at most travel agents and information centres throughout New Zealand. In general, the further you book in advance the better the discount.

The faster *Lynx* (☎ 0800 802 802) operates only from December to April, doing the trip to Picton in less than two hours; it leaves from both ends three times daily. Fares follow the same dubious four-tiered discount system as the *Interislander*: standard fares for adults/children are $59/35 ($30/18 super saver); cars are $190 ($95 super saver); campervans are $220 ($185 economy); motorcycles cost $59 ($30 super saver); and bicycles are $12. There are also 'one-dayer' and 'combo' return discounted fares.

A free shuttle-bus service is provided for ferry sailings on both sides of the strait. In Wellington it operates between the ferry and train station (where long-distance buses also depart), departing from the train station 35 minutes before each sailing. The shuttle meets all arriving ferries. On the Picton side, a free shuttle runs between the ferry and the Picton-Christchurch *Coastal Pacific Express* train.

Vehicle Storage If you need to store your vehicle while you go across on the ferry, Wellington has some reputable vehicle-storage services. The ferry terminal has an overnight lock-up service. Securaport (☎ (04) 387 3700; 57-61 Kingsford Smith St, Lyall Bay) and Car Storage (☎ (04) 472 3215; 138 Old Hutt Rd, Kaiwharawhara) charge around $10 per day and pick up and drop off at the ferry and airport terminals.

Getting Around
To/From the Airport The airport is 7km south-east of the city centre. Johnstons Shuttle (☎ (04) 569 9017) and Super Shuttle (☎ (04) 387 8787) provide door-to-door shuttle buses between the city and the airport at $8 for one person, $10 for two and $12 for three.

Both companies also operate scheduled shuttles ($5 per person) from the train station to the airport, with stops at Lambton Quay, Cuba St and elsewhere. Johnstons Shuttle runs half-hourly from 8 am to 5.30 pm daily;

Super Shuttle runs every half to one hour between 7.15 am and 5.45 pm on weekdays.

A taxi between the city centre and airport costs around $15.

Bus Wellington has a good local bus system, with frequent buses operating daily from around 7 am to 11.30 pm on most routes. Most depart from beside the train station and from the major bus stop on Courtenay Place at the intersection with Cambridge Terrace. Useful colour-coded bus route maps and timetables are available at the information centre.

Phone Ridewell (☎ 0800 801 7000) for timetable and fare information from Monday to Saturday from 7.30 am to 8.30 pm and on Sunday from 9 am to 3 pm.

Bus fares are determined by zones. The 'Miracle Mile', between the train station and the Courtenay Place/Cambridge Terrace bus stops, costs $1; otherwise it's $1.10 to ride in one section and $1.70 for two sections.

An all-day Daytripper Pass for $5 allows unlimited rides on Stagecoach Wellington buses (most local buses) after 9 am. They are available from bus drivers only and two children can ride free with each adult.

Train Four suburban electric train routes, with frequent trains daily from around 6 am to midnight, leave the Wellington train station. These routes are: Johnsonville, via Khandallah and Ngaio; Paraparaumu, via Porirua and Paekakariki; Melling, via Petone and Lower Hutt; and Upper Hutt, going on to Masterton. Phone Ridewell (☎ 0800 801 7000) or pick up timetables from the train station or visitor information centre.

In addition to the regular fares there is also a day pass ($15) available which allows two adults and two children (or one adult and three children) to ride these suburban trains anywhere, all day long.

Car Wellington has a number of hire car operators (check the Yellow Pages and shop around by phone), but the prices are nowhere near as competitive as Auckland. Prices start at around $40 a day for an older car. If you

are landing in Wellington and heading to the South Island, it is cheaper and easier to hire a car in Picton. Prices are around the same as in Wellington but you don't have to pay the ferry charges.

Bicycle The Penny Farthing Cycle Shop (☎ (04) 385 2279) at 89 Courtenay Place and Pins Cycles (☎ (04) 472 4591), on the corner of Willis and Boulcott Sts, hire mountain bikes at $25 per day, and do longer term rentals. Both shops offer a full range of bicycle gear, clothing, bicycle repairs, and bicycles for sale.

Around Wellington

HUTT VALLEY

The Hutt River acts as the western boundary for land-starved Wellington's dormitory cities, Lower Hutt (population 95,000) and Upper Hutt (population 36,000). Apart from some attractive forest parks for picnics and a few museums, they are just suburbs. Both cities are easily reached by train from Wellington.

Lower Hutt has the **Petone Settlers Museum** on the Esplanade, Petone, which is open from noon to 4 pm from Tuesday to Friday and from 1 to 5 pm on weekends. For more information contact the Lower Hutt Visitor Information Centre (☎ (04) 570 6699) in the Pavilion shopping mall, 25 Laings Rd.

In Upper Hutt, the **Silver Stream Railway Museum** on Eastern Rd has NZ's largest collection of working steam locomotives. the museum also runs train rides on Sunday and public holidays ($5, children $3). The drive from Upper Hutt to Waikanae on the scenic Akatarawa road passes the **Staglands Wildlife Reserve**. The Upper Hutt Visitor Information Centre (☎ (04) 527 6041) is on Main Rd.

To the south are the towns of Wainuiomata and Eastbourne. Wainuiomata has a **heritage trail** with 14 points of interest. At Eastbourne there's a pavilion popular with

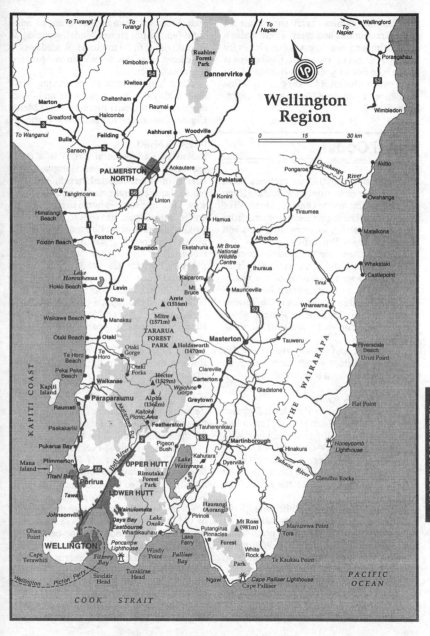

Wellington Region

0   15   30 km

families for picnics, craft shops, an art gallery, restaurants and cafes. There's also a good swimming beach, kayaks and bikes for hire, and fishing off the wharf. Eastbourne is a 7km bike ride or walk from Burdan's Gate at the end of Muritai Rd to the country's first permanent lighthouse, **Pencarrow Lighthouse**.

Kapiti Coast

The picturesque Kapiti Coast stretches 30km along the west coast from Paekakariki (45km north of Wellington) to Otaki (75km north of Wellington). The region takes its name from large Kapiti Island, an interesting bird and marine sanctuary 5km offshore.

The coast has fine white-sand beaches, good swimming and other water activities, and is a summer playground of the windy city, as well as a suburban extension of Wellington. The other attractions is the Tararua Forest Park in the Tararua Range, which forms a backdrop to the coastline all along its length.

The Kapiti Coast is easily visited as a day trip from Wellington but also has good accommodation for a few restful days.

Getting There & Away

Paraparaumu airport also has direct flights to Nelson in the South Island for $59 (including pick-up), and direct flights to Auckland with Associated Airlines (☎ 0800 650 400).

Getting from Wellington to the west coast is a breeze – the coast is on the major route (SH1) from Wellington to the rest of the North Island.

InterCity, Newmans, White Star, Kiwi Experience and Magic buses all stop at Paraparaumu and Otaki on their north-south routes to/from Wellington. From Wellington it's about an hour to Otaki and 45 minutes to Paraparaumu, much of it by motorway.

Trains between Wellington and the coast are easier and more frequent than buses. Electric trains between Wellington and Paraparaumu ($7.50; one hour) run hourly in

both directions from around 6 am to midnight (until 8 pm on weekends), stopping at Paekakariki ($6; 50 minutes). Weekday off-peak fares (available from 9 am to 3 pm) are slightly cheaper.

Three long-distance trains serving Wellington also stop at Paraparaumu and Otaki daily, as does the early morning Tranz Metro *Capital Connection* to Palmerston North.

PAEKAKARIKI

Paekakariki (population 1700) is a quiet seaside village spread out along a lovely stretch of often-deserted beach, just two blocks from the train station and the highway. This little town is home to a number of artists and is a pleasant spot to relax within striking distance of Wellington. Paekakariki means 'the perch (*pae*) of the parakeet (*kakariki*)'.

Fly by Wire (☎ 025 300 366) provides an adrenalin-buzz activity in the hills just behind Paekakariki. You fly yourself in a bullet-shaped contraption with a turbo fan at back, hanging from a cable that dangles 55m from an overhead suspension point. You can reach speeds of up to 120km/h. A seven-minute flight costs $99, including a video. Book at the Southern Lights Cafe or telephone direct.

Steam Inc (☎ (04) 292 8662), by the train station and almost on SH1, contains restored steam locomotives, a must for those that love the screech of steam and the smell of smoke. It's open on Saturday from 8.30 am to 6 pm.

About 5km north of Paekakariki at MacKay's Crossing, just off SH1, the **Wellington Tramway Museum** (☎ (04) 292 8361) has restored wooden trams that ran in Wellington until its tram system was shut down in 1964, plus interesting photographs of old-time Wellington. A 2km track runs from the museum down to the beach with good swimming, a playground and walking tracks through the dunes. A return ride is $4 (children $2). The museum is open from 11 am to 5 pm on weekends and holidays (daily over the Christmas holidays).

An alternative way to travel between Wellington and Paekakariki is over the scenic

Paekakariki Hill Rd. If you're cycling south, it's a steep climb for about 3km and then smooth sailing all the way after that.

Places to Stay & Eat

Paekakariki Holiday Park (☎ (04) 292 8292) is about 1.5km north of the town, right on the beach in Queen Elizabeth Park. Tent or powered sites are $19 for two, cabins are $38 for two people and tourist flats are $55 for two. *Belvedere Motel* (☎ (04) 292 8478) is on SH1.

Up on a hill just one block from the beach and one block from the train station and highway turn-off, *Paekakariki Backpackers* (☎ (04) 292 8749) at 11 Wellington Rd is a small, friendly and relaxed hostel with a magnificent view of the sea and sunset. Free use of surfboards and bicycles is included in the cost of $14 in share rooms, or $35 in twin/double rooms.

The main street, Beach Rd, has a takeaway fish and chip shop, a pub for counter meals and the *Southern Cafe* for coffee, light meals and breakfast. The *Paekakariki Cafe*, on Wellington St near the steps up to the backpackers, has more substantial and innovative meals and is open for dinner from Wednesday to Saturday.

PARAPARAUMU

Paraparaumu (population 8800) is the principal town of the Kapiti Coast, forming almost a suburban satellite of Wellington, which is within commuting distance. This modern town is made up of Paraparaumu on the main highway, Paraparaumu Beach on the coast 3km west, and Raumati Beach further south. The beach is the coast's most developed, with a beachside park and plenty of water activities. Boat trips to Kapiti Island depart from Paraparaumu Beach.

The name Paraparaumu is rather a mouthful, and locally it is shortened to 'para-par-AM', although this is a politically incorrect corruption of the original. Radio announcers and the culturally aware now use the correct pronunciation ('para-para-umu'), but the locals won't budge. The name means 'scraps from an oven' and is said to have originated

when a Maori war party attacked the settlement and found only scraps of food in the oven.

Most things you'll need in Paraparaumu are on the highway. The Kapiti Visitor Information Centre (☎ (04) 298 8195) in the big shopping centre is open daily from 9 am to 4 pm. The airport on the road to the beach has flights to Auckland and Nelson, and tandem skydiving (☎ (04) 298 6600), while the Kapiti Aero Club has Tiger Moth aerobatic flights from $69.

Things to See & Do

Paraparaumu Beach, with its beachside park, good swimming and other water activities (waterslide, jet-skiing, windsurfing etc) is the main attraction.

On SH1, 2km north of Paraparaumu, the **Lindale Centre** (☎ (04) 297 0916) is a large tourist complex open daily from 9 am to 5 pm. Here you'll find the Lindale Farm Park with weekend farm shows ($6, children $4), and an outlet for the region's famous cheese and ice cream – drop in for a taste. Helicopter tours, craft shops and cafes complete the scene. Inquire at the NZ Geographic Shop in the centre about visiting **Nikau Gardens** further along the highway. Entry is $9 to these landscaped gardens and butterfly park, where NZ's prehistoric insect, the weta, is on display.

Another kilometre north, just off SH1, the **Southward Car Museum** has one of the largest collections of antique and unusual cars in Australasia. Its more than 130 cars include the oldest in New Zealand, an array of motorbikes, three-wheeled cars, inventive homemade vehicles, some antique airplanes, and bicycles. See also Marlene Dietrich's Rolls Royce, the 1895 Benz 'horseless carriage' and a gull-winged Mercedes Benz. It's open from 9 am to 4.30 pm daily ($5, children $2).

Nyco Chocolates, on SH1 about 1km south of town, is open from 9 am to 5 pm daily, with all kinds of chocolates and other confections for sale; tours ($1) leave at 10.30 am and 2.30 pm on weekdays.

WELLINGTON REGION

Places to Stay & Eat

The *Lindale Motor Park* (☎ (04) 298 8046) is about 2km north of the town near SH1, just south of the Lindale Centre. Rates are $17/19 for two for tent/powered sites, $28 for single cabins and from $40 to $56 for double cabins.

Opposite the beachside park at Paraparaumu Beach, *Barnacles Seaside Inn* (☎ (04) 298 4856), 3 Marine Parade, has views of the sea and is convenient to everything. It has dorms for $15 but most of the rooms are singles ($20) or doubles and twins for $35 and $40. The location and the rooms are good but it doesn't have a backpackers atmosphere.

There are plenty of motels in the town and at the beach; most charge around $65 to $75 a double. At Paraparaumu Beach there's the *Ocean Motel* (☎ (04) 298 6458) at 42-44 Ocean Rd, *Wright's by the Sea* (☎ (04) 298 7646) at 387-389 Kapiti Rd, *Kapiti Court* (☎ (04) 298 7982) at 341 Kapiti Rd, and the *Golf View* (☎ (04) 298 6089) at 16 Golf Rd.

Restaurants, cafes and takeaways are plentiful near Paraparaumu Beach. Out on the highway, just south of town, *Pizza Hut*, *McDonald's* and *KFC* are all strategically located to ensnare passing motorists.

KAPITI ISLAND

About 10km long and 2km wide, Kapiti Island is the coastline's dominant feature. Its name is short for Te-Waewae-Kapiti-o-Tara-raua-ko-Rangitane, meaning 'the place where the boundaries of Tara and Rangitane divide'; historically it formed the boundary between the Ngati Tara and Rangitane tribal lands. In the early 1800s the island was the base for Te Rauparaha, a mighty warrior who came down from Kawhia with his forces and took over the entire region. Later that century, the main island and the three small islands between it and the mainland became bases for seven whaling stations.

Since 1897 the island has been a protected wildlife reserve. Many species of birds that are now rare or extinct on the mainland still thrive on Kapiti Island.

The island is maintained by DOC and access is limited to 50 people per day. To visit you must obtain a permit ($8, children $4) from the DOC office in Wellington (☎ 0900 52 748) in the government buildings on Lambton Quay. You can book up to three months in advance. You might be able to arrange something on the coast at the last minute if a booking is cancelled, but don't count on it. Transport is booked separately (DOC can advise you). Kapiti Tours (☎ (06) 364 5042) is the main operator and has a ferry from Paraparaumu Beach to the island ($30 return).

Although access to the island itself is restricted, boat and diving trips can go *around* the island. A variety of tours around the island are offered by Kapiti Tours and Kapiti Marine Charter (☎ (04) 297 2585). Tamarillo Sea Kayaking (☎ 025 244 1616) has all-day kayaking trips for $125.

WAIKANAE

About 5km north of Paraparaumu, Waikanae (population 6600) is another town with two sections, one on SH1 and another by the beach. The Waikanae Field Centre (☎ (04) 293 2191) at 10 Parata St is the main DOC office for the Kapiti Coast.

Waikanae's main attraction is the **Nga Manu Sanctuary**, a 15-hectare bird sanctuary with habitats including ponds, swamp, scrubland, coastal and swamp forest, and birds such as mute swans, keas, pied stilts, parakeets, ducks and wood pigeons. Other features include picnic areas, bushwalks and a nocturnal house with kiwis, owls and tuataras.

To reach the sanctuary, turn seaward from SH1 onto Te Moana Rd and then follow the signs; the sanctuary is several kilometres from the turn-off. It's open from 10 am to 5 pm daily ($3, children $1.50).

Places to Stay

Waikanae has several motels including the *Kapiti Gateway Motel* (☎ (04) 293 6053) on SH1; the beachside *Sand Castle Motel* (☎ (04) 293 6072) on Paetawa Rd; the *Toledo Park Motel* (☎ (04) 293 6199) at 95 Te Moana Rd and the *Ariki Lodge Motel*

(☎ (04) 293 6592) at 4 Omahi St. Of the many B&Bs, *Waimoana* (☎ (04) 293 7158), 63 Kakariki Grove, has been recommended. Singles/doubles are $60/100 to $90/140 and dinner is $45 per person. This place has a swimming pool, garden and waterfall all under the one roof.

OTAKI

Otaki (population 5600) is primarily a gateway to the Tararua ranges. It has a strong Maori history and influence: the little town has nine maraes and a Maori college. The historic Rangiatea Church, built under the guidance of Ngati Toa chief Te Rauparaha nearly 150 years ago, was tragically burnt to the ground in 1995. This was the original burial site of Te Rauparaha and also the burial place of the opera singer Inia Te Wiata.

Most services, including the train station where buses stop, are on SH1. The main centre of Otaki, with the post office and more shops, is 2km seawards. Three kilometres further on the same road brings you to Otaki's windswept beach.

Otaki means 'the place of sticking in' – a story tells that Otaki was where Hau stuck his staff in the ground when he was pursuing his wife, though the story seems to have lost something in the translation.

Otaki Forks

Two kilometres south of the town, Otaki Gorge Rd takes off inland from SH1 and leads 19km to Otaki Forks, the main western entrance to the Tararua Forest Park. The scenic half-hour drive up through the Otaki Gorge to the Forks has a number of posted walking tracks along the way.

Otaki Forks has picnic and swimming areas, camping areas and a hut, and a resident conservation officer (☎ (06) 364 3111) who has maps and information on the Tararua Forest Park. Bushwalks from 30 minutes to 3½ hours long are around the immediate area; longer tracks lead to huts. Ask for advice on longer tracks in the park – you can walk across the Tararuas, but must bring adequate clothing and be well equipped and

prepared for adverse weather. Sign the intentions book.

On Otaki Gorge Rd, **Tararua Outdoor Recreation Centre** (☎ (06) 364 3110) has guided kayak and rafting trips on the Otaki River (grade 2 to 3) for $35. Night (evening) rafting trips are very popular. You can hire river equipment or mountain bikes for $30 a day, and be dropped off by 4WD for an extra $10; abseiling is also offered. The centre is open from October to April.

Places to Stay

Otaki's two motor camps are just a block from the beach. *Byron's Resort* (☎ (06) 364 8121) at 20 Tasman Rd has tent/powered sites at $17/20 for two, and tourist flats and motels units from $55 to $100. Facilities include a licensed restaurant, swimming pool, spa, sauna, tennis and playgrounds. The *Otaki Beach Motor Camp* (☎ (06) 364 7107) on Moana St is a more simple place with tent/powered sites at $14/19 and cabins and on-site caravans at $25 to $30.

Coming into Otaki from Wellington, *Toad Hall* (☎ (06) 364 6906), 4 Addington Rd, is just off SH1 about 3km before the town. This friendly backpackers is in an impressive two-storey wooden house and is surrounded by farmland. Dorms are $15 and doubles are $36. Free bikes and pick-up from town are offered.

Otaki Oasis (☎ (06) 364 6860) at 33 Rahui Rd is a small hobby farm on the inland side of the railway tracks, about a block south of the train station. The well-kept backpackers lodge next to the house charges $15 for dorms or $35 for a double room. Pony treks are offered for $15 per hour.

The *Otaki Motel* (☎ (06) 364 8469) on SH1 has units from $60 and *Waitohu Lodge B&B* (☎ (06) 364 5389) a few doors along charges $50/70 for singles/doubles.

The Wairarapa

The large region east and north-east of Wellington is known as the Wairarapa, taking its

WELLINGTON REGION

name from Lake Wairarapa (literally 'shimmering waters'), a shallow but vast 8000 hectare lake. This region, very much the apotheosis of rural New Zealand, is principally a sheep-raising district – it boasts that it has three million sheep within a 16km radius of Masterton, the region's main town. It also has a few interesting attractions for visitors, including the Mt Bruce National Wildlife Centre, wineries at Martinborough, and very good tramping and camping in several regional and forest parks. Get a copy of the free, excellent *Wairarapa: Capital Country Escape* from the visitor information centre. The route through the Wairarapa along SH2 is a pleasant, much less frenetic alternative to busy SH1 on the west coast.

MASTERTON

The main town of the Wairarapa, Masterton (population 19,700) is not a particularly exciting place, although it's a fair-sized town and can be used as a base for the surrounding area. Its main claim to fame is the international Golden Shears competition held annually during the first week in March, in which sheep shearing is raised to the level of sport and art, with the world's top shearers competing for finesse as well as speed.

Tourism Wairarapa (☎ (06) 378 7373; fax 378 7042) at 5 Dixon St has information on the Wairarapa region; it's open on weekdays from 9 am to 5 pm and on weekends from 10 am to 4 pm.

The DOC field office (☎ (06) 378 2061) on South Rd, 2km south of the town centre, is open on weekdays from 8.30 am to 5 pm. The AA (☎ (06) 378 2222) is on the corner of Chapel and Jackson Sts.

Things to See & Do

The large 32 hectare **Queen Elizabeth Park** has sportsgrounds, an aviary, aquarium, deer park, small lake where boats are hired out, children's playgrounds and a miniature railway where trains run on weekends and holidays.

The **Museum of Early Childhood**, 40 Makora Rd, has a fascinating collection of antique dolls, toys, games, books and clothing and an array of teddy bears (admission by donation). Ring for an appointment (☎ (06) 377 4743).

Places to Stay

The *Mawley Park Motor Camp* (☎ (06) 378 6454) is on Oxford St on the bank of the Waipoua River. Tent/powered sites are $15/16, and cabins are $27 and $35 for two.

The associate YHA *Masterton Backpackers* (☎ (06) 377 2228) at 22 Victoria St in the centre of town is a homey, colonial-style hostel. A bed in this friendly place is $14 per night or $32 in a twin room. The *Victoria House Guesthouse* (☎ (06) 377 0186) opposite offers B&B for $39/60 for singles/doubles. A standout B&B is the delightful *Essex House* (☎ (06) 378 6252), 29 Essex St, charging $65/95.

Inexpensive hotels and motels include the *Station Hotel* (☎ (06) 378 9319) at 145 Perry St charging $35/50, the *Colonial Cottage Motel* (☎ (06) 377 0063) at 122 Chapel St with singles/doubles at $58/67 and the *Cornwall Park Motel* (☎ (06) 378 2939) at 119 Cornwall St with units for $70 and $78.

The *Masterton Motor Lodge* (☎ (06) 378 2585) on SH2 in South Masterton has units for $95 to $155. The upmarket *Solway Park Hotel* (☎ (06) 377 5129) on High St charges from $95 to $156, plus GST, for a double or twin. Just about every sporting whim is satisfied here – there's even a jogging track.

The information centre has referrals for farmstays and homestays in the Wairarapa; singles/doubles start at $30/60.

Places to Eat

Cobb & Co on High St South is open seven days, *Burridges* on Queen St North has its own in-house brewery and the *Slug & Lettuce* at 94 Queen St doesn't (fortunately!) serve the first item of its name.

McDonald's is on the corner of Lincoln Rd and Chapel St. The cafe to laze in is *Bloomfields*, also on the corner of Lincoln Rd and Chapel St, and the *Arts Cafe* opposite the information centre down Bruce St has good coffee and light meals.

Getting There & Away

From Wellington, the Tranz Metro train is faster, cheaper and more frequent than the buses, with four trains daily on weekdays and two daily on weekends. An adult day excursion ticket is $15.

Tranzit Coachlines (☎ (06) 377 1227) has one bus daily to/from Wellington, but only on weekdays. It also has two weekday buses and a Sunday bus to/from Palmerston North, passing Mt Bruce ($6) on the way.

MT BRUCE

Thirty kilometres north of Masterton on SH2, the **Mt Bruce National Wildlife Centre** is an important sanctuary for native NZ wildlife, mostly birds. Large aviaries and outdoor reserves feature some of the country's most rare and endangered species, which you probably won't get to see elsewhere, in addition to more common species and an impressive nocturnal house with kiwis (sightings are not guaranteed), tuataras and other endangered reptiles. There are breeding programs of endangered species. Each species is given as natural a habitat as possible, so you have to look closely in the dense growth to find the birds.

The centre is open from 9 am to 4.30 pm daily ($6, children $1.50). Facilities include a cafe and displays; a good audiovisual is screened. The last admissions to the centre are at 4 pm; get there much earlier as there's a lot to see.

The private **Mt Bruce Pioneer Museum** on SH2, 10km south of the wildlife centre, has a huge collection, including gramophones, farming equipment and relics of NZ's pioneering days. It is open daily from 9 am to 4.30 pm; admission is $3 (children 50c).

Tranzit Coachlines (Wellington; ☎ (04) 387 2018) buses between Masterton and Palmerston North pass the wildlife centre and the museum, but stop only for pre-booked passengers because Tranzit also runs tours to the wildlife centre from Wellington ($34) and elsewhere in the Wairarapa ($18). It's easy to hitchhike.

CARTERTON, GREYTOWN & FEATHERSTON

A number of rural communities line SH2. Carterton has the **Paua Shell Factory** at 54 Kent St, open daily. You can see shellfish in a live paua aquarium and buy tacky and tasteful shell souvenirs.

Greytown was the country's first planned inland town and good examples of Victorian architecture line the main street. Pick up a heritage trail brochure from the tourist office for self-guided historic walks in the region. The quaint Cobblestones Museum at 169 Main St is open from 9 am to 4.30 pm daily. North-west of Greytown is the scenic **Waiohine Gorge** with a vast choice of outdoor activities conducted in an amphitheatre of native forests of rimu, kahikatea, beech and rata.

In Featherston, the **Fell Engine Museum** on the corner of Lyon and Fitzherbert Sts is worth a look. It houses the only remaining Fell locomotive in the world which once ran on three rails to climb 265m up the Rimutaka Incline. The museum is open on weekends from 10 am to 4 pm (from 1 to 4 pm on Sunday in winter). The information centre (☎ /fax (06) 308 8051) is in the courthouse on Fitzherbert St. The *Leeway Motel* (☎ (04) 308 9811) has backpackers beds for $20 ($15 for two nights or more) as well as motel units for $80 a double.

Tranzit Coachlines buses from Wellington pass through all three towns and the train stops at Featherston and Carterton. Cyclists can avoid the worst of the horrors of the Rimutaka Hills on SH2 by taking the **Rimutaka Incline**, the old railway line now converted to a walking and mountain bike track. It starts 10km from Featherston along Western Lake Rd and comes out on SH2 at Kaitoke, where there is a YHA hostel, 9km before Upper Hutt.

MARTINBOROUGH

Off SH2 and south of Greytown, Martinborough (population 1500) is the centre for tourism in the Wairarapa. Once just a sleepy town (although it still is on weekdays), it has become very popular with Wellingtonians as a weekend retreat because of the many vineyards in the area. On weekends, Gucci replaces gumboots and the town's fashionable dining establishments fill up.

Some 16 **wineries** are close to the town and are outlined in the free *Winemakers of Martinborough* pamphlet. The region produces only 2% of New Zealand's grapes but a wide variety of styles can be tasted. Martinborough is particularly known for its pinot noir. Local tour operators that do winery tours include Laura's Tours (☎ (06) 377 3534), South Wairarapa Tours (☎ (06) 308 9352) and U Name It Tours (☎ (06) 308 9878). Tours also run from Wellington: Wally Hammond Tours (☎ (04) 472 0869) and Tranzit Coachlines (☎ (04) 387 2018) include Martinborough in their Wairarapa itineraries. Tranzit also has a transport-only option to Martinborough for $30 return (less for YHA members).

Other sights around Martinborough include the impressive **Patuna Chasm Walkway** through native bush and a limestone gorge. It goes through private property and can be booked ($10) through the information centre (☎ (06) 306 9043; fax 306 8033) at 18 Kitchener St, which also has a full rundown on other activities, including glow-worm cave visits. One of the more bizarre activities is a canoeing trip that includes a visit to a taxidermy gallery, run by Kahutara Canoes (☎ (06) 308 8453).

Places to Stay & Eat
Budget accommodation is nonexistent unless you count the very basic *Martinborough Camp Ground* (☎ (06) 306 9336) on the corner of Princes and Dublin Sts. Tent/powered sites are $10/12.50 for two and there is a small amenities block.

The information centre has a big list of B&Bs, farmstays and self-contained cottages in the area, and will book them. Cottages are popular and cost from around $60 to $120 a night.

A good B&B in the town is *Oak House Homestay* (☎ (06) 306 9198) at 45 Kitchener St, in a 70-year-old Californian bungalow. Run by a local winemaker, it charges $45/80

for singles/doubles with shared facilities. Others of note are *Mangapari* (☎ (06) 306 9440) on White Rock Rd ($40/65) and the more luxurious *Shadyvale* (☎ (06) 306 9374) on Hinakura Rd ($90/120). Cottages include *Vintage Cottage* (☎ (06) 306 9482) at 48 Princess St ($120 a double) and *Hiwinui* (☎ (06) 308 9581) off Te Maire Rd ($90 a double, $25 per extra adult).

Dining options include the bistro at the magnificently restored *Martinborough Hotel* in the square. The menu is innovative, the chef is French and meals start at around $20 a main. Local wines are offered by the glass. On the opposite corner, the *Zodiac* in the old post office has a reputation as one of Martinborough's top dining spots. *Cafe Medici*, 9 Kitchener, is very fashionable and crowded on weekends. The wineries don't have restaurants, but the *Grape Vine* at 48 Kitchener St is a pleasant winery cafe for antipasto, cheeses and wine from 11 am to 5 pm.

WAIRARAPA COAST
The Wairarapa coast from Palliser Bay to Castlepoint is one of the most remote and intriguing in the North Island and well worth exploring. The road to Cape Palliser is really scenic, hemmed in as it is by the sea and the Aorangi Mountains. It also offers grand views across to the South Island, a spectacular sight in winter when the far-off hills are cloaked in snow. On the way, you pass the Wairarapa Wetlands and the Spit at Onoke – both good birdwatching sites. The coast is also the best surfing destination around Wellington.

The **Putangirua Pinnacles**, formed by rain washing silt and sand away and exposing the underlying bedrock, stand like giant organ pipes. Well worth a visit, they're accessible by a track near the car park on the Cape Palliser road. It's a one-hour return walk along a stream bed to the pinnacles, or the three-hour loop track takes in the hills and coastal views.

Not far to the south is the archetypal fishing village of **Ngawi**. The first thing that will impress you is the bulldozers pulling the fishing boats ashore. Continue on to the Cape Palliser **seal colony**, the North Island's largest breeding area. Whatever you do in your quest for that *National Geographic* shot, don't get between the seals and the sea.

There are 252 steps up to the Cape Palliser **lighthouse**, from where there are even more breathtaking views of the South Island on a clear day. Occasionally you will see surfers enjoying the southerly and south-easterly swells.

Castlepoint, with its reef and the lofty 162m-high Castle Rock, is an awesome place, with good protected swimming and plenty of walking tracks. There is a 45-minute return walk across the reef to the lighthouse, with over 70 species of fossil shells in the rock you pass over. Another 1½-hour walk goes to a huge limestone cave, or take the two-hour track from Deliverance Cove to Castle Rock. Keep well away from the lower reef when heavy seas are running; many lives have been lost here.

Places to Stay

Lake Ferry, a short detour off the road to Cape Palliser, has black sand dunes, lake fishing and surf casting, and accommodation. *Lake Ferry Motor Camp* (☎ (06) 307 7873) has tent/powered sites for $7.50/8 and cabins from $15 per person. Overlooking the water, *Lake Ferry Hotel* (☎ (06) 307 7831) has doubles for $40 and $50.

At Ngawi, the local shop and cafe, the *Top House Tea Garden* (☎ (06) 307 8229), has one room with en suite, TV and fridge for $55 and a fully self-contained unit for $65 a double.

FOREST PARKS

Good opportunities for tramping in the Wairarapa are in the Tararua, Rimutaka and Haurangi (Aorangi) forest parks. There are some fine coastal walks too. Maps and infor-

mation are available from DOC offices in Wellington and Masterton.

A favourite spot for tramping is at **Holdsworth**, the main eastern entrance to the Tararua Forest Park, where mountain streams run through some beautiful virgin forest. The park entrance has swimming, picnic and camping areas ($4 per night), a good hut ($8) and fine walks including short, easy family walks; excellent one or two-day walks; and longer, more challenging treks for experienced trampers right across to the west coast, coming out near Otaki.

A resident conservation officer (☎ (06) 377 0022) has maps and information on tramping in the area, and an intentions book for you to sign. Ask about current weather and track conditions before setting off, and come prepared for all types of weather – the Tararua Forest Park has a notoriously changeable climate. The turn-off to Holdsworth is on SH2, 35km south of Masterton; from there it's 15km to the park entrance.

Closer to Wellington, the **Rimutaka Incline** walk is a five to seven-hour walk (it can also be biked) each way along a historic old railway line which carried trains between Wellington and the Wairarapa between 1878 and 1955. The walk begins from SH2 (look for the signpost) 9km north of Upper Hutt. A little further north, 16km north of Upper Hutt on SH2, the **Kaitoke Regional Park** is good for swimming, rafting, camping, picnicking and walking; it has walks ranging from 20 minutes to six hours long.

The *Black Stump YHA Hostel* (☎ (04) 526 4626) is at Kaitoke, 42km north of Wellington at the top of the Hutt Valley. On Marchant Rd, just off SH2, the hostel is in hill country at the edge of the Tararua Forest Park. It's 1.5km from bushwalking tracks, swimming holes, horse and kayak hire, and 45 minutes drive from Wellington (or you can take the Tranzit bus to Masterton). This rather basic hostel charges $10 a night.

WELLINGTON REGION

South Island

Marlborough & Nelson

Crossing Cook Strait from Wellington to Picton in the South Island is like entering a new country – the landscapes and people are similar yet different, and the Maori influence is almost nonexistent. Many visitors strike out further afield immediately after crossing, but there is much of interest in this area, in particular the inlets and bays of Marlborough Sounds.

To the west is the Nelson region, with great tramping possibilities in its national parks. Nelson is a great city to relax in, as are the towns of Motueka and Takaka. If you are lucky and make it over to the far west, you can tour up to Farewell Spit.

Marlborough Region

The first sight of the South Island for many visitors on the ferry is the convoluted waterways of the Marlborough Sounds. Picton is the gateway to the South Island and the many hideaways in the Marlborough Sounds, where you can set up a base and go walking, fishing, sailing and kayaking. To the south of Picton is the sedate city of Blenheim and many nearby vineyards. Further south is the marine wildlife centre of Kaikoura, and inland there are mountainous regions with good walking possibilities.

History
The first European to come across the Marlborough district was Abel Tasman, who spent five days sheltering on the eastern coast of D'Urville Island in 1642. It was to be over 100 years before the next European, British explorer Captain James Cook, turned up – in January 1770, remaining there for 23 days. Between 1770 and 1777 Cook made four visits to the stretch of water he named Queen Charlotte's (now Charlotte) Sound. Near the entrance to Ship Cove a monument

HIGHLIGHTS

- Boating, walking and relaxing on the waterways of the Marlborough Sounds
- Walking the Heaphy, Leslie-Karamea and Wangapeka tracks and taking in the rugged scenery of Kahurangi National Park
- Whale-watching, dolphin and seal swimming at Kaikoura – one of the best ecotourism destinations anywhere
- Taking the ferry from Wellington to Picton, across Cook Strait and through the Tory Channel
- Relaxing and holidaying in Nelson
- Walking the Abel Tasman Coastal Track – undoubtedly and deservedly the most popular in the country
- Making the trip to the gannet colony and the lighthouse at the end of Farewell Spit
- Walking, boating or fishing in the Nelson Lakes National Park

Map Index

Marlborough Sounds p452

Heaphy Track p494

Abel Tasman National Park p489

Motueka p485

Nelson p475

Picton p458

Blenheim p462

Kaikoura p468

Marlborough and Nelson phone numbers have the ☎ 03 area code

commemorates the explorer's visits. Because of Cook's detailed reports, the area became the best-known haven in the southern

449

Cape Farewell
Farewell Spit
Wharariki Beach
Puponga
Pakawau
Paturau
Collingwood
Golden Bay
Takaka
Totaranui
Marlborough Sounds Maritime Park
Cook Strait
Aorere
D'Urville Island
Kahurangi Point
Bainham
60
Pupu Springs
Marlborough Sounds
TASMAN SEA
KAHURANGI NATIONAL PARK
Devil River Peak (1775m)
Marahau
ABEL TASMAN NATIONAL PARK
Heaphy Track
Mt Domett (1615m)
Leslie-Karamea Track
Cobb River
Upper Takaka
Kaiteriteri
Riwaka
Tasman Bay
Maungatapu Saddle
TASMAN MOUNTAINS
Motueka
Lower Moutere
Rai Valley
Karamea
Karamea Bight
Motueka Valley Highway
Mapua
Rabbit Island
6
Karamea Bight
Little Wanganui
Mt Kendall (1751m)
Woodstock
Stoke
Nelson
Pinedale (Canvastown)
Havelock
Wangapeka Track
Tapawera
Richmond
Brightwater
Wakefield
Mt Richmond Forest Park
Cloudy Bay
Waikawa
Picket
67
Seddonville
Mt Owen (1875m)
Hope Saddle
St Arnaud
Tophouse
RICHMOND RANGE
Renwick
6
Wairau River
65
Wairau Lagoons
Westport
Murchison
Kawatiri
Gowan Bridge
Blenheim
Seddon
Buller Gorge
6
Lake Rotoroa
Rainbow Valley Ski Area (entrance)
Lake Rotoiti
Molesworth
Grassmere
Ward
Cape Campbell
To Greymouth (via Coastal Route)
Inangahua Junction
69
NELSON LAKES NATIONAL PARK
Severn (2027m)
INLAND KAIKOURA RANGE
Tapuaenuku (2891m)
65
Victoria Forest Park
Mt Travers (2338m)
Awatere River
Reefton
SPENCER MTS
St Bernard
Clarence River
Manakau (2610m)
Clarence
Mt Una (2301m)
Dillon Cone (2173m)
To Greymouth (via Grey Valley)
7
Faerie Queen (2237m)
HANMER SPRINGS NATIONAL PARK
Clarence River
SEAWARD KAIKOURAS
Kaikoura
Springs Junction
Maruia Springs
Lewis Pass
Amuri Ski Area
Kaikoura Peninsula
Lake Sumner Forest Park
LEWIS PASS NATIONAL PARK
Hanmer Springs
70
Oaro
Goose Bay
Mt Longfellow (1898m)
Waiau River
Waiau
Parnassus
Conway River
SOUTH PACIFIC OCEAN
ARTHUR'S PASS NATIONAL PARK
Hurunui River
Culverden
Cheviot
Gore Bay
Craigeburn Forest Park
7
Waipara

Marlborough & Nelson

0   40   80 km

Christchurch
1

hemisphere. In 1827 the French navigator Jules Dumont d'Urville discovered the narrow strait now known as French Pass, and his officers named the island just to the north in his honour.

In the same year a whaling station was set up at Te Awaiti in Tory Channel, which brought about the first permanent European settlement in the district. In June 1840 Governor Hobson's envoy, Major Bunbury, arrived on the HMS *Herald* on the hunt for Maori signatures to the Treaty of Waitangi. On 17 June Bunbury proclaimed the British Queen's sovereignty over the South Island at Horahora Kakahu Island. Towards the end of that year a Wesleyan mission was set up at Ngakuta Bay in the north-western corner of the port.

Despite this, the Marlborough area was not the site of an organised company settlement; it was more an overflow of the Nelson colony. Around 1840 the opportunistic and unscrupulous New Zealand Company tried to settle part of the Wairau Plain after buying the alleged rights from the widow of a trader, John Blenkinsopp. He claimed he bought the land from the Maori for a 16-pound cannon, and had obtained a dubious deed signed by Maori chiefs who couldn't read English. The cannon is on display in Blenheim.

By 1843 the pressure for land from the Nelson settlers was so great that it led to conflict with the Maori, who denied all knowledge that any part of Wairau was sold. Two Maori chiefs, Te Rauparaha and Te Rangihaeata, arrived from Kapiti to resist survey operations. The Pakeha sent out a hurriedly co-opted armed party led by Arthur Wakefield and Police Magistrate Thompson to arrest the chiefs. The party was met peacefully by the Maori at Tuamarina, but the Pakeha precipitated a brief skirmish, during which Te Rangihaeata's wife was shot. The Pakeha were then forced to surrender and Rangihaeata, mad with rage, demanded vengeance. Twenty-two of the party, including Wakefield and Thompson, were clubbed to death or shot; the rest escaped through the scrub and over the hills. The whole event came to be known as the Wairau Massacre.

Te Rauparaha was a formidable Ngati Toa chief who was, indirectly, a major reason for the British government taking control of New Zealand. He cultivated the captains and crews of visiting whaling ships (they nicknamed him the 'old sarpint') and, with muskets and other weapons he acquired, set out on the wholesale and horrific slaughter of other South Island tribes. In his most gruesome raid he was aided by a Pakeha trader, who transported his warriors and decoyed the opposing chiefs on board, where they were set upon by Te Rauparaha's men. The ensuing slaughter virtually wiped out the local tribe. When news of this event and the captain's part in it reached Sydney, the British Government finally decided to bring some law and order to New Zealand and to their unruly citizens operating there. (For a detailed account of Te Rauparaha's life see the biography *Te Rauparaha: A New Perspective* by Patricia Burns.)

In March 1847 Wairau was finally bought and added to the Nelson territory. It was not long before the place was deluged by settlers from Nelson and elsewhere. However, when the Wairau settlers realised that revenue from land sales in their area was being used to develop the Nelson district, they petitioned for independence. The appeal was successful and the colonial government called the new region Marlborough and approved one of the two settlements, Waitohi (now Picton) as the capital. At the same time, the other settlement known as 'The Beaver' was renamed Blenheim. After a period of intense rivalry between the two towns, including legal action, the capital was transferred peacefully to Blenheim in 1865.

MARLBOROUGH SOUNDS

The convoluted waters of the Marlborough Sounds have many delightful bays, islands, coves and waterways, formed by the sea invading its deep valleys after the Ice ages. Parts of the sounds are now included in the Marlborough Sounds Maritime Park, which is actually many small reserves separated by private land. The small paperback *Marlborough Sounds Maritime Park* ($8) is a

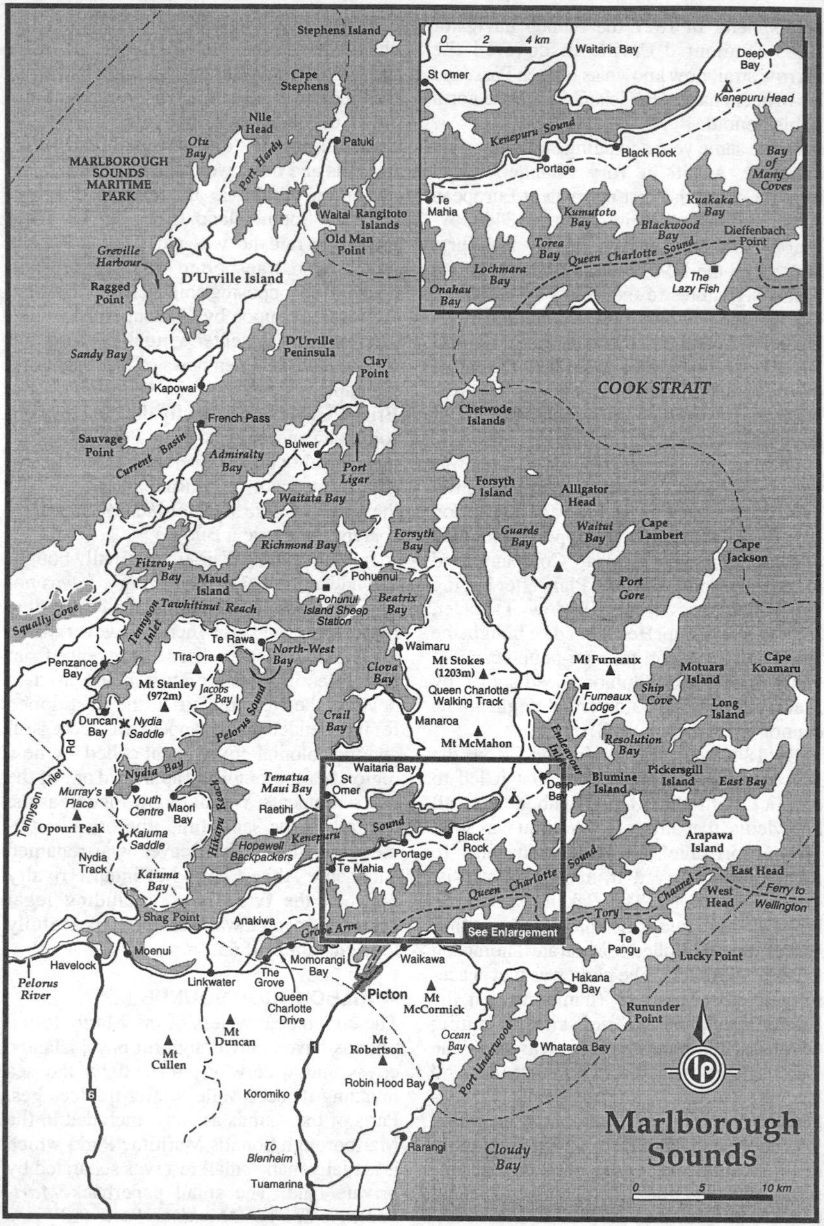

Marlborough & Nelson

Enlargement (inset, top right):

0 2 4 km

St Omer
Waitaria Bay
Deep Bay
Kenepuru Head
Kenepuru Sound
Black Rock
Portage
Bay of Many Coves
Te Mahia
Kumutoto Bay
Ruakaka Bay
Blackwood Bay
Dieffenbach Point
Torea Bay
Queen Charlotte Sound
Lochmara Bay
Onahau Bay
The Lazy Fish

Main map:

Stephens Island
Cape Stephens
Nile Head
Patuki
Otu Bay
Port Hardy
MARLBOROUGH SOUNDS MARITIME PARK
Waitai
Rangitoto Islands
Old Man Point
Greville Harbour
Ragged Point
D'Urville Island
Sandy Bay
D'Urville Peninsula
Clay Point
Kapowai
French Pass
COOK STRAIT
Chetwode Islands
Sauvage Point
Current Basin
Admiralty Bay
Bulwer
Port Ligar
Forsyth Island
Waitata Bay
Alligator Head
Waitui Bay
Cape Lambert
Cape Jackson
Richmond Bay
Forsyth Bay
Guards Bay
Fitzroy Bay
Maud Island
Pohuenui
Beatrix Bay
Port Gore
Squally Cove
Tawhitinui Reach
Pohuenui Island Sheep Station
Waimaru
Mt Furneaux
Motuara Island
Cape Koamaru
Penzance Bay
Te Rawa
North-West Bay
Clova Bay
Mt Stokes (1203m)
Ship Cove
Long Island
Tira-Ora
Jacobs Bay
Queen Charlotte Walking Track
Fumeaux Lodge
Mt Stanley (972m)
Crail Bay
Manaroa
Resolution Bay
Duncan Bay
Nydia Saddle
Mt McMahon
Endeavour Inlet
Pickersgill Island
East Bay
Rd
Nydia Bay
Tematua Maui Bay
Waitaria Bay
St Omer
Blumine Island
Murray's Place
Youth Centre
Maori Bay
Raetihi
Deep Bay
Arapawa Island
Opouri Peak
Kaiuma Saddle
Hopewell Backpackers
Kenepuru Sound
Black Rock
Portage
Nydia Track
Kaiuma Bay
Te Mahia
East Head
Ferry to Wellington
Shag Point
Anakiwa
Queen Charlotte Sound
Tory Channel
West Head
Havelock
Moenui
Momorangi Bay
Grove Arm
Waikawa
Te Pangu
Lucky Point
Pelorus River
Linkwater
The Grove
Queen Charlotte Drive
Picton
Mt McCormick
Hakana Bay
Rununder Point
Mt Cullen
Mt Duncan
Mt Robertson
Ocean Bay
Port Underwood
Whataroa Bay
6
1
Koromiko
Robin Hood Bay
To Blenheim
Cloudy Bay
Tuamarina
Rarangi

See Enlargement

Marlborough Sounds

0 5 10 km

good introduction to the area. To get an idea of how convoluted the sounds are, Pelorus Sound is 42km long but has 379km of shoreline.

The Queen Charlotte Track attracts most visitors, but accommodation is scattered throughout the sounds, offering delightful scenic retreats with an emphasis on water-based activities or simply relaxing.

Information

The best way to get around the sounds is still by boat, although the road system has been extended. Permits are required for hunting or camping and there's plenty of good swimming, tramping and fishing. Information on the park is available in Picton from the visitor centre and DOC.

Queen Charlotte Track

Those put off by the hordes doing the Abel Tasman Track may wish to try this increasingly popular alternative. Though it doesn't have the beaches of the Abel Tasman, it has similarly wonderful coastal scenery. It is a 67km-long track that connects historic Ship Cove with Anakiwa. You pass through privately owned land and DOC reserves. The coastal forest is lush, and from the ridges you can look down on either side to Queen Charlotte and Kenepuru sounds.

You can do the walk in sections using local boat services or do the whole three to four-day journey. There are many camp sites for those tenting it, as well as hostels and hotels. The route relies on the cooperation of local landowners, so respect their property and carry out what you carry in.

The track is well defined and suitable for people of all ages and average fitness. Ship Cove is the usual starting point, simply because it is easier to arrange a boat from Picton to Ship Cove than vice versa, but the walk can also be started from Anakiwa. Between Camp Bay and Torea Saddle you'll find the going toughest. For more information, get a copy of the *The Queen Charlotte Track* pamphlet from DOC in Picton. It is possible to do a leg of the trip by sea kayak; contact Marlborough Sounds Adventure Company (☎ 573 6078) for advice. Estimated distances and conservative walking times are:

	Distance	Time
Ship Cove-		
Resolution Bay	4.5km	two hours
Resolution Bay-		
Endeavour Inlet	10.5km	three hours
Endeavour Inlet-		
Camp Bay/		
Punga Cove	11.5km	four hours
Camp Bay/Punga Cove-		
Torea Saddle/Portage	20.5km	nine hours
Torea Saddle/		
Portage-Mistletoe Bay	7.5km	four hours
Mistletoe Bay-Anakiwa	12.5km	four hours

Getting There & Away A number of boat operators drop off at Ship Cove. Cougar Line (☎ 573 7925), Endeavour Express (☎ 579 8465) and Beachcomber Cruises (☎ 573 6175), all at the Town Wharf in Picton, charge $25 to $35 to Ship Cove, and you can arrange to be dropped off at other destinations such as Resolution Bay, Camp Bay or Torea Bay (for Portage). Boats from Picton leave around 9 to 10 am and then around 1.30 pm. Pick-up from Ship Cove is around one hour later.

At the Anakiwa end, Sounds Connection (☎ 573 8843), Knightline (☎ 547 4734) and the Mail Run (☎ 573 7389) pick up at the Anakiwa Kiosk and bus you to Picton for around $10. West Bay Water Transport (☎ 573 5597) covers the southern end of the track by boat, leaving from the southern side of the ferry terminal to Anakiwa ($16) and other southern bays such as Lochmara ($12) at 9.45 am and 3.15 pm. Endeavour Express also covers Anakiwa in summer.

Endeavour Express has a good round-trip special for $40 that includes transferring your pack between accommodation daily, allowing you to walk with a day-pack only. For a day-trip walk, it'll drop you off at Ship Cove and pick you up in the afternoon at Furneaux Lodge for $30. Cougar Line also has a wide range of day-walk options. West Bay has good one and two-day specials with walks from Torea Saddle or Mistletoe Bay to Anakiwa.

Sea Kayaking

The Marlborough Sounds Adventure Company (☎ 573 6078) in Picton organises sea-kayak trips and bush walks around the sounds. The kayak trips range from one day ($70) to four days ($450). It also hires out kayaks for solo trips at a daily cost of $40 for a single kayak (minimum of two days) or $65 for a double kayak. For $70 they will drive you and your kayaks to Tennyson Inlet.

Other operators running similar sea-kayaking trips out of Picton are: Sea Kayaking Adventure Tours (☎ 574 2765), Waikawa Sea Kayaks (☎ 573 6800) and Sounds Kayaks (☎ 573 8128).

Places to Stay & Eat

Accommodation is scattered throughout the sounds and, though some places are accessible only by boat, they are delightfully isolated and in some beautiful settings. Prices are usually reasonable and practically all places offer free use of dinghies and other facilities.

Most popular are those on or just off the Queen Charlotte Track – even with people not walking the trail – but there are many other options.

Queen Charlotte Track Starting at Ship Cove (where camping is not permitted), the first camping is the DOC camp site at Resolution Bay. A little further along the track is *Resolution Bay Cabins* (☎ 579 9411), with backpackers beds for $15 and self-contained cabins for $40 and $80. Nearby is *Kamahi Lodge* (☎ 579 9415), a homestay charging $65 per person including all meals.

A couple of hours' walk further on is *Furneaux Lodge* (☎ 579 8259) on Endeavour Inlet. This century-old place is set amid lovely gardens; chalets for two are $80, backpacker accommodation is $15 and $25 per person and camping is $5. The lodge has a shop, bar and restaurant. A further 10-minute walk is *Endeavour Resort* (☎ 579 8381), which is comfortable with backpackers beds at $20, cabins for $60 and $80 or you can camp.

On the western side of Endeavour Inlet is the DOC camping ground at Camp Bay, and other good accommodation options are a short walk off the track. These places are accessible by car as well as boat. Top of the range *Punga Cove Resort* (☎ 579 8561) has expensive A-frame chalets for $100 to $250 but special packages may be on offer. The older backpackers lodge has twin rooms for $25 per person with linen. The resort has a pool, shop and an excellent but expensive restaurant. A 10-minute walk around the bay is *Homestead Backpackers* (☎ 579 8373), open from the end of November to mid-April. This old farmhouse has a variety of beds for $16 per person, extra with linen. Five minutes further up the hill is *Noeline's* (☎ 579 8375), a friendly place with great views. This well-kept homestay has beds in comfortable twin rooms for $15 per person.

Next along, the Bay of Many Coves has a DOC camping ground on the saddle above the track. You can walk for one hour down to the bay (and a long way back up) to stay at Craglee Lodge (☎ 579 9223), which has backpackers beds at $25. Rooms are $98 per person or $110 with en suite including all meals. *Gem Resort* (☎ 579 9771) is further south on the bay and charges $20 for backpackers and from $65 to $85 for units. The resort has a shop and licensed restaurant. Access to the Bay of Many Coves is only by boat or on foot.

DOC's Black Rock camp is further along the trail above Kumutoto Bay or you can continue on to the Torea Saddle and down to Portage. The well-known *Portage Hotel* (☎ 573 4309) on Kenepuru Sound has double rooms from $100 per night. Improved bunkroom facilities cost $25 per person and you can cook. The hotel has sailboats, windsurfers, fishing, a spa, gym and tennis courts. The Portage Bay Shop (☎ 573 4445) also rents out yachts, dinghies, kayaks and bikes. Just around the bay from the Portage Hotel is the DOC Cowshed Bay camp site. Portage can easily be reached by road from Picton or Havelock.

The new *Lochmara Lodge* (☎ 573 4554) on Lochmara Bay promises to be a popular backpackers retreat, with good facilities and dorm beds for $20 per night. It's off the Queen Charlotte Track to the south and only 15 minutes by boat from Picton.

Towards the southern end of the track, the *Mistletoe Bay Reserve* (☎ 573 7582) is the pick of the DOC accommodation. As well as the camp site ($4), three farm cottages have beds for $10 per night. North of the track, just off the main road and in a beautiful bay facing Kenepuru Sound, *Te Mahia Bay Resort* (☎ 573 4089) has backpackers beds for $20 and self-contained units for $90. Camping is also possible and there's a store.

Right at the end of the trail, *Anakiwa Backpackers* (☎ 574 2334) has a good self-contained backpackers unit with just four beds for $15 per person, but the sprawl of beds upstairs in the main house is less inviting in the busy season.

Other Sounds Accommodation DOC also has almost 30 camping grounds scattered throughout the sounds, providing water and toilet facilities but not a lot else – pick up a list in Picton. The *Marlborough Sounds Parkmap* ($11) shows camping locations. The only fully serviced DOC camping ground near the water is the pleasant *Momorangi Bay Motor Camp* (☎ 573 7865), 15km from Picton on the road to Havelock. Tent/powered sites are $7/8 per person and cabins are $15/25 for singles/doubles.

The most popular backpackers is the stylish *Lazy Fish* (☎ 579 9049) on Queen Charlotte Sound, 12km from Picton and accessible only by boat. This renovated homestead-turned-hostel charges $20 per person for dorms and $45 for doubles. This includes free use of the windsurfer, dinghy, canoe, fishing gear, snorkels etc. The hostel has its own secluded beach and a spa pool underneath the palm trees. It is popular so book ahead before you catch a boat out there.

On Kenepuru Sound, *Mary's Holiday Cottage* (☎ 573 4660) at Waitaria Bay, 95km from Picton via Linkwater, is a YHA associate hostel. You'll probably have the old farmhouse to yourself at $14 per person, unless a family or group rents out the whole house for $70. Further along the same road,

Hopewell (☎ 573 4341) is the place to choose if you really want to stay in a remote part of Kenepuru Sound. Doubles and twins are $34, and the price lets you use a full range of equipment such as rowing boats, fishing lines and table tennis. Access by road is possible but it's a long, tedious drive along an unmade road. A better option is taking a water taxi from Portage.

Other accommodation at Kenepuru Sound (accessible by road) includes the *Raetihi Lodge* (☎ 573 4300), with budget rooms for $40/60 and a variety of lodge rooms for up to $115 a double. Meals are available. The old-fashioned *St Omer House* (☎ 573 4086) has bunkroom accommodation from $25 per person, cottages from $60 a double and full board in the main buildings for $80 per person with excellent meals.

The *Te Pangu Bay Lodge* (☎ 579 9755) on Te Pangu Bay, Tory Channel, rents out self-contained units for two to seven people for $25 per person (minimum unit charge $40). The *Tira-Ora Lodge* (☎ 579 8253) on Northwest Bay, Pelorus Sound, is more expensive at $112.50 a double. Both lodges can only be reached by boat. *Te Rawa Boatel* (☎ 579 8285), 27km by launch from Havelock, is cheaper at $50 for two people.

Pohuenui Island Sheep Station (☎ 597 8161) at Pohuenui, 30km north of Havelock, comes recommended by readers and has accommodation ranging from a bunkroom at $18 to full board in the homestead for $200 including boat trips, with the bonus of staying on a working sheep station.

The Picton Visitor Information Centre can advise on many other accommodation options in the sounds.

Getting There & Away
Scheduled boats service most of the accommodation on the Queen Charlotte Track (see that section) and are the cheapest way to get around the sounds. The Cougar Line also runs to the Lazy Fish hostel on Queen Charlotte Sound at least two days a week for a $25 return special. A water taxi costs about the same if you have a group of four or five to split the fare.

Arrow Water Taxis (☎ 573 8229) is one well-known operator at Town Wharf in Picton servicing Queen Charlotte Sound. In Havelock, the Havelock Outdoors Centre (☎ 574 2114) books water taxis. On Kenepuru Sound are Daniel Water Taxis (☎ 573 4238), Kenepuru Tours (☎ 573 4203) and the Portage Bay Shop (☎ 573 4445). As an example, a water taxi from Picton to Onahau or Torea bays will cost around $50, while from Havelock to Portage will cost around $100.

No scheduled buses service the sounds but much of it is accessible by car. The road to Portage is sealed, but beyond that you have to endure forever-winding, gravel roads.

PICTON

The ferry from the North Island comes into Picton (population 4000), a pretty little port at the head of Queen Charlotte Sound. Picton, originally called Waitohi, is a small borough. It's a hive of activity when the ferry is in and during the peak of summer, but rather slow and sleepy any other time.

Information

The Picton Visitor Information Centre (☎ 573 7477; fax 573 8362), 200m from the ferry terminal, has good maps, information on boats and walking in the sounds area, and books transport and accommodation. It is open from 8.30 am to 5 pm daily in winter and until 7.30 pm in summer. DOC also has a booth in the centre and the main office (☎ 573 7582) is in the same building. The Railway Station (☎ 573 8857) in the Picton train station also has information on almost everything.

The ferry terminal in Picton has a rare convenience for NZ – a laundrette. The Marlin Motel (☎ 573 6784) at 33 Devon St is the Automobile Association (AA) agent.

The Edwin Fox

Between the information centre and the ferry wharf is the battered, but still floating, hull of the old East Indiaman *Edwin Fox*. Built of teak in Bengal, the 157ft (48m), 760-ton vessel was launched in 1853 and in its long

and varied career carried convicts to Perth (Australia), troops to the Crimean War and immigrants to NZ.

The *Edwin Fox* is slowly being restored and the metal-sheathed hull is open to visitors from 8.45 am to 5 pm daily and closing at 4.30 pm in winter ($4, children $1). Enter through the small museum which has a few maritime exhibits and local crafts.

Other Attractions

The excellent little **Picton Museum** is on the foreshore, right below London Quay. Interesting exhibits include whaling items such as a harpoon gun, and a Dursley Pederson bicycle built around 1890. The museum is open from 10 am to 4 pm daily ($3, children 50c).

On the eastern side of Shakespeare Bay, across the inlet from the town centre via the footbridge, is the scow (barge) **Echo**, which now houses the Maritime History Gallery. Built on the Wairau River in 1905, the *Echo* shipped around 14,000 tons of freight a year between Blenheim and Wellington, and was only retired in 1965 after the railway ferries were introduced. Entry is $3, children $1.

Tuamarina, 19km south of Picton, is historically interesting as the site of the **Wairau Massacre**. The tree near where the skirmish started still stands on the riverbank. In the cemetery, just above the road, is a Pakeha monument designed by Felix Wakefield, youngest brother of Arthur Wakefield, who was killed in the affray.

Walking

The information centre has a map showing several good walks in and near town, as well as others further afield in the sounds and the maritime park. DOC also has plenty of maps and leaflets on walks in the area.

An easy 1km track runs along the eastern side of Picton Harbour to Bob's Bay, where there's a BBQ area in a sheltered cove. The **Snout Walkway** carries on along the ridge from the Bob's Bay path and has great views of the length of Queen Charlotte Sound. Allow three hours for the walk.

The **Tirohanga Walkway**, beginning on

Newgate St behind the hospital, takes about 45 minutes each way and features panoramic views of Picton and the sounds.

Organised Tours

The main access around Queen Charlotte Sound is by water, serviced by innumerable cruises and fishing trips.

Round-the-bay cruises include the Beachcomber Fun Cruises' (☎ 573 6175) all-day mail-run cruise around Pelorus Sound on Tuesday, Thursday and Friday for $66, and a Queen Charlotte Sound Cruise on Wednesday and Saturday. Other options are its Round the Bays and Portage Luncheon Cruise.

Dolphin Watch Marlborough (☎ 573 8040), beside the train station, has a variety of eco boat tours taking in the seals, seabirds and dolphins of Queen Charlotte Sound with departures at 8.45 am and 1.45 pm.

On land, Sounds Connection (☎ 573 8843) and the Corgi Bus Company (☎ 573 7125) are local tour operators; winery visits are a speciality. Deluxe Coach-lines (☎ 578 5467) operates all day wine-trail tours from Blenheim but also picks up in Picton.

Diver's World (☎ 573 7323) on the corner of London Quay and Auckland St and Picton Underwater Centre at 41 Wellington St hire out equipment and organise charters.

See the Marlborough Sounds section for kayaking trips out of Picton.

Places to Stay

Camping & Cabins The *Blue Anchor Holiday Park* (☎ 573 7212) on Waikawa Rd, only 500m from the town centre, has tent/powered sites at $18/20, various cabins for around $32 to $40 and tourist flats at $55 to $60; prices are for two. The ageing *Alexander's Holiday Park* (☎ 573 6378) is 1km out on Canterbury St and has sites at $18 for two, plus a variety of cabins at $30 to $40 for two. *Picton Campervan Park* (☎ 573 8875) is a small, new and well-equipped slice of suburbia with powered sites at $18 for two.

The neat *Parklands Marina Holiday Park* (☎ 573 6343) is on Beach Rd at Waikawa

Bay, 3km from town. Other possibilities include *Waikawa Bay Holiday Park* (☎ 573 7434) and *Momorangi Bay Motor Camp* (☎ 573 7865) by the water 13km from Picton (see the Marlborough Sounds section).

Hostels The *Villa* (☎ 573 6598) at 34 Auckland St is a well-equipped, popular hostel in a fine renovated villa. Dorm beds cost $16 and $17, and doubles or twins are $42. It books various activities, breakfast is included in the price and it has a spa. The attentive owners make this place special.

The *Bavarian Lodge Backpackers* (☎ 573 6536), 42 Auckland St, is next to the Villa and, though not as stylish, it's comfortable and well-run. Dorm beds cost $15 per person, doubles cost $34 and $36 and twins cost $40, all including breakfast. German is spoken and mountain bikes are free.

Around the corner is *Wedgwood House* (☎ 573 7797), a YHA associate hostel at 10 Dublin St. It's a converted guesthouse with two, four or six beds to a room; the cost is $15 per person or $34 for twin rooms. It is open until 11 pm for passengers from the late ferry.

The closest accommodation to the ferry terminal is *Baden's Picton Lodge* (☎ 573 7788) at 3 Auckland St. Dorms are $15 per person, and twins and doubles are $36. The facilities in this large place are good and there's a smokers terrace with harbour views. It is 200m from the ferry and next to the train station.

The *Juggler's Rest* (☎ 573 5570), 8 Canterbury St, about five minutes walk south of town, is a backpackers with a difference. It is run by professional jugglers and juggling lessons are offered free. The house has a nice garden and dorm beds are $14 and doubles $32.

Just along, *Sounds Backpackers* (☎ 573 8126), 2 Canterbury St, is a tidy place with dorm beds for $15 and singles/doubles for $25/36. They also run kayaking trips on the sounds – accommodation is free if you take their trip.

On Waikawa Bay, *Bayview Backpackers* (☎ 573 7668), 318 Waikawa Rd, indeed has

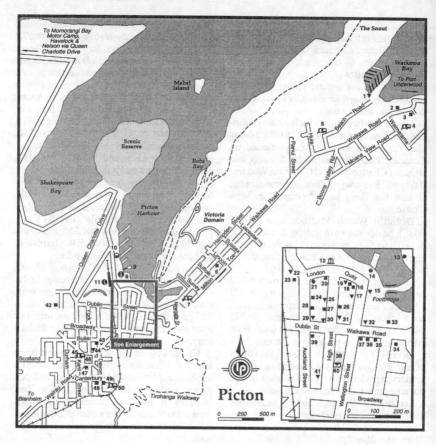

Picton

0   250   500 m

0   100   200 m

bay views and pleasant porch areas from which to enjoy them. It's 4km from central Picton but offers free pick-up and drop-off. Doubles and twins are $34, and the dorms cost from $13.50 to $15 per person. There are heaters in all the rooms, two kitchens, two lounges, and watersports equipment and bicycles are free for guests.

B&Bs & Guesthouses Picton has a number of B&Bs and guesthouses, including *Cottage International* (☎ 573 7935), 25 Gravesend Place, in a comfortable private house. It's halfway between a backpackers

and a B&B – rooms are $30/50 with linen or $23/30 without, and breakfast is an extra $5 or $7. German, French and English are spoken.

Marineland Guesthouse & Motels (☎ 573 6429), 28 Waikawa Rd, has a pool. Singles/ doubles are $38/55, up to $45/65 in the peak season with breakfast, and motel units are $70 for two. The staff are friendly and helpful.

The *Admiral's Lodge* (☎ 573 6590) at 22 Waikawa Rd has B&B rooms for $55/85 and offers low-season discounts. Next door at 20 Waikawa Rd, the *Gables* (☎ 573 6772) is

MARLBOROUGH & NELSON

PLACES TO STAY
2 Bay Vista Motel
3 Bayview Backpackers
4 Waikawa Bay Holiday
    Park
5 Parklands Marina
    Holiday Park
6 Bell Bird Motel
7 Blue Anchor Holiday
    Park
16 Oxleys Hotel
18 Federal Hotel
20 Terminus Hotel
23 Baden's Picton Lodge
24 The Villa
26 Americano Motor Inn
    & Restaurant
27 Tourist Court Motel
28 Bavarian Lodge
    Backpackers
33 Picton Beachcomber
    Inn
34 Harbour View Motel
35 Marineland
    Guesthouse &
    Motels
36 Admiral's Lodge
37 The Gables

39 Wedgewood House
    Youth Hostel
42 Cottage International
43 Marlin Motel
45 Picton Campervan
    Park
48 Juggler's Rest
49 Sounds Backpackers
50 Alexander's Holiday
    Park

PLACES TO EAT
1 Jolly Roger Bar & Cafe
15 Kiwi Takeaways
17 Bollies Cafe
19 Seaspray Cafe
22 Stoker's Bar;
    Toot 'n' Whistle
25 Ships Cove; Le Cafe;
    Marlborough
    Terranean
29 Picton Bakery
30 Holty's
31 Kentucky Eat Aways
32 Ancient Mariner
41 Lord Thompson
44 Wiseway's
    Supermarket

47 Crow Tavern

OTHER
8 Visitor Information
    Centre & DOC
9 Edwin Fox
10 Cook Strait Ferry
    Terminal &
    Laundrette
11 Railway Station,
    Booking Office &
    Dolphin Watch
    Marlborough
12 Picton Museum
13 Echo
14 Town Wharf
    (Marlborough
    Sounds Adventure
    Company, Cougar
    Line, Beachcomber
    Fun Cruises &
    Marlborough
    Sounds Yacht
    Charter)
21 Diver's World
38 Mariners Mall
40 Post Office
46 Nelson Square

similarly priced and serves some good breakfasts.

Motels & Hotels Picton has plenty of motels, many of them on Waikawa Rd just east of the city centre. Most are priced at around $70 for two and low-season discounts usually apply. The very central *Tourist Court Motel* (☎ 573 6331), 45 High St, is a simple place with studio units from $54 for two or two-bedroom units for $69. The *Bell Bird Motel* (☎ 573 6912), 96 Waikawa Rd, is another cheapie with units for $55. The *Bay Vista Motel* (☎ 573 6733), 4km out at Waikawa Bay, is also good value at $69 to $74 for two. The *Harbour View Motel* (☎ 573 6259), 30 Waikawa Rd, is notable for its great views. Units cost from $65 to $75.

The *Americano Motor Inn* (☎ 573 6398), 32 High St, is a better class of motel with a spa, pool, restaurant and bar. Units cost from $69 to $84. *Picton Beachcomber Inn* (☎ 573 8899), 27 Waikawa Rd, is at the top of the range, with units from $75 to $115.

The central *Terminus Hotel* (☎ 573 6452), 1 High St, has good pub rooms with private facilities costing $45/75 for singles/doubles. Many of the rooms have great sea views. The *Federal Hotel* (☎ 573 6077), 12 London Quay, is a notch down the scale but also central and with sea views. Rooms are $25/50 or $70 a double with en suite.

Places to Eat

Restaurants *Holty's*, on the corner of High and Dublin Sts, has straightforward food and provides kids meals. Along London Quay, the *Terminus*, *Federal* and *Oxley* hotels all have pub food, with bistro meals from about $8 to $10. The Terminus has sticky carpets and laminex tables but fine bay views and good food. On the south side of Nelson Square, the *Crow Tavern* has pub fare and fresh seafood. *Toot 'n' Whistle* is a much classier pub with reasonably priced snacks and meals, and *Stoker's Bar* next door has cheap buffets.

Picton's best cluster of restaurants is on

MARLBOROUGH & NELSON

High St. The *Marlborough Terranean*, 31 High St, is a sophisticated place with a good wine selection. The European, not just Mediterranean, inspired menu features many seafood dishes at around $9 an entrée and $23 a main. Next door, the artistic *Le Cafe* is very popular for its reasonable prices – mains are around $16. Strand Arcade, beside Le Cafe, houses *Ships Cove* with nautical décor and good old-fashioned steaks (around $16) as well as seafood selections.

The town's better motels have highly regarded restaurants: the *Americano Restaurant* at 32 High St has main courses from $14 to $25; the *Ancient Mariner* on the corner of Wellington St and Waikawa Rd has mains for about $23; and *Whalers* in the Picton Beachcomber Inn has cheaper steaks and seafood.

Fast Food Ever popular for fast food, *Kiwi Takeaways* is near the corner of the Quay and Wellington St. *Kentucky Eat Aways* on High St is similar. Further down High St, *Lord Thompson* has good fish and chips and is open late.

The *Picton Bakery*, on the corner of Dublin and Auckland Sts, has been recommended by an enthusiastic German traveller for its 'dark long-baked rye bread ... real German style'.

Along the waterfront, the little *Seaspray Cafe* has standard Kiwi coffee-shop fare and cheap breakfasts. *Bollies Cafe* on Wellington St has similarly plain but cheap and hearty meals.

The best supermarket is in Mariners Mall on High St. Wiseway's supermarket is on Nelson Square.

Getting There & Away

Air Soundsair (☎ 573 6184) has a regular service across the strait to and from Wellington. The short flight costs $55 and operates about six times a day. The courtesy shuttle bus from the airstrip at Koromiko, 8km out of town, is included in the price.

There are flights from nearby Blenheim.

Bus Numerous buses go south to Christchurch and beyond, and west to Nelson, from where connections go through the island's centre to the West Coast.

InterCity (☎ 573 7025), at the ferry terminal, has a service to Christchurch with connections to Dunedin and Invercargill, and another route east to Nelson via Blenheim and Havelock with connections to Greymouth and the glaciers. At least one bus daily on each of these routes connects with a ferry sailing to and from Wellington.

Newmans has one bus daily between Nelson and Christchurch, in either direction, stopping at the ferry terminal in Picton, and in Blenheim.

A 'confusion' of small shuttle buses head south to Christchurch and beyond. You can choose from Atomic Shuttles (☎ 573 6855), Nationwide Shuttles (☎ 379 5531), South Island Connections (☎ 578 9904), Compass Coachlines (☎ 578 7102), Ko-op Shuttles (☎ 366 6633), Southern Link Shuttles (☎ 573 7477) and 3-D Express (☎ 0800 113 850). They charge around $25 to $30. You can book through the information centres.

To Nelson, the main shuttles are Kiwilink (☎ 577 8332) and Knightline, both running Blenheim-Picton-Nelson. Sounds to Coast (☎ 0800 802 225) has shuttles three days a week to Greymouth via St Arnaud. Nelson Lakes Transport (☎ 521 1877) also runs to St Arnaud and on to Westport in summer.

All buses serving Picton operate from the ferry terminal or the information centre.

Train The *Coastal Pacific* train between Picton and Christchurch, via Blenheim and Kaikoura, operates daily in each direction. The train connects with the ferry and a free shuttle service is provided between the train station and ferry terminal on both sides of the strait. This trip is highly recommended for its coastal scenery.

Hitching Hitching out on SH1 towards Blenheim is possible, but may take a few hours. Most traffic is on the road as soon as the ferry docks – there is not much between sailings. Most cars are off the ferry before you can get your thumb out and you'll have to compete with other hitchhikers.

Heading west, Queen Charlotte Drive between Picton and Havelock is the shortest way to Nelson but has little traffic. It's easier to hitch via Blenheim on the Spring Creek bypass: follow the Blenheim road (SH1) for 22km to Spring Creek, where you turn right towards Renwick. On average it will take a day to reach Christchurch or Nelson.

Boat *Interislander* ferries (☎ 0800 802 802) shuttle back and forth between Wellington and Picton four or five times daily; the crossing takes three hours. The faster *Lynx* operates in summer three times daily. (See the Wellington section of the Wellington Region chapter for details.)

Getting Around
Avis, Hertz, Thrifty, Budget and Avon Cars (Shoestring Rentals) have rental offices at the ferry terminal. Pegasus (☎ 573 7733), near the train station, and other cheaper car rentals are also represented in Picton.

Nifty-fifty (50cc) motorbikes (for which you need a current car licence) can be hired from the kiosk beside the MV *Beachcomber* office.

See the Marlborough Sounds section for details of cruises, boat connections and water taxis to the sounds. Check at the wharf in Picton, at the station information office or at the visitor information centre.

BLENHEIM
The largest town in the Marlborough Sounds region, Blenheim (population 26,000) is 29km south of Picton on the Wairau Plains, a contrasting landscape to the sounds. The flatness of the town, at the junction of the Taylor and Opawa rivers, was a problem in the early days and it grew up around a swamp, now the reclaimed Seymour Square with its attractive lawns and gardens.

Blenheim doesn't have Picton's picturesque setting but does have a large array of services and is at the centre of New Zealand's most famous wine-growing district. During the second weekend in February Blenheim hosts the now famous Marlborough Food & Wine Festival at Montana's Brancott Estate.

Get a copy of the comprehensive *A Taste of Marlborough: Gourmet Paradise*, which tells of the festival, outlines restaurants and wineries, and has profiles of the winemakers.

Information
The Blenheim Information Centre (☎ 578 9904; fax 578 6084) is in the Forum Building on Queen St. It has a number of DOC maps and leaflets on the many walkways around the Marlborough Sounds and environs. The centre is open from 8.30 am to 6.30 pm daily in summer and for shorter hours in winter (closed on Sunday). The AA office (☎ 578 3399) is at 23 Maxwell Rd, on the corner of Seymour St.

Things to See
The 5.5-hectare **Brayshaw Museum Park**, off New Renwick Rd, has several attractions, including a reconstructed colonial village of old Blenheim, early farming equipment, a miniature railway and the Museum & Archives Building. The park is open during daylight hours (admission is free). As regional museums go, this is a good one.

Pollard Park & Waterlea Gardens, off Parker St, have a childrens playground and a fitness trail; flowers bloom all year here.

Near Seymour Square are relics of Blenheim's violent early history, including **Blenkinsopp's cannon** in front of the council offices on Seymour St. Originally from the whaling ship *Caroline*, which Blenkinsopp captained, this is reputedly the cannon for which Te Rauparaha was persuaded to sign over the Wairau Plains and, therefore, one of the causes of the subsequent massacre at Tuamarina.

Recreation Areas DOC's pamphlet *Central Marlborough Recreation Areas* outlines a number of rural retreats with a variety of landforms and flora, such as native broom or prostrate kowhai. The Robertson Range and Whites Bay near Port Underwood north of Blenheim have great vistas of Cloudy Bay. **Wairau Lagoons**, to the east of Blenheim, are home to more than 70 bird species.

The coastal road from Blenheim to Picton

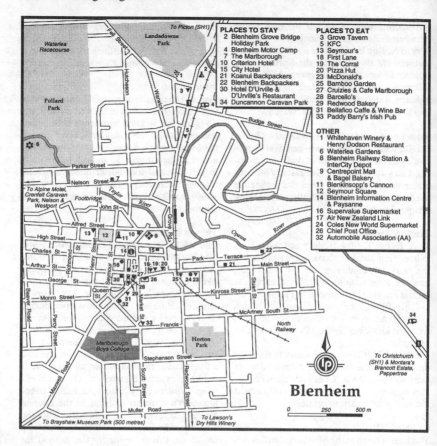

PLACES TO STAY
2 Blenheim Grove Bridge Holiday Park
4 Blenheim Motor Camp
7 The Marlborough
10 Criterion Hotel
15 City Hotel
21 Koanui Backpackers
22 Blenheim Backpackers
30 Hotel D'Urville & D'Urville's Restaurant
34 Duncannon Caravan Park

PLACES TO EAT
3 Grove Tavern
5 KFC
13 Seymour's
18 First Lane
19 The Corral
20 Pizza Hut
23 McDonald's
25 Bamboo Garden
27 Cruizies & Cafe Marlborough
28 Barcello's
29 Redwood Bakery
31 Bellafico Caffe & Wine Bar
33 Paddy Barry's Irish Pub

OTHER
1 Whitehaven Winery & Henry Dodson Restaurant
6 Waterlea Gardens
8 Blenheim Railway Station & InterCity Depot
9 Centrepoint Mall & Bagel Bakery
11 Blenkinsopp's Cannon
12 Seymour Square
14 Blenheim Information Centre & Paysanne
16 Supervalue Supermarket
17 Air New Zealand Link
24 Coles New World Supermarket
26 Chief Post Office
32 Automobile Association (AA)

Blenheim

is a good two-hour drive but has spectacular coastal views and remnants of early European history. Good spots for picnics are Robin Hood Bay, Ocean Bay and at the head of Port Underwood (Hakahaka Bay). The narrow winding road from Waikawa to Rarangi has superb views of the North Island silhouetted on the horizon.

Wineries The big attraction around Blenheim is the wineries, of which there are around 20. They produce a variety of wines, but the Marlborough region is particularly famous for its floral sauvignon blancs. Pick up a copy of the *Marlborough Winemakers Wine Trail Guide* from the information centre. Most wineries are open daily and some, such as Highfield, Hunter's and Allan Scott, have restaurants.

If you really want to finish yourself off, Prenzel Distillery on Sheffield St, 6km south-east of Blenheim, produces liqueurs, schnapps, fruit wines and brandies. The Cork & Keg in Renwick, 10km west of Blenheim, is a ye olde English pub that brews its own malt beers. Ponder Estate, 2km south of Renwick, produces olives as well as wine.

Deluxe Coachlines (☎ 578 5467) has a

MARLBOROUGH & NELSON

six-hour 'Scenic Wine Trail' tour of local wineries which costs $34 ($38 from Picton). Highlight Tours (☎ 578 9904) offers personalised tours for between $35 and $45 per person. Back Country Safaris (☎ 575 7525) also puts together well-regarded personalised tours for a minimum of two people.

Activities

There is **skiing** at the Rainbow Valley ski area (☎ 521 1861), 130km (1½ hours) west of Blenheim. Back Country Safaris (☎ 575 7525) and JJs Ski Transport (☎ 544 7081) buses go right to the ski field.

The more adventurous could try **white-water rafting** in some of the nearby rivers. Action in Marlborough (☎ 578 4531) at 59 Lakings Rd, Blenheim, can get you wet any time. The costs range from about $65 for a half-day trip to $450 for three-day expeditions. Its trips focus on the Buller and Gowan rivers.

Horse-trekking operators include Loddon Horse Riding (☎ 572 2561).

Places to Stay

Camping & Cabins The *Blenheim Grove Bridge Holiday Park* (☎ 578 3667) at the northern end of town at 78 Grove Rd (SH1) is the pick of the camping places. It has sites by the river at $20 for two, cabins from $35 to $50 for two and tourist flats from $60. The neat and fastidious *Blenheim Motor Camp* (☎ 578 7419) is nearby at 27 Budge St, just off SH1. Tent/powered sites are $18/20 for two but there's not much grass for campers. It has mostly cabins at $30 to $55 a double, and the new backpackers lodge at $14.50 per person has good facilities but not much atmosphere.

Camping grounds further out include *Duncannon Caravan Park* (☎ 578 8193), 2km east of the town centre, where sites cost $18 and on-site caravans and cabins are $26 to $30 for two. The *Spring Creek Holiday Park* (☎ 570 5893), on Rapaura Rd 6km out towards Picton and about 500m off SH1, has camp sites ($18) and cabins ($26 to $38). It is peaceful and near a good fishing creek.

Hostels *Blenheim Backpackers* (☎ 578 6062) is at 29 Park Terrace, in an old maternity home. Doubles are $36 and dorms are $15 per person. The Opawa River runs behind the house and you can borrow canoes. At 33 Main St, *Koanui Backpackers* (☎ 578 7487) has bunks at $14 per person and twins/doubles for $32/36. This is a friendly place popular with itinerant fruit pickers. It has a pool table, BBQ and electric blankets on all the beds.

At Renwick, 10km west of Blenheim in the heart of the wine-growing district, *Watson's Way Backpackers* (☎ 572 8228), 56 High St, is an excellent purpose-built hostel in a quiet garden setting. Shared rooms are $18 per person and the one double room is $40. Breakfast is included in the price.

Guesthouses, Motels & Hotels The information centre has a big list of B&Bs, homestays and self-contained accommodation. Recommended B&Bs are *Peppertree* (☎ 578 7009) on SH1 south of town in a beautiful garden setting, with doubles for $164, and *Stonehaven* (☎ 572 9730) on Rapaura Rd north-west of town, where doubles are $95 to $110. Those on vineyards are particularly popular and include *Black Birch Lodge* (☎ 572 8876), 13km from Blenheim, and *Thainstone* (☎ 572 8823) on Giffords Rd, 14km north-west of Blenheim. Both have pools and singles/doubles for around $60/95. The similarly priced *Le Grys* (☎ 572 9490) on Conders Bend Rd is 20km from town in a mudbrick house with a spa. It also has a self-contained cottage for $130.

Reasonably priced motels include the *Raymar Motor Inn* (☎ 578 5104) at 164 High St, where double rooms cost $55 to $62, and the similarly priced *Alpine Motel* (☎ 578 1604) at 148 Middle Renwick Rd. At most other motels, doubles cost $59 to $65.

Rooms at the *Criterion Hotel* (☎ 578 3299) on Market St cost $60/75 for singles/twins. The smaller *City Hotel* (☎ 578 5029), 25 High St, charges $40/50. Upmarket hotels include the *Marlborough* (☎ 577 7333) at 20 Nelson St, close to Pollard Park, with rooms from $169 and the boutique *Hotel D'Urville*

(☎ 577 9945) on Queen St with just eight rooms for $259/276.

Places to Eat

Restaurants For pub food, the *Criterion* on the corner of Market and Alfred Sts has a large carvery. *Paddy Barry's* is an Irish-style place on Scott St for seafood and steaks washed down with Guinness.

The Corral at 3 Main St has innovative mains with a French touch for around $20. For Chinese food head to the *Bamboo Garden* on Main St.

At the top of the dining tree are *D'Urville's* at 52 Queen St, serving international cuisine (mains are about $22) and a big selection of local wines; the award-winning *Seymour's* on the corner of Henry and Alfred Sts, where the Captain Cook seafood platter at $39.50 for two and the Sunday evening smorgasbord at $22 are great value; *Bellafico Caffe & Wine Bar* at 17 Maxwell Place, with an interesting, varied menu; and *Paysanne* upstairs in the Forum building on Market St, with a blackboard menu, a selection of pizzas, and mains from $16 to $25.

Wineries Several of the wineries around Blenheim also serve meals. The *Henry Dodson Restaurant* in the Whitehaven Winery north of town on Dodson St (off Grove Rd) has tasty food. The Hunters and Merlen wineries on Rapaura Rd also serve food. At Merlen you can enjoy your German-style meal and wine in the Weingarten. Also recommended is the *Twelve Trees Restaurant* at Allan Scott's winery on Jacksons Rd. Lawson's Dry Hills also serves meals, usually enjoyed after a wine tour.

Out in Renwick, 10km west of Blenheim, is the *Cork & Keg*, where you can lunch and relax with a beer if you tire of wine.

Fast Food & Self-Catering Takeaways around the centre include *McDonald's* and *Pizza Hut* on Main St and *KFC* on the northern side of town.

Cruizies, 10 Maxwell Rd, is an old-style cafe with filled rolls, bagels and giant muffins. The *Redwood Bakery* on Queen St bakes continental bread for those tired of the usual Kiwi loaf.

Barcello's at 67 Queen St is a small cafe and bar with ambience, good coffee and great hot chocolate served in a huge cup. *First Lane* on Main St is another salubrious cafe with good delicatessen fare.

For self-caterers, the Supervalue supermarket on the corner of Charles and Queen Sts, and Coles New World on Main St are open daily until late.

Getting There & Around

Air New Zealand (☎ 578 4059; 0800 737 000) at 29 Queen St has direct flights to Wellington with connections to other centres. Ansett (☎ 0800 800 146) has direct flights between Blenheim, Wellington and Palmerston North. Straits Air (☎ 0800 115 522) also has two flights a day to Wellington. Soundsair (☎ 573 6184) in Picton also flies the Wellington-Blenheim route twice a week for $65.

The Blenheim airport is on Middle Renwick Rd, about 6km west of town. Supershuttle Blenheim (☎ 572 9910) has a door-to-door service for $8.

Deluxe Coachlines (☎ 578 5467) at 45 Main St has regular services between Blenheim and Picton. Newmans (☎ 578 2713) and InterCity (☎ 577 2890) pass through Blenheim on their way to Christchurch and Nelson and stop at the train station. InterCity has connections on to the West Coast. A plethora of shuttle buses (see the Picton section) run to Nelson, Christchurch and other destinations; the information centre makes booking.

Sounds to Coast (☎ 0800 802 225) has a shuttle three days a week to Greymouth ($44) via St Arnaud ($10). Nelson Lakes Transport (☎ 521 1877) also runs to St Arnaud and on to Westport in summer.

The *Coastal Pacific* Picton-Christchurch train stops daily at Blenheim. The reservations number is ☎ 0800 802 802.

You can also hire mountain bikes for $25 per day in town from Spokesman Cycles on Queen St and Blenheim Hire Cycle.

HAVELOCK

Founded around 1860 and named after Sir Henry Havelock of Indian Mutiny fame, this small town of 500 people is at the confluence of the Pelorus and Kaiuma rivers, 43km west of Blenheim.

Havelock was once the hub of the timber milling and export trade, and later became the service centre for gold-mining in the area. Today it has a thriving small-boat harbour and is the place to catch a boat to more remote parts of Marlborough Sounds. Otherwise, the town's title as the 'green-shelled mussel capital of the world' pretty much sums it up.

Information

The Havelock Outdoors Centre (☎ /fax 574 2114) on the main street is the main booking centre for transport, accommodation and activities in and around town. It is open daily from around 8 am to 5 pm. Across the road, Havelock Fishing Charters (☎ 574 2190) organises charter boats and water taxis.

DOC (☎ 574 2019) has a small office on Mahakipawa Rd.

The tiny museum on the main street is a good source of information on local history.

Walking

There's not much to do in the town itself, but good walks include the four-hour return walk to **Takorika Summit** behind the township and the half-hour walk to Cullen Point for good views of Havelock and the sunset.

Extended walks include the **Mt Stokes** walk. From the 1204m summit, the highest point in the Marlborough Sounds, you can see the Kaikouras, Tararuas (in the North Island) and the sounds below. Another walk is the three-day **Pelorus Track** to Nelson. This follows the Pelorus River, then heads over Dun Saddle via a historic railway line. Mountain bikers can test their pedal strength on the **Maungatapu Track**, which passes through scenic Maitai Reserve.

The **Nydia Track** starts at Kaiuma and ends at Duncan Bay. The suggested walking time is two days or 10½ hours. DOC has camping grounds and the *Nydia Lodge* ($12). About halfway along, Murray Timms (Murray's Place) and Marty Quinn both offer accommodation for around the same price. Nydia Bay was originally the site of a Maori *pa* (fortified village) and its Maori name meant 'place of sadness' – the DOC pamphlet explains why. The walk passes through different habitats of various species of birds.

It is best to get dropped off at Shag Point by water taxi as it is only a five-minute trip past the mudflats, and you can arrange a water taxi for around $60 at the other end. Pelorus Sounds Water Taxi (☎ 574 2151) is one of the main operators; you can phone the water taxi or shuttle service from Murray's Place. You can attempt the track in either direction.

Sea Kayaking

Maritime Park Wilderness Company (☎ 574 2114) has full-day sea-kayaking trips on the delightful Marlborough Sounds for $70, leaving from Havelock. They rent out all equipment for one day for $40 up to four days for $140. Sea Kayaking Adventure Tours (☎ 574 2765) operates from Anakiwa at the end of the Queen Charlotte Walkway and has kayaks ($40 per day), mountain bikes ($25) and one-day guided kayak tours for $60 per person.

Organised Tours

Beachcomber Cruises takes passengers on the Pelorus mail boat, stopping at isolated homesteads to deliver mail and supplies. It can drop off and pick up later anywhere along the way if you want to camp or tramp. Take supplies, though fresh water is available in some places; ask the locals.

The trips depart from Havelock at 9.30 am on Tuesday, Thursday and Friday, and return between 5 and 6 pm. The round-trip mail-run fare is $66.

The Mussel Run visits the mussel farms where you can sample the product. Classic Cruises also has very popular boat tours of the sounds in a 40ft kauri launch. Both can be booked at the Havelock Outdoors Centre.

Many water taxis operate out of Havelock and nature cruises can be organised to Maud

Island, abode of the takahe, kakapo and Hamilton frog.

Places to Stay & Eat

Havelock Motor Camp (☎ 574 2339) on Inglis St has tent/powered sites for $7/8 per person, and cabins for $25 a double. The *Chartridge Park* (☎ 574 2129), 6km south of Havelock at Kaiuma Bridge on SH6, has camp sites at $16 for two and budget beds at $10 per person in a basic bunkroom. It has a pool, six-hole golf course and a river running through it.

The well equipped *Havelock YHA Hostel* (☎ 574 2104) on the corner of Lawrence St and Main Rd charges $15 per person in dorms, and $32 and $34 for doubles. The hostel is in an 1881 schoolhouse once attended by Lord Ernest Rutherford, who discovered the atomic nucleus. The manager has information on walks and other local activities including fishing, farmstays and explorations around the sounds.

Havelock has a couple of small motels, both on the main road through town. The *Havelock Garden Motel* (☎ 574 2387) has units at $55 to $73 for two, with low-season discounts available. The *Pelorus Tavern* (☎ 574 2412), which has a restaurant and pub, has motel units for $60.

The *Pelorus Jack Tearooms* on the main road has snacks and light meals. The *Darling Dill Cafe* is a little more upmarket. The *Pelorus Tavern*, overlooking the Havelock marina, has counter or restaurant meals.

Getting There & Away

Both InterCity and Newmans have Picton-Blenheim-Nelson buses at least once each day. Kiwilink has two services a day to Blenheim ($8), Picton ($11) and Nelson ($11). Knightline has a similar service.

HAVELOCK TO NELSON

The SH6 from Havelock to Nelson is 75km of scenic highway, passing the Wakamarina Valley, Pinedale (also known as Canvastown), the Pelorus Bridge Scenic Reserve and Rai Valley.

Pinedale

The tiny township of Pinedale, in the Wakamarina Valley 8km west of Havelock, got the nickname Canvastown back in the 1860s, when gold was discovered in the river. By 1864 thousands of canvas tents had sprung up as miners flocked to the prosperous working goldfield, one of the richest in the country. By 1865 the boom was over. Nevertheless, gold is still found in the area and in 1986 a tourist panned a 5g nugget from the river.

Visits to the interesting indoor-outdoor gold-mining museum, gold panning, horse trekking, bushwalking and trout fishing are all popular activities. The **Wakamarina Track**, an old gold-miners trail which passes through the Mt Richmond State Forest Park, begins from Butchers Flat, 15km into the Wakamarina Valley on the metalled road from Pinedale.

The *Trout Hotel* (☎ 574 2120) at the entrance to the Wakamarina Valley has doubles and motel units from $50. The *Pinedale Motor Camp* (☎ 574 2349) has tent/powered sites for $14/16 for two and cabins from $25 to $35 for two; you can hire gold pans and other equipment here and lessons can be arranged. Butchers Flat, Roadend, Wakamarina Valley is a local DOC camping ground.

Pelorus Bridge

The Pelorus Bridge Scenic Reserve, 18km west of Havelock, has interesting walks of between 30 minutes and three hours on the Pelorus and Rai rivers, with waterfalls, a suspension bridge and the Pelorus Bridge itself. Within the reserve are tearooms, tent/caravan sites at $14/18 for two and cabins at $24 for two. Ask for the ranger at the Pelorus Bridge Tearoom (☎ 571 6019).

The *Lord Lionel* (☎ 574 2770) is on SH6 near the Pelorus Bridge Scenic Reserve; the German-speaking owners offer single/double B&B for $60/100 and budget beds.

Rai Valley

At Carluke, 1.5km from the Rai Valley township on the road leading to Tennyson Inlet, is the Rai Valley Pioneer Cottage, built in 1881 when the area was still virgin bush. The cottage was home to its owner for 28 years and had been used as a sheep shed and chicken house before being restored in 1969 and given to the Historic Places Trust in 1980. There's no charge to see the cottage, but donations are appreciated.

South Marlborough

Many travellers head west or north-west from Picton to the walking tracks or the West Coast glaciers, but there are also a number of points of interest along the route south from the Marlborough district across the Seaward Kaikoura foothills to Christchurch.

KAIKOURA

This small town of 2200 people, 133km south of Blenheim on SH1, is a mecca for wildlife enthusiasts.

Until relatively recently, Kaikoura was just a sleepy little fishing town noted mainly for its crayfish (lobster) – Kaikoura means 'to eat crayfish' in Maori. Then, during Christmas 1987, Nature Watch Charters began whale-watching trips, the first such commercial operation in NZ. The tours quickly became famous and put Kaikoura on the tourist map.

Kaikoura is also the home of dolphin swimming, another activity now popular in many parts of NZ. Besides seeing whales and dolphins, the area has a host of other activities and Kaikoura has a superb setting on a beautiful bay backed by the steeply rising foothills of the Seaward Kaikouras, snow-capped in winter.

History

In Maori legend, the tiny Kaikoura Peninsula (Taumanu-o-te-waka-a-Maui) was the seat upon which the demigod Maui sat when he fished the North Island up from the depths of the sea. The area was heavily settled before Europeans came – at least 14 Maori pa sites have been identified.

Excavations near the Fyffe House show that the area was a moa-hunter settlement about 800 to 1000 years ago. In 1857 George Fyffe came upon an early moa-hunter burial site near the present Fyffe House and among other things he found an almost complete moa eggshell, the largest moa egg ever found (240mm long, 178mm in diameter).

Captain Cook passed by here on 15 February 1770, but did not land. His journal states that 57 Maori in four double-hulled canoes came out from shore towards the *Endeavour*, but 'would not be prevail'd upon to put along side'. Cook called the peninsula 'Lookers on', a name which was later mistakenly ascribed to the Seaward Kaikouras.

In 1828 the beachfront of Kaikoura, now the site of the Garden of Memories, was the scene of a tremendous battle when a Ngati Toa war party led by the chief Te Rauparaha from Kapiti Island, in the south of the North Island, bore down on Kaikoura armed with muskets, killing or capturing several hundred of the local Ngai Tahu tribe.

The first European to settle in Kaikoura was Robert Fyffe, who established a whaling station in 1842. Kaikoura was a whaling centre from 1843 until 1922, and sheep-farming and agriculture flourished. After whaling ended, the sea and the farmland continued to support the community.

Information

The Kaikoura Visitor Information Centre (☎ 319 5641; fax 319 6819) on the Esplanade by the car park (on the beach side) is open from 8 am to 6.30 pm daily in summer and 9 am to 5 pm in winter. The staff are very helpful and can make bookings for any tour. They screen an excellent 20-minute audiovisual ($2) on the marine environment around Kaikoura.

DOC has a field centre (☎ 319 5714) on Ludstone Rd which is not always staffed.

Things to See

George Fyffe, cousin of NZ's first European settler, Robert Fyffe, came to Kaikoura from Scotland in 1854 and built **Fyffe House** around 1860. The house, about 2km east of

MARLBOROUGH & NELSON

Kaikoura

PLACES TO STAY
7 Maui Youth Hostel
8 Panorama Motel
9 Pacific Palms
10 Blue Seas Motels
11 Anchor Inn Motel
13 Cray Cottage
15 Backpacker 116 Torquay
17 Seaview Motel
18 Fortuna Rocks
19 Esplanade Holiday Park
20 New Commercial Hotel
21 Norfolk Pine Motor Inn
26 Blue Pacific Hotel
28 Nikau Guesthouse
31 Dolphin Lodge
34 Topspot Backpackers
38 The Planet Backpackers
38 K's Backpackers
41 Adelphi Hotel
46 Searidge Holiday Park
47 A1 Kaikoura Motels & Holiday Park
53 Moby Dix's Backpackers

PLACES TO EAT
4 Green Dolphin
5 Pier Hotel
16 Finz
24 White Morph Restaurant & Motel
29 Sonic
37 Why Not Cafe; The Craypot
44 Aromas
49 Act-One
50 Hislops Cafe
54 Kaikoura Bakery

OTHER
1 Seal Colony & Seal Swimming
2 Start of Peninsula Walk
3 Fyffe House
6 Sea Aquarium
12 Swimming Pool
14 Nga Niho Pa
23 Four Square Supermarket
25 Takahanga Domain
27 Garden of Memories
30 Post Office
32 Hospital
33 Walkway to Deal St
35 Visitor Information Centre
36 InterCity; Newmans
39 Dolphin Encounter
40 DOC
42 Kaikoura Supermarket
43 Whale Watch Air; Allsports Adventure Centre
45 Whale Watch
48 Museum
51 Kaikoura Helicopters
52 Kaikoura Dive & Sports Centre

Point Kean
Wildlife Refuge
Gull Colony
Whalers Bay
East Head
Seal Colony
Sea Caves
Seal Colony
South Bay
Promenade Clifftop Walk
Promenade Shoreline Walk
Recreation Reserve
Jimmy Harmer's Beach
Quay
Fyffe
Ward St
Lookout
Dempseys Track
Wharf
Margate St
Ramsgate St
Brighton St
Yarmouth St
Torquay St
Scarborough Terrace
The Esplanade
Takahanga Pa
West End
Beach Road
Torquay St
Parade
South Bay
Racecourse
Rail to Christchurch
Ludstone Road
Mt Fyffe Road
Rotomon Road
Hawthorne Road
To Old Convent
To Maori Leap Cave & Caves Restaurant, Whale Watching & Scenic Flights, Christchurch & Golf Course
To Beachcomber Motel, Blenheim

0   0.5   1 km

the town centre, is the only survivor from the whaling days and is protected by the Historic Places Trust. It is open from 10 am to 4 pm daily. The curator conducts tours for $3.50 (children free).

The **museum** on Ludstone Rd has several big sections out the back, including the old town jail (1910), historical photographs, Maori and colonial artefacts, and an exhibit on the region's whaling era. The museum is open from 2 to 4 pm daily in summer and during school holidays in winter ($2, children $50c).

The tiny **Sea Aquarium**, beside the YHA hostel on the Esplanade, has a single tank of sea animals and a video presentation on Kaikoura's ocean wildlife. It's run by the University of Canterbury Research Centre and is open most days (free).

Up on the hill at the eastern end of town is a water tower with a great **lookout**; you can see both sides of the peninsula and all down the coast. Take the walking track up to the tower from Torquay St or drive up Scarborough Terrace.

Tours of **Maori Leap Cave**, a limestone cave formed by the sea and discovered in 1958, take place around 10.30 am and 12.30 and 2.30 pm daily and depart from the Caves Restaurant, 3km south of the town on SH1. The 45-minute tour costs $7.50 (children $3.50). Book at the restaurant or the visitor information centre.

Marine-Mammal Watching

Thousands of international visitors come for the wildlife every year and during the busy summer months, especially December to March, it pays to book whale-watch tours and dolphin swimming a few days ahead.

The 'Big Five' most likely to be seen are the sperm whale, Hector's dolphin (smallest and rarest of dolphins), the dusky dolphin (found only in the southern hemisphere), the NZ fur seal and the bottlenose dolphin. Other animals frequently seen include the orca (killer whale), common dolphins, pilot whales and blue penguins. Sea birds include shearwaters, fulmars, petrels, and royal and wandering albatross. Seals are readily seen out on the rocks at the seal colony.

There's no guarantee of seeing any specific animal on any one tour, but it's fairly certain something of interest will be sighted. Sperm whales are most likely to be seen from October to August and orcas from December to March. Most other fauna is seen year-round.

Marine animals are abundant at Kaikoura because of the currents and continental shelf formation. From land, the shelf slopes gradually to a depth of about 90m, then plunges to over 800m. Warm and cold currents converge here, and when the southerly current hits the continental shelf it creates an upwelling current, bringing nutrients up from the ocean floor and into the light zone. The waters are often red with great clouds of krill, the sperm whale's favourite food, which attract larger fish and squid.

Whale-Watching Whale Watch Kaikoura (☎ 319 6767, 0800 655 121), at the old train station, sets out to sea in search of the whales and other wildlife in boats equipped with hydrophones (underwater microphones) to pick up the sounds of whales below the surface. Three-hour tours run daily from 5 am to 1.30 pm most of the year for $95 (children $60, or $30 for three to four year olds).

For most people the tour is a thrilling experience – the main attraction is the sperm whale, and Kaikoura is the most accessible spot on the planet to see them (for more information see the colour Fauna & Flora chapter). Other whales sighted include orcas, the minke, humpback and southern right. Dolphins are also usually spotted, as well as sea birds.

There is one hitch to the whale-watch experience – the weather. Nothing is more dismal than heading out for a special encounter with nature, only to have it stopped by the intervention of the uncontrollable. Whale Watch depends on its spotter planes to locate the whales at sea and they can't usually find them in foggy or wet conditions. The Whale Watch office then cancels line after line of disappointed customers. The town benefits each time this happens as many people stay on to try the next day. If this trip is a *must* for you, allow a few days.

You can also see whales from the air by aircraft or helicopter. Air Tours Kaikoura (☎ 319 5986) and Whale Watch Air (☎ 319 6580), both based at the airport, charge $85 each (minimum two, children $50) for a half-hour flight. Kaikoura Helicopters (☎ 319 6609) at the old train station also offers 20 to 30-minute flights out over the whales for $120 to $180. They also guarantee that you see the 'whole whale'.

To learn more before you go whale-watching (or even dolphin swimming), get a copy of the excellent *Whales & Dolphins of Kaikoura, NZ* by Barbara Todd.

Dolphin Swimming The original operator, Dolphin Encounter (☎ 319 6777) at 58 West End, offers swimming with huge pods of dusky dolphins. It provides wetsuits (essential in this water), masks and snorkels for $80 for a three-hour 'dolphin encounter' ($48 if you are just a spectator). The Kaikoura Wildlife Centre (☎ 319 6622) opposite the information centre also operates dolphin swimming trips for the same price.

Seal Swimming Seals may appear threatening if approached on land, but under water,

---

Dolphin Swimming

I didn't quite know what to expect when I went dolphin swimming. At the Dolphin Encounter office I was fitted out with a good-quality wetsuit, flippers, face mask and snorkel. The early hour added to the confusion and the only hint of what I was about to experience was given by the numerous photographs and postcards scattered around the office.

We went out in a powered catamaran to an area between Oaro and Goose Bay, the preferred feeding ground of the pods of dusky dolphins. There was no guarantee that the dolphins would be there but the skipper had successfully located many in the previous days. When the first pod was sighted, the atmosphere on board the boat was electric. The skipper manoeuvred in front of the pod, which was feeding on squid, and advised us to enter the water. The eight of us donned our masks and flippers and jumped into the cold water. The initial shock was quickly overcome as streaks of quicksilver flashed by. Before I knew it, a curious dusky circled below me and I gasped for air through my snorkel: I was witness to one of the most beautiful, streamlined creatures of the sea. I raised my head out of the water to see another dolphin performing, circus-like, back flip after back flip – not one or two, but 10, 11, 12 ...

I dived down to show more of me to the curious dolphins and for a brief instant I was an interloper in their underwater world. I now had a better view of their graceful forms as they darted by. It made me feel that there really is some inexplicable spiritual communication between human and dolphin.

Three pods of dusky dolphins – numbering some 450 in total – had joined together for mass feeding on that day. Later they were joined by a pod of common dolphins, and on the way back to Kaikoura, a lone bottlenose dolphin, Maui, came up to the boat. Three dolphin species in one day. The encounter was over and my satisfaction complete. I don't think I have ever experienced anything quite like it before.

Jeff Williams

in their element, they are completely passive. Graeme's Seal Swim (☎ 319 6182) arranges snorkelling with NZ fur seals. These two-hour guided snorkelling tours from the shore are a great opportunity to view your mammalian cousins at close hand. The cost is $35 (children $25). Dave at Topspot Backpackers (☎ 319 5440) also arranges similar trips.

You can also snorkel with the seals from a boat. From September to May, the Kaikoura Wildlife Centre (☎ 319 6622) organises seal swimming and supplies all equipment for $45 ($25 for observers).

Walking
The Kaikoura Peninsula has many good walkways. There are two **Peninsula walkways** starting from the seal colony, one along the seashore and one above it along the cliff top, which take 2½ hours. If you go on the seashore trail, check the tides beforehand. Both walks afford excellent views of the NZ fur seal and red-billed seagull colonies. A trail from South Bay Rd leads over farmland and back to the town. A walks pamphlet is available from the information centre.

Other good walks in the area are at Mt Fyffe Forest, 9km from Kaikoura; the Puhi Puhi Scenic Reserve, 18km from town; and the Omihi Lookout, 19km from town.

The **Mt Fyffe Walking Track** centres on Mt Fyffe (1602m), an outlier of the Seaward Kaikoura Range, which dominates the narrow Kaikoura plain and the town. The eastern face of Fyffe is cloaked in forest. Information about history, vegetation, birds and the walking tracks is in the *Mt Fyffe Forest: Kaikoura* pamphlet.

A popular day or overnight walk is to the summit of Fyffe and the hut of the same name for impressive views of the peninsula and plains. On a clear day you can see Banks Peninsula to the south and Cape Palliser on the North Island. The forest is accessed from the end of Mt Fyffe Rd, which leads to the short forest walk, or from the western end of Postmans Rd, the access route to the Hinau Picnic area.

The **Kaikoura Coast Track** is a three-day walk through private farmland and along the Amuri coast, 50km south of Kaikoura. The walk has spectacular coastal views and accommodation is in comfortable farm cottages – the Staging Post at Hawkswood (☎ 319 2708), where you get information on the walk, Ngaroma near the sea, and Medina on the Conway River Flats. You can get a shuttle from Kaikoura and the cost is $90. Bring your own sleeping bag and food.

Other Activities
In winter, Mt Lyford has **skiing**. Daily lift charges are quite reasonable. Sea to Summit Safaris (☎ 319 6182) runs to the field in winter only for $20 return at 8 am, returning at 6.30 pm.

The **golf course** is on the highway south of the racecourse. The beach in front of the Esplanade has safe **swimming** and a swimming pool. Other beaches are on the peninsula's north-east (eg Jimmy Harmers) and at South Bay. The whole coastline, with its rocky formations and abundant marine life, is good for snorkelling and diving. Mangamanu Beach, about 15km north of Kaikoura, has good surfing.

Fishing is popular off the new and old wharves, at the Kahutara river mouth, or by surfcasting on the many beaches. Fishing charters can be arranged. Rock Lobster Fishing Charters (☎ 319 5712) has crayfishing trips for around $60.

The Kaikoura Dive & Sports Centre (☎ 319 6444), 61 Beach Rd, does **diving** trips.

Four Wheeler Safaris (☎ 319 6424) operates **quad bike rides** on and around Mt Fyffe and the Kowhai River where you drive through rivers, hill country and bush. The cost for a three-hour trip is $85 up to $140 for a full-day trip.

Fyffe View Horse Treks (☎ 319 5069) has half-day guided **horse treks** for $35.

Lake Rotorua Bird-Watch Cruises (☎ 319 5985) has **birdwatching** tours for the avid twitcher that take in hideouts of the pied shag, an inland nesting colony of little black cormorants and, occasionally, groups of royal spoonbills. The two-hour trip is $44.

Places to Stay

Camping & Cabins *A1 Kaikoura Motels &
Holiday Park* (☎ 319 5999) at 11 Beach Rd,
near the railway overpass, has tent/powered
sites for $18/20, cabins from $30 and tourist
flats from $50 ($11 each extra adult); all
prices are for two. There's also a backpackers
upstairs for $15 per person.

The *Searidge Holiday Park* (☎ 319 5362),
34 Beach Rd, beside the train station, has
tent/powered sites for $18/20 and a standard
two-berth cabin for $33. The only problem
is noise from the whale-watch helicopters.
The *Esplanade Holiday Park* (☎ 319 5947),
126 the Esplanade, also has sites and cabins.

Seaside camping grounds near Kaikoura
include the *Peketa Camping Ground* (☎ 319
6299), 8km south, with tent and powered
sites, cabins and a camp shop; and *Goose
Bay Camping Ground* (☎ 319 5348), 18km
south. The Goose Bay camp is actually
several camping areas spread over a 5km
stretch of coastline. Generally, the sites at
each camping ground cost $7 per adult ($8
for power) and the cabins cost around $24 to
$28 for two.

Hostels The *Maui YHA Hostel* (☎ 319 5931)
at 270 the Esplanade is an attractive, modern
hostel beside the sea about 1.5km from the
town centre. The common room has superb
views along the bay to the mountains
beyond. Dorms cost $16 per person, twins
$38 and doubles $40.

Topspot Backpackers (☎ 319 5540) at 22
Deal St has plenty of space and is a non-
smokers haven. There is a BBQ, sundeck and
a courtesy van. The clean and tidy share
rooms are $16 per person and doubles are
$40. There's a sign near the post office indi-
cating the path to this place. *Dolphin Lodge*
(☎ 319 5842) at 15 Deal St, almost directly
across the road from the Topspot, is a homey
well-equipped place where dorm beds are
$16 per person, and twins and doubles are
$40.

The most central is the laid-back *Planet
Backpackers* (☎ 319 5538) at 85 West End.
This new place has a large, open dorm

upstairs costing $15 and new doubles and
twins downstairs for $36 and $38.

The very friendly *Cray Cottage* (☎ 319
5152), 190 the Esplanade, is one of Kaikoura's most popular backpackers (it pays to
book). The well-equipped little hostel
behind the house charges $16 in the dorms
and $36 in good twin rooms. Fishing trips
and other free activities are organised.

K's Backpackers (☎ 319 5538), 11 Churchill St, is small, homey and a short walk
from town. The comfortable beds are a
change from the old sleeping bag and there
is a nice lounge and kitchen with tea and
coffee-making facilities. The cost is $40 for
twins or doubles with linen.

At 65 Beach Rd, *Moby Dix's Backpackers*
(☎ 319 6699) has dorms for $14.50 per
person, and twins and doubles for $33. It has
all the necessary facilities, a volleyball court,
sundeck with a BBQ and a creek at the back.

The A1 Kaikoura Motels & Holiday Park
and the Blue Pacific Hotel (see under the
Motels & Hotels heading) also have backpackers beds. The information centre has
listings of other budget options, such as
Glentree Station Backpackers (☎ 319 5189),
25km south of Kaikoura at Oaro, where beds
cost $14. At 116 Torquay St (☎ 319 6321),
the family has a self-contained backpackers
unit with just four beds for $15 per person;
ring ahead.

B&Bs & Guesthouses The *Old Convent*
(☎ 319 6603), out on Mt Fyffe Rd (near the
junction with Mill Rd) and about three minutes from town, is a highly regarded B&B.
Its advertising says: 'Get in the habit ... nun
can compare.' A wide variety of singles/
doubles start at $50/70 and doubles with en
suite are $90 to $115. Three-course French
dinners are $35.

Another good choice right in town is the
renovated, two-storey *Nikau Guesthouse*
(☎ 319 6973) at 53 Deal St. B&B doubles
with en suite in this pleasant establishment
cost $65 to $75. *Pacific Palms* (☎ 319 5857),
218 the Esplanade, overlooks the harbour
and has B&B doubles for $70.

The information centre has other B&B

listings and makes bookings. It also has a large selection of self-contained units and houses, which can be very good value and start from around $50.

Motels & Hotels Kaikoura has many motels, especially along the Esplanade. Most charge around $65 to $80 per night for two, including the *A1 Kaikoura Motels & Holiday Park* ($55 to $70). *Panorama Motel* (☎ 319 5053) at 266 the Esplanade, *Blue Seas Motels* (☎ 319 5441) at 222 the Esplanade and *Beachcomber* (☎ 319 5623) at 169 Beach Rd are similarly priced. *Fortuna Rocks*, 158 the Esplanade, has just a few simple units behind a house but it is very friendly and good value at $45 and $50.

The *Norfolk Pine Motor Inn* (☎ 319 5120), 124 the Esplanade, has studio units for $68 and other units from $80.

The *White Morph Motor Inn* (☎ 319 5014), 92-94 the Esplanade, next to the restaurant of the same name, is one of the better motels. The *Anchor Inn Motel* (☎ 319 5426), 208 the Esplanade, is new and at the top of heap with units from $100 to $130.

The *Adelphi Hotel* (☎ 319 5141) on West End has twins and doubles from $50 to $55 with private facilities. The *Blue Pacific Hotel* (☎ 319 5017), 114 the Esplanade, has backpackers beds at $15 and budget rooms, including linen, for $20 per person.

Places to Eat
In season, crayfish is often featured in Kaikoura restaurants and even the local takeaways. Before the whale-watching boom, the crayfish alone made Kaikoura a worthwhile stop.

Takeaways and coffee shops around town include the *Why Not Cafe* in the town centre for homemade food, takeaways, pizza and sandwiches. *Act-One* is a standard place for a wide variety of fast food to take away or eat there. The *Kaikoura Bakery* out on Beach Rd (on the corner of Hawthorne Rd) is a good place to pick up a quick snack before eco-touring.

Aromas in the town centre is more stylish

and the place for coffee, quiche and cake. *Hislops Cafe* on Beach Rd is a smart cafe, very popular for wholefood meals and snacks.

Various hotels serve standard pub fare including the *Pier Hotel* near the wharf, *Adelphi Hotel*, *Blue Pacific* and *New Commercial Hotel*.

The *Craypot* on West End is a long-running restaurant-bar and is the place for a good feed of crayfish; a half crayfish is $27.50 but it may be frozen rather than fresh. The *White Morph* at 94 the Esplanade is in a stately old home and has both indoor and outdoor garden tables. With local seafood so plentiful, what better place to try a paella ($25)?

The *Green Dolphin* is at 12 Avoca St opposite the Pier Hotel near the wharf. The food is continental and delicious with mains for around $15.

The *Sonic* is Kaikoura's current hot spot, with a bar, dining area and tables outside. All-day light meals such as pasta and burgers are around $12 to $14 and fancier dinner mains cost around $20. The food is good and it is open till late.

Out at South Bay is *Finz*, a predominantly seafood place with a bar, open daily from 6 pm till late.

Getting There & Away
Kaikoura Air Services (☎ 0800 524 568) has flights to/from Wellington for $95 or only $55 stand-by. Schedules can change and only two flights per week operate in winter. It also has flights to Blenheim ($65) and Hanmer Springs ($40).

The daily InterCity and Newmans bus services operating between Nelson, Picton and Christchurch all stop at Kaikoura. Buses arrive and depart from the town car park; tickets for both are sold at the information centre next door.

Over a dozen shuttle buses service Kaikoura, including Compass Coachlines, South Island Connections, Southern Link, Ko-op and Nationwide. They charge around $15 to Christchurch, Blenheim or Picton.

The information centre takes bookings. Hanmer Springs costs around $25 by shuttle. Touch of Class has a daily door-to-door service to/from Christchurch for $20.

One northbound and one southbound *Coastal Pacific* train between Picton and Christchurch stop at Kaikoura daily. The northbound arrives at 10.30 am and the southbound at 4.10 pm.

Nelson Region

The Nelson region is one of the top destinations for travellers to NZ. In addition to its equable climate and some good beaches, it is home to some of the best and most popular national parks in the country – Kahurangi, Nelson Lakes and Abel Tasman parks offer a wealth of walking and other outdoor activities. The city of Nelson and the towns of Motueka, Takaka and Collingwood are great places to 'lay back' for a while.

NELSON

The city of Nelson (population 51,000) is pleasant, bright and active. The surrounding area has some of the finest beaches in New Zealand and more sunshine than any other part of the country so it's a popular holiday area. Apart from beaches and bays, Nelson is noted for its fruit-growing industry and its energetic local arts and crafts community.

Nelson stages many noteworthy events throughout the year. One of the most interesting, the Wearable Art Award, is held in September and the annual Arts Festival is held around the same time. In early February the Taste Nelson Festival features locally produced food and beverages.

History

The Maori began to migrate to the South Island during the 16th century, and among the first to arrive in Nelson were the Ngati Tumatakokiri. By 1550 this tribe occupied most of the province, as Abel Tasman found out to his cost when he turned up in 1642 at what he later named Murderers' Bay. Other tribes followed the Tumatakokiri, settling at the mouth of the Waimea River. The Tumatakokiri remained supreme in Tasman Bay until the 18th century, when the Ngati-apa from Wanganui and the Ngai Tahu – the largest tribe in the South Island – got together in a devastating attack on the Tumatakokiri, who virtually ceased to exist as an independent tribe after 1800.

The Ngati-apa's victory was short-lived because between 1828 and 1830 they were practically annihilated by armed tribes from Taranaki and Wellington who sailed into the bay in the largest fleet of canoes ever assembled in New Zealand.

By the time the European settlers arrived no Maori lived at Te Wakatu – the nearest pa being at Motueka – and the decimated population that remained in the area put up no resistance. The first Pakeha settlers sailed in response to advertisements by the New Zealand Company, set up by Edward Gibbon Wakefield to systematically colonise the country. His grandiose scheme was to transplant a complete slice of English life from all social classes. In reality 'too few gentlemen with too little money' took up the challenge and the new colony almost foundered in its infancy from lack of money.

The settlement was planned to consist of small but workable farms grouped around central towns. However, the New Zealand Company's entitlement to the land was disputed and it was almost a year before this problem was sorted out. Town land was distributed early, but farmland remained unallocated for so long that landowners and labourers were forced to live in town and whittle away their capital to survive.

The Wairau Massacre (described at the beginning of the Marlborough Region section) resulted in the deaths of 22 of Nelson's most able citizens, including Captain Wakefield whose leadership was irreplaceable, and plunged the colony into deep gloom. To make matters worse the New Zealand Company was declared bankrupt in April 1844 and, since nearly three-quarters of the population were dependent on it in some

Nelson

To Picton & Blenheim

To Founders Park

Queen Elizabeth II Drive

Trafalgar Park

Weka Street

Tasman Street

Milton Street

Cambria Street

Rutherford Park

Maitai

River

Panpanu Road

Haven Road

Grove Street

To Tahunanui Beach, Wakefield Quay

Ajax Avenue

Halifax Street

Halifax Street

Anzac Park

Haven

Achilles Avenue

Wakatu Lane

New Street

Bridge Street

Avon Terrace

Vanguard St

To Nelson Cabins & Caravan Park, Post Boy

Alma Street

Trafalgar Street

Queen's Gardens

Hardy Street

To Botanic Gardens & Centre of New Zealand

Tasman Street

To Matai Valley Motor Camp

Selwyn Place

Sussex Street

Collingwood Street

Alton Street

Nile Street East

To Alan's Place & Brook Valley Motor Camp

Rutherford Street

Nile St West

South Street

Shelbourne St

Mount Street

Trafalgar Square

0   250   500 m

Examiner Street

MARLBOROUGH & NELSON

Renwick Place

Bronte Street

Brougham Street

Wainea Road

To Broadgreen House, Brightwater Stoke, Airport & Golden Bay

Fairfield Park

Van Dieman Street

PLACES TO STAY
1 Tasman Towers
2 Paradiso Backpackers
3 Cambria House
4 Trafalgar Lodge Motel
5 California House
6 Riverlodge Motel
9 AA Motor Lodge
11 Waimarie Motel
17 Boots Backpackers
18 Senecio Backpackers
22 Centre of New Zealand Backpackers
23 Sussex House
26 Wakatu Hotel & Cobb & Co
34 Bumbles Hostel
36 Nelson Central YHA
39 Mid City Motor Lodge
53 Palace Backpackers
54 Club Nelson
55 Dominion House
57 Hotel Rutherford
60 Nelson Backpackers 125

61 Trampers Rest
62 Collingwood House
63 Lynton Lodge Motel

PLACES TO EAT
13 Metro Café
15 Valeno's Cafe Bar
16 Roadside Diner
20 Little Rock Bar & Cafe
27 Ciao Restaurant
29 Food with Attitude
30 Ak Baba's
32 Penguino
33 Fifeshire Fare
41 Faces
42 Ploy Siam
43 Burgerholics
46 Land of the Pharoahs
47 Zippy's Vegetarian
48 Victorian Rose
50 Chez Eelco; Pomeroy's
51 McDonald's
64 Pizza Hut

OTHER
7 Library
8 Nelson Visitor Centre; Transit Centre
10 Automobile Association (AA)
12 Chief Post Office
14 InterCity Depot & Suburban Bus Lines
19 Molly McGuire's
21 Riverside Pool
24 Suter Art Gallery
25 DOC & Land Information NZ
28 Royal Hotel & O'Reilly's Bar
31 Air New Zealand
33 Rollo's BBQ & Camping
35 Natural High
38 New World Supermarket
40 Zhivago's
44 Black Fly Bar
45 Alp Sports Centre
48 Nelson Ferrari Collection
52 Shell Petrol Station
56 South Street Gallery
58 Cathedral
59 Bishop's School

way, particularly for sustenance, the situation was so grim as to be near famine. Only the later arrival of hard-working German immigrants saved the region from economic ruin.

Information

The Nelson Visitor Information Centre (☎ 548 2304; fax 546 9008) on the corner of Trafalgar and Halifax Sts is open from 8.30 am to 6 pm daily in summer (from 8.30 am to 5 pm on weekdays and 10 am to 4 pm on weekends in winter). Pick up copies of *Your Guide to Nelson City* and the *Nelson Region Guide* here. It is also Nelson's Transit Centre – all buses arrive and depart from this office. Trafalgar St, which crosses the river just before the information centre and runs straight up to the cathedral, is the main street in Nelson.

A DOC officer is at the information centre in summer for inquiries about national parks and walks, and a full range of literature is available. The main DOC office (☎ 546 9335) is in the Monroe Building at 186 Bridge St. The AA office is at 45 Halifax St.

Camping gear can be hired from most of the hostels or from Natural High (☎ 546 6936), 52 Rutherford St, which also has bicycles and kayaks. Others with camping gear for sale or hire are Alp Sports (☎ 546 8536) at 220 Hardy St, Basecamp (☎ 548 1710) at 295 Trafalgar St and Rollo's BBQ & Camping (☎ 548 2363) at 12 Bridge St. Hire prices are reasonable at around $5 a day for packs and boots, and $10 a day for tents.

Fruit picking and other agricultural work is available from February to May – contact the Employment NZ office or individual growers. Fish processors down at the port sometimes have casual daily work.

Historic Buildings

The traditional symbol of Nelson is its Art Deco **cathedral** at the top of Trafalgar St. Work began in 1925 but was delayed and arguments raged in the 1950s over whether the building should be completed to its original design. Finally completed in 1965 to a modified design, it was consecrated in 1972, 47 years after the foundation stone was laid! The cathedral is open from 8 am to 7 pm daily.

Close to the cathedral, **South St** is home to a row of restored workers cottages dating from 1863 to 1867. Of prime interest is the South St Gallery on the corner of Nile St West, noted for its extensive collection of fine pottery. It's open daily.

For about 90 years from 1840, **Bishop's School** served Nelson as a school. On display are the notes and textbooks used in the old days. It's on Nile St East and open by appointment only (☎ 548 0821).

Broadgreen House at 276 Nayland Rd in Stoke is a historic two-storey cob house built about 1855 and carefully furnished in the period. It is open daily except Monday in summer, Wednesday and weekend afternoons in winter ($3, children 50c).

Beaches

Five kilometres west of the town centre, **Tahunanui** is an old-fashioned Kiwi holiday resort with mini golf, a playground, waterslide and a motley little zoo called Natureland. Now a suburb of Nelson, it's had a slight update, with a few fashionable cafes. A stroll along the foreshore and wide, greysand beach with shallow waters is pleasant. Paddle trikes can be hired in summer. It's reached on a Nelson Suburban bus.

Rabbit Island, some 20km west of Nelson, has 13km of undeveloped, much better beach backed by plantation forest. The bridge to the island is closed after 9 pm daily and camping is not allowed; opening hours depend on the fire risk.

Founders Park

This replica colonial village on Atawhai Drive reflects the town's early history. It's near the waterfront (look for the big windmill), 1km north-west of the city centre, and open from 10 am to 4 pm daily ($5, children $2). Next door are the attractive Miyazu Japanese Gardens (free).

Museums & Galleries

The **Suter Art Gallery** adjoins Queen's Gardens on Bridge St and is named after Bishop Suter, founder of the Bishopdale Sketching Club in 1889. It has a few interesting lithographs and paintings and is the city's main repository of high art, with changing exhibitions, musical and theatrical performances, films, a craft shop and restaurant. It's open from 10.30 am to 4.30 pm daily ($1).

The **Nelson Ferrari Collection**, 132 Collingwood St, has six of the red devils for aficionados of Italian racing design. It's open from 10 am to 5 pm daily ($6, children $3).

The small **Nelson Provincial Museum** at Isel Park, 6km south of Nelson in Stoke, has a permanent Maori collection and tries hard with rotating exhibits that sometimes draw on the museum's large photographic collection. It's open from 10 am to 4 pm on weekdays and noon to 4 pm on weekends ($2, children $1). The beautiful Isel Park gardens are worth a visit in their own right, and also in the grounds is historic **Isel House**, open from 2 to 4 pm on weekends ($1, children 50c). Get there on the bus to Stoke.

Nelson is famous for its pottery and the quality of local clay, but glass-blowing, furniture, woodcarving, paintings and other arts and crafts are represented. The Nelson Potters' Association has a leaflet, or pick up the excellent *Nelson Regional Guide Book: Art in its Own Place* with maps showing numerous studios and galleries.

Gardens

Nelson has some fine gardens, including the Botanic Gardens and Queens Gardens. The **Botanic Gardens** has a good lookout at the top of Botanical Hill, with a spire proclaiming it NZ's exact geographical centre.

Activities

The Rapid River Adventure Company (☎ 545 0332) and Ultimate Descents (☎ 546 6212) both do **white-water rafting** on the Buller and Gowan rivers for around $65 for a half-day trip and $105 for the full day.

You can go **parapenting** with Airborn (☎ 543 2669) or Active Air Paragliding (☎ 544 1182). For a little extra try a tandem parachute jump with Tandem Skydive Nelson (☎ 548 7652). It costs $185 per person including transport, 10 minutes' instruction and a certificate.

Nelson's most popular activity is a **quad bike** tour along farmland and high-country trails with Happy Valley Tours (☎ 545 0304), a 10-minute drive north-west along SH6. The ride takes in native bush and great views for $65 (2½ hours), including refreshments at the cafe. Inexperienced riders can do a farm fun ride for $35. Also being built is the Skywire, a 1.6km free-fall ride on flying fox swing.

The Nelson Visitor Centre has walking pamphlets and information on many other activities around Nelson. Of the many **walks** and tramps, the riverside footpath makes a pleasant stroll through the city and the Maitai Valley Walkway is particularly restful and beautiful.

Organised Tours

Many tours around Nelson can be booked through the visitor centre. Some of the more popular are Wine Trail Tours ($35 to $57) and Craft & Scenic Tours (from $25). Day trips from Nelson to the Abel Tasman National Park are popular and good value (see the Abel Tasman National Park section for details).

Places to Stay

Camping & Cabins *Tahuna Beach Holiday Park* (☎ 548 5159), 70 Beach Rd near the airport, is a huge motor camp accommodating thousands, but there are plenty of secluded tent and powered sites for $18, cabins and lodges from $28 to $39, tourist flats ($50) and motels ($60) – prices are for two. The site is 5km from the city centre and has its own supermarket.

Brook Valley Motor Camp (☎ 548 0399) at the end of Tasman St in the upper Brook Valley is in a superb forested setting by a stream. It's the same distance from the centre as Tahuna, but rather smaller and more personal. Tent/powered sites are $15/16, very basic two-bunk cabins are $22 and better cabins are $28 to $36; all prices are for two.

The simpler *Maitai Valley Motor Camp* (☎ 548 7729) on Maitai Valley Rd is in a similarly delightful setting on the riverbank, 6km west of the centre; tent/powered sites are $15/16 and cabins $22.

The central *Nelson Cabins & Caravan Park* (☎ 548 1445) at 230 Vanguard St has powered sites at $17 for two, but no tent sites. Cabins with own kitchens are $42 and you can hire linen. Tourist flats with shower and toilet are $52 for two.

Other sites in the area include the *Richmond Motel & Holiday Park* (☎ 544 7323), 13km south of Nelson at 26 Gladstone Rd in Richmond, and the *Waimea Town & Country Club* (☎ 544 6476), 345 Queen St, also in Richmond.

Hostels Hostels have been popping up like mushrooms around Nelson – plenty of good choice in this small city.

The very central, purpose-built *Nelson Central YHA* (☎ 548 8817) at 57 Rutherford St has excellent new rooms and facilities. It has several quiet areas and good common rooms in a sound-proofed environment, and the expansive kitchen/dining room opens onto a terrace garden. A dorm bed is $18 per person and singles/doubles are $28/40.

A close second in the facilities stakes is the renovated *Paradiso Backpackers* (☎ 546 6703), 42 Weka St, in a lovely old building with spacious grounds. It's perhaps a little cramped for the number of rooms but has a pool, spa, sauna and a wonderful glassed-in dining room. Seven or eight-bed dorms with mezzanines cost $16, four-bed dorms are $17 and twins and doubles are $38.

Nearby at 10 Weka St, *Tasman Towers* (☎ 548 7950) is another large, purpose-built hostel with very good rooms and facilities. Dorms (mostly quads) are $17, and twins and doubles are $38.

The central *Palace Backpackers* (☎ 548 4691) at 114 Rutherford St is in an old turn-of-the-century villa set above the street with views from the balconies. The house is surrounded by garden and there are plenty of areas to sit and relax. It has a wide variety of rooms, with dorms costing $16 and $17, and doubles and twins costing $38.

Boots Backpackers (☎ 548 9001), right in the centre of town on the corner of Trafalgar and Bridge Sts, is not the fanciest but it's clean and roomy enough. Dorms are $16 per person and doubles cost $38. There's a special sound-proofed 'Party Room' and pool table. Not far away is the *Senecio Backpackers* (☎ 546 6962), 28 New St, above the former Metropolitan Hotel, charging $16 in dorms, $38 for doubles.

In the centre at 8 Bridge St, *Bumbles* (☎ 548 2771) is a former hotel turned backpackers. It has a big common room, plenty of information and helpful staff. Dorm beds are $16 to $18 per person and twins and doubles are $36 or $40 with en suite.

An uphill walk away is the rambling *Club Nelson* (☎ 548 3466) at 18 Mount St. This big hostel has large dorms for $12, small dorms for $16 and a big selection of singles/doubles for $20/38 including linen. Small and cosy it ain't but it's quiet, has plenty of parking and the old institutional building and gardens are impressive.

More hostels can be found just east of the centre. For a small, homestay-style backpackers it's hard to beat *Trampers Rest* (☎ 545 7477), 31 Alton St. The friendly owner is a keen tramper and cyclist and provides information on both activities, as well as free bikes. The small, attractive house has only a few beds for $16 and $36 a double.

Nelson Backpackers 125 (☎ 548 7576), 125 Tasman St, is another smaller hostel in an old house with dorms for $15 and $16, and doubles for $34. It's a little worn but friendly.

Alan's Place (☎ 548 4854) at 42 Westbrook Terrace is a bit further out, but not far from town. It's also an older house but has a good atmosphere and Alan, one of the 'originals' in the backpacker industry, offers pick-up, free bikes and other services. Dorm beds cost $16, twins $32 and doubles $36.

The *Centre of New Zealand Backpackers* (☎ 546 6667), 193 Milton St, occupies a beautiful large manor house, built in 1881, with ample space inside and around the grounds. It is perched on the side of a hill (access is via a long driveway) and has magnificent views. The cost is $16 and $17 in dorms, and $40 in doubles and twins. It also has its own little gorge camping area ($10 per person).

Beach Hostel (☎ 548 6817), 25 Muritai St, is 4km out at Tahunanui Beach, a pleasant area to stay with restaurants, a pub and the airport nearby. It's friendly, laid back and roomy with good communal areas. Free pick-up and bikes are offered. Dorms are $15, twins $34 and doubles $36.

B&Bs, Guesthouses & Cottages Nelson has plenty of B&Bs, but they may be full in the high season. The best-known and probably most expensive is *Cambria House* (☎ 548 4681), 7 Cambria St, for luxury-plus at $165 to $255. *California House* (☎ 548 4173) at 29 Collingwood St is just across the river from the town centre. The cost is from $115/135 for singles/doubles, which includes a hearty, home-baked Californian breakfast.

Further south along the same street, at No 174, is *Collingwood House* (☎ 548 4481) where rooms cost $55/75. *Sussex House* (☎ 548 9972) at 238 Bridge St charges $50/80 or $90 a double with en suite.

Opposite the beach at Tahunanui, *Aloha Lodge* (☎ 546 4000), 19 Beach Rd, is a large, modern guesthouse with strange Chinese architecture and good rooms with en suite, TV and coffee-making facilities for $50/90 B&B. *Willowbank* (☎ 548 5041) at 71 Golf Rd is another B&B in Tahunanui and *Pepper Tree Place* (☎ 542 3376), 126 Lord Rutherford Rd, is in Brightwater.

Historic South St has some delightful cottages for rent. *14 South St* (☎ 546 7628) has two self-contained bungalows in the garden for $55/75 B&B. *South St Cottages* (☎ 540 2769) rents out complete workers cottages at No 1 and No 12 for $107 a double, including a simple, self-serve breakfast. Inquire at South St Gallery on the corner of Nile St West if no one is around, but it pays to book.

Motels & Hotels Many of Nelson's motels, mostly of higher standard, are near the beach at Tahunanui on Beach Rd and Muritai St. Central and reasonably priced motels include the *Lynton Lodge Motel* (☎ 548 7112) at 25 Examiner St with double rooms for $70 to $79. The *Riverlodge Motel* (☎ 548 3094), 31 Collingwood St, on the Grove St corner, has units for $79 to $105. At the *Trafalgar Lodge Motel* (☎ 548 3980), 46 Trafalgar St, units cost $68 to $78 for doubles (less in winter), while B&B in the guesthouse section is $35 per person.

The *Waimarie Motel* (☎ 548 9418), 45 Collingwood St, is very central and has units for $75 to $95. The *Mid City Motor Lodge* (☎ 546 9063) in the centre of town at 218 Trafalgar St has rooms priced from $70 to $88 for doubles. By the river at 8 Ajax Ave, the *AA Motor Lodge* (☎ 548 8214) is conveniently located with rooms costing around $88 for two people.

Regular hotels include the *Dominion* (☎ 548 4984) at 2 Nile St West, where singles cost from $30 to $35 and doubles $40 to $45; and the *Wakatu Hotel* (☎ 548 4299) at 83 Collingwood St, with singles/doubles at $39/59.50. The expensive 115-room *Hotel Rutherford* (☎ 548 2299) is on Nile St West and has everything from a sauna and swimming pool to a spa and gym. The cheapest rooms cost $130 to $295, with discounts on weekends.

Places to Eat

The wealth of local produce, particularly seafood, makes dining out in Nelson a pleasure. Over 70% of the country's fishing quota is owned by Nelson businesses. Deep sea fish such as orange roughie and hoki, scallops from Tasman and Golden Bays, and mussels and oysters are available in the town's restaurants, complemented by locally produced wines and beers.

Make a point of trying the local beer. The appropriately named Pink Elephant – reminiscent of some Belgian Trappist varieties – is worth a try, and Bay's beer is the latest of the local brews. Mac's is Nelson's own independently brewed beer, popular throughout

New Zealand. Sunshine Tours (☎ 544 1240) includes Mac's Brewery in its winery tour, or you can arrange to join the tour at the brewery at 2 pm for $5.

Restaurants & Cafes *Chez Eelco*, near the cathedral at 296 Trafalgar St, is a Nelson institution and still the place to find out about the 'alternative' scene. This relaxed place is open from 6 am to 11 pm daily and serves everything from strong coffee, croissants, sandwiches and fruit juices to regular restaurant meals. It's a popular meeting place and the front window is an equally popular local notice board. Next door, at No 276, the place with a pervasive smell of fresh roasted coffee is *Pomeroys*, where you can get cakes, croissants and coffee. The *Metro Café* also on Trafalgar St is another trendy little place for good coffee and has regular art exhibitions. The cafe at the *Suter Art Gallery* is worth considering for a more expensive but pleasant lunch – it's open daily.

For vegetarian selections, *Zippy's* at 276 Hardy St, with its decor based on the 1970s cartoon character, and the very popular *Broccoli Row* at 5 Buxton Square are the best choices. At the latter, bookings are essential and mains are around $20.

The *Land of the Pharaohs* at 270 Hardy St is appropriately run by an Egyptian who knows how to serve a bevy of Middle Eastern delights for under $15. *Ak Baba's* at 130 Bridge St is run by Turks and you dine at low tables surrounded by Turkish rugs and carpets; three courses will set you back $15. Both do takeaways.

For excellent seafood by the sea and a touch of the Côte d'Azur in sunny Nelson, head for *Quayside*, *Coasters* or the *Boatshed* at Wakefield Quay on the road to Tahunanui. The wonderful Boatshed at No 350 is on stilts over the sea and serves superb chilli crab for $22.50. Other seafood selections include crayfish and it has a cheaper lunch menu.

Across the road from the Wakatu Hotel is the *Little Rock Bar & Cafe* serving pizza and budget meals to good music. The cost of the original wrought iron sculpture is added to the wide range of cocktails. *Ploy Siam*, 142 Hardy St, has good Thai food.

Ciao Restaurant, 94 Collingwood St, has expensive but good Italian food for lunch and dinner, Monday to Saturday. *Faces* on Hardy St is a bit more raunchy and has tasty Italian food for around $18. It has a good selection of local and international wines. *Valeno's Cafe Bar* on Bridge St is a great place for cheap food; meals are less than $15.

Pub Food There's a *Cobb & Co* in the Wakatu Hotel on the corner of Collingwood and Bridge Sts. At 281 Trafalgar St, *Victorian Rose* is a pastiche of English/Irish pub styles in airy premises. The Guinness is served with care and there is a varied selection of beers. Meals are cheap and backpackers specials are offered.

Out past the airport at Nayland, on Point Rd, the *Honest Lawyer* is a stylish pub overlooking the estuary with outdoor tables and reasonably priced meals.

Fast Food There are plenty of sandwich specialists around the centre and Rutherford St has a *Pizza Hut* and a *McDonald's*. The *Roadside Diner* is a big white pie cart that has been serving fast food in Nelson since 1933 and is reputed to have the 'biggest burgers in NZ'. It is parked on Trafalgar St near Bridge St after 6 pm daily except Sunday and is open until late most nights (until 3.30 am on Friday and Saturday).

Food with Attitude on Bridge St serves greasy burgers to alleviate the late-night hunger horrors. On Hardy St is *Burgerholics*, described by a traveller as 'fantastic'. Try the delicious chargrilled beef and bacon burger with wholegrain mustard. Sadly for 'holics, both places are closed on Monday.

For delicious ice cream and coffee try *Penguino* down an arcade off Trafalgar St facing the car park. *Fifeshare Fare* on Hardy St is a small food court for cheap, mostly Asian, meals.

Entertainment

Suter Art Gallery has theatre, music and dance, and its Stage Two theatre shows a selection of popular and international art films.

Various pubs have entertainment including the *Ocean Lodge Hotel* at Tahunanui with a disco and *O'Reilly's Bar* at the Royal Hotel.

The local band scene can be summed up as: *Molly McGuire's* for Irish, folk and country; the *Victorian Rose* for blues and pop; and *O'Reilly's* for pop, blues and dance music.

Zhivago's in the City Centre shopping arcade is a clean, tidy and safe nightclub. The *Black Fly* on the corner of Hardy and Trafalgar Sts is a backpackers bar popular with bus groups.

Getting There & Away

Air The Air New Zealand (Air Nelson Ltd) office (☎ 546 6242) is on the corner of Trafalgar and Bridge Sts. Direct flights go to Wellington, Auckland, Christchurch and New Plymouth, with connections to other cities. Ansett (☎ 0800 267 388) has direct flights to Wellington and Auckland. Flight Corporation (☎ 547 8175) flies from Nelson to Wellington daily except Saturday for $80; book at the visitor centre.

Bus All buses serving Nelson stop and pick up from the Nelson Visitor Centre on the corner of Trafalgar and Halifax Sts, where you can also buy tickets. The main depot for InterCity (☎ 548 1539) and Newmans (☎ 548 2581) is at 27 Bridge St.

InterCity buses run daily to Picton and Christchurch and to Greymouth via Murchison and Westport, with connections to the Franz Josef and Fox glaciers. The latter is an interesting route to Greymouth via the Buller Gorge and the scenic Coast Road, with a stop at Punakaiki.

Newmans also has daily buses from Nelson to Picton, which continue to Christchurch.

White Star (☎ 546 8687) runs daily between Nelson and Picton, and Nelson and Christchurch via the Lewis Pass. To Westport, White Star takes the quicker route through Springs Junction, where you change buses. Brett's Budget Bus (☎ 547 8393) has

a shuttle service to Greymouth ($35) and Christchurch ($25).

Abel Tasman Coachlines (☎ 548 0285) at 27 Bridge Rd provides transport from Nelson, Motueka and Takaka to the Abel Tasman Track (see the Abel Tasman National Park section for details) and to the Heaphy Track. To Picton and Blenheim, the main shuttles are Kiwilink and Knightline. Bayways Book-a-Bus (☎ 0800 259 864) has daily services to Collingwood ($32), Takaka ($20) and Motueka ($9).

To the Nelson Lakes National Park, Wadsworths Motors (☎ 522 4248) has buses from Nelson to Tapawera and St Arnaud on weekdays. Nelson Lakes Transport (☎ 548 6858) runs to St Arnaud and on to Murchison from Monday to Saturday. For trampers heading to the Heaphy and Wangapeka tracks, the Mt Arthur Tablelands, Cobb Valley and Mt Richmond forest park there is Transport for Trampers (☎ 545 1055 for costs, timetable and minimum numbers).

A backpackers bus, the West Coast Express, departs from Nelson for six-day trips down the 'Coast' to Queenstown, with plenty of stops along the way. Since hitching is notoriously slow and you don't see all the sights by public bus, this is a good option. See the Getting Around chapter for details.

Hitching Getting out of Nelson is not easy as the city sprawls so far. It's best to take a bus to the outskirts. Hitching to the West Coast can be hard going.

Getting Around

Super Shuttle Nelson (☎ 547 5782) offers door-to-door service to and from the airport (6km south-west) for $6. A taxi to the airport costs about $15. You can also use the shuttle to get to Tahunanui, from the visitor centre or the Hotel Rutherford.

Nelson Suburban Bus Lines (☎ 548 3290) operates local services from its terminal in Lower Bridge St. They run out to Richmond via Tahunanui and Stoke, and also to Wakefield. Buses operate until about 5 or 6 pm on weekdays, with one later bus at about 7 pm on Friday.

Bicycles can be hired from Stewart Cycle City (☎ 548 1666) at 114 Hardy St, by the half-day, day, week or month, from Fraine Cycles Ltd (☎ 548 3877) at 105 Bridge St and Natural High (☎ 546 6936), 52 Rutherford St. Thunderbike Engineering (☎ 548 7888) on Achilles Ave hires out touring motorbikes.

AROUND NELSON
Brightwater & Wakefield
The small town of Brightwater, the birthplace of Lord Rutherford, is a pleasant place to stay. Brightwater is 9km south of Richmond on the SH6, and there are farmstays and homestays in the region. Also south of Nelson, at Pigeon Valley, Wakefield, is the **Pigeon Valley Steam Museum**, with an interesting collection of vintage steam-driven machinery. It's open daily from 9 am to 4.30 pm.

Wineries
Many vineyards on the Nelson Wine Trail can be visited by doing a loop from Nelson through Richmond to Motueka, following the SH60 coast road in one direction and the inland Moutere River road in the other. Some wineries are open for visitors, including Ruby Bay Wines, Neudorf Vineyards, Seifried Estate, Redwood Cellars, Pelorus Vineyard, Robinson Brothers, Glover's Vineyard and Laska Cellars. McCashin's Brewery & Malthouse is also nearby if you wish to sample the legendary Black Mac. Information centres in Nelson or Motueka have a wine trail map.

NELSON LAKES NATIONAL PARK
Nelson Lakes National Park is 118km southwest of Nelson. Two beautiful glacial lakes are fringed by beech forest and flax, with a backdrop of forested mountains. There's good tramping, walking, lake scenery and also skiing (in winter) at the Rainbow Valley and Mt Robert ski fields. Information on the park is available at the Park Visitors Centre (☎ 521 1806) in St Arnaud or at the Lake Rotoroa Ranger Station (☎ 523 9369) near the northern end of Lake Rotoroa.

The park is accessible from two different areas, lakes Rotoiti and Rotoroa. St Arnaud village, at Lake Rotoiti, is the main centre, while Rotoroa receives far fewer visitors (mainly trampers and fishing groups). An excellent three-day tramp from St Arnaud takes you south along the eastern shore of Lake Rotoiti to Lake Head, across the Travers River and up the Cascade Track to Angelus Hut on beautiful alpine Lake Angelus. The trip back to St Arnaud goes along Roberts Ridge to the Mt Robert ski field. On a clear day this ridge walk affords magnificent alpine views all along its length. The track descends steeply to the Mt Roberts car park, from where it's a 7km road walk back to St Arnaud. Other walks at Rotoiti include the Peninsula Nature walk (1½ hours), Black Hill track (1½ hours return), Mt Robert Lookout (20 minutes), St Arnaud Range Track (five hours), Loop Track (1½ hours return) and Lakehead Track around the Lake (six hours).

There are a number of walks around Lake Rotoroa. Two short ones are the Short Loop Track (20 minutes) and the Flower Walk (10 minutes), while medium-length ones include Porika Lookout (two to three hours), Lakeside Track (six hours) and Braeburn Walk (two hours). The track along the eastern shore of the lake connects with the Sabine, Blue Lake and Lake Constance area of the walk described under Lake Rotoiti. For more information get a copy of the publications *Lake Rotoroa, Lake Rotoiti, Mt Robert* and *Peninsula Nature Walks* – these have condensed much of the information you need to know about NZ's forests into tiny, excellent volumes. For information on other walks in the Nelson Lakes region, ask at the ranger stations or refer to LP's *Tramping in New Zealand*.

Places to Stay & Eat
Lake Rotoiti DOC camping grounds (☎ 521 1806) are at the edge of the lake in West and Kerr bays. Tent/powered sites cost $7/8 per person. There are toilets, coin-operated hot showers and a kitchen.

The *Yellow House* (☎ 521 1887) in St

Arnaud is a YHA associate hostel charging $15 per person in a dorm, and $34 for doubles. It has a spa pool, hires out tramping equipment, and is only a five-minute walk to Lake Rotoiti. The self-contained *St Arnaud Log Chalets* (☎ 521 1887), which cost $80 for two people, are next door.

The *Alpine Lodge* (☎ 521 1869), a 10-minute walk from the lake, has doubles for $95 to $130. Across the car park is its *Alpine Chalet* backpackers accommodation. This is a large, clean and European-style 'alpine' building costing $16 per person in dorms and $45 for a double. Guests are left to themselves.

St Arnaud Homestay (☎ 521 1028) has rooms for $50/80.

There are also several camping grounds and lodges within the park itself – contact the Park Visitors Centre. There's a restaurant at the Alpine Lodge, and a snack bar at the petrol station, which also sells limited grocery supplies. The *Tophouse* (☎ 521 1848), 8km from St Arnaud, dates from the 1880s, when it was a hotel. It is now a comfortable B&B with self-contained cottages, all $80 a double.

Lake Rotoroa There is not much accommodation here. A basic DOC camping ground ($4 per person) by the lake has only a toilet and water point. The *Retreat Camping Ground*, towards Gowan Bridge, is a centre for white-water rafting but you can camp for $7 per person ($8 with power) and cabins are $13 per person. The small *Gowan River Holiday Camp* (☎ 523 9921), 5km from SH6 on Gowan Valley Rd, is scenic and has tent/powered sites for $7/8 and cute railway carriage cabins for $12 ($13 with en suite). Other options include the simple *Dizzy's Corner B&B* at Gowan Bridge and the exclusive *Rotoroa Lodge* and *Braeburn Lodge*.

Getting There & Around

See the Nelson, Blenheim and Picton sections for details of buses to St Arnaud.

Nelson Lakes Shuttles (☎ 521 1887) operates in the region to Lake Rotoroa, Mt Roberts and Kawatiri; inquire at the Yellow House. JJ's Ski Transport (☎ 544 7081) operates from Nelson to the Rainbow Valley ski field and the Mt Robert car park in winter. Nelson Lakes Transport (☎ 548 6858) also does charters.

Water taxis operate on lakes Rotoiti and Rotoroa; these can be booked on (☎ 521 1894; Lake Rotoiti) or (☎ 523 9199; Lake Rotoroa).

NELSON TO MOTUEKA

From Richmond, south of Nelson, SH60 heads west to Motueka. The region fringing Tasman Bay is very popular with local holidaymakers, with plenty of accommodation, art and craft outlets, vineyards, yacht charters, fishing and swimming.

The picturesque Waimea Inlet and the twin villages of **Mapua** and **Ruby Bay** are at the mouth of the Waimea River. Facing them is Rabbit Island with great swimming beaches, boating, fishing and forest walks. *Mapua Nature Smoke*, right on Mapua wharf, is a great cafe with delicious wood-smoked fish such as groper, tarakihi, moki and snapper.

On the back road route along Wilsons Rd from Nelson to Motueka are the **tame eels** of the Moutere River that will slither out of the water to take bits of meat from your hand. The eels are about 11km from Upper Moutere village – look for the signpost. Entry is $3 (children $1).

Places to Stay

The *Mapua Leisure Park* (☎ 540 2666) at 33 Toru St, Mapua, is 'NZ's first clothes-optional leisure park'. Not for the shy perhaps, but you don't have to bare all and the position (next to the beach and river) and facilities are superb – nine-hole golf course, tennis and volleyball courts, swimming pool, sauna and spa, childrens playground and waterfront cafe. Tent/powered sites are $9.50/10.50 per person, cabins are $15 per person, on-site caravans are $44 for two or good chalets and tourist flats are $50 to $85 (with off-season reductions).

McKee Memorial Reserve, 2km north of the leisure park, is a very basic camping ground at the water's edge costing $6 for two. Water, toilets and barbecue pits are the only amenities.

Bush Lodge Holiday Camp (☎ 540 3542) is off SH60, north of Ruby Bay, 2km from the coast. It has tent/powered sites at $9/10 and twin cabins at $15 per person.

There are many homestays and farmstays in the region. Out at Thorpe, accessible from Motueka, Richmond or Mapua, *Rerenga Farm* (☎ 543 3825) on the Dovedale-Woodstock Rd is a rural retreat. In this 80-year-old homestead B&B costs $45/65 for singles/doubles and there is a self-contained cottage for $45. Dinners with the hosts (one from Holland and the other from the USA) are $20 per person. Nearby is *Doone Cottage* (☎ 526 8740), Woodstock, which has singles/doubles with private bathrooms for $70/95. It is close to some great fishing spots.

MOTUEKA

Motueka (population 6600) is the centre of a green tea, hops and fruit-growing area. The main picking season for apples, grapes and kiwi fruit is March to June and Motueka is also a base for trampers en route to the walks in the Abel Tasman and Kahurangi national parks. The inhabitants are very cosmopolitan and include many craftspeople. In summer it's a bustling place, but in winter they say you could shoot a gun down the main street and not hit a thing!

Information

The helpful Motueka Visitor Information Centre (☎ 528 6543; fax 528 6563), 236 High St, sells tickets for most things, including tours, kayaks, launches and transport. It's open from 8.30 am to 7 pm daily in summer (until 5 pm in winter). It is also the AA agent. Pick up a copy of the *Motueka Valley Craft Trail* guide for local crafts and a *Wine Trail* map. Abel Tasman National Park Enterprises (☎ 528 7801), next door at No 234, sells a profusion of national park trips.

DOC (☎ 528 9117) is on the corner of High and King Edward Sts. The office is an excellent source of information on the Abel Tasman and Kahurangi national parks. DOC and the information centre sell passes for the Abel Tasman Track. Also check with the visitor centre and DOC for tidal information.

Coppins Great Outdoor (☎ 528 7296) at 255 High St hires out tents and backpacks for use on the tracks. Hostels rent out sleeping bags and cooking gear.

Activities

The best beaches are outside Motueka at Kaiteriteri and Marahau. The beaches along the Abel Tasman National Park coast can be easily reached on day launch trips. You can hire **sea kayaks** from a number of places in the area. See the Abel Tasman National Park section for launch and kayak information.

Ultimate Descents (☎ 0800 748 377), based in Motueka, does **white-water rafting** trips on the Buller and Gowan rivers for $65 (half-day) and $100 (full day). There's also an easier 1½-hour family trip on the Motueka River for $40 (children $30).

Places to Stay

Camping & Cabins *Fernwood Holiday Park* (☎ 528 7488) is sandwiched between SH60 and High St South at the southern end of town. Tent/powered sites in this well-equipped park are $13/16 for two and good four-person cabins are $30 and $10 per extra adult.

Spacious *Fearon's Bush Motor Camp* (☎ 528 7189), 10 Fearon St, at the northern end of town, has tent or powered sites at $17 for two and comfortable cabins with one double and one single bed for $34 a double. This is also a YHA associate with beds in the cabins for $17 per person. New two-bedroom motel units are $70.

Vineyard Tourist Units (☎ 528 8550), 328 High St, has a variety of simple but good value cabins and flats, each with its own kitchen and en suite for $38 to $56 a double.

Hostels The *White Elephant* (☎ 528 6208), 55 Whakarewa St, is a good backpackers with room for 20 people in a big, comfortable old house on almost one hectare of land. It charges $16 per person in dorms, and $40 for doubles including linen. It also has tent sites,

PLACES TO STAY
2 Fearon's Bush Motor Camp
3 Abel Tasman Motel
4 Twin Oaks Cottage
6 Motueka Hotel
11 Post Office Hotel
21 Equestrian Lodge Motel
23 Swan Hotel
25 White Elephant
26 Vineyard Tourist Units
29 Motueka Garden Motel
30 The Troubadour Motel & B&B
31 Elianse Tourist Units
32 Motueka (YMCA) Hostel
33 Fernwood Holiday Park

PLACES TO EAT
7 Hot Mama's
8 Theatre Cafe; Rolling
Pin Bakery
12 Annabelle's; The Wheelhouse
13 Joyanne Bakery; Grain and
Grape
14 Gothic Gourmet
15 The Eaterie
16 Bakehouse Cafe & Pizzeria

OTHER
1 Ultimate Descents
5 Police Station
9 Supervalue Supermarket
10 Post Office
17 Abel Tasman National Park
Enterprises
18 Visitor Information Centre
19 Motueka Hire Centre
20 Coppins Great Outdoor
22 New World Supermarket
24 Swimming Pool
27 Recreation Centre
28 DOC
34 Saltwater Swimming Pool

Motueka

0   0.5   1 km

To Pretty's Tours,
Old Cederman House,
Takaka (55 km), Kaiteriteri &
Marahau (Abel Tasman
National Park)

Riwaka

Umukuri Road

River Road

Main Road

Lodder Lane

High Street North

Staples Street

Thorp Street

Parker Street

Fearon Street

Saxon St

Poole Street

Pah Street

Greenwood Street

Grey Street

Tudor Street

Harbour Road

Whakarewa Street

Motueka Quay

High Street

Woodland Avenue

To A Melting Pot
Backpackers; Woodstock

King Edward Street

Old Wharf Road

Thorp Street

Trewavas Street

Courtney St

*Tasman
Bay*

South Street

Coastal Highway

Courtney St

Wharf Road

*Moutere
Inlet*

*George
Quay*

*Port
Motueka*

To Richmond (41 km) &
Riverside Community

MARLBOROUGH & NELSON

so the communal areas can come under strain in the picking season.

The friendly *Twin Oaks Cottage* (☎ 528 7882) at 25 Parker St has dorms for $15 per person, twins for $36 and a caravan for $30. The backpackers is a good, if cramped, cottage in a spacious garden.

Motueka YMCA Hostel (☎ 528 8652) is at 500 High St on the southern edge of town. Nightly costs in this pleasant and modern hostel are $15 per person ($18 with linen), mostly in twin rooms. It also has tent sites at $8 person, but it has a large kitchen and the facilities to handle the numbers.

Only if you're desperate, the shabby *Motueka Backpackers* is at 200 High St near the Gothic Gourmet restaurant.

Five kilometres south-west of town, *A Melting Pot Backpackers* (☎ 528 9423) is on College St, which is the SH61 highway to Woodstock. This large, former institutional premises has a variety of rooms costing $11 in the dorm, $12.50 for partitioned singles and $36 for double rooms.

The *Riverside Community* (☎ 526 7805), 7km out of Motueka on the Moutere Rd, has been going since 1941 (it was set up by pacifists during WWII). It has a hostel where visitors can stay and sample communal living, but it pays ring in advance.

Also on the way to Woodstock and 18km south of Motueka at Ngatimoti is the *Fisherman's Rest* (☎ 526 8086). Run by an avid fisherman, this large house has rural views and twins/doubles for $36/40.

B&Bs, Motels & Hotels *The Troubadour Motel & B&B* (☎ 528 7318) at 430 High St is a friendly B&B in what used to be a nunnery. All rooms have a washbasin and there's a lounge with pleasant views. The cost is $52/72 for singles/doubles with breakfast. Motel units cost $70 to $85 a double.

The rough *Post Office Hotel* (☎ 528 9890) in the centre of town has basic rooms at $30/45. Other alternatives include the *Abel Tasman Motel* (☎ 528 6688) at 45 High St with units for $75, which also has a new, good-value lodge with rooms from $40.

Elianse Tourist Units (☎ 528 6629) at 432 High St charges $70 for a double. *Motueka Garden Motel* (☎ 528 9299), 71 King Edward St, near the clock tower, has units from $60 to $90. The town's best motel is the *Equestrian Lodge Motel* (☎ 528 9369) on Tudor St with units from $75 to $90.

Places to Eat

Motueka's seemingly endless main street has the usual string of takeaways and sandwich bars, including the *Wheelhouse*, opposite the post office, *Rolling Pin Bakery* at No 105, *Joyanne Bakery* at No 180 or the fancier the *Eaterie* at No 219.

Pub food is served at the *Post Office Hotel* for lunch and dinner daily except Sunday. The *Grain and Grape*, 218 High St, is a cafe with food such as Cajun burger and plough-mans lunch.

This Kiwi country town has some surprisingly good restaurants. The *Gothic Gourmet* in the town centre was a Gothic-style Methodist church. Walk in the side door and you enter the bar. The gourmet-style meat and vegetarian dishes would be notable anywhere.

Annabelle's, in the museum building in the centre of town, is both a cafe and an art gallery, with dining inside or out on the covered patio. They have particularly good salads, desserts and coffee, with plenty for both meat-eaters and vegetarians.

Hot Mama's on High St is a hip(py) cafe with good coffee and reasonably priced light meals. It's licensed and has live music on weekends. The *Theatre Cafe* on High St is small but has good pizza.

In a laneway off Wallace St, just behind High St, the *Bakehouse Cafe & Pizzeria* is a European-style cafe with a bar, and has excellent pizza and Italian food. It's the town favourite and highly recommended.

Getting There & Around

Takaka Valley Air Service (☎ 0800 501 901) flies to Wellington from Wednesday to Sunday in summer for $135.

Abel Tasman Coachlines (☎ 528 8850) buses stop at the information centre. There are services from Motueka to Nelson, Takaka, Collingwood and the Abel Tasman National Park (both ends of the track all year round). It also operates a charter service into the Heaphy Track. Buses also link Motueka and Nelson with Kaiteriteri, to connect with the coastal launch that follows the Abel Tasman Track, but you *must* book ahead.

Bayways Book-a-Bus (☎ 0800 259 864) has daily buses from Takaka to Nelson which pass through Motueka; you can catch them at the visitor centre. It also runs to and from Totaranui by arrangement. See the Abel Tasman National Park section for more information on transport to and from the track.

This area is ideal to explore on bike, especially if you are going to the wineries or craft places. Think twice, however, about cycling up Takaka Hill for the views.

MOTUEKA TO TAKAKA

From Motueka, SH60 continues over Takaka Hill to Takaka and Collingwood. Before ascending Takaka Hill, on the right is the turn-off to Kaiteriteri and the southern end of Abel Tasman National Park, then a turn-off on your left to Riwaka Valley, a good area for picnicking, swimming in river pools and walks. You can walk to the spring that is the source of the Riwaka River.

Takaka Hill, 791m high, separates Tasman Bay from Golden Bay. Near the summit are the **Ngarua Caves** (☎ 528 8093) where you can see moa bones. Just before the Ngarua Caves is the Hawkes Lookout, from where there are great views of the source of the Riwaka River. The caves are open from 10 am to 4 pm daily except Friday but are closed from mid-June to August.

Also in the area is the biggest *tomo* (entrance or cave) in the southern hemisphere, **Harwood's Hole**. It is 400m deep and 70m wide. It will take you half a day to get there from Motueka, as it is a half-hour walk one way from the car park at the end of Canaan Rd, off SH60. Exercise caution as you approach the lip of the hole – accidents have occurred.

There are many homestays and farmstays in the region. On the way up Takaka Hill, 17km north-west of Motueka, *Kairuru* (☎ 528 8091) is a comfortable homestay, charging $100 for two with breakfast and $25 per person for dinner. A little further up the road and nestled amid the karst formations is *Marble Park* (☎ 528 8061) where single/double B&B costs from $60/105; dinner is $25 extra.

As you cross the crest of the hill, Harwood Lookout has fine views down the Takaka River Valley to Takaka and Golden Bay. The lookout has interesting explanations of the geography and geology of the area, from the North-west Nelson peneplain to the Anatoki Ranges. A peneplain, you ask? It is an area worn almost flat by erosion.

From the lookout you wind down through the beautiful Takaka Hill Scenic Reserve to the river valley, through Upper Takaka and on to Takaka itself.

Kaiteriteri Beach

This is one of the most popular and beautiful beaches in the area, just 13km from Motueka on a sealed road. The beach has genuine golden sand and clear, green waters. All water sports are available as well as a great childrens playground complete with mini golf. Behind the camping ground is **Withells Walk**, a 45-minute excursion into native bush from where great views look out across the bay. Otherwise walk to Kaka Pah Point at the end of the beach and find some of the secluded little coves and hideaways.

Launch and kayak trips run to the Able Tasman National park from Kaiteriteri, though Marahau is the usual base for the national park.

Places to Stay & Eat Summer brings many holidaymakers to Kaiteriteri, mainly locals, but accommodation is limited.

The large and well-equipped *Kaiteriteri Beach Camp* (☎ 527 8010), across the road from the beach, has numerous sites at $18 for two. Cabins cost from $24 to $32 for two.

The *Kimi Ora Holiday & Health Resort* (☎ 527 8027), above the beach on Martin Farm Rd, has good facilities including a vegetarian restaurant, pool, sauna, gym, tennis courts and more. Good units range from $65 a double to $95 with kitchen and some units sleep up to six. Prices are up to 20% higher from Christmas to the end of February.

Kaiteriteri also has a motel and some private units for hire.

Apart from the restaurant at Kimi Ora and the *Seafarers* near the beach, dining choices are limited.

Getting There & Away Abel Tasman Coachline buses run from Nelson and Motueka to connect with Abel Tasman National Park Enterprises cruises to the park. With sufficient numbers the hire of a water taxi can be economical. Water-Taxi Charter (☎ 528 7497) at Kaiteriteri Beach can drop off at various parts of the national park or even provide transport for diving trips.

Marahau
Further north along the coast from Kaiteriteri, tiny Marahau, 18km north of Motueka, is the main gateway to the Abel Tasman National Park. It has a growing number of accommodation possibilities, as well as water taxis, kayak hire, seal swimming and regular bus connections (see the Abel Tasman National Park section).

It's a pleasant spot and other activities include horse treks for $20 per hour with Abel Tasman Stables (☎ 527 8181) and, believe it or not, llama safaris from Old Macdonald's Farm.

Places to Stay The *Marahau Beach Camp* (☎ 527 8176) at Marahau has tent/powered sites for $15/18, cabins for $35 for two and a self-contained backpackers lodge costing $12 in eight or five-bed dorms and one double for $28. The camp has a shop, rents out kayaks and has a water taxi service.

Marahau Lodge (☎ 527 8250), 500m past the camp, has very comfortable units with en suite for $98 a double. Nearby, the *Ocean View Chalets* (☎ 527 8232) has excellent cottages with en suite on the hill for $84 and

cottages with kitchen for $97. Prices drop considerably in the off-season.

Further along near the start of the Abel Tasman Track and the park information kiosk, the excellent *Park Cafe* has good food and a great atmosphere. Gorge on cakes, muffins, blueberry crumble and milkshakes before heading out on the track. It's open for breakfast, lunch and dinner and sometimes has entertainment.

From the cafe, Harveys Rd heads away from the beach to the *Barn Backpackers* (☎ 527 8043), where dorm beds are $14 per person, and doubles are $35; there are 15 camp sites at $8 per person. The bus service from Nelson drops you off at the Barn.

Old MacDonald's Farm (☎ 527 8288), further along Harveys Rd, is a simple camping ground but more facilities are being built. Tent/powered sites cost $14/18 or onsite vans are $30 and $40 a double. Very basic backpackers huts are $12 per person or homestay accommodation is $35 bed-only up to $70 for full board.

Other options include the *Abel Tasman Stables* (☎ 527 8181) on Marahau Valley Rd, which offers B&B.

ABEL TASMAN NATIONAL PARK
The coastal Abel Tasman National Park is a very popular tramping area. The park is at the northern end of a range of marble and limestone hills extending from Kahurangi National Park, and the interior is honeycombed with caves and potholes. There are various tracks in the park, including an inland track, although the coastal track is the most popular – but beware of the sandflies

Abel Tasman Coastal Track
This 51km, three to four-day track is one of the most beautiful in the country, passing through pleasant bush overlooking beaches of golden sand lapped by bright blue water. The numerous bays, small and large, make it like a travel brochure come to life.

Once little-known outside the immediate area, this track has now been 'discovered' and in summer hundreds of backpackers may be on the track at any one time – far more

Abel Tasman National Park

than can be accommodated in the huts, so bringing a tent is a good idea. At other times of the year it's not so crowded. The park has become so popular that DOC intends to introduce a booking system, as on the Routeburn and Milford tracks. Check with DOC.

Information The track operates on a Great Walks Pass system – the cost is $12 per person in the huts and $6 for camp sites or, from June to October, $6 for huts or camp sites. You can obtain the pass from DOC or information centres in Nelson, Motueka and Takaka. All these DOC offices are sources of track information, and there's also a National Park Visitors Centre at Totaranui, open seasonally from late November to February, otherwise the latest bus and boat schedules are posted there. The huts (Anchorage, Bark Bay Awaroa and Whariwharangi Homestead) have bunks for 20 or more people and are equipped with wood stoves.

Walking the Track Several sections of the main track are tidal, with long deviations during high tides, particularly at Awaroa. As the tidal stretches are all just on the northern side of huts, it is important to do the track in a southerly direction if the low tides are in the afternoons, and from south to north if they are in the mornings. Check the newspaper, subtracting 20 minutes from the Nelson tidal times. Tide tables and advice are available at the DOC office in Motueka.

Take additional food so that you can stay longer should you have the inclination. Bays around all the huts are beautiful but the sandflies are a problem, except at the tiny, picturesque beach of Te Puketea near the Anchorage Hut.

Excess luggage can be sent very cheaply by the various buses between Nelson, Motueka and Takaka. Abel Tasman National Park Enterprises has expensive, all-inclusive guided walks for $1100. Or you could parallel the track in a sea kayak. Estimated walking times are as follows, south to north:

Marahau to Anchorage Hut	3½ hours
Anchorage Hut to Bark Bay Hut	three hours
Bark Bay Hut to Awaroa Hut	three hours
Awaroa Hut to Totaranui	1½ hours

Most walkers stop at Totaranui, the final stop for the boat services, but it is possible to keep walking around the headland from Totaranui to Whariwharangi (two hours) and then on to Wainui (1½ hours), where buses service the car park.

Sea Kayaking

Sea kayaking is very popular and allows you to avoid overcrowded huts and camp sites. It is a stunning way to see the coast and be with nature, but don't expect to be on your own – even the water can be crowded at times.

The Ocean River Adventure Company (☎ 527 8266) on Main Rd, Marahau, rents out sea kayaks for $95 per person for two days (two day, two-person minimum). It also has one to five-day guided trips from $90 to $536 per person, depending on duration. Another operator out of Marahau is Abel Tasman Kayaks (☎ 527 8022), with prices similar to Ocean River. Planet Earth Adventures (☎ 5259095) in Pohara rents out kayaks. Even operators in Nelson, such as Natural High, will rent out kayaks and arrange transport.

Seal Swimming

Abel Tasman Seal Swim (☎ 527 8136) in

Sea Kayaking in Abel Tasman National Park

A lot of people choose to sea kayak around the relatively safe and definitely scenic waters of Abel Tasman National Park. A popular starting-point is Marahau at the southern end of the Abel Tasman Track. The peak season is from November to Easter but you can paddle year-round. Winter is a really good time as you will see more birdlife. Instruction is given to first-timers. For those going on a day trip, enough guidance is provided – ie basic strokes – for you to manage a day's paddling. If renting, you will be given a couple of hours' briefing on tides, weather and basic strokes.

Firstly, you could try a day trip. Typically, from Marahau you are on the water by 9.30 am (depending on the tides). You can hope to get to Fisherman and Adele islands in about one hour of paddling. On the way you will see lagoons, an important wildlife habitat, and several species of wading birds. If you are lucky, when you head into the open sea you will spot penguins, black shags, Australasian gannets, black-backed gulls, crested and white-fronted terns, and sometimes black-fronted and Caspian terns. Often a delicious lunch is caught – mussels, pipis and scallops – complemented by pitta bread, salad, kebabs, orange juice, tea, coffee and cake from the Park Cafe.

Longer trips, operated by the two main companies at Marahau, are typically two nights and three days; the cost is around $250. It may be a base-camp trip returning to the same camp each night, say North Head or Bark Bay. From the base you will paddle out to Tonga Island to see fur seals and, tide permitting, into the lagoons. It would not be unusual to see a dolphin. The other type of trip would cover a set distance, eg Marahau to Onetahuti Beach, with two overnight stops at Te Puketea Bay/Anchorage and then Mosquito Bay/Tonga Quarry. Return is by water taxi to Marahau. Again, the paddlers see Tonga Island and fern-lined lagoons.

Save your feet for the bigger walks down south and paddle Abel Tasman National Park. ■

Marahau organises swimming trips with seals off Tonga Island; it has the DOC licence for this activity. It will supply snorkel, mask, flippers and a snack for $65. If you prefer to just watch as the swimmers frolic with the seals it costs $40.

Organised Tours

Cruises & Water Taxis Abel Tasman National Park Enterprises (☎ 528 7801) has launch services departing from Kaiteriteri at 9 am (also 12.30 pm in the high season), picking up and dropping off trampers at Torrent Bay, Bark Bay, Tonga Bay, Awaroa and finally Totaranui (the northern end of the track), arriving back at Kaiteriteri 5½ hours later. It also picks up in Marahau but boats can't dock and you are shuttled out on a tractor trailer to meet the boat.

The launch service doubles as trampers transport and is also a pleasant day cruise. A 5½-hour cruise is $46 (children $16) or the 3½-hour cruise to Bark Bay is $34. You can easily combine a walk along part of the Abel Tasman Track with the cruise, being dropped off at one bay and picked up later at another. There are several such options, the most popular being to disembark at Torrent Bay, walk the track for two hours to Bark Bay, have time on the beach for swimming and be picked up from there for $37 (children $16).

The launch operates scheduled routes all year, but cancellations occur and they are not 100% reliable. All trips should be booked in advance, either directly with Abel Tasman National Park Enterprises or at the information centres in Nelson or Motueka. Abel Tasman Coachlines has a bus service from Nelson and Motueka which connects with the launch, making it an easy day trip from either town.

Alternatively, Abel Tasman Seafaris (☎ 527 8083) operates an excellent trampers service from Marahau to Torrent Bay ($15), Bark Bay ($18), Tonga ($20), Awaroa ($25) and Totaranui ($28) and return. It also offers three-hour cruises for $40, an Awaroa return day trip for $45 and a variety of walk-cruise options.

The catamaran *Spirit of Golden Bay II*

(☎ 525 9135) in Takaka offers trampers transport and has a variety of walk-cruises leaving Tarakohe at 8.30 am (bus from Takaka is included). You can be dropped off at Mutton Cove and walk to Totaranui ($20), spend the day at Arawoa ($28) or be dropped off at Kaiteriteri ($50). Twilight Cruises ($30) are also offered.

Places to Stay & Eat

At the southern edge of the park, Marahau is the main jumping off point. The nearest towns with accommodation at the northern end are Pohara and Takaka.

On the trail at Awaroa Bay, *Awaroa Lodge & Cafe* (☎ 025 433 135) is only 300m from the water. At this place, 200m off the track, seven-bed dorms are $20 per person and have kitchen facilities, doubles are $65 and family units are $95 to $145. The cafe offers a range of health food and the proprietors will also pack lunches. Stay a while to look at the birds – white-faced herons, pied stilts, Caspian terns, tuis, bellbirds and moreporks are all found here. You can get to Awaroa Lodge by water taxi, walking part of the Abel Tasman Track from Totaranui, or driving to the Awaroa car park and then walking.

The *Totaranui Beach Camp* (☎ 525 8026) at Totaranui, 33km from Takaka in the northern part of the national park, is administered by DOC and has no power or hot water. Camp sites are $6.50 per person. The Christmas holidays should be booked.

Getting There & Away

Abel Tasman Coachlines operates buses from Nelson (☎ 548 0285) to Motueka (☎ 528 8805) and on to Marahau, leaving Nelson at 7.20 am and 3.25 pm daily, picking up in Motueka one hour later. The 7.20 am bus also goes to Totaranui and the Wainui car park at the northern end of the track, returning at 1.15 pm from Totaranui. Open-dated Motueka-Marahau return tickets cost $10, while Nelson-Marahau-Nelson costs $18; loop tickets and one-way fares are available. Buses also go to Kaiteriteri but only when the launches operate, ie for a launch cruise, which will cost $58 return from Nelson.

MARLBOROUGH & NELSON

Bayways Book-a-Bus (☎ 0800 259 864) also has a scheduled summer service between Takaka and Totaranui/Wainui.

TAKAKA

The small centre of Takaka (population 1250) is the last town of any size as you head towards the north-west corner of the South Island. It's the main centre for the beautiful Golden Bay area. It's also quite a hip little community – lots of 'children of the 60s' and artistic types have settled here.

Information

Just about everything in Takaka is along Commercial St, the main road through town. On the Motueka side of town, the helpful information centre (☎ 525 9136) is open from 9 am to 5 pm daily in summer and 10 am to 4 pm in winter.

DOC (☎ 525 8026), 1 Commercial St, has information on the Abel Tasman and Kahurangi national parks, the Heaphy and Kaituna tracks, Farewell Spit, Cobb Valley, the Aorere goldfield and the Pupu Springs Scenic Reserve. It's open from 8.30 am to 4 pm on weekdays.

Passes for the Abel Tasman Track are available in Takaka from the DOC office and Tickets & Trips at 49 Commercial St.

Pupu Springs

These springs (the full Maori name is Waikoropupu, but everyone calls it simply Pupu) are the largest freshwater springs in NZ. Many springs are dotted around the Pupu Springs Scenic Reserve, including one with 'dancing boulders' thrown upwards by the great volume of incredibly clear water emerging from the ground.

Walking tracks through the reserve take you to the springs and a glassed viewing area, passing by gold-mining works from last century – gold was discovered in Golden Bay in 1856. DOC has an excellent leaflet about the reserve. To reach Pupu from Takaka, go 4km north-west on SH60, turn inland at Waitapu Bridge and continue for 3km.

Other Attractions

Takaka has a small **museum**, open daily ($1, children 50c). The **Begonia House** in Clifton, 8km east of town, is open in summer to show off its colourful flowers.

Many artists and craftspeople are based in the Golden Bay area, including painters, potters, blacksmiths, screenprinters, silversmiths and knitwear designers. The large **Artisans' Shop** cooperative on Commercial St, next to the Village Theatre, displays their wares. Many other artists and craftspeople are tucked away all around the bay. The *Golden Bay Craft Trail* leaflet gives directions to the galleries and workshops. The Whole Meal Trading Company and the Golden Bay Gallery (in the old post office) also have local art on display.

Windsurfing

Windsurfing is a popular activity on Golden Bay – all the local beaches are excellent – and windsurfers are available at the Shady Rest and the Pohara Beach Camp.

Places to Stay

Takaka has a reasonable selection of accommodation, though the nearby beach resort of Pohara has more choices and is more popular.

Camping & Cabins Pohara has the closest camping ground, or the *Golden Bay Holiday Park* (☎ 525 9742) is at Tukurua Beach, 18km north of Takaka and 8km south of Collingwood. Tent/powered sites are $18/19, on-site caravans are $35 and cabins are $32; all prices are for two.

Hostels In a big historic home on the main road, the *Shady Rest Hostel*, 141 Commercial St, is friendly enough but basic, with a large dorm costing $15 per person. There's no sign and it is 'Telecom-free'. The *River Inn* (☎ 525 8501), 3km west of town on the road to Collingwood, is an old pub-turned-backpackers with better standards of accommodation and charging $15/30 for singles/doubles.

About 15km west is the *Shambhala Beach*

Farm Hostel (☎ 525 8463), spectacularly set overlooking the beach at Onekaka. The Bayway Book-a-Bus can drop you at the Mussel Inn at Onekaka. If you're driving take the right turn 50m before the Inn (coming from Takaka), but it is then about 3km along a dirt road. Costs are only $15 per person in share rooms, and $35 in twins and doubles in the house and cottages around. There is a great German-language book exchange and much of the owner's artwork adorns the walls. A big attraction is the free use of horses.

B&Bs, Motels & Hotels Many B&Bs and homestays are in the area and are listed at the information centres. The *Golden Bay Motel* (☎ 525 9428), 113 Commercial St, charges $70 to $85 a double, or *Anotaki Lodge* (☎ 525 8047) at No 147 is the town's best at $74 to $110. The old *Junction Hotel* (☎ 525 9207), 15 Commercial St, has old pub singles/doubles with character for $32/50.

Places to Eat

The *Whole Meal Trading Company* in the town centre is a local institution, an enjoyable wholefood cafe, restaurant and art gallery which also sells bulk natural foods, has a bulletin board and sometimes has live music in the evenings.

Milliways further down the main road is a fancier restaurant (mains $18 to $28) with a relaxed atmosphere; it is licensed and open daily in summer. The *Takaka Tearooms* is next to an inexpensive Chinese and fish and chip takeaway.

Getting There & Away

Takaka Valley Air Service (☎ 0800 501 901) flies to Wellington from Wednesday to Sunday for $135 (Friday and Sunday only in winter).

A Bayways Book-a-Bus service (☎ 0800 259 864) goes from Takaka to Collingwood ($12) and to Nelson ($20) daily. Abel Tasman Coachlines also operates from Nelson to Takaka. Both buses have daily services to Totaranui at the northern end of the Abel Tasman National Park, passing Pohara on the way.

The catamaran *Spirit of Golden Bay II* (☎ 525 9135) has cruises to the park.

POHARA

Small Pohara is a popular summer resort, 10km north-east of Takaka. The beach is beautiful and it's on the way to the northern end of the Abel Tasman Track. The road to the park is unsealed but scenic and passes a lookout with a pillar dedicated to Abel Tasman, the first European to enter Golden Bay in 1642.

The **Rawhiti Caves** (☎ 525 9061) near Pohara have the largest entrance of any cave in NZ, well worth a look (*ra* is the Maori sun god and *whiti* is the morning sun). A three-hour return guided tour of the caves costs $14 (children $6). To reach the caves you walk for 45 minutes past 400-year-old totara. It's an enjoyable and popular tour.

Planet Earth Adventures (☎ 525 9095) rents out kayaks, windsurfers, snorkelling gear and bicycles.

Places to Stay & Eat

The *Pohara Beachside Holiday Park* (☎ 525 9500) is right on the beach and has sites for $18, cabins for $35 or $48 with cooking facilities and motel units for $80.

The *Nook* (☎ 525 8501) is an excellent backpackers in a new, rendered hay-bale house. Share rooms cost $16, twins and doubles are $32 to $40 and tents sites are available. Many people come to Pohara just to stay here. It's on the main road as you enter Pohara, five minutes walk from the beach.

The *Sans Souci Inn* (☎ 525 8663) at Pohara Beach is an attractive rammed-earth building with a sod roof, done in Mediterranean style. This very chic place charges $65 for doubles (shared bathrooms) and there are also family rooms. It has a good licensed restaurant (mains $15 to $18) and guests can use the kitchen.

Pohara Beachfront Motel (☎ 525 9660) has pokey units from $55 or better units up to $85 in the peak Christmas season. Cheaper at $52 is the *Sunflower Motel* (☎ 525 9075) on Selwyn St. *Marina Motel* (☎ 525 9428) is the best and has units from $55 to $75. It has a tavern attached with good, if slightly expensive, seafood meals.

Tata Beach Motel (☎ 525 9712), on Tata Beach, the next beach north, charges $74.

KAHURANGI NATIONAL PARK

Formerly the North-West Nelson Forest Park, this is the newest and second-largest of NZ's national parks and, undoubtedly, one of the greatest. Within its 500,000 hectares is an ecological wonderland – over 100 bird species, 50% of all NZ's plant species, 80% of its alpine plant species, a karst landscape and the largest known cave system in the southern hemisphere. Kahurangi means 'treasured possession'. Few keen trampers will disagree, as the many fine tracks and rugged country attracts them in droves, most of them to walk the Heaphy Track.

Information

Detailed information, park maps and Great Walks Passes for the Heaphy Track are available from these DOC offices:

Karamea Field Centre (☎ 782 6852), Main Rd
Nelson Conservancy (☎ 546 9335), Munro State Building, 186 Bridge St
Nelson Visitor Information Centre (☎ 548 2304), corner of Trafalgar and Halifax Sts
Motueka Field Centre (☎ 528 9117), corner of King Edward and High Sts
Takaka Field Centre (☎ 525 8026), 1 Commercial St

For those who need a guide in this region, Bush & Beyond (☎ 528 9054) has guided walks throughout the park. As well as longer tramps, it does an interesting one-day walk to less-visited Mt Arthur, south-west of Motueka, climbing to the peak and returning via Flora Hut for $85, including transport and lunch.

Heaphy Track

The four to six-day Heaphy Track is one of the best-known tracks in NZ. The track doesn't have the spectacular scenery of the Routeburn, but it still has its own beauty. Surprisingly, some people find it a disappointment if done immediately after the nearby Abel Tasman Coastal Track.

The track lies almost entirely within the Kahurangi National Park. Highlights include the view from the summit of Mt Perry (two-hour return walk from Perry Saddle Hut) and the coast, especially around the Heaphy Hut. It's worth spending a day or two resting at the Heaphy Hut, something appreciated by those travelling south from Collingwood. It is possible to cross the Heaphy River at its mouth at low tide.

Huts are geared for 20 or more people. They all have gas stoves, except Heaphy and Gouland Downs which have wood stoves,

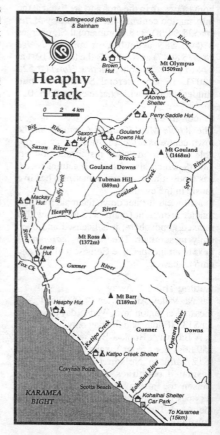

and nightly hut fees are $8 (children $4); camping is permitted ($6 per person).

Walking the Track Most people travel south-west from Collingwood to Karamea. From Brown Hut the track passes through beech forest to Perry Saddle (but don't take the shortcut uphill, unless you are fit). The country opens up to the swampy Gouland Downs, then closes in with sparse bush all the way to Mackay Hut. The bush becomes more dense towards the Heaphy Hut with the beautiful nikau palm growing at lower levels.

The final section is along the coast through heavy bush and partly along the beach. Unfortunately, the sandflies are unbearable along this, the most beautiful part of the track. The climate here is surprisingly mild, but do not swim in the sea as the undertows and currents are vicious. The lagoon at Heaphy Hut is good for swimming though, and fishing is possible in the Heaphy River.

The Heaphy has kilometre markers along its length; the zero marker is at the start of the track at the Kohaihai River near Karamea and the total length is 76km.

Estimated walking times are as follows:

Brown Hut to Perry Saddle Hut	five hours
Perry Saddle Hut to Gouland Downs Hut	two hours
Gouland Downs Hut to Saxon Hut	1½ hours
Saxon Hut to Mackay Hut	three hours
Mackay Hut to Lewis Hut	three to four hours
Lewis Hut to Heaphy Hut	two to three hours
Heaphy Hut to Kohaihai River	five hours

Wangapeka & Leslie-Karamea Tracks
It is possible to return to the Nelson/Golden Bay region by the more scenic, if harder, **Wangapeka Track** (three to five days) starting just south of Karamea. Although not as well known as the Heaphy, the Wangapeka, also in Kahurangi National Park, is thought by many to be a more enjoyable walk. The track starts some 25km south of Karamea at Little Wanganui (on the West Coast side) and runs 52km east to the Rolling River near

Tapawera. It takes about five days and there is a good chain of huts ($4 to $8 per night, children $2 to $4) along the track.

The 90km **Leslie-Karamea Track** is a medium to hard tramp of five to seven days. It connects the Cobb Valley near Takaka with Little Wanganui, south of Karamea, on the West Coast (thus including part of the Wangapeka Track on the final two days).

Cobb Valley & Mt Arthur Tablelands
The areas outlined in the DOC pamphlets, *Cobb Valley* and *Mt Arthur Tablelands Walks*, offer plenty of scope for walkers. The Cobb Valley is 28km from the Upper Takaka turn-off. You first drive up to the power station and from there it's another 13km drive to the valley. Once in the valley there are a number of walks to choose from. These range from the 45-minute Mytton's Forest Walk to others of a few hours' duration, eg Cobb Ridge to Peat Flat and Trilobite Hut to Chaffey Hut. Chaffey Hut, built in 1954, is constructed of split beech slabs.

To get to the Mt Arthur Tablelands you drive from Motueka south to Pokororo. Take the Graham Rd into the Flora car park, and from here there are a great number of walking possibilities. Walks include Mt Arthur Hut (3km, one hour), Mt Arthur (8km, three hours), Mt Lodestone (5km, two hours) and Flora Hut (2km, 30 minutes).

Kaituna Track
This track is west of Collingwood and the user is provided with two choices: a return walk of two to three hours through the old gold workings and bush scenery, or a longer track (five to seven hours, 12km) which takes you to the West Coast at Whanganui Inlet. The *Kaituna Track* pamphlet is most informative, outlining in detail the flora and fauna seen along the way, including the nikau, the world's most southerly occurring palm, and the crown fern.

The Inn-let (☎ 524 8040) guides a one-day walk through the beautiful Wakamarama Range for $65 (see the Collingwood section for details of the Inn-let backpackers).

Aorere Goldfield

The Aorere goldfield was the first major goldfield in New Zealand. In February 1857 five ounces (142g) of Collingwood gold were auctioned in Nelson, precipitating a gold rush which lasted three years, although various companies continued to wrest gold from the soil by sluicing and stamping batteries right up until WWI. The old goldfields are now overgrown but terraces, water races and mine shafts can still be seen.

The DOC office in Takaka has an excellent publication, *Aorere Goldfields/Caves Walk*, detailing the history of the goldfield and guiding you on a historical walk, beginning from Collingwood. The walk takes most of the day to complete. You can learn more about the local history at the small museum in town. The Inn-let backpackers also does tours.

Getting There & Away

Abel Tasman Coachlines (☎ 528 8805) has a service from Collingwood and Takaka to the track entrance in summer ($15 and $20 respectively); in winter it is on demand and expensive. Bayways Book-a-Bus (☎ 0800 259 864) provides transport to the track on demand, as will Bickley Motors in Takaka. Takaka to the Heaphy costs $22.50 each for a minimum of four. There's a phone at the trailhead to call buses. Wadsworth Motors (☎ 522 4248) services the Wangapeka and Leslie-Karamea tracks. For details on the Karamea end of the tracks see the Karamea section in the West Coast chapter.

Transport for Trampers (☎ 547 9603) in Nelson specialises in providing transport to and from other walking tracks in Kahurangi National Park. From Nelson it runs to Cobb Valley, Mt Arthur Tablelands, Wangapeka Track and the Heaphy Track for around $25 to $35 (minimum of four for all trailheads).

Hitchhiking to either the Karamea or Bainham end of the Heaphy Track is very difficult.

COLLINGWOOD

Tiny Collingwood (population 250) is almost at the end of the line, which is one of its main attractions. For many it's simply one jumping-off point for the Heaphy Track in the Kahurangi National Park. For others who wish to explore, there are many rewards such as the natural wonderland of Farewell Spit.

As befits a frontier town, there is a place where you can get a horse. Cape Farewell Horse Treks (☎ 524 8031) based in Puponga; a one-hour ride is $15 and a three-hour trip to Wharariki is $50. And a kayak? A full-day trip in Whanganui Inlet with Aorere Adventure Tramps, Walks & Kayaks (☎ 524 8040) is $65 to $85, depending on the number of people.

Farewell Spit

Farewell Spit is a wetland of international importance and a renowned bird sanctuary. It's the summer home to thousands of migratory waders from the Arctic tundra. On the 26km beach run there are huge crescent-shaped sand dunes from where you get panoramic views of the Spit, Golden Bay and, at low tide, the vast salt marsh.

At the Puponga car park (before the restricted section of road) there are bones from a sperm whale which beached here. You can look out over the eel grass flats and see many waders and seabirds such as pied and variable oystercatchers, turnstones, Caspian terns, eastern bar-tailed godwits, black and white-fronted terns, and big black shags. The Puponga visitors centre provides information as well as refreshments, and powerful binoculars are set up to view the wetlands and the many species of wading birds.

The crossing to the north side of the Spit is made by the tour companies. The trucks grind up over the beach to about 1km from Cape Farewell. Down towards the start of the sand are a number of fossilised shellfish. From this point it is 27km to the end of the sandy spit. Again many species of birds are seen along the way and, often, a stranded pilot whale carcass. The normal trip ends at the old lighthouse compound. The 100-year-old metal lighthouse has an eight-sided light which flashes every 15 seconds.

Further east, up on the blown shell banks which comprise the far extremity of the Spit are colonies of Caspian terns and Australasian gannets.

Two guided tours go to the remarkable Farewell Spit region. These are the only licensed vehicles allowed to visit the Spit, otherwise you'll have to walk.

Collingwood Safari Tours (☎ 524 8257) pioneered travel up the sandy beach to the lighthouse. The five-hour Farewell Spit Safari Tour costs $52 and you go up the beach in a 4WD vehicle. Tours leave daily on demand, timed to the tides. Farewell Spit Nature Tours (☎ 524 8188) also goes to the lighthouse for $60 (children $35).

Collingwood Safari Tours is also licensed by DOC to visit the gannet colony, a 1km walk from the lighthouse. The 5½-hour tour costs $55. Its wader-watch tour on the inside of the sandy spit (the estuarine side) is a must for twitchers.

In addition to a Farewell Spit tour, Collingwood Bus Service offers a good Scenic Mail Run tour that visits isolated farming settlements and communities around Cape Farewell and the West Coast. The driver points out many points of historical and contemporary interest along the way. Five-hour tours depart from the Collingwood post office at 9.30 am on weekdays and cost $35 ($20 for children under 12), including lunch.

Whariariki Beach

This beach is 29km to the north of Collingwood and involves a 20-minute walk to the beach from the car park. It is a wild introduction to the West Coast, with unusual dune formations, two looming, rock islets just out from shore, and a seal colony at its eastern end. A special place to get away entirely from the 'rat race' of Collingwood.

Places to Stay

The Collingwood Motor Camp (☎ 524 8149) on William St, near the centre of the tiny township, has tent and powered sites at $18 for two and cabins from $32 for two. The Pakawau Beach Park (☎ 524 8327) is 13km north of Collingwood, which means it's even closer to the end of the road. Sites are $20 for

two, large cabins with cooking facilities are $44 and motel units are $79.

The Collingwood Motel (☎ 524 8224) on Haven Rd has units for $65 to $70 for two. On Tasman St, the Collingwood Beachcomber Motels (☎ 524 8499) has units at $55 to $65 for two ($10 for each extra adult). The newer Pioneer Motels (☎ 524 8109) on Tasman St charges $55 to $65.

Skara Brae (☎ 524 8464) on Elizabeth St is a small B&B with two self-contained units costing $50 ($60 B&B). Northwest Lodge (☎ 524 8108) is an upmarket B&B 10km south of Collingwood; doubles are $120 with en suite. In Pakawau, the Old School House Café (☎ 524 8457) has a small pool, a couple of very good units for $70 a double, and cabins.

The friendly Inn-let (☎ 524 8040) is on the way to Pakawau, about 10km from Collingwood. Jonathan and Katie are attuned to their environment and are full of details about the surrounding area. Comfortable beds in renovated share rooms are $16 and double rooms are $40. Another fully self-contained cottage sleeping six is $90. The owners pick up from Collingwood and also arrange kayaking, caving and guided walks. Incidentally, Opua means 'terrace', so sit on theirs above the river of that name, have a BBQ and relax in native bush surroundings.

Places to Eat

The Collingwood Cafe, a dairy and cafe, is open from 7.30 am to 8 or 9 pm daily. The bistro at the tavern opposite the post office serves passable food, but meals may finish early.

About halfway between Takaka (15km) and Collingwood is a new (modelled on a turn-of-the-century) alehouse, the Mussel Inn. Good seafood, steak and salad meals are reasonably priced. The visitor centre at Puponga has great views of Farewell Spit but average food.

The Old School House Café in Pakawau is the best restaurant in the area. The building's decor matches its former calling and scallops and other local seafood are featured on the menu (mains around $20).

Getting There & Away

Bayways Book-a-Bus (☎ 0800 259 864) has a daily bus service from Collingwood to Takaka and Nelson.

Abel Tasman National Coachlines (☎ 528 8850) has daily services from Nelson to Motueka, Takaka and Collingwood (and the Heaphy in summer).

The West Coast

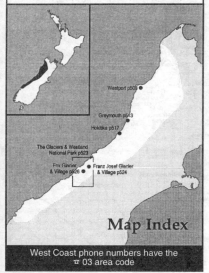

Westport p505
Greymouth p513
Hokitika p517
The Glaciers & Westland National Park p523
Fox Glacier & Village p526
Franz Josef Glacier & Village p524

Map Index

West Coast phone numbers have the ☎ 03 area code

The West Coast (Westland) is a rugged land of wild, pebbled and rocky beaches, and bush-clad hills sweeping up to towering icy peaks. Often the narrow coastal strip is *pakihi* (dried-up) swamp or second-class farmland, and the region is studded with jewel-like lakes mirroring the peaks above.

Pioneers hacked back the coastal bush half-successfully. Patches of native forest have escaped the axe and fire, and the rest of the scrubby farming land is always in danger of being reclaimed. The hills are still largely untamed, and scattered throughout the thick bush and by the rivers is the rusted debris of 100 years of exploitative industry – gold and coal mining, and timber milling.

The two glaciers, Fox and Franz Josef, are the major drawcards, but the stretch from Karamea to Jackson Bay is worth exploring.

The road hugs the coastline most of the way from Westport in the north to Hokitika, then runs inland until it finally joins the coast again between Knights Point and Haast, before turning east and heading over the Haast Pass. Near the coast, but a long way by road, are Mts Cook and Tasman.

Most visit the region in summer, especially from December to January. From May to September the days can often be warm and clear, with views of snow-capped peaks, no crowds and off-peak accommodation rates. The area is worth a visit any time of year.

Westland could aptly be called 'Wetland'. Average annual rainfall is around 5m (200 inches). This said, the West Coast receives as many sunshine hours as the Christchurch region. An early and poetically inspired visitor to Hokitika summed up the West Coast weather situation pretty well:

It rained and rained and rained
The average fall was well maintained
And when the tracks were simply bogs
It started raining cats and dogs
After a drought of half an hour
We had a most refreshing shower
And then the most curious thing of all
A gentle rain began to fall
Next day also was fairly dry
Save for a deluge from the sky
Which wetted the party to the skin
And after that the rain set in

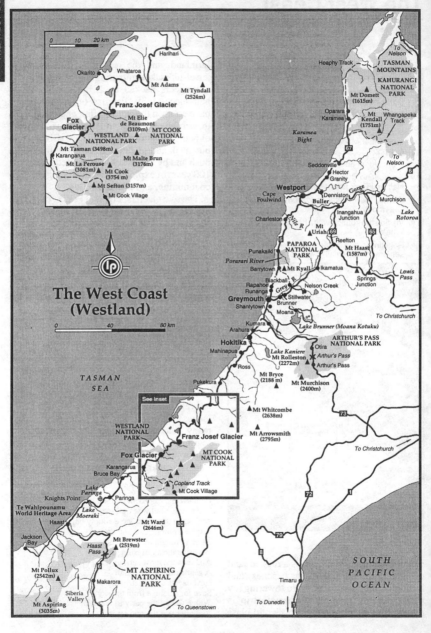

The West Coast (Westland)

BULLER GORGE AREA

The road across from Nelson to the coast via the Buller Gorge is interesting and scenic. The Buller area is still scarred from the 1929 Murchison and 1968 Inangahua earthquakes. From Inangahua Junction you can head through the lower Buller Gorge to the coast, or go on to Greymouth via Reefton on the inland route. The coastal route has more to offer but is longer.

Murchison

Murchison is on the Buller Gorge Heritage Highway, some 125km south of Nelson. With a population of 600, 'Murch' is an important service centre for the surrounding region and the starting point for a number of adventure activities. It is actually in the Nelson region but included here as it is very much the gateway to the West Coast if you are coming from the north.

The Murchison information centre (☎ 523 9350) on Waller St is open daily from 10 am to 5 pm, from 1 October to 30 April. The small **museum**, open from 10 am to 4 pm daily, has interesting exhibits on the 1929 earthquake.

Activities Activities in the Murchison area including fishing, rafting, kayaking, tramping, gold panning, boating, mountain biking, caving and rock climbing.

Hundreds of kayakers descend on Murchison in summer to **kayak** the Buller and its tributaries, which have easy road access. The New Zealand Kayak School (☎ 523 9611) rents out kayaks for $25, including gear, and offers four-day courses.

Go West Rafting (☎ 523 9161), based at the Riverview Motor Camp, offers **whitewater rafting** options. These include a Fun Run on the Gowan and Buller (two to three hours for $75). Buller Experience (☎ 523 9696) offers 20-minute **jet-boating** trips on the Matakitaki, Mangles and Buller rivers for $40 or $120 for two adults and three kids.

Mountain-bike trails dot the area and popular rides include the west bank of the Matakitaki (16km return) and the Upper Matakitaki (76km return). The Tutaki Valley

has good **horse trekking** and Tiraumea Horse Treks (☎ 523 9341) runs trips from one hour to a full day. The **fishing** in the scenic rivers nearby is rightly said to be 'unbelievable', but a guided day out to hook a trout is not cheap – from $500 up. The information centre lists guides.

Gold panning in Lyell Creek, the Buller River and the Howard Valley is popular. The information centre rents out pans and shovels for $5, with a $20 bond.

Places to Stay *Riverview Holiday Park* (☎ 523 9591), 2km from town on the road to Nelson, is right by the river and has tent sites at $6/10 for one/two people, powered sites at $8/12 and well-kept cabins at $14/25. This is also a YHA associate hostel – beds are in the cabins. Self-contained tourist flats are $50 and motel units $65. Showers cost $2 because the park is right next to the domain, where camping is free and the many kayakers in summer sneak in and use the facilities.

The well-run *Kiwi Park Motels & Motor Camp* (☎ 523 9248), 170 Fairfax St, has tent/powered sites at $15/16 for two and an old backpackers lodge costing $15 per person. Tourist cabins are $40 a double, flats $50 and excellent motel units $80 (less in the low season).

The basic *Lions Club Aorangi Hall Hostel* (☎ 523 9415 or 523 9103) is at the end of Hampden St next to the sportsground. It charges $10 per person and is only open from 1 December to the end of February, when it's managed by a retired American professor, who makes it interesting.

The *Commercial Hotel* (☎ 523 9490) on the main street has shabby backpackers rooms for $15 per person, but the regular pub rooms for only $18/36 a single/double are much better. The *Hampden Hotel* (☎ 523 9008), opposite on Fairfax St, charges $25/40.

Motels include the *Murchison* (☎ 523 9026) and the *Mataki* (☎ 523 9088); expect to pay from $65 for two.

Places to Eat There are two of the ubiquitous tearooms in town – *Collins* and the *Murchison*. The *Hampden* and *Commercial* serve pub meals such as steak and fish for about $15 a main. The pleasant *Beechwoods* cafe, on the southern edge of town, is open from 6 am until about 11 pm. A feast at the luxury *Moonlight Lodge*, 32km south of Murchison on SH65, will set you back about $50 a head.

Getting There & Away A number of bus services pass through Murchison on the way to the West Coast, Nelson, St Arnaud, Blenheim and Picton. These include Nelson Lakes Transport, White Star, Sounds to Coast and InterCity. These buses stop either at Collins Tearooms on Fairfax St or outside Beechwoods on SH6.

Buller Gorge
Travelling from Murchison to Westport takes about 1½ hours. To get on to the Buller Gorge road (SH6) you turn off at Sullivan's Bridge at the junction with SH65 to Maruia Springs and the Lewis Pass. Just past the bridge, look up the valley to the left to see **Old Man Mountain**. With some imagination you see a pot-bellied supine fellow – the cloud above is smoke from his hidden pipe. Further on is a long swingbridge. The homestay-style *Brian's Backpackers* (☎ 523 9453) is on SH65, just 200m from the junction with SH6. A bed costs $13 in the small farmhouse or camping is $9.

The road winds through the gorge to Inangahua Junction. This was the epicentre of a major earthquake in 1968 – over seven on the Richter scale. The scarred hillsides still bear testimony to the power of nature. There's a DOC camping ground on SH6 at Lyell, Upper Buller Gorge, 10km north of Inangahua. Another option for cyclists is *Inwood Farm Backpackers* (☎ 789 0205) on Inwoods Road at Inangahua Junction where a bed costs $12 or the twin room is $26.

The Buller Gorge itself is dark and forbidding, especially on a murky day – primeval ferns and cabbage trees cling to steep cliffs, and toi toi flanks the road between gorge and river. A drive through the gorge's scenic reserve is picturesque in any weather.

At **Hawks Crag** the road has been literally hacked out of the rock. Buses pass through it very slowly as the rock overhang comes extremely close to the top of the vehicle. It is named not after the birds but a goldminer, Robert Hawks, who prospected in the area.

WESTPORT
Westport, the major town at the northern end of the West Coast, has a population of 4250 and is developing a reputation for outdoor activities. Its prosperity is based on coal mining although the mining activity takes place some distance from town. Westport is 5km north from the turn-off to Greymouth on the main coast road, SH6. The SH67 passes through Westport and ends beyond Karamea at the start of the Heaphy Track.

Information
The Westport Visitor Information Centre (☎ 789 6658; fax 789 6668) is on Brougham St, a couple of doors off Palmerston St. It's open from 9 am to 7 pm daily in summer, and from 9 am to 5 pm on weekdays and 10 am to 3 pm on weekends in winter. It has information on the seal colony and the many tracks and walkways in the area. It also operates the laundrette on Brougham St. The DOC office (☎ 789 7742) on Russell St is open from 9 am to 5 pm on weekdays. The AA agency (☎ 789 8002) is on Marine Parade, Carters Beach. The post office is on the corner of Brougham and Palmerston Sts.

Seal Colony & Cape Foulwind
Depending on the time of year, anything from 20 to over 100 seals may be down on the rocks at the Tauranga Bay seal colony, 12km from Westport. Pups are born from late November to early December and for about a month afterwards the mothers stay on the rocks to tend the young before setting off to sea on feeding forays. Don't venture past the marked areas, as the cliffs can be dangerous.

The 90-minute one-way **Cape Foulwind Walkway** extends along the coast 4km past the seal colony to Cape Foulwind, passing a replica of Abel Tasman's astrolabe (a navigational aid) and a lighthouse site. The information centre has a good brochure. The

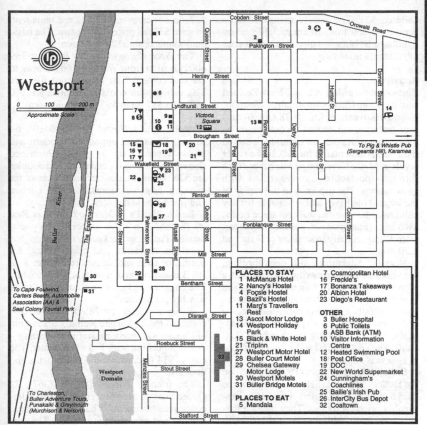

Westport

0   100   200 m
Approximate Scale

PLACES TO STAY
1 McManus Hotel
2 Nancy's Hostel
4 Focsle Hostel
9 Bazil's Hostel
11 Marg's Travellers
   Rest
13 Ascot Motor Lodge
14 Westport Holiday
   Park
15 Black & White Hotel
21 Tripinn
27 Westport Motor Hotel
28 Buller Court Motel
29 Chelsea Gateway
   Motor Lodge
30 Westport Motels
31 Buller Bridge Motels

PLACES TO EAT
5 Mandala

7 Cosmopolitan Hotel
16 Freckle's
17 Bonanza Takeaways
20 Albion Hotel
23 Diego's Restaurant

OTHER
3 Buller Hospital
6 Public Toilets
8 ASB Bank (ATM)
10 Visitor Information
   Centre
12 Heated Swimming Pool
18 Post Office
19 DOC
22 New World Supermarket
24 Cunningham's
   Coachlines
25 Bailie's Irish Pub
26 InterCity Bus Depot
32 Coaltown

Maori knew the cape as Tauranga, meaning 'a sheltered anchorage or landing place'. The first European to reach the cape was Abel Tasman, who sighted it in December 1642 and named it Glyphaygen Hock (Rocky Point). When Captain Cook anchored in March 1770 his ship, the *Endeavour*, was rocked by a furious storm, so he gave it the apt name it retains today.

From the Tauranga Bay car park (where pukekos and wekas abound) it is a five-minute walk to the seal colony. Karaka Tours (☎ 789 5080) runs two-hour tours to the seal colony for $15 per person (minimum two),

including a scenic drive. They can also drop you off at the seal colony and pick you up at the other end of the walkway for $20 per person.

Coaltown

This well laid-out museum on Queen St reconstructs aspects of coal-mining life, including a walk through a simulated mine complete with authentic sound effects. There is also a one-hour film, coal and gold-mining artefacts, and some excellent photographic exhibits. It's open from 9 am to 4.30 pm daily (with extended hours over Christmas; $6,

THE WEST COAST

children \$3). The locally owned Miner's Brewery (open from 10 am to 5.30 pm) on Lyndhurst St is a good place to quench your thirst after a mine tour.

Activities

Black-water rafting is a real New Zealand activity. From Charleston, south of Westport, Norwest Adventures Ltd (☎ 789 6686) runs trips underground into what could easily be the reaches of Xanadu on Coleridge's sacred river (the Nile actually) for \$70. In the lower levels of Metro Cave you paddle rubber rafts through spectacular caverns filled with glow-worms. The trip ends in the rapids of the larger Nile River and is suitable for any child over 10 who can walk for three hours. Two trips (maximum 36 passengers) depart from Westport daily in summer at 9 am and 2.30 pm.

Norwest Adventures also does thrilling, four-hour **adventure caving**, starting with a 30m abseil into the Te Tahi *tomo* (hole). You then worm your way through rock squeezes and waterfalls, exploring prehistoric fossils and formations as you go (stalactites, stalagmites, straws, columns and a whale skeleton). The cost is \$150 and a good standard of fitness is required.

Buller Adventure Tours (☎ 789 7286) on the Buller Gorge Rd (SH6), 4km east of the Greymouth turn-off, offers a variety of reasonably priced activities. They include particularly good **white-water rafting** with Grade IV trips on the Buller (\$70 half-day) and Mokihinui (\$295 two days), and Grade V rapids on the Karamea (\$195 one day). Other activities include **jet-boating** on the Buller River (\$45/70 for one/two hours) and **horse trekking**.

The information centre has brochures on good **bush walks** in the region, many of which pass through old gold and coal-mining areas.

Places to Stay

Camping & Cabins The *Westport Holiday Park* (☎ 789 7043) is on Domett St, only 1km from the post office. Tent/powered sites are \$16/18, chalets (most with fridge) are

\$27, on-site caravans are \$32 and units with en suite \$37; all prices are for two. The basic bunkrooms costs \$12 per person.

The *Seal Colony Tourist Park* (☎ 789 8002) is 6km from Westport, on the way to the seal colony. Tent or powered sites are \$20, cabins with cooking facilities are \$40 and units \$87 up to \$93 (three bedroom).

Hostels *Bazil's Hostel* (☎ 789 6410), 54 Russell St, is well appointed, modern and highly regarded by its guests. Furnished shared rooms are \$16, and twins and doubles are \$36. There is a sheltered area of lawn for relaxing, new bathrooms, a stylish kitchen and free herbs and spices.

Beside Bazil's is *Marg's Travellers Rest* (☎ 789 8627), a YHA associate and guest-house. The new backpackers section has excellent standards and costs \$16.50 for dorms, or twin and double rooms are \$40. B&B is also offered in units at \$68 a double. The complex includes a restaurant with reasonably priced meals.

Nancy's Hostel (☎ 789 6565) on the corner of Pakington and Romilly Sts is a big old house with predominant lead-lighting – down at heel but with lots of character. The cost is \$14 in dorms and \$32 for twins and doubles.

The friendly *TripInn* (☎ 789 7367), 72 Queen St, is an even bigger old house undergoing refurbishment. It has a new kitchen, laundry and new units at the side. The cost in dorms (from four to 14 beds) is \$15, and twins and doubles are \$34.

The *Foçsle Hostel* (☎ 789 6226), 48 Cobden St, is in a big old, institutional building with zero atmosphere but lots of single rooms for \$20.

Motels & Hotels *Westport Motels* (☎ 789 7575), 32 the Esplanade, has units at \$58/65 for singles/doubles; at this price, they are as good as anywhere. The *Westport Motor Hotel* (☎ 789 7889) at 207 Palmerston St has doubles from \$69 to \$85 and a restaurant; the *Buller Bridge* (☎ 789 7519) on the Esplanade – recommended by 'Coasters' – has singles/doubles for \$67.50/75; the *Buller*

Court (☎ 789 7979) at 235 Palmerston St charges from $70 for two; the *Ascot* (☎ 789 7832), 74 Romilly St, charges $75 to $90 for two; and the new *Chelsea Gateway* (☎ 789 6835) on the corner of Palmerston and Bentham Sts is at the top of the heap and charges $80 to $140 with spa bath.

Palmerston St has the *McManus Hotel* (☎ 789 6304), where singles/doubles cost $25/45 and, opposite the post office, the *Black & White Hotel* (☎ 789 7959), which charges $25/50.

Places to Eat

Palmerston St is crammed with takeaways and sandwich shops, including *Bonanza Takeaways*, near the Wakefield St corner, which also has tables. *Freckle's* on Palmerston St is a good little cafe serving espresso, muffins and homemade food. Standard pub food is available in the evenings from Thursday to Sunday at the *McManus Hotel* and the *Pig & Whistle*, while the *Black & White* and *Cosmopolitan* have better restaurants.

The party scene centres on *Bailie's Irish Pub* on Palmerston St, with live Irish music on Friday night, Guinness and very reasonable prices for BBQ meals, huge nachos and other snacks. This is where most travellers will gravitate to after bush walks or rafting trips.

The *Mandala* on Palmerston St is a standard restaurant, while *Diego's* at 18 Wakefield St is the town's culinary oasis with an innovative menu. In summer it is open daily from 6 pm until late.

At Tauranga Bay, around the bay from the seal colony, the stylish *Bay House Cafe* has great food and ocean views. The á la carte menu is interesting (mains are around $20) and the Wednesday pasta and pizza night really packs them in. It's also open for coffee, cake and light meals during the day after seeing the seals.

Getting There & Around

Air New Zealand Link (☎ 789 7209) has daily direct flights to Wellington. A taxi to the airport costs around $15.

InterCity (☎ 789 7819) runs daily between Nelson and the glaciers via Westport, and other buses make return trips between Westport and Greymouth (two hours) with a rest stop at the Punakaiki every day. InterCity buses leave from Craddock's Service Station on Palmerston St.

White Star, based at the Cunningham depot, has a Nelson-Westport-Christchurch service (via Springs Junction). This bus leaves for Springs Junction at 10.05 am every day except Saturday; the cost to Christchurch is $33, to Nelson $27.

East-West Express has a shuttle to Christchurch ($39) at 8 am from the InterCity depot. The shuttle leaves from the Christchurch station at 1.30 pm and returns to Westport at 6.30 pm.

Heading north to Karamea for the Heaphy Track, Cunningham's buses make the return trip from Monday to Friday, leaving Karamea in the morning and returning from Westport in the afternoon at 3.10 pm ($15).

For getting around Westport, you can hire bicycles from Beckers Cycles & Sports and Anderson Sports on Palmerston St, and also from Bazil's and other hostels.

WESTPORT TO KARAMEA

This trip north along SH67 passes through a number of interesting towns. The first reached is Waimangaroa and the turn-off to **Denniston**. This town was once the largest producer of coal in NZ and can be reached by the Denniston Walkway. The track follows the original path to the town and has great views of the Denniston Incline. In its day this was a great engineering feat, as empty coal trucks were hauled back up the incline by the weight of the descending loaded trucks, sometimes at a gradient of one in one. Four kilometres north of Waimangaroa is the **Britannia Track**, a six-hour return walk to the Britannia battery and other remnants of the gold-mining era.

At Granity, head uphill for 5km to the ghost towns of Millerton and Stockton. The **Millerton Incline Walk** is 40 minutes return and takes in the old railway, a tunnel and an old dam. Just near Granity is another interesting walk at **Charming Creek**. This all-weather, five-hour return track follows an old coal line through the picturesque Ngakawau River Gorge. You can also walk the track all the way to **Seddonville**, a small town surrounded by bush covered hills on the Mohikinui River. Accommodation is at the *Motor Camp* (☎ 782 1816) or *Motor Hotel* (☎ 782 1828).

Gentle Annie Beach, 3km along the gravel De Manchester Rd from the highway, has a charming little restaurant, the *Cowshed Cafe* (☎ 782 1826), at the mouth of the Mohikinui. Muffins, salads and steaks are specialities. It's NZ's only cowshed restaurant – 'No shit!'. It also has a rustic backpackers made of hand-hewn timbers for $15 per person, and a three-bedroom bach near the beach costing $45 per night for one, then $15 per extra adult. Big Raft Outdoor Activities (☎ 782 1866) rents out canoes and has guided canoe trips for $35.

Between Mohikinui and Little Wanganui you pass over the **Karamea Bluff**, a slow but magnificent scenic drive through rata and matai forest with views of the Tasman Sea below.

KARAMEA

From Westport, SH67 continues 100km north to Karamea, an 'end of the road' town near the Heaphy and the Wangapeka tracks. Information is available at the Karamea information centre (☎ /fax 782 6652), the DOC office (☎ 782 6852) or the Last Resort (☎ 782 6617).

Oparara Basin & Honeycomb Caves

North of Karamea are spectacular limestone arch formations and the unique Honeycomb Caves, ancient home to the moa. Of equal interest is the area's primitive rainforest growing over the karst landscape. Moss-laden trees droop over the tannin-coloured Oparara River, illuminated by light filtering through the dense forest canopy.

Halfway along the road to the start of the Heaphy Track, turn off and go 15km past the sawmill along a rough road to the arches. From the road it is an easy 20-minute walk to the huge Oparara Arch spanning the

Oparara River. The smaller but equally beautiful Moria Gate is a harder 40-minute walk along a muddy track that is not always easy to follow – take care not to get lost in the dense forest. Another arch, the Honeycomb, can only be reached by canoe.

Other interesting formations are the Mirror Tarn, and the Crazy Paving and Box Canyon Caves at the end of the road. Beyond is the magnificent Honeycomb Caves, with bones of moa and other extinct species. See the bones of three of the five moa species –

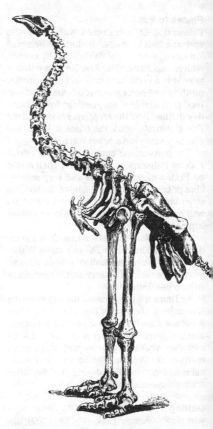

Bone remains of the now-extinct moa show the bird grew to over 3m tall.

the slender *Megalapteryx didinus*, small *Pachyornis elephantopus* and giant *Dinornis giganteus*. This is also the cave where bones of the now-extinct giant Haast eagle, the world's largest, were discovered. This eagle, with a 3 to 4m wingspan, preyed on the moa.

Also here is the cave-dwelling spider, *gradungula*, unique to this area; it has a body length of 2.5cm and leg span of 10cm. If you're lucky you will also see the carnivorous snail (*Powelliphanta hochstetteri*), favourite food of the weka.

Access to the cave is restricted and it can only be visited on a tour. The Last Resort organises 5½-hour tours to the cave and other features for $60 (minimum four people). Bus only to the Oparara Basin is $20. A full-day trip including canoeing to the Honeycomb Arch is $160.

Activities

The Karamea River offers good swimming, fishing and canoeing. The Wanganui, Oparara and Kohaihai rivers also have good swimming holes. Tidal lagoons, 1km north and 3km south of Karamea, are sheltered and good for swimming at high tide, otherwise swimming in the sea is dangerous. The only drawback at the beautiful beaches around Karamea is the millions of sandflies. A local saying is that 'sandflies work in pairs – one pulls back the sheets, while the other eats you alive'.

Many good day **walks** are found in this area, including the five-hour Fenian Track into Adams Flat, the eight-hour return trek to 1084m Mt Stormy and the walk to Lake Hanlon. The first leg of the Wangapeka Track also makes a good day walk.

Those not keen on walking the whole **Heaphy Track** can walk all or part-way to the Heaphy Hut and return. This takes in the walk along the beach, considered by many to be the best part. Scotts Beach is 1½ hours return and passes beautiful nikau palm groves. The separate Nikau Grove loop at the start of the track takes half an hour. For more information on the Heaphy and Wangapeka tracks, see the Kahurangi National Park

section in the Marlborough & Nelson chapter.

Places to Stay & Eat

The *Karamea Holiday Park* (☎ 782 6758) has sites for $16, cabins for $27 and units for $50; all prices are for two. At Kohaihai, 15km north of Karamea, is a DOC camping ground.

The *Last Resort* (☎ 782 6617) is a beautiful complex with rooms connected by walkways to the impressive central building. The buildings have sod roofs and feature massive beams of local timbers – eco-architecture at its best. Modern twin and share rooms are simple but good value at $15 per person, or lodge rooms are $50 a double with linen. Other units with en suite are $75 and cottages are $120. The complex has a licensed restaurant and a bar serving cheaper meals.

The old and fading *Township Motels* (☎ 782 6838) on Wharf Rd has single/double units at $40/50, or the self-contained cabins at $15 per person are good value.

The *Karamea Village Hotel* (☎ 782 6800) has new motel units for $65 and $75, as well as a backpackers house across the road where single rooms are $15 ($25 with linen) or doubles with linen are $40.

The hotel has excellent food; a whitebait patty with chips is about $5. Otherwise the *Karamea Tearooms* has standard fare to take away or eat in.

Getting There & Away

A Cunningham's bus (☎ 789 7717) departs from Karamea at 8.45 am to Westport ($15; 1½ hours). The bus to Karamea departs from Cunningham's depot on Palmerston St at 3.10 pm.

The ends of the Heaphy and Wangapeka tracks have phones to arrange transport out to Karamea. The Last Resort and Karamea Motors (☎ 782 6757) run on demand for $25. Cheaper, scheduled summer services may be offered. Ring the Karamea information centre for the latest operators. Karaka Tours (☎ 789 6658) will go from Westport to the Heaphy for $50 for one person, then $25 for each additional person. It is also possible to fly from Karamea to Takaka and then walk back.

WESTPORT TO PUNAKAIKI

This is an interesting stretch of road. Nowadays the towns along the way are extremely small – 10 or so inhabitants. It was a different story 130 years ago, when the gold rush was in full swing. **Charleston** was a booming town with shanties all along the pack route and gold-diggers moving out to their claims on the Nile River. Today, the raucous pubs are all closed but you can find sanctuary in the *Charleston Motel* (☎ 728 7599) or *Motor Camp* (☎ 728 6773) – units cost $60 to $65 for two. Norwest Adventures has an office next to the pub and runs its 'Underworld' black-water rafting and tomo exploring trips from here. **Constant Bay**, once the busy port for the mining settlement, is a pleasant picnic area nearby.

The coast from Fox River to Runanga is rugged and the road will remind west-coast Americans of California's Big Sur – with similarly spectacular views. Woodpecker Bay, Tiromoana, Punakaiki, Barrytown, 14-mile, Motukiekie, 10-mile, Nine-mile and Seven-mile are all beaches sculpted by the relentless fury of the Roaring Forties.

Punakaiki & Paparoa National Park

Almost midway between Westport and Greymouth, the small settlement of Punakaiki and the Paparoa National Park have the finest coastal scenery on the West Coast and a good beach. Pressure for many years resulted in this area being declared a national park in December 1987, when the 30,000-hectare Paparoa National Park became NZ's 12th national park.

Punakaiki is centred around the well-known **Pancake Rocks & Blowholes**. These limestone rocks at Dolomite Point have formed into what looks like stacks of pancakes, through a weathering process known as stylobedding. When a good tide is running, the water surges into caverns below the rocks and squirts out in impressive geyser-like blowholes. A 15-minute loop walk from the road goes around the rocks

and blowholes. It's best to go at high or king tide, when the blowholes perform. Heed the warning signs to keep on the track.

In addition to the rocks at Punakaiki, the park has many other natural attractions: mountains (the Paparoa Range), rivers, wilderness areas, limestone formations including cliffs and caves, diverse vegetation, and a Westland black petrel colony – the only nesting area of this rare sea bird.

Interesting walks in the park include the 30km **Inland Pack Track**. This is a two-day track along a route established by miners around 1867 to circumvent the more rugged coastal walk. Also notable is the **Croesus Track**, a full day or two-day tramp over the Paparoa Range from Blackball to Barrytown, passing through historic gold-mining areas. There are also many shorter river and coastal walks. If you're planning on walking, register your intentions at the park's visitor centre. Many of the tracks were closed after the Cave Creek tragedy in 1995, when several visitors were killed after a viewing platform collapsed, and the status of tracks is still under review; check at the park's visitor centre.

The Punakaiki Visitor Centre (☎ 731 1895; fax 731 1888) next to the highway is open from 8.30 am to 6 pm daily in summer (sometimes later) and 9 am to 4 pm in winter. It has interesting displays on the park, pamphlets and maps on all the park's walks and attractions, and can supply information on tides and current conditions throughout the park. Many of the inland walks are subject to river flooding and other conditions, so check before setting out.

Organised Tours Paparoa Nature Tours (☎ 731 1826) has tours to the world's only breeding colony of the Westland black petrel (*Procellaria westlandica*), the largest burrowing petrel. Tours commence 30 minutes before sunset and cost $15 per person. It also arranges other tours.

Kiwa Sea Adventures (☎ 731 1893) combines natural history and geology with an adrenalin-inducing boat ride. Hector's dolphins, seals and spotted shags may be seen.

A two-hour trip to Seal Island is $85 (children $45).

Paparoa Horse Treks (☎ 731 1839) organises horse trekking at $50 for two hours. Punakaiki Canoe Hire (☎ 731 1870) is based near the bridge over the Pororari River and hires out canoes from $10 for one hour up to $40 all day.

Places to Stay & Eat Tiny Punakaiki is a popular destination with more accommodation being built all the time. Plans are afoot to build a huge tourist complex and tavern (bye-bye paradise?).

Punakaiki Camping Ground (☎ 731 1894) next to the beach has tent/powered sites at $17/20, cabins from $28 to $33 (prices are for two) and a five-bed bunkroom at $12 per person. *Punakaiki Cottages* (☎ 731 1008) has studio and family units from $85 and $95 for two.

Te Nikau Retreat (☎ 731 1111) is a magnificent place, replete with 'bush' character in its thick forest setting. The cost is $15 in dorms and $36 for twin and double rooms. There is a sleepout, the *Tui*, which is $50 per couple. Te Nikau is 3km north of Punakaiki on the seaward side of the road, 200m past the entry to the Truman Track. Follow the rough no-exit drive for 450m.

The comfortable *Punakaiki Beach Hostel* (☎ 731 1852) on Webb Terrace is in a converted motel near the village, 1km from the visitor centre and only a stone's throw from the beach. A shared room is $16 per person and singles and doubles are $37. A separate house with three doubles and two bunkrooms can be rented for $150 or a double room with linen costs $40.

Hydrangea Cottage (☎ 731 1839) is a self-contained cottage backed by rainforest and overlooking pancake rocks. It costs $80 a double. *Punakaiki Cottage Motels* (☎ 731 1008) is near the beach and well-appointed units cost $100 (high season). *Mamakau Lodge* (☎ 731 1853) near Te Nikau has doubles for $60 and $70.

The *Pancake Tearooms*, opposite the Pancake Rocks, are open year-round from 9 am. Just along, the pleasant *Nikau Palms*

Cafe, open from 9 am to 5 pm, serves natural food.

Getting There & Away InterCity buses between Westport and Greymouth stop at Punakaiki every day. Kea West Coast Tours (☎ 768 9292) has an 18-seater bus which goes from Greymouth to Punakaiki for $30 per person return.

THE COAST ROAD

The coast road from Punakaiki to Greymouth is scenic. There are white-capped breakers and rugged rocks out at sea and the steep, bush-clad Paparoa Ranges force you to drive almost on the precipice. If you're looking for solitude, you'll find a number of accommodation possibilities along this coastline.

At **Barrytown**, 16km south of Punakaiki, the *All Nations (Barrytown) Tavern* (☎ 731 1812) has doubles for $50 and a bunkroom for $15 per person. There's a kitchen for guests, or takeaways and bistro meals. It's a good option at the end of the Croesus Track. A couple of kilometres south of the tavern and off the main road, the *Hexagon* (☎ 731 1827) is just that – a hexagonal building where for $12 ($15 with linen) you get a mattress on the floor. It's quite basic but in a beautiful setting and very relaxing.

The township of **Runanga**, about 7km north of Greymouth, is the archetypal mining village. It is not far from Rapahoe (Seven-Mile) Beach and there is a 90-minute return walk to nearby Coal Creek falls.

The windswept *Rapahoe Hotel* (☎ 762 7701) is 2km north of Runanga at the northern terminus of the Point Elizabeth Track. It's a good for a drink at tables outside fronting the driftwood-covered beach, or basic pub rooms are $28/38. Rapahoe also has the *Rapahoe Motor Camp* (☎ 762 7337).

THE GREY VALLEY

From Murchison, an alternative route to the West Coast is to turn off at Inangahua Junction and travel inland via Reefton in the Inangahua Valley, then over the mountains into the Grey Valley. Despite the best efforts

Whitebait

Whitebait is a translucent, elongated small fish, which is the imago (immature) stage of the river smelt. They swarm up the West Coast rivers in dense schools and are caught in set seine-net traps or large, round scoop nets. Many an argument has been had along a riverbank or near a river mouth about the best rock to position yourself on to catch the biggest haul.

The season has been limited in recent years in an attempt to allow the declining stocks to breed. Usually it is September to mid-November, but may vary from year to year. Cooked in batter, these small fish are delicious and highly prized by locals.

One of the West Coast's doyennes of culinary expertise provided this perfect recipe for whitebait patties:

Take a pint of whitebait (about half a litre – yes, the fish are measured as a liquid rather than a solid, as they used to be loaded into glass pint milk bottles for sale) and pour it into a bowl. For the batter take one egg, about three tablespoons of flour, a pinch of salt and a little milk to make a smooth paste. Mix this and then pour over the whitebait; cook in smoking hot fat until golden brown and serve straight away with mint sauce and hot potato chips. Pickled onions are a fine accompaniment. ■

of a century of plunderers, abundant rainfall has fuelled regenerating bush on the green-cloaked hills and the paddocks have fast become overgrown. The small towns provide a reminder of those futile attempts to tame the land.

Reefton

Reefton (population 1050) is a pleasant little town in the heart of great walking country. Reefton's name comes from the gold-bearing quartz reefs in the region. As early as 1888, Reefton had its own electricity supply and street lighting, beating all other towns in NZ. Two old buildings worth exploring are the **School of Mines** and **Blacks Point Museum**.

The enthusiastic and helpful Reefton Visitor Centre (☎ 732 8391; fax 732 8616), 67 Broadway, has lots of information on the many walks in the region and books coal mine tours ($25). It is open from 8.30 am to 6 pm in summer (9 am to 4 pm in winter). DOC is in the same building. The visitor

centre houses an interesting re-creation of the Quartzopolis Mine.

The surrounding area has many fine **walks** and great possibilities for mountain biking on the Big River Track. The walks include short ones around town such as the Powerhouse Walk, Reefton Walkway and the historic Reefton Walk. The Blacks Point Walk (two to three hours) goes to abandoned coal mines. The Energetic Mine (one hour) is the closest.

There is a wealth of walking in **Victoria Forest Park**, the largest forest park in the country. The two-day Big River and three-day Kirwans, Blue Grey River and Robinson Valley tracks are all exciting possibilities. Reefton is close to the Lewis Pass and more excellent walking tracks (and superb trout fishing along the way).

Places to Stay & Eat The *Reefton Domain Camp* (☎ 732 8477) on Main St has tent/powered sites for $10/14 and cabins at $30 for two. The DOC camping ground is nearby at Slab Hut Creek, on SH7, 7km south-west of Reefton.

The cute *Reef Cottage* (☎ 732 844) on Broadway has B&B singles/doubles from $30/55 and the *Quartz Lodge* (☎ 732 8383) on the corner of Shiel and Sinnamon Sts has backpackers B&B for $20 in addition to regular rooms for $35/70. *Dawsons Hotel* (☎ 732 8406), 74 Broadway, has motel units for $50 and *Reefton Motels* (☎ 732 8574), 11 Smith St, charges the same.

Broadway has a proliferation of take-aways and tearooms, *CCs* for better cafe fare and the *Electric Light Cafe* in Dawsons. The *Al Fresco* on Broadway is, as its name suggests, an outdoor eatery with à la carte and takeaway pizzas.

Getting There & Away White Star operates a Westport-Springs Junction-Christchurch bus service and East West Express runs a Christchurch to Westport service – both pass through Reefton. The Sounds to Coast Shuttle (Picton to Greymouth) passes through Reefton on Monday and Friday (and Wednesday in summer).

SH7 to Greymouth
At Hukarere, 21km south of Reefton, turn east to visit **Waiuta**, now a ghost town but once the focus of a rich gold mine. Get the excellent DOC pamphlet *Waiuta: Victoria Forest Park*. The drive through beech forest to Waiuta is scenic and the views from the ghost town are well worth the time spent travelling there; watch out for cars coming in the other direction on the narrow dirt road. The *Waiuta Lodge* is a 30-bunk lodge – book at the Reefton Visitor Centre.

Further south at **Ikamatua**, the *Ikamuka Hotel* (☎ 732 3555) has a host of accommodation – bunkroom, camp sites and hotel rooms – from $12.50 to $40 per person. It is 50km from Greymouth, a world away from anywhere. There's no better introduction to the hidden delights of the Grey Valley.

Just before Ngahere, and 32km from Greymouth, you can turn off to beautiful **Nelson Creek** and a great swimming hole. This area is full of reminders of the gold-mining era, with a number of walks, including Callaghans which heads to a lookout. Nelson Creek has a DOC camping ground and a pub.

Blackball This town, 25km north of Greymouth on the road to Reefton, was established in 1866 as a service centre for the gold diggers. It was then a coal-mining centre from the late 1880s until 1964. The national Federation of Labour (organisation of trade unions) was born here after two cataclysmic strikes in 1908 and 1931.

The *Formerly the Blackball Hilton* (☎ 732 4705) offers hostel shared rooms for $15 and B&B rooms. Once a hotel, the building is full of character and designated a New Zealand Historic Place. The 'formerly' has been added, as this humble backpackers was such a threat to the giant hotel chain that it mounted a challenge to force a change of name. The owners are friendly and have lots of information on the history of the hotel, the town, and things to do around Blackball. Organised activities include tramping over the Croesus Track, gold panning, horse riding and a historic walk. If you ring from Greymouth they may be able to organise transport with locals.

After passing through the sawmilling town of Stillwater, the former coal-mining town of Dobson and pastoral Kaiata, you arrive at the mouth of the Grey River near the Cobden Bridge and the Cobden Gap.

Lake Brunner At Stillwater you can make a detour to Lake Brunner (also known as Moana Kotuku, 'Lake Heron'). The other points of access to the lake are near Jacksons on the Arthur's Pass road or near Kumara on the same road. If you have never baited a hook or gaffed an eel, then Lake Brunner offers you the big chance. They say the trout here die of old age. Fishing guides can be hired at Lake Brunner Lodge to show you the spots where the big ones shouldn't get away.

The **Moana Kiwi House & Conservation Park** (☎ 738 0009) has kiwi viewing and a large area devoted to indigenous bird species such as the white heron (kotuku) and other exotic animals. The nearby Velenski Walk, which starts near the camping ground, leads through a remarkable tract of native bush consisting of totara, rimu and kahikatea.

In Moana township, the *Moana Camping Ground* (☎ 337 0572) is on the shores of Lake Brunner and the *Moana Hotel* (☎ 738 0083) has pub rooms, cabins and motel units. The *Station House Cafe* on the lake shore comes recommended. Across the lake at Mitchells is the upmarket *Lake Brunner Lodge* (☎ 738 0163).

GREYMOUTH

Greymouth was once the site of a Maori *pa* and known as Mawhera, meaning 'widespread river mouth'. To the Ngai Tahu people, the Cobden Gap to the north of the town is where their ancestor Tuterakiwhanoa broke the side of Te Waaka o Aoraki (the canoe of Aoraki), releasing trapped rainwater out to sea.

Greymouth has a long gold-mining history and still has a hint of gold-town flavour today. Although it has a small population (10,200), Greymouth is the largest town on the West Coast. It's at the mouth of the Grey River – hence its name – and despite the high protective wall along the Mawhera Quay the river still manages to flood the town after periods of heavy rain. The Grey River meets the sea at the 'bar' (an accumulation of sand just below the waterline) between Cobden and Blaketown headlands.

The seascapes are phenomenal: to the south you can see a large sweep of beach culminating in the faint outlines of Mts Cook and Tasman and, to the north, the rocky promontory of Point Elizabeth and Big Rock at the far end of Cobden Beach.

Information

The Greymouth Information Centre (☎ 768 5101; fax 768 0317) is in the Art Deco Regent Theatre on the corner of Herbert and Mackay Sts. In summer it's open from 9.30 am to 5.30 pm daily and, in winter, 9 am to 5 pm on weekdays and 10 am to 4 pm on weekends. It organises free tours of Westland

Breweries. The AA office (☎ 768 4300) is at 84 Tainui St.

Things to See

The **History House Museum**, open from 10 am to 4 pm from Monday to Saturday, has a fabulous photo collection and other bric-a-brac detailing the town's history ($2, children $1).

At the **Jade Boulder Gallery** on the corner of Guinness and Tainui Sts, original jade sculpture and jewellery is crafted. The gallery is open daily from 8.30 am to 5 pm and until 9 pm in summer (it has lots of information if the information centre is closed).

Westland Breweries is the home of Monteith's Extra Bitter Brown. Free tours at 10.30 am and 1.30 pm from Monday to Thursday are much better than the ones you pay for in larger cities and you get a free beer.

Interesting nearby **mining** areas include the Brunner Mine Site, the Rewanui Mine Site near Runanga and Nelson Creek. The information centre can give directions and historical information on all these sites, and advise on good spots for gold panning.

Activities

Good walks in the region include the three-hour return **Point Elizabeth Track**, 6km north of Greymouth, which passes through the Rapahoe Range Scenic Reserve and interesting old gold-mining areas. The quay walk from Cobden Bridge towards Blaketown is well worth doing; get a copy of the informative *Great Wall of Greymouth* from the visitor centre.

Wild West Adventures (☎ 0800 223 456) has designed a subterranean adventure into the **Taniwha Cave** which is not for the fainthearted. The trip begins with a 30-minute walk through native beech forest. You then float on inflated tubes down through a subterranean glow-worm gallery, and end the trip by sliding down a 30m natural hydroslide. The cost of this 5½-hour trip is $89.

Heritage Jet Tours (☎ 0800 668 355) has exhilarating **jet-boat rides** up the Grey River to the Brunner Mine site (60 to 90

HOLGER LEUE

JEFF WILLIAMS

JEFF WILLIAMS

VICKI BEALE

A	
B	C
D	

Marlborough & Nelson
A: The mail boat makes a delivery near Picton
B: Truck home, Nelson
C: Dune formation, Farewell Spit, Nelson
D: Wainui Inlet, Golden Bay, Marlborough

HOLGER LEUE

HOLGER LEUE

The West Coast
Top: The Pancake Rocks & Blowholes, Punakaiki
Bottom: Fox Glacier, Westland National Park

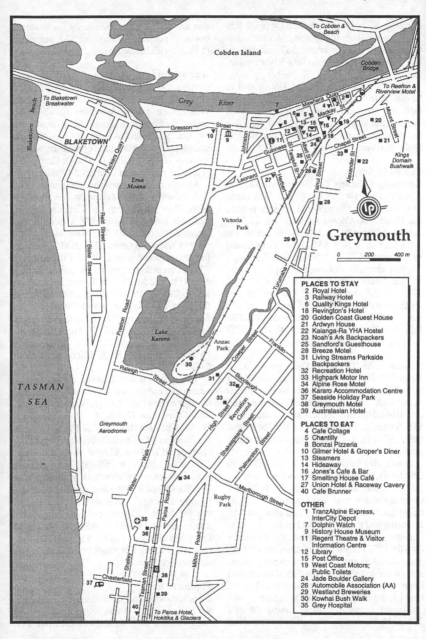

Greymouth

PLACES TO STAY
2   Royal Hotel
3   Railway Hotel
6   Quality Kings Hotel
18 Revington's Hotel
20 Golden Coast Guest House
21 Ardwyn House
22 Kaianga-Ra YHA Hostel
23 Noah's Ark Backpackers
25 Sandford's Guesthouse
28 Breeze Motel
31 Living Streams Parkside
    Backpackers
32 Recreation Hotel
33 Highpark Motor Inn
34 Alpine Rose Motel
36 Kararo Accommodation Centre
37 Seaside Holiday Park
38 Greymouth Motel
39 Australasian Hotel

PLACES TO EAT
4   Cafe Collage
5   Chantilly
8   Bonzai Pizzeria
10 Gilmer Hotel & Groper's Diner
13 Steamers
14 Hideaway
16 Jones's Cafe & Bar
17 Smelting House Café
27 Union Hotel & Raceway Cavery
40 Cafe Brunner

OTHER
1   TranzAlpine Express,
    InterCity Depot
7   Dolphin Watch
9   History House Museum
11 Regent Theatre & Visitor
    Information Centre
12 Library
15 Post Office
19 West Coast Motors;
    Public Toilets
24 Jade Boulder Gallery
26 Automobile Association (AA)
29 Westland Breweries
30 Kowhai Bush Walk
35 Grey Hospital

minutes, $50). Dolphin Watch (☎ 0800 929 991) has sea tours for spotting Hector's dolphins and seals (1½ hours, $67), as well as Lake Brunner ($90) and Grey River cruises ($50).

There's surfing at Cobden Beach and at Seven-Mile Beach in Rapahoe. Fishing safaris are especially popular activities from Greymouth and there's good fishing at Lake Brunner, and in the Arnold, Orangepuke and Hohonu rivers.

Places to Stay

Camping & Cabins The *Greymouth Seaside Holiday Park* (☎ 768 6618) is 2.5km south of the centre on Chesterfield St, right next to the beach. Tent/powered sites are $17/19, cabins are from $32 to $40, on-site caravans are $32, tourist flats $54 and self-contained motel units $72 (all prices are for two). There's also a bunkroom at $12 per person.

The *South Beach Motor Park* (☎ 762 6768) about 5km south of Greymouth has tent/powered sites at $16/18 for two, on-site vans for $25 and motel units from $75. The *Rapahoe Beach Motor Camp* (☎ 762 7025) is 11km north on the coast road.

Hostels The friendly *Kaianga-Ra YHA Hostel* (☎ 768 4951) at 15 Alexander St is a large, spacious former Marist brother's residence with four-bed dorms at $16 per person or a 10-bed dorm that used to be a chapel for $16. Twins and doubles are $36. The hostel has a BBQ area, TV and video room, and a piano.

Noah's Ark Backpackers (☎ 768 4868), 16 Chapel St, occupies a huge edifice built in 1912 as the monastery for St Patrick's Church, which was once next door. It is being tastefully renovated and charges $15 in dorms and doubles or $35 in twins.

Living Streams Parkside Backpackers (☎ 768 7272) is a large, modern hostel with good facilities and dorms at $15 per person, and twins and doubles for $35. Duvets and linen are supplied in the doubles. Use of kayaks, the dinghy and BBQs is free.

Kararo Accommodation Centre (☎ 768 7686), 16 Tasman St, is another option if the rest are full. It caters primarily for students but it is possible to stay for $12 per night ($16.50 with breakfast).

Guesthouses, Motels & Hotels The *Golden Coast Guesthouse* (☎ 768 7839) at 10 Smith St overlooking the river is good value with singles/doubles for $45/70, including breakfast. *Sandfords Guesthouse* (☎ 768 5605), 62 Albert St, has singles/doubles for $30/60 with a cooked breakfast. *Ardwyn House* (☎ 768 6107), 48 Chapel St, is a good option and charges $40/60.

Motels are numerous but expensive. The *Willowbank Pacifica Lodge* (☎ 768 5339) on SH6, 3km north from the Cobden Bridge, has two studio units at $78 a double, but larger units cost $90. The *Riverview Motel* (☎ 768 6884) on Omoto Rd, also 2km from the centre, has a pool and units from $65 to $75. Other possibilities are the central *Breeze Motel* (☎ 762 5068), 125 Tainui St, charging $80 to $95 and the *Greymouth Motel* (☎ 768 6090) at 195 High St, with units for $70 to $80. Top of the motel range is the *Highpark Motor Inn* (☎ 768 4846), 90 High St, charging $90 to $125, or the new *Alpine Rose* (☎ 768 7586), 139 High St, charges $85 to $110.

The gold-mining history shows in the number of hotels around central Greymouth, though none of them is particularly special. The *Recreation Hotel* (☎ 768 5154) at 68 High St has singles/doubles for $55/65, or the *Railway* (☎ 768 7023) on Mawhera Quay charges $17/34 or $27/54 with breakfast. *Revington's Hotel* (☎ 768 7055) on Tainui St has doubles with attached bathroom for $71.50. Queen Elizabeth II stayed here once (a long time ago) and now backpackers can too for from $20 per person. The *Quality Kings Hotel* (☎ 768 5085) on Mawhera Quay has classy rooms for $108 and classier rooms for $130. For other places, ask at the information centre.

Places to Eat

Standard cafes and sandwich places include the *Hideaway* on Albert St and the *Chantilly* sandwich bar on Mackay St on the Mall. The

Bonzai Pizzeria at 29 Mackay St is a pleasant little place with 16 varieties of pizza. The *Smelting House Café* on Mackay St is much more stylish, with good coffee and light meals in renovated surrounds.

At the Union Hotel on Herbert St, near the railway line, the *Raceway Carvery* is something of a local institution. The front is unpromising but it's quite reasonable inside. The accent is on low prices and big quantities; cuisine highlights are a definite second. Quite a few other pubs offer food, including the *Royal Hotel* on Mawhera Quay and *Ham's* at the Paroa Hotel. The Gilmer Hotel on Gresson St is home to *Groper's Diner* for excellent, inexpensive seafood. The fisherman's basket costs $15.50 and scallops, oysters, prawns and crayfish are also available. Fish meals in the bar are even cheaper.

Other good places are the *Cafe Brunner* in the Ashley Motor Inn on Tasman St, Karoro, where main meals cost about $15. *Steamers* on Mackay St near the library is in a former shipping company office. This pleasant cafe and bar has a good selection of beers.

For a fancier night out try *Cafe Collage*, 115 Mackay St. This is a BYO and quite expensive at $20 to $25 for a main course, but offers a good range of international cuisines.

Greymouth's glitterati head to *Jones's Cafe & Bar* at 37 Tainui St for fish of the day ($17), steaks ($17.50) and kebabs ($16).

Getting There & Away

Air New Zealand Link flights operate only from Hokitika, 40km from Greymouth. Greymouth Taxis (☎ 768 7078) go to Hokitika airport for $15.

InterCity buses depart from the train station (☎ 768 1435). It has daily services to Westport and Nelson, and to the glaciers.

The Coast to Coast Shuttle (☎ 0800 800 847) and Alpine Coach & Courier (☎ 762 6332) operate between Greymouth and Christchurch ($35) via Arthur's Pass ($15) and also go to Hokitika. Ko-op Shuttles (☎ 366 6633) also goes to Christchurch.

The *TranzAlpine Express* operates daily between Christchurch and Greymouth. The trip, which costs an exorbitant $74, takes about five hours and is notable for its spectacular scenery – it crosses some remarkable gorges on its climb through the Southern Alps, passing over numerous viaducts and bridges and through 19 tunnels, including the 8.5km Otira Tunnel. Between Arthur's Pass and Greymouth the road and railway line take quite different routes. For bookings contact NZ Rail (☎ 0800 802 802). If you can get it (numbers are limited), a Super Saver will cost $37 one way or backpackers discounts are available.

Getting Around

Value Rentals (☎ 762 7503) hires out cars for $65 per day inclusive of kilometres (much cheaper for long rentals). Car hire sometimes works out cheaper than some of the tours. Tracy Mann (☎ 768 0255), 25 Mackay St, and Graeme Peters Cycle & Sport (☎ 768 6559), 37 Mackay St, rent out bicycles ($25 per day), stock a full range of components and carry out repairs.

SHANTYTOWN & PAROA BEACH

Greymouth to Hokitika has great views of the wild West Coast. If you deviate from the main road to the beach you will see miles of salt spray and endless lines of driftwood.

Shantytown, 8km south of Greymouth and 3km inland from the main road, is Greymouth's most famous attraction. It recreates an 1880s West Coast town in the gold rush and is well done. It's good family entertainment and for many the prime attraction is a ride on the 1897 steam locomotive.

You can also try gold panning; there's an old fellow who'll give you pointers. Everyone is assured of coming up with at least a few flakes of gold to take away.

Shantytown is open daily from 8.30 am to 5 pm (until 7 pm in summer) and entry, including train rides and gold panning, costs $11 (children $5) or $8 without the panning.

You can't go past the *Paroa Hotel & Motel* (☎ 762 6860) for good old-fashioned West Coast hospitality. It is on the beach opposite the turn-off to Shantytown. Motel units cost $63/75 for singles/doubles and good hearty meals are available from *Ham's* restaurant (the scallops are highly recommended). It's worth staying just for an evening stroll along unspoilt Paroa Beach, 100m away.

HOKITIKA

Hokitika (population 3800), or Hoki as it is affectionately known, is 40km south of Greymouth. It was settled in the 1860s after the discovery of gold and became a busy port.

Hokitika is now a major centre for the working of greenstone but the region offers more to do than just look at stone being mass-produced into bookends, *tiki* and *taniwha*. Hoki is rich in history and nearby is a wealth of native forests, lakes and rivers.

Trivia? Hoki was the first place in NZ to have a scheduled air service. Air Travel (NZ) started flying de Havilland Fox Moths to airstrips in South Westland 60 years ago and continued doing so in biplanes until 1967.

Information

The Westland Visitor Information Centre (☎ 755 8322; fax 755 8026) on the corner of Weld and Sewell Sts is open from 9 am to 5 pm on weekdays. From mid-December to March it's also open on weekends from 9 am to 6 pm.

Hokitika has several banks which you might want to use as there are no banks further south until you reach Wanaka.

Things to See

Hokitika's newest tourist attraction is **Westland's Water World** on Sewell St. The small aquarium has a variety of fish and other West Coast marinelife, including giant whitebait, but the main attraction is at 10 am, noon, 3 and 5 pm, when a diver descends into the eel tank to feed the voracious giant eels. Steelmesh gloves have to be worn to keep fingers intact. Entry is $10 (children $5) and it's open from 9 am to 5.30 pm daily (until 4.30 pm in winter).

Take the time to do the historical walk outlined in the museum pamphlet *Hokitika Historic Walk*. The **Custom House** and **Gibson Quay** are well worth having a look at – it is not hard to imagine the river and wharf choked with sailing ships many years ago. The local Heritage Hokitika group has renovated the historic wharf along Gibson Quay.

The **West Coast Historical Museum** on Tancred St has many gold-mining relics. Medal collectors will revel in the wealth of items here. It's open daily from 9 am to 5 pm ($3, children $1), including an audiovisual presentation about the gold rush. You can pan for gold at the museum for $5.

Phelp's Goldmine is 2km south of Hoki on SH6. Open-cast methods are used and visitors can pan for gold. It's open daily from 8.30 am to 4.30 pm or later ($5, plus $5 to pan).

Greenstone

Greenstone is big in Hoki. Historically, greenstone – or jade – was much treasured by the Maori who used it for decorative jewellery (tiki) and for carving their lethal weapons (the flat war clubs known as *mere*). Since greenstone is found predominantly on the West Coast, expeditions undertaken by the Maori to collect it not only took months but were also dangerous. Working the stone with their primitive equipment was no easy task either, but they managed to produce some exquisite items.

The legend of Tamatea explains why there are differing types of greenstone in the South Island. Tamatea's three wives were either abducted by Poutini (a taniwha) or they deserted him. At Anita Bay he found one wife, Hinetangiwai, turned into greenstone, and when he wept his tears entered it, giving it its flecked appearance, hence the name of *tangiwai* (water of weeping) given to the stone. When travelling north he heard voices in the Arahura Valley and went to investigate. His companion, Tumuaki, breached *tapu* (sacred law) by putting his burnt fingers in his mouth while cooking, so Tamatea was not able to find his other wives. Like Hinetangiwai, the other wives were turned into greenstone – *auhanga* and *pounamu*. ■

Hokitika

There's a **glow-worm dell** right beside the road on the northern edge of the town.

Activities
Alpine Rafts (☎ 755 8156) offers various **white-water rafting** trips, including all-day 'thrill seeker' trips down some of NZ's steepest rafting rivers. Helicopters are used for access to the upper parts of the rivers, making the experience doubly exciting. Alpine Rafts does thrilling heli-rafting to the Frisco Canyon down one of NZ's steepest rivers for $195. A full-day trip down the Whanganui River includes a dip in the hot pools on the riverbank and a BBQ at the end ($285). A half-day trip on the Taipo is $155 (including a helicopter ride).

WestAir (☎ 755 7767) and Wilderness Wings (☎ 755 8118) run **scenic flights** from Hokitika over Mt Cook and the glaciers for around $150 (minimum two passengers) and local flightseeing.

Skydive NZ (☎ 755 8711) in Hokitika and Greymouth has **tandem skydiving** for from $195 (7000ft) up to $265 (12,000ft).

The information centre and DOC have detailed brochures on the many **walks** in the area. A number of walks are near Lake

Kaniere. Dorothy Falls, Kahikatea Forest and Canoe Cove are all short walks, but the Lake Kaniere Walkway is 13km and takes about four hours. Longer walks include Mt Tahua and Mt Brown, both of seven hours duration. The Mahinapua Walkway (two hours, 5.5km) goes through the scenic reserve to a swamp teeming with wildlife and to sand dunes. For the more sedentary, the *Takutai Belle*, a **paddle steamer**, operates on Mahinapua Creek to the lake and back for $20 per person.

Places to Stay

Camping, Cabins & Hostels The *Hokitika Holiday Park* (☎ 755 8172), 242 Stafford St, has tent/powered sites for $16/18, cabins for $26 to $40 and tourist flats for $52 to $60 (all for two). There are DOC camping grounds at Goldsborough (17km) and Shanghai Bay, Lake Mahinapua (16km) – distances are from Hoki.

Beach House Backpackers (☎ 755 6859), 137 Revell St, has dorm beds for $15 and doubles for $36. It's a friendly place with a lively bar/restaurant attached, but unfortunately the bar seems to take precedence over the backpackers, which needs attention.

Seaside Backpackers (☎ 755 6859), 163 Revell St, is a small, homestay-style backpackers with just one four-bed dorm at $15 and one double at $32. A bonus is that the owner is a jade carver and runs popular courses.

The new, purpose-built *Mountain Jade Backpackers* (☎ 755 8007), 41 Weld St, is very central and above the souvenir shop of the same name, with a cafe downstairs. Standards are very high in dorms for $16 and doubles for $40.

The *Blue Spur Lodge* (☎ 755 8445) is 5km east from town on the Cement Lead Rd and is reached via the Hau Hau Rd. It is well-equipped and peaceful with dorm beds for $15, and twins and doubles for $36. They offer free pick-up from Hokitika, free bikes, and for $35 they will give you a kayak and transport to and from Lake Kaniere. They can also advise on good tramps in the nearby hills.

Motels & Hotels Hokitika has a number of motels and the *Jade Court Motor Lodge* (☎ 755 8855) at 85 Fitzherbert St comes recommended; a unit costs from $80 to $92. The pleasant *Teichelmann's B&B* (☎ 755 8232) at 20 Hamilton St is a cosy place with singles from $60 to $76 and doubles from $76 to $96; prices include a big continental breakfast. The visitor information centre has listings for farmstays in Hokitika and South Westland.

The big *Westland Hotel* (☎ 755 8411) on the corner of Weld and Revell Sts has twins from $40 to $70. The *Club Hotel* (☎ 755 8170) at 131 Revell St has rooms for $30/52. The *Southland Hotel* (☎ 755 8334) at 111 Revell St has budget singles/doubles at $32/42, as well as more expensive 'deluxe' rooms at $65/75. The *Pioneer Hotel* (☎ 755 8641) on the corner of Gibson Quay and Bealey St has budget rooms from $30/40 ($35/45 B&B).

Places to Eat

For snacks and sandwiches you can try *Preston's Bakery* on Revell St, *PR's Coffee Shop* on Tancred St and *Millie's Place*, 135 Weld St, which has an all-you-can-eat, four-course carvery for $20. *Porky's Takeaway* on Weld St does fish and chips.

The *Beach House Cafe* at the Beach House Backpackers has cheap breakfasts and reasonably priced meals and is a popular watering hole. *Cafe 41* at Mountain Jade has pizzas.

Overlooking Hokitika's windswept and grey beach (the attraction for a lot of diners) is the *Tasman View* à la carte restaurant; it has a smorgasbord on Friday which is popular with locals. The French-style food at the *Cafe de Paris* on Tancred St near the corner of Hamilton St is recommended – its menus includes venison, lamb, mussels and whitebait with just a little hint of 'la rive gauche'.

Trappers at 79 Revell St serves venison, buffalo, wild pig, rabbit, duck and even kangaroo; three-course set meals are $25 or you can dine à la carte.

Things to Buy

Hoki's biggest attraction is the profusion of art and craft outlets, open from 8 am to 5 pm daily. Most of them are on Tancred St. Greenstone is the main attraction but, even with modern tools and electric power, working greenstone is not simple and good greenstone pieces will not be cheap. Westland Greenstone on Tancred St has a big selection of jewellery, tikis and other greenstone ornaments. Mountain Jade on Weld St specialises in jade sculpture as well as jewellery. You can see it being carved at both.

Quades House of Wood and the Hokitika Craft Gallery on Tancred St have other crafts. Next door, the Gold Room sells handcrafted gold jewellery made from locally mined gold; there are many specimens of gold nuggets found in the region. Also on Tancred St is the Hokitika Glass Studio. On Weld St is Revelations and Ocean Paua. The Sheep Station on Sewell St has a most unusual entrance – be engorged by a giant ram before you buy its outer coat.

Getting There & Away

Air New Zealand (☎ 0800 652 881) has daily direct flights to Christchurch, with connections to other centres.

The InterCity services travelling from Greymouth to Fox Glacier pass through Hokitika daily. Travel time is 40 minutes to Greymouth and four hours to Fox Glacier. The InterCity agent is Hokitika Travel Centre at 65 Tancred St. The Coast to Coast Shuttle and Alpine Coach & Courier (☎ 762 6332) run to Christchurch via Arthur's Pass; book at the visitor centre.

SOUTH FROM HOKITIKA

It's about 140km south from Hokitika to the Franz Josef Glacier, but you can make a few stops on the way. Hitching along this coast is notoriously bad, so go by bus – the InterCity buses from Greymouth to the glaciers will stop anywhere along the highway.

Ross

Ross, 30km south of Hokitika, is a small, historic gold-mining town and gold is still mined today. NZ's largest gold nugget, the 99oz 'Honourable Roddy', was found here in 1907. Grimmond House – in the goldrush era home to the Bank of New Zealand – is now the information centre and you can visit the small **Miner's Cottage** museum.

The cottage stands at the beginning of two historic goldfield **walkways**, the Jones Flat Walk and the Water Race Walk. Each takes about one to two hours and passes by interesting features from the gold rush era.

Near the car park in front of the cottage is a new working gold mine – you can look down on the operations. In the centre of town is a display of old gold-mining equipment and buildings.

The atmospheric *Empire Hotel* (☎ 755 4005), 19 Aylmer St, has tent sites at $16, cabins at $30 and shared/en suite rooms at $50/55; all prices are for two. Around the corner the *Ross Motel* (☎ 755 4022) on Gibson St has motel units at $58 a double. The *Empire Hotel* has bar meals, the *City Hotel* has a dining room and there's also the *Nicada Tearooms*.

Pukekura to Okarito

From Ross it's another 109km to Franz Josef, but there are plenty of bush tracks and lakes along the way if you want to break the journey and can cope with the sandflies. Heading southwards the rainforest becomes more dense and in many parts looks as if it would be easier to walk over the top of it than to find a way through!

Many places along here provide low-cost accommodation. About 20km south of Ross, *Lake Ianthe Cabins* (☎ 755 4032) near Pukekura has cabins at $30 for two, with activities including boating, sailing and fishing. About 100m south of the lake on the eastern side of the road is a giant matai tree. The short track to it is marked.

The **Bushmen's Centre** has a restaurant which serves up West Coast wild foods – this effectively excludes vegetarians – and entry to the West Coast's Castle Machismo costs $5 (children $2). Horse treks can be arranged from here.

The region has interesting **walks**. About

two hours from Greens Beach is a seal colony, and the adventurous can head down to Saltwater Lagoon, a truly beautiful and remote place. The **Coastal Pack Track** goes to the end of La Fontaine Creek; get details from the 'Bush-persons' Centre.

Harihari The small town of Harihari is 22.5km south of Lake Ianthe. Harihari made headlines in 1931, when Aussie Guy Menzies completed the first solo flight across the Tasman Sea from Sydney. The landing was anything but smooth as he crash-landed *Southern Cross Junior* in the La Fontaine swamp. The aircraft turned over and when he undid his safety straps he fell head-first into the mud. He had made the trip in 11¾ hours, 2½ hours less than fellow Australian Charles Kingsford Smith and his crew in 1928.

The two to three-hour **Harihari Coastal Walkway** (also called the Doughboy Walk) is a popular local attraction, with a lookout over the coastline, forest and mountains. You can also walk up into the Wilberg Range near the town (20 minutes return). Other possibilities are an old goldminers' pack track, rivermouth fishing for trout and salmon, or exploring the estuaries and wetlands of the Poerua and Wanganui rivers. Go **birdwatching** and try to spot native parakeets, herons, penguins, kakas and a number of migratory wading birds.

The *Harihari Motor Inn* (☎ 753 3026) has motel units at $70 for two, bunk beds at $15 per person and a hot spa pool. Across the road, *Tomasi Motel* (☎ 753 3116) has cabins with private bathroom at $30 for two and motel units at $60 a double. Neither has kitchen facilities, but Harihari has a tearoom, fish and chip shop and the Motor Inn has pub meals, a restaurant and takeaways.

Whataroa & the Kotuku Sanctuary Near Whataroa, 35km south of Harihari, is a sanctuary for the kotuku (white heron), which nests from November to the end of February; it is the only NZ nesting site of this species. The herons then fly off individually to spend winter throughout the country. Access is possible only with a permit from DOC.

White Heron Sanctuary Tours (☎ 753 4120) at Whataroa operates jet-boat tours to the kotuku colony beside the Waitangi-taona River. Don't panic, bird lovers – the jet-boat doesn't enter the nesting area. You walk along a boardwalk to the hide, where you spend 30 to 40 minutes. The cost is $75 (children $37.50) including a permit for the 2½-hour return trip.

The tours office also has expensive motel units (from $75), cabins ($35 and $40) and tent and powered sites (but no kitchen). The *Whataroa Hotel* (☎ 753 4076) has rooms and serves meals. Across the road from the tours office is the *White Heron Store & Tea Rooms*.

Okarito

Another 15km south of Whataroa is the Forks and the turn-off to peaceful Okarito, 13km away on the coast. Much of Keri Hulme's bestseller *The Bone People* is set in this wild, isolated region. There are lots of walks along the coast from Okarito – get hold of leaflets from the visitor centres in Hokitika or Franz Josef.

Okarito Nature Tours (☎ 753 4014) on the Strand organises popular kayaking trips into the beautiful **Okarito Lagoon**, a feeding ground for the kotuku and a good place for watching all kinds of birds. The lagoon is New Zealand's largest unmodified wetland and consists of shallow open water and tidal flats. The lake is surrounded by rimu and kahikatea rainforest. Half or full-day trips to the Okarito River delta cost $30 and $35 per person to see birds up close or overnight trips to Lake Windemere cost $60 and it is possible to get permits to the White Heron sanctuary. Trips are unguided but include all gear and transport. Guides are available.

The small *Okarito YHA Hostel* (☎ 753 4124) charges $10 per night. Hot showers are available from the nearby caravan park for multiples of 50c. The hostel was a schoolhouse, built in the 1870s when Okarito was a thriving gold town. Opposite the hostel is a very basic camping ground with BBQs and toilets. The ground is in a pleasant location and camp sites cost $5.

The very friendly and good value *Royal Motel & Hostel* (☎ 753 4080) nearby has a backpackers with two twins and one double at $13 per person. Self-contained 'motel' units are $40 and $50. Okarito has no shop so bring your own food.

Back towards the Forks turn-off, 3km in from the highway, the *Forks Lodge* (☎ 753 4122) is a simple, self-contained little lodge costing $10 per person or $25 for a double room. Bring your own bedding and food. It also has tent and powered sites.

THE GLACIERS

The two most famous glaciers in the Westland National Park – the Fox and the Franz Josef – are among the major attractions in New Zealand. Nowhere else in the world, at this latitude, have glaciers advanced so close to the sea. Unlike the Tasman Glacier, on the other side of the dividing range in Mt Cook National Park, these two are just what glaciers should be – mighty rivers of ice, tumbling down a valley towards the sea.

The reason for the glaciers' development is threefold. The West Coast is subject to the prevailing rain-drenched westerlies which fall as snow high up in the névés. The snow crystals fuse to form clear ice at a depth of about 20m. Secondly, the zones where the ice accumulates on the glacier are very large, so there's a lot of ice to push down the valley. Finally, they're very steep glaciers – the ice can get a long way before it finally melts.

The rate of descent is staggering: a plane that crashed on the Franz Josef in 1943, 3.5km from the terminal face, made it down to the bottom 6½ years later – a speed of 1.5m per day. At times the glacier can move at up to 5m a day, over 10 times as fast as glaciers in the Swiss Alps. Generally, it moves at the rate of about 1m a day.

The heavy tourist traffic – most staying only one night – is catered for in the two twin towns of Franz Josef and Fox, 23km apart. These small, modern, tourist villages have plenty of accommodation and enough facilities at higher than average prices. Change money before you reach the glaciers (there are no banks between Hokitika and Wanaka) and fill up on petrol if you're driving.

Franz Josef Glacier

The Franz Josef was first explored in 1865 by Austrian Julius Haast, who named it after the Austrian emperor. Apart from short advances from 1907-09, 1921-34, 1946-59 and 1965-67, the glacier has generally been in retreat since 1865, although in 1985 it started advancing again. It has progressed well over 1.7km since 1985, moving forward by about 70cm a day, although it is still several kilometres back from the terminal point Haast first recorded.

The glacier is 5km from the town. Kamahi Tours (☎ 752 0699) has a shuttle to the car park for $5 (minimum two). It is a 10-minute walk to the glacier from the car park. Hope for a fine day and great views to the snow-capped peaks behind. The glaciers are roped off to stop people getting close to where there is a risk of ice fall, but the ropes are a ridiculously long way back.

For $35 (children $17.50) you can walk up onto the glacier ice with an experienced guide. In the high season, guided walks (3½ hours, with 1½ hours on the glacier) depart twice daily from the Franz Josef Glacier Guides office (☎ 752 0763) in the village; equipment, including boots, is included in the price.

Information The Franz Josef Information Centre (☎ 752 0796; fax 752 0797) is open from 8.15 am to 7 pm daily in summer (until 6 pm in winter). The centre has leaflets on the many short walks around the glacier. In the summer it operates a program of evening lectures and slide shows.

There is an EFTPOS facility at the local petrol station, Glacier Motors, which has the most expensive petrol in New Zealand. DA's Restaurant acts as the local postal agency.

Walking Ask at the information centre for one of its excellent walk leaflets. There are several good glacier viewpoints close to the road leading to the glacier car park.

Advance & Retreat

Glaciers always advance, they never really retreat. Sometimes, however, the ice melts even faster than it advances, and in that case the terminal, or end, face of the glacier moves back up the mountain and appears to be retreating.

The great mass of ice higher up the mountain pushes the ice down the Fox and Franz Josef valleys at prodigious speeds but – like most glaciers in the world – this past century has been a story of steady retreat and only the odd short advance.

The last great Ice age of 15,000 to 20,000 years ago saw the glaciers reach right down to the sea. Then warmer weather came and they may have retreated even further than their current position. In the 14th century a new 'mini Ice age' started and for centuries the glaciers advanced, reaching their greatest extent around 1750. At both Fox and Franz Josef, the terminal moraines from that last major advance can be clearly seen. In the nearly 250 years since then, the glaciers have steadily retreated and the terminal face is now several kilometres back from its first recorded position in the late 19th century or even from its position in the 1930s.

From 1965 to 1968 the Fox and Franz Josef glaciers made brief advances of about 180m, and in 1985 they once again started to advance and have been moving forward steadily and fairly dramatically ever since. Nobody is quite sure why this advance is taking place. It could be cooler or more overcast summers, or it could be the result of heavy snowfalls 10 or 15 years ago, which are now working their way down to the bottom of the glacier.

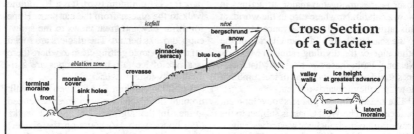

Cross Section of a Glacier

Useful Terminology

ablation zone – where the glacier melts

accumulation zone – where the snow collects

bergschrund – large crevasse in the ice near the headwall or starting point of the glacier

blue ice – as the accumulation zone or névé snow is compressed by subsequent snowfalls, it becomes firn and then blue ice

crevasses – as the glacial ice moves down the mountain it bends and cracks open in crevasses as it crosses obstacles

dead ice – as a glacier retreats, isolated chunks of ice may be left behind (sometimes these can remain for many years)

firn – partly compressed snow on the way to becoming glacial ice

glacial flour – the river of melted ice that flows off glaciers is a milky colour from the suspension of finely ground rocks

icefall – when a glacier descends so steeply that the upper ice breaks up in a jumble of iceblocks

kettle lake – lake formed by the melt of an area of isolated dead ice

lateral moraine – walls of debris formed at the sides of the glacier

névé – snowfield area where firn is formed

seracs – ice pinnacles formed, like crevasses, by the glacier passing over obstacles

terminal – the final ice face at the end of the glacier

terminal moraine – mass of boulders and rocks marking the end point of the glacier, its final push down the valley ■

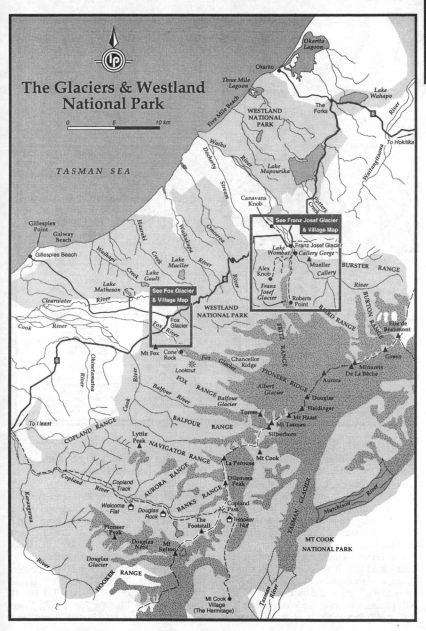

The Glaciers & Westland National Park

0   5   10 km

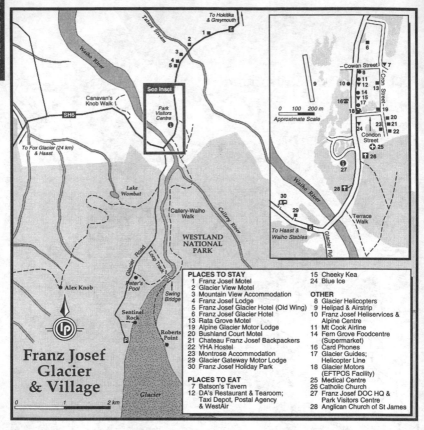

Franz Josef Glacier & Village

PLACES TO STAY
1 Franz Josef Motel
2 Glacier View Motel
3 Mountain View Accommodation
4 Franz Josef Lodge
5 Franz Josef Glacier Hotel (Old Wing)
6 Franz Josef Glacier Hotel
13 Rata Grove Motel
19 Alpine Glacier Motor Lodge
20 Bushland Court Motel
21 Chateau Franz Josef Backpackers
22 YHA Hostel
23 Montrose Accommodation
29 Glacier Gateway Motor Lodge
30 Franz Josef Holiday Park

PLACES TO EAT
7 Batson's Tavern
12 DA's Restaurant & Tearoom;
   Taxi Depot, Postal Agency
   & WestAir
15 Cheeky Kea
24 Blue Ice

OTHER
8 Glacier Helicopters
9 Helipad & Airstrip
10 Franz Josef Heliservices &
   Alpine Centre
11 Mt Cook Airline
14 Fern Grove Foodcentre
   (Supermarket)
16 Card Phones
17 Glacier Guides;
   Helicopter Line
18 Glacier Motors
   (EFTPOS Facility)
25 Medical Centre
26 Catholic Church
27 Franz Josef DOC HQ &
   Park Visitors Centre
28 Anglican Church of St James

Other walks require a little worthwhile footslogging. The **Douglas Walk**, off the Glacier Access Rd, is an hour's stroll by the terminal moraine from the 1750 advance and Peter's Pool, a small 'kettle lake'. It's a longer walk (3½ hours) to **Roberts Point**, which overlooks and is quite close to the terminal face.

The **Terrace Track** makes a pleasant one-hour round trip. It starts on the old Callery Track, a former gold-mining area, and leads up onto a terrace at the back of the village, with pleasant views of the Waiho River. The **Callery-Waiho Walk** is about four hours return. The **Canavan's Knob Walk**, closer to town, is about 40 minutes return.

Aerial Sightseeing The hills are alive with the sound of buzzing helicopters and planes doing runs over the glaciers (from $100; $175 to $250 including Mt Cook). Many flights include a snow landing, and heli-hiking is a variation on the theme.

Companies include Glacier Helicopters (☎ 0800 800 732), Mt Cook Airline (☎ Franz Josef 752 0714; Fox 751 0812), The Helicopter Line (☎ 752 0767), Franz Josef Heliservices (☎ 751 0866) and West

Air Safaris (☎ 752 0716). Flights up and over the glaciers are expensive but they're a superb experience.

Other Activities Waiho Stables (☎ 752 0747) conducts 2½-hour **horse riding** tours through rainforest for $35. Fishing trips and small launch cruises can be enjoyed on Lake Mapourika, a 10-minute drive north of Franz Josef.

Places to Stay The *Franz Josef Holiday Park* (☎ 752 0766) is 1km south of the township, right beside the river. Tent/powered sites are $18/19, tourist cabins and flats are $49 to $59 and motels are $89; all prices are for two. New owners have seen an improvement in atmosphere and the addition of the well-equipped *Black Sheep* hostel, which charges $13.50 in the 10-bed bunkhouse, $17 in quad rooms and $35 for doubles.

Hostels generally have good facilities but are large and cater to short-term numbers, so they're not always chatty, cosy hostels. Hostel row is on Cron St, just off the main road. The *Franz Josef Glacier YHA Hostel* (☎ 752 0754) at No 2-4 is a pleasant hostel with friendly managers and charges $16 per person in dorms and $36 for doubles. It has a small shop, pool table and videos in the evenings.

Next door is the *Chateau Franz Josef Backpackers* (☎ 752 0738), where shared rooms are $16 per person and doubles/twins are $35/40. It's large with rooms leading off everywhere but pleasant and well-equipped.

Montrose Accommodation (☎ 752 0188) opposite is in a refurbished house with large dorms for $15.50 and doubles for $40. Facilities and atmosphere are stretched.

On SH6 is *Franz Josef Lodge* (☎ 752 0712), former staff housing for the adjoining Franz Josef Glacier Hotel. It's a more basic sort of backpackers but the common areas are good. Share rooms are $17.50, and twin bunkrooms and a couple of doubles are $35.

Nearby, *Mountain View Accommodation* (☎ 752 0735) has an older, self-contained budget cottage at $16 per person in share rooms or $40 for a double. Very good, new motel units are $65 to $80.

The older *Bushland Court Motel* (☎ 752 0757) at 10 Cron St has units from $70 and also owns the very flash *Alpine Glacier Motor Lodge* across the street with a variety of new units, some with a spa, for $100 to $170. Other motels cost around $75 to $85 a night. *Franz Josef Glacier Hotel* (☎ 752 0729) has a large motel-style complex just north of Cowan St and the older resort-hotel wing about 1km north of the township on SH6. Rooms cost $180 to $225.

Places to Eat The shops at Franz Josef have a good selection of food supplies. *DA's* has a cafe and takeaway section and a restaurant, all offering much the same menu. Main courses in the coffee shop at the *Franz Josef Glacier Hotel* are also in the $14 to $20 range.

Good cafes with some interesting dinner menus include the *Cheeky Kea* and the *Blue Ice*. *Batson's Tavern* on the corner of Cowan and Cron Sts has a good range of bistro meals from $10 to $15 and the BBQ area is overlooked by rainforest, often cloaked in flowering rata.

Getting There & Away North and southbound InterCity buses cross between the two glaciers, with daily buses south to Fox Glacier and Queenstown and north to Greymouth. The connections are such that Nelson to Queenstown (or vice versa) by bus along the West Coast takes a minimum of two days. In the high season (summer) these buses can be heavily booked, so plan well ahead or be prepared to wait until there's space.

Along the West Coast, hitching prospects can be bleak. If you're lucky you might do Greymouth to Queenstown in three days – if not you could well stand on the same spot for a couple of days.

Fox Glacier

If time is short, seeing one glacier may be enough, but if you have time it's interesting to see both. Basically the same activities are offered at both glaciers – glacier walks, flights and so on. Despite consistent retreat

THE WEST COAST

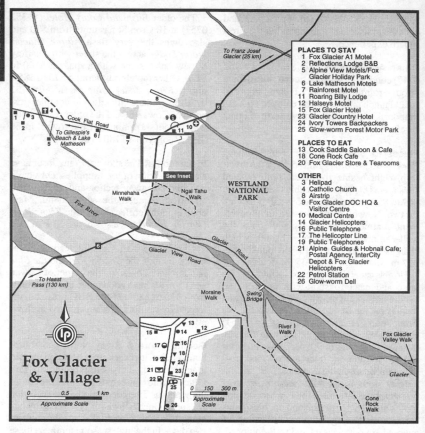

Fox Glacier & Village

PLACES TO STAY
1 Fox Glacier A1 Motel
2 Reflections Lodge B&B
5 Alpine View Motels/Fox Glacier Holiday Park
6 Lake Matheson Motel
7 Rainforest Motel
11 Roaring Billy Lodge
12 Halseys Motel
15 Fox Glacier Hotel
23 Glacier Country Hotel
24 Ivory Towers Backpackers
25 Glow-worm Forest Motor Park

PLACES TO EAT
13 Cook Saddle Saloon & Cafe
18 Cone Rock Cafe
20 Fox Glacier Store & Tearooms

OTHER
3 Helipad
4 Catholic Church
8 Airstrip
9 Fox Glacier DOC HQ & Visitor Centre
10 Medical Centre
14 Glacier Helicopters
16 Public Telephone
17 The Helicopter Line
19 Public Telephones
21 Alpine Guides & Hobnail Cafe; Postal Agency, InterCity Depot & Fox Glacier Helicopters
22 Petrol Station
26 Glow-worm Dell

throughout much of this century, the Fox Glacier, like the Franz Josef, has been advancing since 1985. In the last 10 years it has advanced almost 1km, and now averages about 40cm per day. Its name was given in 1872 after a visit by the New Zealand prime minister, Sir William Fox.

Information The Fox Glacier Visitor Centre (☎ 751 0807; fax 751 0858) is open from 8.15 am to 7 pm daily in summer, until 6 pm in winter, and has evening slide shows in summer. The centre has displays on the glaciers and the natural environment as well

as leaflets on a number of short walks around the ice.

There's a petrol station in the village – the last fuel stop until you reach Haast, 120km further on. Alpine Guides is the local postal agency and sells phone cards.

Walking The shortest and most popular walk at the Fox Glacier is the couple of minutes stroll from the centre to the **glow-worm dell** (entry $2). Of course, you have to go at night to see them glowing.

Head towards the coast from the township for a lookout with a superb vista of the glacier and the Southern Alps. Before this lookout is the turn-off to **Lake Matheson** and one of the most famous panoramas in NZ. It's an hour's walk around the lake and at the far end are those unforgettable calendar and postcard views of the mountains and their reflection in the lake. The best time to see the famed reflection is very early in the morning, when the lake is at its most mirror-like calm. There is a cafe at the lake.

An almost equally famous viewpoint can be found off Glacier View Rd, by making the short climb up to **Cone Rock** or the easier walk to Chalet lookout. **Mt Fox**, off SH6 to Haast, is another excellent viewpoint – a three-hour walk one way.

Other interesting walks around the glacier include the short moraine walk over the advance of 200 years ago, forest walks on the Ngai Tahu Track, the short Minnehaha Walk or the River Walk. It takes just over an hour to walk from the village to the glacier – it's 1.5km from Fox to the turn-off and the glacier is another 5km back from the main road.

Gillespie's Beach has a handful of houses and a three-hour return walk along the beach to a seal colony. The first half-hour goes through cut back scrub to an old gold dredge, which is nothing more than a rusting junk heap, before it leads on to the beach. As this is one of NZ's most boring walks, skip it and just walk along the wild, black-sand beach the whole way.

Aerial Sightseeing If you don't fancy walking on the ice, flightseeing may be your best option. Glacier Helicopters (☎ 0800 800 732), Mt Cook Airline (☎ 751 0812), the Helicopter Line (☎ 751 0767) and Fox Glacier Helicopter Services (☎ 751 0866) have much the same flights and prices as at Franz Josef. These trips are expensive but provide a superb experience with amazing views.

Horse Riding Glacier Horse Treks (☎ 751 0707) offers one-hour ($25) and two-hour ($45) horse treks.

Organised Tours As at Franz Josef you can take guided walks up onto the glacier ice

with Alpine Guides (☎ 751 0825). Tours leave at 9.30 am and 2 pm daily from the village, and boots and other equipment are included in the $36 (children $24) cost. They also have full-day guided glacier walks. Of course, you can just follow the marked track to the glacier from the car park, but the glacier is roped off as at Franz Josef.

Alpine Guides has three-hour ($155 each for three people) and full-day heli-hikes ($390), and an overnight trip to Chancellor Hut. The overnight trip includes hut fees, food and the flight up for $495 each for three people, $645 each for two, including a helicopter trip on each end. It also offers mountaineering instruction and full-day glacier skiing – this costs $445, which includes hut fees and a helicopter lift for the 10km ski run.

Places to Stay The *Fox Glacier Holiday Park* (☎ 751 0821) is a motor camp down the Lake Matheson road from the township. Tent/powered sites are $18/20 for two, bunkroom accommodation is $12 per person, cabins are $35 and $40 for two, and tourist flats are $55 for two. *Glow-worm Forest Motor Park* (☎ 751 0888) has no tent sites, only powered sites for $20 in a pretty setting.

The *Ivory Towers* (☎ 751 0838) on Sullivans Rd behind the Golden Glacier Motor Inn is tidy and well equipped. It charges $16 a night in dorms or $40 for a twin or double. As yet unseen, a new backpackers is due to open and may provide welcome competition: the *Fox Glacier Inn & Backpackers* (☎ 751 0022) is at 39 Sullivan Rd.

B&Bs and farmstays in the area charge around $60 to $75. *Reflections Lodge* (☎ 751 0707) has B&B doubles for $80, *Roaring Billy Lodge* (☎ 751 0815) charges $65 and *Homestyle* (☎ 751 0895) charges $65.

The elderly *Fox Glacier Hotel* (☎ 751 0839) in the centre of the village on Cook Flat Rd has budget rooms for $38 or $55 with en suite or a better annexe with en suite doubles for $115. Close by, on the Lake Matheson road, is *Lake Matheson Motels* (☎ 751 0830), where a double is $75 to $80. At the *Alpine View Motels* (☎ 751 0821), by the motor camp, units cost $64 for two. The new *Rainforest Motel* (☎ 751 0140) on Cook Flat Rd has units for $70 to $95.

Places to Eat The *Fox Glacier Store* in the town centre has a reasonable selection of essentials, although not as wide a choice as at Franz Josef. You can eat good vegetarian food at the *Cone Rock Cafe*, and the *Hobnail Cafe* in the Alpine Guides building has good sandwiches and light meals. The locals flock to the Tex-Mex-style *Cook Saddle Saloon & Cafe* on the corner of SH6 and the Cook Flat Rd; main meals of seafood, steak and venison are from $16 to $22. Good meals are also available in the restaurant at the *Glacier Country Hotel*, which has an open fire and cosy atmosphere.

Unlike the pub at the Franz Josef Glacier, the *Fox Glacier Hotel* is wonderfully central and you can sit with a jug of beer and talk about the day's activities.

Getting There & Away The InterCity bus services overlap – southbound services from Greymouth start and finish at Fox Glacier, while northbound ones from Queenstown continue on to Franz Josef. Buses run every day to and from Greymouth (four hours) and Queenstown (eight hours). From Greymouth there are onward connections to Westport, Nelson and Picton.

See the Franz Josef section for the sad news on hitchhiking and a warning about the heavily booked bus services.

SOUTH TO HAAST

Heading south from the glaciers, the rainforest is so dense on both sides of the road (SH6) that you can barely see a couple of metres into it. Further on, it opens up to reveal broad sweeps of coastline before Haast.

Just 26km south of Fox Glacier is the **Copland Valley**. This is at the end of the Copland Track, coming over from Mt Cook. It's a very pleasant six-hour walk up the valley from the highway here to the last hut at Welcome Flat, where there are hot springs. A sign on the road marks the entrance to the valley and the track. The excellent modern

hut at Welcome Flat sleeps 40 and should be paid for at the DOC visitor centre in Haast or Fox. InterCity buses pass by the Copland Valley entrance.

There are a few places to stay between Fox Glacier and Haast if you wish to break up the journey. The *Pinegrove Motels* (☎ 751 0898), 36km south of Fox Glacier, has a variety of accommodation including powered sites at $16, basic cabins at $30, and units at $60; all prices are for two people.

Lake Paringa

Lake Paringa, about 70km south of Fox Glacier and 50km north of Haast, is a tranquil little trout-filled lake surrounded by forest, right beside the road. The friendly *Paringa Lodge* (☎ 751 0894) is on the lake shore and has boats and canoes for hire. Fading, self-contained cabin units cost only $20 per person, but kitchens have no stoves or cooking utensils. Motel units are $75 for two. About 1km further south, still on the lakefront, is a free DOC camping area with basic facilities – toilets and picnic areas. Beside Paringa Lodge is the excellent *Lake Paringa Cafe*. It serves everything from sandwiches to venison pie ($9) for lunch and dinner mains for $20 to $25 are surprisingly innovative for this isolated spot.

The historic **Haast-Paringa Cattle Track** starts from the main road 43km north of Haast and comes out at the coast by the Waita River, just a few kilometres north of Haast. Before the Haast Pass road was opened in 1965, this trail was the only link between Otago/Southland and the West Coast. The first leg of the track makes a pleasant day hike. Information on the track is available from the visitor centre in Haast.

Lake Moeraki

Lake Moeraki, 31km north of Haast, not far off the highway, is another peaceful forest lake with good fishing. It's also not far from the coast – just a 40-minute walk along a stream brings you to **Monro Beach**, where there's a breeding colony of Fiordland crested penguins; they can be found there from July to November. Also at Monro Beach are fur seals and good snorkelling. There are many other good short and long walks around the lake and the Moeraki River which runs from the lake to the sea.

The *Wilderness Lodge Lake Moeraki* (☎ 750 0881), right on the highway and just 20m from the lakeside, is a special place where visitors can fully enjoy a wilderness experience. It has rooms at $140/175 per person in low/high season for dinner B&B. Daily outdoor and nature activities, such as walks to Fiordland crested penguin colonies and canoe safaris, are organised; short activities of up to 90 minutes' duration are free for guests and half-day trips cost $48. The *Riverside Restaurant*, with its superb views of the massive trees growing outside, specialises in fish and game dishes. The canoe safaris are also open to the public.

Past Moeraki is the much-photographed **Knight's Point**, where the Haast road was eventually opened in 1965; there is an information shelter here. And Knight? He was a surveyor's dog.

THE HAAST REGION

The Haast region is the centre of a major wildlife refuge, where some of the biggest stands of rainforest survive alongside some of the most extensive wetlands. The kahikatea swamp forests, sand dune forests, seal and penguin colonies, the kaka, Red Hills and vast sweeps of beach have ensured the listing of this hauntingly beautiful place as a World Heritage area.

In the forests you will see the flaming red rimu in flower and kahikatea thriving in swampy lagoons. Birdlife abounds and the observant twitcher might see fantail, bellbird, native pigeon (kereru), falcon, kaka, kiwi and morepork. On the beaches you are likely to see blue penguins and Fiordland crested penguins. This is the home turf of the legendary Arawata Bill, who roamed this domain as a self-styled prospector and explorer. Walk through his incredible country and take a trip back hundreds of years – raupo, ferns and cabbage trees inhibit progress if you stray off the beaten track.

Haast

The tiny community of Haast is on the coast where the wide Haast River meets the sea, 120km south of Fox Glacier. After the magnificent scenery of the Haast Highway or the glaciers, this modern little frontier settlement comes as something of a blight on the landscape, but it makes a convenient stop and the area has been targeted for tourist development; it is now a World Heritage area.

A series of tracks has been developed, including the **Hapuka Estuary Walk** leading from the motor camp, and a rainforest, seacoast and wetland walk along **Ship Creek**, halfway between Haast and Lake Moeraki.

The South West New Zealand World Heritage Visitor Centre (☎ 750 0809; fax 750 0832), at the junction of SH6 and Jackson Bay Rd on the southern bank of the Haast River, has wonderful displays and information on the area. Activities in the area include scenic flights, canoeing, fishing, diving for crayfish and South West Penguin (☎ 750 0824) has tours ($50) to see Fiordland crested penguins.

Places to Stay & Eat The *Haast Beach Holiday Park* (☎ 750 0860) is at Okuru, 11km south of Haast township on the road to Jackson Bay. Tent/powered sites cost $16/17 for two and cabins $30 to $46 for two, with linen for hire if needed. On the same road, 4km from Haast, *Erewhon Motels* (☎ 750 0817) has units for $79 and $80.

The township, 3km east of the visitor centre and 200m from SH6, has a small supermarket and accommodation. *Wilderness Backpackers* (☎ 0800 750 029) is a neat and tidy new place. It has dorm beds from $15 per person and doubles for $34. *Heritage Park Lodge* (☎ 750 0868) next door has new motel units for $79 and $90. *Haast Highway Accommodation* (☎ 750 0703) is a YHA associate backpackers ($15 to $18 per person) and also has more expensive options. The standards are good but this place is in need of a Kiwi Host course. The township also has *Smithy's Tavern* and the *Fantail Tearooms* for light meals.

The *Haast World Heritage Hotel* (☎ 750 0828) near the bridge has doubles from $89, two-bedroom suites from $140 and a few budget rooms from $40. There is a public bar nearby, a house bar and a restaurant with a good selection of à la carte dishes. The pub meals are really good value and $10 will see you well satisfied.

Haast to Jackson Bay & the Cascade

A road heads south from the SH6 at Haast to the Arawata River and Jackson Bay. Near Okuru is a walk to the tidal Hapuka Estuary.

On the south side of the Arawata bridge, turn off onto the gravel road that follows the Jackson River to the start of the scenic **Lake Ellery** track, a one-hour return walk. Continue to Martyr Saddle, with its views of the incredible Red Hills and the Cascade River valley. The distinctive colour of the **Red Hills** is due to high concentrations of magnesium and iron in the rock forced up by the meeting of the Australo and Pacific tectonic plates at this point. Continue on from Martyr Saddle to the flats of the Cascade River, a true wilderness region.

The main road continues west from the bridge to the fishing hamlet of **Jackson Bay**, a real end of the road town and perhaps the most remote in NZ. The views north to the Southern Alps are memorable and there are colonies of Fiordland crested penguins close to the road. Migrants settled here in 1875 under an assisted immigrant program that was doomed. Dreams to start a farming district were shattered by rain and the lack of a wharf, which was not built until 1938. Today, fishing boats seek lobster, tuna, tarakihi, gurnard and grouper.

Interesting short **walks** here include the three-hour Smoothwater Bay Track, the 15-minute Jackson Viewpoint Walk and the 20-minute Wharekai Te Kau Walk, which has great coastal rock formations. Keener trampers can walk to Stafford Bay Hut, which is a long day walk or an easier two-day walk with an overnight stop at the hut. Check tidal information with the visitor centre in Haast.

HAAST PASS

Turning inland at Haast, snaking along beside the wide Haast River and climbing up the pass, you soon enter Mt Aspiring National Park and the scenery changes again – further inland the vegetation becomes much more sparse until beyond the 563m summit, when you reach snow country covered only in tussock and scrub. Along the Haast Pass are many picturesque waterfalls, most of them just a couple of minutes walk off the road.

The roadway over Haast Pass was opened in 1965. Prior to that the only southern link to the West Coast was by the Haast-Paringa Cattle Track, walking or on horseback. En route to Wanaka, the **Fantail** and **Thunder Creek** waterfalls are close to the road. See the DOC booklet *Haast Pass Highway: Short Walks*.

Heading south after Haast, the next town of any size is Wanaka, 145km or 3½ hours away. If driving north, check your fuel gauge: the petrol station at Haast is the last before the Fox Glacier, 120km north.

Makarora & the Siberia Valley

When you reach Makarora you have left the West Coast, but it still has a West Coast frontier feel and it is the gateway to the Haast Pass and the coast for north-bound traffic.

An early traveller gave the region some terrible names. He called one of the world's most beautiful valleys Siberia and named the nearby Matterhornesque peaks Dreadful and Awful – he is not to be believed. In the Siberia Valley you can walk in one of the last refuges of the blue duck and the rare orange-wattled South Island kokako (thought to be nearly extinct).

Makarora's permanent population is only around 30 but it can accommodate about 140 people, mostly trampers and adventure-seekers. There isn't much else in this township – which is part of its charm. The DOC Makaroa Visitor Centre (☎ 443 8365) on the highway has information on the Haast and should be consulted before undertaking any tramps.

'Siberia Experience' Makarora is the base for one of NZ's great outdoor adventures – the Siberia Experience. This is one of those Kiwi extravaganzas that combines sundry thrill-seeking activities – in this case a small-plane flight (20 minutes), a three-hour bush walk through a remote mountain valley and a jet-boat trip (45 minutes) down a river valley. Make sure you follow the markers as you descend from Siberia; people have become lost and have had to spend the night in the open.

Southern Alps Air (☎ 443 8372) operates the 'experience' from mid-October to mid-April ($135, minimum of three passengers). It also has 40-minute trips over Mt Aspiring ($80 per person), 70-minute trips to Mt Cook and the glaciers ($150) and landings at Milford Sound ($180).

Jet-Boating A 50km, one-hour jet-boating trip into Mt Aspiring National Park costs $45 (minimum five people) with Wilkin River Jets (☎ 443 8351), much cheaper than Shotover jet-boat trips.

For trampers, jet-boats go to Kerin Forks at the top of the Wilkin River for $40 and a ferry service goes across the Young River mouth when the Makarora floods for $17. Inquire on ☎ 443 8351 or at DOC.

Walking The area has many walks. Shorter ones include the Old Bridal Track (1½ hours), which heads from the top of the Haast pass to Davis Flat; a 20-minute nature walk around Makarora; and the Blue Pools River Walk, where you can see huge rainbow trout.

Longer tramps go through magnificent countryside but are not to be undertaken lightly. Alpine conditions, flooding and the possibility of avalanches mean that you must be well-prepared and consult with DOC before heading off. DOC's *Tramping Guide to the Makarora Region* ($2.50) is a good investment.

The three-day **Gillespies Pass** tramp goes via the Young, Siberia and Wilkin rivers but this is a high pass with avalanche danger.

With a jet-boat ride down the Wilkin to complete it, this surely could rate alongside the Milford Track as one of the great tramps. The **Wilkin Valley Track** heads off from Kerin Forks Hut, reached by jet-boat, or you can also fly in to Top Forks, Siberia Hut and others. From Kerin Forks the track leads to Top Forks Hut, then the north branch of the Wilkin. Here you will see the picturesque lakes Diana, Lucidus and Castalia. These are one hour, 1½ hours and three to four hours respectively from Top Forks Hut.

Places to Stay & Eat The *Makarora Tourist Centre* (☎ 443 8372) behind the tearooms has good accommodation in a bush setting. The cost is $60 for two people in the self-contained chalets, $38 for two in the A-frame cabins and $7.50 per person for a tent site (powered $9.50).

The *Larrivee Homestead* (☎ 443 9177) is not far from the Makarora Tourist Service – take the road closest to the DOC office and drive up until you reach the octagonal masterpiece at the end of the drive. The cost for homestay B&B is $60 for singles and $90 to $120 for doubles. The very comfortable, self-contained cottage costs $60 for two and $15 for each extra person (maximum of six). The house and cottage are made of stone and hand-split cedar. Dinners are prepared for $25 per person.

The nearest DOC camping grounds are on SH6 at Cameron Flat and Davis Flat, 14km and 17km north of Makarora respectively.

The 10-bed hut in Siberia Valley costs $8 per person and other huts are scattered around the park.

The tearooms, open from 8.30 am to 8.30 pm in summer, has light meals and snacks and a grocery store for basic supplies.

Getting There & Away West Coast Express, Magic Bus and Kiwi Experience buses regularly stop here. InterCity has one northbound (to the glaciers) and one southbound (to Hawea, Wanaka and Queenstown) bus per day.

Canterbury

Canterbury is the hub of the South Island and contains the South Island's largest city, Christchurch. The large Canterbury region extends from near Kaikoura in the north to near Oamaru in the south, and from the Pacific to Arthur's Pass and Mt Cook in the Southern Alps.

This is one of the driest and flattest areas of New Zealand. The moisture-laden westerlies from the Tasman Sea hit the Southern Alps and dump their rainfall on the West Coast before reaching Canterbury, which has an annual rainfall of only 0.75m compared with 5m on the West Coast.

The region is dominated by the expansive Canterbury Plains, dead-flat farming land backed by the Southern Alps. The Alps, however, are also part of Canterbury and contain New Zealand's highest mountains – Mts Cook (Aoraki), Tasman, Sefton. This striking geographical contrast is *the* New Zealand of postcards – rural, sheep-strewn fields backed by rugged, snow-capped mountains.

Christchurch Region & the North

Christchurch is the focal point of Canterbury, centrally located on the coast midway between Kaikoura and Timaru. It is a large, ordered city with a population of 309,000. To the west, beyond the extensive alluvial plain, are the imposing Southern Alps and Arthur's Pass National Park; to the north, beyond the rolling hills, are Hanmer and more forest parks; and to the south-east is the absorbing Banks Peninsula.

CHRISTCHURCH
Christchurch is often described as the most English of New Zealand's cities. Punts glide down the picturesque River Avon, a grand

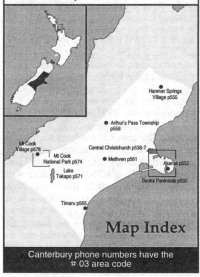

HIGHLIGHTS

- Experiencing the beautiful city of Christchurch and seeing the fascinating Canterbury Museum – one of the best regional museums anywhere
- Visiting the charming settlement of Akaroa
- Walking in and watching the fabulous mountainscapes of Arthur's Pass National Park
- Exploring the Port Hills and Banks Peninsula region by car or on foot
- Being amazed by the grandeur of Mt Cook (Aoraki) and the glaciers in Mt Cook National Park
- Discovering the Lewis Pass region and the getaway town of Hanmer with its hot springs
- Seeing Lake Tekapo – an azure blue lake surrounded by mountains

Hanmer Springs Village p555

Arthur's Pass Township p558

Mt Cook Village p578

Mt Cook National Park p574

Central Christchurch p536-7

Methven p561

Akaroa p552

Lake Tekapo p571

Banks Peninsula p550

Timaru p565

Map Index

Canterbury phone numbers have the ☎ 03 area code

Anglican cathedral dominates the city square and trams rattle past streets with oh-so English names. To the west, tranquil suburbs such as Fendalton, Avonhead, Bryndwr, Burnside and Ilam contain the exquisite

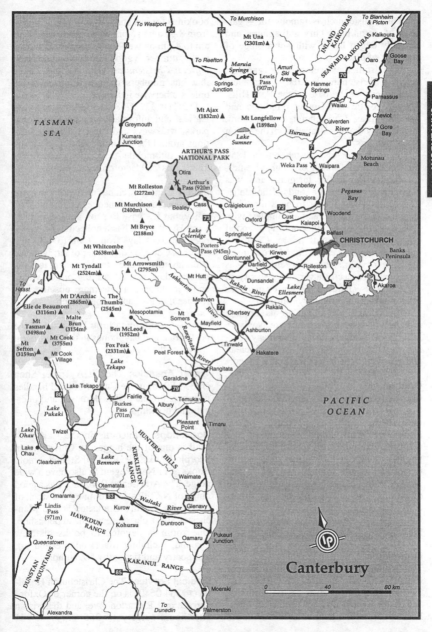

Canterbury

gardens Christchurch is famous for – gardens of geraniums, chrysanthemums and carefully edged lawns with not a blade of grass out of place.

Away from the river and the gardens, much of Christchurch is a flat, typical New Zealand city at the base of the Port Hills. Though it still has Gothic buildings and wooden villas, Christchurch is a modern, thriving city that has strayed from the vision of its founders.

The settlement of Christchurch in 1850 was an ordered Church of England enterprise, and the fertile farming land was deliberately placed in the hands of the gentry. Christchurch was meant to be a model of England in the South Pacific, complete with class system, not another scruffy colonial outpost of small landholders. Churches rather than pubs were built and wool made the elite of Christchurch wealthy. It was incorporated as a city, a very English city, in 1862, but its character slowly changed as other migrants and industry followed.

Christchurch still clings to its English affectations – even the trams are newly re introduced – largely because so many tourists are attracted to this well-ordered, clean and green city, the hub of the South Island.

Orientation

Cathedral Square is very much the centre of town. To find it, just look for the spire and, once there, climb to the top to get your orientation. Christchurch is compact and walking around is easy, although made slightly complicated by the river which twists and winds through the centre and crosses your path in disconcertingly varied directions. The network of one-way streets adds even more excitement if you're driving. Colombo St, running north-south through the square, is the main shopping street.

Information

Tourist Offices The busy Christchurch/ Canterbury Visitor Centre (☎ 379 9629; fax 377 2424) is by the river on the corner of Worcester St and Oxford Terrace. It has a host of advertising brochures and takes bookings for just about everything. It's open from 8.30 am to 5 pm on weekdays and 8.30 am to 4 pm on weekends; it stays open later in the summer. A good free publication is the *Official Christchurch Visitors Guide*. Note that bus numbers refer to Canride buses unless otherwise indicated.

DOC (☎ 379 9758) at 133 Victoria St has leaflets and information on most national parks, walkways and other outdoor attractions around the South Island.

The Automobile Association (AA; ☎ 379 1280) is at 210 Hereford St.

Money Christchurch has plenty of banks for changing travellers cheques or foreign currency, but it's wise to shop around as rates vary. Hereford St has a collection of banks, open on weekdays from 9 am to 4.30 pm. Thomas Cook, on the corner of Armagh and Colombo Sts, is open from 8.30 am to 5 pm on weekdays and 10 am to 4 pm on weekends; it changes a few more obscure currencies that the banks won't touch.

Post & Communications You will find the post office and payphones in the south-west corner of the Square.

Travel Agencies The YHA Travel Shop (☎ 379 8046) in the Cashel St Mall handles membership and makes domestic and international bookings.

Bookshops Whitcoulls in the Cashel St Mall is one of the biggest in Christchurch. Scorpio Books, 79 Hereford St, and Arnold Books at 11 New Regent St also have a wide range. The Arts Centre Bookshop has a good range of NZ titles, including a good stock of LP guides. Smith's Bookshop at 133 Manchester St is a classic secondhand bookshop. One room is devoted to books on New Zealand, including Maori culture and art, and poetry and fiction by NZ authors.

Medical Services The Christchurch Hospital (☎ 364 0640) is on the corner of Oxford Terrace and Riccarton Ave, and there is an after-hours surgery (☎ 365 7777) at 931

Colombo St, on the corner of Bealey Ave, open from 5 pm to 8 am on weekdays and 24 hours on weekends and public holidays.

Cathedral Square

Cathedral Square is the heart of Christchurch and the best place to start exploring the city. The square is dominated by **Christ Church Cathedral**, consecrated in 1881. For $4, you can see the historical display and climb 133 steps to the viewing balconies 30m up the 63m-high spire of the cathedral. Study the cathedral bells and take in the views from the spire which has been damaged by earthquakes on several occasions, once sending the very top into Cathedral Square.

One of the city's most-visited attractions, the church has embraced tourism and the free market with secular zeal. The cathedral has a souvenir shop, screens videos ($2), charges for cameras (another $2) and has a good cafe open on weekdays. What would the pious founding fathers say? But the proceeds help maintain this wonderful Gothic building, you can view the interior for free (donations gratefully accepted) or attend Sunday services. The cathedral is open from 8.30 am to 8 pm on weekdays, 9 am to 5 pm on Saturday and 7.30 am to 8 pm on Sunday. Free tours usually go at 11 am and 2 pm.

Guided City Walks (☎ 342 7691) runs two-hour **guided walks** of the city, departing from its kiosk in the south-western section of the square. Tours leave at 10 am and 2 pm daily, cost $8 and are most informative. Independent walkers can get a copy of the free brochure *Central City Walks*.

The Wizard This latter-day Merlin attempts to conquer gravity through levity and can be heard spouting in Cathedral Square on fine days in the summer months. One of New Zealand's more amusing eccentrics, he dresses the part – long black velvet robes and cape in winter and white robes in summer – and plays it to the hilt. Extremely eloquent, the Wizard has a line of glib patter – pet subjects are bureaucracy, Americans, priests, insurance com- panies and feminism – and a skilful way of playing with the hecklers. His politics belong with the flat earth theory but, whether you like what he has to say or not, it's a production you shouldn't miss.

Southern Encounter Aquarium Cathedral Square's newest attraction in a pseudo-landscaped warehouse has fish in acrylic tanks. There's touch tanks, a fly fishing simulator (costs extra), divers feeding the eels and other oddities including a re-creation of a fishing lodge. The aquarium is well presented but quite small and, with entry at $12.50 (children $6), nothing to get too excited about. It is open from 9 am to 9 pm daily (until 6 pm in winter).

The Banks of the Avon

The invitingly calm and picturesque **Avon River** is a delight just to walk along. If you want to row down it, head to the Antigua Boatsheds by the footbridge at the southern end of Rolleston Ave. Canoes are $5 an hour, paddle boats $10 an hour and row boats $20 an hour. The boatsheds are open from 9 am to 5 pm daily.

Or you can relax and be punted along the river. **Punts** depart from behind the visitor centre, with departures and landings also from the Antigua boatsheds, or opposite the Town Hall Restaurant and the Thomas Edmonds Restaurant. A 20-minute trip costs $10 per person, 30 minutes is $12 and for 45 minutes it's $15 (children under 12 half-price). The punts ply the river from 9 am to dusk daily (10 am to 4 pm in winter).

Beside the museum off Rolleston Ave the **Botanic Gardens**, open from 7 am to one hour before sunset, are 30 hectares of greenery beside the Avon River. The garden's information centre, many floral show houses and the popular fern house are open from 10.15 am to 4 pm daily. Tours leave from the cafe between 11 am and 4 pm from August to April when the weather is fine. The garden restaurant is open for lunch.

Enchanting **Mona Vale**, an Elizabethan-style riverside homestead with 5.5 hectares of richly landscaped gardens, ponds and fountains, is open from 8 am to 7.30 pm daily from October to March, and from 8.30 am to

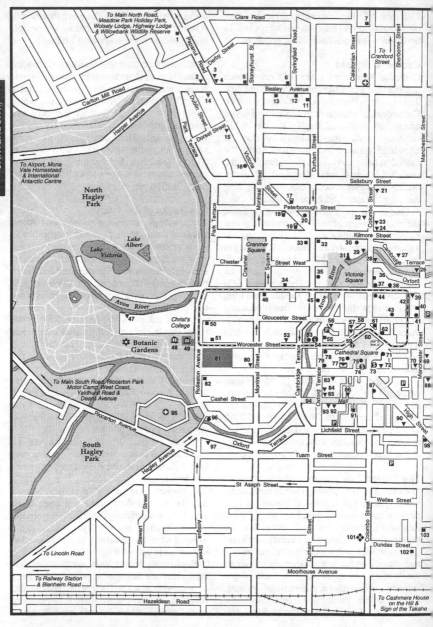

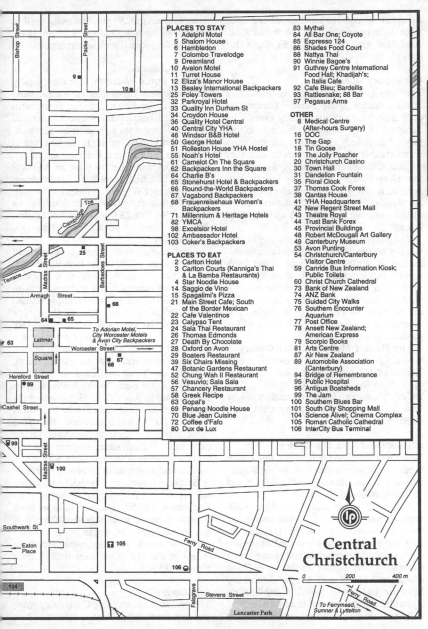

CANTERBURY

PLACES TO STAY
1 Adelphi Motel
5 Shalom House
6 Hambledon
7 Colombo Travelodge
9 Dreamland
10 Avalon Motel
11 Turret House
12 Eliza's Manor House
13 Bealey International Backpackers
25 Foley Towers
32 Parkroyal Hotel
33 Quality Inn Durham St
34 Croydon House
36 Quality Hotel Central
40 Central City YHA
46 Windsor B&B Hotel
50 George Hotel
51 Rolleston House YHA Hostel
55 Noah's Hotel
61 Camelot On The Square
62 Backpackers Inn the Square
64 Charlie B's
65 Stonehurst Hotel & Backpackers
66 Round-the-World Backpackers
67 Vagabond Backpackers
68 Frauenreisehaus Women's
   Backpackers
71 Millennium & Heritage Hotels
82 YMCA
98 Excelsior Hotel
102 Ambassador Hotel
103 Coker's Backpackers

PLACES TO EAT
2 Carlton Hotel
3 Carlton Courts (Kanniga's Thai
   & La Bamba Restaurants)
4 Star Noodle House
14 Saggio de Vino
15 Spagalimi's Pizza
21 Main Street Cafe; South
   of the Border Mexican
22 Cafe Valentinos
23 Calypso Tent
24 Sala Thai Restaurant
26 Thomas Edmonds
27 Death By Chocolate
28 Oxford on Avon
29 Boaters Restaurant
39 Six Chairs Missing
47 Botanic Gardens Restaurant
52 Chung Wah II Restaurant
56 Vesuvio; Sala Sala
57 Chancery Restaurant
58 Greek Recipe
63 Gopal's
69 Penang Noodle House
70 Blue Jean Cuisine
72 Coffee d'Fafo
80 Dux de Lux

83 Mythai
84 All Bar One; Coyote
85 Expresso 124
86 Shades Food Court
88 Nattya Thai
90 Winnie Bagoe's
91 Guthrey Centre International
   Food Hall; Khadijah's;
   In Italia Cafe
92 Cafe Bleu; Bardellis
93 Rattlesnake; 88 Bar
97 Pegasus Arms

OTHER
8 Medical Centre
   (After-hours Surgery)
16 DOC
17 The Gap
18 Tin Goose
19 The Jolly Poacher
20 Christchurch Casino
30 Town Hall
31 Dandelion Fountain
35 Floral Clock
37 Thomas Cook Forex
38 Qantas House
41 YHA Headquarters
42 New Regent Street Mall
43 Theatre Royal
44 Trust Bank Forex
45 Provincial Buildings
48 Robert McDougall Art Gallery
49 Canterbury Museum
53 Avon Punting
54 Christchurch/Canterbury
   Visitor Centre
59 Canride Bus Information Kiosk;
   Public Toilets
60 Christ Church Cathedral
73 Bank of New Zealand
74 ANZ Bank
75 Guided City Walks
76 Southern Encounter
   Aquarium
77 Post Office
78 Ansett New Zealand;
   American Express
79 Scorpio Books
81 Arts Centre
87 Air New Zealand
89 Automobile Association
   (Canterbury)
94 Bridge of Remembrance
95 Public Hospital
96 Antigua Boatsheds
99 The Jam
100 Southern Blues Bar
101 South City Shopping Mall
104 Science Alive; Cinema Complex
105 Roman Catholic Cathedral
106 InterCity Bus Terminal

Central Christchurch

0   200   400 m

5.30 pm from April to September. For guided tours of the homestead book on ☎ 348 9660. It's 1.5km from the city at 63 Fendalton Rd (bus No 9).

Canterbury Museum

This very good museum, on Rolleston Ave at the entrance to the Botanic Gardens, is open from 9 am to 5.30 pm daily. Entry is by donation ($5 is suggested, but not obligatory). Particularly interesting are the early colonist exhibits and the Antarctic discovery section. Christchurch is the HQ for 'Operation Deep Freeze', the supply link to Antarctica. It has good historical exhibits on Antarctic exploration and the natural history of the Antarctic, subantarctic and Chatham islands.

The Maori gallery is very good, as is the slightly repugnant but very informative collection of stuffed birds, right across NZ's species list, including the now-extinct moa. While you're at it, check out the pull-out draws of mounted insects for a look at NZ's unique wetas, as well as huge tarantulas. The museum has a good cafe with views of the gardens on the 4th floor.

The **Robert McDougall Art Gallery** is behind the museum. It has an extensive collection of NZ and international art and is open from 10 am to 4.30 pm daily. The gallery's annexe, featuring contemporary New Zealand art, is in the nearby Arts Centre on Rolleston Ave.

International Antarctic Centre

Near the airport, on Orchard Rd, this centre is part of a huge complex built for the administration and warehousing of the NZ, US and Italian Antarctic programs.

The centre has hands-on exhibits, video presentations and the 'sights and sounds' of the vast continent. Special effects dazzle the kids and the new Snow and Ice Experience allows you to freeze while you slide down a snow slope and explore a snow cave. Good educational family stuff, but the Canterbury Museum has better historical exhibits on Antarctic exploration and is a lot cheaper.

The centre is open from October to March

from 9.30 am to 8.30 pm, and from April to September from 9.30 am to 5.30 pm ($12, children $6). Reach it on an airport bus.

Other Museums

The **Air Force Museum** is exceptionally well presented. On display are aircraft used by the NZ Air Force over the years, with figures and background scenery. Antarctic aircraft sit in the snow, aircraft are serviced, a Canberra bomber of the 1950s taxis out at night, a WWII fighter is hidden in the jungle. You can even pretend to pilot an A4 Skyhawk jet in a flight simulator. The museum is at the former Wigram air base, a 15-minute drive south of the city on Main South Rd, or take bus No 8 or 25 from Cathedral Square. It's open from 10 am to 5 pm daily ($9, children $4).

South-east of the city centre is **Ferrymead Historic Park** at 269 Bridle Path Rd, Heathcote. This historical village is a working museum of transport and technology with electric and steam locomotives, old household appliances, cars, machinery etc. It's open from 10 am to 4.30 pm daily ($6, children $3; steam train and tram rides are $2). Catch Canride bus No 3 from the square.

The **Yaldhurst Transport Museum**, opposite the Yaldhurst Hotel on the Main West Rd, 11km from the city centre, is open from 10 am to 5 pm daily. Displayed in the grounds of an attractive 1876 homestead is some of NZ's earliest transport, including horse-drawn vehicles, vintage cars, racing cars, motorcycles, steam engines and aircraft; admission is $6.50 (children $2.50).

In the old train station, on Moorhouse Ave, is **Science Alive!**, an interesting hands-on science exhibit featuring numerous interactive stations ($6.50, children $5). Open from 9 am to 5 pm on weekdays and 10 am to 6 pm on weekends, its slogan is: 'If I wasn't meant to touch anything, what are these things on the end of my arms for?' A great place for kids.

Arts Centre

The former University of Canterbury town site has been transformed into the Arts

Centre, a great place to browse. The beautiful old Gothic buildings are now an arts, craft and entertainment complex with a good selection of cafes and restaurants thrown in. Tours ($5) of the complex are conducted by the Christchurch town crier at 11 am and 2 pm – buy tickets at the Arts Centre's information centre.

The Galleria, open from 10.30 am to 4.30 pm, has dozens of craft shops with everything from fine pottery, jewellery, weaving, woollen goods and Maori carvings to handmade toys – not cheap but one of the best craft centres in New Zealand and in some cases you can see the craftspeople at work. A craft market is also held on weekends.

National Marae
The largest marae in New Zealand is at 250 Pages Rd, 6km north-east of the city. Nga Hau e Wha (the four winds) is a multicultural facility open to all people – 'Nau mai haere mai' (all are welcome). You can see the carvings, weavings and paintings in the *whare nui* (meeting house) and *whare whananga* (house of learning).

Tours (☎ 388 7685) at 11 am and 2 pm are $5.50 (children $3.50) for a minimum of four. Evening tours and concert cost $25 or $55 with a hangi (bookings essential). Reach the marae on bus No 5.

Christchurch Tramway
Trams, first introduced to Christchurch streets in 1905, only lasted as a means of transport for 60 years. Restored green and cream trams have been reintroduced as part of a 2.5km inner-city loop around many of the city's best features and shopping areas. The trams operate from 8 am to 11 pm daily. Tickets cost $5 for one hour, $6 for four hours and $7 for a full day (children $2/3/4). It's probably quicker (certainly cheaper) to walk. One plus is that it passes through the historic **New Regent St** precinct, with many examples of Spanish architecture.

Christchurch Gondola
For a cost of $12 (children $6, families $29) you can be whisked up from the Heathcote Valley terminal on a 4½-minute ride to a point somewhere above the Lyttelton Rd tunnel. There are great views at the top (Mt Cavendish, around 500m) right across to the Southern Alps on a fine day.

The gondola operates from 10 am until late daily; the free Gondola bus leaves regularly from the visitor centre or take the No 28 Lyttelton bus. At the top, there's a cafe, restaurant, shop and heritage show to spend more money on. Walkways lead on to the Crater Rim Walkway (see under Walking). You can mountain-bike down with the Mountain Bike Adventure Company (☎ 381 4044) or paraglide down with Nimbus Paragliding (☎ 332 2233).

Christchurch Casino
NZ's first casino is in the heart of town on Victoria and Kilmore Sts. Las Vegas comes to sleepy hollow, but draconian dress standards (no jeans, tramping boots etc) apply and it relies on pensioners from the countryside who come in on the free casino buses. It is open 24 hours. All the traditional methods of losing your money are provided.

Wildlife Reserves
The **Orana Park Wildlife Trust** has an excellent walk-through aviary of native birds and a nocturnal kiwi house, as well as tuataras. Most of the extensive grounds, however, are devoted to the 'African Plains' of lions, rhino, giraffe, zebra, oryx and cheetah. Animal feeding times are scheduled daily. It's open from 10 am to 5 pm daily (last admission at 4.30 pm; $12, children $6) and includes a shuttle bus tour. It's on McLeans Island Rd, Harewood, beyond the airport, and about 20 minutes from the city.

The **Willowbank Wildlife Reserve** has exotic and local animals, including a variety of domestic animals. The selection of native wildlife is extensive and there is a large nocturnal kiwi house. The reserve is open from 10 am to 10 pm daily and entry is $11 (children $5). The reserve is on Hussey Rd. The City Circuit bus runs there from the visitor centre.

Other Attractions

The **Queen Elizabeth II Park** (☎ 383 4313) on Travis Rd, North Beach, 8km north-east of the centre, is a huge sports complex, with indoor pools, water-slides and squash courts, and was the venue for the 1974 Commonwealth Games. The adjacent fun park has a variety of amusement park attractions. Take Canride bus No 10 or 19 from the square.

Riccarton House, an imposing Victorian mansion, is at 16 Kahu Rd, 3km west of the centre. The house is open from 1 to 4 pm on weekdays and 2 to 4 pm on Sunday, but of most interest is the six-hectare stand of native bush in the estate, a remnant of the long-since cleared Canterbury plains.

Swimming & Surfing

The closest beaches to the city are North Beach (10km; bus No 19), South Brighton Beach (10km; bus No 5), Sumner (11km; bus No 3), Waimairi (10km; bus No 10), New Brighton (8km; bus No 5) and Taylors Mistake – a pleasant beach further out from Sumner, popular for surfing.

Walking

The Christchurch/Canterbury Visitor Centre has details and leaflets about walks around Christchurch.

Starting in the city are the **Riverside Walk** (the leaflet on this is packed with information) and various historical walks. For great views of the city, there is a walkway from the **Sign of the Takahe**. The various 'Sign of the ...' places in this area were originally roadhouses built during the depression as rest stops. Now they vary from the impressive tearooms at the Sign of the Takahe to a simple shelter at the Sign of the Bellbird and are referred to primarily as landmarks. This walk leads up to the **Sign of the Kiwi** through Victoria Park and then along near the Summit Rd to Scott Reserve, with several lookout points along the way. The walk is accessible by bus No 2 from Victoria Square near the Town Hall.

You can walk to Lyttelton on the **Bridle Path**. It starts from Heathcote Valley (take bus No 28) and takes one to 1½ hours at an easy pace. The **Godley Head Walkway** is a two-hour round trip from Taylors Mistake, crossing then recrossing Summit Rd with beautiful views on a clear day. The **Rapaki Track** is an excellent walk taking just a couple of hours and offering fine views of the whole city and of Lyttelton.

The **Crater Rim Walkway** around Lyttelton Harbour goes some 14km from the Bridle Path to the Ahuriri Scenic Reserve, passing through a number of scenic reserves along the way, plus the Sign of the Bellbird and the Sign of the Kiwi. The walkway can easily be done in several short stages.

There are a number of shorter walks in and around **Nicholson Park and Sumner Head**, about 25 minutes by car from the square, or catch a No 3 bus. Here you'll see many inshore birds, such as the eastern bar-tailed godwit, gulls, shags and black swans.

Skiing

Several ski areas are within a two-hour drive of Christchurch. For more information see Skiing in the Outdoor Activities chapter and individual entries for each of the resorts in this chapter. The Christchurch/Canterbury Visitor Information Centre has information on all ski areas.

Organised Tours

The City Circuit bus departs on the hour from the visitor centre (see Getting Around in this section).

Gray Line (☎ 343 3874) has a three-hour morning highlights tour which includes Mona Vale and the Port Hills ($30, children $15), and an afternoon sights tour to Sumner, Lyttelton Harbour (launch cruise) and the Port Hills ($34, children $17).

Travel Pioneer (☎ 388 2042) has interesting trips which offer activities that other bus trips don't. Akaroa via the coastal back roads is $58; Arthur's Pass and the Otira Gorge is $78; and Hanmer Springs via the Waipara Gorge back road is $58. All trips leave at about 8.30 am and return about 6 pm. There's courtesy pick-up from inner-city hostels.

Christchurch Sightseeing Tours (☎ 366 9660) offers half-day city tours ($25) and three-hour garden tours to the city's leading gardens on Tuesday, Thursday and Saturday from November to March ($20).

Canterbury Leisure Tours (☎ 0800 484 485) has half and full-day golfing tours and tours further afield to Mt Cook, Kaikoura and Hanmer Springs. A number of readers recommend Canterbury Trails (☎ 337 1185), which offers personalised tours to various parts of the province in a 4WD vehicle.

Places to Stay

Camping & Cabins The *Showground Motor Camp* (☎ 338 9770) at 47-51 Whiteleigh Rd off Lincoln Rd is 3km south-west of the city centre and has tent/powered sites at $13.40/15.40 for two. It also has a variety of cabins from as little as $25 to $46 for self-contained cabins. It's conveniently located and cheap, but not somewhere you'd want to spend a lot of time. Get there on bus No 7.

The *Meadow Park Holiday Park* (☎ 352 9176) at 39 Meadow St off the Main North Rd is 5km north. Camping, with power, costs $20 for two, cabins are from $33, tourist flats are $50 to $57 for two and a lodge with 22 units sleeping two to five is $47 for two. The camping ground has a heated swimming pool, a spa, children's playground and a recreation hall. Take bus No 4.

Russley Park Motor Camp (☎ 342 7021) is at 372 Yaldhurst Rd, opposite Riccarton Racecourse about 10km north-west of the square or 5km from the airport. Tent/powered sites cost $16/19, chalet cabins are from $30 to $39 and there are some fancier tourist flats from $55; all prices are for two. Take bus No 8.

South Brighton Motor Camp (☎ 388 9844), 59 Halsey St off Estuary Rd, 10km north-east, is another attractive park. Tent/powered sites are $15/17 for two and cabins are $25. Take bus No 5. The *All Seasons Holiday Park* (☎ 384 9490) is at 5 Kidbrooke St, Linwood, about 4km east of the city. In this park tent/powered sites are $16/18, on-site vans are $33 and cabins are $28; all prices are for two.

Amber Park Caravan Park (☎ 348 3327) is at 308 Blenheim Rd, only 4km west of the

square. Tent/powered sites cost $18/19 and tourist flats, which share the camp kitchen facilities but have en suites, are from $46 to $56; prices are for two. Take bus No 25. The *North South Airport Holiday Park* (☎ 359 5993) is on the corner of Johns and Sawyers Arms Rds, on the North-South Bypass, 2.5km from the airport. Tent/powered sites are $14/18, basic cabins are $30 and tourist cabins are $40 and $50; all prices are for two.

Out-of-town parks include the *Prebbleton Holiday Park* (☎ 349 7861) at 18 Blakes Rd, Prebbleton, 12km south of the city; and *Spencer Park Holiday Camp* (☎ 329 8721) on Heyders Rd, Spencerville, 14km north.

Hostels Christchurch has two YHA hostels and some popular backpackers. Some of the big, older backpackers offer very cheap rates in the off season – as low as $10 for a dorm bed.

Rolleston House YHA Hostel (☎ 366 6564), 5 Worcester St, is in an excellent position opposite the Arts Centre and only 700m from the square. A dorm bed is $17 per person and twins are $38.

The larger *Central City YHA* (☎ 379 9535), 273 Manchester St, has four-bed rooms for $18 per person and twins/doubles for $40/42. It has a spacious common room, excellent kitchen facilities and quiet, tidy rooms with heating.

The ever popular *Foley Towers* (☎ 366 9720), 208 Kilmore St near Madras St, is a large but spacious backpackers with a pleasant little garden out the back. A dorm or shared room costs $15 per person and the twin and double rooms are $30/38 without/with en suite.

Bealey International Backpackers (☎ /fax 366 6760) at 70 Bealey Ave (between Montreal and Durham Sts) is a smaller place with a friendly atmosphere, an outdoor garden and BBQ area, and a cosy log fire in winter. It offers luggage storage and can book activities. Rates are $15 for a shared room or $34 for twins and doubles.

The *Backpackers Inn the Square* (☎ 366 5158), right on Cathedral Square, is one of Christchurch's once-famous hotels, now fallen on hard times. The only plus is the location. Dorms are $14.50 per person (plus $5 key deposit) and twin and double rooms are $35 and $40 with en suite.

The large and well-equipped *Coker's Backpackers* (☎ 379 8580) is at 52 Manchester St. This former pub is an older, labyrinthine place with a huge kitchen, dining room and lounge areas, and a bar next door. There are dorms for $16 per person, and twins and doubles for $44 (all have en suites).

Dreamland (☎ 366 3519), 21 Packe St, is a relaxed, homey backpackers in a comfortable old house. The cost for shared rooms is $14 and $15 per person and $34 for twins or doubles. The owner is a keen cyclist and maintains visitors' bikes ($1) in his workshop. It has open fireplaces, lots of information and a nice atmosphere.

Charlie B's (☎ 379 8429), on the corner of Madras and Gloucester Sts, is very central. This large backpackers is shabby in parts, but it has all the facilities, including a games room, videos, BBQ and off-street parking. A bed in the huge dorms costs $11 – you get what you pay for. Smaller shared rooms cost $14 per person, and it has a large selection of singles ($25) and twin and double rooms ($32).

Frauenreisehaus – The Homestead (☎ 366 2585), 272 Barbadoes St, is a well-equipped women-only backpackers. It has a full kitchen and laundry, TV and video, games room, library and free linen. Tastefully furnished rooms cost $13 for dorms, $20 for singles and $30 for twins.

Further north, at 314 Barbadoes St, is the purpose built *Round-the-World Backpackers* (☎ 365 4363). It is well set up and has excellent fixtures and fittings. A dorm is $15 per person and twins or doubles are $36.

The popular *Vagabond* (☎ 379 9677) at 232 Worcester St is one of the newest and smallest hostels close to the city centre. It has a homey feel, has been attractively refurbished and has a sunny outdoor garden. Bunk beds are $12.50, shared rooms are $15 per person, twins and doubles are $30 and there is one single for $19. Further along at

563 Worcester St, 2.5km from the city, *Avon City Backpackers* (☎ 389 6876) is another small place but not with the same atmosphere as Vagabond. Dorms are $15 and doubles $36.

The *Shalom House* (☎ 366 6770) at 69 Bealey Ave is a Christian guesthouse-cum-backpackers. This old house has well-presented, comfortable rooms but a cramped kitchen and lounge. Advertised rates are $15 for dorms and $25/34 for singles/doubles, but they may charge more.

The *Stonehurst Hotel* (☎ 379 4620) at 241 Gloucester St is very close to the city centre. Rates are $13 per person in the dorms (provide your own bedding) or doubles are $30 to $39 and some have an en suite. Hostellers can use the pub facilities next door. Room rates in the hotel are from $50 for doubles and breakfast is from $5.

The *YMCA* (☎ 366 0689), 12 Hereford St, is a few steps from the Arts Centre and Canterbury Museum. The hostel, open 24 hours, takes both men and women and the cafeteria serves cheap meals. During the school terms most of the cheaper rooms are full of students, but there should always be room for casuals. Bunkrooms are $17 per person, cheaper rooms are $37/50, motel-style rooms with en suite are $60/85 and apartments are $100 to $120.

Lyttelton, only a half-hour by bus from Christchurch, also has a good hostel if you want to escape the city.

B&Bs & Guesthouses A cheap option is the *Thistle Guesthouse* (☎ 348 1499), 21 Main South Rd near the junction of Riccarton and Yaldhurst Rds, about 6km from the city square. Singles/doubles are $30/50. Breakfast is available ($7) and there's a kitchen, laundry and off-street parking. The *Windsor B&B Hotel* (☎ 366 1503) at 52 Armagh St is just five to 10 minutes walk from the city centre. It's meticulously clean and orderly, and rooms with shared bath cost $60/90. On the same street at No 63, *Croydon House* (☎ 366 5111) is similar and charges $56/88.

Two kilometres north-west of the square, the *Wolseley Lodge* (☎ 355 6202) at 107

Papanui Rd is a big, old-fashioned house in a quiet setting with rooms at $40/70 including breakfast. A few doors down at No 121 the *Highway Lodge* (☎ 355 5418) has rooms for $35/50 or $49/65 and continental breakfast is available. This leafy area is very pleasant, with restaurants nearby and easy access to the centre (walk or take bus No 1).

Built in 1885, *Turret House* (☎ 365 3900), 435 Durham St (North), has been elegantly restored. Rooms cost from $65/85, which includes continental breakfast and en suite. At 82 Bealey Ave is the elegantly restored *Eliza's Manor House* (☎ 366 8584) with bedrooms from $90 to $145 (winter rates from $65). It has a fully licensed restaurant and a bar. *Hambledon* (☎ 379 0723) at 103 Bealey Ave is a gracious old place; singles are from $65 to $90 and doubles from $85 to $145. The gardens are delightful.

At 141 Hackthorne Rd, at the foot of the hills of the same name, is *Cashmere House on the Hill* (☎ 332 7864), an elegantly restored mansion on Cashmere Hill. It has almost half a hectare of gardens and views over the city. Singles/doubles cost from $110/140.

Motels Christchurch is well endowed with motels, most of them charging from $70 to $90 a double. Motels can be found all around the city, but Bealey Ave has a few close to the centre and Papanui Rd has a string of mostly more upmarket motels. Better priced motels include:

Achilles Motel (☎ 379 9688), 118 Sherbourne St, St Albans (on SH1); doubles $55 to $70
Adelphi Motel (☎ 355 6037), 49 Papanui Rd; doubles $80 to $100
Adorian Motel (☎ 366 7626), 347 Worcester St, Linwood; singles/doubles $69/79
Airport Lodge Motel (☎ 358 5119), 105 Roydvale Ave, Burnside; doubles $79 to $89
Avalon Motel (☎ 379 9680), on the corner of Bealey Ave and Geraldine St; doubles $75 to $85
Avon City Motel (☎ 352 6079), 402 Main North Rd; doubles/triples $60 to $75
Avonhead Lodge Motel (☎ 348 1309), 168 Yaldhurst Rd; doubles $75 to $95 during holidays
Belle Bonne Motel (☎ 348 8458), 95 Yaldhurst Rd, Riccarton; singles/doubles $72/80

Cashel Court Motel (☎ 389 2768), 457 Cashel St; doubles $58 to $70
City Worcester Motels (☎ 366 4491), 336 Worcester St; doubles from $55 to $79
Colombo Travelodge (☎ 366 3029), 965 Colombo St; doubles $62 to $69
Cranford Court Motel (☎ 379 2406), 63 Cranford St, St Albans; doubles $74 to $98
Earnslaw Motel (☎ 348 6387), 288 Blenheim Rd, Riccarton; singles/doubles $68/75
Golden Mile Motor Lodge (☎ 349 6153), Main South Rd, Riccarton; doubles $73
Golden Sands Beach Motel (☎ 388 7996), 121 Estuary Rd, New Brighton; doubles $70
Hagley Motel (☎ 348 7683), 13 Darvel St, Riccarton; doubles $70 to $100
Holiday Lodge Motel (☎ 366 6584), 862 Colombo St; doubles $65 to $75
Middlepark Motel (☎ 348 7320), 120 Main South Rd, Upper Riccarton; doubles $59 to $85
Riccarton Motel (☎ 348 7127), 92 Main South Rd, Upper Riccarton; singles/doubles $65/75
Tall Trees Motel (☎ 352 6681), 454 Papanui Rd, Papanui; doubles $69 to $89

Hotels The Stonehurst Hotel (see under Hostels) has cheap rooms or the *Ambassador Hotel* (☎ 366 7808) at 19 Manchester St is a 10-minute walk south of the city centre. It's quite a flash old hotel, with leadlight windows. Singles/doubles are $40/60, including continental breakfast. The *Excelsior Hotel* (☎ 366 9489), on the corner of High and Manchester Sts, has old pub rooms for $35/45 or $55 a double with en suite.

Top-bracket Christchurch hotels include the *Chateau on the Park* (☎ 348 8999) on the corner of Deans Ave and Kilmarnock St at the edge of Hagley Park, the *Quality Hotel Durham* (☎ 365 4699) on the corner of Durham and Kilmore Sts, the *Quality Hotel Central* (☎ 379 5880) at 776 Colombo St, *Noah's* (☎ 379 4700) on the corner of Worcester St and Oxford Terrace, and, out at the airport, the *Airport Plaza* (☎ 358 3139). In these hotels doubles are from $150 (and up).

On Cathedral Square, *Camelot On The Square* (☎ 337 5757) is a mid-range hotel with rooms from $150, and the *Millennium* (☎ 365 1111) and *Heritage* are much flasher hotels with rooms from around $200.

The *George Hotel* (☎ 379 4560), 50 Park

Terrace, is a small boutique hotel out of the mould and definitely in the luxury class. Rooms cost $275 to $300 and suites $345 to $550.

Right at the top of the price scale is the imaginatively designed and wonderfully located *Parkroyal Hotel* (☎ 365 7799), on the corner of Durham and Kilmore Sts, where a double with great views costs $345.

Places to Eat

Restaurants The *Gardens Restaurant* in the wonderful Botanic Gardens is renowned for excellent smorgasbords ($12.50 including coffee) from noon to 2 pm daily. The restaurant is open from 10 am to 4.30 pm for snacks and other light meals.

More expensive options along the riverside include *Thomas Edmonds*, in a former band rotunda on Cambridge Terrace. It's a great position and you could complement the romantic atmosphere by arriving by punt! Light main courses for lunch start at around $10 (dinner from $20), with both meat and vegetarian selections. It's open for lunch from Sunday to Friday and dinner from Monday to Saturday. The riverside setting of the expensive *Boaters Restaurant* restaurant in the town hall makes it a popular place to eat. Best value are the lunch buffets.

Across the plaza at the ultra-expensive Parkroyal Hotel, the elegant *Victoria Street Cafe* is in the inner courtyard and is not as expensive as it looks – main courses, meat and vegetarian, cost around $20 and there's a salad bar. The wine list is extensive. Also in the Parkroyal is the very upmarket and award-winning *Canterbury Tales* and the *Yamagen*, an expensive Japanese place.

Sala Sala, 184-186 Oxford Terrace near the corner of Gloucester St, is another good Japanese restaurant open every night for dinner. Further south, Oxford Terrace is lined with bar-restaurants, spilling around into Cashel Mall, but the food may take second place to the drinking.

Blue Jean Cuisine, 205 Manchester St, is a bar-restaurant in a sand-blasted warehouse and is very popular for its reasonably priced fish, chicken and steak mains at around $18.

Penang Noodle House, 172 Manchester St, is a no-frills place with good Malaysian meals ($5 to $6) and is open daily except Tuesday for lunch and dinner. *Six Chairs Missing* at 36 New Regent St sounds like a best movie candidate at Cannes, but is a good little cafe with innovative mains for around $23 – the rack of lamb is excellent. It's open from 10 am to 6 pm daily except Sunday and for dinner from Wednesday to Sunday.

Fans of Thai food will not be disappointed with the authentic cuisine at *Mythai*, 84 Hereford St. The dowdy but cheap *Sala Thai* is on the corner of Colombo and Kilmore Sts, or the better *Nattya Thai*, 196 Hereford St, has an extensive menu with mains for around $12 to $14 and vegetarian selections for $10. There are plenty of Chinese restaurants, including the imposing *Chung Wah II* at 63 Worcester St.

Carlton Courts on the corner of Bealey Ave and Papanui Rd has a small cluster of good restaurants, including *Kanniga's Thai* for reasonably priced Thai food. Next door, *La Bamba*, a South American, Cajun and Mexican restaurant, has mains from $20, up to $25 for the seafood jambalaya.

For something different, *Calypso Tent* on Colombo St is a Caribbean restaurant open Monday to Saturday for dinner and has gumbo ($17) and other similarly priced mains. *South of the Border*, 834 Colombo St, is a reasonably priced Tex-Mex restaurant.

Christchurch has a good selection of quality Italian restaurants. *Cafe Valentino's* at 813 Colombo St is a casual place with spacious wooden beam-and-brick décor. It is open daily from noon until late and dinner mains are around $20, less for pasta. *Spagalimi's Pizza* at 155 Victoria St is a very popular place in the Pizza Hut mould that also does takeaways. The upmarket *Saggio di Vino*, 185 Victoria St (corner of Bealey Ave), has a great wine selection, available by the glass, and light meals. At 83 Lichfield St is *Winnie Bagoe's*, a lively hostelry which is also open until late serving pizza until 3 am. *Bardelli's* in the city centre at 98 Cashel St specialises in Mediterranean food. It has blackboard and à la carte menus and pasta

Canterbury
Top: Lake Tekapo
Bottom: Lyttelton Harbour, Christchurch's port

Canterbury
Top: Lake Tekapo in winter
Middle: Lake Pukaki and Mt Cook from the air
Bottom: Wide open road, near Twizel

night specials ($9) from Monday to Thursday.

To finish yourself off, *Death by Chocolate* tempts in Faustian fashion at 209 Cambridge Terrace. This dessert restaurant has sinfully rich offerings for around $15.

Vegetarian *Gopal's* at 143 Worcester St is another of the Hare Krishna-run restaurants. It's open for lunch ($3.50) on weekdays and dinner ($6) on Friday night.

Exceptionally good vegetarian food can be found at the relaxed and popular *Main Street Cafe*, 840 Colombo St, with an open-air courtyard at the back. Imaginative main courses are around $10, the salads are good and the desserts mouthwatering. It's open from 10 am to late daily.

Dux de Lux is a very popular gourmet restaurant specialising in seafood but also features vegetarian taste treats. It's close to the Arts Centre, on Montreal St near Hereford St. There's an outdoor courtyard and a bar and brewery, with live music several nights a week. It's open from around 10 am until midnight.

Cafes The Arts Centre has some very pleasant cafes, including *Le Café* and the *Boulevard Bakehouse*, as well as more expensive dining options.

A reader, describing himself as one of 'the fussiest and most hopelessly addicted drinkers of gourmet speciality coffees', recommends *Coffee d'Fafo*, 137 Hereford St, for its authentic products. The very popular *Vesuvio* at 182 Oxford Terrace is another street-front cafe and also boasts an impressive selection of wines by the glass. The *Star Noodle House* is a small but chic takeaway and restaurant on Papanui Rd near the corner of Bealey Ave. Thai noodles and other dishes are cheap.

Pub Food On Colombo St, the *Oxford on Avon* plays the ye olde pub theme to the hilt and is in a lovely setting right by the river with an outside garden bar. It is popular for huge, hearty and cheap meals. Big English breakfasts are $9.95 and three-course dinner

roasts are similarly oversized and cost $14.95. It's open daily from 6.30 am to midnight.

Other possibilities include the *Carlton Hotel* on the corner of Papanui Rd and Bealey Ave, with cheap bar meals and a rugby clientele; the *Pegasus Arms*, 14 Oxford Terrace near the hospital, for a bistro lunch; and the *Chancery* at 98 Gloucester St, which features roasts and steaks at around $12 a main.

Fast Food A good variety of food stalls is set up in Cathedral Square with benches and tables to eat. The *Greek Recipe* at 55 Cathedral Square, beside the West End Theatre, has authentic, inexpensive Greek takeaways and is open from 10 am to 10 pm daily except Sunday.

The *Guthrey Centre International Food Hall* on Cashel Mall has Chinese, Greek and other good food stalls. *Khadijah's*, upstairs above the food hall area, is slightly more restaurant-like and has cheap, excellent Malaysian food. The more expensive *In Italia Cafe* at the entrance to the Guthrey Centre has good pasta (around $12), antipasto, espresso etc and tables outside in the mall for people watching.

On the other side of Cashel Mall in Shades Arcade, *Shades Food Court* also has a good selection of food stalls.

Entertainment

Cinema & Performing Arts Christchurch is the cultural centre of the South Island. The focus is the Town Hall (☎ 366 8899) on Kilmore St by the riverside where you can hear a chamber or symphony orchestra. The James Hay Theatre in the town hall and the Theatre Royal in Gloucester St are the centres of live theatre. There is a big cinema complex in the old train station.

Bars, Music & Dancing Christchurch has a big selection of cafe-bars for a night on the town, and nightlife in this small city is very active on weekends.

An old favourite is *Bailies* at Backpackers Inn the Square. Smoke fills the room, the

Guinness is carefully decanted into pint glasses, and snacks are left on the bar for patrons.

Christchurch's liveliest area at night is around the Bridge of Remembrance where the Cashel Mall meets Oxford Terrace. Guys in check shirts and gangs of youths too young to drink cruise the mall, but inside the cafes and bars are very fashionable. On the mall, *Bardellis*, *Cafe Bleu* and *88 Bar* are popular with a more moneyed crowd. *Rattlesnake* and *Espresso 124* are similar but even more crowded on weekends. Around the corner, Oxford Terrace is a constant procession of bar patrons and *All Bar One* and *Coyote* are standing room only.

Those in search of the seedy can head to the other end of the Mall and south to Lichfield St in the red-light/bathhouse enclave. Polynesian techno and hip-hop clubs dominate, or a bit further east the *Jam* has bands in the upper decibel range. The best place for aficionados of good blues music is the *Southern Blues Bar* on the corner of Madras and Tuam Sts. The bouncers are oversized, but it gets a mixed crowd of workers and the city's elite.

Of course, you can always have a drink at the casino while you lose your money, but before you reach that stage, some good bars are nearby. For a good old-fashioned night out that lingers well into the 'wee' hours, the *Jolly Poacher* is opposite the casino on Victoria St. It is less pretentious than the chic *Tin Goose* nearby on the corner of Peterborough St. Diagonally opposite, set back from Peterborough St, the *Gap* has good jazz bands and a relaxed atmosphere.

The *Dux de Lux* restaurant has its own brewery, bar and bands (see under Vegetarian). The *Carlton* on the corner of Bealey Ave and Papanui Rd is a straightforward pub with weekend entertainment. Plenty of other pubs in the suburbs have bands.

Getting There & Away

Air Christchurch is the main international gateway to the South Island. Overseas airlines with offices in Christchurch are:

British Airways
    (☎ 379 2503), Level 18, Price Waterhouse Building, 119 Armagh Street
Japan Airlines
    (☎ 365 5879), Level 11, Clarendon Towers, 78 Worcester Street
Qantas Airways
    (☎ 0800 808 767), Price Waterhouse Building, 119 Armagh Street
Singapore Airlines
    (☎ 366 8003), Level 13, Forsyth Barr Building, on the corner of Armagh and Colombo Sts
United Airlines
    (☎ 366 1736), 152 Hereford St

Air New Zealand is the main international and domestic carrier. Its main Christchurch office (☎ 353 4899) is at the Triangle Centre, 702 Colombo St. Daily direct flights go between Christchurch and Auckland, Blenheim, Dunedin, Hokitika, Invercargill, Mt Cook, Nelson, Queenstown, Te Anau, Timaru and Wellington, with connections to most other centres. It can also book Air Chatham flights to the Chatham Islands.

Ansett New Zealand (☎ 371 1146) on the corner of Worcester St and Oxford Terrace has direct flights to Auckland, Dunedin, Invercargill, Palmerston North, Queenstown, Rotorua and Wellington.

Bus InterCity (☎ 379 9020) is the main South Island carrier and buses depart from the corner of Moorhouse and Fitzgerald Aves. To the north, buses go to Kaikoura (three hours), Blenheim and Picton (5½ hours) with connections to Nelson. Daily buses go to Queenstown (10½ hours) via Mt Cook (5½ hours), with connections to Wanaka. To the south, three daily buses run along the coast via the towns of the SH1 to Dunedin (six hours) with connections to Invercargill, Te Anau and Queenstown.

Newmans (☎ 374 6149) buses stop at the visitor information centre on Oxford Terrace. It has daily buses to Dunedin and to Nelson via Picton and Kaikoura.

Mt Cook Landline (☎ 348 2099) is at 47 Riccarton Rd, 2km west of the city centre. Daily buses go to Queenstown via Mt Cook.

The West Coast is sadly neglected by the major bus companies, but Coast to Coast

Shuttle (☎ 0800 800 847) and Alpine Coach & Courier (☎ 0800 274 888) have daily services to Greymouth or Hokitika, both $35, via Arthur's Pass. Other shuttles are Ko-Op (☎ 366 6633) to Greymouth and East West (☎ 0800 500 251) to Westport.

Myriad shuttle buses run to most destinations including Picton, Queenstown, Wanaka, Dunedin, Akaroa, Hanmer Springs and points in between. See under those towns for details. Most can be booked at the visitor information centre or the bus information kiosk on Cathedral Square. See the Getting Around chapter for details on the backpacker buses.

Train The train station (☎ 0800 802 802) is on Clarence St in Addington, some way out of the city, and there is a free morning bus service; ask at the visitor centre.

Trains run daily each way between Christchurch and Picton, connecting with the 1.30 pm *Interislander* ferry to Wellington. There is also a daily *Southerner* service each way between Christchurch and Invercargill via Dunedin. The *TranzAlpine Express* train runs daily between Christchurch and Greymouth via Arthur's Pass. Crossing over to the west coast the section of railway through the Waimakariri Gorge (above Springfield) has interesting scenery, but the road follows a different and even more spectacular route.

Hitching It's pretty good hitching on the whole but Christchurch to Dunedin can be a long day, and tends to get harder further south until you approach Dunedin. Catch a Templeton bus (No 25 or 8) to get out of the city. Christchurch to Picton can be done in a day, although there can be long waits. Hitching north, bus No 1 or 4 will get you to Redwood on SH74, a couple of kilometres before it joins SH1.

To hitch west take bus No 8 (Yaldhurst) – then keep your fingers crossed; it can be a long, hard haul, as much as two days. Pick up the train along the way if you become despondent. The first part is easily hitched, but once you leave SH1 it gets harder to find a lift.

Getting Around

To/From the Airport Christchurch airport is 11km north-west of the city centre. Airport banks change money, but this international airport is not particularly well-stocked with facilities. Information centres (☎ 358 5029) are in both the domestic and international terminals. Queues are long when flights arrive and customs here seems to think that every second person is a carrier of drugs or mad cow disease and has a reputation for unnecessary searches. Departure tax on international flights is $25.

The public bus to the airport ($2.70) leaves from Cathedral Square. On weekdays buses leave every half-hour from 7.10 am to 6.40 pm, then every hour until 9.40 pm. They run every hour from 8.25 am to 9.25 pm on Saturday and until 7.25 pm on Sunday.

Door-to-door airport shuttle bus companies, such as Super Shuttle (☎ 365 5655) and Carrington (☎ 352 6369), operate 24 hours and charge from $8 per person. A taxi to or from the airport will cost about $20.

Bus Most city buses are operated by Canride and run from Cathedral Square. Unlike most NZ urban bus services, Christchurch's is good, cheap and well organised. For bus information phone Bus Info (☎ 366 8855). Fares are 90c, $1.80 and a maximum of $2.70. An all-day Big Red Bus Pass is $5 ($10 family). Pick up the pamphlet for the useful bus information.

The City Circuit bus (☎ 385 5386) has two circuits (Plains and Port), both leaving from the visitor centre and costing $25 for eight hours of travel or $15 on one circuit only. Plains Circuit buses leave in the morning and take in Willowbank, the International Antarctic Centre, Air Force Museum and Mona Vale. The afternoon Port Circuit runs to Lyttelton via the gondola and other points of interest.

Car & Motorcycle The major rental companies all have offices in Christchurch, as do numerous smaller local companies. The yellow pages lists over 50 operators. Competition keeps the prices down and, though not as good as Auckland, Christchurch is the best place in the South Island to rent a car. Operators with national networks often want cars to be shifted from Christchurch to Auckland because most renters travel in the opposite direction. Special rates may apply.

With the smaller operators, unlimited kilometres rates start from around $50 a day, but can be much less for longer rentals if you shop around by phone. Christchurch is also a good place to rent a motor home – prices fluctuate but recent price wars have seen big discounts on the normally high rates.

Avis
    (☎ 379 6133), 26 Lichfield St
*Brits New Zealand Rental
    (☎ 358 0973), 33 Orchard Rd
Economy Rental Cars
    (☎ 359 7410), 518 Wairakei Rd, Burnside
Hertz
    (☎ 358 6789), 801 Wairakei Rd
*Kombi Kampa Rentals
    (☎ 384 4751), 1013 Ferry Rd
*Maui
    (☎ 358 4159), 530-544 Memorial Ave
National
    (☎ 366 5574), 134 Victoria St
Pegasus Rental Cars
    (☎ 365 1100), 127 Peterborough St
Renny Rentals
    (☎ 366 6790), 156 Tuam St
Shoestring Rentals
    (☎ 385 3647), 19 Bideford Pl, Burwood

*Campervan specialists

Wheels ChCh – Sales (☎ 366 4855), 20 Manchester St, hires cars and also has a sale and buy-back scheme.

Motorcycles can be hired from Eric Wood Motorcycles (☎ 366 0129) at 35 Manchester St for around $70 a day for a new bike.

Taxi Christchurch has plenty of taxis. Catch them at ranks (there's one on the north-west side of Cathedral Square) or phone: Blue Star (☎ 379 9799), First Direct (☎ 377 5555) or Gold Band (☎ 379 5795). Flagfall is $1.90, each kilometre costs $1.70, waiting time is 60c per minute and a $1 airport surcharge applies.

Bicycle Trailblazers (☎ 366 6033; fax 366 6173) at 86 Worcester Boulevard rents out bikes for $5 an hour or $20 a day; it has good mountain bikes.

AROUND CHRISTCHURCH
Lyttelton
To the south-east of Christchurch are the prominent Port Hills and, behind them Lyttelton Harbour, Christchurch's port. Christchurch's first settlers landed at Lyttelton in 1850 and then made the historic trek over the hills to their new promised land.

Only 12km from Christchurch, Lyttelton is an attractive small port town, with historic buildings and cafe-bars popular with Christchurch daytrippers on weekends. It makes a good day trip, especially if you have a car and go via the scenic **Port Hills**. Drive along the narrow Summit Rd of the hills for breathtaking views of the azure waters of the harbour, the golden brown sweep of the bare hillsides and vistas of Christchurch and the Southern Alps. The route is outlined in the free *Port Hills Drive* pamphlet. Alternatively, Lyttelton is reached more quickly from Christchurch by a road tunnel, an impressive piece of engineering with gleaming tiles reminiscent of a huge, elongated public toilet.

The **Lyttelton Museum** on Gladstone Quay has colonial displays, a maritime gallery and an Antarctic gallery. It is open weekends from 2 to 4 pm, also from Tuesday and Thursday in summer.

On Reserve Terrace, the **Timeball Station** is one of the few remaining in the world. Built in 1876, it once fulfilled an important maritime duty. Daily for 58 years, the huge timeball was hoisted on a mast and then dropped at exactly 1 pm, Greenwich Mean Time, allowing ships in the harbour to set their clocks and thereby accurately calculate longitude. It's open from 10 am to 5 pm daily ($3, children $1).

The helpful Lyttelton Information Office (☎ 328 9093) is at 20 Oxford St. Pick up a copy of the self-guided historic walk pamphlet, or the office can book guided walking tours.

Activities Most popular are the **harbour cruises**. Lyttelton Harbour Cruises (☎ 328 8368) operates a 2.45 pm harbour cruise ($8, children half-price) and a passenger service from B Jetty in Lyttelton to Diamond Harbour ($7.20 return), Quail Island ($8) and Ripapa Island Historic Reserve ($12) throughout the day in summer (weekends only in winter).

The turn-of-the-century steam tug *Lyttelton* (☎ 322 8911) also has harbour cruises on weekends in summer, and Canterbury Sea Tours (☎ 326 5607) has a jet-boat style craft departing from Lyttelton or nearby Sumner for harbour tours that also visit pods of Hector's dolphins.

Phoenix Paragliding (☎ 326 7634) sets sail from the Gondola/Summit Rd directly above Lyttelton, and Nimbus (☎ 328 8383) is also based in Lyttelton. Tandem flights start from $80.

Places to Stay & Eat *Tunnel Vision Backpackers* (☎ 328 7576), 44 London St, is only half an hour by bus from Christchurch if you want to stay out of the city. This attractive, refurbished old building is right in the centre, close to the harbour and cafes. The eight-bed dorm costs $13 per person, four-bed rooms are $15 and twins are $32.

Otherwise Lyttelton has basic pub accommodation or *Randolf House* (☎ 328 8877), 49 Sumner Rd, has B&B singles/doubles from $65/80 to $80/105.

Lyttelton has plenty of dining choices for lunch or dinner, most of them on the main street, London St, once the scene of the Great Fire of Lyttelton – on 24 October 1870 fire demolished the business area of town. Now the only thing burning along this street is (occasionally) the food. Along London St are *Volcano Cafe*, *Harbour Light Theatre & Cafe Bar*, *Deluxe Cafe*, *Waterfront Wholefoods* and *Smail's Wine Bar & Cafe*.

The *Volcano* is a quaint place with artwork adorning the walls and the quirkiest toilet entry you are likely to see. Relax with a drink or enjoy a good range of food. Next door, the *Lava Bar* erupts every night at 5 pm and the Black Mac flows.

Down on the waterfront (Norwich Quay), the *Lyttelton Brasserie* adds a touch of class to a street well accustomed to the nocturnal roaming of sailors (from all world ports).

For a drink with a view try the *Wunderbar*, rather hidden and with a convoluted stairway entry through a doorway on London St. The *Backroom* is a music venue a couple of fire escapes away; the Wunder-barbarians will direct you there.

Getting There & Away Bus No 28 from Cathedral Square goes to Lyttelton every half-hour (hourly on weekends) via the road tunnel (12km). Alternatively, drive via the bayside suburb of Sumner and Evans Pass (19km) or head straight down Colombo St from the Square and go up over Dyers Pass and along scenic Summit Rd (22km).

From Lyttelton by car you can continue around Lyttelton Harbour and eventually on to Akaroa. This is a very scenic but narrow and much longer route than via SH75 between Christchurch and Akaroa.

BANKS PENINSULA

Near Christchurch, Banks Peninsula makes an interesting side trip. A change from the flat area around the city itself, this hilly peninsula was formed by two giant volcanic eruptions. Small harbours such as Le Bons, Pigeon and Little Akaroa bays radiate out from the peninsula's centre giving it a cogwheel shape. The historic town of Akaroa is the main highlight.

The peninsula has a chequered history of settlement. Captain Cook first sighted the peninsula in 1770, although he thought it was an island. He named it after naturalist Sir Joseph Banks. The Maori Ngai Tahu tribe, who then occupied the peninsula, were attacked by Te Rauparaha in 1831 and suffered a severe decline in numbers.

A few years later, in 1836, the British established a whaling station at Peraki. The most notable settlement was at Akaroa, where French immigrants arrived in 1840, spurring the British to annex all New Zealand under the Treaty of Waitangi, signed just before the arrival of the French settlers.

CANTERBURY

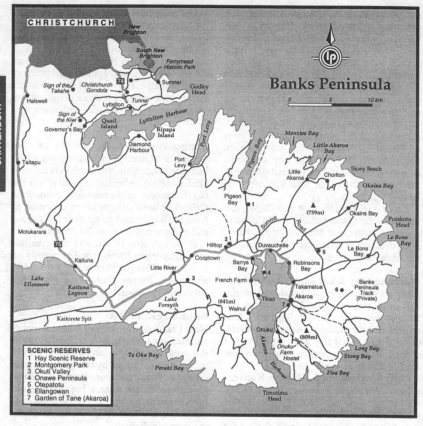

Banks Peninsula

0   5   10 km

SCENIC RESERVES
1 Hay Scenic Reserve
2 Montgomery Park
3 Okuti Valley
4 Onawe Peninsula
5 Otepatotu
6 Ellangowan
7 Garden of Tane (Akaroa)

The French did settle at Akaroa, but in 1849 the French land claim was sold to the New Zealand Company and the following year the French were joined by a large group of British settlers.

Originally heavily forested, the land was cleared for timber, and dairy farming, later supplanted by sheep farming, became the main industry of the peninsula.

Akaroa
Akaroa (population 650), meaning 'long harbour' in Maori, is the site of the first French settlement in New Zealand. This charming town, 82km from Christchurch, lies on a scenic harbour and strives to re-create the feel of a French provincial village.

In 1838 Jean Langlois, a whaling captain, negotiated the sale of Banks Peninsula from local Maori and returned to France to form a trading company. With the backing of the French government, 63 settlers emigrated in 1840 under escort of the warship *L'Aube* but only days before they arrived panicked British officials sent their own warship to raise the flag at Akaroa, claiming British sovereignty under the Treaty of Waitangi. Had the settlers arrived two years earlier, the

South Island may well have become a French colony.

The original French colonists stayed on and have clearly stamped their mark. Streets (rues Lavaud, Balguerie, Jolie) and houses (Langlois-Eteveneaux) have French names, and descendants of the original French settlers reside in the town. It is a delight just to walk the streets, and Akaroa is a popular day trip from Christchurch or it has good facilities and activities for a longer stay.

Information The Akaroa Information Centre (☎ 377 1755) in the post office building on the corner of rues Lavaud and Balguerie is open from 9 am to 4 pm daily.

Things to See & Do The **Akaroa Museum** on Rue Lavaud has a 15-minute audiovisual on the history of the Banks Peninsula, and assorted colonial memorabilia. The old courthouse and **Langlois-Eteveneaux Cottage**, one of the oldest houses in New Zealand and partly fabricated in France, are part of the museum complex, as is the tiny **Customs House** by Daly's Wharf. The museum is open from 10.30 am to 4.30 pm daily (until 4 pm in winter; $3, children $1).

It is a short walk via a forest trail or paved road to the **Old French Cemetery**, but the gravestones were removed in 1925 and a rather dull memorial marks the spot. Continue further up L'Aube Hill for views across town.

For an excellent **walking tour**, pick up a copy of the *Akaroa Historic Village Walk* pamphlet. The tour starts at Waeckerle Cottage at the northern end of town and finishes at the lighthouse. The walk takes in all the wonderful old wooden buildings and churches that give the town so much of its character.

Activities Daily **harbour cruises** on the *Canterbury Cat* depart from the Main Wharf at 11 am and 1.30 pm (1.30 pm only from April to November). The cost is $27 (children $13 to $19). Buy tickets from the office on the wharf (☎ 304 7641) next to the Main Wharf Cafe. The same company has outer

bays tours at 2 pm on the *Canterbury Clipper*, an inflatable naiad, from where you may see Hector's dolphins, little blue penguins and NZ fur seals. The cost is $35 (children $20). Dolphin swimming tours are also offered at noon ($65, children $45).

Dolphin Experience (☎ 304 7207) also has popular 'swim with the dolphins' tours ($67, children $47).

Advertised as 'Four nights, four days, four beaches, four bays', the **Banks Peninsula Track** is a two to four-day walk from Onuku Farm Hostel to the Mt Vernon Lodge across private farmland and then around the dramatic coastline of Banks Peninsula. It costs $120 including transport from Akaroa and hut accommodation. The two-day option is $75. Stand-by rates are available. Prior booking is essential (☎ 304 7612).

Other private tracks include the Southern Bays Track (☎ 329 0007) which begins and ends at Little River and Le Bons Bay Track (☎ 304 8533).

A quiet, peaceful way to cruise the waters around Akaroa is in a **sea kayak** with Sea Kayak Banks Peninsula.

Places to Stay Most of the places to stay on the Banks Peninsula are in or near Akaroa, but a few possibilities are scattered around the various bays.

Akaroa Akaroa Holiday Park (☎ 304 7471) on Morgans Rd, off Old Coach Rd, has fine views of the harbour and town. Sites cost $18, on-site caravans $32, cabins from $42 and tourist flats $56; all prices are for two.

The one backpackers, the very central *Chez la Mer* (☎ 304 7024), Rue Lavaud, is in a small historic house with a beautiful garden. Dorms are $16 per person ($15 if you book yourself and pay cash), while singles/doubles are $22/36.

Mt Vernon Lodge & Stables (☎ 304 7180; PO Box 51), about 2km from town on Rue Balguerie, is a combination hostel and guest lodge. Rates are $45 ($5 each extra adult) for two in a four-bed unit if you supply your own bedding. Chalets and cabins cost $70 a double. There's a swimming pool, BBQ and

CANTERBURY

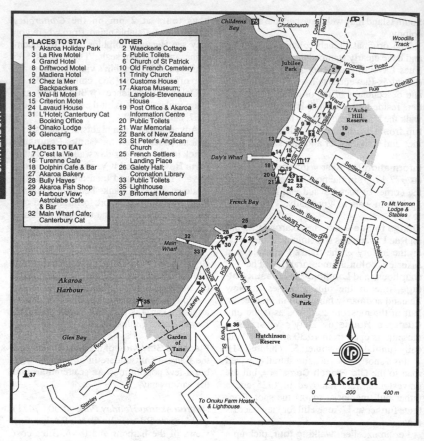

PLACES TO STAY
1 Akaroa Holiday Park
3 La Rive Motel
4 Grand Hotel
8 Driftwood Motel
9 Madiera Hotel
12 Chez la Mer
   Backpackers
13 Wai-iti Motel
15 Criterion Motel
24 Lavaud House
31 L'Hotel; Canterbury Cat
   Booking Office
34 Oinako Lodge
36 Glencarrig

PLACES TO EAT
7 C'est la Vie
16 Turenne Cafe
18 Dolphin Cafe & Bar
27 Bully Hayes
28 Akaroa Bakery
29 Akaroa Fish Shop
30 Harbour View;
   Astrolabe Cafe
   & Bar
32 Main Wharf Cafe;
   Canterbury Cat

OTHER
2 Waeckerle Cottage
5 Public Toilets
6 Church of St Patrick
10 Old French Cemetery
11 Trinity Church
14 Customs House
17 Akaroa Museum;
   Langlois-Eteveneaux
   House
19 Post Office & Akaroa
   Information Centre
20 Public Toilets
21 War Memorial
22 Bank of New Zealand
23 St Peter's Anglican
   Church
25 French Settlers
   Landing Place
26 Gaiety Hall;
   Coronation Library
35 Public Toilets
35 Lighthouse
37 Britomart Memorial

Akaroa

0   200   400 m

a large comfortable common room with an open fire and horse-trekking is offered. In the hostel section dorm beds are \$15, and doubles or twins are \$36.

The *Grand Hotel* (☎ 304 7011) at 6 Rue Lavaud has pub rooms with shared facilities for \$25 per person.

A good spotless B&B is *Lavaud House* (☎ 304 7121), 83 Rue Lavaud; singles/ doubles are \$50/70. The *Oinako Lodge* (☎ 304 8787), 99 Beach Rd, is a fabulous retreat in a grand old building near the beach with B&B from \$165 to \$200 for two. *Glencarrig* (☎ 304 7008), 7 Percy St, is one

of Akoroa's most historic buildings and has B&B from \$80/100. The information centre has details of other B&Bs and farmstays.

Cheaper motels include *La Rive Motel* (☎ 304 7651) at 1 Rue Lavaud with rooms from \$50/65 and the *Wai-iti Motel* (☎ 304 7292) on the waterfront at 64 Rue Jolie with rooms from \$60/80. The *Driftwood* (☎ 304 7484) and the *Criterion* (☎ 304 7775), both on Rue Jolie, and *L'Hotel* (☎ 304 7559) at 75 Beach Rd have units for around \$100.

Other Areas At the *Duvauchelle Reserve Motor Camp* (☎ 304 5777), 8km before

Akaroa off SH75 on Seafield Rd, tent and powered sites cost $7 per person. The *Le Bons Bay Motor Camp* (☎ 304 8533) on Le Bons Bay Valley Rd about 22km from Akaroa has tent/powered sites at $9/10 per person and cabins for $38 for two. The *Okains Bay Domain* also has tent sites, kitchen and shower facilities. The nearby Okains Bay museum has a sacred god stick from the 1400s, an Akaroa *heitiki* and a war canoe ($4, children $1).

Six kilometres south of Akaroa at Onuku, the friendly and relaxed *Onuku Farm Hostel* (☎ 304 7612) is beside the bay on a 400-hectare sheep farm. Nightly costs are $15 in the house, $10 in summer huts or $8 for camp sites. It operates the Banks Peninsula Walk and is a good place to get away from it all. It is closed from June to August.

Le Bons Bay Backpackers (☎ 304 8582) is out of the way – on the right-hand side of the hill about 6km before Le Bons Bay. The farmhouse is in a great location with commanding views down the valley. The cost is $14 and $16 in dorms and $36 in doubles, all including breakfast. An evening meal costs $9. Book ahead as places are limited. It suits people with cars but you can phone for pick-up from Akaroa. Boat trips and walks can be organised.

Places to Eat The biggest and most fashionable selection of eateries is on Beach Road near the main wharf. Cheap eats are scarce, but the *Akaroa Bakery* is a pleasant and cheap spot for pastries, filled rolls and coffee from 7.30 am to 4 pm. The *Akaroa Fish Shop* has excellent fish and chips and you can eat them on tables out the front overlooking the harbour.

More salubrious restaurants on Beach Rd include the chic and sunny *Bully Hayes* (No 57) with a changing blackboard menu and a good bar. The *Harbour View* (No 69) has mixed lunch fare, while the *Astrolabe Cafe & Bar* (No 71) has an Italian-inspired menu with focaccia, calzone and pizza. *L'Hotel* has a pleasant bar overlooking the water and a better class of pub fare (mains $16 to $20).

The *Main Wharf Cafe* on the pier is the place for light meals and good coffee with a view.

In the centre of town, the *Turenne Cafe*, across from the information centre, is good for breakfast (until 11 am) and reasonably priced lunches. *C'est La Vie* on Rue Lavaud caters for vegetarians and has a BYO licence. The *Dolphin Cafe & Bar* has expensive fish and steak dishes. Pick of the crop for good-value seafood is the *Jolly Roger* in the Grand Hotel. It serves fish, garlic prawns and other seafood for $17 a main and lobster crops up on the menu from time to time.

Getting There & Away The Akaroa Shuttle (☎ 0800 500 929) departs from the Christchurch/Canterbury Visitor Centre at 10.30 am and 4 pm, and the Akaroa Information Centre at 8.30 am and 2.15 pm from November to April (only once daily in winter). A day excursion fare is $25, one-way is $15 and the trip takes 1½ hours.

The French Connection (book with Inter-City ☎ 377 0951) leaves the InterCity depot at 8.45 am (the Christchurch Information Centre at 9.10 am) and returns from Akaroa at 3.30 pm. The tour includes commentary and stops at a craft shop and cheese factory. The cost is $19 one-way.

Bayline Services (☎ 304 7207), 108 Rue Jolie, operates the Eastern Bays Scenic Mail Run, a 110km rural delivery service, Monday to Saturday. You visit remote parts of the peninsula, isolated communities and seven bays. It departs from the information centre at 8.30 am and returns at 1 pm ($20); bookings are essential.

NORTH OF CHRISTCHURCH
SH1 heads north from Christchurch through the towns of Belfast, Kaiapoi and Woodend. The large market town of Rangiora is 6km west of Woodend. At Waipara, 57km north of Christchurch, SH1 splits – the left highway, SH7, heads via Hurunui and Culverden to the Red Post Corner where it too splits. The westerly choice leads to the Lewis Pass, Maruia Springs, and eventually either the West Coast or Nelson. If you proceed north from Red Post Corner you will reach

Kaikoura either by the inland or coastal routes. About 23km from Red Post, on the Lewis Pass route, there is a right-hand turn to Hanmer Springs, a well-known thermal area and resort. The *Hurunui Triangle Heritage Trail*, free from information centres, outlines all the things to see and do in this region.

At Waipara, about 75km from Hanmer, the *Waipara Sleepers* (☎ 314 6708) has novel accommodation; the 'fare' in the four-bed guard's vans is $15 person, a double is $50, a railway hut with wheelchair access is $20 for a single and tent sites are also available.

Kaiapoi

This part-provincial, part-suburban town is on the coast 20km north of Christchurch, just off SH1. It takes its name from a famous *pa* site of the Ngai Tahu tribe.

The main attraction is the *Tuhoe*, an **old steamer**, which sails most Sundays down the river to Kairaki on the coast and back (just over an hour). It doesn't sail every Sunday so check on ☎ 327 8645; sailings are subject to weather conditions. Tickets cost $8 (children $4). The Kaiapoi River has trout, salmon and whitebait fishing.

Kaiapoi has accommodation but no reason to stay. A good place for lunch is the *Bridge Tavern* on Williams St overlooking the river, with $6 lunch specials.

Kaiapoi is 35 minutes from Christchurch on bus No 1 or 4. For times and points of departure, phone Bus Info (☎ 366 8855).

Hanmer Springs

Hanmer Springs, the main thermal resort on the South Island, is about 10km off SH7, the highway to the West Coast. Apart from the excellent hot pools, it's popular for outdoor activities including forest walks, horse treks, river and lake fishing, jet-boating, rafting, bungy jumping from the Waiau ferry bridge, skiing in winter and golfing at the 18-hole course. The permanent population is only 600, but visitors swell the population year-round.

Information The Hurunui Visitor Information Centre (☎/fax 315 7128), run with DOC assistance, is on the corner of Amuri and Jacks Pass Rds. It's open from 9 am to 6 pm daily in summer. Winter hours are 10 am to 4.30 pm on weekdays and 10 am to 5 pm on weekends.

Change money at the BNZ in the shopping mall on Conical Hill Rd.

Thermal Reserve For over a hundred years, Hanmer Springs has been renowned for its thermal waters. Legend has it that the springs are a piece of the fires of Tamatea dropped from the sky after an eruption of Mt Ngauruhoe's volcanic ridge. Centuries later it has metamorphosed into the excellent Hanmer Springs Thermal Reserve (☎ 315 7511).

Open from 10 am to 9 pm daily, hot spring water mixes with fresh water to produce pools of varying temperatures. There are 'relaxer' pools, landscaped rock pools, private pools, a freshwater 25m pool, sauna and steam room, a toddlers pool and a restaurant. Admission is $7 (children $3) and a day pass is $9 (come and go as much as you like). Per half-hour, private pools are $20 for two and the sauna or steam room is $10 per person.

Activities There are two main **skiing** areas near Hanmer Springs. Amuri is the closest, 27km from Hanmer, and Lyford is 75km away. They are not nearly as expensive as the larger resorts. (See Skiing in the Outdoor Activities chapter for more details.)

The *Hanmer Forest Walks* pamphlet outlines a number of pleasant **walks** near the town, mostly through exotic forest. The easy Woodland Walk starts from Jollies Pass Rd, 1km from the town, and goes through Douglas fir, poplar and redwood stands. It joins the Majuba Walk, which leads to Conical Hill Lookout and than back to Conical Hill Rd – about one hour all up. The Hurunui Visitor Information Centre has information on longer tramps in the area, including Lake Sumner Forest Park.

Thrillseekers Canyon is Hanmer Springs' adrenalin centre, and is the closest to

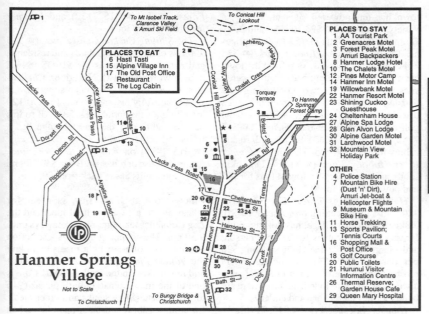

PLACES TO STAY
1 AA Tourist Park
2 Greenacres Motel
3 Forest Peak Motel
5 Amuri Backpackers
8 Hanmer Lodge Hotel
10 The Chalets Motel
12 Pines Motor Camp
14 Hanmer Inn Motel
19 Willowbank Motel
22 Hanmer Resort Motel
23 Shining Cuckoo
   Guesthouse
24 Cheltenham House
27 Alpine Spa Lodge
28 Glen Alvon Lodge
30 Alpine Garden Motel
31 Larchwood Motel
32 Mountain View
   Holiday Park

OTHER
4 Police Station
7 Mountain Bike Hire
   (Dust 'n' Dirt),
   Amuri Jet-boat &
   Helicopter Flights
9 Museum & Mountain
   Bike Hire
11 Horse Trekking
13 Sports Pavilion;
   Tennis Courts
16 Shopping Mall &
   Post Office
18 Golf Course
20 Public Toilets
21 Hurunui Visitor
   Information Centre
26 Thermal Reserve;
   Garden House Cafe
29 Queen Mary Hospital

PLACES TO EAT
6 Hasti Tasti
15 Alpine Village Inn
17 The Old Post Office
   Restaurant
25 The Log Cabin

Hanmer Springs Village
Not to Scale

CANTERBURY

Christchurch for **bungy jumping** off the Waiau ferry bridge where it crosses the river of the same name. It costs $89 to hurl yourself from this bridge (37m high). **Jet-boating** ($60), **white-water rafting** ($60) and **river bugs** (individual fun rafts; $65) are also offered at the Thrillseekers Canyon centre (☎ 315 7046), next to the bridge where the Hanmer Springs turn-off meets SH7. It operates from 9 am to 5 pm.

Rainbow Adventures (☎ 315 7444) at The Stables, Jacks Pass Rd, takes **horse treks** around Hanmer costing from $25 for one hour to $90 for a full day. They offer a variety of other exciting activities including **canyoning** ($39), where you slide down cascades and river pools, **fun yak canoeing** ($58), white-water rafting and tandem paragliding. Hurunui Horse Treks (☎ 314 4204) in Hawarden has treks from a half-day to eight days.

A fun way to see the surrounding countryside is on a **four-wheel motorbike safari** on a high-country sheep and cattle station. After introductory instruction, you tackle the trails on farm quad bikes up into the hills for magnificent views. Len Earl (☎ 315 7545) takes the trips which cost $79 for three hours ($95 for the more demanding four-hour trip).

This region is very popular for **mountain biking**. Dust and Dirt (☎ 315 7233) operates two-hour guided trips for $19 and a full-day Molesworth Station ride for $75. Bike hire costs from $9 for one hour to $25 for a day; a map of all the tracks is provided.

Organised Tours Trailways Safaris (☎ 315 7401) has trips to Molesworth Station, the largest in NZ's high country, for $58 for a half-day and $98 for a full-day tour (lunch is provided on the latter). Flight-seeing tours, Harley tours and other farm tours are available – contact the information centre.

Places to Stay The *Mountain View Holiday Park* (☎ 315 7113) on the southern edge of town has tent/powered sites at $17/19, a variety of cabins at $33 to $43 and fully equipped tourist flats at $57 to $65; prices are for two. The *AA Tourist Park* (☎ 315 7112) on Jacks Pass Rd, 3km from the town centre, is the best equipped. Tent/powered sites cost $15/17 for two, good cabins are $40 and tourist flats $52; AA members get a discount. Also on Jacks Pass Rd, next to the golf course, the *Pines Motor Camp* (☎ 315 7152) has tent/powered sites for $13/16 and cabins for $32 for two. The small *Hanmer River Holiday Park* (☎ 315 7111), 6km south, has cabins for $35, tourist flats for $45 and powered sites for $15.

Hanmer Springs Forest Camp (☎ 315 7202) in a pretty setting on Jollies Pass Rd, 2.8km east of the village, has dozens of old forestry workers cabins for $13 per person, and a large self-contained lodge costing $20 per person. This YHA associate caters mostly to school groups, but one kitchen is always set aside for independents. There are bonds for keys, crockery and cutlery.

Hanmer Backpackers (☎ 315 7196), 41 Conical Hill Rd, is a small, comfortable wooden chalet (a winter ski lodge) with two bunkrooms for $15 per person ($18 with linen) and one double for $36.

The *Hanmer Lodge Hotel* (☎ 315 7021) is a grand old resort hotel fallen on hard times, but extensive renovations are planned. Until then, singles/doubles cost $48/58 and $65/84 with en suite.

Numerous motels cost from $70 per night. The *Willowbank* (☎ 315 7211) on Argelins Rd is the cheapest with units from $55 to $72 for two. The new and very central *Hanmer Inn* (☎ 315 7516), 16 Jacks Pass Rd, has excellent units from $85 to $125. The *Alpine Garden* (☎ 315 7332) on Leamington St is another good, new motel with units from $79 to $105. The zenith of motel luxury are the tower units in the *Alpine Spa Lodge* (☎ 315 7311) on the corner of Amuri Rd and Harrogate St which have circular beds and spa baths, for a cool $185. Other units cost from $79 to $95 for two.

Other motels include the *Greenacres* (☎ 315 7125), *Larchwood* (☎ 315 7281),

Forest Peak (☎ 315 7132) and *Hanmer Resort* (☎ 315 7362).

The *Shining Cuckoo Guest House* (☎ 315 7905) is old, both in standards and residents, and has singles/doubles for $19/38 ($46 a double with breakfast). Next door, *Cheltenham House* (☎ 315 7545) is a superb B&B with beautifully restored rooms for $90/120 including a substantial breakfast. All rooms have en suite and the guest lounge has a full-sized billiard table. *Glen Alvon Lodge* (☎ 315 7475) on Amuri Ave is also in a restored house and has B&B for $50/70 and new motel units at the back from $95.

Places to Eat *Hasti Tasti* is great for takeaways or a sit-down light meal and the *Log Cabin* has tearooms and takeaways until 9.30 pm. The shopping mall has a selection of cafes for coffee or light meals including the *Village Plus* and *Aromas* for breakfast and lunch. Also in the mall, *Jaywalk Cafe* is one of the most upmarket with pizzas ($16 to $18), pasta ($15), steaks and other meals for around $20. It is usually open late when all else shuts early with a bang. The *Garden House Cafe* in the hot pools complex has snacks and winebar dining in pleasant surrounds but the meals are average.

The *Old Post Office* is one of the best restaurants in town and serves tasty NZ fare but mains will set you back around $24. Noted for its beef and lamb dishes, it is open from Thursday to Monday from 6 pm.

The *Alpine Village Inn*, near the mall on Jacks Pass Rd, is the local boozer and has reasonably priced bistro meals for around $12.

Getting There & Away Hanmer Connection (☎ 315 7575; 0800 377378) runs daily between Hanmer Springs and Christchurch ($22, two hours), and from October to April it also goes three days a week to Kaikoura ($25, two hours). Hanmer Springs Alpine Experience (☎ 366 0398) does day trips to Hanmer Springs from Christchurch for $40 return, including a tour of the attractions, and will also drop you off at hotels for $20 one way.

White Star and East West buses from Christchurch to the West Coast stop at the Hanmer turn-off, but the junction is 10km from town.

Hanmer Springs to the West Coast

SH7 continues west from the Hanmer Springs turn-off to Lewis Pass, Maruia Springs and Springs Junction. This is a beautiful route but, lying at the northern end of the Southern Alps, the **Lewis Pass** (907m) is not as steep or the forest as dense as the routes through the Arthur's and Haast passes. The forest near Lewis Pass is mainly red and silver beech. The kawhais which grow along the river terraces are spectacular in spring. The informative pamphlet *Hanmer Springs to the West Coast: A guide to the Lewis Pass Highway* outlines points of interest along the way.

The Lewis Pass area has a number of interesting walks – pick up the *Lewis Pass Region* pamphlet and the *Lake Sumner Forest Park* Infomap. Most of the tracks pass through beech forest, snow-capped mountains form the backdrop and there are lakes, alpine tarns and mountain rivers. The most popular tramps are those around Lake Sumner in the Lake Sumner Forest Park and the St James Walkway in the Lewis Pass National Reserve. Subalpine conditions apply – contact DOC in Hanmer Springs for advice before heading off.

Maruia Springs is 69km from the Hanmer turn-off. The lovely *Maruia Springs Thermal Resort* (☎ 523 8840) has natural thermal water pumped into a sex-segregated Japanese bathhouse and outdoor rock pools that are magic in winter when the snow flakes drift down while you relax in the hot water. The complex is open from 9 am to 9 pm ($6, children $4). Private spa units (open from 11 am to 5 pm) cost $20 per hour. Accommodation at the resort ranges from the run-down backpackers costing $20 per person to good hotel units from $95 to $110. Tent camping costs $17 for two, but there are no cooking facilities. All accommodation includes entry to the pools and bathhouse, and the resort has a cafe.

From Maruia the road continues to Springs Junction where it splits. SH65 heads north to SH6 and on to Nelson. SH7 continues west to Reefton, then down the Grey Valley to Greymouth and the West Coast. *Lewis Pass Motels* (☎ 523 8863), between Maruia Springs and Springs Junction, has single/double units for $55/75. In Springs Junction, *Springs Junction Village* (☎ 523 8813) has chalets for $30/50 and motel units for $70 a double. DOC camping grounds in the area include: Marble Hill, 6.5km east of Springs Junction (start of the Lake Daniells walk); and Deer Valley, Lewis Pass, 25km east of Springs Junction

At Maruia, about 20km north of Springs Junction on SH65, *Reids Store Backpacker* (☎ 523 8869) has bunk beds for $15, and doubles and twins for $38, and they can advise on various walks and activities in the area.

WEST OF CHRISTCHURCH

Heading west from Christchurch on SH73, it's about a two-hour trip to Arthur's Pass and the Arthur's Pass National Park. The crossing from Christchurch to Greymouth, over the pass, is a very scenic route covered by both bus and the *TranzAlpine Express* train.

Nowhere in New Zealand do you get a better picture of the climb from the sea to the mountains than the Arthur's Pass crossing. From Christchurch and almost at sea level, the road cuts through the flat Canterbury Plains, through rural towns such as Kirwee, Darfield, Racecourse Hill, Sheffield and Springfield. It then winds up into the skiing areas of Porters Heights and Craigieburn before following the Waimakariri and Bealey rivers to Arthur's Pass. Picturesque lakes are passed on the way, including lakes Pearson and Grassmere.

To the south-west of Christchurch and reached by SH73 and SH77 is the Mt Hutt ski resort and the adventure centre, Methven.

Craigieburn Forest Park

This forest park is 110km north-west of Christchurch and 42km south of Arthur's Pass, on SH73. A good system of walking tracks cross the park, and in the valleys west of the Craigieburn Range longer tramps are possible. The nearby country is suitable for rock climbing and skiing. The predominant vegetation types are beech, alpine tussock, snow totara, mountain toatoa and turpentine scrub. If you are lucky you may see patches of South Island edelweiss *Leucogenes grandiceps*. Get a copy of the DOC pamphlet *Craigieburn Forest Park Walks* for more information.

The *Flock Hill Resort* (☎ 318 8196) is a high-country sheep station 44km east of Arthur's Pass on SH73, adjacent to Lake Pearson and the Craigieburn Forest Park. Bunk and twin rooms cost from $22 to $40 per person, there's a fully equipped communal kitchen and a restaurant. Activities include swimming, fishing, skiing, walking and mountain biking.

Craigieburn is one of the best **skiing** areas in the country, as it has a rise of 503m. It is set in wild country and suits the advanced skier (see also Broken River, Porters Heights and Mt Cheeseman under Skiing in the Outdoor Activities chapter).

Twelve kilometres east of Arthur's Pass at **Bealey** is the now legendary *Bealey Hotel* (☎ 318 9277), famous for its hoax which led people across the nation to believe that a live moa had been sighted in the area, 'confirmed' by two German tourists. Motel units cost $75 and the budget lodge costs $18 per person in double rooms.

Arthur's Pass

The small settlement of Arthur's Pass is 4km from the pass of the same name. The 924m pass was on the route used by the Maori to reach Westland, but its European discovery was made by Arthur Dobson in 1864, when the Westland gold rush created enormous pressure to find a crossing over the Southern Alps from Christchurch. A coach road was completed within a year of Dobson's discovery. Later on, the coal and timber trade demanded a railway, which was completed in 1923.

The town is a fine base for walks, climbs, views and winter-time skiing (at Temple

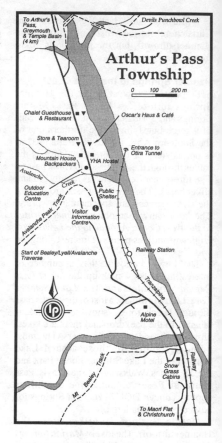

Basin) in Arthur's Pass National Park or to visit on a day trip from Greymouth or Christchurch.

Information The Arthur's Pass Visitor Centre (☎ 318 9211; fax 318 9271) in the town is open from 8 am to 5 pm daily. It has information on all the park walks, topographical maps and route guides for longer tramps with huts. The staff can also offer invaluable advice on the park's often savagely changeable weather conditions – check here before you go on any walk, and fill out an intentions card. Be sure to sign out again when you leave, otherwise they'll send a search party to find you!

The visitors centre is also a park museum, with excellent displays. In January there's a summer program of guided walks and evening talks, discussions, films and slide shows.

Arthur's Pass National Park Day walks in the park offer 360° views of the snow-capped peaks. Many of these peaks are over 2000m, the highest being Mt Murchison (2400m). One of the most spectacular views from the road is of the Bealey Face of Mt Rolleston.

The park has huts on the tramping tracks and several areas suitable for camping. The day walks leaflet from the visitor centre lists half-day walks of one to four hours and day walks of five to eight hours. The four-hour return walk to Temple Basin provides superb views of the surrounding peaks. For skiing at Temple Basin, see Skiing in the Outdoor Activities chapter.

Longer tramps with superb alpine scenery include the two-day Goat Pass Track and the difficult Harman Pass and Harpers Pass tracks. Tracks require previous tramping experience, flooding can make rivers dangerous to cross and the weather can be extreme – always seek advice from DOC first.

Places to Stay & Eat You can camp at the basic public shelter for $3 per night, which has running water (must be treated) and a flush toilet. Camping is also available at the YHA hostel ($8) and Mountain House ($9). Camping is free at Klondyke Corner, 8km east of Arthur's Pass, and Kelly Shelter, 17km west. Both have toilets and water that must be treated.

From November to March all accommodation is in demand; it is advisable to book ahead. The *Sir Arthur Dudley Dobson Memorial YHA Hostel* (☎ 318 9230) has bunks at $15 per night or $36 a double. Across the road is *Mountain House* (☎ 318 9258), a good backpackers which has shared

and dorms for $15 – from May to September stay three nights for the price of two.

The *Alpine Motel* (☎ 318 9233) has doubles at $75 and some simpler rooms from $65. The *Chalet* (☎ 318 9236) offers B&B for $90 for a double with shared facilities or $100 a double with private facilities. *Snowy Peaks Holiday Cottages* (☎ 318 9266) on School Rd are self-contained cottages for $85 and there's a spa.

Outside town, the *Otira Hotel* (☎ 738 2802) in the township of Otira, 14.5km west of Arthur's Pass, has cheap rooms. There are some great walks in the area including the Goat Pass trip which forms part of the Coast to Coast endurance race. Also nearby is the start of the Harpers Pass Track.

Eat at the *Arthur's Pass Store & Tearoom* or in the *Chalet Restaurant*, which has a cheaper coffee bar beyond its restaurant area. *Oscar's Haus* has a cafe and bar serving good value meals and it is the social focus of the town.

Getting There & Around Arthur's Pass is on the main run for buses between Christchurch ($25) and Greymouth ($15). Coast to Coast, Ko-Op Shuttles and Alpine Coach & Courier (☎ 0800 274 888) stop at Arthur's Pass.

The *TranzAlpine* Express train runs between Greymouth ($33) and Christchurch ($52); discounts for backpackers and others may be available. Bus and train tickets are sold at the Arthur's Pass Store. Between Arthur's Pass and Christchurch, the *Tranz-Alpine* train takes the more scenic route incorporating the Waimakariri Gorge. On to Greymouth, they both offer great views, although the road goes over the top of the pass while the train goes through the less scenic 8.5km Otira tunnel immediately upon leaving town. The road over the pass is winding and very steep – the most tortuous of all the passes – but new works will make the trip easier.

Arthur's Pass Taxi Service (☎ 318 9266) offers trampers transport service to the walking tracks, eg Greyneys Shelter ($10), Klondyke Corner ($20) and Cass ($30).

Central & South Canterbury

From Christchurch, two routes go through the South Canterbury region. Take SH1 south along the coast to Ashburton, Timaru, Oamaru and then Dunedin. Or head inland, crossing the Mackenzie Country to the spectacular lakes and the Southern Alps.

CHRISTCHURCH TO OTAGO

SH1, south of Christchurch, is very flat and boring as you cross the Canterbury Plains, but better in an elevated bus, allowing you to see over the nearby hedges and obstructions. In clear weather there are magnificent views of the distant Southern Alps.

South of Christchurch, the road crosses many wide, glacial-fed rivers – quite a sight in flood, though the water is low at other times. The 2km-long Rakaia River Bridge is popular for jet-boating, the Rangitata River attracts white-water rafters, and salmon fishing is possible in many streams in South Canterbury. The first sizeable town is Ashburton.

Ashburton

Ashburton (population 15,800) is very much the service centre for the surrounding district. It is 85km south of Christchurch and lies between the Rakaia and Rangitata rivers. Tour buses stop at the renovated **train station**, which has expensive knitwear, souvenirs and a good cafe.

If **museums** are your thing, six of them are in or around this town – the Historical, Station, Aviation, Railway & Preservation, Vintage Car and Historical Woodworking museums. The town has some good craft galleries – Ashford Crafts on East St is worth a look.

The Ashburton Information Centre (☎ /fax 308 1064) is on the main road, East St, in the centre of town and handles bookings for just about everything. The AA area office (☎ 308 7128) is at 119 Tancred St. Change money at the BNZ, 295 Stafford St.

Places to Stay & Eat The *Coronation Holiday Park* (☎ 308 6603), 780 East St, has tent or powered sites for $18 for two, on-site caravans for $28, cabins for $45 and motel units. Next door is the *Academy Lodge Motel* (☎ 308 5503) with rooms from $72 for two. Seven other motels, all on the highway, typically charge from $60 to $70 for a unit. Inquire at the information centre for more accommodation and farmstays in the region.

Turangi Backpackers (☎ 308 4444), about 4km from the information centre on Turangi Rd and on the north-eastern outskirts of town, charges $15 per person. It is housed in a large institutional building shared with other public offices.

Don't expect gourmet food – this town is just discovering that there's more to life than mutton and lamb – but some reasonable dining options exist. The *Railway Station Cafe* is a pleasant spot for a light meal and *Cactus Jack's*, 509 Wills St, has Mexican food. The *Royal Oak* on West St is a good old-fashioned family restaurant or *Kelly's* on East St near the tourist office has varied fare and is one of Ashburton's best restaurants.

Getting There & Away InterCity (☎ 308 5179), Mt Cook Landline (☎ 308 5178) and Newmans (☎ 0800 777 707) stop at the train station in Ashburton on their way to Dunedin, Christchurch or Queenstown. Ashburton Shuttle (☎ 308 4889) runs three times a week between Ashburton and Christchurch for $15, or hop aboard the free bus to the Christchurch Casino, leaving the day after pension cheque day.

Methven

Inland from Ashburton on SH77 is Methven (population 1100), a good centre for the Canterbury Plains or the mountains. A small town, Methven is quiet for most of the year, coming alive in winter when it fills up with skiers using it as a base for Mt Hutt and other ski areas. There is a world-class 18-hole golf course nearby.

Information The Methven Information Centre (☎/fax 302 8955) on Main Rd is a private travel agent that makes bookings for accommodation, skiing packages and other activities in this area.

There are two banks near the mall and the medical centre is opposite, on the corner of Chertsey and Mt Hutt Rds.

Activities The Mt Hutt Forest, an area of predominantly mountain beech, is 14km west of Methven. It is adjoined by the Awa Awa Rata Reserve and the Pudding Hill Scenic Reserve.

There are two access roads: Pudding Hill Rd leads to foot access for Pudding Hill Stream, and McLennan's Bush Rd leads to Pudding Hill Reserve and Awa Awa Rata Reserve. There are many **walking trails**: the Pudding Hill Stream Route, which requires many stream crossings, takes 2½ hours, and the Awa Awa Rata Reserve Loop Track takes 1½ hours. In the rata reserve many short walks show the diverse vegetation within the surrounding forest.

It is **skiing** that has really set Methven on an upward growth curve. Nearby Mt Hutt offers six months of skiing, perhaps the longest ski season of any resort in NZ. The skiable area is 365 hectares and snow-making facilities ensure adequate cover for the whole season. All levels of alpine skiing, snow-boarding, telemarking and recreational racing are catered for. *Beaches Restaurant* on the mountain is the highest dining establishment in Australasia. (See Skiing in the Outdoor Activities chapter for more details.)

White Water Jets (☎ 318 6574) and Rakaia Gorge Scenic Jet (☎ 318 6515) zip up to the Rakaia Gorge on **jet-boats** for around $35 per person. As you can only see the gorge from the river, a jet-boat is the best means of transport on this braided river system.

The Parachute Centre (☎ mobile (025) 321 135) at Pudding Hill, 5km from Methven, has **tandem skydiving**. More sedate is a **balloon flight** organised through Aoraki

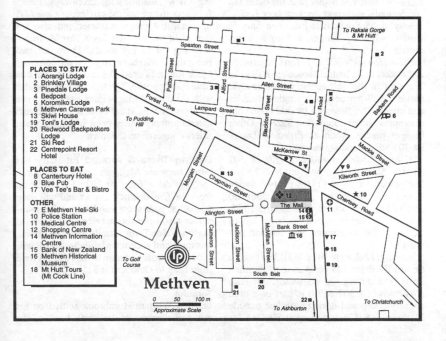

PLACES TO STAY
1 Aorangi Lodge
2 Brinkley Village
3 Pinedale Lodge
4 Bedpost
5 Koromiko Lodge
6 Methven Caravan Park
13 Skiwi House
19 Toni's Lodge
20 Redwood Backpackers Lodge
21 Ski Red
22 Centrepoint Resort Hotel

PLACES TO EAT
8 Canterbury Hotel
9 Blue Pub
17 Vee Tee's Bar & Bistro

OTHER
7 E Methven Heli-Ski
10 Police Station
11 Medical Centre
12 Shopping Centre
14 Methven Information Centre
15 Bank of New Zealand
16 Methven Historical Museum
18 Mt Hutt Tours (Mt Cook Line)

Methven

0   50   100 m
Approximate Scale

Balloon Safaris (☎ 302 8172); the $195 flights include a champagne breakfast.

Tandem paragliding, heli-skiing in winter and horse trekking are also available.

Places to Stay In winter Methven has over 2000 beds to cater for skiers on Mt Hutt, but many places are closed in summer. The following are open year-round unless otherwise indicated.

Methven Caravan Park (☎ 302 8005) on Barkers Rd has tent/powered sites at $13/16 for two and basic cabins at $13 per person. Bedding and cooking utensils can be hired. The *Bedpost* (☎ 302 8508) near the corner of Main Rd and Lampard St in central Methven has hostel-style accommodation from $18 and new, well-appointed units from $55.

Ski Red (☎ 302 8964), 5 Wayne Place, is a well-appointed lodge with a communal/ kitchen area and good four-bed rooms with en suite for $15 per person in summer and $25 in winter. The owner runs the older but comfortable *Redwood Backpackers Lodge*, nearby at 25 South Belt Rd, open only in winter, when it charges $15 to $18 per person.

Skiwi House (☎ 302 8772) on Chapman St is the other main budget choice open all year. The cost in this self-contained, older-style house is $17 per person in singles, doubles and quads. The *Blue Pub* (☎ 302 8046) has reasonable hotel rooms for $22/44. Other budget places, such as *Pinedale Lodge* (☎ 302 8621), operate in winter.

Kohuia Lodge of Pudding Hill (☎ 302 8416), 5km from town on SH72, has tent/powered sites at $14/18 for two, lodge rooms from $40, studio apartments from $60 and backpackers accommodation from $15. Rates are higher in winter. There are lots of extras, including a sauna, spa, bar and restaurant.

Aorangi Lodge (☎ 302 8482), 38 Spaxton St, has B&B for $25 per person in summer, up to $48 during the ski season. *Mt Hutt Homestead* (☎ 302 8130) is part of a high country sheep and deer station just outside Methven. B&B is not cheap at $90/115 for singles/doubles, but the food is excellent and it's an interesting place to stay.

Motel-style lodges include the comfortable *Koromiko Lodge* (☎ 302 8165) on SH77 (Main Rd), where B&B is $75 a double in summer, closer to $100 in winter. *Toni's Lodge* (☎ 302 8875), 74 Main Road, is another in the ski lodge mould with lots of wood panelling, sauna, spa and a pleasant bar-restaurant. Rooms with en suite cost $50/60 in summer ($95/100 in winter).

The *Centrepoint Resort Hotel* (☎ 302 8724) on Rakaia Gorge is one of the flashest in town; a double is $105 to $155 ($20 less in summer). *Brinkley Village* (☎ 302 8862) is a new, luxurious apartment complex catering to the ski crowds with rooms from $110 to $180 in winter ($80 to $140 in summer). The visitor centre has a list of many more places.

Places to Eat The main shopping centre has a selection of dining establishments including *Uncle Dominic's* for takeaways, *Pam's* for tearoom fare and the salubrious *Cafe 131*, open until 4 pm in summer and also for dinner in winter. *Vee Tee's Bar & Bistro* serves good family meals. There are two pubs: the *Canterbury Hotel*, on the corner of Main Rd and Forest Drive, and the famous *Blue Pub* opposite. The latter is very popular with ski bums during winter, but both serve good pub meals. Many more restaurants and entertainment venues open in winter when skiers converge on the town.

Getting There & Around InterCity has buses between Methven and Christchurch for $14. Value Tours (☎ 302 8112) picks up from the Christchurch airport and will drop you off at your accommodation; other companies also offer this service during the ski season. Value Tours usually include ski hire, transport and accommodation in a package.

Many shuttles operate to Mt Hutt ski field from May to October for $15 to $17.

Temuka

In 1853 William Hornbrook settled on his run Arowhenua, on the south bank of the

Temuka River. His wife, who settled there a year later, was the first female European pioneer in South Canterbury. Arowhenua had long been a pa site of the Ngai Tahu people. Their earth ovens, *te umu kaha* (fierce strong ovens), gave Tumukaha, later Temuka, its name.

A number of relics of early settlement survive, including middens, Old Hope Cottage, Mendelssohn House and the magnificent redwood trees on the corner of King St and Wilmhurst Rd. The site of pioneer aviator Richard Pearse's first attempted flight and a replica of his plane is out on Main Waitohi Rd, 13.5km from Temuka towards Hanging Rock Bridge. He took off from the road but crashed into a long-since removed hedge. Five kilometres south of Waitohi, **Pleasant Point**, 18km west of Timaru towards Fairlie, has an interesting railway museum (☎ 686 2269) at the old train station and a collection of steam locomotives and carriages that run along 3km of track on weekends and holidays.

The District Council Service Centre (☎ 615 9537) on Domain Ave acts as an information centre.

Places to Stay & Eat The *Temuka Holiday Park* (☎ 615 7241), 2 Fergusson Drive, has tent/powered sites for $14/15 and cabins at $28 for two. Temuka has five hotels and four motels. The *Royal Hotel* (☎ 615 7507) has singles/doubles for $40/50 and the *A & A Motel* (☎ 615 8004), 54 King St, has reasonable units for $45/55.

Along King St are pubs serving meals, a number of takeaways and the omnipresent tearooms. The local cheeses are superb.

Timaru

Timaru is a thriving port city of 27,500 people, halfway between Christchurch and Dunedin. It is a small city, but a convenient stopping point with an attractive beach at Caroline Bay. The Caroline Bay Christmas Carnival, beginning on 26 December and running for about 10 days, is a lot of fun.

Timaru comes from the Maori name Te Maru, meaning 'the place of shelter', but no permanent settlement existed when the first Europeans, the Weller brothers of Sydney, set up a whaling station in 1839. The *Caroline*, a sailing ship that picked up whale oil, gave the picturesque bay its name.

The town really began to boom when a landing service was established at the foot of Strathallan St. It moved in 1868 to George St and has been renovated into a boutique brewery pub. After about 30 vessels were wrecked attempting to berth near Timaru between the mid-1860s and 1880s, an artificial harbour was built. The result is today's excellent port and Caroline Bay's beach, a result of the construction of breakwaters. The port is an important shipping point for the surrounding agricultural region. You may see one of the huge sheep 'liners' – five-storey-high ships crammed with live sheep on a death cruise bound for the Middle East.

Information Timaru's main road, SH1, is a road of many names – the Hilton Highway north of town, Evans St as it enters town and then it bypasses the central business district along Theodosia St and Craigie Ave. The CBD centres on Stafford St. Continuing south, the highway becomes King St and then SH1 as it emerges from town.

The Timaru Visitor Information Centre (☎ 688 6163; fax 688 6162) at 14 George St, diagonally across from the train station, has enthusiastic staff. It's open from 8.30 am to 5 pm on weekdays and from 10 am to 3 pm on weekends (summer hours may be extended). Pick up a street map and the interesting pamphlet *Timaru City Historic Walk*. The AA is on the corner of Church and Bank Sts.

Things to See & Do One of the few safe, sheltered beaches on the east coast is **Caroline Bay**. The park along the beach has a walk-through aviary, a maze, a pleasant walkway and other attractions, including a new landscaped piazza. A good walk heads north from town along Caroline Bay, past the Benvenue Cliffs and on to the Dashing Rocks and rock pools at the north end of the

CANTERBURY

Three Great Champions

The Timaru region has produced three great sporting champions – two human, the third a horse.

In the centre of Timaru, next to the ANZ Bank, is a statue of Robert Fitzsimmons, three-time world boxing champion with a record barely matched today. Fitzsimmons was born in 1862 and developed his impressive physique at his father's blacksmith's forge. He defeated Jack Dempsey (the Irish Jack Dempsey, not the illustrious 1920s American boxer of the same name) in 1891 to take the world middleweight crown and Jim Corbett in 1897 in 14 rounds to win the heavyweight crown (held until 1899). Four years later, he took the world light-heavyweight championship. He died in 1917, three years after the last of his 350 or so professional bouts.

Dr John Edward (Jack) Lovelock, born in 1910, was the world record holder for the one mile. In 1936, in front of a crowd of 120,000 at the Berlin Olympics, he broke the record for the 1500m and took the gold medal. Hitler presented him with an oak tree, which is still growing in the grounds of Timaru Boys' High School on North St.

The racecourse at Washdyke is named after New Zealand's most famous galloper, Phar Lap, who was born at nearby Seadown. In the late 1920s and early 1930s Phar Lap swept all challengers before him. After winning Australia's top horse race, the Melbourne Cup, in 1930, he was later taken to the USA,

Phar Lap – New Zealand's most famous horse – came from the Timaru area

where he continued his winning streak. Here he died, apparently poisoned, soon after winning the richest race in the world, the Agua Caliente Handicap in Mexico. Despite racing in the Depression years, Phar Lap was for many years the greatest stakes winner in the world. Today, Phar Lap's stuffed skin is held by the National Museum in Melbourne (Australia), his skeleton is in the Auckland Museum and his heart is preserved at the Institute of Anatomy in Canberra (also in Australia). ■

---

bay. Caroline Bay is sheltered and calm but there's good surfing south of town (Patiti Point) where you might also see sea lions. An easy 45-minute walk around the bay is outlined in a map available from the information centre.

Timaru has other good parks including Centennial Park along the Otipua Creek with a pleasant 3.5km walkway along the stream bed. The information centre has leaflets outlining a scenic drive.

The **South Canterbury Museum**, in the Pioneer Hall on Perth St, is the main regional museum, with exhibits on the whalers and early settlers. Admission is free and it's open from 1.30 to 4.30 pm daily except Monday. One fascinating exhibit is a replica of the aeroplane designed and flown by early South

Canterbury aviator, Richard Pearse, in 1903 (some nine months before Orville Wright in the USA). Pearse died in a psychiatric hospital in Christchurch in 1953, virtually unknown to the outside world.

Over 900 works of art, plus changing exhibits, feature at the **Aigantighe Art Gallery** at 49 Wai-iti Rd, open from 11 am to 4.30 pm from Tuesday to Friday and 2 to 4.30 pm on weekends (admission is free but donations are welcome).

The **DB Brewery** (☎ 688 2059) at Sheffield St, 6km north of town at Washdyke, has free tours at 10.30 am from Monday to Thursday. Enclosed footwear must be worn.

Places to Stay The *Selwyn Holiday Park* (☎ 684 7690) on Selwyn St, 2km north of the

CANTERBURY

town centre, has tent/powered sites for $16/18, cabins for $25 and $29 or $39 with own kitchen and tourist flats for $52 to $60; all prices are for two. The *Glenmark Motor Camp* (☎ 684 3682) on Beaconsfield Rd, 3km south of the town centre, has sites at $16 and cabins for $25.

The *Seadown Holiday Village* (☎ 688 2657), on the corner of Divan Rd and SH1, 6km north of Timaru, has tent/powered sites for $14/16 ($20 with en suite) for two, cabins for $25 and motel units for $65 for two.

DOC camping grounds are at Mt Nimrod, Back Line Rd, 32km south-west, and Otaio

Gorge, Back Line Rd, 29km south-west of Timaru. They cost $3 per adult; drinking water, toilets and BBQs are provided.

At 44 Evans St in the Anchor Motel is the YHA-associate *Timaru Backpackers* (☎ 684 5067). It is small (10-person capacity), homey and the management go out of their way to look after you. A bed costs $17 per person, or comfortable and well-appointed singles/doubles are $25/40. The *Old Bank Backpackers* (☎ 686 9098), 232 Stafford St, above the Old Bank bar, is a new addition to the backpackers scene with dorm beds for $14 and doubles for $36.

Jan's Place Guesthouse (☎ 688 4589) at 4A Rose St offers B&B for $30/55 and there is one backpackers twin room for $15 per person. *Kosta's Scone* (☎ 688 0871), 24 Evans St, is one of the most basic backpackers in NZ, but at least you can always find a room. It offers dorm beds for $12 and $14, and doubles for $30.

Ashbury House (☎ 684 3396) at 30 Te Weka St has B&B for $30/65, but is closed in winter. The *Hibernian Hotel* (☎ 688 8125), 6 Latter St, has units at $70 for two. The *Hotel Benvenue* (☎ 688 4049), 18 Evans St, is a better class of hotel with rooms for $92 ($85 on weekends). It has an intimate bar and a good restaurant. The *Hydro Grand* (☎ 684 7059), 10 Bay Hill, is a traditional old hotel with singles/doubles for $30/40 or $40/50 with en suite.

Timaru has numerous motels, especially along Evans St (SH1) at the northern end of town. Most cost from around $70 a night but the *Anchor Motel* (☎ 684 5067) at 42 Evans St has single/double units for $50/60. Also reasonable are the *Bay Motel* (☎ 684 3267), 9 Hewlings St; *Al Casa* (☎ 684 7071), 131 Evans St; the *Caroline* (☎ 684 4155), 48 Evans St; *White Star Motel* (☎ 684 7509), 12 White St; and *Wai-iti Court* (☎ 688 8447), 5 Preston St. The *Baywatch Motor Lodge* (☎ 688 1886), 7 Evans St, is more upmarket and charges $80 to $110. The new units have bay views. The new *Ashley Motor Lodge* (☎ 688 9939), 97 King St, on the south side of town, is also a cut above the rest and charges $85.

The information centre has extensive listings for private homestays and farmstays.

Places to Eat On Stafford St, the *Stafford Mall* has a food court for cheap kebabs, Chinese food or filled rolls during the day.

Good value, pub-style meals can be found at *McGinty's*, down an arcade near the corner of George and Stafford Sts, and at the *Sail & Anchor* in the Royal Arcade nearby. Both are also popular nightspots.

The *Old Bank* (see Places to Stay) is another popular night venue also serving meals. The *Loaded Hog Brewery* is a boutique brewery, in the former Landing Service building in George St, with food and a veritable trough of selections for the beer lover.

Casa Italia on Strathallan St, in a beautiful historic building, has an excellent wine list and serves authentic Italian food. Pasta mains cost around $15 to $17, although more expensive dishes are offered.

Passions, in an old church on Theodosia St, is a very good wine bar with a wood-fired oven for pizza. *Park Hill Estate* (☎ 614 7925) at Levels, 12km west of Timaru on SH8, is a vineyard with a restaurant for fine dining in pleasant surrounds.

Good-value eats can be found around the Northland Mall. *South of the Border*, fronting Evans St, is a small restaurant/bar for cheap Tex-Mex food. *Absolutely Fatty's* in the Northern Tavern has big serves and low prices. The mall also has a Pack 'N Save supermarket, and *McDonald's* is across the road.

Things to Buy Aficionados of 'Swannies', the check woollen shirts famed throughout New Zealand, should flock to the Alliance Textiles Factory Shop, 23 Bank St. Other woollen clothing, duvets and oilskins are also sold. Goods are seconds, but high quality and cheaper than in the shops.

Getting There & Around Air New Zealand (☎ 0800 652 881) has daily flights to Christchurch and Wellington. Timaru's airport is 12km north-west of town, just off SH1. Timaru Taxis (☎ 688 8899) has an airport shuttle for $7 or a taxi (ring Call A Cab ☎ 688 8811) will cost about $15.

InterCity and Newmans buses stop at the train station, where the Travellers Rest & Bookings Centre (☎ 688 3597) handles bookings. InterCity passes through Timaru on the Christchurch-Dunedin-Queenstown and Christchurch-Dunedin-Te Anau routes. Newmans' Christchurch-Dunedin buses stop in Timaru.

Shuttle buses between Christchurch and Dunedin pass through Timaru, such as Catch-a-Bus (☎ 453 1480), Atomic (☎ 322 8883), Ko-op Shuttles (☎ 366 6633), Southern Link (☎ 379 9991) and Eaziway/Nationwide (☎ 0508 504050). The fare is around $20 to Christchurch or Dunedin.

The *Southerner* train (ChristchurchInvercargill) passes through Timaru daily: at 10.35 am going south and 3.10 pm going north.

For hitching north get a Canride Grantlea bus to Jellicoe St and save yourself a walk.

Waimate

This town, 45km south of Timaru, is reached by a deviation off SH1 onto SH82. It is possible to do a loop and rejoin SH1 near the Waitaki River. The town's name translates as 'stagnant water' although there is little hint of it today. The town has a **museum** and the historic **Cuddy**, a thatched cottage constructed from a single totara tree – contact the Waimate Information Centre (☎ 689 8079) on Queen St. Waimate is the gateway to the hydro lakes of the Waitaki Valley, noted for Quinnat salmon fishing.

Don't be surprised if you see wallabies in the nearby hills, as they have bred like rabbits since being introduced from Australia.

At the *Victoria Park Motor Camp* (☎ 689 8079), 5 Tennant St, a tent/powered site is $10/14 for two and basic cabins are $8 per person. A room in the *New Criterion* (☎ 689 8069), on the corner of Mill Rd and Queen St, will cost $35/60 for a single/double. The *Lochiel Motel* (☎ 689 7570), 100 Shearman St, has units at $50 to $60 for two and also offers rooms in a simple guest house.

Queen St has plenty of dining possibilities, including the *Country Kitchen* tearooms and the *Dolphin Restaurant* for cheap meals and takeaways.

TO THE MACKENZIE COUNTRY

Those heading to Queenstown and the lakes from Christchurch will probably turn off SH1 onto SH79. This scenic route passes through the towns of Geraldine and Fairlie before joining with SH8, which heads over Burkes Pass to Lake Tekapo.

Geraldine

On the road inland to Mt Cook is Geraldine (population 2200), a picturesque town with a country village atmosphere. Geraldine was not settled until 1854, when Samuel Hewlings built the first bark hut in Talbot St; a totara tree planted at that time still survives. A number of early settlers cottages remain.

The **Vintage Car & Machinery Museum** on Lower Talbot St has over 30 vintage and veteran cars dating from 1905. A huge shed at the back houses tractors dating back to the 1920s. The tractors are entered in the annual Geraldine tractor races and competitions. The museum is open from October to Easter daily from 10 am to noon and 1.30 to 4.30 pm, and by arrangement (☎ 693 8700) at other times ($4).

Buses between Christchurch and Queenstown stop in Geraldine, and the Berry Barn tourist complex in the centre of town sells souvenirs for the bus trade. Of primary interest is the Barker's Wines shop specialising in fruit wines, mulled wine, jams and preserves. Geraldine is also noted for its beautiful private gardens and active craft scene, culminating in the November Festival of Arts & Plants.

The information centre (☎/fax 693 8597) on Talbot St is open from 8 am to 5 pm weekdays and 10 am to 2 pm on weekends.

Places to Stay & Eat The *Geraldine Motor Camp* (☎ 693 8147) on Hislop Rd has tent and powered sites for $8 and cabins for $15 per person. The *Farmyard Holiday Park* (☎ 693 9355), 7km from Geraldine, has tent/powered sites for $15/17 and cabins for $28 for two. The neat and tidy *Olde Presbytery* (☎ 693 9644), 13 Jollie St, is a homestaystyle backpackers with friendly owners. A bed here costs $20 per person in double and twin rooms.

The *Crossing* (☎ 693 9689) on Woodbury Rd is a luxurious B&B with a licensed restaurant. Singles/doubles cost $80/96 and $106/134 with en suite. Geraldine has plenty of other B&Bs for around $70 a double. On Talbot St, the *Crown Hotel* (☎ 693 8458) offers B&B twins for $55 or $65 with en suite and has two backpackers singles for $20. The *Geraldine Motel* (☎ 693 8501), 97 Talbot St, charges $60 for two; the *Andorra* (☎ 693 8622), 16 McKenzie St, is $65 to $75 for a unit; and the *Four Peaks* (☎ 693 8339), 28 McKenzie St, charges $69.

For a good breakfast go to *Robbie's Tearooms & Restaurant* on Talbot St. *Berry Barn Bakery* on Talbot St has good, cheap fare, or *Plums Cafe* has Chinese food and fish and chips.

Peel Forest & Mt Somers

The Peel Forest, 19km north of Geraldine, is one of NZ's most important areas of indigenous podocarp forest. Mt Peel station is nearby and the road from it leads to Mesopotamia, once the run of the English writer Samuel Butler in the 1860s.

Get information, including *Peel Forest Park: Track Information*, at the Peel Forest Store (☎ /fax 696 3567). The store has tearooms (open from 8 am to 7.30 pm) and also manages the excellent, fully serviced DOC camping ground on the banks of the Rangitata River ($6.50 each adult and an extra $2.50 for power). Ask at the store about baches to rent. Other, more basic DOC camping grounds in this region are at Orari Gorge on Yates Rd, 12km north of Geraldine; Waihi Gorge on Waihi Gorge Rd, 14km north of Geraldine; and Pioneer Park on Home Bush Rd, 14km west of Geraldine.

The magnificent native podocarp (conifer) forest consists of totara, kahikatea and matai. One fine example of totara on the **Big Tree Walk** is 9m in circumference and over 1000 years old. Birdlife attracted to this forest includes the rifleman, kereru (native pigeon), bellbird, fantail and grey warbler. Nesting New Zealand falcons are on the higher reaches of Mt Peel. There are also picturesque waterfalls in the park – Emily Falls (1½ hour), Rata Falls (two hours) and Acland Falls (20 minutes).

Mt Peel-based Rangitata Rafts (☎ 0800 251 251) operates **white-water rafting** on the nearby Rangitata River; it has budget accommodation at Mt Peel, where you can get a basic bunk bed for $10. Rangitata Gorge is one of the best, because of the exhilarating Grade V rapids at all water levels. The cost is $105 per person for the Rangitata Gorge, including lunch and a BBQ dinner. The trips depart from Christchurch between 9 and 9.30 am and arrive at the river base at 11.30 am. The trip on the river is about three hours and returns to Christchurch about 7 to 8 pm. Rangitata Rafts is a 10-minute drive past Peel Forest.

The 10-hour **Mt Somers Subalpine Walkway** traverses the northern face of Mt Somers, linking the Sharplin Falls with Woolshed Creek. The highlight is walking through several altitudinal plant sequences, although there is also plenty of regenerating beech forest. Two huts, the Pinnacles and Mt Somers, on the walk cost $4 each adult. Be warned that this route is subject to sudden changes in weather and all tramping precautions should be taken. Hut tickets are available at the general store in Mt Somers township. The *Mt Somers Holiday Park* (☎ 303 9719) in town has tent and powered sites from $15 and cabins. *Stronechrubie* (☎ 303 9814) has motel units for $80 and a superb, award-winning restaurant.

Fairlie

Fairlie (population 850) is often described as 'the gateway to the Mackenzie' because, just west of here, the landscape changes dramatically as the road mounts Burkes Pass to the open spaces of the Mackenzie Country. It was named after the town of Fairlie in Ayrshire, Scotland, the birthplace of the town's first hotel owner in 1865.

One legacy of the early residents is the tree-lined avenues. The colonial **Mabel Binney cottage** and **Vintage Machinery Museum** are on the main highway, just west of the town centre. A few minutes drive west of Fairlie is the historic limestone **woolshed** of the Three Springs Sheep Station.

A good 1½-hour, 38km scenic drive from Fairlie takes in the spectacular Opihi Gorge. It goes to Allandale, then along Middle Valley Rd and Spur Rd to Opihi, and back to Fairlie. The Sunflower Centre (☎ 685 8258),

31 Main St, has information on Fairlie and the surrounding area.

Nearby **skiing** is at Fox Peak (☎ 685 8539), in the Two Thumb Range 37km north-west of Fairlie, a club ski area with a vertical run of 680m. Mt Dobson (☎ 685 8039), 26km north-west of Fairlie, is in a basin 3km wide, accessed from the highest car park in NZ (1692m). Mt Cook and the Southern Alps are clearly viewed. Daily transport is offered from the Ski Shack in Fairlie. For more information see the Skiing section in the Outdoor Activities chapter.

Places to Stay & Eat The *Gateway Holiday Park* (☎ 685 8375) on Allandale Rd has tent/powered sites for $8/9 per person, and cabins for $30 a double or $35 with own cooking facilities. It also has a spic-and-span backpackers lodge with two dorms and a kitchen/living area for $15 per person. The *Allandale Lodge*, 10 Allandale Rd, is predominantly a B&B but also has dorm beds for $10 per person in a fully equipped backpackers lodge.

The *Gladstone Grand Hotel* (☎ 685 8140), 43 Main St, charges $25/40 and serves meals.

The *Aorangi Motel* (☎ 685 8340), 26 Denmark St, and the *Rimuwhare Country Retreat* (☎ 685 8058), 53 Mt Cook Rd, have units from $60; the latter has a restaurant.

The *Sunflower Centre* serves tearoom fare or the *Old Library* is a better bet for a good meal. *Fairlie Stores* and *Tom's*, both on Main St, cater for the fast food and fish and chip cravers.

Getting There & Away InterCity's depot is the BB Stop (☎ 685 8139), 81 Main St. Atomic Shuttles also passes through Fairlie between Christchurch and Queenstown.

MACKENZIE COUNTRY

The high country from which the Mt Cook park rises is known as the Mackenzie country after the legendary Jock McKenzie, who is said to have run his stolen flocks in this uninhabited region around 1843 (see the boxed text entitled The Legend of Jock McKenzie). When he was finally caught, other settlers realised the potential of the land and followed in his footsteps. The first people to traverse the Mackenzie were the Maori, who used to trek from Banks Peninsula to Otago hundreds of years ago.

Lake Tekapo

At the southern end of Lake Tekapo, the small settlement of Lake Tekapo has sweeping views across the turquoise lake with the hills and snow-capped mountains as a backdrop. The turquoise colour of the lake is created by 'rock flour', finely ground particles of rock held in suspension in the glacial melt water. Tekapo derives its name from *taka* (sleeping mat) and *po* (night).

Lake Tekapo is a popular first stop on a tour of the Southern Alps. The buses heading to or from Mt Cook or Queenstown stop at the cluster of tourist shops by the main road and create chaos when they arrive.

The picturesque little **Church of the Good Shepherd** beside the lake was built of stone and oak in 1935. Further along is a statue of a collie dog, a touching tribute to the sheep dogs which helped develop the Mackenzie country. It is not, as a lot of

CANTERBURY

The Legend of Jock McKenzie

A legend this rightly is – many subsequent investigations have only helped to cloud or confuse the truth. It is thought that James (Jock) McKenzie was born in 1820 in Scotland. In his short time in this country (date of arrival unknown), possibly only two years, he achieved great notoriety. In March 1855 he was caught near present-day Mackenzie Pass in possession of 1000 sheep which had been stolen from the Levels run, north-west of Timaru.

It was believed at the time that he had stolen the sheep to stock a run he had purchased in Otago and that he was aided only by his remarkable dog, Friday. He was captured near the pass by the Levels overseer and two Maori shepherds. He escaped and made his way to Lyttelton where, while hiding in a loft, he was recaptured by a police sergeant. He was then tried for sheep stealing and sentenced to five years imprisonment. Throughout the trial McKenzie had pleaded not guilty, and nine months after the trial he was granted a pardon. He had, reputedly, escaped from prison three times during his nine-month incarceration, always proclaiming his innocence. Even the then Superintendent of Canterbury, James Fitzgerald, remarked: 'I am inclined to believe his story.' Popular myth has it that he was then ordered to leave the country, but there is no evidence to back this belief.

Lyttelton's town clock now covers the foundations of the gaol that once held McKenzie; he was interned here after the only Supreme Court trial ever held in the town. It is believed by some that McKenzie's 'treasure' – well, his savings anyway – are concealed in a bush near Edendale, 39km north of Invercargill. He supposedly selected the bush as it was *tapu* (sacred) to the local Maori. As legend has it, McKenzie was only pardoned on the condition that he leave New Zealand for ever – so he never returned to pick up his savings.

If you're heading to Timaru via Mackenzie Pass you will see a monument erected near the spot where McKenzie was apprehended, although no-one really knows the exact spot. The pass is said to be named after McKenzie as the discoverer, but it is now believed that it had appeared on an earlier map in the late 1840s. Similarly, there is no proof that he had ever purchased land in Otago to stock with either stolen or bought sheep. Little is known of his later life and the date of his death is a mystery. ∎

---

people believe, the infamous dog Friday of James Mackenzie. Visit after the last bus leaves.

The Hide Shop on the main road acts as an information office.

Activities Popular activities around Lake Tekapo include fishing, boating, kayaking, water skiing, bicycle touring and horse trekking. The Alpine Inn is the main operator and booking agent. In winter, Lake Tekapo is the base for downhill **skiing** at Mt Dobson or cross-country skiing on Two Thumb Range. There's ski area transport and ski hire in season. Lake Tekapo also has an open-air ice-skating rink, open from June to September.

Alpine Recreation (☎ 680 6736) offers mountaineering and climbing courses and guided treks in the Mt Cook National Park.

The region has a number of good **walks**. Most popular is the one-hour walk to the top of Mt John, and you can continue on to lakes Alexandrina and McGregor, an all-day walk. Other walks are along the eastern side of the lake to the ski area road: the one-hour return walk to the Tekapo Lookout and 1½ hours to the power station.

Tailor-made-Tekapo Backpackers (☎ 680 6700) also operates interesting 4WD trips on demand (minimum four people).

Organised Tours Air Safaris (☎ 680 6880) operates aerial sightseeing flights from Lake Tekapo over Mt Cook and its glaciers for $150 (children $105). Backpackers with cards can get a 10% discount. The flights do not land on the glacier, but Air Safari's spectacular 'Grand Traverse' takes you up the Tasman Glacier, over the upper part of the Fox and Franz Josef glaciers, and by Mts Cook, Tasman and Elie de Beaumont.

Air Safaris operates the same flights from Glentanner, near Mt Cook, for the same price. These flights are much cheaper than similar flights offered by other airlines from

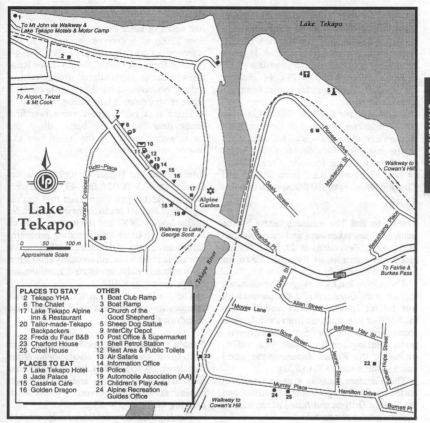

Lake Tekapo

0   50   100 m
Approximate Scale

PLACES TO STAY
2 Tekapo YHA
6 The Chalet
17 Lake Tekapo Alpine Inn & Restaurant
20 Tailor-made-Tekapo Backpackers
22 Freda du Faur B&B
23 Charford House
25 Creel House

PLACES TO EAT
7 Lake Tekapo Hotel
8 Jade Palace
15 Cassinia Cafe
16 Golden Dragon

OTHER
1 Boat Club Ramp
3 Boat Ramp
4 Church of the Good Shepherd
5 Sheep Dog Statue
9 InterCity Depot
10 Post Office & Supermarket
11 Shell Petrol Station
12 Rest Area & Public Toilets
13 Air Safaris
14 Information Office
18 Police
19 Automobile Association (AA)
21 Children's Play Area
24 Alpine Recreation Guides Office

Mt Cook itself. It is the most comprehensive aerial coverage of the national park, including the Godley River.

Places to Stay In a beautiful setting by the lake, the efficient *Lake Tekapo Motels & Motor Camp* (☎ 680 6825) has tent/powered sites at $16/18, cabins at $30, cottages with cooking facilities at $55 and comfortable units from $70; all prices are for two.

The *Tekapo YHA Hostel* (☎ 680 6857; PO Box 38) is on the Mt Cook side of town, beyond the post office and shops, down towards the water. It's a well-equipped,

friendly little hostel with great views across the lake to the mountains beyond. It arranges many activities and the dorm cost is $15 per person, twins are $36 or there are limited tent sites for $9 per person. Bicycles can be hired for $15 per day.

Wilma and Michael run *Tailor-made-Tekapo Backpackers* (☎ 680 6700), where dorms $15 per person, doubles and twins are $34 (duvets are supplied). It has full kitchen facilities, a laundry and, importantly, caring owners. It is on Aorangi Crescent, not far from the highway where the buses stop.

The *Lake Tekapo Alpine Inn* (☎ 680 6848)

is the largest hotel, favoured by tour groups. Singles/doubles, all with en suite, cost from $60/85 to $125/155 for the lakeview rooms. Rates include a cooked breakfast. It has a swimming pool and a range of restaurants.

The *Chalet* (☎ 680 6774), 14 Pioneer Drive, has units and holiday homes from $85 to $120 for two.

Freda du Faur B&B (☎ 680 6513) – the name commemorates one of the first great woman mountaineers – is at 1 Esther Hope St; the cost is $80 for a double. Other B&Bs on Murray Place include *Creel House* (☎ 680 6516) with B&B from $60/85 and *Charford House* (☎ 680 6888) with doubles for $85.

Places to Eat The business centre by the main road has takeaways and cafes, as well as a bakery. *Reflections* at the Lake Tekapo Hotel has bistro meals for around $16 for lunch or dinner daily.

The Alpine Inn has a range of restaurants, including the *Garden Buffet Restaurant* with hot buffet lunches ($15) and dinners ($28.50) or you can dine from the à la carte menu. The Alpine Inn has two other restaurants catering for the Asian bus traffic, including the *Kohan Japanese* for good value sashimi sets ($20 to $22).

The *Cassinia Cafe* is a more upmarket coffee shop with vegetarian alternatives, and the *Golden Dragon* and *Jade Palace* are two cheap Chinese restaurants.

Getting There & Away InterCity and Mt Cook Landline southbound services to Queenstown, Wanaka and Mt Cook come through daily, as do the northbound services to Christchurch. The InterCity (☎ 680 6895) depot is at High Country Crafts on Main St and the Mt Cook Landline agent is Tekapo Services (☎ 680 6809) at the Shell station.

Nationwide, Southern Link, Kiwi Discovery (takes bikes for free) and Atomic Shuttles include Lake Tekapo on their route; it is $20 to Christchurch and $25 to Queenstown.

Hitching in or out of Lake Tekapo can sometimes be difficult, but once you've got a ride it will probably be going a fair way.

Twizel

Just south of Lake Pukaki, Twizel (population 1200) is a convenient base for the surrounding area. By car it's only about 40 minutes from Mt Cook. Nearby Lake Ruataniwha has an international rowing centre, fishing, boating and windsurfing. In the Ben Ohau ranges there is heli-skiing in winter.

There is a black stilt captive breeding centre near Twizel. The black stilt is the rarest wader species in the world (see the colour Fauna & Flora section).

Information The Twizel Visitor Information Centre (☎ 435 0802; fax 435 0852) on Wairepo Rd is open from 9 am to 4 pm on weekdays and 10 am to 3 pm on weekends. It also houses DOC and the headquarters of the important black stilt breeding program. Informative tours to the black stilt hide leave from here at 10.30 am on weekdays and 2 pm on weekends ($10, children $5, minimum charge for a tour $20).

The National Bank in the Twizel Mall changes money and has an ATM for Visa withdrawals.

Places to Stay Right beside the lake, 4km from town, the spacious *Ruataniwha Holiday Park* (☎ 435 0613) has tent/powered sites at $17/18 for two and cheap, basic cabins at $13 per person. Cabins with cooking facilities cost $35.

The *High Country Holiday Lodge* (☎ 435 0671) on Mackenzie Drive has all sorts of accommodation in cabins originally built for the hydro scheme workers, starting with hostel-style bunks (only two beds to a room) at $15 per person, and singles/doubles and twins at $33/48. Rooms with private facilities cost $60 and motel units are $70 a double. The lodge has a restaurant.

Another cheap alternative is *Mountain Chalet Motels* (☎ 435 0785) on Wairepo Rd; the 13-person lodge has bunkrooms, twins and doubles for $15 per person ($5 extra with linen). This is a very comfortable place and would work out cheaply for a group. Motel units are $80 to $90 a double.

The *Colonial Motels* (☎ 435 0100) on

Mackenzie Drive near the service station has well-appointed units for $85. At the edge of town the flash *MacKenzie Country Inn* (☎ 435 0869) has rooms at $145 a double.

Glenbrook Station (☎ 438 9407) is a high-country sheep station 8km south of Twizel and 22km north of Omarama. Dinner, bed and breakfast is $96/152 for singles/doubles, but there are also some bunkhouse beds for $14 per person. It's an interesting place to stay, with horse riding, cross-country trail riding and bush walks.

Homestead B&B accommodation on the 72 sq km *Rhoborough Downs Sheep Station* (☎ 435 0509), 15km from Twizel near the SH8 and SH80 junction, costs $50/80.

There's a DOC camping ground in Temple Forest on Lake Ohau Rd, 50km west of Twizel.

Places to Eat Twizel Mall in the centre of town has a range of eateries. The *Black Stilt Restaurant & Cafe* offers takeaways, burgers and breakfast, and meals at around $10. The *Altiplano Cafe* has slightly more innovative coffeeshop fare, or the *Golden Palace* has Chinese food. The more salubrious *Hunter's Bar & Cafe*, 2 Market Place, is open from 11 am until late and has a blackboard menu from 6 pm offering steak, fish, salmon and other mains for around $14 to $19.

At 13 Tasman Rd, the *Top Hut Cafe & Bar*, open daily from 10 am, has a sit-down bistro and takeaways. The restaurant at the *Mackenzie Country Inn* has higher class dining and less expensive bistro meals.

Getting There & Away InterCity and Mt Cook Landline buses serving Mt Cook stop at Twizel, with additional buses shuttling between Twizel and Mt Cook (50 minutes). The Mt Cook depot is at the High Country Holiday Lodge. Christchurch-Queenstown shuttles, such as Atomic and Southern Link, also stop in Twizel. GTS (☎ 0800 487 287) links Twizel with Timaru and Oamaru, but only on Thursday or Friday.

Lake Ohau & Ohau Forests
Six forests in the Lake Ohau area (Dobson,

Hopkins, Huxley, Temple, Ohau and Ahuriri) are administered by DOC. The walks in this vast area are too numerous to mention but are outlined in the DOC pamphlet *Ohau Forests Recreation Guide*. Huts are scattered throughout the region for the more adventurous trampers.

Lake Ohau Lodge (☎ 438 9885) on the western shore of Lake Ohau has good facilities and luxurious units from $140 to $180; backpackers rates in the older wing are $44 per person.

MT COOK NATIONAL PARK
Mt Cook National Park, along with Fiordland, Aspiring and Westland national parks, has been incorporated into a World Heritage area which extends from the Cook River in Westland down to the base of Fiordland. The Mt Cook National Park is 700 sq km in area and one of the most spectacular in a country famous for its parks. Encompassed by the main divide, the Two Thumb, Liebig and Ben Ohau ranges, more than one-third of the park is in permanent snow and glacial ice.

Of the 27 New Zealand mountains over 3050m, 22 are in this park, including the mighty Mt Cook – at 3755m the highest peak in Australasia.

Known to the Maori as Aoraki, after a deity from Maori mythology, the tent-shaped Mt Cook was named after Captain James Cook by Captain Stokes of the survey ship HMS *Acheron*. It was first climbed on Christmas Day 1894 (by local mountaineers Jack Clarke, Tom Fyfe and George Graham) and many famous climbers, including Sir Edmund Hillary, have sharpened their skills on this formidable peak. Dominating the park, it is the centrepiece of the vista from the Hermitage.

In the early hours of 14 December 1991, a substantial piece of the east face (around 14 million cubic metres) fell away in a massive landslide. Debris spewed out over the surrounding glaciers for 7.3km, following a path down the Grand Plateau and Hochstetter Icefall and reaching as far as the Tasman Glacier.

The national park is on most itineraries of

CANTERBURY

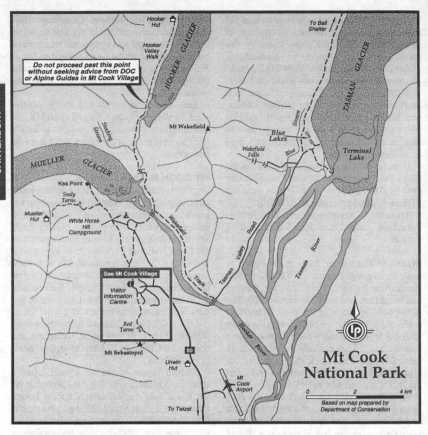

Do not proceed past this point without seeking advice from DOC or Alpine Guides in Mt Cook Village

Mt Cook National Park

0   2   4 km

Based on map prepared by Department of Conservation

the South Island and Mt Cook is certainly an impressive sight – if you can get clear views. Most visitors to the park come on tour buses for a quick stop at the Hermitage and photos, and are then off again, but the park has a number of accommodation options, though most are expensive and rooms are limited. The park has some excellent short walks, but is not a major tramping destination.

Information

The National Park Visitor Centre (☎ 435 1818; fax 435 1895), open daily from 8 am to 6 pm, will advise you on guided tours and tramping routes. For advance information write to: the field centre manager, PO Box 5, Mt Cook. They screen a 20-minute audiovisual on the history, mountaineering and human occupation in the Mt Cook region hourly from 9 am to 4 pm ($2.50).

A post office and general store (open 9 am to 6 pm) are not far from the visitor centre. Mt Cook has no banking facilities.

The Alpine Guides Mountain Shop (☎ 435 1834) sells equipment for skiing and mountaineering, and rents out equipment including, ice axes, crampons, day packs and sleeping bags.

The best introduction to this park is the beautifully illustrated *Alpine World of Mt Cook National Park* by Andy Dennis & Craig Potton. It has details of flora and fauna, walks and the park's history.

The Hermitage

The Hermitage is the most famous hotel in New Zealand, principally for its location and the fantastic views of Mt Cook. Originally constructed in 1884, when the trip up from Christchurch took several days, the first hotel was destroyed in a flash flood in 1913. You can see the foundations about 1km from the current Hermitage. Rebuilt, it survived until 1957 when it totally burnt out; the present Hermitage was built on the same site.

Even if it is beyond your budget to stay, you can sample the bar and restaurants and look out the huge windows straight up to Mt Cook.

Tasman Glacier

Higher up, the Tasman Glacier is a spectacular sweep of ice just like a glacier should be, but further down it's ugly. Glaciers in New Zealand (and elsewhere in the world) have generally been retreating this century, although they are advancing now. Normally as a glacier retreats it melts back up the mountain, but the Tasman is unusual because its last few kilometres are almost horizontal. In the process, over the last 75-or-so years it has melted from the top down, leaving stones, rocks and boulders on top as the ice around them melts. So the Tasman in its 'ablation zone' (the region it melts in) is covered in a more or less solid mass of debris, which slows down its melting rate and makes it unsightly.

Despite this considerable melt, the ice by the site of the old Ball Hut is still estimated to be over 600m thick. In its last major advance, 17,000 years ago, the glacier crept right down to Pukaki, carving out Lake Pukaki in the process. A later advance didn't reach out to the valley sides, so the Ball Hut Rd runs between the outer valley walls and the lateral moraines of this later advance.

Like the Fox and Franz Josef glaciers on the other side of the divide, the glaciers from Mt Cook move fast. The Alpine Memorial, near the old Hermitage site on the Hooker Valley Walk, illustrates the glaciers' speed. The memorial commemorates Mt Cook's first climbing disaster, when three climbers were killed by an avalanche in 1914. Only one of the bodies was recovered at the time but 12 years later a second body melted out of the bottom of the Hochstetter Icefall, 2000m below where the party was buried.

Alpine Guides organises sightseeing trips from September to May to the Tasman Glacier viewpoint. It costs $26 for 1½-hour trips and $30 for two-hour trips (children half-price).

Walking

Various easy walks from the Hermitage area are outlined in the *Walks in Mt Cook National Park* leaflet ($1) from the visitor centre. Be prepared for sudden changes in climate.

In summer look for the large mountain buttercup, often called the Mt Cook lily, as well as mountain daisies, gentians and edelweiss. Animals include the thar, a goat-like mammal and excellent climber; the chamois, smaller and of lighter build than the thar but an agile climber; and red deer.

The trail to **Kea Point** is an easy two to three-hour return walk with much native plant life and fine views of Cook, the Hooker Valley and the ice faces of Mt Sefton and the Footstool. You will probably see cheeky keas on this walk.

The walk to **Sealy Tarns** is a three to four-hour return walk from the village, branching off the Kea Point track. If the weather is warm and you're feeling brave you can swim in the tarns. The Sealy Tarns track continues up the ridge to Mueller Hut. If you intend staying up here register your intentions at the DOC visitor centre and pay the hut fee ($18 per person per night).

A good way to spend two to three hours (return) is to walk to **Red Tarns**. Climb another half-hour for spectacular views of Mt Cook and the valley.

It is a four-hour return walk up the **Hooker**

Valley across a couple of swingbridges to Stocking Stream and the terminus of the Hooker Glacier. After the second swing bridge Mt Cook totally dominates the valley. For those who have never seen a glacier 'calving' ice blocks into the azure blue glacial lake, this is a must. From here the alpine route to the Hooker Hut deteriorates rapidly and walkers without equipment (and sound advice) should go no further. Check with DOC and make sure you sign an intentions form at park headquarters.

The 3½-hour return **Wakefield Track** follows the route used by early mountaineers and sightseers, then returns by the southern section of the Hooker Valley track. This walk has deteriorated – seek advice from DOC before heading off. **Governors Bush** is a short one-hour walk through one of the last stands of silver beech in the park. A brochure on the native plants found in Governors Bush is available at the visitor centre.

Shorter walks include the 10-minute **Bowen Bush Walk** through a small patch of totara trees near the Alpine Guides shop. The 15-minute **Glencoe Walk**, beginning from the rear of the Hermitage, ascends through totara forest to a lookout point facing Mt Cook and the Hooker Valley.

The **Tasman Valley** walks are popular for a view of the Tasman Glacier. The walks start at the end of unsealed Tasman Valley Rd, 8km from the village. It is only a 15-minute walk up from the car park to the Tasman Glacier viewpoint, passing the Blue Lakes on the way. The views of Mt Cook and the surrounding area are spectacular, but the view of the glacier is limited mostly to the icy, grey sludge of the Terminal Lake and the Tasman River. To get close to the snub of the glacier, take the Ball Shelter Track (three to four hours return) from the car park, but this track is subject to flooding (consult DOC). A few hundred metres before the car park is the side road to the **Wakefield Falls Track**, an easy 30-minute return walk to the waterfall.

Longer Walks Longer walks are only for those with mountaineering experience. Advice must be sought from DOC and inten-

tions registered. Conditions at higher altitudes are severe, the tracks dangerous and many people have died. The majority of walkers shouldn't even consider tackling them (see Mountaineering).

The well-known Copland Pass Route is now almost a thing of the past. The three to four-day route crosses over the Southern Alps and down to the West Coast, but collapsing moraine walls and other changes have made this route dangerous. Even experienced mountaineers should think twice before tackling this one.

Guided Walks Alpine Recreation (☎ 680 6736), based in Lake Tekapo, offers high-altitude guided walks in the area. The Ball Pass trip is a two to three-day crossing over Ball Pass (2130m) from the Tasman to the Hooker valleys; it allows you to get close to Mt Cook without requiring mountaineering experience (with a group of six to eight people it costs $500 each).

Alpine Guides in Mt Cook Village also offers short guided walks along the tracks.

Mountaineering
There is unlimited scope here for climbing for the experienced, but beware: there have been over 175 people killed in climbing accidents in the park, with an average of five deaths each year.

The highly changeable weather is an important factor around here – Mt Cook is only 44km from the Tasman coast, catching the weather conditions blowing in over the Tasman Sea. The weather can change abruptly and you can suddenly find yourself in a storm. Unless you are experienced in such conditions, don't attempt to climb anywhere without a guide.

It's important to check with the park rangers before attempting any climb, and not only to check with them, but also to heed their advice! Fill in a climber's intentions card before starting out on any climb, so they can check on you if you are overdue coming out.

Alpine Guides (☎ 435 1834) has ski-touring and mountaineering courses but they are costly. Alpine Recreation (☎ 680 6736) in Lake Tekapo also has mountaineering courses.

Heli-Skiing & Heli-Hiking
In the winter months, Alpine Guides (☎ 435 1834), with Mt Cook Line, offers ski-touring trips and ski-mountaineering courses, but the speciality is glacier heli-skiing. Day-trips on the Tasman Glacier are $595 (three skiplane flights) and their Wilderness Heli-Skiing trip takes in the Liebig or Malte Brun ranges on four runs with a minimum of 3000 vertical metres of skiing for $650.

Another possibility is the half-day heli-hike for $325, an expensive option that takes you by helicopter up the Liebig Range for a walk and play around in the snow.

Aerial Sightseeing
The skies above Mt Cook are alive with the sound of aircraft. This is the antipodean equivalent of the Grand Canyon in the USA. The views are superb and glacier landings are a great experience – a must on any NZ adventure.

Trips are operated by Mt Cook Airlines (☎ 435 1849) from Mt Cook, by Air Safaris from Lake Tekapo (see the Lake Tekapo section earlier in this chapter) and Glentanner, the Helicopter Line (☎ 435 1801) from Glentanner, and Southern Lakes Helicopters (☎ 435 0370) in Twizel.

The Mt Cook skiplane landing flights are the most expensive but still worthwhile. The 30-minute Skiplane flight is $151; the 40-minute Glacier Highlights flight is $210; and a 55-minute Grand Circle flight is $300. Flights without landing range from $94 (15 minutes) to $225 (40 minutes). It also offers helicopter flights with snow landings from $135 to $285.

From Glentanner, the Helicopter Line (☎ 435 1801) has a 20-minute Alpine Vista flight at $125; an exhilarating 30-minute flight over the Richardson Glacier with a landing at $210; and a 45-minute Mountains High flight over the Tasman Glacier and by Mt Cook with a glacier landing for $285.

Southern Lakes Helicopters (☎ 435 0370) has chopper flights from Twizel for $195 (35 minutes) to $365 (70 minutes).

Organised Tours
Alpine Guides' interesting (but, at $30, rather expensive) two-hour Tasman Glacier Guided Tours go two or three times a day in season – check at the Hermitage about bookings and tour times. The rocky road follows the lateral moraines of the Tasman Glacier and the bus stops several times to see this mighty river of ice. Part of the tour involves an optional 15-minute walk to the glacier viewpoint.

If you want to go boating on a glacial lake then contact the Hermitage booking desk. You go out in a small motorised inflatable with about six people. Trips are over two hours and cost $60 (children $30).

From Glentanner (☎ 435 1855) you can go on horse treks over this high-country station from $30 for half an hour to $120 for three hours. There are 4WD trips for $25 per person ($15 for children), lasting about 90 minutes, which climb up to the highest point of the station at about 1500m.

Another good 4WD trip is Alan's 4WD Tours (☎ 435 1809) where it is guaranteed that all 'will rub knees, shoulders and bums' as the vehicle climbs up to Husky Flat above the glacier. Alan points out interesting alpine flora. The 2½-hour trip costs $60.

Places to Stay
Camping is allowed at the *White Horse Hill Camping Ground* at the old Hermitage site, the starting point for the Hooker Valley track, 1.8km from Mt Cook Village. There's running water and toilets but no electricity, showers or cooking facilities. It's run by DOC on a first-come, first-served basis and the cost is $3 per night. Contact the visitor centre.

The nearest motor camp to the park is 23km down the valley on the shores of Lake Pukaki at *Glentanner Park* (☎ 435 1855). The facilities are good, it is spacious and there are great views of Mt Cook. Tent/powered sites are $16 for two, basic cabins are $35 and deluxe cabins are $60 for two.

The restaurant, open from 8 am to 5.30 pm, sells milk and bread, but the nearest store is at Mt Cook Village. There is a booking service in the complex for Air Safaris, Helicopter Line, and Glentanner Horse Trekking.

About 3.5km before the village is the NZ Alpine Club's *Unwin Hut* (☎ 435 1102). Members get preference but beds are usually available ($20 per person) for intrepid travellers who wish to meet spider-person ascensionists. Feel privileged. It's basic bunk accommodation but there is a big common room with fireplace, showers, well-equipped kitchen and excellent views up the Tasman Glacier to the Minarets and Elie de Beaumont.

The excellent *Mt Cook YHA Hostel* (☎ 435 1820), on the corner of Bowen and Kitchener Drives, is comfortable and well-equipped with a sauna, shop and a good video collection. It's conveniently located and open all day. It can get crowded in the high season, from December to April, so try to book at least four days in advance. The cost in dorms is $20 per person and $46/52 for twins/doubles.

Apart from the YHA, all accommodation in the village itself is controlled by the one company and should be booked by phoning ☎ 435 1809. Some of the accommodation options may be closed in winter. *Big Rock Backpackers* is part of the complex and you may be able to get a bed for $20, but this place caters primarily for bus groups and is often full.

Mt Cook Chalets costs $112.50 for up to four people. It has two mini-bedrooms and a fold-out double sofabed, so between four people it can be reasonably economical. Well-equipped kitchens and a dining table add to the convenience.

Other accommodation around here is expensive. *Mt Cook Motels* charges $135 a double and the *Mt Cook Travelodge* charges $191; the rooms have no cooking facilities but the price includes breakfast. The *Hermitage* has prices and services in line with its fame and position, not the standard of its rooms – from $275 to $315 for a double or twin.

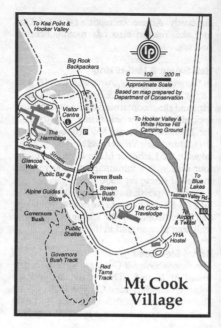

Mt Cook Village

Places to Eat

The store is well stocked for self-catering, but prices are higher than elsewhere. There is a cafe at Glentanner and a little coffee shop at the Mt Cook airport.

The Hermitage base line is the coffee shop for cheap cafeteria-style meals, pies and coffee. Then there is the *Alpine Room*, where unexciting main courses are around $17 to $25 (vegetables or a salad cost extra) and desserts are around $6. Buffets are also offered. The *Mt Cook Travelodge* has a similarly priced restaurant for dinner. Finally, at the Hermitage's *Panorama Room* two people can easily spend well over $100, but the view from here must be up there with the best in the world – you see Sefton to your left, Cook in the centre and the Ben Ohau ranges, dark brown and forbidding, to your right.

The *Mt Cook Tavern*, open until 1 am (midnight on Sundays), has pizza ($7.50), pies and BBQ meals ($9) and is the place to drink, sit and talk. Entertainment is often featured during the busy season.

Getting There & Away

Air Mt Cook Airlines (☎ 435 1848) has daily direct flights to/from Queenstown and Christchurch, with connections to other centres. Mt Cook provides bus services to and from the airport for $4.

There's no scheduled air service to the West Coast but Air Safaris can fly between Glentanner and Franz Josef for $150 one-way (minimum of two). It's a way of combining transport with a scenic flight, but the flights are weather-dependent.

Bus Mt Cook Landline (☎ 435 1849) has daily buses year-round between Christ-church, Wanaka, Queenstown and Te Anau. These buses stop in Twizel, from where you transfer to Mt Cook, 70km (a 50-minute drive) away.

InterCity buses on the daily Christchurch-Wanaka route go directly to Mt Cook, where they stop for one hour. The InterCity buses stop at the YHA hostel and at the Hermitage, both of which also handle bookings.

Hitching Hitching is hard – expect long waits once you leave SH1 if coming from Christchurch or Dunedin, and long waits all the way if coming from Queenstown. Hardest of all is simply getting out of Mt Cook itself, since the road is a dead end. It's worth considering taking the bus down to Twizel, where there's much more traffic.

Otago

Queenstown and Wanaka with their adrenalin activities, the Otago Peninsula, New Zealand's first real foray into ecotourism, and Dunedin, the capital of the region with its fine architecture, make Otago a must for any visitor to NZ. Otago's history featured a major goldrush and many aspects of the region's geography hark back to an era of prosperity when rivers and creeks swarmed with prospectors.

Otago occupies a central position on the South Island. The main entry route is SH1 from Christchurch along the east coast. From Southland you can approach Otago via the southern scenic route, through the Catlins or via SH1 from Invercargill. The most scenic way, however, is via the West Coast (SH6) and across Haast Pass.

Dunedin & the Otago Peninsula

Otago Harbour's long fiord-like inlet is the hub for many ecotourism activities, especially on the Otago Peninsula and in nearby coastal areas. The fauna-rich peninsula is close to Dunedin, a quaint city with many historic buildings and a convenient base for trips further afield to Central Otago and the Catlins.

DUNEDIN
Dunedin is the second city of the South Island, home of NZ's first university and during the gold-rush days it was the largest city in the country. Founded by Scottish settlers (Dunedin is Celtic for Edinburgh), Dunedin has a statue of Robert Burns guarding its city centre, produces whisky at a local distillery and still has haggis ceremonies.

Dunedin's ostentatious wealth in the latter half of the 19th century produced a grand Victorian city in the South Pacific. Though

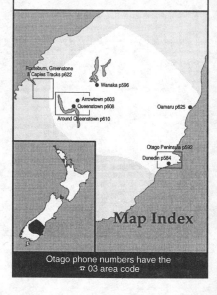

HIGHLIGHTS

- Enjoying activities on water, land and air at Queenstown, Lake Wakatipu and Lake Wanaka
- Tackling the Glenorchy, Routeburn and Rees-Dart tracks amid spectacular mountain scenery
- Skiing on any of the ranges near Queenstown (The Remarkables and Coronet Peak), Wanaka (Treble Cone) and Cardrona
- Marvelling at the historic towns of the Manuherikia and Maniototo valleys and the goldfields of Central Otago
- Enjoying architecturally rich Dunedin and the best nightlife on the South Island
- Seeing albatross, rare penguins and sea lions on the Otago Peninsula

Routeburn, Greenstone & Caples Tracks p622
Wanaka p596
Arrowtown p603
Queenstown p608
Around Queenstown p610
Oamaru p625
Otago Peninsula p592
Dunedin p584

Map Index

Otago phone numbers have the ☎ 03 area code

central Dunedin now has modern intrusions, much of the Victorian architecture survives: solid public buildings dot the city and wooden villas are scattered across the hilly suburbs. Preservation was as much a matter

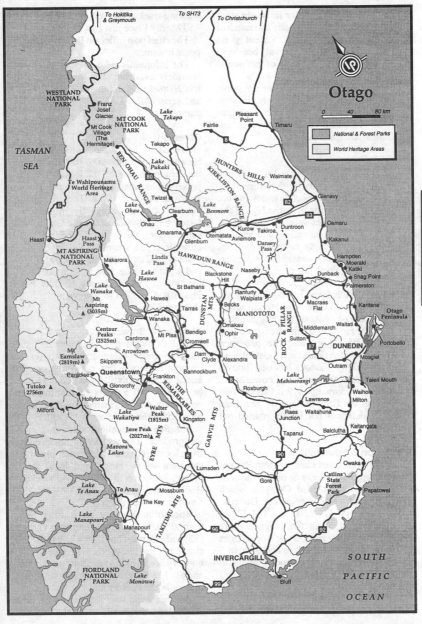

OTAGO

of fate as of planning. After its heady start, Dunedin declined economically and much of its population drifted away. Recent years have witnessed a slight revival, but local papers still lament the lack of economic opportunities.

Though Dunedin's boom years are gone, it is cultured, graceful and lively for its size. The 17,000 tertiary students out of the population of 118,000 drive the local arts, entertainment, cafe and pub scenes.

History

The early Maori history of the Dunedin area was particularly bloody, with a three-way feud between Otago Peninsula tribes and *utu* (revenge) followed attack as the Ngai Tahu and Ngatimamoe tribes' feud escalated at the end of the 1800s. Then sealing and whaling along the coast brought ravaging diseases and by 1848 the once considerable population of Otakau Pa was just over 100.

The first permanent European settlers arrived at Port Chalmers in March 1848, six years after the plan for a Presbyterian settlement on the east coast of the South Island was initially mooted. Soon after, gold was discovered in Otago and the province quickly became the richest and most influential in the colony. Famous business houses were established and it was the powerhouse of the NZ economy. In 1879 it was the first city outside the USA to have its own tram system, which was not finally phased out until 1957.

Orientation & Information

Dunedin's main street changes from Princes St on the south to George St on the north as it crosses the eight-sided Octagon which marks the centre of Dunedin. The Dunedin Visitor Centre (☎ 474 3300; fax 474 3311), 48 the Octagon, is in the magnificently restored municipal chambers. It's open from 8.30 am to 5 pm on weekdays and 9 am to 5 pm on weekends, with extended hours in summer. The centre has a busy activities and tour booking desk.

The DOC Shop (☎ 477 0677), 77 Lower Stuart St, has pamphlets and information on

walking tracks. The AA (☎ 477 5945) is at 450 Moray Place just east of Princes St.

The chief post office on Princes St handles poste restante.

The informative, free *Focus on Dunedin* is widely available. The visitor centre also has *Historic Dunedin*, *Walk the City* ($1), and *Accessibility for People with Disabilities* pamphlets.

Olveston

Designed by a London architect and built between 1904 and 1906, this fine turn-of-the-century house at 42 Royal Terrace is preserved as when lived in by the Theomin family in the early 1900s. Though the building is not as extravagantly impressive as Larnach Castle (see under the Otago Peninsula section), the lavish furnishings and art collections are stunning. One-hour guided tours at 9.30 and 10.45 am, noon, 1.30, 2.45 and 4 pm are a fascinating glimpse into the lifestyle of this fabulously wealthy family. Phone ☎ 477 3320 to reserve a place ($10, children $3).

Distillery & Breweries

Dunedin's most famous and popular factory tour has gone – Cadbury's no longer has chocolate tours – but breweries and **Wilson's Whisky Distillery** on George St can be visited. All aspects of distillation are covered in the informative one-hour guided tour ($5) of the southernmost distillery in the world. See the excellent video and sample the product. The whisky is made entirely from local products – pure water piped from the Lammerlaw range, and local malting barley. Tours run at 2.45 pm on weekdays. Book at the visitor centre (☎ 474 3300). Enjoy your 'wee dram'.

Speight's Brewery on Rattray St has tours at 10.30 am from Monday to Thursday ($5) and you must book (☎ 477 9480). Tours start from the brewery's visitor centre. The brewery is one of the smallest in the country and the 1¾-hour tour concludes with a glass of beer in the board room.

Another good tour ($5) is run by **Emerson's Brewery** (☎ 477 1812) at 4 Grange St, a boutique brewery specialising in good dark malt beers. Make sure you try the excellent London Porter or the India Pale Ale. Bookings are essential.

Museums

The **Otago Museum**, on the corner of Great King and Union Sts, has a large and varied collection, including Maori and South Pacific exhibits, a marine and maritime hall and a good Asian collection. The natural history displays of penguins, moas and extinct birds are particularly good and there is a hands-on Discovery World science centre for children. It's open from 10 am to 5 pm on weekdays and from noon to 5 pm on weekends (admission is free), and has a cafe and craft shop.

The **Early Settlers Museum**, 220 Cumberland St near the train station, has a photographic collection of the region's early settlers, balanced by politically correct exhibits on the loss of Maori land and the role of Chinese miners. The transport section has a variety of old vehicles. Steam locomotives in glassed-in display rooms at the train station end of the museum include *Josephine*, the first engine to run between Dunedin and Port Chalmers. The museum is open from 10 am to 5 pm on weekdays and 1 to 5 pm on weekends ($4, children free).

In the Octagon, the **Dunedin Public Art Gallery** is the oldest art gallery in NZ. Its international collection is small but has some big names – Gainsborough, Reynolds, Constable, Turner, Durer and Monet – even if some of the paintings are minor works. Excellent visiting exhibitions are staged. It's open from 10 am to 6 pm daily, except Friday (10 am to 8 pm) and Sunday (10 am to 5 pm).

The **Geology Museum** (☎ 479 1100) at the University of Otago has displays of mineral types and NZ fossils. Admission is free and during term it's open from 9 am to 5 pm on weekdays. Also in the university, the **Hocken Library**, founded by Dr TM Hocken (1836-1910), has an extensive collection of books, manuscripts, paintings and photographs relating to NZ and the Pacific.

The university itself was founded in 1869,

25 years after the settlement of Otago, with 81 students. It has an interesting variety of old and new styles of architecture. The old administration building is the most photographed building in Dunedin.

Other Attractions

Dunedin parks include the extensive **Botanical Gardens** at the northern end of the city on the lower slopes of Signal Hill. There is a hothouse and an aviary with keas and other native birds.

It's possible to stargaze at the **Beverly Begg Observatory** (☎ 477 7683), in the Robin Hood Ground – it's off to your left across the lawn at the top (western end) of Rattray St. Viewing is on clear Sunday nights an hour or so after dusk.

A short but definitely strenuous walk is up **Baldwin St**, listed in the *Guinness Book of Records* as the steepest street in the world with a gradient of 1 in 1.266. From the city centre, head north up Great King St for 2km to where the road branches left to Timaru – veer right along North Rd for another kilometre. The Gut Buster race, held every year during the Dunedin Festival around February, sees the winners run up and back in around two minutes.

Swimming & Walking

The heated outdoor saltwater pool on the headland at the end of St Clair Beach is open in summer – catch bus No 34 from the Octagon. St Clair and St Kilda are good beaches for walking but on the shortest day (the middle of winter) you can join the famous Shortest Day Swim (in the sea, not the heated pool!).

There is a 1.5km walkway to **Tunnel Beach**, south-west of the city centre. Catch a Corstorphine bus from the Octagon to Stenhope Crescent and walk 1.4km along Blackhead Rd to Tunnel Beach Rd. It is then 400m to the start of the trail which leads down through farmland for 20 minutes to the hand-hewn stone tunnel built by John Cargill so that his family could enjoy picnics on the small, secluded beach just over the headland. The sandstone cliffs are impressive and

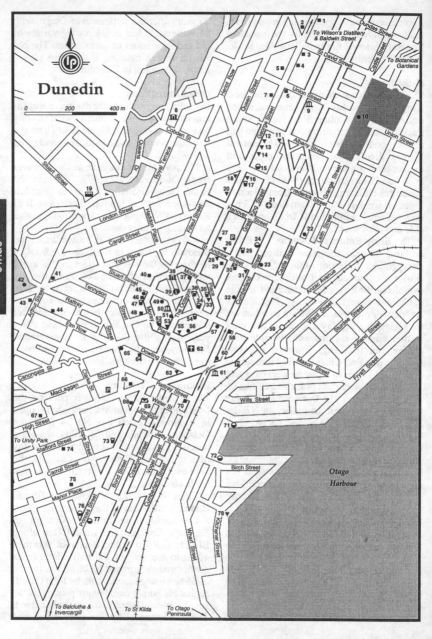

OTAGO

OTAGO

contain fossils if you look closely. The walkway is closed from August to October for the lambing season.

Catch a Normandy Citibus No 34 from the Octagon to the start of Norwood Rd, then walk two hours uphill (90 minutes down) to the **Mt Cargill-Bethunes Gully Walkway**, north-east of town. The highlight is the view from Mt Cargill, which is accessible by car. In Maori legend the three peaks of Cargill represent the petrified head and feet of a princess of an early Otakau tribe. Captain William Cargill was a leader of the early Otago colonists. Take warm clothes – it gets very windy at the top. From Mt Cargill a trail continues down to the 10 million-year-old Organ Pipes (half an hour), formed by cooling lava flows that left behind a crop of giant granite crystals. From here it is half an hour to the Mt Cargill Rd on the other side of the mountain.

North of Dunedin, the 5km **Pineapple Flagstaff Walk** is not accessible by public transport but offers great views of the harbour, coastline and inland ranges.

The visitor centre has leaflets and directions to these walks.

Other Activities

Other Dunedin activities include golf (three 18-hole courses), tennis and tenpin bowling. The Otago Aero Club (☎ 489 6158), Helicopters Otago (☎ 486 1784) and Mainland Air Services (☎ 486 2200) offer **flightseeing**.

The Otago Tramping & Mountaineering Club has regular meetings at 3 Young St, St

Kilda; the Wilderness Shop (☎ 477 3679), 101 Stuart St, has information on these activities.

Trojan Horseriding (☎ 465 7013) has rides along the beach north of Dunedin from $25 to $75, and Bums 'n' Saddles (☎ 488 0097) is based south of Dunedin at Blackhead. Horse treks also go to Larnach Castle.

Silverpeaks Tours (☎ 489 6167) has jetboating and white-water rafting trips on the Taieri River.

Organised Tours

Taieri Gorge Railway Some visitors rate this as one of the great train journeys, similar to the Silverton to Durango line in Colorado. From October to April, four-hour excursions depart from Dunedin Station on set days at 2.30 pm and, from May to August, at 1.30 pm. The 58km trip to Pukerangi costs $49 return (students $39; one child free per adult). Some trains continue 19km further to Middlemarch. Tickets are available from Dunedin Station (☎ 477 4449).

Most take the train as a day trip, but you can continue on to Queenstown by bus with Pacific Tourways for a steep $99. Or take your bike on the train and cycle the Otago Central Rail Trail to Alexandra, an excellent trip following the rail-line extension that has been ripped up and converted into a mountain bike-walking track (see under Central Otago for more details).

Cruises Otago Harbour Cruises (☎ 477 4276) is the main operator and has daily cruises from one to five hours long on the MV *Monarch* from Rattray St wharf. The half-day Otago Harbour cruise for $45 (children half-price) passes fur seal, shag and gull colonies and the albatross colony at Taiaroa Head. The hour-plus cruise from Wellers Rock takes in Taiaroa Head for $20, or the six-hour cruise-coach option is $79. There also are evening supper cruises with a smorgasbord.

The 57ft (17.5m) *Southern Spirit* (☎ 477 1031) operates five-hour cruises to Taiaroa Head from the Harbour Board Basin Marina in Birch St for $44. It also runs salmon-fishing trips. Blue Wave Cruise (☎ 471 0804) has two-hour wildlife trips to Taiaroa Head and three-hour fishing trips.

Bus Tours Newton Tours (☎ 477 5577) has 1½-hour double-decker Citisights tours at 10 am and 3.30 pm from the visitor centre taking in historic buildings, the university, Baldwin St and the Botanic Gardens for $15 (children $8). See also Organised Tours in the Otago Peninsula section.

Gold Trail Mini Tours (☎ 455 3139) go via Pig Root to the Macraes gold mine and the historic Golden Point Battery with lunch at Stanleys Hotel in Macraes Flat. The tour returns on the Taieri Gorge train and costs $71.50.

Places to Stay

Camping & Cabins The large, efficiently run *Tahuna Motor Park* (☎ 455 4690), 41 Victoria Rd, is near the showgrounds and beach at St Kilda. Tent/powered sites cost $18/18.50, cabins are $32 to $42 with en suite (prices are for two). The check-out call over the loudspeakers will get you moving in the morning. St Kilda bus No 47 from the Octagon stops nearby.

The well-tended *Aaron Lodge Motor Camp* (☎ 476 4725), 162 Kaikorai Valley Rd, has tent/powered sites at $18/20, cabins at $30 to $33 and tourist flats at $51 to $58 (again, for two). It is 2.5km north-west of the city; take a Bradford or Brockville bus from the Octagon.

The attractive *Leith Valley Touring Park* (☎ 467 9936) at 103 Malvern St, Woodhaugh, has tent and powered sites at $18 for two, on-site caravans at $30 and tourist flats for $55.

The *Farmlands Caravan Park* (☎ 482 2730) is on Waitati Valley Rd, 15km north of Dunedin off SH1. Powered sites are $18 and cabins cost $28 for two. There's an adventure playground with pony rides, a flying fox and farm animals.

The *Brighton Motor Camp* (☎ 481 1404), 1044 Brighton Rd, Brighton, by the beach 10km south of Dunedin, charges $16 for tent or powered sites for two and $30 for on-site caravans for two.

Hostels The *Stafford Gables YHA Hostel* (☎ 474 1919) is at 71 Stafford St, only a five-minute walk from the post office. It's an elegant and sprawling old building, once used as a private hotel. The cost is $16 in dorm rooms and $24/38 for singles/doubles.

At 296 High St, the central *Chalet Backpackers* (☎ 479 2075) is a former hospital with lots of character. Shared rooms cost $15 per person, singles $25, and twins and doubles $35, all including linen. There is plenty of information and some comfortable spots in the building's nooks and crannies to get away from it all.

The new *Adventurer Backpackers Lodge* (☎ 477 7367), 37 Dowling St, is close to the action and offers the highest standards. This large old building has been extensively renovated and the large common area with a small bar-kitchen is very chic. The rooms are immaculate and cost $14 in dorms, $32 for twin bunkrooms and $36 for doubles. The only drawback is that many of the rooms are small and windowless.

Elm Lodge (☎ 474 1872), 74 Elm Row, 10 minutes uphill (five back down) from the Octagon, is a fine old family home with a cosy atmosphere and fantastic harbour views. It charges $13.50/14.50 per person in dorm/shared rooms and $34 for twins and doubles. This good backpackers also offers excellent wildlife tours of Otago Peninsula. It picks up and drops off visitors (within reason) and rents out bicycles. Its overflow building nearby, *Elm Lodge Too* on Arthur St, is another fine old house with the same rates.

In one of Dunedin's old stately homes, the busy *Manor House Backpackers* (☎ 477 0484) at 28 Manor Place has dorm/shared rooms at $13.50/14.50 per person, twins for $32 and doubles for $35. It operates a courtesy vehicle and has a comfortable TV common room.

Right in the centre, *Penguin Palace Backpackers* (☎ 479 2175) on the corner of Rattray and Vogel Sts is old but has all the facilities, including a TV room, sitting room with pool table and a pleasant dining/kitchen area upstairs. The helpful management is a definite plus. This city-style hostel has beds for $13.50, or $15 in less-cramped dorms. A single, when available, is $22 and doubles and twins are $32.

Most central of all, *Next Stop Dunedin Backpackers* (☎ 477 0447), 2 View St, is just a short walk from the Octagon up a steep street. This hostel is a converted church hall, with most rooms fronting the cavernous common room. Kitchen and bathroom facilities are good, but more work is needed. There are dorm/shared rooms for $13.50/15 per person, and twins and doubles for $34.

B&Bs, Guesthouses & Motels Close to the city centre at 619 George St, the *Sahara Guesthouse & Motels* (☎ 477 6662) is a grand old house with worn singles/doubles from $50/77 or a better room in en suite costs $81. Motel units cost $69. Nearby is the superbly renovated *Albatross Inn* (☎ 477 2727), 770 George St. Luxurious doubles with en suite and TV range from $95 to $125 for those with kitchen (less in winter).

Castlewood (☎ 477 0526), 50 Arthur St, is in a fine house and costs $35/65 up to $50/85 for more luxurious rooms. *Magnolia House* (☎ 467 5999), 18 Grendon St, Maori Hill, 2km from the city centre, has been recommended by readers and charges $50/75. The *Baldwin St B&B* (☎ 473 0215), on the steepest street in the world, has rooms in a cottage for $55/90.

On SH1, 18km from Dunedin in East Taieri, the *Silverpeaks Lodge* (☎ 489 6167) is a working farm with sheep, cattle and goats. Doubles cost from $100 for B&B.

Dunedin's most convenient motel row is along George St. The *Argyle Court Motel* (☎ 477 5129) on the corner of Duke and George Sts has units for $69. The *Owens Motel* (☎ 477 7156), 745 George St, has units from $68 to $89. Motels on George St charging around $90 include: *Farrys* (☎ 477 9333) at No 575, *Allan Court* (☎ 477 7526) at No 590 and *Academy Court & Dunedin Motels* (☎ 477 7692) at No 624.

OTAGO

Moray Place Motel (☎ 477 2050), 97 Moray Place, is the most central. Good, new units cost from $79 to $110.

Moderately priced motels along Musselburgh Rise, on the Otago Peninsula side of town, include the *Arcadian Motel* (☎ 455 0992) at Nos 85-89, the *Chequers Motel* (☎ 455 0778) at No 119 and the *Bayfield Motel* (☎ 455 0756) at No 210. Double rooms cost $60 and $65. The *St Kilda Motel* (☎ 455 1151) on the corner of Victoria Rd and Queens Drive near St Kilda Beach charges from $55/65.

Hotels Relatively cheap hotels include the small *Statesman* (☎ 477 8411) at 91 St Andrew St. Singles/doubles cost $30/60 including breakfast. The very central *Law Courts Hotel* (☎ 477 8036), 65 Stewart St, has rooms with shower for $50/75.

The *Beach Hotel* (☎ 455 4642), 134 Prince Albert Rd in St Kilda, has rooms with en suite for $40/60. *Wains Boutique Hotel* (☎ 477 1155) at 310 Princes St is a great-looking old place close to the city centre with doubles at $95.

The solid, reliable, old-fashioned and central *Leviathan Hotel* (☎ 477 3160) on the corner of Cumberland and High Sts is a Dunedin landmark. Its budget twin rooms are $59, the standard rate is $83, and studio units are $93. At the top of the Dunedin listings are the *Quality Hotel Dunedin* (☎ 477 6784) on Upper Moray Place and the *Southern Cross* (☎ 477 0752), with its excellent DeliCafe, at 118 High St. Prices at both start at around $190. *Cargill's Hotel* (☎ 477 7983), 678 George St, charges $112 to $195. The five-star Grand Hotel is under construction at the old post office site on Princes St.

Places to Eat

Restaurants *Palms Cafe* on the corner of Dowling and Lower High Sts is a pleasant and deservedly popular place open for dinner. Mains are around $20.

For Italian food, the stylish and very popular *Etrusco at the Savoy*, 8A Moray Place, is fully licensed and open from Tuesday to Sunday from 5.30 pm. Small pastas are reasonably priced at around $12, pizzas are $14 and the desserts are excellent. *Casa Italia Ristorante*, in the municipal building on the Octagon (next to the visitor centre), is an elegant restaurant with fine cuisine, priced accordingly.

A great Indian eatery is the tandoori *Little India* at 82 St Andrew St. Curry mains are around $16 and set meals are offered. Get there early to be sure of a table.

Steak-lovers can't go wrong at the *Huntsman Chargrill Steak House*, 311 George St, with 20 steak dishes and a fantastic selection of salads at reasonable prices. More steak (and other dishes) are on offer at *Bentley's*, near the corner of Cumberland and St Andrew Sts.

Blades, 450 George St, has a reputation as one of Dunedin's best restaurants. The food is certainly innovative. Entrees include grilled crocodile and kangaroo ($9), and, as well as more usual mains, venison mignon on fried haggis ($21) is featured. Nearby *Cafe Cena*, 466 George St, also has very good, innovative NZ fare with mains costing around $21.

High Tide, 29 Kitchener St, is another excellent restaurant down by the waterfront with views of the harbour and peninsula. The blackboard menu features local produce, including seafood.

Cafes Cafe society is well catered for in and around the Octagon. *Cafe Nova* at the Dunedin Public Art Gallery on the Octagon has good coffee, all day breakfasts and sumptuous cakes. The *Metro Espresso* bar-cafe on Stuart St adds a touch of European style, and the *Percolator* across the road specialises in good coffee. Both have reasonably priced meals and snacks, are open during the day and are popular night venues.

Paasha, 31 St Andrew St, is an excellent little Turkish cafe open from 11.30 am to midnight (until 2 am on Friday and Saturday). Large mains are only $6.50 up to $9.50 for the Turkish Mixed Grill, and it does takeaways.

Top of the cafe tree is *Parisettes*, 368 Moray Place, where they seem to have got the cafe/eatery mix just right; they have a full blackboard menu. *Botanica* in the botanical gardens has good service and food in a delightful setting and is open from 10 am to 4 pm daily.

Pub Food The London Lounge upstairs in the *Albert Arms Tavern* on the corner of George and London Sts is open daily for hearty pub meals – steak and seafood – for under $10. The weekday lunch roasts are only $5.50. Serves are huge and piled with chips to satisfy student appetites, and Emerson's fine brews are on tap.

The *Captain Cook Hotel* is another popular student pub and has good food upstairs – if you can get in the door – and a beer garden. It's at the intersection of Albany and Great King Sts.

JW's Bar at *Wains Hotel* is slightly more salubrious and does great-value smorgasbords for $14.50.

Fast Food Many of Dunedin's sandwich or lunch places are along George St and around Moray Place. Try the BYO *Cafe Zambezi*, 480 Moray Place, for an excellent selection of sandwiches and light meals. *Potpourri*, 97 Stuart St, is a good wholefood place with salads, vegetarian burritos, quiche and other light meals. It's open from 9 am to 8 pm on weekdays and 10 am to 2 pm on Saturday. *Mega Bite* at 388 George St has a similar menu, and desserts topped with frozen yoghurt.

Governors, 438 George St, is something of an institution for student meals (big breakfasts, steaks, pies etc) and low prices. Open from 8 am until midnight, it is decorated with student notices and ads. The Union Building in the university has a cheap cafeteria, a bar and *Cousin Vinnies*, offering good pizza by the slice or pasta and salad for only $4.50.

Entertainment

Theatre & Folk Music Dunedin has the professional Fortune Theatre and several amateur companies. The New Edinburgh Folk Club meets at 6 Carroll St on Friday at 8 pm. The Saturday *Otago Daily Times* lists what's on around the city.

Pubs, Music & Dancing Dunedin is a drinkers' town and a good place for a pub

OTAGO

The Dunedin Sound

Dunedin was once the most active place in the New Zealand music scene. In the past dozen or so years it has produced a number of successful bands, many of which have achieved international recognition. A lot of this has had to do with the success of the Flying Nun (FN) record label and its successful overseas promotion. Although the label has now moved to Auckland, it has been replaced with the Port Chalmers-based Xpressway label.

So many of the Dunedin 'gig goers' have affiliations with musicians that one American observer once said that Dunedin was 'just a town full of band members'. A lot of really good bands evolve in this town, make an album which receives a small local following, perhaps get recognition overseas, then disband. As soon as they have gone, the vast resource pool of student musicians and songwriters in town throws up another band to fill the void.

Some North Americans equate Dunedin, a relatively small city, with Athens, Georgia, home of the B-52s and mega band REM. Bands from Dunedin which have been or are popular on the college airwaves in the USA include the Verlaines, Straitjacket Fits, the Clean and, perhaps most popular of all, the Chills.

Ten years of Flying Nun and a large chunk of the Dunedin band scene was celebrated with the release of *Getting Older*, which featured the four bands mentioned earlier, along with other well-known acts such as the Able Tasmans, the Bats and the Headless Chickens. Another compilation album, *Pink Flying Saucers over the Southern Alps*, covered a more recent selection and included Dunedin's 3Ds, which in the early 90s was getting good press overseas.

So, while in Dunedin, head out to one of the pubs where a band is playing. Maybe one of next year's supergroups will be there, and you will have seen it for the price of a couple of beers. ■

crawl. Many of the pubs and bars cater to students and are packed during term but die in the university holidays.

The *Captain Cook*, or simply the 'Cook', on the corner of Albany and Great King Sts near the university, is *the* student pub, often so hopelessly crowded you can hardly get in the door. Bands often play. The *Albert Arms* on George St is another less-crowded student pub that comes into its own on Monday and Tuesday nights when bands play. Monday night's Irish band is very popular.

Other student bars are the *Woolshed* on Moray Place, a smaller place with a good atmosphere, and *Diva* on Great King St, a cafe-bar with music. *Ruby in the Dust* on the Octagon gets a mixed crowd and has acoustic and other music.

Dunedin has few bands playing original music, despite its reputation as NZ's alternative music capital. The *Empire Hotel* on Princes St is the only regular venue for innovative music and body piercing. Otherwise it is mostly standard rhythm and blues fare (try *Crossroads* in Great King St) or inevitable Irish music (try *Rosie O'Grady's* at the intersection of Cumberland and St Andrew Sts).

Some of the liveliest drinking holes are the many bar/cafe/restaurants. *Metro Espresso* on Stuart St is one of the best and often has interesting music on weekends, starting late. *Percolator* opposite is favoured by an arty, less boozy crowd. *Bennu* on Moray Place is an incredibly popular place with a yuppie crowd, especially on Friday and Saturday nights in the downstairs Ra Bar, which has house music.

Then there's *Abbey Road*, 110 Moray Place, or the *Robbie Burns* if you still have the energy or inclination.

Getting There & Away

Air Air New Zealand (☎ 477 5769) on the corner of Princes St and the Octagon has daily direct flights to/from Auckland, Christchurch and Wellington, with connections to other centres. Ansett (☎ 0800 800 146), 1 George St (on the Octagon), has direct flights to/from Auckland, Christchurch and Wellington, and from (but not to) Invercargill. Southern Air flies to Invercargill and on to Stewart Island ($69 stand-by).

International flights are limited to Freedom Air's direct Sydney and Brisbane flights (as low as $429 return through travel agents), but it remains to be seen how long they will last. Korean Air is planning direct flights to Seoul. Departure tax on international flights is $20.

Bus InterCity (☎ 477 8860), 599 Princes St, has services to Christchurch, Invercargill, Wanaka, Queenstown and Te Anau. Newmans'(☎ 479 0958) Christchurch leaves from the same location.

A number of door-to-door shuttles service Dunedin. Atomic Shuttles (☎ 474 3300) runs to Christchurch ($24) and Queenstown ($25). Catch-a-Bus (☎ 443 1480) has services from Dunedin to Christchurch, Invercargill, Queenstown, Te Anau and Wanaka. Southern Link (book at the visitor centre) also runs to Christchurch.

Train Dunedin's magnificent train station (☎ 477 4449) is on Anzac Ave. The *Southerner* (Christchurch-Invercargill) passes through in both directions daily, except Saturday. Tickets are sold at the train station and the visitor centre.

The Taieri Gorge Railway is a scenic return day trip to Pukerangi and Middlemarch, but it is also possible to go one way and continue on to Queenstown by bus or bicycle (see Organised Tours earlier).

Hitching To hitch northwards get a Pinehill bus to SH1 before the motorway or a Normandy bus to the Botanical Gardens from the Octagon, or walk in 30 to 40 minutes. Hitching south, take an Otago Road Services bus from Princes to Fairfield.

Getting Around

Dunedin Airport Shuttles (☎ 477 7777), Gold Star Super (☎ 489 5184), Johnson's Express (☎ 476 2519), City Airport (☎ 477 1771) and Ritchies Airport (☎ 477 9238) offer door-to-door airport services for $10 per person (children $5). The 27km trip takes 40 minutes.

Citibus buses leave from the Octagon area and buses to districts around Dunedin leave from Cumberland St. Buses run regularly during the week, but routes combine on weekends to form limited services or they simply stop running. The visitor centre has timetables and the average trip costs $1.50 to $1.80.

OTAGO PENINSULA

You can spend a pleasant day, or longer, tripping around the Otago Peninsula, the most accessible wildlife area on the South Island. Stops can be made at Larnach Castle, Glenfalloch Woodland Gardens, the Portobello Aquarium and Otakou Marae, where there's a Maori church and meeting house with a small museum, but there are many other historical sites, walkways and natural formations. The *Otago Peninsula* brochure and map is available at both the Dunedin and Taiaroa visitors centres and lists over 40 sights and activities.

Wildlife

For many people the peninsula's wealth of interesting fauna is the main reason for visiting. As well as albatross and yellow-eyed penguin tours, little blue penguins and especially fur seals can be seen easily in many locations on the peninsula.

Albatross Taiaroa Head, at the end of the peninsula, has the only northern royal albatross colony in the world close to human habitation. The birds arrive at the nesting site in September, court and mate in October, lay eggs in November, then incubate the eggs until January, when the chicks hatch. Between March and September parents leave their chicks while collecting food, returning only for feeding. By September the fledged chicks leave.

The visitor centre at the Taiaroa has excellent displays on the albatross and other wildlife, with regular screenings of videos. From the centre, tours head up the hill to the glassed-in viewing area overlooking the albatross nesting sites. The tour costs $20, including a 30-minute introduction at the visitor centre and then 30 minutes viewing the birds. In calm weather it's unlikely you'll see an albatross flying but chances are better later in the day when the wind picks up. Ask if the birds are around before you pay, although the centre has been offering a $10 refund if no birds are sighted. Entry to just the visitor centre is $2 and well worth it.

The head is also home to the tunnels of **Fort Taiaroa**, built in 1886 and featuring a 150mm Armstrong Disappearing Gun. The gun was installed during the late 19th century to counter the improbable threat of attack from Tsarist Russia. Tours go to the fort for $10, or the 1½ hour combined albatross and fort tour costs $25.

The visitor centre (☎ 478 0499) is open from 9 am to 8 pm daily (9 am to 5 pm in winter). Tours go hourly until 1 pm, then roughly every half-hour. Tours run from Dunedin (see Organised Tours in this section) or catch a Portobello bus and hitch the remaining 11km through beautiful scenery. The *Monarch* cruise allows you to see these birds from the water.

Penguins The yellow-eyed penguin (Maori: hoiho), one of the rarest penguin species, can be seen at close quarters on the peninsula. Tours run from Dunedin but you have more options with your own transport.

From Penguin Place (☎ 478 0286), just off the Portobello Rd, 1½-hour tours run to its unique hoiho wildlife conservation project. A talk on penguins and their conservation is included, and the system of trenches and hides allows viewing of the penguins from just a few metres. This is as close as you'll get anywhere, so the tours are very popular. Tours cost $20 and go throughout the day in peak times, though prime viewing time is a couple of hours before dark. The project is funded entirely through profits from these tours. For tour times and bookings, phone Penguin Place or the Dunedin Visitor Centre.

The operators of Penguin Place have replanted the breeding habitat, built nesting sites, cared for sick and injured birds and,

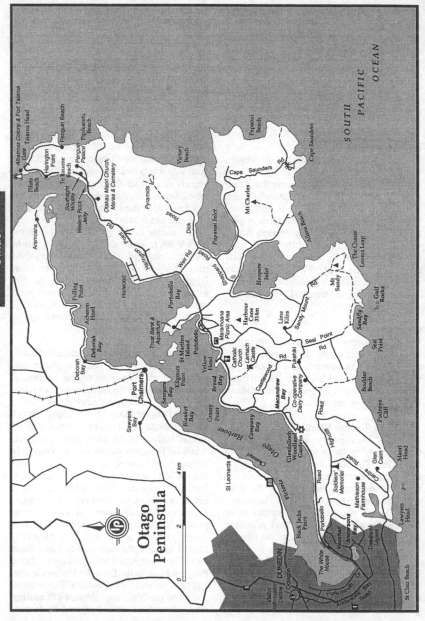

OTAGO

importantly, trapped predators. The hoiho's greatest threat is loss of habitat, especially the low-lying coastal vegetation in which they nest. Sadly, many farmers in Southland and Otago allow cattle to trample remaining patches of vegetation favoured by the hoiho.

If you have a car, Southlight Wildlife (☎ 478 0287), 200m past the turn-off to Penguin Place, can give you a key ($7.50, family $15) that opens the gate to a farm road starting right next to the albatross colony and leading to Penguin Beach. This beach has the largest colony of yellow-eyed penguins, viewed from high on a cliff (bring some binoculars or there are coin-operated telescopes). Fur seals and cormorants can also be viewed at very close range nearby.

A number of tour operators (see Organised Tours in this section) go to other hoiho beaches through private 'conservation reserves', ie land owned by farmers who charge for the privilege. Hoiho also nest at other, public beaches but numbers are small and sightings less certain. Sandfly Bay has a small colony which can be viewed from a DOC hide at the far end of the beach. Follow

Conservation efforts focus on restoring the nesting habitat of the rare yellow-eyed penguin on the Otgao Peninsula

all signs, don't approach the penguins and view only from the hide.

Hooker's Sea Lions The Hooker's sea lions can only be seen on a tour (see Organised Tours) to a 'secret' beach where the first pup was born on the NZ mainland after a breeding absence of 700 years. You will usually see six or more animals. The sea lions, visitors from Campbell Island and the Auckland Islands, are predominantly bachelor males.

Things to See
Larnach Castle (☎ 476 1616) is Dunedin's best-known building, a symbol of the indecent wealth that once resided in the city. This private 'castle' is a conglomeration of architectural styles and fantasies on the highest point of the peninsula. Built by JWM Larnach in 1871, its construction cost £125,000, about $25 million by today's standards. Proving that money can't buy happiness, Larnach, a merchant and politician, committed suicide in a Parliament House committee room in 1898.

Larnach Castle is 15km from central Dunedin and can be reached by tour or by taking the Portobello bus to Company Bay and walking 4km uphill. Horse treks are operated from Broad Bay to Larnach Castle with Castle Discovery Horse Treks (☎ 478 0592) for $35, including castle admission. The castle is open from 9 am to 5 pm. Entry to the castle and gardens is $10 (children $3.50) and you can explore the castle at will, or it is $5 (children $1) to visit only the gardens, stable and ballroom. Accommodation is also available.

The **Glenfalloch Woodland Gardens**, 430 Portobello Rd, 9km from Dunedin, are noted for their rhododendrons and azaleas and for the domestic birds freely wandering in the grounds. The gardens are open from 9.30 am until dusk daily. There's a tearoom, and a restaurant popular with wedding parties. The Portobello bus stops at the front.

The University of Otago's **Trust Bank Aquarium** is on Hatchery Rd, at the end of a small peninsula near Portobello. The small room has fish and invertebrates from a

OTAGO

variety of local marine habitats, and 'touch tanks' with animals and plants found in shallow waters and rock pools. The aquarium is open from noon to 4.30 pm, from 1 December to 1 March and during school holidays. The rest of the year it's open on weekends at the same hours. Admission is $5 (children $2, family $10).

Walking
The peninsula has a number of scenic farmland and beach walks, though you really need your own transport to get to the trails. It is a half-hour walk from the car park at the end of Seal Point Rd down huge sand dunes to the beautiful beach at Sandfly Bay.

From the end of Sandymount Rd it is a 40-minute round-trip walk to the impressive cliff scenery of The Chasm and Lovers Leap. A one-hour side trail leads to Sandfly Bay.

Other walks include those to the Pyramids and Mt Charles (through private land). Try to find a copy of the *Otago Peninsula Tracks* pamphlet.

Organised Tours
From Dunedin, Newton Tours (☎ 477 5577), 595 Princes St, has bus tours to Larnach Castle along the Highcliff Rd for $28 (children $15), and Wildlife Tours to Taiaroa with options to view the albatross on land or with the *Monarch* cruise, or to see the hoiho at Penguin Place. It costs $43 (children $22) or $79 (children $40), including the penguins and a *Monarch* cruise.

Otago Peninsula Express (☎ 474 3300) provides shuttle transport to Taiaroa, Penguin Place and Southlight Wildlife for $20 return, but not Larnach Castle. It departs from the Dunedin Visitor Centre and hotel pick-up can be arranged.

Wildlife tour companies Elm Wildlife Tours (☎ 474 1872; $39), South Coast Nature Tours (☎ 455 8527; $42) and Back to Nature Tours (☎ 477 0484; $39) have interesting tours of five to six hours, which usually see the royal albatross (visitor centre tours not included), little blue penguins, fur seals, hoiho and Hooker's sea lions. Viewing sites are at private beaches. Many other species of birds are spotted on the way, especially waders in the peninsula's eastern estuaries.

For small group ecotours, Wings of Kotuku (☎ 454 5169) is recommended and has a German-speaking guide. Dawn trips include the Sandfly Bay hoiho for $35.

You can catch the *Monarch* wildlife cruises at Wellers Rock Jetty, 1km before the turn-off to Penguin Place, for a one-hour cruise to the albatross colony (see Organised Tours in the Dunedin section for more details).

Places to Stay & Eat
The small *Portobello Village Tourist Park* (☎ 478 0359) at 27 Hereweka St in Portobello township has tent/powered sites at $17/19 for two. Cabins and on-site vans are $29 to $45.

The excellent *Penguin Place Lodge* (☎ 478 0286), at the Penguin Place tour office on Harrington Point Rd, has a lounge, fully equipped kitchen and laundry for $15 per person in twin rooms (linen $5 extra).

Nearby, the *Harrington Point Village Motel* (☎ 478 0287) on the main road near Southlight Wildlife has self-contained units sleeping four for $85. Broad Bay has B&B accommodation and there are other homestays on the peninsula.

In the grounds of the famous castle, *Larnach Lodge* (☎ 476 1616) has double rooms in the historic stable building at $49 and hotel-style rooms in the new lodge from $120. Meals are available.

Portobello's *1908 Cafe & Bar* is an excellent, if expensive, restaurant. The changing blackboard menu has a wide variety of delights, including seafood – blue cod, bay clams and mussels. Entrees cost around $9, mains around $25. Portobello also has a fish and chip shop, while Macandrew Bay has fish and chips and the *Harbour Lights Cafe*.

PORT CHALMERS
On the opposite side of Otago Harbour from the peninsula, Port Chalmers was founded in 1844 and became Dunedin's port. The modern container port is no great attraction,

but the town's historic streetscapes have hardly changed since its heyday as the centre of the frozen meat trade in the 19th century. The **museum**, open from 1.30 to 4.30 pm on weekends, has nautical displays but the main interest is the collection of old photograph albums. **Flagstaff Lookout** has expansive views of the town and harbour.

Pub accommodation is available, though Port Chalmers is primarily a day-trip destination. Stop for a drink at one of the old stone pubs, such as Carey's Bay Hotel overlooking the yacht harbour. The Port Stables Bar & Cafe is a trendier alternative on the main street.

From Port Chalmers the narrow road hugs the coast all the way to **Aramoana**, a small bach settlement with a white-sand surf beach where hoiho nest.

Wanaka Region

Entering Otago via the Haast Pass, the first sizeable towns are Hawea and Wanaka, after passing between lakes Wanaka and Hawea at the Neck. The central feature of this region is Mt Aspiring, surrounded by the national park of the same name.

WANAKA

Wanaka is nirvana for adrenalin buzz seekers, with fine living and an overdose on scenery and the outdoors. Just over 100km from Queenstown, at the southern end of Lake Wanaka, Wanaka is the gateway to the Mt Aspiring National Park and the Treble Cone, Cardrona, Harris Mountains and Pisa Range ski areas. This laid-back town of just 2200 people offers a sharp contrast to the hype of Queenstown.

Long a Kiwi summer resort famous for its New Year revelries and popular ski town in winter, Wanaka has a host of activities and natural splendour attracting international visitors year-round.

Information

The Wanaka Visitor Information Centre

(☎ 443 1233; fax 443 9238) in the Mt Aspiring National Park Visitor Centre (☎ 443 7660) on Ardmore St is open from 8 am to 4.45 pm on weekdays and 9 am to 4.30 pm on weekends. It has displays and audiovisuals, and the DOC counter is the place to inquire about walks and tramps.

The Adventure Centre (☎ 443 9422), 99 Ardmore St, books most of the adventure activities including kayaking, parapenting, rock climbing, white-water sledging and rafting, skiing and canyoning. In summer it's open from 8.30 am to 6 pm; in winter it becomes Harris Mountain Heli-Ski & Treble Cone Ski Field.

Lakeland Adventures (☎ 443 7495), beside the jetty, books lake activities, rents out canoes, bikes and cars, and is open from 9 am to 6 pm daily.

Puzzling World Maze

Three-dimensional mazes have become a NZ craze and an export activity. This maze was the original. The idea is to find your way along the 1.5km of passages to the towers at each corner and then back to the exit. And it's more difficult than you think. The Tilted House, built on a 15° angle, is designed to confuse the senses. The maze complex is open from 8.30 am to 5.30 pm ($6, children $3.50) and includes a Puzzle Centre, with a variety of puzzles to try, and the Hologram Hall. It's on the road to Cromwell, 2km from Wanaka.

Museums

Wanaka airport, 8km from town, is quite an aviation centre. As well as offering many aerial activities, it has the well-presented **New Zealand Fighter Pilots Museum**, open from 9.40 am to 4 pm ($6, children $2). It chronicles the history and exploits of NZ's fighter pilots, but the real treasures are the war planes, lovingly restored and most in working order. Planes include a Mustang, Spitfire, Kittyhawk, SE5A biplane, Gruman Avenger, and Japanese and Russian aircraft.

Just outside the airport, **Wanaka Transport Museum** has aircraft ranging from a Russian Antonov to the tiny Flying Flea,

OTAGO

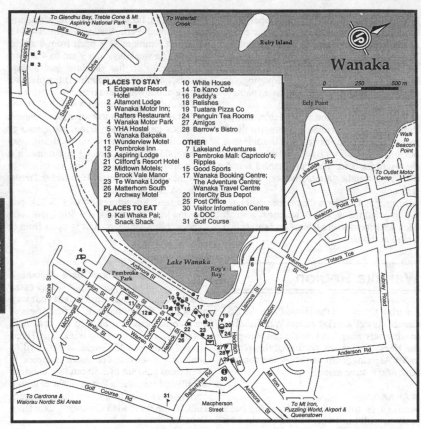

PLACES TO STAY
1 Edgewater Resort Hotel
2 Altamont Lodge
3 Wanaka Motor Inn; Rafters Restaurant
4 Wanaka Motor Park
5 YHA Hostel
6 Wanaka Bakpaka
11 Wunderview Motel
12 Pembroke Inn
13 Aspiring Lodge
21 Clifford's Resort Hotel
22 Midtown Motels; Brook Vale Manor
23 Te Wanaka Lodge
26 Matterhorn South
29 Archway Motel

PLACES TO EAT
9 Kai Whaka Pai; Snack Shack

10 White House
14 Te Kano Cafe
16 Paddy's
18 Relishes
19 Tuatara Pizza Co
24 Penguin Tea Rooms
27 Amigos
28 Barrow's Bistro

OTHER
7 Lakeland Adventures
8 Pembroke Mall: Capriccio's; Ripples
15 Good Sports
17 Wanaka Booking Centre; The Adventure Centre; Wanaka Travel Centre
20 InterCity Bus Depot
25 Post Office
30 Visitor Information Centre & DOC
31 Golf Course

motorbikes and other vehicles. It also has a collection of old British cars that until recently were very much in evidence on NZ roads. It is open from 8 am to 6 pm daily (9 am to 5 pm in winter). Admission is $5 (children $2).

Mt Aspiring National Park
In 1964, 200 hectares in north-western Otago and southern Westland were earmarked as a national park, named after its highest peak, 3027m Mt Aspiring, the highest outside the Mt Cook region. The park now extends over 3500 sq km along the

Southern Alps from the Haast river in the north to its border with the Fiordland National Park in the south.

The park has wide valleys, secluded flats, over 100 glaciers and towering mountains. The southern end of the park around Glenorchy is the most trafficked and includes popular tramps such as the Routeburn, but there are good short walks and more demanding tramps in the Matukituki Valley close to Wanaka.

Tracks are reached from Raspberry Creek at the end of the mostly gravel Mt Aspiring Rd, 54km from Wanaka. The Mt Aspiring

Express (☎ 443 8802) runs to Raspberry Creek for $25 one-way ($40 return).

The popular three-hour return **Rob Roy** walk has good views. From Raspberry Creek follow the West Matukituki Valley, from where the walk goes up the Rob Roy Stream to a point below the Rob Roy Glacier.

The **West Matukituki Valley** track continues on to Aspiring Hut, a scenic four-hour return walk over mostly grassy flats. Overnight or longer tramps continue up the valley to French Ridge Hut and Liverpool Bivvy for great views of Mt Aspiring, or over the very scenic but difficult Cascade Saddle to link up with the Rees-Dart Track north of Glenorchy.

Longer tramps are subject to snow and can be treacherous in adverse weather. The icy slopes of the Cascade Saddle killed a tramper recently. Register intentions and seek advice from the DOC counter at the Mt Aspiring National Park Visitor Centre in Wanaka before heading off.

Mountain Recreation (☎ 443 7330) offers guided treks. The four day West Matukituki Valley trek goes to the comfortable Shovel Flat base camp, treks up to the valley head to see glaciers and waterfalls, stops overnight in the French Ridge Hut and climbs on Mt French, with superb views of the Bonar Glacier and Mt Aspiring ($750). An easier three-day option costs $495. All equipment, accommodation and food is provided.

With all those snowy peaks, the park is popular for **mountaineering** and alpine climbing courses. Mount Aspiring Guides (☎ 443 9422) and Mountain Recreation offer beginners courses, guided ascents of Mt Aspiring for the more experienced and ski-mountaineering tours.

Walking
DOC's *Wanaka Walks* brochure has a rough map and outlines 11 walks around the town, including the easy 30-minute lakeside walk to Eely Point and on to Beacon Point, and the Waterfall Creek walk.

The fairly gentle climb up **Mt Iron** (549m), near the maze, takes 45 minutes to the top with views of rivers, lakes and mountains.

The more exhausting trek up **Mt Roy** (1578m), starting 6km from Wanaka on the Mt Aspiring Rd, takes about three hours to the top if you're fit. The 8km track winds every step of the way, but the view of Mt Aspiring is a knockout. Mountain bikes can also use this track. The **Diamond Lake** track, a 25-minute drive from town, offers a three-hour walk to the great views from the top of Rocky Hill.

Aerial Activities
Tandem Skydive Wanaka (☎ 443 7207) does **tandem skydiving** from 9000ft for $225 ($195 for backpackers) and from 12,000ft for $265. As well as the adrenalin buzz, the views of the Southern Alps and Mt Aspiring are stunning.

Wanaka is ideally suited for **paragliding** and attracts paragliders from all over the world. Wanaka Paragliding School (☎ 443 9193) has full-day introductory courses for $138 (by the end of which you will be doing 100m flights from Mt Iron) and tandem flights from Treble Cone for $98.

Kayaking
Alpine River Guides (☎ 443 9023, 443 9422) at the Adventure Centre, 99 Ardmore St, offers kayak trips on the Matukituki or Makarora rivers taking the better part of a day. The Matukituki trip put-in point is Raspberry Creek, after the guides have gone through the rudiments of kayaking. A full day (well, about seven hours) costs $96 and is well worth it. Other trips are also offered.

Canyoning
Those with a sense of adventure and a smattering of 'derring-do' will love this unique summertime-only activity involving tobogganing, swimming and waterfall abseiling through confined, steep and wild gorges. Transport to the canyon, a picnic lunch, instruction and equipment are included for $145. These thrilling trips through three canyons are operated by Deep Canyon Experience (☎ 443 7922) and can be booked at the Adventure Centre.

OTAGO

Aerial Sightseeing

Aspiring Air (☎ 443 7943) at the airport has scenic flights ranging from 45 minutes over Mt Aspiring, the glacier and alpine country for $120 to a Mt Cook flight for $230 or Milford Sound for $210. A launch trip on the sound takes the cost to $248.

Combining adventure with sightseeing, Biplane Adventures (☎ 443 1000) at Wanaka Airport will take you up in a Pitts Special stunt plane and roll, stall, fly upside down and loop with the force of four Gs for a cost of $150 for 15 minutes. More sedate flights in a Tiger Moth cost the same, or warplane aficionados with $2000 to burn can scorch the heavens in a P51 Mustang.

Other Activities

The Wanaka and Hawea lakes (16km away) are good for trout and salmon **fishing**. Lakeland Adventures has 2½-hour guided trips for $200, including boat hire for three people. Alternatively, on your own, hire a motorised runabout for $50 per hour, a rod for $12 per day while a licence will cost another $12.

Alpine Mountain Biking (☎ 443 8943) does just that – high altitude **mountain biking** in summer. Half-day trips ($70) start with a 4WD ride to 1100m and then downhill back to town. More demanding full-day trips ($89) go to 1800m in the Waiorau Nordic ski area for fabulous views. With your own bike it is around $15 less. Overnight trips ($125) and heli-biking ($165) from 2000m are also offered.

Frogz Have More Fun (☎ 0800 338 737) has **white-water sledging** on individual boogey board-styled rafts with wet suits and flippers. Four to five-hour trips on the Clutha, Hawea and Kawarau, in ascending order of grade, are $75 to $90. Pioneer Rafting (☎ 443 1246) has easy **white-water rafting** trips with an eco bent for $75 a half-day, $95 a full day.

NZ Backcountry Saddle Expeditions (☎ 443 8151), 26km from Wanaka on the Cardrona Valley Rd (SH89), offers two-hour **horse treks** for $45 (children $30) and overnight wilderness trips from $130. Mt Iron Saddle Adventures (☎ 443 7581) has two-hour treks to the top of the mountain for $55.

Out on a Thread (☎ 443 9418) offers a full day of **rock climbing** instruction (including the essential skills of belaying and protection placement) for $125 ($85 half-day).

A 50-minute **jet-boat** trip with Lakeland Adventures across the lake and then up the Clutha River costs $50 (children $25). Jet Boat Charters (☎ 443 9126) has rides on the Clutha ($65) and Matukituki ($75) rivers. Edgewater Adventures (☎ 443 8422) at the Edgewater Resort Hotel has jet-boat trips on the Clutha River for $50, as well as cruises, boat hire, fishing and other activities.

Good **skiing** areas nearby include Treble Cone, Cardrona, the Waiorau Nordic Ski Area (for cross-country skiing), and Harris Mountain for heli-skiing (see Skiing in the Outdoor Activities chapter).

Other seasonal activities on the lake in summer include windsurfing, water-skiing and jet-skiing. Good Sports (☎ 443 7966) on Dunmore St hires out a vast array of sports equipment.

Organised Tours

Lakeland Adventures by the waterfront has lake cruises from $15 for 30 minutes up to $50 for its three-hour Sanctuary Island cruise (including a 30-minute walk).

For something different, Aspiring Images (☎ 443 8358) and Photo Nature Tours (☎ 443 7951) offer nature/photographic tours that teach you how to snap all that wonderful scenery for around $50 per hour.

Places to Stay

Camping & Cabins The *Wanaka Motor Park* (☎ 443 7883), 212 Brownston St, is only 1km from the town centre and has lake views and treed areas. Sites cost $18 for two, cabins are $30 and tourist flats are $50 to $58. The *Pleasant Lodge Holiday Park* (☎ 443 7360), 3km from Wanaka on Glendhu Bay Rd, has cabins and tourist flats at similar prices and a swimming pool.

Right on Lake Wanaka, 13km from town on Mt Aspiring Rd, the ageing *Glendhu Bay Camp* (☎ 443 7243) has tent/powered sites for $7/8 per person and cabins for $13 per person. The *Outlet Motor Camp* (☎ 443 7478), 6km north of Wanaka, is at the source of the Clutha River for fishing and has wonderful lake and mountain views. Tent sites cost $8 per person and power is $3 per site.

DOC camping grounds are at Boundary Creek Reserve, adjacent to SH6, at the head of Lake Wanaka; at Kidds Bush Reserve, Mead Rd, west of the Neck between lakes Hawea and Wanaka; and at Albert Town reserve, adjacent to SH6, 5km north-east of Wanaka.

Hostels The *Wanaka YHA Hostel* (☎ 443 7405), 181 Upton St, has a relaxed, friendly atmosphere and is open all day. It charges $15 per person in dorms or doubles are $34. Mountain bikes are available and there are many other activities.

At 56 Brownston St *Matterhorn South* (☎ 443 1119) is a small homey hostel with a cosy log fire. Dorm and shared rooms are $15 per person, doubles and twins are $35. The owners are friendly and informative and also have new units (with en suite) sleeping up to four at $65 a double ($10 per extra person).

The friendly *Wanaka Bakpaka* (☎ 443 7837) at 117 Lakeside Rd is opposite the jetty on the northern side of Roy's Bay, with great views of the lake and mountains. It is well set up for travel and tramping information. Mountain bikes, kayaks and canoes can be hired. Dorms or shared rooms cost $15 per person, twins are $34 and doubles are $36.

B&Bs & Guesthouses *Altamont Lodge* (☎ 443 8864) on Mt Aspiring Rd is on the edge of town towards Treble Cone, making it popular with skiers in winter. It's also open in summer and is good value with very comfortable singles/doubles for $30/48. Facilities include a modern kitchen, tennis court, TV-video room, playground, BBQ and spa pool.

More luxurious ski lodges, also open in summer, are the stylish *Te Wanaka Lodge* (☎ 433 9224) at 23 Brownston St charging $90 to $120 including breakfast, and *Aspiring Lodge* (☎ 443 7816) on Dunmore St charging $75 to $120 a double.

A dozen or so B&B-style places (singles/doubles starting from $45/70) are in and around Wanaka; contact the visitor information centre.

Motels & Hotels The no frills *Midtown Motels* (☎ 443 8333), 51 Brownston St, is the cheapest in town, with units for $55. The modern *Brook Vale Manor* (☎ 443 8333), 31 Brownston St, has rooms from $78 for two.

The cheaper *Archway Motel* (☎ 433 7968), 64 Hedditch St, has doubles from $68. The more central but similarly priced *Wunderview Motel* (☎ 433 7480) and *Pembroke Inn* (☎ 433 7296) are both on Brownston St.

The excellent *Bayview Motel* (☎ 433 7766) is 3km from town on Glendhu Bay Rd. All rooms have great views and cost $80 to $97 for two and the complex is surrounded by beautiful, spacious gardens.

Clifford's Resort Hotel (☎ 433 7826) on Ardmore St has doubles from $79 to $135, depending on the season, while the *Wanaka Motor Inn* (☎ 443 8216) on Mt Aspiring Rd is a swish establishment with doubles from $108. The flash *Edgewater Resort Hotel* (☎ 433 8311) on Sargood Drive charges $145 to $225 and has an excellent range of activities and facilities.

Places to Eat

Penguin Tea Rooms on Ardmore St has pies, fish and chips and other fast food to eat in or take away; it's open in the evenings. The *Snack Shack* on Ardmore St by the Mall has pizzas and the usual takeaway food. Next door is the highly recommended *Kai Whaka Pai*, a pleasant cafe with good cheap food such as doner kebabs.

Paddy's on Dunmore St is a popular family restaurant with low prices. No-nonsense fare such as lamb, steak and vegetarian meals cost $10 to $15.

Barrow's Bistro in the tavern of the same name on Ardmore St is a popular ski hangout and serves good pub fare at reasonable

OTAGO

prices. *Cliffords Resort Hotel* has all-you-can-eat buffets for $20.

Wanaka is surprisingly well equipped with restaurants, like the *Te Kano Cafe* on Brownston St, a little cottage with imaginative, filling and delicious vegetarian food and pizzas. *Amigos* on Ardmore St is a pleasant place to dine inside or outside and has reasonably priced Mexican food and a more varied dinner menu.

The *Tuatara Pizza Co* on Ardmore St is an interesting little place with friendly owners and pizzas from $15 to $25. Enjoy a game of pool while you wait. The prize-winning *Relishes* on Ardmore St is the pick of the cafes with main courses for around $15 and cheaper lunches. It is great for a piece of country-style cake, muffins and a frothy cappuccino.

In the Mall, the upmarket *Ripples* offers alfresco dining on the verandah, with good views of the lake and mountains. It's open for lunch and dinner (closed Sunday) and its menu features seafood. *Capriccio's* has pasta mains for around $14 to $20 but this award-winning Italian restaurant also has lamb, venison and salmon dishes for around $23.

Around the corner on Dungarvon St, the much recommended *White House* is a chic dining establishment with a bar and interesting menu.

Getting There & Away
Air Aspiring Air (☎ 0800 100943) has up to three flights daily to Queenstown, connecting with other airlines to other centres. Full fare is $95, dropping to $67 if booked more than seven days in advance.

Bus The InterCity bus depot at the Paper Place (☎ 443 7885), 84 Ardmore St opposite Clifford's, has daily buses from Queenstown, stopping at Wanaka on the way to Franz Josef via Haast Pass. Buses from Queenstown to Christchurch via Mt Cook stop in Wanaka and a daily bus to Cromwell connects with the Queenstown to Dunedin route.

Mt Cook Landline buses operate from the Wanaka Travel Centre (☎ 443 7414) on Ardmore St. Buses run daily to Tarras for connections to Queenstown and Christchurch.

Wanaka is well serviced by door-to-door shuttles, most of which can be booked at the Wanaka Travel Centre. Southern Link goes to Queenstown ($15) and Christchurch ($35), while Kiwi Discovery (☎ 0800 505 504) does the same run, Wanaka Connection (☎ 0800 879 926) goes just to Queenstown and Catch-a-Bus (☎ 453 1480) goes to Dunedin.

Car & Motorcycle Although the Cardrona Road to Queenstown looks much shorter on the map than the route via Cromwell, it's a winding, climbing, unsealed mountain road past Cardrona. Travel is slower and rental cars, campervans and caravans are banned from this road.

Hitching The Haast Pass Road branches off the Cromwell road 2km from Wanaka, just beyond the Maze. Traffic is light and hitching is difficult to the Haast Pass and glacier country. Most traffic heads to Cromwell (for Queenstown), though you could still be in for a wait. Hitchhikers have written on stones by the roadside the sorry stories of their long waits.

Getting Around
Mt Aspiring Express (☎ 443 8802) offers regular transport to the national park for $25/40 one way/return. Numerous places around town rent out mountain bikes, such as the YHA hostel (for nonguests also) at $15 per day or $10 for half a day, Good Sports and Lakeland Adventures; the latter two also rent out cars.

HAWEA
Lake Hawea, separated from Lake Wanaka by a narrow isthmus, is 35km long and 410m deep. The lake was raised 20m in 1958 to provide those important cusecs for power stations downriver. Trout and landlocked salmon can be caught in its waters. Harry Urquhart (☎ 443 1535) has recommended fishing trips on the lake.

The small town of Hawea has yet more spectacular lake and mountain views, but is mostly just a collection of holiday and retiree homes. At the lake shore, *Lake Hawea Motor Camp* (☎ 443 1767) has tent/powered sites for $16/18 and cabins for $27; prices are for two people. The *Lake Hawea Hotel* (☎ 443 1224) has a spartan hostel with beds in four-bed dorms for $20; its units are $85. Doubles at the *Glenruth Lakeview Motel* (☎ 443 1440) are $74. The pub does good food and will cook the fish you catch.

Central Otago

Most Central Otago towns owe their origin to 40 years of gold-mining last century. The goldfields area extends from Wanaka down to Queenstown and Glenorchy, east through Alexandra to the coast at Palmerston, and south-east from Alexandra to Milton. Interpretative pamphlets such as *Goldfields: Heritage Trail* show towns and gold-mining areas. Stone buildings, gold-mining equipment and machinery, and miles of tailings (waste left over from mining) are found throughout the area, while Queenstown, an important town during Otago's golden days, maintains its glory in the modern gold rush – tourism.

Most of Central Otago lies on a rugged and dry plateau, sheltered by the Southern Alps. In summer, days are warm to hot and rainfall is very low. In winter, temperatures can drop to well below freezing.

CROMWELL

This modern little town of 2600 people is on the main route between Wanaka and Queenstown. Cromwell is the heart of stone fruit country – as testified by the giant Carmen Miranda's hat display in front of the town. Roadside stalls sell apricots, peaches, nectarines, plums, cherries, apples and pears. January and February are the best months for picking work.

The Visitor Information Centre (☎ 445 0212; fax 445 1319) in the Cromwell Mall handles bookings and has displays on the hydroelectric projects in the Clutha Valley. It's open from 10 am to 4 pm daily. The information centre also houses the town **museum** with artefacts of local mining, including a section on the Chinese miners.

On Melmore Terrace, **Old Cromwell** is a row of historic buildings housing craft shops overlooking Dunstan Dam. They were painstakingly removed and restored from the original Cromwell, now flooded by the waters of the dam.

Gold-mining sites around Cromwell include Bannockburn, Bendigo and the Kawarau. Across a footbridge spanning the Kawarau Gorge, the **Goldfields Mining Centre**, 5km towards Queenstown, has tours of the tailings and old mine machinery for $14 – easily skipped at that price. **Bendigo**, 18km from Cromwell on the Bendigo Loop Rd, is a classic ghost town. A hunt around in the scrub will turn up the ruins of stone cottages, but stick to obvious tracks as there are many deep mine shafts.

The Kawarau Gorge between here and Queenstown is spectacular and you can watch **bungy jumping** at the interesting old Kawarau suspension bridge. Built in 1880 for access to the Wakatipu goldfields, it was used until 1963.

Places to Stay & Eat

The *Cromwell Holiday Park* (☎ 445 0164) on Alpha St, about 2km from the town centre, has tent and powered sites at $17 and cabins from $25 to $38 for two.

The *Chalets* (☎ 445 1399), 102 Barry Ave, owned by the local polytechnic, was once the quarters for the dam workers. Each chalet has its own lounge and kitchen and a number of well-equipped singles/doubles with washbasin for $20/30 (linen $5 extra). It's good value.

Hotels and motels include the *Golden Gate Lodge* (☎ 445 1777) on Barry Ave with restaurant, lounge, public bars and doubles from $80. The *Twin Rivers Motel* (☎ 445 0035) at 69 Inniscort St has rooms for $55/68.

The Cromwell Mall has coffee lounges and restaurants. The *Ploughmans* is licensed and has a takeaway section.

ARROWTOWN

Between Cromwell and Queenstown (not far past the bungy bridge) is the loop road turn-off to Arrowtown. The faithfully restored early gold-mining settlement has a population of 1400 and a beautiful avenue of deciduous trees. Lined with wooden buildings, the main street looks a lot like a movie set for a western, except for all the tourist shops.

The **Lake District Museum** has displays on gold-mining and local history, and also acts as the local information office (☎ 442 1824). It's open from 9 am to 5 pm ($4, children 50c). Get copies of *Historic Arrowtown* and *Arrowtown Walks* from the museum – the latter has information about getting to Macetown as well as historic notes about the area.

The best example of a gold-era **Chinese settlement** in NZ is near Bush Creek, at the top end of Buckingham St. A store and two huts have been restored as a reminder of the role played by Chinese 'diggers' during and after the gold rush. The Chinese were subjected to prejudice, especially during the 1880s economic depression. They often did not seek new claims but worked through the tailings looking for the fine gold undetected by earlier miners.

Macetown

Just north of Arrowtown is Macetown, a ghost town reached only by going down a long, unimproved and flood-prone road – the original miners' wagon track – which crosses the Arrow River 44 times! Trips are made from Queenstown on horseback or by 4WD vehicle, and allow time to do some gold panning. The main operator is Nomad Safaris (☎ 442 6699); the five hour trip costs $59 ($35 for children).

Places to Stay & Eat

At the *Arrowtown Camping Ground* (☎ 442 1876), with an entrance off Suffolk St, sites are $8 per person, and cabins $30 for two. Sites are $18 at the *Arrowtown Caravan Park* (☎ 442 1838) at 47 Devon St.

Arrowtown's motels have units from $75 to $85 for doubles: the *Golden View* (☎ 442 1833) at 48 Adamson Drive; the *Mace* (☎ 442 1825) at 13 Cardigan St; *Viking Lodge* (☎ 442 1765), 21 Inverness Crescent; and top of the range *Settlers Motel* (☎ 442 1734) at 20-22 Hereford St. The *New Orleans Hotel* (☎ 442 1745), 27 Buckingham St, has singles/doubles for $35/60, and a simple backpackers bunkroom for $12 per bed. The *Royal Oak Hotel* (☎ 442 1700), 42 Buckingham St, charges $25/45.

Along Buckingham St, the *Arrowtown Bakery* has excellent pies, rolls and German-style bread. The *Arrowtown Burger Bar* has great fish and chips. The *New Orleans* and *Royal Oak* hotels have bistros with the usual pub fare. The *Wind in the Willows Cafe & Bookshop* on Ramshaw Lane is a very pleasant spot for coffee and snacks.

In gold-era dwellings are *Granny's Kitchen* for tearoom fare, or the *Stables* and the *Stone Cottage* for fine dining.

About 400m from the Kawarau Bridge, the *Gibbston Valley Winery* has a cellar restaurant and outdoor courtyard set among the vines. The blackboard menu is changed daily and the food receives rave reviews. Dine here *after* your bungy jump.

Getting There & Away

From Queenstown, the red Double Decker bus makes a 2½-hour trip to Arrowtown at 10 am and 2 pm daily for $27 (children $10). Arrow Express (☎ 442 1535) has scheduled services that can be picked up outside the library in Buckingham St, at the top of the Mall in Queenstown. The 25-minute journey costs $5.

Circuit Shuttles (☎ 025 449 314) leaves from Camp St in Queenstown hourly from 9 am to 4 pm and does a loop via the Arthurs Point Rd to Arrowtown, then to the Kawarau bungy bridge and Gibbston Valley Wines on SH6 and back to Queenstown. A day pass costs $25.

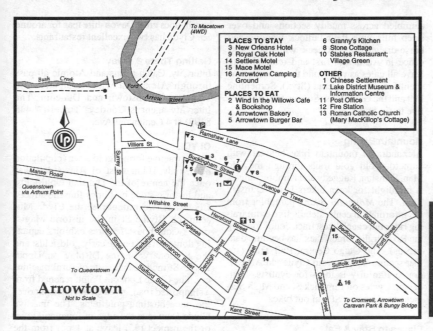

PLACES TO STAY
3 New Orleans Hotel
9 Royal Oak Hotel
14 Settlers Motel
15 Mace Motel
16 Arrowtown Camping Ground

PLACES TO EAT
2 Wind in the Willows Cafe & Bookshop
4 Arrowtown Bakery
5 Arrowtown Burger Bar

6 Granny's Kitchen
8 Stone Cottage
10 Stables Restaurant; Village Green

OTHER
1 Chinese Settlement
7 Lake District Museum & Information Centre
11 Post Office
12 Fire Station
13 Roman Catholic Church (Mary MacKillop's Cottage)

Arrowtown
Not to Scale

OTAGO

InterCity buses to Wanaka and Dunedin also can stop at Arrowtown for pre-booked passengers.

It can be easy to reach Arrowtown by nifty-fifty (motorbikes) from Queenstown, or even by bicycle. The back road via Arthurs Point is steep and hard going just outside Queenstown but flat for most of the way and scenic.

ALEXANDRA

East of Cromwell is Alexandra (population 4600), the hub of Central Otago. The lure of gold brought thousands of diggers to the Dunstan goldfields but the town owes its permanence to the post-rush dredging boom of the 1890s. The orchardists followed and Alexandra owes its current prosperity to them. This pretty town is an oasis of trees among barren, rocky hills.

The Central Otago Visitor Information office (☎ 448 9515; fax 448 9516), 22 Centennial Ave, provides maps and plenty of local information like its excellent *Walk – Central Otago*, a series of eight free pamphlets outlining interesting walks in the town and nearby region. The huge clock on the hill above town, Alexandra's answer to the Hollywood Hills sign, can be reached by a walking track or you can drive to a nearby viewpoint. The DOC office (☎ 448 8874) is at 45 Centennial Ave.

The **Alexandra Historical Museum** (☎ 448 7077), on the corner of Thompson and Walton Sts, houses a comprehensive collection of mining and pioneering relics; it is open from 11 am to 5 pm on weekdays and 1 to 4 pm on weekends. The free *Central Otago Vineyards* map has details on a dozen **vineyards**, the southernmost in the world.

Four-wheel driving enthusiasts can attempt the **Dunstan Trail**, a magnificent rugged mountain road from Alexandra to SH87 near Outram, an hour's drive from Dunedin. The trail leaves you in awe of the tenacity of the early gold prospectors who stumbled across muddy sections and over steep hills with their bullock wagons and horse-drawn drays. Check with the DOC office in Alexandra first and remember to leave all gates as you found them. With time spent for stops at Paerau (Styx), Serpentine Flat and the Great Moss Swamp the trip takes five to six hours.

Mountain Biking

Alexandra is mountain bike heaven with numerous old gold trails through the Old Man, Dunstan, Raggedy and Knobby ranges. A highlight for keen bikers is the Dunstan Trail. The *Mountain Biking* pamphlet from the information centre details five exhilarating rides but check latest track conditions (eg the Roxburgh Gorge Track has become dangerous). The Otago Central Rail Trail (see that section below) from Clyde via Alexandra to Ranfurly is ideal for cyclists. Henderson Cycles on Limerick St and MCS Services on Shannon St rent out bikes.

Places to Stay & Eat

Alexandra has plenty of accommodation or you can stay in nearby Clyde. The *Alexandra Holiday Camp* (☎ 448 8297) on Manuherikia Rd has sites for $16 for two and basic cabins from $20 to $35 for two. The *Pine Lodge Holiday Camp* (☎ 448 8861) on Ngapara St has sites for $16.50, basic cabins from $27 to $31 (all for two).

The excellent YHA associate *Two Bob Backpackers* (☎ 448 8152), 4 Dunorling St, overlooks the Clutha River and is a great source of information on walks, mountain biking, kayaking and other activities. Dorm beds cost $15, there is one double for $36 and a family room.

Of the town's seven motels, the *Kiwi Motel* (☎ 448 8258), 115 Centennial Ave, is one of the cheapest with units from $63.

Centennial Ave has the *Avenue* and the *Bakery* bakeries, the *Kiwi Milk Bar* is in the Centrepoint Mall and a number of takeaways are on Tarbert St. Pub food is served at the *Bendigo Hotel* on Tarbert St. *Fruitlands Cafe*, 10 minutes out of town towards Rox-

burgh, does great Devonshire teas for around $5. Clyde has two excellent restaurants.

Getting There & Away

InterCity, Catch-a-Bus and Atomic all pass through Alexandra with connections to Wanaka, Queenstown and Dunedin. The InterCity agent is Gourleys Travel (☎ 448 8198) at 4 Centennial Ave.

CLYDE

This attractive former gold town (population 850), only 10km west of Alexandra, was once the centre of the Dunstan Goldfields, and historic stone buildings line the streets. Clyde has two **museums**: the Clyde Museum on Blythe St in the historic Magistrate's Courthouse features exhibits depicting domestic life on the early goldfields; and the Stationary Engine Display on Upper Fraser St includes all sorts of rural machinery. The Clyde Lookout Point, reached from a signposted road, gives great views out over the once bustling goldfields. The massive Clyde Dam is at the edge of town and tours of the project ($5) leave at 1 pm from the Clyde information centre (☎ 449 2056); bookings are essential.

Places to Stay & Eat

There's not much to Clyde but good accommodation caters for the regular tourist traffic. The *Clyde Holiday Park* (☎ 449 2713) has tent/powered sites for $13/15, and on-site vans and cabins for $30. *Dunstan House* *B&B* on the main road in a beautiful old stone building is a fine place to stay and charges $39/60 for singles/doubles. A couple of doors along, the equally historic *Dunstan Hotel* (one of the few left in a town that once boasted 70 pubs) has rooms from $35/50 and meals. Clyde also has motels.

The *Post Office Cafe & Bar* near the information centre is a fine dining establishment as is the delightful, award-winning *Oliver's Restaurant*, 34 Sunderland St.

OTAGO CENTRAL RAIL TRAIL

Combined with the scenic Taieri Gorge rail trip from Dunedin to Middlemarch (see under Dunedin for details), this track makes an excellent traffic-free route for cyclists. The former railway line from Middlemarch to Alexandra and Clyde has been taken over by DOC, the tracks ripped up and resurfaced, and the trail uses the old rail bridges, viaducts and tunnels. The Middlemarch to Ranfurly (62km) and Lauder to Clyde (45km) sections are open. Until Ranfurly to Lauder (50km) is complete, cyclists have to use SH85 or the Ida Valley Rd on this section.

The trail can also be used by horses or walked, but the rolling farmland and rocky hill scenery is not enough to maintain interest for walkers over the entire length.

ALEXANDRA TO PALMERSTON

To the north-east of Alexandra the Manuherikia Valley bears rich evidence of Otago's golden age. At Blackstone Hill the SH85 swings south-east to the Maniototo plain and via the Pig Root to the sea and Palmerston.

Today's peacefulness belies the bustling past of the small township of **Ophir**, 27km north of Alexandra and a short sidetrip from Omakau on the main highway. The Manuherikia River is still spanned by the 1870s Dan O'Connell bridge and there is a restored 1886 post and telegraph building. The town has the widest temperature range of any in NZ: from -20°C in winter to 35°C in summer. *Ophir Lodge Backpackers* (☎ 447 3339) on Macdonald St is handy if you're cycling the rail trail and they will pick up from Omakau. Cabin accommodation costs $12.50 (share), twins are $28 and doubles are $26. It is closed from June to August.

The road forks at Becks, where there is a great old pub. The left fork leads to **St Bathans**, once a thriving gold-mining town with a population of 2000 – today there are less than 20 inhabitants. This is a real getaway sort of place and has original buildings like the 'haunted' *Vulcan Hotel* (☎ 447 3629), a quaint living museum and the only survivor of the town's 14 hotels. Rooms cost $30/50 and meals are available. In winter curling teams compete on frozen ponds near the town. The **Blue Lake**, formed entirely by

sluicing activity, is a popular nearby picnic spot.

Back on SH85, eastbound past Blackstone Hill, **Naseby** was once the largest goldmining town on the Maniototo. There's a museum and the surrounding area is great walking country. From May to September the Maniototo Ice Rink (☎ 444 9270) is used for skating, curling and ice hockey. The *Ancient Briton Hotel & Motel* (☎ 444 9992) on Lever St has rooms for $22 per person or motel rooms for $68 for two. The *Larchview Camping Ground* (☎ 444 9904) has sites for $15, cabins for $28 and self-contained cottages from $35 to $45 for two.

Danseys Pass, 39km north of Naseby, is another goldfields town with a great 1860s pub where it's said the stonemason was paid a pint of beer for each stone laid! The *Danseys Pass Coach Inn* (☎ 444 9048), strategically located between the Maniototo and the Waitaki Valley, has been extensively refurbished. An en suite double costs $108.

Ranfurly

This small town (population 850) is the hub of the vast inland Maniototo plain which is the site of a number of stud farms. Nearby Naseby with its goldfields and the more luckless Hamiltons goldfields near Waipiata were the original reasons for European settlement. When the railway line was closed in 1990, it came as another nail in the town's coffin, but the conversion of the line into the walking-cycling Otago Central Rail Trail brings a promise of tourism. The **Display Centre** at the old train station has interesting exhibits and audiovisuals on the history of the line.

At the *Ranfurly Motor Camp* (☎ 444 9144) on Read St tent/powered sites are $10/15 and cabins are $20 for two. The *Ranfurly Lion Hotel* (☎ 444 9140) at 10 Charlemont St East on the main street has good pub rooms for $30/50 or $35/60 with en suite. It also runs the *Dew Drop Inn* backpackers opposite, a blockhouse building next to a rail line that charges $10 per person ($15 with linen). The pub's restaurant is the best in town.

Peter's Farm Hostel (☎ 444 9083) is in an old farmhouse, 3km from Waipiata and 12km from Ranfurly off the highway. Apart from the peace and quiet of the farm, the main attractions are the free horse treks and kayaking that Peter conducts, and the walking loop nearby. Dorm beds cost $14 per night, while doubles and twins are $32. You can arrange pick-up or drop-off with Catch-A-Bus and Southern Explorer which pass through Ranfurly between Dunedin and Wanaka.

Macraes Flat

Not all of the gold has disappeared, and the small town of Macraes Flat is the gateway to the huge Macraes Gold Mine. From Ranfurly it is 63km east along SH85 to Dunback and then 17km south to Macraes Flat. The open-cut mine is the largest in New Zealand, and tours on the first weekend of the month can be arranged through *Stanley's Hotel* (☎ 465 2400) in Macraes Flat. The hotel has singles/doubles for $25/40. Gold Trail Mini Tours (☎ 455 3139) also has tours from Dunedin.

ALEXANDRA TO DUNEDIN

South-east from Alexandra via SH8 to Dunedin there's more evidence of last century's gold-seekers and spectacular scenery. First there's **Fruitlands**, a restored 1866 pub where food and crafts are sold. One kilometre away, via Symes Rd, the restored **Mitchells Cottage** is a fine example of the Shetland Islands stonemasons' building skills.

The next town of any size is **Roxburgh**, in an area known for fruit growing. Sales begin in early December, continuing until early winter. This small town has a camp and a couple of motels. The *Villa Rose Backpackers* (☎ 485 9101), 79 Scotland St, is a tidy converted house with all facilities; a dorm or shared room is $14, or twins and doubles (if not taken up by itinerant fruit pickers) are $32.

Between Roxburgh and Milton, near Lawrence, is **Gabriels Gully**, the site of a frenzied stampede for gold by 10,000 miners

in July 1861, after Gabriel Read discovered gold in the Tuapeka River. Interesting walks near the town include Gabriels Gully to Jacobs Ladder. In Lawrence the *Oban Guest House – Backpackers* (☎ 485 9600), 1 Oban St, has beds for $15 in shared or dorm rooms and twins and doubles for $34. There is a takeaway and bistro in the *Coach & Horses Tavern* on Ross Place.

At Lawrence the road splits to the coast and SH1 to Dunedin via Milton or by Lake Mahinerangi and the Waipori goldfield (and Waipori Falls) with more relics of the gold rushes. Dunedin is 55km north of Milton or about half that distance from where the Waipori Falls road meets SH1.

THE CLUTHA DISTRICT

The mighty Clutha River, through the Clutha district's collection of small communities, is not NZ's longest (the Waikato is 16km longer) but it carries the most water. Clutha is Gaelic for Clyde, alluding to that river in Scotland; to the Maori it is Mata-au (surface current).

The Clutha drains a huge area including lakes Hawea, Wanaka and Wakitipu. In a number of places the river has been dammed to feed hydroelectric power stations. The Clyde Dam holds back the waters of Lake Dunstan, and generated great controversy at the drowning of such natural beauty.

The towns of Clinton, Lawrence, Milton, Waihola, Owaka, Tapanui and Balclutha are all part of the region. Owaka is covered in the Catlins section of the Southland chapter.

Balclutha

The largest town in South Otago, Balclutha (population 4200) is dominated by an impressive arched concrete bridge across the Clutha River. The Clutha Information Centre (☎ 418 0388; fax 418 1877), 63 Clyde St, is open from 10 am to 4 pm on weekdays and 1 to 4 pm on Sunday. The **museum** at 1 Renfrew St can also provide information. The scattered collection of 10,000 old farming and household implements indicates just how much things have changed over the years.

The *Naish Park Motor Camp* (☎ 418 0088), 56 Charlotte St, has sites for $16 and cabins for $22 to $30 for two. The flashest place in town is the *Rosebank Lodge* (☎ 418 1490) at 265 Clyde St; a double or twin costs $80. The information centre has a list of regional accommodation.

The *265 Restaurant* in the Rosebank Lodge has a menu featuring locally caught salmon and trout. The *Hotel South Otago* and a string of takeaways are along the main street.

Lake Wakatipu

Queenstown is the self-styled 'adventure capital of the world' but when the party ends the Wakatipu region, with its stunning lake and surrounding mountain scenery, materialises as the real attraction. The aptly name Remarkables and the Eyre Mountains form a breathtaking backdrop. Words hardly do The Remarkables justice – they're pure magic capped with snow, at sunrise or in the afterglow of dusk.

QUEENSTOWN

Queenstown, on the shores of Lake Wakatipu, is nestled in what is surely one of the most scenic spots in the world. Queenstown is *the* resort town of the South Island and every tour stops here. There is plenty of hustling for the tourist dollar and overdevelopment threatens the town's character, but it has a fabulous range of facilities, activities, restaurants and nightlife.

There is great skiing in winter and plenty of substitute adrenalin activities in summer. Most activities are centred around the lake and many rivers nearby, especially the Dart, Shotover and Kawarau. White-water rafting and sledging, jet-boating and boogey boarding are all great ways to get wet. Bungy jumping, tandem parachuting and parapenting are similarly exciting ways to fly. But Queenstown also is a superbly equipped resort for more urbane pursuits.

Those wishing to move at a much more leisurely pace can take a trip on the TSS *Earnslaw*, stroll through golden Arrowtown in autumn, play golf on beautiful Millbrook, or shop in Queenstown's many (expensive) boutiques.

History

When the first Pakeha arrived in the mid-1850s the region was deserted, although there is evidence of Maori settlement. Sheep farmers came first, but in 1862 two shearers, Thomas Arthur and Harry Redfern, discovered gold on the banks of the Shotover, precipitating a rush of prospectors to the area. A year later Queenstown was a mining town with streets and permanent buildings. Then the gold petered out and by 1900 the population had dropped from several thousand to a mere 190.

The lake was the principal means of transport and at the height of the mining boom there were four paddle steamers and 30 other craft plying the waters. The Queenstown-Glenorchy Road along the lake was only completed in 1962.

Orientation & Information

Queenstown is a compact town sloping up the steep hills from the lakeside. It is relatively small with a permanent population of only 7500, but visitor numbers swell the town considerably. The main streets are the pedestrian-only mall and Shotover St, with its activity booking offices offering 'information' but their main purpose is to remove money from your pocket.

The Queenstown Travel & Visitor Centre (☎ 442 4100; fax 442 8907), close to the lake in the Clocktower Centre on the corner of Shotover and Camp Sts, is open from 7 am to 7 pm in summer (until 6 pm in winter). This very busy office does provide information and is also the biggest booking agent in town.

DOC (☎ 442 7933) on Shotover St opposite the Trust Bank is the place for information on the many natural attractions of the area, and on long and short drives and walks. It is open daily, except Sunday, from 8 am to 7 pm (to 5 pm in winter).

OTAGO

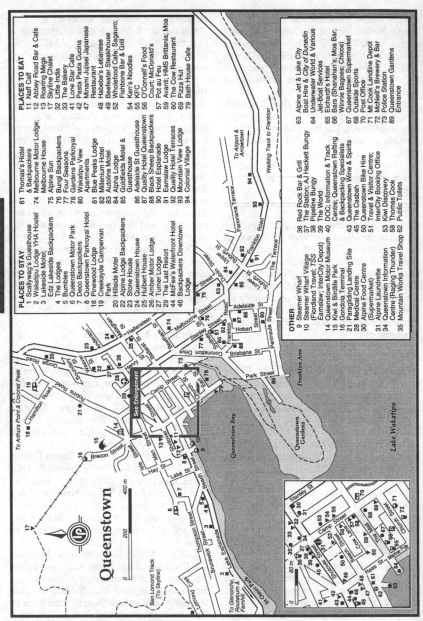

Queenstown

PLACES TO STAY

1 Scallywag's Guesthouse
2 Wakatipu Lodge YHA Hostel
3 Lakeside Motel;
   Edz Lakeside Backpackers
4 The Lodges
5 Bumbles
6 Queenstown Motor Park
7 Deco Backpackers
8 Queenstown Parkroyal Hotel
9 Pinewood Lodge
19 Creekside Campervan
   Park
20 Hillside Motel
23 Alpine Lodge Backpackers
24 Stone House
25 Queenstown House
26 Hulbert House
27 Amber Motor Lodge
29 Turner Lodge
44 The Last Resort
45 McFee's Waterfront Hotel
46 Backpackers Downtown
   Lodge

61 Thomas's Hotel
   & Backpackers
74 Melbourne Motor Lodge;
   Melbourne House
75 Alpine Sun
76 Bungi Backpackers
77 Four Seasons
78 Gardens Parkroyal
80 Wakatipu View
   Apartments
81 Blue Peaks Lodge
82 Millenium Hotel
83 Autoline Motel
84 Alpha Lodge
85 Goldfields Motel &
   Guesthouse
86 Adelaide St Guesthouse
87 Quality Hotel Queenstown
88 Black Sheep Backpackers
90 Hotel Esplanade
91 Earnslaw Lodge
92 Quality Hotel Terraces
93 Mountain View Lodge
94 Colonial Village

PLACES TO EAT

11 Naff Caff
12 Abbey Road Bar & Cafe
13 Roaring Megs
17 Skyline Chalet
32 Little India
33 The Bakery
41 Lone Star Cafe
42 Pasta Pasta Cucina
47 Minami Jujisei Japanese
   Restaurant
48 Habebe's Lebanese
49 Beefeater Steakhouse
52 Wholefood Cafe; Sagauro;
   Fishbone Bar & Grill
54 Ken's Noodles
55 KFC
56 O'Connell's Food
   Court; McDonald's
57 Pot au Feu
59 Avanti; HMS Britannia; Moa
60 The Cow Restaurant
69 Pizza Hut
79 Bath House Cafe

OTHER

9 Steamer Wharf Village
10 Steamer Wharf Village
   (Fiordland Travel; TSS
   Earnslaw; InterCity Depot)
14 Queenstown Motor Museum
15 Kiwi & Birdlife Park
16 Gondola Terminal
21 Paragliding Landing Site
28 Medical Centre
30 Alpine Food Centre
   (Supermarket)
31 Alpine Laundrette
34 Queenstown Information
   Centre (Raging Thunder)
35 Mountain Works Travel Shop

36 Red Rock Bar & Grill
37 The Station; AJ Hackett Bungy
38 Pipeline Bungy
39 The World
40 DOC; Information & Track
   Centre; Queenstown Rafting
   & Backpacking Specialists
43 Queenstown Wine & Spirits
45 The Casbah
51 Queenstown Bike Hire
   Travel & Visitor Centre;
   InterCity Booking Office
53 Kiwi Discovery
58 Thomas Cook
62 Public Toilets

63 Alpine Jet & Lake City
   Boat Hire & City of Dunedin
64 Underwater World & Various
   Jet-Boat Services
65 Eichardt's Hotel
66 Bars (Shanahan's; Moa Bar;
   Winnie Bagoes; Chicos)
67 Queenstown Supermarket
68 Outside Sports
70 Post Office
71 Mt Cook Landline Depot
72 McNeill's Brewery & Bar
73 Police Station
89 Queenstown Gardens
   Entrance

Otago
Top: Hot air ballooning, near Queenstown
Middle: Skiing at Treble Cone above Lake Wanaka
Bottom: Lake Wanaka

HOLGER LEUE

HOLGER LEUE

HOLGER LEUE

HOLGER LEUE

A	C
B	
D	

Otago
A: Sheep country, Otago Peninsula
B: Apples for sale, Clyde, central Otago

C: The Otago Peninsula is a good place to see yellow-eyed penguins
D: The Skyline Gondola shuttles to and from Bob's Peak, Queenstown

Next door, the Information & Track Centre (☎ 442 9708) handles most of the transport to the trail heads for the Routeburn, Greenstone-Caples, Kepler, Milford and Rees-Dart tracks. It is open in summer from 8 am to 8 pm (to 7 pm in winter). Kiwi Discovery (☎ 0800 505 504) on Camp St also has track transport, ski transport and hire in winter, and books other tours and transport.

Activity booking offices on Shotover St include The Station (☎ 442 5252), a video jungle that also houses AJ Hackett, while its competitor, Pipeline Bungy (☎ 442 5455), is next door. The misleadingly named Queenstown Information Centre is actually Raging Thunder rafting. Queenstown Rafting & Backpacking Specialists is at No 35. Backpacking Specialists (☎ 442 8178) is an agent for many cheap activities and shuttle buses.

Fiordland Travel (☎ 0800 656 501) in the Steamer Wharf Village on the waterfront takes bookings for lake trips and trips to Doubtful and Milford Sounds.

There is a 24-hour information service, Infophone (☎ 442 5024), listing a variety of activities and services. The post office on Camp St (with poste restante facilities) is open from 9 am to 5 pm on weekdays.

Queenstown has branches of all the major banks and plenty of moneychangers are open for longer hours. Thomas Cook is on the corner of the Mall and Camp St, and Queenstown has note changing machines, including one on the Mall.

Things to See

Start at the top by catching the **Skyline Gondola** to the summit of the hill overlooking the town for incredible views over the lake. The hefty return fee is $12 (children $4). If the view isn't enough then look at *Kiwi Magic*, a hi-tech film which screens on the hour from 10 am to 8 pm. It's a chance to get rid of more change from your pocket ($7, children $3). The more energetic can walk up the vehicle track to Skyline from Lomond Crescent, but the ride is worth experiencing. The gondola operates from 10 am to 10 pm (until 9 pm in winter).

For views in the other direction, drive up to the back of the ski field. A short track leads past Lake Alta to a viewpoint at the top of The Remarkables, looking down over the lake to a diminutive Queenstown.

The private **Queenstown Motor Museum**, just below the lower gondola terminal, has a collection of old cars, motorcycles and a MiG 21 on show. The museum is open from 9.30 am to 5.30 pm daily (shorter hours in winter). Admission is $7 (children $3).

Right next to the gondola terminal is the **Kiwi & Birdlife Park**. It has the New Zealand standard – a nocturnal kiwi house – and a small but growing program of raising endangered species. Kea and the rare black stilt are on display in this attractive, landscaped park in the pine forest. It is open from 9 am to 5 pm daily (later in summer) and admission is $9.50 (children $3.50).

On the pier at the end of the Mall, near the centre of Queenstown, is the interesting **Underwater World**, a submerged observation gallery where you can see eels and trout in the clear waters of the lake. The agile little scaup or 'diving' ducks also make periodic appearances outside the windows. Entry costs $7 (children $3.50), or you might see them by just peering into the water from the jetty.

There are also **garden tours** which include the Speight Gardens ($55), escorted tours, winery tours and Farm Scene for the kids. Queenstown even has a tourist-oriented Maori concert and hangi-style feast (a rarity in the South Island) for $45 (☎ 442 8878).

Bungy Jumping

The Queenstown activity which probably sparks the most interest is bungy jumping and there is no shortage of 'jumping' options. AJ Hackett (☎ 442 7100) is in the Station on the corner of Shotover and Camp Sts. Hackett, world famous for his jump off the Eiffel Tower in 1986, began operating at Queenstown in November 1988.

Most jumpers are attracted to the historic **Kawarau Suspension Bridge**, 23km from Queenstown on SH6. It's 43m from the bungy jump platform down to the river.

OTAGO

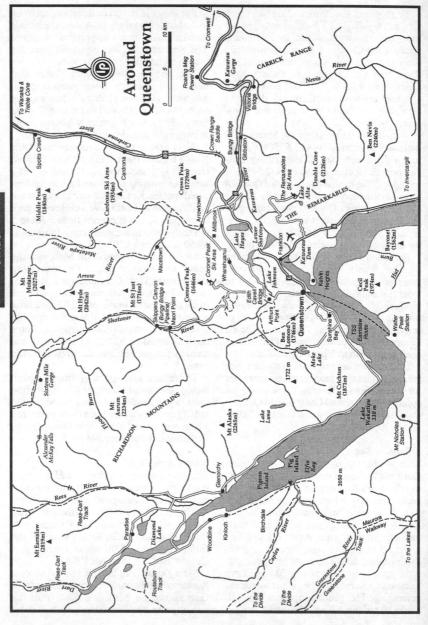

Observation platforms accommodate spectators. The Kawarau jump costs $129, including a video of your leap.

The **Skippers Canyon Bridge**, towering 71m over the narrow Shotover River gorge, is a more spectacular site and more difficult to reach, about an hour down a tortuous road from Queenstown. It costs $110 including a T-shirt.

Neither of these high enough? Then throw yourself from the **Pipeline**, the highest of the adrenalin 'highs' at 102m. Pipeline Bungy (☎ 442 5455) built the single-span suspension bridge across Skippers Canyon on the site of an 1864 gold sluicing water pipeline. The pipeline has been reinstated and now incorporates a walkway. From the Pipeline office on Shotover St, the cost is $130 including transport to Skippers. Food and drinks are available on-site and there's a museum. Videos, photographs and T-shirts cost extra.

Hackett and Pipeline offer combination packages which include jet-boating, helicopter flights, rafting, jumping and psychological counselling. Let's face it, after the jump the other options are chicken feed but, if you must do it all in one day, Hackett's Action Culture will charge $289. For those who want to do the highest and biggest, Pipeline offers its Shotover Assault incorporating a helicopter ride, bungy jump, jet-boating and rafting for $299.

Jet-Boating

Hurtling up and down the rivers around Queenstown in jet-boats is a popular activity. The Shotover and Kawarau are the preferred rivers, with the Dart River less travelled, lengthy and far more scenic (see the Glenorchy section later in this chapter).

Trips either depart straight from Queenstown or go by minibus to the river to board the jet. You can combine helicopter and jet-boat rides (from $89) or helicopter, jet-boat and raft rides ($199 on the Shotover). The busiest trip (but not necessarily the best value for money) is the Shotover Jet. Companies include:

Dart River Jet-boat Safaris (☎ 442 7318; see Glenorchy); $129 from Queenstown
Kawarau Jet (☎ 442 6142) and Alpine Jet (☎ 442 8832); depart from main pier for the Kawarau and lower Shotover; $55
Projet (☎ 442 3034) and Helijet (☎ 442 3034); courtesy coach to Kawarau bridge; $55 to $89
Shotover Jet (☎ 442 8570); 30 minutes in the canyon; $65
Skippers Canyon Jet (☎ 442 9434); top of the canyon and a land tour; $69
Twin Rivers Jet (☎ 442 3257); leaves from Frankton marina for Kawarau and Shotover; $55

White-Water Rafting

The rivers are equally good for rafting and again the Shotover and Kawarau rivers are the main locations. Rivers are graded, for rafting purposes, from I to VI or 'unraftable'. The Shotover canyon varies from III to V+, depending on the time of year. The Kawarau River is a IV. On the rougher stretches there's usually a minimum age of 12 or 13 years. Rafting companies supply all equipment – it's like *Apocalypse Now* as you are lined up and uniform rafting gear is doled out; groups are marshalled into minibuses as others disembark from jet-boats and helicopters buzz overhead.

Trips on the Shotover typically take 4½ hours or longer, but half of this time is getting there and back by minibus. Trips on the Kawarau take about an hour less. On the Shotover you can do rafting only ($99), a jet-boat and raft combination ($160 to $180) or, on both rivers, three-in-one jet-boat, raft and helicopter combination trips ($199).

Rafting companies include:

Extreme Green Adventure Co (☎ 442 7100); attached to the Hackett empire (involves bungy jumps)
Kiwi Discovery Tours (☎ 442 7340) on Camp St
Queenstown Rafting (☎ 442 9792), 35 Shotover St
Raging Thunder (☎ 442 7318) on the corner of Shotover and Camp Sts

White-Water Sledging & River Surfing

Perhaps the most exciting things you can do in the water near Queenstown are white-water sledging or river surfing in the Kawarau River (near the Bungy Bridge).

Frogz Have More Fun (☎ 442 7640) and Mad Dogs (☎ 442 9792) take sledge trips through the churning Chinese Dogleg rapid. The great thing about this trip is that you actually get to steer the highly manoeuvrable polystyrene sleds through the rapids ($95); it's the best adrenalin buzz in town.

You can surf the same 7km section of the Kawarau with Serious Fun (☎ 442 5262) using modified boogey boards. The first trip costs $95.

Parapenting & Parachuting

If you are up to it, try a tandem aerial parapente jump from Bob's Peak. Operators include Max Air (☎ 442 9792), Queenstown Tandems (☎ 442 7318), Renegade Tandems (☎ 442 7640) and Flying Cow (☎ 442 5455); all charge $110. Book or get hustled for business at the top of the gondola. The Freeflight Parapenting School (☎ 442 6311) has a one-day introductory course for $180 and a three-day PG1 course for $400. For those who prefer a delta wing there is Skytrek Hanggliding (☎ 442 6311) for $135. G-Force (☎ 442 9708) and Icarus are other operators that do Coronet Peak for $120.

For $245 the Ultimate Jump (☎ 021 325 961) lets you tandem freefall to 'terminal' velocity before your parachute is opened and you are nursed safely to ground. The sign on its loo declares: 'The Ultimate Dump!'

Paraflying on the lake is another way to see the sights from the air. Contact Paraflying (☎ 442 8507); an eight-minute flight behind its boat is $65.

Skiing

In winter The Remarkables and Coronet Peak ski fields operate from Queenstown. Those who prefer motorised mobility to skis can churn up the white stuff with Summit Snowmobiling (☎ 0800 766 662) for $110. Heli-skiing is also popular and a full day with three runs will cost around $525. See Skiing in the Outdoor Activities chapter for more details or tune into 92 MHz FM.

Mountain Biking

The Queenstown region has great mountain biking. If you are not that fit, avoid the strenuous uphill pedalling with an operator who takes you and your bike to a suitable high point. Gravity Action (☎ 442 8178) has a 'mega' trip into Skippers Canyon ($50).

Motorcycling

The region around Queenstown is perfect for off-road bikes, bigger touring bikes or four-wheelers on wild country tracks. Some Europeans find the freedom of these tracks a pleasant change from the restricted roads in their countries.

The rides combine thrills with a chance to see inaccessible historical areas amid the canyons and hills of Central Otago. Three hours of the best biking you are ever likely to experience costs around $160. Dennis at Guided Motorcycle Adventure Tours (☎ 442 7858) has information, prices and (especially) ideas.

Walking

Many of Queenstown's activities are decidedly expensive but the walks cost nothing. Stroll along the waterfront through town and keep going to the peaceful park on the peninsula. The lakeside walkway from Queenstown's Peninsula St takes just over an hour each way through beautiful parkland.

One of the shortest climbs around Queenstown is up Queenstown Hill (900m), overlooking the town. It's a comfortable two to three hours up and back with good views. For a more spectacular view, climb Ben Lomond (1746m) – a difficult walk requiring a good level of fitness as it takes six hours return. Follow the Skyline vehicle track for half an hour until you get to a small rock cairn marking a turn-off on your left. When you reach the saddle, head west to the top of Ben Lomond.

There are many other walks in the area, especially from Arthurs Point and Arrowtown, areas rich in history – consult the DOC office for information. For longer walks you can hire camping equipment at Mountain Works (☎ 442 7329) on Camp St; R&R Sports (☎ 442 7791) on the Mall, and Kiwi Discovery (☎ 442 7340) at 37 Camp St.

Queenstown Heli-Hike (☎ 442 6386) has an all-day backpackers special including one helicopter flight, guided walk, lunch and transfer for $225. A half-day walk in the mountains with two scenic flights is $280.

Aerial Sightseeing

No possibility is ignored in Queenstown – if you can't boat up it, down it or cross it, walk around it, or get a chairlift over it, then you can fly over it. Options range from short helicopter flights over The Remarkables with a landing (from $100) to flights to Milford Sound (from $165). More expensive flights to Milford include a brief landing, or a one or two-hour launch cruise on the sound. Mt Cook Airline, Fiordland Travel, Air Fiordland and Air Wakatipu all fly this route for $195 to $265.

Other Activities

Still not enough activities in Queenstown? Well there's fishing, water-skiing, windsurfing, yachting, catamarans, horses, rock climbing, water-bikes, mopeds or you can just collapse in a heap.

Organised Tours

Lake Cruises The stately steel-hulled TSS (Twin Screw Steamer) *Earnslaw* is the most famous of the lake's many cruise boats. Measuring 51m in length and 7.3m across the beam, it is licensed to carry 810 passengers, churns across the lake at 13 knots, burns a tonne of coal an hour and was once the major means of transport on the lake. The development of modern roads ended its career with NZ Railways. Since 1969 it has been used for lake cruises and now works harder than ever – check this schedule:

Walter Peak Sheep Station morning tour
    from October to April, leaves at 9 am ($45, children $10); three hours long; see sheep dogs and sheep shearing at the station
Walter Peak Sheep Station afternoon tour
    leaves at 2 pm year-round, except June (cost same as the morning tour)
Four-hour horseriding option at Walter Peak Sheep Station with Moonlight Stables
    take *Earnslaw* at 9 am or 2 pm and after farm tour take scenic one-hour horse ride before returning ($95, children $47.50)

Short lunch-time cruise
    leaves at 12.30 pm year-round, except June ($22, children $10, lunch $5 to $10)
Evening cruise
    leaves at 5.30 pm ($27, children $10); 1½ hours long; boat stops at Walter Peak with buffet dinner option for $65 (children $32.50), including cruise

The *City of Dunedin* sailed around the world in 1982, taking nine months to complete the 43,500km voyage. The *City* does two-hour sailings with every passenger (maximum 19) participating as part of the crew. The yacht sails from the water-taxi jetty opposite the Parkroyal Hotel ($45, children $20, food costs $10 extra). The best deal is the overnight cruise for $49, which includes a sail, dinner and overnight on the boat.

Other lake cruises include Sail South (☎ 442 6946) and the owner is none other than Graeme Hull! You act as part of the crew for $65 or two-hour sail-only trips are $49. Sail South departs from the pier at the end of The Mall.

Bus Tours There are all sorts of buses for a pleasant trip to nearby **Arrowtown** (see under Arrowtown).

Very popular **Skippers Canyon** trips take the winding 4WD road from Arthurs Point towards Coronet Peak and then above the Shotover River passing many sights from the gold-mining days. The scenery is spectacular, the road is hair-raising, and there's plenty of historical interest. Riches of Skippers Canyon (☎ 442 9434) and Outback Tours (☎ 442 7386) do 4WD trips for around $49 (children $22), including a stop to try panning for gold. For $69 you also see Winky's Museum and have a jet-boat ride.

Day trips via Te Anau to **Milford Sound** take 12 to 13 hours and cost around $140 (children about half-price), including a two-hour launch cruise on the sound. Bus-plane options are also available. The main operators are Fiordland Travel, Mt Cook, Great Sights and InterCity. Milford Sound is a long way from Queenstown and Te Anau is a better departure point. The same is true for trips to Doubtful Sound, which cost $186

OTAGO

OTAGO

(children $93) from Queenstown or $155 ($40) from Manapouri.

Some smaller buses catering primarily for backpackers also do day trips to Milford and include a cruise. Kiwi Discovery (☎ 442 7340) charges $90, the Milford Bus (☎ 0800 800 287) charges $95, Alpine Tours (☎ 442 7250) charges $109, including lunch, and the BBQ Bus (☎ 442 1045) charges $130, including a BBQ lunch.

From October to March, Fiordland Travel has two-day 'backpackers alternative' trips to Milford for $149. On the first day you go to Walter Peak by boat, then a bus takes you to Te Anau via the back road and on to Milford where you overnight on the *Milford Wanderer*. On the second day you return by bus and the TSS *Earnslaw* across Lake Wakatipu.

Places to Stay
Despite Queenstown's 15,000 beds, finding a room at peak periods can be difficult. Prices go sky high during the summer and ski season peaks. Prices given are for the high season.

Camping & Cabins The *Queenstown Motor Park* (☎ 442 7252) is less than 1km from the town centre at the end of Man St. A tent/powered site is $18/20, cabins cost from $30 and tourist flats from $56 (all for two). The camp is convenient and very well equipped – good kitchen, coin-operated laundry, TV room and even email facilities.

The *Creeksyde Campervan Park* (☎ 442 9447) on Robins Rd is a modern, neat place with a few tent sites and powered sites for $22, lodge rooms for $20 per person, tourist flats and motels for $65 to $75 a double.

The tired *Frankton Motor Camp* (☎ 442 2079), by the lake 6km from town, has tent/powered sites at $17/19 for two, cabins for $32 and tourist flats for $40 to $50. The *Kawarau Falls Lakeside Holiday Park* (☎ 442 3510) is past the airport at Frankton in a beautiful setting by the lake. Tent/powered sites cost $8.50/9.50 per person, cabins are from $24 to $37 for two and a hostel-style lodge is $15 per person.

A DOC camping ground at 12-Mile Creek Reserve, Glenorchy Rd, is just 5km from Queenstown.

Hostels The *Wakatipu Lodge YHA Hostel* (☎ 442 8413) is right by the lake at 80 Lake Esplanade. The cost is $18 per person in four to eight-bed dorms and $40 for twins and doubles. It has recently been renovated with good rooms, and even has email facilities. The evening cafe has tasty food – a huge lasagne with salad is $9. The only drawback is that it is a large hostel (capacity 140 people).

Further along Lake Esplanade, *Bumbles* (☎ 442 6298) on the corner of Brunswick and Beach Sts has dorm/twin bunkrooms for $16/18 per person, twins and doubles for $40 and good communal areas with views across the lake. It gets mixed reviews and a mixed clientele but all-in-all this is a good place. *Edz Lakeside Backpackers* (☎ 442 8976), 18 Lake Esplanade, is a dowdy lodge attached to the Lakeside Motel but it's well-kept, comfortable and reasonably priced. Dorm beds are $15 and singles/twins are $18/35.

Just a short walk to town, *Black Sheep* (☎ 442 7289), 13 Frankton Rd, is a former motel and has a spa pool, a deck and good outside areas. A favourite with bus groups, it is a new place and standards are quite high. Dorms come in a variety of sizes (up to 10-bed) and cost $18; doubles are $42 and $44.

In the town itself, *Backpackers Downtown Lodge* (☎ 442 6395), 48 Shotover St, is a rambling former hotel with dorm beds for $16 ($18 in the high season), and twins and doubles for $40 and $42. Many of the dorms and rooms have attached bathrooms, but some have showers only. The communal areas are cramped, but it's very central.

Also central, the *Last Resort* (☎ 442 4320) at the east end of Man St is a stylish place approached across a small bridge over a stream. All rooms are shared – there are three four-bed dorms and one six-bed dorm – and the cost is $18 per person, including linen and towels. It is friendly, small and very popular.

Alpine Lodge Backpackers (☎ 442 7220), 13 Gorge Rd, is cosy with a ski-lodge feel. It charges $16 per person in four to six-bed dorms; twins and doubles are $40, or a group can take over the complete upstairs area for $125.

A short walk from town, *Deco Backpackers* (☎ 442 7384), 52 Man St, is in a restored Art Deco building (hence its name), and has shared rooms for $16 per person and twins and doubles for $36. It gets mixed reviews.

Bungi Backpackers (☎ 442 8725) on the corner of Sydney and Melbourne Sts looks dilapidated from the outside but is quite presentable inside. You may or may not get a hospitable reception. Dorms are only $12 and singles/doubles are $25/35. Bikes can be hired for $20 per day.

Pinewood Lodge (☎ 442 8273) is a little further from the centre at 48 Hamilton Rd. Budget accommodation costs $16 in dorms or rooms are $25/40, and there's a spa. It has a variety of old lodges and the new chalet backpackers with four six-bed dorms has excellent facilities.

The small *Scallywags Guesthouse* (☎ 442 7083), 27A Lomond Crescent, is a fair hike uphill from town but has good standards of accommodation. Shared rooms are $20 and doubles and twins are $50.

Two hotels, *Thomas's* and *McFee's*, also offer good-value backpackers rooms and are very central (see under Hotels).

B&Bs & Guesthouses The upmarket and central *Queenstown House* (☎ 442 9043), 69 Hallenstein St on the corner of Malaghans St, has B&B singles/doubles from $145/165. There are good views over the town and lake from the balcony. B&B at the nearby *Melbourne House* (☎ 442 9043), 35 Melbourne St, charges $50/78 or $106/128 with en suite. It's friendly and well-organised with laundry and kitchen facilities and a guest lounge. Just off Gorge Rd at 2 Turner St the *Turner Lodge* (☎ 442 9432) charges $60/90.

Between Melbourne House and Queenstown House, the wonderful old *Hulbert House* (☎ 442 8767) at 68 Ballarat St offers upper-class B&B for $130/160 in a handful of gracious rooms with wonderful views. The *Stone House* (☎ 442 9812) at 47 Hallenstein St is a great B&B in a historic building with doubles at $195.

The *Adelaide St Guesthouse* (☎ 442 6207), 15 Adelaide St, is not far from town, has good views and costs from $60/85 ($110 with en suite). The *Goldfields Motel & Guesthouse* (☎ 442 7211) at 41 Frankton Rd has chalet units from $50/65.

Wakatipu View Apartments (☎ 442 7180) at 14 Frankton Rd has studio units at $82 up to $125 for two-bedroom apartments.

Queenstown Lodge (☎ 442 7107) is on Sainsbury Rd in Fernhill, 2km east of the centre, with a magnificent view of the lake. This huge place is like a cross between a ski lodge and student college housing with dozens of rooms on different levels down the hillside. It caters mostly to cheap tour groups. The lodge has budget meals, a licensed restaurant and bar, games and TV room. Rooms cost $40/58 or $50/74 with en suite. Quad shared rooms are available for $20 per person.

Motels Queenstown motels are expensive but prices fluctuate with the seasons. Some offer a variety of accommodation. The *Mountain View Lodge* (☎ 442 8246) on Frankton Rd is a good example – there are cabin-style units at $50/60 for singles/ doubles and motel-style rooms from $100.

Some of the more reasonably priced motels and their prices for double units include:

Alpha Lodge (☎ 442 6095), 42 Frankton Rd, $85
Alpine Sun (☎ 442 8482), 14 Hallenstein St, $75
Amber Motor Lodge (☎ 442 8480), on the corner of Shotover St and Gorge Rd, $85 to $95
Autoline (☎ 442 8734), on the corner of Frankton Rd and Dublin St, $88
Blue Peaks Lodge (☎ 442 9224), on the corner of Stanley and Sydney Sts, $95 and $115
Colonial Village (☎ 442 7629), 100 Frankton Rd, $75 to $100
Four Seasons (☎ 442 8953), 12 Stanley St, $100
Hillside (☎ 442 9280), 35 Gorge Rd, $80
Lakeside (☎ 442 8976), 18 Lake Esplanade, $100

OTAGO

OTAGO

Hotels *Thomas's Hotel & Backpackers* (☎ 442 7180) at 50 Beach St is popular for its backpackers rooms. Dorms cost $16.50 and $18 ($23 with linen) or doubles with TV and telephone are a cut above the usual backpackers and cost $49. All rooms are heated and have their own bathrooms. Regular, better-equipped hotel rooms cost from $69/82. It has a first-floor kitchen and lounge with views of Lake Wakatipu.

McFee's Waterfront Hotel (☎ 442 7400) at 48a Shotover St also has four-bed backpackers dorms for $18 and twin and doubles for $49. All have ensuite bathrooms and TV. Bigger and better-equipped hotel rooms cost $70 and $79. The kitchen/lounge area on the 3rd floor has great lake views.

At the *Hotel Esplanade* (☎ 442 8611), overlooking the lake at 32 Peninsula St, tired singles/doubles with bath cost $45/65. It has a bar and a good dining area for breakfast.

The *Sherwood Manor Hotel* (☎ 442 8032), Goldfield Heights on Frankton Rd, has a great setting next to the lake, good facilities and well-appointed doubles from $115 to $135.

Other top-range establishments are the *Earnslaw Lodge* (☎ 442 8728) at 53 Frankton Rd; *Novotel Queenstown* (☎ 0800 655 557) on Sainsbury Rd, Fernhill; the *Quality Hotel Queenstown* (☎ 442 8123) at 27 Frankton Rd; the *Lodges* (☎ 442 7552) at 8 Lake Esplanade; *Quality Hotel Terraces* (☎ 442 7950) at 48 Frankton Rd; and the *Queenstown Parkroyal* (☎ 442 7800) on Beach St has cheaper weekend rates.

Pick of the crop is the magnificent *Millbrook* (☎ 442 1563) on Malaghans Rd between Queenstown and Arrowtown. It has beautiful scenery, luxurious accommodation and restored historic buildings. There are myriad things to do nearby and the golf course is superlative, but count on $300 plus a double.

Places to Eat

Queenstown has a thriving restaurant scene, with the South Island's best dining outside Christchurch and Dunedin.

Restaurants The *Cow Restaurant* on Cow Lane is something of a Queenstown institution but very busy. The pasta and pizza are good if you get the time to digest them. *Pasta Pasta Cucina*, 6 Brecon St, near the Lone Star, receives rave reviews for its pasta and pizza for around $18 and the delicious dips with house bread. On the Mall *Avanti* is a straightforward Italian BYO with pizza, pasta for around $15 and Italian main courses for around $19 – good value and with a pleasant courtyard.

Another mall establishment is *HMS Britannia*, set up as an English galleon. The wide-ranging menu has a seafood emphasis. Next door is the *Moa* where the blackboard menu features fresh seafood, pasta dishes and good salads. At the *Pot au Feu* (☎ 442 8333) on Camp St the innovative NZ cuisine is consistently good. Mains cost $20 to $28 and reservations are essential.

Little India upstairs at 11 Shotover St has good curries and reasonable prices, and with a little imagination The Remarkables will take on the appearance of the Hindu Kush or Himalaya.

The *Lone Star Cafe* at 14 Brecon St is a great place to dine and enjoy a drink. The food is Tex-Mex and a plate of nachos is large enough for two people. Upstairs in the Trust Bank Arcade on Beach St, *Saguaro* is another reasonable Mexican restaurant.

More expensive restaurants include *Roaring Megs*, one of the town's better restaurants noted for its lamb cuisine. It is in an old miner's cottage at 57 Shotover St, with main courses in the $20 to $25 range.

Japanese food is well represented in Queenstown. *Minami Jujisei*, 45 Beach St, has mains from $20 and good sushi/sashimi platters for $22. The *Red Snapper* on the boardwalk in the Steamer Wharf Village is stylish and one of the best for Japanese fare. Sushi will set you back $15 to $20, while sashimi and reasonably priced mains are around $17. Upstairs in wharf village, the *Boardwalk* has good, if expensive, seafood.

Steak-lovers will be seen at the BYO *Beefeater*, 40 Shotover St, which has been around for over 20 years. Steaks for around $20 are served with a baked potato and there is a free salad bar.

The large resort hotels have numerous restaurants for fine dining. *Kiwa Kiwa* at the Millennium on Frankton Rd serves good seafood and other NZ produce. The Millbrook out towards Arrowtown has two excellent restaurants, including the less expensive *Italian Cafe* for good pizza and mains from $15.

Or ride the gondola to the *Skyline Chalet* where there's entertainment with dinner nightly and impressive views back down to the lights of Queenstown. Buffets for $37 are reasonably priced for the locale.

Cafes & Fast Food *Wholefood Cafe* down an arcade between Beach and Shotover Sts has natural foods, a sandwich bar and sells sweets.

Ken's Noodles on Camp St near Kiwi Discovery is a local favourite where the hungry go for all types of udon (noodles) and sushi at reasonable prices.

If you want the definitive cup of coffee, go to *Naff Caff* at 62 Shotover St – it has its own coffee roaster. Fresh croissants make the perfect accompaniment or there are reasonably priced breakfasts. *Abbey Road* at 66 Shotover St also does a good full breakfast for $8 and has reasonably priced meals into the evening.

The *Bath House Cafe* is a little more expensive for a coffee and light meal, but is in a delightful setting next to the lake, gardens and a children's playground.

For a good fish lunch go to the *Fishbone Bar & Grill* at 7 Beach St – the fish is fresh and they will cook fish that you have caught.

The *Bakery* at 11 Shotover St just beyond Camp St has baked food, sandwiches and pizzas and is open 24 hours. The tiny *Habebe's Lebanese* is near the waterfront in the arcade on the corner of Rees and Beach Sts (opposite McFee's Waterfront Hotel).

Pizza Hut and *KFC* are on Camp St, and *McDonald's* is in O'Connell's Shopping Centre on Beach St. *O'Connell's Food Hall* inside the shopping centre is open from 9 am

to 9 pm daily and has an excellent collection of stalls, including Thai and Japanese.

Self-Catering For self-catering, Queenstown still doesn't have a large supermarket. *Queenstown Supermarket* is on the Mall or the *Alpine Food Centre* on Shotover St has the best range and prices. The cheapest and largest supermarket is out at Frankton. Buy booze at *Queenstown Wine & Spirits* on Shotover St.

Entertainment
Queenstown is a small place but has a raging nightlife every night of the week.

The Mall is a good place to start a pub crawl. Near the waterfront is long-running *Eichardt's Hotel*, where, during the 1879 floods, hard-drinking miners are said to have paddled up to the bar in rowing boats. During the Franco-Prussian war (1870-71), Herr Eichardt, being a good Prussian nationalist, ran the Prussian flag up the flagpole after every Prussian victory. Meanwhile, down the road at Monsieur Francois St Omer's bakery, the tricolour flew every time the French won. The public bar is a popular local meeting and drinking place. The *Lava Lounge* upstairs is a quiet nightclub.

On the Mall a couple of doors from Eichardt's is *Shanahan's*, a Guinness bar which drags in the crowds on the weekends when live entertainment is featured. Next door, the *Moa Bar* is more upmarket and sedate but can still pack them in. Next along, *Winni Bagoes* is one of Queenstown's more happening places with a good crowd and the dance floor can get very lively. It also has good late-night pizzas to line the stomach. A few doors further along, *Chicos* can take a while to get going but builds up into the early hours when the dance floor starts jumping.

Around the corner on Church St is *McNeill's Brewery & Bar*. Apart from reasonably priced pub fare, it has good beer including a number of its own brews. Bands play on weekends but this place tends to peter out as the night wears on.

On Upper Camp St, *Red Rock Bar & Grill* is very popular in the ski season, but even in

OTAGO

summer ski bunnies linger on, reminiscing and watching snowboarding videos.

Bus-bound backpackers congregate at *Abbey Road* on Shotover St, where the emphasis is on cheap beer. When that closes, the *Casbah* further down Shotover St is as noisy, smelly, smoky, bustling, boozy and colourful as befits a real kasbah.

Nearby at the top end of Rees St, the *Lone Star* is a rowdy place, both upstairs and downstairs, as it brings out the nocturnal twitchings of the town's vast battalions of adrenalin junkies. Last but not least, the *World*, 27 Shotover St, is usually wall-to-wall with punters and undoubtedly Queenstown's most popular venue. You might strike one of their foam parties, when the bar is filled thigh deep with foam.

Teetotallers can just wander the streets and browse through souvenir shops and outrageously expensive tourist boutiques, many of which stay open until around 11 pm. The small Embassy Cinema (☎ 442 9994) on the Mall next to Winnie Bagoes sometimes has good movies for around $10.

Despite objections from most of the town's residents, Queenstown is likely to get a casino in the near future.

Getting There & Away

Air Air New Zealand/Mt Cook Airline (☎ 442 4600) on Camp St has daily direct flights to Auckland, Christchurch, Te Anau, Milford Sound, Wanaka and Mt Cook, with a number of connecting flights from Christchurch.

Ansett New Zealand (☎ 0800 800 146), 76 Shotover St, has daily direct flights to Christchurch, Rotorua and Auckland. Tranzair flies on its behalf to Te Anau and Milford.

Bus The InterCity booking office (☎ 442 8238) is in the visitor centre on the corner of Shotover and Camp Sts. InterCity buses have several daily routes to and from Queenstown. The route to Christchurch goes via Mt Cook. The other routes are to Te Anau and Milford Sound, Invercargill and Dunedin. InterCity also has a daily West Coast service to the glaciers via Wanaka and Haast

Pass. To continue up the coast from the glaciers and on to Nelson you have to overnight at Fox or Franz Josef.

'Alternative' bus tours such as the West Coast Express, Kiwi Experience, Magic Bus or the Flying Kiwi also go up the West Coast to Nelson. See the Getting Around chapter for details.

Mt Cook Landline (☎ 442 4640) on Church St has daily buses to Te Anau, Milford and Christchurch with connections to Wanaka and Mt Cook. The morning bus to Christchurch goes directly to Mt Cook and stops long enough to take a scenic flight with a glacier landing.

A good way of getting around Southland is in the 16-seater bus Southern Explorer; book in Queenstown at the Backpacking Specialists (☎ 442 8178). It has a fixed weekly itinerary and departs from Queenstown each Wednesday, returning on Tuesday. A full circuit is $170 or you can do selected sections. One-day sections are: Queenstown-Te Anau via the back road ($45, direct $25); Te Anau-Milford return ($45); Te Anau-Invercargill and Bluff ($40); Invercargill-Dunedin via the Catlins ($45); and Dunedin through the Central Otago goldfields to Queenstown ($45).

The Bottom Bus – book at the Information & Track Centre (☎ 442 9708) – offers a similar service, with a Queenstown-Te Anau-Milford leg provided by Kiwi Experience (see The Catlins section in the Southland chapter for details).

Myriad shuttle buses operate from out of Queenstown. Backpacking Specialists (☎ 442 8178) books most of them, as does the visitor centre. Atomic Shuttles goes to Christchurch ($35) and Dunedin ($25). Southern Link goes to Christchurch via Wanaka ($20). Catch-a-Bus goes to Dunedin and Topline Tours goes to Te Anau. Kiwi Discovery (☎ 442 7340) runs on weekdays between Queenstown and Christchurch for $40, dropping off at Christchurch airport and the city square, and also to Te Anau ($25) and Milford ($59). Southern Air (☎ 442 0099) has a daily shuttle to Invercargill ($38) connecting with its flights to Stewart Island.

Trampers Transport Backpacker Express (☎ 442 9939) runs to and from the Routeburn, Greenstone, Caples, and Rees-Dart tracks, all via Glenorchy. Main Divide (☎ 442 8889) also covers these runs. Kiwi Discovery (☎ 442 7340) services the Routeburn and Greenstone from the east and the Routeburn and Milford from west of The Divide via Te Anau. Backpacker Express departs from the Track Centre on Shotover St, and Kiwi Discovery from its office in Camp St. Approximate prices are:

Queenstown to Glenorchy	$10
Queenstown to the Routeburn	$20
Queenstown to the Greenstone-Caples	$25
Routeburn to Greenstone-Caples	$15
Queenstown to the Rees	$25
Dart to Glenorchy	$15
Greenstone-Caples to Glenorchy	$15
Queenstown to The Divide	$45

Services between Queenstown and Milford via Te Anau can be used for track transport or simply as a way to get to or from Milford. Buses generally run two or three times weekly but the schedule varies according to demand, with extra trips in summer and possibly none at all in winter.

Hitching Hitching into Queenstown is usually easy, but getting out may require real patience. Big wet backpacks are a real deterrent.

Getting Around
To/From the Airport The airport is at Frankton, 8km from town. Super Shuttle (☎ 442 9803) and Johnsons Shuttle (☎ 442 3639) pick up and drop off for $5 per person. Taxis cost around $15 – phone Alpine Taxis (☎ 442 6666) or Queenstown Taxis (☎ 442 7788).

Bicycle & Moped Queenstown Bike Hire, 23 Beach St opposite Whitcoulls book shop, has a big variety of bikes, including tandems, from $14 to $28 per day. Mopeds are $35 a day and scooters are $45. Outside Sports (☎ 442 8883) on the corner of The Mall and Camp St also has scooters for $45 a day and suspension mountain bikes for $40 to $70 a day.

GLENORCHY
At the head of Lake Wakatipu the picturesque, tiny hamlet of Glenorchy is 47km (a 40 minute drive) from Queenstown and offers a tranquil escape. Many pass through briefly in their rush to knock off the Routeburn Track, and thus bypass perhaps one of the greatest tramping opportunities – the Rees and Dart river valleys.

Those with a car can explore the superb valleys north of Glenorchy. If you've always been searching for **Paradise**, it lies some 20km north-west of Glenorchy at the start of the Rees-Dart Track. Paradise is just a paddock but the gravel road there runs through beautiful farmland surrounded by majestic mountains. About halfway the road passes through dripping forest where it is a five-minute walk to a small mossy waterfall. Alternatively, explore the Rees Valley or take the road to Routeburn, which goes via the Dart River Bridge, where the jet-boats congregate. Near the start of the Routeburn Track in Mt Aspiring National Park there is a day hut and a couple of short walks – the Double Barrel and the Lake Sylvan walks – if you are not tackling the Routeburn.

The town has a small museum, golf course and pleasant walks around the lake. DOC (☎ 442 9937) has an office in Glenorchy for the latest track conditions, hut tickets and general information. It is open from 8.30 am to 5 pm daily in summer and on weekdays only in winter. The Chocolate Fish (Glenorchy General Store) stocks general food supplies or the Glenorchy Holiday Park has a good selection of dehydrated food. Don't expect to find much in the way of camping gear for hire – get it in Queenstown or Te Anau.

Jet-Boating
The Dart River jet-boat trip offers a scenic trip into the heart of the Dart River wilderness, one of NZ's most beautiful places. Savour the grandeur of the slopes of Mt Earnslaw and the bush-clad mountain walls

OTAGO

on both sides of the river. The breathtaking scenery lasts for 2½ hours plus a stop to take a walk through the beech forest at Beansburn, downriver from the turnaround point. Of course, the driver will also spin the boat and pretend to almost crash into river obstacles.

Dart River Jet-boat Safaris (☎ 442 9992) depart from Queenstown at 8 and 11 am, and 2 pm in summer; check departure times in winter. If coming from Queenstown the five-hour trip costs $129 or it is $119 from Glenorchy. The office is Glenorchy is next to the general store.

Kayaking

A novel way to finish the Rees-Dart Track is to kayak the last day of the walk. Eric Billoud's Dart River Fun Yaks (☎ 442 7374) gets you to the start of the Rees (saving you normal transport costs), you then walk independently for three days through the Rees and Upper Dart valleys. On day four you are met at Sandy Bluff and travel in an inflatable canoe down the Dart to the Dart River bridge near Glenorchy, to meet the vehicle back to Queenstown. The cost is $89 from Queenstown, $79 from Glenorchy.

You can also take a jet-boat up with Dart River Jet-boat Safaris and canoe down via the Rockburn Chasm. No experience is necessary and the return cost from Queenstown is $149.

Other Activities

Dart Stables (☎ 442 9968) has guided **horse treks** in the spectacular high country for $40 per hour and High Country Horse Treks (☎ 442 9915) also has rides on the flats and around the lake. Glenorchy Air (☎ 442 2207) has a 20-minute local **flightseeing** trip around Mt Earnslaw and the Routeburn for $80. Mt Aspiring and the Olivine Ice Plateau are included in 45 minutes for $149. To Milford Sound the price is $195, including a cruise.

Places to Stay & Eat

The *Glenorchy Holiday Park* (☎ 442 9939) at 2 Oban St has camp sites for $7 per person, power sites for $8, hostel beds for $12 per person and cabins for $28 a double. It is well set up for trampers and runs Backpackers Express for transport to the tracks.

The *Glenorchy Hotel* (☎ 442 9902) has doubles for $55 and $75 with en suite plus a restaurant and bars. Out the back, its *Glenorchy Backpackers Retreat* consists of a 10-bed lodge and a four-bed hut for $14 per person, if you're desperate. Close by is the *Glen Roydon Lodge* (☎ 442 9968), with well-appointed doubles for $80 and $90.

Shirley's (☎ 442 8307) on Oban St has comfortable B&B singles/doubles in the house for $55/95 and a budget hut outside with four beds for $16 per person.

The delightful *Glenorchy Cafe* has $8 full breakfasts, focaccia bakes and a range of home-cooked meals. For a fuller meal try the Glenorchy Hotel or the Glen Roydon Lodge.

The area has a few more accommodation options. On the Glenorchy-Queenstown Rd, 28km from Queenstown, *Round-the-Bend Farmstay* (☎ 442 6196) has delightful gardens, farms walks, kayaking and fishing. A variety of rooms in the eclectically styled farmhouse cost around $60. The *Routeburn Farm Motel* (☎ 442 9901) is on the road to the Routeburn Track, 6km before the start of the walk and 21km from Glenorchy. The self-contained cottage is good value for $65 a double and $10 each extra person. *Greenstone Farmstay* is at Greenstone Wharf (see under Greenstone Track).

Getting There & Away

The scenic Glenorchy-Queenstown Rd is now sealed almost all the way, but its constant hills are a killer for cyclists. In summer there are almost daily trampers' buses such as Backpacker Express, based at the Glenorchy Holiday Park, and Kiwi Discovery (see Getting There & Away in the Queenstown section). When the weather is fine, Backpacker Express operates boats rather than buses to the Caples track. It can also arrange boat trips to Pigeon Island and Pig Island in the middle of Lake Wakatipu.

LAKE WAKATIPU REGION TRAMPS

The mountainous region at the northern head of Lake Wakatipu combines some of the greatest scenery in NZ with a number of the best tramping tracks – the famous Routeburn and lesser known Greenstone, Caples and Rees-Dart tracks are all here. Glenorchy is a convenient base, with excellent facilities, for all these tramps. See Getting There & Away in the Queenstown section.

Track Information

For accommodation details, transport to and from all trailheads and the location of DOC information offices and ranger stations, see the Queenstown and Glenorchy sections in this chapter and Te Anau in the Southland chapter.

DOC staff will advise on the best maps to use, outline track conditions and sell hut and Great Walks passes. For more detailed information on the tracks see Lonely Planet's *Tramping in New Zealand*.

The Routeburn Track

The great variety of country and scenery makes the three to four-day Routeburn Track one of the best rainforest/subalpine tracks in the country. Unfortunately, it has become the surrogate for those that miss out on the Milford Track and pressures on the track have necessitated the introduction of a booking system, as on the Milford. No one is allowed to commence the Routeburn until they have arranged their accommodation. In summer, huts (Routeburn Flats, Routeburn Falls, Mackenzie and Howden) are $28 and camp sites are $9 per person. The track is extremely popular in January and should be booked weeks in advance, but advance bookings are required throughout the main season. DOC in Te Anau is the main booking office, or counter bookings can be made in Queenstown and Glenorchy.

From May to October huts and camp sites are $4 but the Routeburn is often closed by snow in the winter and a stretch of the track between Harris Saddle and Lake Mackenzie is very exposed and dangerous in bad weather. This section has even been closed by snow in the middle of summer, so check with DOC in Glenorchy, Te Anau or Queenstown.

There is a guided four-day walk on the Routeburn (including return transport, accommodation and meals); inquire at the visitor information centres.

There are car parks at The Divide and the Glenorchy end of Routeburn but they are not attended so don't leave valuables in your car. The Glenorchy Holiday Park will store gear for free if you use its transport but otherwise charges $2.50 per day.

Walking the Track The track can be started from either end. Many people travelling from the Queenstown end attempt to reach The Divide in time to catch the bus to Milford, connecting with the launch trip across Milford Sound. Highlights of the track are the view from the Harris Saddle and from the top of nearby Conical Hill. You can see the waves breaking on the West Coast beach at Martins Bay. The view is almost as good as the view from Key Summit, which offers a panorama not only of the Hollyford Valley but also of the Eglinton and Greenstone River valleys.

Estimated walking times are:

Routeburn Shelter to Flats Hut	2½ hours
Flats Hut to Falls Hut	one hour
Falls Hut to Harris Saddle	1½ hours
Harris Saddle to Mackenzie Hut	3½ hours
Mackenzie Hut to Howden Hut	three hours
Howden Hut to The Divide	one hour

Routeburn, Greenstone & Caples Tracks

The Routeburn can be combined with the Caples or Greenstone tracks for a round trip. Access at the Caples and Greenstone end is at Greenstone Wharf. The road from Kinloch to Greenstone Wharf is unsealed and rough. The Caples and Greenstone tracks together form a loop track. The huts on these tracks are Mid-Greenstone, McKellar, Mid-Caples and Upper Caples (all $8 per person per night) and Sly Burn ($4).

OTAGO

Estimated walking times are:

Greenstone Wharf to Mid-Caples Hut	three hours
Mid-Caples Hut to Upper Caples Hut	2½ hours
Upper Caples Hut to McKellar Saddle	3½ hours
McKellar Saddle to Howden Hut	three hours

The McKellar Saddle to Howden Hut walk leads on to the Routeburn as mentioned earlier. Other options from McKellar Saddle include turning off for The Divide before reaching Howden Hut, or turning onto the Greenstone Track.

Greenstone Track

This track is often used as a means of returning to Queenstown from the Routeburn, or as a loop with the Caples Track. It is a 13½-hour walk down the broad, easy Greenstone Valley to Lake Wakatipu from Lake Howden. You can meet Lake Wakatipu at Greenstone Wharf (where the Caples Track also begins) from where the Glenorchy Holiday Park has a boat to Glenorchy and there are minibuses. *Greenstone Farmstay* (☎ 442 7068) at Greenstone Wharf has backpackers accommodation for $15 per person.

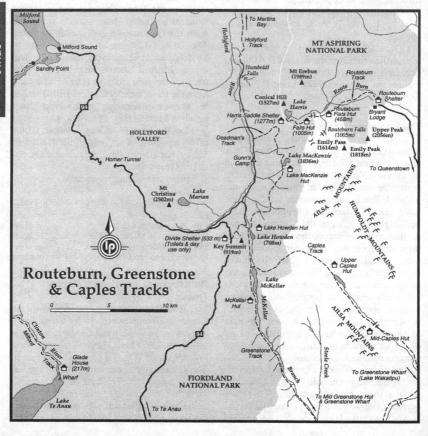

Routeburn, Greenstone & Caples Tracks

Estimated walking times are:

Greenstone Wharf to Sly Burn Hut	four hours
Sly Burn Hut to Mid-Greenstone Hut	one hour
Mid-Greenstone Hut to McKellar Hut	five hours
McKellar Hut to Howden Hut	two hours

Rees-Dart Track

This difficult four to five day circular route goes from the head of Lake Wakatipu by way of the Dart River, Rees Saddle and Rees River valley, with the possibility of a side trip to the Dart Glacier if you're suitably equipped. Access by vehicle is possible as far as Muddy Creek on the Rees side, from where it is two hours to 25-Mile Hut.

You can park at Muddy Creek, or transport is available to and from the tracks. Most people go up the Rees first and then back down the Dart. The three DOC huts (Shelter Rock, Dart and Daleys Flat) are serviced and cost $8 per person a night.

Estimated walking times are:

Muddy Creek to Shelter Rock Hut	six hours
Shelter Rock Hut to Dart Hut	five to seven hours
Dart Hut to Daleys Flat Hut	six to eight hours
Daleys Flat Hut to Paradise	six to eight hours

North Otago

The Waitaki River, south of Waimate, marks North Otago. Continuing south from the Waitaki is Oamaru, the largest town in North Otago. Follow either SH82 from Waimate or SH83 from Pukeuri Junction (just north of Oamaru), to reach Kurow and the Waitaki Valley. From here SH83 continues to Omarama via the hydroelectric lakes of Waitaki, Aviemore and Benmore.

WAITAKI VALLEY

The Waitaki Valley has interesting towns between the turn-offs on SH1 and Omarama: Glenavy, Duntroon, Kurow and Otematata. **Duntroon** was established in 1859 by Robert Campbell, owner of Otekaieke Station, as a village for his workers. Named after Duntroon Castle in Scotland, it has an authentic blacksmith shop, trout and salmon fishing nearby and jet-boating on the Waitaki. Accommodation is available at the motor camps (including Dansey Pass) and food at the Duntroon tavern.

There are Maori rock drawings at **Takiroa**, 50km west of Oamaru on SH83. The sandstone cliff drawings were done with red ochre and charcoal and may date back to the moa-hunting period (1000 to 1500 AD). Other rock art sites in the region are mostly on private land and can only be visited with permission from the owners. The Oamaru Visitor Information Centre can give directions.

Kurow, at the junction of the Waitaki and Hakataramea rivers, loosely translates as a 'hundred mists', as nearby Mt Bitterness is often covered with fog. From 1928, when the Waitaki power station was built, Kurow has been a service centre for Waitaki hydroelectric schemes like Benmore power station (constructed from 1956 to 1965) and Aviemore (1968) and there is fishing, boating and snow skiing nearby. Visits to the huge Benmore power station must be arranged through the Benmore Information Centre (☎ 438 9212). Check with the Kurow Community Centre (☎ 436 0812) about motels in the town and nearby farm stays.

Omarama

Omarama (population 400) is at the head of the Waitaki Valley, 119km north-west of Oamaru, at the junction of SH8 and SH83. Not far from Omarama are the Paritea or **Clay Cliffs**, formed by the active Osler fault line which continually exposes clay and gravel cliffs. These clay pinnacles are quite interesting but they are 15km from Omarama down a dirt road and entry is $5. Similar formations can be seen from SH8, a few kilometres south of town.

Omarama has a world-wide reputation for gliding due to the area's north-west thermals – the world championships were held here. Alpine Soaring (☎ 438 9600) has flights costing around $135 for 20 minutes.

The Omarama Information Centre (☎ 438 9610; fax 438 9694) is open daily from 10 am to 4 pm, but closed from May to August.

OTAGO

Places to Stay *Omarama Holiday Park* (☎ 438 9875) has tent/powered sites for $8.50/9 per person, basic cabins at $16/30 for singles/doubles, tourist flats for $45 and motels for $47. Glenburn, 7km away, also has a motor camp. The *Omarama Hotel* (☎ 438 9713) has rooms for $30/55 and the town has motels.

Eight kilometres north of Omarama on SH8, *Buscot Station* (☎ 438 9646) has a good backpackers on a merino sheep and Hereford cattle farm. Beds in shared rooms cost $12 and twins are $30; it is closed from mid-May to mid-August. Fifteen kilometres south of Omarama on SH8, *Killermont Station* (☎ 438 9864) has a similarly peaceful backpackers lodge and also closes in winter. Singles, twins and doubles are all $12 per person.

Fishing

The fishing season in Waitaki's rivers, hydro lakes and tributaries is usually from 1 October to 30 April but lasts all year in some rivers. Rainbow and brown trout are caught in the Waitaki, Hakataramea, Otematata and Maerewhenua rivers, Deep Stream and Waitaki, Aviemore and Benmore lakes; and quinnat salmon are taken from the Waitaki. Anglers can toss in a Tylo, a Pheasant tail nymph, a Royal Wulff or Craig's Nighttime and wait for that elusive bite. At night, a caddis imitation will be just the ticket. The locals may reveal some of their secrets (for a few cans of beer).

OAMARU

Oamaru is a pretty town of 13,500 people. First settled by Europeans in 1853 Oamaru was the seventh largest town in NZ by the 1870s and early 1880s. Refrigerated meat shipping made it prosperous, and the local sandstone was the favoured material for the many imposing buildings that still grace the town.

The town comes alive during the Heritage Celebrations in mid-November with penny farthing races and other events. Oamaru also has fine public gardens and colonies of little blue and the rare yellow-eyed penguins.

The Oamaru Information Centre (☎ 434 1656; fax 434 1657) on the corner of Thames and Itchen Sts has extremely helpful staff and is open from 9 am to 5 pm on weekdays and 10 am to 4 pm on weekends. There's an AA agent on the corner of Thames and Usk Sts.

Harbour-Tyne Historic Precinct

Oamaru boasts the best preserved collection of historic commercial buildings in NZ, particularly in the Harbour-Tyne Street Precinct with 22 classified buildings. The town's architecture is a mosaic of styles from Gothic revival to Neoclassical Italianate and Greek. The local limestone could be sawn, but hardened when exposed to the air so it was a convenient and enduring building material. The free *Historic Oamaru* pamphlet describes the historic precinct. Walking tours ($5) leave from the visitor centre.

A number of small businesses have set up in the precinct, including a bookbinder, book shop, antique shops, cafes and the Criterion hotel, open on Friday for an old-fashioned ale. The Woolstore has souvenirs and a car museum. A good market is held on Sunday and a steam train operates on holidays.

The **North Otago Museum** on Thames St is open from 1 to 4.30 pm on weekdays and has historic and general exhibits.

Public Gardens

Floraphiles will adore the 1876 public gardens with a red Japanese bridge across Oamaru Creek, an Oriental Garden, Fragrant Garden, Rhododendron Dell, Cactus House and Azalea Lawn. The main entrance gates are on Severn St where SH1 crosses the railway line. Weekends from October to March feature Clydesdale and Wagon Tours for $3 (children $1.50).

Penguin Watching

You can actually walk to the yellow-eyed penguin (Maori: hoiho) and little blue penguin (Maori: koroa) colonies from the town centre.

Little blue penguins are numerous and nest right in the town around the Oamaru

Oamaru

0   250   500 m

OTAGO

PLACES TO STAY
1 Thames Court Motel
2 Alpine Motel
11 Red Kettle YHA
   Seasonal Hostel
12 Oamaru Gardens
   Holiday Park
23 Criterion Hotel
25 Swaggers Backpackers

PLACES TO EAT
4 McDonald's
5 KFC
15 Brydone Hotel
16 Last Post Restaurant
17 Bridge Cafe
18 Zephyr Cafe
21 Star & Garter

OTHER
3 Automobile Association (AA)
6 InterCity Depot
7 Railway Station
8 Taxis
9 Post Office
10 Police Station
13 Library
14 North Otago Museum
19 Forrester Art Gallery
20 Visitor Information Centre
22 The Woolstore
24 Penguin Club
26 Lookout Point
27 Little Blue Penguin
   Reserve
28 Graves Walkway
29 Yellow-eyed Penguin Hide

Harbour. Once considered a pest – they would nest under buildings and on council reserves – they are now the mascot for Oamaru and the town's biggest tourist attraction. At the end of Waterfront Rd, a nesting site has been fenced to keep out predators, and nesting boxes and a small grandstand have been built. This is a country town version of the Phillip Island complex in Australia, the most famous site for viewing little blue (or fairy) penguins. The small visitor centre has souvenirs and entry costs $8 (children free). The penguins waddle ashore around dusk in the nesting season from Sep-

tember to February, but can also be seen at other times. Commentary is provided in the grandstand.

The loss of coastal forest for breeding has made **yellow-eyed penguins** among the world's rarest penguins. The Bushy Beach nesting site has good natural vegetation and a hide allows undisturbed observation of these beautiful birds. The yellow-eyeds are best seen a couple of hours before sunset, when they come ashore to feed their chicks, but they are shy and easily upset, so avoid loud noises and stick to the trail and hide. It is well worth taking a tour ($5), operated under a DOC concession, that allows closer viewing. Tours leave from the car park on Bushy Beach Rd in the early evening (the information centre has times).

Places to Stay & Eat

The *Oamaru Gardens Holiday Park* (☎ 434 7666) on Chelmer St, adjacent to the large public gardens, has tent or powered sites at $18 for two and various cabins for $28 to $50 for two. At the southern side of the Waitaki bridge, on SH1, the *Waitaki Mouth Motor Camp* (☎ 431 3880) has tent/powered sites at $12/16 for two or cabins at $12.50 per person. There's a DOC camping ground at Glencoe Reserve, adjacent to SH1, 2km west of Herbert, 22km south of Oamaru.

The old but well-kept *Red Kettle YHA Seasonal Hostel* (☎ 434 5008) on the corner of Reed and Cross Sts is open from 1 October to May/June. Dorm beds are $14 and twins are $32. *Swaggers* (☎ 434 1656), 25 Wansbeck St, is a small, homey backpackers with a good atmosphere. Dorms cost $15 or the twin room is $34.

The conveniently located *Alpine Motel* (☎ 434 5038), 285 Thames St, has units sleeping one to seven for $65 to $85 for two. *Thames Court Motel* (☎ 434 6963), 252 Thames St, charges $68 for two; *Avenue Motel* (☎ 437 0091), 473 Thames Highway, has doubles for $55 to $65; and *Tui Motels* (☎ 437 1443), 469 Thames Highway, has basic doubles for $50.

The information centre's *Waitaki District Accommodation Guide* lists many homestays and farmstays in and around Oamaru, which typically charge from $25 to $35 per person.

Oamaru's restaurants, tearooms and takeaways are concentrated along Thames St and the Thames Highway. The *Zephyr Cafe* is home to Oamaru's cafe society and has the best coffee in town. *Bridge Cafe* next door is a popular tearoom that attracts the lawn bowls set. Numerous fast food options include *McDonald's* and *KFC*. On Thames St, the town's first post office is revived as the fashionable *Last Post* with main courses at about $20. The *Star & Garter* on Itchen St

is an interesting restaurant with a heritage theme, a pianola and changing blackboard menu with mains around $20.

The *T Bar* in the Brydon Hotel has good-value meals (steaks $12.50 and pizzas around $14.50). The *Criterion* is the town's best watering hole but is only open on Friday. From there ask for directions to the *Penguin Club*, a hot little club run by local musos that gets some top name bands on Friday and other special nights.

Getting There & Around

InterCity and Newmans buses between Christchurch and Dunedin stop in Oamaru.

Shuttles which pass through are generally cheaper but not as reliable. Eaziway, Atomic (☎ 0800 322 888) and Catch-a-Bus (☎ 0800 508 000) charge about $15 to Dunedin. To Christchurch it costs $20 from the visitor centre and $35 for door-to-door. The only bus to Central Otago is the Canride bus to Twizel on Friday or there is a bus to Geraldine.

The Christchurch-Invercargill rail service stops at Oamaru, with a train in each direction daily except Saturday and Sunday. Trains leave for Invercargill at 11.32 am and for Christchurch at 2.10 pm.

There is a taxi service (☎ 434 1234) but the best way to see the old part of town is on foot.

OAMARU TO MOERAKI

The coast road south from Oamaru provides a peaceful break from SHI with fine coastal views, good beaches and resident dolphins. It joins the highway again about half way to Moeraki. Past Kakanui township, *Coastal Backpackers* (☎ 439 5411), 18km south of Oamaru at All Day Bay, is on a hill with great coastal views. Dorms are $12, doubles $30 and it provides a number of activities – canoes for paddling in the adjacent wetland bird sanctuary, surf boards for the nearby beach and bikes.

MOERAKI

At Moeraki, 30km south of Oamaru, there are extraordinary spherical boulders rather

Moeraki boulders

like giant marbles. There are others further south at Katiki and Shag Point. The Ngai Tahu people tell how the canoe *Arai Te Uru*, on a voyage in search of prized *te wai pounamu* (greenstone), was wrecked near Shag Point. The round boulders are baskets and gourds (*te kai hinaki* or food baskets), and the irregularly shaped boulders to the south are kumara (sweet potatoes). The reef which extends seaward from Shag Point is the wreck of the canoe.

Scientists have a less romantic explanation that the boulders were not washed up onto the beach, but eroded from the mudstone cliffs behind. They were not moulded by the surf but formed into their spherical shape in the mudstone. Geologists refer to the boulders as septarian concretions, formed when minerals crystallised equally in all directions from an organic nuclei. Subse-

quent erosion often exposes an internal network of veins, which look like a turtle's shell, hence the name 'turtle back'. Further down the beach two concretions have been found to contain the bones of a 7m plesiosaur and a smaller mosasaur.

The township of Moeraki is 3km further south, off SH1 on a sheltered bay. From the back of the town a gravel road leads to the lighthouse for great views of the coast and trails lead down the cliffs to a seal colony and a yellow-eyed penguin hide.

Places to Stay & Eat

The friendly *Moeraki Motor Camp* (☎ 439 4759), 37km south of Oamaru and less than an hour's walk from the boulders, has tent/powered sites for $15/16, other cabins for $30 to $35, and tourist flats from $45; all prices are for two. The German-speaking managers will find room for weary cyclists and have a cabin for $12/20 a single/double. The nearby *Motel Moeraki* (☎ 439 4862) has units at $60.

Lighthouse Backpackers (☎ 439 4834) out on the lighthouse road near the lighthouse provides very good standards of accommodation for $15 per person on the windswept hills overlooking the sea.

Meals are available from the tourist complex near the boulders.

MOERAKI TO DUNEDIN

The phallic-shaped symbol atop **Puketapu**, the high, pointed hill past Shag Point, is a monument to the member of parliament responsible for splitting large farms into smaller holdings. There's a track to the top signposted from the northern end of **Palmerston**. *Locomotion No 1* at the train station and *McGregor's Bakery* at 126 Ronaldsay St have food for the road.

From Palmerston the **Pig Root** to Central Otago leaves SH1; the name probably concerns the early road's condition. Gold miners preferred this route into the Maniototo as it was far more sheltered than the Old Dunstan Trail. The much improved road makes a great scenic trip into Central Otago.

The town of **Karitane**, 34km north of

OTAGO

Dunedin, overlooks part of the Waikouaiti estuary. The Plunket Society, whose nurses continue to care for the country's babies, was founded in 1907 by Sir Truby King in King's Cliff, the two-storey house on the cliff. King revolutionised child care and in his lifetime saw infant mortality in NZ drop by two-thirds.

Southland

Southland is famous for the Milford Sound, but while many visit Milford on day trips from Queenstown, they get no further into this frontier province of rugged fiords, mountains, fine coastal scenery and abundant flora and fauna.

There are three main routes into Southland: via Queenstown to Fiordland; from Queenstown down SH6 to Invercargill; or from Dunedin to Invercargill on SH1. All three, however, miss spectacular scenery, so some interesting local routes are described in this chapter.

Southland has a predominantly Scottish heritage and many of its inhabitants speak with a distinctive rolling of their 'r's. There is also a considerable Maori population, whose maraes are being re-established.

Fiordland

The spectacular Fiordland National Park and World Heritage area includes some of New Zealand's most famous walks, including the best-known of the lot, the Milford Track. The tracks, however, barely penetrate this raw, powerful region. The immensity of it all can only really be appreciated from the air or from a boat or kayak out on the sounds.

TE ANAU

Lake Te Anau, and its three arms that penetrate into the mountainous forested shore, was gouged out by a huge glacier. It is 417m at its deepest, 53km long and 10km across at its widest, making it NZ's second-largest lake after Taupo in the North Island. The lake takes its name from the caves discovered on its western shore, Te Ana-au (cave of rushing water).

The township of 1800 people is beautifully situated on the lake shore and is the main tourist centre of the region – a smaller, low-key version of Queenstown. It has all

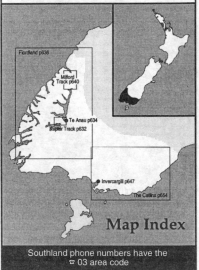

HIGHLIGHTS

- Cruising on lakes Te Anau and Manapouri to the Te Ana-au Caves and Doubtful Sound
- Walking in Fiordland National Park, especially on the famed Milford and Kepler tracks
- Sea kayaking on magnificent Milford Sound (or cruising and flightseeing for the less adventurous)
- Driving from Te Anau to Milford via Lake Te Anau, the Eglinton Valley, Homer Tunnel and Cleddau Canyon
- Taking the Southern Scenic Route from Manapouri to Invercargill
- Seeing the displays at the Southland Museum in Invercargill, especially the tuataras
- Exploring the fauna-rich Catlins and finding many surprises – ancient fossilised forests, native bushland, Hector's dolphins, penguins and rare birds

Map Index

Southland phone numbers have the ☎ 03 area code

manner of activities and trips to keep you busy, although for many visitors the town is just a jumping-off point for Milford.

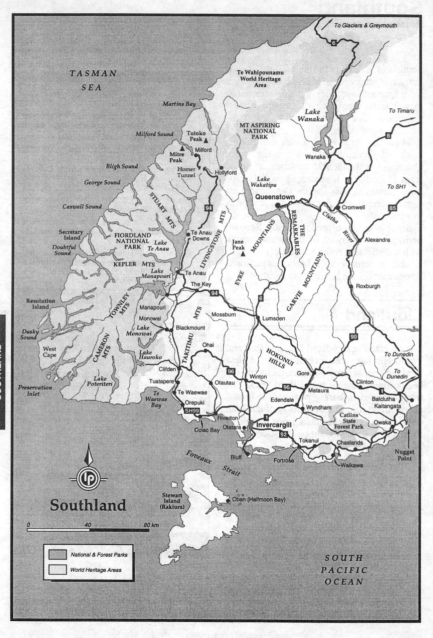

SOUTHLAND

Southland

National & Forest Parks

World Heritage Areas

0   40   80 km

Information

DOC's Fiordland National Park Visitor Centre (☎ 249 7921) is on Lake Front Drive near the turn-off to Manapouri. It has a museum, park exhibits and information on tramping or shorter walks. It's open from 8 am to 8 pm daily in summer and from 9 am to 4.30 pm in winter. Independent walkers for the Milford and Routeburn tracks should book here (☎ 249 8514; fax 249 8515).

The Te Anau Visitor Information Centre (☎ 249 9900; fax 249 7022) is in the Fiordland Travel office by the waterfront on the corner of Te Anau Terrace and Milford Rd. Fiordland Travel (☎ 0800 656 501) operates lake cruises and tours. Mt Cook Airline is also on Te Anau Terrace by the Te Anau Travelodge. The post office is in the centre of town on Milford Rd, and there are banks near the corner of Mokonui St and Milford Rd.

Te Anau is the jumping-off point for the Milford Track and many other walks – the Kepler, Dusky, Routeburn and Hollyford. If you need a guide for remote walks, try Southwest NZ Wilderness Guiding (☎ 249 7832) or Deepwater Cruises (☎ 249 7737). Bev's Tramping Gear (☎ 249 7389), 16 Homer St, and Te Anau Sportsworld (☎ 249 8195), 38/40 Town Centre, rent out camping equipment.

Te Anau Wildlife Centre

This DOC-run centre is just outside Te Anau on the road to Manapouri. The landscaped grounds and mostly natural enclosures house numerous birds including the rare takahe, one of NZ's flightless birds considered extinct until a colony was discovered in 1948 (see the colour Fauna & Flora chapter). This is a good opportunity to identify birds you may see on the tramps (admission is free, but donations are welcome).

A long way behind in the wildlife stakes is the **Underground Trout Aquarium** on Lake Front Drive ($1).

Te Ana-au Caves

These impressive caves, on the western side of the lake, were mentioned in Maori legends but only rediscovered in 1948. On the shores of the lake and accessible only by boat, the 200m of active cave system is magical with waterfalls, whirlpools and a glow-worm grotto in the inner reaches. The heart of the caves is reached by a system of walkways and two short punt journeys. The 2½-hour trip costs $35 (children $10); departures are at 2 and 8.15 pm daily. Book at Fiordland Travel.

Kepler Track

This Great Walk starts just outside Te Anau and goes to the Kepler Mountains at the southern end of Lake Te Anau. Like any Fiordland track, the walk depends on the weather; when it's wet, it's very, very wet. The track is top quality, well-graded and gravelled, and the three large huts are well equipped, with heating and gas stoves. Hut fees are $15 per night and hut wardens are on hand from the end of October to late April. Camping ($6 per person per night) is available at Iris Burn and Brod Bay only (not the Mt Luxmore Hut).

The alpine sections of the track may be closed in winter due to weather conditions (the cost in winter is $4 per night); these sections also require a good level of fitness. Other sections are much easier.

The walk can be done over four days and features a variety of vegetation and terrain including lakeside and riverside sections (good trout fishing), then climbing up out of the beech forest to the treeline and panoramic views. The alpine stretch between Iris Burn Hut and Mt Luxmore Hut goes along a high ridge line, well above the bush with fantastic views when it's clear. Other sections cross U-shaped glacier-carved valleys. It's recommended that the track be done in the Mt Luxmore-Iris Burn-Moturau direction. Estimated walking times are as follows:

Fiordland National Park Visitor	
Centre to control gates	45 minutes
Control gates to Brod Bay	1½ hours
Brod Bay to Mt Luxmore Hut	3½ to 4½ hours
Mt Luxmore to Iris Burn Hut	five to six hours
Iris Burn Hut to Moturau Hut	five to six hours
Moturau Hut to Rainbow Reach	1½ hours
Rainbow Reach to control gates	2½ to 3½ hours

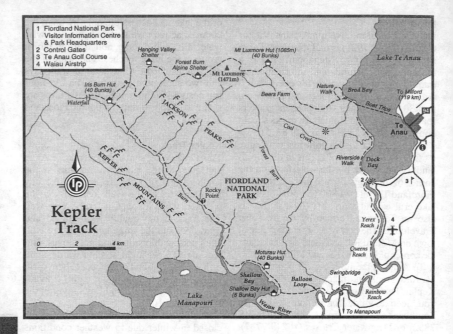

1 Fiordland National Park
  Visitor Information Centre
  & Park Headquarters
2 Control Gates
3 Te Anau Golf Course
4 Waiau Airstrip

Kepler
Track

0   2   4 km

FIORDLAND
NATIONAL
PARK

Plenty of other shorter walks in the Te Anau area are outlined in the DOC *Te Anau Walks* pamphlet. Deepwater Cruises (☎ 249 7737) has a range of guided walks, tailor-made for your requirements, including the remote George Sound Track.

Kayaking

Kayaking trips in this enthralling natural environment are offered by Fiordland Wilderness Experiences (☎ 249 7700) at 66 Quintin Drive, Te Anau, and Fiordland Kayaks (☎ 249 8275), also in Te Anau. Both offer guided trips and independent rentals. All trips are in the World Heritage area and could include lakes Te Anau and Manapouri, or Doubtful and Milford sounds. The view of the bush, lakes, waterfalls and fiords from this vantage point will overwhelm you.

Fiordland Wilderness Experiences has kayaking trips to the Milford Track trail ends and day paddles on Milford Sound ($80 including transport from Te Anau). The two-day, guided trips on serene Doubtful Sound ($220) receive rave reviews from travellers. This trip can be extended with another two days of independent paddling back across Lake Manapouri ($280). Three-day combined Milford and Doubtful sound trips cost $280 and a few trips to remote Dusky Sound are held each year. Independent rental costs around $40 per day.

Aerial Sightseeing

Waterwings Airways (☎ 249 7405) has float-plane flights from right off Te Anau Terrace in the town centre. There's a quick zip around the area for $39, a flight to Dusky and Doubtful sounds for $210, another over the Kepler Track for $72 and to Doubtful Sound for $139. Waterwings Airways also has a variety of Milford flights, including morning and afternoon Milford Sound Overheads ($170). Children's fares are 60% of adult fares. All flights are either by floatplane or normal plane.

SOUTHLAND

Air Fiordland (☎ 249 7505) has short scenic flights from Milford ($48), flights to Milford Sound from Te Anau ($75 one way) and to Doubtful Sound ($115), or a 1½-hour tour over both sounds and the Fiordland National Park ($250). A coach-cruise trip to Milford with a flight back is $225, but if you fly-cruise-coach it's only $151 because they need to fill planes on the way in to Milford. Again, children's fares are 60% of adult fares. The flight to Milford Sound goes over the Milford Track, with views of the amazing drop of the Sutherland Falls and Lake Quill.

Air Fiordland has cheaper scenic flights from Milford in summer: a 25-minute flight to Sutherland Falls is $72. Charters are also available – Milford or Hollyford to Martins Bay is $265 (for four people with packs).

Southern Lakes Helicopters (☎ 249 7167) also has flights around the area. On one combination trip, similar to but not as good as the Siberia Experience (see Makarora & the Siberia Valley section in the West Coast chapter), you can 'heli-trek-sail' for $100. Southern Lakes takes you up to Mt Luxmore, then you walk to Brod Bay (about three hours) and then sail back to Te Anau on the *Manuska*.

Organised Tours

Boat & Bus Tours Cruises on Lake Te Anau are popular. As well as Te Ana-au Caves trips, Fiordland Travel has trips to Milford and Doubtful sounds from Te Anau. See the Milford Sound and Manapouri sections for details.

From November to April, when the Milford Track is open, Fiordland Travel's MV *Tawera* runs from Te Anau Downs to Glade House ($40, children $10), the starting point for the Milford Track. It runs at 2 pm daily during the season, connecting with Mt Cook buses to Te Anau. Deepwater Cruises (☎ 249 7737), based at Te Anau Motor Park, also goes to Glade House at 9.30 am ($50, including coach to Te Anau Downs). It also offers Milford Track day trips for $85.

Yacht charters, scenic cruises and trampers transport are also provided on the lake by Sinbad Cruises (☎ 249 7106). Its gaff ketch

Manuska sails to Glade House for $50 or Brod Bay for $15 ($25 return); scenic lake or evening cruises are $45. Lakeland Boat Hire (☎ 249 8364) rents out rowing boats, outboard motors, pedal boats, catamarans, canoes or jet skis from a little caravan beside the lake. Boat transfer to Brod Bay costs $15, going on demand. Trips 'n' Tramps (☎ 249 7081) offers a variety of things to do around Te Anau, including half-day and all-day guided walks.

Places to Stay

Camping & Cabins The *Te Anau Motor Park* (☎ 249 7457), opposite the lake and just 1km from Te Anau on the road to Manapouri, has tent/powered sites for two for $18/21, standard cabins for $35, tourist cabins for $46 and motel units for $75. Beds in the large bunkhouse cost $14 and $16. It's a large, well-equipped camping ground with attractive surroundings; staff can organise track and boat transfers. Car, van and gear storage is available for trampers.

The central *Mountain View Holiday Park* (☎ 249 7462) on Te Anau Terrace is in a neat little slice of suburbia with well-tended power sites for $21 for two and a few tent sites for $20. Cabins are $38 ($57 with en suite), motel units are $72 to $77. About 1.5km from town on the Milford Rd is the *Fiordland Holiday Park* (☎ 249 7059). Camp sites are $14 for two (power is $1 extra), basic cabins are $20, better cabins are from $35 to $58 and on-site caravans are $28.

There are over a dozen basic DOC camping grounds in this region, all adjacent to SH94 (see the Te Anau to Milford section).

Hostels The friendly, large *Te Anau Backpackers* (☎ 249 7713) at 48 Lake Front Drive is set among the town's prime real estate with great lake views. Dorms are $14 and $16 per person and twins and doubles are $36 and $40. It has gear storage and free cooking utensils for trampers, and its staff help arrange transport to the tracks. Next door at 50 Lake Front Drive, the new *Lakefront Backpackers Lodge* (☎ 249 7974) is similar

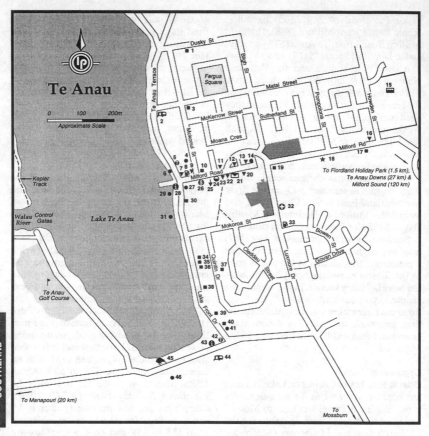

Te Anau

0   100   200m
Approximate Scale

Kepler Track

Walau River   Control Gates

Lake Te Anau

Te Anau Golf Course

To Manapouri (20 km)

Dusky St
Fergus Square
Bligh St
Matai Street
Te Anau Terrace
McKerrow Street
Sutherland St
Pompolona St
Howden St
Mokonui St
Moana Cres
Milford Rd
Milford Road
To Fiordland Holiday Park (1.5 km),
Te Anau Downs (27 km) &
Milford Sound (120 km)
Mokoroa St
Cleddau Street
Bowen St
Luxmore Dr
Govan Drive
Quintin Dr
Lake Front Dr

To Mossburn

SOUTHLAND

but smaller and charges $16.50 for dorms and $36 and $40 in twins and doubles.

The *Te Anau YHA Hostel* (☎ 249 7847), about 800m out of town on Milford Rd, has dorms for $16 per person, and twins and doubles for $38. It is also well set up for trampers and will store gear. There is a takeaway and small shop across the road.

B&Bs & Guesthouses There are a couple of well-kept B&B places. *Shakespeare House* (☎ 249 7349) at 10 Dusky St offers B&B accommodation with a substantial breakfast. Quiet and pleasant rooms cost $70

for a single and $96 to $112 for doubles with en suite, less in the off season.

The *Matai Lodge* (☎ 249 7360) on the corner of Matai and Mokonui Sts is central; B&B costs $55/76 for singles/doubles with share bathrooms. The *Cats Whiskers* (☎ 249 8112), 2 Lake Front Drive, is opposite the DOC centre and has B&B singles for $55 and ensuite doubles for $95.

Motels & Hotels At the *Lynwood Lodge* (☎ 249 8538) on the corner of Luxmore Drive and Milford Rd, doubles are $95 ($20 for each extra person). The *Edgewater XL*

Motel (☎ 249 7258) at 52 Te Anau Terrace has doubles for $78 and $85 per night. The *Lakeside Motel* (☎ 249 7435) at 36 Lake Front Drive is in a prime position and has units for $80 to $90. Another moderately priced motel is the *Anchorage Hotel* (☎ 249 7256) at 47 Quintin Drive, with double rooms for $80. There are numerous other motels at similar or higher prices.

At the top end, *Te Anau Travelodge* (☎ 249 7411) on Te Anau Terrace in the town centre has rooms from $120. The *Luxmore Resort Hotel* (☎ 249 7526) on Milford Rd near the corner of Mokonui St and *Quality Hotel* (☎ 249 7421) on Lake Front Drive are other upmarket options.

Places to Eat

The *Pop Inn* near the lakefront has light snacks and sandwiches, and is often crammed with forlorn and starved bus travellers. Several places along Milford Rd and on Jailhouse Mall in the town centre serve snacks and takeaways. Try the *Jailhouse Café*, which has good light meals or hearty grills for around $14 or the popular *Te Anau Dairy* or *Snack Attack*. *Baileys,* on the corner of Mokonui St, serves breakfast all day, bistro lunches, and morning and afternoon teas.

Te Anau has a good restaurant scene for its size. *Keplers* on Milford Rd features venison, lamb and seafood on its menu, with main courses costing around $15 to $20. On Milford Rd in the town centre, the Italian *La Toscana* is one of Te Anau's best dining spots. Pasta mains are around $15 and pizzas are $18; it serves excellent desserts.

Henry's at the Te Anau Travelodge is a pub-style bistro for dinner and offers cheap Sunday evening buffets. *Hollywood Boulevard Cafe* on Milford Rd looks expensive but the wide menu is reasonably priced. The *Settlers Steakhouse* on Milford Rd is the local hunting ground for carnivores and the *Ranch* is similar, with huge steaks for $22.50 or good-value grill meals for $12.50.

The *Ming Gardens Restaurant* on Milford Crescent has reasonable Chinese food, while the licensed *China City*, next to the library, is more upmarket.

Getting There & Away

Air Mt Cook Airline (☎ 249 7516) has daily direct flights to Queenstown and on to Mt Cook, Christchurch and other centres. Waterwings Airways (☎ 249 7405), an agent for Ansett New Zealand, has flights to Queenstown and Milford. Air Fiordland

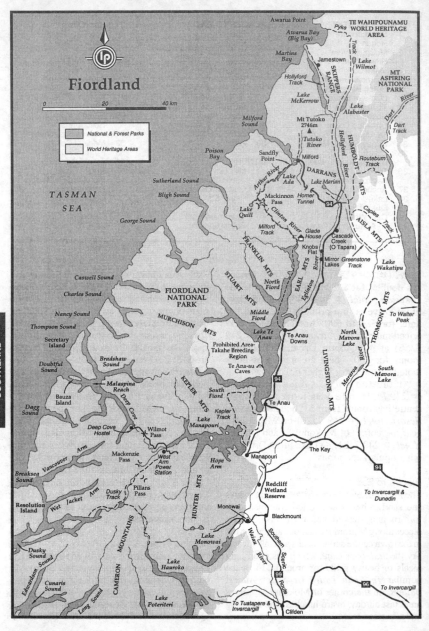

SOUTHLAND

(☎ 249 7505) also has flights from Milford to Te Anau and Queenstown.

Bus InterCity (☎ 249 7559) has daily services between Queenstown and Milford via Te Anau. Daily services also go to Invercargill (three hours), involving a transfer stop in Lumsden, and Dunedin (four hours) continuing on to Christchurch. Buses arrive at and depart from the InterCity depot on Milford Rd. Mt Cook Landline (☎ 249 7516) has daily buses to/from Milford, Queenstown and Christchurch.

Topline Tours (☎ 249 8059) operates a daily shuttle service between Te Anau and Queenstown ($35, discount $25), departing from Te Anau at 10 am and Queenstown at 2 pm. Spitfire Shuttle (☎ 249 7505) departs from Te Anau daily for Invercargill at 8.30 am, returning at 1 pm ($40, discount $34). Catch-a-Bus (☎ 214 6243) runs to Dunedin.

Fiordland Travel (☎ 249 7419) on the lakefront has buses to Queenstown and Milford. Southern Explorer (☎ 249 7820) and Bottom Bus are good services for backpackers to get around this region. See the Queenstown section in the Otago chapter.

Trampers Transport Track Net (☎ 249 7777), operating out of Te Anau Motor Park, has shuttle buses from October to May for the Kepler, Routeburn and Hollyford tracks and to Milford. The Kepler shuttle runs to the control gates and the swingbridge. The shuttle to Milford ($35) passes The Divide ($20) at the start/end of the Routeburn. To the Hollyford costs $30.

Kiwi Discovery (☎ 249 7505) from Queenstown also provides trampers' transport, passing through Te Anau at 10 am on the way to Milford. Mt Cook has three services a day to Milford, via The Divide, and InterCity has one.

Hitching Hitching in and out of Te Anau is a bit easier than to Milford, though still fairly hard. Hitching between Manapouri and Te Anau is usually good.

Getting Around
You can hire bicycles ($20 per day) from Mini Golf & Bike Hire (☎ 249 7959) on Mokonui St and the Te Anau Motor Park.

TE ANAU TO MILFORD
It is 119km from Te Anau to Milford on one of the most scenic roads you could hope for. The first part is through relatively undulating farmland which sits atop the lateral moraine of the glacier that once gouged out Lake Te Anau. At 16km the road enters a patch of mountain beech forest, passes the **Te Anau Downs Harbour** at 29km and heads towards the entrance of Fiordland National Park and the Eglinton Valley. Again, you pass patches of beech – red, silver and mountain, as well as alluvial flats and meadows.

Two interesting sights on the way are the **Avenue of the Disappearing Mountain** and the **Mirror Lakes** (58km from Te Anau, about halfway to Milford). **Knobs Flat**, 5km past Mirror Lakes, is home to a new visitor centre with exhibits on the area, toilets, a dumping station and water for campers.

At the 77km mark is the area now referred to as O Tapara, but known more commonly as **Cascade Creek**. O Tapara is the original name of nearby Lake Gunn and refers to a Ngai Tahu ancestor, Tapara. The lake was a stopover for parties heading to Anita Bay in search of greenstone. A 40-minute walking track passes through tall red beech forest that shelters a variety of birdlife, such as fantails, tomtits, bellbirds, parakeets, kereru and riflemen. Paradise ducks and New Zealand scaup are often seen on the lake. Lake Gunn is the largest of the Eglinton Valley lakes but Fergus and Lochie are higher in altitude. The forest floor is an array of mosses, ferns and lichens. In Cascade Creek you may see longtail bats, NZ's only native land mammal.

The vegetation alters significantly as **The Divide** is approached. The size of the bush is reduced and ribbonwood and fuchsia are prominent. The Divide is the lowest east-west pass in the Southern Alps; there is a good shelter for walkers either finishing or starting the Routeburn and Greenstone tracks. About a 1½-hour walk along the

Routeburn brings you to **Key Summit**, where there are numerous tarns and patches of alpine bog. Three river systems – the Hollyford, Greenstone/Clutha and Eglinton/Waiau – start from the sides of this feature and radiate out to the west, east and south coasts of the island.

From the divide, the road falls into the beech forest of the **Hollyford Valley** and there is an interesting turn-off to Hollyford (Gunn's) Camp and the start of the Hollyford Track to Martins Bay. At the end of the unsealed road it is a 10-minute walk to the high **Humbolt Falls**. One kilometre down the Lower Hollyford Rd from Marian Corner is a track leading to **Lake Marian** with splendid views; you can take the three-hour return, hard tramp or a pleasant short walk to view the rapids.

Back at the corner, the road to Milford rises up to the east portal of the **Homer Tunnel**, 101km from Te Anau. The tunnel is named after Harry Homer, who discovered the Homer Saddle in 1889; work on the tunnel didn't begin until 1935 (to provide relief work for unemployed people after the Depression) and it wasn't finished until 1952. Rough-hewn, it has a steep east to west gradient, but emerges after 1207m into the spectacular **Cleddau Canyon** on the Milford side. At the portals are short nature walks, describing alpine species found here. Cheeky kea greet buses.

The road is normally open all year, but may be closed in winter by high snowfalls and avalanches.

About 10km before Milford is the **Chasm Walk**. The Cleddau River plunges through eroded boulders in a narrow chasm, the Upper Fall, which is 22m deep. About 16m lower it cascades under a natural rock bridge to another waterfall.

There are views of **Mt Tutoko** (2746m), Fiordland's proudest and highest peak, glimpsed above the beech forest just before you arrive in Milford. The majestic Darrans are in this area. A track leads off from the western side of the bridge over Tutoko River. After a two-hour walk through bush, the scenery here is overpowering. Don't venture

any further unless you are a competent tramper and very well equipped. There is no development in this region – nature, swarms of gigantic sandflies and abundant rainfall seem to retort 'Just you try'.

Hollyford Track (to Martins Bay)

This is a well-known track along the broad Hollyford Valley through rainforest to the Tasman Sea at Martins Bay. Because of its length (four days one way), it should not be undertaken lightly. Check at Fiordland National Park Visitor Centre (☎ 249 7921), Te Anau, for detailed information and the latest track and weather conditions.

Hollyford Valley Walk Ltd (☎ 442 3760) in Queenstown has guided walks from Te Anau with transfers, including a flight out to Milford Sound and a jet-boat trip on Lake McKerrow, avoiding the hardest and most tedious part of the walk, Demon Trail. A three-day trip is $950 (four-day trip $1175).

Tracknet (☎ 249 7777) has a shuttle from Te Anau ($30) to the start of the trail. Air Fiordland (☎ 249 7505) flies from Milford to Martins Bay for $265. DOC has six huts (Hidden Falls, Alabaster, McKerrow Island, Demon Trail, Hokuri and the new Martins Bay Hut), all costing $4.

Estimated walking times are:

Lower Hollyford Rd car park to	
Hidden Falls	2½ to three hours
Hidden Falls to Lake Alabaster	3½ to four hours
Lake Alabaster to Lake McKerrow	three hours
Lake McKerrow to Demon Trail	1½ hours
Demon Trail to Hokuri River	five hours
Hokuri River to Martins Bay	five hours

Places to Stay & Eat

Along SH94 are many DOC camping grounds. Their distances from Te Anau are:

Location	Km	Location	Km
Ten Mile Bush	17	Deer Flat	62
Henry Creek	25	Kiosk Creek	65
Boyd Creek	45	Smithy Creek	67
Walker Creek	49	Upper Eglinton	71
McKay Creek	53	Cascade Creek	78
Totara Creek	53	Lake Gunn	81
East Branch Eglinton	56		

SOUTHLAND

Te Anau Downs Motor Inn (☎ 249 7811) is at Te Anau Downs, 27km on the road to Milford, where boats depart for Glade House and the Milford Track. Hotel rooms cost $70 a double or $90 B&B, while the motel units are $100. The hotel section also houses *Grumpy's Backpackers* (☎ 0800 4786797), providing good share rooms for $16, or doubles/twins with bathroom and TV for $40/45. The backpackers has good facilities, including a pool table, laundry and kitchen.

Hollyford Camp, formerly Gunn's Camp, in the Hollyford Valley has rustic cabins (with innerspring mattresses, wood and coal-burning stoves, separate kitchen and hand basins) from $16/28 for one/two people or $14 per person share. Camping is possible but there are no kitchen facilities for campers. The camp also has a shop with basic trampers supplies (sorted into 'pack-friendly' bags). The interesting little museum is the very personal creation of owner Murray Gunn, who has been finding things in the hills around here for over 40 years and saving mementoes of the area's history; entry is free if you stay in his cabins.

Just before the Homer Tunnel is a turn-off to the hidden *Homer Hut*, the property of the NZ Alpine Club. The club takes casual guests during the week for a minimal fee; check with the caretaker at the hut – if there is one.

MILFORD SOUND

One of New Zealand's most famous tourist destinations, Milford Sound is the most visited of all the fiords, and the most instantly breathtaking. The 22km-long fiord is dominated by the beautiful, 1695m-high Mitre Peak. The calm water mirrors the sheer peaks that rise all around.

Though remote, Milford Sound has thousands of visitors each year, some coming via the Milford Track, which ends at the sound, but most by the buses that pull into the cruise wharf. The wharf resembles an international air terminal and is as busy when all the buses arrive. A cruise on Milford Sound is a must.

In the morning and late afternoon, Milford is serene again. It is definitely worth visiting,

---

Annoying Weather & Wildlife

Once you leave Te Anau, you hit two of the menaces of Fiordland: rain and sandflies. Rain in this area is very heavy – Milford gets over 6m annually! Sandflies, for those who haven't met them, are nasty little biting insects, smaller than mosquitoes, with a similar bite – you will see clouds of them at Milford. Don't be put off sightseeing by rain; the masses of water hurtling down the sheer walls of Milford Sound are an incredible sight and the rain tends to keep the sandflies away. For walking and tramping it is a different story, as the rain means flooded rivers and poor visibility. ■

---

but don't expect blue skies. Milford is synonymous with rain: 5.5m of it a year is only average. Consider yourself lucky if you strike a fine day, otherwise take in the spectacular waterfalls.

In the foyer of Mitre Peak Lodge is a small display with photographs and stories relating to the history, geology and the glacial formation of the fiords, and Donald Sutherland (1843-1919), 'the Hermit of Milford', who ran the first accommodation at Milford Sound. The Sutherland Falls are named after him and his grave lies behind the hotel.

Milford Track

Described by some as the finest walk in the world, this four-day walk is along a very scenic track. It is the country's best-known walk and one that most Kiwis dream of doing, even if it's the *only* track they ever walk. Many overseas visitors also make a special effort to do the track though, sadly, they often leave NZ without realising that many other great tracks exist.

The number of walkers is limited each year, accommodation is only in huts, camping is not allowed and you have to follow a set itinerary. Some walkers resent the restrictions, but the benefits outweigh the inconvenience: keeping numbers down protects the environment and, though it is a hassle to book, you are guaranteed the track won't be overcrowded.

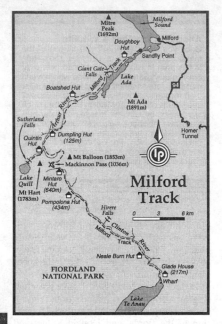

The track must be booked from late October to mid-April. In the off season it is still possible to walk the track, but there is no trail transport, the huts are not staffed and some of the bridges are removed. In the height of winter, snow and avalanches make it unwise, but it is accessible a few weeks either side of the main season.

Expect lots of rain, but when it does rain in this country of granite the effect is an experience not to be missed. Water cascades *everywhere* and small streams become raging torrents within minutes. Remember your raincoat and pack your belongings in an extra plastic bag.

Bookings You can walk the track as an independent tramper or as part of a guided tour. The track can only be done in one direction – from Lake Te Anau to Milford. A permit is required from the DOC visitor centre in Te Anau, allowing you to enter the track on a particular day and no other. Book-

ings can be heavy and it pays to book as far ahead as possible – even several months in advance, especially for December-January. For independent bookings contact: Great Walks Booking Desk, Fiordland National Park Visitor Centre, Lakefront Drive, Te Anau (☎ 249 8514; fax 249 8515).

If you are already in the country, you can also enquire about permits at other DOC offices.

For independent walkers, a permit costs $90 (children $45), which includes three nights in the huts. The booking desk can also book transport: a bus to Te Anau Downs ($11), ferry to Glade House ($40), launch from Sandfly Point to the cruise terminal ($20) and bus back to Te Anau ($35). All up the cost is $196 per person (children $95). There are 30% family discounts for two adults and children.

Milford Track Guided Walk (☎ 249 7590; fax 249 7411) takes bookings for guided walks. These organised parties stay at a different chain of huts from the 'independents', so there is little mingling of the two. The guided walk costs $1324, (children, 10 to 15 years, $750) all inclusive for six days/five nights ex Te Anau, but walkers still only get three days on the trail.

Walking the Track The trail starts at Glade House, at the northern end of Lake Te Anau, accessed by boat from Te Anau Downs or Te Anau. The track follows the fairly flat Clinton River valley up to the Mintaro Hut, passing through rainforest. From Mintaro it passes over the scenic Mackinnon Pass, down to the Quintin Hut and through the rainforest in the Arthur River valley to Milford Sound. You can leave your pack at the Quintin Hut while you make the return walk to Sutherland Falls, NZ's highest. If the pass appears clear on arrival at Mintaro Hut make the effort to climb it, after a hot drink, as it may not be clear the next day. The highlights of Milford are the beautiful views from the Mackinnon Pass, the 630m Sutherland Falls, the rainforest and the crystal-clear streams, swarming with clever trout and eels. An amazingly intricate and very unnatural

Southland
Milford Sound

Outer Islands
Top: Fishing Boat, Paterson Inlet, Stewart Island
Bottom: Little Mangere Island, Chatham Islands

staircase has been built down beside the rapids on the descent from Mackinnon Pass.

Estimated walking times are as follows:

Glade House to Neale Burn Hut	one hour
Neale Burn Hut to Mintaro Hut	5.5 hours
Mintaro Hut to Dumpling Hut	six hours
Side trip to Sutherland Falls	1.5 hours return
Dumpling Hut to Sandfly Point	5.5 hours

Guided walkers stop at their own huts – Glade House, Pompolona and Quintin – and for their money they have a longer walk than independent walkers on the last day (from Quintin Hut out to Sandfly Point).

Transport to Glade House Mt Cook Landline's 1.15 pm bus from Te Anau to Milford stops at Te Anau Downs ($11; 27km) to connect with Fiordland Travel's 2 pm boat to Glade House ($40). Western Safaris (☎ 249 7226) has early or late boat departures from Te Anau Downs to Glade House and can arrange transport to Te Anau for $45 all up.

Alternatively, Deepwater Cruises and Sinbad Cruises go from Te Anau to Glade House by boat for $50. You can also fly with Waterwings Airways for $99 or kayak from Te Anau. See the Te Anau section for more details.

Transport from Sandfly Point Ferries leave Sandfly Point at 2 and 3 pm for the Milford Sound cruise wharf ($20). Deepwater Cruises in Te Anau has a late 4.30 pm pick-up from Sandfly Point and will drop you off at the Milford Sound Lodge ($15).

Or you could kayak to Milford. Rosco Gaudin (see under the following Sea Kayaking heading) has guided kayaking from Sandfly Point to Milford for $18 ($45 including the bus back to Te Anau). Fiordland Wilderness Experiences in Te Anau offers the same service.

Many operators offer complete packages covering both ends of the walk for $98.

Sea Kayaking

The most spectacular way to see Milford Sound is at water level in a sea kayak. In a plastic shell, you fully realise your insignificance in the sound's huge natural amphitheatre. Whatever the weather, looking up to the towering bulk of the bush-clad mountains is nothing short of awesome.

Rosco Gaudin (☎ 249 8840) has summer sea-kayak trips of around six hours that include: Stirling Falls, Harrison Cove beneath the bulk of the Pembroke Glacier, Bowen Falls and flora and fauna from an almost 'reach-out-and-touch-it' vantage point. Trips are great value at $69 and well within the bounds of someone with average fitness. Rosco can also arrange transport to and from Te Anau and kayaking from the end of the Milford Track.

Milford Sound Cruises

Day Cruises Cruises on Milford Sound are popular, so it's a good idea to book a few days ahead. On all trips you can expect to see Bowen Falls, Mitre Peak, Anita Bay, The Elephant and Stirling Falls. More expensive cruises include the **underwater observatory** moored at Harrison Cove that explains and allows viewing of the reef system.

All cruises leave from the huge wharf complex, a five-minute walk from the cafe and car park on a covered and elevated walkway through a patch of Fiordland bush.

Fiordland Travel (☎ 249 7419) has 1½ hour cruises for $40 (children $10) or $45 (children $18) including the underwater observatory. *Milford Wanderer* day cruises are longer (2½ hours) and cost $45. Buffet lunch costs $22 (children $14.50), a packed lunch is $9.50, or you can bring your own. Tea and coffee are served on all cruises.

Red Boat Cruises (☎ 0800 657 444) is the biggest operator in Milford and takes basically the same route as the Fiordland Travel boats, charges the same and also offers lunch. It has more cruises that take in the underwater observatory. The three-hour *Milford Adventurer* cruise at 12.25 pm includes the observatory and ventures out into the Tasman Sea.

The two operators between them have over a dozen cruises a day in summer between 9 am and 3.15 pm.

Overnight Cruises Fiordland Travel's *Milford Wanderer*, modelled on an old trading scow, carries 70 passengers overnight from 1 October to 30 April. The overnight cruise allows you to appreciate the fiord when all the other traffic has ceased. Kayaking, shore visits, fishing and swimming are offered as the boat sails the full length of the sound. You'll see wildlife like dolphins, seals and penguins. The *Wanderer* is impressive when the sails are unfurled and it heaves its way through the Tasman swell out from Milford Sound. Staying overnight in four-bunk cabins costs $199 per person from Queenstown, $153 from Te Anau or $120 from Milford (linen and meals are provided). The *Wanderer* is a YHA-associate hostel on the water and small YHA discounts are offered.

Red Boat Cruises also has a similar but slightly more upmarket cruise on the *Lady of the South Pacific* costing $129 and $199 in twin-share cabins from Milford.

Places to Stay & Eat

Independent walkers seeking a bit of luxury after completing the Milford Track will be disappointed. The old Milford Hotel is now the Mitre Peak Lodge, catering only to those who do the guided walk.

The only other place to stay is the hostel-style *Milford Lodge* (☎ 249 8071). Tent/powered sites cost $8/9 per person, but don't count on power – the generator can't handle it and it's lights off at 10.30 pm for everyone. A bed in the musty, cramped bunkhouse is $18, or the singles/twins for $30/40 are better; doubles with linen cost $45. Accommodation is fairly basic, as are the shared bathrooms, but there is a good sitting/dining area where cheap meals are served and there's a kitchen for guests' use. Coming from Te Anau, the lodge is a couple of kilometres before the ferry wharf, off the main road.

Down on the sound near the wharf, the Mitre Peak Lodge runs the *Mitre Peak Cafe*, which has good coffee and snacks but closes around 5 pm. The *Shark in the Bar* next door

is the local pub. It has pies and beer but not much else.

Getting There & Away

You can reach Milford Sound by four methods, all interesting: hike, fly, bus or drive. The most spectacular is flying from Queenstown or Te Anau (see the Queenstown section in the Otago chapter and the Te Anau section earlier in this chapter). A good combination trip is to go to Milford by bus and return by air. Scenic flights are also offered in Milford, starting at $50 to go to the head of the sound.

The 120km trip by road and through the Homer tunnel is also spectacular. Mt Cook Landline and InterCity run daily bus services from Queenstown and Te Anau for around $35 (discount $25), but most passengers come on day trips that include a cruise. Tramping buses also operate from Te Anau and Queenstown and will pick you up at the Milford Lodge. All these buses pass The Divide (the start/end of the Routeburn and Greenstone tracks).

Many visitors make the return trip from Queenstown in one long 12-hour day. Te Anau is a better starting point as it is only five hours by bus. Fiordland Travel's coach-cruise-coach excursion, leaving Te Anau at 8 am and returning at 5 pm, costs $85 (children $42.50). InterCity has basically the same excursion at the same price, except the cruise is on the Red Boats. From Queenstown, the cost is around $140 but a number of smaller operators do it for much less (see the Queenstown section in the Otago chapter). It's essential to book in advance for the Milford cruises during the high season.

By car, the drive should take about 2½ hours, not allowing for stops.

Hitching on the Milford road is possible but hard going. There's little traffic and nearly all of it is tourist traffic which is unlikely to stop.

MANAPOURI

Just 19km south of Te Anau, on the shores of the lake of the same name, Manapouri is a popular centre for trips, cruises and walking expeditions into the Fiordland area. The lake, the second deepest lake in NZ after Hauroko, is in a spectacular setting, surrounded by mountains covered by native bush in their lower reaches. The town exists on a combination of hydroelectricity generation and tourism, an uneasy mix at the best of times. Now greenies work hand in hand with rednecks – the damage has been done and all are attempting to preserve their livelihoods.

Information

Fiordland Travel (☎ 0800 656 502; fax 249 6603) is the main information and tour centre. The office at Pearl Harbour organises most of the trips, but is very busy just prior to boat departures. Buses from Te Anau connect with the West Arm Power Station and Doubtful Sound trips.

Doubtful Sound

Milford Sound, dominated by Mitre Peak, may be more immediately spectacular, but Doubtful Sound is larger, gets much less tourist traffic and is also a magnificent wilderness area of rugged peaks, dense forest and thundering waterfalls after rain.

Until relatively recently, only the most intrepid tramper or sailor entered the inner reaches of Doubtful Sound. Even Captain Cook, who named it, did not enter. Observing it from off the coast in 1770, he was 'doubtful' whether the winds in the sound would be sufficient to blow the ship back out to sea and sailed on. In 1793 the Spanish entered the sound; Malsapina Reach is named after one of the leaders of this expedition, Bauza Island after another.

Doubtful Sound became accessible when the road over the Wilmot Pass was built in 1959 to facilitate construction of the West Arm Power Station, which was built to provide electricity for the aluminium smelter near Bluff. A tunnel was dug through the mountain from Lake Manapouri to Doubtful Sound, and the massive flow of water into the sounds drives the power station turbines. The project sparked intense environmental battles and in the 1970s plans to considerably raise the level of the Lake Manapouri was defeated by the Save Manapouri Petition – the longest petition in NZ history. The lake is described as 'New Zealand's loveliest lake' – it's hard to imagine that anyone would want to destroy it.

Today, Doubtful Sound is exquisitely peaceful. Bottlenose and dusky dolphins and fur seals can be seen in its waters, and Fiordland crested penguins nest in October and November. Below the surface, black coral and other deep sea life exist at unusually shallow depths because sunlight is filtered out by a permanent 3 to 4m layer of fresh water on top of the sea water. As well as the water pumped down from Lake Manapouri, Doubtful Sound receives some 6m of rain per year.

Activities

Adventure Charters (☎ 249 6626), next to the garage, rents out **kayaks** and gear at $35 per day for paddling on Lake Manapouri and can also arrange Doubtful Sound trips. Dinghies can be hired for $5 per person per day.

With a dinghy you can cross the Waiau River for the best **walks** close to town – the three-hour Circle Track or further out to Hope Arm. Though Te Anau is the usual access point for the Kepler Track, the trail touches the top end of Lake Manapouri. Part of the Kepler can also be done as a day walk from Manapouri – access is via the swingbridge about 10km north of town. Manapouri is also a staging point for the remote, five-day Dusky Track, a real walk into the wilderness of Dusky Sound. This challenging walk is only for experienced trampers prepared for plenty of rain. See Lonely Planet's *Tramping in New Zealand* for more details. Access to the track is by ferry to West Arm ($25), from where it is a half-hour walk to the start of the trail (you may be able to get a seat on the tour buses). Many walkers fly from Te Anau to Supper Cove, the end of the track, and then walk back. Waterwings Airways (☎ 249 7405) in Te Anau can arrange flights from $148 per person.

Deep Cove Charters (☎ 249 6828) has

SOUTHLAND

boat, diving and fishing charters and there are a number of specialist fishing guides.

Organised Tours

Fiordland Travel has cruises from Manapouri to Doubtful Sound. After a half-hour cruise across Lake Manapouri, the next leg is by bus to Doubtful Sound with a side trip venturing 2km underground by road to the West Arm Power Station. After a tour of the power station, you get back on the bus and over Wilmot Pass to the sea, and then explore Doubtful Sound on a three-hour cruise.

The eight-hour trip costs $155 (children $40). You can visit only as far as the power station for $44 (children $10), but that is the most boring part of the trip. Add around $10 for a bus transfer from Te Anau ($30 from Queenstown). You can order lunch or take your own.

Fiordland Ecology Holidays (☎ 249 6600), 1 Home St, offers a unique experience to a small number of clients. These tours are run by Lance and Ruth Shaw, who are very familiar with the flora and fauna of the area. They sail their superbly equipped yacht into parts of the World Heritage area that are only now being discovered. Experienced divers have the chance to dive in the fiords, as many visiting marine biologists do, plunging below the fresh water to see deep-water species you couldn't hope to see elsewhere. Non-divers are given many opportunities to explore the flora and fauna of this unique area.

Four-day trips on Doubtful Sound cost around $600 to $700; other interesting trips include ones to Dusky Sound, Bluff and return, and scientific trips to the subantarctic islands that interested visitors can join. Ring for sailing dates.

Places to Stay & Eat

The small *Manapouri Glade Motor Park* (☎ 249 6623), in a stunning location next to the river and lake, has sites for $15 for two, cabins from $30 and motel units for $70.

The friendly and rather eccentric *Lakeview Motor Park* (☎ 249 6624), 1km from the post office on the Te Anau Road, has tent/powered sites for $17/18 for two and

backpacker cabins from $15 per person. Other cabins from $32 for two include the cute 'doll's houses' for $39. Motel units cost $60 and the motor park has a sauna ($3).

Relaxing *Possum Lodge* (☎ 249 6660), 3 Waiau St, provides fine backpacker accommodation, free bikes, gear storage, and transport to the Kepler Track. Dorms cost $16, while doubles and twins are $36.

Deep Cove Hostel (☎ 216 1340) on Doubtful Sound charges $17 per person. It caters mostly for school groups and is well set up for sea and walking activities. Independent arrangements must be made in advance through the hostel.

The *Cottage* (☎ 249 6838) on Waiau St near the river has just two, very good B&B rooms for $75 a double. *Fiordland Ecology Holidays* (☎ 249 6600), 1 Home St, has onshore B&B accommodation for $65 a double. The fine *Murrell's Grand View House* (☎ 249 6642), built in 1889, has four comfortable double ensuite rooms for $160 to $180.

The *Lakeview Motor Inn* (☎ 249 6652) has motels units from $60 to $80 and a restaurant with great lake views. *Cathedral Cafe*, attached to the general store/post office, has a good range of home-cooked meals and snacks. The *Pearl Harbour Coffee Bar* is underneath the Fiordland Travel office and has good sandwiches and other snacks – handy for a cheap lunch for a cruises.

Getting There & Away

Public transport options are limited. Spitfire Shuttle (☎ 249 7505) runs in the morning to Invercargill ($29) and in the afternoon to Te Anau ($8). Otherwise ask at Fiordland Travel if there are any spare seats on its coaches to Te Anau.

The hitching between Te Anau and Manapouri is OK if you don't rely on it to make a connection with the Doubtful Sound cruises.

THE SOUTHERN SCENIC ROUTE

The Southern Scenic Route starts in Te Anau and goes via Manapouri, Blackmount and Clifden to Tuatapere. At Tuatapere, SH99 goes to Invercargill via Colac Bay and

Riverton. From Invercargill to Dunedin you can take the scenic east-coast route through the Catlins (see the Catlins section). Public transport is limited but the Bottom Bus proves a good backpacker shuttle (see the Catlins section).

Between Manapouri and Blackmount watch out for the one sign indicating the **Redcliff Wetland Reserve** – birdwatchers will be particularly pleased to see a predatory bush falcon in action. Just before Blackmount there is a turn-off to the right (west) to **Lake Monowai** and Borland Lodge (☎ 225 5464), which caters primarily for school groups but individuals can stay there. Lake Monowai stands today as testament to blunder – it was flooded in 1925 for a very small power station and the lake is still unsightly.

The town of **Clifden** has a cave system nearby and the Clifden Suspension Bridge, built in 1902. The mystical Clifden (Waiau) Caves can be explored but heed all warnings. You will need at least two torches. The caves are 17km from Tuatapere; turn left towards Eastern Bush at Lime Works and continue 1km up the road. Ladders are provided in steep sections.

About 16km from Clifden there is a walk to 1000-year-old totara trees. From Clifden you can drive out on 30km of unsealed road to **Lake Hauroko**, the deepest in NZ. Hauroko lies in a beautiful bush setting, with precipitous slopes on its sides. Out on Mary Island in 1967 a good example of a Maori cave burial was discovered. In this tapu place a woman of high rank was buried, sitting upright, in about 1660.

The **Dusky Track** starts at Hauroko Burn and leads to Supper Cove on Dusky Sound and then to the Wilmot Pass road and Lake Manapouri. This is a rugged but rewarding eight-day tramp for the well prepared. Consult DOC and LP's *Tramping in New Zealand*. Lake Hauroko Tours (☎ 226 6681) organises four and eight-day tramps from Hauroko to Lake Manapouri.

The Southern Coastal Track and the Hump Track are described in the DOC pamphlet *Waitutu Tracks*; both start at Te Waewae Bay.

The coastal track goes via Port Craig (where there is an old schoolhouse) to Lake Hakapoua. The Hump goes to Teal Bay at the southern end of Hauroko, and then via the lake's eastern shore to the Hauroko roadhead.

Tuatapere

Once a timber milling town, Tuatapere (population 740) is a farming centre on the banks of the Waiau River, now famous as the 'sausage capital' of NZ. It can be used as a base for trips to Lake Hauroko or Te Waewae Bay and beyond. See how effective the woodchoppers were, look at the small remnant of native forest in the town's domain – once most of the area looked like this.

The Tuatapere information centre (☎ 226 6349) on the main road in town has information on many activities and provides a map to the Clifden Caves. Jet-boats operate on the Wairaurahiri River, and helicopter tours and trampers transport can be arranged through the centre. The town also has a DOC field centre (☎ 226 6475).

Places to Stay & Eat Tuatapere has two tiny, very basic motor camps but the *Tuatapere Motor Camp* (☎ 226 6397) in the domain is in a beautiful position next to the river. Tent/powered sites are $6/8 and cabins $12 for two. The *Mickaela Motor Camp* (☎ 226 6626) on Peace St is just a suburban block with sites for $12/14 for two and a $25 cabin.

Five Mountains Park (☎ 226 6418), 14 Clifden Rd, has ordinary budget twins for $26 and tent sites. B&B doubles at the *Waiau Hotel* (☎ 226 6409), 47 Main St, cost $80; the *Tuatapere Motel* (☎ 226 6250) is at 41 Orawia Rd. The information centre lists B&Bs and farmstays.

The Waiau Hotel has good solid country fare and great Tuatap sausages, while Main St has takeaways.

Tuatapere to Riverton

About 10km south of Tuatapere the scenic route reaches the cliffs above **Te Waewae Bay**, where Hector's dolphins and southern right whales are sometimes seen. At the eastern end of the bay is Monkey Island, or Te Poka a Takatimu (anchor stone of the *Taka-timu* canoe). Nearby is **Orepuki**, where strong southerlies have had a dramatic effect on the growth of macrocarpas, trees wind-blown so that they grow in a direction away from the shore.

The next point of interest is **Colac Bay**, an old Maori settlement and now a popular holiday spot for Southlanders. It has a good beach and Isobel's Weaving Studio for homespun and knitted woollen wear. *Camp Orama* lodge attached to the Colac Bay Tavern (☎ 234 8399) has good-value budget accommodation for $12 per person; it has a kitchen, laundry and BBQ.

On the highway and 7km past Orepuki, *Hillcrest* (☎ 234 5129) is a good little sheep farm with a backpackers. Horse riding and interesting walks can be organised. The backpackers house costs $14 per person, mostly in doubles and twins, or the outside cabin costs $10 per person. Camping sites are $8.

Riverton

Riverton (population 1500), 38km west of Invercargill and at the mouths of the Aparima and Pourakino rivers, is considered to be one of the oldest settlements in NZ, dating from the sealing and whaling days. This pretty town has good beaches and proclaims itself the 'Riviera of the South'.

The **Early Settlers Museum** on Palmerston St is open daily in the afternoon. The town of **Thornbury**, close by, has a Vintage Machinery Museum. The Riverton Rocks area is a popular (if cold) local beach and Taramea Bay is a safe place to swim. Look for the 'big paua' on Bath Rd, where a paua factory turns out all sorts of shell souvenirs and jewellery.

The town's information centre is the Riverton Rock. It also runs the Bottom Bus, which overnights in Riverton.

Places to Stay & Eat At the *Riverton Motor Camp* (☎ 234 8526), off Roy and Hamlet Sts, sites are $15 for two, cabins and on-site

vans are $25 to $30 for two and the cottages are $40. The *Riverton Beach Motel* (☎ 234 8181), 4 Marne St, has singles/doubles for $50/60.

The *Riverton Rock* (☎ 234 8886), 136 Palmerston St, is a beautifully renovated backpackers and guesthouse in the centre of town. It has plenty of character and lots of information on the area. The six-bed dorm costs $19 per person and guesthouse doubles are $44 ($78 with en suite).

The town's eateries are on Palmerston St and include *Ricardo's Pizzeria* at No 135 and the *Pioneer Food Bar* at No 118. The pick of the crop is *Country Nostalgia*, which has homemade pies and an interesting dinner blackboard menu.

Central Southland

SH1, from Invercargill to Gore, in effect cuts the province of Southland into two. To the west of it is Fiordland and to the south-east is the Catlins. Most of Southland's population is concentrated in the centre of the province along SH1 and in the city of Invercargill.

INVERCARGILL

This is the southernmost city in NZ, the main city (population 53,000) of Southland and very much a farm-service community. It is often claimed to be the southernmost city in the world, conveniently forgetting Ushuaia in Argentina and the rest of South American Patagonia.

Invercargill has missed out on a lot of the tourism wealth you'll find in many South Island towns. Instead of a host of smart cafes and urban regeneration, Invercargill still has check shirts and bad haircuts. However, an increasing number of travellers are stopping over on the way to the tramping tracks of Stewart Island, the nearby Catlins and the wild areas of southern Fiordland. It is a remarkably ordered city based on a grid pattern criss-crossing a 'flat as a tack' plain.

The locals staunchly defend their city,

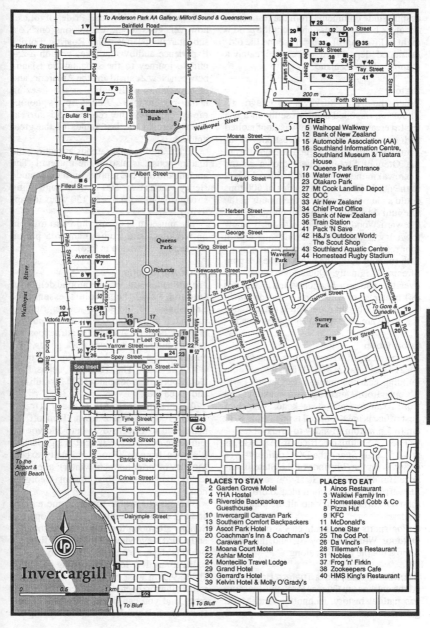

Invercargill

OTHER
5 Waihopai Walkway
12 Bank of New Zealand
15 Automobile Association (AA)
16 Southland Information Centre, Southland Museum & Tuatara House
17 Queens Park Entrance
18 Water Tower
23 Otakaro Park
27 Mt Cook Landline Depot
32 DOC
33 Air New Zealand
34 Chief Post Office
35 Bank of New Zealand
36 Train Station
41 Pack 'N Save
42 H&J's Outdoor World; The Scout Shop
43 Southland Aquatic Centre
44 Homestead Rugby Stadium

PLACES TO STAY
2 Garden Grove Motel
4 YHA Hostel
6 Riverside Backpackers Guesthouse
10 Invercargill Caravan Park
13 Southern Comfort Backpackers
19 Ascot Park Hotel
20 Coachman's Inn & Coachman's Caravan Park
21 Moana Court Motel
22 Ashlar Motel
24 Montecillo Travel Lodge
29 Grand Hotel
30 Gerrard's Hotel
39 Kelvin Hotel & Molly O'Grady's

PLACES TO EAT
1 Ainos Restaurant
3 Waikiwi Family Inn
7 Homestead Cobb & Co
8 Pizza Hut
9 KFC
11 McDonald's
14 Lone Star
25 The Cod Pot
26 Da Vinci's
28 Tillerman's Restaurant
31 Nobles
37 Frog 'n' Firkin
38 Zookeepers Cafe
40 HMS King's Restaurant

SOUTHLAND

despite snide comments from the rest of NZ about its backwardness and ennui. Spend a night in Invercargill, wander around the old-fashioned department stores and catch a glimpse of Old Zealand.

History

When the Chief Surveyor of Otago, JT Thomson, travelled south to settle on a site for Invercargill, the region was uninhabited and covered in a dense forest known as Taurakitewaru Wood, which stretched from the Otepuni Stream (then known as the Otarewa) in the south to the Waihopai River in the north. Realising that ships of 500 tons could sail up the estuary to the mouth of the Otepuni Stream, Thomson chose Taurakitewaru Wood as the best site for the new town. It was laid out over 'a mile square' with four reserves just inside its boundaries and a fifth running down the banks of the Otepuni Stream. Originally, Queens Park was just over the northern boundary and 200 acres (80 hectares) of forest was set aside for it. Today the only part of the forest that remains is a small area known as Thomsons Bush.

Information

The Invercargill Visitor Information Centre (☎ 214 6243; fax 218 9753) is in the museum building near the entrance to Queens Park. It's open from 9 am to 5 pm on weekdays and from 10 am to 5 pm on weekends. The chief post office is in Don St and is open from 8.30 am to 5 pm from Monday to Friday.

The AA Southland office (☎ 218 9033) is at 47-51 Gala St and the DOC office (☎ 214 4589) is on the 7th floor of the State Insurance Building on Don St. If you're going to Stewart Island, it's a good idea to drop in at the DOC office to pick up all the details on walks.

For sports equipment, check out H&J's Outdoor World, 27 Tay St, and the Scout Shop a couple of doors along.

Southland Museum & Tuatara House

At the entrance to Queens Park, this museum has natural history, technology and Maori galleries, and art galleries with temporary and touring exhibitions. Pride of place, however, goes to the exhibitions on NZ's subantarctic islands. The Roaring Forties Experience audiovisual takes you on a 25-minute journey to the subantarctic islands between New Zealand and the Antarctic, and other exhibits outline life in the freezing nether-regions of NZ. Andris Apse's photography captures the remote and surreal atmosphere of the last stands of the great untouched.

Invercargill's most famous attraction, the tuatara house, is also in the museum. The ancient and rare NZ reptiles on show include Henry, who is over 100 years old and going strong (tuataras can live to 150 years in captivity).

The museum is open from 9 am to 5 pm on weekdays and from 10 am to 5 pm on weekends (admission is free).

Other Attractions

From the museum, wander around delightful **Queens Park**, the absolute essence of Englishness. If there was a river running through it you would see punts and punters in straw boaters. Among its attractions are various animals, an aviary, duck ponds, rose gardens and a tea kiosk open from 10 am to 4.30 pm daily. The 18-hole Queens Park Golf Course is good value at $25 for club hire and green fees.

Anderson Park Art Gallery (☎ 215 7432) is 7km north of town. Turn off the main road to Queenstown onto McIvor Rd and drive down it for 3km; it is signposted. It's open from 1.30 to 5 pm daily except Monday (shorter hours in winter); afternoon tea is available at this elegant Georgian house.

The curious **water tower** at the eastern end of Leet St was built in 1889. It's open on Sunday afternoon for a climb to the top ($1) and a bird's-eye view of the town's flatness; on other days, go next door to fetch a key.

Invercargill's long, sweeping beach is **Oreti**, 9.5km west of the city. The water is milder than expected because of warm currents, and you can drive on the hard sands (take care). If you're not up to braving the sea, the Southland Aquatic Centre on Elles Rd is a huge swimming pool complex with slides, wave machine etc.

Activities

For local sites of interest, pick up a walking-tour leaflet of Invercargill's historical places from the museum. Thomson's Bush, on Queens Drive, is the last remnant of Taurakitewaru Wood, the forest that once covered Invercargill. It is about 3.5km north of the CPO. The best of the area's short **walks** are at the Sandy Point Domain, near Oreti Beach, with a mixture of totara scrub forest, fern gullies, coastal views and birdlife. There are several other walks, scenic flights and tandem skydiving; ask at the visitor information centre.

Blue Taxis (☎ 218 6078) has city tours, and tours to Oreti Beach, Bluff and Riverton.

Places to Stay

Camping & Cabins The *Invercargill Caravan Park* (☎ 218 8787) is at the A&P Showgrounds on Victoria Ave, only 1km north-west of the centre. This gulag of long-termers is closed during showtime (the first two weeks in December), but during the rest of the year tent/powered sites are $14/16 for two, cabins are from $24 to $30 for two and there's a bunkroom at $10 per person.

The *Coachman's Caravan Park* (☎ 217 6046), 705 Tay St, is little more than a back-yard strip behind the Coachman's Inn, with sites at $15 for two and a few cabins.

The simple *Beach Road Motor Camp* (☎ 213 0400) is 6km west of town on Dunns Rd, 1km before Oreti Beach. Tent/powered sites are $12/16 and cabins are $24 to $38.

The pick of the camping grounds is the small *Lorneville Lodge* (☎ 235 8031), 352 Lorne Dacre Rd. From town, head north along SH6 for 8km, then turn right and travel for 4km. This peaceful, friendly farmlet has tent/powered sites for $10/17, cabins for $36 and a tourist flat for $55; all prices are for two. B&B in the house is $45 per person.

Hostels The *Southern Comfort Backpackers* (☎ 218 3838) at 30 Thomson St, consistently rated one of the best in the country, is housed in a turn-of-the-century Art Nouveau villa, with beautifully manicured gardens and tasteful decor. Pleasant, clean dorms are $16, and twins and doubles are $36. To many travellers this place is the highlight of Invercargill.

Riverside Backpackers Guesthouse (☎ 0800 302 277) is at 70 Filleul St, in the city's north by the Waihopai River. It is a poor cousin in comparison to the Southern Comfort. Dorms cost $15, or the cabin at the back is $10 per person, and a single is $25. This old house is down a lane off Filleul St.

The world's southernmost *YHA Hostel* (☎ 215 9344) is at 122 North Rd (on the corner of Bullar St), Waikiwi, about 3km north of the town centre. It is neat and tidy with a variety of dorms for $15 per person and one double for $36.

B&Bs, Motels & Hotels There are a couple of good B&Bs. The pleasant *Aarden House* (☎ 214 8825) at 193 North Rd charges $40/65 for singles/doubles ($50/75 with en suite). The *Oak Door* (☎ 213 0633) at 22 Taiepa Rd, Otatara, is another good place at $60/80.

The straightforward but well-kept *Montecillo Lodge* (☎ 218 2503) at 240 Spey St is an old guesthouse that's had a facelift and also has motel rooms. Rooms are $76/97 including a cooked breakfast in the old dining room; motel units are $65/79.

Invercargill has over 30 motels. The *Coachman's Inn* (☎ 217 6046), 705 Tay St, has units for $75. Similarly priced motels include the *Ashlar Motel* (☎ 217 9093) at 81 Queens Drive, *Garden Grove Motel* (☎ 215 9555) at 161 North Rd, *Moana Court Motel* (☎ 217 8443) at 554 Tay St and the *Queens Park* (☎ 214 4504) at 85 Alice St. The slightly more expensive but good *Tower Lodge* (☎ 217 6729) is at 119 Queens Drive.

Gerrard's Hotel (☎ 218 3406) on the corner of Esk and Leven Sts, opposite the train station, is an ornate 1896 building with a good restaurant. Singles/doubles are $40/60 ($50/70 with a big breakfast) or renovated doubles with en suite are $85 to $90.

On Dee St and opposite the west end of Don St is the imposing old *Grand Hotel* (☎ 218 8059), where small singles are $45 or larger rooms are $65/70, all with en suite. The pretty ordinary *Kelvin Hotel* (☎ 218 2829) on Kelvin St in the town centre is the largest of its ilk in Invercargill. It's well kept but bland and charges a hefty $108 for doubles.

The town's best is the *Ascot Park Hotel* (☎ 217 6195) on the corner of Tay St and Racecourse Rd (it's next to the racecourse). It has an indoor pool and charges $92 for motel units or $145 for deluxe hotel rooms. Check for weekend discounts.

Places to Eat

Restaurants & Cafes Invercargill does have a few fashionable cafes, the pick of which is the cool little *Zookeepers Cafe* at 50 Tay St. Light meals, such as lasagne, cost around $12 and steaks are around $16. *Rocks Cafe* on Courtville Place, just off Dee St, is similar to the Zookeepers. *Tillerman's Restaurant*, 16 Don St, is another good local gathering spot with a wider menu, including sushi and vegetarian selections. Mains are around $16 and there is also an Art Deco bar.

You could try the simple and straightforward *Ainos Restaurant* on North Rd in Waikiwi, seven blocks north of the YHA hostel. *China City* at 232 Dee St, next to the Pizza Hut, is an attractive licensed Chinese restaurant with six-course meals for $14 at lunch time and around $20 to $24 in the evening.

If you want to sample some of the local seafood, try *HMS King's Restaurant* at 83 Tay St. It is decked out like an old sailing ship and its menu (mains $20 to $25) features oysters, whitebait, blue cod and salmon. It is open daily for lunch and dinner.

The *Lone Star*, on the corner of Dee and Leet Sts, is open from 5.30 pm until late. It has two parts – a back bar and dining area. It has huge nachos, all you can eat ribs and other Tex-Mex inspired food at reasonable prices. The *Frog 'n' Firkin* is next to the cinema complex at 31 Dee St. It is open daily except Sunday for lunch and dinner until late. There is a restaurant and bar and you can pick up a meal for under $10. Its fiery potato wedges make the perfect accompaniment to the fine selection of ales.

Pub Food & Fast Food Invercargill has plenty of pubs serving food. The *Homestead Cobb & Co* on the corner of Dee and Avenal Sts, Avenal, serves consistent fare at reasonable prices. It's open for lunch and dinner daily. The *Waikiwi Family Inn*, north of the town centre, also has good pub food. *Molly O'Grady's* in the Kelvin Hotel on Kelvin St is classier than most and has cafe fare for lunch and à la carte dining for dinner.

Along Dee St and around the town centre there's the usual collection of fast-food and sandwich places. *Nobles* at 47 Dee St serves good 'mousetraps' (onion, cheese and bacon on toast) and weak cappuccinos. The *Cod Pot* on Dee St turns out consistently good fish and chips, and offers delicious Bluff oysters in season.

Da Vinci's at 300 Dee St is the pick of the pizza places in town; a large pizza will cost about $16 and an extra large $18. Further north up Dee St, there's a *Pizza Hut*, *McDonald's*, *KFC* and several other big drive-in takeaway places.

Entertainment

Although the town centre closes with a bang after 9 pm, there *is* entertainment if you are willing to search it out. The odd nightclub buzzes until the early hours, and a lot is happening out in the suburbs, but you need to ask around.

Lively places with the best atmosphere for a drink include *Zookeepers Cafe* at 50 Tay St. The Zoo has laid-back staff, some of Invercargill's brighter party animals, and corrugated iron statuary. The *Rocks Cafe* on Courtville Place, folksy *Tillerman's* at 16 Don St, the Tex-Mex *Lone Star* on the corner of Dee and Lee Sts and the 'hits and memories' *Frog 'n' Firkin* on Dee St are of a similar ilk.

The *Rafters Bar* at the Whitehouse Hotel is possibly the best place to go for music, but it's right out at Lorneville, 8km north of

Waikiwi (a left turn west towards Riverton); there's a cover charge. The weekend editions of the *Southland Times* will indicate what's on elsewhere. In Invercargill for Labour Day long weekend? You can catch the Trucking and Country Music Convention.

Getting There & Away

Air Air New Zealand (☎ 214 4737) at 46 Esk St and Ansett New Zealand (☎ 214 4644) at Invercargill airport have daily direct flights to Dunedin, Christchurch and Wellington, with connections to other centres.

Southern Air (☎ 0800 658 876) makes flights to Stewart Island (see the Stewart Island section in the Outer Islands chapter). Southern Air and Southeast Air (SEA; ☎ 214 5522) can be chartered to remote parts such as Mason's Bay. Southern Air also flies to Dunedin twice daily on weekdays for $90 or $45 stand-by.

Bus InterCity buses are based at the train station (☎ 218 1837, 214 0598). Daily buses run from Invercargill to Te Anau and Christchurch, with more frequent buses to Dunedin. Southern Air (☎ 218 9129) does the leg to Queenstown for InterCity daily for $36.

Catch-a-Bus (☎ 214 6243) has scheduled services to Dunedin and Wanaka at 8.30 am. Spitfire Shuttle (☎ 214 1851) operates from Invercargill to Te Anau and return (see the Te Anau section). Knightrider (☎ 202 5338) has coach services to Dunedin and Christchurch.

Two services pass through the Catlins (see the Catlins section).

Train The *Southerner* Christchurch to Invercargill train operates daily, departing from each end at 8.30 am and arriving at the other end around 5.20 pm. Phone ☎ 0800 802 802 for bookings and information.

Hitching Hitching between Dunedin and Invercargill is usually fairly simple and should only take about half a day. Queenstown or Te Anau gets steadily harder the further you go, and many people get stuck overnight in Lumsden. The Catlins coastal route between Dunedin and Invercargill is pretty hard – public transport is almost non-existent and there's little traffic for hitching.

Getting Around

The airport is 2.5km from the centre, $8 by taxi, or $3 with Spitfire Shuttle (☎ 214 1851) which will pick you up from accommodation. There are two taxi companies: Taxi Co (☎ 214 4478) and Blue Star (☎ 218 6079).

City buses (☎ 218 7108) run on weekdays from around 7 am to 6 pm or until around 9 or 10 pm on late shopping nights. Local bus trips cost $1.20.

Wensley's Cycles (☎ 218 6206) on the corner of Tay and With Sts hires out bicycles.

BLUFF

Invercargill's port, and departure point for the Stewart Island catamaran, Bluff is 27km to the south. A small place of 2100 people, its Maori name is Motupohue ('motu' because it looks like an island and 'pohue' from the white convolvulus flower).

Popular folklore has it that Bluff is the land's end of New Zealand, though it is not the South Island's southernmost point. 'From Cape Reinga to Bluff' is an oft-quoted phrase signifying the entire length of New Zealand. The country's main highway, SH1, runs between the two and terminates at the **Stirling Point signpost**, which indicates distances to the South Pole and elsewhere in the world.

Foveaux Walk is a good 6.6km, 2½ hour coastal walkway from the signpost to Ocean Beach, where there's a smelly freezing works. Alternatively, take the trail for about 1km and then return by the 1.5km Glory Track, as good a short walk as you'll find, uphill and then down through superb bush and ponga groves.

You can drive or walk for half an hour to the observation point at the top of 265m **Bluff Hill** for unobstructed views of the flat surrounding area and across to Stewart Island.

The **Bluff Maritime Museum** ($2) at the wharf is open from 10 am to 4.30 pm on weekdays and from 1 to 5 pm on weekends.

Fred & Myrtle's Paua Shell House, 258 Marine Parade, has an amazing array of kitsch statuary (check out the fountain) and shells from all over the world. Visitors are welcome from 9 am to 5 pm daily (entry by donation). The nonagenarian couple enjoy their celebrity status.

Across the harbour from Bluff is the huge **Tiwai aluminium smelter**, a major source of employment for Invercargill's citizens. They get mighty sensitive to any hint of criticism of it. Aluminium is an important NZ export. Free tours at 10 am on weekdays can be arranged by phoning ☎ 218 5494 well in advance.

Places to Stay & Eat
The small *Bluff Motor Camp* (☎ 212 8704) on Gregory St has tent/powered sites for $10/12. *Flynn's Club Hotel* (☎ 212 8124), 100 Gore St, and the *Bayview* (☎ 212 8615), 48 Gore St, have pub singles/doubles for around $30/50. The untidy *Property Arcade Backpackers* (☎ 212 8074) at 120 Gore St, opposite the ferry wharf, has dorms for $12 per person.

Land's End NZ (☎ 212 7575), a B&B at the end of SH1 opposite the signpost, is the pick of the local accommodation and charges $95 a double. The cafe has a wide selection of meals and wine. The nearby *Stirling Point* restaurant/tearooms keeps variable hours.

Plump Bluff oysters, the best in NZ, can be bought in season at outlets in town.

Getting There & Away
Campbelltown Passenger Services (☎ 212 7404) has a door-to-door service from Invercargill ($6, $7.50 from the YHA) to Bluff to meet the Stewart Island ferry. See the Stewart Island section of the Outer Islands chapter for ferry details.

INVERCARGILL TO DUNEDIN
From Invercargill to Dunedin, SH1 via Gore and Balclutha is the quick, direct route. Much more scenic is the continuation of the Southern Scenic Route, SH92, via the coastal road through the Catlins.

SH1 passes through Mataura, site of a huge freezing works; Gore, home of the Big Brown Trout and country music; and Balclutha (in Otago), with a good little regional museum. The scenery is rural, which you may just have had enough of by now. If so, read about the Catlins and plan to spend some extra time there – you won't regret it.

Gore
This farming service town (population 10,600), Southland's second largest, spans the Mataura River and has the Hokonui Hills as a great backdrop. In June, Gore hosts the NZ Gold Guitars, an annual country and western festival, when the town is booked out.

Find the trout and you will find the Gore Information Centre (☎ /fax 208 9908), on Ordsal St near the Mataura River. It's open from 9 am to 7 pm on weekdays and 10 am to 7 pm on weekends (shorter hours in winter).

The **Eastern Southland Museum & Art Gallery** on Hokonui Drive is open from 10 am to 5 pm on weekdays and 2 to 4 pm on Sunday. The **Croydon Aircraft Company** (☎ 208 9755) at Mandeville, 16km towards Queenstown, restores vintage aircraft and offers Tiger Moth flights.

With luck, you will catch a trout the size of the 'big one' in one of the many (40 or so) excellent streams, including the Pomahaka, Mataura, Waimea, Otamita and Waipahi. For further information get the *Anglers' Access* pamphlet from the information centre.

Places to Stay & Eat At the southern end of town at 35 Broughton St, *Gore Motor Camp* (☎ 208 4919) has sites for $9 per person and cabins for $30 for two. *Charlton Motel* (☎ 208 9733) at 9 Charlton Rd and the *Oakleigh Motel* (☎ 208 4863) at 70 Hokonui Drive both have rooms for around $65 to $80 a double. The *Croydon Lodge Motor Hotel* (☎ 208 9029), Main Queenstown Highway (Waimea St), has twin rooms for $105 and a nine-hole golf course. The *O Te Ika Rama Marae* at McNab, a short drive north of Gore on SH1, is a special place to stay because travellers get a chance to experience Maori culture first hand.

Main St has a number of places to keep the wolf from the door. They range from the *Gore Pie Cart*, next to the United Video shop, to the *Guangzhou Restaurant* to the successful *Table Talk Cafe* and the BYO *Cafe 1901*.

The Catlins

If you're travelling between Invercargill and Dunedin with your own transport, take the longer Catlins coastal route, allowing a couple of days for stopovers. The distance is similar to the inland route but you travel much slower as some 50km is unsealed. The route goes through the region known as the Catlins, which stretches from Waipapa Point in Southland to Nugget Point in South Otago. It includes the Western Catlins Forest (22,250 hectares) and a number of other forests and scenic reserves. The Catlins is a totally absorbing area.

History
The area was once inhabited by the moa hunters and evidence of their camp sites and middens have been found at Papatowai. Between 1600 and 1800 the Maori population thinned out because of the decline of the moa, the lack of kumara cultivation and fear of the Maeroero – the wild, yeti-like creature of the Tautuku bush, reputed to snatch children and young women.

Later, whalers occupied sites along the shoreline such as at Waikawa Harbour, Tautuku Peninsula and Port Molyneaux. Then timber millers, serving the Dunedin market, moved into the dense stands of beech forest in the 1860s. At the height of logging there were about 30 mills in the area. The railway was started in 1879 but did not reach Owaka for another 25 years. It reached Tahakopa, where it terminated, 36 years later; it was closed in 1971. As in many other parts of New Zealand, the pastoralists constituted the final wave of settlement.

Flora & Fauna
There are still reserves of podocarp forests in the Catlins, containing trees such as kahikatea, totara, rimu and miro. Behind the sand dunes of Tahakopa and Tautuku bays there are excellent examples of native forest that extend several kilometres inland. The vegetation zones are best seen at Tautuku: sand-dune plants (marram, lupin, flax) are found near the beach; behind these are low trees such as rata, kamahi and five-finger; in the peaty sands behind the dunes is young podocarp forest; and then there is mature forest with emergent rimu and miro and a main canopy of kamahi. A good example of young forest is found near Lake Wilkie, where growth has occurred on the sediments that have gradually filled in the lagoon.

The fauna as much as the flora attracts visitors. New Zealand fur seals and Hooker's sea lion are abundant. Elephant seals breed at The Nuggets, a series of remarkable wave-like pinnacles. The variety of birdlife is an ornithologist's delight, with many sea, estuary and forest birds. Included are the endangered yellow-eyed penguin (hoiho), the kaka, blue ducks and the rare mohua (yellowhead).

Organised Tours
Catlins Wildlife Trackers' (☎ 415 8163; 474 3300) highly recommended tour is a specialist eco-experience. Natural history, landforms and geology are interwoven with recent history, the secrets of the sea, littoral, rainforest, wetlands and sky, while nature's rare, timid creatures are revealed. Food, land, water transport, all equipment (wet suit, snorkels etc) and a bed in its holiday home at Papatowai is included. The two-day tour costs $180 (ex Balclutha, including pick-up) and car storage and onward transport can be arranged.

Getting There & Away
Two buses pass through the Catlins and allow independent travellers to stop off and see the sights. See the Queenstown section of the Otago chapter for details of the Southern Explorer (☎ 249 7820).

SOUTHLAND

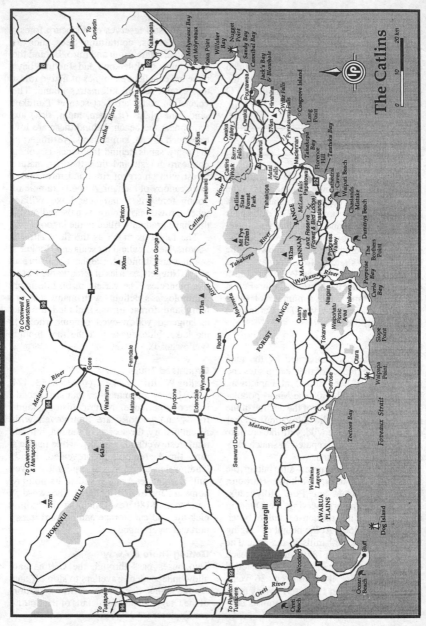

Another good service is the Bottom Bus (☎ 471 0292), specialising in the Catlins/ Southern Scenic Route. It stops at all main points of interest and you can get off it and catch the next bus coming through. It runs three days a week between Dunedin and Te Anau via the Catlins, Invercargill and the Southern Scenic Route. Connections between Te Anau and Dunedin via the inland route through Gore complete the circuit. Passes are available in conjunction with Kiwi Experience for Queenstown-Te Anau-Milford travel. Dunedin-Te Anau (or vice versa) costs $109 (minimum 1½ days), and various options range up to $199 for a full loop including Queenstown, Milford and back to Dunedin or Te Anau.

INVERCARGILL TO PAPATOWAI

The road from Invercargill, SH92, meets the coast at Fortrose. Before Fortrose, to the south of SH92, is the significant 14,000-hectare **Awarua Wetlands** region consisting of the Waituna, Seaward Moss and Toetoes scientific reserves. The reserves support wading bird species in Awarua Bay and Waituna Lagoon, and many vegetation types, including magnificent cushion bogs in the Waituna Wetlands, red tussock grasslands and estuarine and salt marsh communities.

At Fortrose, take a turn-off to the south to **Waipapa Point**. The lighthouse here was erected in 1884, after the second-worst maritime disaster in NZ's history. In 1881 the SS *Tararua* struck the Otara Reef, 1km offshore. Of the 151 passengers and crew only 20 survived; in the nearby graveyard lie the graves of 65 victims.

The next detour is to **Slope Point**, the most southerly point on the South Island. A small and hard-to-see beacon lies across private land. It can also be approached from Tokanui.

Curio Bay is the next point of interest. At low tide you can see one of the most extensive fossil forests in the world – it is 160 million years old. The petrified stumps and fallen log fossils are evidence of New Zealand's location in the ancient supercontinent Gondwanaland and the plant species identified here are similar to those found in South America – cycads, tree ferns and matai-like and kauri-like trees.

Just around the corner in **Porpoise Bay** you may see Hector's dolphins surfing in the waves breaking on the beach, and you can swim with them. Be careful not to touch or otherwise harry the dolphins, which come close into shore over summer to rear their young. Yellow-eyed penguins, fur seals and sea lions also inhabit the area.

In the old church at **Waikawa**, Dolphin Magic (☎ 246 8444) organises boat trips to see the dolphins. Its two cruises cost $45 and $65; the latter price includes a trip to the Brothers Point, where NZ fur seals and Hooker's sea lions are often seen. A study is being conducted on the effect of human contact on the dolphins. Waikawa also has a small district museum (open from 1 to 4 pm daily in summer) and a good backpackers, but nothing else.

The **Cathedral Caves** on Waipati Beach, so-named for their resemblance to an English cathedral, are only accessible at low tide (tide tables are posted at the turn-off from SH92). From the road it is 2km to the car park, then a 15-minute walk to the beach and a further 25 minutes to the caves.

Next along is Lenz Reserve, with a bird lodge and remains of the old Tuatuku sawmill just a short walk from the road. At **Tautuku Bay** there is a 15-minute walk to the beach, a stunning sweep of sand punctuated by drifts of seaweed, and a five-minute walk to **Lake Wilkie**, where there are some unique forms of plant life. Just past Tautuku there is a good vantage point at **Florence Hill** from where you can distinguish the different vegetation types and other points of interest.

Papatowai, at the mouth of the Tahakopa River, is the next tiny town reached. This is the base for Catlins Wildlife Trackers and some amazing forays into the close forests.

Places to Stay & Eat

At Tokanui, the turn-off to the coast leads 1.7km to *Pope's Place* (☎ 246 8420), a friendly farm backpackers with dorms for

$14 and doubles and twins for $30. Right next door is the Little Shop, indeed little and proudly the southernmost shop on the South Island. It's geared to the tourist trade with a sauna in the garage. On SH92, halfway between Tokanui and the turn-off to Waikawa, is the *Egilshay Farmstay* (☎ 246 8703).

The *Curio Bay Camping Ground* (☎ 246 8897) is right on the beach at Curio Bay and tent/powered sites cost $6/10 for two.

At Waikawa is the *Waikawa Holiday Lodge* (☎ 246 8552) opposite the dolphin centre, which has a small shop and cafe. A dorm bed costs $15 and twins/doubles are $34/36 in this comfortable house. Halfway along the route, this lodge is a popular place to stop.

One of the nicest places to stay is the *Catlins Farmstay* (☎ 246 8843) on Progress Valley Rd, which starts just past the turn-off to Waikawa. A great B&B costs $40/70 for singles/doubles in a very comfortable house. Dinners cost $25.

Further along the main road and closer to Papatowai, *Chaslands Farm Motor Lodge* (☎ 415 8501) has motel-style cabins at $50 for two. The *Tautuku Lodge* (☎ 415 8024), 6km south of Papatowai in the Lenz Reserve, is owned by the Royal Forest & Bird Protection Society. It is possible to stay for around $20 per night – ring in advance or arrange it in Papatowai.

At the *Papatowai Motor Camp* (☎ 415 8500) a tent/powered site is $12/14 for two, cabins are $30 and the backpackers is $12 per person. At the entrance to the motor camp, attached to the shop, is the *Scenic Highway Motels* (☎ 415 8147), where excellent new units cost $50/60 for a single/double.

A place with fantastic views and great sunsets is the friendly *Hilltop* (☎ 415 8028), a backpackers reached on the Tahakopa Rd just before the bridge near Papatowai. It is a little over 1km from the main road and then another 500m up a steep hill. The farmhouse offers very high standards for $18 in a four-bed dorm or $40 for doubles.

The *Papatowai Trading Post* organises meals, sandwiches and tea or coffee.

PAPATOWAI TO BALCLUTHA

Between Papatowai and the regional centre of Owaka there are many interesting places to visit. First, follow SH92 east to **Matai Falls** on the Maclennan River. After looking at these, head south on the signposted road to the more scenic **Purakaunui Falls**. It is only a short walk through bush to these tiered falls best viewed from a platform at their base.

In the **Catlins State Forest Park** you can do the river walk, a good day trip out of Owaka. There is a track to Tawanui from the Wisp camping area – observant walkers may see the rare mohua (yellowhead) here. Out near the mouth of the Catlins River, on the western side, is **Jack's Blowhole**, a 55m-deep hole in the middle of paddocks. It is 200m from the sea but connected by a subterranean cavern.

On the eastern side of the river, south-east of Owaka, is the **Pounawea Nature Walk**, a 45-minute loop through kahikatea, ferns, kamahi, rimu, totara and southern rata. There is a salt marsh near the Catlins River estuary.

Owaka

Owaka (population 400) is the main town of the Catlins area. The Catlins Information Centre (☎ 415 8392) in the Catlins Diner has information on the whole area and accommodation listings. Like the diner, it is open in the evening. The DOC field office (☎ 415 8341) is on the corner of Ryley and Campbell Sts. The Owaka Museum is open from 1.30 to 4 pm on Sunday or by appointment.

Places to Stay & Eat The *Pounawea Motor Camp* (☎ 415 8483) is a few kilometres south-east of town on the river. It's quite basic but is in a lovely setting adjoining the Pounawea Scenic Reserve. Tent/powered sites cost $12/14 for two and cabins are $30.

Catlins Backpackers (☎ 415 8392) on Main Rd belongs to the diner and is behind the information centre. It has three and four-bed share rooms and one double, all $14 per person, and hires out bicycles.

The friendly *Highview Motel & Candy Cone Backpackers* (☎ 415 8636), 23 Royal

Terrace, has motel units for $55 and a well-equipped backpackers costing $12/30 in the dorm/doubles. It arranges tours/transport from Invercargill or Dunedin for $30.

Owaka Lodge Motel (☎ 415 8728) on the corner of Ryley and Campbell Sts has units for $60 to $65. *Catlins Retreat Guesthouse* (☎ 415 8830) in a restored house at 27 Main Rd has rooms for $60. You can eat out at the *Catlins Diner* on Main St, the *Catlins Inn*, 21 Ryley St, or the *Lumberjack Cafe & Bar*, the biggest thing to hit Owaka in years.

There are DOC camping grounds at the following areas in the Catlins, all in southeast Otago: Tawanui (Catlins State Forest Park) and Purakaunui Bay.

Owaka to Balclutha

East of Owaka, **Cannibal Bay** is home to a Hooker's sea lion breeding ground, but is difficult to reach. Before Punawea, cross the bridge and take the Newhaven Rd to Newhaven, from where you walk around the beach to Cannibal Bay. The bay gets its name from the surveyor Hector, who discovered human bones in a midden here and assumed it was part of a feast. Te Rauparaha exacted revenge here, which may have included acts of cannibalism.

To the east of Owaka at **Tunnel Hill** there is a short track that leads to NZ's most southerly railway tunnel, excavated by hand in 1893 as part of the Catlins Branch Railway.

Further around the coast, on a not-to-be-missed sidetrack from the Kaka Point road, is **Nugget Point**, one of NZ's special places. The islands sitting out from the lighthouse promontory seem to lead off to the very edge of the world. Fur seals bask below on the rocks, as do Hooker's sea lions and elephant seals on occasions; it is the only place on the NZ mainland where these species coexist. There is a wealth of birdlife: yellow-eyed and little blue penguins, gannets, shags and sooty shearwaters breed here and many other pelagic species, such as the cape pigeon, pass by. The stone lighthouse was built in 1869.

Avoid the temptation to leave the track – observe only from above with binoculars so as not to disturb the birds. Look down on the huge bladderkelp forests in the water that fringe the Nuggets' reefs.

Only 2km from the lighthouse, *Nuggets Lodge* (☎ 412 8783) has a self-contained flat for $65 and homestay B&B at $70 a double.

From Nugget Point the road loops back around through Kaka Point and Port Molyneaux to SH92 and Balclutha (see the Otago chapter). **Kaka Point** is a pleasant little town on a good beach and the *Kaka Point Camping Ground* (☎ 412 8814), above the town on Tarata Rd, has tent/powered sites for $8/10 per person and cabins for $14/25 for one/two people. Near the beach, *Fernlea Backpackers* (☎ 412 8834) is a cute cottage up the steps from Moana St. A bed costs $15 per person in the two bunkrooms or the one double.

Outer Islands

New Zealand is often mistakenly believed to consist of just the two islands, North and South. In fact there are a number of island groups off its shores and these contain fascinating culture, unique flora and fauna, magnificent scenery and isolation and solitude for those who want to escape.

Stewart Island

Called Rakiura by the Maori, New Zealand's third-largest island is an increasingly popular destination for getting away from it all. Rakiura means 'land of the glowing skies' in Maori, perhaps referring to the aurora australis that is often seen in this southern sky, or the spectacular blood red sunrises and sunsets. The island is often thought of as being isolated and suffering the battering of harsh southern winds – actually Stewart Island is not as inhospitable as that, but it most definitely is an unspoilt, get-away-from-it-all place.

The minuscule population of 420 is congregated in the only town of any size, Oban, on Halfmoon Bay. Half an hour's walk away you enter a sanctuary of forest, beaches and hills. The hardy and independent people have a healthy suspicion of the law and bureaucracy. The weather is incredibly changeable – brilliant sunshine one minute, pouring rain the next. Conditions can be very muddy underfoot and you will need boots and waterproof clothing, but the temperature is much milder than you would expect. As one islander has pointed out, the island's rainforest *is* more beautiful in the rain – and mud is 'great character-building stuff'!

History

There is evidence that parts of Rakiura were occupied by moa hunters as early as the 13th century AD. According to Polynesian mythology New Zealand was hauled up from

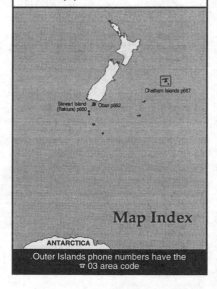

HIGHLIGHTS

- Kiwi spotting on Ocean Beach, Stewart Island
- Walking on any of Stewart Island's tracks – truly a remote walking experience
- Enjoying the isolation and peace of the getaway centre of Halfmoon Bay on Stewart Island
- Seeing the rich birdlife of Stewart and Ulva islands
- Exploring Chatham Island, its isolated lagoons, ramshackle fishing settlements and wild landscapes
- Tracing Moriori culture on Chatham Island, especially the tree carvings (dendroglyphs) at Te Hapupu

Chatham Islands p667

Stewart Island (Rakiura) p660 • Oban p662

Map Index

ANTARCTICA

Outer Islands phone numbers have the ☎ 03 area code

the depths of the South Pacific Ocean by Maui who said 'Let us go out of sight of land and when we have quite lost sight of it, then let the anchor be dropped; but let it be very far off – quite out in the open sea'. One interpretation of this myth is that the North

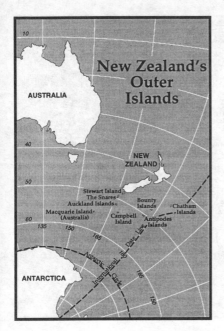

to an increase in settlement but the rush didn't last long and today the island's economy is based on fishing – crayfish, paua (abalone), salmon and cod – and tourism.

Flora & Fauna

Unlike the North and South islands, there is no beech forest on Stewart Island. The predominant lowland vegetation is hardwood but there are also lots of tree ferns, a variety of ground ferns and several different kinds of orchid, including a lady's slipper orchid, two earinas and a number of spider orchids. Along the coast the vegetation consists of muttonbird scrub, grass tree, tree daisies, supplejack and leatherwood. But you are warned not to go tramping off the beaten track, as the bush is impenetrable in most places.

Stewart Island is an ornithologist's delight. Apart from the many seabirds that breed here, bush birds such as tuis, parakeets, kakas, bellbirds, fernbirds, robins (the last two are seen near Freshwater Flats), dotterels and kiwis abound. The weka can sometimes be spotted, and the Fiordland crested, yellow-eyed and little blue penguins are also seen (see Ulva Island later in this section).

Two species of deer were introduced to the island early in the 20th century. They are the red deer, found mainly around Mt Anglem, in the Freshwater and Rakeahua valleys and at Toi Toi Flat in the south-east, and the Virginia (whitetail) deer which inhabits the coastal areas of the island. Also introduced were brush-tailed possums, which are very numerous in the northern half of the island and rather destructive to the native bush. Stewart Island has lots of NZ fur seals too.

Around the shores are clusters of bull kelp, common kelp, fine red weeds, delicate green thallus and bladders of all shapes and sizes.

Orientation

Stewart Island is 64km long and 40km across at its widest, has less than 20km of roads and a rocky coastline incised by numerous inlets, the largest of these being Paterson. The highest point on the island is Mt Anglem at 980m. The principal settlement is Oban

Island was a great flat fish caught by Maui; the South Island his canoe and Rakiura the anchor – 'Te Punga o te Waka a Maui' being the legendary name for the latter.

The first European visitor was Captain Cook, who sailed around the eastern, southern and western coasts in 1770 but could not make up his mind whether it was an island or a peninsula. Deciding it was part of the South Island mainland he called it Cape South. Several decades later the sealing vessel *Pegasus*, under the command of Captain Chase, circumnavigated Stewart Island and proved it to be an island. It was named after William Stewart, first officer of the *Pegasus*, who charted the southern coast of the island in detail.

In June 1864 Stewart and the adjacent islands were bought from the Maori for the sum of £6000. Early industries consisted of sealing, timber milling, fish curing and ship building. The discovery of gold and tin towards the end of the 19th century also led

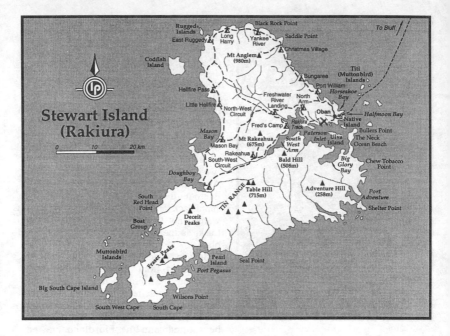

Stewart Island (Rakiura)

(which takes its name from a place in Scotland), on the shores of Halfmoon Bay, with roads extending a few kilometres further out from there.

Information

The Stewart Island Visitor Information Centre (☎ 219 1218; fax 219 1555) is at the DOC Visitors Centre just a few minutes walk from the wharf. In addition to practical information on the island it has good displays on flora, fauna, walks and so on, and a summer activities program in January. The friendly staff have many ideas on how you could spend your time on the island.

Several handy and cheap pamphlets on tramps on the island, including *Halfmoon Bay Walks*; *Rakiura Track* and *North West Circuit* (all $1 each) can be purchased here. You can store gear at the DOC centre while you're walking ($2.50 small locker, $5 large).

The Adventure Centre (☎ 219 1134) at the

end of the wharf is a booking agency for activities on the island and the Agency (☎ 219 1171), also near the wharf, has information on a wide range of accommodation.

The general store, Ship to Shore, at Halfmoon Bay has a wide variety of supplies such as dried foods, gas canisters, fresh fruit and vegetables and hardware, as well as EFTPOS. Stewart Island Travel also has EFTPOS, fax and photocopying facilities.

The postal agency is at the Southern Air depot on Elgin Terrace, about five minutes walk from the wharf. Stewart Island is a local (not long-distance) phone call from Invercargill. There are card phones outside Stewart Island Travel, at the Shearwater Inn and coinphones in the hotel foyer and, after hours, on the wharf at the Adventure Centre. There are public toilets at DOC, the South Sea Hotel, the wharf and the public hall.

Essential companions (if you can get them) are *Stewart Island Explored* by John Hall-Jones, *The Last Refuge* by Erwin

Brinkmann & Neville Peat and *Rakiura* by Basil Howard.

Ulva Island

Ever dreamed of paradise? It may well be Ulva Island. It is only 260 hectares, but a lot is packed into it. An early naturalist, Charles Traill, was honorary postmaster here. He would hoist a flag to signal to other islands, including Stewart, that the mail had arrived and hopefuls would come from everywhere. It fell out of favour, however, being replaced by a postal service at Oban. A year later, in 1922, the island was declared a bird sanctuary.

Ulva is a joy for birders. As soon as you get off the launch the air is alive with the song of tuis and bellbirds. You see kaka, weka, kakariki and kereru (native pigeon). This has a lot to do with the absence of predators on the island.

The island's forest has a mossy floor and many tracks intersect the stands of rimu, miro, totara and rata – all of which, added to the delight of the birdsong, create a setting you won't forget. The birds come so close that you don't even need a telephoto lens.

A number of tour operators pass here on their way to view salmon farms. If you would rather follow tracks to quiet, private beaches than visit a commercial salmon farm in Big Glory Bay, alight here while the launch excursion visits the farms. They will pick you up when they stop on the return trip to let the other passengers briefly explore the island.

You can get to Ulva by water taxi from Golden Bay wharf; expect to pay about $15 to $20 for a return trip. You can arrange the length of your stay with booking agencies.

Things to See

The **Rakiura Museum** on Ayr St is no Victoria & Albert but it's worth a visit if you're interested in the history of the island – it features whaling, sealing, tin mining, timber milling and fishing. The collection of shipping memorabilia includes scrimshaw and photographs of the many ferries that plied across Foveaux Strait.

Particularly interesting is the section dealing with Maori heritage. It is believed that Maori have lived on Rakiura for 800 years or more. The muttonbirds (titi) on the islands adjacent to Rakiura were an important seasonal food source for the southern Maori. Today's southern Maori population is predominantly Ngai Tahu, with earlier lineages to Kati Mamoe and Waitaho. There is a dolphin teeth necklace on display, alongside a collection of adzes and barter goods traded between Maori and whalers, such as pipes from The Neck.

The museum is open from 10 am to noon Monday to Saturday, noon to 2 pm on Sunday ($1, children 50c).

The **library** is on Ayr St and a craft shop and gallery, **The Fernery** (☎ 219 1453), is 400m south from town in a bush setting, and housed in a new building designed to look like an original island cottage. Here, tiny fernlets from the hen-and-chicken fern, *Aplenium bulbiferum*, are placed in small egg-shaped containers and grow, ultimately to four or five feet tall. There are a number of other tasteful items for sale.

At Harrold Bay, about 3km north-east of town, is an **old stone house** built by Lewis Acker around 1835. It's one of the oldest stone buildings in New Zealand.

Walking

If you want to visit Stewart Island, plan on spending a few days so you can enjoy the beaches, seals and rare bird and plant life. There are many walks on the island; although some take only a couple of hours, a day trip to Stewart Island is hardly worthwhile as it is tramper's heaven. You could spend weeks tramping here.

There is a good network of tracks and huts in the northern part of the island, but the southern part is undeveloped and can be very desolate and isolated. At the DOC office, buy your Great Walks pass and pay your hut fees for the more distant walks. Get their pamphlets before you set off – they have detailed

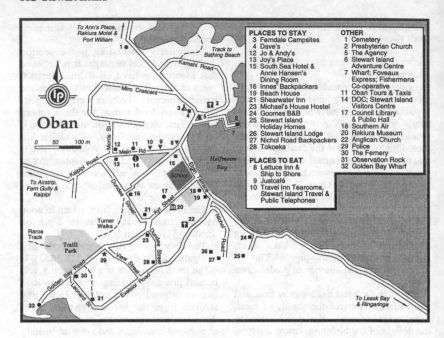

PLACES TO STAY
3 Ferndale Campsites
4 Dave's
13 Jo & Andy's
13 Joy's Place
15 South Sea Hotel &
   Annie Hansen's
   Dining Room
16 Innes' Backpackers
19 Beach House
21 Shearwater Inn
23 Michael's House Hostel
24 Goomes B&B
25 Stewart Island
   Holiday Homes
26 Stewart Island Lodge
27 Nichol Road Backpackers
28 Tokoeka

PLACES TO EAT
8 Lettuce Inn &
   Ship to Shore
9 Justcafé
10 Travel Inn Tearooms,
   Stewart Island Travel &
   Public Telephones

OTHER
1 Cemetery
2 Presbyterian Church
5 The Agency
6 Stewart Island
   Adventure Centre
7 Wharf; Foveaux
   Express; Fishermens
   Co-operative
11 Oban Tours & Taxis
14 DOC; Stewart Island
   Visitors Centre
17 Council Library
   & Public Hall
18 Southern Air
20 Rakiura Museum
22 Anglican Church
29 Police
30 The Fernery
31 Observation Rock
32 Golden Bay Wharf

information on the walks, the time they take, when to go and hut facilities.

You are advised not to go off on your own, particularly from the established walks, unless you have discussed your itinerary with someone beforehand. Foam rubber mattresses, wood stoves and billies are provided at each hut but you need to take food, sleeping bags, ground sheets, eating and cooking utensils, first-aid equipment and so on with you. If you have them, a tent and portable gas stove are very useful as the huts can get packed out at certain times of the year. A stove is also a boon when firewood is wet.

The **Rakiura Track**, starting from Oban, makes an interesting three-day circular tramp. Huts at Port William and North Arm have space for 30 trampers and cost $8 per night or camping is $6. (There's a maximum stay of two nights in a hut.) Huts and camping cost $4 from April to October. This is one of the Great Walks which requires a

pass. The track is well defined (as it has been extensively boardwalked) and it's an easy walk, the major drawback being that it gets very crowded in summer.

The northern portion of the island has the **North-West Circuit Track** but it is long, some eight to 10 days. Fees for most of the North-West Circuit huts are $4 (children $2). The tracks further away from Halfmoon Bay can be very muddy and quite steep in places. These two longer walks are detailed in Lonely Planet's *Tramping in New Zealand*.

Around Halfmoon Bay there are a number of shorter walks. Take the 15-minute walk to Observation Rock which affords good views over Paterson Inlet. You can continue past the Stone House at Harrold Bay to Ackers Point, where there are good views of Foveaux Strait. Seals and penguins can be seen near the rocks and this is the site of a shearwater colony. There are many other possible walks outlined in DOC's *Halfmoon Bay Walks*.

OUTER ISLANDS

Organised Tours

In summer there are minibus tours around Halfmoon Bay, Horseshoe Bay and various other places. They are zippy little one-hour trips for around $15 because there really isn't very far you can drive on Stewart Island! Check with Stewart Island Travel (☎ 219 1269) or the notice boards next to the store.

Bravo Adventure Cruises (☎ 219 1144) has daily trips to Ulva Island and salmon farms for $45. Moana Charters (☎ 219 1202) runs half-day fishing and sightseeing trips for up to 21 people for $40 a head. Thorfinn Charters (☎ 219 1210) has a 30ft (9m) launch available for half-day ($45) and full-day ($65) cruises; nature tours are their speciality and they also run fishing trips. The *Southern Isle* (☎ 219 1133) does half-day fishing trips for $45 per person and also visits salmon farms and Ulva Island.

Kayaks can be rented for around $45 a day for independent exploring of Paterson Inlet, and guided kayaking is also offered; see the visitors centre for information. The inlet is 100 sq km of bush-clad sheltered waterways, with 20 islands, DOC huts and two navigable rivers. A popular trip is a paddle to Freshwater River Landing (7km upriver from the inlet) followed by a three to four-hour walk to Mason Bay to see kiwis in the wild.

Kiwi Spotting This is one of the best eco-activities of New Zealand. The search for *Apteryx australis lawryi* would be a difficult one if you did not know where to look. The Stewart Island kiwi is a distinct sub-species of the brown kiwi, with larger legs and beak than its northern cousins. These kiwis are common over much of the island, particularly around beaches where they forage for sandhoppers under washed-up kelp. Unusually, *A. australis lawryi* is active during the day as well as at night – the birds are forced to forage for longer to attain breeding condition. Many trampers on the North-West Circuit spot them, especially at Mason Bay.

On any one night in summer you will probably see about three to five kiwis on Ocean Beach. Nowadays, they are quite used to human voyeurs and they even let people come close enough to take video footage.

Numbers are limited for the kiwis' protection. Only 15 people can travel to Ocean Beach on the MV *Volantis* to view this flightless marvel. The demand outstrips supply, and they don't go every day, so make sure you book ahead with Bravo Adventure Cruises (☎ 249 1144) to avoid disappointment. The tours cost $55.

Places to Stay

The DOC Stewart Island Visitors Centre (☎ 219 1218) has information on all accommodation options. There is a free camping ground at Apple Bridge and Kaipipi Rd, but it's definitely basic, with a fireplace, wood and water supply and pit toilets only. It's about a half-hour walk from the wharf along Main Rd.

Ferndale Campsites (☎ 219 1176) at Halfmoon Bay has tent sites for $5; it has an ablution block with coin-operated showers ($2 for six minutes), toilets, picnic tables and rubbish collection.

Ann Pullen of *Ann's Place* (☎ 219 1065) offers tramping-style accommodation in a small house behind the main house for $10 per night. It's very basic, but then so is the price, and it's a supremely friendly place to stay. *Nichol Rd Backpackers* (☎ 219 1328) is a little more in the backpackers mould and has twin rooms for $36 and folding beds at $16 per person.

Several homes on the island offer hostel-style accommodation at hostel (or lower) rates. The visitor centre has the latest lists. *Jo & Andy's B&B* (☎ 219 1230), on the corner of Main Rd and Morris St, has one twin and one double for $32 (linen $3 extra). *Joy's Place* (☎ 219 1376) has bunkroom beds for $15, and there is definitely no drinking or smoking here.

There are a number of converted bachelor pads on the island. *Michael's House Hostel* (☎ 219 1425) can accommodate up to six people in his house at the start of the Golden Bay Rd. The cost is $15; bring your own sleeping bag and food. *Dave's* (☎ 219 1078) is another place at $15. *Innes' Backpackers*

(☎ 219 1080) is another possibility at $15, dropping to $10 on the 3rd night. The visitors centre will show you photos of all these places and direct you to them.

The *Shearwater Inn* (☎ 219 1114) on Ayr St, in the centre of the township, has singles/doubles (linen included) at $36/60, or $24 per person in larger shared rooms (three or four people). More basic backpacker rooms are $14 in the dorm, or $32 for twins. The inn has a restaurant serving breakfast and dinner, and there are limited kitchen facilities for guests.

The *South Sea Hotel* (☎ 219 1059), close to the wharf, costs $40/80 for singles/twins, or $95 for a room with a sea view. A room at the *Rakiura Motel* (☎ 219 1096), 1.5km from the township, costs $80 for two ($15 each extra adult). The central *Beach House* (☎ 219 1059) overlooking the bay has three-bedroom motel-style units for $120 a double and $15 per extra adult. The glamorous *Stewart Island Lodge* (☎ 219 1085) is much more expensive. Its four rooms all have private facilities and cost about $197 per person in twin share rooms (or $237 for a single), including all meals, or around $90 less for B&B only.

Another option on Stewart Island is to hire one of the many self-contained flats or holiday homes. Jeanette and Peter Goomes (☎ 217 6585; 219 1057) of *Stewart Island Holiday Homes* have two houses, each sleeping up to 10 people, about a five-minute walk from the town. The cost is $95 for two plus $15 for an extra adult (children $7.50). The Goomes also have the pick of the B&B options, charging $65/120 for singles/doubles. Other B&Bs outside the town include *The Retreat* (☎ 219 1071) on Horseshoe Bay, which has doubles for $60.

The self-contained *Gibb's House* (☎ 219 1135) is $90 a double, and $15 per extra adult. Heti Atkins (☎ 219 1274), who enjoys the company of travellers, rents out a self-contained flat at $48 for four people.

Other houses include *Tokoeka* (☎ 219 1143), which costs $85 for two and $15 each extra adult, and *Tenola* (☎ 219 1133) which costs $60 and $15 per extra. For details of other rental houses contact the visitor centre or the Agency (☎ 219 1171).

Places to Eat

Dining options are limited. The South Sea Hotel has *Annie Hansen's* which features local seafood on the menu. The *Shearwater Inn* has a blackboard menu every night and is open from September until April. *Justcafé* fills the void for coffee and light meals, a good alternative to the *Travel Inn*. Over on Horseshoe Bay, the *Retreat* has a cafe.

You can get basic necessities from the general store, buy fresh fish and crayfish from the locals, catch your own fish or bring food across from Invercargill and prepare meals yourself. Often the Fishermen's Coop on the Halfmoon Bay wharf and Southern Seafoods at Horseshoe Bay have fresh fish and crayfish for sale.

The only place for nightlife is the pub, the Shearwater Inn – observe the evening life cycle of the endangered, white-gumbooted Stewart Islander.

Getting There & Away

For a quick look at Stewart Island, inquire at the Invercargill visitors centre about packages, which can be good value and include airfares, accommodation and tours.

Air Southern Air (☎ 0800 658 876) flies from Invercargill to Stewart Island for $68 one way and $123 return (children half-price). The student/YHA stand-by fare of $37 (return $70) is as cheap as the ferry. Be at the airport 30 minutes before departure; it's a good idea to telephone ahead to see if any discounted seats are available – Invercargill hostels can do this for you. Flights go three times a day and take 20 minutes to hop over the narrow strait. Southern Air also has connections from Dunedin to Stewart Island for $95 one-way.

The bus from the Ryans Creek airstrip to 'town' on Stewart Island is included in the airfare. Baggage allowance is only 15kg per person, and excess luggage rates are charged.

Boat Stewart Island Marine's (☎ 212 7660)

Foveaux Express runs from Bluff to Stewart Island for $37/74 one-way/return (children half-price). There are departures twice daily at 9.30 am and 5 pm in summer (once on Sunday at 5 pm). In winter, there are no sailings on Saturday. Book at least a few days ahead in summer – the ferry only takes 62 passengers. The crossing takes one hour across Foveaux Strait, noted for its often stormy weather – it can be a rough trip.

Campbelltown Passenger (☎ 212 7404) connects with the ferry and picks up from anywhere in Invercargill.

Getting Around

Stewart Island Travel (☎ 219 1269) arranges bus tours, taxis, accommodation and rental cars. Go there for travel advice, especially air and boat charters. With a lack of roads, a boat trip is a good option to get a feel for the island.

Oban Taxis & Tours (☎ 219 1456) near the wharf provides a 24-hour taxi service and runs bus tours. A couple of places on the island have mountain bikes for hire.

A number of charter boats are available for pick-ups and drop-offs on remote parts of the island. The Stewart Island Water Taxi's (☎ 219 1394) *Flyer* takes six passengers; to Ulva Island costs $20 return for one person ($15 for two or more) and a half-day sightseeing trip costs about $80 per person. Seaview Tours (☎ 219 1014) also has Ulva Island trips for up to eight passengers and offers a water taxi charter service.

Chatham Islands

The Chathams are an isolated, mysterious and wild group of islands, very much off the beaten track. Given the name Rekohu (Misty Sun) by the Moriori, they are way out in the Pacific, about 770km east of Christchurch. There are 10 islands in the group but apart from the 50 or so people on Pitt Island, only Chatham Island, with 700 people, is significantly populated.

The islands offer a world of contrast – rugged coastlines and towering cliffs, volcanic peaks, lagoons and peat bogs, sweeping beaches devoid of human habitation, isolated farms, wind-stunted vegetation and dense patches of forest. Apart from farming and tourism, the other main industry is crayfish processing and there are plants at Waitangi, Kaingaroa, Owenga and Port Hutt. These four towns look like neglected junk heaps choking in the flotsam and jetsam of their *raison d'être*. They may not be flash, but they exude a nuggety, dilapidated charm.

History

Chatham Island is renowned for being the last home of the Moriori, an isolated group of Polynesians. They were here before the Maori settlement of New Zealand, but with the arrival of Europeans things rapidly began to go wrong.

A British expedition commanded by Lieutenant Broughton first arrived at the island in 1791 and even that initial visit resulted in a clash, at aptly named Skirmish Bay (now Kaingaroa), and one Moriori was killed. Two memorials remain at the spot to this day. In the 1820s and 1830s European and American whalers and sealers began to arrive and then, in 1835, a Maori tribe, the Ngati-awa, was resettled in the Chathams. The impact on the peaceable Moriori was dramatic as the Ngati-awa, under Chief Pomare, established themselves by right of conquest; the Moriori population crashed from around 2000 at the time of the first European arrival in 1791 to only about 100 in the 1860s. By the beginning of the 20th century there were just 12 full-blooded Moriori left.

The Maori leader and prophet Te Kooti was imprisoned here in the 19th century, after he had eluded the British troops and officials on the mainland for many years. He turned to peace and established the Ringatu faith while incarcerated.

Fauna

There are 18 species of bird unique to the islands and, because of their isolation, there is a large degree of endemism, as with the local tomtit, pigeon and robin. Entry to the

OUTER ISLANDS

The Last Moriori?

One of the most fascinating aspects of the Chathams is the cultural legacy of the Moriori. There are still Moriori descendants on the islands and there are a few remnants of the once flourishing culture.

There has been much speculation as to where the Moriori came from. It is now generally accepted that they were Polynesians, like the Maori, who sailed to the Chathams from New Zealand. The date of their arrival is in dispute, however, as there is little archaeological evidence, but it was some time between 900 AD and 1500 AD.

Once in the Chathams they began to develop a separate identity from the mainland Maori. They did not have rigid social divisions, they forbade tribal warfare and settled disputes on a one-to-one basis with hand-to-hand combat, and their language developed subtle differences. Most importantly, they carved their symbols into trees (dendroglyphs) and into the rocks which fringe Te Whanga Lagoon (petroglyphs). When the HMS *Chatham* visited the island in 1791 there were believed to be about 2000 Moriori on the islands.

From about November 1835, groups of Maori began to arrive in the Chathams and soon there were about 900 new residents made up of the Ngati Tama and Ngati Mutunga of the Taranaki Ati Awa. They began to occupy the land in a process known as *takahi*, killing about 300 Moriori who resisted, and enslaving others. By 1841 there were believed to be only 160 Moriori and over 400 Maori and it was not until two years later that the Maori released the last of the Moriori slaves. In 1870 the Native Land Court Hearings recognised that the Maori had sovereignty over 97% of the Chathams by right of conquest; small reserves were created for the surviving 90 Moriori. The Moriori and Maori intermarried in time and slowly the unique identity of the Moriori faded. Their language died with the last great Moriori scholar, Hirawanu Tapu, in 1900. There were only 12 full-blooded Moriori left at this stage.

The last full-blooded Moriori was Tommy Solomon, who died in 1933. His passing was seen at the time as the extinction of a particular race but it was far from that. His three sons and two daughters are identified as Moriori and there were many other families on the island who claimed Moriori ancestry.

There are now believed to be over 300 Moriori descendants and there has been a revival of Moriori consciousness, particularly strong after the building of the Solomon monument at Manukau Point near Owenga in the south-east of the island. Today Moriori, Pakeha and Maori live side by side as Chatham Islanders. ■

OUTER ISLANDS

sanctuaries, such as those at Pitt and Rangatira (South East) Island, is prohibited but many species can still be seen. DOC staff will outline the best viewing spots for bird-watchers. Rare and unusual birds include the endangered black robin, which at one stage was perilously close to extinction in its last refuge, Little Mangere Island near Pitt Island (read more about the black robin story in the Fauna & Flora colour section). The rare taiko (*Pterodroma magentae*) was recently rediscovered nesting in the Tuku River region of the south coast of Chatham. Black swans, pukekos, wekas and many species of ducks are common.

There is a fur seal colony near Kaingaroa in the north-east of Chatham Island.

Information

Waitangi is the only sizeable town on the islands. There are a couple of shops, a hotel, motel, tourist lodge and a post office with savings bank facilities. The free fortnightly *Chatham Islander* carries the local news. The islands also have their own radio station, Radio Weka, and TV station (Chathams Television) run in conjunction with TVNZ. There is an STD and fax link with the mainland. The signposted DOC office (☎ 305 0098) is in Te One; ring before you go as it is likely to be unattended.

Information on the islands is available from Air Chathams or the local information centre (☎ 305 0443). *A Land Apart*, by Michael King & Robin Morrison, provides a wealth of information about the islands.

The Chatham Islands are very exposed but they have a temperate climate. Average daily temperatures vary from 12°C to 18°C in February and 6°C to 10°C in July. The best time to visit is in December and January; often the temperatures then reach 23°C to 24°C.

Chatham Islands time is 45 minutes ahead of mainland New Zealand time.

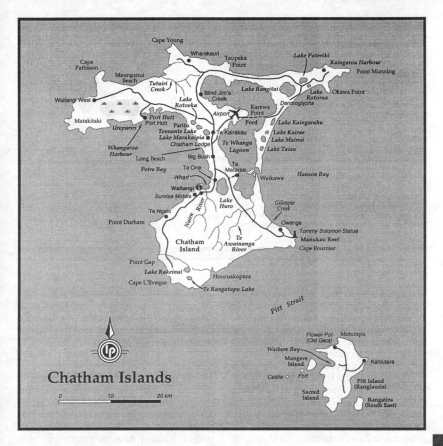

Chatham Islands

0   10   20 km

Things to See & Do

The islands have plenty of fine beaches popular for fishing and particularly for catching crayfish. Crayfish are a major industry in the Chatham Islands, and they're exported to North America and Japan. Six crayfish can be caught per person per day and 10 paua are allowed each person; check with DOC in Te One. Scuba divers can explore the shipwrecks around the islands while trampers will also find interesting country to explore, particularly at the southern end of Chatham Island. DOC has set up six formal reserves, developed with walking tracks of anything from an hour to a full day in duration. The northern end of Chatham is flat and windswept. There's a small museum with Moriori artefacts in the council offices.

Three unusual attractions are the tree carvings, rock engravings and fossilised black sharks' teeth. The 200-year-old Moriori **tree carvings** (dendroglyphs) can be found in a grove adjacent to the old Te Hapupu aerodrome, in a signposted and fenced-off area. These mysterious carvings are gradually disappearing. The **rock engravings** (petroglyphs) are found on the shores of Te Whanga Lagoon, not far from the airstrip.

A Paua Recipe

First things first – what is a paua? It is quite a large shellfish with a green-black body and a concave shell which is rough on the outside and rather beautiful on the inside. In other countries it is called abalone.

There are parts of NZ where you can pick up unprepared paua quite cheaply. It is then up to you to prepare it in a fashion that would cost about $45 for two in a restaurant.

Try the following recipe (provided by the Goomes family of Oban, Rakiura):

First, stir-fry the onion rings from one brown onion with one minced clove of garlic and a dab (teaspoon) of butter. Cut the skirt off the paua then beat the flesh until tender (with a meat mallet) – the shell can be cleaned later and used as a receptacle for knick-knacks. Slice the paua into 5mm-thick slices and cook with the onion rings for exactly three minutes. Serve on a lettuce leaf with lemon and tomato wedges. Voilà! ∎

The **fossilised sharks' teeth** can be found at Blind Jim's Creek, also on the shores of Te Whanga Lagoon. The teeth are about 40 million years old and a local heritage – please leave them where you see them. Their appearance here, pushed up by the waves of the lagoon, has not yet been fully explained.

One unusual sight is the **statue** of the 'last Moriori', Tommy Solomon, at Manukau Point. Tommy's eyes seem to follow you as you scramble around the rocks below (see the boxed text earlier in this section).

Manukau Point will host a special party on 31 December 1999. Because of the kink in the International Dateline it claims to be the first land to see in the year 2000.

Places to Stay & Eat

Note that prices for accommodation and meals are invariably quoted *without* GST included. Add 12.5% to all prices.

The *Hotel Chathams* (☎ 305 0048), Waterfront Rd, Waitangi, has singles for $55, twins and doubles for $85. The hotel also has a small souvenir shop (where you can get the highly sought-after Chathams T-shirt). It also hires out cars and organises trips. Meals are served and breakfast is $10, lunch $15

and an excellent three-course dinner is $28. The same owners run *Travellers Rest Guesthouse* (☎ 305 0492) next door, offering more luxurious accommodation at $100/110 for singles/doubles with en suite.

Rooms at the *Sunrise Motels* (☎ 305 0157), about 500m south of Waitangi, cost $45 for singles and a self-contained unit is $65 for two. Meals are available or there are kitchens to prepare your own meals, unlike at the hotel and the lodge. The owners also run the good *Roo's Roost Backpackers*, in central Waitangi near the community hall, which costs $25 per person.

The more upmarket *Chatham Lodge* (☎ 305 0196), north of the Kaingaroa and Airport Roads junction and well signposted, has singles/doubles for $75/80 or $130/190 with all meals. There are package tour rates and a self-contained cottage (sleeps four) costs $100 per day. The lodge hires out 4WDs and boats and activities offered include diving, fishing, boating, horse riding, tramping in nearby Henga Reserve and the world's most easterly windsurfing. Meals are $15 for breakfast and lunch, and $25 for dinner.

Homestays with locals are also possible,

especially when all other accommodation is booked up. The Smith family farmstay *Te Matarae* (☎ 305 0144), near the shores of Te Whanga Lagoon, is surrounded by natural bush and has a small pool. They have singles/doubles with en suite for $65/75 B&B per person and prepare great dinners for $15.

Ask permission from the locals before camping anywhere. If you ask around, it may be possible to camp at the Norm Kirk Centre, just north of Waitangi on the road to the airport. The centre has showers and cooking facilities.

A new addition to the dining scene is the *Waitangi Cafe* between the post office and police station. It has standard takeaway and tearoom fare.

You can buy crayfish and blue cod at the packaging factory in Waitangi. Flounder and whitebait can be caught in the lagoon, and paua and kina gathered just offshore. For the true gourmets there are swan egg omelettes and weka (in season) – yes the weka is consumed here as it is not native to the islands. Entertainment – bring your own or head to the Hotel Chathams, the local, to listen to a few yarns and trade friendly jibes.

Getting There & Away

Apart from a periodic freight-only cargo ship, the only transport to the islands is by air with Air Chathams (☎ 305 0209), which can also be booked through Air New Zealand. Air Chathams flies to/from Wellington on Monday, Wednesday and Friday, and Christchurch on Monday and Thursday. One-way fares from either destination are $354 or Super Thrifty fares booked one month in advance are $212, which put the Chathams within reach of many more travellers. The flight takes three hours and since there are only minimal seats available it's wise to book well ahead.

Getting Around

Beyond Waitangi most roads are unsealed and there is no public transport. Accommodation owners will pick you up from Karewa airport if they know of your arrival, other-

wise on occasion visitors have been left stranded at the airport. Chatham Motors (☎ 305 0093) hires out 4WDs, starting at around $60 per day (kilometres not included). Chathams Lodge, Te Matarae and Hotel Chathams hire out vehicles – expect to pay around $75 for a car, around $100 for a 4WD, inclusive of kilometres. It's also quite easy to hitch around the island.

Air Chathams operates a light aircraft (five-seat Cessna) for flightseeing and for trips to Pitt Island. It may be possible to hitch a ride with fishing vessels across to Pitt Island, but the seas are very rough, often with mountainous waves.

Tours are available from Chathams Lodge; prices are on application. It is relatively easy to hire a car and see most of the island's sights by yourself. Walking is a popular form of transport but check with DOC about access across private land.

Subantarctic Islands

New Zealand administers a number of subantarctic islands – the Snares, Campbell, Auckland, Bounty and Antipodes islands – where there are established nature reserves. Entry is restricted to three of the five island groups and is by permit only. To get some idea of this wild environment go to the Southland Museum & Art Gallery in Invercargill and watch the *Roaring Forties Experience* audiovisual.

The islands have a colourful human history – sealing, shipwrecks and forlorn attempts at farming. Now the islands are important as a reserve for remaining areas of vegetation unmodified by humans and breeding grounds for seabirds, penguins and mammals such as the elephant seal.

Few are fortunate enough to visit these remote islands but increasing eco-tourism possibilities, well-managed and guided, are possible by boat but expensive. A 15-day cruise, which takes in all the islands, will cost $2500 or more, all inclusive. Fiordland Ecology Holidays (☎/fax (03) 249 6600) in

Manapouri takes scientific trips to the subantarctic islands every year and sells left-over berths to help fund the trips. Southern Heritage Expeditions (☎ (03) 359 7711), PO Box 20219, Bishopdale, Christchurch has a large range of tours. If you have the money you will consider it well spent, because of the rich variety of flora and fauna encountered.

SNARES ISLANDS

The Snares are famous for the incredible number of sooty shearwaters (muttonbirds) which breed there. It has been estimated that on any one evening during the season there will be six million in the air before they crash land to find their burrows. Other birds found here are the endemic Snares crested penguin, cape pigeon and Bullers mollymawks.

AUCKLAND ISLANDS

These are probably the most accessible of the islands, especially Enderby Island, but it was closed to visitors in 1998 (along with Campbell Island) because a mystery illness was killing sea lions. At Sandy Bay on Enderby you can see Hooker's sea lions. Many species of birds also make Enderby their home (either temporary or permanent), including endemic shags, the flightless teal and the royal albatross. Skuas (gull-like birds) are ever present in the skies above the sea lion colony. Settlement was attempted in Erebus Cove, and it was not until 1992 that the last introduced cattle were destroyed. On Disappointment Island there are some 50,000 white-capped mollymawks.

CAMPBELL ISLAND

This is the only inhabited island in the New Zealand subantarctic islands, as there is a contingent from the NZ meteorological service stationed here. Apart from a few humans it is the true domain of pelagic bird species. It is estimated that there are over 7500 pairs of southern royal albatross here, as well as colonies of greyheaded and black-browed mollymawks.

ANTIPODES ISLANDS

These islands get their name from the fact that they are opposite latitude 0° at Greenwich, England. The real treat on this island is the endemic Antipodes Island parakeet, which is found with, but does not breed with, the red-crowned parakeet (similar to the NZ species of parakeet). In the short grass at the top of the islands, wandering albatross nest.

BOUNTY ISLANDS

Landing is not permitted on any of the 13 Bounty Islands – there is a good chance that you would step on the wildlife anyway, as the 135 hectares of land that makes up these granite islands is covered with mammals or birds. There are literally thousands of erect crested penguins, fulmar prions and salvins mollymawks clustered in crevices, near the lower slopes and on all other available pieces of real estate.

OUTER ISLANDS

Glossary

This glossary is a list of Maori and English terms you will come across in New Zealand.

AA – New Zealand Automobile Association; the organisation which provides road information and roadside assistance

afghan – popular homemade chocolate biscuit

All Black – a member of NZ's revered national rugby union team (the name comes from 'All Backs', which the press called the NZ rugby team on an early visit to England)

Aoraki – Maori name for Mt Cook, meaning 'the cloud piercer'

Aotearoa – Maori name for NZ; literally 'land of the long white cloud'; jokingly translated as 'land of the wrong white crowd'

atua – spirit or gods

bach – a holiday home, usually a wooden cottage (pronounced 'batch'); see also *crib*

Barrier, the – local name for Great Barrier Island in the Hauraki Gulf

baths – swimming pool, often referred to as municipal baths

Beehive – Parliament House in Wellington, so-called because of its distinctive shape

black-water rafting – rafting or tubing underground in a cave or *tomo*

boozer – a public bar

box of birds – an expression meaning 'on top of the world', usually in response to 'How are you?'

bro – literally 'brother'; usually meaning mate, as in 'just off to see the bros'

bush – heavily forested areas

Buzzy Bee – a child's toy as essential to NZ child development as dinosaur models; a wooden bee dragged along by a string to produce a whirring noise

BYO – bring your own (drinks and/or alcohol)

Captain Cooker – a large feral pig, introduced by Captain Cook and now roaming wild over most of NZ's rugged bush land

CHE – not the revolutionary but Crown Health Enterprise (regional, privatised health authorities)

chillie bin – cooler; esky; large insulated box for keeping food and drink cold

choice – fantastic; great

ciggies – cigarettes

crib – the name for a *bach* in Otago and Southland

cuzzies – cousins; relatives

dairy – a small corner store which sells just about everything, especially milk, bread, the newspaper and ice cream; a convenience store

Dalmatian – a term applied to the predominantly Yugoslav gum diggers who fossicked for kauri gum (used as furniture polish) in the gum fields of Northland

DOC – Department of Conservation (or *Te Papa Atawhai*); the government department which administers national parks and thus all tracks and huts

domain – an open grassed area in a town or city, often the focus of the civic amenities such as gardens, picnic areas and bowling clubs

DOSLI – former name of Land Information NZ

doss house – temporary accommodation

farmstay – accommodation on a typical Kiwi farm where you are encouraged to join with in the day-to-day activities

fiscal envelope – money set aside by the NZ government to make financial reparation for injustices to Maori people since the Treaty of Waitangi

football – rugby, either union or league

freezing works – slaughterhouse

Gilbert – the most popular brand of rugby football

Godzone – New Zealand (God's own country)

good as gold, good as – very good

greenstone – jade, pounamu

haka – the traditional challenge; war dance
hakari – feast
handle – a beer glass with a handle
hangi – oven made by digging a hole and steaming food in baskets over embers in the hole; a feast of traditional Maori food
hapu – sub-tribe or smaller tribal grouping
hard case – an unusual or strong-willed character
Hawaiki – the unknown place in the Pacific from where the Maori tribes (the original seven waka) came
heitiki – carved, stylised human figure worn around the neck, often a carved representation of an ancestor; also called a *tiki*
hoa – friend
hokey pokey – a delicious variety of ice cream with butterscotch chips
hoki – a fish common in fish and chip shops
homestay – accommodation in a family house where you are treated (temporarily, thank God) as one of the family
hongi – Maori greeting; the pressing of noses and sharing of life breath
hui – gather; meeting
huntaway – a loud-barking sheep-herding dog, usually a sturdy black-and-brown hound

Ika a Maui, Te – the North Island
Instant Kiwi – state-run lottery
Interislander – the ferry which makes the crossing across Cook Strait between the North and South islands
'Is it what!' – strong affirmation or agreement; 'Yes isn't it!'
iwi – a large tribal grouping with lineage to the original migration from Hawaiki; people; tribe

jandals – sandals; flip-flops; thongs; usually rubber footwear
jersey – a jumper, usually woollen (also the shirt worn by rugby players, eg grab him by the jersey)
judder bars – bumps in the road to make you drive slowly; speed humps

K Rd – Karangahape Rd in Auckland
kai – food; any word with kai in it has some food connection
kainga – village; pre-European unfortified Maori village
ka pai – good; excellent
karakia – prayer
kaumatua – highly respected members of a tribe; the people you would ask for permission to enter a marae.
kina – sea urchins; a Maori delicacy
kiwi – the flightless, nocturnal brown bird with a long beak which is the national symbol; the New Zealand dollar; a New Zealander; a member of the national rugby league team; an adjective to mean anything of or relating to NZ
kiwi bear – the introduced Australian ringtailed possum; also called an opossum
kiwi fruit – a small, succulent fruit with fuzzy brown skin and juicy green flesh; a Chinese gooseberry
koe – you (singular)
koha – a donation
kohanga reo – schools where Maori language and culture are at the forefront of the education process; also called 'language nest' schools
koutou – you (plural)
kumara – Polynesian sweet potato; a Maori staple food
kunekune – another type of wild pig introduced by Chinese gold-diggers in the 19th century
Kupe – an early Polynesian navigator, from Hawaiki, credited with the discovery of the islands that are now NZ

league – rugby league football
lounge bar – a more upmarket bar than a public bar; called a 'ladies bar' in some countries

mana – the spiritual quality of a person or object; authority of a chief or priest
manaia – a traditional carving design; literally means 'bird-headed man'
manuhiri – visitor; guest
Maori – indigenous people of New Zealand
Maoritanga – Maori culture

marae – sacred ground in front of the Maori meeting house; also used to refer to the traditional ancestral village of a tribe

Maui – an important figure in Maori mythology

mere – flat, greenstone war club

metal/metalled road – gravel road

MMP – Mixed Member Proportional; a cumbersome electoral system used in NZ and Germany; a limited form of proportional voting

moko – facial tattoo

Mongrel Mob – a large, well-organised and mainly Maori bikie gang

Moriori – an isolated Polynesian group; inhabitants of the Chatham Islands

motor camp – well-equipped camping grounds with tent sites, caravan and camper-van sites, on-site caravans, cabins and tourist flats

motorway – freeway or expressway

naiad – a rigid hull inflatable boat (used for dolphin swimming, whale-watching etc)

ngati – people; tribe (in the South Island; Ngai)

nifty-fifty – 50cc motorcycle

nui – carved ceremonial poles of peace and war

NZ – the universal appellation for New Zealand; pronounced 'enzed'

o – of

pa – fortified Maori village, usually on a hill top

Pacific Rim – a term used to describe modern NZ cuisine; cuisine with an innovative use of local produce, especially seafood, with imported styles

Pakeha – Maori for a white or European person; once derogatory, and still considered so by some, this term is now widely used for white New Zealanders

pakihi – unproductive and often swampy land on South Island's west coast; pronounced 'par-kee'

papa – large blue-grey mudstones; the word comes from the Maori for the Earth Mother

parapenting – paragliding

paua – abalone; tough shellfish pounded, minced, then made into patties (fritters), which are available in almost every NZ fish and chip shop

peneplain – area worn almost flat by erosion

pig islander – derogatory term used by a person from one island for someone from the other island

pillocking – 'surfing' across mud flats on a rubbish-bin lid

Plunket – an adjective to describe the Plunket Society's services to promote the health of babies eg Plunket rooms (baby clinics), Plunket nurses (baby nurses)

polly – politician

ponga – the silver tree fern; called a bungy (pronounced 'bungee', with a soft 'g', in parts of the South Island)

powhiri – a traditional Maori welcome onto the marae

quad bikes – four-wheel farm bikes

Rakiura – literally 'land of glowing skies'; Maori name for Stewart Island, which is important in Maori mythology as the anchor of Maui's canoe

rap jump – face-down abseil

Ratana – a Protestant Maori church; adherents of the Ratana faith

raupo – bullrush

Rheiny – affectionate term for Rheineck beer

rigger – a refillable half-gallon plastic bottle for holding draught beer

scrap – a fight, not uncommon at the pub

section – a small block of land

silver fern – the symbol worn by the All Blacks on their jerseys, representative of the underside of a ponga leaf

Steinie – affectionate term for Steinlager beer

Syndicate, the – the NZ defenders of the America's Cup in 2000

Tamaki-makau-rau – Maori name for Auckland

tane – man

tangata – the people

tangata whenua – people of the land; local people

taniwha – fear-inspiring water spirit

taonga – something of great value; a treasure

tapu – sacred; forbidden; taboo

tarseal – sealed road; bitumen

te – the

Te Kooti – a prominent Maori rebellion leader

Te Papa Atawhai – Maori name for *DOC*

tiki – short for *heitiki*

tohunga – priest; wizard; general expert

tomo – hole; entrance to a cave

tramp – walk; trek; hike; a more serious undertaking than an ordinary walk, requiring some experience and/or special equipment

tua tua – shellfish

tuatara – a prehistoric reptile dating back to the age of the dinosaurs (perhaps 260 million years)

tukutuku – wall panellings in marae and churches

tuna – eel

varsity – university

VIN – Visitor Information Network; the umbrella organisation of the visitor information centres and offices

wahine – woman

wai – water

waiata – song

Wai Pounamu, Te – Maori for the South Island

Waitangi – short way of referring to the Treaty of Waitangi

waka – war canoe

Watties – the NZ food and canning giant; New Zealand's answer to Heinz, until Heinz took over the company

whakapapa – genealogy

whare – house

whare runanga – meeting house

whare taonga – a treasure house; a museum

whare whakairo – carved house

whenua – the land

whitebait – a small elongated transluscent fish which is scooped up in nets and eaten whole (head, eyes and all!) or made into patties

wopwops – remote ('in the wopwops' is out in the middle of nowhere)

Index

Abbreviations

North Island – NI   South Island – SI   Outer Islands – OI

Maps

TEXT

Thanks

Many thanks to the travellers who used the last edition and wrote to us with helpful hints, useful advice and interesting anecdotes. Your names follow:

David & Carol Adams, Ernst Aebi, Julia Alabaster, Louise Alder, Dr Jennifer Alexander, Tom & Lindsay Alker, John Allen, Dominic Amey, M Andersson, Elizabeth Ashley, Rachel Askam

Georgina Bade, Ton Bakker, Lys-Ann Bale, Jon Barber, P Barclay, Cath & Pete Barlow, Christian Barnett, Les Barnett, Philippa Barrett, Dr Sarah Bartlett, Pauline Bates, Paul Bayard, Jeremy & Su Beare, A Beck, Erik Becker, Ben & Jennie, Joachim Bender, Phyllis Benham, Sylvia Bennion, Judy & Mort Berman, Kristin Bervig-Alentine, Steve Best, James Bettles, R Bhadresa, Oliver Bingcang, S Bird, Anthony Birtwistle, Helle Bjerre, Mike Blake, Penny Blakestone, N Blaton, Evi Blueth, Jorg Blum, Birgitte Bonn, Sarah Booth, Roy Bourne, Neil Bowen, Maria Bowers, Robert Bowie, John Boxall, Michael Bradbury, Karen Bradford, T Bradford-Hunter, Danielle Braun, Uschi Braun, J Brauneiser, Tom & Chris Brayton, Angelique Breaat, Justine Bridge, Jude Bridgland, Kathy Brierley, Tim Brill, Dan Brod, Mary Brogan, Kathy Brooks, Richard Brooks, Georgina Brown, Graham Brown, Carolyn Browse, Daniel Brumm, M Buchholz, Lee Bumsted, Dominik Burget, William Burles, Lenny & Wendy Burnett, J M Butcher, Jean Byworth

Jan Calkins, J Callander, Christine Cameron, Steve Campion, Daniel Carey, Ellie & Ron Carleton, Dr P B Carslake, Michael Casey, Peter Caspar, Marjory Cassells, Elly & Jan Cassiers, Michel Centi, Ian Chamberlain, Ryan Chapman, H B Charman, Anna Chipchase, Adam Cohen, Richard Colbey, Dave Cole, Dr J E Collins, Stock & Jan Colt, Carmela Conroy, Patrick Cotter, James Coulson, David Cowan, Paul Cowan, Alison Craig, David Cripps, Alfred Crook, Barry Cuthbertson

Peter Darby, K F Davies, Ruth & Rob Davies, Darren Davis, P De Clerck, Jessie Dennett, Judith denOuden, J Deschepper, Dr Mark De Souza, Andries de Vries, L J Diver, Jan Doms, Jochen Domscheit, D Downes, Nick Doyle, A Draper, Colin & Amber Draper, J Du Bois, P Duffield, Keith Duffy, A Duflos, Nadia Duguay, Joy Durighello, Paul Dyer

Ron Ebert, Rebecca Elder, Ulf Ellervik, Alicia Eppler, Norman Erlichman, Peter Evans

Stefan Fairweather, Henry Fan, Zoya Fansler, David Farnham, Denis Farrelly, Shaun Fay, Andrew Fearnside, M & Simon Feiler, Lucia Fell, P & T Ferris, Ulrich Fischer, Chris Foggin, Marcelo Follari, Nigel Foster, Helene Frankel, Ingo Friese, Kara Fuller, Larry & Jean Fureigh, Markus Fussel

M Gallagher, Siobhan Gallagher, Dominic Galvin, James Garrett, Dan Gawlik, Mathias Geisen, Tony George, Kay Gienow, Ranulf Glanville, Jon Glosser, Ruth Goldhor, Alison Gray, Vicki Gray, Richard Green, C Grierson, Tracy Griffin, C L Grimshaw, Helen Grinstead, Roger Guillaume, Richard Gutermuth

Jean Hackett, Nicholas Haddow, Gina Han, Peter Handley, Darcey Harding, Anne Harkin, Peter Harlow, Claire Hawkins, J He, Jonathon Heath, Clifford Heather, Ingrid Hecht, A Heitsch, Dr E G Hellewell, Paula Heritage, Elisabeth Herreria, Lucilla Herrmann, Dr Elaina Hershowitz, Matthias Hessler, Christine Heusner, Iain Hill, Trevor & Sheila Hills, Julie Hilton, Ursula Hilton-Jones, D & S Hirschhorn, Marian Hodge, M Holdsworth, Michelle House, Mark Howes, John & Alison Howie, C A Hunter, Dave Huntzinger, Lynn Hurton, Yoong Hwee

M Incles, Al Inglis, June Injiam, Takanobu Iwamatsa

Dr Emma Jackson, Paul Jacobs, Ami Jamael, Erika Jarvis, Rachel Jelfs, Mandy Johnson, J Johnson, Brian Johnston, V & S Johnston, Chris Jones, Jean Luc Jourdan

Gunnel Kallus, I Kates, Alison Kauffman, Mel Kay, Sandra Kellett, Shawn Kelley, Sheila & John Kemse, Lachlan Kennedy, M Kennedy, Marjorie Kerr, Phil & Julie Key, Dorothy Kidd, Robin Kilroy, Nick Kimber, Robert King, Dr Barbara Klein, Jeffrey Knorr, Leif Kongstad, William Koolhaas, Shirley Kootstra, Ute Koppmann, M Kraetier, Chris & Danielle Kraus, Brigitte Kroge, Heike Kupfer, Marion Kusserow & Friends, Kylie & Jodie

Van Laere-Marroyen, Kathryn Lamble, M Lankhorst, S Lannenmaki, Andreas Larsson, Jim Lawaich, George Lawson, Jody Lawson, Adam Leader, Lucien Leape, Adam Leavesley, Elizabeth Leboe, Kathryn Leishman, Simon Levi, Jonathan Lightman, Vivienne Lim, Philip Lisamer, Helen Lloyd, Peter Lops, Ben & Tamara Lord, Elke Lorenzen, Helen Lucas, Jenny Lucas, Georgina Lucocq

Anita Mangels, Guy Manova, Dan & Amy Marcus, Marilyn Marsh-Booth, Mike & Ginny Mathews, S Matmon, Triolo Maurizio, Elizabeth McAusland, Heather McCauley, D McCormack, Mabel McDonald, Michael McEvoy, Mr & Mrs McLoughlin, Marcelle McManus, F & C McNicol, C McPherson, G Meindl, Manfred Meyer, Ulrike Michiels, O Middleton, Andreas Minchsner, John Moddy, Annette Montague, Jan & James Montague, Sue Moody, Philip Mooney, Frances Morries, Annalie Morris, Peter Morris, Susan Morrissey, Jennifer Moy, Kathryn & Maria Murphy, Kathleen Murphy

Sydney Newell, Steve Nichols, Helene Nilsson, Elizabeth Nolan, Hans Nouwem, Janet Nussmann

Chris Ogilvie, Judy O'Kane, Mark O'Kane, Carley Olley, Barb & Frank O'Neal, S Ostergaard, Vera Osterhan, Ingrid Otten, Jake Overton, K Oxenham

Birlie Paber, S & A Pagliantini, Stephen Palmer, A Parienty, N Partamian, Margaret Pavitt, Trixi Pech & Family , John Peirce, Pat Penning, C J Penny, Adam Penwarden, Denise Petch, Kathryn Phelps, Pam & Rob Pickens, Roy Piepers, Jo Pilkington-Down, David Pindar, Peter Plaskitt, Nigel Poole, John & Helen Porteous, O E Power, Barbara Price, Debbie Price, Heather Proctor, Steven Proctor, Dr Thomas Proft, Mark & Tracy Purkiss

R Raderstorf, Keith Rakow, Hans Ramlou, Peter Ratcliffe, Madeleine Rawlence, Ian Read, Maureen Real, J Redfern, Lynette Regan, David Reid, Graham Reid, Oliver Reinhard, Dirk Reiser, Thomas Rice, Kim Richardson, Wayne Riddlehoover, Andy Rigby, Daniel Roberts, John Roberts, Dawn Robinson, E Robinson, Margaret Robinson, Carlos Rodriguez, Elizabeth Rogers, Ernesto Romero, Clare Ronald, Guy Roper-Lowe, Daniel Ross, S Ross, Stephanie Rowatt, Paul & Carol Rust, Merril Rylance

Kurt Salloux, Jill Salvin, Gavin Sandercoe, Lex Sarah, J Saunders, Phil & Teresa Savage, John Schlamm, Christine Schlegelmilch, Benny Schlesinger, Frances Schmechel, Audrey Scholl, Angela Schorah, M Schulze, Karen Schur-Narula, Carol Schwille, Ian Scott, J Scott-Russell, Syd Searle, Tim Searle, Steve Seifert, Aniha Sengers, Dorothea Senior, Aimee Serafini, Julie & Bob Shanahan, Cynny Sharp, Lorraine Shears, Jenny Shiel, Steve Shipway, Richard Shive, Y Shwarts-Kates, Ira Silverman, Craig & Melanie Simpson, John Simpson, Stella Sims, Duncan Simth, Jean Sinclair, Claire Skinner, Elaine Slade, Jody Slade, Rebecca Slinger, Jan Smith, Kathleen Smith, Michael Smith, R Smith, Stuart Smith, H Smyrl, Richard South, George Spark, Sue Spear, Willemine Speh, Arthur Spencer, R Spooner,

Yvonne Spreckelmeyer, Nina Stalmann, Keith Stansfield, Keith Stead, R E Steed, Grace Steele, Cyril Stephan, M Stephens, Joyce Stevenson, Antony Stockwell, Iris Stone, Cindy Stork, Robert Strenski, Roland Stuckardt, Urs Studer, S Susino, Dora Svavarsdottir, Mark Swain, Kate Swinburn

D Tabibi, Alison Taylor, Nick Taylor, Tony Taylor, Jean & John Telfour, Hila Tene, Chang-Kwong Thai, M Thesseling, Simon Thomas, Mr & Mrs A & E Thompson, C Thompson, Jodi Tilley, Stephen & Lois Tonnison, JesusAyuso Toral, Brett Townsend, Shannon Tribble, Andy Trist, John Truran, Denise Turner, Nicola Turner

Kevin Underwood

Bervig Valentine, Connie VanDerHulst, Lidy van der Ploeg, Ralf van Essen, Stefan van Wildemeersch, Ana Vaurek, Kirsty Vickerstaff, N J Vincent, Chris Vinegra, Martin Volkening

H Wachter, Elizabeth Wagstaff, Alex Walker, Guy Walker, Janet Walker, Tracy Walker, Louise Walls, Kathy Walsh, Patricia Walsh, Dr F J M Walters, Mike Ward, A Wason, John & Joanna Watney, Deidre Watson, Maurice Watson, Elizabeth Watts, Jenny Watt, Amanda Webb, Dorit Weissberg, Ian & Bev Wentworth, Neil Wheadon, Barbara Whitcher, Elaine White, N & O Wikeley, Miss E Wilding, Brendan Wilkins, Sophie Williams, Nathan & Jackie Williamson, Sally Willis, Tim Willment, Anne Wilshin, Mark, Lucy, Emma & Peter Wilson, N Wilson, Norm Wilson, Regula Windlinger, Petra Wink, Timo Wolf, Peter Wolfenden, Vicky Wood, Tracey Woods, Styart Worrell, Celia Wright, Rainer Wurth

Elihu York

Norbert Zach, Reg Zima.

Phrasebooks

Lonely Planet phrasebooks are packed with essential words and phrases to help travellers communicate with the locals. With colour tabs for quick reference, an extensive vocabulary and use of script, these handy pocket-sized language guides cover day-to-day travel situations.

- handy pocket-sized books
- easy to understand Pronunciation chapter
- clear & comprehensive Grammar chapter
- romanisation alongside script to allow ease of pronunciation
- script throughout so users can point to phrases for every situation
- full of cultural information and tips for the traveller

'...vital for a real DIY spirit and attitude in language learning'
– *Backpacker*

'the phrasebooks have good cultural backgrounders and offer solid advice for challenging situations in remote locations'
– *San Francisco Examiner*

Arabic (Egyptian) ● Arabic (Moroccan) ● Australian *(Australian English, Aboriginal and Torres Strait languages)* ● Baltic States *(Estonian, Latvian, Lithuanian)* ● Bengali ● Brazilian ● British ● Burmese ● Cantonese ● Central Asia ● Central Europe *(Czech, French, German, Hungarian, Italian, Slovak)* ● Eastern Europe *(Bulgarian, Czech, Hungarian, Polish, Romanian, Slovak)* ● Ethiopian (Amharic) ● Fijian ● French ● German ● Greek ● Hebrew phrasebook ● Hill Tribes ● Hindi/Urdu ● Indonesian ● Italian ● Japanese ● Korean ● Lao ● Latin American Spanish ● Malay ● Mandarin ● Mediterranean Europe *(Albanian, Croatian, Greek, Italian, Macedonian, Maltese, Serbian, Slovene)* ● Mongolian ● Nepali ● Pidgin ● Pilipino (Tagalog) ● Quechua ● Russian ● Scandinavian Europe *(Danish, Finnish, Icelandic, Norwegian, Swedish)* ● South-East Asia *(Burmese, Indonesian, Khmer, Lao, Malay, Tagalog Pilipino, Thai, Vietnamese)* ● South Pacific Languages ● Spanish (Castilian) *(also includes Catalan, Galician and Basque)* ● Sri Lanka ● Swahili ● Thai ● Tibetan ● Turkish ● Ukrainian ● USA *(US English, Vernacular, Native American languages, Hawaiian)* ● Vietnamese ● Western Europe *(Basque, Catalan, Dutch, French, German, Greek, Irish)*

Lonely Planet Journeys

J OURNEYS is a unique collection of travel writing – published by the company that understands travel better than anyone else. It is a series for anyone who has ever experienced – or dreamed of – the magical moment when they encountered a strange culture or saw a place for the first time. They are tales to read while you're planning a trip, while you're on the road or while you're in an armchair in front of a fire.

These outstanding titles explore our planet through the eyes of a diverse group of international writers. JOURNEYS books catch the spirit of a place, illuminate a culture, recount a crazy adventure or introduce a fascinating way of life. They always entertain, and always enrich the experience of travel.

IN RAJASTHAN
Royina Grewal

As she writes of her travels through Rajasthan, Indian writer Royina Grewal takes us behind the exotic facade of this fabled destination: here is an insider's perceptive account of India's most colourful state, conveying the excitement and challenges of a region in transition.

SHOPPING FOR BUDDHAS
Jeff Greenwald

In his obsessive search for the perfect Buddha statue in the backstreets of Kathmandu, Jeff Greenwald discovers more than he bargained for ... and his souvenir-hunting turns into an ironic metaphor for the clash between spiritual riches and material greed. Politics, religion and serious shopping collide in this witty account of an enlightening visit to Nepal.

BRIEF ENCOUNTERS
Stories of Love, Sex & Travel
edited by Michelle de Kretser

Love affairs on the road, passionate holiday flings, disastrous pick-ups, erotic encounters ... In this seductive collection of stories, 22 authors from around the world write about travel romances. A tourist in Peru falls for her handsome guide; a writer explores the ambiguities of his relationship with a Japanese woman; a beautiful young man on a train proposes marriage ... Combining fiction and reportage, *Brief Encounters* is must-have reading – for everyone who has dreamt of escape with that perfect stranger.

Includes stories by Pico Iyer, Mary Morris, Emily Perkins, Mona Simpson, Lisa St Aubin de Terán, Paul Theroux and Sara Wheeler.

LONELY PLANET

Lonely Planet Travel Atlases

Lonely Planet has long been famous for the number and quality of its guidebook maps. Now we've gone one step further and produced a handy companion series: Lonely Planet travel atlases – maps of a country produced in book form.

Unlike other maps, which look good but lead travellers astray, our travel atlases have been researched on the road by Lonely Planet's experienced team of writers. All details are carefully checked to ensure the atlas corresponds with the equivalent Lonely Planet guidebook.

- full-colour throughout
- maps researched and checked by Lonely Planet authors
- place names correspond with Lonely Planet guidebooks
- no confusing spelling differences
- legend and travelling information in English, French, German, Japanese and Spanish
- size: 230 x 160 mm

Available now: Chile & Easter Island ● Egypt ● India & Bangladesh ● Israel & the Palestinian Territories ● Jordan, Syria & Lebanon ● Kenya ● Laos ● Portugal ● South Africa, Lesotho & Swaziland ● Thailand ● Turkey ● Vietnam ● Zimbabwe, Botswana & Namibia

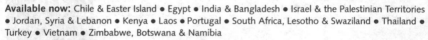

Lonely Planet TV Series & Videos

Lonely Planet travel guides have been brought to life on television screens around the world. Like our guides, the programs are based on the joy of independent travel, and look honestly at some of the most exciting, picturesque and frustrating places in the world. Each show is presented by one of three travellers from Australia, England or the USA and combines an innovative mixture of video, Super-8 film, atmospheric soundscapes and original music.

Videos of each episode – containing additional footage not shown on television – are available from good book and video shops, but the availability of individual videos varies with regional screening schedules.

Video destinations include: Alaska ● American Rockies ● Australia – The South-East ● Baja California & the Copper Canyon ● Brazil ● Central Asia ● Chile & Easter Island ● Corsica, Sicily & Sardinia – The Mediterranean Islands ● East Africa (Tanzania & Zanzibar) ● Ecuador & the Galapagos Islands ● Greenland & Iceland ● Indonesia ● Israel & the Sinai Desert ● Jamaica ● Japan ● La Ruta Maya ● Morocco ● New York ● North India ● Pacific Islands (Fiji, Solomon Islands & Vanuatu) ● South India ● South West China ● Turkey ● Vietnam ● West Africa ● Zimbabwe, Botswana & Namibia

The Lonely Planet TV series is produced by: Pilot Productions
The Old Studio
18 Middle Row
London W10 5AT, UK

LONELY PLANET

Mail Order

Lonely Planet products are distributed worldwide. They are also available by mail order from Lonely Planet, so if you have difficulty finding a title please write to us. North and South American residents should write to 150 Linden St, Oakland, CA 94607, USA; European and African residents should write to 10a Spring Place, London NW5 3BH, UK; and residents of other countries to PO Box 617, Hawthorn, Victoria 3122, Australia.

ISLANDS OF THE INDIAN OCEAN Madagascar & Comoros • Maldives • Mauritius, Réunion & Seychelles

MIDDLE EAST & CENTRAL ASIA Arab Gulf States • Central Asia • Central Asia phrasebook • Hebrew phrasebook • Iran • Israel & the Palestinian Territories • Israel & the Palestinian Territories travel atlas • Istanbul • Istanbul to Cairo • Jerusalem • Jordan & Syria • Jordan, Syria & Lebanon travel atlas • Lebanon • Middle East on a shoestring • Syria • Turkey • Turkish phrasebook • Turkey travel atlas • Yemen
Travel Literature: The Gates of Damascus • Kingdom of the Film Stars: Journey into Jordan

NORTH AMERICA Alaska • Backpacking in Alaska • Baja California • California & Nevada • Canada • Chicago • Chicago city map • Deep South • Florida • Hawaii • Honolulu • Las Vegas • Los Angeles • Miami • New England • New Orleans • New York City • New York city map • New York, New Jersey & Pennsylvania • Pacific Northwest USA • Puerto Rico • Rocky Mountain States • San Francisco • San Francisco city map • Seattle • Southwest USA • Texas • USA • USA phrasebook • Vancouver • Washington, DC & the Capital Region • Washington DC city map
Travel Literature: Drive Thru America

NORTH-EAST ASIA Beijing • Cantonese phrasebook • China • Hong Kong • Hong Kong city map • Hong Kong, Macau & Guangzhou • Japan • Japanese phrasebook • Japanese audio pack • Korea • Korean phrasebook • Kyoto • Mandarin phrasebook • Mongolia • Mongolian phrasebook • North-East Asia on a shoestring • Seoul • South-West China • Taiwan • Tibet • Tibetan phrasebook • Tokyo
Travel Literature: Lost Japan

SOUTH AMERICA Argentina, Uruguay & Paraguay • Bolivia • Brazil • Brazilian phrasebook • Buenos Aires • Chile & Easter Island • Chile & Easter Island travel atlas • Colombia • Ecuador & the Galapagos Islands • Latin American Spanish phrasebook • Peru • Quechua phrasebook • Rio de Janeiro • Rio de Janeiro city map • South America on a shoestring • Trekking in the Patagonian Andes • Venezuela
Travel Literature: Full Circle: A South American Journey

SOUTH-EAST ASIA Bali & Lombok • Bangkok • Bangkok city map • Burmese phrasebook • Cambodia • Hanoi • Healthy Travel Asia & India • Hill Tribes phrasebook • Ho Chi Minh City • Indonesia • Indonesia's Eastern Islands • Indonesian phrasebook • Indonesian audio pack • Jakarta • Java • Laos • Lao phrasebook • Laos travel atlas • Malay phrasebook • Malaysia, Singapore & Brunei • Myanmar (Burma) • Philippines • Pilipino (Tagalog) phrasebook • Singapore • South-East Asia on a shoestring • South-East Asia phrasebook • Thailand • Thailand's Islands & Beaches • Thailand travel atlas • Thai phrasebook • Thai audio pack • Vietnam • Vietnamese phrasebook • Vietnam travel atlas

ALSO AVAILABLE: Antarctica • The Arctic • Brief Encounters: Stories of Love, Sex & Travel • Chasing Rickshaws • Lonely Planet Unpacked • Not the Only Planet: Travel Stories from Science Fiction • Sacred India • Travel with Children • Traveller's Tales

LONELY PLANET

Guides by Region

Lonely Planet is known worldwide for publishing practical, reliable and no-nonsense travel information in our guides and on our Web site. The Lonely Planet list covers just about every accessible part of the world. Currently there are thirteen series: travel guides, shoestring guides, walking guides, city guides, phrasebooks, audio packs, city maps, travel atlases, diving and snorkeling guides, restaurant guides, first-time travel guides, healthy travel and travel literature.

AFRICA Africa – the South • Africa on a shoestring • Arabic (Egyptian) phrasebook • Arabic (Moroccan) phrasebook • Cairo • Cape Town • Cape Town city map• Central Africa • East Africa • Egypt • Egypt travel atlas • Ethiopian (Amharic) phrasebook • The Gambia & Senegal • Healthy Travel Africa • Kenya • Kenya travel atlas • Malawi, Mozambique & Zambia • Morocco • North Africa • South Africa, Lesotho & Swaziland • South Africa, Lesotho & Swaziland travel atlas • Swahili phrasebook • Tanzania, Zanzibar & Pemba • Trekking in East Africa • Tunisia • West Africa • Zimbabwe, Botswana & Namibia • Zimbabwe, Botswana & Namibia travel atlas
Travel Literature: The Rainbird: A Central African Journey • Songs to an African Sunset: A Zimbabwean Story • Mali Blues: Traveling to an African Beat

AUSTRALIA & THE PACIFIC Auckland • Australia • Australian phrasebook • Bushwalking in Australia • Bushwalking in Papua New Guinea • Fiji • Fijian phrasebook • Islands of Australia's Great Barrier Reef • Melbourne • Melbourne city map • Micronesia • New Caledonia • New South Wales & the ACT • New Zealand • Northern Territory • Outback Australia • Out To Eat – Melbourne • Papua New Guinea • Papua New Guinea (Pidgin) phrasebook • Queensland • Rarotonga & the Cook Islands • Samoa • Solomon Islands • South Australia • South Pacific Languages phrasebook • Sydney • Sydney city map • Tahiti & French Polynesia • Tasmania • Tonga • Tramping in New Zealand • Vanuatu • Victoria • Western Australia
Travel Literature: Islands in the Clouds • Kiwi Tracks • Sean & David's Long Drive

CENTRAL AMERICA & THE CARIBBEAN Bahamas and Turks & Caicos • Bermuda • Central America on a shoestring • Costa Rica • Cuba • Dominican Republic & Haiti • Eastern Caribbean • Guatemala, Belize & Yucatán: La Ruta Maya • Jamaica • Mexico • Mexico City • Panama • Puerto Rico
Travel Literature: Green Dreams: Travels in Central America

EUROPE Amsterdam • Amsterdam city map • Andalucía • Austria • Baltic States phrasebook • Barcelona • Berlin • Berlin city map • Britain • British phrasebook • Brussels, Bruges & Antwerp • Budapest city map • Canary Islands • Central Europe • Central Europe phrasebook • Corsica • Croatia • Czech & Slovak Republics • Denmark • Dublin • Eastern Europe • Eastern Europe phrasebook • Edinburgh • Estonia, Latvia & Lithuania • Europe • Finland • France • French phrasebook • Germany • German phrasebook • Greece • Greek phrasebook • Hungary • Iceland, Greenland & the Faroe Islands • Ireland • Italian phrasebook • Italy • Lisbon • London • London city map • Mediterranean Europe • Mediterranean Europe phrasebook • Norway • Paris • Paris city map • Poland • Portugal • Portugal travel atlas • Prague • Prague city map • Provence & the Côte d'Azur • Romania & Moldova • Rome • Russia, Ukraine & Belarus • Russian phrasebook • Scandinavian & Baltic Europe • Scandinavian Europe phrasebook • Scotland • Slovenia • Spain • Spanish phrasebook • St Petersburg • Switzerland • Trekking in Spain • Ukrainian phrasebook • Vienna • Walking in Britain • Walking in Ireland • Walking in Italy • Walking in Switzerland • Western Europe • Western Europe phrasebook
Travel Literature: The Olive Grove: Travels in Greece

INDIAN SUBCONTINENT Bangladesh • Bengali phrasebook • Bhutan • Delhi • Goa • Hindi/Urdu phrasebook • India • India & Bangladesh travel atlas • Indian Himalaya • Karakoram Highway • Kerala • Mumbai • Nepal • Nepali phrasebook • Pakistan • Rajasthan • Read This First: Asia & India • South India • Sri Lanka • Sri Lanka phrasebook • Trekking in the Indian Himalaya • Trekking in the Karakoram & Hindukush • Trekking in the Nepal Himalaya
Travel Literature: In Rajasthan • Shopping for Buddhas

The Lonely Planet Story

L onely Planet published its first book in 1973 in response to the numerous 'How did you do it?' questions Maureen and Tony Wheeler were asked after driving, bussing, hitching, sailing and railing their way from England to Australia.

Written at a kitchen table and hand collated, trimmed and stapled, *Across Asia on the Cheap* became an instant local bestseller, inspiring thoughts of another book.

Eighteen months in South-East Asia resulted in their second guide, *South-East Asia on a shoestring*, which they put together in a backstreet Chinese hotel in Singapore in 1975. The 'yellow bible', as it quickly became known to backpackers around the world, soon became *the* guide to the region. It has sold well over half a million copies and is now in its 9th edition, still retaining its familiar yellow cover.

Today there are over 350 titles, including travel guides, walking guides, language kits & phrasebooks, travel atlases, diving guides and travel literature. The company is the largest independent travel publisher in the world. Although Lonely Planet initially specialised in guides to Asia, today there are few corners of the globe that have not been covered.

The emphasis continues to be on travel for independent travellers. Tony and Maureen still travel for several months of each year and play an active part in the writing, updating and quality control of Lonely Planet's guides.

They have been joined by over 120 authors and 280 staff at our offices in Melbourne (Australia), Oakland (USA), London (UK) and Paris (France). Travellers themselves also make a valuable contribution to the guides through the feedback we receive in thousands of letters each year and on our web site.

The people at Lonely Planet strongly believe that travellers can make a positive contribution to the countries they visit, both through their appreciation of the countries' culture, wildlife and natural features, and through the money they spend. In addition, the company makes a direct contribution to the countries and regions it covers. Since 1986 a percentage of the income from each book has been donated to ventures such as famine relief in Africa; aid projects in India; agricultural projects in Central America; Greenpeace's efforts to halt French nuclear testing in the Pacific; and Amnesty International.

LONELY PLANET OFFICES

Australia
PO Box 617, Hawthorn, Victoria 3122
☎ 03 9819 1877 fax 03 9819 6459
email: talk2us@lonelyplanet.com.au

USA
150 Linden St, Oakland, CA 94607
☎ 510 893 8555 TOLL FREE: 800 275 8555
fax 510 893 8572
email: info@lonelyplanet.com

UK
10a Spring Place, London NW5 3BH
☎ 020 7428 4800 fax 020 7428 4828
email: go@lonelyplanet.co.uk

France
1 rue du Dahomey, 75011 Paris
☎ 01 55 25 33 00 fax 01 55 25 33 01
email: bip@lonelyplanet.fr
www.lonelyplanet.fr

World Wide Web: www.lonelyplanet.com *or* **AOL keyword: lp**
Lonely Planet Images: lpi@lonelyplanet.com.au